W9-CYD-941

LIQUIDITY RATIOS

Ratio	Formula	Description	Reference
Current ratio	$\frac{\text{Current Assets}}{\text{Current Liabilities}}$	Measures short-term debt-paying ability	Chapter 4, LO5
Quick ratio	$\frac{\text{Cash + Marketable Securities + Receivables}}{\text{Current Liabilities}}$	Measures short-term debt-paying ability	Chapter 28, LO3
Receivable turnover	$\frac{\text{Net Sales}}{\text{Average Accounts Receivable}}$	Average number of times receivables are turned into cash during an accounting period	Chapter 7, LO1
Days' sales uncollected	$\frac{\text{Days in Year}}{\text{Receivable Turnover}}$	Average number of days a company must wait to receive payment for credit sales or to collect accounts receivable	Chapter 7, LO1
Inventory turnover	$\frac{\text{Costs of Goods Sold}}{\text{Average Inventory}}$	Number of times a company's average inventory is sold during an accounting period	Chapter 6, LO1
Days' inventory on hand	$\frac{\text{Days in Year}}{\text{Inventory Turnovers}}$	Average number of days taken to sell inventory on hand	Chapter 6, LO1
Payables turnover	$\frac{\text{Costs of Goods Sold +/− Change in Inventory}}{\text{Average Accounts Payable}}$	Average number of times a company pays its accounts payable in an accounting period	Chapter 8, LO1
Days' payable	$\frac{\text{Days in Year}}{\text{Payables Turnover}}$	Average number of days a company takes to pay accounts payable	Chapter 8, LO1

PROFITABILITY RATIOS

Ratio	Formula	Description	Reference
Profit margin	$\frac{\text{Net Income}}{\text{Net Sales}}$	Percentage of each sales dollar that contributes to net income	Chapter 4, LO5
Asset turnover	$\frac{\text{Net Sales}}{\text{Average Total Assets}}$	How efficiently assets are used to produce sales	Chapter 4, LO5
Return on assets	$\frac{\text{Net Income}}{\text{Average Total Assets}}$	How efficiently a company uses its assets to produce income, or the amount earned on each dollar of assets invested	Chapter 4, LO5
Return on equity	$\frac{\text{Net Income}}{\text{Average Owner's Equity}}$	Relates the amount earned by a business to the owner's investment in the business	Chapter 4, LO5

LONG-TERM SOLVENCY RATIOS

Ratio	Formula	Description	Reference
Debt to equity ratio	$\frac{\text{Total Liabilities}}{\text{Owner's Equity}}$	Proportion of a company's assets financed by creditors and the proportion financed by the owner	Chapter 4, LO5
Interest coverage ratio	$\frac{\text{Income Before Income Taxes + Interest Expense}}{\text{Interest Expense}}$	Degree of protection a company has from default on interest payments	Chapter 10, LO1

CASH FLOW ADEQUACY RATIOS

Ratio	Formula	Description	Reference
Cash flow yield	$\frac{\text{Net Cash Flows from Operating Activities}}{\text{Net Income}}$	Measures a company's ability to generate operating cash flows in relation to net income	Chapter 14, LO2
Cash flows to sales	$\frac{\text{Net Cash Flows from Operating Activities}}{\text{Net Sales}}$	Ratio of net cash flows from operating activities to sales	Chapter 14, LO2
Cash flows to assets	$\frac{\text{Net Cash Flows from Operating Activities}}{\text{Average Total Assets}}$	Measures the ability of assets to generate operating cash flows	Chapter 14, LO2
Free cash flow	Net Cash Flows from Operating Activities − Dividends − Net Capital Expenditures	Measures the amount of cash that remains after deducting the funds a company must commit to continue operating at its planned level	Chapter 9, LO1

MARKET STRENGTH RATIOS

Ratio	Formula	Description	Reference
Price/earnings ratio	$\frac{\text{Market Price per Share}}{\text{Earnings per Share}}$	Measures investors' confidence in a company's future; a means of comparing stock values	Chapter 11, LO1
Dividends yield	$\frac{\text{Dividends per Share}}{\text{Market Price per Share}}$	Measures a stock's current return to an investor or stockholder	Chapter 11, LO1

Financial and Managerial Accounting

NINTH EDITION

Belverd E. Needles, Jr., Ph.D., C.P.A., C.M.A.
DePaul University

Marian Powers, Ph.D.
Northwestern University

Susan V. Crosson, M.S. Accounting, C.P.A
Santa Fe College

Australia • Brazil • Canada • Mexico • Singapore • Spain • United Kingdom • United States

Financial and Managerial Accounting, Ninth Edition

Belverd Needles, Marian Powers, Susan Crosson

Vice President of Editorial, Business: Jack W. Calhoun

Editor in Chief: Rob Dewey

Executive Editor: Sharon Oblinger

Supervising Developmental Editor: Katie Yanos

Sr. Marketing Manager: Kristen Hurd

Marketing Coordinator: Heather Mooney

Sr. Marketing Communications Manager: Libby Shipp

Content Project Manager: Darrell Frye

Media Editor: Bryan England

Editorial Assistant: Julie Warwick

Frontlist Buyer, Manufacturing: Doug Wilke

Production Service: S4Carlisle Publishing Services

Sr. Art Director: Stacy Jenkins Shirley

Cover and Internal Designer: Grannan Graphic Design

Cover Image: ©Getty Images/Image Bank

Permissions Account Manager: John Hill

© 2011, 2008 South-Western, Cengage Learning

Photo Credits: p. 3, Scott Olson/Staff/Getty Images News/Getty Images; p. 91, TEH ENG KOON/AFP/Getty Images; p., Justin Sullivan/Stringer/Getty Images News/Getty Images; p. 209, Zuma Press/Newscom; p. 261, AP Photo/Don Ryan; p. 311, Tom Boyle/Getty Images News/Getty Images; p. 353, Ron Vesely/MLB Photos via Getty Images; p. 393, STAN HONDA/AFP/Getty Images; p. 435, Rommel Pecson/The Image Works; p. 481, Viennaphoto/allOver photography/Alamy; p. 533, Chris Hondros/Getty Images; p. 579, AP Photo/Jae C. Hong; p. 621, Peter Cade/Getty Images; p. 667, Scott Eells/Bloomberg News/Landov; p. 719, Dorling Kindersley/Getty Images; p. 761, Caro/Alamy; p. 807, Lori Adamski Peek /Workbook Stock/Getty Images; p. 845, Tim Boyle/Newsmakers/Getty Images; p. 883, AP Photo/Carlos Osorio; p. 923, Ben Bloom/Getty images; p. 965, Laura Doss/Fancy/PhotoLibrary; p.1017, Ben Blankenburg/istockphoto; p. 1061, UPI Photo/Kevin Dietsch/Newscom; p. 1109, Jupiterimages; p. 1149, Monkey Business Images ,2009/Used under license from Shutterstock.com; p. 1187, AP Photo/Mark Lennihan; p. 1233, © Richard Levine/Alamy; p. 1271 AP Photo/Martin Mejia

ALL RIGHTS RESERVED. No part of this work covered by the copyright herein may be reproduced, transmitted, stored, or used in any form or by any means graphic, electronic, or mechanical, including but not limited to photocopying, recording, scanning, digitizing, taping, web distribution, information networks, or information storage and retrieval systems, except as permitted under Section 107 or 108 of the 1976 United States Copyright Act, without the prior written permission of the publisher.

For product information and technology assistance, contact us at
Cengage Learning Customer & Sales Support, 1-800-354-9706

For permission to use material from this text or product,
submit all requests online at **www.cengage.com/permissions**
Further permissions questions can be emailed to
permissionrequest@cengage.com

Exam*View*® is a registered trademark of eInstruction Corp. Windows is a registered trademark of the Microsoft Corporation used herein under license. Macintosh and Power Macintosh are registered trademarks of Apple Computer, Inc. used herein under license.

© 2011 Cengage Learning. All Rights Reserved.

Cengage Learning WebTutor™ is a trademark of Cengage Learning.

Library of Congress Control Number: 2009943378

Student Edition ISBN 10: 1-4390-3780-9
Student Edition ISBN 13: 978-1-4390-3780-5

Instructors Edition ISBN 10: 0-538-74282-8
Instructors Edition ISBN 13: 978-0-538-74282-5

South-Western Cengage Learning
5191 Natorp Boulevard
Mason, OH 45040
USA

Cengage Learning products are represented in Canada by Nelson Education, Ltd.

For your course and learning solutions, visit **www.cengage.com**
Purchase any of our products at your local college store or at our preferred online store **www.cengagebrain.com**

Printed in the United States of America
1 2 3 4 5 6 7 14 13 12 11 10

BRIEF CONTENTS

CONTENTS

CHAPTER 4 Financial Reporting and Analysis 208

SUPPLEMENT TO CHAPTER 4 The Annual Report Project 258

CHAPTER 5 The Operating Cycle and Merchandising Operations 260

CHAPTER 6 Inventories 310

CHAPTER 7 Cash and Receivables 352

CHAPTER 8 Current Liabilities and Fair Value Accounting 392

CHAPTER 11 Contributed Capital 532

CHAPTER 12 Investments 578

CHAPTER 13 The Corporate Income Statement and the Statement of Stockholders' Equity 620

CHAPTER 16 Cost Concepts and Cost Allocation 760

CHAPTER 17 Costing Systems: Job Order Costing 806

CHAPTER 18 Costing Systems: Process Costing 844

CHAPTER 21 The Budgeting Process 964

CHAPTER 22 Performance Management and Evaluation 1016

CHAPTER 23 Standard Costing and Variance Analysis 1060

CHAPTER 26 Pricing Decisions, Including Target Costing and Transfer Pricing 1186

CHAPTER 27 Quality Management and Measurement 1232

CHAPTER 28 Financial Analysis of Performance 1270

Accounting in Motion!

This revision of *Financial and Managerial Accounting* is based on an understanding of the nature, culture, and motivations of today's undergraduate students and on extensive feedback from many instructors who use our book. These substantial changes meet the needs of these students, who not only face a business world increasingly complicated by ethical issues, globalization, and technology but who also have more demands on their time. To assist them to meet these challenges, the authors carefully show them how the effects of business transactions, which are the result of business decisions, are recorded in a way that will be reflected on the financial statements. Instructors will find that building on the text's historically strong pedagogy, the authors have strengthened transaction analysis and its link to the accounting cycle.

Updated Content, Organization and Pedagogy

Strengthened Transaction Analysis

Maintaining a solid foundation in double-entry accounting, we increased the number of in-text journal entries and have used T accounts linked to these journal-entry illustrations throughout the financial accounting chapters. In Chapter 2, "Analyzing Business Transactions," for example, we clarified the relationship of transaction analysis to the accounting cycle. In Chapter 5, "The Operating Cycle and Merchandising Accounting," we include transaction illustrations for all transactions mentioned in the chapter. At the same time, we reduced excessive detail, shortened headings, simplified explanations, and increased readability in an effort to reduce the length of each chapter.

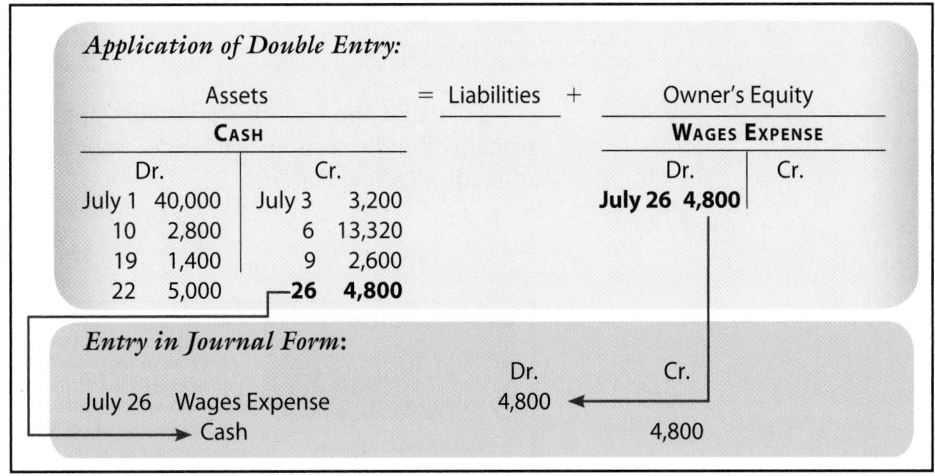

Strong Pedagogical System

Financial and Managerial Accounting originated the pedagogical system of ***Integrated Learning Objectives.*** The system supports both learning and teaching by providing flexibility in support of the instructor's teaching of first-year accounting. The chapter review and all assignments identify the applicable learning objective(s) for easy reference.

Each learning objective refers to a specific content area, usually either conceptual content or procedural techniques, in short and easily understandable segments. Each segment is followed by a "**Stop and Apply**" section that illustrates and solves a short exercise related to the learning objective.

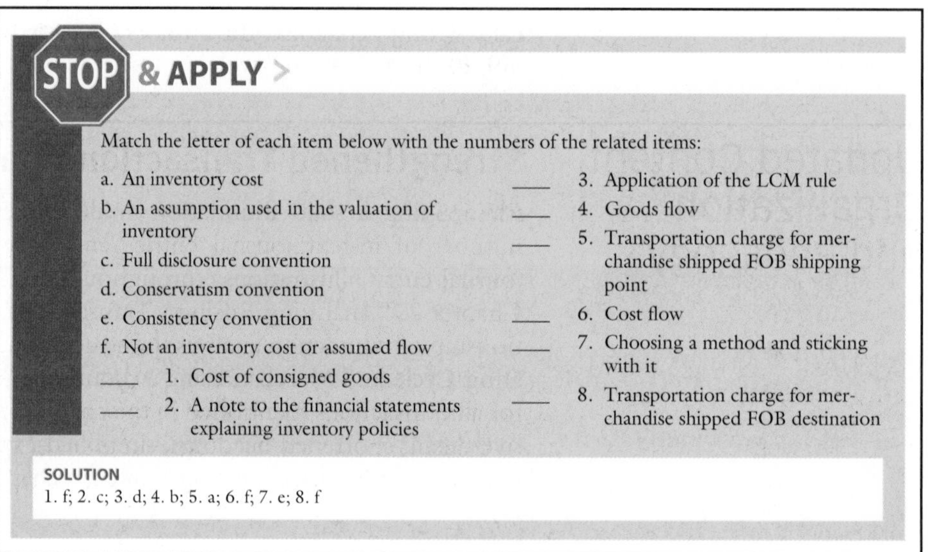

STOP & APPLY >

Match the letter of each item below with the numbers of the related items:

a. An inventory cost
b. An assumption used in the valuation of inventory
c. Full disclosure convention
d. Conservatism convention
e. Consistency convention
f. Not an inventory cost or assumed flow

____ 1. Cost of consigned goods
____ 2. A note to the financial statements explaining inventory policies
____ 3. Application of the LCM rule
____ 4. Goods flow
____ 5. Transportation charge for merchandise shipped FOB shipping point
____ 6. Cost flow
____ 7. Choosing a method and sticking with it
____ 8. Transportation charge for merchandise shipped FOB destination

SOLUTION
1. f; 2. c; 3. d; 4. b; 5. a; 6. f; 7. e; 8. f

To make the text more visually appealing and readable, it is divided into student-friendly sections with brief bulleted lists, new art, photographs, and end-of-section review material.

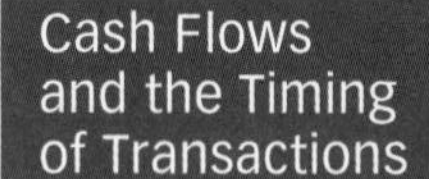

LO5 Show how the timing of transactions affects cash flows and liquidity.

To avoid financial distress, a company must be able to pay its bills on time. Because the timing of cash flows is critical to maintaining adequate liquidity to pay bills, managers and other users of financial information must understand the difference between transactions that generate immediate cash and those that do not. Consider the transactions of Miller Design Studio shown in Figure 2-3. Most of them involve either an inflow or outflow of cash.

As you can see in Figure 2-3, Miller's Cash account has more transactions than any of its other accounts. Look at the transactions of July 10, 15, and 22:

- July 10: Miller received a cash payment of $2,800.
- July 15: The firm billed a customer $9,600 for a service it had already performed.
- July 22: The firm received a partial payment of $5,000 from the customer, but it had not received the remaining $4,600 by the end of the month.

Because Miller incurred expenses in providing this service, it must pay careful attention to its cash flows and liquidity.

One way Miller can manage its expenditures is to rely on its creditors to give it time to pay. Compare the transactions of July 3, 5, and 9 in Figure 2-3.

Study Note

After Step 1 has been completed, the Income Summary account reflects the account balance of the Design Revenue account before it was closed.

Further, to reduce distractions, the margins of the text include only **Study Notes**, which alert students to common misunderstandings of concepts and techniques; key ratio and cash flow icons, which highlight discussions of profitability and liquidity; and accounting equations. Icons and equations appear in the financial chapters (Chapters 1–14).

Enhanced Real-World Examples Demonstrate Accounting in Motion

IFRS, Fair Value, and Other Updates

International Financial Reporting Standards and fair value have been integrated throughout the book where accounting standards have changed and also in the **Business Focus** features where applicable. All current events, statistics, and tables have been updated with the latest data.

FOCUS ON BUSINESS PRACTICE IFRS

IFRS: The Arrival of International Financial Reporting Standards in the United States

Over the next few years, international financial reporting standards (IFRS) will become much more important in the United States and globally. The International Accounting Standards Board (IASB) has been working with the Financial Accounting Standards Board (FASB) and similar boards in other nations to achieve identical or nearly identical standards worldwide. IFRS are now required in many parts of the world, including Europe. The Securities and Exchange Commission (SEC) recently voted to allow foreign registrants in the United States. This is a major development because in the past, the SEC required foreign registrants to explain how the standards used in their statements differed from U.S. standards. This change affects approximately 10 percent of all public U.S. companies. In addition, the SEC may in the near future allow U.S. companies to use IFRS.[11]

Use of Diverse Companies

Each chapter begins with a **Decision Point**, a real-world scenario about a company that challenges students to see the connection between accounting information and management decisions.

DECISION POINT ▸ **A USER'S FOCUS THE BOEING COMPANY**

In April 2006, the Chinese government announced that it had ordered 80 **Boeing** commercial jet liners, thus fulfilling a commitment it had made to purchase 150 airplanes from Boeing. Valued at about $4.6 billion, the order for the 80 airplanes was one of many events that brought about Boeing's resurgence in the stock market. After Boeing received this order, as well as orders from other customers, its stock began trading at an all-time high.

Typically, it takes Boeing almost two years to manufacture an airplane. In this case, the aircraft delivery cycle was expected to peak in 2009.[1]

- An order for airplanes is obviously an important economic event for both the buyer and the seller. Is there a difference between an economic event and a business transaction that should be recorded in the accounting records?
- Should Boeing record the order in its accounting records?
- How important are liquidity and cash flows to Boeing?

These company examples come full circle at the end of the chapter by linking directly to the **A Look Back At** diverse company examples illustrate accounting concepts and encourage students to apply what they have learned.

A LOOK BACK AT ▸ **THE BOEING COMPANY**

The Decision Point at the beginning of the chapter described the order for 80 airplanes that the Chinese government placed with **Boeing**. It posed the following questions:

- An order for airplanes is obviously an important economic event to both the buyer and the seller. Is there a difference between an economic event and a business transaction that should be recorded in the accounting records?
- Should Boeing record the order in its accounting records?
- How important are liquidity and cash flows to Boeing?

Despite its importance, the order did not constitute a business transaction, and neither the buyer nor the seller should have recognized it in its accounting records. At the time the Chinese government placed the order, Boeing had not yet built the airplanes. Until it delivers them and title to them shifts to the Chinese government, Boeing cannot record any revenue.

Use of Well-Known Public Companies

This textbook also offers examples from highly recognizable public companies, such as CVS Caremark, Southwest Airlines, Dell Computer, and Netflix, to relate basic accounting concepts and techniques to the real world. **Chapter 4, "Financial Reporting and Analysis,"** helps students interpret financial information. The latest available data is used in exhibits to incorporate the most recent FASB pronouncements. The authors illustrate current practices in financial reporting by referring to data from *Accounting Trends and Techniques* (AICPA) and integrate international topics wherever appropriate.

Consolidated means that data from all companies owned by CVS are combined.

CVS Caremark Corporation
Consolidated Statements of Operations

CVS's fiscal year ends on the Saturday closest to December 31.

	Fiscal Year Ended		
(In millions, except per share amounts)	**Dec. 31, 2008 (52 weeks)**	**Dec. 29, 2007 (52 weeks)**	**Dec. 30, 2006 (53 weeks)**
Net revenues	$87,471.9	$76,329.5	$43,821.4
Cost of revenues	69,181.5	60,221.8	32,079.2
Gross profit	18,290.4	16,107.7	11,742.2
Total operating expenses	12,244.2	11,314.4	9,300.6
Operating profit[1]	6,046.2	4,793.3	2,441.6
Interest expense, net[2]	509.5	434.6	215.8
Earnings before income tax provision	5,536.7	4,358.7	2,225.8
Loss from discontinued operations, net of income tax benefit of $82.4	(132)	—	—
Income tax provision	2,192.6	1,721.7	856.9
Net earnings[3]	3,212.1	2,637.0	1,368.9
Preference dividends, net of income tax benefit[4]	14.1	14.2	13.9
Net earnings available to common shareholders	$ 3,198.0	$ 2,622.8	$ 1,355.0
BASIC EARNINGS PER COMMON SHARE:[5]			
Net earnings	$ 2.23	$ 1.97	$ 1.65
Weighted average common shares outstanding	1,433.5	1,328.2	820.6
DILUTED EARNINGS PER COMMON SHARE:			
Net earnings	$ 2.18	$ 1.92	$ 1.60
Weighted average common shares outstanding	1,469.1	1,371.8	853.2

Revised and Expanded Assignments

Assignments have been carefully scrutinized for direct relevancy to the learning objectives in the chapters. Names and numbers for all Short Exercises, Exercises, and Problems have been changed except those used on videos. We have reversed the alternate and main problems from the previous edition. Most importantly, alternative problems have been expanded so that there are ample problems for any course.

All of the cases have been updated as appropriate and the number of cases in each chapter has been reduced in response to user preferences. The variety of cases in each chapter depends on their relevance to the chapter topics, but throughout the text there are cases involving conceptual understanding, ethical dilemmas, interpreting financial reports, group activities, business communication, and the Internet. Annual report cases based on CVS Caremark and Southwest Airlines can be found at the end of the chapter.

Specific Chapter Changes

The following chapter-specific changes have been made in this edition of *Financial and Managerial Accounting:*

Chapter 1 Uses of Accounting Information and the Financial Statements

- Discussion of performance measures revised using CVS and General Motors as examples of how these measures relate to profitability and liquidity
- Discussion of the statement of cash flows revised to relate the statement to business activities and goals
- Updated and enhanced coverage of the roles of the Financial Accounting Standards Board (FASB) and the International Accounting Standards Board (IASB)
- New Focus on Business Practice box on SEC's decision to let foreign companies registered in the United States use international financial reporting standards (IFRS)
- New study note on the role of the Public Company Accounting Oversight Board (PCAOB)

Chapter 2 Analyzing Business Transactions

- Section on valuation in Learning Objective (LO) 1 revised to address fair value and IFRS
- New Focus on Business Practice box on fair value accounting in an international marketplace
- New example of recognition violation focusing on Computer Associates
- LO3 revised to emphasize and clarify the role of T accounts, journal form, and their relationship to the general ledger
- Cash flow discussion in LO5 edited for clearer delineation of the sequence of transactions

Chapter 3 Measuring Business Income

- New company (Netflix) used as example in the Decision Point
- Discussion of the matching rule and cash basis of accounting in LO1 revised for greater clarity
- New example of earnings management focusing on Dell Computer
- New Focus on Business Practice box describing the FASB's rules for revenue recognition and the one broad IFRS that the IASB uses
- Inclusion of journal entries, along with T accounts and explanatory comments, in the discussion of the adjustment process in LO3

Chapter 4 Financial Reporting and Analysis

- First section in LO1 revised to reflect the FASB's emphasis on the needs of capital providers and other users of financial reports
- Coverage of qualitative characteristics simplified and shortened
- Topics in LO2 reorganized to reflect changes in LO1
- New Focus on Business Practice box on convergence of U.S. GAAP and IFRS and their effect on accounting conventions
- New Focus on Business Practice box on the IASB's proposed changes in the format of financial statements
- New Focus on Business Practice box on how the convergence of U.S. GAAP and IFRS has made financial analysis more difficult
- New Focus on Business Practice box on the use of ratios in measuring performance and determining executives' compensation

Chapter 5 The Operating Cycle and Merchandising Operations

- Discussion of the operating cycle in LO1 revised for greater clarity
- New Focus on Business Practice box on the effectiveness of the Sarbanes-Oxley Act in preventing fraud
- Journal entries used to illustrate accounting for merchandising transactions under both the perpetual and periodic inventory systems (LO3 and LO4)
- Clearer differentiation in LO4 between the cost of goods available for sale and the cost of goods sold
- New Focus on Business Practice box on methods of preventing shoplifting
- Material in LO6 reformatted to clarify discussion of documents used in an internal control plan for purchases and cash disbursements

Chapter 6 Inventories

- New company (Toyota) used as example in the Decision Point
- Discussion in LO1 of disclosure of inventory methods shortened for greater clarity
- New Focus on Business Practice box on the lower-of-cost-or-market rule
- New Focus on Business Practice box on the use of LIFO inside and outside the United States
- New Focus on Business Practice box on how IFRS and U.S. standards define fair value

Chapter 7 Cash and Receivables

- New coverage of subprime loans, including a new Focus on Business Practice box in LO1
- Concept of fair value introduced at various points throughout the chapter
- Revised Focus on Business Practice box on estimating cash collections

Chapter 8 Current Liabilities and Fair Value Accounting

- New company (Microsoft) used as example in the Decision Point
- Chapter revised to include coverage of fair value accounting
- Discussions and assignments related to future value deleted to emphasize present value and fair value, which are more directly related to this course

Chapter 9 Long-Term Assets

- Tables added in LO1 and LO3 to enhance and clarify discussions of acquisition of long-term assets and methods of computing depreciation
- Revised Focus on Business Practice box on accelerated methods of accounting for depreciation

- Coverage of tax laws in LO3 revised to address the Economic Stimulus Act of 2008
- Coverage of intangible assets in LO6 revised to reflect current standards
- Revised Focus on Business Practice box on the amortization of customer lists

Chapter 10 Long-Term Liabilities

- Discussion in LO1 of accounting for defined benefit plans updated
- Section on cash flow information added to LO1
- New Focus on Business Practice box on postretirement liabilities
- Bonds interest rates changed so that they are more realistic than in previous edition

Chapter 11 Contributed Capital

- Revised Focus on Business Practice box on how political pressure affected the FASB's ruling on stock options
- Section on cash flow information added to LO1
- Updated Focus on Business Practice box on share buybacks

Chapter 12 Investments

- Discussion of measuring investments at fair value added to valuation section in LO1
- New Focus on Business Practice box on the role of fair value accounting in the subprime mortgage collapse

Chapter 13 The Corporate Income Statement and the Statement of Stockholders' Equity

- New Focus on Business Practice box on looking beyond the bottom line
- Revised Focus on Business Practice box on pro forma earnings
- Discontinued operations and extraordinary items, which were covered in LO3 in previous edition, now discussed in section on nonoperating items in LO1

Chapter 14 The Statement of Cash Flows

- New company (Amazon.com) used as example in the Decision Point
- Clarification of required disclosure of noncash investing and financing activities in LO1
- Sections on the risks of having too much cash and on interpreting the statement of cash flows added to LO2
- New Focus on Business Practice box on the IASB's support of the direct method

Chapter 15 The Changing Business Environment: A Manager's Perspective

- Updated definition of management accounting in LO1
- *Lean production* introduced as a key term in LO3
- Sections on total quality management and activity based management in LO3 revised
- Updated Focus on Business Practice box on how to blow the whistle on fraud

Chapter 16 Cost Concepts and Cost Allocation

- New company (Hershey's) used as example in the Decision Point
- Discussions of costs in LO2 in previous edition incorporated in LO1

- Introduction to methods of product cost measurement added and section on computing service unit cost shortened in new LO4
- LO7 and LO8 in previous edition (the traditional and ABC approaches to allocating overhead) streamlined and incorporated in new LO5

Chapter 17 Costing Systems: Job Order Costing

- Chapter 17 in previous edition separated into two chapters, with new Chapter 17 focusing on job order costing and new Chapter 18 focusing on process costing
- *Operations costing system* introduced as a key concept
- Discussions of manufacturer's job order cost card, computation of unit cost, and job order costing in a service organization included in new LO4

Chapter 18 Costing Systems: Process Costing

- New chapter (part of Chapter 17 in previous edition)

Chapter 19 Value-Based Systems: ABM and Lean

- Chapter revised to emphasize value-based systems
- LO1, LO2, and LO3 in last edition revised and incorporated in new LO1
- New listing of the disadvantages of activity-based costing in LO2
- New focus on lean operations in LO3 and section on accounting for product costs added

Chapter 20 Cost Behavior Analysis

- New company (Flickr) used as example in the Decision Point
- Sections on variable, fixed, and mixed costs, which were in LO2 in last edition, now included in LO1
- Concept of a *step cost* introduced in discussion of fixed costs in LO1
- Methods used to separate the components of mixed costs and the contribution margin income statement now the focus of LO2
- Material in LO4 reformatted to clarify concepts

Chapter 21 The Budgeting Process

- New company (Framerica Corporation) used as example in the Decision Point
- LO1 reorganized, revised, and shortened
- Section on advantages of budgeting and three new key terms—*static budget, continuous budget,* and *zero-based budgeting* added to LO1

Chapter 22 Performance Management and Evaluation

- LO1 and LO2 in last edition combined and revised

Chapter 23 Standard Costing and Variance Analysis

- New company (iRobot Corporation) used as example in the Decision Point
- LO1 and LO2 in last edition combined and revised
- New Focus on Business Practice box titled "What Do You Get When You Cross a Vacuum Cleaner with a Gaming Console?"

Chapter 24 Short-Run Decision Analysis

- Chapter revised to focus on the use of incremental analysis in making short-run decisions; capital investment analysis and time value of money now covered in Chapter 25

Chapter 25 Capital Investment Analysis

- New chapter

Chapter 26 Pricing Decisions, Including Target Costing and Transfer Pricing

- LO1 reorganized and shortened
- Updated Focus on Business Practice box on Internet fraud
- Discussions of steps followed in gross margin pricing and return on assets pricing in LO3 reformatted for greater clarity
- Discussion of the differences between cost-based pricing and target costing in LO4 revised and made more succinct
- Section on developing a transfer price in LO5 revised

Chapter 27 Quality Management and Measurement

- In LO2, formula for computing delivery cycle time added and displayed; formula for computing waste time also displayed
- In LO4, discussion of Motorola's Sigma Six quality goal revised, with disadvantages noted

Chapter 28 Financial Analysis of Performance

- Section on the management process in LO1 revised to increase the focus on management's objectives
- Revised Focus on Business Practice box on pro forma earnings
- In LO3, two-year coverage of the comprehensive ratio analysis extended to three years
- Revised Focus on Business Practice box on performance measurement and management compensation

Online Solutions for Every Learning Style

South-Western, a division of Cengage Learning, offers a vast array of online solutions to suit your course and your students' learning styles. Choose the product that best meets your classroom needs and course goals. Please check with your sales representative for more details and ordering information.

CengageNOW™

CengageNOW for Needles/Powers *Financial and Managerial Accounting*, 9e is a powerful and fully integrated online teaching and learning system that provides you with flexibility and control. This complete digital solution offers a comprehensive set of digital tools to power your course. CengageNOW offers the following:

- Homework, including algorithmic variations
- Integrated e-book
- Personalized study plans, which include a variety of multimedia assets (from exercise demonstrations to videos to iPod content) for students as they master the chapter materials
- Assessment options, including the full test bank and algorithmic variations
- Reporting capability based on AACSB, AICPA, and IMA competencies and standards
- Course Management tools, including grade book
- WebCT and Blackboard Integration

Visit www.cengage.com/tlc for more information.

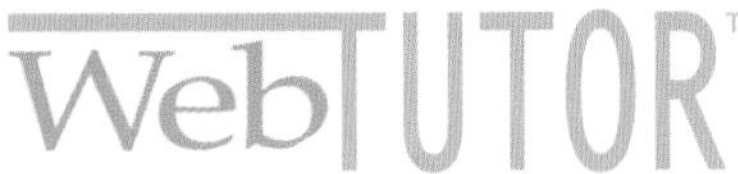

WebTutor™ on Blackboard® and WebCT™

WebTutor™ is available packaged with Needles/Powers *Financial and Managerial Accounting*, 9e or for individual student purchase. Jump-start your course and customize rich, text-specific content with your Course Management System.

- **Jump-start:** Simply load a WebTutor cartridge into your Course Management System.
- **Customize content:** Easily blend, add, edit, reorganize, or delete content. Content includes media assets, quizzing, test bank, web links, discussion topics, interactive games and exercises, and more.

Visit www.cengage.com/webtutor for more information.

Teaching Tools for Instructors

- **Instructor's Resource CD-ROM:** Included on this CD set are the key supplements designed to aid instructors, including the Solutions Manual, ExamView Test Bank, Word Test Bank, and Lecture PowerPoint slides.
- **Solutions Manual:** The Solutions Manual contains answers to all exercises, problems, and activities that appear in the text. As always, the solutions are author-written and verified multiple times for numerical accuracy and consistency with the core text.
- **ExamView® Pro Testing Software:** This intuitive software allows you to easily customize exams, practice tests, and tutorials and deliver them over a network, on the Internet, or in printed form. In addition, ExamView comes with searching capabilities that make sorting the wealth of questions from the printed test bank easy. The software and files are found on the IRCD.
- **Lecture PowerPoint® Slides:** Instructors will have access to PowerPoint slides online and on the IRCD. These slides are conveniently designed around learning objectives for partial chapter teaching and include art for dynamic presentations. There are also lecture outline slides for each chapter for those instructors who prefer them.
- **Instructor's Companion Website:** The instructor website contains a variety of resources for instructors, including the Instructor's Resource Manual (which has chapter planning matrices, chapter resource materials and outlines, chapter reviews, difficulty and time charts, etc.), and PowerPoint slides. www.cengage.com/accounting/needles

- **Klooster & Allen's General Ledger Software:** Prepared by Dale Klooster and Warren Allen, this best-selling, educational, general ledger package introduces students to the world of computerized accounting through a more intuitive, user-friendly system than the commercial software they will use in the future. In addition, students have access to general ledger files with information based on problems from the textbook and practice sets. This context allows them to see the difference between manual and computerized accounting systems firsthand. Also, the program is enhanced with a problem checker that enables students to determine if their entries are correct. Klooster & Allen emulates commercial general ledger packages more closely than other educational packages. Problems that can be used with Klooster/Allen are highlighted by an icon. The Inspector Files found on the IRCD allow instructors to grade students' work. A free Network Version is available to schools whose students purchase Klooster/Allen's General Ledger Software.

Learning Resources for Students

CengageNOW™

CengageNOW for Needles/Powers *Financial and Managerial Accounting*, 9e is a powerful and fully integrated online teaching and learning system that provides you with flexibility and control. This complete digital solution offers a comprehensive set of digital tools to power your course. CengageNOW offers the following:

- Homework, including algorithmic variations
- Integrated e-book
- Personalized study plans, which include a variety of multimedia assets (from exercise demonstrations to videos to iPod content) for students as they master the chapter materials
- Assessment options, including the full test bank and algorithmic variations
- Reporting capability based on AACSB, AICPA, and IMA competencies and standards
- Course Management tools, including grade book
- WebCT and Blackboard Integration

Visit www.cengage.com/tlc for more information.

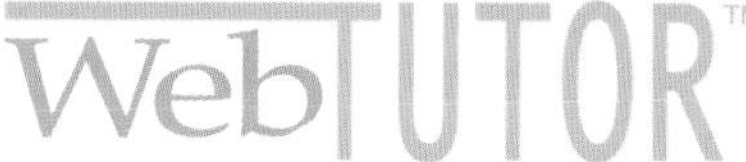

WebTutor™ on Blackboard® and WebCT™

- WebTutor™ is available packaged with Needles/Powers *Financial and Managerial Accounting*, 9e or for individual student purchase. Jump-start your course and customize rich, text-specific content with your Course Management System.
- **Jump-start:** Simply load a WebTutor cartridge into your Course Management System.
- **Customize content:** Easily blend, add, edit, reorganize, or delete content. Content includes media assets, quizzing, test bank, web links, discussion topics, interactive games and exercises, and more.

Visit www.cengage.com/webtutor for more information.

Klooster & Allen's General Ledger Software: This best-selling, educational, general ledger software package introduces you to the world of computerized accounting through a more intuitive, user-friendly system than the commercial software you'll use in the future. Also, the program is enhanced with a problem checker that provides feedback on selected activities and emulates commercial general ledger packages more closely than other educational packages. Problems that can be used with Klooster/Allen are highlighted by an icon.

Working Papers (Printed): A set of preformatted pages allow students to more easily work end-of-chapter problems and journal entries.

Student CD-ROM for Peachtree®: You will have access to Peachtree so you can familiarize yourself with computerized accounting systems used in the real world. You will gain experience from working with actual software, which will make you more desirable as a potential employee.

Electronic Working Papers in Excel® Passkey Access (for sale online): Students can now work end-of-chapter assignments electronically in Excel with easy-to-follow, preformatted worksheets. This option is available via an online download with a passkey.

Companion Website: The student website contains a variety of educational resources for students, including online quizzing, the Glossary, Flashcards, and Learning Objectives.

www.cengage.com/accounting/needles

Acknowledgements

A successful textbook is a collaborative effort. We are grateful to the many professors, other professional colleagues, and students who have taught and studied from our book, and we thank all of them for their constructive comments. In the space available, we cannot possibly mention everyone who has been helpful, but we do want to recognize those who made special contributions to our efforts in preparing the eleventh edition of *Financial and Managerial Accounting.*

We wish to express deep appreciation to colleagues at DePaul University, who have been extremely supportive and encouraging.

Very important to the quality of this book are our proofreaders, Margaret Kearney and Cathy Larson, to whom we give special thanks. We also appreciate the support of our Supervising Development Editor, Katie Yanos; Executive Editor, Sharon Oblinger; Senior Marketing Manager, Kristen Hurd; and Content Project Manager, Darrell Frye.

Others who have had a major impact on this book through their reviews, suggestions, and participation in surveys, interviews, and focus groups are listed below. We cannot begin to say how grateful we are for the feedback from the many instructors who have generously shared their responses and teaching experiences with us.

Daneen Adams, Santa Fe College
Sidney Askew, Borough of Manhattan Community College
Nancy Atwater, College of St. Scholastica
Algis Backaitis, Wayne County Community College
Abdul Baten, Northern Virginia Community College
Robert Beebe, Morrisville State College
Teri Bernstein, Santa Monica College
Martin Bertisch, York College
Tes Bireda, Hillsborough Community College
James Bryant, Catonsville Community College
Earl Butler, Broward Community College
Lloyd Carroll, Borough of Manhattan Community College
Stanley Carroll, New York City College of Technology
Roy Carson, Anne Arundel Community College
Janet Caruso, Nassau Community College
Sandra Cereola, Winthrop University
James J. Chimenti, Jamestown Community College
Carolyn Christesen, SUNY Westchester Community College
Stan Chu, Borough of Manhattan Community College
Jay Cohen, Oakton Community College
Sandra Cohen, Columbia College
Scott Collins, The Pennsylvania State University
Joan Cook, Milwaukee Area Tech College—Downtown
Barry Cooper, Borough of Manhattan Community College
Michael Cornick, Winthrop University
Robert Davis, Canisius College
Ron Deaton, Grays Harbor College
Jim Delisa, Highline Community College
Tim Dempsey, DeVry College of Technology

Vern Disney, University of South Carolina Sumter
Eileen Eichler, Farmingdale State College
Mary Ewanechko, Monroe Community College
Cliff Frederickson, Grays Harbor College
John Gabelman, Columbus State Community College
Lucille Genduso, Kaplan University
Nashwa George, Berkeley
Rom Gilbert, Santa Fe College
Janet Grange, Chicago State University
Tom Grant, Kutztown
Tim Griffin, Hillsborough Community College—Ybor City Campus
Sara Harris, Arapahoe Community College
Lori Hatchell, Aims Community College
Roger Hehman, Raymond Walters College/University of Cincinnati
Sueann Hely, West Kentucky Community & Technical College
Many Hernandez, Borough of Manhattan Community College
Michele Hill, Schoolcraft College
Cindy Hinz, Jamestown Community College
Jackie Holloway, National Park Community College
Phillip Imel, Southwest Virginia Community College
Jeff Jackson, San Jacinto College
Irene Joanette-Gallio, Western Nevada Community College
Vicki Jobst, Benedictine University
Doug Johnson, Southwest Community College
Jeff Kahn, Woodbury University
John Karayan, Woodbury University
Miriam Keller-Perkins, University of California-Berkeley
Randy Kidd, Longview Community College
David Knight, Borough of Manhattan Community College
Emil Koren, Saint Leo University
Bill Lasher, Jamestown Business College
Jennifer LeSure, Ivy Tech State College
Archish Maharaja, Point Park University
Harvey Man, Borough of Manhattan Community College
Robert Maxwell, College Of The Canyons
Stuart McCrary, Northwestern University
Noel McKeon, Florida Community College—Jacksonville
Terri Meta, Seminole Community College
Roger Moore, Arkansas State University—Beebe
Carol Murphy, Quinsigamond Community College
Carl Muzio, Saint John's University
Mary Beth Nelson, North Shore Community College
Andreas Nicolaou, Bowling Green State University
Patricia Diane Nipper, Southside Virginia Community College
Tim Nygaard, Madisonville Community College
Susan L. Pallas, Southeast Community College
Clarence Perkins, Bronx Community College
Janet Pitera, Broome Community College
Eric Platt, Saint John's University
Shirley Powell, Arkansas State University—Beebe
LaVonda Ramey, Schoolcraft College
Michelle Randall, Schoolcraft College
Eric Rothenburg, Kingsborough Community College
Rosemarie Ruiz, York College—CUNY

Michael Schaefer, Blinn College
Sarah Shepard, West Hills College Coalinga
Linda Sherman, Walla Walla Community College
Deborah Stephenson, Winston-Salem State University
Ira Stolzenberg, SUNY—Old Westbury
David Swarts, Clinton Community College
Linda Tarrago, Hillsborough Community College—Main Campus
Thomas Thompson, Savannah Technical College
Peter Vander Weyst, Edmonds Community College Lynnwood
Dale Walker, Arkansas State University—Beebe
Doris Warmflash, Westchester Community College
Wanda Watson, San Jacinto College—Central
Andy Williams, Edmonds Community College—Lynnwood
Josh Wolfson, Borough of Manhattan Community College
Paul Woodward, Santa Fe College
Allen Wright, Hillsborough Community College—Main Campus
Jian Zhou, SUNY at Binghamton

ABOUT THE AUTHORS

Belverd E. Needles, Jr., Ph.D., C.P.A., C.M.A.
DePaul University

Belverd Needles is an internationally recognized expert in accounting education. He has published in leading journals and is the author or editor of more than 20 books and monographs. His current research relates to international financial reporting, performance measurement, and corporate governance of high-performance companies in the United States, Europe, India, and Australia. His textbooks are used throughout the world and have received many awards, including the 2008 McGuffey Award from the Text and Academic Authors Association. Dr. Needles was named Educator of the Year by the American Institute of CPAs, Accountant of the Year for Education by the national honorary society Beta Alpha Psi, and Outstanding International Accounting Educator by the American Accounting Association. Among the numerous other awards he has received are the Excellence in Teaching Award from DePaul University and the Illinois CPA Society's Outstanding Educator Award and Life-Time Achievement Award. Active in many academic and professional organizations, he has served as the U.S. representative on several international accounting committees, including the Education Committee of the International Federation of Accountants (IFAC). He is currently vice president of education of the American Accounting Association.

Marian Powers, Ph.D.
Northwestern University

Internationally recognized as a dynamic teacher in executive education, Marian Powers specializes in teaching managers how to read and understand financial reports, including the impact that international financial reporting standards have on their companies. More than 1,000 executives per year from countries throughout the world, including France, the Czech Republic, Australia, India, China, and Brazil, attend her classes. She has taught at the Kellogg's Allen Center for Executive Education at Northwestern University since 1987 and at the Center for Corporate Financial Leadership since 2002. Dr. Powers's research on international financial reporting, performance measurement, and corporate governance has been published in leading journals, among them *The Accounting Review; The International Journal of Accounting; Issues in Accounting Education; The Journal of Accountancy; The Journal of Business, Finance and Accounting;* and *Financial Management.* She has also coauthored three interactive multimedia software products: Fingraph Financial Analyst™ (financial analysis software); Financial Analysis and Decision Making, a goal-based learning simulation focused on interpreting financial reports; and Introduction to Financial Accounting, a goal-based simulation that uses the Financial Consequences Model to introduce financial accounting and financial statements to those unfamiliar with accounting. Dr. Powers is a member of the American Accounting Association, European Accounting Association, International Association of Accounting Education and Research, and Illinois CPA Society. She currently serves on the board of directors of the Illinois CPA Society and the board of the CPA Endowment Fund of Illinois. She has served as vice president of Programs and secretary of the Educational Foundation.

Susan V. Crosson,
Santa Fe College

Susan V. Crosson is the accounting program coordinator and a professor of accounting at Santa Fe College, Gainesville, FL. Susan has also enjoyed teaching at the University of Florida, Washington University in St. Louis, University of Oklahoma, Johnson County Community College in Kansas, and Kansas City Kansas Community College. She is known for her innovative application of pedagogical strategies online and in the classroom. She is a recipient of the Outstanding Educator Award from the American Accounting Association's Two Year College Section, an Institute of Management Accountants' Faculty Development Grant to blend technology into the classroom, the Florida Association of Community Colleges Professor of the Year Award for Instructional Excellence, and the University of Oklahoma's Halliburton Education Award for Excellence. Susan is active in many academic and professional organizations. She served in the American Institute of CPA Pre-certification Education Executive Committee and is on the Florida Institute of CPAs Relations with Accounting Educators committee and the Florida Association of Accounting Educators Steering Committee. She has served as the American Accounting Association's Vice President for Sections and Regions and as a council member-at-large, chairperson of the Membership Committee, and was chairperson of the Two-Year Accounting Section. Previously she served as chairperson of the Florida Institute of CPAs Accounting Careers and Education Committee and was chair of the Florida Institute of CPAs Relations with Accounting Educators Committee. Susan was on the American Institute of CPAs' Core Competencies Best Practices Task Force also. Susan co-authors accounting textbooks for Cengage Learning: *Principles of Accounting*, *Financial and Managerial Accounting*, and *Managerial Accounting* with Bel Needles and Marian Powers. Susan holds a BBA in Economics and Accounting from Southern Methodist University and a MS in Accounting from Texas Tech University.

Financial and Managerial Accounting

NINTH EDITION

CHAPTER

1

Uses of Accounting Information and the Financial Statements

Focus on Financial Statements

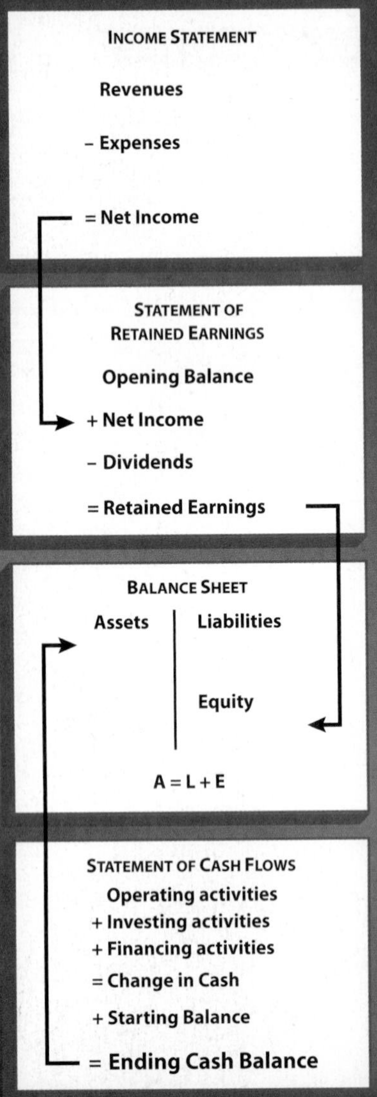

INCOME STATEMENT

Revenues

− Expenses

= Net Income

STATEMENT OF RETAINED EARNINGS

Opening Balance

+ Net Income

− Dividends

= Retained Earnings

BALANCE SHEET

Assets	Liabilities
	Equity

A = L + E

STATEMENT OF CASH FLOWS

Operating activities

+ Investing activities

+ Financing activities

= Change in Cash

+ Starting Balance

= Ending Cash Balance

Although each financial statement gives a unique view of a company's results, all four are interrelated.

Today, more people than ever before recognize the importance of accounting information to a business, its owners, its employees, its lenders, and the financial markets. In this chapter, we discuss the importance of ethical financial reporting, the uses and users of accounting information, and the financial statements that accountants prepare. We end the chapter with a discussion of generally accepted accounting principles.

LEARNING OBJECTIVES

LO1 **Define *accounting* and describe its role in making informed decisions, identify business goals and activities, and explain the importance of ethics in accounting.** (pp. 4–9)

LO2 **Identify the users of accounting information.** (pp. 10–13)

LO3 **Explain the importance of business transactions, money measure, and separate entity.** (pp. 13–15)

LO4 **Describe the characteristics of a corporation.** (pp. 15–18)

LO5 **Define *financial position,* and state the accounting equation.** (pp. 19–21)

LO6 **Identify the four basic financial statements.** (pp. 21–26)

LO7 **Explain how generally accepted accounting principles (GAAP) relate to financial statements and the independent CPA's report, and identify the organizations that influence GAAP.** (pp. 26–29)

DECISION POINT ▶ A USER'S FOCUS CVS CAREMARK

CVS Caremark operates a chain of more than 6,000 stores. Its pharmacies fill more than 1 billion prescriptions each year. Over the last five years, CVS has opened or purchased 2,100 new stores and more than doubled its sales and profits. This performance places it among the fastest-growing retail companies.

Why is CVS considered successful? Customers give the company high marks because of the quality of the products that it sells and the large selection and good service that its stores offer. Investment firms and others with a stake in CVS evaluate the company's success in financial terms.

Whether a company is large or small, the same financial measures are used to evaluate its management and to compare it with other companies. In this chapter, as you learn more about accounting and the business environment, you will become familiar with these financial measures.

- ▶ Is CVS meeting its goal of profitability?
- ▶ As a manager at CVS, what financial knowledge would you need to measure progress toward the company's goals?
- ▶ As a potential investor or creditor, what financial knowledge would you need to evaluate CVS's financial performance?

Accounting as an Information System

LO1 Define *accounting* and describe its role in making informed decisions, identify business goals and activities, and explain the importance of ethics in accounting.

Accounting is an information system that measures, processes, and communicates financial information about an economic entity.[1] An economic entity is a unit that exists independently, such as a business, a hospital, or a governmental body. Although the central focus of this book is on business entities, we include other economic units at appropriate points in the text and in the end-of-chapter assignments.

Accountants focus on the needs of decision makers who use financial information, whether those decision makers are inside or outside a business or other economic entity. Accountants provide a vital service by supplying the information decision makers need to make "reasoned choices among alternative uses of scarce resources in the conduct of business and economic activities."[2] As shown in Figure 1-1, accounting is a link between business activities and decision makers.

1. Accounting measures business activities by recording data about them for future use.
2. The data are stored until needed and then processed to become useful information.
3. The information is communicated through reports to decision makers.

In other words, data about business activities are the input to the accounting system, and useful information for decision makers is the output.

Business Goals and Activities

A **business** is an economic unit that aims to sell goods and services to customers at prices that will provide an adequate return to its owners. The list that follows contains the names of some well-known businesses and the principal goods or services that they sell.

FIGURE 1-1
Accounting as an Information System

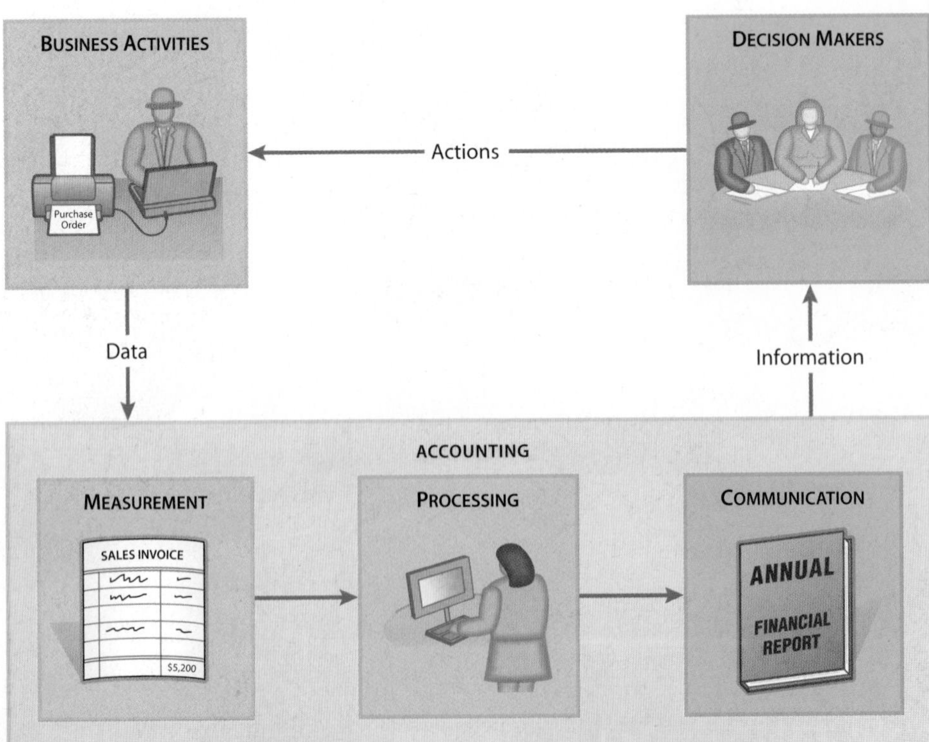

Wal-Mart Corp.	Comprehensive discount store
Reebok International Ltd.	Athletic footwear and clothing
Best Buy Co.	Consumer electronics, personal computers
Wendy's International Inc.	Food service
Starbucks Corp.	Coffee
Southwest Airlines Co.	Passenger airline

Despite their differences, these businesses have similar goals and engage in similar activities, as shown in Figure 1-2.

The two major goals of all businesses are profitability and liquidity.

- **Profitability** is the ability to earn enough income to attract and hold investment capital.
- **Liquidity** is the ability to have enough cash to pay debts when they are due.

> **Study Note**
> Users of accounting information focus on a company's profitability and liquidity. Thus, more than one measure of performance is of interest to them. For example, lenders are concerned primarily with cash flow, and owners are concerned with earnings and dividends.

For example, **Toyota** may meet the goal of profitability by selling many cars at a price that earns a profit, but if its customers do not pay for their cars quickly enough to enable Toyota to pay its suppliers and employees, the company may fail to meet the goal of liquidity. If a company is to survive and be successful, it must meet both goals.

All businesses, whether they are retailers, manufacturers, or service providers, pursue their goals by engaging in operating, investing, and financing activities.

- **Operating activities** include selling goods and services to customers, employing managers and workers, buying and producing goods and services, and paying taxes.
- **Investing activities** involve spending the capital a company receives in productive ways that will help it achieve its objectives. These activities include buying land, buildings, equipment, and other resources that are needed to operate the business and selling them when they are no longer needed.

FIGURE 1-2
Business Goals and Activities

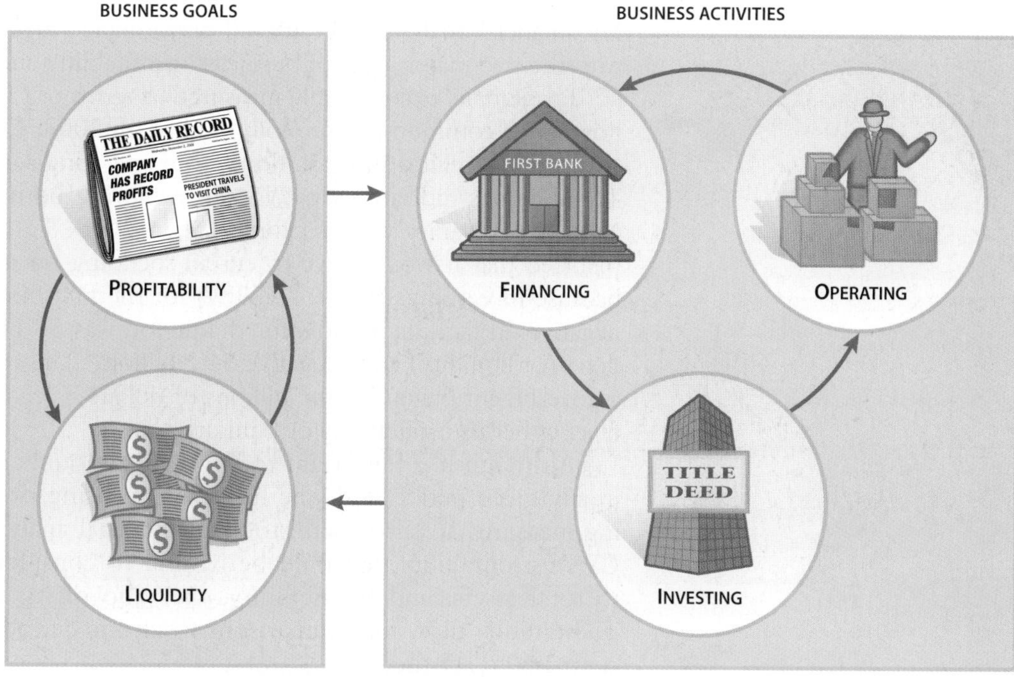

FOCUS ON BUSINESS PRACTICE

What Does CVS Have to Say About Itself?

In its annual report, **CVS's** management describes the company's goals in meeting the major business objectives:

- Liquidity: "Along with our strong free cash flow generation, . . . we faced virtually none of the liquidity issues that sent shockwaves across so much of the business landscape in 2008. CVS Caremark has a solid balance sheet and an investment grade credit rating, and we maintain a commercial paper program currently backed by $4 billion in committed bank facilities."
- Profitability: "CVS Caremark generated record revenue and earnings, achieved industry-leading same-store sales growth, and continued to gain share across our businesses."[3]

CVS's main business activities are shown at the right.

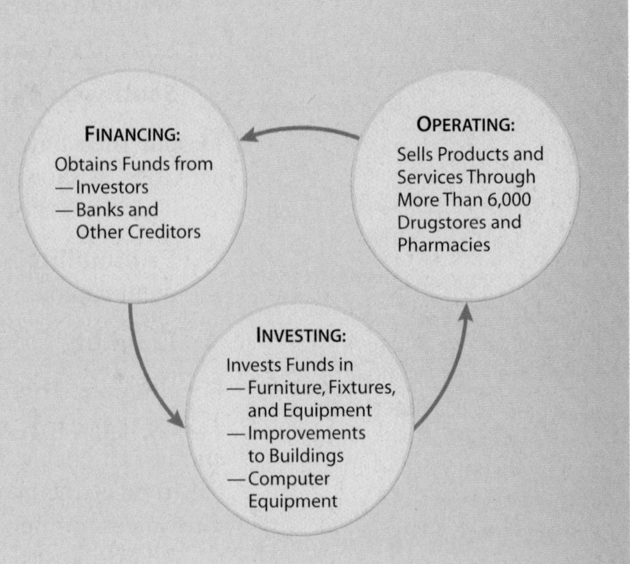

- **Financing activities** involve obtaining adequate funds, or capital, to begin operations and to continue operating. These activities include obtaining capital from creditors, such as banks and suppliers, and from owners. They also include repaying creditors and paying a return to the owners.

An important function of accounting is to provide **performance measures**, which indicate whether managers are achieving their business goals and whether the business activities are well managed. The evaluation and interpretation of financial statements and related performance measures is called **financial analysis**. For financial analysis to be useful, performance measures must be well aligned with the two major goals of business—profitability and liquidity.

Profitability is commonly measured in terms of earnings or income, and cash flows are a common measure of liquidity. In 2008, **CVS** had earnings or income of $3,212.1 million and cash flows from operating activities of $3,947.1 million. These figures indicate that CVS was achieving both profitability and liquidity. Not all companies were so fortunate in 2008. For instance, **General Motors** reported that it would have to curtail spending on new auto and truck models because its earnings (or profitability) for the first nine months of the year were negative; in fact, its net loss for the period was $3 billion. Even worse, its cash flows (or liquidity) were negative $4.2 billion.[4] This result led to bankruptcy and a government bailout in the billions of dollars. Clearly, General Motors did not meet either its profitability or liquidity goals.

Although it is important to know the amounts of earnings and cash flows in any given period and whether they are rising or falling, ratios of accounting measures are also useful tools of financial analysis. For example, to assess CVS's profitability, it would be helpful to consider the ratio of its earnings to total assets, and for liquidity, the ratio of its cash flows to total assets. These ratios allow for comparisons from one period to another and from one company to another.

FOCUS ON BUSINESS PRACTICE

Cash Bonuses Depend on Accounting Numbers!

Nearly all businesses use the amounts reported in their financial statements as a basis for rewarding management. Because managers act to achieve these accounting measures, selecting measures that are not easily manipulated is important. Equally important is maintaining a balance of measures that reflect the goals of profitability and liquidity.[5]

Financial and Management Accounting

Accounting's role of assisting decision makers by measuring, processing, and communicating financial information is usually divided into the categories of management accounting and financial accounting. Although the functions of management accounting and financial accounting overlap, the two can be distinguished by the principal users of the information that they provide.

Management accounting provides *internal* decision makers who are charged with achieving the goals of profitability and liquidity with information about operating, investing, and financing activities. Managers and employees who conduct the activities of the business need information that tells them how they have done in the past and what they can expect in the future. For example, **The Gap**, a retail clothing business, needs an operating report on each outlet that tells how much was sold at that outlet and what costs were incurred, and it needs a budget for each outlet that projects the sales and costs for the next year.

Financial accounting generates reports and communicates them to *external* decision makers so they can evaluate how well the business has achieved its goals. These reports are called **financial statements**. **CVS**, whose stock is traded on the New York Stock Exchange, sends its financial statements to its owners (called *stockholders*), its banks and other creditors, and government regulators. Financial statements report directly on the goals of profitability and liquidity and are used extensively both inside and outside a business to evaluate the business's success. It is important for every person involved with a business to understand financial statements. They are a central feature of accounting and a primary focus of this book.

Processing Accounting Information

It is important to distinguish accounting from the ways in which accounting information is processed by bookkeeping, computers, and management information systems.

Study Note

Computerized accounting information is only as reliable and useful as the data that go into the system. The accountant must have a thorough understanding of the concepts that underlie accounting to ensure the data's reliability and usefulness.

Accounting includes the design of an information system that meets users' needs, and its major goals are the analysis, interpretation, and use of information. **Bookkeeping**, on the other hand, is mechanical and repetitive; it is the process of recording financial transactions and keeping financial records. It is a small—but important—part of accounting.

Today, computers collect, organize, and communicate vast amounts of information with great speed. They can perform both routine bookkeeping chores and complex calculations. Accountants were among the earliest and most enthusiastic users of computers, and they now use computers in all aspects of their work.

Computers make it possible to create a management information system to organize a business's many information needs. A **management information system (MIS)** consists of the interconnected subsystems that provide the

FOCUS ON BUSINESS PRACTICE

How Did Accounting Develop?

Accounting is a very old discipline. Forms of it have been essential to commerce for more than 5,000 years. Accounting, in a version close to what we know today, gained widespread use in the 1400s, especially in Italy, where it was instrumental in the development of shipping, trade, construction, and other forms of commerce. This system of double-entry bookkeeping was documented by the famous Italian mathematician, scholar, and philosopher Fra Luca Pacioli. In 1494, Pacioli published his most important work, *Summa de Arithmetica, Geometrica, Proportioni et Proportionalita*, which contained a detailed description of accounting as practiced in that age. This book became the most widely read book on mathematics in Italy and firmly established Pacioli as the "Father of Accounting."

information needed to run a business. The accounting information system is the most important subsystem because it plays the key role of managing the flow of economic data to all parts of a business and to interested parties outside the business.

Ethical Financial Reporting

Ethics is a code of conduct that applies to everyday life. It addresses the question of whether actions are right or wrong. Actions—whether ethical or unethical, right or wrong—are the product of individual decisions. Thus, when an organization acts unethically by using false advertising, cheating customers, polluting the environment, or treating employees unfairly, it is not the organization that is responsible—it is the members of management and other employees who have made a conscious decision to act in this manner.

Ethics is especially important in preparing financial reports because users of these reports must depend on the good faith of the people involved in their preparation. Users have no other assurance that the reports are accurate and fully disclose all relevant facts.

The intentional preparation of misleading financial statements is called **fraudulent financial reporting**.[6] It can result from the distortion of records (e.g., the manipulation of inventory records), falsified transactions (e.g., fictitious sales), or the misapplication of various accounting principles. There are a number of motives for fraudulent reporting—for instance, to cover up financial weakness in order to obtain a higher price when a company is sold, to meet the expectations of stockholders and financial analysts, or to obtain a loan. The incentive can also be personal gain, such as additional compensation, promotion, or avoidance of penalties for poor performance.

Whatever the motive for fraudulent financial reporting, it can have dire consequences, as the accounting scandals that erupted at **Enron Corporation** and **WorldCom** attest. Unethical financial reporting and accounting practices at those two major corporations caused thousands of people to lose their jobs, their investment incomes, and their pensions. They also resulted in prison sentences and fines for the corporate executives who were involved.

In 2002, Congress passed the **Sarbanes-Oxley Act** to regulate financial reporting and the accounting profession, among other things. This legislation ordered the Securities and Exchange Commission (SEC) to draw up rules requiring the chief executives and chief financial officers of all publicly traded U.S. companies to swear that, based on their knowledge, the quarterly statements and annual reports that their companies file with the SEC are accurate and complete. Violation can result in criminal penalties.

A company's management expresses its duty to ensure that financial reports are not false or misleading in the management report that appears in the company's annual report. For example, in its management report, **Target Corporation** makes the following statement:

> Management is responsible for the consistency, integrity and presentation of the information in the Annual Report.[7]

However, it is accountants, not management, who physically prepare and audit financial reports. To meet the high ethical standards of the accounting profession, they must apply accounting concepts in such a way as to present a fair view of a company's operations and financial position and to avoid misleading readers of their reports. Like the conduct of a company, the ethical conduct of a profession is a collection of individual actions. As a member of a profession, each accountant has a responsibility—not only to the profession but also to employers, clients, and society as a whole—to ensure that any report he or she prepares or audits provides accurate, reliable information.

The high regard that the public has historically had for the accounting profession is evidence that an overwhelming number of accountants have upheld the ethics of the profession. Even as the Enron and WorldCom scandals were making headlines, a Gallup Poll showed an increase of 28 percent in the accounting profession's reputation between 2002 and 2005, placing it among the most highly rated professions.[8]

Accountants and top managers are, of course, not the only people responsible for ethical financial reporting. Managers and employees at all levels must be conscious of their responsibility for providing accurate financial information to the people who rely on it.

STOP & APPLY >

Match the terms below with the definitions (some answers may be used more than once):

____ 1. Management accounting
____ 2. Liquidity
____ 3. Financial accounting
____ 4. Investing activities
____ 5. Operating activities
____ 6. Financing activities
____ 7. Profitability
____ 8. Fraudulent financial reporting

a. An unethical practice
b. A business goal
c. Engaged in by all businesses
d. Major function of accounting

SOLUTION

1. d; 2. b; 3. d; 4. c; 5. c; 6. c; 7. b; 8. a

Decision Makers: The Users of Accounting Information

LO2 Identify the users of accounting information.

As shown in Figure 1-3, the people who use accounting information to make decisions fall into three categories:

1. Those who manage a business
2. Those outside a business enterprise who have a direct financial interest in the business
3. Those who have an indirect financial interest in a business

These categories apply to governmental and not-for-profit organizations as well as to profit-oriented ventures.

Management

Management refers to the people who are responsible for operating a business and meeting its goals of profitability and liquidity. In a small business, management may consist solely of the owners. In a large business, managers must decide what to do, how to do it, and whether the results match their original plans. Successful managers consistently make the right decisions based on timely and valid information.

Study Note

Managers are internal users of accounting information.

To make good decisions, managers at **CVS** and other companies need answers to such questions as:

- What were the company's earnings during the past quarter?
- Is the rate of return to the owners adequate?
- Does the company have enough cash?
- Which products or services are most profitable?

Because so many key decisions are based on accounting data, management is one of the most important users of accounting information.

In its decision-making process, management performs functions that are essential to the operation of a business. The same basic functions must be performed in all businesses, and each requires accounting information on which to base decisions. The basic management functions are:

Financing the business—obtaining funds so that a company can begin and continue operating

FIGURE 1-3
The Users of Accounting Information

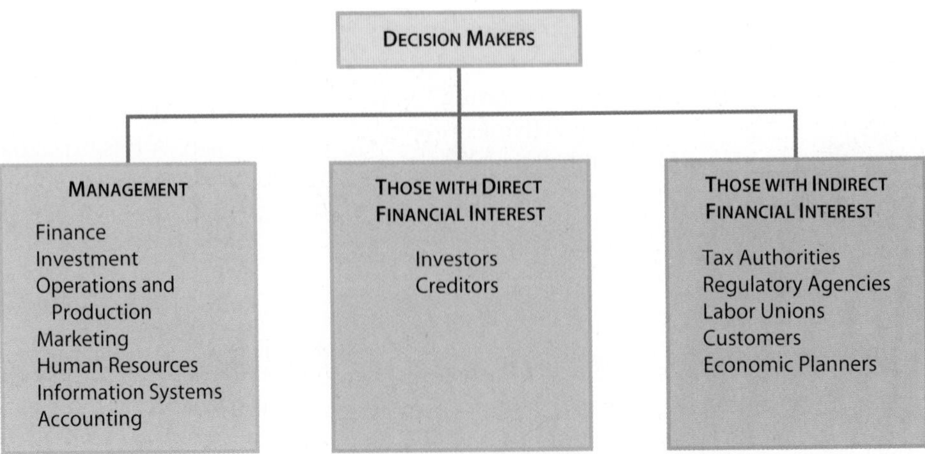

FOCUS ON BUSINESS PRACTICE

What Do CFOs Do?

According to a survey, the chief financial officer (CFO) is the "new business partner of the chief executive officer" (CEO). CFOs are increasingly required to take on responsibilities for strategic planning, mergers and acquisitions, and tasks involving international operations, and many of them are becoming CEOs of their companies. Those who do become CEOs are finding that "a financial background is invaluable when they're saddled with the responsibility of making big calls."[9]

Investing resources—investing assets in productive ways that support a company's goals

Producing goods and services—managing the production of goods and services

Marketing goods and services—overseeing how goods or services are advertised, sold, and distributed

Managing employees—overseeing the hiring, evaluation, and compensation of employees

Providing information to decision makers—gathering data about all aspects of a company's operations, organizing the data into usable information, and providing reports to managers and appropriate outside parties. Accounting plays a key role in this function.

Users with a Direct Financial Interest

Most businesses periodically publish a set of general-purpose financial statements with accompanying information that report their success in meeting the goals of profitability and liquidity. These statements show what has happened in the past, and they are important indicators of what will happen in the future. Many people outside the company carefully study these financial reports. The providers of capital in the form of investments in or loans to a business have a direct financial interest in its success and depend on the financial statements to evaluate how the business has performed. These important providers of capital are investors and creditors.

> **Study Note**
> The primary external users of accounting information are investors and creditors.

Investors Those, such as **CVS**'s stockholders, who invest or may invest in a business and acquire a part ownership in it are interested in its past success and its potential earnings. A thorough study of a company's financial statements helps potential investors judge the prospects for a profitable investment. After investing, they must continually review their commitment, again by examining the company's financial statements.

Creditors Most companies borrow money for both long- and short-term operating needs. Creditors, those who lend money or deliver goods and services before being paid, are interested mainly in whether a company will have the cash to pay interest charges and to repay the debt on time. They study a company's liquidity and cash flow as well as its profitability. Banks, finance companies, mortgage companies, securities firms, insurance firms, suppliers, and other lenders must analyze a company's financial position before they make a loan.

Users with an Indirect Financial Interest

In recent years, society as a whole, through governmental and public groups, has become one of the largest and most important users of accounting information. Users who need accounting information to make decisions on public issues include tax authorities, regulatory agencies, and various other groups.

Tax Authorities Government at every level is financed through the collection of taxes. Companies and individuals pay many kinds of taxes, including federal, state, and city income taxes; Social Security and other payroll taxes; excise taxes; and sales taxes. Each tax requires special tax returns and often a complex set of records as well.

Proper reporting is generally a matter of law and can be very complicated. The Internal Revenue Code, for instance, contains thousands of rules governing the preparation of the accounting information used in computing federal income taxes.

Regulatory Agencies Most companies must report periodically to one or more regulatory agencies at the federal, state, and local levels. For example, all publicly traded corporations must report periodically to the **Securities and Exchange Commission (SEC)**. This body, set up by Congress to protect the public, regulates the issuing, buying, and selling of stocks in the United States. Companies listed on a stock exchange also must meet the special reporting requirements of their exchange.

Other Groups Labor unions study the financial statements of corporations as part of preparing for contract negotiations; a company's income and costs often play an important role in these negotiations. Those who advise investors and creditors—such as financial analysts, brokers, underwriters, lawyers, economists, and the financial press—also have an indirect interest in the financial performance and prospects of a business. Consumer groups, customers, and the general public have become more concerned about the financing and earnings of corporations as well as about the effects that corporations have on inflation, the environment, social issues, and the quality of life. And economic planners—among them the President's Council of Economic Advisers and the Federal Reserve Board—use aggregated accounting information to set and evaluate economic policies and programs.

Governmental and Not-for-Profit Organizations

More than 30 percent of the U.S. economy is generated by governmental and not-for-profit organizations (hospitals, universities, professional organizations, and charities). The managers of these diverse entities perform the same functions as managers of businesses, and they therefore have the same need for accounting information and a knowledge of how to use it. Their functions include raising funds from investors, creditors, taxpayers, and donors and deploying scarce resources. They must also plan how to pay for operations and to repay creditors on a timely basis. In addition, they have an obligation to report their financial performance to legislators, boards, and donors, as well as to deal with tax authorities, regulators, and labor unions.

Although most of the examples that we present in this text focus on business enterprises, the same basic principles apply to governmental and not-for-profit organizations.

STOP & APPLY >

Match the terms on the left with the type of user of accounting information on the right (some answers may be used more than once):

____ 1. Tax authorities	a. Internal user
____ 2. Investors	b. Direct external user
____ 3. Management	c. Indirect user
____ 4. Creditors	
____ 5. Regulatory agencies	
____ 6. Labor unions and consumer groups	

SOLUTION

1. c; 2. b; 3. a; 4. b; 5. c; 6. c

Accounting Measurement

LO3 Explain the importance of business transactions, money measure, and separate entity.

In this section, we begin the study of the measurement aspects of accounting—that is, what accounting actually measures. To make an accounting measurement, the accountant must answer four basic questions:

1. What is measured?
2. When should the measurement be made?
3. What value should be placed on what is measured?
4. How should what is measured be classified?

Accountants in industry, professional associations, public accounting, government, and academic circles debate the answers to these questions constantly, and the answers change as new knowledge and practice require. But the basis of today's accounting practice rests on a number of widely accepted concepts and conventions, which are described in this book. We begin by focusing on the first question: What is measured? We discuss the other three questions (recognition, valuation, and classification) in the next chapter.

Every system must define what it measures, and accounting is no exception. Basically, financial accounting uses money to gauge the impact of business transactions on separate business entities.

Business Transactions

Business transactions are economic events that affect a business's financial position. Businesses can have hundreds or even thousands of transactions every day. These transactions are the raw material of accounting reports.

A transaction can be an exchange of value (a purchase, sale, payment, collection, or loan) between two or more parties. A transaction also can be an economic event that has the same effect as an exchange transaction but that does not involve an exchange. Some examples of "nonexchange" transactions are losses from fire, flood, explosion, and theft; physical wear and tear on machinery and equipment; and the day-by-day accumulation of interest.

To be recorded, a transaction must relate directly to a business entity. Suppose a customer buys toothpaste from **CVS** but has to buy shampoo from a competing store because CVS is out of shampoo. The transaction in which the toothpaste was sold is entered in CVS's records. However, the purchase of the shampoo from the competitor is not entered in CVS's records because even though it indirectly affects CVS economically, it does not involve a direct exchange of value between CVS and the customer.

Money Measure

Study Note

The common unit of measurement used in the United States for financial reporting purposes is the dollar.

All business transactions are recorded in terms of money. This concept is called **money measure**. Of course, nonfinancial information may also be recorded, but it is through the recording of monetary amounts that a business's transactions and activities are measured. Money is the only factor common to all business transactions, and thus it is the only unit of measure capable of producing financial data that can be compared.

The monetary unit a business uses depends on the country in which the business resides. For example, in the United States, the basic unit of money is the dollar. In Japan, it is the yen; in Europe, the euro; and in the United Kingdom, the pound. In international transactions, exchange rates must be used to translate from one currency to another. An **exchange rate** is the value of one currency in terms of another. For example, a British person purchasing goods from a U.S. company like **CVS** and paying in U.S. dollars must exchange British pounds for U.S. dollars before making payment. In effect, currencies are goods that can be bought and sold.

Table 1-1 illustrates the exchange rates for several currencies in dollars. It shows the exchange rate for British pounds as $1.63 per pound on a particular date. Like the prices of many goods, currency prices change daily according to supply and demand. For example, a year and a half earlier, the exchange rate for British pounds was $1.98. Although our discussion in this book focuses on dollars, some examples and assignments involve foreign currencies.

Separate Entity

Study Note

For accounting purposes, a business is always separate and distinct from its owners, creditors, and customers.

For accounting purposes, a business is a **separate entity**, distinct not only from its creditors and customers but also from its owners. It should have its own set of financial records, and its records and reports should refer only to its own affairs.

For example, Just Because Flowers Company should have a bank account separate from the account of Holly Sapp, the owner. Holly Sapp may own a home, a car, and other property, and she may have personal debts, but these are not the resources or debts of Just Because Flowers. Holly Sapp may own another business, say a stationery shop. If she does, she should have a completely separate set of records for each business.

TABLE 1-1
Examples of Foreign Exchange Rates

Country	Price in $ U.S.	Country	Price in $ U.S.
Australia (dollar)	0.82	Hong Kong (dollar)	0.13
Brazil (real)	0.53	Japan (yen)	0.0106
Britain (pound)	1.63	Mexico (peso)	0.077
Canada (dollar)	0.90	Russia (ruble)	0.03
Europe (euro)	1.41	Singapore (dollar)	0.69

Source: The Wall Street Journal, August 17, 2009.

STOP & APPLY >

Match the terms on the left with the type of user of accounting information on the right:

____ 1. Requires an exchange of value between two or more parties	a. Business transaction
____ 2. Requires a separate set of records for a business	b. Money measure
____ 3. An amount associated with a business transaction	c. Separate entity

SOLUTION

1\. a; 2. c; 3. b

The Corporate Form of Business

LO4 Describe the characteristics of a corporation.

The three basic forms of business enterprise are the sole proprietorship, the partnership, and the corporation. The characteristics of corporations make them very efficient in amassing capital, which enables them to grow extremely large. As Figure 1-4 shows, even though corporations are fewer in number than sole proprietorships and partnerships, they contribute much more to the U.S. economy in monetary terms. For example, in 2007, **ExxonMobil** generated more revenues than all but 30 of the world's countries. Because of the economic significance of corporations, this book emphasizes accounting for the corporate form of business.

Characteristics of Corporations, Sole Proprietorships, and Partnerships

A **sole proprietorship** is a business that is owned by one person. The owner takes all the profits or losses of the business and is liable for all its obligations. Sole

FIGURE 1-4
Number and Receipts of U.S. Proprietorships, Partnerships, and Corporations

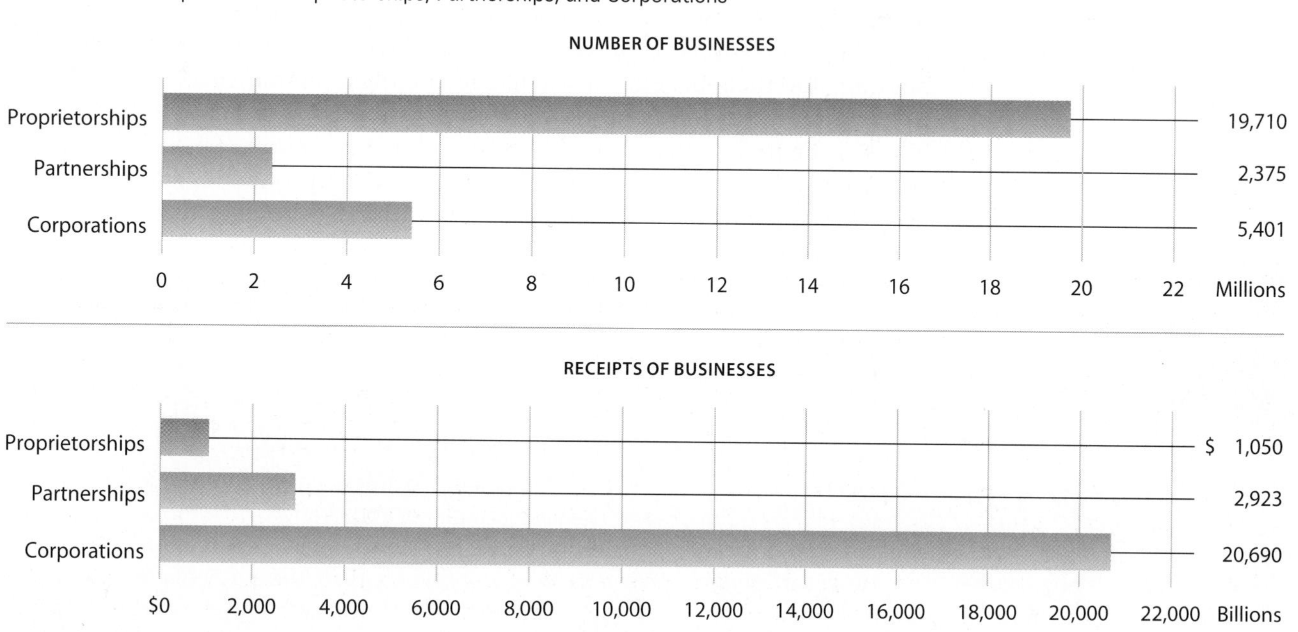

Source: U.S. Treasury Department, Internal Revenue Service, *Statistics of Income Bulletin*, Winter 2006.

This fashion merchandising operation is a partnership. Because it is a partnership, the owners share the profits and losses of the business, and their personal resources can be called on to pay the obligations of the business.

Courtesy of Neil Beckerman/Stone/Getty Images.

proprietorships represent the largest number of businesses in the United States, but typically they are the smallest in size.

A **partnership** is like a sole proprietorship in most ways, but it has two or more owners. The partners share the profits and losses of the business according to a prearranged formula. Generally, any partner can obligate the business to another party, and the personal resources of each partner can be called on to pay the obligations. A partnership must be dissolved if the ownership changes, as when a partner leaves or dies. If the business is to continue as a partnership after this occurs, a new partnership must be formed.

Study Note

A key disadvantage of a partnership is the unlimited liability of its owners. Unlimited liability can be avoided by organizing the business as a corporation or, in some states, by forming what is known as a limited liability partnership.

Both the sole proprietorship and the partnership are convenient ways of separating the owners' commercial activities from their personal activities. Legally, however, there is no economic separation between the owners and the businesses.

A **corporation**, on the other hand, is a business unit chartered by the state and legally separate from its owners (the *stockholders*). The stockholders, whose ownership is represented by shares of stock, do not directly control the corporation's operations. Instead, they elect a board of directors to run the corporation for their benefit. In exchange for their limited involvement in the corporation's operations, stockholders enjoy limited liability; that is, their risk of loss is limited to the amount they paid for their shares. Thus, stockholders are often willing to invest in risky, but potentially profitable, activities. Also, because stockholders can sell their shares without dissolving the corporation,

FOCUS ON BUSINESS PRACTICE

Are Most Corporations Big or Small Businesses?

Most people think of corporations as large national or global companies whose shares of stock are held by thousands of people and institutions. Indeed, corporations can be huge and have many stockholders. However, of the approximately 4 million corporations in the United States, only about 15,000 have stock that is publicly bought and sold. The vast majority of corporations are small businesses privately held by a few stockholders. Illinois alone has more than 250,000 corporations. Thus, the study of corporations is just as relevant to small businesses as it is to large ones.

the life of a corporation is unlimited and not subject to the whims or health of a proprietor or a partner.

Formation of a Corporation

To form a corporation, most states require individuals, called incorporators, to sign an application and file it with the proper state official. This application contains the **articles of incorporation**. If approved by the state, these articles, which form the company charter, become a contract between the state and the incorporators. The company is then authorized to do business as a corporation.

Organization of a Corporation

The authority to manage a corporation is delegated by its stockholders to a board of directors and by the board of directors to the corporation's officers (see Figure 1-5). That is, the stockholders elect a board of directors, which sets corporate policies and chooses the corporation's officers, who in turn carry out the corporate policies in their management of the business.

Stockholders A unit of ownership in a corporation is called a **share of stock**. The articles of incorporation state the maximum number of shares that a corporation is authorized to issue. The number of shares held by stockholders is the outstanding stock; this may be less than the number authorized in the articles of incorporation. To invest in a corporation, a stockholder transfers cash or other resources to the corporation. In return, the stockholder receives shares of stock representing a proportionate share of ownership in the corporation. Afterward, the stockholder may transfer the shares at will. Corporations may have more than one kind of stock, but in the first part of this book, we refer only to **common stock**—the most universal form of stock.

Board of Directors As noted, a corporation's board of directors decides on major business policies. Among the board's specific duties are authorizing contracts, setting executive salaries, and arranging major loans with banks. The declaration of dividends is also an important function of the board of directors. **Dividends** are distributions of resources, generally in the form of cash, to stockholders, and only the board of directors has the authority to declare them. Paying dividends is one way of rewarding stockholders for their investment when the corporation has been successful in earning a profit. (The other way is through a rise in the market value of the stock.) Although there is usually a delay of two or three weeks between the time the board declares a dividend and the date of the actual payment, we assume in the early chapters of this book that declaration and payment are made on the same day.

The composition of the board of directors varies from company to company, but generally it includes several officers of the corporation and several outsiders. The outsiders are called *independent directors* because they do not directly participate in managing the business.

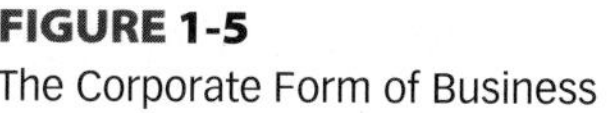

FIGURE 1-5
The Corporate Form of Business

Management Management, appointed by the board of directors to carry out corporate policies and run day-to-day operations, consists of the operating officers—generally the president, or chief executive officer; vice presidents; chief financial officer; and chief operating officer. Besides being responsible for running the business, management has the duty of reporting the financial results of its administration to the board of directors and the stockholders. Though management must, at a minimum, make a comprehensive annual report, it generally reports more often. The annual reports of large public corporations are available to the public. Excerpts from many of them appear throughout this book.

Corporate Governance

The financial scandals at **Enron**, **WorldCom**, and other companies highlighted the importance of **corporate governance**, which is the oversight of a corporation's management and ethics by its board of directors. Corporate governance is growing and is clearly in the best interests of a business. A survey of 124 corporations in 22 countries found that 78 percent of boards of directors had established ethical standards, a fourfold increase over a 10-year period. In addition, research has shown that, over time, companies with codes of ethics tend to have higher stock prices than those that have not adopted such codes.[10]

To strengthen corporate governance, a provision of the Sarbanes-Oxley Act required boards of directors to establish an **audit committee** made up of independent directors who have financial expertise. This provision was aimed at ensuring that boards of directors would be objective in evaluating management's performance. The audit committee is also responsible for engaging the corporation's independent auditors and reviewing their work. Another of the committee's functions is to ensure that adequate systems exist to safeguard the corporation's resources and that accounting records are reliable. In short, the audit committee is the front line of defense against fraudulent financial reporting.

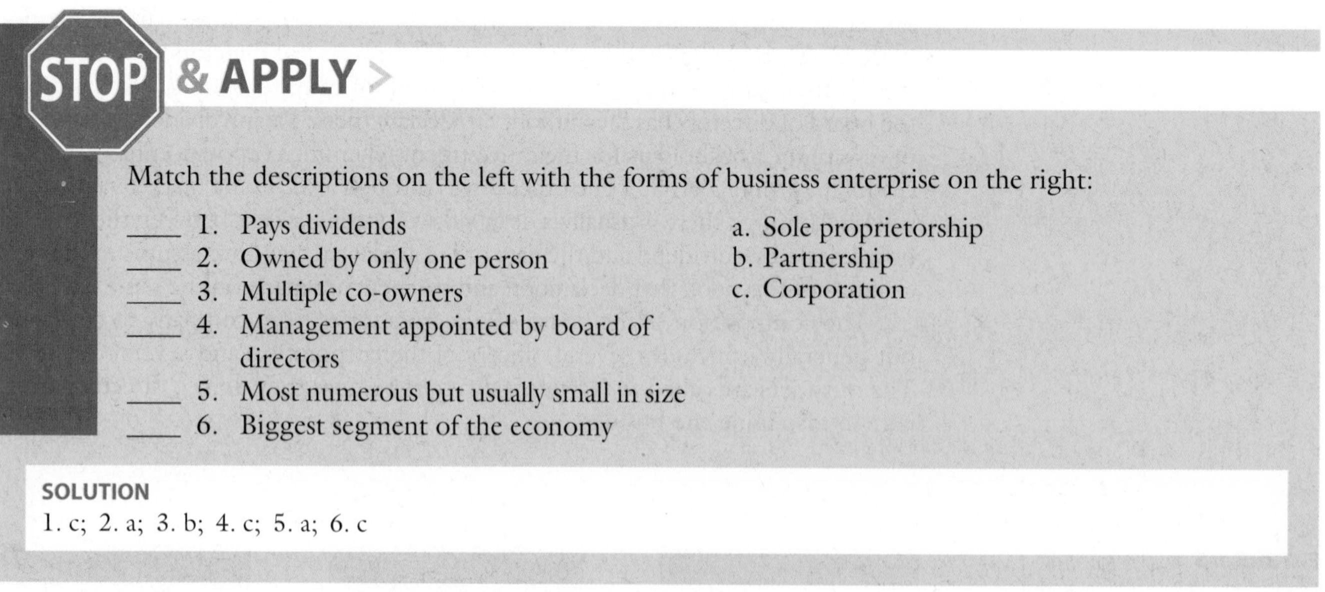

Match the descriptions on the left with the forms of business enterprise on the right:

____ 1. Pays dividends		a. Sole proprietorship
____ 2. Owned by only one person		b. Partnership
____ 3. Multiple co-owners		c. Corporation
____ 4. Management appointed by board of directors		
____ 5. Most numerous but usually small in size		
____ 6. Biggest segment of the economy		

SOLUTION

1. c; 2. a; 3. b; 4. c; 5. a; 6. c

Financial Position and the Accounting Equation

LO5 Define *financial position*, and state the accounting equation.

Financial position refers to a company's economic resources, such as cash, inventory, and buildings, and the claims against those resources at a particular time. Another term for claims is *equities*.

Every corporation has two types of equities: creditors' equities, such as bank loans, and stockholders' equity. (In the case of sole proprietorships and partnerships, which do not have stockholders, stockholders' equity is called *owners' equity*.) The sum of these equities equals a corporation's resources:

Economic Resources = Creditors' Equities + Stockholders' Equity

In accounting terminology, economic resources are called *assets*, and creditors' equities are called *liabilities*. So the equation can be written like this:

Assets = Liabilities + Stockholders' Equity

This equation is known as the **accounting equation**. The two sides of the equation must always be equal, or be "in balance," as shown in Figure 1-6. To evaluate the financial effects of business activities, it is important to understand their effects on this equation.

Assets

Assets are the economic resources of a company that are expected to benefit the company's future operations. Certain kinds of assets—for example, cash and money that customers owe to the company (called *accounts receivable*)—are monetary items. Other assets—inventories (goods held for sale), land, buildings, and equipment—are nonmonetary, physical items. Still other assets—the rights granted by patents, trademarks, and copyrights—are nonphysical.

Liabilities

Liabilities are a business's present obligations to pay cash, transfer assets, or provide services to other entities in the future. Among these obligations are amounts owed to suppliers for goods or services bought on credit (called *accounts payable*), borrowed money (e.g., money owed on bank loans), salaries and wages owed to employees, taxes owed to the government, and services to be performed.

As debts, liabilities are claims recognized by law. That is, the law gives creditors the right to force the sale of a company's assets if the company fails to pay its debts. Creditors have rights over stockholders and must be paid in full before the stockholders receive anything, even if payment of the debt uses up all the assets of the business.

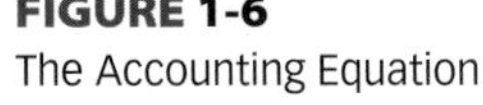

FIGURE 1-6
The Accounting Equation

Stockholders' Equity

Stockholders' equity (also called *shareholders' equity*) represents the claims of the owners of a corporation (the shareholders) to the assets of the business. Theoretically, it is what would be left over if all liabilities were paid, and it is sometimes said to equal **net assets** (also called *net worth*).

By rearranging the accounting equation, we can define stockholders' equity this way:

Stockholders' Equity = Assets − Liabilities

Stockholders' equity has two parts, contributed capital and retained earnings:

Stockholders' Equity = Contributed Capital + Retained Earnings

Contributed capital is the amount that stockholders invest in the business. As noted earlier, their ownership in the business is represented by shares of capital stock.

Typically, contributed capital is divided between par value and additional paid-in capital. **Par value** is an amount per share that when multiplied by the number of common shares becomes the corporation's common stock amount; it is the minimum amount that can be reported as contributed capital. When the value received is greater than par value, the amount over par value is called **additional paid-in capital**.*

Retained earnings represent stockholders' equity that has been generated by the business's income-producing activities and kept for use in the business. As you can see in Figure 1-7, retained earnings are affected by three kinds of transactions: revenues, expenses, and dividends.

Simply stated, **revenues** and **expenses** are the increases and decreases in stockholders' equity that result from operating a business. For example, the amount a customer pays (or agrees to pay in the future) to **CVS** in return for a product or service is a revenue to CVS. CVS's assets (cash or accounts receivable) increase, as does its stockholders' equity in those assets. On the other hand, the amount CVS must pay out (or agree to pay out) so that it can provide a product or service is an expense. In this case, the assets (cash) decrease or the liabilities (accounts payable) increase, and the stockholders' equity decreases.

Generally, a company is successful if its revenues exceed its expenses. When revenues exceed expenses, the difference is called **net income**. When expenses exceed revenues, the difference is called **net loss**. As noted earlier, dividends are distributions to stockholders of assets (usually cash) generated by past earnings. It is important not to confuse expenses and dividends, both of which reduce retained earnings. In summary, retained earnings are the accumulated net income (revenues − expenses) less dividends over the life of the business.

FIGURE 1-7
Three Types of Transactions That Affect Retained Earnings

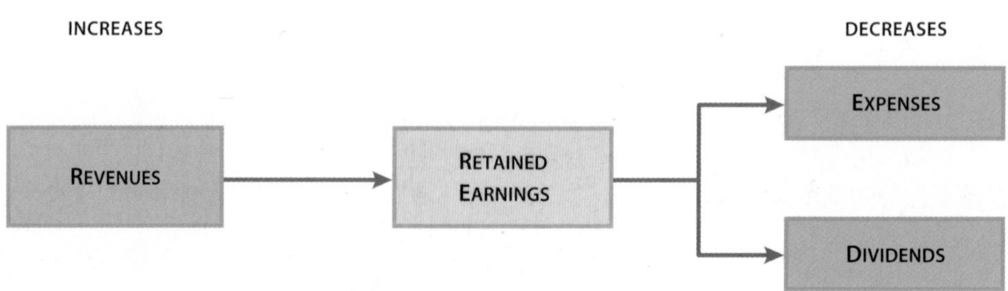

*We assume in the early chapters of this book that common stock is listed at par value.

STOP & APPLY >

Johnson Company had assets of $140,000 and liabilities of $60,000 at the beginning of the year and assets of $200,000 and liabilities of $70,000 at the end of the year. During the year, $20,000 was invested in the business, and dividends of $24,000 were paid. What amount of net income did the company earn during the year?

Beginning of the year				
Assets	=	Liabilities	+	Stockholders' Equity
$140,000	=	$60,000	+	**$ 80,000**
During year				
		Investment	+	20,000
		Dividends	−	(24,000)
		Net income		?
End of year				
$200,000	=	$70,000	+	**$130,000**

SOLUTION

Net income = $54,000

Start by finding the stockholders' equity at the beginning of the year. (Check: $140,000 − $60,000 = $80,000)

Then find the stockholders' equity at the end of the year. (Check: $200,000 − $70,000 = $130,000)

Then determine net income by calculating how the transactions during the year led to the stockholders' equity amount at the end of the year. (Check: $80,000 + $20,000 − $24,000 + $54,000 = $130,000)

Financial Statements

LO6 Identify the four basic financial statements.

Financial statements are the primary means of communicating important accounting information about a business to those who have an interest in the business. These statements are models of the business enterprise in that they show the business in financial terms. As is true of all models, however, financial statements are not perfect pictures of the real thing. Rather, they are the accountant's best effort to represent what is real. Four major financial statements are used to communicate accounting information about a business: the income statement, the statement of retained earnings, the balance sheet, and the statement of cash flows.

Study Note

Businesses use four basic financial statements to communicate financial information to decision makers.

Income Statement

The **income statement** summarizes the revenues earned and expenses incurred by a business over an accounting period (see Exhibit 1-1). Many people consider it the most important financial report because it shows whether a business achieved its profitability goal—that is, whether it earned an acceptable income. Exhibit 1-1 shows that Weiss Consultancy, Inc., had revenues of $14,000 earned from consulting fees. From this amount, total expenses of $5,600 were deducted (equipment rental expense of $2,800, wages expense of $1,600, and utilities expense of $1,200) to arrive at income before income taxes of $8,400. Income taxes of $1,200 were deducted to arrive at net income of

EXHIBIT 1-1
Income Statement for Weiss Consultancy, Inc.

Weiss Consultancy, Inc.
Income Statement
For the Month Ended December 31, 2010

Revenues		
Consulting fees		$14,000
Expenses		
Equipment rental expense	$2,800	
Wages expense	1,600	
Utilities expense	1,200	
Total expenses		5,600
Income before income taxes		$ 8,400
Income taxes expense		1,200
Net income		$ 7,200

$7,200. To show the period to which it applies, the statement is labeled "For the Month Ended December 31, 2010."

Statement of Retained Earnings

The **statement of retained earnings** shows the changes in retained earnings over an accounting period. In Exhibit 1-2, beginning retained earnings are zero because Weiss began operations in this accounting period. During the month, the company earned an income (as shown on the income statement) of $7,200. Deducted from this amount are the dividends for the month of $2,400, leaving an ending balance of $4,800 of earnings retained in the business.

The Balance Sheet

Study Note

The date on the balance sheet is a single date, whereas the dates on the other three statements cover a period of time, such as a month, quarter, or year.

The purpose of a **balance sheet** is to show the financial position of a business on a certain date, usually the end of the month or year (see Exhibit 1-3). For this reason, it often is called the *statement of financial position* and is dated as of a specific date.

The balance sheet presents a view of the business as the holder of resources, or assets, that are equal to the claims against those assets. The claims consist of

EXHIBIT 1-2
Statement of Retained Earnings for Weiss Consultancy, Inc.

Weiss Consultancy, Inc.
Statement of Retained Earnings
For the Month Ended December 31, 2010

Retained earnings, December 1, 2010	$ 0
Net income for the month	7,200
Subtotal	$7,200
Less dividends	2,400
Retained earnings, December 31, 2010	$4,800

EXHIBIT 1-3 Balance Sheet for Weiss Consultancy, Inc.

Weiss Consultancy, Inc. Balance Sheet December 31, 2010				
Assets		**Liabilities**		
Cash	$ 61,200	Accounts payable		$ 2,400
Accounts receivable	4,000			
Supplies	2,000	**Stockholders' Equity**		
Land	40,000	Common stock	$200,000	
Building	100,000	Retained earnings	4,800	
		Total stockholders' equity		204,800
Total assets	$207,200	Total liabilities and stockholders' equity		$207,200

the company's liabilities and the stockholders' equity in the company. Exhibit 1-3 shows that Weiss Consultancy, Inc. has several categories of assets, which total $207,200. These assets equal the total liabilities of $2,400 (accounts payable) plus the ending balance of stockholders' equity of $204,800. Notice that the amount of retained earnings on the balance sheet comes from the ending balance on the statement of retained earnings.

Statement of Cash Flows

Whereas the income statement focuses on a company's profitability, the **statement of cash flows** focuses on its liquidity (see Exhibit 1-4). **Cash flows** are the inflows and outflows of cash into and out of a business. Net cash flows are the difference between the inflows and outflows. As you can see in Exhibit 1-4, the statement of cash flows is organized according to the three major business activities described earlier in the chapter.

> **Study Note**
> The statement of cash flows explains the change in cash in terms of operating, investing, and financing activities over an accounting period. It provides valuable information that cannot be determined in an examination of the other financial statements.

- **Cash flows from operating activities:** The first section of Exhibit 1-4 shows the cash produced by business operations. Weiss's operating activities produced cash flows of $3,600 (liquidity) compared to net income of $7,200 (profitability). The company used cash to increase accounts receivable and supplies. However, by borrowing funds, it increased accounts payable. This is not a good trend, which Weiss should try to reverse in future months.
- **Cash flows from investing activities:** Weiss used cash to expand by purchasing land and a building.
- **Cash flows from financing activities:** Weiss obtained most of its cash from stockholders and paid a small dividend.

Overall, Weiss's had a net increase in cash of $61,200, due in large part to the investment by stockholders. In future months, Weiss must generate more cash through operations.

The statement of cash flows is related directly to the other three financial statements. Notice that net income comes from the income statement and that dividends come from the statement of retained earnings. The other items in the statement represent changes in the balance sheet accounts: accounts receivable,

EXHIBIT 1-4 Statement of Cash Flows for Weiss Consultancy, Inc.

Weiss Consultancy, Inc.
Statement of Cash Flows
For the Month Ended December 31, 2010

Cash flows from operating activities		
Net income		$ 7,200
Adjustments to reconcile net income to net cash flows from operating activities		
Increase in accounts receivable	($ 4,000)	
Increase in supplies	(2,000)	
Increase in accounts payable	2,400	(3,600)
Net cash flows from operating activities		$ 3,600
Cash flows from investing activities		
Purchase of land	($ 40,000)	
Purchase of building	(100,000)	
Net cash flows from investing activities		(140,000)
Cash flows from financing activities		
Issued common stock	$200,000	
Paid dividends	(2,400)	
Net cash flows from financing activities		197,600
Net increase (decrease) in cash		$ 61,200
Cash at beginning of month		0
Cash at end of month		$ 61,200

Note: Parentheses indicate a negative amount.

supplies, accounts payable, land, building, and common stock. Here we focus on the importance and overall structure of the statement. Its construction and use are discussed in a later chapter.

Relationships Among the Financial Statements

Study Note

Notice the sequence in which these financial statements must be prepared. The statement of retained earnings is a link between the income statement and the balance sheet, and the statement of cash flows is prepared last.

Exhibit 1-5 illustrates the relationships among the four financial statements by showing how they would appear for Weiss Consultancy, Inc. The period covered is the month of December 2010.

Notice the similarity of the headings at the top of each statement. Each identifies the company and the kind of statement. The income statement, the statement of retained earnings, and the statement of cash flows indicate the period to which they apply; the balance sheet gives the specific date to which it applies. Much of this book deals with developing, using, and interpreting more complete versions of these statements.

EXHIBIT 1-5 Income Statement, Statement of Retained Earnings, Balance Sheet, and Statement of Cash Flows for Weiss Consultancy, Inc.

Weiss Consultancy, Inc.
Income Statement
For the Month Ended December 31, 2010

Revenues		
Consulting fees		$14,000
Expenses		
Equipment rental expense	$2,800	
Wages expense	1,600	
Utilities expense	1,200	
Total expenses		5,600
Income before income taxes		$ 8,400
Income taxes expense		1,200
Net income		$ 7,200

Weiss Consultancy, Inc.
Statement of Retained Earnings
For the Month Ended December 31, 2010

Retained earnings, December 1, 2010	$ 0
Net income for the month	7,200
Subtotal	$ 7,200
Less dividends	2,400
Retained earnings, December 31, 2010	$ 4,800

Weiss Consultancy, Inc.
Balance Sheet
December 31, 2010

Assets		**Liabilities**	
Cash	$ 61,200	Accounts payable	$ 2,400
Accounts receivable	4,000		
Supplies	2,000	**Stockholders' Equity**	
Land	40,000	Common stock	$200,000
Building	100,000	Retained earnings	4,800
		Total stockholders' equity	$204,800
Total assets	$207,200	Total liabilities and stockholders' equity	$207,200

Weiss Consultancy, Inc.
Statement of Cash Flows
For the Month Ended December 31, 2010

Cash flows from operating activities		
Net income		$ 7,200
Adjustments to reconcile net income to net cash flows from operating activities		
Increase in accounts receivable	($ 4,000)	
Increase in supplies	(2,000)	
Increase in accounts payable	2,400	(3,600)
Net cash flows from operating activities		$ 3,600
Cash flows from investing activities		
Purchase of land	($ 40,000)	
Purchase of building	(100,000)	
Net cash flows from investing activities		(140,000)
Cash flows from financing activities		
Issued common stock	$200,000	
Paid dividends	(2,400)	
Net cash flows from financing activities		197,600
Net increase (decrease) in cash		$ 61,200
Cash at beginning of month		0
Cash at end of month		$ 61,200

Complete the following financial statements by determining the amounts that correspond to the letters. (Assume no new investments by stockholders.)

Income Statement

Revenues	$2,775
Expenses	(a)
Net income	$ (b)

Statement of Retained Earnings

Beginning balance	$7,250
Net income	(c)
Less dividends	500
Ending balance	$7,500

Balance Sheet

Total assets	$ (d)
Liabilities	$4,000
Stockholders' equity	
Common stock	5,000
Retained earnings	(e)
Total liabilities and stockholders' equity	$ (f)

SOLUTION

Net income links the income statement and the statement of retained earnings. The ending balance of retained earnings links the statement of retained earnings and the balance sheet.

Thus, start with (c), which must equal $750 (check: $7,250 + $750 − $500 = $7,500). Then, (b) equals (c), or $750. Thus, (a) must equal $2,025 (check: $2,775 − $2,025 = $750). Because (e) equals $7,500 (ending balance from the statement of retained earnings), (f) must equal $16,500 (check: $4,000 + $5,000 + $7,500 = $16,500). Now, (d) equals (f), or $16,500.

Generally Accepted Accounting Principles

LO7 Explain how generally accepted accounting principles (GAAP) relate to financial statements and the independent CPA's report, and identify the organizations that influence GAAP.

To ensure that financial statements are understandable to their users, a set of practices, called **generally accepted accounting principles (GAAP)**, has been developed to provide guidelines for financial accounting. "Generally accepted accounting principles encompass the conventions, rules, and procedures necessary to define accepted accounting practice at a particular time."[11] In other words, GAAP arise from wide agreement on the theory and practice of accounting at a particular time. These "principles" are not like the unchangeable laws of nature in chemistry or physics. They evolve to meet the needs of decision makers, and they change as circumstances change or as better methods are developed.

In this book, we present accounting practice, or GAAP, as it is today, and we try to explain the reasons or theory on which the practice is based. Both theory and practice are important to the study of accounting. However, accounting is a discipline that is always growing, changing, and improving. Just as years of research are necessary before a new surgical method or lifesaving drug can be

TABLE 1-2
Large International Certified Public Accounting Firms

Firm	Home Office	Some Major Clients
Deloitte & Touche	New York	General Motors, Procter & Gamble
Ernst & Young	New York	Coca-Cola, McDonald's
KPMG	New York	General Electric, Xerox
PricewaterhouseCoopers	New York	ExxonMobil, IBM, Ford

introduced, it may take years for new accounting practices to be implemented. As a result, you may encounter practices that seem contradictory. In some cases, we point out new directions in accounting. Your instructor also may mention certain weaknesses in current theory or practice.

GAAP and the Independent CPA's Report

Because financial statements are prepared by management and could be falsified for personal gain, all companies that sell shares of their stock to the public and many companies that apply for sizable loans have their financial statements audited by an independent **certified public accountant (CPA)**. *Independent* means that the CPA is not an employee of the company being audited and has no financial or other compromising ties with it. CPAs are licensed by all states for the same reason that lawyers and doctors are—to protect the public by ensuring the quality of professional service. The firms listed in Table 1-2 employ about 25 percent of all CPAs.

An **audit** is an examination of a company's financial statements and the accounting systems, controls, and records that produced them. The purpose of the audit is to ascertain that the financial statements have been prepared in accordance with generally accepted accounting principles. If the independent CPA is satisfied that this standard has been met, his or her report contains the following language:

> In our opinion, the financial statements... present fairly, in all material respects... in conformity with generally accepted accounting principles....

Study Note

The audit lends credibility to a set of financial statements. The auditor does not attest to the absolute accuracy of the published information or to the value of the company as an investment. All he or she renders is an opinion, based on appropriate testing, about the fairness of the presentation of the financial information.

This wording emphasizes that accounting and auditing are not exact sciences. Because the framework of GAAP provides room for interpretation and the application of GAAP necessitates the making of estimates, the auditor can render only an opinion about whether the financial statements *present fairly* or conform *in all material respects* to GAAP. The auditor's report does not preclude minor or immaterial errors in the financial statements. However, a favorable report from the auditor does imply that on the whole, investors and creditors can rely on the financial statements.

Historically, auditors have enjoyed a strong reputation for competence and independence. The independent audit has been an important factor in the worldwide growth of financial markets.

Organizations That Issue Accounting Standards

Study Note

The FASB is the primary source of GAAP, but the IASB is increasing in importance.

Two organizations issue accounting standards that are used in the United States: the FASB and the IASB. The **Financial Accounting Standards Board (FASB)** is the most important body for developing rules on accounting practice. This independent body has been designated by the Securities and Exchange Commission (SEC) to issue the *Statements of Financial Accounting Standards.*

With the growth of financial markets throughout the world, global cooperation in the development of accounting principles has become a priority. The **International Accounting Standards Board (IASB)** has approved more than

FOCUS ON BUSINESS PRACTICE 

The Arrival of International Financial Reporting Standards in the United States

Over the next few years, international financial reporting standards (IFRS) will become much more important in the United States and globally. The International Accounting Standards Board (IASB) has been working with the Financial Accounting Standards Board (FASB) and similar boards in other nations to achieve identical or nearly identical standards worldwide. IFRS are now required in many parts of the world, including Europe. The Securities and Exchange Commission (SEC) recently voted to allow foreign registrants in the United States to use IFRS. This is a major development because in the past, the SEC required foreign registrants to explain how the standards used in their statements differed from U.S. standards. This change affects approximately 10 percent of all public U.S. companies. In addition, the SEC may in the near future allow U.S. companies to use IFRS.[12]

40 **international financial reporting standards (IFRS)**. Foreign companies may use these standards in the United States rather than having to convert their statements to U.S. GAAP as called for by the FASB standards.

Other Organizations That Influence GAAP

Study Note

The PCAOB regulates audits of public companies registered with the Securities and Exchange Commission.

Study Note

The AICPA is the primary professional organization of certified public accountants.

Many other organizations directly or indirectly influence GAAP and so influence much of what is in this book.

The **Public Company Accounting Oversight Board (PCAOB)**, a governmental body created by the Sarbanes-Oxley Act, regulates the accounting profession and has wide powers to determine the standards that auditors must follow and to discipline them if they do not.

The **American Institute of Certified Public Accountants (AICPA)**, the professional association of certified public accountants, influences accounting practice through the activities of its senior technical committees. In addition to endorsing standards issued by the FASB, the AICPA has determined that standards issued by the IASB are also of high quality.*

The **Securities and Exchange Commission (SEC)** is an agency of the federal government that has the legal power to set and enforce accounting practices for companies whose securities are offered for sale to the general public. As such, it has enormous influence on accounting practice.

The **Governmental Accounting Standards Board (GASB)**, which is under the same governing body as the FASB, issues accounting standards for state and local governments.

The tax laws that govern the assessment and collection of revenue for operating the federal government also influence accounting practice. Because a major source of the government's revenue is the income tax, the tax laws specify the rules for determining taxable income. The **Internal Revenue Service (IRS)** interprets and enforces these rules. In some cases, the rules conflict with good accounting practice, but they are nonetheless an important

*Established in January 2007, the Private Company Financial Reporting Committee of the AICPA is charged with amending FASB accounting standards so that they better suit the needs of private companies, especially as they relate to the cost or benefit of implementing certain standards. This initiative could ultimately result in two sets of standards, one for private companies and one for public companies.

influence on practice. Cases in which the tax laws affect accounting practice are noted throughout this book.

Professional Conduct

The code of professional ethics of the American Institute of Certified Public Accountants (adopted, with variations, by each state) governs the conduct of CPAs. Fundamental to this code is responsibility to clients, creditors, investors, and anyone else who relies on the work of a CPA. The code requires CPAs to act with integrity, objectivity, and independence.

- **Integrity** means the accountant is honest and candid and subordinates personal gain to service and the public trust.
- **Objectivity** means the accountant is impartial and intellectually honest.
- **Independence** means the accountant avoids all relationships that impair or even appear to impair his or her objectivity.

The accountant must also exercise **due care** in all activities, carrying out professional responsibilities with competence and diligence. For example, an accountant must not accept a job for which he or she is not qualified, even at the risk of losing a client to another firm, and careless work is unacceptable. These broad principles are supported by more specific rules that public accountants must follow; for instance, with certain exceptions, client information must be kept strictly confidential. Accountants who violate the rules can be disciplined or even suspended from practice.

Study Note

The IMA is the primary professional association of management accountants.

The **Institute of Management Accountants (IMA)** also has a code of professional conduct. It emphasizes that management accountants have a responsibility to be competent in their jobs, to keep information confidential except when authorized or legally required to disclose it, to maintain integrity and avoid conflicts of interest, and to communicate information objectively and without bias.[13]

STOP & APPLY >

Match the following acronyms with their descriptions:

____ 1. GAAP
____ 2. IFRS
____ 3. CPA
____ 4. FASB
____ 5. IASB
____ 6. PCAOB
____ 7. AICPA
____ 8. SEC

a. Sets U.S. accounting standards
b. Audits financial statements
c. Established by the Sarbanes-Oxley Act
d. Sets international accounting standards
e. Established by the FASB
f. Established by the IASB
g. Influences accounting standards through member CPAs
h. Receives audited financial statements of public companies

SOLUTION

1. e; 2. f; 3. b; 4. a; 5. d; 6. c; 7. g; 8. h

A LOOK BACK AT ▸ CVS CAREMARK

The Decision Point at the beginning of this chapter focused on **CVS Caremark**, a successful nationwide chain of more than 6,000 stores. It posed these questions:

- Is CVS meeting its goal of profitability?
- As a manager at CVS, what financial knowledge would you need to measure progress toward the company's goals?
- As a potential investor or creditor, what financial knowledge would you need to evaluate CVS's financial performance?

As you've learned in this chapter, managers and others with an interest in a business measure its profitability in financial terms, such as net sales, net income, total assets, and stockholders' equity. Managers report on the progress they have made toward their financial goals in their company's financial statements.

As you can see in the highlights from CVS's financial statements presented below, the company's net sales, net earnings (net income), total assets, and stockholders' equity have increased over the years.[14] But how do we use these data to determine if CVS is meeting its goal of profitability?

Study Note

Most companies list the most recent year of information in the first column, as shown here.

CVS'S FINANCIAL HIGHLIGHTS

(In millions)	**2008**	2007	2006
Net sales	**$87,471.9**	$76,329.5	$43,821.4
Net earnings	**3,212.1**	2,637.0	1,368.9
Total assets	**60,959.9**	54,721.9	20,574.1
Stockholders' equity	**34,574.4**	31,321.9	9,917.6

As mentioned earlier in the chapter, one way to measure financial performance is through ratios. Ratios are used to compare a company's financial performance from one year to the next and to make comparisons among companies. The ratio that tells us if CVS is meeting its goal of profitability is the **return on assets** ratio. This ratio shows how efficiently a company is using its assets to produce income.

We use two values to calculate return on assets: net income, which is what is left after expenses are subtracted from revenues (see the income statement in Exhibit 1-1), and average total assets. Average total assets are the total of this year's assets plus last year's assets divided by 2 (see the balance sheet in Exhibit 1-3).

The return on assets ratio for CVS is calculated as follows (amounts are in millions):

	2008	**2007**
$\frac{\text{Net Income}}{\text{Average Total Assets}}$	$\frac{\$3,212.1}{(\$60,959.9 + \$54,721.9) \div 2}$	$\frac{\$2,637.0}{(\$54,721.9 + \$20,574.1) \div 2}$
K/R	$\frac{\$3,212.1}{\$57,840.9}$	$\frac{\$2,637.0}{\$37,648.0}$
Return on Assets:	$0.056 \times 100 = 5.6\%$	$0.070 \times 100 = 7.0\%$

We can draw several conclusions from this ratio. First, CVS earned 5.6 to 7.0 cents on each dollar it invested in assets. Second, from 2007 to 2008, its profitability declined from 7.0 to 5.6 percent. Third, CVS is a growing company as demonstrated by the increases

in its net sales, net earnings, total assets, and stockholders' equity in every year of the three-year period presented in CVS's Financial Highlights. These amounts indicate that CVS is a profitable and successful company but faces challenges in maintaining its profitability. You will learn much more about ratios in the chapters that follow.

If you aspire to be a manager of a business, an accountant, an investor, a business owner, or just a good employee, you will need to be familiar with measures like the return on assets ratio. You will also need to master other accounting concepts and terminology and know how financial information is produced, interpreted, and analyzed. The purpose of this book is to help you acquire that knowledge.

Review Problem

Preparation and Interpretation of Financial Statements

LO6

The following accounts and amounts are from the records of Jackson Realty for the year ended April 30, 2010, the company's first year of operations:

Accounts payable	$ 19,000
Accounts receivable	104,000
Cash	90,000
Commissions earned	375,000
Common stock	100,000
Dividends	10,000
Equipment	47,000
Income taxes expense	27,000
Income taxes payable	6,000
Marketing expense	18,000
Office and equipment rental expense	91,000
Salaries and commission expense	172,000
Salaries payable	78,000
Supplies	2,000
Utilities expense	17,000

Required

1. Prepare an income statement, statement of retained earnings, and balance sheet for Jackson Realty. For examples, refer to Exhibit 1-5.
2. User insight: How are the statements related to each other?

Answers to Review Problem

1.

	A	B	C	D
1		**Jackson Realty**		
2		**Income Statement**		
3		**For the Year Ended April 30, 2010**		
4				
5	**Revenues**			
6		Commissions earned		$375,000
7	**Expenses**			
8		Marketing expense	$ 18,000	
9		Office and equipment rental expense	91,000	
10		Salaries and commission expense	172,000	
11		Utilities expense	17,000	
12		Total expenses		298,000
13	Income before income taxes			$ 77,000
14	Income taxes expense			27,000
15	**Net income**			$ 50,000
16				

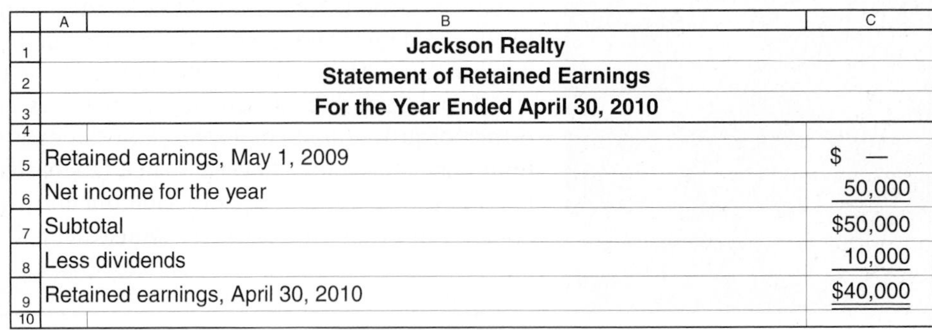

Jackson Realty Statement of Retained Earnings For the Year Ended April 30, 2010	
Retained earnings, May 1, 2009	$ —
Net income for the year	50,000
Subtotal	$50,000
Less dividends	10,000
Retained earnings, April 30, 2010	$40,000

Jackson Realty Balance Sheet April 30, 2010				
Assets		**Liabilities**		
Cash	$ 90,000	Accounts payable	$ 19,000	
Accounts receivable	104,000	Salaries payable	78,000	
Supplies	2,000	Income taxes payable	6,000	
Equipment	47,000	Total liabilities		$103,000
		Stockholders' Equity		
		Common stock	$100,000	
		Retained earnings	40,000	
		Total stockholders' equity		140,000
		Total liabilities and		
Total assets	$243,000	stockholders' equity		$243,000

2. Net income from the income statement appears on the statement of retained earnings. The ending balance (on April 30, 2010) on the statement of retained earnings appears on the balance sheet.

LO1 Define *accounting* and describe its role in making informed decisions, identify business goals and activities, and explain the importance of ethics in accounting.

Accounting is an information system that measures, processes, and communicates financial information about an economic entity. It provides the information necessary to make reasoned choices among alternative uses of scarce resources in the conduct of business and economic activities. A business is an economic entity that engages in operating, investing, and financing activities to achieve the goals of profitability and liquidity.

Management accounting focuses on the preparation of information primarily for internal use by management. Financial accounting is concerned with the development and use of reports that are communicated to those outside the business as well as to management. Ethical financial reporting is important to the well-being of a company; fraudulent financial reports can have serious consequences for many people.

LO2 Identify the users of accounting information.

Accounting plays a significant role in society by providing information to managers of all institutions and to individuals with a direct financial interest in those institutions, including present or potential investors and creditors. Accounting information is also important to those with an indirect financial interest in the business—for example, tax authorities, regulatory agencies, and economic planners.

LO3 Explain the importance of business transactions, money measure, and separate entity.

To make an accounting measurement, the accountant must determine what is measured, when the measurement should be made, what value should be placed on what is measured, and how to classify what is measured. The objects of accounting measurement are business transactions. Financial accounting uses money measure to gauge the impact of these transactions on a separate business entity.

LO4 Describe the characteristics of a corporation.

Corporations, whose ownership is represented by shares of stock, are separate entities for both legal and accounting purposes. The stockholders own the corporation and elect the board of directors. The board is responsible for determining corporate policies and appointing corporate officers, or top managers, to operate the business in accordance with the policies that it sets. The board is also responsible for corporate governance, the oversight of a corporation's management and ethics. The audit committee, which is appointed by the board and is made up of independent directors, is an important factor in corporate governance.

LO5 Define *financial position*, and state the accounting equation.

Financial position refers to a company's economic resources and the claims against those resources at a particular time. The accounting equation shows financial position as Assets = Liabilities + Stockholders' Equity. (In the case of sole proprietorships and partnerships, stockholders' equity is called *owners' equity*.) Business transactions affect financial position by decreasing or increasing assets, liabilities, and stockholders' (or owners') equity in such a way that the accounting equation is always in balance.

LO6 Identify the four basic financial statements.

The four basic financial statements are the income statement, the statement of retained earnings, the balance sheet, and the statement of cash flows. They are the primary means by which accountants communicate the financial condition and activities of a business to those who have an interest in the business.

LO7 Explain how generally accepted accounting principles (GAAP) relate to financial statements and the independent CPA's report, and identify the organizations that influence GAAP.

Acceptable accounting practice consists of the conventions, rules, and procedures that make up generally accepted accounting principles at a particular time. GAAP are essential to the preparation and interpretation of financial statements and the independent CPA's report. Foreign companies registered in the United States may use international financial reporting standards (IFRS).

Among the organizations that influence the formulation of GAAP are the Financial Accounting Standards Board, the Public Company Accounting Oversight Board, the American Institute of Certified Public Accountants, the Securities and Exchange Commission, and the Internal Revenue Service.

All accountants must follow a code of professional ethics, which is based on responsibility to the public. Accountants must act with integrity, objectivity, and independence, and they must exercise due care in all their activities.

REVIEW of Concepts and Terminology

The following concepts and terms were introduced in this chapter:

Accounting 4 (LO1)

Accounting equation 19 (LO5)

Additional paid-in capital 20 (LO5)

American Institute of Certified Public Accountants (AICPA) 28 (LO7)

Articles of incorporation 17 (LO4)

Assets 19 (LO5)

Audit 27 (LO7)

Audit committee 18 (LO4)

Balance sheet 22 (LO6)

Bookkeeping 7 (LO1)

Business 4 (LO1)

Business transactions 13 (LO3)

Cash flows 23 (LO6)

Certified public accountant (CPA) 27 (LO7)

Common stock 17 (LO4)

Contributed capital 20 (LO5)

Corporate governance 18 (LO4)

Corporation 16 (LO4)

Dividends 17 (LO4)

Due care 29 (LO7)

Ethics 8 (LO1)

Exchange rate 14 (LO3)

Expenses 20 (LO5)

Financial accounting 7 (LO1)

Financial Accounting Standards Board (FASB) 27 (LO7)

Financial analysis 6 (LO1)

Financial position 19 (LO5)

Financial statements 7 (LO1)

Financing activities 6 (LO1)

Fraudulent financial reporting 8 (LO1)

Generally accepted accounting principles (GAAP) 26 (LO7)

Governmental Accounting Standards Board (GASB) 28 (LO7)

Income statement 21 (LO6)

Independence 29 (LO7)

Institute of Management Accountants (IMA) 29 (LO7)

Integrity 29 (LO7)

Internal Revenue Service (IRS) 28 (LO7)

International Accounting Standards Board (IASB) 27 (LO7)

International financial reporting standards (IFRS) 28 (LO7)

Investing activities 5 (LO1)

Liabilities 19 (LO5)

Liquidity 5 (LO1)

Management 10 (LO2)

Management accounting 7 (LO1)

Management information system (MIS) 7 (LO1)

Money measure 14 (LO3)

Net assets 20 (LO5)

Net income 20 (LO5)

Net loss 20 (LO5)

Objectivity 29 (LO7)

Operating activities 5 (LO1)

Partnership 16 (LO4)

Par value 20 (LO5)

Performance measures 6 (LO1)

Profitability 5 (LO1)

Public Company Accounting Oversight Board (PCAOB) 28 (LO7)

Retained earnings 20 (LO5)

Revenues 20 (LO5)

Sarbanes-Oxley Act 8 (LO1)

Securities and Exchange Commission (SEC) 12, 28 (LO2, LO6, LO7)

Separate entity 14 (LO3)

Share of stock 17 (LO4)

Sole proprietorship 15 (LO4)

Statement of cash flows 23 (LO6)

Statement of retained earnings 22 (LO6)

Stockholders' equity 20 (LO5)

Key Ratio

Return on assets 30

CHAPTER ASSIGNMENTS

BUILDING Your Basic Knowledge and Skills

Short Exercises

LO1 Accounting and Business Enterprises

SE 1. Match the terms on the left with the definitions on the right:

____ 1. Accounting
____ 2. Profitability
____ 3. Liquidity
____ 4. Financing activities
____ 5. Investing activities
____ 6. Operating activities
____ 7. Financial accounting
____ 8. Management accounting
____ 9. Ethics
____ 10. Fraudulent financial reporting

a. The process of producing accounting information for the internal use of a company's management
b. Having enough cash available to pay debts when they are due
c. Activities management engages in to obtain adequate funds for beginning and continuing to operate a business
d. The process of generating and communicating accounting information in the form of financial statements to decision makers outside the organization
e. Activities management engages in to spend capital in ways that are productive and will help a business achieve its objectives
f. The ability to earn enough income to attract and hold investment capital
g. An information system that measures, processes, and communicates financial information about an identifiable economic entity
h. The intentional preparation of misleading financial statements
i. Activities management engages in to operate the business
j. A code of conduct that applies to everyday life

LO3 Accounting Concepts

SE 2. Indicate whether each of the following words or phrases relates most closely to (a) a business transaction, (b) a separate entity, or (c) a money measure:

1. Partnership
2. U.S. dollar
3. Payment of an expense
4. Corporation
5. Sale of an asset

LO4 Forms of Business Enterprises

SE 3. Match the descriptions on the left with the forms of business enterprise on the right:

____ 1. Most numerous
____ 2. Commands most revenues
____ 3. Two or more co-owners
____ 4. Has stockholders
____ 5. Owned by only one person
____ 6. Has a board of directors

a. Sole proprietorship
b. Partnership
c. Corporation

LO5 The Accounting Equation

SE 4. Determine the amount missing from each accounting equation below.

	Assets	=	Liabilities	+	Stockholders' Equity
1.	?		$50,000		$ 70,000
2.	$156,000		$84,000		?
3.	$292,000		?		$192,000

LO5 The Accounting Equation

SE 5. Use the accounting equation to answer each question below.

1. The assets of Aaron Co. are $240,000, and the liabilities are $90,000. What is the amount of the stockholders' equity?
2. The liabilities of Oak Company equal one-fifth of the total assets. The stockholders' equity is $40,000. What is the amount of the liabilities?

LO5 The Accounting Equation

SE 6. Use the accounting equation to answer each question below.

1. At the beginning of the year, Fazio Company's assets were $45,000 and its stockholders' equity was $25,000. During the year, assets increased by $30,000 and liabilities increased by $5,000. What was the stockholders' equity at the end of the year?
2. At the beginning of the year, Gal Company had liabilities of $50,000 and stockholders' equity of $96,000. If assets increased by $40,000 and liabilities decreased by $30,000, what was the stockholders' equity at the end of the year?

LO5 The Accounting Equation and Net Income

SE 7. Carlton Company had assets of $280,000 and liabilities of $120,000 at the beginning of the year, and assets of $400,000 and liabilities of $140,000 at the end of the year. During the year, there was an investment of $40,000 in the business and the company paid dividends of $48,000. What amount of net income did the company earn during the year?

LO6 Preparation and Completion of a Balance Sheet

SE 8. Use the following accounts and balances to prepare a balance sheet with the accounts in proper order for Global Company at June 30, 2009, using Exhibit 1-3 as a model:

Accounts Receivable	$ 1,600
Wages Payable	700
Retained Earnings	4,700
Common Stock	24,000
Building	22,000
Cash	?

LO6 Preparation of Financial Statements

SE 9. Tarech Corporation engaged in activities during the first year of its operations that resulted in the following: service revenue, $4,800; total expenses, $2,450; and dividends, $410. In addition, the year-end balances of selected accounts were as follows: Cash, $1,890; Other Assets, $1,000; Accounts Payable, $450; and Common Stock, $500. In proper format, prepare the income statement, statement of retained earnings, and balance sheet for Tarech Corporation (assume the year ends on December 31, 2010). (**Hint:** You must solve for the beginning and ending balances of retained earnings for 2010.)

Return on Assets

SE 10. Orbit Machine had net income of $15,000 in 2010. Total assets were $80,000 at the beginning of the year and $140,000 at the end of the year. Calculate return on assets.

Exercises

LO1 LO2 LO3 LO4

Discussion Questions

E 1. Develop a brief answer to each of the following questions.

1. What makes accounting a valuable discipline?
2. Why do managers in governmental and not-for-profit organizations need to understand financial information as much as managers in profit-seeking businesses do?
3. Are all economic events business transactions?
4. Sole proprietorships, partnerships, and corporations differ legally; how and why does accounting treat them alike?

LO5 LO6 LO7

Discussion Questions

E 2. Develop a brief answer to each of the following questions.

1. How are expenses and dividends similar, and how are they different?
2. In what ways are **CVS** and **Southwest Airlines** comparable? Not comparable?
3. How do generally accepted accounting principles (GAAP) differ from the laws of science?
4. What are some unethical ways in which a business may do its accounting or prepare its financial statements?

LO1 LO2 LO7

The Nature of Accounting

E 3. Match the terms below with the descriptions in the list that follows:

____ 1. Bookkeeping
____ 2. Creditors
____ 3. Money measure
____ 4. Financial Accounting Standards Board (FASB)
____ 5. Business transactions
____ 6. Financial statements
____ 7. Communication
____ 8. Securities and Exchange Commission (SEC)
____ 9. Investors
____ 10. Sarbanes-Oxley Act
____ 11. Management
____ 12. Management information system

a. The recording of all business transactions in terms of money
b. A process by which information is exchanged between individuals through a common system of symbols, signs, or behavior
c. The process of identifying and assigning values to business transactions
d. Legislation ordering CEOs and CFOs to swear that any reports they file with the SEC are accurate and complete
e. Shows how well a company is meeting its goals of profitability and liquidity
f. Collectively, the people who have overall responsibility for operating a business and meeting its goals
g. People who commit money to earn a financial return
h. The interconnected subsystems that provide the information needed to run a business
i. The most important body for developing and issuing rules on accounting practice, called *Statements of Financial Accounting Standards*

j. An agency set up by Congress to protect the public by regulating the issuing, buying, and selling of stocks
k. Economic events that affect a business's financial position
l. People to whom money is due

LO2 LO4 Users of Accounting Information and Forms of Business Enterprise

E 4. Gottlieb Pharmacy has recently been formed to develop a new type of drug treatment for cancer. Previously a partnership, Gottlieb has now become a corporation. Describe the various groups that will have an interest in the financial statements of Gottlieb. What is the difference between a partnership and a corporation? What advantages does the corporate form have over the partnership form of business organization?

LO3 Business Transactions

E 5. Velu owns and operates a minimart. Which of Velu's actions described below are business transactions? Explain why any other actions are not considered transactions.

1. Velu reduces the price of a gallon of milk in order to match the price offered by a competitor.
2. Velu pays a high school student cash for cleaning up the driveway behind the market.
3. Velu fills his son's car with gasoline in payment for his son's restocking the vending machines and the snack food shelves.
4. Velu pays interest to himself on a loan he made to the business three years ago.

LO3 LO4 Accounting Concepts

E 6. Financial accounting uses money measures to gauge the impact of business transactions on a separate business entity. Tell whether each of the following words or phrases relates most closely to (a) a business transaction, (b) a separate entity, or (c) a money measure:

1. Corporation
2. Euro
3. Sales of products
4. Receipt of cash
5. Sole proprietorship
6. U.S. dollar
7. Partnership
8. Stockholders' investments
9. Japanese yen
10. Purchase of supplies

LO3 Money Measure

E 7. You have been asked to compare the sales and assets of four companies that make computer chips to determine which company is the largest in each category. You have gathered the following data, but they cannot be used for direct comparison because each company's sales and assets are in its own currency:

Company (Currency)	Sales	Assets
US.Chip (U.S. dollar)	2,750,000	1,300,000
Nanhai (Hong Kong dollar)	5,000,000	2,800,000
Tova (Japanese yen)	350,000,000	290,000,000
Holstein (Euro)	3,500,000	3,900,000

Use the exchange rates in Table 1-1 to convert all the figures to U.S. dollars and determine which company is the largest in sales and which is the largest in assets.

LO5 The Accounting Equation

E 8. Use the accounting equation to answer each question that follows. Show any calculations you make.

1. The assets of Rasche Corporation are $380,000, and the stockholders' equity is $155,000. What is the amount of the liabilities?
2. The liabilities and stockholders' equity of Lee Corporation are $65,000 and $79,500, respectively. What is the amount of the assets?
3. The liabilities of Hurka Corporation equal one-third of the total assets, and stockholders' equity is $180,000. What is the amount of the liabilities?
4. At the beginning of the year, Jahis Corporation's assets were $310,000 and its stockholders' equity was $150,000. During the year, assets increased $45,000 and liabilities decreased $22,500. What is the stockholders' equity at the end of the year?

LO5 LO6 Identification of Accounts

E 9. 1. Indicate whether each of the following accounts is an asset (A), a liability (L), or a part of stockholders' equity (SE):

a. Cash
b. Salaries Payable
c. Accounts Receivable
d. Common Stock
e. Land
f. Accounts Payable
g. Supplies

2. Indicate whether each account below would be shown on the income statement (IS), the statement of retained earnings (RE), or the balance sheet (BS).

a. Repair Revenue
b. Automobile
c. Fuel Expense
d. Cash
e. Rent Expense
f. Accounts Payable
g. Dividends

LO6 Preparation of a Balance Sheet

E 10. Listed in random order below are some of the account balances for the Uptime Services Company as of December 31, 2010.

Accounts Payable	$ 25,000	Accounts Receivable	$31,250
Building	56,250	Cash	12,500
Common Stock	62,500	Equipment	25,000
Supplies	6,250	Retained Earnings	43,750

Place the balances in proper order and prepare a balance sheet similar to the one in Exhibit 1-3.

LO6 Preparation and Integration of Financial Statements

E 11. Proviso Corporation had the following accounts and balances during the year: Service Revenue, $26,400; Rent Expense, $2,400; Wages Expense, $16,680; Advertising Expense, $2,700; Utilities Expense, $1,800; Income Taxes Expense, $400; and Dividends, $1,400. In addition, the year-end balances of selected accounts were as follows: Cash, $3,100; Accounts Receivable, $1,500; Supplies, $200; Land, $2,000; Accounts Payable, $900; and Common Stock, $2,000.

In proper format, prepare the income statement, statement of retained earnings, and balance sheet for Proviso Corporation (assume the year ends on December 31, 2010). (**Hint:** You must solve for the beginning and ending balances of retained earnings for 2010.)

LO5 **Stockholders' Equity and the Accounting Equation**

E 12. The total assets and liabilities at the beginning and end of the year for Schupan Company are listed below.

	Assets	Liabilities
Beginning of the year	$180,000	$ 68,750
End of the year	275,000	150,500

Determine Schupan Company's net income or loss for the year under each of the following assumptions:

1. The stockholders made no investments in the business, and no dividends were paid during the year.
2. The stockholders made no investments in the business, but dividends of $27,500 were paid during the year.
3. The stockholders invested $16,250 in the business, but no dividends were paid during the year.
4. The stockholders invested $12,500 in the business, and dividends of $29,000 were paid during the year.

LO6 **Statement of Cash Flows**

E 13. Martin Service Corporation began the year 2009 with cash of $55,900. In addition to earning a net income of $38,000 and paying a cash dividend of $19,500, Martin Service borrowed $78,000 from the bank and purchased equipment with $125,000 of cash. Also, Accounts Receivable increased by $7,800, and Accounts Payable increased by $11,700.

Determine the amount of cash on hand at December 31, 2009, by preparing a statement of cash flows similar to the one in Exhibit 1-4.

LO4 LO5 LO6 **Statement of Retained Earnings**

E 14. Below is information from the statement of retained earnings of Mrs. Kitty's Cookies, Inc. for a recent year.

Dividends	$ 0
Net income	?
Retained earnings, January 31, 2010	$159,490
Retained earnings, January 31, 2009	$105,000

Prepare the statement of retained earnings for Mrs. Kitty's Cookies in good form. You will need to solve for the amount of net income. What are retained earnings? Why would the company's board of directors decide not to pay any dividends to its owners?

LO7 **Accounting Abbreviations**

E 15. Identify the accounting meaning of each of the following abbreviations: AICPA, SEC, PCAOB, GAAP, FASB, IRS, GASB, IASB, IMA, and CPA.

Return on Assets

E 16. Saxon wants to know if its profitability performance has increased from 2009 to 2010. The company had net income of $48,000 in 2009 and $50,000 in 2010. Total assets were $400,000 at the end of 2008, $480,000 at the end of 2009, and $560,000 at the end of 2010. Calculate return on assets for 2009 and 2010 and comment on the results.

Problems

LO6 **Preparation and Interpretation of the Financial Statements**

P 1. Below is a list of financial statement items.

___	Utilities expense	___	Accounts payable
___	Building	___	Rent expense
___	Common stock	___	Dividends
___	Net income	___	Income taxes expense
___	Land	___	Fees earned
___	Equipment	___	Cash
___	Revenues	___	Supplies
___	Accounts receivable	___	Wages expense

Required

1. Indicate whether each item is found on the income statement (IS), statement of retained earnings (RE), and/or balance sheet (BS).

User insight ▶ 2. Which of the financial statements is most closely associated with the goal of profitability?

LO6 **Integration of Financial Statements**

P 2. The following three independent sets of financial statements have several amounts missing:

	Set A	Set B	Set C
Income Statement			
Revenues	$5,320	$ 8,600	$ m
Expenses	a	g	2,010
Net income	$ 510	$ h	$ n
Statement of Retained Earnings			
Beginning balance	$1,780	$15,400	$ 200
Net income	b	i	450
Less dividends	c	1,000	o
Ending balance	$ d	$16,000	$ p
Balance Sheet			
Total assets	$ e	$ j	$1,900
Liabilities	$ f	$ 2,000	$1,300
Stockholders' equity			
Common stock	200	8,000	50
Retained earnings	2,100	k	q
Total liabilities and stockholders' equity	$2,700	$ l	$ r

Required

1. Complete each set of financial statements by determining the amounts that correspond to the letters.

User insight ▶ 2. Why is it necessary to prepare the income statement prior to the balance sheet?

LO6 **Preparation and Interpretation of the Income Statement, Statement of Retained Earnings, and Balance Sheet**

KA KLOOSTER & ALLEN CASH FLOW

P 3. On the next page are the financial accounts of Special Assets, Inc. The company has just completed its 10th year of operations ended December 31, 2011.

Accounts Payable	$ 3,600
Accounts Receivable	4,500
Cash	57,700
Commissions Expense	225,000
Commissions Payable	22,700
Commissions Revenue	400,000
Common Stock	29,000
Dividends	33,000
Equipment	59,900
Income Taxes Expense	27,000
Income Taxes Payable	13,000
Marketing Expense	20,100
Office Rent Expense	36,000
Retained Earnings, December 31, 2010	35,300
Supplies	700
Supplies Expense	2,600
Telephone and Computer Expenses	5,100
Wages Expense	32,000

Required

1. Prepare the income statement, statement of retained earnings, and balance sheet for Special Assets, Inc.

User insight ▶

2. The owners of Special Assets, Inc., are considering expansion. What other statement would be useful to the owners in assessing whether the company's operations are generating sufficient funds to support the expansion? Why would it be useful?

LO1 LO6 **Preparation and Interpretation of Financial Statements**

P 4. The following are the accounts of Unique Ad, Inc., an agency that develops marketing materials for print, radio, and television. The agency's first year of operations ended on January 31, 2010.

Accounts Payable	$ 19,400
Accounts Receivable	24,900
Advertising Service Revenue	165,200
Cash	1,800
Common Stock	5,000
Dividends	0
Equipment Rental Expense	37,200
Income Taxes Expense	560
Income Taxes Payable	560
Marketing Expense	6,800
Office Rent Expense	13,500
Salaries Expense	86,000
Salaries Payable	1,300
Supplies	1,600
Supplies Expense	19,100

Required

1. Prepare the income statement, statement of retained earnings, and balance sheet for Unique Ad, Inc.

User insight ▶

2. Review the financial statements and comment on the financial challenges Unique Ad, Inc. faces.

LO1 LO6 LO7

Use and Interpretation of Financial Statements

P 5. The financial statements for Oros Riding Club, Inc. follow.

Oros Riding Club, Inc.
Income Statement
For the Month Ended November 30, 2010

Revenues		
Riding lesson revenue	$4,650	
Locker rental revenue	1,450	
Total revenues		$6,100
Expenses		
Salaries expense	$1,125	
Feed expense	750	
Utilities expense	450	
Total expenses		2,325
Income before income taxes		$3,775
Income taxes expense		600
Net income		$3,175

Oros Riding Club, Inc.
Statement of Retained Earnings
For the Month Ended November 30, 2010

Retained earnings, October 31, 2010	$5,475
Net income for the month	3,175
Subtotal	$8,650
Less dividends	2,400
Retained earnings, November 30, 2010	$6,250

Oros Riding Club, Inc.
Balance Sheet
November 30, 2010

Assets		**Liabilities**		
Cash	$ 6,700	Accounts payable		$13,350
Accounts receivable	900			
Supplies	750	**Stockholders' Equity**		
Land	15,750	Common stock	$34,500	
Building	22,500	Retained earnings	6,250	
Horses	7,500	Total stockholders' equity		40,750
		Total liabilities and		
Total assets	$54,100	stockholders' equity		$54,100

Oros Riding Club, Inc.
Statement of Cash Flows
For the Month Ended November 30, 2010

Cash flows from operating activities		
Net income		$3,175
Adjustments to reconcile net income to net cash flows from operating activities		
Increase in accounts receivable	($ 400)	
Increase in supplies	(550)	
Increase in accounts payable	400	(550)
Net cash flows from operating activities		$2,625
Cash flows from investing activities		
Purchase of horses	($1,000)	
Sale of horses	2,000	
Net cash flows from investing activities		1,000
Cash flows from financing activities		
Issue of common stock	$5,000	
Payment of cash dividends	(2,400)	
Net cash flows from financing activities		2,600
Net increase in cash		$ 6,225
Cash at beginning of month		475
Cash at end of month		$6,700

Required

User insight ▶ 1. Explain how the four statements for Oros Riding Club, Inc., are related to each other.

User insight ▶ 2. Which statements are most closely associated with the goals of liquidity and profitability? Why?

User insight ▶ 3. If you were the owner of this business, how would you evaluate the company's performance? Give specific examples.

User insight ▶ 4. If you were a banker considering Oros Riding Club, Inc. for a loan, why might you want the company to get an audit by an independent CPA? What would the audit tell you?

Alternate Problems

LO6 Integration of Financial Statements

P 6. The following three independent sets of financial statements have several amounts missing.

	Set A	Set B	Set C
Income Statement			
Revenues	$1,200	$ g	$240
Expenses	a	5,000	m
Net income	$ b	$ h	$148
Statement of Retained Earnings			
Beginning balance	$2,900	$15,400	$132
Net income	c	1,600	n
Less dividends	200	i	o
Ending balance	$3,090	$ j	$ p

Balance Sheet	Set A	Set B	Set C
Total assets	$ d	$30,000	$ q
Liabilities	$1,600	$ 5,000	$ r
Stockholders' equity			
Common stock	2,000	9,000	100
Retained earnings	e	k	280
Total liabilities and stockholders' equity	$ f	$ l	$580

Required

1. Complete each set of financial statements by determining the amounts that correspond to the letters.

User insight ▶ 2. In what order is it necessary to prepare the financial statements? Why is that order necessary?

LO1 LO6 **Preparation and Interpretation of the Income Statement, Statement of Retained Earnings, and Balance Sheet**

P 7. Below are the financial accounts of Metro Labs. The company has just completed its third year of operations ended November 30, 2011.

Accounts Payable	$ 7,400
Accounts Receivable	51,900
Cash	115,750
Common Stock	15,000
Dividends	40,000
Income Taxes Expense	38,850
Income Taxes Payable	13,000
Marketing Expense	19,700
Office Rent Expense	25,000
Retained Earnings, November 30, 2010	55,400
Salaries Expense	96,000
Salaries Payable	2,700
Supplies	800
Supplies Expense	5,500
Testing Service Revenue	300,000

Required

1. Prepare the income statement, statement of retained earnings, and balance sheet for Metro Labs.

User insight ▶ 2. Evaluate the company's ability to meet its bills when they come due.

LO4 LO6 **Preparation and Interpretation of Financial Statements**

P 8. Below are the accounts of Gino's Painting Specialists, Inc. The company has just completed its first year of operations ended September 30, 2010.

Accounts Payable	$10,500	Income Taxes Payable	$ 3,000
Accounts Receivable	13,200	Marketing Expense	1,500
Cash	2,600	Painting Service Revenue	82,000
Common Stock	2,000	Salaries Expense	56,000
Dividends	1,000	Salaries Payable	700
Equipment	6,300	Supplies	400
Equipment Rental Expense	2,900	Supplies Expense	4,100
Income Taxes Expense	3,000	Truck Rent Expense	7,200

Required

1. Prepare the income statement, statement of retained earnings, and balance sheet for Gino's Painting Specialists, Inc.

Users insight ▶ 2. Why would the owners of Gino's Painting Specialists, Inc., set their business up as a corporation and not a partnership?

LO1 LO6 Preparation and Interpretation of Financial Statements

P 9. Below are the financial accounts of Brad Realty, Inc. The company has just completed its 10th year of operations ended December 31, 2011.

Accounts Payable	$ 3,500
Accounts Receivable	10,700
Cash	57,700
Commissions Expense	230,000
Commissions Payable	21,500
Commissions Revenue	450,000
Common Stock	31,000
Dividends	40,000
Equipment	44,200
Income Taxes Expense	35,700
Income Taxes Payable	13,000
Marketing Expense	29,200
Office Rent Expense	40,000
Retained Earnings, December 31, 2010	15,200
Supplies	900
Supplies Expense	2,700
Telephone and Computer Expenses	6,300
Wages Expense	36,800

Required

1. Prepare the income statement, statement of retained earnings, and balance sheet for Brad Realty, Inc.
2. The owners of Brad Realty, Inc. are considering expansion. What other statement would be useful to the owners in assessing whether the company's operations are generating sufficient funds to support the expenses? Why would it be useful?

ENHANCING Your Knowledge, Skills, and Critical Thinking

LO1 LO2 **Business Activities and Management Functions**

C 1. Costco Wholesale Corporation is America's largest membership retail company. According to its letter to stockholders:

> Our mission is to bring quality goods and services to our members at the lowest possible price in every market where we do business... A hallmark of Costco warehouses has been the extraordinary sales volume we achieve.[15]

To achieve its strategy, Costco must organize its management by functions that relate to the principal activities of a business. Discuss the three basic activities Costco will engage in to achieve its goals, and suggest some examples of each. What is the role of Costco's management? What functions must its management perform to carry out these activities?

LO3 **Concept of an Asset**

C 2. Southwest Airlines Co. is one of the most successful airlines in the United States. Its annual report contains this statement: "We are a company of People, not Planes. That is what distinguishes us from other airlines and other companies. At Southwest Airlines, People are our most important asset."[16] Are employees considered assets in the financial statements? Why or why not? Discuss in what sense Southwest considers its employees to be assets.

LO7 **Generally Accepted Accounting Principles**

C 3. Fidelity Investments Company is a well-known mutual fund investment company. It makes investments worth billions of dollars in companies listed on the New York Stock Exchange and other stock markets. Generally accepted accounting principles (GAAP) are very important for Fidelity's investment analysts. What are generally accepted accounting principles? Why are financial statements that have been prepared in accordance with GAAP and audited by an independent CPA useful for Fidelity's investment analysts? What organizations influence GAAP? Explain how they do so.

LO6 **Nature of Cash, Assets, and Net Income**

C 4. Research in Motion Limited (RIM) is not well known, but it produces a well-known product: the Blackberry mobile phone. Information for 2008 and 2007 from the company's annual report appears at the top of the next page.[18] (All numbers are in thousands.) Three students who were looking at RIM's annual report were overheard making the following comments:

> *Student A:* What a great year RIM had in 2008! The company earned income of \$2,422,238 because its total assets increased from \$3,088,949 to \$5,511,187.
>
> *Student B:* But the company didn't do that well because the change in total assets isn't the same as net income! The company had a net income of only \$507,254 because its cash increased from \$677,144 to \$1,184,398.
>
> *Student C:* I see that retained earnings went from \$359,227 to \$1,653,094. Don't you have to take that into consideration when analyzing the company's performance?

User insight ▶ 1. Comment on the interpretations of Students A and B, and then answer Student C's question.

User insight ▶ 2. Estimate RIM's net income for 2008. (*Note:* RIM did not pay any cash dividends.)

RIM Limited
Condensed Balance Sheets
March 1, 2008, and March 3, 2007
(In thousands)

	2008	2007
Assets		
Cash	$1,184,398	$ 677,144
Other assets	4,326,789	2,411,805
Total assets	$5,511,187	$3,088,949
Liabilities		
Total liabilities	$1,577,621	$ 605,449
Stockholders' Equity		
Common stock and other	2,280,472	2,124,273
Retained earnings	1,653,094	359,277
Total liabilities and stockholders' equity	$5,511,187	$3,088,949

LO6 **Analysis of Four Basic Financial Statements**

C 5. Refer to the **CVS** annual report in the Supplement to Chapter 1 to answer the questions below. Keep in mind that every company, while following basic principles, adapts financial statements and terminology to its own special needs. Therefore, the complexity of CVS's financial statements and the terminology in them will differ somewhat from the financial statements in the text.

1. What names does CVS give to its four basic financial statements? (Note that the word *consolidated* in the names of the financial statements means that these statements combine those of several companies owned by CVS.)
2. Prove that the accounting equation works for CVS on December 31, 2008 by finding the amounts for the following equation: Assets = Liabilities + Stockholders' Equity.
3. What were the total revenues of CVS for the year ended December 31, 2008?
4. Was CVS profitable in the year ended December 31, 2008? How much was net income (loss) in that year, and did it increase or decrease from the year ended December 29, 2007?
5. Did the company's cash and cash equivalents increase from December 29, 2007 to December 31, 2008? If so, by how much? In what two places in the statements can this number be found or computed?
6. Did cash flows from operating activities, cash flows from investing activities, and cash flows from financing activities increase or decrease from years 2007 to 2008?
7. Who is the auditor for the company? Why is the auditor's report that accompanies the financial statements important?

LO1 LO5 LO7 **Performance Measures and Financial Statements**

C 6. Refer to the **CVS** annual report and the financial statements of **Southwest Airlines Co.** in the Supplement to Chapter 1 to answer these questions:

1. Which company is larger in terms of assets and in terms of revenues? What do you think is the best way to measure the size of a company?
2. Which company is more profitable in terms of net income? What is the trend of profitability over the past three years for both companies?

3. Compute the return on assets for each company for 2008. By this measure, which company is more profitable? Is this a better measure than simply comparing the net income of the two companies? Explain your answer.
4. Which company has more cash? Which increased its cash the most in the last year? Which has more liquidity as measured by cash flows from operating activities?

LO7 **Professional Ethics**

C 7. Discuss the ethical choices in the situations below. In each instance, describe the ethical dilemma, determine the alternative courses of action, and tell what you would do.

1. You are the payroll accountant for a small business. A friend asks you how much another employee is paid per hour.
2. As an accountant for the branch office of a wholesale supplier, you discover that several of the receipts the branch manager has submitted for reimbursement as selling expenses actually stem from nights out with his spouse.
3. You are an accountant in the purchasing department of a construction company. When you arrive home from work on December 22, you find a large ham in a box marked "Happy Holidays—It's a pleasure to work with you." The gift is from a supplier who has bid on a contract your employer plans to award next week.
4. As an auditor with one year's experience at a local CPA firm, you are expected to complete a certain part of an audit in 20 hours. Because of your lack of experience, you know you cannot finish the job within that time. Rather than admit this, you are thinking about working late to finish the job and not telling anyone.
5. You are a tax accountant at a local CPA firm. You help your neighbor fill out her tax return, and she pays you $200 in cash. Because there is no record of this transaction, you are considering not reporting it on your tax return.
6. The accounting firm for which you work as a CPA has just won a new client, a firm in which you own 200 shares of stock that you received as an inheritance from your grandmother. Because it is only a small number of shares and you think the company will be very successful, you are considering not disclosing the investment.

LO2 LO7 **Users of Accounting Information**

C 8. Public companies report quarterly and annually on their success or failure in making a net income. The following appeared in Walgreen's annual report: "We continue to expand into new markets and increase penetration in existing markets. . . . The net earnings increase resulted from increased sales. . ."[19]

Your instructor will divide the class into groups representing the following users. Discuss why the user your group is representing needs accounting information. Be prepared to discuss in class.

1. The management of Walgreens
2. The stockholders of Walgreens
3. The creditors of Walgreens
4. Potential stockholders of Walgreens
5. The Internal Revenue Service
6. The Securities and Exchange Commission
7. The Teamsters' union
8. A consumers' group called Public Cause
9. An economic adviser to the president of the United States

SUPPLEMENT TO CHAPTER

1

How to Read an Annual Report

More than 4 million corporations are chartered in the United States. Most of them are small, family-owned businesses. They are called *private* or *closely held corporations* because their common stock is held by only a few people and is not for sale to the public. Larger companies usually find it desirable to raise investment funds from many investors by issuing common stock to the public. These companies are called *public companies.* Although they are fewer in number than private companies, their total economic impact is much greater.

Public companies must register their common stock with the Securities and Exchange Commission (SEC), which regulates the issuance and subsequent trading of the stock of public companies. The SEC requires the management of public companies to report each year to stockholders on their companies' financial performance. This report, called an *annual report*, contains the company's annual financial statements and other pertinent data. Annual reports are a primary source of financial information about public companies and are distributed to all of a company's stockholders. They must also be filed with the SEC on a Form 10-K.

The general public may obtain an annual report by calling or writing the company or accessing the report online at the company's website. If a company has filed its 10-K electronically with the SEC, it can be accessed at *www.sec.gov/edgar.shtml.* Many libraries also maintain files of annual reports or have them available on electronic media, such as *Compact Disclosure.*

This supplement describes the major components of the typical annual report. We have included many of these components in the annual report of **CVS Caremark Corporation**, one of the country's most successful retailers. Case assignments in many chapters refer to this annual report. For purposes of comparison, the supplement also includes the financial statements and summary of significant accounting policies of **Southwest Airlines Co.**, one of the largest and most successful airlines in the United States.

The Components of an Annual Report

In addition to listing the corporation's directors and officers, an annual report usually contains a letter to the stockholders (also called *shareholders*), a multiyear summary of financial highlights, a description of the company, management's discussion and analysis of the company's operating results and financial condition, the financial statements, notes to the financial statements, a statement about management's responsibilities, and the auditors' report.

Letter to the Stockholders

Traditionally, an annual report begins with a letter in which the top officers of the corporation tell stockholders about the company's performance and prospects. In CVS's 2008 annual report, the chairman and chief executive officer wrote to the stockholders about the highlights of the past year, the key priorities for the new year, and other aspects of the business. He reported as follows:

> Today, we are the nation's largest pharmacy health care company. With U.S. health care costs expected to reach more than $4 trillion annually over the next decade, we are beginning to deliver healthy outcomes for patients and driving down costs in ways that no other company in our industry can.

Financial Highlights

The financial highlights section of an annual report presents key statistics for at least a five-year period but often for a ten-year period. It is often accompanied by graphs. CVS's annual report, for example, gives key figures for sales, operating profits, and other key measures. Note that the financial highlights section often includes nonfinancial data and graphs, such as the number of stores in CVS's case.

Description of the Company

An annual report contains a detailed description of the company's products and divisions. Some analysts tend to scoff at this section of the annual report because it often contains glossy photographs and other image-building material, but it should not be overlooked because it may provide useful information about past results and future plans.

Management's Discussion and Analysis

In this section, management describes the company's financial condition and results of operations and explains the difference in results from one year to the next. For example, CVS's management explains the effects of its strategy to relocate some of its stores:

> Total net revenues continued to benefit from our active relocation program, which moves existing in-line shopping center stores to larger, more convenient, freestanding locations. Historically, we have achieved significant improvements in customer count and net revenue when we do this. As of December 31, 2008, approximately 62% of our existing stores were freestanding, compared to approximately 64% and 61% at December 29, 2007 and December 30, 2006, respectively. During 2008, the decrease in the percentage of freestanding stores resulted from the addition of the Longs Drug Stores.

CVS's management also describes the increase in cash flows from investing activities:

> Net cash used in investing activities increased to $4.6 billion in 2008. This compares to $3.1 billion in 2007 and $4.6 billion in 2006. The increase in net cash used in investing activities during 2008 was primarily due to the Longs Acquisition. The $3.1 billion of net cash used in investing activities during 2007 was primarily due to the Caremark Merger. The increase in net cash used in investing activities during 2006 was primarily due to the Albertson's Acquisition.

Financial Statements

All companies present the same four basic financial statements in their annual reports, but the names they use may vary. As you can see in Exhibits S-1 to S-4, CVS presents statements of operations (income statements), balance sheets, statements of cash flows, and statements of shareholders' equity (includes retained earnings). (Note that the numbers given in the statements are in millions, but the last six digits are omitted. For example, $4,793,300,000 is shown as $4,793.3.)

The headings of CVS's financial statements are preceded by the word *consolidated*. A corporation issues *consolidated* financial statements when it consists of more than one company and has combined the companies' data for reporting purposes.

CVS provides several years of data for each financial statement: two years for the balance sheet and three years for the others. Financial statements presented in this fashion are called *comparative financial statements*. Such statements are in accordance with generally accepted accounting principles and help readers assess the company's performance over several years.

CVS's fiscal year ends on the Saturday nearest the end of December (December 31, 2008 in the latest year). Retailers commonly end their fiscal years during a slow period, usually the end of January, which is in contrast to CVS's choosing the end of December.

Income Statements CVS uses a multistep form of the income statement in that results are shown in several steps (in contrast to the single-step form illustrated in the chapter). The steps are gross profit, operating profit, earnings before income tax provision, and net earnings (see Exhibit S-1). The company also shows net earnings available to common shareholders, and it discloses the basic earnings per share and diluted earnings per share. Basic earnings per share is used for most analysis. Diluted earnings per share assumes that all rights that could be exchanged for common shares, such as stock options, are in fact exchanged. The weighted average number of shares of common stock, used in calculating the per share figures, are shown at the bottom of the income statement.

Balance Sheets CVS has a typical balance sheet for a retail company (see Exhibit S-2). In the assets and liabilities sections, the company separates out the current assets and the current liabilities. Current assets will become available as cash or will be used up in the next year; current liabilities will have to be paid or satisfied in the next year. These groupings are useful in assessing a company's liquidity.

Several items in the shareholders' equity section of the balance sheet may need explanation. Common stock represents the number of shares outstanding at par value. Capital surplus (additional paid-in capital) represents amounts invested by stockholders in excess of the par value of the common stock. Preferred stock is capital stock that has certain features that distinguish it from common stock. Treasury stock represents shares of common stock the company repurchased.

Statements of Cash Flows Whereas the income statement reflects CVS's profitability, the statement of cash flows reflects its liquidity (see Exhibit S-3). This statement provides information about a company's cash receipts, cash payments, and investing and financing activities during an accounting period.

The first major section of CVS's consolidated statements of cash flows shows cash flows from operating activities. It shows the cash received and paid for various items related to the company's operations. The second major section is cash flows from investing activities. Except for acquisitions in 2006, 2007, and 2008, the largest outflow in this category is additions for property and equipment. This figure demonstrates that CVS is a growing company. The third major section is cash

EXHIBIT S-1 CVS's Income Statements

Consolidated means that data from all companies owned by CVS are combined.

CVS Caremark Corporation
Consolidated Statements of Operations

CVS's fiscal year ends on the Saturday closest to December 31.

	Fiscal Year Ended		
(In millions, except per share amounts)	**Dec. 31, 2008 (52 weeks)**	**Dec. 29, 2007 (52 weeks)**	**Dec. 30, 2006 (53 weeks)**
Net revenues	$87,471.9	$76,329.5	$43,821.4
Cost of revenues	69,181.5	60,221.8	32,079.2
Gross profit	18,290.4	16,107.7	11,742.2
Total operating expenses	12,244.2	11,314.4	9,300.6
Operating profit[1]	6,046.2	4,793.3	2,441.6
Interest expense, net[2]	509.5	434.6	215.8
Earnings before income tax provision	5,536.7	4,358.7	2,225.8
Loss from discontinued operations, net of income tax benefit of $82.4	(132)	—	—
Income tax provision	2,192.6	1,721.7	856.9
Net earnings[3]	3,212.1	2,637.0	1,368.9
Preference dividends, net of income tax benefit[4]	14.1	14.2	13.9
Net earnings available to common shareholders	$ 3,198.0	$ 2,622.8	$ 1,355.0
BASIC EARNINGS PER COMMON SHARE:[5]			
Net earnings	$ 2.23	$ 1.97	$ 1.65
Weighted average common shares outstanding	1,433.5	1,328.2	820.6
DILUTED EARNINGS PER COMMON SHARE:			
Net earnings	$ 2.18	$ 1.92	$ 1.60
Weighted average common shares outstanding	1,469.1	1,371.8	853.2
DIVIDENDS DECLARED PER COMMON SHARE:	$ 0.25800	$ 0.22875	$ 0.15500

1. This section shows earnings from ongoing operations.
2. CVS shows interest expense and income taxes separately.
3. The net earnings figure moves to the statements of shareholders' equity.
4. CVS shows the dividends distributed to preferred shareholders. This distribution is not an expense.
5. CVS discloses various breakdowns of earnings per share.

flows from financing activities. You can see here that CVS's largest cash inflows are for borrowing of long-term and short-term debt.

At the bottom of the statements of cash flows, you can see a reconciliation of net earnings to net cash provided by operating activities. This disclosure is important to the user because it relates the goal of profitability (net earnings) to liquidity (net cash provided). Most companies substitute this disclosure for the operating activities at the beginning of their statement of cash flows, as illustrated in Chapter 1.

Statements of Shareholders' Equity Instead of a simple statement of retained earnings, CVS presents consolidated statements of shareholders' equity (see Exhibit S-4). These statements explain the changes in components of stockholders' equity, including retained earnings.

EXHIBIT S-2 CVS'S Balance Sheets

CVS Caremark Corporation
Consolidated Balance Sheets

(In millions, except shares and per share amounts)	Dec. 31, 2008	Dec. 29, 2007
ASSETS:		
Cash and cash equivalents	$ 1,352.4	$ 1,056.6
Short-term investments	—	27.5
Accounts receivable, net	5,384.3	4,579.6
Inventories	9,152.6	8,008.2
Deferred income taxes	435.2	329.4
Other current assets	201.7	148.1
Total current assets	$ 16,526.2	14,149.4
Property and equipment, net	$ 8,125.2	$ 5,852.8
Goodwill	25,493.9	23,922.3
Intangible assets, net	10,466.2	10,429.6
Deferred income taxes	—	—
Other assets	368.4	367.8
Total assets	$ 60,959.9	$ 54,721.9
LIABILITIES:		
Accounts payable	$ 3,800.7	$ 3,593.0
Claims and discounts payable	2,814.2	2,484.3
Accrued expenses	3,177.6	2,556.8
Short-term debt	3,044.1	2,085.0
Current portion of long-term debt	653.3	47.2
Total current liabilities	13,489.9	10,766.3
Long-term debt	8,057.2	8,349.7
Deferred income taxes	3,701.7	3,426.1
Other long-term liabilities	1,136.7	857.9
Commitments and contingencies (Note 12)		
SHAREHOLDERS' EQUITY:		
Preferred stock, $0.01 par value: authorized 120,619 shares; no shares issued or outstanding	—	—
Preference stock, series one ESOP convertible, par value $1.00: authorized 50,000,000 shares; issued and outstanding 3,583,000 shares at December 31, 2008 and 3,798,000 shares at December 29, 2007	191.5	203.0
Common stock, par value $0.01: authorized 3,200,000,000 shares; issued 1,603,267,000 at December 31, 2008 and 1,590,139,000 shares at December 29, 2007	16.0	15.9
Treasury stock, at cost: 164,502,000 shares at December 31, 2008 and 153,682,000 shares at December 30, 2007	(5,812.3)	(5,620.4)
Shares held in trust, 1,700,000 shares at December 31, 2008 and 9,224,000 shares at December 29, 2007	(55.5)	(301.3)
Guaranteed ESOP obligation	—	(44.5)
Capital surplus	27,279.6	26,831.9
Retained earnings	13,097.8	10,287.0
Accumulated other comprehensive loss	(142.7)	(49.7)
Total shareholders' equity	34,574.4	31,321.9
Total liabilities and shareholders' equity	$ 60,959.9	$ 54,721.9

CVS categorizes certain assets as current assets.

These are noncurrent or long-term assets.

CVS categorizes certain liabilities as current liabilities.

These are noncurrent or long-term liabilities.

Balances in the shareholders' equity section are from the statements of shareholders' equity.

EXHIBIT S-3 CVS's Statements of Cash Flows

CVS Corporation
Consolidated Statements of Cash Flows

Cash flows are shown for operating activities, investing activities, and financing activities.

(In millions)	Fiscal Year Ended Dec. 31, 2008 (52 weeks)	Dec. 29, 2007 (52 weeks)	Dec. 30, 2006 (53 weeks)
CASH FLOWS FROM OPERATING ACTIVITIES:			
Cash receipts from revenues	$69,493.7	$61,986.3	$43,273.7
Cash paid for inventory	(51,374.7)	(45,772.6)	(31,422.1)
Cash paid to other suppliers and employees	(11,832.0)	(10,768.6)	(9,065.3)
Interest and dividends received	20.3	33.6	15.9
Interest paid	(573.7)	(468.2)	(228.1)
Income taxes paid	(1,786.5)	(1,780.8)	(831.7)
NET CASH PROVIDED BY OPERATING ACTIVITIES	3,947.1	3,229.7	1,742.4
CASH FLOWS FROM INVESTING ACTIVITIES:			
Additions to property and equipment	(2,179.9)	(1,805.3)	(1,768.9)
Proceeds from sale-leaseback transactions	203.8	601.3	1,375.6
Acquisitions (net of cash acquired) and other investments	(2,650.7)	(1,983.3)	(4,224.2)
Cash outflow from hedging activities	—	—	(5.3)
Sale of short-term investments	27.5	—	—
Proceeds from sale or disposal of assets	18.7	105.6	29.6
NET CASH USED IN INVESTING ACTIVITIES	(4,580.6)	(3,081.7)	(4,593.2)
CASH FLOWS FROM FINANCING ACTIVITIES:			
Additions to/(reductions in) short-term debt	959.0	242.3	1,589.3
Repayment of debt assumed in acquisition	(352.8)	—	—
Additions to long-term debt	350.0	6,000.0	1,500.0
Reductions in long-term debt	(1.8)	(821.8)	(310.5)
Dividends paid	(383.0)	(322.4)	(140.9)
Proceeds from exercise of stock options	327.8	552.4	187.6
Excess tax benefits from stock based compensation	53.1	97.8	42.6
Repurchase of common stock	(23.0)	(5,370.4)	—
NET CASH PROVIDED BY (USED IN) FINANCING ACTIVITIES	929.3	377.9	2,868.1
Net increase in cash and cash equivalents	295.8	525.9	17.3
Cash and cash equivalents at beginning of year	1,056.6	530.7	513.4
CASH AND CASH EQUIVALENTS AT END OF YEAR	$ 1,352.4	$ 1,056.6	$ 530.7
RECONCILIATION OF NET EARNINGS TO NET CASH PROVIDED BY OPERATING ACTIVITIES			
Net earnings	$ 3,212.1	$ 2,637.0	$ 1,368.9
Adjustments required to reconcile net earnings to net cash provided by operating activities:			
Depreciation and amortization	1,274.2	1,094.6	733.3
Stock based compensation	92.5	78.0	69.9
Deferred income taxes and other non-cash items	(3.4)	40.1	98.2
Change in operating assets and liabilities providing/(requiring) cash, net of effects from acquisitions:			
Accounts receivable, net	(291.0)	279.7	(540.1)
Inventories	(448.1)	(448.0)	(624.1)
Other current assets	12.5	(59.2)	(21.4)
Other assets	19.1	(26.4)	(17.2)
Accounts payable	(63.9)	(181.4)	396.7
Accrued expenses	182.5	(168.2)	328.9
Other long-term liabilities	0.6	(16.5)	(50.7)
NET CASH PROVIDED BY OPERATING ACTIVITIES	$ 3,947.1	$ 3,229.7	$ 1,742.4

Cash and cash equivalents move to balance sheets.

This section explains the difference between net earnings and net cash provided by operating activities.

EXHIBIT S-4 CVS's Statements of Stockholders' Equity

Each component of shareholders' equity is explained.

CVS Caremark Corporation
Consolidated Statements of Shareholders' Equity

(In millions)	Shares			Dollars		
	Dec. 31, 2008	Dec. 29, 2007	Dec. 30, 2006	Dec. 31, 2008	Dec. 29, 2007	Dec. 30, 2006
PREFERENCE STOCK:						
Beginning of year	3.8	4.0	4.2	$ 203.0	$ 213.3	$ 222.6
Conversion to common stock	(0.2)	(0.2)	(0.2)	(11.5)	(10.3)	(9.3)
End of year	3.6	3.8	4.0	191.5	203.0	213.3
COMMON STOCK:						
Beginning of year	1,590.1	847.3	838.8	15.9	8.5	8.4
Common stock issued for Caremark Merger	—	712.7	—	—	7.1	—
Stock options exercised and awards	13.2	30.1	8.5	0.1	0.3	0.1
End of year	1,603.3	1,590.1	847.3	16.0	15.9	8.5
TREASURY STOCK:						
Beginning of year	(153.7)	(21.5)	(24.5)	(5,620.4)	(314.5)	(356.5)
Purchase of treasury shares	(6.5)	(135.0)	0.1	(33.0)	(5,378.7)	(0.1)
Transfer from Trust	(7.5)	—	—	(272.3)	—	—
Conversion of preference stock	1.0	0.9	0.8	35.2	24.7	11.7
Employee stock purchase plan issuance	2.2	1.9	2.1	78.2	48.1	30.4
End of year	(164.5)	(153.7)	(21.5)	(5,812.3)	(5,620.4)	(314.5)
GUARANTEED ESOP OBLIGATION:						
Beginning of year				(44.5)	(82.1)	(114.0)
Reduction of guaranteed ESOP Obligation				44.5	37.6	31.9
End of year				—	(44.5)	(82.1)
SHARES HELD IN TRUST:						
Beginning of year	(9.2)	—	—	(301.3)	—	—
Transfer to treasury stock	7.5	—	—	245.8	—	—
Shares acquired through Caremark Merger	—	(9.2)	—	—	(301.3)	—
End of year	(1.7)	(9.2)		(55.5)	(301.3)	—
CAPITAL SURPLUS:						
Beginning of year				26,831.9	2,198.4	1,922.4
Common stock issued for Caremark Merger, net of issuance costs				—	23,942.4	—
Conversion of shares held in Trust to treasury stock				26.5		
Stock option activity and awards				391.8	607.7	235.8
Tax benefit on stock options and awards				53.1	97.8	42.6
Conversion of preference stock				(23.7)	(14.4)	(2.4)
End of year				27,279.6	26,831.9	2,198.4
ACCUMULATED OTHER COMPREHENSIVE LOSS:						
Beginning of year				(49.7)	(72.6)	(90.3)
Recognition of unrealized gain/(loss) on derivatives, net of income tax				3.4	3.4	(0.3)
Pension liability adjustment				(96.4)	19.5	23.6
Pension liability adjustment to initially apply SFAS No. 158, net of tax benefit				—	—	(5.6)
End of year				(142.7)	(49.7)	(72.6)

EXHIBIT S-4 *(continued)*

RETAINED EARNINGS:			
Beginning of year	10,287.0	7,966.6	6,738.6
Net earnings ← Net earnings are from the income statement.	3,212.1	2,637.0	1,368.9
Common stock dividends	(369.7)	(308.8)	(127.0)
Preference stock dividends	(14.0)	(14.8)	(15.6)
Tax benefit on preference stock dividends	0.6	1.2	1.7
Adoption of EITF 06-04 and EITF 06-10	(18.2)	—	—
Adoption of FIN 48	—	5.8	—
End of year	13,097.8	10,287.0	7,966.6
TOTAL SHAREHOLDERS' EQUITY	$34,574.4	$31,321.9	$9,917.6
COMPREHENSIVE INCOME:			
Net earnings	$ 3,212.1	$ 2,637.0	$1,368.9
Recognition of unrealized gain/(loss) on derivatives, net of income tax	3.4	3.4	(0.3)
Pension liability, net of income tax	(96.4)	19.5	23.6
COMPREHENSIVE HOME	$ 3,119.1	$ 2,659.9	$1,392.2

Notes to the Financial Statements

To meet the requirements of full disclosure, a company must add notes to the financial statements to help users interpret some of the more complex items. The notes are considered an integral part of the financial statements. In recent years, the need for explanation and further details has become so great that the notes often take more space than the statements themselves. The notes to the financial statements include a summary of significant accounting policies and explanatory notes.

Summary of Significant Accounting Policies Generally accepted accounting principles require that the financial statements include a *Summary of Significant Accounting Policies.* In most cases, this summary is presented in the first note to the financial statements or as a separate section just before the notes. In this summary, the company tells which generally accepted accounting principles it has followed in preparing the statements. For example, in CVS's report, the company states the principles followed for revenue recognition:

> The RPS [Retail Pharmacy Segment] recognizes revenue from the sale of merchandise (other than prescription drugs) at the time the merchandise is purchased by the retail customer. Revenue from the sale of prescription drugs is recognized at the time the prescription is filled, which is or approximates when the retail customer picks up the prescription. Customer returns are not material. Revenue generated from the performance of services in the RPS' healthcare clinics is recognized at the time the services are performed.... The PSS [Pharmacy Services Segment] recognizes revenues from prescription drugs sold by its mail service pharmacies and under national retail pharmacy network contracts where the PSS is the principal using the gross method at the contract prices negotiated with its customers.

Explanatory Notes Other notes explain some of the items in the financial statements. For example, CVS describes its commitments for future lease payments as follows:

Following is a summary of the future minimum lease payments under capital and operating leases as of December 31, 2008:

(In millions)	Capital Leases	Operating Leases
2009	17.0	1,744.2
2010	17.2	1,854.4
2011	17.2	1,609.0
2012	17.6	1,609.0
2013	17.9	1,682.6
Thereafter	83.0	14,821.0
	$169.9	$23,294.6

Information like this is very useful in determining the full scope of a company's liabilities and other commitments.

Supplementary Information Notes In recent years, the FASB and the SEC have ruled that certain supplemental information must be presented with financial statements. Examples are the quarterly reports that most companies present to their stockholders and to the SEC. These quarterly reports, called *interim financial statements,* are in most cases reviewed but not audited by a company's independent CPA firm. In its annual report, CVS presents unaudited quarterly financial data from its 2008 quarterly statements. The quarterly data also includes the high and low price for the company's common stock during each quarter.

Reports of Management's Responsibilities

Separate statements of management's responsibility for the financial statements and for internal control structure accompany the financial statements as required by the Sarbanes-Oxley Act of 2002. In its reports, CVS's management acknowledges its responsibility for the consistency, integrity, and presentation of the financial information and for the system of internal controls.

Reports of Certified Public Accountants

The *registered independent auditors' report* deals with the credibility of the financial statements. This report, prepared by independent certified public accountants, gives the accountants' opinion about how fairly the statements have been presented. Because management is responsible for preparing the financial statements, issuing statements that have not been independently audited would be like having a judge hear a case in which he or she was personally involved. The certified public accountants add the necessary credibility to management's figures for interested third parties. They report to the board of directors and the stockholders rather than to the company's management.

In form and language, most auditors' reports are like the one shown in Figure S-1. Usually, such a report is short, but its language is very important. It normally has four parts, but it can have a fifth part if an explanation is needed.

1. The first paragraph identifies the financial statements that have been audited. It also identifies responsibilities. The company's management is responsible for the financial statements, and the auditor is responsible for expressing an opinion on the financial statements based on the audit.
2. The second paragraph, or *scope section,* states that the examination was made in accordance with standards of the Public Company Accounting Oversight Board (PCAOB). This paragraph also contains a brief description of the objectives and nature of the audit.

3. The third paragraph, or *opinion section,* states the results of the auditors' examination. The use of the word *opinion* is very important because the auditor does not certify or guarantee that the statements are absolutely correct. To do so would go beyond the truth, because many items, such as depreciation, are based on estimates. Instead, the auditors simply give an opinion about whether, overall, the financial statements "present fairly," in all material respects, the company's financial position, results of operations, and cash flows. This means that the statements are prepared in accordance with generally accepted accounting principles. If, in the auditors' opinion, the statements do not meet accepted standards, the auditors must explain why and to what extent.
4. The fourth paragraph identifies a new accounting standard adopted by the company.
5. The fifth paragraph says the company's internal controls are effective.

FIGURE S-1 Auditor's Report for CVS Caremark Corporation

Report of Independent Registered Public Accounting Firm
The Board of Directors and Shareholders

CVS Caremark Corporation

1. We have audited the accompanying consolidated balance sheets of CVS Caremark Corporation as of December 31, 2008 and December 29, 2007, and the related consolidated statements of operations, shareholders' equity and cash flows for the fiscal years ended December 31, 2008 and December 29, 2007. These financial statements are the responsibility of the Company's management. Our responsibility is to express an opinion on these financial statements based on our audits.
2. We conducted our audits in accordance with the standards of the Public Company Accounting Oversight Board (United States). Those standards require that we plan and perform the audit to obtain reasonable assurance about whether the financial statements are free of material misstatement. An audit includes examining, on a test basis, evidence supporting the amounts and disclosures in the financial statements. An audit also includes assessing the accounting principles used and significant estimates made by management, as well as evaluating the overall financial statement presentation. We believe that our audits provide a reasonable basis for our opinion.
3. In our opinion, the financial statements referred to above present fairly, in all material respects, the consolidated financial position of CVS Caremark Corporation at December 31, 2008 and December 29, 2007, and the consolidated results of its operations and its cash flows for the fiscal years ended December 31, 2008 and December 29, 2007, in conformity with U.S. generally accepted accounting principles.
4. As discussed in Note 1 to the consolidated financial statements, effective December 31, 2006, CVS Caremark Corporation adopted Financial Accounting Standards Board (FASB) Interpretation No. 48, *Accounting for Uncertainty in Income Taxes—an interpretation of FASB Statement No. 109* and effective December 30, 2007, CVS Caremark Corporation adopted Emerging Issues Task Force (EITF) No. 06-4, *Accounting for Deferred Compensation and Postretirement Benefit Aspects of Endorsement Split-Dollar Life Insurance Arrangements* and EITF No. 06-10, *Accounting for Collateral Assignment Split-Dollar Life Insurance Arrangements.*
5. We also have audited, in accordance with the standards of the Public Company Accounting Oversight Board (United States), CVS Caremark Corporation's internal control over financial reporting as of December 31, 2008, based on criteria established in *Internal Control—Integrated Framework* issued by the Committee of Sponsoring Organizations of the Treadway Commission and our report dated February 26, 2009 expressed an unqualified opinion thereon.

Ernst & Young LLP
Boston, Massachusetts
February 26, 2009

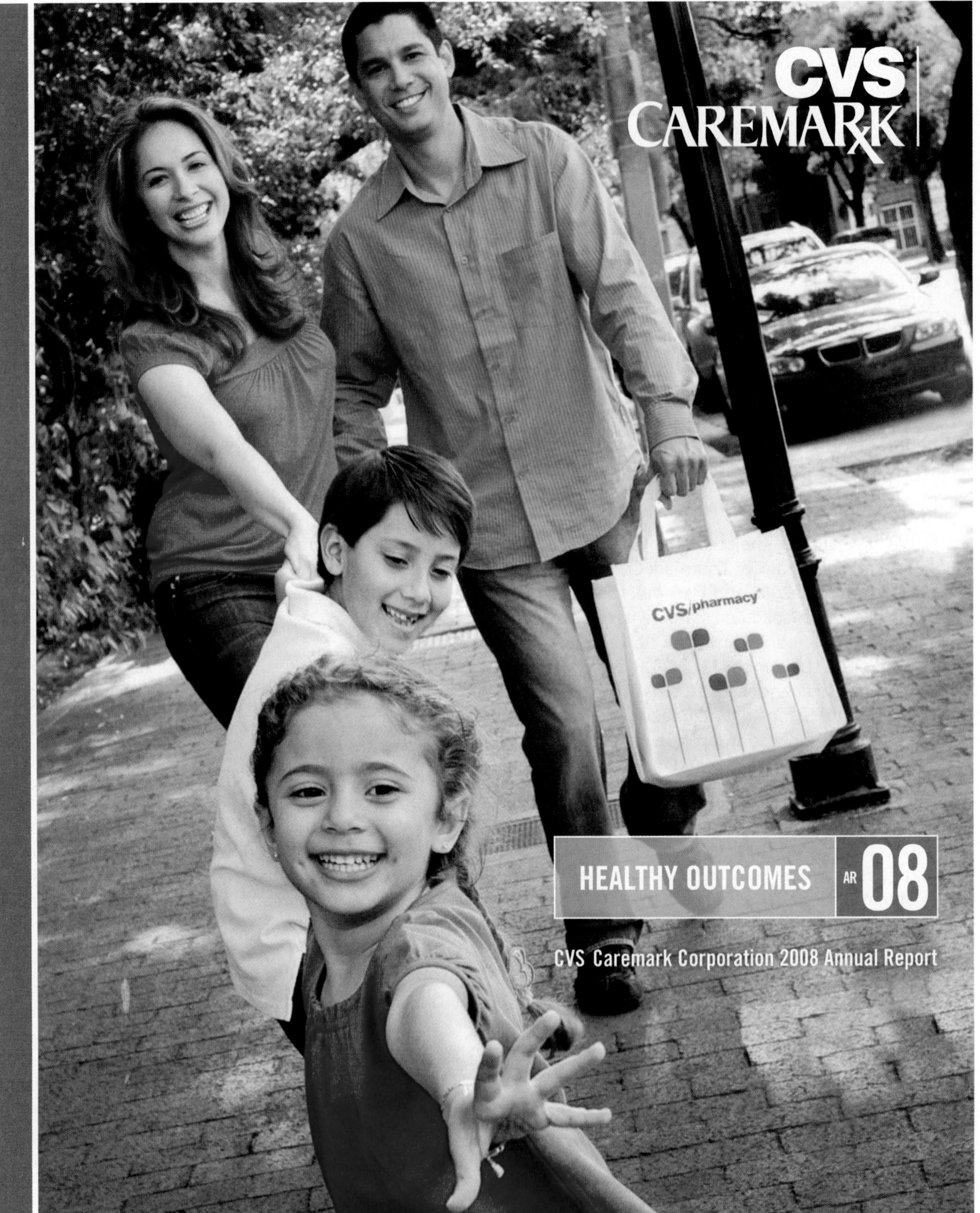
CVS
CAREMARK
CVS/pharmacy
HEALTHY OUTCOMES
AR 08
CVS Caremark Corporation 2008 Annual Report

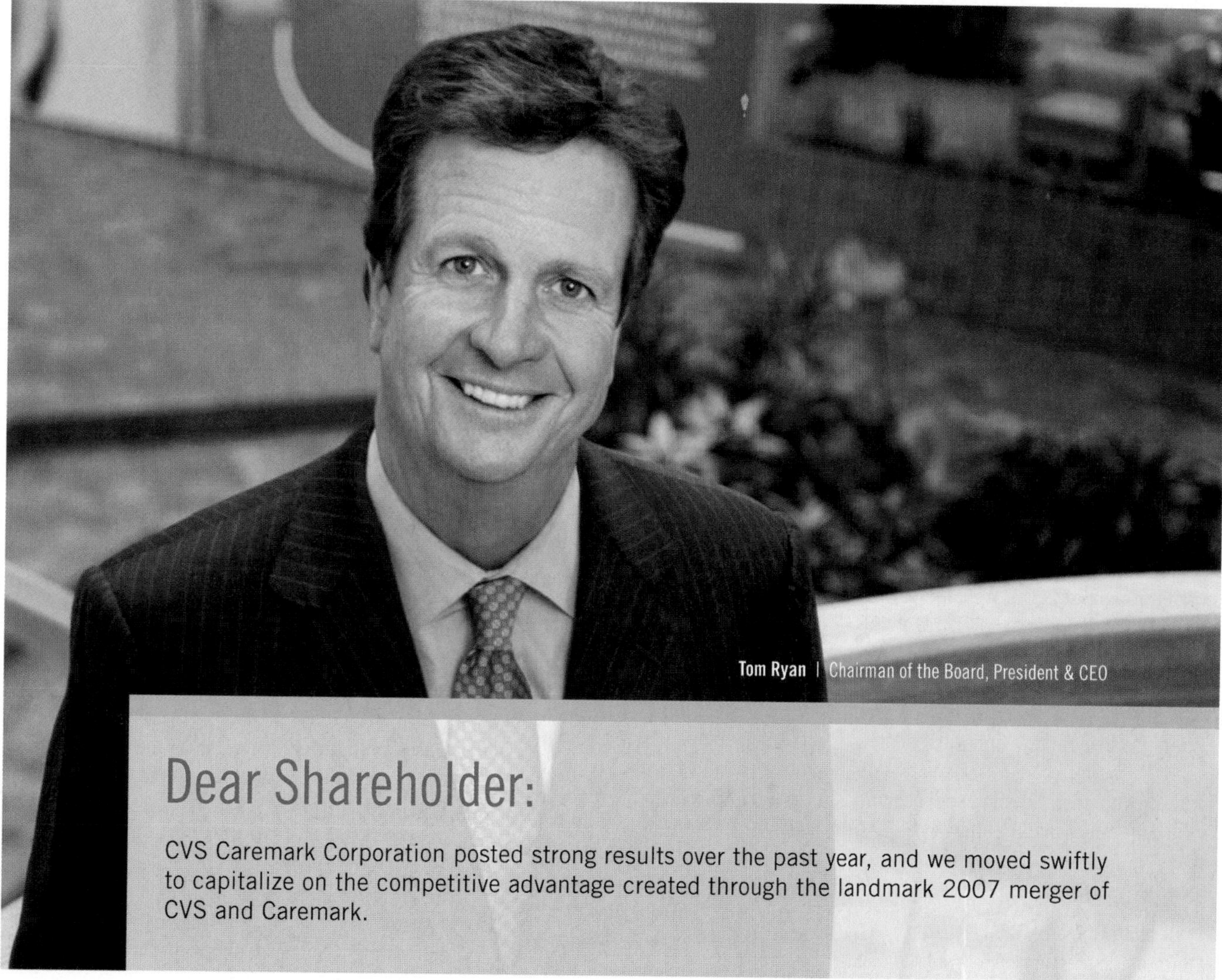

Tom Ryan | Chairman of the Board, President & CEO

Dear Shareholder:

CVS Caremark Corporation posted strong results over the past year, and we moved swiftly to capitalize on the competitive advantage created through the landmark 2007 merger of CVS and Caremark.

Today, we are the nation's largest pharmacy health care company. With U.S. health care costs expected to reach more than $4 trillion annually over the next decade, we are beginning to deliver healthy outcomes for patients and driving down costs in ways that no other company in our industry can.

Here are just a few of the year's many accomplishments:

- CVS Caremark generated record revenue and earnings, achieved industry-leading same-store sales growth, and continued to gain share across our businesses.
- We introduced our Proactive Pharmacy Care offerings, which are designed to make pharmacy care more accessible and lower overall health care costs for patients and payors.
- Our PBM added more than 90 new clients during our latest selling season, which will generate approximately $7 billion in revenue for us in 2009.
- We completed the acquisition of Longs Drug Stores and its PBM, RxAmerica®, in October 2008 and also opened 317 new or relocated CVS/pharmacy stores.

Although we are not immune to the recession, we continued to enjoy strong growth in 2008. Total revenues rose 14.6 percent to $87.5 billion. Driven in part by record operating margins, net earnings increased 21.8 percent. A number of factors fueled our margin gains, with continued growth in generic drugs leading the way.

Along with our strong free cash flow generation, I'm happy to report that we faced virtually none of the liquidity issues that sent shockwaves across so much of the business landscape

"CVS Caremark is adding clients across the PBM spectrum – from large- and small-cap companies to government entities and private insurers. We're achieving this by offering payors and patients everything they have come to expect from a top-rated PBM; however, we're also offering plan design options and services that no standalone PBM can match."

in 2008. CVS Caremark has a solid balance sheet and an investment grade credit rating, and we maintain a commercial paper program currently backed by $4 billion in committed bank facilities.

As noted, the U.S. economy is definitely in a recession and it will likely last throughout 2009. We'll feel its effect to some degree, with growth in script utilization slowing industry-wide. Lower utilization, layoffs, and job loss will affect our PBM business; however, in a landscape where control of health care spending is urgently needed, our proven cost-reducing services and the cost-effective care offered through MinuteClinic should prove more valuable than ever.

Our share price certainly wasn't immune to the turmoil in the financial markets during the past year, but we still outperformed the broad market averages. Our shares fell 27.7 percent in 2008, compared with the 38.5 percent decline of the S&P 500 Index and the 33.8 percent drop in the Dow Jones Industrial Average (DJIA). Over the past five years, on average CVS Caremark shares returned 10.4 percent annually. The S&P 500 and DJIA had negative returns of 2.2 percent and 1.1 percent, respectively, over the same period.

Our Proactive Pharmacy Care Offerings Are Gaining Traction with PBM Clients

Looking at our PBM business, we're very pleased with the broad-based enthusiasm among customers for the groundbreaking new products and services we have brought to market. This was reflected in the number of sizable new contracts we won in the latest selling season.

CVS Caremark is adding clients across the PBM spectrum – from large- and small-cap companies to government entities and private insurers. We're achieving this by offering payors and patients everything they have come to expect from a top-rated PBM; however, we're also offering plan design options and services that no standalone PBM can match. Through the Proactive Pharmacy Care offerings we began rolling out in 2008, we're giving consumers easier access to their medications and to the counseling they need, whether it is through one of our mail pharmacies or at one of our more than 6,900 stores. By helping patients adhere to their drug therapies, we're lowering overall health care costs and improving outcomes.

You can read about specific Proactive Pharmacy Care offerings, such as Maintenance Choice and integrated specialty, elsewhere in this report. Let me note, though, how pleased we are that over 200 clients have already committed to offering Maintenance Choice to their more than 2 million covered lives.

Specialty pharmacy and our Medicare Part D Prescription Drug Plan (PDP) business are also part of our PBM segment. The past year marked our 30th anniversary in specialty pharmacy, our industry's fastest-growing sector. In fact, specialty pharmacy accounts for approximately 20 percent of the money spent on prescription drugs in the United States even though these medications are used by only a small fraction of the population. Payors need help managing these costs and CVS Caremark is the clear category leader. Based on prescriptions we fill or manage, we have a 27 percent share of the $38 billion specialty market addressable by PBMs and drug retailers. Still, we currently provide specialty services to only 60 percent of our PBM customers. The ability to cross sell to the remaining 40 percent represents an important opportunity for growth.

Medicare Part D continues to play a key role in ensuring that seniors can afford the prescriptions they need. We're a major factor in this arena through our SilverScript® and RxAmerica proprietary PDP plan offerings and as a provider of PBM services to these plans and to PDPs sponsored by others. Through our PDPs and related PBM activities, we expect to cover approximately 1.5 million lives in 2009.

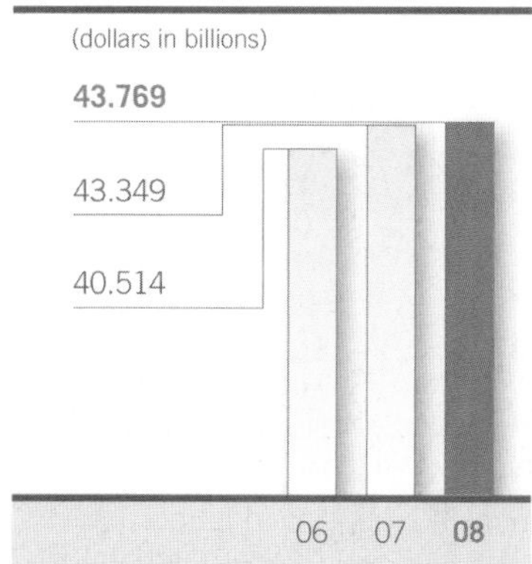

*Comparable data

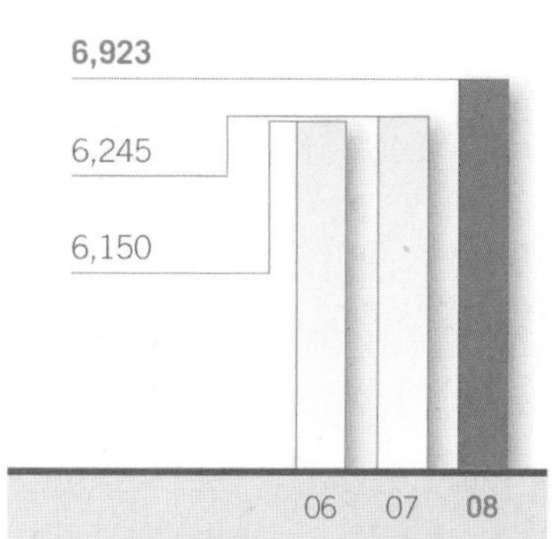

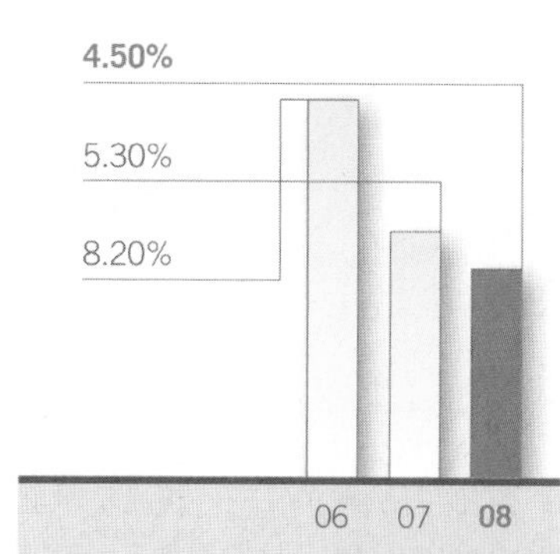

We're Moving Quickly to Integrate Longs Drug Stores and Improve Their Performance

In our retail business, I'm delighted to welcome over 20,000 Longs' colleagues to our company. The Longs acquisition has given us a high-quality network of more than 500 drugstores – primarily in Central and Northern California and Hawaii – as well as Longs' RxAmerica PBM. Commercial real estate values in California and Hawaii are among the highest in the country, and it would have taken at least a decade to assemble the prime locations we acquired had we instead opted exclusively for organic growth in these markets. We had only a modest presence in Central and Northern California and none in Hawaii. By acquiring Longs, we have become the leader in both markets virtually overnight. In fact, we now have over 800 stores in California, more than any other drugstore chain.

We've also begun to integrate RxAmerica – and its 8 million plan participants – with our PBM business. More importantly, our greater presence on the West Coast and in Hawaii plays an important strategic role for our PBM as it pursues new contracts. We can extend our Proactive Pharmacy Care offerings to plan sponsors with active or retired employees living in these markets.

I've often said that we don't acquire stores for growth. Rather, we acquire stores that we can grow. The Longs deal is no exception. Our existing stores outperform the Longs locations significantly in sales per square foot, gross margins, and other important measures. We intend to leverage our systems, our focus on private label and exclusive brands, our category mix, and the ExtraCare loyalty card to turn good stores into great ones. We recognize that the recession is impacting the California economy, and it may take us a while to accomplish this. When the economy rebounds, though, we will have outstanding, well-run assets in place.

We've had a lot of experience in making the most of the opportunities inherent in our acquisitions. Just take a look at the stores we acquired from JCPenney in 2004 and from Albertsons in 2006. We've been able to increase their sales per square foot considerably and have realized healthy margin gains as well. Moreover, we still see significant opportunities to improve the profitability of both acquisitions.

We Led the Industry in Same-Store Sales Growth In Both the Pharmacy and Front of the Store

Even as we completed the Longs acquisition, we continued to execute our organic growth strategy at retail. Retail square footage increased by 3.6 percent, in line with our annual target. We opened a total of 317 new or relocated stores. Factoring in closings, organic net unit growth increased by 150 stores.

Our CVS/pharmacy-Retail business had an outstanding year, with same-store sales rising an industry-leading 4.5 percent. Pharmacy same-store sales increased by 4.8 percent, even with the adoption of new generics. We're gratified by early consumer response to the Health Savings Pass for prescription drugs we introduced in November for the uninsured and underinsured. Given the current state of the economy, this is one of the ways in which we can help make health care more affordable for the general public. We are also in the process of rolling out our new pharmacy system, RxConnect™, which will reengineer the way pharmacists communicate and fill prescriptions.

"With strong execution across our businesses, we have good reason to feel optimistic about the future. We expect a number of long-term industry trends to work in our favor as well, including rising use of generic drugs and the aging of the U.S. population."

Same-store sales in the front of the store increased by 3.6 percent, and we gained share in 85 percent of our front-store categories. Since non-discretionary items account for the majority of front-end sales, that part of our business should prove relatively recession-resistant. And given the state of the economy, customers have been more willing to try our private-label and proprietary products. Sales of private-label and CVS-exclusive brands rose faster than in prior years to more than 16 percent of our front-end total at year-end. Much like generics in the pharmacy, these offerings also yield greater margins.

MinuteClinic's Expanded Offerings Bolster Our Health Care Strategy

As part of our broader health care strategy, we've continued to open MinuteClinic locations and expand their range of services. They now include wellness and prevention screenings, and a larger selection of vaccinations. We also launched pilot programs to incorporate MinuteClinic into our PBM offerings. For example, some of our PBM plan participants can now stop in for health assessments at convenient locations.

We've noted since MinuteClinic's acquisition that its competitive price can help us lower costs for health plans and self-insured employers. They have begun to embrace this model, and we've been able to contract with more payors as a result. In fact, visits paid for by third parties amounted to more than 70 percent of our total in 2008.

Our expanded health care focus can also be seen in the appointment of Troyen Brennan, M.D., in November 2008 to the newly created role of chief medical officer. Dr. Brennan, a practicing physician, former hospital administrator and, most recently, chief medical officer at Aetna, has assumed responsibility for MinuteClinic, Accordant Health Care, clinical and medical affairs, and our health care strategy.

Broad Industry Trends Will Contribute to Our Long-Term Performance

With strong execution across our businesses, we have good reason to feel optimistic about the future. We expect a number of long-term industry trends to work in our favor as well, including rising use of generic drugs and the aging of the U.S. population. Well over 60 percent of all drugs dispensed in 2008 across our industry were generics. That figure is likely to rise to 75 percent by 2012 as several blockbuster drugs lose patent protection.

Looking at the U.S. population, approximately 38 million people are 65 or older today. That number is projected to climb to 47 million by 2015, and prescription drug use is expected to rise substantially within this demographic. With leading market positions in California, Florida, and other sun-belt states, we stand to benefit from this trend to a greater extent than most other pharmacy players.

Other changes are likely to unfold in the coming years that should benefit CVS Caremark, patients, and payors alike. Among them, the Obama administration has already begun exploring ways in which health insurance can be broadened to cover a larger portion of the population. The resulting increase in access to prescription drugs would be good for CVS Caremark and good for the country. Legislation paving the way for a biogeneric approval process as well as growth in e-prescribing is also on the horizon. We look forward to working with the new administration on health care reform.

On behalf of the board of directors and CVS Caremark's 215,000 colleagues across the country, thank you for your confidence in our company and our vision. We are just beginning to realize the benefits of our broader pharmacy health care mission.

Thomas M. Ryan
Chairman of the Board,
President & CEO

Consolidated Statements of Operations

	Fiscal Year Ended		
In millions, except per share amounts	**Dec. 31, 2008**	Dec. 29, 2007	Dec. 30, 2006
Net revenues	**$ 87,471.9**	$ 76,329.5	$ 43,821.4
Cost of revenues	**69,181.5**	60,221.8	32,079.2
Gross profit	**18,290.4**	16,107.7	11,742.2
Total operating expenses	**12,244.2**	11,314.4	9,300.6
Operating profit	**6,046.2**	4,793.3	2,441.6
Interest expense, net	**509.5**	434.6	215.8
Earnings before income tax provision	**5,536.7**	4,358.7	2,225.8
Income tax provision	**2,192.6**	1,721.7	856.9
Earnings from continuing operations	**3,344.1**	2,637.0	1,368.9
Loss from discontinued operations, net of income tax benefit of $82.4	**(132.0)**	–	–
Net earnings	**3,212.1**	2,637.0	1,368.9
Preference dividends, net of income tax benefit	**14.1**	14.2	13.9
Net earnings available to common shareholders	**$ 3,198.0**	$ 2,622.8	$ 1,355.0
BASIC EARNINGS PER COMMON SHARE:			
Earnings from continuing operations	**$ 2.32**	$ 1.97	$ 1.65
Loss from discontinued operations	**(0.09)**	–	–
Net earnings	**$ 2.23**	$ 1.97	$ 1.65
Weighted average common shares outstanding	**1,433.5**	1,328.2	820.6
DILUTED EARNINGS PER COMMON SHARE:			
Earnings from continuing operations	**$ 2.27**	$ 1.92	$ 1.60
Loss from discontinued operations	**(0.09)**	–	–
Net earnings	**$ 2.18**	$ 1.92	$ 1.60
Weighted average common shares outstanding	**1,469.1**	1,371.8	853.2
Dividends declared per common share	**$ 0.25800**	$ 0.22875	$ 0.15500

See accompanying notes to consolidated financial statements.

Consolidated Balance Sheets

In millions, except shares and per share amounts	Dec. 31, 2008	Dec. 29, 2007
ASSETS:		
Cash and cash equivalents	$ 1,352.4	$ 1,056.6
Short-term investments	–	27.5
Accounts receivable, net	5,384.3	4,579.6
Inventories	9,152.6	8,008.2
Deferred income taxes	435.2	329.4
Other current assets	201.7	148.1
Total current assets	16,526.2	14,149.4
Property and equipment, net	8,125.2	5,852.8
Goodwill	25,493.9	23,922.3
Intangible assets, net	10,446.2	10,429.6
Other assets	368.4	367.8
Total assets	$ 60,959.9	$ 54,721.9
LIABILITIES:		
Accounts payable	$ 3,800.7	$ 3,593.0
Claims and discounts payable	2,814.2	2,484.3
Accrued expenses	3,177.6	2,556.8
Short-term debt	3,044.1	2,085.0
Current portion of long-term debt	653.3	47.2
Total current liabilities	13,489.9	10,766.3
Long-term debt	8,057.2	8,349.7
Deferred income taxes	3,701.7	3,426.1
Other long-term liabilities	1,136.7	857.9
Commitments and contingencies (Note 12)	–	–
SHAREHOLDERS' EQUITY:		
Preferred stock, $0.01 par value: authorized 120,619 shares; no shares issued or outstanding	–	–
Preference stock, series one ESOP convertible, par value $1.00: authorized 50,000,000 shares; issued and outstanding 3,583,000 shares at December 31, 2008 and 3,798,000 shares at December 29, 2007	191.5	203.0
Common stock, par value $0.01: authorized 3,200,000,000 shares; issued 1,603,267,000 shares at December 31, 2008 and 1,590,139,000 shares at December 29, 2007	16.0	15.9
Treasury stock, at cost: 164,502,000 shares at December 31, 2008 and 153,682,000 shares at December 29, 2007	(5,812.3)	(5,620.4)
Shares held in trust, 1,700,000 shares at December 31, 2008 and 9,224,000 shares at December 29, 2007	(55.5)	(301.3)
Guaranteed ESOP obligation	–	(44.5)
Capital surplus	27,279.6	26,831.9
Retained earnings	13,097.8	10,287.0
Accumulated other comprehensive loss	(142.7)	(49.7)
Total shareholders' equity	34,574.4	31,321.9
Total liabilities and shareholders' equity	$ 60,959.9	$ 54,721.9

See accompanying notes to consolidated financial statements.

Consolidated Statements of Cash Flows

	Fiscal Year Ended		
In millions	**Dec. 31, 2008**	Dec. 29, 2007	Dec. 30, 2006
CASH FLOWS FROM OPERATING ACTIVITIES:			
Cash receipts from revenues	**$ 69,493.7**	$ 61,986.3	$ 43,273.7
Cash paid for inventory	**(51,374.7)**	(45,772.6)	(31,422.1)
Cash paid to other suppliers and employees	**(11,832.0)**	(10,768.6)	(9,065.3)
Interest and dividends received	**20.3**	33.6	15.9
Interest paid	**(573.7)**	(468.2)	(228.1)
Income taxes paid	**(1,786.5)**	(1,780.8)	(831.7)
Net cash provided by operating activities	**3,947.1**	3,229.7	1,742.4
CASH FLOWS FROM INVESTING ACTIVITIES:			
Additions to property and equipment	**(2,179.9)**	(1,805.3)	(1,768.9)
Proceeds from sale-leaseback transactions	**203.8**	601.3	1,375.6
Acquisitions (net of cash acquired) and other investments	**(2,650.7)**	(1,983.3)	(4,224.2)
Cash outflow from hedging activities	**–**	–	(5.3)
Sale of short-term investments	**27.5**	–	–
Proceeds from sale or disposal of assets	**18.7**	105.6	29.6
Net cash used in investing activities	**(4,580.6)**	(3,081.7)	(4,593.2)
CASH FLOWS FROM FINANCING ACTIVITIES:			
Net additions to short-term debt	**959.0**	242.3	1,589.3
Repayment of debt assumed in acquisition	**(352.8)**	–	–
Additions to long-term debt	**350.0**	6,000.0	1,500.0
Reductions in long-term debt	**(1.8)**	(821.8)	(310.5)
Dividends paid	**(383.0)**	(322.4)	(140.9)
Proceeds from exercise of stock options	**327.8**	552.4	187.6
Excess tax benefits from stock-based compensation	**53.1**	97.8	42.6
Repurchase of common stock	**(23.0)**	(5,370.4)	–
Net cash provided by financing activities	**929.3**	377.9	2,868.1
Net increase in cash and cash equivalents	**295.8**	525.9	17.3
Cash and cash equivalents at beginning of year	**1,056.6**	530.7	513.4
Cash and cash equivalents at end of year	**$ 1,352.4**	$ 1,056.6	$ 530.7
RECONCILIATION OF NET EARNINGS TO NET CASH PROVIDED BY OPERATING ACTIVITIES:			
Net earnings	**$ 3,212.1**	$ 2,637.0	$ 1,368.9
Adjustments required to reconcile net earnings to net cash provided by operating activities:			
Depreciation and amortization	**1,274.2**	1,094.6	733.3
Stock-based compensation	**92.5**	78.0	69.9
Deferred income taxes and other non-cash items	**(3.4)**	40.1	98.2
Change in operating assets and liabilities providing/(requiring) cash, net of effects from acquisitions:			
Accounts receivable, net	**(291.0)**	279.7	(540.1)
Inventories	**(488.1)**	(448.0)	(624.1)
Other current assets	**12.5**	(59.2)	(21.4)
Other assets	**19.1**	(26.4)	(17.2)
Accounts payable	**(63.9)**	(181.4)	396.7
Accrued expenses	**182.5**	(168.2)	328.9
Other long-term liabilities	**0.6**	(16.5)	(50.7)
Net cash provided by operating activities	**$ 3,947.1**	$ 3,229.7	$ 1,742.4

See accompanying notes to consolidated financial statements.

Consolidated Statements of Shareholders' Equity

	Shares			Dollars		
In millions	**Dec. 31, 2008**	Dec. 29, 2007	Dec. 30, 2006	**Dec. 31, 2008**	Dec. 29, 2007	Dec. 30, 2006
PREFERENCE STOCK:						
Beginning of year	**3.8**	4.0	4.2	**$ 203.0**	$ 213.3	$ 222.6
Conversion to common stock	**(0.2)**	(0.2)	(0.2)	**(11.5)**	(10.3)	(9.3)
End of year	**3.6**	3.8	4.0	**191.5**	203.0	213.3
COMMON STOCK:						
Beginning of year	**1,590.1**	847.3	838.8	**15.9**	8.5	8.4
Common stock issued for Caremark Merger	**–**	712.7	–	**–**	7.1	–
Stock options exercised and awards	**13.2**	30.1	8.5	**0.1**	0.3	0.1
End of year	**1,603.3**	1,590.1	847.3	**16.0**	15.9	8.5
TREASURY STOCK:						
Beginning of year	**(153.7)**	(21.5)	(24.5)	**(5,620.4)**	(314.5)	(356.5)
Purchase of treasury shares	**(6.5)**	(135.0)	0.1	**(33.0)**	(5,378.7)	(0.1)
Conversion of preference stock	**1.0**	0.9	0.8	**35.2**	24.7	11.7
Transfer from Trust	**(7.5)**	–	–	**(272.3)**	–	–
Employee stock purchase plan issuance	**2.2**	1.9	2.1	**78.2**	48.1	30.4
End of year	**(164.5)**	(153.7)	(21.5)	**(5,812.3)**	(5,620.4)	(314.5)
GUARANTEED ESOP OBLIGATION:						
Beginning of year				**(44.5)**	(82.1)	(114.0)
Reduction of guaranteed ESOP obligation				**44.5**	37.6	31.9
End of year				**–**	(44.5)	(82.1)
SHARES HELD IN TRUST:						
Beginning of year	**(9.2)**	–	–	**(301.3)**	–	–
Transfer to treasury stock	**7.5**	–	–	**245.8**	–	–
Shares acquired through Caremark Merger	**–**	(9.2)	–	**–**	(301.3)	–
End of year	**(1.7)**	(9.2)		**(55.5)**	(301.3)	–
CAPITAL SURPLUS:						
Beginning of year				**26,831.9**	2,198.4	1,922.4
Common stock issued for Caremark Merger, net of issuance costs				**–**	23,942.4	–
Conversion of shares held in Trust to treasury stock				**26.5**	–	–
Stock option activity and awards				**391.8**	607.7	235.8
Tax benefit on stock options and awards				**53.1**	97.8	42.6
Conversion of preference stock				**(23.7)**	(14.4)	(2.4)
End of year				**27,279.6**	26,831.9	2,198.4

Consolidated Statements of Shareholders' Equity

	Shares			Dollars		
In millions	**Dec. 31, 2008**	Dec. 29, 2007	Dec. 30, 2006	**Dec. 31, 2008**	Dec. 29, 2007	Dec. 30, 2006
ACCUMULATED OTHER COMPREHENSIVE LOSS:						
Beginning of year				**(49.7)**	(72.6)	(90.3)
Recognition of unrealized gain/(loss) on derivatives, net of income tax				**3.4**	3.4	(0.3)
Pension liability adjustment, net of income tax				**(96.4)**	19.5	23.6
Pension liability adjustment to initially apply SFAS No.158, net of income tax				**–**	–	(5.6)
End of year				**(142.7)**	(49.7)	(72.6)
RETAINED EARNINGS:						
Beginning of year				**10,287.0**	7,966.6	6,738.6
Net earnings				**3,212.1**	2,637.0	1,368.9
Common stock dividends				**(369.7)**	(308.8)	(127.0)
Preference stock dividends				**(14.0)**	(14.8)	(15.6)
Tax benefit on preference stock dividends				**0.6**	1.2	1.7
Adoption of EITF 06-04 and EITF 06-10				**(18.2)**	–	–
Adoption of FIN 48				**–**	5.8	–
End of year				**13,097.8**	10,287.0	7,966.6
Total shareholders' equity				**$ 34,574.4**	$ 31,321.9	$ 9,917.6
COMPREHENSIVE INCOME:						
Net earnings				**$ 3,212.1**	$ 2,637.0	$ 1,368.9
Recognition of unrealized gain/(loss) on derivatives, net of income tax				**3.4**	3.4	(0.3)
Pension liability, net of income tax				**(96.4)**	19.5	23.6
Comprehensive income				**$ 3,119.1**	$ 2,659.9	$ 1,392.2

See accompanying notes to consolidated financial statements.

Notes to Consolidated Financial Statements

NO 1 SIGNIFICANT ACCOUNTING POLICIES

Description of business. CVS Caremark Corporation (the "Company") operates one of the largest pharmacy services businesses and the largest retail pharmacy business (based on revenues and store count) in the United States.

Pharmacy Services Segment (the "PSS"). The PSS provides a full range of prescription benefit management services including mail order pharmacy services, specialty pharmacy services, plan design and administration, formulary management and claims processing. The Company's customers are primarily employers, insurance companies, unions, government employee groups, managed care organizations and other sponsors of health benefit plans and individuals throughout the United States.

As a pharmacy benefits manager, the PSS manages the dispensing of pharmaceuticals through our mail order pharmacies and national network of approximately 60,000 retail pharmacies (which include our CVS/pharmacy® and Longs Drug® stores) to eligible participants in the benefits plans maintained by our customers and utilizes its information systems to perform, among other things, safety checks, drug interaction screenings and brand to generic substitutions.

The PSS's specialty pharmacies support individuals that require complex and expensive drug therapies. The specialty pharmacy business includes mail order and retail specialty pharmacies that operate under the Caremark® and CarePlus CVS/pharmacy™ names.

The PSS also provides health management programs, which include integrated disease management for 27 conditions, through our Accordant® health management offering.

In addition, through our SilverScript Insurance Company ("SilverScript") and Accendo Insurance Company ("Accendo") subsidiaries, the PSS is a national provider of drug benefits to eligible beneficiaries under the Federal Government's Medicare Part D program. The PSS acquired Accendo in the Longs Acquisition (see Note 2 later in this document), and, effective January 1, 2009, Accendo replaced RxAmerica® as the Medicare-approved prescription drug plan for the RxAmerica Medicare Part D drug benefit plans.

Our pharmacy services business generates net revenues primarily by contracting with clients to provide prescription drugs to plan participants. Prescription drugs are dispensed by our mail order pharmacies, specialty pharmacies and national network of retail pharmacies. Net revenues are also generated by providing additional services to clients, including administrative services such as claims processing and formulary management, as well as health care related services such as disease management.

The pharmacy services business operates under the Caremark Pharmacy Services®, Caremark®, CVS Caremark™, CarePlus CVS/pharmacy™, CarePlus™, RxAmerica®, Accordant Care™ and TheraCom® names. As of December 31, 2008, the Pharmacy Services Segment operated 58 retail specialty pharmacy stores, 19 specialty mail order pharmacies and 7 mail service pharmacies located in 26 states, Puerto Rico and the District of Columbia.

Retail Pharmacy Segment (the "RPS"). The RPS sells prescription drugs and a wide assortment of general merchandise, including over-the-counter drugs, beauty products and cosmetics, photo finishing, seasonal merchandise, greeting cards and convenience foods through our CVS/pharmacy and Longs Drug retail stores and online through CVS.com®.

The RPS also provides health care services through its MinuteClinic health care clinics. These health care clinics utilize nationally recognized medical protocols to diagnose and treat minor health conditions and are staffed by nurse practitioners and physician assistants.

As of December 31, 2008, our retail pharmacy business included 6,923 retail drugstores (of which 6,857 operated a pharmacy) located in 41 states and the District of Columbia operating primarily under the CVS/pharmacy® or Longs Drug® names, our online retail website, CVS.com® and 560 retail health care clinics operating under the MinuteClinic® name (of which 534 were located in CVS/pharmacy stores).

Basis of presentation. The consolidated financial statements include the accounts of the Company and its wholly-owned subsidiaries. All material intercompany balances and transactions have been eliminated.

Fiscal year change. On December 23, 2008, the Board of Directors of the Company approved a change in the Company's fiscal year end from the Saturday nearest December 31 of each year to December 31 of each year to better reflect the Company's position in the health care, rather than the retail industry. The fiscal year change was effective beginning with the fourth quarter of fiscal 2008. Prior to Board approval of this change, the Saturday nearest December 31, 2008 would have resulted in a 53-week fiscal year that would have ended January 3, 2009.

Following is a summary of the impact of the fiscal year change:

Fiscal Year	Fiscal Year-End	Fiscal Period	Fiscal Period Includes
2008	December 31, 2008	December 30, 2007 – December 31, 2008	368 days
2007	December 29, 2007	December 31, 2006 – December 29, 2007	364 days
2006	December 30, 2006	January 1, 2006 – December 30, 2006	364 days

Unless otherwise noted, all references to years relate to the above fiscal years.

Reclassifications. Certain reclassifications have been made to the consolidated financial statements of prior years to conform to the current year presentation.

Use of estimates. The preparation of financial statements in conformity with generally accepted accounting principles requires management to make estimates and assumptions that affect the reported amounts in the consolidated financial statements and accompanying notes. Actual results could differ from those estimates.

Cash and cash equivalents. Cash and cash equivalents consist of cash and temporary investments with maturities of three months or less when purchased.

Short-term investments. The Company's short-term investments consisted of auction rate securities with initial maturities of greater than three months when purchased. These investments, which were classified as available-for-sale, were carried at historical cost, which approximated fair value at December 29, 2007. The Company had no short-term investments at December 31, 2008.

Accounts receivable. Accounts receivable are stated net of an allowance for uncollectible accounts of $188.8 million and $107.8 million as of December 31, 2008 and December 29, 2007, respectively. The balance primarily includes amounts due from third party providers (e.g., pharmacy benefit managers, insurance companies and governmental agencies) and vendors as well as clients, participants and manufacturers.

Fair value of financial instruments. As of December 31, 2008, the Company's financial instruments include cash and cash equivalents, accounts receivable, accounts payable and short-term debt. Due to the short-term nature of these instruments, the Company's carrying value approximates fair value. The carrying amount and estimated fair value of long-term debt was $7.9 billion and $6.9 billion, respectively as of December 31, 2008. The carrying amount and estimated fair value of long-term debt was $8.2 billion as of December 29, 2007. The fair value of long-term debt was estimated based on rates currently offered to the Company for debt with similar terms and maturities. The Company had outstanding letters of credit, which guaranteed foreign trade purchases, with a fair value of $7.0 million as of December 31, 2008 and $5.7 million as of December 29, 2007. There were no outstanding investments in derivative financial instruments as of December 31, 2008 or December 29, 2007.

Inventories. Inventories are stated at the lower of cost or market on a first-in, first-out basis using the retail method of accounting to determine cost of sales and inventory in our CVS/pharmacy stores, average cost to determine cost of sales and inventory in our mail service and specialty pharmacies and the cost method of accounting to determine inventory in the Longs Drug Stores and our distribution centers. The Longs Drug Stores will be conformed to the retail method of accounting when their accounting systems are converted in 2009. Physical inventory counts are taken on a regular basis in each store and a continuous cycle count process is the primary procedure used to validate the inventory balances on hand in each distribution center to ensure that the amounts reflected in the accompanying consolidated financial statements are properly stated. During the interim period between physical inventory counts, the Company accrues for anticipated physical inventory losses on a location-by-location basis based on historical results and current trends.

Property and equipment. Property, equipment and improvements to leased premises are depreciated using the straight-line method over the estimated useful lives of the assets, or when applicable, the term of the lease, whichever is shorter. Estimated useful lives generally range from 10 to 40 years for buildings, building improvements and leasehold improvements and 3 to 10 years for fixtures and equipment. Repair and maintenance costs are charged directly to expense as incurred. Major renewals or replacements that substantially extend the useful life of an asset are capitalized and depreciated.

Following are the components of property and equipment:

In millions	**Dec. 31, 2008**	Dec. 29, 2007
Land	**$ 1,304.1**	$ 586.4
Building and improvements	**1,343.1**	896.0
Fixtures and equipment	**6,216.1**	4,947.4
Leasehold improvements	**2,581.3**	2,133.2
Capitalized software	**665.6**	474.6
Capital leases	**181.7**	181.7
	12,291.9	9,219.3
Accumulated depreciation and amortization	**(4,166.7)**	(3,366.5)
	$ 8,125.2	$ 5,852.8

Notes to Consolidated Financial Statements

The Company capitalizes application development stage costs for significant internally developed software projects. These costs are amortized over the estimated useful lives of the software, which generally range from 3 to 5 years. Unamortized costs were $70.0 million as of December 31, 2008 and $74.2 million as of December 29, 2007.

Goodwill. The Company accounts for goodwill and intangibles under Statement of Financial Accounting Standards ("SFAS") No. 142, "Goodwill and Other Intangible Assets." As such, goodwill and other indefinite-lived assets are not amortized, but are subject to impairment reviews annually, or more frequently if necessary. See Note 3 for additional information about goodwill.

Intangible assets. Purchased customer contracts and relationships are amortized on a straight-line basis over their estimated useful lives of up to 20 years. Purchased customer lists are amortized on a straight-line basis over their estimated useful lives of up to 10 years. Purchased leases are amortized on a straight-line basis over the remaining life of the lease. See Note 3 for additional information about intangible assets.

Impairment of long-lived assets. The Company accounts for the impairment of long-lived assets in accordance with SFAS No. 144, "Accounting for Impairment or Disposal of Long-Lived Assets." As such, the Company groups and evaluates fixed and finite-lived intangible assets excluding goodwill, for impairment at the lowest level at which individual cash flows can be identified. When evaluating assets for potential impairment, the Company first compares the carrying amount of the asset group to the individual store's estimated future cash flows (undiscounted and without interest charges). If the estimated future cash flows used in this analysis are less than the carrying amount of the asset group, an impairment loss calculation is prepared. The impairment loss calculation compares the carrying amount of the asset group to the asset group's estimated future cash flows (discounted and with interest charges). If required, an impairment loss is recorded for the portion of the asset group's carrying value that exceeds the asset group's estimated future cash flows (discounted and with interest charges).

Revenue Recognition:

Pharmacy Services Segment. The PSS sells prescription drugs directly through its mail service pharmacies and indirectly through its national retail pharmacy network. The PSS recognizes revenues from prescription drugs sold by its mail service pharmacies and under national retail pharmacy network contracts where the PSS is the principal using the gross method at the contract prices negotiated with its customers. Net revenue from the PSS includes: (i) the portion of the price the customer pays directly to the PSS, net of any volume-related or other discounts paid back to the customer (see "Drug Discounts" later in this document), (ii) the portion of the price paid to the PSS ("Mail Co-Payments") or a third party pharmacy in the PSS' national retail pharmacy network ("Retail Co-Payments") by individuals included in its customers' benefit plans and (iii) administrative fees for national retail pharmacy network contracts where the PSS is not the principal as discussed later in this document.

SEC Staff Accounting Bulletin 104, "Revenue Recognition, corrected copy" ("SAB 104") provides the general criteria for the timing aspect of revenue recognition, including consideration of whether: (i) persuasive evidence of an arrangement exists, (ii) delivery has occurred or services have been rendered, (iii) the seller's price to the buyer is fixed or determinable and (iv) collectability is reasonably assured. The Company has established the following revenue recognition policies for the PSS in accordance with SAB 104:

- Revenues generated from prescription drugs sold by mail service pharmacies are recognized when the prescription is shipped. At the time of shipment, the Company has performed substantially all of its obligations under its customer contracts and does not experience a significant level of reshipments.
- Revenues generated from prescription drugs sold by third party pharmacies in the PSS' national retail pharmacy network and associated administrative fees are recognized at the PSS' point-of-sale, which is when the claim is adjudicated by the PSS' online claims processing system.

The PSS determines whether it is the principal or agent for its national retail pharmacy network transactions using the indicators set forth in Emerging Issues Task Force ("EITF") Issue No. 99-19, "Reporting Revenue Gross as a Principal versus Net as an Agent" on a contract by contract basis. In the majority of its contracts, the PSS has determined it is the principal due to it: (i) being the primary obligor in the arrangement, (ii) having latitude in establishing the price, changing the product or performing part of the service, (iii) having discretion in supplier selection, (iv) having involvement in the determination of product or service specifications and (v) having credit risk. The PSS' obligations under its customer contracts for which revenues are reported using the gross method are separate and distinct from its obligations to the third party pharmacies included in its national retail pharmacy network contracts. Pursuant to these contracts, the PSS is contractually required to pay the third party pharmacies in its national retail pharmacy network for products sold, regardless of whether the PSS is paid by its customers. The PSS' responsibilities under its customer contracts typically include validating eligibility and coverage levels, communicating the prescription price and the co-payments due to the third party retail pharmacy, identifying possible adverse drug interactions for the pharmacist to address with the physician prior to dispensing, suggesting clinically appropriate generic alternatives where appropriate and approving the prescription for dispensing. Although the PSS does not have credit risk with respect to Retail Co-Payments, management believes that all of the other indicators of gross revenue reporting are present. For contracts under which the PSS acts as an agent, the PSS records revenues using the net method.

Drug Discounts. The PSS deducts from its revenues any discounts paid to its customers as required by EITF No. 01-9, "Accounting for Consideration Given by a Vendor to a Customer (Including a Reseller of the Vendor's Products)" ("EITF 01-9"). The PSS pays discounts to its customers in accordance with the terms of its customer contracts, which are normally based on a fixed discount per prescription for specific products dispensed or a percentage of manufacturer discounts received for specific products dispensed. The liability for discounts due to the PSS' customers is included in "Claims and discounts payable" in the accompanying consolidated balance sheets.

Medicare Part D. The PSS began participating in the Federal Government's Medicare Part D program as a Prescription Drug Plan ("PDP") on January 1, 2006. The PSS' net revenues include insurance premiums earned by the PDP, which are determined based on the PDP's annual bid and related contractual arrangements with the Centers for Medicare and Medicaid Services ("CMS"). The insurance premiums include a beneficiary premium, which is the responsibility of the PDP member, but is subsidized by CMS in the case of low-income members, and a direct premium paid by CMS. Premiums collected in advance are initially deferred in accrued expenses and are then recognized in net revenues over the period in which members are entitled to receive benefits.

In addition to these premiums, the PSS' net revenues include co-payments, deductibles and co-insurance (collectively, the "Member Co-Payments") related to PDP members' actual prescription claims in its net revenues. In certain cases, CMS subsidizes a portion of these Member Co-Payments and pays the PSS an estimated prospective Member Co-Payment subsidy amount each month. The prospective Member Co-Payment subsidy amounts received from CMS are also included in the PSS' net revenues. The Company assumes no risk for these amounts, which represented 1.3% and 0.8% of consolidated net revenues in 2008 and 2007, respectively. If the prospective Member Co-Payment subsidies received differ from the amounts based on actual prescription claims, the difference is recorded in either accounts receivable or accrued expenses.

The PSS accounts for CMS obligations and Member Co-Payments (including the amounts subsidized by CMS) using the gross method consistent with its revenue recognition policies for Mail Co-Payments and Retail Co-Payments (discussed previously in this document), which include the application of EITF 99-19. See Note 7 for additional information about Medicare Part D.

Retail Pharmacy Segment. The RPS recognizes revenue from the sale of merchandise (other than prescription drugs) at the time the merchandise is purchased by the retail customer. Revenue from the sale of prescription drugs is recognized at the time the prescription is filled, which is or approximates when the retail customer picks up the prescription. Customer returns are not material. Revenue generated from the performance of services in the RPS' health care clinics is recognized at the time the services are performed. See Note 13 for additional information about the revenues of the Company's business segments.

Cost of Revenues:

Pharmacy Services Segment. The PSS' cost of revenues includes: (i) the cost of prescription drugs sold during the reporting period directly through its mail service pharmacies and indirectly through its national retail pharmacy network, (ii) shipping and handling costs and (iii) the operating costs of its mail service pharmacies and customer service operations and related information technology support costs (including depreciation and amortization). The cost of prescription drugs sold component of cost of revenues includes: (i) the cost of the prescription drugs purchased from manufacturers or distributors and shipped to participants in customers' benefit plans from the PSS' mail service pharmacies, net of any volume-related or other discounts (see "Drug Discounts" previously in this document) and (ii) the cost of prescription drugs sold (including Retail Co-Payments) through the PSS' national retail pharmacy network under contracts where it is the principal, net of any volume-related or other discounts.

Retail Pharmacy Segment. The RPS' cost of revenues includes: the cost of merchandise sold during the reporting period and the related purchasing costs, warehousing and delivery costs (including depreciation and amortization) and actual and estimated inventory losses. See Note 13 for additional information about the cost of revenues of the Company's business segments.

Vendor Allowances and Purchase Discounts:

The Company accounts for vendor allowances and purchase discounts under the guidance provided by EITF Issue No. 02-16, "Accounting by a Customer (Including a Reseller) for Certain

Notes to Consolidated Financial Statements

Consideration Received from a Vendor," and EITF Issue No. 03-10, "Application of EITF Issue No. 02-16 by Resellers to Sales Incentives Offered to Consumers by Manufacturers."

Pharmacy Services Segment. The PSS receives purchase discounts on products purchased. The PSS' contractual arrangements with vendors, including manufacturers, wholesalers and retail pharmacies, normally provide for the PSS to receive purchase discounts from established list prices in one, or a combination of, the following forms: (i) a direct discount at the time of purchase, (ii) a discount for the prompt payment of invoices or (iii) when products are purchased indirectly from a manufacturer (e.g., through a wholesaler or retail pharmacy), a discount (or rebate) paid subsequent to dispensing. These rebates are recognized when prescriptions are dispensed and are generally calculated and billed to manufacturers within 30 days of the end of each completed quarter. Historically, the effect of adjustments resulting from the reconciliation of rebates recognized to the amounts billed and collected has not been material to the PSS' results of operations. The PSS accounts for the effect of any such differences as a change in accounting estimate in the period the reconciliation is completed. The PSS also receives additional discounts under its wholesaler contract if it exceeds contractually defined annual purchase volumes.

The PSS earns purchase discounts at various points in its business cycle (e.g., when the product is purchased, when the vendor is paid or when the product is dispensed) for products sold through its mail service pharmacies and third party pharmacies included in its national retail pharmacy network. In addition, the PSS receives fees from pharmaceutical manufacturers for administrative services. Purchase discounts and administrative service fees are recorded as a reduction of "Cost of revenues" as required by EITF 02-16.

Retail Pharmacy Segment. Vendor allowances received by the RPS reduce the carrying cost of inventory and are recognized in cost of revenues when the related inventory is sold, unless they are specifically identified as a reimbursement of incremental costs for promotional programs and/or other services provided. Funds that are directly linked to advertising commitments are recognized as a reduction of advertising expense (included in operating expenses) when the related advertising commitment is satisfied. Any such allowances received in excess of the actual cost incurred also reduce the carrying cost of inventory. The total value of any upfront payments received from vendors that are linked to purchase commitments is initially deferred. The deferred amounts are then amortized to reduce cost of revenues over the life of the contract based upon purchase volume. The total value of any upfront payments received from vendors that are not linked to purchase commitments is also initially deferred. The deferred amounts are then amortized to reduce cost of revenues on a straight-line basis over the life of the related contract. The total amortization of these upfront payments was not material to the accompanying consolidated financial statements.

Shares held in trust. As a result of the Caremark Merger (see Note 2 for additional information about the Caremark Merger), the Company maintains grantor trusts, which held approximately 1.7 million and 9.2 million shares of its common stock at December 31, 2008 and December 29, 2007, respectively. These shares are designated for use under various employee compensation plans. Since the Company holds these shares, they are excluded from the computation of basic and diluted shares outstanding.

Insurance. The Company is self-insured for certain losses related to general liability, workers' compensation and auto liability. The Company obtains third party insurance coverage to limit exposure from these claims. The Company is also self-insured for certain losses related to health and medical liabilities. The Company's self-insurance accruals, which include reported claims and claims incurred but not reported, are calculated using standard insurance industry actuarial assumptions and the Company's historical claims experience.

Store opening and closing costs. New store opening costs, other than capital expenditures, are charged directly to expense when incurred. When the Company closes a store, the present value of estimated unrecoverable costs, including the remaining lease obligation less estimated sublease income and the book value of abandoned property and equipment, are charged to expense. The long-term portion of the lease obligations associated with store closings was $398.6 million and $370.0 million in 2008 and 2007, respectively.

Advertising costs. Advertising costs are expensed when the related advertising takes place. Advertising costs, net of vendor funding, (included in operating expenses), were $323.8 million in 2008, $290.6 million in 2007 and $265.3 million in 2006.

Interest expense, net. Interest expense was $529.8 million, $468.3 million and $231.7 million, and interest income was $20.3 million, $33.7 million and $15.9 million in 2008, 2007 and 2006, respectively. Capitalized interest totaled $27.8 million in 2008, $23.7 million in 2007 and $20.7 million in 2006.

Accumulated other comprehensive loss. Accumulated other comprehensive loss consists of changes in the net actuarial gains and losses associated with pension and other post retirement benefit plans, unrealized losses on derivatives and an adjustment to initially apply SFAS No. 158. In accordance with SFAS No. 158, the amount included in accumulated other comprehensive income related to the Company's pension and post retirement plans was $216.9 million pre-tax ($132.3 million after-tax) as of December 31, 2008 and $58.7 million pre-tax ($35.9 million after-tax) as of December 29, 2007. The unrealized loss on derivatives totaled $16.6 million pre-tax ($10.5 million after-tax) and $21.9 million pre-tax ($13.8 million after-tax) as of December 31, 2008 and December 29, 2007, respectively.

Stock-based compensation. On January 1, 2006, the Company adopted SFAS No. 123(R), "Share-Based Payment," using the modified prospective transition method. Under this method, compensation expense is recognized for options granted on or after January 1, 2006 as well as any unvested options on the date of adoption. As allowed under the modified prospective transition method, prior period financial statements have not been restated. Prior to January 1, 2006, the Company accounted for its stock-based compensation plans under the recognition and measurement principles of Accounting Principles Board ("APB") Opinion No. 25, "Accounting for Stock Issued to Employees," and related interpretations. As such, no stock-based employee compensation costs were reflected in net earnings for options granted under those plans since they had an exercise price equal to the fair market value of the underlying common stock on the date of grant. See Note 10 for additional information about stock-based compensation.

Income taxes. The Company provides for federal and state income taxes currently payable, as well as for those deferred because of timing differences between reported income and expenses for financial statement purposes versus tax purposes. Federal and state tax credits are recorded as a reduction of income taxes. Deferred tax assets and liabilities are recognized for the future tax consequences attributable to differences between the carrying amount of assets and liabilities for financial reporting purposes and the amounts used for income tax purposes. Deferred tax assets and liabilities are measured using the enacted tax rates expected to apply to taxable income in the years in which those temporary differences are expected to be recoverable or settled. The effect of a change in tax rates is recognized as income or expense in the period of the change. See Note 11 for additional information about income taxes.

Loss from discontinued operations. In connection with certain business dispositions completed between 1991 and 1997, the Company continues to guarantee store lease obligations for a number of former subsidiaries, including Linens 'n Things. On May 2, 2008, Linens Holding Co. and certain affiliates, which operate Linens 'n Things, filed voluntary petitions under Chapter 11 of the United States Bankruptcy Code in the United States Bankruptcy Court for the District of Delaware. Pursuant to the court order entered on October 16, 2008, Linens Holding Co. is in the process of liquidating the entire Linens 'n Things retail chain. The Company's loss from discontinued operations includes $132.0 million of lease-related costs ($214.4 million, net of an $82.4 million income tax benefit), which the Company believes it will likely be required to satisfy pursuant to its Linens 'n Things lease guarantees. These amounts, which are expected to change as each lease is resolved, were calculated in accordance with SFAS No. 146, "Accounting for Costs Associated with Exit or Disposal Activities."

Earnings per common share. Basic earnings per common share is computed by dividing: (i) net earnings, after deducting the after-tax Employee Stock Ownership Plan ("ESOP") preference dividends, by (ii) the weighted average number of common shares outstanding during the year (the "Basic Shares").

When computing diluted earnings per common share, the Company assumes that the ESOP preference stock is converted into common stock and all dilutive stock awards are exercised. After the assumed ESOP preference stock conversion, the ESOP Trust would hold common stock rather than ESOP preference stock and would receive common stock dividends ($0.25800 per share in 2008, $0.22875 per share in 2007 and $0.15500 per share in 2006) rather than ESOP preference stock dividends (currently $3.90 per share). Since the ESOP Trust uses the dividends it receives to service its debt, the Company would have to increase its contribution to the ESOP Trust to compensate it for the lower dividends. This additional contribution would reduce the Company's net earnings, which in turn, would reduce the amounts that would be accrued under the Company's incentive compensation plans.

Diluted earnings per common share is computed by dividing: (i) net earnings, after accounting for the difference between the dividends on the ESOP preference stock and common stock and after making adjustments for the incentive compensation plans, by (ii) Basic Shares plus the additional shares that would be issued assuming that all dilutive stock awards are exercised and the ESOP preference stock is converted into common stock. Options to purchase 20.9 million, 10.7 million, and 4.7 million shares of common stock were outstanding as of December 31, 2008, December 29, 2007 and December 30, 2006, respectively, but were not included in the calculation of diluted earnings per share because the options' exercise prices were greater than the average market price of the common shares and, therefore, the effect would be antidilutive. See Note 8 for additional information about the ESOP.

Notes to Consolidated Financial Statements

New accounting pronouncements. In the first quarter of 2008, the Company adopted EITF Issue No. 06-4, "Accounting for Deferred Compensation and Postretirement Benefit Aspects of Endorsement Split-Dollar Life Insurance Arrangements" ("EITF 06-4"). EITF 06-4 requires the application of the provisions of SFAS No. 106, "Employers' Accounting for Postretirement Benefits Other Than Pensions" ("SFAS 106") (if, in substance, a postretirement benefit plan exists), or Accounting Principles Board Opinion No. 12 (if the arrangement is, in substance, an individual deferred compensation contract) to endorsement split-dollar life insurance arrangements. SFAS 106 requires the recognition of a liability for the discounted value of the future premium benefits that will be incurred through the death of the underlying insureds. The adoption of this statement did not have a material effect on the Company's consolidated results of operations, financial position and cash flows.

In the first quarter of 2008, the Company adopted EITF No. 06-10 "Accounting for Collateral Assignment Split-Dollar Life Insurance Agreements" ("EITF 06-10") effective fiscal 2008. EITF 06-10 provides guidance for determining a liability for the postretirement benefit obligation as well as recognition and measurement of the associated asset on the basis of the terms of the collateral assignment agreement. The adoption of this statement did not have a material effect on the Company's consolidated results of operations, financial position and cash flows.

In the first quarter of 2008, the Company adopted Financial Accounting Standards Board ("FASB") Staff Position No. FAS 157-3, "Determining the Fair Value of a Financial Asset When the Market for That Asset Is Not Active," which clarifies the application of SFAS No. 157 in a market that is not active. The adoption of this statement did not have a material impact on the Company's consolidated results of operations, financial position and cash flows.

In December 2007, the FASB issued SFAS No. 141 (revised 2007), Business Combinations ("SFAS 141R"), which replaces SFAS 141. SFAS 141R establishes the principles and requirements for how an acquirer recognizes and measures in its financial statements the identifiable assets acquired, the liabilities assumed, any noncontrolling interest in the acquiree and the goodwill acquired. The Statement also establishes disclosure requirements which will enable users to evaluate the nature and financial effects of business combinations. SFAS 141R is effective for fiscal years beginning after December 15, 2008.

been treated as an adjustment to the purchase price allocation if they had been recognized under SFAS 141. It is possible that a significant portion of these benefits will be recognized within the next twelve months. To the extent these benefits are recognized

they had been recognized under SFAS 141. It is possible that a significant portion of these benefits will be recognized within the next twelve months. To the extent these benefits are recognized after the adoption of SFAS 141R, their recognition would affect the Company's effective income tax rate rather than being treated as an adjustment to the purchase price allocation of the acquiree.

In February 2008, the FASB issued FASB Staff Position ("FSP") No. SFAS 157-2, "Effective Date of FASB Statement No. 157," which defers the effective date of SFAS 157 for nonfinancial assets and nonfinancial liabilities, except those that are recognized or disclosed at fair value in the financial statements on a recurring basis (at least annually), to fiscal years and interim periods within those fiscal years, beginning after November 15, 2008. The Company does not believe the adoption of this statement will have a material effect on its consolidated results of operations, financial position and cash flows.

In April 2008, the FASB issued FSP No. FAS 142-3, "Determining the Useful Life of Intangible Assets," which amends the factors an entity should consider in developing renewal or extension assumptions used in determining the useful lives of recognized intangible assets. This statement is effective for fiscal years beginning after December 15, 2008. The Company does not believe the adoption of this statement will have a material effect on its consolidated results of operations, financial position and cash flows.

In June 2008, the FASB reached consensus on EITF Issue No. 08-3, "Accounting by Lessees for Nonrefundable Maintenance Deposits" ("EITF 08-3"). Under EITF 08-3, lessees should account for nonrefundable maintenance deposits as deposit assets if it is probable that maintenance activities will occur and the deposit is therefore realizable. Amounts on deposit that are not probable of being used to fund future maintenance activities should be expensed. EITF 08-3 is effective for fiscal years beginning after December 15, 2008. Early application is not permitted. The Company does not believe the adoption of this statement will have a material effect on its consolidated results of operations, financial position and cash flows.

In December 2008, the FASB issued FSP No. FAS 132(R)-1, "Employers' Disclosures about Postretirement Benefit Plan Assets," which enhances the required disclosures about plan assets in an employer's defined benefit pension or other postretirement plan, including investment allocations decisions, inputs and valuations techniques used to measure the fair value of plan assets and significant concentrations of risks within plan assets. This statement is effective for financial statements issued for fiscal years ending after December 15, 2009. The Company is currently evaluating the potential impact the adoption of this statement may have on its consolidated financial statement disclosures.

Notes to Consolidated Financial Statements

NO 15 QUARTERLY FINANCIAL INFORMATION (UNAUDITED)

In millions, except per share amounts	First Quarter	Second Quarter	Third Quarter	Fourth Quarter	Fiscal Year
2008:[1]					
Net revenues	$ 21,326.0	$ 21,140.3	$ 20,863.4	$ 24,142.2	$ 87,471.9
Gross profit	4,293.0	4,373.2	4,400.6	5,223.6	18,290.4
Operating profit	1,370.1	1,478.1	1,466.2	1,731.8	6,046.2
Earnings from continuing operations	748.5	823.5	818.8	953.3	3,344.1
Loss from discontinued operations, net of income tax benefit	–	(48.7)	(82.8)	(0.5)	(132.0)
Net earnings	748.5	774.8	736.0	952.8	3,212.1
Earnings per share from continuing operations, basic	0.52	0.57	0.57	0.66	2.32
Loss per common share from discontinued operations	–	(0.03)	(0.06)	–	(0.09)
Net earnings per common share, basic	0.52	0.54	0.51	0.66	2.23
Earnings per common share from continuing operations, diluted	0.51	0.56	0.56	0.65	2.27
Loss per common share from discontinued operations	–	(0.03)	(0.06)	–	(0.09)
Net earnings per common share, diluted	0.51	0.53	0.50	0.65	2.18
Dividends per common share	0.06000	0.06000	0.06900	0.06900	0.25800
Stock price: (New York Stock Exchange)					
High	41.53	44.29	40.14	34.90	44.29
Low	34.91	39.02	31.81	23.19	23.19
2007:					
Net revenues	$ 13,188.6	$ 20,703.3	$ 20,495.2	$ 21,942.4	$ 76,329.5
Gross profit	3,303.2	4,158.5	4,195.2	4,450.8	16,107.7
Operating profit	736.5	1,309.8	1,271.1	1,475.9	4,793.3
Net earnings	408.9	723.6	689.5	815.0	2,637.0
Net earnings per common share, basic	0.45	0.48	0.47	0.56	1.97
Net earnings per common share, diluted	0.43	0.47	0.45	0.55	1.92
Dividends per common share	0.04875	0.06000	0.06000	0.06000	0.22875
Stock price: (New York Stock Exchange)					
High	34.93	39.44	39.85	42.60	42.60
Low	30.45	34.14	34.80	36.43	30.45

(1) On December 23, 2008, our Board of Directors approved a change in our fiscal year-end from the Saturday nearest December 31 of each year to December 31 of each year to better reflect our position in the health care, rather than the retail industry. The fiscal year change was effective beginning with the fourth quarter of fiscal 2008. Prior to Board approval of this change, the Saturday nearest December 31, 2008 would have resulted in a 53-week fiscal year that would have ended January 3, 2009. As you review our operating performance, please consider that fiscal years 2008 and 2007 and fiscal quarters 2008 and 2007 include 368 days, 364 days, 95 days and 91 days, respectively.

Five-Year Financial Summary

In millions, except per share amounts	**2008[1]**	2007[2]	2006	2005	2004
Statement of operations data:					
Net revenues	**$ 87,471.9**	$ 76,329.5	$ 43,821.4	$ 37,006.7	$ 30,594.6
Gross profit	**18,290.4**	16,107.7	11,742.2	9,694.6	7,915.9
Operating expenses[3][4]	**12,244.2**	11,314.4	9,300.6	7,675.1	6,461.2
Operating profit[5]	**6,046.2**	4,793.3	2,441.6	2,019.5	1,454.7
Interest expense, net	**509.5**	434.6	215.8	110.5	58.3
Income tax provision[6]	**2,192.6**	1,721.7	856.9	684.3	477.6
Earnings from continuing operations	**3,344.1**	2,637.0	1,368.9	1,224.7	918.8
Loss from discontinued operations, net of tax benefit[7]	**(132.0)**	–	–	–	–
Net earnings	**$ 3,212.1**	$ 2,637.0	$ 1,368.9	$ 1,224.7	$ 918.8
Per common share data:					
Basic earnings per common share:					
Earnings from continuing operations	**$ 2.32**	$ 1.97	$ 1.65	$ 1.49	$ 1.13
Loss from discontinued operations	**(0.09)**	–	–	–	–
Net earnings	**$ 2.23**	$ 1.97	$ 1.65	$ 1.49	$ 1.13
Diluted earnings per common share:					
Earnings from continuing operations	**$ 2.27**	$ 1.92	$ 1.60	$ 1.45	$ 1.10
Loss from discontinued operations	**(0.09)**	–	–	–	–
Net earnings	**$ 2.18**	$ 1.92	$ 1.60	$ 1.45	$ 1.10
Cash dividends per common share	**0.25800**	0.22875	0.15500	0.14500	0.13250
Balance sheet and other data:					
Total assets	**$ 60,959.9**	$ 54,721.9	$ 20,574.1	$ 15,246.6	$ 14,513.3
Long-term debt (less current portion)	**$ 8,057.2**	$ 8,349.7	$ 2,870.4	$ 1,594.1	$ 1,925.9
Total shareholders' equity	**$ 34,574.4**	$ 31,321.9	$ 9,917.6	$ 8,331.2	$ 6,987.2
Number of stores (at end of period)	**6,923**	6,301	6,205	5,474	5,378

(1) On December 23, 2008, our Board of Directors approved a change in our fiscal year-end from the Saturday nearest December 31 of each year to December 31 of each year to better reflect our position in the health care, rather than the retail industry. The fiscal year change was effective beginning with the fourth quarter of fiscal 2008. Prior to Board approval of this change, the Saturday nearest December 31, 2008 would have resulted in a 53-week fiscal year that would have ended January 3, 2009. As you review our operating performance, please consider that fiscal 2008 includes 368 days, compared to each of the remaining fiscal years presented, which include 364 days.

(2) Effective March 22, 2007, pursuant to the Agreement and Plan of Merger dated as of November 1, 2006, as amended (the "Merger Agreement"), Caremark Rx, Inc. was merged with and into a newly formed subsidiary of CVS Corporation, with the CVS subsidiary, Caremark Rx, L.L.C. ("Caremark"), continuing as the surviving entity (the "Caremark Merger"). Following the Caremark Merger, the name of the Company was changed to "CVS Caremark Corporation." By virtue of the Caremark Merger, each issued and outstanding share of Caremark common stock, par value $0.001 per share, was converted into the right to receive 1.67 shares of CVS Caremark's common stock, par value $0.01 per share. Cash was paid in lieu of fractional shares.

(3) In 2006, the Company adopted the Securities and Exchange Commission (SEC) Staff Accounting Bulletin ("SAB") No. 108, "Considering the Effects of Prior Year Misstatements when Qualifying Misstatements in Current Year Financial Statements." The adoption of this statement resulted in a $40.2 million pre-tax ($24.7 million after-tax) decrease in operating expenses for 2006.

(4) In 2004, the Company conformed its accounting for operating leases and leasehold improvements to the views expressed by the Office of the Chief Accountant of the Securities and Exchange Commission to the American Institute of Certified Public Accountants on February 7, 2005. As a result, the Company recorded a non-cash pre-tax adjustment of $65.9 million ($40.5 million after-tax) to operating expenses, which represents the cumulative effect of the adjustment for a period of approximately 20 years. Since the effect of this non-cash adjustment was not material to 2004, or any previously reported fiscal year, the cumulative effect was recorded in the fourth quarter of 2004.

(5) Operating profit includes the pre-tax effect of the charge discussed in Note (3) and Note (4) above.

(6) Income tax provision includes the effect of the following: (i) in 2006, a $11.0 million reversal of previously recorded tax reserves through the tax provision principally based on resolving certain state tax matters, (ii) in 2005, a $52.6 million reversal of previously recorded tax reserves through the tax provision principally based on resolving certain state tax matters, and (iii) in 2004, a $60.0 million reversal of previously recorded tax reserves through the tax provision principally based on finalizing certain tax return years and on a 2004 court decision relevant to the industry.

(7) In connection with certain business dispositions completed between 1991 and 1997, the Company continues to guarantee store lease obligations for a number of former subsidiaries, including Linens 'n Things. On May 2, 2008, Linens Holding Co. and certain affiliates, which operate Linens 'n Things, filed voluntary petitions under Chapter 11 of the United States Bankruptcy Code in the United States Bankruptcy Court for the District of Delaware. Pursuant to the court order entered on October 16, 2008, Linens Holding Co. is in the process of liquidating the entire Linens 'n Things retail chain. The loss from discontinued operations includes $132.0 million of lease-related costs ($214.4 million, net of an $82.4 million income tax benefit), which the Company believes it will likely be required to satisfy pursuant to its Linens 'n Things lease guarantees. These amounts, which are expected to change as each lease is resolved, were calculated in accordance with SFAS No. 146, "Accounting for Costs Associated with Exit or Disposal Activities."

Report of Independent Registered Public Accounting Firm

The Board of Directors and Shareholders
CVS Caremark Corporation

We have audited the accompanying consolidated balance sheets of CVS Caremark Corporation as of December 31, 2008 and December 29, 2007, and the related consolidated statements of operations, shareholders' equity and cash flows for the fiscal years ended December 31, 2008 and December 29, 2007. These financial statements are the responsibility of the Company's management. Our responsibility is to express an opinion on these financial statements based on our audits.

We conducted our audits in accordance with the standards of the Public Company Accounting Oversight Board (United States). Those standards require that we plan and perform the audit to obtain reasonable assurance about whether the financial statements are free of material misstatement. An audit includes examining, on a test basis, evidence supporting the amounts and disclosures in the financial statements. An audit also includes assessing the accounting principles used and significant estimates made by management, as well as, evaluating the overall financial statement presentation. We believe that our audits provide a reasonable basis for our opinion.

In our opinion, the financial statements referred to above present fairly, in all material respects, the consolidated financial position of CVS Caremark Corporation at December 31, 2008 and December 29, 2007, and the consolidated results of its operations and its cash flows for the fiscal years ended December 31, 2008 and December 29, 2007, in conformity with U.S. generally accepted accounting principles.

As discussed in Note 1 to the consolidated financial statements, effective December 31, 2006, CVS Caremark Corporation adopted Financial Accounting Standards Board (FASB) Interpretation No. 48, *Accounting for Uncertainty in Income Taxes – an interpretation of FASB Statement No. 109* and effective December 30, 2007, CVS Caremark Corporation adopted Emerging Issues Task Force (EITF) No. 06-4, *Accounting for Deferred Compensation and Postretirement Benefit Aspects of Endorsement Split-Dollar Life Insurance Arrangements* and EITF No. 06-10, *Accounting for Collateral Assignment Split-Dollar Life Insurance Arrangements.*

We also have audited, in accordance with the standards of the Public Company Accounting Oversight Board (United States), CVS Caremark Corporation's internal control over financial reporting as of December 31, 2008, based on criteria established in *Internal Control – Integrated Framework* issued by the Committee of Sponsoring Organizations of the Treadway Commission and our report dated February 26, 2009 expressed an unqualified opinion thereon.

Ernst & Young LLP

The Board of Directors and Shareholders
CVS Caremark Corporation

We have audited the accompanying consolidated statements of operations, shareholders' equity and cash flows of CVS Caremark Corporation (formerly CVS Corporation) and subsidiaries for the fiscal year ended December 30, 2006. These consolidated financial statements are the responsibility of the Company's management. Our responsibility is to express an opinion on these consolidated financial statements based on our audit.

We conducted our audit in accordance with the standards of the Public Company Accounting Oversight Board (United States). Those standards require that we plan and perform the audit to obtain reasonable assurance about whether the financial statements are free of material misstatement. An audit includes examining, on a test basis, evidence supporting the amounts and disclosures in the financial statements. An audit also includes assessing the accounting principles used and significant estimates made by management, as well as evaluating the overall financial statement presentation. We believe that our audit provides a reasonable basis for our opinion.

In our opinion, the consolidated financial statements referred to above present fairly, in all material respects, the results of operations and cash flows of CVS Caremark Corporation and subsidiaries for the fiscal year ended December 30, 2006, in conformity with U.S. generally accepted accounting principles.

KPMG LLP

KPMG LLP
Providence, Rhode Island
February 27, 2007

SOUTHWEST
NO-HIDDEN-FEE ZONE
SOUTHWEST AIRLINES CO. 2008 ANNUAL REPORT

Item 8. ***Financial Statements and Supplementary Data***

SOUTHWEST AIRLINES CO.

CONSOLIDATED BALANCE SHEET

	December 31, 2008	December 31, 2007
	(In millions, except share data)	
ASSETS		
Current assets:		
Cash and cash equivalents	**$ 1,368**	$ 2,213
Short-term investments	**435**	566
Accounts and other receivables	**209**	279
Inventories of parts and supplies, at cost	**203**	259
Fuel derivative contracts	**—**	1,069
Deferred income taxes	**365**	—
Prepaid expenses and other current assets	**3 13**	57
Total current assets	**2,893**	4,443
Property and equipment, at cost:		
Flight equipment	**13,722**	13,019
Ground property and equipment	**1,769**	1,515
Deposits on flight equipment purchase contracts	**380**	626
	15,871	15,160
Less allowance for depreciation and amortization	**4,831**	4,286
	11,040	10,874
Other assets	**375**	1,455
	$14,308	$16,772
LIABILITIES AND STOCKHOLDERS' EQUITY		
Current liabilities:		
Accounts payable	**$ 668**	$ 759
Accrued liabilities	**1,012**	3,107
Air traffic liability	**963**	931
Current maturities of long-term debt	**163**	41
Total current liabilities	**2,806**	4,838
Long-term debt less current maturities	**3,498**	2,050
Deferred income taxes	**1,904**	2,535
Deferred gains from sale and leaseback of aircraft	**105**	106
Other deferred liabilities	**1,042**	302
Commitments and contingencies		
Stockholders' equity:		
Common stock, $1.00 par value: 2,000,000,000 shares authorized; 807,611,634 shares issued in 2008 and 2007	**808**	808
Capital in excess of par value	**1,215**	1,207
Retained earnings	**4,919**	4,788
Accumulated other comprehensive income (loss)	**(984)**	1,241
Treasury stock, at cost: 67,619,062 and 72,814,104 shares in 2008 and 2007, respectively	**(1,005)**	(1,103)
Total stockholders' equity	**4,953**	6,941
	$14,308	$16,772

See accompanying notes.

SOUTHWEST AIRLINES CO.

CONSOLIDATED STATEMENT OF INCOME

	Years Ended December 31,		
	2008	**2007**	**2006**
	(In millions, except per share amounts)		
OPERATING REVENUES:			
Passenger	**$10,549**	$9,457	$8,750
Freight	**145**	130	134
Other	**329**	274	202
Total operating revenues	**11,023**	9,861	9,086
OPERATING EXPENSES:			
Salaries, wages, and benefits	**3,340**	3,213	3,052
Fuel and oil	**3,713**	2,690	2,284
Maintenance materials and repairs	**721**	616	468
Aircraft rentals	**154**	156	158
Landing fees and other rentals	**662**	560	495
Depreciation and amortization	**599**	555	515
Other operating expenses	**1,385**	1,280	1,180
Total operating expenses	**10,574**	9,070	8,152
OPERATING INCOME	**449**	791	934
OTHER EXPENSES (INCOME):			
Interest expense	**130**	119	128
Capitalized interest	**(25)**	(50)	(51)
Interest income	**(26)**	(44)	(84)
Other (gains) losses, net	**92**	(292)	151
Total other expenses (income)	**171**	(267)	144
INCOME BEFORE INCOME TAXES	**278**	1,058	790
PROVISION FOR INCOME TAXES	**100**	413	291
NET INCOME	**$ 178**	$ 645	$ 499
NET INCOME PER SHARE, BASIC	**$ .24**	$ .85	$ .63
NET INCOME PER SHARE, DILUTED	**$ .24**	$ .84	$ .61

See accompanying notes.

SOUTHWEST AIRLINES CO.

CONSOLIDATED STATEMENT OF STOCKHOLDERS' EQUITY

	Common Stock	Capital in excess of par value	Retained earnings	Accumulated other comprehensive income (loss)	Treasury stock	Total
	Years Ended December 31, 2008, 2007, and 2006					
	(In millions, except per share amounts)					
Balance at December 31, 2005	$802	$ 963	$4,018	$ 892	$ —	$ 6,675
Purchase of shares of treasury stock	—	—	—	—	(800)	(800)
Issuance of common and treasury stock pursuant to Employee stock plans	6	39	(196)	—	410	259
Tax benefit of options exercised	—	60	—	—	—	60
Share-based compensation	—	80	—	—	—	80
Cash dividends, $.018 per share	—	—	(14)	—	—	(14)
Comprehensive income (loss)						
Net income	—	—	499	—	—	499
Unrealized (loss) on derivative instruments	—	—	—	(306)	—	(306)
Other	—	—	—	(4)	—	(4)
Total comprehensive income						189
Balance at December 31, 2006	$808	$1,142	$4,307	$ 582	$ (390)	$ 6,449
Purchase of shares of treasury stock	—	—	—	—	(1,001)	(1,001)
Issuance of common and treasury stock pursuant to Employee stock plans	—	—	(150)	—	288	138
Tax benefit of options exercised	—	28	—	—	—	28
Share-based compensation	—	37	—	—	—	37
Cash dividends, $.018 per share	—	—	(14)	—	—	(14)
Comprehensive income (loss)						
Net income	—	—	645	—	—	645
Unrealized gain on derivative instruments	—	—	—	636	—	636
Other	—	—	—	23	—	23
Total comprehensive income						1,304
Balance at December 31, 2007	$808	$1,207	$4,788	$ 1,241	$(1,103)	$ 6,941
Purchase of shares of treasury stock	—	—	—	—	(54)	(54)
Issuance of common and treasury stock pursuant to Employee stock plans	—	—	(34)	—	152	118
Tax benefit of options exercised	—	(10)	—	—	—	(10)
Share-based compensation	—	18	—	—	—	18
Cash dividends, $.018 per share	—	—	(13)	—	—	(13)
Comprehensive income (loss)						
Net income	—	—	178	—	—	178
Unrealized (loss) on derivative instruments	—	—	—	(2,166)	—	(2,166)
Other	—	—	—	(59)	—	(59)
Total comprehensive income (loss)						(2,047)
Balance at December 31, 2008	**$808**	**$1,215**	**$4,919**	**$ (984)**	**$(1,005)**	**$ 4,953**

See accompanying notes.

SOUTHWEST AIRLINES CO.

CONSOLIDATED STATEMENT OF CASH FLOWS

	Years Ended December 31,		
	2008	2007	2006
		(In millions)	
CASH FLOWS FROM OPERATING ACTIVITIES:			
Net income	**$ 178**	$ 645	$ 499
Adjustments to reconcile net income to net cash provided by operating activities:			
Depreciation and amortization	**599**	555	515
Deferred income taxes	**56**	328	277
Amortization of deferred gains on sale and leaseback of aircraft	**(12)**	(14)	(16)
Share-based compensation expense	**18**	37	80
Excess tax benefits from share-based compensation arrangements	**—**	(28)	(60)
Changes in certain assets and liabilities:			
Accounts and other receivables	**71**	(38)	(5)
Other current assets	**(384)**	(229)	87
Accounts payable and accrued liabilities	**(1,853)**	1,609	(223)
Air traffic liability	**32**	131	150
Other, net	**(226)**	(151)	102
Net cash provided by (used in) operating activities	**(1,521)**	2,845	1,406
CASH FLOWS FROM INVESTING ACTIVITIES:			
Purchases of property and equipment, net	**(923)**	(1,331)	(1,399)
Purchases of short-term investments	**(5,886)**	(5,086)	(4,509)
Proceeds from sales of short-term investments	**5,831**	4,888	4,392
Debtor in possession loan to ATA Airlines, Inc.	**—**	—	20
Other, net	**—**	—	1
Net cash used in investing activities	**(978)**	(1,529)	(1,495)
CASH FLOWS FROM FINANCING ACTIVITIES:			
Issuance of long-term debt	**1,000**	500	300
Proceeds from credit line borrowing	**91**	—	—
Proceeds from revolving credit agreement	**400**	—	—
Proceeds from sale and leaseback transactions	**173**	—	—
Proceeds from Employee stock plans	**117**	139	260
Payments of long-term debt and capital lease obligations	**(55)**	(122)	(607)
Payments of cash dividends	**(13)**	(14)	(14)
Repurchase of common stock	**(54)**	(1,001)	(800)
Excess tax benefits from share-based compensation arrangements	**—**	28	60
Other, net	**(5)**	(23)	—
Net cash provided by (used in) financing activities	**1,654**	(493)	(801)
NET INCREASE (DECREASE) IN CASH AND CASH EQUIVALENTS	**(845)**	823	(890)
CASH AND CASH EQUIVALENTS AT BEGINNING OF PERIOD	**2,213**	1,390	2,280
CASH AND CASH EQUIVALENTS AT END OF PERIOD	**$ 1,368**	$ 2,213	$ 1,390
SUPPLEMENTAL DISCLOSURES			
Cash payments for:			
Interest, net of amount capitalized	**$ 100**	$ 63	$ 78
Income taxes	**$ 71**	$ 94	$ 15

See accompanying notes.

47

NOTES TO CONSOLIDATED FINANCIAL STATEMENTS
December 31, 2008

1. Summary of Significant Accounting Policies

Basis of Presentation

Southwest Airlines Co. (the Company) is a major domestic airline that provides point-to-point, low-fare service. The Consolidated Financial Statements include the accounts of the Company and its wholly owned subsidiaries. All significant intercompany balances and transactions have been eliminated. The preparation of financial statements in conformity with generally accepted accounting principles in the United States (GAAP) requires management to make estimates and assumptions that affect the amounts reported in the financial statements and accompanying notes. Actual results could differ from these estimates.

Certain prior period amounts have been reclassified to conform to the current presentation. In the Consolidated Statement of Income for the years ended December 31, 2007 and 2006, jet fuel sales taxes and jet fuel excise taxes are both presented as a component of "Fuel and oil" instead of being included in "Other operating expenses" as previously presented. For the years ended December 31, 2007 and 2006, the Company reclassified a total of $154 million and $146 million, respectively, in jet fuel sales taxes and jet fuel excise taxes as a result of this change in presentation. For the year ended December 31, 2008, "Fuel and oil" includes $187 million in jet fuel sales taxes and jet fuel excise taxes.

Cash and cash equivalents

Cash in excess of that necessary for operating requirements is invested in short-term, highly liquid, income-producing investments. Investments with maturities of three months or less are classified as cash and cash equivalents, which primarily consist of certificates of deposit, money market funds, and investment grade commercial paper issued by major corporations and financial institutions. Cash and cash equivalents are stated at cost, which approximates market value.

Short-term investments

Short-term investments consist of investments with maturities of greater than three months but less than twelve months. These are primarily money market funds and investment grade commercial paper issued by major corporations and financial institutions, short-term securities issued by the U.S. Government, and certain auction rate securities with auction reset periods of less than 12 months for which auctions have been successful or are expected to be successful within the following 12 months. All of these investments are classified as available-for-sale securities and are stated at fair value, except for $17 million in auction rate securities that are classified as trading securities as discussed in Note 11. For all short-term investments, at each reset period, the Company accounts for the transaction as "Proceeds from sales of short-term investments" for the security relinquished, and a "Purchase of short-investments" for the security purchased, in the accompanying Consolidated Statement of Cash Flows. Unrealized gains and losses, net of tax, are recognized in "Accumulated other comprehensive income (loss)" in the accompanying Consolidated Balance Sheet. Realized net gains on specific investments, which totaled $13 million in 2008, $17 million in 2007, and $17 million in 2006, are reflected in "Interest income" in the accompanying Consolidated Statement of Income.

The Company's cash and cash equivalents and short-term investments as of December 31, 2007 included $2.0 billion in collateral deposits received from a counterparty of the Company's fuel derivative instruments. As of December 31, 2008, the Company did not hold any cash collateral deposits from counterparties, but had $240 million of its cash on deposit with a counterparty. Although amounts provided or held are not restricted in any way, investment earnings from these deposits generally must be remitted back to the entity that provided the deposit. Depending on the fair value of the Company's fuel derivative instruments, the amounts of collateral deposits held or provided at any point in time can fluctuate significantly. Therefore, the Company generally excludes cash collateral deposits held, but includes deposits provided, in its decisions related to long-term cash planning and forecasting. See Note 10 for further information on these collateral deposits and fuel derivative instruments.

Accounts and other receivables

Accounts and other receivables are carried at cost. They primarily consist of amounts due from credit card companies associated with sales of tickets

NOTES TO CONSOLIDATED FINANCIAL STATEMENTS — (Continued)

for future travel and amounts due from counterparties associated with fuel derivative instruments that have settled. The amount of allowance for doubtful accounts as of December 31, 2008, 2007, and 2006 was immaterial. In addition, the provision for doubtful accounts and write-offs for 2008, 2007, and 2006 were immaterial.

Inventories

Inventories primarily consist of flight equipment expendable parts, materials, aircraft fuel, and supplies. All of these items are carried at average cost, less an allowance for obsolescence. These items are generally charged to expense when issued for use. The reserve for obsolescence was immaterial at December 31, 2008, 2007, and 2006. In addition, the Company's provision for obsolescence and write-offs for 2008, 2007, and 2006 was immaterial.

Property and equipment

Property and equipment is stated at cost. Depreciation is provided by the straight-line method to estimated residual values over periods generally ranging from 23 to 25 years for flight equipment and 5 to 30 years for ground property and equipment once the asset is placed in service. Residual values estimated for aircraft are generally 10 to 15 percent and for ground property and equipment range from zero to 10 percent. Property under capital leases and related obligations is recorded at an amount equal to the present value of future minimum lease payments computed on the basis of the Company's incremental borrowing rate or, when known, the interest rate implicit in the lease. Amortization of property under capital leases is on a straight-line basis over the lease term and is included in depreciation expense.

When appropriate, the Company evaluates its long-lived assets used in operations for impairment. Impairment losses would be recorded when events and circumstances indicate that an asset might be impaired and the undiscounted cash flows to be generated by that asset are less than the carrying amounts of the asset. Factors that would indicate potential impairment include, but are not limited to, significant decreases in the market value of the long-lived asset(s), a significant change in the long-lived asset's physical condition, and operating or cash flow losses associated with the use of the long-lived asset. Excluding the impact of cash collateral deposits with counterparties based on the fair value of the Company's fuel derivative instruments, the Company continues to experience positive cash flow associated with its aircraft fleet, and there have been no impairments of long-lived assets recorded during 2008, 2007, or 2006.

Aircraft and engine maintenance

The cost of scheduled inspections and repairs and routine maintenance costs for all aircraft and engines are charged to maintenance expense as incurred. Modifications that significantly enhance the operating performance or extend the useful lives of aircraft or engines are capitalized and amortized over the remaining life of the asset.

Intangible assets

Intangible assets primarily consist of leasehold rights to airport owned gates. These assets are amortized on a straight-line basis over the expected useful life of the lease, approximately 20 years. The accumulated amortization related to the Company's intangible assets at December 31, 2008, and 2007, was $12 million and $9 million, respectively. The Company periodically assesses its intangible assets for impairment in accordance with SFAS 142, *Goodwill and Other Intangible Assets*; however, no impairments have been noted.

Revenue recognition

Tickets sold are initially deferred as "Air traffic liability". Passenger revenue is recognized when transportation is provided. "Air traffic liability" primarily represents tickets sold for future travel dates and estimated refunds and exchanges of tickets sold for past travel dates. The majority of the Company's tickets sold are nonrefundable. Tickets that are sold but not flown on the travel date (whether refundable or nonrefundable) can be reused for another flight, up to a year from the date of sale, or refunded (if the ticket is refundable). A small percentage of tickets (or partial tickets) expire unused. The Company estimates the amount of future refunds and exchanges, net of forfeitures, for all unused tickets once the flight date has passed.

NOTES TO CONSOLIDATED FINANCIAL STATEMENTS — (Continued)

The Company is also required to collect certain taxes and fees from Customers on behalf of government agencies and remit these back to the applicable governmental entity on a periodic basis. These taxes and fees include U.S. federal transportation taxes, federal security charges, and airport passenger facility charges. These items are collected from Customers at the time they purchase their tickets, but are not included in Passenger revenue. The Company records a liability upon collection from the Customer and relieves the liability when payments are remitted to the applicable governmental agency.

Frequent flyer program

The Company records a liability for the estimated incremental cost of providing free travel under its Rapid Rewards frequent flyer program at the time an award is earned. The estimated incremental cost includes direct passenger costs such as fuel, food, and other operational costs, but does not include any contribution to overhead or profit.

The Company also sells frequent flyer credits and related services to companies participating in its Rapid Rewards frequent flyer program. Funds received from the sale of flight segment credits are accounted for under the residual value method. Under this method, the Company has determined the portion of funds received for sale of flight segment credits that relate to free travel, currently estimated at 81 percent of the amount received per flight segment credit sold. These amounts are deferred and recognized as "Passenger revenue" when the ultimate free travel awards are flown or the credits expire unused. The remaining 19 percent of the amount received per flight segment credit sold, which is assumed not to be associated with future travel, includes items such as access to the Company's frequent flyer program population for marketing/ solicitation purposes, use of the Company's logo on co-branded credit cards, and other trademarks, designs, images, etc. of the Company for use in marketing materials. This remaining portion is recognized in "Other revenue" in the period earned.

Advertising

The Company expenses the costs of advertising as incurred. Advertising expense for the years ended December 31, 2008, 2007, and 2006 was $199 million, $191 million, and $182 million, respectively.

Share-based Employee compensation

The Company has share-based compensation plans covering the majority of its Employee groups, including a plan covering the Company's Board of Directors and plans related to employment contracts with the Chairman Emeritus of the Company. The Company accounts for share-based compensation utilizing the fair value recognition provisions of SFAS No. 123R, "Share-Based Payment." See Note 14.

Financial derivative instruments

The Company accounts for financial derivative instruments utilizing Statement of Financial Accounting Standards No. 133 (SFAS 133), "Accounting for Derivative Instruments and Hedging Activities," as amended. The Company utilizes various derivative instruments, including crude oil, unleaded gasoline, and heating oil-based derivatives, to attempt to reduce the risk of its exposure to jet fuel price increases. These instruments primarily consist of purchased call options, collar structures, and fixed-price swap agreements, and upon proper qualification are accounted for as cash-flow hedges, as defined by SFAS 133. The Company has also entered into interest rate swap agreements to convert a portion of its fixed-rate debt to floating rates and one floating-rate debt issuance to a fixed-rate. These interest rate hedges are accounted for as fair value hedges or as cash flow hedges, as defined by SFAS 133.

Since the majority of the Company's financial derivative instruments are not traded on a market exchange, the Company estimates their fair values. Depending on the type of instrument, the values are determined by the use of present value methods or standard option value models with assumptions about commodity prices based on those observed in underlying markets. Also, since there is not a reliable forward market for jet fuel, the Company must estimate the future prices of jet fuel in order to measure the effectiveness of the hedging instruments in offsetting changes to those prices, as required by SFAS 133. Forward jet fuel prices are estimated through utilization of a statistical-based regression

NOTES TO CONSOLIDATED FINANCIAL STATEMENTS — (Continued)

equation with data from market forward prices of like commodities. This equation is then adjusted for certain items, such as transportation costs, that are stated in the Company's fuel purchasing contracts with its vendors.

For the effective portion of settled hedges, as defined in SFAS 133, the Company records the associated gains or losses as a component of "Fuel and oil" expense in the Consolidated Statement of Income. For amounts representing ineffectiveness, as defined, or changes in fair value of derivative instruments for which hedge accounting is not applied, the Company records any gains or losses as a component of "Other (gains) losses, net", in the Consolidated Statement of Income. Amounts that are paid or received associated with the purchase or sale of financial derivative instruments (i.e., premium costs of option contracts) are classified as a component of "Other (gains) losses, net", in the Consolidated Statement of Income in the period in which the instrument settles or expires. All cash flows associated with purchasing and selling derivatives are classified as operating cash flows in the Consolidated Statement of Cash Flows, within "Changes in certain assets and liabilities." See Note 10 for further information on SFAS 133 and financial derivative instruments.

Software capitalization

The Company capitalizes certain costs related to the acquisition and development of software in accordance with Statement of Position 98-1, "Accounting for the Costs of Computer Software Developed or Obtained for Internal Use." The Company amortizes these costs using the straight-line method over the estimated useful life of the software which is generally five years.

Income taxes

The Company accounts for deferred income taxes utilizing Statement of Financial Accounting Standards No. 109 (SFAS 109), "Accounting for Income Taxes", as amended. SFAS 109 requires an asset and liability method, whereby deferred tax assets and liabilities are recognized based on the tax effects of temporary differences between the financial statements and the tax bases of assets and liabilities, as measured by current enacted tax rates. When appropriate, in accordance with SFAS 109, the Company evaluates the need for a valuation allowance to reduce deferred tax assets.

The Company's policy for recording interest and penalties associated with audits is to record such items as a component of income before taxes. Penalties are recorded in "Other (gains) losses, net," and interest paid or received is recorded in interest expense or interest income, respectively, in the statement of income. For the year ended December 31, 2008, the Company recorded no interest related to the settlement of audits for certain prior periods.

Concentration Risk

Approximately 77 percent of the Company's Employees are unionized and are covered by collective bargaining agreements. Historically, the Company has managed this risk by maintaining positive relationships with its Employees and its Employee's Representatives. The following Employee groups are under agreements that have become amendable and are currently in negotiations: Pilots, Flight Attendants, Ramp, Operations, Provisioning, and Freight Agents, Stock Clerks, and Customer Service and Reservations Agents. The Company reached a Tentative Agreement with its Mechanics during fourth quarter 2008, and the agreement was ratified by this group during January 2009. The Company's Aircraft Appearance Technicians and its Flight Dispatchers are subject to agreements that become amendable during 2009.

The Company attempts to minimize its concentration risk with regards to its cash, cash equivalents, and its investment portfolio. This is accomplished by diversifying and limiting amounts among different counterparties, the type of investment, and the amount invested in any individual security or money market fund.

To manage risk associated with financial derivative instruments held, the Company selects and will periodically review counterparties based on credit ratings, limits its exposure to a single counterparty, and monitors the market position of the program and its relative market position with each counterparty. The Company also has agreements with

NOTES TO CONSOLIDATED FINANCIAL STATEMENTS — (Continued)

counterparties containing early termination rights and/or bilateral collateral provisions whereby security is required if market risk exposure exceeds a specified threshold amount or credit ratings fall below certain levels. At December 31, 2008, the Company had provided $240 million in cash collateral deposits to one of its counterparties under these bilateral collateral provisions. The cash collateral provided to the counterparty has been recorded as a reduction to "Cash and cash equivalents" and an increase to "Prepaid expenses and other current assets." Cash collateral deposits serve to decrease, but not totally eliminate, the credit risk associated with the Company's hedging program. See Note 10 for further information.

The Company operates an all-Boeing 737 fleet of aircraft. If the Company was unable to acquire additional aircraft from Boeing, or Boeing was unable or unwilling to provide adequate support for its products, the Company's operations could be adversely impacted. However, the Company considers its relationship with Boeing to be excellent and believes the advantages of operating a single fleet type outweigh the risks of such a strategy.

CHAPTER

2 Analyzing Business Transactions

Focus on Financial Statements

INCOME STATEMENT

Revenues
– Expenses
= Net Income

STATEMENT OF RETAINED EARNINGS

Opening Balance
+ Net Income
– Dividends
= Retained Earnings

BALANCE SHEET

Assets	Liabilities
	Equity

A = L + E

STATEMENT OF CASH FLOWS

Operating activities
+ Investing activities
+ Financing activities
= Change in Cash
+ Starting Balance
= Ending Cash Balance

Business transactions can affect all the financial statements.

All business transactions require the application of three basic accounting concepts: recording a transaction at the right time, placing the right value on it, and calling it by the right name. Most accounting frauds and mistakes violate one or more of these basic accounting concepts. What you learn in this chapter will help you avoid making such mistakes. It will also help you recognize correct accounting practices.

LEARNING OBJECTIVES

LO1 Explain how the concepts of recognition, valuation, and classification apply to business transactions and why they are important factors in ethical financial reporting. (pp. 92–96)

LO2 Explain the double-entry system and the usefulness of T accounts in analyzing business transactions. (pp. 96–100)

LO3 Demonstrate how the double-entry system is applied to common business transactions. (pp. 101–108)

LO4 Prepare a trial balance, and describe its value and limitations. (pp. 109–111)

LO5 Show how the timing of transactions affects cash flows and liquidity. (pp. 111–113)

SUPPLEMENTAL OBJECTIVE

SO6 Define the *chart of accounts,* record transactions in the general journal, and post transactions to the ledger. (pp. 114–119)

DECISION POINT ▸ A USER'S FOCUS THE BOEING COMPANY

In April 2006, the Chinese government announced that it had ordered 80 **Boeing** commercial jet liners, thus fulfilling a commitment it had made to purchase 150 airplanes from Boeing. Valued at about $4.6 billion, the order for the 80 airplanes was one of many events that brought about Boeing's resurgence in the stock market. After Boeing received this order, as well as orders from other customers, its stock began trading at an all-time high.

Typically, it takes Boeing almost two years to manufacture an airplane. In this case, the aircraft delivery cycle was expected to peak in 2009.[1]

- ▸ An order for airplanes is obviously an important economic event for both the buyer and the seller. Is there a difference between an economic event and a business transaction that should be recorded in the accounting records?
- ▸ Should Boeing record the order in its accounting records?
- ▸ How important are liquidity and cash flows to Boeing?

Measurement Issues

LO1 Explain how the concepts of recognition, valuation, and classification apply to business transactions and why they are important factors in ethical financial reporting.

Business transactions are economic events that affect a company's financial position. As shown in Figure 2-1, to measure a business transaction, you must decide when the transaction occurred (the recognition issue), what value to place on the transaction (the valuation issue), and how the components of the transaction should be categorized (the classification issue).

These three issues—recognition, valuation, and classification—underlie almost every major decision in financial accounting today. They are at the heart of accounting for pension plans, mergers of giant companies, and international transactions. In discussing these issues, we follow generally accepted accounting principles (GAAP) and use an approach that promotes an understanding of basic accounting concepts. Keep in mind, however, that measurement issues can be controversial, and resolutions to them are not always as cut-and-dried as the ones presented here.

Recognition

Study Note

In accounting, *recognize* means to record a transaction or event.

The **recognition** issue refers to the difficulty of deciding *when* a business transaction should be recorded. The resolution of this issue is important because the date on which a transaction is recorded affects amounts in the financial statements.

To illustrate some of the factors involved in the recognition issue, suppose a company wants to purchase an office desk. The following events take place:

1. An employee sends a purchase requisition for the desk to the purchasing department.
2. The purchasing department sends a purchase order to the supplier.
3. The supplier ships the desk.
4. The company receives the desk.
5. The company receives the bill from the supplier.
6. The company pays the bill.

Study Note

A purchase should usually not be recognized (recorded) before title is transferred because until that point, the vendor has not fulfilled its contractual obligation and the buyer has no liability.

According to accounting tradition, a transaction should be recorded when title to merchandise passes from the supplier to the purchaser and creates an obligation to pay. Thus, depending on the details of the shipping agreement for the

FIGURE 2-1
The Role of Measurement Issues

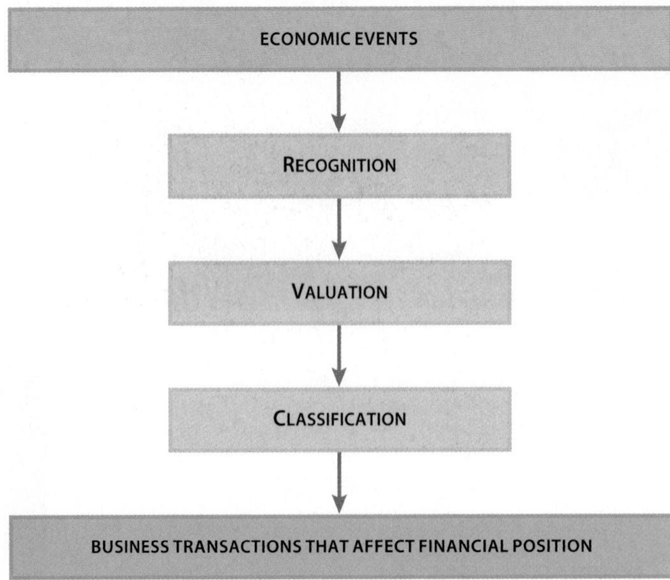

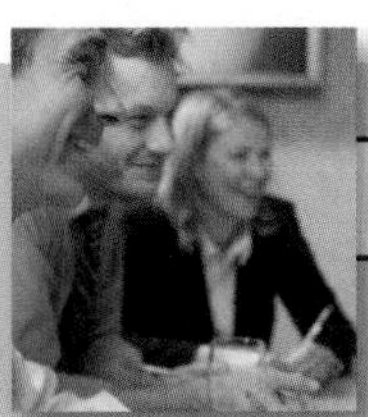

FOCUS ON BUSINESS PRACTICE

Accounting Policies: Where Do You Find Them?

As the text explains, the order of 80 **Boeing** jet liners by the Chinese government, which is the focus of this chapter's Decision Point, was not an event that either the buyer or the seller should have recorded as a transaction. But when do companies record sales or purchase transactions? The answer to this question and others about companies' accounting policies can be found in the Summary of Significant Accounting Policies in their annual reports. For example, in that section of its annual report, Boeing states: "We recognize sales for commercial airplane deliveries as each unit is completed and accepted by the customer."[2]

desk, the transaction should be recognized (recorded) at the time of either event **3** or **4**. This is the guideline we generally use in this book. However, many small businesses that have simple accounting systems do not record a transaction until they receive a bill (event **5**) or pay it (event **6**) because these are the implied points of title transfer. The predetermined time at which a transaction should be recorded is the **recognition point**.

Although purchase requisitions and purchase orders (events **1** and **2**) are economic events, they do not affect a company's financial position, and they are not recognized in the accounting records. Even the most important economic events may not be recognized in the accounting records. For example, the order of 80 airplanes described in the Decision Point was a very important economic event for the Chinese government and **Boeing**, but the recognition point for the transaction for both the buyer and the seller is several years in the future—that is, when the planes are delivered and title to them transfers from Boeing to the Chinese government.

Here are some more examples of economic events that should and should not be recorded as business transactions:

Events That Are Not *Recorded as Transactions*	*Events That* Are *Recorded as Transactions*
A customer inquires about the availability of a service.	A customer buys a service.
A company hires a new employee.	A company pays an employee for work performed.
A company signs a contract to provide a service in the future.	A company performs a service.

The recognition issue can be a difficult one to resolve. For example, consider an advertising agency that is planning a major advertising campaign for one of its clients. Employees may work on the plan several hours a day for a number of weeks. They add value to the plan as they develop it. Should this added value be recognized as the plan is being developed or at the time it is completed? In most cases, the increase in value is recorded at the time the plan is finished and the client is billed for it. However, if a plan is going to take several months to develop, the agency and the client may agree that the client will be billed at key points during its development. In that case, a transaction is recorded at each billing.

FOCUS ON BUSINESS PRACTICE

IFRS

The Challenge of Fair Value Accounting

The measurement of fair value is a major challenge in merging international financial reporting standards (IFRS) with U.S. GAAP. Both the International Accounting Standards Board (IASB) and the Financial Accounting Standards Board (FASB) are committed to this effort. Fair value is the price to sell an asset or transfer a liability in an orderly market by an arm's-length transaction. Fair value represents a hypothetical transaction that in many cases is difficult to measure: It represents the selling price of an asset or the payment price of a liability. It does not represent the price of acquiring the asset or assuming the liability. In practice, the potential selling price of equipment used in a factory or an investment in a private company for which no ready market exists may not be easy to determine.

Valuation

The **valuation** issue focuses on assigning a monetary value to a business transaction and accounting for the assets and liabilities that result from the business transaction. Generally accepted accounting principles state that all business transactions should be valued at *fair value* when they occur. **Fair value** is defined as the *exchange price* of an actual or potential business transaction between market participants.[3] This practice of recording transactions at exchange price at the point of recognition is commonly referred to as the **cost principle.** It is used because the cost, or exchange price, is verifiable. For example, when the order referred to in the Decision Point is finally complete and **Boeing** delivers the airplanes to the Chinese government, the two entities will record the transaction in their respective records at the price they have agreed on.

Study Note

The value of a transaction usually is based on a business document—a canceled check or an invoice.

Normally, the value of an asset is held at its initial fair value or cost until the asset is sold, expires, or is consumed. However, if there is evidence that the fair value of the asset or liability has changed, an adjustment to the initial value may be required. There are different rules for the application of fair value to different classes of assets. For example, a building or equipment remains at cost unless there is convincing evidence that the fair value is less than cost. In this case, a loss should be recorded to reduce the value from its cost to fair value. Investments,

FOCUS ON BUSINESS PRACTICE

No Dollar Amount: How Can That Be?

Determining the value of a sale or purchase transaction isn't difficult when the value equals the amount of cash that changes hands. However, barter transactions, in which exchanges are made but no cash changes hands, can make valuation more complicated. Barter transactions are quite common in business today. Here are some examples:

- A consulting company provides its services to an auto dealer in exchange for the loan of a car for a year.
- An office supply company provides a year's supply of computer paper to a local weekly newspaper in exchange for an advertisement in 52 issues of the paper.
- Two Internet companies each provide an advertisement and link to the other's website on their own websites.

Determining the value of these transactions is a matter of determining the fair value of the items being traded.

on the other hand, are often accounted for at fair value, regardless of whether fair value is greater or less than cost. Because these investments are available for sale, the fair value is the best measure of the potential benefit to the company. In its annual report, **Intel Corporation** states: "Investments designated as available-for-sale on the balance sheet date are reported at fair value."[4]

Classification

> **Study Note**
> If CVS buys paper towels to resell to customers, the cost would be recorded as an asset in the Inventory account. If the paper towels are used for cleaning in the store, the cost is an expense.

The **classification** issue has to do with assigning all the transactions in which a business engages to appropriate categories, or 96. Classification of debts can affect a company's ability to borrow money, and classification of purchases can affect its income. For example, purchases of tools may be considered repair expenses (a component of stockholders' equity) or equipment (asset).

As noted in the Decision Point, it will take **Boeing** several years to manufacture the 80 airplanes that the Chinese government ordered. Over those years, many classification issues will arise. One of the most important is how to classify the numerous costs that Boeing will incur in building the airplanes. As you will see, generally accepted accounting principles require that these costs be classified as assets until the sale is recorded at the time the airplanes are delivered. At that time, they will be reclassified as expenses. In this way, the costs will offset the revenues from the sale. It will then be possible to tell whether Boeing made a profit or loss on the transaction.

As we explain later in the chapter, proper classification depends not only on correctly analyzing the effect of each transaction on a business but also on maintaining a system of accounts that reflects that effect.

Ethics and Measurement Issues

Recognition, valuation, and classification are important factors in ethical financial reporting, and generally accepted accounting principles provide direction about their treatment. These guidelines are intended to help managers meet their obligation to their company's owners and to the public. Many of the most egregious financial reporting frauds over the past several years have resulted from violations of these guidelines.

Unethical accounting practices at Enron led to the collapse of the company and the loss of thousands of jobs and pensions. This photograph shows the former Enron building in Houston, Texas.

Courtesy of Paul S. Wolf, 2009/Used under license from Shutterstock.com.

- **Computer Associates** violated the guidelines for recognition when it kept its books open a few days after the end of a reporting period so revenues could be counted a quarter earlier than they should have been. In all, the company prematurely reported $3.3 billion in revenues from 363 software contracts. When the SEC ordered the company to stop the practice, Computer Associates' stock price dropped by 43 percent in a single day.
- Among its many other transgressions, **Enron Corporation** violated the guidelines for valuation when it valued assets that it transferred to related companies at far more than their actual value.
- By a simple violation of the guidelines for classification, **WorldCom** (now **MCI**) perpetrated the largest financial fraud in history, which resulted in the largest bankruptcy in history. Over a period of several years, the company recorded as assets expenditures that should have been classified as expenses; this had the effect of understating the company's expenses and overstating its income by more than $10 billion.

STOP & APPLY >

Four major issues underlie every accounting transaction: recognition, valuation, classification, and ethics. Match each of these issues to the statements below that are most closely associated with the issue. A company

1. Records a piece of equipment at the price paid for it.
2. Records the purchase of the equipment on the day on which it takes ownership.
3. Records the equipment as an expense in order to show lower earnings.
4. Records the equipment as an asset because it will benefit future periods.

SOLUTION

1. valuation; 2. recognition; 3. ethics; 4. classification

Double-Entry System

LO2 Explain the double-entry system and the usefulness of T accounts in analyzing business transactions.

The double-entry system, the backbone of accounting, evolved during the Renaissance. The first systematic description of double-entry bookkeeping appeared in 1494, two years after Columbus discovered America, in a mathematics book by Fra Luca Pacioli. Goethe, the famous German poet and dramatist, referred to double-entry bookkeeping as "one of the finest discoveries of the human intellect." Werner Sombart, an eminent economist-sociologist, believed that "double-entry bookkeeping is born of the same spirit as the system of Galileo and Newton."

What is the significance of the double-entry system? The system is based on the *principle of duality,* which means that every economic event has two aspects—effort and reward, sacrifice and benefit, source and use—that offset, or balance, each other. In the **double-entry system,** each transaction must be recorded with at least one debit and one credit, and the total amount of the debits must equal the total amount of the credits. Because of the way it is designed, the whole system is always in balance. All accounting systems, no matter how sophisticated, are based on the principle of duality.

Study Note

Each transaction must include at least one debit and one credit, and the debit totals must equal the credit totals.

Accounts

Accounts are the basic storage units for accounting data and are used to accumulate amounts from similar transactions. An accounting system has a separate account for each asset, each liability, and each component of stockholders' equity, including revenues and expenses. Whether a company keeps records by hand or by computer, managers must be able to refer to accounts so that they can study their company's financial history and plan for the future. A very small company may need only a few dozen accounts; a multinational corporation may need thousands.

An account title should describe what is recorded in the account. However, account titles can be rather confusing. For example, *Fixed Assets, Plant and Equipment, Capital Assets,* and *Long-Lived Assets* are all titles for long-term assets. Moreover, many account titles change over time as preferences and practices change.

When you come across an account title that you don't recognize, examine the context of the name—whether it is classified in the financial statements as an asset, liability, or component of stockholders' equity—and look for the kind of transaction that gave rise to the account.

The T Account

Study Note

Many students have preconceived ideas about what debit and credit mean. They think debit means "decrease" (or implies something bad) and credit means "increase" (or implies something good). It is important to realize that debit simply means "left side" and credit simply means "right side."

The **T account** is a good place to begin the study of the double-entry system. Such an account has three parts: a title, which identifies the asset, liability, or stockholders' equity account; a left side, which is called the **debit** side; and a right side, which is called the **credit** side. The T account, so called because it resembles the letter *T*, is used to analyze transactions. It looks like this:

Title of Account	
Debit (left) side	Credit (right) side

Any entry made on the left side of the account is a debit, and any entry made on the right side is a credit. The terms *debit* (abbreviated Dr., from the Latin *debere*) and *credit* (abbreviated Cr., from the Latin *credere*) are simply the accountant's words for "left" and "right" (*not* for "increase" or "decrease"). We present a more formal version of the T account, the ledger account form, later in this chapter.

The T Account Illustrated

Suppose a company had several transactions that involved the receipt or payment of cash. These transactions can be summarized in the Cash account by recording receipts on the left (debit) side of a T account and payments on the right (credit) side.

	Cash	
	100,000	70,000
	3,000	400
		1,200
	103,000	**71,600**
Bal.	**31,400**	

The cash receipts on the left total $103,000. (The total is written in bold figures so that it cannot be confused with an actual debit entry.) The cash payments on the right side total $71,600. These totals are simply working totals, or **footings**. Footings, which are calculated at the end of each month, are an easy way to determine cash on hand. The difference in dollars between the total debit footing and the total credit footing is called the **balance**, or *account balance*. If the balance is a debit, it is written on the left side. If it is a credit, it is written on the right side. Notice that the Cash account has a debit balance of $31,400 ($103,000 − $71,600). This is the amount of cash the business has on hand at the end of the month.

Rules of Double-Entry Accounting

The two rules of the double-entry system are that every transaction affects at least two accounts and that total debits must equal total credits. In other words, for every transaction, one or more accounts must be debited, or entered on the left side of the T account, and one or more accounts must be credited, or entered on the right side of the T account, and the total dollar amount of the debits must equal the total dollar amount of the credits.

Look again at the accounting equation:

Assets = Liabilities + Stockholders' Equity

You can see that if a debit increases assets, then a credit must be used to increase liabilities or stockholders' equity because they are on opposite sides of the equal sign. Likewise, if a credit decreases assets, then a debit must be used to decrease liabilities or stockholders' equity. These rules can be shown as follows:

Assets		=	Liabilities		+	Stockholders' Equity	
Debit for increases (+)	Credit for decreases (−)		Debit for decreases (−)	Credit for increases (+)		Debit for decreases (−)	Credit for increases (+)

1. Debit increases in assets to asset accounts. Credit decreases in assets to asset accounts.
2. Credit increases in liabilities and stockholders' equity to liability and stockholders' equity accounts. Debit decreases in liabilities and stockholders' equity to liability and stockholders' equity accounts.

One of the more difficult points to understand is the application of double-entry rules to the components of stockholders' equity. The key is to remember that dividends and expenses are deductions from stockholders' equity. Thus, transactions that *increase* dividends or expenses *decrease* stockholders' equity. Consider this expanded version of the accounting equation:

				Stockholders' Equity						
Assets	=	Liabilities	+	Common Stock	+	Retained Earnings	−	Dividends	+	Revenues	−	Expenses

Assets		Liabilities		Common Stock		Retained Earnings		Dividends		Revenues		Expenses	
+	−	−	+	−	+	−	+	+	−	−	+	+	−
(Dr.)	(Cr.)	(Dr.)	(Cr.)	(Dr.)	(Cr.)	(Dr.)	(Cr.)	(Dr.)	(Cr.)	(Dr.)	(Cr.)	(Dr.)	(Cr.)

TABLE 2-1
Normal Account Balances of Major Account Categories

	Increases Recorded by		Normal Balance	
Account Category	**Debit**	**Credit**	**Debit**	**Credit**
Assets	x		x	
Liabilities		x		x
Stockholders' equity:				
Common stock		x		x
Retained earnings		x		x
Dividends	x		x	
Revenues		x		x
Expenses	x		x	

Normal Balance

The **normal balance** of an account is its usual balance and is the side (debit or credit) that increases the account. Table 2-1 summarizes the normal account balances of the major account categories. If you have difficulty remembering the normal balances and the rules of debit and credit, try using the acronym ADE: Asset accounts, Dividends, and Expenses are always increased by debits. All other accounts are increased by credits.

Study Note

Although dividends are a component of stockholders' equity, they normally appear only in the statement of retained earnings. They do not appear in the stockholders' equity section of the balance sheet.

Stockholders' Equity Accounts

Figure 2-2 illustrates how stockholders' equity accounts relate to each other and to the financial statements. The distinctions among these accounts are important for both legal purposes and financial reporting.

- Stockholders' equity accounts represent the legal claims of stockholders to the assets of a corporation. The Common Stock account represents stockholders' claims arising from their investments in the business, and the Retained Earnings account represents stockholders' claims arising from profitable operations.

FIGURE 2-2
Relationships of Stockholders' Equity Accounts

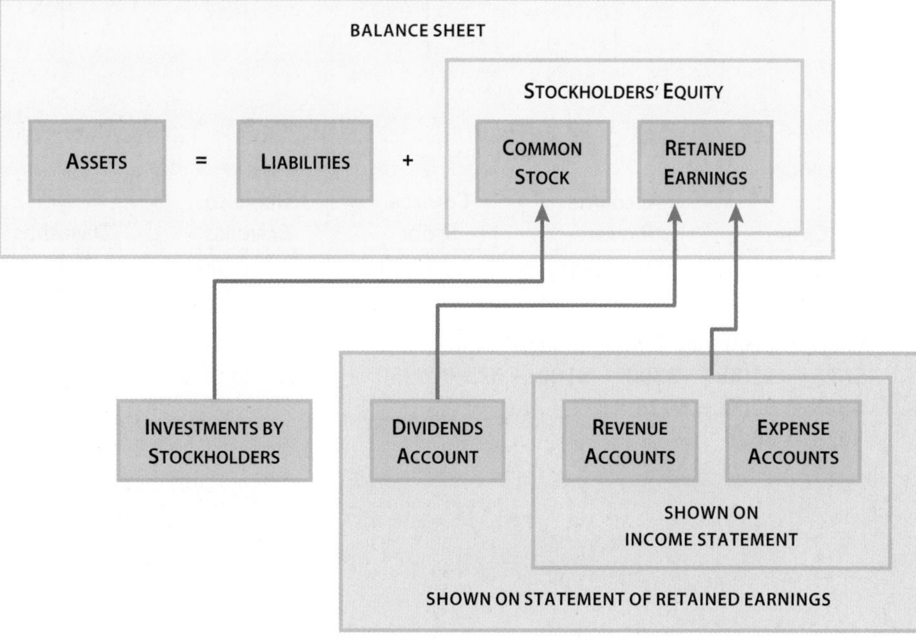

Study Note

Although revenues and expenses are components of stockholders' equity, they appear on the income statement, not in the stockholders' equity section of the balance sheet. Figure 2-2 illustrates this point.

Both are claims against the general assets of the company, not against specific assets. Dividends are deducted from the stockholders' claims on retained earnings and are shown on the statement of retained earnings.

- By law, investments by stockholders and dividends must be separated from revenues and expenses for both income tax purposes and financial reporting purposes.
- Managers need a detailed breakdown of revenues and expenses for budgeting and operating purposes. From the Revenue and Expense accounts on the income statement, they can identify the sources of all revenues and the nature of all expenses. In this way, accounting gives managers information about whether they have achieved a primary business goal—that is, whether they have enabled their company to earn a net income.

& APPLY >

You are given the following list of accounts with dollar amounts:

Dividends	$ 75	Common Stock	$300
Accounts Payable	200	Fees Revenue	250
Wages Expense	150	Retained Earnings	100
Cash	625		

Insert the account title at the top of its corresponding T account and enter the dollar amount as a normal balance in the account. Then show that the accounting equation is in balance.

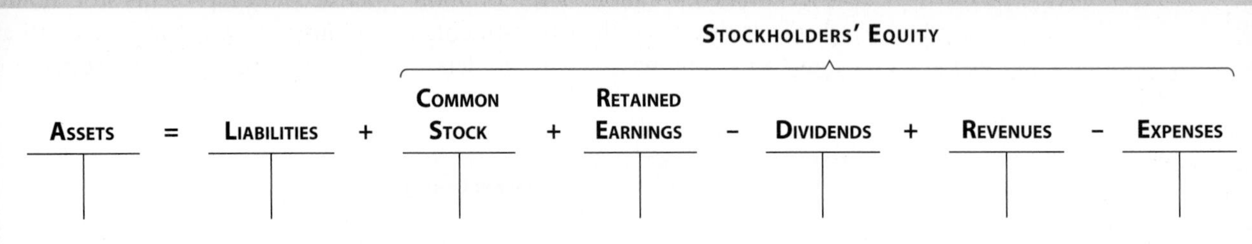

SOLUTION

Cash	Accounts Payable	Common Stock	Retained Earnings	Dividends	Fees Revenue	Wages Expense
625 (debit)	200 (credit)	300 (credit)	100 (credit)	75 (debit)	250 (credit)	150 (debit)

Assets = Liabilities + Stockholders' Equity
$625 = $200 + ($300 + $100 − $75 + $250 − $150)
$625 = $200 + $425
$625 = $625

Business Transaction Analysis

LO3 Demonstrate how the double-entry system is applied to common business transactions.

In the next few pages, we show how to apply the double-entry system to some common business transactions. **Source documents**—invoices, receipts, checks, or contracts—usually support the details of a transaction. We focus on the transactions of a small firm, Miller Design Studio, Inc. For each transaction, we follow these steps:

1. State the transaction.
2. Analyze the transaction to determine which accounts are affected.
3. Apply the rules of double-entry accounting by using T accounts to show how the transaction affects the accounting equation. It is important to note that *this step is not part of the accounting records* but is undertaken *before* recording a transaction in order to understand the effects of the transaction on the accounts.
4. Show the transaction in **journal form.** The journal form is a way of recording a transaction with the date, debit account, and debit amount shown on one line, and the credit account (indented) and credit amount on the next line. The amounts are shown in their respective debit and credit columns. *This step represents the initial recording of a transaction in the records* and takes the following form:

		Dr.	Cr.
Date	Debit Account Name	Amount	
	Credit Account Name		Amount

5. Provide a comment that will help you apply the rules of double entry.

Owner's Investment in the Business

July 1: To begin the business, Joan Miller files articles of incorporation with the state to receive her charter and invests $40,000 in Miller Design Studio, Inc., in exchange for 40,000 shares of $1 par value common stock.

Analysis: An owner's investment in the business *increases* the asset account *Cash* with a debit and *increases* the stockholders' equity account *Common Stock* with a credit.

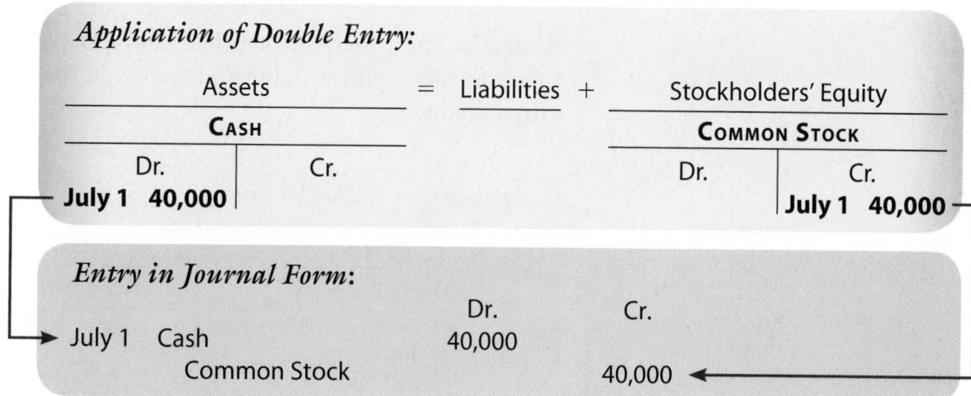

Application of Double Entry:

Assets = Liabilities + Stockholders' Equity

Cash Dr.	Cash Cr.	Common Stock Dr.	Common Stock Cr.
July 1 40,000			July 1 40,000

Entry in Journal Form:

		Dr.	Cr.
July 1	Cash	40,000	
	Common Stock		40,000

Comment: If Joan Miller had invested assets other than cash in the business, the appropriate asset accounts would be increased with a debit.

Economic Event That Is Not a Business Transaction

July 2: Orders office supplies, $5,200.

Comment: When an economic event does not constitute a business transaction, no entry is made. In this case, there is no confirmation that the supplies have been shipped or that title has passed.

Prepayment of Expenses in Cash

July 3: Rents an office; pays two months rent in advance, $3,200.

Analysis: The prepayment of office rent in cash *increases* the asset account *Prepaid Rent* with a debit and *decreases* the asset account *Cash* with a credit.

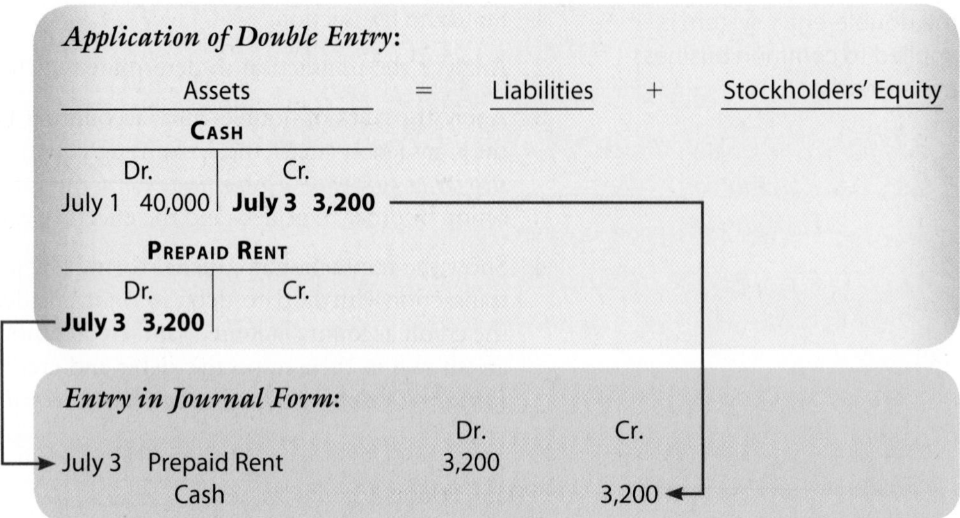

Comment: A prepaid expense is an asset because the expenditure will benefit future operations. This transaction does not affect the totals of assets or liabilities and stockholders' equity because it simply trades one asset for another asset. If the company had paid only July's rent, the stockholders' equity account *Rent Expense* would be debited because the total benefit of the expenditure would be used up in the current month.

Purchase of an Asset on Credit

July 5: Receives office supplies ordered on July 2 and an invoice for $5,200.

Analysis: The purchase of office supplies on credit *increases* the asset account *Office Supplies* with a debit and *increases* the liability account *Accounts Payable* with a credit.

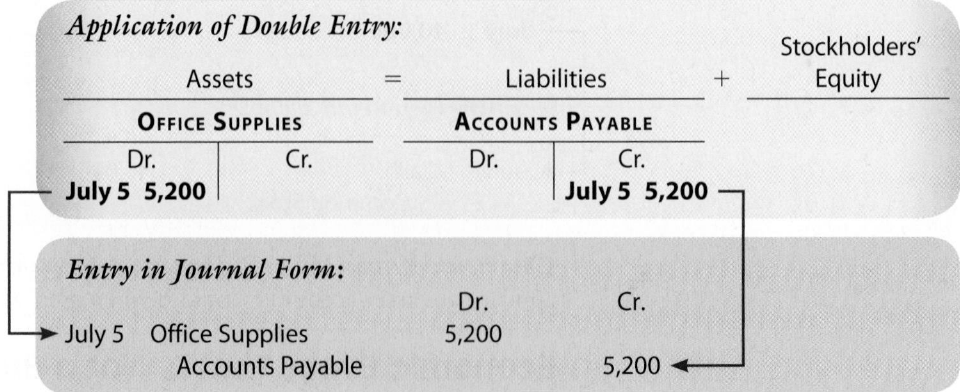

Comment: Office supplies are considered an asset (prepaid expense) because they will not be used up in the current month and thus will benefit future periods. Accounts Payable is used when there is a delay between the time of the purchase and the time of payment.

Purchase of an Asset Partly in Cash and Partly on Credit

July 6: Purchases office equipment, $16,320; pays $13,320 in cash and agrees to pay the rest next month.

Analysis: The purchase of office equipment in cash and on credit *increases* the asset account *Office Equipment* with a debit, *decreases* the asset account *Cash* with a credit, and *increases* the liability account *Accounts Payable* with a credit.

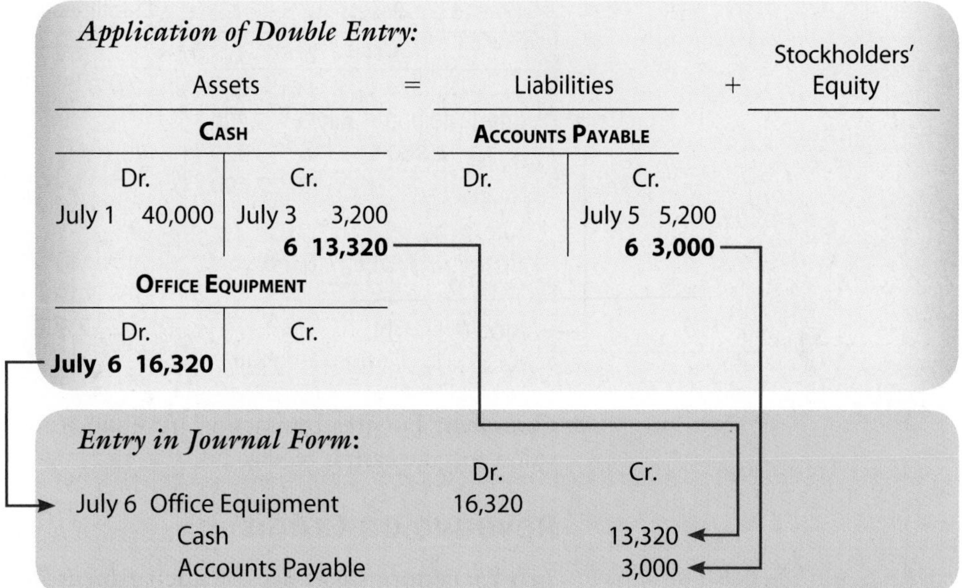

Comment: As this transaction illustrates, assets may be paid for partly in cash and partly on credit. When more than two accounts are involved in a journal entry, as they are in this one, it is called a **compound entry.**

Payment of a Liability

July 9: Makes a partial payment of the amount owed for the office supplies received on July 5, $2,600.

Analysis: A payment of a liability *decreases* the liability account *Accounts Payable* with a debit and *decreases* the asset account *Cash* with a credit.

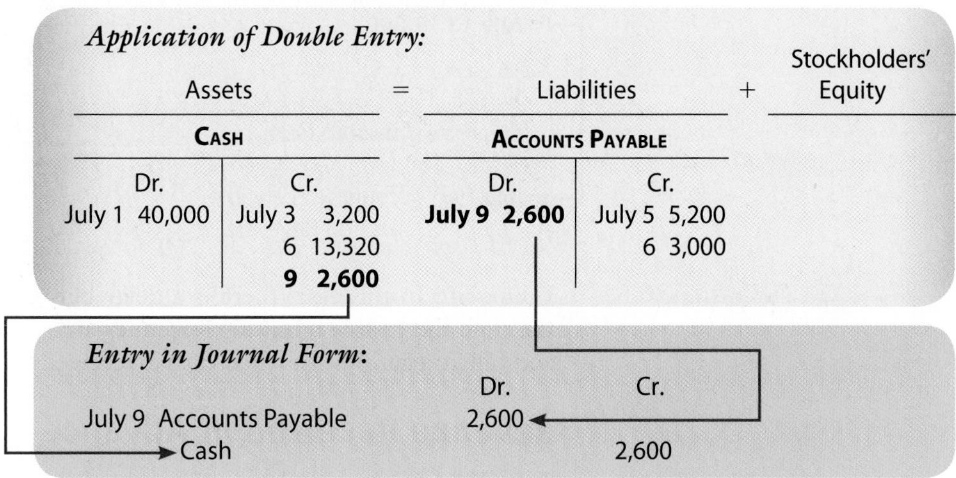

Comment: Note that the office supplies were recorded when they were purchased on July 5.

Revenue in Cash

July 10: Performs a service for an investment advisor by designing a series of brochures and collects a fee in cash, $2,800.

Analysis: A revenue received in cash *increases* the asset account *Cash* with a debit and *increases* the stockholders' equity account *Design Revenue* with a credit.

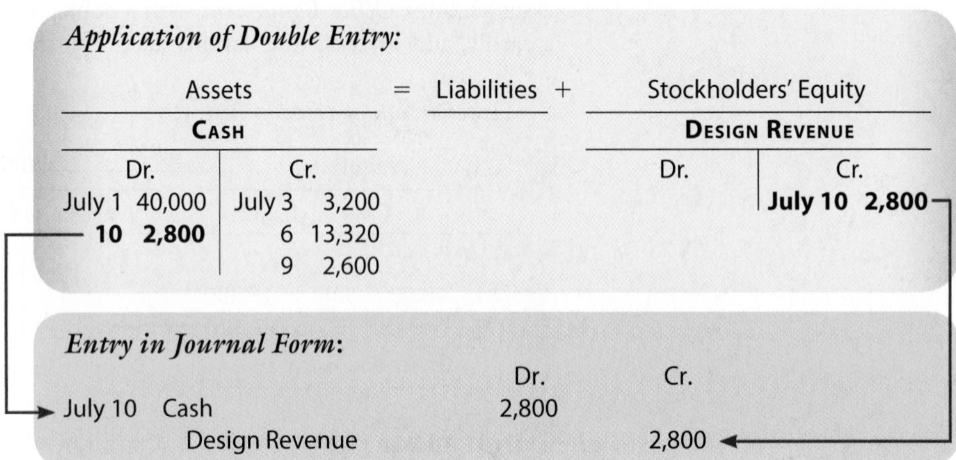

Comment: For this transaction, revenue is recognized when the service is provided and the cash is received.

Revenue on Credit

July 15: Performs a service for a department store by designing a TV commercial; bills for the fee now but will be paid later, $9,600.

Analysis: A revenue billed to a customer *increases* the asset account *Accounts Receivable* with a debit and *increases* the stockholders' equity account *Design Revenue* with a credit. Accounts Receivable is used to indicate the customer's obligation until it is paid.

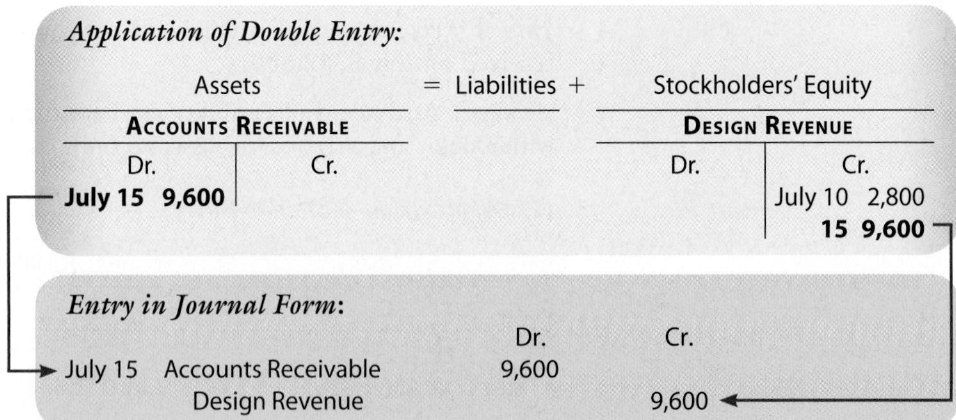

Comment: In this case, there is a delay between the time revenue is earned and the time the cash is received. Revenues are recorded at the time they are earned and billed regardless of when cash is received.

Revenue Received in Advance

July 19: Accepts an advance fee as a deposit on a series of brochures to be designed, $1,400.

Analysis: A revenue received in advance *increases* the asset account *Cash* with a debit and *increases* the liability account *Unearned Design Revenue* with a credit.

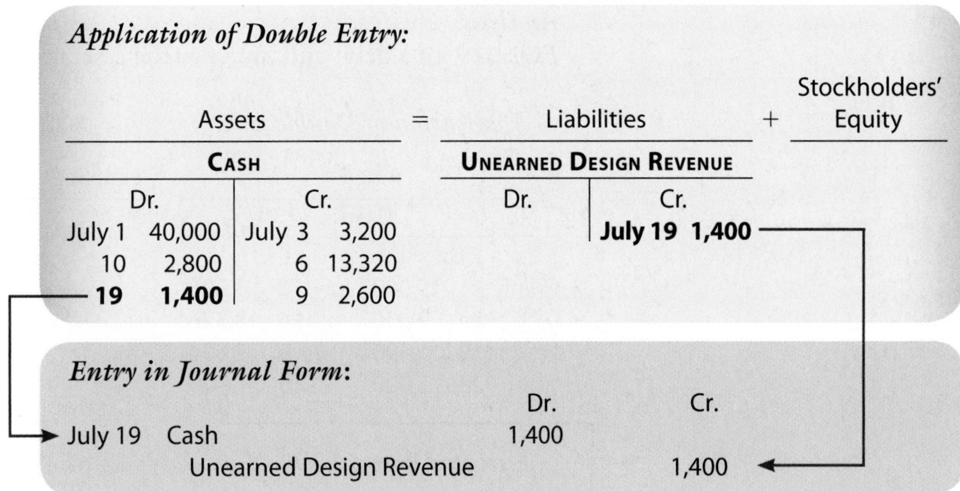

Comment: In this case, payment is received before the fees are earned. Unearned Design Revenue is a liability because the firm must provide the service or return the deposit.

Collection on Account

July 22: Receives partial payment from customer billed on July 15, $5,000.

Analysis: Collection of an account receivable from a customer previously billed *increases* the asset account *Cash* with a debit and *decreases* the asset account *Accounts Receivable* with a credit.

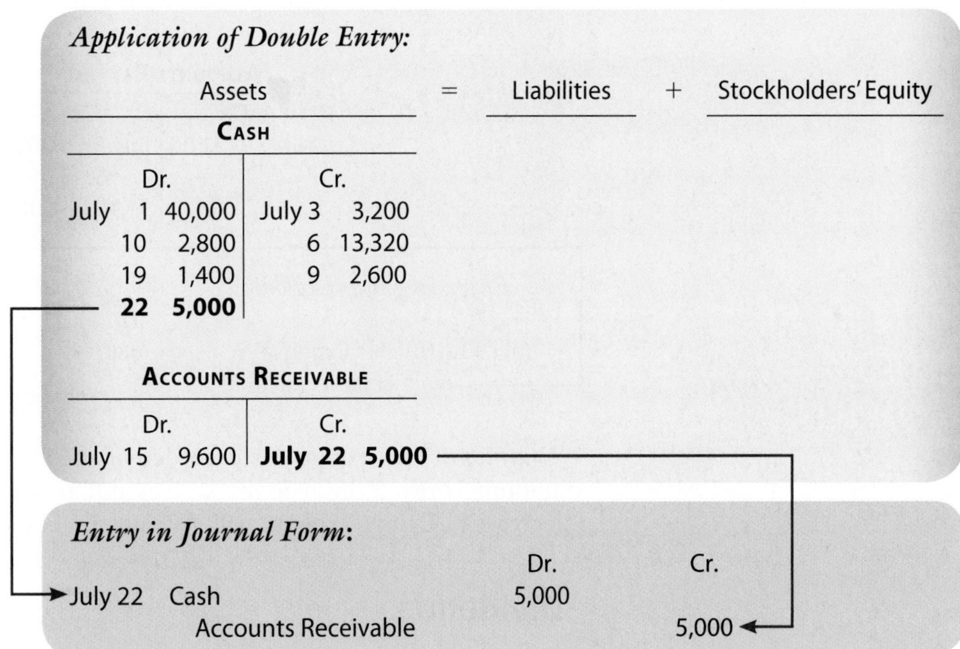

Comment: Note that the revenue related to this transaction was recorded on July 15. Thus, no revenue is recorded at this time.

Expense Paid in Cash

July 26: Pays employees four weeks' wages, $4,800.

Analysis: This cash expense *increases* the stockholders' equity account *Wages Expense* with a debit and *decreases* the asset account *Cash* with a credit.

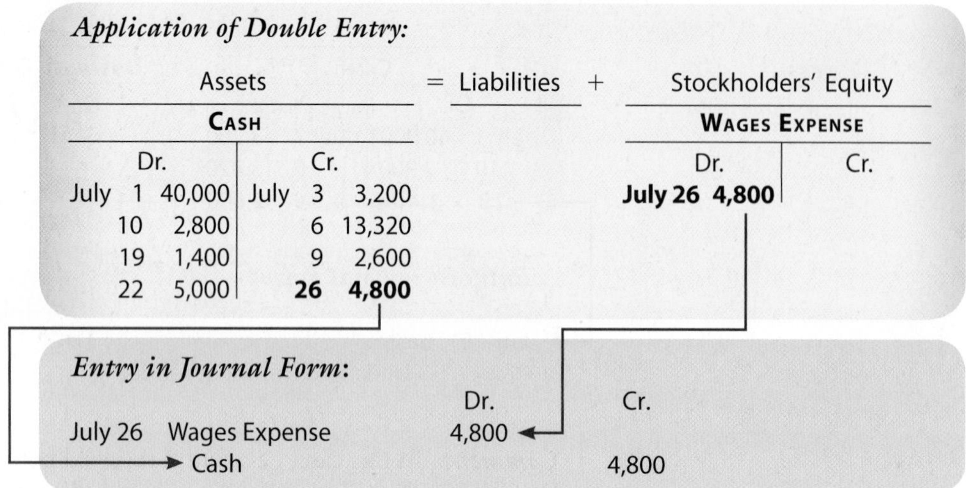

Application of Double Entry:

Assets = Liabilities + Stockholders' Equity

CASH

Dr.		Cr.	
July 1	40,000	July 3	3,200
10	2,800	6	13,320
19	1,400	9	2,600
22	5,000	**26**	**4,800**

WAGES EXPENSE

Dr.		Cr.
July 26	**4,800**	

Entry in Journal Form:

		Dr.	Cr.
July 26	Wages Expense	4,800	
	Cash		4,800

Comment: The increase in Wages Expense will *decrease* stockholders' equity.

Expense to Be Paid Later

July 30: Receives, but does not pay, the utility bill which is due next month, $680.

Analysis: This cash expense *increases* the stockholders' equity account *Utilities Expense* with a debit and *increases* the liability account *Accounts Payable* with a credit.

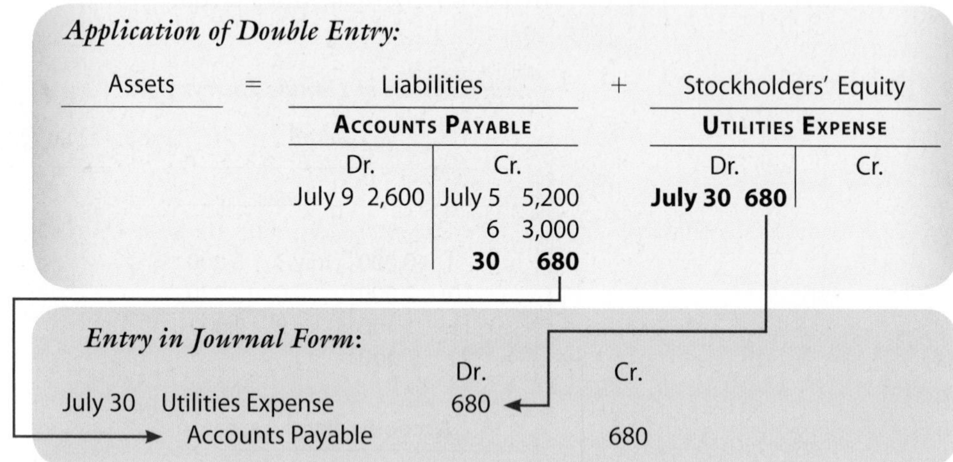

Application of Double Entry:

Assets = Liabilities + Stockholders' Equity

ACCOUNTS PAYABLE

Dr.		Cr.	
July 9	2,600	July 5	5,200
		6	3,000
		30	**680**

UTILITIES EXPENSE

Dr.		Cr.
July 30	**680**	

Entry in Journal Form:

		Dr.	Cr.
July 30	Utilities Expense	680	
	Accounts Payable		680

Comment: The expense is recorded if the benefit has been received and the amount is owed, even if the cash is not to be paid until later. Note that the increase in Utility Expense will *decrease* stockholders' equity.

Dividends

July 31: Declares and pays a dividend, $2,800.

Analysis: Payment of a cash dividend *increases* the stockholders' equity account *Dividends* with a debit and *decreases* the asset account *Cash* with a credit.

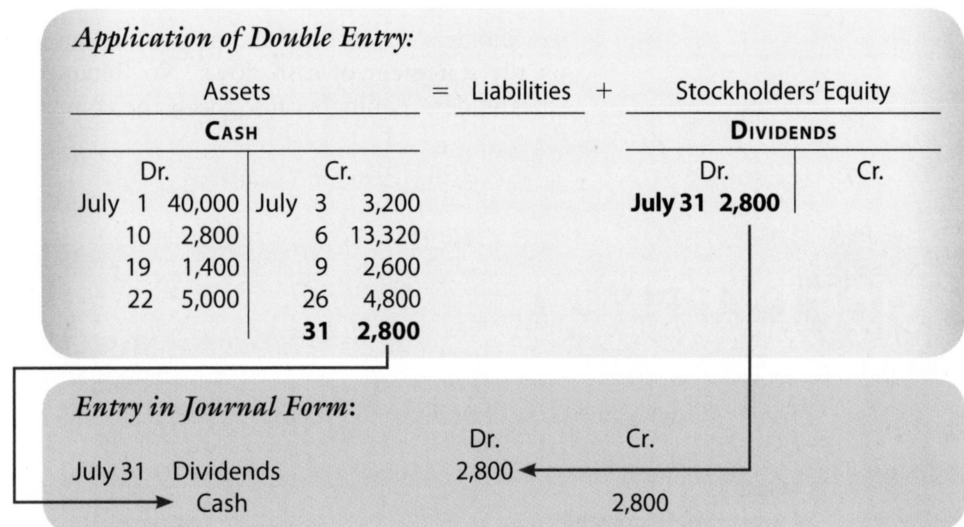

Comment: Note that the increase in Dividends will result in a *decrease* in stockholders' equity.

Summary of Transactions

Exhibit 2-1 uses the accounting equation to summarize the transactions of Miller Design Studio, Inc. Note that the income statement accounts appear under

EXHIBIT 2-1 Summary of Transactions of Miller Design Studio, Inc.

Assets = Liabilities + Stockholders' Equity

Cash

Dr.		Cr.	
July 1	40,000	July 3	3,200
10	2,800	6	13,320
19	1,400	9	2,600
22	5,000	26	4,800
		31	2,800
	49,200		26,720
Bal.	22,480		

This account links to the statement of cash flows.

Accounts Receivable

Dr.		Cr.	
July 15	9,600	July 22	5,000
Bal.	4,600		

Office Supplies

Dr.		Cr.	
July 5	5,200		

Prepaid Rent

Dr.		Cr.	
July 3	3,200		

Office Equipment

Dr.		Cr.	
July 6	16,320		

Accounts Payable

Dr.		Cr.	
July 9	2,600	July 5	5,200
		6	3,000
		30	680
	2,600		8,880
		Bal.	6,280

Unearned Design Revenue

Dr.		Cr.	
		July 19	1,400

Common Stock

Dr.		Cr.	
		July 1	40,000

Dividends

Dr.		Cr.	
July 31	2,800		

Design Revenue

Dr.		Cr.	
		July 10	2,800
		15	9,600
		Bal.	12,400

Wages Expense

Dr.		Cr.	
July 26	4,800		

Utilities Expense

Dr.		Cr.	
July 30	680		

These accounts link to the income statement.

Assets	=	Liabilities	+	Stockholders' Equity
$51,800	=	$7,680	+	$44,120

stockholders' equity and that the transactions in the Cash account will be reflected on the statement of cash flows. No Retained Earnings account appears under stockholders' equity because this is the company's first month of operation.

STOP & APPLY >

The following accounts are for Leona's Nail Salon, Inc., a company that provides manicures and pedicures:

1. Cash
2. Accounts Receivable
3. Supplies
4. Equipment
5. Accounts Payable
6. Services Revenue
7. Wages Expense
8. Rent Expense

In the transaction list that follows, enter the account number in the appropriate debit or credit column.

	Debit	Credit
a. Made a rent payment for the current month.	8	1
b. Received cash from customers for current services.	____	____
c. Agreed to accept payment next month from a client for current services.	____	____
d. Purchased supplies on credit.	____	____
e. Purchased a new chair and table for cash.	____	____
f. Made a payment on accounts payable.	____	____

SOLUTION

	Debit	Credit
a. Made a rent payment for the current month.	8	1
b. Received cash from customers for current services.	1	6
c. Agreed to accept payment next month from a client for current services.	2	6
d. Purchased supplies on credit.	3	5
e. Purchased a new chair and table for cash.	4	1
f. Made a payment on accounts payable.	5	1

The Trial Balance

LO4 Prepare a trial balance, and describe its value and limitations.

For every amount debited, an equal amount must be credited. This means that the total of debits and credits in the T accounts must be equal. To test this, the accountant periodically prepares a **trial balance**. Exhibit 2-2 shows a trial balance for Miller Design Studio, Inc. It was prepared from the accounts in Exhibit 2-1.

Preparation and Use of a Trial Balance

Although a trial balance may be prepared at any time, it is usually prepared on the last day of the accounting period. These are the steps involved in preparing a trial balance:

1. List each account that has a balance, with debit balances in the left column and credit balances in the right column. Accounts are listed in the order in which they appear in the financial statements.
2. Add each column.
3. Compare the totals of the columns.

Once in a while, a transaction leaves an account with a balance that isn't "normal." For example, when a company overdraws its bank account, its Cash account (an asset) will show a credit balance instead of a debit balance. The "abnormal" balance should be copied into the trial balance columns as it stands, as a debit or a credit.

The trial balance proves whether the accounts are in balance. *In balance* means that the total of all debits recorded equals the total of all credits recorded. But the trial balance does not prove that the transactions were analyzed correctly or recorded in the proper accounts. For example, there is no way of determining from the trial balance that a debit should have been made in the Office Supplies account rather than in the Office Equipment account. And the trial balance does not detect whether transactions have been omitted, because equal debits and credits will have been omitted. Also, if an error of the same amount is made in both a debit and a credit, it will not be evident in the trial

Study Note

A trial balance is usually prepared at the end of an accounting period. It is an initial check that the accounts are in balance.

EXHIBIT 2-2
Trial Balance

Miller Design Studio, Inc.
Trial Balance
July 31, 2010

Cash	$22,480	
Accounts Receivable	4,600	
Office Supplies	5,200	
Prepaid Rent	3,200	
Office Equipment	16,320	
Accounts Payable		$ 6,280
Unearned Design Revenue		1,400
Common Stock		40,000
Dividends	2,800	
Design Revenue		12,400
Wages Expense	4,800	
Utilities Expense	680	
	$60,080	$60,080

FOCUS ON BUSINESS PRACTICE

Are All Trial Balances Created Equal?

In computerized accounting systems, posting is done automatically, and the trial balance can be easily prepared as often as needed. Any accounts with abnormal balances are highlighted for investigation. Some general ledger software packages for small businesses list the trial balance amounts in a single column and show credit balances as minuses. In such cases, the trial balance is in balance if the total is zero.

balance. The trial balance proves only that the debits and credits in the accounts are in balance.

Finding Trial Balance Errors

If the debit and credit balances in a trial balance are not equal, look for one or more of the following errors:

1. A debit was entered in an account as a credit, or vice versa.
2. The balance of an account was computed incorrectly.
3. An error was made in carrying the account balance to the trial balance.
4. The trial balance was summed incorrectly.

Other than simply adding the columns incorrectly, the two most common mistakes in preparing a trial balance are:

1. Recording an account as a credit when it usually carries a debit balance, or vice versa. This mistake causes the trial balance to be out of balance by an amount divisible by 2.
2. Transposing two digits when transferring an amount to the trial balance (for example, entering $23,459 as $23,549). This error causes the trial balance to be out of balance by a number divisible by 9.

So, if a trial balance is out of balance and the addition of the columns is correct, determine the amount by which the trial balance is out of balance and divide it first by 2 and then by 9. If the amount is divisible by 2, look in the trial balance for an amount that is equal to the quotient. If you find such an amount, chances are it's in the wrong column. If the amount is divisible by 9, trace each amount back to the T account balance, checking carefully for a transposition error. If neither of these techniques is successful in identifying the error, first recompute the balance of each T account. Then, if you still have not found the error, retrace each posting to the journal or the T account.

STOP & APPLY >

Prepare a trial balance from the following list of accounts of the Jasoni Company as of March 31, 2011. Compute the balance of cash.

Accounts Payable	$ 9	Equipment	2
Accounts Receivable	5	Land	6
Building	10	Retained Earnings	8
Cash	?	Supplies	3
Common Stock	13		

SOLUTION

Jasoni Company
Trial Balance
March 31, 2011

Accounts Payable		$ 9
Accounts Receivable	$ 5	
Building	10	
Cash	4	
Common Stock		13
Equipment	2	
Land	6	
Retained Earnings		8
Supplies	3	
	$30	$30

Cash Flows and the Timing of Transactions

LO5 Show how the timing of transactions affects cash flows and liquidity.

To avoid financial distress, a company must be able to pay its bills on time. Because the timing of cash flows is critical to maintaining adequate liquidity to pay bills, managers and other users of financial information must understand the difference between transactions that generate immediate cash and those that do not. Consider the selected transactions of Miller Design Studio, Inc., shown in Figure 2-3. Most of them involve either an inflow or outflow of cash.

As you can see in Figure 2-3, Miller's Cash account has more transactions than any of its other accounts. Look at the transactions of July 10, 15, and 22:

- July 10: Miller received a cash payment of $2,800.
- July 15: The firm billed a customer $9,600 for a service it had already performed.
- July 22: The firm received a partial payment of $5,000 from the customer, but it had not received the remaining $4,600 by the end of the month.

Because Miller incurred expenses in providing this service, it must pay careful attention to its cash flows and liquidity.

One way Miller can manage its expenditures is to rely on its creditors to give it time to pay. Compare the transactions of July 3, 5, and 9 in Figure 2-3.

- July 3: Miller prepaid rent of $3,200. That immediate cash outlay may have caused a strain on the business.
- July 5: The firm received an invoice for office supplies in the amount of $5,200. In this case, it took advantage of the opportunity to defer payment.

Study Note

Recording revenues and expenses when they occur will provide a clearer picture of a company's profitability on the income statement. The change in cash flows will provide a clearer picture of the company's liquidity on the statement of cash flows.

FIGURE 2-3
Selected Transactions of Miller Design Studio, Inc.

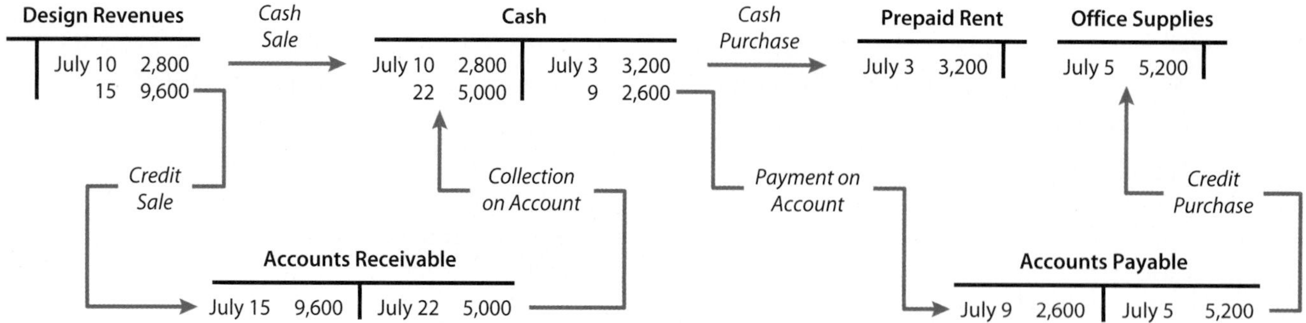

- July 9: The firm paid $2,600, but it deferred paying the remaining $2,600 until after the end of the month.

Of course, Miller expects to receive the rest of the cash from the customer that it billed on July 15, and it must eventually pay the rest of what it owes on the office supplies. In the meantime, the firm must perform a delicate balancing act with its cash flows to ensure that it achieves the goal of liquidity so that it can grow and be profitable.

Large companies face the same challenge, but often on a much greater scale. Recall from the Decision Point that **Boeing** takes years to plan and make the airplanes that the Chinese government and other customers order. At the end of 2006, Boeing had orders for 8,274 airplanes totaling $174.3 billion, or about $21 million per airplane.[5] Think of the cash outlays Boeing must make before it delivers the airplanes and collects payment for them. To maintain liquidity so that Boeing can eventually reap the rewards of delivering the airplanes, Boeing's management must carefully plan the company's needs for cash.

Because car manufacturers take years to plan and make a new model of car, their management must carefully plan the company's needs for cash. The timing of cash flows is critical to maintaining adequate liquidity.

Courtesy of Ricardo Azoury/iStockphoto.com.

FOCUS ON BUSINESS PRACTICE

Should Earnings Be Aligned with Cash Flows?

In 2005, **Electronic Data Systems Corporation (EDS),** the large computer services company, announced that it was reducing past earnings by $2.24 billion to implement a new accounting rule that would more closely align its earnings with cash flows. Analysts had been critical of EDS for recording revenue from its long-term contracts when the contracts were signed rather than when the cash was received. In fact, about 40 percent of EDC's revenue had been recognized well before the cash was to be received. Analysts' response to the change in EDC's accounting was very positive. "Finally, maybe, we'll see cash flows moving in line with earnings," said one.[6] Although there are natural and unavoidable differences between earnings and cash flows, it is best if accounting rules do not exaggerate these differences.

STOP & APPLY >

A company engaged in the following transactions:

Oct. 1 Performed services for cash, $1,050.
2 Paid expenses in cash, $550.
3 Incurred expenses on credit, $650.
Oct. 4 Performed services on credit, $900.
5 Paid on account, $350.
6 Collected on account, $600.

Enter the correct titles in the following T accounts, and enter the above transactions in the accounts. Determine the cash balance after these transactions, the amount still to be received, and the amount still to be paid.

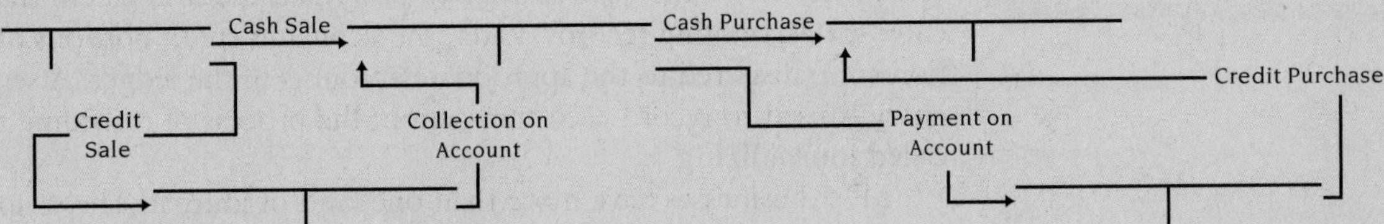

SOLUTION

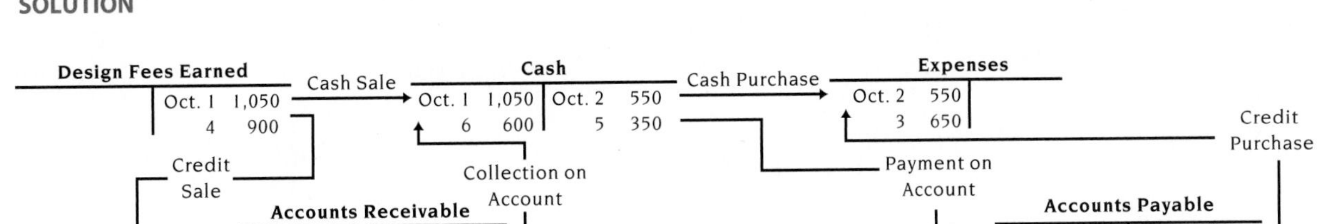

Cash balance after transactions: $1,050 + $600 − $550 − $350 = $750
Amount still to be received: $900 − $600 = $300
Amount still to be paid: $650 − $350 = $300

Recording and Posting Transactions

SO6 Define the *chart of accounts,* record transactions in the general journal, and post transactions to the ledger.

Earlier in the chapter, we described how transactions are analyzed according to the rules of double entry and how a trial balance is prepared. As Figure 2-4 shows, transaction analysis and preparation of a trial balance are the first and last steps in a four-step process. The two intermediate steps are recording the entry in the general journal and posting the entry to the ledger. In this section, we demonstrate how these steps are accomplished in a manual accounting system.

Chart of Accounts

Study Note

A chart of accounts is a table of contents for the ledger. Typically, it lists accounts in the order in which they appear in the ledger, which is usually the order in which they appear in the financial statements. The numbering scheme allows for some flexibility.

In a manual accounting system, each account is kept on a separate page or card. These pages or cards are placed together in a book or file called the **general ledger.** In the computerized systems that most companies have today, accounts are maintained electronically. However, as a matter of convenience, accountants still refer to the group of company accounts as the *general ledger,* or simply the *ledger.*

To help identify accounts in the ledger and make them easy to find, the accountant often numbers them. A list of these numbers with the corresponding account titles is called a **chart of accounts.** A very simple chart of accounts appears in Exhibit 2-3. The first digit in the account number identifies the major financial statement classification—that is, an account number that begins with the digit 1 means that the account is an asset account, an account number that begins with a 2 means that the account is a liability account, and so forth. The second and third digits identify individual accounts. The gaps in the sequence of numbers allow the accountant to expand the number of accounts.

General Journal

Study Note

The journal is a chronological record of events.

Although transactions can be entered directly into the ledger accounts, this method makes identifying individual transactions or finding errors very difficult because the debit is recorded in one account and the credit in another. The solution is to record all transactions chronologically in a **journal.** The journal is sometimes called the *book of original entry* because it is where transactions first enter the accounting records. Later, the debit and credit portions of each transaction are transferred to the appropriate accounts in the ledger. A separate **journal entry** is used to record each transaction; the process of recording transactions is called **journalizing.**

Most businesses have more than one kind of journal. The simplest and most flexible kind is the **general journal,** the one we focus on here. Businesses will

FIGURE 2-4
Analyzing and Processing Transactions

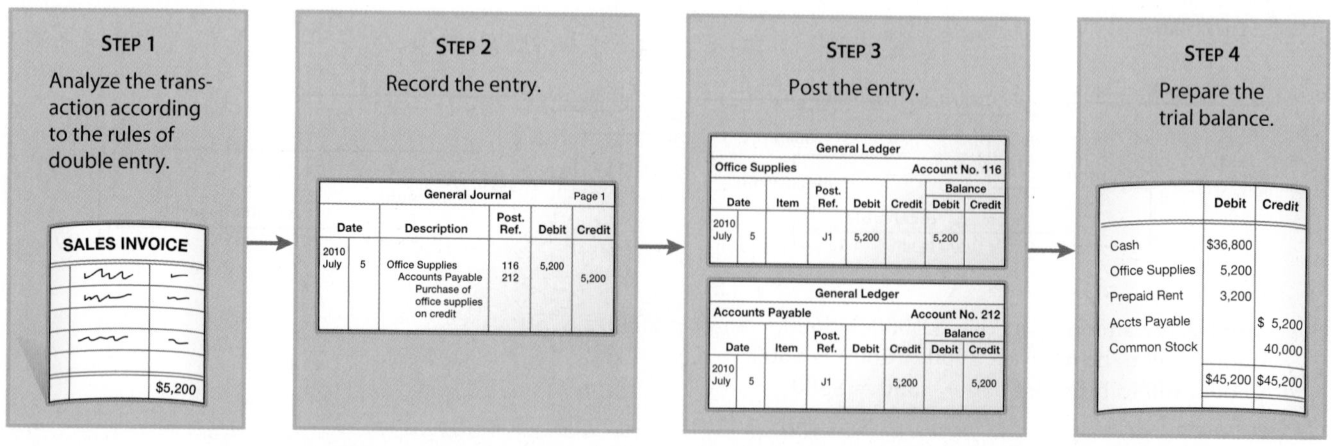

EXHIBIT 2-3
Chart of Accounts for a Small Business

Account Number	Account Name	Description
		Assets
111	Cash	Money and any medium of exchange (coins, currency, checks, money orders, and money on deposit in a bank)
112	Notes Receivable	Promissory notes (written promises to pay definite sums of money at fixed future dates) due from others
113	Accounts Receivable	Amounts due from others for revenues or sales on credit (sales on account)
116	Office Supplies	Prepaid expense; office supplies purchased and not used
117	Prepaid Rent	Prepaid expense; rent paid in advance and not used
118	Prepaid Insurance	Prepaid expense; insurance purchased and not expired
141	Land	Property owned for use in the business
142	Buildings	Structures owned for use in the business
143	Accumulated Depreciation–Buildings	Periodic allocation of the cost of buildings to expense; deducted from Buildings
146	Office Equipment	Office equipment owned for use in the business
147	Accumulated Depreciation–Office Equipment	Periodic allocation of the cost of office equipment to expense; deducted from Office Equipment
		Liabilities
211	Notes Payable	Promissory notes due to others
212	Accounts Payable	Amounts due to others for purchases on credit
213	Unearned Design Revenue	Unearned revenue; advance deposits for website design to be provided in the future
214	Wages Payable	Amounts due to employees for wages earned and not paid
215	Income Taxes Payable	Amounts due to government for income taxes owed and not paid
		Stockholders' Equity
311	Common Stock	Stockholders' investments in a corporation for which they receive shares of stock
312	Retained Earnings	Stockholders' claims against company assets derived from profitable operations
313	Dividends	Distributions of assets (usually cash) that reduce retained earnings
314	Income Summary	Temporary account used at the end of the accounting period to summarize the revenues and expenses for the period
		Revenues
411	Design Revenue	Revenues derived from website design services
		Expenses
511	Wages Expense	Amounts earned by employees
512	Utilities Expense	Amounts for utilities, such as water, electricity, and gas, used
513	Telephone Expense	Amounts of telephone services used
514	Rent Expense	Amounts of rent on property and buildings used
515	Insurance Expense	Amounts for insurance expired
517	Office Supplies Expense	Amounts for office supplies used
518	Depreciation Expense–Buildings	Amount of buildings' cost allocated to expense
520	Depreciation Expense–Office Equipment	Amount of office equipment cost allocated to expense
521	Income Taxes Expense	Amount of tax on income

also have several special-purpose journals, each for recording a common transaction, such as credit sales, credit purchases, cash receipts, and cash disbursements. At this point, we cover only the general journal. Exhibit 2-4, which displays two of the transactions of Miller Design Studio, Inc. that we discussed earlier, shows the format for recording entries in a general journal. As you can see in Exhibit 2-4, the entries in a general journal include the following information about each transaction:

1. The date. The year appears on the first line of the first column, the month on the next line of the first column, and the day in the second column opposite the month. For subsequent entries on the same page for the same month and year, the month and year can be omitted.
2. The names of the accounts debited and credited, which appear in the Description column. The names of the accounts that are debited are placed next to the left margin opposite the dates; on the line below, the names of the accounts credited are indented.
3. The debit amounts, which appear in the Debit column opposite the accounts that are debited, and the credit amounts, which appear in the Credit column opposite the accounts that are credited.
4. An explanation of each transaction, which appears in the Description column below the account names. An explanation should be brief but sufficient to explain and identify the transaction.
5. The account numbers in the Post. Ref. column, if they apply.

At the time the transactions are recorded, nothing is placed in the Post. Ref. (posting reference) column. (This column is sometimes called LP or *Folio.*) Later, if the company uses account numbers to identify accounts in the ledger, the account numbers are filled in. They provide a convenient cross-reference from the general journal to the ledger and indicate that the entry has been posted to the ledger. If the accounts are not numbered, the accountant uses a checkmark (✓) to signify that the entry has been posted.

General Ledger

The general journal is used to record the details of each transaction. The general ledger is used to update each account.

EXHIBIT 2-4
The General Journal

A	=	L	+ SE
+ 3,200			
− 3,200			

A	=	L	+ SE
+ 5,200		+ 5,200	

General Journal — **Page 1**

Date		Description	Post. Ref.	Debit	Credit
2010					
July	3	Prepaid Rent		3,200	
		Cash			3,200
		Paid two months' rent in advance			
	5	Office Supplies		5,200	
		Accounts Payable			5,200
		Purchase of office supplies on credit			

Study Note

A T account is a means of quickly analyzing a set of transactions. It is simply an abbreviated version of a ledger account. Ledger accounts, which provide more information, are used in the accounting records.

The Ledger Account Form The T account is a simple, direct means of recording transactions. In practice, a somewhat more complicated form of the account is needed to record more information. The **ledger account form**, which contains four columns for dollar amounts, is illustrated in Exhibit 2-5.

The account title and number appear at the top of the account form. As in the journal, the transaction date appears in the first two columns. The Item column is rarely used to identify transactions because explanations already appear in the journal. The Post. Ref. column is used to note the journal page on which the original entry for the transaction can be found. The dollar amount is entered in the appropriate Debit or Credit column, and a new account balance is computed in the last two columns opposite each entry. The advantage of this account form over the T account is that the current balance of the account is readily available.

Posting After transactions have been entered in the journal, they must be transferred to the ledger. The process of transferring journal entry information from the journal to the ledger is called **posting**. Posting is usually done after several entries have been made—for example, at the end of each day or less frequently, depending on the number of transactions. As Exhibit 2-6 shows, in posting, each amount in the Debit column of the journal is transferred to the Debit column of the appropriate account in the ledger, and each amount in the Credit column of the journal is transferred to the Credit column of the appropriate account in the ledger. The steps in the posting process are as follows:

1. In the ledger, locate the debit account named in the journal entry.
2. Enter the date of the transaction in the ledger and, in the Post. Ref. column, the journal page number from which the entry comes.
3. In the Debit column of the ledger account, enter the amount of the debit as it appears in the journal.
4. Calculate the account balance and enter it in the appropriate Balance column.
5. Enter in the Post. Ref. column of the journal the account number to which the amount has been posted.
6. Repeat the same five steps for the credit side of the journal entry.

Notice that Step 5 is the last step in the posting process for each debit and credit. As noted earlier, in addition to serving as an easy reference between the journal entry and the ledger account, this entry in the Post. Ref. column of the journal indicates that the entry has been posted to the ledger.

EXHIBIT 2-5
Accounts Payable in the General Ledger

General Ledger

Accounts Payable — **Account No. 212**

Date		Item	Post. Ref.	Debit	Credit	Balance Debit	Balance Credit
2010							
July	5		J1		5,200		5,200
	6		J1		3,000		8,200
	9		J1	2,600			5,600
	30		J2		680		6,280

EXHIBIT 2-6
Posting from the General Journal to the Ledger

General Journal — **Page 2**

Date		Description	Post. Ref.	Debit	Credit
2010					
July	30	Utilities Expense	512	680	
		Accounts Payable	212		680
		Received bill from utility company			

General Ledger

Accounts Payable — **Account No. 212**

Date		Item	Post. Ref.	Debit	Credit	Balance	
						Debit	Credit
2010							
July	5		J1		5,200		5,200
	6		J1		3,000		8,200
	9		J1	2,600			5,600
	30		J2		680		6,280

General Ledger

Utilities Expense — **Account No. 512**

Date		Item	Post. Ref.	Debit	Credit	Balance	
						Debit	Credit
2010							
July	30		J2	680		680	

Some Notes on Presentation

A ruled line appears in financial reports before each subtotal or total to indicate that the amounts above are added or subtracted. It is common practice to use a double line under a final total to show that it has been verified.

Dollar signs ($) are required in all financial statements and in the trial balance and other schedules. On these reports, a dollar sign should be placed before the first amount in each column and before the first amount in a column following a ruled line. Dollar signs in the same column are aligned. Dollar signs are not used in journals and ledgers.

On normal, unruled paper, commas and decimal points are used when recording dollar amounts. On the paper used in journals and ledgers, commas and decimal points are unnecessary because ruled columns are provided to properly align dollars and cents. Commas, dollar signs, and decimal points are also unnecessary in electronic spreadsheets. In this book, because most problems and illustrations are in whole dollar amounts, the cents column usually is omitted. When accountants deal with whole-dollars, they often use a dash in the cents column to indicate whole dollars rather than taking the time to write zeros.

Account names are capitalized when referenced in text or listed in work documents like the journal or ledger. In financial statements, however, only the first word of an account name is capitalized.

Record the following transactions in proper journal form, and use the following account numbers—Cash, 111; Supplies, 114; and Accounts Payable, 212—to show in the Post. Ref. columns that the entries have been posted:

June 4 Purchased supplies for $40 on credit.
8 Paid for the supplies purchased on June 4.

SOLUTION

Date	Description	Post. Ref.	Debit	Credit
June 4	Supplies	114	40	
	Accounts Payable	212		40
	Purchased supplies on credit			
8	Accounts Payable	212	40	
	Cash	111		40
	Paid amount due for supplies			

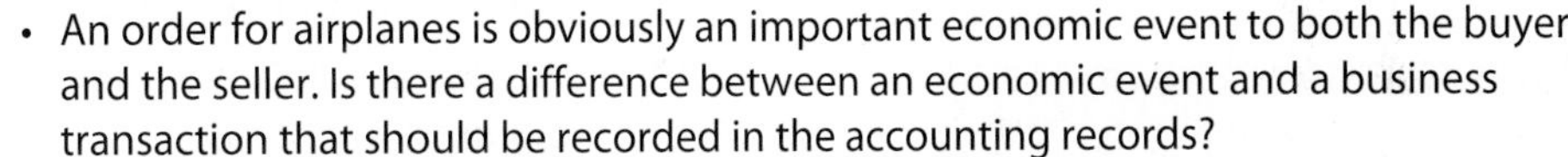

A LOOK BACK AT ▸ THE BOEING COMPANY

The Decision Point at the beginning of the chapter described the order for 80 airplanes that the Chinese government placed with **Boeing**. It posed the following questions:

- An order for airplanes is obviously an important economic event to both the buyer and the seller. Is there a difference between an economic event and a business transaction that should be recorded in the accounting records?
- Should Boeing record the order in its accounting records?
- How important are liquidity and cash flows to Boeing?

Despite its importance, the order did not constitute a business transaction, and neither the buyer nor the seller should have recognized it in its accounting records. At the time the Chinese government placed the order, Boeing had not yet built the airplanes. Until it delivers them and title to them shifts to the Chinese government, Boeing cannot record any revenue.

Even for "firm" orders like this one, Boeing cautions that "an economic downturn could result in airline equipment requirements less than currently anticipated, resulting in requests to negotiate the rescheduling or possible cancellation of firm orders."[7] In fact, in the period following the 9/11 attacks on the World Trade Center and the war in Iraq, many airlines canceled or renegotiated orders they had placed with Boeing. The ongoing energy crisis is also causing airlines to rethink their orders.

Because it takes almost two years to manufacture an airplane, Boeing must pay close attention to its liquidity and cash flows. One measure of liquidity is the **cash return on assets** ratio, which shows how productive assets are in generating cash flows from operations. In other words, it shows how much cash is generated by each dollar of assets invested in operations. This ratio is different from the return on assets ratio, a profitability measure that we introduced in Chapter 1. Using amounts (in millions) from

Boeing's balance sheet and statement of cash flows in its annual report, we can calculate the company's cash return on assets as follows:[8]

K/R

		2008	2007
Cash Return on Assets =	Net Cash Flows from Operating Activities / Average Total Assets	($401) / ($53,779 + $58,986) ÷ 2	$9,584 / ($58,986 + $51,794) ÷ 2
		($401) / $56,383	$9,584 / $55,390
		−0.007(−0.7%)	0.173(17.3%)

What do these results tell us? First, in 2008, each dollar of assets that Boeing invested in operations lost about 0.7 percent, and that was a lot worse than the 17.3 percent generated a year earlier. Second, cash flows from operations decreased from $9,584 million to negative $401 million, while average total assets increased slightly from $55,390 to $56,383. This trend indicates a weak cash-generating ability and makes Boeing's position uncertain in a growing global market for aircraft.

Review Problem

Transaction Analysis, T Accounts, Journalizing, and the Trial Balance

LO1 LO3
LO4 SO6

After completing yoga school, Tobias Raza started a private practice. The transactions of his company in July are as follows:

2010

July	1	Tobias Raza invested $4,000 for 4,000 shares of $1 par value common stock in his newly chartered company, Yoga Center, Inc.
	3	Paid $600 in advance for two months' rent of an office.
	9	Purchased supplies for $400 in cash.
	12	Purchased $800 of equipment on credit; made a 25 percent down payment.
	15	Gave a yoga lesson for a fee of $70 on credit.
	18	Made a payment of $100 on the equipment purchased on July 12.
	27	Paid a utility bill of $80.

Required

1. Record the company's transactions in journal form.
2. Post the transactions to the following T accounts: Cash, Accounts Receivable, Supplies, Prepaid Rent, Equipment, Accounts Payable, Common Stock, Yoga Fees Earned, and Utilities Expense.
3. Prepare a trial balance as of July 31, 2010.
4. How does the transaction of July 15 relate to recognition and cash flows? How do the transactions of July 9 and July 27 relate to classification?

Answers to Review Problem

1. Transactions recorded in journal form:

	A	B	C	D	E	F	G	H
1	July	1		Cash			4,000	
2					Common Stock			4,000
3						Issued 4,000 shares of $1 par		
4						value common stock		
5		3		Prepaid Rent			600	
6					Cash			600
7						Paid two months' rent in advance		
8						for an office		
9		9		Supplies			400	
10					Cash			400
11						Purchased supplies for cash		
12		12		Equipment			800	
13					Accounts Payable			600
14					Cash			200
15						Purchased equipment on credit,		
16						paying 25 percent down		
17		15		Accounts Receivable			70	
18					Yoga Fees Earned			70
19						Fee on credit for yoga lesson		
20		18		Accounts Payable			100	
21					Cash			100
22						Partial payment for equipment		
23						purchased July 12		
24		27		Utilities Expense			80	
25					Cash			80
26						Paid utility bill		
27								

2. Transactions posted to T accounts:

Cash

July	1	4,000	July	3	600
				9	400
				12	200
				18	100
				27	80
		4,000			*1,380*
Bal.		*2,620*			

Accounts Receivable

July	15	70			

Supplies

July	9	400			

Prepaid Rent

July	3	600			

Equipment

July	12	800			

Accounts Payable

July	18	100	July	12	600
			Bal.		*500*

Common Stock

			July	1	4,000

Yoga Fees Earned

			July	15	70

Utilities Expense

July	27	80			

3. Trial balance:

Yoga Center, Inc.
Trial Balance
July 31, 2010

Cash	$2,620	
Accounts Receivable	70	
Supplies	400	
Prepaid Rent	600	
Equipment	800	
Accounts Payable		$ 500
Common Stock		4,000
Yoga Fees Earned		70
Utilities Expense	80	
	$4,570	$4,570

4. The transaction of July 15 is recorded, or recognized, on that date even though the company received no cash. The company earned the revenue by providing the service, and the customer accepted the service and now has an obligation to pay for it. The transaction is recorded as an account receivable because the company allowed the customer to pay for the service later. The transaction of July 9 is classified as an asset, Supplies, because these supplies will benefit the company in the future. The transaction of July 27 is classified as an expense, Utilities Expense, because the utilities have already been used and will not benefit the company in the future.

LO1 Explain how the concepts of recognition, valuation, and classification apply to business transactions and why they are important factors in ethical financial reporting.

To measure a business transaction, you must determine when the transaction occurred (the recognition issue), what value to place on the transaction (the valuation issue), and how the components of the transaction should be categorized (the classification issue). In general, recognition should occur when title passes, and a transaction should be valued at the exchange price—the fair value or cost at the time the transaction is recognized. Classification refers to assigning transactions to the appropriate accounts. Generally accepted accounting principles provide guidance about the treatment of these three basic measurement issues. Failure to follow these guidelines is a major reason some companies issue unethical financial statements.

LO2 Explain the double-entry system and the usefulness of T accounts in analyzing business transactions.

In the double-entry system, each transaction must be recorded with at least one debit and one credit, and the total amount of the debits must equal the total amount of the credits. Each asset, liability, and component of stockholders' equity, including revenues and expenses, has a separate account, which is a device for storing transaction data. The T account is a useful tool for quickly analyzing the effects of transactions. It shows how increases and decreases in assets, liabilities, and stockholders' equity are debited and credited to the appropriate accounts.

LO3 Demonstrate how the double-entry system is applied to common business transactions.

The double-entry system is applied by analyzing transactions to determine which accounts are affected and by using T accounts to show how the transactions affect the accounting equation. The transactions may be recorded in journal form with the date, debit account, and debit amount shown on one line, and the credit account (indented) and credit amount on the next line. The amounts are shown in their respective debit and credit columns.

LO4 Prepare a trial balance, and describe its value and limitations.

A trial balance is used to check that the debit and credit balances are equal. It is prepared by listing each account balance in the appropriate Debit or Credit column. The two columns are then added, and the totals are compared. The major limitation of a trial balance is that even when it shows that debit and credit balances are equal, it does not guarantee that the transactions were analyzed correctly or recorded in the proper accounts.

LO5 Show how the timing of transactions affects cash flows and liquidity.

Some transactions generate immediate cash. For those that do not, there is a holding period in either Accounts Receivable or Accounts Payable before the cash is received or paid. The timing of cash flows is critical to a company's ability to maintain adequate liquidity so that it can pay its bills on time.

Supplemental Objective

SO6 Define the *chart of accounts*, record transactions in the general journal, and post transactions to the ledger.

The chart of accounts is a list of account numbers and titles; it serves as a table of contents for the ledger. The general journal is a chronological record of all transactions; it contains the date of each transaction, the titles of the accounts involved, the amounts debited and credited, and an explanation of each entry. After transactions have been entered in the general journal, they are posted to the ledger. Posting is done by transferring the amounts in the Debit and Credit columns of the general journal to the Debit and Credit columns of the corresponding account in the ledger. After each entry is posted, a new balance is entered in the appropriate Balance column.

REVIEW of Concepts and Terminology

The following concepts and terms were introduced in this chapter:

Accounts 97 (LO2)

Balance 98 (LO2)

Chart of accounts 114 (SO6)

Classification 95 (LO1)

Compound entry 103 (LO3)

Cost principle 94 (LO1)

Credit 97 (LO2)

Debit 97 (LO2)

Double-entry system 96 (LO2)

Fair Value 94 (LO1)

Footings 98 (LO2)

General journal 114 (SO6)

General ledger 114 (SO6)

Journal 114 (SO6)

Journal entry 114 (SO6)

Journal form 101 (LO3)

Journalizing 114 (SO6)

Ledger account form 117 (SO6)

Normal balance 99 (LO2)

Posting 117 (SO6)

Recognition 92 (LO1)

Recognition point 93 (LO1)

Source documents 101 (LO3)

T account 97 (LO2)

Trial balance 109 (LO4)

Valuation 94 (LO1)

Key Ratio

Cash return on assets 119

CHAPTER ASSIGNMENTS

BUILDING Your Basic Knowledge and Skills

Short Exercises

LO1 **Recognition**

SE 1. Which of the following events would be recognized and entered in the accounting records of Kazuo Corporation? Why?

Jan. 10	Kazuo Corporation places an order for office supplies.
Feb. 15	Kazuo Corporation receives the office supplies and a bill for them.
Mar. 1	Kazuo Corporation pays for the office supplies.

LO1 LO3 **Recognition, Valuation, and Classification**

SE 2. Tell how the concepts of recognition, valuation, and classification apply to this transaction:

Cash		Supplies	
	June 1 1,000	June 1 1,000	

LO1 **Classification of Accounts**

SE 3. Tell whether each of the following accounts is an asset, a liability, a revenue, an expense, or none of these:

a. Accounts Payable
b. Supplies
c. Dividends
d. Fees Earned
e. Rent Expense
f. Accounts Receivable
g. Unearned Revenue
h. Equipment

LO2 **Normal Balances**

SE 4. Tell whether the normal balance of each account in **SE 3** is a debit or a credit.

LO3 **Transaction Analysis**

SE 5. For each transaction that follows, indicate which account is debited and which account is credited.

May	2	Leon Bear started a computer programming business, Bear's Programming Service, Inc., by investing $5,000 in exchange for common stock.
	5	Purchased a computer for $2,500 in cash.
	7	Purchased supplies on credit for $300.
	19	Received cash for programming services performed, $500.
	22	Received cash for programming services to be performed, $600.
	25	Paid the rent for May, $650.
	31	Billed a customer for programming services performed, $250.

LO3 **Recording Transactions in T Accounts**

SE 6. Set up T accounts and record each transaction in **SE 5**. Determine the balance of each account.

LO4 **Preparing a Trial Balance**

SE 7. From the T accounts created in **SE 6**, prepare a trial balance dated May 31, 2010.

LO5 **Timing and Cash Flows**

SE 8. Use the T account for Cash below to record the portion of each of the following transactions, if any, that affect cash. How do these transactions affect the company's liquidity?

Cash

Jan. 2 Provided services for cash, $1,200
4 Paid expenses in cash, $700
8 Provided services on credit, $1,100
9 Incurred expenses on credit, $800

SO6 **Recording Transactions in the General Journal**

SE 9. Prepare a general journal form like the one in Exhibit 2-4 and label it Page 4. Record the following transactions in the journal:

Sept. 6 Billed a customer for services performed, $3,800.
16 Received partial payment from the customer billed on Sept. 6, $1,800.

SO6 **Posting to the Ledger Accounts**

SE 10. Prepare ledger account forms like the ones in Exhibit 2-5 for the following accounts: Cash (111), Accounts Receivable (113), and Service Revenue (411). Post the transactions that are recorded in **SE 9** to the ledger accounts, at the same time making the proper posting references. Also prepare a trial balance.

SO6 **Recording Transactions in the General Journal**

SE 11. Record the transactions in **SE 5** in the general journal.

Cash Return on Assets

SE 12. Calculate cash return on assets for 2010 using the following data: A company has net cash flows from operating activities of $1,500 in 2010, beginning total assets of $13,000, and ending total assets of $14,000.

Exercises

LO1 LO2 LO3 **Discussion Questions**

E 1. Develop a brief answer to each of the following questions.

1. Which is the most important issue in recording a transaction: recognition, valuation, or classification?
2. What is an example of how a company could make false financial statements through a violation of the recognition concept?
3. How are assets and expenses related, and why are the debit and credit effects for assets and expenses the same?
4. In what way are unearned revenues the opposite of prepaid expenses?

LO4 LO5 SO6 **Discussion Questions**

E 2. Develop a brief answer to each of the following questions.

1. Which account would be most likely to have an account balance that is not normal?
2. A company incurs a cost for a part that is needed to repair a piece of equipment. Is the cost an asset or an expense? Explain.
3. If a company's cash flows for expenses temporarily exceed its cash flows from revenues, how might it make up the difference so that it can maintain liquidity?
4. How would the asset accounts in the chart of accounts for Miller Design Studio, Inc., differ if it were a retail company that sells advertising products instead of a service company that designs ads?

LO1 **Recognition**

E 3. Which of the following events would be recognized and recorded in the accounting records of Villa Corporation on the date indicated?

Jan. 15	Villa Corporation offers to purchase a tract of land for $140,000. There is a high likelihood that the offer will be accepted.
Feb. 2	Villa Corporation receives notice that its rent will increase from $500 to $600 per month effective March 1.
Mar. 29	Villa Corporation receives its utility bill for the month of March. The bill is not due until April 9.
June 10	Villa Corporation places an order for new office equipment costing $21,000.
July 6	The office equipment Villa Corporation ordered on June 10 arrives. Payment is not due until August 1.

LO1 **Application of Recognition Point**

E 4. Torez Flower Shop, Inc., uses a large amount of supplies in its business. The following table summarizes selected transaction data for supplies that Torez Flower Shop, Inc. purchased:

Order	Date Shipped	Date Received	Amount
a.	June 26	July 5	$300
b.	July 10	15	750
c.	16	22	450
d.	23	30	600
e.	27	Aug. 1	700
f.	Aug. 3	7	500

Determine the total purchases of supplies for July alone under each of the following assumptions:

1. Torez Flower Shop, Inc., recognizes purchases when orders are shipped.
2. Torez Flower Shop, Inc., recognizes purchases when orders are received.

LO2 **T Accounts, Normal Balance, and the Accounting Equation**

E 5. You are given the following list of accounts with dollar amounts:

Rent Expense	$ 450
Cash	1,725
Service Revenue	750
Retained Earnings	300
Dividends	375
Accounts Payable	600
Common Stock	900

Insert each account name at the top of its corresponding T account and enter the dollar amount as a normal balance in the account. Then show that the accounting equation is in balance.

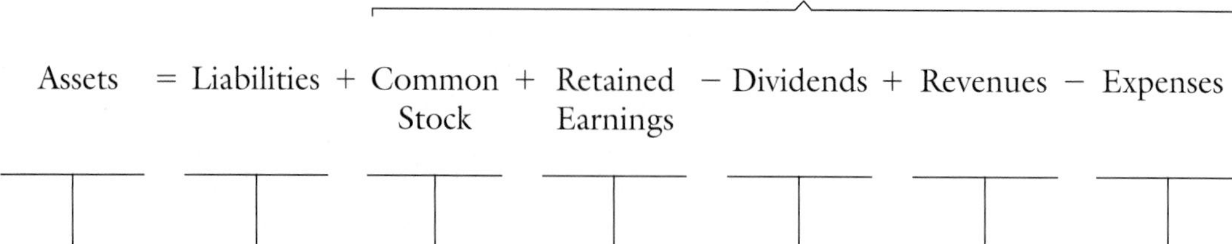

LO2 **Classification of Accounts**

E 6. The following ledger accounts are for the Tuner Service Corporation:

a. Cash
b. Wages Expense
c. Accounts Receivable
d. Common Stock
e. Service Revenue
f. Prepaid Rent
g. Accounts Payable
h. Investments in Securities
i. Income Taxes Payable
j. Income Taxes Expense
k. Land
l. Advertising Expense
m. Prepaid Insurance
n. Utilities Expense
o. Fees Earned
p. Dividends
q. Wages Payable
r. Unearned Revenue
s. Office Equipment
t. Rent Payable
u. Notes Receivable
v. Interest Expense
w. Notes Payable
x. Supplies
y. Interest Receivable
z. Rent Expense

Complete the following table, using X's to indicate each account's classification and normal balance (whether a debit or a credit increases the account).

	Type of Account						Normal Balance (increases balance)	
			Stockholders' Equity					
			Common	Retained Earnings				
Item	**Asset**	**Liability**	**Stock**	**Dividends**	**Revenue**	**Expense**	**Debit**	**Credit**
a.	X						X	

LO3 **Transaction Analysis**

E 7. Analyze transactions **a–g**, as in the example below for transaction **a**.

a. Sarah Lopez established Sarah's Beauty Parlor, Inc., by incorporating and investing $2,500 in exchange for 250 shares of $10 par value common stock.
b. Paid two months' rent in advance, $1,680.
c. Purchased supplies on credit, $120.
d. Received cash for hair services, $700.
e. Paid for supplies purchased in c.
f. Paid utility bill, $72.
g. Declared and paid a dividend of $100.

Example

a. The asset account Cash was increased. Increases in assets are recorded by debits. Debit Cash $2,500. A component of stockholders' equity, Common Stock, was increased. Increases in stockholders' equity are recorded by credits. Credit Common Stock $2,500.

LO3 **Transaction Analysis**

E 8. The following accounts are applicable to Dale's Lawn Service, Inc., a company that maintains condominium grounds:

1. Cash
2. Accounts Receivable
3. Supplies
4. Equipment
5. Accounts Payable
6. Lawn Services Revenue
7. Wages Expense
8. Rent Expense

Dale's Lawn Service, Inc., completed the following transactions:

	Debit	Credit
a. Paid for supplies purchased on credit last month.	5	1
b. Received cash from customers billed last month.		
c. Made a payment on accounts payable.		
d. Purchased supplies on credit.		
e. Billed a client for lawn services.		
f. Made a rent payment for the current month.		
g. Received cash from customers for current lawn services.		
h. Paid employee wages.		
i. Ordered equipment.		
j. Received and paid for the equipment ordered in **i**.		

Analyze each transaction and show the accounts affected by entering the corresponding numbers in the appropriate debit or credit columns as shown in transaction **a.** Indicate no entry, if appropriate.

LO3 **Recording Transactions in T Accounts**

E 9. Open the following T accounts: Cash; Repair Supplies; Repair Equipment; Accounts Payable; Common Stock; Dividends; Repair Fees Earned; Salaries Expense; and Rent Expense. Record the following transactions for the month of June directly in the T accounts; use the letters to identify the transactions in your T accounts. Determine the balance in each account.

a. Tony Ornega opened Ornega Repair Service, Inc., by investing $4,300 in cash and $1,600 in repair equipment in return for 5,900 shares of the company's $1 par value common stock.
b. Paid $800 for the current month's rent.
c. Purchased repair supplies on credit, $1,100.
d. Purchased additional repair equipment for cash, $600.
e. Paid salary to a helper, $900.
f. Paid $400 of amount purchased on credit in **c**.
g. Accepted cash for repairs completed, $3,720.
h. Declared and paid a dividend of $1,000.

LO4 **Trial Balance**

E 10. After recording the transactions in **E 9**, prepare a trial balance in proper sequence for Ornega Repair Service, Inc., as of June 30, 2010.

LO3 **Analysis of Transactions**

E 11. Explain each transaction (a–h) in the T accounts that follow.

Cash			
a.	20,000	b.	7,500
g.	750	e.	1,800
h.	450	f.	2,250

Accounts Receivable			
c.	4,000	g.	750

Equipment			
b.	7,500	h.	450
d.	4,500		

Accounts Payable			
f.	2,250	d.	4,500

Common Stock			
		a.	20,000

Service Revenue			
		c.	4,000

Wages Expense			
e.	1,800		

LO4 **Preparing a Trial Balance**

E 12. The list that follows presents the accounts (in alphabetical order) of the Dymarski Corporation as of March 31, 2010. The list does not include the amount of Accounts Payable.

Accounts Payable	?
Accounts Receivable	$ 2,800
Building	20,400
Cash	5,400
Common Stock	12,000
Equipment	7,200
Land	3,120
Notes Payable	10,000
Prepaid Insurance	660
Retained Earnings	6,870

Prepare a trial balance with the proper heading (see Exhibit 2-2) and with the accounts listed in the chart of accounts sequence (see Exhibit 2-3). Compute the balance of Accounts Payable.

LO4 **Effects of Errors on a Trial Balance**

E 13. Which of the following errors would cause a trial balance to have unequal totals? Explain your answers.

a. A payment to a creditor was recorded as a debit to Accounts Payable for $129 and as a credit to Cash for $102.
b. A payment of $150 to a creditor for an account payable was debited to Accounts Receivable and credited to Cash.
c. A purchase of office supplies of $420 was recorded as a debit to Office Supplies for $42 and as a credit to Cash for $42.
d. A purchase of equipment for $450 was recorded as a debit to Supplies for $450 and as a credit to Cash for $450.

LO4 **Correcting Errors in a Trial Balance**

E 14. The trial balance for Marek Services, Inc., at the end of July appears at the top of the next page. It does not balance because of a number of errors. Marek's accountant compared the amounts in the trial balance with the ledger, recomputed the account balances, and compared the postings. He found the following errors:

a. The balance of Cash was understated by $800.
b. A cash payment of $420 was credited to Cash for $240.
c. A debit of $120 to Accounts Receivable was not posted.
d. Supplies purchased for $60 were posted as a credit to Supplies.
e. A debit of $180 to Prepaid Insurance was not posted.

Marek Services, Inc. Trial Balance July 31, 2010		
Cash	$ 3,440	
Accounts Receivable	5,660	
Supplies	120	
Prepaid Insurance	180	
Equipment	7,400	
Accounts Payable		$ 4,540
Common Stock		3,000
Retained Earnings		7,560
Dividends		700
Revenues		5,920
Salaries Expense	2,600	
Rent Expense	600	
Advertising Expense	340	
Utilities Expense	26	
	$20,366	$21,720

f. The Accounts Payable account had debits of $5,320 and credits of $9,180.
g. The Notes Payable account, with a credit balance of $2,400, was not included on the trial balance.
h. The debit balance of Dividends was listed in the trial balance as a credit.
i. A $200 debit to Dividends was posted as a credit.
j. The actual balance of Utilities Expense, $260, was listed as $26 in the trial balance.

Prepare a corrected trial balance.

LO5 Cash Flow Analysis

E 15. A company engaged in the following transactions:

Dec.	1	Performed services for cash, $750
	1	Paid expenses in cash, $550
	2	Performed services on credit, $900
	3	Collected on account, $600
	4	Incurred expenses on credit, $650
	5	Paid on account, $350

Enter the correct titles on the following T accounts and enter the above transactions in the accounts. Determine the cash balance after these transactions, the amount still to be received, and the amount still to be paid.

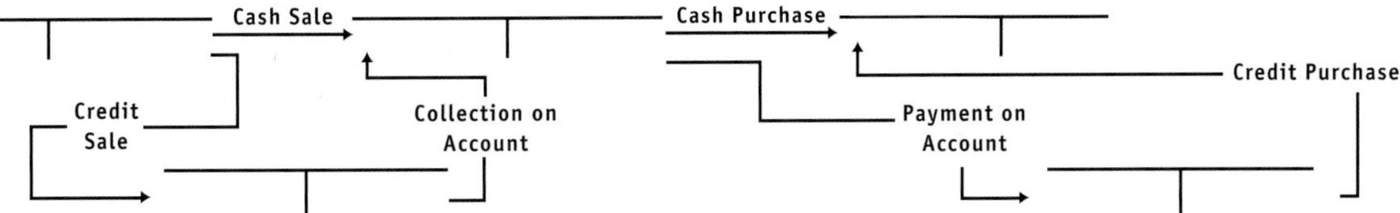

SO6 Recording Transactions in the General Journal

E 16. Record the transactions in **E 9** in the general journal.

LO3 SO6 **Analysis of Unfamiliar Transactions**

E 17. Managers and accountants often encounter transactions with which they are unfamiliar. Use your analytical skills to analyze and record in journal form the following transactions, which have not yet been discussed in the text.

May 1	Purchased merchandise inventory on account, $1,200.
2	Purchased marketable securities for cash, $3,000.
3	Returned part of merchandise inventory for full credit, $250.
4	Sold merchandise inventory on account, $800 (record sale only).
5	Purchased land and a building for $300,000. Payment is $60,000 cash, and there is a 30-year mortgage for the remainder. The purchase price is allocated as follows: $100,000 to the land and $200,000 to the building.
6	Received an order for $12,000 in services to be provided. With the order was a deposit of $3,500.

SO6 **Recording Transactions in the General Journal and Posting to the Ledger Accounts**

E 18. Open a general journal form like the one in Exhibit 2-4, and label it Page 10. After opening the form, record the following transactions in the journal:

Dec. 14	Purchased equipment for $6,000, paying $2,000 as a cash down payment.
28	Paid $3,000 of the amount owed on the equipment.

Prepare three ledger account forms like the one shown in Exhibit 2-5. Use the following account numbers: Cash, 111; Equipment, 144; and Accounts Payable, 212. Post the two transactions from the general journal to the ledger accounts, being sure to make proper posting references. The Cash account has a debit balance of $8,000 on the day prior to the first transaction.

Cash Return on Assets

E 19. Waksal Company wants to know if its liquidity performance has improved. Calculate cash return on assets for 2009 and 2010 using the following data:

Net cash flows from operating activities, 2009	$ 4,300
Net cash flows from operating activities, 2010	5,000
Total assets, 2008	36,000
Total assets, 2009	40,000
Total assets, 2010	46,000

By this measure has liquidity improved? Why is it important to use average total assets in the calculation?

Problems

LO2 **T Accounts, Normal Balance, and the Accounting Equation**

P 1. Delux Design Corporation creates radio and television advertising for local businesses in the twin cities. The following alphabetical list shows Delux Design's account balances as of January 31, 2010:

Accounts Payable	$ 3,210	Loans Payable	$ 5,000
Accounts Receivable	39,000	Rent Expense	5,940
Cash	9,200	Retained Earnings	22,000
Common Stock	15,000	Telephone Expense	480
Design Revenue	105,000	Unearned Revenue	9,000
Dividends	18,000	Wages Expense	62,000
Equipment	?		

Required

Insert the account title at the top of its corresponding T account and enter the dollar amount as a normal balance in the account. Determine the balance of Equipment and then show that the accounting equation is in balance.

Stockholders' Equity

Assets = Liabilities + Common Stock + Retained Earnings − Dividends + Revenues − Expenses

LO3 **Transaction Analysis**

P 2. The following accounts are applicable to Tom's Chimney Sweeps, Inc.:

1. Cash
2. Accounts Receivable
3. Supplies
4. Prepaid Insurance
5. Equipment
6. Notes Payable
7. Accounts Payable
8. Common Stock
9. Retained Earnings
10. Dividends
11. Service Revenue
12. Rent Expense
13. Repairs Expense

Tom's Chimney Sweeps, Inc., completed the following transactions:

		Debit	Credit
a.	Paid for supplies purchased on credit last month.	7	1
b.	Billed customers for services performed.		
c.	Paid the current month's rent.		
d.	Purchased supplies on credit.		
e.	Received cash from customers for services performed but not yet billed.		
f.	Purchased equipment on account.		
g.	Received a bill for repairs.		
h.	Returned part of equipment purchased in **f** for a credit.		
i.	Received payments from customers previously billed.		
j.	Paid the bill received in **g**.		
k.	Received an order for services to be performed.		
l.	Paid for repairs with cash.		
m.	Made a payment to reduce the principal of the note payable.		
n.	Declared and paid a dividend.		

Required

Analyze each transaction and show the accounts affected by entering the corresponding account numbers in the appropriate debit or credit column as shown in transaction **a**. Indicate no entry, if appropriate.

LO3 LO4 LO5

Transaction Analysis, T Accounts, and Trial Balance

P 3. Carmen Dahlen opened a secretarial school called Star Secretarial Training, Inc.

a. Dahlen contributed the following assets to the business in exchange for 14,300 shares of $1 par value common stock:

Cash	$5,700
Computers	5,000
Office Equipment	3,600

b. Paid the first month's rent, $260.
c. Paid for an advertisement announcing the opening of the school, $190.
d. Received applications from three students for a four-week secretarial program and two students for a ten-day keyboarding course. The students will be billed a total of $1,300.
e. Purchased supplies on credit, $330.
f. Billed the enrolled students, $2,040.
g. Purchased a second-hand computer, $480, and office equipment, $380, on credit.
h. Paid for the supplies purchased on credit in e, $330.
i. Paid cash to repair a broken computer, $40.
j. Received partial payment from students previously billed, $1,380.
k. Paid the utility bill for the current month, $90.
l. Paid an assistant one week's salary, $440.
m. Declared and paid a dividend of $300.

Required

1. Set up the following T accounts: Cash; Accounts Receivable; Supplies; Computers; Office Equipment; Accounts Payable; Common Stock; Dividends; Tuition Revenue; Salaries Expense; Utilities Expense; Rent Expense; Repair Expense; and Advertising Expense.
2. Record the transactions directly in the T accounts, using the transaction letter to identify each debit and credit.
3. Prepare a trial balance using today's date.
4. (User insight ▶) Examine transactions **f** and **j**. What were the revenues and how much cash was received from the revenues? What business issues might you see arising from the differences in these numbers?

LO1 LO3 LO4

Transaction Analysis, Journal Form, T Accounts, and Trial Balance

P 4. Melvin Patel bid for and won a concession to rent bicycles in the local park during the summer. During the month of June, Patel completed the following transactions for his bicycle rental business:

June 2	Began business by placing $7,200 in a business checking account in the name of the corporation in exchange for 7,200 shares of $1 par value common stock.
3	Purchased supplies on account for $150.
4	Purchased 10 bicycles for $2,500, paying $1,200 down and agreeing to pay the rest in 30 days.
5	Paid $2,900 in cash for a small shed to store the bicycles and to use for other operations.
8	Paid $400 in cash for shipping and installation costs (considered an addition to the cost of the shed) to place the shed at the park entrance.
9	Hired a part-time assistant to help out on weekends at $7 per hour.
10	Paid a maintenance person $75 to clean the grounds.

June 13 Received $970 in cash for rentals.
17 Paid $150 for the supplies purchased on June 3.
18 Paid a $55 repair bill on bicycles.
23 Billed a company $110 for bicycle rentals for an employee outing.
25 Paid the $100 fee for June to the Park District for the right to operate the bicycle concession.
27 Received $960 in cash for rentals.
29 Paid the assistant wages of $240.
30 Declared and paid a dividend of $500.

Required

1. Prepare entries to record these transactions in journal form.
2. Set up the following T accounts and post all the journal entries: Cash; Accounts Receivable; Supplies; Shed; Bicycles; Accounts Payable; Common Stock; Dividends; Rental Revenue; Wages Expense; Maintenance Expense; Repair Expense; and Concession Fee Expense.
3. Prepare a trial balance for Patel Rentals, Inc., as of June 30, 2010.

User insight ▶

4. Compare and contrast how the issues of recognition, valuation, and classification are settled in the transactions of June 3 and 10.

LO3 LO4 LO5 SO6

Transaction Analysis, General Journal, Ledger Accounts, and Trial Balance

P 5. Alpha Pro Corporation is a marketing firm. The company's trial balance on July 31, 2010, appears below.

Alpha Pro Corporation
Trial Balance
July 31, 2010

Cash (111)	$10,590	
Accounts Receivable (113)	5,500	
Supplies (115)	610	
Office Equipment (141)	4,200	
Accounts Payable (212)		$ 2,600
Common Stock (311)		12,000
Retained Earnings (312)		6,300
	$20,900	$20,900

During the month of August, the company completed the following transactions:

Aug. 2 Paid rent for August, $650.
3 Received cash from customers on account, $2,300.
7 Ordered supplies, $380.
10 Billed customers for services provided, $2,800.
12 Made a payment on accounts payable, $1,300.
14 Received the supplies ordered on August 7 and agreed to pay for them in 30 days, $380.
17 Discovered some of the supplies were not as ordered and returned them for full credit, $80.
19 Received cash from a customer for services provided, $4,800.
24 Paid the utility bill for August, $250.
26 Received a bill, to be paid in September, for advertisements placed in the local newspaper during the month of August to promote Alpha Pro Corporation, $700.

Aug. 29 Billed a customer for services provided, $2,700.
30 Paid salaries for August, $3,800.
31 Declared and paid a dividend of $1,200.

Required

1. Open accounts in the ledger for the accounts in the trial balance plus the following accounts: Dividends (313); Marketing Fees (411); Salaries Expense (511); Rent Expense (512); Utilities Expense (513); and Advertising Expense (515).
2. Enter the July 31, 2010, account balances from the trial balance.
3. Enter the above transactions in the general journal (Pages 22 and 23).
4. Post the journal entries to the ledger accounts. Be sure to make the appropriate posting references in the journal and ledger as you post.
5. Prepare a trial balance as of August 31, 2010.

Users insight ▶

6. Examine the transactions for August 3, 10, 19, and 29. How much were revenues and how much cash was received from the revenues? What business issues might you see arising from the differences in these numbers?

Alternate Problems

LO2 T Accounts, Normal Balance, and the Accounting Equation

P 6. The Stewart Construction Corporation builds foundations for buildings and parking lots. The following alphabetical list shows Stewart Construction's account balances as of April 30, 2010:

Accounts Payable	$ 1,950	Rent Expense	$3,600
Accounts Receivable	5,060	Retained Earnings	5,000
Cash	?	Revenue Earned	8,700
Common Stock	15,000	Supplies	3,250
Dividends	3,500	Utilities Expense	210
Equipment	13,750	Wages Expense	4,400
Notes Payable	10,000		

Required

Insert the account at the top of its corresponding T account and enter the dollar amount as a normal balance in the account. Determine the balance of cash and then show that the accounting equation is in balance.

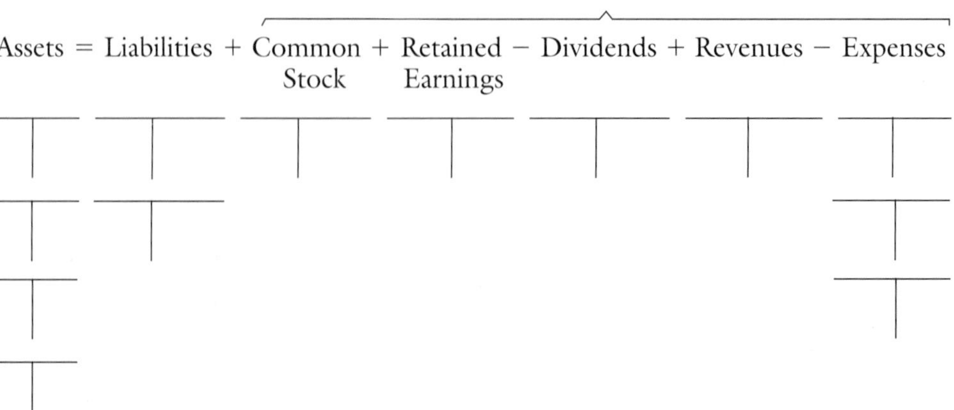

LO1 LO3 LO4

Transaction Analysis, T Accounts, and Trial Balance

P 7. Brad Cupello began an upholstery cleaning business on October 1 and engaged in the following transactions during the month:

Oct.	1	Began business by depositing $15,000 in a bank account in the name of the corporation in exchange for 15,000 shares of $1 par value common stock.
	2	Ordered cleaning supplies, $3,000.
	3	Purchased cleaning equipment for cash, $2,800.
	4	Made two months' van lease payment in advance, $1,200.
	7	Received the cleaning supplies ordered on October 2 and agreed to pay half the amount in 10 days and the rest in 30 days.
	9	Paid for repairs on the van with cash, $1,080.
	12	Received cash for cleaning upholstery, $960.
	17	Paid half the amount owed on supplies purchased on October 7, $1,500.
	21	Billed customers for cleaning upholstery, $1,340.
	24	Paid cash for additional repairs on the van, $80.
	27	Received $600 from the customers billed on October 21.
	31	Declared and paid a dividend of $700.

Required

1. Set up the following T accounts: Cash; Accounts Receivable; Cleaning Supplies; Prepaid Lease; Cleaning Equipment; Accounts Payable; Common Stock; Dividends; Cleaning Revenue; and Repairs Expense.
2. Record transactions directly in the T accounts. Identify each entry by date.
3. Prepare a trial balance for Cupello Upholstery Cleaning, Inc., as of October 31, 2010.

Users insight ▶

4. Compare and contrast how the issues of recognition, valuation, and classification are settled in the transactions of October 7 and 9.

LO3 LO4 LO5 SO6

Transaction Analysis, General Journal, Ledger Accounts, and Trial Balance

P 8. The Golden Nursery School Corporation provides baby-sitting and child-care programs. On January 31, 2010, the company had the following trial balance:

Golden Nursery School Corporation
Trial Balance
January 31, 2010

Cash (111)	$ 2,070	
Accounts Receivable (113)	1,700	
Equipment (141)	1,040	
Buses (143)	17,400	
Notes Payable (211)		$15,000
Accounts Payable (212)		1,640
Common Stock (311)		4,000
Retained Earnings (312)		1,570
	$22,210	$22,210

During the month of February, the company completed the following transactions:

Feb.	2	Paid this month's rent, $400.
	3	Received fees for this month's services, $650.
	4	Purchased supplies on account, $85.
	5	Reimbursed the bus driver for gas expenses, $40.
	6	Ordered playground equipment, $1,000.
	8	Made a payment on account, $170.
	9	Received payments from customers on account, $1,200.
	10	Billed customers who had not yet paid for this month's services, $700.
	11	Paid for the supplies purchased on February 4.
	13	Received and paid cash for playground equipment ordered on February 6, $1,000.
	17	Purchased equipment on account, $290.
	19	Paid this month's utility bill, $145.
	22	Received payment for one month's services from customers previously billed, $500.
	26	Paid part-time assistants for services, $460.
	27	Purchased gas and oil for the bus on account, $325.
	28	Declared and paid a dividend of $200.

Required

1. Open accounts in the ledger for the accounts in the trial balance plus the following ones: Supplies (115); Dividends (313); Service Revenue (411); Rent Expense (511); Gas and Oil Expense (512); Wages Expense (513); and Utilities Expense (514).
2. Enter the January 31, 2010, account balances from the trial balance.
3. Enter the above transactions in the general journal (Pages 17 and 18).
4. Post the entries to the ledger accounts. Be sure to make the appropriate posting references in the journal and ledger as you post.
5. Prepare a trial balance as of February 28, 2010.

Users insight ▶

6. Examine the transactions for February 3, 9, 10, and 22. What were the revenues and how much cash was received from the revenues? What business issue might you see arising from the differences in these numbers?

ENHANCING Your Knowledge, Skills, and Critical Thinking

LO1 LO3 **Valuation and Classification of Business Transactions**

C 1. Tower Garden Center has purchased two pre-owned trucks for delivery of plants and flowers to its customers. The trucks were purchased at a cash-only auction for 15 percent below current market value. The owners have asked you to record these purchases in the financial records at current market value. You don't think that is correct. In response to the owners, write a brief business memorandum in good form based on your knowledge of Chapter 2. Explain how the purchase of the pre-owned trucks will affect the balance sheet, include the entry to record the transaction, and explain why the amount must be at the price paid for the trucks.

LO3 **Recording of Rebates**

C 2. Is it revenue or a reduction of an expense? That is the question companies that receive manufacturer's rebates for purchasing a large quantity of product must answer. Food companies like **Sara Lee**, **Kraft Foods**, and **Nestlé** give supermarkets special manufacturer's rebates of up to 45 percent, depending on the quantities purchased. Some firms were recording these rebates as revenue, whereas others were recording them as a reduction of the cost until the SEC said that only one way is correct. What, then, is the correct way for supermarkets to record these rebates? Would your answer change net income?

LO2 LO3 **Interpreting a Bank's Financial Statements**

C 3. **Mellon Bank** is a large bank holding company. Selected accounts from the company's 2008 annual report are as follows (in millions):[9]

Cash and Due from Banks	$ 4,881
Loans to Customers	42,979
Securities Available for Sale	32,064
Deposits by Customers	159,673

1. Indicate whether each of the accounts just listed is an asset, a liability, or a component of stockholders' equity on Mellon Bank's balance sheet.
2. Assume that you are in a position to do business with this large company. Show how Mellon Bank's accountants would prepare the entry in T account form to record each of the following transactions:
   a. You sell securities in the amount of $2,000 to the bank.
   b. You deposit in the bank the $2,000 received from selling the securities.
   c. You borrow $5,000 from the bank.

LO5 **Cash Flows**

C 4. You have been promoted recently and now have access to the firm's monthly financial statements. Business is good. Revenues are increasing rapidly, and income is at an all-time high. The balance sheet shows growth in receivables, and accounts payable have declined. However, the chief financial officer is concerned about the firm's cash flows from operating activities because they are decreasing. What are some reasons why a company with a positive net income may fall short of cash from its operating activities? What could be done to improve this situation?

LO1 **Recognition, Valuation, and Classification**

C 5. Refer to the Summary of Significant Accounting Policies in the notes to the financial statements in the **CVS** annual report in the Supplement to Chapter 1 to answer these questions:

1. How does the concept of recognition apply to advertising costs?
2. How does the concept of valuation apply to inventories?
3. How does the concept of classification apply to cash and cash equivalents?

Cash Return on Assets

C 6. Refer to the financial statements of **CVS** and **Southwest Airlines Co.** in the Supplement to Chapter 1. Compute cash return on assets for the past two years for both companies and comment on the results. Total assets in fiscal 2006 were $20,574.1 million for CVS and $13,460 million for Southwest.

LO1 Recognition Point and Ethical Considerations

C 7. Robert Shah, a sales representative for Quality Office Supplies Corporation, is compensated on a commission basis and received a substantial bonus for meeting his annual sales goal. The company's recognition point for sales is the day of shipment. On December 31, Shah realizes he needs sales of $2,000 to reach his sales goal and receive the bonus. He calls a purchaser for a local insurance company, whom he knows well, and asks him to buy $2,000 worth of copier paper today. The purchaser says, "But Jerry, that's more than a year's supply for us." Shah says, "Buy it today. If you decide it's too much, you can return however much you want for full credit next month." The purchaser says, "Okay, ship it." The paper is shipped on December 31 and recorded as a sale. On January 15, the purchaser returns $1,750 worth of paper for full credit (approved by Shah) against the bill. Should the shipment on December 31 be recorded as a sale? Discuss the ethics of Shah's action.

LO1 Financial Measurement Concepts

C 8. Go to the website of any major company. Find the "Investor Relations" or "About Our Company" section and access either the company's annual report or its Form 10-K. Find the financial statements and look at the notes that follow the financial statements. The first note should relate to significant accounting policies. Find an example of an accounting policy that is an application of each of the following financial measurement concepts: recognition, valuation, and classification. Write a brief report of your findings and be prepared to discuss them in class.

LO1 LO3 Valuation and Classification Issues for Dot-Coms

C 9. The dot-com business has raised many issues about accounting practices, some of which are of great concern to both the SEC and the FASB. Important ones relate to the valuation and classification of revenue transactions. Many dot-com companies seek to report as much revenue as possible because revenue growth is seen as a key performance measure for these companies. **Amazon.com** is a good example. Consider the following situations:

a. An Amazon.com customer orders and pays $28 for a video game on the Internet. Amazon sends an email to the company that makes the product, which sends the video game to the customer. Amazon collects $28 from the customer and pays $24 to the other company. Amazon never owns the video game.
b. Amazon agrees to place a banner advertisement on its website for another dot-com company. Instead of paying cash for the advertisement, the other company agrees to let Amazon advertise on its website.
c. Assume the same facts as in situation **b** except that Amazon agrees to accept the other company's common stock in this barter transaction. Over the next six months, the price of that stock declines.

Your instructor will divide the class into three groups. Each group will be assigned one of the above situations. Each group should discuss the valuation and classification issues that arise in the assigned situation, including how Amazon should account for each transaction.

LO1 Valuation Issue

C 10. Nike, Inc., manufactures athletic shoes and related products. In one of its annual reports, Nike made this statement: "Property, plant, and equipment are recorded at cost."[10] Given that the property, plant, and equipment undoubtedly were purchased over several years and that the current value of those assets is likely to be very different from their original cost, what authoritative basis is there for carrying the assets at cost? Does accounting generally recognize changes in value after the purchase of property, plant, and equipment? Assume you are an accountant for Nike. Write a memo to management explaining the rationale underlying Nike's approach.

CHAPTER

3 Measuring Business Income

Focus on Financial Statements

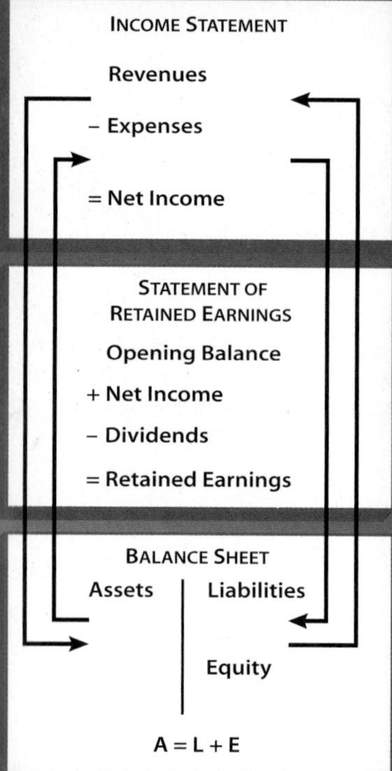

Adjusting entries bring balance sheet and income statement accounts up-to-date at end of period.

Income, or earnings, is the most important measure of a company's success or failure. Thus, the incentive to manage, or misstate, earnings by manipulating the numbers can be powerful, and because earnings are based on estimates, manipulation can be easy. For these reasons, ethical behavior is extremely important when measuring business income.

LEARNING OBJECTIVES

LO1 Define *net income*, and explain the assumptions underlying income measurement and their ethical application. (pp. 144–147)

LO2 Define *accrual accounting*, and explain how it is accomplished. (pp. 148–150)

LO3 Identify four situations that require adjusting entries, and illustrate typical adjusting entries. (pp. 150–160)

LO4 Prepare financial statements from an adjusted trial balance. (pp. 160–163)

LO5 Describe the accounting cycle, and explain the purposes of closing entries. (pp. 163–167)

LO6 Use accrual-based information to analyze cash flows. (pp. 167–168)

DECISION POINT ▸ A USER'S FOCUS NETFLIX, INC.

Netflix is the world's largest online entertainment subscription service. For a monthly fee, its subscribers have access to more than 90,000 DVD titles, which are shipped free of charge; with certain plans, they also have access to more than 5,000 movies online. At the end of any accounting period, Netflix has many transactions that will affect future periods.[1] Two examples appear in the Financial Highlights below: *prepaid expenses*, which, though paid in the period just ended, will benefit future periods and are therefore recorded as assets; and *accrued expenses*, which the company has incurred but will not pay until a future period. If prepaid expenses and accrued expenses are not accounted for properly at the end of a period, Netflix's income will be misstated. Similar misstatements can occur when a company has received revenue that it has not yet earned or has earned revenue that it has not yet received. If misstatements are made, investors will be misled about the company's financial performance.

▸ What assumptions must Netflix make to account for transactions that span accounting periods?

▸ How does Netflix assign its revenues and expenses to the proper accounting period so that net income is properly measured?

▸ Why are the adjustments that these transactions require important to Netflix's financial performance?

NETFLIX'S FINANCIAL HIGHLIGHTS: SELECTED BALANCE SHEET ITEMS (in thousands)

Assets	**2008**	**2007**
Prepaid expenses	$ 8,122	$ 6,116
Liabilities		
Accrued expenses	$31,394	$36,466

Profitability Measurement Issues and Ethics

LO1 Define *net income*, and explain the assumptions underlying income measurement and their ethical application.

As you know, profitability and liquidity are the two major goals of a business. For a business to succeed, or even to survive, it must earn a profit. **Profit**, however, means different things to different people. Accountants prefer to use the term **net income** because it can be precisely defined from an accounting point of view as the *net increase in stockholders' equity that results from a company's operations.*

Net income is reported on the income statement, and management, stockholders, and others use it to measure a company's progress in meeting the goal of profitability. Readers of income statements need to understand what net income means and be aware of its strengths and weaknesses as a measure of a company's performance.

Net Income

Net income is accumulated in the Retained Earnings account. In its simplest form, it is measured as the difference between revenues and expenses when revenues exceed expenses:

$$\text{Net Income} = \text{Revenues} - \text{Expenses}$$

When expenses exceed revenues, a **net loss** occurs.

Study Note
The essence of revenue is that something has been *earned* through the sale of goods or services. That is why cash received through a loan does not constitute revenue.

Revenues are *increases in stockholders' equity* resulting from selling goods, rendering services, or performing other business activities. When a business delivers a product or provides a service to a customer, it usually receives cash or a promise from the customer to pay cash in the near future. The promise to pay is recorded in either Accounts Receivable or Notes Receivable. The total of the increases in these accounts and the total cash received from customers in an accounting period are the company's revenues for that period.

Study Note
The primary purpose of an expense is to generate revenue.

Expenses are *decreases in stockholders' equity* resulting from the costs of selling goods or rendering services and the costs of the activities necessary to carry on a business, such as attracting and serving customers. In other words, expenses are the cost of the goods and services used in the course of earning revenues. Examples include salaries expense, rent expense, advertising expense, utilities expense, and depreciation (allocation of cost) of a building or office equipment. These expenses are often called the *costs of doing business* or *expired costs.*

Not all increases in stockholders' equity arise from revenues, nor do all decreases in stockholders' equity arise from expenses. Stockholders' investments increase stockholders' equity but are not revenues, and dividends decrease stockholders' equity but are not expenses.

Income Measurement Assumptions

Users of financial reports should be aware that estimates and assumptions play a major role in the measurement of net income and other key indicators of performance. **Netflix**'s management acknowledges this in its annual report, as follows:

> The preparation of financial statements in conformity with accounting principles generally accepted in the United States requires . . . estimates and assumptions that affect the reported amounts of assets and liabilities, disclosures of contingent assets and liabilities at the date of the financial statements, and the reported accounts of revenues and expenses during the reporting periods.[2]

The major assumptions made in measuring business income have to do with continuity, periodicity, and matching.

Continuity Measuring business income requires that certain expense and revenue transactions be allocated over several accounting periods. Choosing the number of accounting periods raises the issue of **continuity**. What is the expected life of the business? Many businesses last less than five years, and in any given year, thousands of businesses go bankrupt. The majority of companies present annual financial statements on the assumption that the business will continue to operate indefinitely—that is, that the company is a **going concern**. The continuity assumption is as follows:

> Unless there is evidence to the contrary, the accountant assumes that the business will continue to operate indefinitely.

Justification for all the techniques of income measurement rests on the assumption of continuity. Consider, for example, the value of assets on the balance sheet. The continuity assumption allows the cost of certain assets to be held on the balance sheet until a future accounting period, when the cost will become an expense on the income statement. When a firm is facing bankruptcy, the accountant may set aside the assumption of continuity and prepare financial statements based on the assumption that the firm will go out of business and sell all of its assets at liquidation value—that is, for what they will bring in cash.

Periodicity Measuring business income requires assigning revenues and expenses to a specific accounting period. However, not all transactions can be easily assigned to specific periods. For example, when a company purchases a building, it must estimate the number of years the building will be in use. The portion of the cost of the building assigned to each period depends on this estimate and requires an assumption about **periodicity**. The assumption is as follows:

> Although the lifetime of a business is uncertain, it is nonetheless useful to estimate the business's net income in terms of accounting periods.

Study Note

Accounting periods are of equal length so that one period can be compared with the next.

Financial statements may be prepared for any time period, but generally, to make comparisons easier, the periods are of equal length. A 12-month accounting period is called a **fiscal year**; accounting periods of less than a year are called **interim periods**. The fiscal year of many organizations is the calendar year, January 1 to December 31. However, retailers often end their fiscal years during a slack season, and in this case, the fiscal year corresponds to the yearly cycle of business activity.

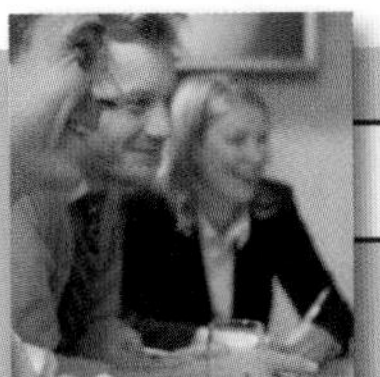

FOCUS ON BUSINESS PRACTICE

Fiscal Years Vary

The fiscal years of many schools and governmental agencies end on June 30 or September 30. The table at the right shows the last month of the fiscal year of some well-known companies.

Company	*Last Month of Fiscal Year*
Apple Computer	September
Caesars World	July
Fleetwood Enterprises	April
H.J. Heinz	March
Kelly Services	December
MGM-UA Communications	August
Toys "R" Us	January

Matching Rule To measure net income adequately, revenues and expenses must be assigned to the accounting period in which they occur, regardless of when cash is received or paid. This is an application of the **matching rule**:

> Revenues must be assigned to the accounting period in which the goods are sold or the services performed, and expenses must be assigned to the accounting period in which they are used to produce revenue.

In other words, expenses should be recognized in the same accounting period as the revenues to which they are related. However, a direct cause-and-effect relationship between expenses and revenues is often difficult to identify. When there is no direct means of connecting expenses and revenues, costs are allocated in a systematic way among the accounting periods that benefit from the costs. For example, a building's cost is expensed over the building's expected useful life, and interest on investments is recorded as income even though it may not yet have been received.

The **cash basis of accounting** differs from the matching rule in that it is the practice of accounting for revenues in the period in which cash is received and for expenses in the period in which cash is paid. Some individuals and businesses use this method to account for income taxes. With this method, taxable income is calculated as the difference between cash receipts from revenues and cash payments for expenses.

Although the cash basis of accounting works well for some small businesses and many individuals, it does not meet the needs of most businesses.

Ethics and the Matching Rule

As shown in Figure 3-1, applying the matching rule involves making assumptions. It also involves exercising judgment. Consider the assumptions and judgment involved in estimating the useful life of a building. The estimate should be based on realistic assumptions, but management has latitude in making that estimate, and its judgment will affect the final net income that is reported.

The manipulation of revenues and expenses to achieve a specific outcome is called **earnings management**. Research has shown that companies that manage their earnings are much more likely to exceed projected earnings targets by a little than to fall short by a little. Why would management want to manage earnings to keep them from falling short? It may want to

- Meet a previously announced goal and thus meet the expectations of the market.

FIGURE 3-1
Assumptions and the Matching Rule

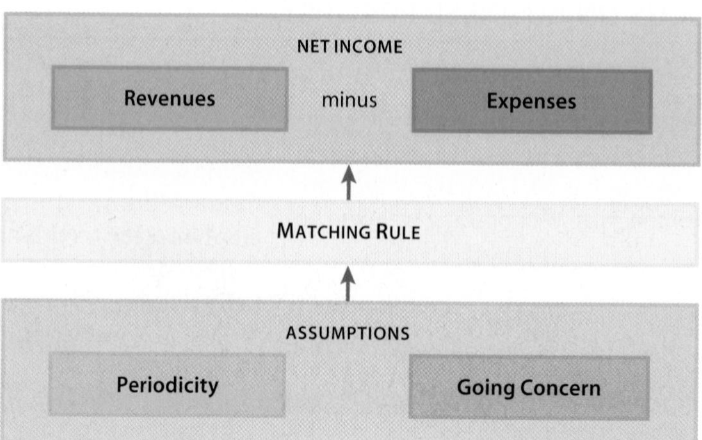

FOCUS ON BUSINESS PRACTICE

Are Misstatements of Earnings Always Overstatements?

Not all misstatements of earnings are overstatements. For instance, privately held companies, which do not have to be concerned about the effect of their earnings announcements on stockholders or investors, may understate income to reduce or avoid income taxes. In an unusual case involving a public company, the SEC cited and fined **Microsoft** for understating its income. Microsoft, a very successful company, accomplished this by overstating its unearned revenue on the balance sheet. The company's motive in trying to appear less successful than it actually was may have been that it was facing government charges of being a monopoly.[3]

- Keep the company's stock price from dropping.
- Meet a goal that will enable it to earn bonuses.
- Avoid embarrassment.

Earnings management, though not the best practice, is not illegal. However, when the estimates involved in earnings management begin moving outside a reasonable range, the financial statements become misleading. For instance, net income is misleading when revenue is overstated by a significant amount or when expenses are understated by a significant amount. As noted earlier in the text, the preparation of financial statements that are intentionally misleading constitutes fraudulent financial reporting.

Most of the enforcement actions that the Securities and Exchange Commission has brought against companies in recent years involve misapplications of the matching rule resulting from improper accrual accounting. For example, **Dell Computer** had to restate four years of its financial results because senior executives improperly applied accrual accounting to give the impression that the company was meeting quarterly earnings targets. After the SEC action, the company conducted an internal investigation that resulted in many changes in its accounting controls.[4] In the rest of this chapter, we focus on accrual accounting and its proper application.

STOP & APPLY >

Match each assumption or action below with the appropriate concept.

_____ 1. Increases in stockholders' equity resulting from selling goods, rendering services, or performing other business activities

_____ 2. Manipulation of revenues and expenses to achieve a specific change in stockholders' equity

_____ 3. Increase in stockholders' equity that results from a company's operations

_____ 4. Decreases in stockholders' equity resulting from the cost of selling goods, rendering services, and other business activities

a. Net income
b. Revenues
c. Expenses
d. Earnings management

SOLUTION

1. b; 2. d; 3. a; 4. c

Accrual Accounting

LO2 Define *accrual accounting*, and explain how it is accomplished.

Accrual accounting encompasses all the techniques accountants use to apply the matching rule. In accrual accounting, revenues and expenses are recorded in the periods in which they occur rather than in the periods in which they are received or paid.

Accrual accounting is accomplished in the following ways:

1. Recording revenues when they are earned.
2. Recording expenses when they are incurred.
3. Adjusting the accounts.

Recognizing Revenues

As you may recall, the process of determining when revenue should be recorded is called **revenue recognition**. The Securities and Exchange Commission requires that all the following conditions be met before revenue is recognized:[5]

- Persuasive evidence of an arrangement exists.
- A product or service has been delivered.
- The seller's price to the buyer is fixed or determinable.
- Collectibility is reasonably assured.

For example, suppose Miller Design Studio, Inc., has created a website for a customer and that the transaction meets the SEC's four criteria: Miller and the customer agree that the customer owes for the service, the service has been rendered, both parties understand the price, and there is a reasonable expectation that the customer will pay the bill. When Miller Design Studio, Inc. bills the customer, it records the transaction as revenue by debiting Accounts Receivable and crediting Design Revenue. Note that revenue can be recorded even though cash has not been collected; all that is required is a reasonable expectation that cash will be paid.

Study Note

Even though certain revenues and expenses theoretically change during the period, there usually is no need to adjust them until the end of the period, when the financial statements are prepared.

Recognizing Expenses

Expenses are recorded when there is an agreement to purchase goods or services, the goods have been delivered or the services rendered, a price has been established or can be determined, and the goods or services have been used to produce revenue. For example, when Miller Design Studio, Inc. receives its utility bill, it recognizes the expense as having been incurred and as having helped produce revenue. Miller Design Studio, Inc. records this transaction by debiting Utilities Expense and crediting Accounts Payable. Until the bill is paid, Accounts Payable serves as a holding account. Note that recognition of the expense does not depend on the payment of cash.

FOCUS ON BUSINESS PRACTICE — IFRS

Revenue Recognition: Principles Versus Rules

Revenue recognition highlights the differences between international and U.S. accounting standards. Although U.S. standards are referred to as generally accepted accounting *principles*, the FASB has issued extensive *rules* for revenue recognition in various situations and industries. The IASB, on the other hand, has one broad IFRS for revenue recognition and leaves it to companies and their auditors to determine how to apply the broad *principle*. As a result, revenue recognition is an issue that will provide a challenge to achieving international convergence of accounting practice.

EXHIBIT 3-1
Trial Balance

Miller Design Studio, Inc. Trial Balance July 31, 2010		
Cash	$22,480	
Accounts Receivable	4,600	
Office Supplies	5,200	
Prepaid Rent	3,200	
Office Equipment	16,320	
Accounts Payable		$ 6,280
Unearned Design Revenue		1,400
Common Stock		40,000
Dividends	2,800	
Design Revenue		12,400
Wages Expense	4,800	
Utilities Expense	680	
	$60,080	$60,080

Adjusting the Accounts

Accrual accounting also involves adjusting the accounts. Adjustments are necessary because the accounting period, by definition, ends on a particular day. The balance sheet must list all assets and liabilities as of the end of that day, and the income statement must contain all revenues and expenses applicable to the period ending on that day. Although operating a business is a continuous process, there must be a cutoff point for the periodic reports. Some transactions invariably span the cutoff point, and some accounts therefore need adjustment.

As you can see in Exhibit 3-1, some of the accounts in Miller Design Studio, Inc.'s trial balance as of July 31 do not show the correct balances for preparing the financial statements. The trial balance lists prepaid rent of $3,200. At $1,600 per month, this represents rent for the months of July and August. So, on July 31, one-half of the $3,200 represents rent expense for July, and the remaining $1,600 represents an asset that will be used in August. An adjustment is needed to reflect the $1,600 balance in the Prepaid Rent account on the balance sheet and the $1,600 rent expense on the income statement.

As you will see, several other accounts in Miller Design Studio, Inc.'s trial balance do not reflect their correct balances. Like the Prepaid Rent account, they need to be adjusted.

Adjustments and Ethics

Accrual accounting can be difficult to understand. The account adjustments take time to calculate and enter in the records. Also, adjusting entries do not affect cash flows in the current period because they never involve the Cash account. You might ask, "Why go to all the trouble of making them? Why worry about them?" For one thing, the SEC has identified issues related to accrual accounting and adjustments as an area of utmost importance because of the potential for abuse and misrepresentation.[6]

All adjustments are important because of their effect on performance measures of profitability and liquidity. Adjusting entries affect net income on the income statement, and they affect profitability comparisons from one accounting period to the next. They also affect assets and liabilities on the balance sheet and thus provide information about a company's *future* cash inflows and outflows.

This information is needed to assess management's performance in achieving sufficient liquidity to meet the need for cash to pay ongoing obligations. The potential for abuse arises because considerable judgment underlies the application of adjusting entries. When this judgment is misused, performance measures can be misleading.

STOP & APPLY >

Four conditions must be met before revenue should be recognized. Identify which of these conditions applies to the following actions by Hastings Corporation:

a. Determines that a client has a good credit rating.
b. Agrees to a price for services before it performs them.
c. Performs services.
d. Signs a contract to perform services.

SOLUTION

a. Collectibility is reasonably assured.
b. The seller's price to the buyer is fixed or determinable.
c. A product or service has been delivered.
d. Persuasive evidence of an arrangement exists.

The Adjustment Process

LO3 Identify four situations that require adjusting entries, and illustrate typical adjusting entries.

When transactions span more than one accounting period, accrual accounting requires the use of **adjusting entries**. Figure 3-2 shows the four situations in which adjusting entries must be made. Each adjusting entry affects one balance sheet account and one income statement account. As we have already noted, adjusting entries never affect the Cash account.

The four types of adjusting entries are as follows:

Type 1. Allocating recorded costs between two or more accounting periods. Examples of these costs are prepayments of rent, insurance, and supplies, and the depreciation of plant and equipment. The adjusting entry in this case involves an asset account and an expense account.

Type 2. Recognizing unrecorded expenses. Examples of these expenses are wages, interest, and income taxes that have been incurred but are not recorded during an accounting period. The adjusting entry involves an expense account and a liability account.

FIGURE 3-2
The Four Types of Adjustments

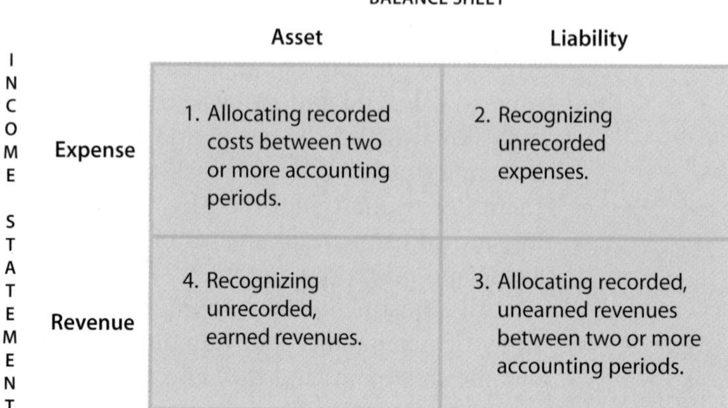

When transactions span more than one accounting period, an adjusting entry is necessary. Depreciation of plant and equipment, such as that found in this warehouse, is a type of transaction that requires an adjusting entry. In this case, the adjusting entry involves an asset account and an expense account.

Courtesy of Timothy Babasade/ istockphoto.com.

Type 3. Allocating recorded, unearned revenues between two or more accounting periods. Examples include payments received in advance and deposits made on goods or services. The adjusting entry involves a liability account and a revenue account.

Type 4. Recognizing unrecorded, earned revenues. An example is revenue that a company has earned for providing a service but for which it has not billed or been paid by the end of the accounting period. The adjusting entry involves an asset account and a revenue account.

Adjusting entries are either deferrals or accruals.

- A **deferral** is the postponement of the recognition of an expense already paid (Type 1 adjustment) or of revenue received in advance (Type 3 adjustment). The cash receipt or payment is recorded before the adjusting entry is made.
- An **accrual** is the recognition of a revenue (Type 4 adjustment) or expense (Type 2 adjustment) that has arisen but not been recorded during the accounting period. The cash receipt or payment occurs in a future accounting period, after the adjusting entry has been made.

Study Note

Adjusting entries provide information about past or future cash flows but never involve an entry to the Cash account.

Type 1 Adjustment: Allocating Recorded Costs (Deferred Expenses)

Companies often make expenditures that benefit more than one period. These costs are debited to an asset account. At the end of an accounting period, the amount of the asset that has been used is transferred from the asset account to an expense account. Two important adjustments of this type are for prepaid expenses and the depreciation of plant and equipment.

Study Note

The expired portion of a prepayment is converted to an expense; the unexpired portion remains an asset.

Prepaid Expenses Companies customarily pay some expenses, including those for rent, supplies, and insurance, in advance. These costs are called **prepaid expenses**. By the end of an accounting period, a portion or all of prepaid services or goods will have been used or have expired. The required adjusting entry reduces the asset and increases the expense, as shown in Figure 3-3. The amount of the adjustment equals the cost of the goods or services used or expired.

FIGURE 3-3
Adjustment for Prepaid (Deferred) Expenses

BALANCE SHEET

Asset

1. Allocating recorded costs between two or more accounting periods.

Asset Account — Adjusting Entry Credit

Expense Account — Adjusting Entry Debit

Amount equals cost of goods or services used up or expired.

Liability

2. Recognizing unrecorded expenses.

3. Allocating recorded, unearned revenues between two or more accounting periods.

4. Recognizing unrecorded, earned revenues.

Revenue

Expense

INCOME STATEMENT

If adjusting entries for prepaid expenses are not made at the end of an accounting period, both the balance sheet and the income statement will present incorrect information. The company's assets will be overstated, and its expenses will be understated. Thus, stockholders' equity on the balance sheet and net income on the income statement will be overstated.

To illustrate this type of adjusting entry and the others discussed below, we refer again to the transactions of Miller Design Studio, Inc.

At the beginning of July, Miller Design Studio, Inc. paid two months' rent in advance. The advance payment resulted in an asset consisting of the right to occupy the office for two months. As each day in the month passed, part of the asset's cost expired and became an expense. By July 31, one-half of the asset's cost had expired and had to be treated as an expense. The adjustment is as follows:

Adjustment for Prepaid Rent

July 31: Expiration of one month's rent, $1,600.

Analysis: Expiration of prepaid rent *decreases* the asset account *Prepaid Rent* with a credit and *increases* the expense account *Rent Expense* with a debit.

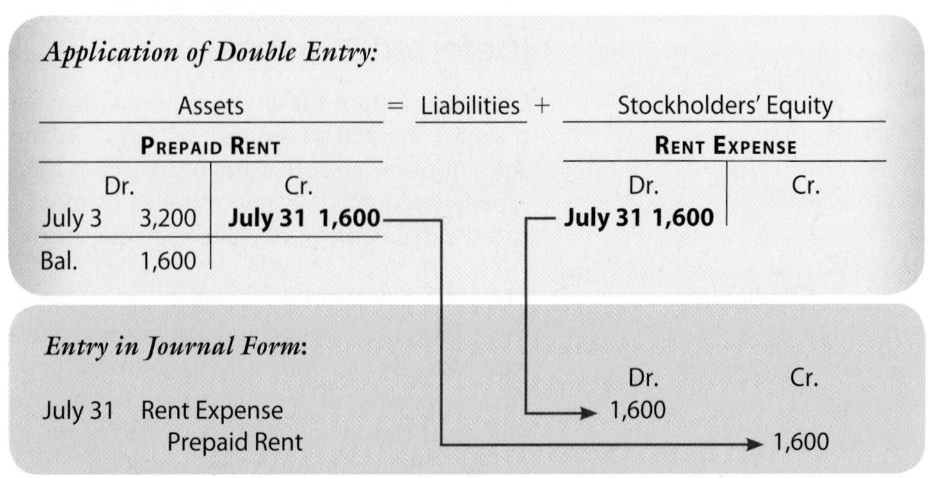

Comment: The Prepaid Rent account now has a balance of $1,600, which represents one month's rent that will be expensed during August. The logic in this analysis applies to all prepaid expenses.

Miller Design Studio, Inc. purchased $5,200 of office supplies in early July. A careful inventory of the supplies is made at the end of the month. It records the number and cost of supplies that have not yet been consumed and are thus still assets of the company. Suppose the inventory shows that office supplies costing $3,660 are still on hand. This means that of the $5,200 of supplies originally purchased, $1,540 worth were used (became an expense) in July. The adjustment is as follows:

Adjustment for Supplies

July 31: Consumption of supplies, $1,540

Analysis: Consumption of office supplies *decreases* the asset account *Office Supplies* with a credit and *increases* the expense account *Office Supplies Expense* with a debit.

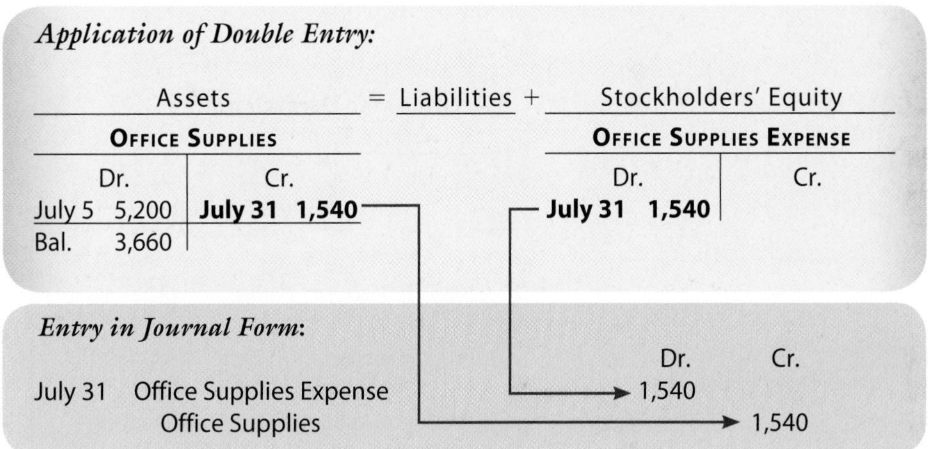

Comment: The asset account Office Supplies now reflects the correct balance of $3,660 of supplies yet to be consumed. The logic in this example applies to all kinds of supplies.

Study Note

In accounting, *depreciation* refers only to the *allocation* of an asset's cost, not to any decline in the asset's value.

Study Note

The difficulty in estimating an asset's useful life is further evidence that the net income figure is, at best, an estimate.

Depreciation of Plant and Equipment When a company buys a long-term asset—such as a building, truck, computer, or store fixture—it is, in effect, prepaying for the usefulness of that asset for as long as it benefits the company. Because a long-term asset is a deferral of an expense, the accountant must allocate the cost of the asset over its estimated useful life. The amount allocated to any one accounting period is called **depreciation**, or *depreciation expense*. Depreciation, like other expenses, is incurred during an accounting period to produce revenue.

It is often impossible to tell exactly how long an asset will last or how much of the asset has been used in any one period. For this reason, depreciation must be estimated. Accountants have developed a number of methods for estimating depreciation and for dealing with the related complex problems. (In the discussion that follows, we assume that the amount of depreciation has been established.)

To maintain historical cost in specific long-term asset accounts, separate accounts—**Accumulated Depreciation accounts**—are used to accumulate the depreciation on each long-term asset. These accounts, which are deducted from their related asset accounts on the balance sheet, are called *contra accounts*. A **contra account** is a separate account that is paired with a related account—in this case, an asset account. The balance of the contra account is shown in the financial statements as a deduction from its related account. The net amount is called the

carrying value, or *book value*, of the asset. As the months pass, the amount of the accumulated depreciation grows, and the carrying value shown as an asset declines.

Adjustment for Plant and Equipment:

July 31: Depreciation of office equipment, $300

Analysis: Depreciation *decreases* the asset account *Office Equipment* by *increasing* the contra account *Accumulated Depreciation–Office Equipment* with a credit and *increasing* the expense account *Depreciation Expense–Office Equipment* with a debit, as shown below.

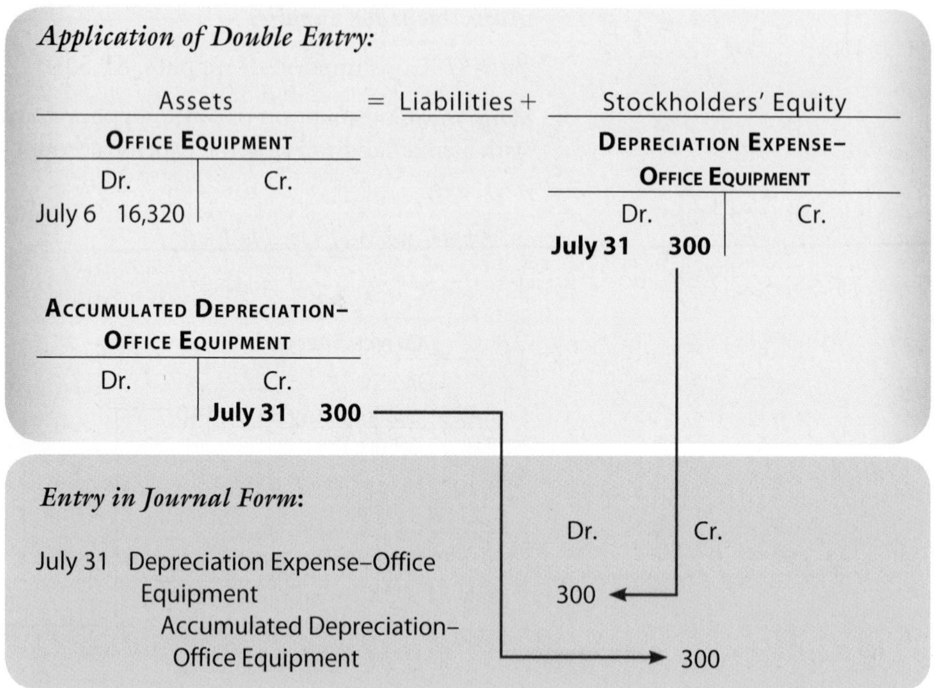

Comment: The carrying value of Office Equipment is $16,020 ($16,320 – $300) and is presented on the balance sheet as follows:

Property, Plant, and Equipment		
Office equipment	$16,320	
Less accumulated depreciation	300	$16,020

Application to Netflix, Inc. Netflix has prepaid expenses and property and equipment similar to those in the examples we have presented. Among Netflix's prepaid expenses are payments made in advance to movie companies for rights to DVDs. By paying in advance, Netflix is able to negotiate lower prices. These fixed payments are debited to Prepaid Expense. When the movies produce revenue, the prepaid amounts are transferred to expense through adjusting entries.[7]

> **Study Note**
> Remember that in accrual accounting, an expense must be recorded in the period in which it is incurred, regardless of when payment is made.

Type 2 Adjustment: Recognizing Unrecorded Expenses (Accrued Expenses)

Usually, at the end of an accounting period, some expenses incurred during the period have not been recorded in the accounts. These expenses require adjusting entries. One such expense is interest on borrowed money. Each day, interest accumulates on the debt. As shown in Figure 3-4, at the end of the accounting period, an adjusting entry is made to record the accumulated interest, which is an

FIGURE 3-4
Adjustment for Unrecorded (Accrued) Expenses

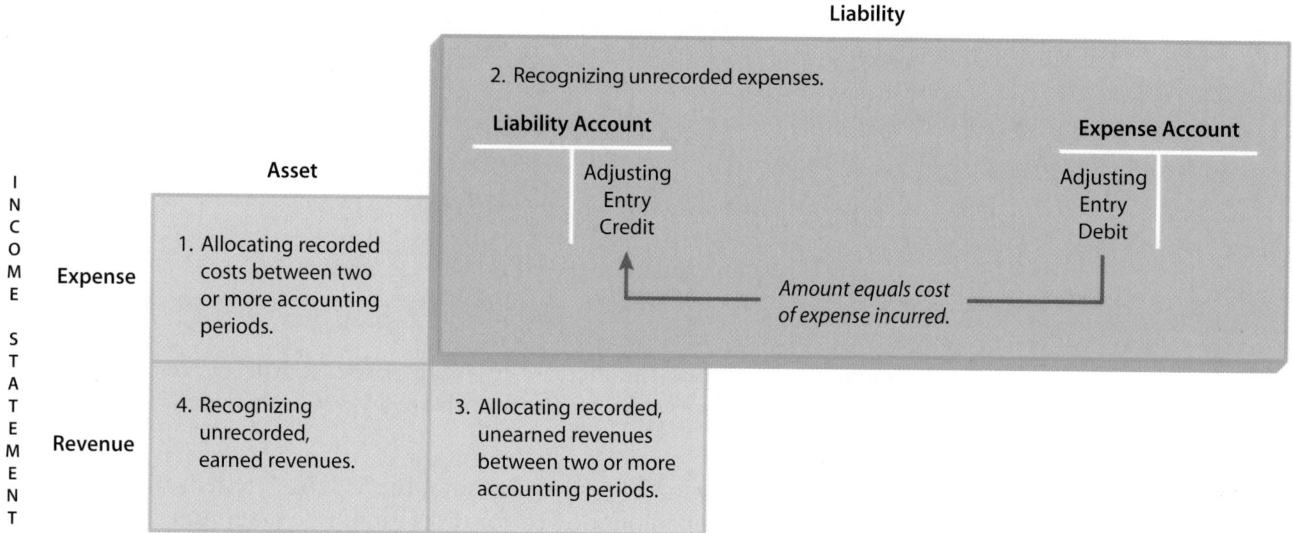

expense of the period, and the corresponding liability to pay the interest. Other common unrecorded expenses are wages, taxes, and utilities. As the expense and the corresponding liability accumulate, they are said to *accrue*—hence, the term **accrued expenses**.

To illustrate how an adjustment is made for unrecorded wages, suppose Miller Design Studio, Inc. has two pay periods a month rather than one. In July, its pay periods end on the 12th and the 26th, as indicated in this calendar:

July

Sun	M	T	W	Th	F	Sa
	1	2	3	4	5	6
7	8	9	10	11	**12**	13
14	15	16	17	18	19	20
21	22	23	24	25	**26**	27
28	29	30	31			

By the end of business on July 31, Miller's assistant will have worked three days (Monday, Tuesday, and Wednesday) beyond the last pay period. The employee has earned the wages for those days but will not be paid until the first payday in August. The wages for these three days are rightfully an expense for July, and the liabilities should reflect that the company owes the assistant for those days. Because the assistant's wage rate is $2,400 every two weeks, or $240 per day ($2,400 ÷ 10 working days), the expense is $720 ($240 × 3 days).

Adjustment for Unrecorded Wages

July 31: Accrual of unrecorded wages, $720

Analysis: Accrual of wages *increases* the stockholders' equity account *Wages Expense* with a debit and *increases* the liability account *Wages Payable* with a credit.

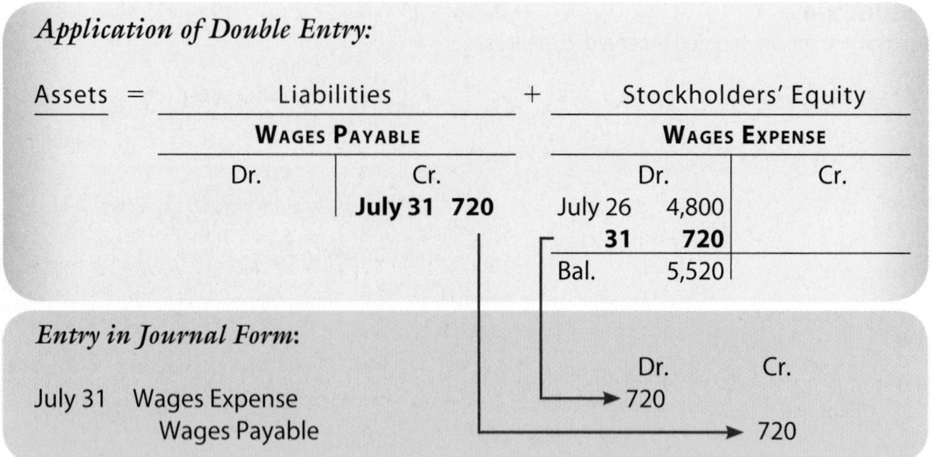

Comment: Note that the increase in Wages Expense will *decrease* stockholders' equity and that total wages for the month are $5,520, of which $720 will be paid next month.

As a corporation, Miller Design Studio, Inc. is subject to federal income taxes. Although the actual amount owed for taxes cannot be determined until after net income is computed at the end of the fiscal year, each month should bear its part of the total year's expense, in accordance with the matching rule. Therefore, the amount of income taxes expense for the current month must be estimated. Assume that after analyzing the firm's operations in its first month of business and conferring with its CPA, the company estimates July's share of income taxes for the year to be $800.

Adjustment for Estimated Income Taxes

July 31: Accrual of estimated income taxes, $800

Analysis: Accrual of income taxes *increases* the stockholders' equity account *Income Taxes Expense* with a debit and *increases* the liability account *Income Taxes Payable* with a credit.

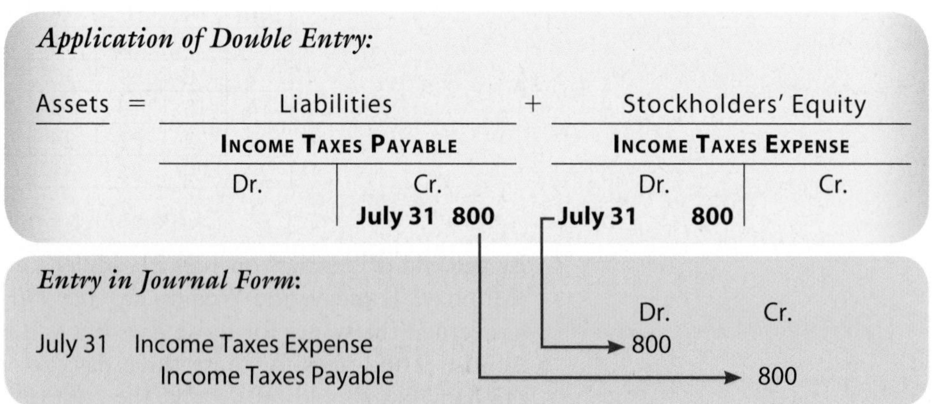

Comment: Note that the increase in Income Taxes Expense will *decrease* stockholders' equity. There are many types of accrued expenses, and the adjustments made for all of them follow the same procedure as the one used for accrued wages and accrued income taxes.

Application to Netflix Inc. In 2008, **Netflix** had accrued expenses of $31,394,000.[8] If the expenses had not been accrued, Netflix's liabilities would be significantly understated, as would the corresponding expenses on Netflix's income statement. The end result would be an overstatement of the company's earnings.

Type 3 Adjustment: Allocating Recorded, Unearned Revenues (Deferred Revenues)

Study Note

Unearned revenue is a liability because there is an obligation to deliver goods or perform a service, or to return the payment. Once the goods have been delivered or the service performed, the liability is transferred to revenue.

Just as expenses can be paid before they are used, revenues can be received before they are earned. When a company receives revenues in advance, it has an obligation to deliver goods or perform services. **Unearned revenues** are therefore shown in a liability account.

For example, publishing companies usually receive payment in advance for magazine subscriptions. These receipts are recorded in a liability account, Unearned Subscriptions. If the company fails to deliver the magazines, subscribers are entitled to their money back. As the company delivers each issue of the magazine, it earns a part of the advance payments. This earned portion must be transferred from the Unearned Subscriptions account to the Subscription Revenue account, as shown in Figure 3-5.

During July, Miller Design Studio, Inc. received $1,400 from another firm as advance payment for a series of brochures. By the end of the month, Miller Design Studio, Inc. had completed $800 of work on the brochures, and the other firm had accepted the work.

Adjustment for Unearned Revenue

July 31: Performance of services paid for in advance, $800

Analysis: Performance of the services for which payment had been received in advance *increases* the stockholders' equity account *Design Revenue* with a credit and *decreases* the liability account *Unearned Design Revenue* with a debit.

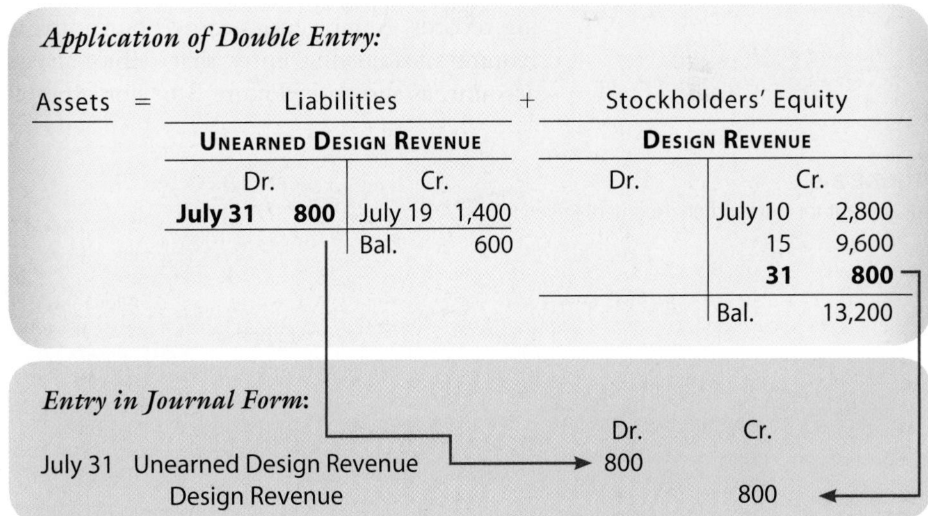

Comment: Unearned Design Revenue now reflects the amount of work still to be performed, $600.

Application to Netflix, Inc. **Netflix** has a current liability account called Deferred (Unearned) Revenue. Deferred revenue consists of subscriptions (monthly payments) billed in advance to customers, for which revenues have not yet been earned. Subscription revenues are recognized ratably over each subscriber's monthly subscription period. As time passes and customers use the service, the revenue is transferred from Netflix's Deferred Revenue account to its Subscription Revenue account.

FIGURE 3-5
Adjustment for Unearned (Deferred) Revenues

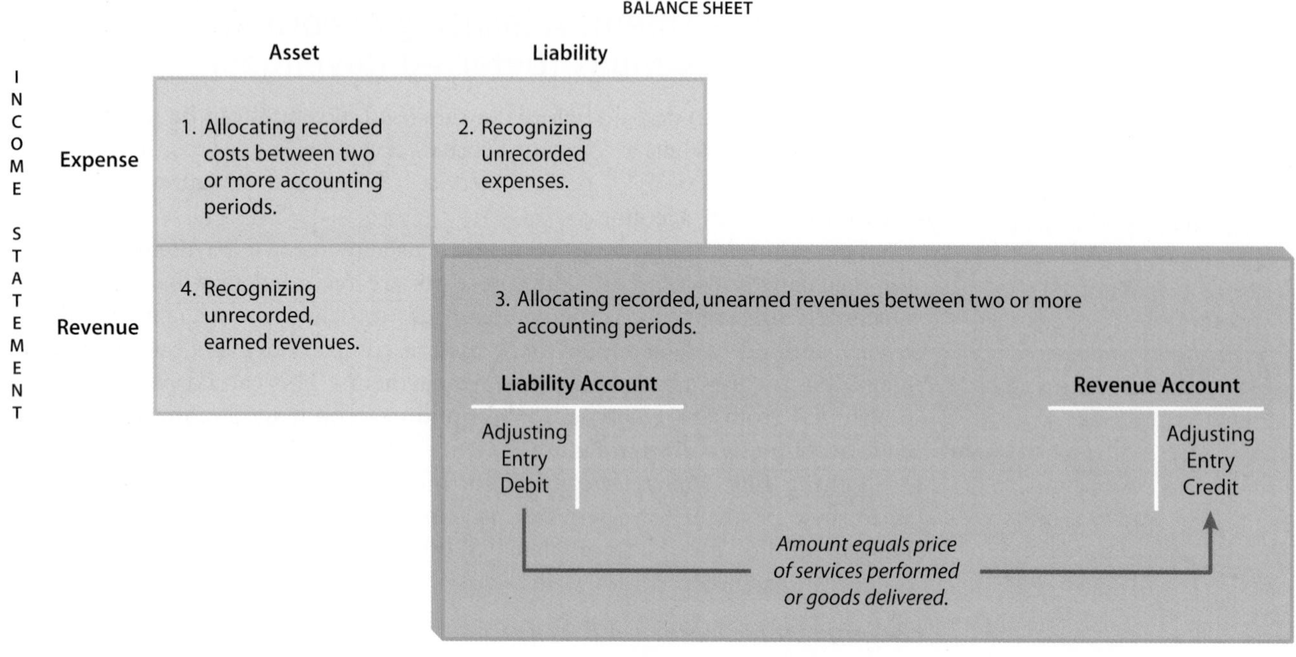

Type 4 Adjustment: Recognizing Unrecorded, Earned Revenues (Accrued Revenues)

Accrued revenues are revenues that a company has earned by performing a service or delivering goods but for which no entry has been made in the accounting records. Any revenues earned but not recorded during an accounting period require an adjusting entry that debits an asset account and credits a revenue account, as shown in Figure 3-6. For example, the interest on a note receivable

FIGURE 3-6
Adjustment for Unrecorded (Accrued) Revenues

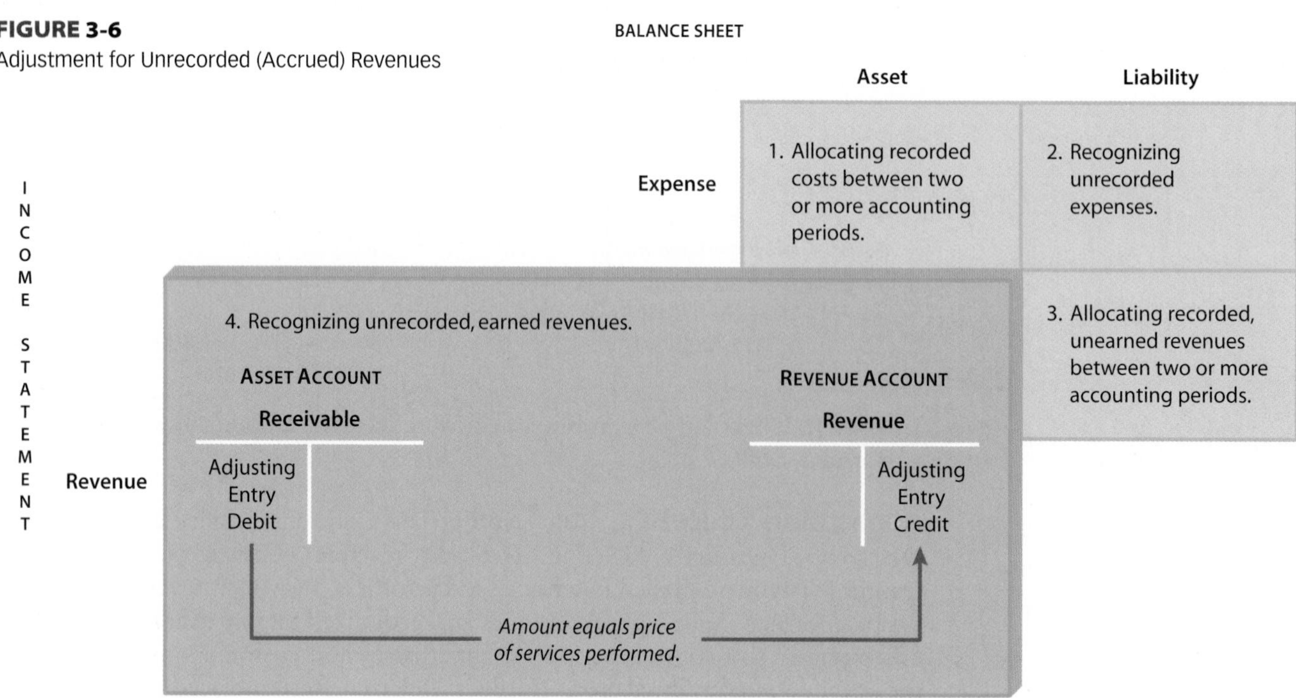

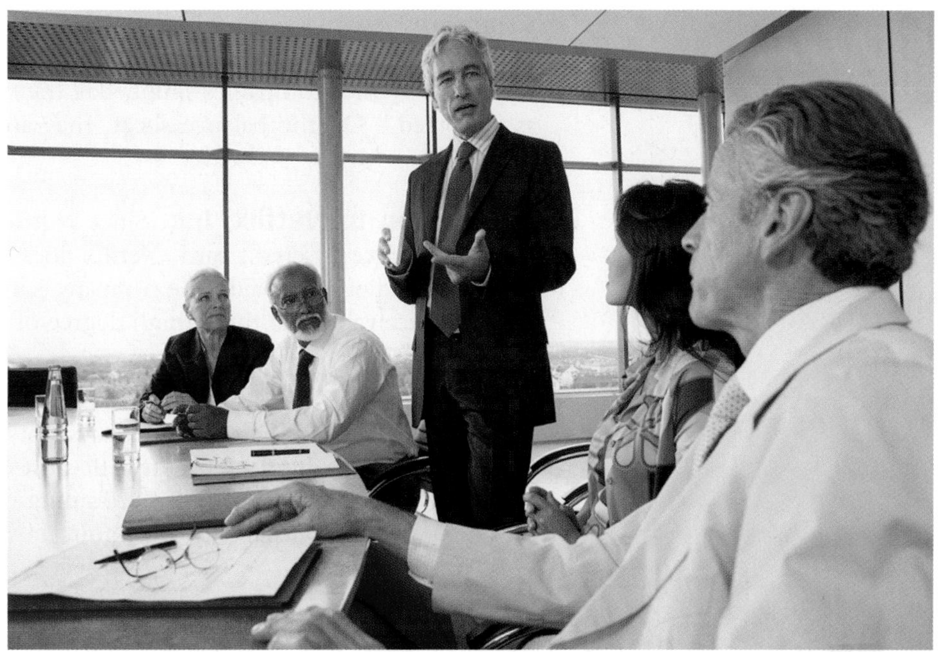

When a company earns revenue by performing a service—such as designing a website or developing marketing plans—but will not receive the revenue for the service until a future accounting period, it must make an adjusting entry. This type of adjusting entry involves an asset account and a revenue account.

Courtesy of Sullivan/Fancy/Corbis.

is earned day by day but may not be received until another accounting period. Interest Receivable should be debited and Interest Income should be credited for the interest accrued at the end of the current period.

During July, Miller Design Studio, Inc. agreed to create two advertisements for Maggio's Pizza Company. It also agreed that the first advertisement would be finished by July 31. By the end of the month, Miller had earned $400 for completing the first advertisement. The client will not be billed until the entire project has been completed.

Adjustment for Design Revenue

July 31: Accrual of unrecorded revenue, $400

Analysis: Accrual of unrecorded revenue *increases* the stockholders' equity account *Design Revenue* with a credit and *increases* the asset account *Accounts Receivable* with a debit.

Application of Double Entry:

Assets = Liabilities + Stockholders' Equity

Accounts Receivable

Dr.		Cr.	
July 15	9,600	July 22	5,000
31	**400**		
Bal.	5,000		

Design Revenue

Dr.	Cr.	
	July 10	2,800
	15	9,600
	31	800
	31	**400**
	Bal.	13,600

Entry in Journal Form:

		Dr.	Cr.
July 31	Accounts Receivable	400	
	Design Revenue		400

Comment: Design Revenue now reflects the total revenue earned during July, $13,600. Some companies prefer to debit an account called Unbilled Accounts Receivable. Other companies simply flag the transactions in Accounts Receivable as "unbilled." On the balance sheet, they are usually combined with accounts receivable.

Application to Netflix, Inc. Since **Netflix**'s subscribers pay their subscriptions in advance by credit card, Netflix does not need to bill customers for services provided but not paid. The company is in the enviable position of having no accounts receivable and thus a high degree of liquidity.

A Note About Journal Entries

Thus far, we have presented a full analysis of each journal entry and showed the thought process behind each entry. Because you should now be fully aware of the effects of transactions on the accounting equation and the rules of debit and credit, we present journal entries without full analysis in the rest of the book.

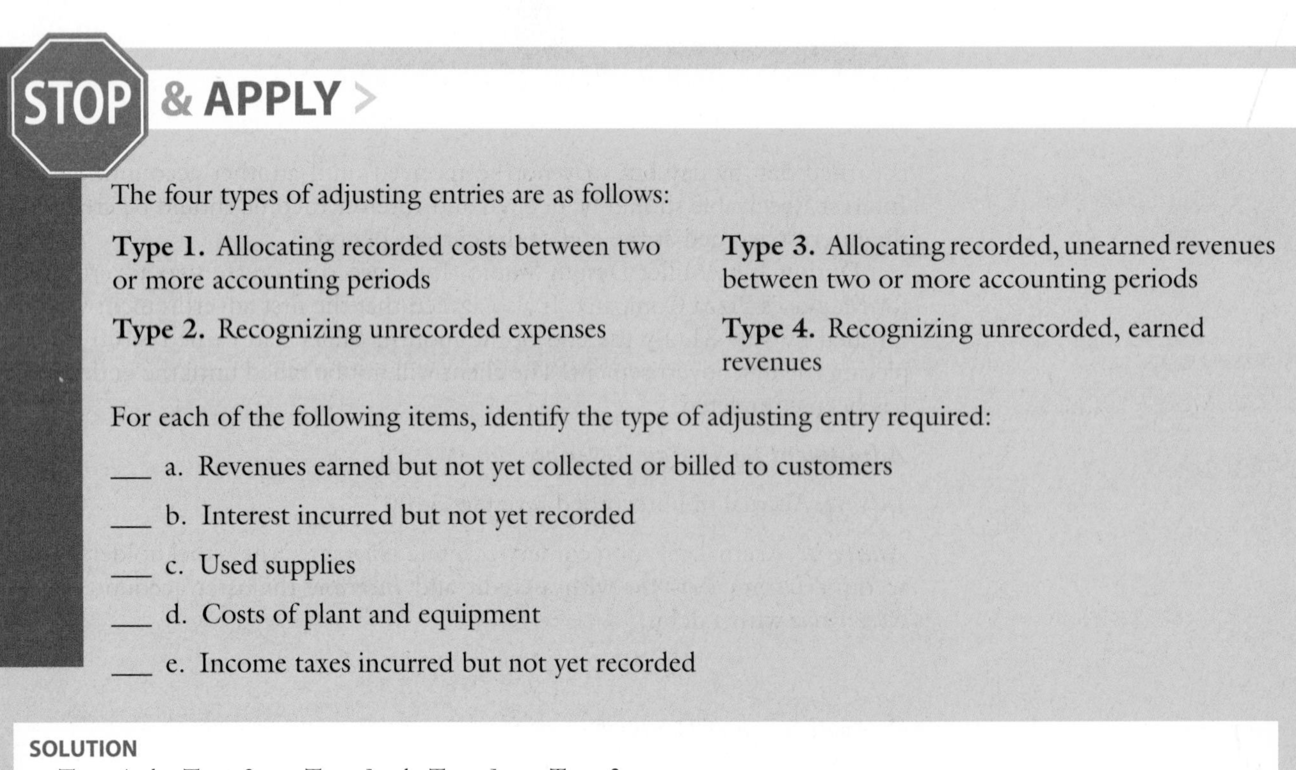

STOP & APPLY >

The four types of adjusting entries are as follows:

Type 1. Allocating recorded costs between two or more accounting periods

Type 2. Recognizing unrecorded expenses

Type 3. Allocating recorded, unearned revenues between two or more accounting periods

Type 4. Recognizing unrecorded, earned revenues

For each of the following items, identify the type of adjusting entry required:

___ a. Revenues earned but not yet collected or billed to customers

___ b. Interest incurred but not yet recorded

___ c. Used supplies

___ d. Costs of plant and equipment

___ e. Income taxes incurred but not yet recorded

SOLUTION

a. Type 4; b. Type 2; c. Type 1; d. Type 1; e. Type 2

Using the Adjusted Trial Balance to Prepare Financial Statements

LO4 Prepare financial statements from an adjusted trial balance.

After adjusting entries have been recorded and posted, an **adjusted trial balance** is prepared by listing all accounts and their balances. If the adjusting entries have been posted to the accounts correctly, the adjusted trial balance will have equal debit and credit totals. The adjusted trial balance for Miller Design Studio, Inc. is shown in Exhibit 3-2.

Notice that some accounts in Exhibit 3-2, such as Cash and Accounts Payable, have the same balances as in the trial balance in Exhibit 3-1 because no adjusting entries affected them. The balances of other accounts, such as Office Supplies and Prepaid Rent, differ from those in the trial balance because adjusting

EXHIBIT 3-2 Relationship of the Adjusted Trial Balance to the Income Statement

Miller Design Studio, Inc.
Adjusted Trial Balance
July 31, 2010

Cash	$22,480	
Accounts Receivable	5,000	
Office Supplies	3,660	
Prepaid Rent	1,600	
Office Equipment	16,320	
Accumulated Depreciation–Office Equipment		$ 300
Accounts Payable		6,280
Unearned Design Revenue		600
Wages Payable		720
Income Taxes Payable		800
Common Stock		40,000
Dividends	2,800	
Design Revenue		13,600
Wages Expense	5,520	
Utilities Expense	680	
Rent Expense	1,600	
Office Supplies Expense	1,540	
Depreciation Expense–Office Equipment	300	
Income Taxes Expense	800	
	$62,300	$62,300

Miller Design Studio, Inc.
Income Statement
For the Month Ended July 31, 2010

Revenues		
Design revenue		$13,600
Expenses		
Wages expense	$5,520	
Utilities expense	680	
Rent expense	1,600	
Office supplies expense	1,540	
Depreciation expense–office equipment	300	
Income taxes expense	800	
Total expenses		10,440
Net income		$ 3,160

Study Note

The net income figure from the income statement is needed to prepare the statement of retained earnings, and the bottom-line figure of that statement is needed to prepare the balance sheet. This dictates the order in which the statements are prepared.

entries did affect them. The adjusted trial balance also has some new accounts, such as depreciation accounts and Wages Payable, which do not appear in the trial balance.

The adjusted trial balance facilitates the preparation of the financial statements. As shown in Exhibit 3-2, the revenue and expense accounts are used to prepare the income statement.

FOCUS ON BUSINESS PRACTICE

Entering Adjustments with the Touch of a Button

In a computerized accounting system, adjusting entries can be entered just like any other transactions. However, when the adjusting entries are similar for each accounting period, such as those for insurance expense and depreciation expense, or when they always involve the same accounts, such as those for accrued wages, the computer can be programmed to display them automatically. All the accountant has to do is verify the amounts or enter the correct amounts. The adjusting entries are then entered and posted, and the adjusted trial balance is prepared with the touch of a button.

EXHIBIT 3-3 Relationship of the Adjusted Trial Balance to the Balance Sheet and Statement of Retained Earnings

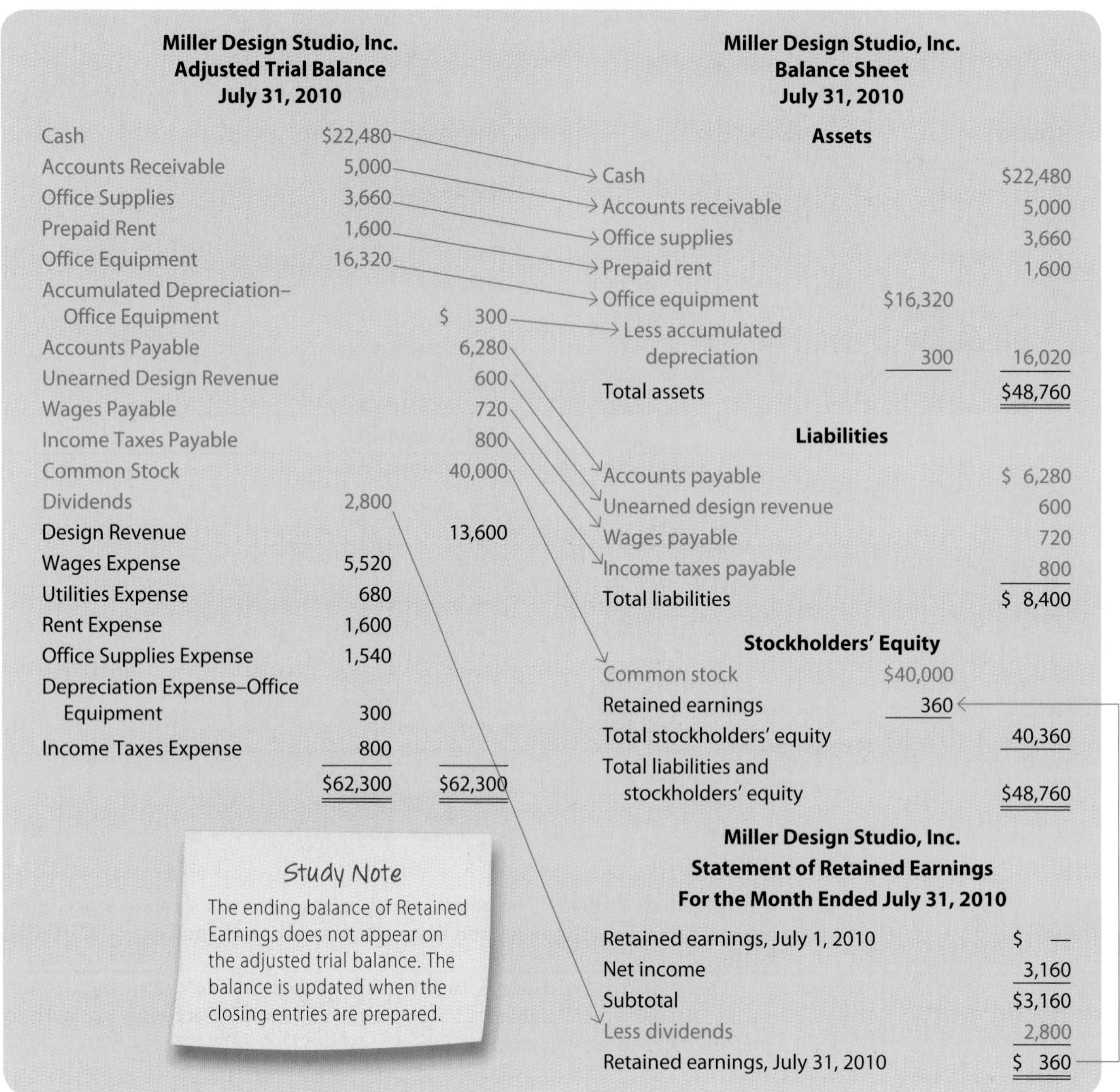

Miller Design Studio, Inc.
Adjusted Trial Balance
July 31, 2010

Cash	$22,480	
Accounts Receivable	5,000	
Office Supplies	3,660	
Prepaid Rent	1,600	
Office Equipment	16,320	
Accumulated Depreciation–Office Equipment		$ 300
Accounts Payable		6,280
Unearned Design Revenue		600
Wages Payable		720
Income Taxes Payable		800
Common Stock		40,000
Dividends	2,800	
Design Revenue		13,600
Wages Expense	5,520	
Utilities Expense	680	
Rent Expense	1,600	
Office Supplies Expense	1,540	
Depreciation Expense–Office Equipment	300	
Income Taxes Expense	800	
	$62,300	$62,300

Miller Design Studio, Inc.
Balance Sheet
July 31, 2010

Assets

Cash		$22,480
Accounts receivable		5,000
Office supplies		3,660
Prepaid rent		1,600
Office equipment	$16,320	
Less accumulated depreciation	300	16,020
Total assets		$48,760

Liabilities

Accounts payable		$ 6,280
Unearned design revenue		600
Wages payable		720
Income taxes payable		800
Total liabilities		$ 8,400

Stockholders' Equity

Common stock	$40,000	
Retained earnings	360	
Total stockholders' equity		40,360
Total liabilities and stockholders' equity		$48,760

Miller Design Studio, Inc.
Statement of Retained Earnings
For the Month Ended July 31, 2010

Retained earnings, July 1, 2010	$ —
Net income	3,160
Subtotal	$3,160
Less dividends	2,800
Retained earnings, July 31, 2010	$ 360

Study Note

The ending balance of Retained Earnings does not appear on the adjusted trial balance. The balance is updated when the closing entries are prepared.

Study Note

The adjusted trial balance is a second check that the ledger is still in balance. Because it reflects updated information from the adjusting entries, it is used in preparing the formal financial statements. It does not mean there are no accounting errors.

Then, as shown in Exhibit 3-3, the statement of retained earnings and the balance sheet are prepared. Notice that the net income from the income statement is combined with dividends on the statement of retained earnings to give the net change in Miller Design Studio, Inc.'s Retained Earnings account.

The resulting balance of Retained Earnings at July 31 is used in preparing the balance sheet, as are the asset and liability account balances in the adjusted trial balance.

The adjusted trial balance for Carroll Corporation on December 31, 2010, contains the following accounts and balances: Retained Earnings, $120; Dividends $100; Service Revenue, $1,100; Rent Expense, $300; Wages Expense, $400; Telephone Expense, $100; and Income Taxes Expense, $50. Compute net income and prepare a statement of retained earnings in proper form for the month of December.

SOLUTION

Net income = $1,100 − $300 − $400 − $100 − $50
= $1,100 − $850
= $250

Carroll Corporation
Statement of Retained Earnings
For the Month Ended December 31, 2010

Retained Earnings, Nov. 30, 2010	$ 120
Net income	250
	$ 370
Less dividends	100
Retained Earnings, Dec. 31, 2010	$ 270

The Accounting Cycle

LO5 Describe the accounting cycle, and explain the purposes of closing entries.

As Figure 3-7 shows, the **accounting cycle** is a series of steps whose ultimate purpose is to provide useful information to decision makers. These steps are as follows:

1. *Analyze* business transactions from source documents.
2. *Record* the transactions by entering them in the journal.
3. *Post* the entries to the ledger, and prepare a trial balance.
4. *Adjust* the accounts, and prepare an adjusted trial balance.
5. *Prepare* financial statements.
6. *Close* the accounts, and prepare a post-closing trial balance.

Note that steps 3, 4, and 6 entail the preparation of trial balances to ensure that the accounts are in balance.

You are already familiar with steps 1 through 5. In this section, we describe step 6, which may be performed before or after step 5.

Closing Entries

Balance sheet accounts, such as Cash and Accounts Payable, are considered **permanent accounts**, or *real accounts*, because they carry their end-of-period balances into the next accounting period. In contrast, revenue and expense accounts, such as Revenues Earned and Wages Expense, are considered **temporary accounts**, or *nominal accounts*, because they begin each accounting period with a zero balance, accumulate a balance during the period, and are then cleared by means of closing entries.

Closing entries are entries made at the end of an accounting period. They have two purposes:

1. Closing entries set the stage for the next accounting period by clearing revenue and expense accounts and the Dividends account of their balances. Recall

FIGURE 3-7
Overview of the Accounting Cycle

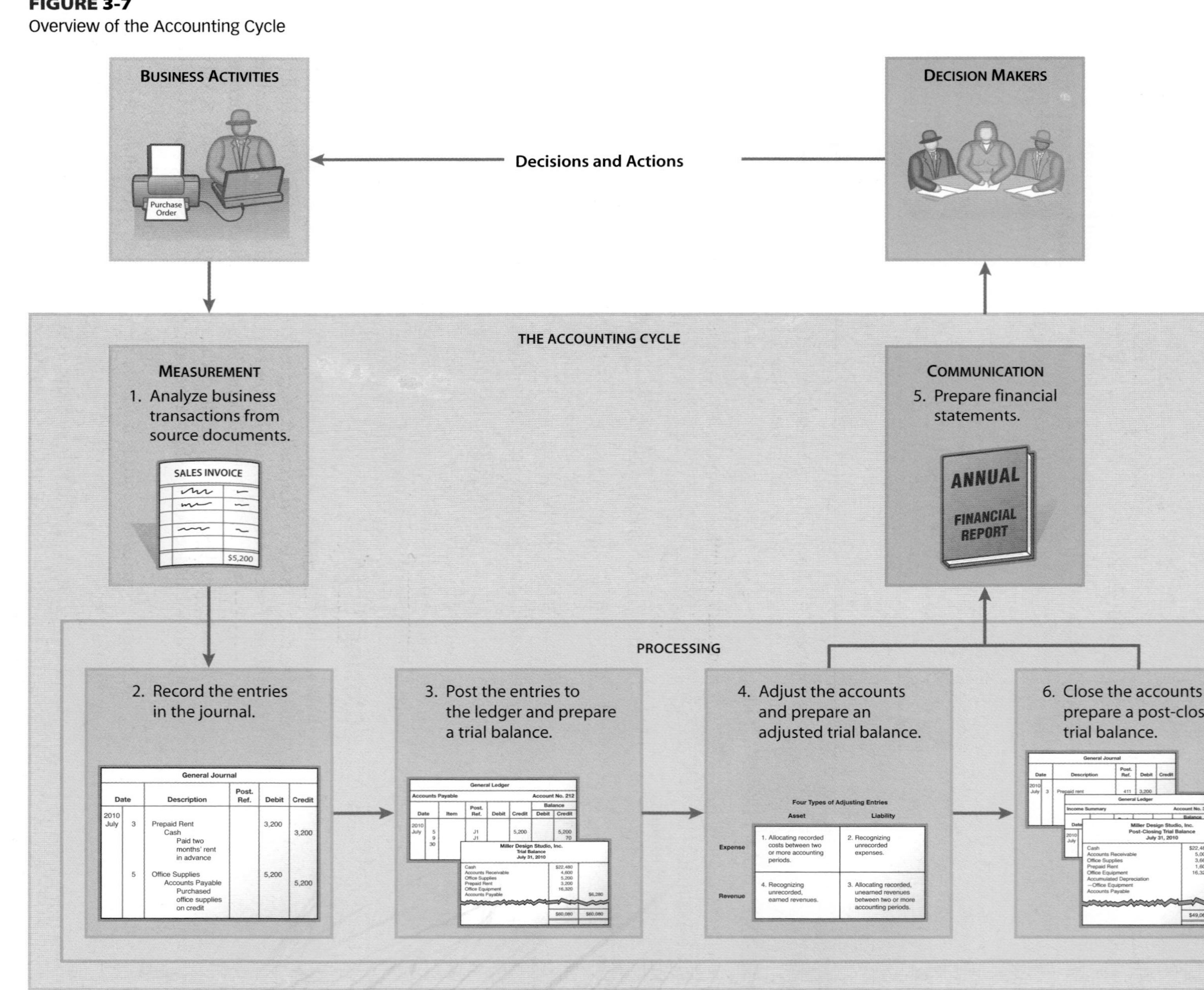

FIGURE 3-8
Overview of the Closing Process*

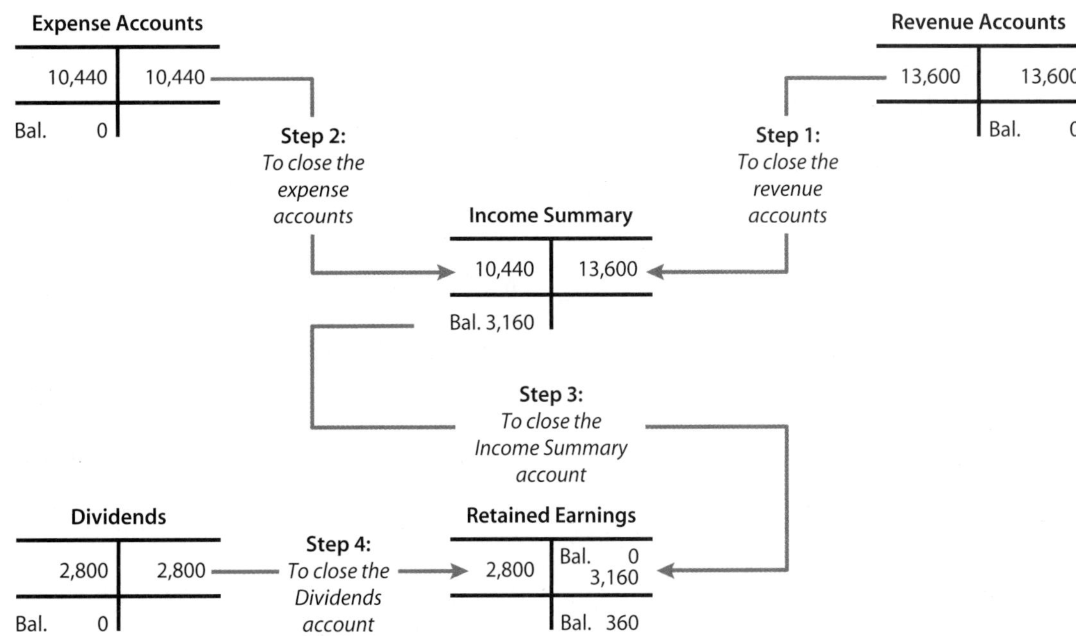

*Amounts are for Miller Design Studio, Inc. See Exhibit S-1 in the Supplement to Chapter 3.

that the income statement reports net income (or loss) for a single accounting period and shows revenues and expenses for that period only.

2. Closing entries summarize a period's revenues and expenses. This is done by transferring the balances of revenue and expense accounts to the Income Summary account. The **Income Summary account** is a temporary account that summarizes all revenues and expenses for the period. It is used only in the closing process—never in the financial statements. Its balance equals the net income or net loss reported on the income statement. The net income or net loss is then transferred to the Retained Earnings account.

The net income or net loss is transferred from the Income Summary account to Retained Earnings because even though revenues and expenses are recorded in revenue and expense accounts, they actually represent increases and decreases in stockholders' equity. Closing entries transfer the net effect of increases (revenues) and decreases (expenses) to stockholders' equity. Figure 3-8 shows an overview of the closing process.

Closing entries are required at the end of any period for which financial statements are prepared. **Netflix** prepares financial statements each quarter, and when it does, it must close its books. Such interim information is helpful to investors and creditors in assessing a company's ongoing financial performance. Many companies close their books monthly to give management a more timely view of ongoing operations.

The Post-Closing Trial Balance

Because errors can be made in posting closing entries to the ledger accounts, it is necessary to prepare a **post-closing trial balance** to determine that all temporary accounts have zero balances and to double-check that total debits equal total credits. This final trial balance contains only balance sheet accounts because the income statement accounts and the Dividends account have all been closed and now have zero balances. We discuss closing entries and the post-closing trial balance further in the Supplement to Chapter 3.

Prepare the necessary closing entries from the following partial adjusted trial balance for MGC Delivery Service, Inc. (except for Retained Earnings, balance sheet accounts have been omitted), and compute the ending balance of retained earnings.

MGC Delivery Service, Inc.
Partial Adjusted Trial Balance
June 30, 2010

Retained Earnings		$12,370
Dividends	$ 9,000	
Delivery Services Revenue		92,700
Driver Wages Expense	44,450	
Fuel Expense	9,500	
Office Wages Expense	7,200	
Packing Supplies Expense	3,100	
Office Equipment Rental Expense	1,500	
Utilities Expense	2,225	
Insurance Expense	2,100	
Interest Expense	2,550	
Depreciation Expense–Trucks	5,020	
Income Taxes Expense	4,500	

SOLUTION

Closing entries prepared:

June 30	Delivery Services Revenue	92,700	
	Income Summary		92,700
	To close the credit balance account		
30	Income Summary	82,145	
	Driver Wages Expense		44,450
	Fuel Expense		9,500
	Office Wages Expense		7,200
	Packing Supplies Expense		3,100
	Office Equipment Rental Expense		1,500
	Utilities Expense		2,225
	Insurance Expense		2,100
	Interest Expense		2,550
	Depreciation Expense–Trucks		5,020
	Income Taxes Expense		4,500
	To close the debit balance accounts		

(*continued*)

June 30	Income Summary	10,555	
	Retained Earnings		10,555
	To close the Income Summary account		
	$92,700 − $82,145 = $10,555		
30	Retained Earnings	9,000	
	Dividends		9,000
	To close the Dividends account		

Ending balance of retained earnings computed:

RETAINED EARNINGS			
June 30	9,000	Beg. Bal.	12,370
		June 30	10,555
		End. Bal.	13,925

Cash Flows from Accrual-Based Information

LO6 Use accrual-based information to analyze cash flows.

Management has the short-range goal of ensuring that its company has sufficient cash to pay ongoing obligations—in other words, management must ensure the company's liquidity. To plan payments to creditors and assess the need for short-term borrowing, managers must know how to use accrual-based information to analyze cash flows.

Almost every revenue or expense account on the income statement has one or more related accounts on the balance sheet. For instance, Supplies Expense is related to Supplies, Wages Expense is related to Wages Payable, and Design Revenue is related to Unearned Design Revenue. As we have shown, these accounts are related by making adjusting entries, the purpose of which is to apply the matching rule to the measurement of net income.

The cash inflows that a company's operations generate and the cash outflows that they require can also be determined by analyzing these relationships. For example, suppose that after receiving the financial statements in Exhibits 3-2 and 3-3, management wants to know how much cash was expended for office supplies. On the income statement, Office Supplies Expense is $1,540, and on the balance sheet, Office Supplies is $3,660. Because July was the company's first month of operation, there was no prior balance of office supplies, so the amount of cash expended for office supplies during the month was $5,200 ($1,540 + $3,660 = $5,200).

Thus, the cash flow used in purchasing office supplies—$5,200—was much greater than the amount expensed in determining income—$1,540. In planning for August, management can anticipate that the cash needed may be less than the amount expensed because, given the large inventory of office supplies, the company will probably not have to buy office supplies in the coming month. Understanding these cash flow effects enables management to better predict the business's need for cash in August.

> **Study Note**
> Income as determined by accrual accounting is important to a company's profitability. Cash flows are related to a company's liquidity. Both are important to a company's success.

The general rule for determining the cash flow received from any revenue or paid for any expense (except depreciation, which is a special case not covered here) is to determine the potential cash payments or cash receipts and deduct the amount not paid or received. As shown below, the application of the general rule varies with the type of asset or liability account:

Type of Account	*Potential Payment or Receipt Not Paid or Received*	*Result*
Prepaid Expense	Ending Balance + Expense for the Period − Beginning Balance	= Cash Payments for Expenses
Unearned Revenue	Ending Balance + Revenue for the Period − Beginning Balance	= Cash Receipts from Revenues
Accrued Payable	Beginning Balance + Expense for the Period − Ending Balance	= Cash Payments for Expenses
Accrued Receivable	Beginning Balance + Revenue for the Period − Ending Balance	= Cash Receipts from Revenues

For instance, suppose that on May 31, a company had a balance of $480 in Prepaid Insurance and that on June 30, the balance was $670. If the insurance expense during June was $120, the amount of cash expended on insurance during June can be computed as follows:

Prepaid Insurance at June 30	$670
Insurance Expense during June	120
Potential cash payments for insurance	$790
Less Prepaid Insurance at May 31	480
Cash payments for insurance during June	$310

The beginning balance is deducted because it was paid in a prior accounting period. Note that the cash payments equal the expense plus the increase in the balance of the Prepaid Insurance account [$120 + ($670 − $480) = $310]. In this case, the cash paid was almost three times the amount of insurance expense. In future months, cash payments are likely to be less than the expense.

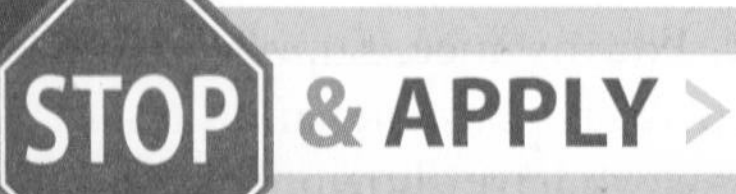

Supplies had a balance of $400 at the end of May and $360 at the end of June. Supplies Expense was $550 for the month of June. How much cash was paid for supplies during June?

SOLUTION

Supplies at June 30	$360
Supplies Expense during June	550
Potential cash payments for supplies	$910
Less Supplies at May 31	400
Cash payments for supplies during June	$510

A LOOK BACK AT ▸ NETFLIX, INC.

In the Decision Point at the beginning of the chapter, we noted that **Netflix** has many transactions that span accounting periods. We asked these questions:

- What assumptions must Netflix make to account for transactions that span accounting periods?
- How does Netflix assign its revenues and expenses to the proper accounting period so that net income is properly measured?
- Why are the adjustments that these transactions require important to Netflix's financial performance?

Two of the assumptions Netflix must make are that it will continue as a going concern for an indefinite time (the continuity assumption) and that it can make useful estimates of its income in terms of accounting periods (the periodicity assumption). These assumptions enable the company to apply the matching rule—that is, revenues are assigned to the accounting period in which goods are sold or services are performed, and expenses are assigned to the accounting period in which they are used to produce revenue.

As you have learned in this chapter, adjusting entries for deferred and accrued expenses and for deferred and accrued revenues have an impact on a company's earnings. By paying close attention to the profit margin ratio, one can assess how well a company is controlling its expenses in relation to its revenues. The **profit margin** shows the percentage of each revenue, or sales dollar, that results in net income. Using data from Netflix's annual report, we can calculate Netflix's profit margin for two successive years as follows (dollars are in thousands):

	2008	2007
Net Income	$83,026	$66,952
Revenues*	$1,364,661	$1,205,340
Profit Margin	6.1%	5.6%

*Also called *net sales.*

These results show that Netflix's revenues and earnings are increasing very rapidly and that its profitability is improving. Because net income equals revenues minus expenses and adjusting entries affect both revenues and expenses, you can see that without adjusting entries, it would be impossible to make a fair assessment of Netflix's financial performance.

Review Problem

Posting to T Accounts, Determining Adjusting Entries, and Using an Adjusted Trial Balance to Prepare Financial Statements

LO3 LO4

The following is the unadjusted trial balance for Reliable Lawn Care, Inc., on December 31, 2010:

	A	B	C	D	E
1			**Reliable Lawn Care, Inc.**		
2			**Trial Balance**		
3			**December 31, 2010**		
4					
5	Cash			$ 4,320	
6	Accounts Receivable			2,500	
7	Office Supplies			360	
8	Prepaid Insurance			480	
9	Office Equipment			6,800	
10	Accumulated Depreciation—Office Equipment				$ 1,200
11	Accounts Payable				1,400
12	Unearned Revenue				920
13	Common Stock				4,000
14	Retained Earnings				5,740
15	Dividends			800	
16	Service Revenue				5,800
17	Wages Expense			3,000	
18	Rent Expense			800	
19				$19,060	$19,060
20					

The following information is also available:

a. Insurance that expired during December amounted to $80.

b. Office supplies on hand on December 31 totaled $150.

c. Depreciation of the office equipment for December totaled $200.

d. Accrued wages on December 31 totaled $240.

e. Revenues earned for services performed in December but not billed by the end of the month totaled $600.

f. Performance of services paid for in advance, $320.

g. Income taxes for December are estimated to be $500.

Required

1. Prepare T accounts for the accounts in the trial balance, and enter the balances.
2. Determine the required adjusting entries, and record them directly in the T accounts. Open new T accounts as needed.
3. Prepare an adjusted trial balance.
4. Prepare an income statement and a statement of retained earnings for the month ended December 31, 2010, as well as a balance sheet at December 31, 2010.

Answers to Review Problem

1. T accounts set up and amounts from trial balance entered:
2. Adjusting entries recorded:

	A	B	C	D	E	F	G	H	I	J	K	L	M	N
1	**Cash**					**Accounts Receivable**					**Office Supplies**			
2	Bal.	4,320				Bal.	2,500				Bal.	360	(b)	210
3						(e)	600				*Bal.*	*150*		
4						*Bal.*	*3,100*							
5														
6											**Accumulated Depreciation—**			
7	**Prepaid Insurance**					**Office Equipment**					**Office Equipment**			
8	Bal.	480	(a)	80		Bal.	6,800						Bal.	1,200
9	*Bal.*	400											(c)	200
10													*Bal.*	*1,400*
11														
12	**Accounts Payable**					**Unearned Revenue**					**Wages Payable**			
13			Bal.	1,400		(f)	320	Bal.	920				(d)	240
14								*Bal.*	*600*					
15														
16	**Income Taxes Payable**					**Common Stock**					**Retained Earnings**			
17			(g)	500				Bal.	4,000				Bal.	5,740
18														
19	**Dividends**					**Service Revenue**					**Wages Expense**			
20	Bal.	800						Bal.	5,800		Bal.	3,000		
21								(e)	600		(d)	240		
22								(f)	320		*Bal.*	*3,240*		
23								*Bal.*	*6,720*					
24														
25	**Rent Expense**					**Insurance Expense**					**Office Supplies Expense**			
26	Bal.	800				(a)	80				(b)	210		
27														
28	**Depreciation Expense—**													
29	**Office Equipment**					**Income Taxes Expense**								
30	(c)	200				(g)	500							
31														

3. Adjusted trial balance prepared:

Reliable Lawn Care, Inc.		
Adjusted Trial Balance		
December 31, 2010		
Cash	$ 4,320	
Accounts Receivable	3,100	
Office Supplies	150	
Prepaid Insurance	400	
Office Equipment	6,800	
Accumulated Depreciation—Office Equipment		$ 1,400
Accounts Payable		1,400
Unearned Revenue		600
Wages Payable		240
Income Taxes Payable		500
Common Stock		4,000
Retained Earnings		5,740
Dividends	800	
Service Revenue		6,720
Wages Expense	3,240	
Rent Expense	800	
Insurance Expense	80	
Office Supplies Expense	210	
Depreciation Expense—Office Equipment	200	
Income Taxes Expense	500	
	$20,600	$20,600

4. Financial statements prepared:

Reliable Lawn Care, Inc.		
Income Statement		
For the Month Ended December 31, 2010		
Revenue		
Service revenue		$6,720
Expenses		
Wages expense	$3,240	
Rent expense	800	
Insurance expense	80	
Office supplies expense	210	
Depreciation expense--office equipment	200	
Income taxes expense	500	
Total expenses		5,030
Net income		$1,690

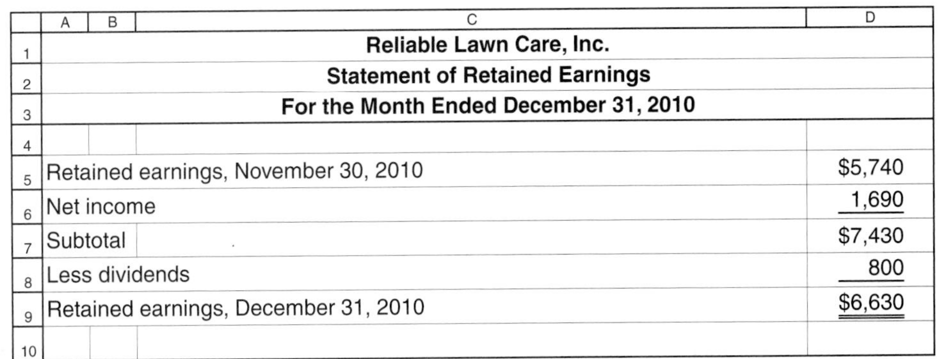

	A	B	C	D
1			**Reliable Lawn Care, Inc.**	
2			**Statement of Retained Earnings**	
3			**For the Month Ended December 31, 2010**	
4				
5	Retained earnings, November 30, 2010			$5,740
6	Net income			1,690
7	Subtotal			$7,430
8	Less dividends			800
9	Retained earnings, December 31, 2010			$6,630
10				

	A	B	C	D	E
1			**Reliable Lawn Care, Inc.**		
2			**Balance Sheet**		
3			**December 31, 2010**		
4					
5			**Assets**		
6	Cash				$ 4,320
7	Accounts receivable				3,100
8	Office supplies				150
9	Prepaid insurance				400
10	Office equipment			$6,800	
11		Less accumulated depreciation		1,400	5,400
12	Total assets				$13,370
13					
14			**Liabilities**		
15	Accounts payable				$ 1,400
16	Unearned revenue				600
17	Wages payable				240
18	Income taxes payable				500
19	Total liabilities				$ 2,740
20					
21			**Stockholders' Equity**		
22	Common stock			$4,000	
23	Retained earnings			6,630	
24	Total stockholders' equity				10,630
25	Total liabilities and stockholders' equity				$13,370
26					

LO1 Define *net income*, and explain the assumptions underlying income measurement and their ethical application.

Net income is the net increase in stockholders' equity that results from a company's operations. Net income equals revenues minus expenses; when expenses exceed revenues, a net loss results. Revenues equal the price of goods sold or services rendered during a specific period. Expenses are the costs of goods and services used in the process of producing revenues.

The continuity assumption recognizes that even though businesses face an uncertain future, without evidence to the contrary, accountants must assume that a business will continue to operate indefinitely. The periodicity assumption recognizes that although the lifetime of a business is uncertain, it is nonetheless useful to estimate the business's net income in terms of accounting periods. The matching rule holds that revenues must be assigned to the accounting period in which the goods are sold or the services performed, and expenses must be assigned to the accounting period in which they are used to produce revenue.

Because applying the matching rule involves making assumptions and exercising judgment, it can lead to earnings management, which is the manipulation of revenues and expenses to achieve a specific outcome. When the estimates involved in earnings management move outside a reasonable range, financial statements become misleading. Financial statements that are intentionally misleading constitute fraudulent financial reporting.

LO2 Define *accrual accounting*, and explain how it is accomplished.

Accrual accounting consists of all the techniques accountants use to apply the matching rule. It is accomplished by recognizing revenues when they are earned, by recognizing expenses when they are incurred, and by adjusting the accounts.

LO3 Identify four situations that require adjusting entries, and illustrate typical adjusting entries.

Adjusting entries are required when (1) recorded costs must be allocated between two or more accounting periods, (2) unrecorded expenses exist, (3) recorded, unearned revenues must be allocated between two or more accounting periods, and (4) unrecorded, earned revenues exist. The preparation of adjusting entries is summarized as follows:

	Type of Account		
Type of Adjusting Entry	**Debited**	**Credited**	**Examples of Balance Sheet Accounts**
1. Allocating recorded costs (previously paid, expired)	Expense	Asset (or contra-asset)	Prepaid rent Prepaid insurance Office supplies Accumulated depreciation–office equipment
2. Accrued expenses (incurred, not paid)	Expense	Liability	Wages payable Income taxes payable
3. Allocating recorded, unearned revenues (previously received, earned)	Liability	Revenue	Unearned design revenue
4. Accrued revenues (earned, not received)	Asset	Revenue	Accounts receivable Interest receivable

LO4 Prepare financial statements from an adjusted trial balance.

An adjusted trial balance is prepared after adjusting entries have been posted to the accounts. Its purpose is to test whether the adjusting entries have been posted correctly before the financial statements are prepared. The balances in the revenue and expense accounts in the adjusted trial balance are used to prepare the income statement. The balances in the asset and liability accounts in the adjusted trial balance and the ending balance from the statement of retained earnings are used to prepare the balance sheet.

LO5 Describe the accounting cycle, and explain the purposes of closing entries.

The accounting cycle has six steps: (1) analyzing business transactions from source documents; (2) recording the transactions by entering them in the journal; (3) posting the entries to the ledger and preparing a trial balance; (4) adjusting the accounts and preparing an adjusted trial balance; (5) preparing the financial statements; and (6) closing the accounts and preparing a post-closing trial balance.

Closing entries have two purposes: (1) they clear the balances of all temporary accounts (revenue, expense, and Dividends accounts) so that they have zero balances at the beginning of the next accounting period, and (2) they summarize a period's revenues and expenses in the Income Summary account so that the net income or net loss for the period can be transferred as a total to Retained Earnings. As a final check on the balance of the ledger and to ensure that all temporary accounts have been closed, a post-closing trial balance is prepared after the closing entries have been posted to the ledger accounts.

LO6 Use accrual-based information to analyze cash flows.

To ensure a company's liquidity, managers must know how to use accrual-based information to analyze cash flows. The general rule for determining the cash flow received from any revenue or paid for any expense (except depreciation) is to determine the potential cash payments or cash receipts and deduct the amount not paid or received.

REVIEW of Concepts and Terminology

The following concepts and terms were introduced in this chapter:

Accounting cycle 163 (LO5)
Accrual 151 (LO3)
Accrual accounting 148 (LO2)
Accrued expenses 155 (LO3)
Accrued revenues 158 (LO3)
Accumulated Depreciation accounts 153 (LO3)
Adjusted trial balance 160 (LO4)
Adjusting entries 150 (LO3)
Carrying value 154 (LO3)
Cash basis of accounting 146 (LO1)
Closing entries 163 (LO5)
Continuity 145 (LO1)
Contra account 153 (LO3)
Deferral 151 (LO3)
Depreciation 153 (LO3)
Earnings management 146 (LO1)
Expenses 144 (LO1)
Fiscal year 145 (LO1)
Going concern 145 (LO1)
Income Summary account 165 (LO5)
Interim periods 145 (LO1)
Matching rule 146 (LO1)
Net income 144 (LO1)
Net loss 144 (LO1)
Periodicity 145 (LO1)
Permanent accounts 163 (LO5)
Post-closing trial balance 165 (LO5)
Prepaid expenses 151 (LO3)
Profit 144 (LO1)
Revenue recognition 148 (LO2)
Revenues 144 (LO1)
Temporary accounts 163 (LO5)
Unearned revenues 157 (LO3)

Key Ratio

Profit margin 169

CHAPTER ASSIGNMENTS

BUILDING Your Basic Knowledge and Skills

Short Exercises

LO1 LO2 **Accrual Accounting Concepts**

SE 1. Match the concepts of accrual accounting on the right with the assumptions or actions on the left:

___ 1. Assumes expenses should be assigned to the accounting period in which they are used to produce revenues	a. Periodicity
___ 2. Assumes a business will last indefinitely	b. Going concern
___ 3. Assumes revenues are earned at a point in time	c. Matching rule
___ 4. Assumes net income that is measured for a short period of time, such as one quarter, is a useful measure	d. Revenue recognition

LO3 **Adjustment for Prepaid Insurance**

SE 2. The Prepaid Insurance account began the year with a balance of $920. During the year, insurance in the amount of $2,080 was purchased. At the end of the year (December 31), the amount of insurance still unexpired was $1,400. Prepare the year-end entry in journal form to record the adjustment for insurance expense for the year.

LO3 **Adjustment for Supplies**

SE 3. The Supplies account began the year with a balance of $760. During the year, supplies in the amount of $1,960 were purchased. At the end of the year (December 31), the inventory of supplies on hand was $880. Prepare the year-end entry in journal form to record the adjustment for supplies expense for the year.

LO3 **Adjustment for Depreciation**

SE 4. The depreciation expense on office equipment for the month of March is $100. This is the third month that the office equipment, which cost $1,900, has been owned. Prepare the adjusting entry in journal form to record depreciation for March and show the balance sheet presentation for office equipment and related accounts after the March 31 adjustment.

LO3 **Adjustment for Accrued Wages**

SE 5. Wages are paid each Saturday for a six-day workweek. Wages are currently running $1,380 per week. Prepare the adjusting entry in journal form required on June 30, assuming July 1 falls on a Tuesday.

LO3 **Adjustment for Unearned Revenue**

SE 6. During the month of August, deposits in the amount of $2,200 were received for services to be performed. By the end of the month, services in the amount of $1,520 had been performed. Prepare the necessary adjustment in journal form for Service Revenue at the end of the month.

LO4 **Preparation of an Income Statement and Statement of Retained Earnings from an Adjusted Trial Balance**

SE 7. The adjusted trial balance for Shimura Company on December 31, 2010, contains the following accounts and balances: Retained Earnings, $4,300; Dividends, $175; Service Revenue, $1,300; Rent Expense, $200; Wages Expense, $450; Utilities Expense, $100; Telephone Expense, $25; and Income Taxes Expense, $175. Prepare an income statement and statement of retained earnings in proper form for the month of December.

LO5 **Preparation of Closing Entries**

SE 8. Using the data in **SE** 7, prepare required closing entries for Shimura Company.

LO6 **Determination of Cash Flows**

SE 9. Unearned Revenue had a balance of $650 at the end of November and $450 at the end of December. Service Revenue was $2,550 for the month of December. How much cash was received for services provided during December?

Profit Margin

SE 10. Calculate profit margin for 2010 using the following data: A company has net income of $14,000 and net sales of $164,000 in 2010.

Exercises

LO1 LO2 LO3 **Discussion Questions**

E 1. Develop a brief answer to each of the following questions.

1. When a company has net income, what happens to its assets and/or to its liabilities?
2. Why must a company that gives a guaranty or warranty with its product or service show an expense in the year of sale rather than in a later year when a repair or replacement is made?
3. Is accrual accounting more closely related to a company's goal of profitability or liquidity?
4. Under normal circumstances, will the carrying value of a long-term asset be equal to its market value?

LO4 **Discussion Questions**

E 2. Develop a brief answer to each of the following questions:

1. Why is Retained Earnings not listed on the trial balance for Miller Design Studio, Inc., in Exhibits 3-1 and 3-2?
2. If, at the end of the accounting period, you were looking at the T account for a prepaid expense like supplies, would you look for the amounts expended in cash on the debit or credit side? On which side would you find the amount expensed during the period?
3. Would you expect profit margin to be a good measure of a company's liquidity? Why or why not?

LO1 LO2 LO3 **Applications of Accounting Concepts Related to Accrual Accounting**

E 3. The accountant for Ronaldo Company makes the assumptions or performs the activities in the list that follows. Tell which of these concepts of accrual accounting most directly relates to each assumption or action: (a) periodicity, (b) going concern, (c) matching rule, (d) revenue recognition, (e) deferral, and (f) accrual.

1. In estimating the life of a building, assumes that the business will last indefinitely
2. Records a sale when the customer is billed
3. Postpones the recognition of a one-year insurance policy as an expense by initially recording the expenditure as an asset
4. Recognizes the usefulness of financial statements prepared on a monthly basis even though they are based on estimates
5. Recognizes, by making an adjusting entry, wages expense that has been incurred but not yet recorded
6. Prepares an income statement that shows the revenues earned and the expenses incurred during the accounting period

LO2 Application of Conditions for Revenue Recognition

E 4. Four conditions must be met before revenue should be recognized. In each of the following cases, tell which condition has *not* been met:

a. Company A accepts a contract from another company to perform services in the future for $2,000.
b. Company B ships products worth $3,000 to another company without an order from the other company but tells the company it can return the products if it does not sell them.
c. Company C performs services for $10,000 for a company that is in financial difficulty.
d. Company D agrees to work out a price later for services that it performs for another company.

LO3 Adjusting Entry for Unearned Revenue

E 5. Fargo Voice, Inc. of Fargo, North Dakota, publishes a monthly magazine featuring local restaurant reviews and upcoming social, cultural, and sporting events. Subscribers pay for subscriptions either one year or two years in advance. Cash received from subscribers is credited to an account called Magazine Subscriptions Received in Advance. On December 31, 2009, the end of the company's fiscal year, the balance of Magazine Subscriptions Received in Advance is $840,000. Expiration of subscriptions revenue is as follows:

During 2009	$175,000
During 2010	415,000
During 2011	250,000

Prepare the adjusting entry in journal form for December 31, 2009.

LO3 Adjusting Entries for Prepaid Insurance

E 6. An examination of the Prepaid Insurance account shows a balance of $16,845 at the end of an accounting period, before adjustment. Prepare entries in journal form to record the insurance expense for the period under the following independent assumptions:

1. An examination of the insurance policies shows unexpired insurance that cost $8,270 at the end of the period.
2. An examination of the insurance policies shows insurance that cost $2,150 has expired during the period.

LO3 Adjusting Entries for Supplies: Missing Data

E 7. Each of the following columns represents a Supplies account:

	a	b	c	d
Supplies on hand at July 1	$264	$346	$196	$?
Supplies purchased during the month	113	?	174	1,928
Supplies consumed during the month	194	972	?	1,741
Supplies on hand at July 31	?	436	85	1,118

1. Determine the amounts indicated by the question marks.
2. Make the adjusting entry in journal form for column **a**, assuming supplies purchased are debited to an asset account.

LO3 **Adjusting Entry for Accrued Salaries**

E 8. Hugo Incorporated has a five-day workweek and pays salaries of $35,000 each Friday.

1. Prepare the adjusting entry in journal form required on May 31, assuming that June 1 falls on a Wednesday.
2. Prepare the entry in journal form to pay the salaries on June 3, including the amount of salaries payable from requirement **1**.

LO3 **Revenue and Expense Recognition**

E 9. Optima Company produces computer software that Tech Comp, Inc., sells. Optima receives a royalty of 15 percent of sales. Tech Comp pays royalties to Optima Company semiannually—on May 1 for sales made in July through December of the previous year and on November 1 for sales made in January through June of the current year. Royalty expense for Tech Comp and royalty income for Optima Company in the amount of $6,000 were accrued on December 31, 2008. Cash in the amounts of $6,000 and $10,000 was paid and received on May 1 and November 1, 2009, respectively. Software sales during the July to December 2009 period totaled $215,000.

1. Calculate the amount of royalty expense for Tech Comp and royalty income for Optima during 2009.
2. Record the adjusting entry in journal form that each company made on December 31, 2009.

LO4 **Preparation of Financial Statements**

E 10. Prepare the monthly income statement, statement of retained earnings, and balance sheet for Alvin Cleaning Company, Inc., from the data provided in the adjusted trial balance at the top of the next page.

LO5 **Preparation of Closing Entries**

E 11. From the adjusted trial balance in **E 10**, prepare the required closing entries for Alvin Cleaning Company, Inc.

LO3 **Adjusting Entries**

E 12. Prepare year-end adjusting entries in journal form for each of the following:

1. Office Supplies has a balance of $336 on January 1. Purchases debited to Office Supplies during the year amount to $1,660. A year-end inventory reveals supplies of $1,140 on hand.
2. Depreciation of office equipment is estimated to be $2,130 for the year.
3. Property taxes for six months, estimated at $1,800, have accrued but have not been recorded.
4. Unrecorded interest receivable on U.S. government bonds is $850.
5. Unearned Revenue has a balance of $1,800. Services for $750 received in advance have now been performed.
6. Services totaling $800 have been performed; the customer has not yet been billed.

Alvin Cleaning Company, Inc.
Adjusted Trial Balance
August 31, 2010

Cash	$ 4,750	
Accounts Receivable	2,592	
Prepaid Insurance	380	
Prepaid Rent	200	
Cleaning Supplies	152	
Cleaning Equipment	3,875	
Accumulated Depreciation–Cleaning Equipment		$ 320
Truck	7,200	
Accumulated Depreciation–Truck		720
Accounts Payable		420
Wages Payable		295
Unearned Janitorial Revenue		1,590
Income Taxes Payable		900
Common Stock		4,000
Retained Earnings		11,034
Dividends	2,000	
Janitorial Revenue		14,620
Wages Expense	5,680	
Rent Expense	1,350	
Gas, Oil, and Other Truck Expenses	580	
Insurance Expense	380	
Supplies Expense	2,920	
Depreciation Expense–Cleaning Equipment	320	
Depreciation Expense–Truck	720	
Income Taxes Expense	800	
	$33,899	$33,899

LO3 **Accounting for Revenue Received in Advanced**

E 13. Robert Shapiro, a lawyer, was paid $84,000 on October 1 to represent a client in real estate negotiations over the next 12 months.

1. Record the entries in journal form required in Shapiro's records on October 1 and at the end of the fiscal year, December 31.
2. How would this transaction be reflected on the income statement and balance sheet on December 31?

LO5 **Preparation of Closing Entries**

E 14. The adjusted trial balance for Burke Consultant Corporation at the end of its fiscal year is at the top of the next page. Prepare the required closing entries.

Office Salaries Expense	13,500
Advertising Expense	2,525

LO4 LO5 **Preparation of a Statement of Retained Earnings**

E 15. The Retained Earnings, Dividends, and Income Summary accounts for New Look Hair Salon, Inc., are shown in T account form below. The closing entries

Burke Consultant Corporation
Trial Balance
December 31, 2010

Cash	$ 7,575	
Accounts Receivable	2,625	
Prepaid Insurance	585	
Office Supplies	440	
Office Equipment	6,300	
Accumulated Depreciation–Office Equipment		$ 765
Automobile	6,750	
Accumulated Depreciation–Automobile		750
Accounts Payable		1,700
Unearned Consulting Fees		1,500
Income Taxes Payable		3,000
Common Stock		10,000
Retained Earnings		4,535
Dividends	7,000	
Consulting Fees Earned		32,550
Office Salaries Expense	13,500	
Advertising Expense	2,525	
Rent Expense	2,650	
Telephone Expense	1,850	
Income Taxes Expense	3,000	
	$54,800	$54,800

have been recorded for the year ended December 31, 2009. Prepare a statement of retained earnings for New Look Hair Salon, Inc.

Retained Earnings

12/31/09	9,500	12/31/08	26,000
		12/31/09	22,000
		Bal.	**38,500**

Income Summary

12/31/09	43,000	12/31/09	65,000
12/31/09	22,000		
Bal.	—		

Dividends

4/1/09	3,000	12/31/09	9,500
7/1/09	3,500		
10/1/09	3,000		
Bal.	—		

LO6 **Determination of Cash Flows**

E 16. After adjusting entries, the balance sheets of Ramiros Company showed the following asset and liability amounts at the end of 2009 and 2010:

	2010	**2009**
Prepaid insurance	$2,400	$2,900
Wages payable	1,200	2,200
Unearned revenue	4,200	1,900

The following amounts were taken from the 2010 income statement:

Insurance expense	$ 3,800
Wages expense	19,500
Fees earned	8,900

Calculate the amount of cash paid for insurance and wages and the amount of cash received for fees during 2010.

LO6 **Relationship of Expenses to Cash Paid**

E 17. The income statement for Sahan Company included the following expenses for 2010:

Rent expense	$ 75,000
Interest expense	11,700
Salaries expense	121,000

Listed below are the related balance sheet account balances at year end for last year and this year.

	Last Year	This Year
Prepaid rent	$1,500	$ 1,350
Interest payable	—	—
Salaries payable	7,500	14,000

1. Compute the cash paid for rent during the year.
2. Compute the cash paid for interest during the year.
3. Compute the cash paid for salaries during the year.

Profit Margin

E 18. Jarvis Company wants to know if its profitability has improved. Calculate its profit margin for 2010 and 2009 using the following data:

Net Income, 2010	$ 10,000
Net Income, 2009	8,600
Net Sales, 2010	192,000
Net Sales, 2009	160,000

By this measure, has profitability improved?

Problems

LO3 **Determining Adjustments**

P 1. At the end of the first three months of operation, the trial balance of City Answering Service, Inc., appears as shown at the top of the next page. Oscar Rienzo, the owner of City Answering Service, has hired an accountant to prepare financial statements to determine how well the company is doing after three months. Upon examining the accounting records, the accountant finds the following items of interest:

a. An inventory of office supplies reveals supplies on hand of $150.
b. The Prepaid Rent account includes the rent for the first three months plus a deposit for April's rent.
c. Depreciation on the equipment for the first three months is $416.
d. The balance of the Unearned Answering Service Revenue account represents a 12-month service contract paid in advance on February 1.
e. On March 31, accrued wages total $105.
f. Federal income taxes for the three months are estimated to be $1,110.

City Answering Service, Inc.
Trial Balance
March 31, 2010

Cash	$ 3,582	
Accounts Receivable	4,236	
Office Supplies	933	
Prepaid Rent	800	
Equipment	4,700	
Accounts Payable		$ 2,673
Unearned Answering Service Revenue		888
Common Stock		5,933
Dividends	2,100	
Answering Service Revenue		9,102
Wages Expense	1,900	
Office Cleaning Expense	345	
	$18,596	$18,596

Required

All adjustments affect one balance sheet account and one income statement account. For each of the above situations, show the accounts affected, the amount of the adjustment (using a + or − to indicate an increase or decrease), and the balance of the account after the adjustment in the following format:

Balance Sheet Account	Amount of Adjustment (+ or −)	Balance after Adjustment	Income Statement Account	Amount of Adjustment (+ or −)	Balance after Adjustment

LO2 LO3 **Preparing Adjusting Entries**

P 2. On November 30, the end of the current fiscal year, the following information is available to assist Caruso Corporation's accountants in making adjusting entries:

a. Caruso Corporation's Supplies account shows a beginning balance of $2,350. Purchases during the year were $4,218. The end-of-year inventory reveals supplies on hand of $1,397.

b. The Prepaid Insurance account shows the following on November 30:

Beginning balance	$4,720
July 1	4,200
October 1	7,272

The beginning balance represents the unexpired portion of a one-year policy purchased the previous year. The July 1 entry represents a new one-year policy, and the October 1 entry represents additional coverage in the form of a three-year policy.

c. The following table contains the cost and annual depreciation for buildings and equipment, all of which Caruso Corporation purchased before the current year:

Account	Cost	Annual Depreciation
Buildings	$298,000	$16,000
Equipment	374,000	40,000

d. On September 1, the company completed negotiations with a client and accepted an advance payment of $18,600 for services to be performed in the next year. The $18,600 was credited to the Unearned Service Revenue account.
e. The company calculated that as of November 30, it had earned $7,000 on an $11,000 contract that would be completed and billed in January.
f. Among the liabilities of the company is a note payable in the amount of $300,000. On November 30, the accrued interest on this note amounted to $18,000.
g. On Saturday, December 2, the company, which is on a six-day workweek, will pay its regular salaried employees $15,000.
h. On November 29, the company completed negotiations and signed a contract to provide services to a new client at an annual rate of $17,500.
i. Management estimates income taxes for the year to be $23,000.

Required

User insight ▶ 1. Prepare adjusting entries in journal form for each item listed above.
2. Explain how the conditions for revenue recognition are applied to transactions **e** and **h**.

LO3 LO4 **Determining Adjusting Entries, Posting to T Accounts, and Preparing an Adjusted Trial Balance**

P 3. The schedule below presents the trial balance for Prima Consultants Corporation on December 31, 2010. The following information is also available:

a. Ending inventory of office supplies, $97.
b. Prepaid rent expired, $500.
c. Depreciation of office equipment for the period, $720.
d. Interest accrued on the note payable, $600.
e. Salaries accrued at the end of the period, $230.
f. Service revenue still unearned at the end of the period, $1,410.
g. Service revenue earned but not billed, $915.
h. Estimated federal income taxes for the period, $2,780.

Prima Consultants Corporation
Trial Balance
December 31, 2010

Cash	$ 13,786	
Accounts Receivable	24,840	
Office Supplies	991	
Prepaid Rent	1,400	
Office Equipment	7,300	
Accumulated Depreciation–Office Equipment		$ 2,600
Accounts Payable		1,820
Notes Payable		10,000
Unearned Service Revenue		2,860
Common Stock		11,000
Retained Earnings		19,387
Dividends	15,000	
Service Revenue		58,500
Salaries Expense	33,400	
Utilities Expense	1,750	
Rent Expense	7,700	
	$106,167	$106,167

Required

1. Open T accounts for the accounts in the trial balance plus the following: Interest Payable; Salaries Payable; Income Taxes Payable; Office Supplies Expense; Depreciation Expense–Office Equipment; Interest Expense; and Income Taxes Expense. Enter the account balances.
2. Determine the adjusting entries and post them directly to the T accounts.
3. Prepare an adjusted trial balance.

User insight ▶

4. What financial statements do each of the above adjustments affect? What financial statement is *not* affected by the adjustments?

LO3 LO4 **Determining Adjusting Entries and Tracing Their Effects to Financial Statements**

P 4. Helen Ortega opened a small tax-preparation service. At the end of its second year of operation, Ortega Tax Service, Inc., had the trial balance shown below. The following information is also available:

a. Office supplies on hand, December 31, 2010, $225.
b. Insurance still unexpired, $100.
c. Estimated depreciation of office equipment, $795.
d. Telephone expense for December, $21; the bill was received but not recorded.
e. The services for all unearned tax fees revenue had been performed by the end of the year.
f. Estimated federal income taxes for the year, $2,430.

Ortega Tax Service, Inc.
Trial Balance
December 31, 2010

Cash	$ 3,700	
Accounts Receivable	1,099	
Prepaid Insurance	240	
Office Supplies	780	
Office Equipment	7,100	
Accumulated Depreciation–Office Equipment		$ 770
Accounts Payable		635
Unearned Tax Fees Revenues		219
Common Stock		3,500
Retained Earnings		3,439
Dividends	6,000	
Tax Fees Revenue		21,926
Office Salaries Expense	8,300	
Advertising Expense	650	
Rent Expense	2,400	
Telephone Expense	220	
	$30,489	$30,489

Required

1. Open T accounts for the accounts in the trial balance plus the following: Income Taxes Payable; Insurance Expense; Office Supplies Expense; Depreciation Expense–Office Equipment; and Income Taxes Expense. Record the balances shown in the trial balance.
2. Determine the adjusting entries and post them directly to the T accounts.

3. Prepare an adjusted trial balance, an income statement, a statement of retained earnings, and a balance sheet.

User insight ▶ 4. Why is it not necessary to show the effects of the above transactions on the statement of cash flows?

LO3 LO4 Determining Adjusting Entries and Tracing Their Effects to Financial Statements

P 5. VIP Limo, Inc., was organized to provide limousine service between the airport and various suburban locations. It has just completed its second year of business. Its trial balance appears below.

VIP Limo, Inc.
Trial Balance
June 30, 2010

Cash (111)	$ 9,812	
Accounts Receivable (112)	14,227	
Prepaid Rent (117)	12,000	
Prepaid Insurance (118)	4,900	
Prepaid Maintenance (119)	12,000	
Spare Parts (141)	11,310	
Limousines (142)	220,000	
Accumulated Depreciation–Limousines (143)		$ 35,000
Notes Payable (211)		45,000
Unearned Passenger Service Revenue (212)		30,000
Common Stock (311)		40,000
Retained Earnings (312)		48,211
Dividends (313)	20,000	
Passenger Service Revenue (411)		428,498
Gas and Oil Expense (511)	89,300	
Salaries Expense (512)	206,360	
Advertising Expense (513)	26,800	
	$626,709	$626,709

The following information is also available:

a. To obtain space at the airport, VIP Limo paid two years' rent in advance when it began the business.
b. An examination of insurance policies reveals that $1,800 expired during the year.
c. To provide regular maintenance for the vehicles, VIP Limo deposited $12,000 with a local garage. An examination of maintenance invoices reveals charges of $10,944 against the deposit.
d. An inventory of spare parts shows $2,016 on hand.
e. VIP Limo depreciates all of its limousines at the rate of 12.5 percent per year. No limousines were purchased during the year.
f. A payment of $11,300 for one full year's interest on notes payable is now due.

g. Unearned Passenger Service Revenue on June 30 includes $17,815 for tickets that employers purchased for use by their executives but which have not yet been redeemed.
h. Federal income taxes for the year are estimated to be $13,250.

Required

1. Determine adjusting entries and enter them in the journal (Page 14).
2. Open ledger accounts for the accounts in the trial balance plus the following: Interest Payable (213); Income Taxes Payable (214); Rent Expense (514); Insurance Expense (515); Spare Parts Expense (516); Depreciation Expense–Limousines (517); Maintenance Expense (518); Interest Expense (519); and Income Taxes Expense (520). Record the balances shown in the trial balance.
3. Post the adjusting entries from the journal to the ledger accounts, showing proper references.
4. Prepare an adjusted trial balance, an income statement, a statement of retained earnings, and a balance sheet.

User insight ▶

5. Do adjustments affect the profit margin? After the adjustments, is the profit margin for the year more or less than it would have been if the adjustments had not been made?

Alternate Problems

LO3 Determining Adjustments

P 6. At the end of its fiscal year, the trial balance for Andy's Cleaners, Inc., appears as shown at the top of the next page:

The following information is also available:

a. A study of the company's insurance policies shows that $680 is unexpired at the end of the year.
b. An inventory of cleaning supplies shows $1,150 on hand.
c. Estimated depreciation on the building for the year is $12,800.
d. Accrued interest on the mortgage payable is $1,000.
e. On September 1, the company signed a contract, effective immediately, with Hope County Hospital to dry-clean, for a fixed monthly charge of $425, the uniforms used by doctors in surgery. The hospital paid for four months' service in advance.
f. The company pays sales and delivery wages on Saturday. The weekly payroll is $3,060. September 30 falls on a Thursday, and the company has a six-day pay week.
g. Estimated federal income taxes for the period are $2,300.

Required

All adjustments affect one balance sheet account and one income statement account. For each of the above situations, show the accounts affected, the amount of the adjustment (using a + or − to indicate an increase or decrease), and the balance of the account after the adjustment in the following format:

Balance Sheet Account	Amount of Adjustment (+ or −)	Balance after Adjustment	Income Statement Account	Amount of Adjustment (+ or −)	Balance after Adjustment

Andy's Cleaners, Inc.
Trial Balance
September 30, 2010

Cash	$ 11,788	
Accounts Receivable	26,494	
Prepaid Insurance	3,400	
Cleaning Supplies	7,374	
Land	18,000	
Building	186,000	
Accumulated Depreciation–Building		$ 45,600
Accounts Payable		18,400
Unearned Cleaning Revenue		1,700
Mortgage Payable		110,000
Common Stock		40,000
Retained Earnings		16,560
Dividends	9,000	
Cleaning Revenue		159,634
Wages Expense	101,330	
Cleaning Equipment Rental Expense	6,100	
Delivery Truck Expense	4,374	
Interest Expense	11,000	
Other Expenses	7,034	
	$391,894	$391,894

LO2 LO3 **Preparing Adjusting Entries**

P 7. On June 30, the end of the current fiscal year, the following information is available to Conti Company's accountants for making adjusting entries:

a. One of the company's liabilities is a mortgage payable in the amount of $260,000. On June 30, the accrued interest on this mortgage was $13,000.
b. On Friday, July 2, the company, which is on a five-day workweek and pays employees weekly, will pay its regular salaried employees $18,700.
c. On June 29, the company completed negotiations and signed a contract to provide services to a new client at an annual rate of $7,200.
d. The Supplies account shows a beginning balance of $1,615 and purchases during the year of $4,115. The end-of-year inventory reveals supplies on hand of $1,318.
e. The Prepaid Insurance account shows the following entries on June 30:

Beginning Balance	$1,620
January 1	2,900
May 1	3,366

The beginning balance represents the unexpired portion of a one-year policy purchased a year ago. The January 1 entry represents a new one-year policy; the May 1 entry represents the additional coverage of a three-year policy.
f. The following table contains the cost and annual depreciation for buildings and equipment, all of which were purchased before the current year:

Account	Cost	Annual Depreciation
Buildings	$170,000	$ 7,300
Equipment	218,000	20,650

g. On June 1, the company completed negotiations with another client and accepted a payment of $21,600, representing one year's services paid in advance. The $21,600 was credited to Services Collected in Advance.

h. The company calculates that as of June 30 it had earned $4,500 on a $7,500 contract that will be completed and billed in August.
i. Federal income taxes for the year are estimated to be $6,300.

Required

1. Prepare adjusting entries in journal form for each item listed above.

User insight ▶ 2. Explain how the conditions for revenue recognition are applied to transactions **c** and **h**.

LO3 **Determining Adjusting Entries, Posting to T Accounts, and Preparing an Adjusted Trial Balance**

P 8. The trial balance for Best Advisors Service, Inc., on December 31 follows.

Best Advisors Service, Inc.
Trial Balance
December 31, 2010

Cash	$ 18,500	
Accounts Receivable	8,250	
Office Supplies	2,662	
Prepaid Rent	1,320	
Office Equipment	9,240	
Accumulated Depreciation–Office Equipment		$ 1,540
Accounts Payable		5,940
Notes Payable		11,000
Unearned Service Revenue		2,970
Common Stock		12,000
Retained Earnings		14,002
Dividends	22,000	
Service Revenue		72,600
Salaries Expense	49,400	
Rent Expense	4,400	
Utilities Expense	4,280	
	$120,052	$120,052

The following information is also available:

a. Ending inventory of office supplies, $300.
b. Prepaid rent expired, $610.
c. Depreciation of office equipment for the period, $526.
d. Accrued interest expense at the end of the period, $570.
e. Accrued salaries at the end of the period, $330.
f. Service revenue still unearned at the end of the period, $1,166.
g. Service revenue earned but unrecorded, $3,100.
h. Estimated income taxes for the period, $4,200.

Required

1. Open T accounts for the accounts in the trial balance plus the following: Interest Payable; Salaries Payable; Income Taxes Payable; Office Supplies Expense; Depreciation Expense–Office Equipment; Interest Expense; and Income Taxes Expense. Enter the balances shown on the trial balance.
2. Determine the adjusting entries and post them directly to the T accounts.
3. Prepare an adjusted trial balance.

User insight ▶ 4. What financial statements do each of the above adjustments affect? What financial statement is *not* affected by the adjustments?

LO3 LO4 Determining Adjusting Entries and Tracing Their Effects to Financial Statements

P 9. Tim Angel opened a small travel agency. At the end of its second year of operation, Angel Travel, Inc., had the trial balance shown below. The following information is also available:

a. Office supplies on hand, at December 31, 2011, $180.
b. Insurance still unexpired, $65.
c. Estimated depreciation of office equipment, $650.
d. Telephone expense for December, $45; the bill was received but not recorded.
e. The services for all unearned travel revenues had been performed by the end of the year.
f. Estimated federal income taxes for the year, $2,385.

Angel Travel, Inc.
Trial Balance
December 31, 2011

Cash	$ 3,650	
Accounts Receivable	970	
Prepaid Insurance	195	
Office Supplies	610	
Office Equipment	6,800	
Accumulated Depreciation–Office Equipment		$ 670
Accounts Payable		590
Unearned Travel Revenues		315
Common Stock		3,300
Retained Earnings		3,117
Dividends	4,200	
Travel Revenue		20,079
Office Salaries Expense	8,300	
Advertising Expense	585	
Rent Expense	2,350	
Telephone Expense	411	
	$28,071	$28,071

Required

1. Open T accounts for the accounts in the trial balance plus the following: Income Taxes Payable; Insurance Expense; Office Supplies Expense; Depreciation Expense–Office Equipment; and Income Taxes Expense. Record the balances shown in the trial balance.
2. Determine the adjusting entries and post them directly to the T accounts.
3. Prepare an adjusted trial balance, an income statement, a statement of retained earnings, and a balance sheet.

User insight ▶ 4. Why is it not necessary to show the effects of the above transactions on the statement of cash flows?

LO3 LO4 Determining Adjusting Entries and Tracing Their Effects to Financial Statements

P 10. Ray Heating & Cooling, Inc., was organized to provide heating and cooling service. It has just completed its second year of business. Its trial balance appears on the next page.

Ray Heating & Cooling, Inc.
Trial Balance
June 30, 2011

Cash (111)	$ 8,120	
Accounts Receivable (112)	13,270	
Prepaid Rent (117)	11,000	
Prepaid Insurance (118)	3,700	
Prepaid Maintenance (119)	11,000	
Spare Parts (141)	15,100	
Vehicles (142)	190,000	
Accumulated Depreciation–Vehicles (143)		$ 25,000
Notes Payable (211)		48,000
Unearned Service Revenue (212)		29,500
Common Stock (311)		27,000
Retained Earnings (312)		53,650
Dividends (313)	19,000	
Service Revenue (411)		419,160
Gas and Oil Expense (511)	95,600	
Salaries Expense (512)	214,320	
Advertising Expense (513)	21,200	
	$602,310	$602,310

The following information is also available:

a. Ray Heating & Cooling paid two years' rent in advance when it began the business.
b. An examination of insurance policies reveals that $1,400 expired during the year.
c. To provide regular maintenance for the vehicles, Ray Heating & Cooling deposited $13,000 with a local garage. An examination of maintenance invoices reveals charges of $9,879 against the deposit.
d. An inventory of spare parts shows $2,580 on hand.
e. Ray Heating & Cooling depreciates its service vehicles at the rate of 12.5 percent per year. No vehicles were purchased during the year.
f. A payment of $11,800 for one full year's interest on notes payable is now due.
g. Unearned Service Revenue on June 30 includes $13,535 for contracts with local restaurants, but the services have not yet been provided.
h. Federal income taxes for the year are estimated to be $12,980.

Required

1. Determine adjusting entries and enter them in the journal (Page 14).
2. Open ledger accounts for the accounts in the trial balance plus the following: Interest Payable (213); Income Taxes Payable (214); Rent Expense (514); Insurance Expense (515); Spare Parts Expense (516); Depreciation Expense–Vehicles (517); Maintenance Expense (518); Interest Expense (519); and Income Taxes Expense (520). Record the balances shown in the trial balance.
3. Post the adjusting entries from the journal to the ledger accounts, showing proper references.

User insight ▶

4. Prepare an adjusted trial balance, an income statement, a statement of retained earnings, and a balance sheet.
5. Do adjustments affect the profit margin? After the adjustments, is the profit margin for the year more or less than it would have been if the adjustments had not been made?

ENHANCING Your Knowledge, Skills, and Critical Thinking

LO1 LO2 LO3

Importance of Adjustments

C 1. Never Flake Company, which operated in the northeastern part of the United States, provided a rust-prevention coating for the underside of new automobiles. The company advertised widely and offered its services through new-car dealers. When a dealer sold a new car, the salesperson attempted to sell the rust-prevention coating as an option. The protective coating was supposed to make cars last longer in the severe northeastern winters. A key selling point was Never Flake's warranty, which stated that it would repair any damage due to rust at no charge for as long as the buyer owned the car.

For several years, Never Flake had been very successful in generating enough cash to continue operations. But in 2008, the company suddenly declared bankruptcy. Company officials said that the firm had only $5.5 million in assets against liabilities of $32.9 million. Most of the liabilities represented potential claims under the company's lifetime warranty. It seemed that owners were keeping their cars longer now than previously. Therefore, more damage was being attributed to rust.

Discuss what accounting decisions could have helped Never Flake to survive under these circumstances.

LO1

Earnings Management and Fraudulent Financial Reporting

C 2. In recent years, the Securities and Exchange Commission (SEC) has been waging a public campaign against corporate accounting practices that manage or manipulate earnings to meet the expectations of Wall Street analysts. Corporations engage in such practices in the hope of avoiding shortfalls that might cause serious declines in their stock price.

For each of the following cases that the Securities and Exchange Commission challenged, tell why each is a violation of the matching rule and how it should be accounted for:

a. **Lucent Technologies** sold telecommunications equipment to companies from which there was no reasonable expectation of payment because of the companies' poor financial condition.
b. **America Online (AOL)** recorded advertising as an asset rather than as an expense.
c. **Eclipsys** recorded software contracts as revenue even though it had not yet rendered the services.
d. **Xerox Corporation** recorded revenue from lease agreements at the time the leases were signed rather than over the lease term.
e. **KnowledgeWare** recorded revenue from sales of software even though it told customers they did not have to pay until they had the software.

LO2 LO3

Application of Accrual Accounting

C 3. The **Lyric Opera of Chicago** is one of the largest and best-managed opera companies in the United States. Managing opera productions requires advance planning, including the development of scenery, costumes, and stage properties and the sale of tickets. To measure how well the company is operating in any given year, management must apply accrual accounting to these and other transactions. At year end, April 30, 2009, Lyric Opera's balance sheet showed deferred production costs and other assets of $1,794,804 and deferred ticket and other revenue of $13,102,512.[9] Be prepared to discuss what accounting policies and adjusting entries are applicable to these accounts. Why are they important to Lyric Opera's management?

LO2 LO3

Analysis of an Asset Account

C 4. **The Walt Disney Company** is engaged in the financing, production, and distribution of motion pictures and television programming. In Disney's 2008 annual report, the balance sheet contains an asset called "film and television costs." Film and television costs, which consist of the costs associated with producing films and television programs less the amount expensed, were $5,394 million. The notes reveal that the amount of film and television costs expensed (amortized) during the year was $3,076 million. The amount spent for new film productions was $3,237 million.[10]

1. What are film and television costs, and why would they be classified as an asset?
2. Prepare an entry in T account form to record the amount the company spent on new film and television production during the year (assume all expenditures are paid for in cash).
3. Prepare an adjusting entry in T account form to record the expense for film and television productions.
4. Suggest a method by which The Walt Disney Company might have determined the amount of the expense in **3** in accordance with the matching rule.

LO3 **Analysis of Balance Sheet and Adjusting Entries**

C 5. In the **CVS** annual report in the Supplement to Chapter 1, refer to the balance sheet and the Summary of Significant Accounting Policies in the notes to the financial statements.

1. Examine the accounts in the current assets, property and equipment, and current liabilities sections of CVS's balance sheet. Which are most likely to have had year-end adjusting entries? Describe the nature of the adjusting entries. For more information about the property and equipment section, refer to the notes to the financial statements.
2. Where is depreciation (and amortization) expense disclosed in CVS's financial statements?
3. CVS has a statement on the "Use of Estimates" in its Summary of Significant Accounting Policies. Read this statement and tell how important estimates are to the determination of depreciation expense. What assumptions do accountants make that allow these estimates to be made?

K/R **Profit Margin**

C 6. Profit margin is an important measure of profitability. Use data from **CVS**'s income statement and the financial statements of **Southwest Airlines Co.** in the Supplement to Chapter 1 to calculate each company's profit margin for the past two years. By this measure, which company is more profitable?

LO1 LO2 LO3 **Importance of Adjustments**

C 7. Main Street Service Co., Inc., has achieved fast growth in the St. Louis area by selling service contracts on large appliances, such as washers, dryers, and refrigerators. For a fee, Main Street agrees to provide all parts and labor on an appliance after the regular warranty runs out. For example, by paying a fee of $200, a person who buys a dishwasher can add two years (years 2 and 3) to the regular one-year (year 1) warranty on the appliance. In 2009, the company sold service contracts in the amount of $1.8 million, all of which applied to future years. Management wanted all the sales recorded as revenues in 2009, contend-ing that the amount of the contracts could be determined and the cash had been received. Discuss whether you agree with this logic. How would you record the cash receipts? What assumptions do you think Main Street should make? Would you consider it unethical to follow management's recommendation? Who might be hurt or helped by this action?

LO3 **Types of Adjusting Entries**

C 8. In this chapter, we discussed adjusting entries for deferred revenue, deferred expense, accrued revenue, and accrued expense. In informal groups in class, discuss how each type of adjusting entry applies to **Netflix**. Be prepared to present your group's findings to the class.

SUPPLEMENT TO CHAPTER

3

Closing Entries and the Work Sheet

Preparing Closing Entries

As you know, closing entries have two purposes: (1) they clear the balances of all temporary accounts (revenue, expense, and Dividends accounts) so that they have zero balances at the beginning of the next accounting period, and (2) they summarize a period's revenues and expenses in the Income Summary account so that the net income or net loss for the period can be transferred as a total to Retained Earnings.

The steps involved in making closing entries are as follows:

Step 1. Close the credit balance accounts on the income statement to the Income Summary account.

Step 2. Close the debit balance accounts on the income statement to the Income Summary account.

Step 3. Close the Income Summary account balance to the Retained Earnings account.

Step 4. Close the Dividends account balance to the Retained Earnings account.

As you will learn in later chapters, not all credit balance accounts are revenues, and not all debit balance accounts are expenses. For that reason, when referring to closing entries, we often use the term *credit balances* instead of *revenue accounts* and the term *debit balances* instead of *expense accounts.*

An adjusted trial balance provides all the data needed to record the closing entries. Exhibit S-1 shows the relationships of the four kinds of closing entries to Miller Design Studio, Inc.'s adjusted trial balance.

> **Study Note**
> Although it is not absolutely necessary to use the Income Summary account when preparing closing entries, it does simplify the procedure.

Step 1: Closing the Credit Balances

On the credit side of the adjusted trial balance in Exhibit S-1, Design Revenue shows a balance of $13,600. To close this account, an entry must be made debiting the account in the amount of its balance and crediting it to the Income Summary account. Exhibit S-2 shows how the entry is posted. Notice that the entry sets the balance of the revenue account to zero and transfers the total revenues to the credit side of the Income Summary account.

> **Study Note**
> The Income Summary account now reflects the account balance of the revenue account before it was closed.

Step 2: Closing the Debit Balances

Several expense accounts show balances on the debit side of the adjusted trial balance in Exhibit S-1. A compound entry is needed to credit each of these expense accounts for its balance and to debit the Income Summary account for the total.

EXHIBIT S-1 Preparing Closing Entries from the Adjusted Trial Balance

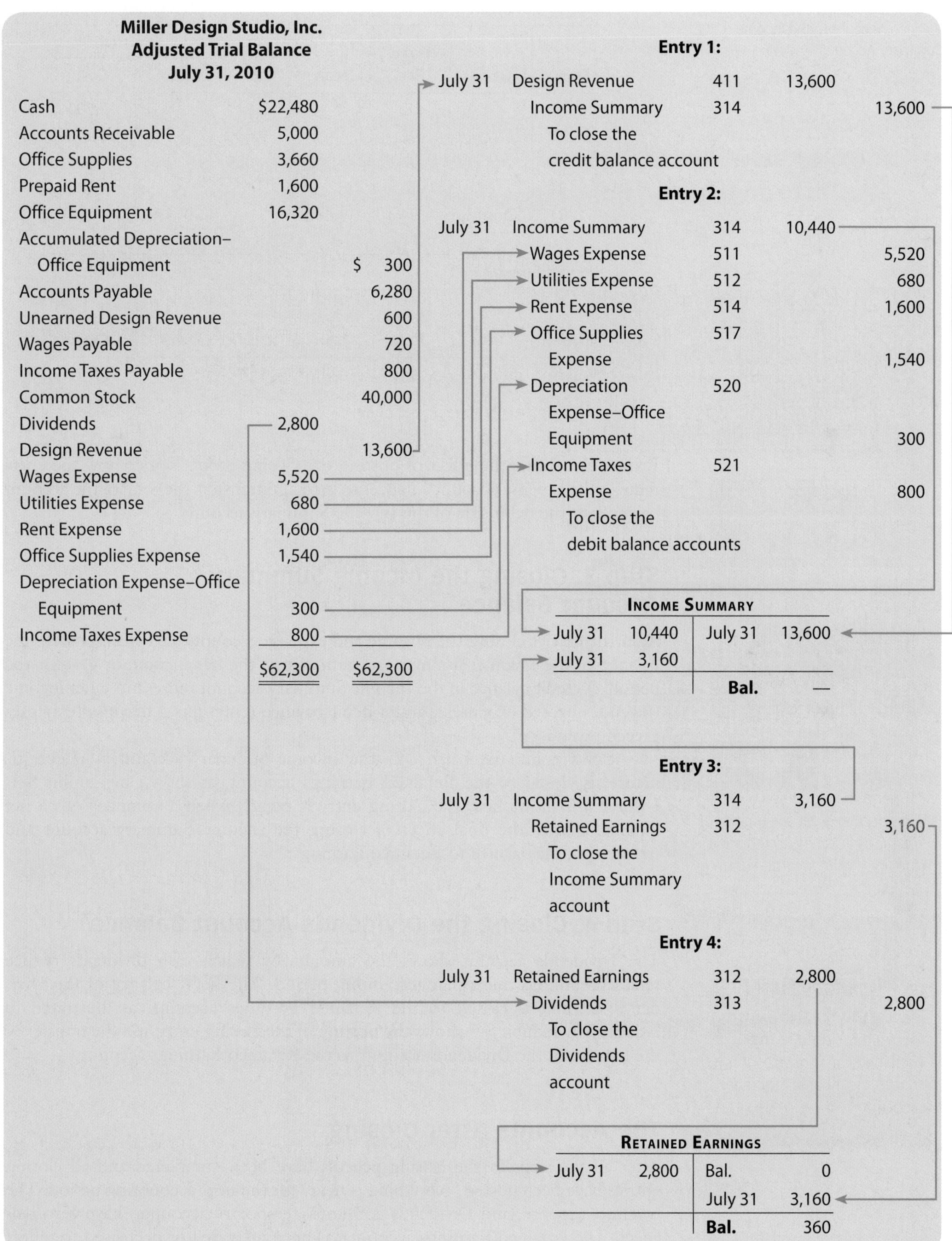

Miller Design Studio, Inc.
Adjusted Trial Balance
July 31, 2010

Cash	$22,480	
Accounts Receivable	5,000	
Office Supplies	3,660	
Prepaid Rent	1,600	
Office Equipment	16,320	
Accumulated Depreciation–Office Equipment		$ 300
Accounts Payable		6,280
Unearned Design Revenue		600
Wages Payable		720
Income Taxes Payable		800
Common Stock		40,000
Dividends	2,800	
Design Revenue		13,600
Wages Expense	5,520	
Utilities Expense	680	
Rent Expense	1,600	
Office Supplies Expense	1,540	
Depreciation Expense–Office Equipment	300	
Income Taxes Expense	800	
	$62,300	$62,300

Entry 1:

July 31	Design Revenue	411	13,600	
	Income Summary	314		13,600
	To close the credit balance account			

Entry 2:

July 31	Income Summary	314	10,440	
	Wages Expense	511		5,520
	Utilities Expense	512		680
	Rent Expense	514		1,600
	Office Supplies Expense	517		1,540
	Depreciation Expense–Office Equipment	520		300
	Income Taxes Expense	521		800
	To close the debit balance accounts			

INCOME SUMMARY

July 31	10,440	July 31	13,600
July 31	3,160		
		Bal.	—

Entry 3:

July 31	Income Summary	314	3,160	
	Retained Earnings	312		3,160
	To close the Income Summary account			

Entry 4:

July 31	Retained Earnings	312	2,800	
	Dividends	313		2,800
	To close the Dividends account			

RETAINED EARNINGS

July 31	2,800	Bal.	0
		July 31	3,160
		Bal.	360

EXHIBIT S-2
Posting the Closing Entry of a Credit Balance Account to the Income Summary Account

DESIGN REVENUE — **ACCOUNT NO. 411**

Date	Item	Post. Ref.	Debit	Credit	Balance Debit	Balance Credit
July 10		J2		2,800		2,800
15		J2		9,600		12,400
31		J3		800		13,200
31		J3		400		13,600
31	Closing	J4	13,600			—

INCOME SUMMARY — **ACCOUNT NO. 314**

Date	Item	Post. Ref.	Debit	Credit	Balance Debit	Balance Credit
July 31	Closing	J4		13,600		13,600

Exhibit S-3 shows the effect of posting the closing entry. Notice how the entry reduces the expense account balances to zero and transfers the total of the account balances to the debit side of the Income Summary account.

Step 3: Closing the Income Summary Account Balance

After the entries closing the revenue and expense accounts have been posted, the balance of the Income Summary account equals the net income or loss for the period. A credit balance in the Income Summary account represents a net income (revenues exceed expenses), and a debit balance represents a net loss (expenses exceed revenues).

At this point, the balance of the Income Summary account, whatever its nature, is closed to the Retained Earnings account, as shown in Exhibit S-1. Exhibit S-4 shows how the closing entry is posted when a company has a net income. Notice the dual effect of closing the Income Summary account and transferring the balance to Retained Earnings.

Study Note

The credit balance of the Income Summary account at this point ($3,160) represents net income—the key measure of performance. When a net loss occurs, debit the Retained Earnings account (to reduce it) and credit the Income Summary account (to close it).

Step 4: Closing the Dividends Account Balance

The Dividends account shows the amount by which cash dividends reduce retained earnings during an accounting period. The debit balance of the Dividends account is closed to the Retained Earnings account, as illustrated in Exhibit S-1. Exhibit S-5 shows the posting of the closing entry and the transfer of the balance of the Dividends account to the Retained Earnings account.

Study Note

Notice that the Dividends account is closed to the Retained Earnings account, not to the Income Summary account.

The Accounts After Closing

After all the steps in the closing process have been completed and all closing entries have been posted, everything is ready for the next accounting period. The revenue, expense, and Dividends accounts (temporary accounts) have zero balances. The Retained Earnings account has been increased or decreased to reflect

EXHIBIT S-3 Posting the Closing Entry of Debit Balance Account to the Income Summary Account

INCOME SUMMARY — ACCOUNT NO. 314

Date	Item	Post. Ref.	Debit	Credit	Balance Debit	Balance Credit
July 31	Closing	J4		13,600		13,600
31	Closing	J4	10,440*			3,160

WAGES EXPENSE — ACCOUNT NO. 511

Date	Item	Post. Ref.	Debit	Credit	Balance Debit	Balance Credit
July 26		J2	4,800		4,800	
31		J3	720		5,520	
31	Closing	J4		5,520	—	

UTILITIES EXPENSE — ACCOUNT NO. 512

Date	Item	Post. Ref.	Debit	Credit	Balance Debit	Balance Credit
July 30		J2	680		680	
31	Closing	J4		680	—	

RENT EXPENSE — ACCOUNT NO. 514

Date	Item	Post. Ref.	Debit	Credit	Balance Debit	Balance Credit
July 31		J3	1,600		1,600	
31	Closing	J4		1,600	—	

OFFICE SUPPLIES EXPENSE — ACCOUNT NO. 517

Date	Item	Post. Ref.	Debit	Credit	Balance Debit	Balance Credit
July 31		J3	1,540		1,540	
31	Closing	J4		1,540	—	

DEPRECIATION EXPENSE–OFFICE EQUIPMENT — ACCOUNT NO. 520

Date	Item	Post. Ref.	Debit	Credit	Balance Debit	Balance Credit
July 31		J3	300		300	
31	Closing	J4		300	—	

INCOME TAXES EXPENSE — ACCOUNT NO. 521

Date	Item	Post. Ref.	Debit	Credit	Balance Debit	Balance Credit
July 31		J3	800		800	
31	Closing	J4		800	—	

*Total of all credit closing entries to expense accounts is debited to the Income Summary account.

EXHIBIT S-4 Posting the Closing Entry of the Income Summary Account Balance to the Retained Earnings Account

INCOME SUMMARY — ACCOUNT NO. 314

Date	Item	Post. Ref.	Debit	Credit	Balance Debit	Balance Credit
July 31	Closing	J4		13,600		13,600
31	Closing	J4	10,440			3,160
31	Closing	J4	3,160			—

RETAINED EARNINGS — ACCOUNT NO. 312

Date	Item	Post. Ref.	Debit	Credit	Balance Debit	Balance Credit
July 31	Closing	J4		3,160		3,160

EXHIBIT S-5 Posting the Closing Entry of the Dividends Account Balance to the Retained Earnings Account

DIVIDENDS — **ACCOUNT NO. 313**

DATE	ITEM	POST. REF.	DEBIT	CREDIT	BALANCE DEBIT	BALANCE CREDIT
July 31		J2	2,800		2,800	
31	Closing	J4		2,800		—

RETAINED EARNINGS — **ACCOUNT NO. 312**

DATE	ITEM	POST. REF.	DEBIT	CREDIT	BALANCE DEBIT	BALANCE CREDIT
July 31	Closing	J4		3,160		3,160
31	Closing	J4	2,800			360

net income or net loss (net income in our example) and has been decreased for dividends. The balance sheet accounts (permanent accounts) show the correct balances, which are carried forward to the next period, as shown in the post-closing trial balance in Exhibit S-6.

The Work Sheet: An Accountant's Tool

Study Note

The work sheet is extremely useful when an accountant must make numerous adjustments. It is not a financial statement, it is not required, and it is not made public.

Accountants must collect relevant data to determine what should be included in financial reports. For example, they must examine insurance policies to calculate how much prepaid insurance has expired, examine plant and equipment records to determine depreciation, and compute the amount of accrued wages. To organize such data and avoid omitting important information that might affect the financial statements, accountants use *working papers.* Because working papers provide evidence of past work, they also enable accountants to retrace their steps when they need to verify information in the financial statements.

The *work sheet* is a special kind of working paper. It is often used as a preliminary step in preparing financial statements. Using a work sheet lessens the possibility of leaving out an adjustment and helps the accountant check the arithmetical accuracy of the accounts. The work sheet is never published and is rarely seen by management. It is a tool for the accountant.

EXHIBIT S-6
Post-Closing Trial Balance

Miller Design Studio, Inc.
Post-Closing Trial Balance
July 31, 2010

Cash	$22,480	
Accounts Receivable	5,000	
Office Supplies	3,660	
Prepaid Rent	1,600	
Office Equipment	16,320	
Accumulated Depreciation–Office Equipment		$ 300
Accounts Payable		6,280
Unearned Design Revenue		600
Wages Payable		720
Income Taxes Payable		800
Common Stock		40,000
Retained Earnings		360
	$49,060	$49,060

Because preparing a work sheet is a mechanical process, many accountants use a computer for this purpose. Some accountants use a spreadsheet program to prepare the work sheet. Others use a general ledger system to prepare financial statements from the adjusted trial balance.

Preparing the Work Sheet

A common form of work sheet has one column for account names and/or account numbers and multiple columns with headings like the ones shown in Exhibit S-7. A heading that includes the name of the company and the period of time covered (as on the income statement) identifies the work sheet. As Exhibit S-7 shows, preparation of a work sheet involves five steps.

Study Note

The Trial Balance columns of a work sheet take the place of the trial balance.

Step 1. Enter and total the account balances in the Trial Balance columns. The debit and credit balances of the accounts as of the last day of an accounting period are copied directly from the ledger into the Trial Balance columns, as shown in Exhibit S-7. When accountants use a work sheet, they do not have to prepare a separate trial balance.

Step 2. Enter and total the adjustments in the Adjustments columns. The required adjustments are entered in the Adjustments columns of the work sheet. As each adjustment is entered, a letter is used to identify its debit and credit parts. For example, in Exhibit S-7, the letter **a** identifies the adjustment made for the rent that Miller Design Studio, Inc. prepaid on July 3, which results in a debit to Rent Expense and a credit to Prepaid Rent. These identifying letters may be used to reference supporting computations or documentation for the related adjusting entries and can simplify the recording of adjusting entries in the journal.

A trial balance includes only accounts that have balances; if an adjustment involves an account that does not appear in the trial balance, the new account is added below the accounts listed on the work sheet. For example, Rent Expense has been added to Exhibit S-7. Accumulated depreciation accounts, which have a zero balance only in the initial period of operation, are the only exception to this rule. They are listed immediately after their associated asset accounts.

When all the adjustments have been made, the two Adjustments columns must be totaled. This procedure proves that the debits and credits of the adjustments are equal, and it generally reduces errors in the work sheet.

Step 3. Enter and total the adjusted account balances in the Adjusted Trial Balance columns. The adjusted trial balance in the work sheet is prepared by combining the amount of each account in the Trial Balance columns with the corresponding amount in the Adjustments columns and entering each result in the Adjusted Trial Balance columns.

Exhibit S-7 contains examples of *crossfooting*, or adding and subtracting a group of numbers horizontally. The first line shows Cash with a debit balance of $22,480. Because there are no adjustments to the Cash account, $22,480 is entered in the debit column of the Adjusted Trial Balance columns. On the second line, Accounts Receivable shows a debit of $4,600 in the Trial Balance columns. Because there is a debit of $400 from adjustment **g** in the Adjustments columns, it is added to the $4,600 and carried over to the debit column of the Adjusted Trial Balance columns as $5,000. On the next line, Office Supplies shows a debit of $5,200 in the Trial Balance columns and a credit of $1,540 from adjustment **b** in the Adjustments columns. Subtracting $1,540 from $5,200 results in a $3,660 debit balance in the Adjusted Trial Balance

EXHIBIT S-7 The Work Sheet

Miller Design Studio, Inc.
Work Sheet
For the Month Ended July 31, 2010

	Trial Balance		Adjustments		Adjusted Trial Balance		Income Statement		Balance Sheet	
Account Name	**Debit**	**Credit**	**Debit**	**Credit**	**Debit**	**Credit**	**Debit**	**Credit**	**Debit**	**Credit**
Cash	22,480				22,480				22,480	
Accounts Receivable	4,600		(g) 400		5,000				5,000	
Office Supplies	5,200			(b) 1,540	3,660				3,660	
Prepaid Rent	3,200			(a) 1,600	1,600				1,600	
Office Equipment	16,320				16,320				16,320	
Accumulated Depreciation–Office Equipment		—		(c) 300		300				300
Accounts Payable		6,280				6,280				6,280
Unearned Design Revenue		1,400	(f) 800			600				600
Common Stock		40,000				40,000				40,000
Dividends	2,800				2,800				2,800	
Design Revenue		12,400		(f) 800 (g) 400		13,600		13,600		
Wages Expense	4,800		(d) 720		5,520		5,520			
Utilities Expense	680				680		680			
	60,080	60,080								
Rent Expense			(a) 1,600		1,600		1,600			
Office Supplies Expense			(b) 1,540		1,540		1,540			
Depreciation Expense–Office Equipment			(c) 300		300		300			
Wages Payable				(d) 720		720				720
Income Taxes Expense			(e) 800		800		800			
Income Taxes Payable				(e) 800		800				800
			6,160	6,160	62,300	62,300	10,440	13,600	51,860	48,700
Net Income							3,160			3,160
							13,600	13,600	51,860	51,860

Note: The columns of the work sheet are prepared in the following order: (1) Trial Balance, (2) Adjustments, (3) Adjusted Trial Balance, and (4) Income Statement and Balance Sheet columns. In the fifth step, the Income Statement and Balance Sheet columns are totaled.

columns. This process is followed for all the accounts, including those added below the trial balance totals. The Adjusted Trial Balance columns are then *footed* (totaled) to check the accuracy of the crossfooting.

Step 4. Extend the account balances from the Adjusted Trial Balance columns to the Income Statement or Balance Sheet columns. Every account in the adjusted trial balance is an income statement account or a balance sheet account. Each account is extended to its proper place as a debit or credit in either the Income Statement columns or the Balance Sheet columns. As shown in Exhibit S-7, revenue and expense accounts are extended to the Income Statement columns, and asset, liability, and the Common Stock and Dividends accounts are extended to the Balance Sheet columns.

To avoid overlooking an account, the accounts are extended line by line, beginning with the first line (Cash) and not omitting any subsequent lines. For instance, the Cash debit balance of $22,480 is extended to the debit column of the Balance Sheet columns; then, the Accounts Receivable debit balance of $5,000 is extended to the debit column of the Balance Sheet columns; and so forth.

Step 5. Total the Income Statement columns and the Balance Sheet columns. Enter the net income or net loss in both pairs of columns as a balancing figure, and recompute the column totals. This last step, shown in Exhibit S-7, is necessary to compute net income or net loss and to prove the arithmetical accuracy of the work sheet.

Net income (or net loss) is equal to the difference between the total debits and credits of the Income Statement columns. It is also equal to the difference between the total debits and credits of the Balance Sheet columns.

Revenues (Income Statement credit column total)	$13,600
Expenses (Income Statement debit column total)	(10,440)
Net Income	$3,3160

In this case, revenues (credit column) exceed expenses (debit column). Thus, Miller Design Studio, Inc. has a net income of $3,160. The same difference occurs between the total debits and credits of the Balance Sheet columns.

The $3,160 is entered in the debit side of the Income Statement columns and in the credit side of the Balance Sheet columns to balance the columns. Remember that the excess of revenues over expenses (net income) increases stockholders' equity and that increases in stockholders' equity are recorded by credits.

When a net loss occurs, the opposite rule applies. The excess of expenses over revenues—net loss—is placed in the credit side of the Income Statement columns as a balancing figure. It is then placed in the debit side of the Balance Sheet columns because a net loss decreases stockholders' equity, and decreases in stockholders' equity are recorded by debits.

As a final check, the four columns are totaled again. If the Income Statement columns and the Balance Sheet columns do not balance, an account may have been extended or sorted to the wrong column, or an error may have been made in adding the columns. Of course, equal totals in the two pairs of columns are not absolute proof of accuracy. If an asset has been carried to the Income Statement debit column (or an expense has been carried to the Balance Sheet debit column) or a similar error with revenues or liabilities has been made, the work sheet will balance, but the net income figure will be wrong.

Using the Work Sheet

Study Note
Theoretically, adjusting entries can be recorded in the accounting records before the financial statements are prepared, or even before the work sheet is completed. However, they always precede the preparation of closing entries.

Accountants use the completed work sheet in performing three principal tasks:

1. **Recording the adjusting entries in the journal**. Because the information needed to record the adjusting entries can be copied from the work sheet, entering the adjustments in the journal is an easy step, as shown in Exhibit S-8. The adjusting entries are then posted to the ledger.
2. **Recording the closing entries in the journal**. The Income Statement columns of the work sheet show all the accounts that need to be closed, except for the Dividends account. Exhibits S-1 through S-5 show how the closing entries are entered in the journal and posted to the ledger.
3. **Preparing the financial statements**. Once the work sheet has been completed, preparing the financial statements is simple because the account balances have been sorted into the Income Statement and Balance Sheet columns.

EXHIBIT S-8 Adjustments from the Work Sheet Entered in the General Journal

General Journal **Page 3**

Date	Description	Post. Ref.	Debit	Credit
2010				
July 31	Rent Expense	514	1,600	
	Prepaid Rent	117		1,600
	To recognize expiration of one month's rent			
	Office Supplies Expense	517	1,540	
	Office Supplies	116		1,540
	To recognize office supplies used during the month			
	Depreciation Expense–Office Equipment	520	300	
	Accumulated Depreciation–Office Equipment	147		300
	To record depreciation of office equipment for a month			
	Wages Expense	511	720	
	Wages Payable	214		720
	To accrue unrecorded wages			
	Income Taxes Expense	521	800	
	Income Taxes Payable	215		800
	To accrue estimated income taxes			
	Unearned Design Revenue	213	800	
	Design Revenue	411		800
	To recognize performance of services paid for in advance			
	Accounts Receivable	113	400	
	Design Revenue	411		400
	To accrue website design fees earned but unrecorded			

Supplement Assignments

Review Questions

1. Can the work sheet be used as a substitute for the financial statements? Explain your answer.
2. Why should the Adjusted Trial Balance columns of the work sheet be totaled before the adjusted amounts are carried to the Income Statement and Balance Sheet columns?
3. What sequence should be followed in extending the amounts in the Adjusted Trial Balance columns to the Income Statement and Balance Sheet columns? Discuss your answer.
4. Do the Income Statement columns and the Balance Sheet columns of the work sheet balance after the amounts from the Adjusted Trial Balance columns are extended? Why or why not?
5. Do the totals of the Balance Sheet columns of the work sheet agree with the totals on the balance sheet? Explain your answer.
6. Should adjusting entries be posted to the ledger accounts before or after the closing entries? Explain your answer.
7. At the end of the accounting period, does the posting of adjusting entries to the ledger precede or follow preparation of the work sheet?

Exercises

Preparation of Closing Entries

E 1. The items below are from the Income Statement columns of the work sheet for Best Repair Shop, Inc., for the year ended December 31, 2010.

	Income Statement	
Account Name	**Debit**	**Credit**
Repair Revenue		25,620
Wages Expense	8,110	
Rent Expense	1,200	
Supplies Expense	4,260	
Insurance Expense	915	
Depreciation Expense–Repair Equipment	1,345	
Income Taxes Expense	1,000	
	16,830	25,620
Net Income	8,790	
	25,620	25,620

Prepare entries in journal form to close the revenue, expense, Income Summary, and Dividends accounts. Dividends of $5,000 were paid during the year.

Completion of a Work Sheet

E 2. The following is a highly simplified list of trial balance accounts and their normal balances for the month ended October 31, 2010, which was the company's first month of operation:

Trial Balance Accounts and Balances

Cash	$4	Unearned Service Revenue	$3
Accounts Receivable	7	Common Stock	5
Prepaid Insurance	2	Retained Earnings	7
Supplies	4	Dividends	6
Office Equipment	8	Service Revenue	23
Accumulated Depreciation–Office Equipment	1	Utilities Expense	2
		Wage Expense	10
Accounts Payable	4		

1. Prepare a work sheet, entering the trial balance accounts in the order they would normally appear and putting the balances in the correct columns.
2. Complete the work sheet using the following information:
   a. Expired insurance, $1.
   b. Of the unearned service revenue balance, $2 has been earned by the end of the month.
   c. Estimated depreciation on office equipment, $1.
   d. Accrued wages, $1.
   e. Unused supplies on hand, $1.
   f. Estimated federal income taxes, $1.

Problems

Closing Entries Using T Accounts and Preparation of Financial Statements

KA KLOOSTER & ALLEN

P 1. The adjusted trial balance for Settles Tennis Club, Inc., at the end of the company's fiscal year appears below.

Settles Tennis Club, Inc.
Adjusted Trial Balance
June 30, 2011

Cash	$ 26,200	
Prepaid Advertising	9,600	
Supplies	1,200	
Land	100,000	
Building	645,200	
Accumulated Depreciation–Building		$260,000
Equipment	156,000	
Accumulated Depreciation–Equipment		50,400
Accounts Payable		73,000
Wages Payable		9,000
Property Taxes Payable		22,500
Unearned Revenue–Locker Fees		3,000
Income Taxes Payable		20,000
Common Stock		200,000
Retained Earnings		271,150
Dividends	54,000	
Revenue from Court Fees		678,100
Revenue from Locker Fees		9,600
Wages Expense	351,000	
Maintenance Expense	51,600	
Advertising Expense	39,750	
Utilities Expense	64,800	
Supplies Expense	6,000	
Depreciation Expense–Building	30,000	
Depreciation Expense–Equipment	12,000	
Property Taxes Expense	22,500	
Miscellaneous Expense	6,900	
Income Taxes Expense	20,000	
	$1,596,750	$1,596,750

Required

1. Prepare T accounts and enter the balances for Retained Earnings, Dividends, Income Summary, and all revenue and expense accounts.
2. Enter the four required closing entries in the T accounts, labeling the components *a*, *b*, *c*, and *d*, as appropriate.
3. Prepare an income statement, a statement of retained earnings, and a balance sheet for Settles Tennis Club, Inc.
4. Explain why it is necessary to make closing entries at the end of an accounting period.

The Complete Accounting Cycle Without a Work Sheet: Two Months

(second month optional)

P 2. On May 1, 2010, Javier Munoz opened Javier's Repair Service, Inc. During the month, he completed the following transactions for the company:

May	1	Began business by depositing $5,000 in a bank account in the name of the company in exchange for 500 shares of $10 par value common stock.
	1	Paid the rent for a store for current month, $425.
	1	Paid the premium on a one-year insurance policy, $480.
	2	Purchased repair equipment from Motley Company, $4,200. Terms were $600 down and $300 per month for one year. First payment is due June 1.
	5	Purchased repair supplies from AWD Company on credit, $468.
	8	Paid cash for an advertisement in a local newspaper, $60.
	15	Received cash repair revenue for the first half of the month, $400.
	21	Paid AWD Company on account, $225.
	31	Received cash repair revenue for the second half of May, $975.
	31	Declared and paid a cash dividend, $300.

Required for May

1. Prepare entries in journal form to record the May transactions.
2. Open the following accounts: Cash (111); Prepaid Insurance (117); Repair Supplies (119); Repair Equipment (144); Accumulated Depreciation–Repair Equipment (145); Accounts Payable (212); Income Taxes Payable (213); Common Stock (311); Retained Earnings (312); Dividends (313); Income Summary (314); Repair Revenue (411); Store Rent Expense (511); Advertising Expense (512); Insurance Expense (513); Repair Supplies Expense (514); Depreciation Expense–Repair Equipment (515); and Income Taxes Expense (516). Post the May entries to the ledger accounts.
3. Using the following information, record adjusting entries in the journal and post to the ledger accounts:
   a. One month's insurance has expired.
   b. The remaining inventory of unused repair supplies is $169.
   c. The estimated depreciation on repair equipment is $70.
   d. Estimated income taxes are $50.
4. From the accounts in the ledger, prepare an adjusted trial balance. (**Note**: Normally a trial balance is prepared before adjustments but is omitted here to save time.)
5. From the adjusted trial balance, prepare an income statement, a statement of retained earnings, and a balance sheet for May.
6. Prepare and post closing entries.
7. Prepare a post-closing trial balance.

(Optional)

During June, Javier Munoz completed these transactions for Javier's Repair Service, Inc.:

June	1	Paid the monthly rent, $425.
	1	Made the monthly payment to Motley Company, $300.
	6	Purchased additional repair supplies on credit from AWD Company, $863.
	15	Received cash repair revenue for the first half of the month, $914.
	20	Paid cash for an advertisement in the local newspaper, $60.
	23	Paid AWD Company on account, $600.
	30	Received cash repair revenue for the last half of the month, $817.
	30	Declared and paid a cash dividend, $300.

8. Prepare and post entries in journal form to record the June transactions.
9. Using the following information, record adjusting entries in the journal and post to the ledger accounts:
   a. One month's insurance has expired.
   b. The inventory of unused repair supplies is $413.
   c. The estimated depreciation on repair equipment is $70.
   d. Estimated income taxes are $50.
10. From the accounts in the ledger, prepare an adjusted trial balance.
11. From the adjusted trial balance, prepare the June income statement, statement of retained earnings, and balance sheet.
12. Prepare and post closing entries.
13. Prepare a post-closing trial balance.

Preparation of a Work Sheet, Financial Statements, and Adjusting and Closing Entries

P 3. Beauchamp Theater Corporation's trial balance at the end of its current fiscal year appears at the top of the next page.

Required

1. Enter Beauchamp Theater Corporation's trial balance amounts in the Trial Balance columns of a work sheet and complete the work sheet using the following information:
   a. Expired insurance, $17,400.
   b. Inventory of unused office supplies, $244.
   c. Inventory of unused cleaning supplies, $468.
   d. Estimated depreciation on the building, $14,000.
   e. Estimated depreciation on the theater furnishings, $36,000.
   f. Estimated depreciation on the office equipment, $3,160.
   g. The company credits all gift books sold during the year to the Gift Books Liability account. A gift book is a booklet of ticket coupons that is purchased in advance as a gift. The recipient redeems the coupons at some point in the future. On June 30 it was estimated that $37,800 worth of the gift books had been redeemed.
   h. Accrued but unpaid usher wages at the end of the accounting period, $860.
   i. Estimated federal income taxes, $20,000.
2. Prepare an income statement, a statement of retained earnings, and a balance sheet.
3. Prepare adjusting and closing entries.

Beauchamp Theater Corporation
Trial Balance
June 30, 2010

Account	Debit	Credit
Cash	$ 31,800	
Accounts Receivable	18,544	
Prepaid Insurance	19,600	
Office Supplies	780	
Cleaning Supplies	3,590	
Land	20,000	
Building	400,000	
Accumulated Depreciation–Building		$ 39,400
Theater Furnishings	370,000	
Accumulated Depreciation–Theater Furnishings		65,000
Office Equipment	31,600	
Accumulated Depreciation–Office Equipment		15,560
Accounts Payable		45,506
Gift Books Liability		41,900
Mortgage Payable		300,000
Common Stock		200,000
Retained Earnings		112,648
Dividends	60,000	
Ticket Sales Revenue		411,400
Theater Rental Revenue		45,200
Usher Wages Expense	157,000	
Office Wages Expense	24,000	
Utilities Expense	112,700	
Interest Expense	27,000	
	$1,276,614	$1,276,614

CHAPTER

4 Financial Reporting and Analysis

Focus on Financial Statements

INCOME STATEMENT

Revenues
– Expenses
= Net Income

STATEMENT OF RETAINED EARNINGS

Opening Balance
+ Net Income
– Dividends
= Retained Earnings

BALANCE SHEET

Assets	Liabilities
	Equity

A = L + E

STATEMENT OF CASH FLOWS

Operating activities
+ Investing activities
+ Financing activities
= Change in Cash
+ Starting Balance
= Ending Cash Balance

Classifying accounts in groups on the financial statements aids financial analysis.

Stockholders, investors, creditors, and other interested parties rely on the integrity of a company's financial reports. A company's managers and accountants therefore have a responsibility to act ethically in the reporting process. However, what is often overlooked is that the users of financial reports also have a responsibility to recognize and understand the types of judgments and estimates that underlie these reports.

LEARNING OBJECTIVES

LO1 **Describe the objective of financial reporting and identify the qualitative characteristics, conventions, and ethical considerations of accounting information.** (pp. 210–213)

LO2 **Define and describe the conventions of *consistency, full disclosure, materiality, conservatism*, and *cost-benefit*.** (pp. 213–217)

LO3 **Identify and describe the basic components of a classified balance sheet.** (pp. 217–223)

LO4 **Describe the features of multistep and single-step classified income statements.** (pp. 223–229)

LO5 **Use classified financial statements to evaluate liquidity and profitability.** (pp. 229–236)

DECISION POINT ▶ A USER'S FOCUS DELL COMPUTER CORPORATION

▶ How should financial statements be organized to provide the best information?

▶ What key measures best capture a company's financial performance?

In a presentation to financial analysts, **Dell**'s management focused on the goals of growth, liquidity, and profitability.[1] In judging whether Dell has achieved those objectives, investors, creditors, managers, and others analyze relationships between key numbers in the financial statements that appear in the company's annual report.

Dell's annual report summarizes the company's financial performance by condensing a tremendous amount of information into a few numbers that managers and external users of financial statements consider most important. As shown in the Financial Highlights below, Dell uses five measures to summarize its operating results and the change in those results from one fiscal year to the next.

DELL'S FINANCIAL HIGHLIGHTS
OPERATING RESULTS
(in millions, except per share)

	2009	2008	Change*
Net revenue	$61,101	$61,133	(0.05)%
Gross margin	10,957	11,671	(6)%
Operating income	3,190	3,440	(7)%
Net income	2,478	2,947	(16)%
Diluted EPS	1.25	1.31	(5)%

*Parentheses indicate a negative percentage.

Foundations of Financial Reporting

LO1 Describe the objective of financial reporting and identify the qualitative characteristics, conventions, and ethical considerations of accounting information.

By issuing stocks and bonds that are traded in financial markets, corporations can raise the cash they need to carry out current and future business activities. Investors in stocks and bonds expect increases in the firm's stock price and returns from dividends. Creditors want to know if the firm can repay a loan plus interest in accordance with specified terms. Very importantly, both investors and creditors need to know if the firm can generate adequate cash flows to maintain its liquidity. Information pertaining to all these matters appears in the financial statements published in a company's annual report.

In the following sections, we describe the objective of financial reporting and the qualitative characteristics, accounting conventions, and ethical considerations that are involved. Figure 4-1 illustrates these factors.

Objective of Financial Reporting

Study Note

Although reading financial reports requires some understanding of business, it does not require the skills of a CPA.

The Financial Accounting Standards Board (FASB) emphasizes the needs of capital providers while recognizing the needs of other users when it defines the objective of financial reporting as follows:

> To provide financial information about the reporting entity that is useful to present and potential equity investors, lenders, and other creditors in making decisions in their capacity as capital providers. Information that is decision-useful to capital providers may also be useful to other users of financial reporting who are not capital providers.[2]

To be useful for decision making, financial reporting must enable the user to do the following:

- **Assess cash flow prospects.** Since the ultimate value of an entity and its ability to pay dividends, interest, and otherwise provide returns to capital providers depends on its ability to generate future cash flows, capital providers and other users need information to help make judgments about the entity's ability to generate cash flows.
- **Assess stewardship.** Since management is accountable for the custody and safekeeping of the entity's economic resources and for their efficient and profitable use, capital providers and others need information about the entity's resources (assets), claims against them (liabilities and stockholders' equity), and changes in these resources and claims as impacted by transactions (earnings and cash flows) and other economic events.

Financial reporting includes the financial statements periodically presented to parties outside the business. The statements—the balance sheet, the income statement, the statement of retained earnings, and the statement of cash flows—are important outputs of the accounting system but not the only output. Management's explanations and other information, including underlying assumptions and significant uncertainties about methods and estimates used in the financial reports, constitute important components of financial reporting by an entity. Because of a potential conflict of interest between managers, who must prepare the statements, and investors or creditors, who invest in or lend money to the business, financial statements usually are audited by outside accountants to ensure their reliability.

Qualitative Characteristics of Accounting Information

Students in their first accounting course often get the idea that accounting is 100 percent accurate. Contributing to this perception is that introductory textbooks like this one present the basics of accounting in a simple form to help students understand them. All the problems can be solved, and all the numbers

FIGURE 4-1
Factors Affecting Financial Reporting

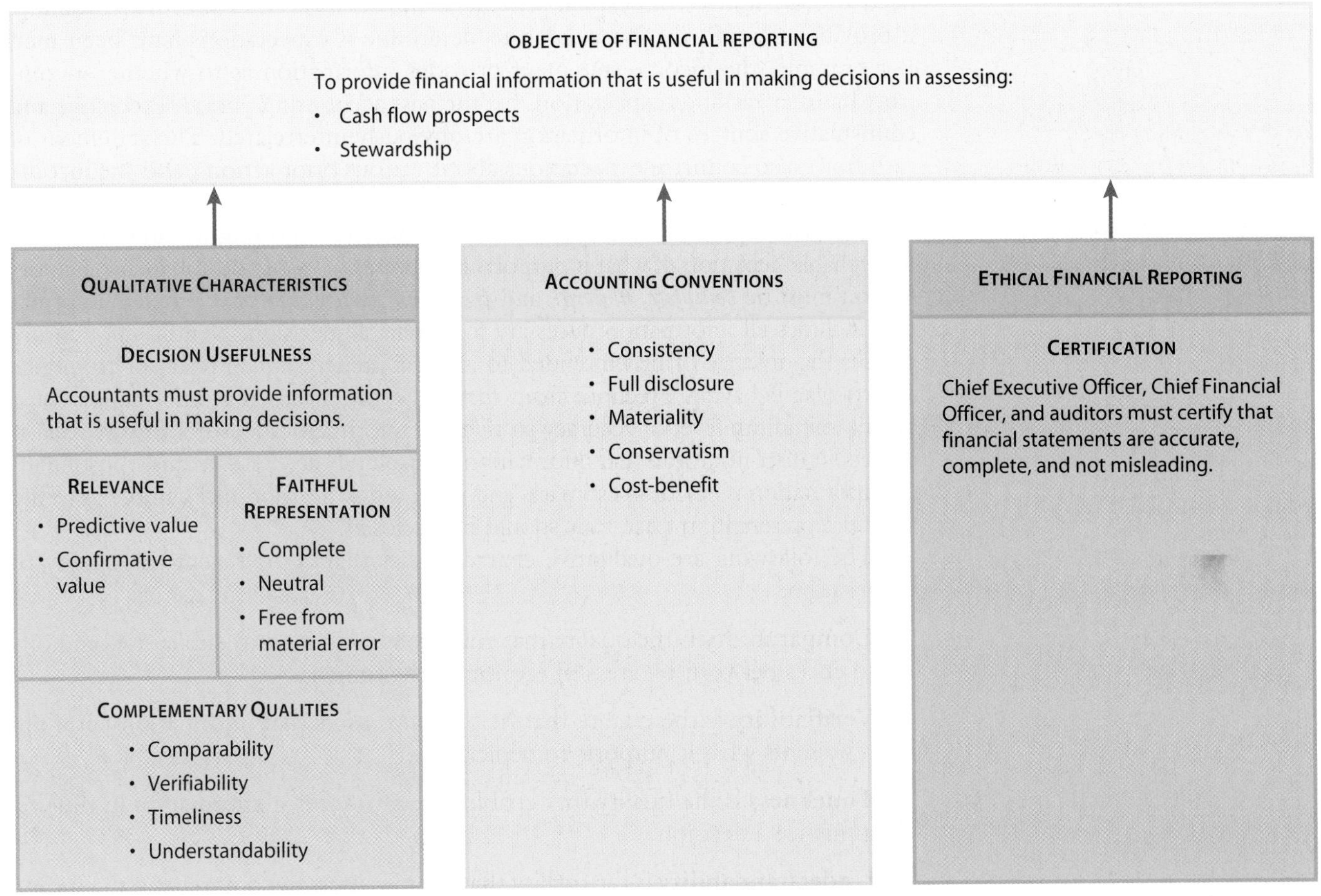

add up; what is supposed to equal something else does. Accounting seems very much like mathematics in its precision. In practice, however, accounting information is neither simple nor precise, and it rarely satisfies all criteria. The FASB emphasizes this fact in the following statement:

> The information provided by financial reporting often results from approximate, rather than exact, measures. The measures commonly involve numerous estimates, classifications, summarizations, judgments and allocations. The outcome of economic activity in a dynamic economy is uncertain and results from combinations of many factors. Thus, despite the aura of precision that may seem to surround financial reporting in general and financial statements in particular, with few exceptions the measures are approximations, which may be based on rules and conventions, rather than exact amounts.[3]

The goal of generating accounting information is to provide data that different users need to make informed decisions for their unique situations. How this goal is achieved provides much of the interest and controversy in accounting. To facilitate interpretation of accounting information, the FASB has established standards, or **qualitative characteristics**, by which to judge the information.[4] The most important or fundamental qualitative characteristics are relevance and faithful representation.

Relevance means that the information has a direct bearing on a decision. In other words, if the information were not available, a different decision would be made. To be relevant, information must have *predictive value, confirmative value,* or both. Information has predictive value if it helps capital providers make decisions about the future. For example, the statement of cash flows can provide information as to whether the company has sufficient funds to expand or if it will need to raise funds from capital providers. Information has confirmative value if it provides the information needed to determine if expectations have been met. For example, the income statement provides information as to whether a company has met earnings expectations for the past accounting period. Predictive and confirmative sources of information are obviously interrelated. The statement of cash flows also confirms expectations about various prior actions, and the income statement helps to determine future earnings.

Faithful representation means that the financial reporting for an entity must be a reliable depiction of what it purports to represent. To be faithful, financial information must be *complete, neutral,* and *free from material error.* Complete information includes all information necessary for a reliable decision. Neutral information implies the absence of bias intended to attain a predetermined result or to induce a particular behavior. Freedom from material error means that information must meet a minimum level of accuracy so that the information does not distort what it depicts. It does not mean that information is absolutely accurate because most financial information is based on estimates and judgments. If major uncertainties as to the faithful representation exist, they should be disclosed.

The following are qualitative characteristics that complement the quality of information:

- **Comparability** is the quality that enables users to identify similarities and differences between two sets of economic phenomena.
- **Verifiability** is the quality that helps assure users that information faithfully represents what it purports to depict.
- **Timeliness** is the quality that enables users to receive information in time to influence a decision.
- **Understandability** is the quality that enables users to comprehend the meaning of the information they receive.

Accounting Conventions

For accounting information to be understandable, accountants must prepare financial statements in accordance with accepted practices. But the decision maker also must know how to interpret the information; in making decisions, he or she must judge what information to use, how to use it, and what it means. Familiarity with the **accounting conventions**, or constraints on accounting, used in preparing financial statements enable the user to better understand accounting information. These conventions, which we discuss later in the chapter, affect how and what information is presented in financial statements.

Ethical Financial Reporting

As we noted earlier in the text, in 2002, in the wake of accounting scandals at **Enron** and **WorldCom**, Congress passed the Sarbanes-Oxley Act. One of the important outcomes of this legislation was that the Securities and Exchange Commission instituted rules requiring the chief executive officers and chief financial officers of all publicly traded companies to certify that, to their knowledge, the quarterly and annual statements that their companies file with the SEC are accurate and complete. Subsequently, an investigation by the audit committee of **Dell**'s board of directors and management disclosed weaknesses in the company's controls and led to restatements of the financial statements for the prior four years. After extensive improvements in control and the restatements, the company's chief executive officer, Michael S. Dell, made the following certifying statement in the company's annual report to the SEC:

> Based on my knowledge, the financial statements, and other financial information included in this report, fairly present in all material respects the financial condition, results of operations and cash flows... for the periods represented in this report.[5]

The chief financial officer may sign a similar certification.

As the Enron and WorldCom scandals demonstrated, fraudulent financial reporting can have high costs for investors, lenders, employees, and customers. It can also have high costs for the people who condone, authorize, or prepare misleading reports—even those at the highest corporate levels. In March 2005, Bernard J. Ebbers, former CEO of WorldCom, was convicted of seven counts of filing false reports with the SEC and one count each of securities fraud and conspiracy.[6] In 2006, both Kenneth Lay, former chairman of Enron Corporation, and Jeffrey Skilling, Enron's former CEO, were convicted on charges similar to the ones of which Ebbers was convicted.

STOP & APPLY >

The lettered items below represent a classification scheme for the concepts of financial accounting. Match each numbered term in the list that follows with the letter of the category in which it belongs.

a. Decision makers (users of accounting information)
b. Objective of accounting information
c. Accounting measurement considerations
d. Accounting processing considerations
e. Qualitative characteristics

1. Furnishing information that is useful in assessing cash flow prospects
2. Verifiability
3. Relevance
4. Assess stewardship
5. Faithful representation
6. Recognition
7. Investors
8. Predictive value
9. Management
10. Valuation
11. Internal accounting control
12. Furnishing information that is useful to investors and creditors

SOLUTION

1. b; 2. e; 3. e; 4. b; 5. e; 6. c; 7. a; 8. e; 9. a; 10. c; 11. d; 12. b

Accounting Conventions for Preparing Financial Statements

LO2 Define and describe the conventions of *consistency, full disclosure, materiality, conservatism*, and *cost-benefit*.

Financial statements are based largely on estimates and the application of accounting rules for recognition and allocation. To deal with the natural constraints on providing financial information, accountants depend on five conventions in recording transactions and preparing financial statements: consistency, full disclosure, materiality, conservatism, and cost-benefit.

Consistency

The **consistency** convention requires that once a company has adopted an accounting procedure, it must use it from one period to the next unless a note to the financial statements informs users of a change in procedure. Generally accepted accounting principles specify what the note must contain:

> The nature of and justification for a change in accounting principle and its effect on income should be disclosed in the financial statements of the period in which the change is made. The justification for the change should explain clearly why the newly adopted accounting principle is preferable.[7]

For example, in the notes to its financial statements, **Goodyear Tire & Rubber Company** disclosed that it had changed its method of accounting for inventories with the approval of its auditors because management felt the new method improved the matching of revenues and costs. Without such an acknowledgment, users of financial statements can assume that the treatment of a particular transaction, account, or item has not changed since the last period. For consistency, all years presented use this new method.

Full Disclosure (Transparency)

The convention of **full disclosure** (or transparency) requires that financial statements present all the information relevant to users' understanding of the statements. That is, the statements must be transparent so that they include any explanation needed to keep them from being misleading. Explanatory notes are therefore an integral part of the financial statements. For instance, as we have already mentioned, the notes should disclose any change that a company has made in its accounting procedures.

A company must also disclose significant events arising after the balance sheet date in the financial statements. Suppose a firm has purchased a piece of land for a future subdivision. Shortly after the end of its fiscal year, the firm is served papers to halt construction because the Environmental Protection Agency asserts that the land was once a toxic waste dump. This information, which obviously affects the users of the financial statements, must be disclosed in the statements for the fiscal year just ended.

Additional note disclosures required by the FASB and other official bodies include the accounting procedures used in preparing the financial statements and important terms of a company's debt, commitments, and contingencies. However, the statements can become so cluttered with notes that they impede rather than help understanding. Beyond the required disclosures, the application of the

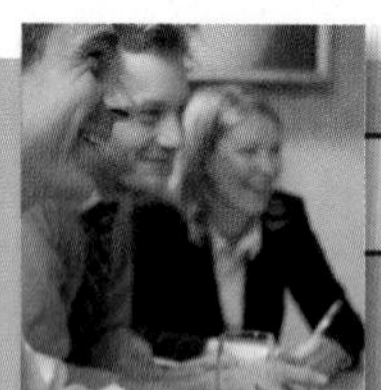

FOCUS ON BUSINESS PRACTICE **IFRS**

How Will Convergence of U.S. GAAP with IFRS Affect Accounting Conventions?

The FASB and the IASB are working toward converging U.S. generally accepted accounting principles (GAAP) with international financial reporting standards (IFRS). Their goal is "to increase the international comparability and the quality of standards used in the United States [which] is consistent with the FASB's obligation to its domestic constituents, who benefit from comparability across national borders."[8] In addition to the comparability convention, other accounting conventions will also be affected by the adoption of IFRS. For instance, conservatism, which has been the bedrock of accounting practice for many decades, would no longer be part of the conceptual framework. The practice of writing up the value of a nonfinancial asset, such as inventory or equipment, that has increased in fair value and recording it as income under IFRS would be considered a violation of the conservatism convention under U.S. GAAP. Such changes will influence the way accountants in the United States analyze financial statements.

FOCUS ON BUSINESS PRACTICE

How Much Is Material? It's Not Only a Matter of Numbers.

The materiality issue was long a pet peeve of the SEC, which contended that companies were increasingly abusing the convention to protect their stocks from taking a pounding when earnings did not reach their targets. In consequence, the SEC issued a rule that put stricter requirements on the use of materiality. In addition to providing quantitative guides, the rule includes qualitative considerations. The percentage assessment of materiality—the rule of thumb of 5 percent or more of net income that accountants and companies have traditionally used—is acceptable as an initial screening. However, the rule states that companies cannot decline to book items in the interest of meeting earnings estimates, preserving a growing earnings trend, converting a loss to a profit, increasing management compensation, or hiding an illegal transaction, such as a bribe.[9]

full-disclosure convention is based on the judgment of management and of the accountants who prepare the financial statements.

In recent years, investors and creditors also have had an influence on full disclosure. To protect them, independent auditors, the stock exchanges, and the SEC have made more demands for disclosure by publicly owned companies. The SEC has pushed especially hard for the enforcement of full disclosure. As a result, more and better information about corporations is available to the public today than ever before.

Materiality

Materiality refers to the relative importance of an item or event. In general, an item or event is material if there is a reasonable expectation that knowing about it would influence the decisions of users of financial statements. Some items or events are so small or insignificant that they would make little difference to decision makers no matter how they are handled. Thus, a large company, like **Dell Computer Corporation**, may decide that expenditures for durable items of less than $500 should be charged as expenses rather than recorded as long-term assets and depreciated.

The materiality of an item normally is determined by relating its dollar value to an element of the financial statements, such as net income or total assets. As a rule, when an item is worth 5 percent or more of net income, accountants treat it as material. However, materiality depends not only on the value of an item but also on its nature. For example, in a multimillion-dollar company, a mistake of $5,000 in recording an item may not be important, but the discovery of even a small bribe or theft can be very important. Moreover, many small errors can add up to a material amount.

Study Note

Theoretically, a $10 stapler is a long-term asset and should therefore be capitalized and depreciated over its useful life. However, the convention of materiality allows the stapler to be expensed entirely in the year of purchase because its cost is small and writing it off in one year will have no effect on anyone's decision making.

Conservatism

When accountants are uncertain about the judgments or estimates they must make, which is often the case, they look to the convention of **conservatism**. This convention holds that when faced with choosing between two equally acceptable procedures or estimates, accountants should choose the one that is least likely to overstate assets and income.

One of the most common applications of the conservatism convention is the use of the lower-of-cost-or-market method in accounting for inventories. Under this method, if an item's market value is greater than its original cost, the more

Study Note

The purpose of conservatism is not to produce the lowest net income and lowest asset value. It is a guideline for choosing among GAAP alternatives, and it should be used with care.

conservative cost figure is used. If the market value is below the original cost, the more conservative market value is used. The latter situation often occurs in the computer industry.

Conservatism can be a useful tool in doubtful cases, but when it is abused, it can lead to incorrect and misleading financial statements. For example, there is no uncertainty about how a long-term asset of material cost should be treated. When conservatism is used to justify expensing such an asset in the period of purchase, income and assets for the current period will be understated, and income in future periods will be overstated. Its cost should be recorded as an asset and spread over the useful life of the asset, as explained in Chapter 3. Accountants therefore depend on the conservatism convention only when uncertain about which accounting procedure or estimate to use.

Cost-Benefit

The **cost-benefit** convention holds that the benefits to be gained from providing accounting information should be greater than the costs of providing it. Of course, minimum levels of relevance and reliability must be reached if accounting information is to be useful. Beyond the minimum levels, however, it is up to the FASB and the SEC, which stipulate the information that must be reported, and the accountant, who provides the information, to judge the costs and benefits in each case.

Firms use the cost-benefit convention for both accounting and non-accounting decisions. Department stores could almost completely eliminate shoplifting if they hired five times as many clerks as they now have and assigned them to watching customers. The benefit would be reduced shoplifting. The cost would be reduced sales (customers do not like being closely watched) and increased wages expense. Although shoplifting is a serious problem for department stores, the benefit of reducing shoplifting in this way does not outweigh the cost.

The costs and benefits of a requirement for accounting disclosure are both immediate and deferred. Judging the final costs and benefits of a far-reaching and costly requirement for accounting disclosure is difficult. For instance, the FASB allows certain large companies to make a supplemental disclosure in their financial statements of the effects of changes in consumer price levels. Most companies choose not to present this information because they believe the costs of producing and providing it exceed its benefits to the readers of their financial statements. Cost-benefit is a question that the FASB, SEC, and all other regulators face. Even though there are no definitive ways of measuring costs and benefits, much of an accountant's work deals with these concepts.

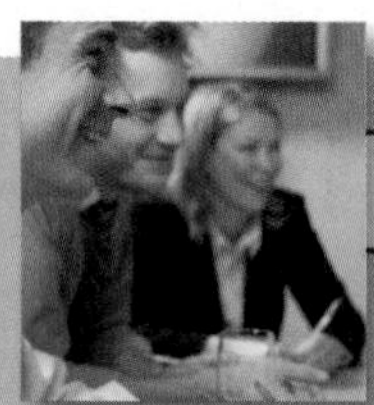

FOCUS ON BUSINESS PRACTICE IFRS

IASB Proposes Change in Format of Financial Statements

In the United States, classified financial statements have been used for more than a century and are second nature to all U.S. businesspeople. However, this may not be true in the near future. The International Accounting Standards Board (IASB) is considering a change that will organize the balance sheet and income statement in a format similar to the statement of cash flows. Under the proposal, each statement will have the categories now found on the statement of cash flows: operating, investing, and financing activities. The balance sheet form that equates total assets with liabilities and stockholders' equity (A = L + SE) would be replaced with a form in which each category of liabilities would be netted against its corresponding asset category. For example, current operating liabilities would be subtracted from current operating assets, and long-term debt would be subtracted from long-term assets on the asset side of the balance sheet.

STOP & APPLY >

Each of the items in the numbered list below pertains to one of the five accounting conventions in the list that follows. Match each item to the letter of the appropriate convention.

1. A note to the financial statements explains the company's method of revenue recognition.
2. Inventory is accounted for at its market value, which is less than its original cost.
3. A company uses the same method of revenue recognition year after year.
4. Several accounts are grouped into one category because the total amount of each account is small.
5. A company does not keep detailed records of certain operations because the information gained from the detail is not deemed useful.

a. Consistency
b. Full disclosure
c. Materiality
d. Conservatism
e. Cost-benefit

SOLUTION

1. b; 2. d; 3. a; 4. c; 5. e

Classified Balance Sheet

LO3 Identify and describe the basic components of a classified balance sheet.

As you know, a balance sheet presents a company's financial position at a particular time. The balance sheets we have presented thus far categorize accounts as assets, liabilities, and stockholders' equity. Because even a fairly small company can have hundreds of accounts, simply listing accounts in these broad categories is not particularly helpful to a statement user. Setting up subcategories within the major categories can make financial statements much more useful. This format enables investors and creditors to study and evaluate relationships among the subcategories.

General-purpose external financial statements that are divided into subcategories are called **classified financial statements**. Figure 4-2 depicts the subcategories into which assets, liabilities, and stockholders' equity are usually broken down.

The subcategories of Cruz Corporation's classified balance sheet, shown in Exhibit 4-1, typify those used by most corporations in the United States. The subcategories under stockholders' equity would, of course, be different if Cruz Corporation, a merchandising company, was a sole proprietorship or partnership rather than a corporation.

Assets

As you can see in Exhibit 4-1, the classified balance sheet of a U.S. company typically divides assets into four categories:

1. Current assets
2. Investments
3. Property, plant, and equipment
4. Intangible assets

FIGURE 4-2
Classified Balance Sheet

ASSETS		LIABILITIES
• Current Assets • Investments • Property, Plant, and Equipment • Intangible Assets	=	• Current Liabilities • Long-Term Liabilities
		STOCKHOLDERS' EQUITY
		• Contributed Capital • Retained Earnings

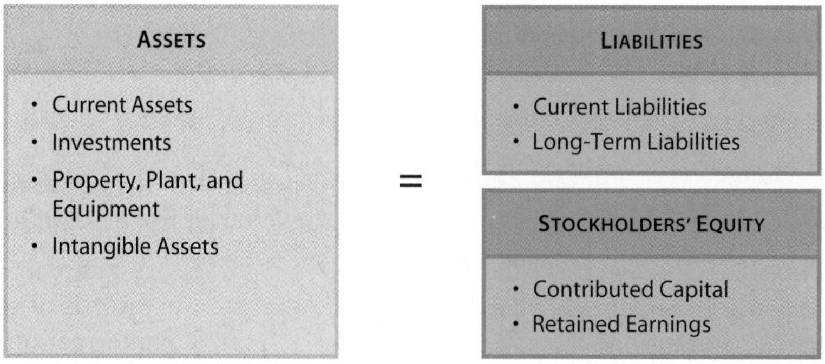

These categories are listed in the order of their presumed ease of conversion into cash. For example, current assets are usually more easily converted to cash than are property, plant, and equipment. For simplicity, some companies group investments, intangible assets, and other miscellaneous assets into a category called **other assets**.

Current Assets **Current assets** are cash and other assets that a company can reasonably expect to convert to cash, sell, or consume within one year or its *normal operating cycle*, whichever is longer. A company's **normal operating cycle** is the average time it needs to go from spending cash to receiving cash. For example, suppose a company uses cash to buy inventory and sells the inventory to a customer on credit. The resulting receivable must be collected in cash before the normal operating cycle ends.

The normal operating cycle for most companies is less than one year, but there are exceptions. For example, because of the length of time it takes **The Boeing Company** to build aircraft, its normal operating cycle exceeds one year. The inventory used in building the airplanes is nonetheless considered a current asset because the planes will be sold within the normal operating cycle. Another example is a company that sells on an installment basis. The payments for a television set or a refrigerator can extend over 24 or 36 months, but these receivables are still considered current assets.

Cash is obviously a current asset. Short-term investments, notes and accounts receivable, and inventory that a company expects to convert to cash within the next year or the normal operating cycle are also current assets. On the balance sheet, they are listed in the order of their ease of conversion to cash.

Prepaid expenses, such as rent and insurance paid in advance, and inventories of supplies bought for use rather than for sale should be classified as current assets. These assets are current in the sense that if they had not been bought earlier, a current outlay of cash would be needed to obtain them.

In deciding whether an asset is current or noncurrent, the idea of "reasonable expectation" is important. For example, Short-Term Investments, also called *Marketable Securities*, is an account used for temporary investments, such as U.S. Treasury bills, of "idle" cash—that is, cash that is not immediately required for operating purposes. Management can reasonably expect to sell these securities as cash needs arise over the next year or within the company's current operating cycle. Investments in securities that management does not expect to sell within the next year and that do not involve the temporary use of idle cash should be shown in the investments category of a classified balance sheet.

> **Study Note**
> For an investment to be classified as current, management must expect to sell it within the next year or the current operating cycle, so it must be readily marketable.

Investments The **investments** category includes assets, usually long term, that are not used in normal business operations and that management does not plan to convert to cash within the next year. Items in this category are securities held for long-term investment, long-term notes receivable, land held for future use,

EXHIBIT 4-1
Classified Balance Sheet for Cruz Corporation

Cruz Corporation
Balance Sheet
December 31, 2010

Assets			
Current assets			
Cash		$ 41,440	
Short-term investments		28,000	
Notes receivable		32,000	
Accounts receivable		141,200	
Merchandise inventory		191,600	
Prepaid insurance		26,400	
Supplies		6,784	
Total current assets			$467,424
Investments			
Land held for future use			50,000
Property, plant, and equipment			
Land		$ 18,000	
Building	$ 82,600		
Less accumulated depreciation	34,560	48,040	
Equipment	$108,000		
Less accumulated depreciation	57,800	50,200	
Total property, plant, and equipment			116,240
Intangible assets			
Trademark			2,000
Total assets			$635,664
Liabilities			
Current liabilities			
Notes payable		$ 60,000	
Accounts payable		102,732	
Salaries payable		8,000	
Total current liabilities			$ 170,732
Long-term liabilities			
Mortgage payable			71,200
Total liabilities			$241,932
Stockholders' Equity			
Contributed capital			
Common stock, $10 par value, 20,000 shares authorized, issued, and outstanding		$200,000	
Additional paid-in capital		40,000	
Total contributed capital		$240,000	
Retained earnings		153,732	
Total stockholders' equity			393,732
Total liabilities and stockholders' equity			$635,664

plant or equipment not used in the business, and special funds established to pay off a debt or buy a building. Also included are large permanent investments in another company for the purpose of controlling that company.

Property, Plant, and Equipment **Property, plant, and equipment** are tangible long-term assets used in a business's day-to-day operations. They represent a place to operate (land and buildings) and the equipment used to produce, sell, and deliver goods or services. They are therefore also called *operating assets* or, sometimes, *fixed assets*, *tangible assets*, *long-lived assets*, or *plant assets*. Through depreciation, the costs of these assets (except land) are spread over the periods they benefit. Past depreciation is recorded in the Accumulated Depreciation account.

To reduce clutter on the balance sheet, property, plant, and equipment are often combined—for example:

Property, plant, and equipment (net) $116,240

The company provides the details in a note to the financial statements.

The property, plant, and equipment category also includes natural resources owned by the company, such as forest lands, oil and gas properties, and coal mines, if they are used in the regular course of business. If they are not, they are listed in the investments category.

Intangible Assets **Intangible assets** are long-term assets with no physical substance whose value stems from the rights or privileges they extend to their owners. Examples are patents, copyrights, goodwill, franchises, and trademarks. These assets are recorded at cost, which is spread over the expected life of the right or privilege. Goodwill, which arises in an acquisition of another company, is an intangible asset that is recorded at cost but is not amortized. It is reviewed each year for possible loss of value, or impairment.

Liabilities

Liabilities are divided into two categories that are based on when the liabilities fall due: current liabilities and long-term liabilities.

Current Liabilities **Current liabilities** are obligations that must be satisfied within one year or within the company's normal operating cycle, whichever is longer. These liabilities are typically paid out of current assets or by incurring new short-term liabilities. They include notes payable, accounts payable, the current portion of long-term debt, salaries and wages payable, taxes payable, and customer advances (unearned revenues).

Long-Term Liabilities Debts that fall due more than one year in the future or beyond the normal operating cycle, which will be paid out of noncurrent assets, are **long-term liabilities**. Mortgages payable, long-term notes, bonds payable, employee pension obligations, and long-term lease liabilities generally fall into this category. Deferred income taxes are often disclosed as a separate category in the long-term liability section of the balance sheet of publicly held corporations. This liability arises because the rules for measuring income for tax purposes differ from those for financial reporting. The cumulative annual difference between the income taxes payable to governments and the income taxes expense reported on the income statement is included in the account Deferred Income Taxes.

Study Note

The portion of a mortgage that is due during the next year or the current operating cycle would be classified as a current liability; the portion due after the next year or the current operating cycle would be classified as a long-term liability.

Stockholders' Equity

As you know, corporations are owned by their stockholders and are separate legal entities. Exhibit 4-1 shows the stockholders' equity section of a corporation's balance sheet. This section has two parts: contributed capital and retained earnings. Generally, contributed capital is shown on a corporate balance sheet as two amounts: the par value of the issued stock, and additional paid-in capital, which is the amount paid in above par value.

Owner's Equity and Partners' Equity

Although the form of business organization does not usually affect the accounting treatment of assets and liabilities, the equity section of the balance sheet of a sole proprietorship or partnership is very different from the equity section of a corporation's balance sheet.

Sole Proprietorship The equity section of a sole proprietorship's balance sheet simply shows the capital in the owner's name at an amount equal to the net assets of the company. It might appear as follows:

Owner's Equity	
Juan Cruz, Capital	$393,732

Because in a sole proprietorship, there is no legal separation between the owner and the business, there is no need to separate contributed capital from earnings retained for use in the business. The Capital account is increased by both the owner's investments and net income. It is decreased by net losses and withdrawals of assets from the business for personal use by the owner. In this kind of business, the formality of declaring and paying dividends is not required.

In fact, the terms *owner's equity*, *proprietorship*, *capital*, and *net worth* are used interchangeably. They all stand for the owner's interest in the company. The first three terms are preferred to *net worth* because most assets are recorded at original cost rather than at current value. For this reason, the ownership section does not represent "worth." It is really a claim against the assets of the company.

Study Note

The only difference in equity between a sole proprietorship and a partnership is the number of Capital accounts.

Partnership The equity section of a partnership's balance sheet is called *partners' equity*. It is much like that of a sole proprietorship's balance sheet. It might appear as follows:

Partners' Equity		
A. J. Martin Capital	$168,750	
Juan Cruz, Capital	224,982	
Total partners' equity		$393,732

Dell's Balance Sheets

Although balance sheets generally resemble the one shown in Exhibit 4-1 for Cruz Corporation, no two companies have financial statements that are exactly alike. The balance sheet of **Dell Computer Corporation** is a good example of some of the variations. As shown in Exhibit 4-2, it provides data for two years so that users can evaluate the change from one year to the next. Note that its major classifications are similar but not identical to those of Cruz Corporation. For instance, Cruz Corporation has asset categories for investments and intangibles, and Dell has an asset category called "other non-current assets," which is a small amount of its total assets. Also note that Dell has a category called "other non-current liabilities." Because this category is listed after long-term debt, it represents longer-term liabilities, due more than one year after the balance sheet date.

EXHIBIT 4-2 Classified Balance Sheets for Dell Computer Corporation

Dell Computer Corporation
Consolidated Statements of Financial Position
(in millions)

	January 30, 2009	February 1, 2008
Assets		
Current assets:		
Cash and cash equivalents	$ 8,352	$ 7,764
Short-term investments	740	208
Accounts receivable, net	4,731	5,961
Financing receivables, net	1,712	1,732
Inventories	867	1,180
Other	3,749	3,035
Total current assets	20,151	19,880
Property, plant, and equipment, net	2,277	2,668
Investments	454	1,560
Other non-current assets	3,618	3,453
Total assets	$26,500	$27,561
Liabilities and Stockholders' Equity		
Current liabilities:		
Short-term borrowings	$ 113	$ 225
Accounts payable	8,309	11,492
Accrued and other	6,437	6,809
Total current liabilities	14,859	18,526
Long-term debt	1,898	362
Other non-current liabilities	5,472	4,844
Total liabilities	22,229	23,732
Stockholders' equity:		
Preferred stock and capital in excess of $.01 par value; shares issued and outstanding: none	—	—
Common stock and capital in excess of $.01 par value; shares authorized: 7,000; shares issued: 3,338* and 3,320*, respectively; shares outstanding: 1,944 and 2,060, respectively	11,189	10,683
Treasury stock, at cost; 919 and 785 shares, respectively	(27,904)	(25,037)
Retained earnings	20,677	18,199
Other comprehensive loss	309	(16)
Total stockholders' equity	4,271	3,829
Total liabilities and stockholders' equity	$26,500	$27,561

*Includes an immaterial amount of redeemable common stock.

Source: Adapted from Dell Computer Corporation, Form 10-K, 2009.

STOP & APPLY >

The following lettered items represent a classification scheme for a balance sheet. The numbered items are account titles. Match each account with the letter of the category in which it belongs, or indicate that it does not appear on the balance sheet.

a. Current assets
b. Investments
c. Property, plant, and equipment
d. Intangible assets
e. Current liabilities
f. Long-term liabilities
g. Stockholders' equity
h. Not on balance sheet

1. Trademark
2. Marketable Securities
3. Land Held for Future Use
4. Taxes Payable
5. Note Payable in Five Years
6. Common Stock
7. Land Used in Operations
8. Accumulated Depreciation
9. Accounts Receivable
10. Interest Expense
11. Unearned Revenue
12. Prepaid Rent

SOLUTION

1. d; 2. a; 3. b; 4. e; 5. f; 6. g; 7. c; 8. c; 9. a; 10. h; 11. e; 12. a

Forms of the Income Statement

LO4 Describe the features of multistep and single-step classified income statements.

In the income statements we have presented thus far, expenses have been deducted from revenue in a single step to arrive at net income. Here, we look at a multistep income statement and a single-step format more complex than the one we presented in earlier chapters.

Multistep Income Statement

A **multistep income statement** goes through a series of steps, or subtotals, to arrive at net income. Figure 4-3 compares the multistep income statement of a service company with that of a **merchandising company**, which buys and sells products, and a **manufacturing company**, which makes and sells products.

As you can see in Figure 4-3, in a service company's multistep income statement, the operating expenses are deducted from revenues in a single step to arrive at income from operations. In contrast, because manufacturing and merchandising companies make or buy goods for sale, they must include an additional step for the cost of goods sold. Exhibit 4-3 shows a multistep income statement for Cruz Corporation, a merchandising company.

Net Sales The first major part of a merchandising or manufacturing company's multistep income statement is **net sales**, often simply called *sales*. Net sales consist of the gross proceeds from sales (gross sales) less sales returns and allowances and any discounts allowed.

- **Gross sales** consist of total cash sales and total credit sales during an accounting period. Even though the cash may not be collected until the following accounting period, under the revenue recognition rule, revenue is recorded as earned when title for merchandise passes from seller to buyer at the time of sale.

FIGURE 4-3
The Components of Multistep Income Statements for Service and Merchandising or Manufacturing Companies

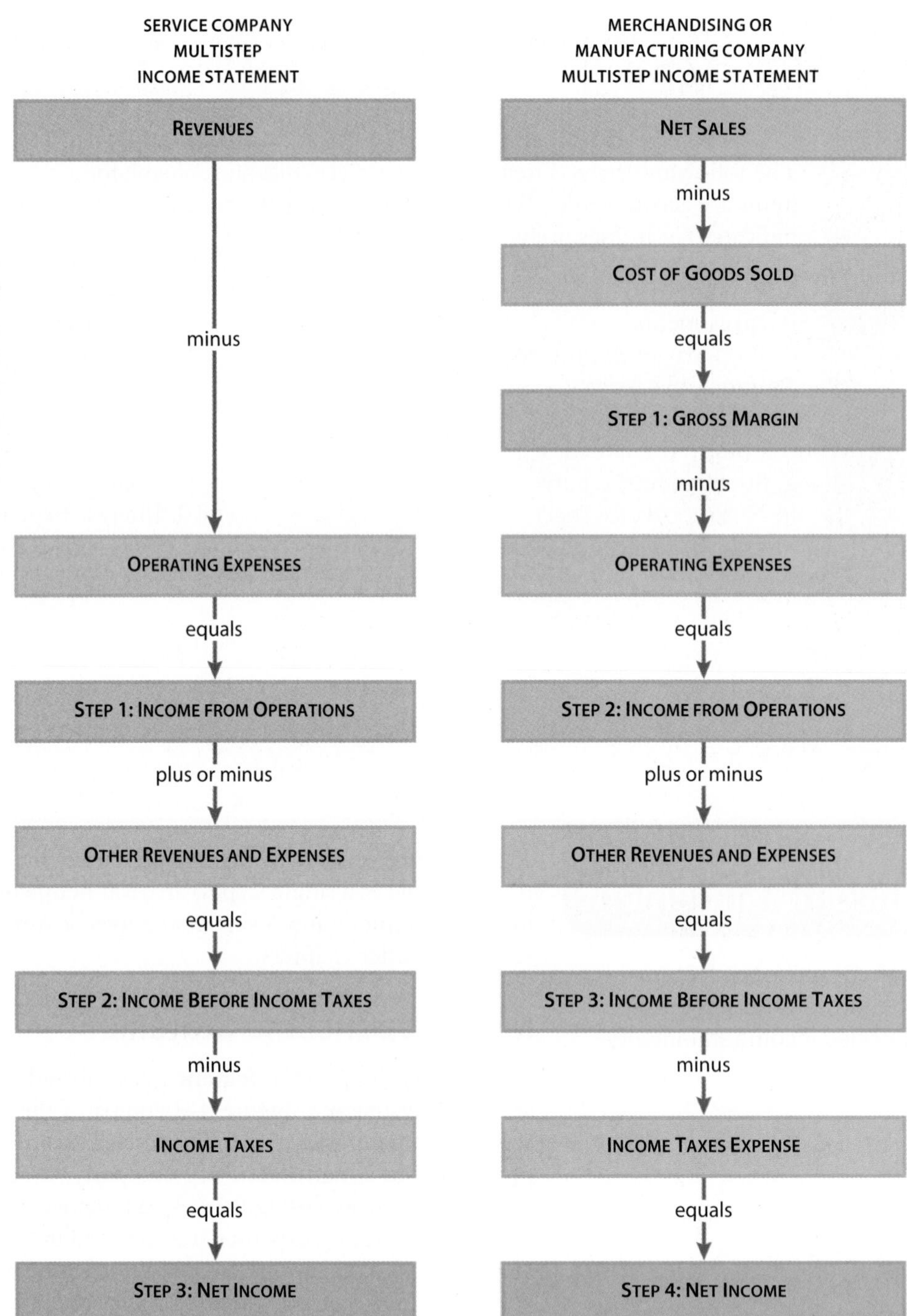

Study Note

The multistep income statement is a valuable analytical tool that is often overlooked. Analysts frequently convert a single-step statement into a multistep one because the latter separates operating sources of income from nonoperating ones. Investors want income to result primarily from operations, not from one-time gains or losses.

- **Sales returns and allowances** are cash refunds, credits on account, and discounts from selling prices made to customers who have received defective products or products that are otherwise unsatisfactory. If other discounts are given to customers, they also should be deducted from gross sales.

Managers, investors, and others often use the amount of sales and trends in sales as indicators of a firm's progress. To detect trends, they compare the net sales of different accounting periods. Increasing sales suggest growth; decreasing sales indicate the possibility of decreased future earnings and other financial problems.

EXHIBIT 4-3
Multistep Income Statement for Cruz Corporation

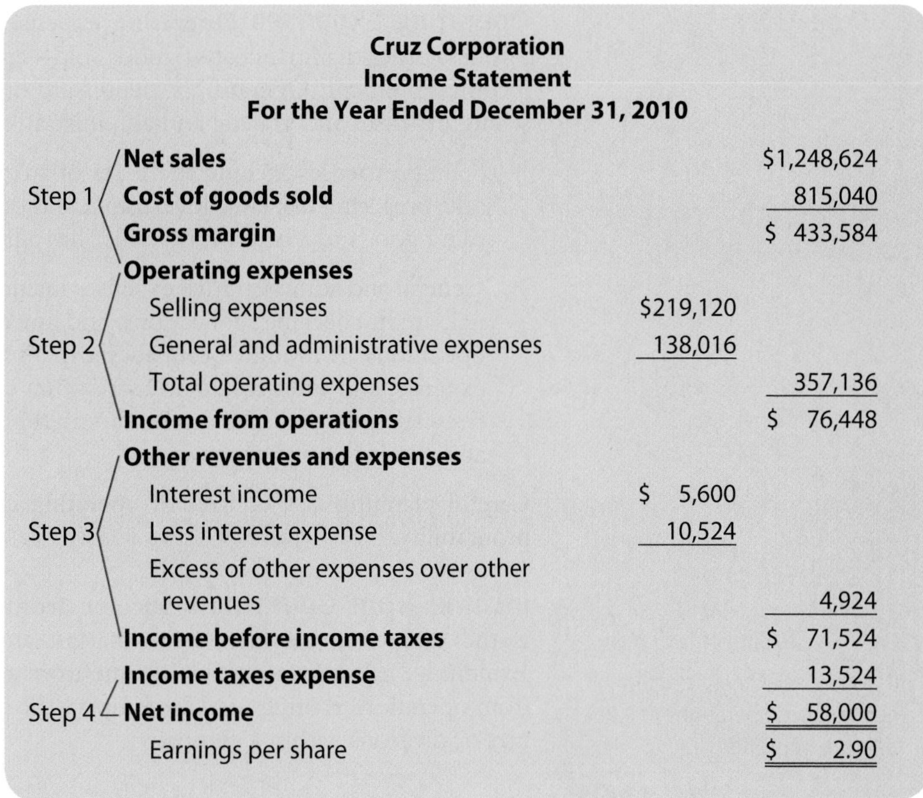

Cruz Corporation
Income Statement
For the Year Ended December 31, 2010

	Net sales		$1,248,624
Step 1	**Cost of goods sold**		815,040
	Gross margin		$ 433,584
	Operating expenses		
	Selling expenses	$219,120	
Step 2	General and administrative expenses	138,016	
	Total operating expenses		357,136
	Income from operations		$ 76,448
	Other revenues and expenses		
	Interest income	$ 5,600	
Step 3	Less interest expense	10,524	
	Excess of other expenses over other revenues		4,924
	Income before income taxes		$ 71,524
	Income taxes expense		13,524
Step 4	**Net income**		$ 58,000
	Earnings per share		$ 2.90

Cost of Goods Sold The second part of a multistep income statement for a merchandiser or manufacturer is **cost of goods sold**, also called *cost of sales*. Cost of goods sold (an expense) is the amount a merchandiser paid for the merchandise it sold during an accounting period. For a manufacturer, it is the cost of making the products it sold during an accounting period.

Study Note
Gross margin is an important measure of profitability. When it is less than operating expenses, the company has suffered a net loss from operations.

Gross Margin The third major part of a multistep income statement for a merchandiser or manufacturer is **gross margin**, or *gross profit*, which is the difference between net sales and the cost of goods sold (Step 1 in Exhibit 4-3). To be successful, companies must achieve a gross margin sufficient to cover operating expenses and provide an adequate after-tax income.

Managers are interested in both the amount and percentage of gross margin. The percentage is computed by dividing the amount of gross margin by net sales. In the case of Cruz Corporation, the amount of gross margin is $433,584, and the percentage of gross margin is 34.7 percent ($433,584 ÷ $1,248,624). This information is useful in planning business operations. For instance, management may try to increase total sales by reducing the selling price. Although this strategy reduces the percentage of gross margin, it will work if the total of items sold increases enough to raise the absolute amount of gross margin. This is the strategy followed by discount warehouse stores like **Sam's Club** and **Costco Wholesale Corporation.**

On the other hand, management may decide to keep a high gross margin from sales and try to increase sales and the amount of gross margin by increasing operating expenses, such as advertising. This is the strategy used by upscale specialty stores like **Neiman Marcus** and **Tiffany & Co.**

Other strategies to increase gross margin from sales include using better purchasing methods to reduce cost of goods sold.

Operating Expenses **Operating expenses**—expenses incurred in running a business other than the cost of goods sold—are the next major part of a multistep income statement. Operating expenses are often grouped into the categories of selling expenses and general and administrative expenses.

- Selling expenses include the costs of storing goods and preparing them for sale; preparing displays, advertising, and otherwise promoting sales; and delivering goods to a buyer if the seller has agreed to pay the cost of delivery.
- General and administrative expenses include expenses for accounting, personnel, credit checking, collections, and any other expenses that apply to overall operations. Although occupancy expenses, such as rent expense, insurance expense, and utilities expense, are often classified as general and administrative expenses, they can also be allocated between selling expenses and general and administrative expenses.

Careful planning and control of operating expenses can improve a company's profitability.

Study Note

Many financial analysts use income from operations as a key measure of profitability.

Income from Operations **Income from operations**, or *operating income*, is the difference between gross margin and operating expenses (Step 2 in Exhibit 4-3). It represents the income from a company's main business. Income from operations is often used to compare the profitability of two or more companies or divisions within a company.

Other Revenues and Expenses **Other revenues and expenses**, also called *nonoperating revenues and expenses*, are not related to a company's operating activities. This section of a multistep income statement includes revenues from investments (such as dividends and interest on stocks, bonds, and savings accounts) and interest earned on credit or notes extended to customers. It also includes interest expense and other expenses that result from borrowing money or from credit extended to the company. If a company has other kinds of revenues and expenses not related to its normal business operations, they, too, are included in this part of the income statement.

An analyst who wants to compare two companies independent of their financing methods—that is, *before* considering other revenues and expenses—would focus on income from operations.

Income Before Income Taxes **Income before income taxes** is the amount a company has earned from all activities—operating and nonoperating—before taking into account the amount of income taxes it incurred (Step 3 in Exhibit 4-3). Because companies may be subject to different income tax rates, income before income taxes is often used to compare the profitability of two or more companies or divisions within a company.

Income Taxes Expense **Income taxes expense**, also called *provision for income taxes*, represent the expense for federal, state, and local taxes on corporate income. Income taxes are shown as a separate item on the income statement. Usually, the word *expense* is not used on the statement. Income taxes do not appear on the income statements of sole proprietorships and partnerships because the individuals who own these businesses are the tax-paying units; they pay income taxes on their share of the business income. Corporations, however, must report and pay income taxes on their earnings.

Because federal, state, and local income taxes for corporations are substantial, they have a significant effect on business decisions. Current federal income tax rates for corporations vary from 15 percent to 35 percent depending on the amount of income before income taxes and other factors. Most other taxes, such as property and employment taxes, are included in operating expenses.

Net Income **Net income** (also called *net earnings*) is the final figure, or "bottom line," of an income statement. It is what remains of gross margin after operating expenses have been deducted, other revenues and expenses have been added or deducted, and income taxes have been deducted (Step 4 in Exhibit 4-3).

Net income is an important performance measure because it represents the amount of earnings that accrue to stockholders. It is the amount transferred to retained earnings from all the income that business operations have generated during an accounting period. Both managers and investors often use net income to measure a business's financial performance over the past accounting period.

Study Note

Because it is a shorthand measure of profitability, earnings per share is the performance measure most commonly cited in the financial press.

Earnings per Share **Earnings per share**, often called *net income per share*, is the net income earned on each share of common stock. Shares of stock represent ownership in corporations, and the net income per share is reported immediately below net income on the income statement. In the simplest case, it is computed by dividing the net income by the average number of shares of common stock outstanding during the year. For example, Cruz Corporation's earnings per share of $2.90 was computed by dividing the net income of $58,000 by the 20,000 shares of common stock outstanding (see the stockholders' equity section in Exhibit 4-1). Investors find the figure useful as a quick way of assessing both a company's profitability and its earnings in relation to the market price of its stock.

Dell's Income Statements

Study Note

If you encounter income statement components not covered in this chapter, refer to the index at the end of the book to find the topic and read about it.

Like balance sheets, income statements vary among companies. You will rarely, if ever, find an income statement exactly like the one we have presented for Cruz Corporation. Companies use both different terms and different structures. For example, as you can see in Exhibit 4-4, in its multistep income statement, **Dell Computer Corporation** provided three years of data for purposes of comparison.

Single-Step Income Statement

Exhibit 4-5 shows a **single-step income statement** for Cruz Corporation. In this type of statement, income before income taxes is derived in a single step by putting the major categories of revenues in the first part of the statement and the major categories of costs and expenses in the second part. Income taxes expense are shown as a separate item, as on the multistep income statement. Both the multistep form and the single-step form have advantages: the multistep form shows the components used in deriving net income, and the single-step form has the advantage of simplicity.

EXHIBIT 4-4 Multistep Income Statements for Dell Computer Corporation

Dell Computer Corporation
Consolidated Statements of Income
(in millions, except per share amounts)

	Fiscal Year Ended		
	January 30, 2009	**February 1, 2008**	**February 2, 2007**
Net revenue	$61,101	$61,133	$57,420
Cost of revenue	50,144	49,462	47,904
Gross margin	10,957	11,671	9,516
Operating expenses:			
Selling, general, and administrative	7,102	7,538	5,948
In-process research and development	2	83	—
Research, development, and engineering	663	610	498
Total operating expenses	7,767	8,231	6,446
Operating income	3,190	3,440	3,070
Investment and other income, net	134	387	275
Income before income taxes	3,324	3,827	3,345
Income tax provision	846	880	762
Net income	$ 2,478	$ 2,947	$ 2,583
Earnings per share*	$ 1.25	$ 1.33	$ 1.15

*Basic
Source: Dell Computer Corporation, Form 10-K, 2009.

EXHIBIT 4-5
Single-Step Income Statement for Cruz Corporation

Cruz Corporation
Income Statement
For the Year Ended December 31, 2010

Revenues		
Net sales		$1,248,624
Interest income		5,600
Total revenues		$1,254,224
Costs and expenses		
Cost of goods sold	$815,040	
Selling expenses	219,120	
General and administrative expenses	138,016	
Interest expense	10,524	
Total costs and expenses		1,182,700
Income before income taxes		$ 71,524
Income taxes expense		13,524
Net income		$ 58,000
Earnings per share		$ 2.90

STOP & APPLY >

A classification scheme for a multistep income statement and a list of accounts appear below. Match each account with the category in which it belongs, or indicate that it is not on the income statement.

a. Net sales
b. Cost of goods sold
c. Selling expenses
d. General and administrative expenses
e. Other revenues and expenses
f. Not on income statement

1. Sales Returns and Allowances
2. Cost of Sales
3. Dividend Income
4. Delivery Expense
5. Office Salaries Expense
6. Wages Payable
7. Sales Salaries Expense
8. Advertising Expense
9. Interest Expense
10. Commissions Expense

SOLUTION

1. a; 2. b; 3. e; 4. c; 5. d; 6. f; 7. c; 8. c; 9. e; 10. c

Using Classified Financial Statements

LO5 Use classified financial statements to evaluate liquidity and profitability.

Study Note

Accounts must be classified correctly before the ratios are computed. If they are not classified correctly, the ratios will be incorrect.

Investors and creditors base their decisions largely on their assessments of a firm's potential liquidity and profitability, and in making those assessments, they often rely on ratios. As you will see in the following pages, ratios use the components of classified financial statements to reflect how well a firm has performed in terms of maintaining liquidity and achieving profitability.

Evaluation of Liquidity

As you know, *liquidity* means having enough money on hand to pay bills when they are due and to take care of unexpected needs for cash. In an earlier chapter, we introduced the cash return on assets ratio, a liquidity measure that is computed by dividing net cash flows from operating activities by average total assets. Here, we introduce two additional measures of liquidity: working capital and the current ratio.

Working Capital **Working capital** is the amount by which current assets exceed current liabilities. It is an important measure of liquidity because current liabilities must be satisfied within one year or one operating cycle, whichever is longer, and current assets are used to pay the current liabilities. Thus, the excess of current assets over current liabilities—the working capital—is what is on hand to continue business operations.

For Cruz Corporation, working capital is computed as follows:

Current assets	$467,424
Less current liabilities	170,732
Working capital	$296,692

Working capital can be used to buy inventory, obtain credit, and finance expanded sales. Lack of working capital can lead to a company's failure.

Current Ratio The current ratio is closely related to working capital. Many bankers and other creditors believe it is a good indicator of a company's ability to pay its debts on time. The **current ratio** is the ratio of current assets to current liabilities. For Cruz Corporation, it is computed like this:

K/R

$$\text{Current Ratio} = \frac{\text{Current Assets}}{\text{Current Liabilities}} = \frac{\$467{,}424}{\$170{,}732} = 2.7$$

Thus, Cruz Corporation has \$2.70 of current assets for each \$1.00 of current liabilities. Is that good or bad? The answer requires a comparison of this year's current ratio with ratios for earlier years and with similar measures for companies in the same industry, which for Cruz Corporation is auto and home supply.

As Figure 4-4 illustrates, the average current ratio varies from industry to industry. For the advertising industry, which has no merchandise inventory, the current ratio is 1.3. The auto and home supply industry, in which companies carry large merchandise inventories, has an average current ratio of 1.9. The current ratio for Cruz Corporation, 2.7, exceeds the average for its industry.

A very low current ratio, of course, can be unfavorable, indicating that a company will not be able to pay its debts on time. But that is not always the case. For example, **McDonald's** and various other successful companies have very low current ratios because they carefully plan their cash flows.

A very high current ratio may indicate that a company is not using its assets to the best advantage. In other words, it could probably use its excess funds more effectively to increase its overall profit.

Evaluation of Profitability

Just as important as paying bills on time is *profitability*—the ability to earn a satisfactory income. As a goal, profitability competes with liquidity for managerial attention because liquid assets, although important, are not the best profit-producing resources. Cash, of course, means purchasing power, but a satisfactory

FIGURE 4-4
Average Current Ratio for Selected Industries

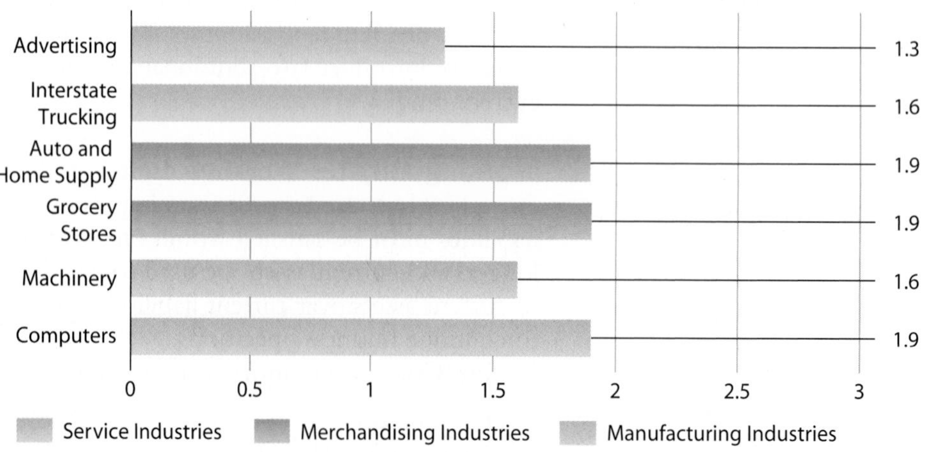

Source: Data from Dun & Bradstreet, *Industry Norms and Key Business Ratios,* 2007–2008.

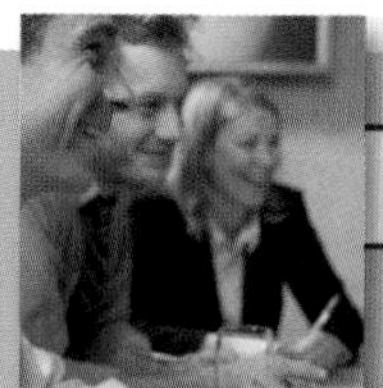

FOCUS ON BUSINESS PRACTICE

IFRS

How Has the Goal of Convergence of U.S. GAAP and IFRS Made Financial Analysis More Difficult?

Although the SEC believes that the ideal outcome of a cooperative international accounting standard-setting process would be worldwide use of a single set of high-quality accounting standards for both domestic and cross-border financial reporting, the reality is that such consistency does not now exist and will be a challenge to implement.[12] For a period of time, users of financial statements will have difficulty comparing companies' performance. Profitability measures of foreign firms that file in the United States using IFRS will not be comparable to profitability measures of companies that file using U.S. GAAP. For instance, consider the reporting earnings of the following European companies under both standards in a recent year:

(Earnings in millions of euros)

	IFRS Earnings	GAAP Earnings	% Diff.
Bayer AG	1,695	269	530.1%
Reed Elsevier	625	399	56.6
Benetton Group	125	100	25.0

Given that assets and equity for these companies are also likely to differ as well as the use of fair value in valuing assets and liabilities, all profitability ratios—profit margin, asset turnover, return of assets, and return on equity—will be affected.

profit can be made only if purchasing power is used to buy profit-producing (and less liquid) assets, such as inventory and long-term assets.

To evaluate a company's profitability, you must relate its current performance to its past performance and prospects for the future, as well as to the averages of other companies in the same industry. The following are the ratios commonly used to evaluate a company's ability to earn income:

1. Profit margin
2. Asset turnover
3. Return on assets
4. Debt to equity ratio
5. Return on equity

In previous chapters, we introduced the profit margin and return on assets ratios. Here, we review these ratios, introduce the other profitability ratios, and show their interrelationships.

Profit Margin The **profit margin** shows the percentage of each sales dollar that results in net income. It should not be confused with gross margin, which is not a ratio but rather the amount by which revenues exceed the cost of goods sold. Cruz Corporation has a profit margin of 4.6 percent. It is computed as follows:

$$\text{Profit Margin} = \frac{\text{Net Income}}{\text{Net Sales}} = \frac{\$58{,}000}{\$1{,}248{,}624} = 0.046\text{, or }4.6\%$$

Thus, on each dollar of net sales, Cruz Corporation makes almost 5 cents. A difference of 1 or 2 percent in a company's profit margin can be the difference between a fair year and a very profitable one.

Asset Turnover The **asset turnover** ratio measures how efficiently assets are used to produce sales. In other words, it shows how many dollars of sales are generated by each dollar of assets. A company with a higher asset turnover uses its assets more productively than one with a lower asset turnover.

The asset turnover ratio is computed by dividing net sales by average total assets. Average total assets are the sum of assets at the beginning of an accounting period and at the end of the period divided by 2. For example, if Cruz Corporation had assets of $594,480 at the beginning of the year, its asset turnover would be computed as follows:

$$\text{Asset Turnover} = \frac{\text{Net Sales}}{\text{Average Total Assets}}$$

$$= \frac{\$1{,}248{,}624}{(\$635{,}664 + \$594{,}480) \div 2} = \frac{\$1{,}248{,}624}{\$615{,}072} = 2.0 \text{ times}$$

Thus, Cruz Corporation would produce $2.00 in sales for each dollar invested in assets. This ratio shows a relationship between an income statement figure (net sales) and a balance sheet figure (total assets).

Return on Assets Both the profit margin and asset turnover ratios have limitations. The profit margin ratio does not consider the assets necessary to produce income, and the asset turnover ratio does not take into account the amount of income produced. The **return on assets** ratio overcomes these deficiencies by relating net income to average total assets. For Cruz Corporation, it is computed like this:

$$\text{Return on Assets} = \frac{\text{Net Income}}{\text{Average Total Assets}}$$

$$= \frac{\$58{,}000}{(\$635{,}664 + \$594{,}480) \div 2} = \frac{\$58{,}000}{\$615{,}072} = 0.094, \text{ or } 9.4\%$$

Study Note

Return on assets is one of the most widely used measures of profitability because it reflects both the profit margin and asset turnover.

For each dollar invested, Cruz Corporation's assets generate 9.4 cents of net income. This ratio indicates the income-generating strength (profit margin) of the company's resources and how efficiently the company is using all its assets (asset turnover).

Return on assets, then, combines profit margin and asset turnover:

$$\frac{\text{Net Income}}{\text{Net Sales}} \times \frac{\text{Net Sales}}{\text{Average Total Assets}} = \frac{\text{Net Income}}{\text{Average Total Assets}}$$

$$\text{Profit Margin} \times \text{Asset Turnover} = \text{Return on Assets}$$

$$4.6\% \times 2.0 \text{ times} = 9.2\%^{*}$$

Thus, a company's management can improve overall profitability by increasing the profit margin, the asset turnover, or both. Similarly, in evaluating a company's overall profitability, a financial statement user must consider how these two ratios interact to produce return on assets.

By studying Figures 4-5, 4-6, and 4-7, you can see the different ways in which various industries combine profit margin and asset turnover to produce return on assets. For instance, by comparing the return on assets for grocery stores and auto and home supply companies, you can see how they achieve that return in very different ways. The grocery store industry has a profit margin of

*The difference between 9.4 and 9.2 percent is due to rounding.

FIGURE 4-5
Average Profit Margin for Selected Industries

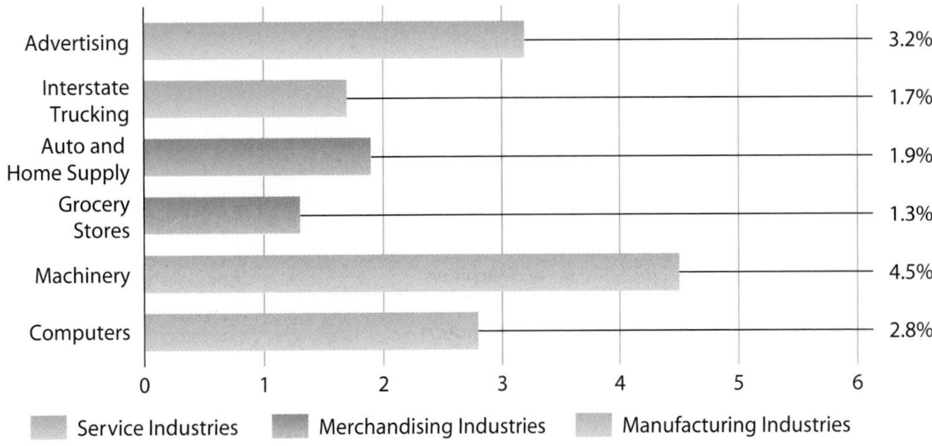

Source: Data from Dun & Bradstreet, *Industry Norms and Key Business Ratios,* 2007–2008

1.3 percent, which when multiplied by an asset turnover of 5.0 times gives a return on assets of 6.4 percent. The auto and home supply industry has a higher profit margin, 1.9 percent, and a lower asset turnover, 2.9 times, and produces a return on assets of 5.4 percent.

Cruz Corporation's profit margin of 4.6 percent is well above the auto and home supply industry's average, but its asset turnover of 2.0 times lags behind the industry average. Cruz is sacrificing asset turnover to achieve a higher profit margin. Clearly, this strategy is working, because Cruz Corporation's return on assets of 9.2 percent exceeds the industry average of 5.4 percent.

Debt to Equity Ratio Another useful measure of profitability is the **debt to equity ratio**, which shows the proportion of a company's assets that is financed by creditors and the proportion that is financed by stockholders. This ratio is computed by dividing total liabilities by stockholders' equity. The balance sheets of most public companies do not show total liabilities; a short way of determining them is to deduct the total stockholders' equity from total assets.

A debt to equity ratio of 1.0 means that total liabilities equal stockholders' equity—that half of a company's assets are financed by creditors. A ratio of 0.5 means that one-third of a company's total assets are financed by creditors. A company with a high debt to equity ratio is at risk in poor economic times because it must continue to repay creditors. Stockholders' investments, on the other hand, do not have to be repaid, and dividends can be deferred when a company suffers because of a poor economy.

FIGURE 4-6
Average Asset Turnover for Selected Industries

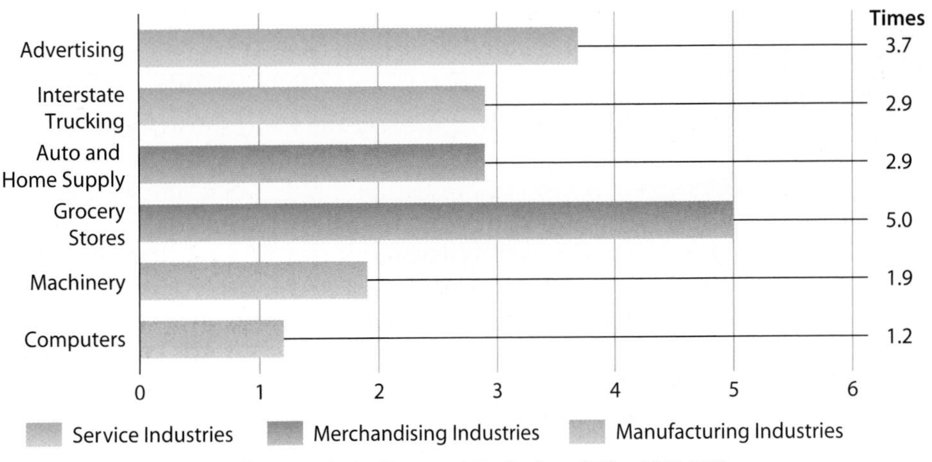

Source: Data from Dun & Bradstreet, *Industry Norms and Key Business Ratios,* 2007–2008

FIGURE 4-7
Average Return on Assets for Selected Industries

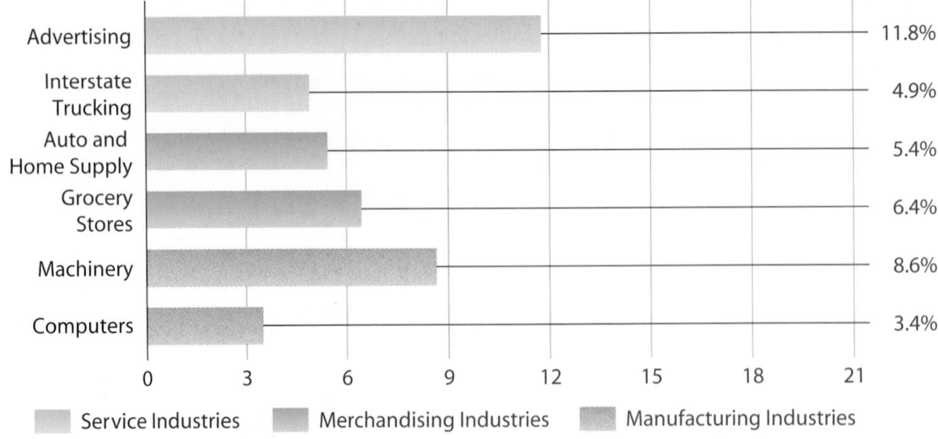

Source: Data from Dun & Bradstreet, *Industry Norms and Key Business Ratios*, 2007–2008

Cruz Corporation's debt to equity ratio is computed as follows:

$$\text{Debt to Equity Ratio} = \frac{\text{Total Liabilities}}{\text{Stockholders' Equity}} = \frac{\$241{,}932}{\$393{,}732} = 0.614, \text{ or } 61.4\%$$

The debt to equity ratio of 61.4 percent means that Cruz Corporation receives less than half its financing from creditors and more than half from investors.

The debt to equity ratio does not fit neatly into either the liquidity or profitability category. It is clearly very important to liquidity analysis because it relates to debt and its repayment. It is also relevant to profitability for two reasons:

1. Creditors are interested in the proportion of the business that is debt-financed because the more debt a company has, the more profit it must earn to ensure the payment of interest to creditors.
2. Stockholders are interested in the proportion of the business that is debt-financed because the amount of interest paid on debt affects the amount of profit left to provide a return on stockholders' investments.

The debt to equity ratio also shows how much expansion is possible through borrowing additional long-term funds.

Figure 4-8 shows that the debt to equity ratio in selected industries varies from a low of 127.8 percent in the grocery industry to a high of 266.3 percent in the advertising industry.

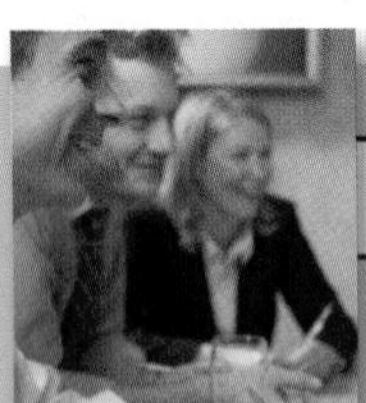

FOCUS ON BUSINESS PRACTICE

What Performance Measures Do Top Companies Use to Compensate Executives?

The boards of directors of public companies often use financial ratios to judge the performance of their top executives and to determine annual bonuses. Public companies must disclose the ratios or performance measures they use in creating these compensation plans. Studies show that the most successful companies over a sustained period of time, like **Dell Computer**, tend to focus the most on profitability measures. For instance, successful companies use earnings goals combined with sales growth 61 percent of the time compared to 43 percent for not so successful companies. Among the most common earnings goals are return on assets (19 percent for the best companies versus 5 percent for other companies) and return on equity (19 percent versus 7 percent). Clearly, successful companies set objectives that will provide incentives to management to increase profitability.[13]

FIGURE 4-8 Average Debt to Equity Ratio for Selected Industries

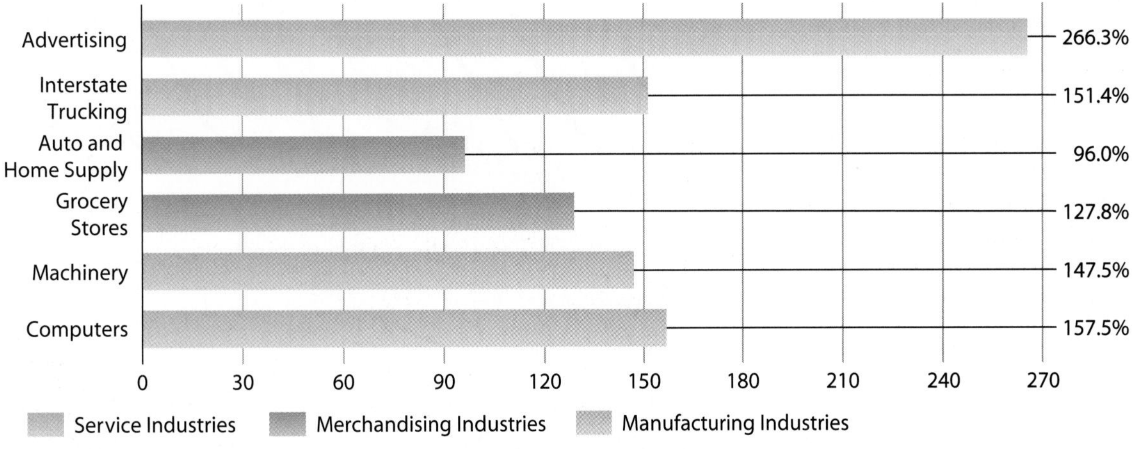

Source: Data from Dun & Bradstreet, *Industry Norms and Key Business Ratios,* 2007–2008

Return on Equity Of course, stockholders are interested in how much they have earned on their investment in the business. Their **return on equity** is measured by the ratio of net income to average stockholders' equity. Taking the ending stockholders' equity from the balance sheet and assuming that beginning stockholders' equity is $402,212, Cruz Corporation's return on equity is computed as follows:

$$\text{Return on Equity} = \frac{\text{Net Income}}{\text{Average Stockholders' Equity}}$$

$$= \frac{\$58{,}000}{(\$393{,}732 + \$402{,}212) \div 2} = \frac{\$58{,}000}{\$397{,}972} = 0.146, \text{ or } 14.6\%$$

Thus, Cruz Corporation earned 14.6 cents for every dollar invested by stockholders. Whether this is an acceptable return depends on several factors, such as how much the company earned in previous years and how much other companies in the same industry earned. As measured by return on equity, the advertising industry is the most profitable of our sample industries, with a return on equity of 47.4 percent (see Figure 4-9). Cruz Corporation's average return on equity of 14.6 percent is the same as the average of 14.6 percent for the auto and home supply industry.

FIGURE 4-9
Average Return on Equity for Selected Industries

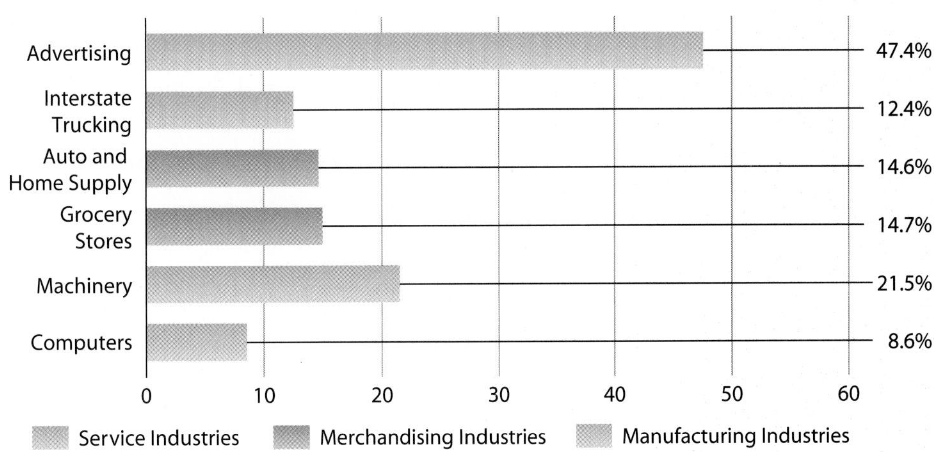

Source: Data from Dun & Bradstreet, *Industry Norms and Key Business Ratios,* 2007–2008

Return on equity—the ratio of net income to average stockholders' equity—is an important measure of a company's profitablility. It indicates how much stockholders have earned on their investments. At one time, Coca-Cola Company was among a few companies that earned a 20 percent return on equity.

Courtesy of STR/AFP/Getty Images.

STOP & APPLY >

The following end-of-year amounts are from the financial statements of Roth Company: Current assets, \$24,000; total assets, \$220,000; current liabilities, \$8,000; total liabilities, \$80,000; stockholders' equity, \$140,000; net sales, \$300,000; net income, \$18,000. One year ago total assets totaled \$180,000 and stockholders' equity totaled \$122,000. Compute the (1) current ratio, (2) profit margin, (3) asset turnover, (4) return on assets, (5) debt to equity ratio, and (6) return on equity.

SOLUTION

(1) Current ratio: $\frac{\$24{,}000}{\$8{,}000} = 3.0$ times

(2) Profit margin: $\frac{\$18{,}000}{\$300{,}000} = 0.06$, or 6.0%

(3) Asset turnover: $\frac{\$300{,}000}{(\$220{,}000 + \$180{,}000) \div 2} = 1.5$ times

(4) Return on assets: $\frac{\$18{,}000}{(\$220{,}000 + \$180{,}000) \div 2} = 0.09$, or 9.0%

(5) Debt to equity ratio: $\frac{\$80{,}000}{\$140{,}000} = 0.571$, or 57.1%

(6) Return on equity: $\frac{\$18{,}000}{(\$140{,}000 + \$122{,}000) \div 2} = 0.137$, or 13.7%

A LOOK BACK AT ▸ DELL COMPUTER CORPORATION

In the Decision Point at the beginning of the chapter, we noted that **Dell**'s management focused on the goals of growth, liquidity, and profitability. We also noted that in judging whether a company has achieved its objectives, investors, creditors, and others analyze relationships between key numbers in the company's financial statements. We asked these questions:

- How should financial statements be organized to provide the best information?
- What key measures best capture a company's financial performance?

As you saw in Exhibits 4-2 and 4-4, Dell uses a classified balance sheet and a multistep income statement to communicate its financial results to users. The Financial Highlights that we presented in the Decision Point show that the company decreased its revenues by 0.05 percent between 2008 and 2009. More significant, its operating income and net income decreased by 7 percent and 16 percent, respectively.

Using data from Dell's balance sheets and income statements, we can analyze how the company achieved this growth by computing its profitability ratios (dollars are in millions):

	2009	2008
Net Income / Net Revenue	$2,478 / $61,101	$2,947 / $61,133
Profit Margin:	4.1%	4.8%
Net Revenue / Average Total Assets	$61,101 / (\$26,500 + \$27,561) ÷ 2	$61,133 / (\$27,561 + \$25,635*) ÷ 2
	$61,101 / $27,031	$61,133 / $26,598
Asset Turnover:	2.3 times	2.3 times
Net Income / Average Total Assets	$2,478 / (\$26,500 + \$27,561) ÷ 2	$2,947 / (\$27,561 + \$25,635*) ÷ 2
	$2,478 / $27,031	$2,947 / $26,598
Return on Assets:	0.092, or 9.2%	0.111, or 11.1%

* From Dell Computer Corporation's 2008 annual report.

The decrease in net income resulted primarily from the increase in profit margin. Asset turnover did not change. The result is a slightly lower return on assets, but we can see by relating Dell's performance to the computer industry averages in Figures 4-5, 4-6, and 4-7, that Dell's profitability is clearly superior to the industry's as follows:

	Profit Margin	×	Asset Turnover	=	Return on Assets
2009:	4.1%	×	2.3 times	=	9.4%*
2008:	4.8%	×	2.3 times	=	11.0%*
Industry Average:	0.5%	×	1.6 times	=	0.8%

* The differences are due to rounding.

Dell also took advantage of debt financing to leverage its profitability into a very high return on equity, as shown by its debt to equity and return on equity ratios:

	2009	2008
Total Liabilities / Total Stockholders' Equity	$22,229 / $4,271	$23,732 / $3,829
Debt to Equity Ratio:	5.20, or 520%	6.20, or 620%
Industry Average:	1.57, or 157%	
Net Income / Average Stockholders' Equity	$2,478 / ($4,271 + $3,829) ÷ 2	$2,947 / ($3,829 + $4,439*) ÷ 2
	$2,478 / $4,050	$2,947 / $4,134
Return on Equity:	61.2%	71.3%
Industry Average:	1.7%	

* From Dell Computer Corporation's Form 10-K, 2008.

Although, Dell transformed a profit margin of 4.1 percent into a return to its stockholders of 61.2 percent—a performance much better than that of its competitors—the large amount of debt may cause difficulty for Dell in the future.

Review Problem

Using Ratios to Analyze Liquidity and Profitability

LO5

Bonalli Shoe Company has been facing increased competition from overseas shoemakers. Its total assets and stockholders' equity at the beginning of 2010 were $690,000 and $590,000, respectively. A summary of the firm's data for 2010 and 2011 follows.

	2011	**2010**
Current assets	$ 200,000	$ 170,000
Total assets	880,000	710,000
Current liabilities	90,000	50,000
Long-term liabilities	150,000	50,000
Stockholders' equity	640,000	610,000
Sales	1,200,000	1,050,000
Net income	60,000	80,000

Required

Use (1) liquidity analysis and (2) profitability analysis to document Bonalli Shoe Company's declining financial position.

Answers to Review Problem

1. Liquidity analysis:

	Current Assets	Current Liabilities	Working Capital	Current Ratio
2010	$170,000	$50,000	$120,000	3.40
2011	200,000	90,000	110,000	2.22
Decrease in working capital			$ 10,000	
Decrease in current ratio				1.18

Both working capital and the current ratio declined between 2010 and 2011 because the $40,000 increase in current liabilities ($90,000 2 $50,000) was greater than the $30,000 increase in current assets.

2. Profitability analysis:

	Net Income	Sales	Profit Margin	Average Total Assets	Asset Turnover	Return on Assets	Average Stockholders' Equity	Return on Equity
2010	$80,000	$1,050,000	7.6%	$700,000[1]	1.50	11.4%	$600,000[3]	13.3%
2011	60,000	1,200,000	5.0%	795,000[2]	1.51	7.5%	625,000[4]	9.6%
Increase (decrease)	($20,000)	$ 150,000	-2.6%	$ 95,000	0.01	-3.9%	$ 25,000	-3.7%

[1] ($710,000 + $690,000) ÷ 2
[2] ($880,000 + $710,000) ÷ 2
[3] ($610,000 + $590,000) ÷ 2
[4] ($640,000 + $610,000) ÷ 2

Net income decreased by $20,000 despite an increase in sales of $150,000 and an increase in average total assets of $95,000. Thus, the profit margin fell from 7.6 percent to 5.0 percent, and return on assets fell from 11.4 percent to 7.5 percent. Asset turnover showed almost no change and so did not contribute to the decline in profitability. The decrease in return on equity, from 13.3 percent to 9.6 percent, was not as great as the decrease in return on assets because the growth in total assets was financed mainly by debt rather than by stockholders' equity, as shown in the capital structure analysis below.

	Total Liabilities	Stockholders' Equity	Debt to Equity Ratio
2010	$100,000	$610,000	16.4%
2011	240,000	640,000	37.5%
Increase	$140,000	$ 30,000	21.1%

Total liabilities increased by $140,000, while stockholders' equity increased by $30,000. Thus, the amount of the business financed by debt in relation to the amount financed by stockholders' equity increased between 2010 and 2011.

LO1 Describe the objective of financial reporting and identify the qualitative characteristics, conventions, and ethical considerations of accounting information.

The objective of financial reporting is to provide financial information about the reporting entity that is useful to present and potential equity investors, lenders, and other creditors in making decisions in their capacity as capital providers. To be decision-useful, financial information must be useful in assessing cash flow prospects and stewardship. Because of the estimates and judgment that go into preparing financial information, such information must exhibit the qualitative characteristics of relevance and faithful representation. To be relevant, information must have predictive value, confirmative value, or both. To be faithful, financial information must be complete, neutral, and free from material error. Complementing the quality of information are the qualities of comparability, verifiability, timeliness, and understandability. It is also important for users to understand the constraints on financial information or accounting conventions used to prepare financial statements. Since the passage of the Sarbanes-Oxley Act in 2002, CEOs and CFOs have been required to certify the accuracy and completeness of their companies' financial statements.

LO2 Define and describe the conventions of *consistency, full disclosure, materiality, conservatism,* and *cost-benefit.*

Because accountants' measurements are not exact, certain conventions are applied to help users interpret financial statements. The first of these conventions is consistency. Consistency requires the use of the same accounting procedures from period to period and enhances the comparability of financial statements. Full disclosure means including all relevant information in the financial statements. The materiality convention has to do with determining the relative importance of an item. Conservatism entails using the procedure that is least likely to overstate assets and income. The cost-benefit convention holds that the benefits to be gained from providing accounting information should be greater than the costs of providing it.

LO3 Identify and describe the basic components of a classified balance sheet.

The basic components of a classified balance sheet are as follows:

Assets	Liabilities
Current assets	Current liabilities
Investments	Long-term liabilities
Property, plant, and equipment	
	Stockholders' Equity
Intangible assets	Contributed capital
(Other assets)	Retained earnings

Current assets are cash and other assets that a firm can reasonably expect to convert to cash or use up during the next year or the normal operating cycle, whichever is longer. Investments are assets, usually long term, that are not used in the normal operation of a business. Property, plant, and equipment are tangible long-term assets used in day-to-day operations. Intangible assets are long-term assets with no physical substance whose value stems from the rights or privileges they extend to stockholders.

A current liability is an obligation due to be paid or performed during the next year or the normal operating cycle, whichever is longer. Long-term liabilities are debts that fall due more than one year in the future or beyond the normal operating cycle.

The equity section of a corporation's balance sheet differs from the balance sheet of a proprietorship or partnership in that it has subcategories for contributed capital (the assets invested by stockholders) and retained earnings (stockholders' claim to assets earned from operations and reinvested in operations).

LO4 Describe the features of multistep and single-step classified income statements. Classified income statements for external reporting can be in multistep or single-step form. The multistep form arrives at income before income taxes through a series of steps; the single-step form arrives at income before income taxes in a single step. A multistep income statement usually has a separate section for other revenues and expenses.

LO5 Use classified financial statements to evaluate liquidity and profitability. In evaluating a company's liquidity and profitability, investors and creditors rely on the data provided in classified financial statements. Two measures of liquidity are working capital and the current ratio. Five measures of profitability are profit margin, asset turnover, return on assets, debt to equity ratio, and return on equity. Industry averages are useful in interpreting these ratios.

REVIEW of Concepts and Terminology

The following concepts and terms were introduced in this chapter:

Accounting conventions 212 (LO1)

Classified financial statements 217 (LO3)

Comparability 212 (LO1)

Conservatism 215 (LO2)

Consistency 213 (LO2)

Cost-benefit 216 (LO2)

Cost of goods sold 225 (LO4)

Current assets 218 (LO3)

Current liabilities 220 (LO3)

Earnings per share 227 (LO4)

Faithful representation 212 (LO1)

Full disclosure 214 (LO2)

Gross margin 225 (LO4)

Gross sales 223 (LO4)

Income before income taxes 226 (LO4)

Income from operations 226 (LO4)

Income taxes expense 226 (LO4)

Intangible assets 220 (LO3)

Investments 218 (LO3)

Long-term liabilities 220 (LO3)

Manufacturing company 223 (LO4)

Materiality 215 (LO2)

Merchandising company 223 (LO4)

Multistep income statement 223 (LO4)

Net income 227 (LO4)

Net sales 223 (LO4)

Normal operating cycle 218 (LO3)

Operating expenses 226 (LO4)

Other assets 218 (LO3)

Other revenues and expenses 226 (LO4)

Property, plant, and equipment 220 (LO3)

Qualitative characteristics 211 (LO1)

Relevance 211 (LO1)

Sales returns and allowances 224 (LO4)

Single-step income statement 227 (LO4)

Timeliness 212 (LO1)

Understandability 212 (LO1)

Verifiability 212 (LO1)

Working capital 229 (LO5)

Key Ratios

Asset turnover 232 (LO5)

Current ratio 230 (LO5)

Debt to equity ratio 233 (LO5)

Profit margin 231 (LO5)

Return on assets 232 (LO5)

Return on equity 235 (LO5)

CHAPTER ASSIGNMENTS

BUILDING Your Basic Knowledge And Skills

Short Exercises

LO1 **Objectives and Qualitative Characteristics**

SE 1. Identify each of the following statements as related to either the objective (O) of financial information or a qualitative (Q) characteristic of accounting information:

1. Information about business resources, claims to those resources, and changes in them should be provided.
2. Decision makers must be able to interpret accounting information.
3. Information that is useful in making investment and credit decisions should be furnished.
4. Accounting information must exhibit relevance and faithful representation.
5. Information useful in assessing cash flow prospects should be provided.

LO2 **Accounting Conventions**

SE 2. State which of the accounting conventions—consistency, materiality, conservatism, full disclosure, or cost-benefit—is being followed in each of the cases listed below.

1. Management provides detailed information about the company's long-term debt in the notes to the financial statements.
2. A company does not account separately for discounts received for prompt payment of accounts payable because few of these transactions occur and the total amount of the discounts is small.
3. Management eliminates a weekly report on property, plant, and equipment acquisitions and disposals because no one finds it useful.
4. A company follows the policy of recognizing a loss on inventory when the market value of an item falls below its cost but does nothing if the market value rises.
5. When several accounting methods are acceptable, management chooses a single method and follows that method from year to year.

LO3 **Classification of Accounts: Balance Sheet**

SE 3. Tell whether each of the following accounts is a current asset; an investment; property, plant, and equipment; an intangible asset; a current liability; a long-term liability; stockholders' equity; or not on the balance sheet:

1. Delivery Trucks
2. Accounts Payable
3. Note Payable (due in 90 days)
4. Delivery Expense
5. Common Stock
6. Prepaid Insurance
7. Trademark
8. Investment to Be Held Six Months
9. Income Taxes Payable
10. Factory Not Used in Business

LO3 **Classified Balance Sheet**

SE 4. Using the following accounts, prepare a classified balance sheet at year end, May 31, 2010: Accounts Payable, $800; Accounts Receivable, $1,100; Accumulated Depreciation–Equipment, $700; Cash, $200; Common Stock, $1,000; Equipment, $3,000; Franchise, $200; Investments (long-term), $500; Merchandise Inventory, $600; Notes Payable (long-term), $400; Retained Earnings, ?; Wages Payable, $100.

LO4 Classification of Accounts: Income Statement

SE 5. Tell whether each of the following accounts is part of net sales, cost of goods sold, operating expenses, or other revenues and expenses, or is not on the income statement:

1. Delivery Expense
2. Interest Expense
3. Unearned Revenue
4. Sales Returns and Allowances
5. Cost of Goods Sold
6. Depreciation Expense
7. Investment Income
8. Retained Earnings

LO4 Single-Step Income Statement

SE 6. Using the following accounts, prepare a single-step income statement at year end, May 31, 2010: Cost of Goods Sold, $840; General Expenses, $450; Income Taxes Expense, $105; Interest Expense, $210; Interest Income, $90; Net Sales, $2,400; Selling Expenses, $555. Ignore earnings per share.

LO4 Multistep Income Statement

SE 7. Using the accounts presented in **SE 6**, prepare a multistep income statement.

LO5 Liquidity Ratios

SE 8. Using the following accounts and balances taken from a year-end balance sheet, compute working capital and the current ratio:

Accounts Payable	$ 7,000
Accounts Receivable	10,000
Cash	4,000
Common Stock	20,000
Marketable Securities	2,000
Merchandise Inventory	12,000
Notes Payable (Due in Three Years)	13,000
Property, Plant, and Equipment	40,000
Retained Earnings expense	28,000

LO5 Profitability Ratios

SE 9. Using the following information from a balance sheet and an income statement, compute the (1) profit margin, (2) asset turnover, (3) return on assets, (4) debt to equity ratio, and (5) return on equity. (The previous year's total assets were $200,000, and stockholders' equity was $140,000.)

Total assets	$240,000
Total liabilities	60,000
Total stockholders' equity	180,000
Net sales	260,000
Cost of goods sold	140,000
Operating expenses	80,000
Income taxes expense	10,000

LO5 Profitability Ratios

SE 10. Assume that a company has a profit margin of 6.0 percent, an asset turnover of 3.2 times, and a debt to equity ratio of 50 percent. What are the company's return on assets and return on equity?

Exercises

LO1 LO2 LO3

Discussion Questions

E 1. Develop a brief answer to each of the following questions:

1. How do the four basic financial statements meet the stewardship objective of financial reporting?
2. What are some areas that require estimates to record transactions under the matching rule?
3. How can financial information be consistent but not comparable?
4. When might an amount be material to management but not to the CPA auditing the financial statements?

LO4 LO5

Discussion Questions

E 2. Develop a brief answer to each of the following questions:

1. Why is it that land held for future use and equipment not currently used are classified as investments rather than as property, plant, and equipment?
2. Which is the better measure of a company's performance—income from operations or net income?
3. Why is it important to compare a company's financial performance with industry standards?
4. Is the statement "Return on assets is a better measure of profitability than profit margin" true or false and why?

LO1 LO2

Financial Accounting Concepts

E 3. The lettered items below represent a classification scheme for the concepts of financial accounting. Match each numbered term in the list that follows with the letter of the category in which it belongs.

a. Decision makers (users of accounting information)
b. Business activities or entities relevant to accounting measurement
c. Objective of accounting information
d. Accounting measurement considerations
e. Accounting processing considerations
f. Qualitative characteristics
g. Accounting conventions
h. Financial statements

1. Conservatism
2. Verifiability
3. Statement of cash flows
4. Materiality
5. Faithful representation
6. Recognition
7. Cost-benefit
8. Predictive value
9. Business transactions
10. Consistency
11. Full disclosure
12. Furnishing information that is useful to investors and creditors
13. Specific business entities
14. Classification
15. Management
16. Neutrality
17. Internal accounting control
18. Valuation
19. Investors
20. Completeness
21. Relevance
22. Furnishing information that is useful in assessing cash flow prospects

LO2 **Accounting Concepts and Conventions**

E 4. Each of the statements below violates a convention in accounting. State which of the following accounting conventions is violated: comparability and consistency, materiality, conservatism, full disclosure, or cost-benefit.

1. Reports that are time-consuming and expensive to prepare are presented to the board of directors each month, even though the reports are never used.
2. A company changes its method of accounting for depreciation.
3. The company in **2** does not indicate in the financial statements that the method of depreciation was changed; nor does it specify the effect of the change on net income.
4. A company's new office building, which is built next to the company's existing factory, is debited to the Factory account because it represents a fairly small dollar amount in relation to the factory.
5. The asset account for a pickup truck still used in the business is written down to what the truck could be sold for, even though the carrying value under conventional depreciation methods is higher.

LO3 **Classification of Accounts: Balance Sheet**

E 5. The lettered items below represent a classification scheme for a balance sheet, and the numbered items in the list are account titles. Match each account with the letter of the category in which it belongs.

a. Current assets
b. Investments
c. Property, plant, and equipment
d. Intangible assets
e. Current liabilities
f. Long-term liabilities
g. Stockholders' equity
h. Not on the balance sheet

1. Patent
2. Building Held for Sale
3. Prepaid Rent
4. Wages Payable
5. Note Payable (Due in Five Years)
6. Building Used in Operations
7. Fund Held to Pay Off Long-Term Debt
8. Inventory
9. Prepaid Insurance
10. Depreciation Expense
11. Accounts Receivable
12. Interest Expense
13. Unearned Revenue
14. Short-Term Investments
15. Accumulated Depreciation
16. Retained Earnings

LO3 **Classified Balance Sheet Preparation**

E 6. The following data pertain to Branner, Inc.: Accounts Payable, \$10,200; Accounts Receivable, \$7,600; Accumulated Depreciation–Building, \$2,800; Accumulated Depreciation–Equipment, \$3,400; Bonds Payable, \$12,000; Building, \$14,000; Cash, \$6,240; Common Stock, \$5 par, 4,000 shares authorized, issued, and outstanding, \$20,000; Copyright, \$1,240; Equipment, \$30,400; Inventory, \$8,000; Investment in Corporate Securities (long-term), \$4,000; Investment in Six-Month Government Securities, \$3,280; Land, \$1,600; Additional Paid-in Capital, \$10,000; Prepaid Rent, \$240; Retained Earnings, \$17,640; and Revenue Received in Advance, \$560.

Prepare a classified balance sheet at December 31, 2010.

LO4 Classification of Accounts: Income Statement

E 7. Using the following classification scheme for a multistep income statement, match each account with the letter of the category in which it belongs.

a. Net sales
b. Cost of goods sold
c. Selling expenses
d. General and administrative expenses
e. Other revenues and expenses
f. Not on the income statement

1. Sales Returns and Allowances
2. Cost of Goods Sold
3. Dividend Income
4. Advertising Expense
5. Office Salaries Expense
6. Freight Out Expense
7. Prepaid Insurance
8. Utilities Expense
9. Sales Salaries Expense
10. Rent Expense
11. Depreciation Expense–Delivery Equipment
12. Income Taxes Payable
13. Interest Expense

LO4 Preparation of Income Statements

E 8. The following data pertain to a corporation: net sales, $202,500; cost of goods sold, $110,000; selling expenses, $45,000; general and administrative expenses, $30,000; income taxes expense, $3,750; interest expense, $2,000; interest income, $1,500; and common stock outstanding, 25,000 shares.

1. Prepare a single-step income statement.
2. Prepare a multistep income statement.

LO4 Multistep Income Statement

E 9. A single-step income statement appears below. Present the information in a multistep income statement, and indicate what insights can be obtained from the multistep form as opposed to the single-step form.

Vision Company
Income Statement
For the Year Ended December 31, 2010

Revenues		
Net sales		$1,207,132
Interest income		5,720
Total revenues		$1,212,852
Costs and expenses		
Cost of goods sold	$787,080	
Selling expenses	203,740	
General and administrative expenses	100,688	
Interest expense	13,560	
Total costs and expenses		1,105,068
Income before income taxes		$ 107,784
Income taxes expense		24,000
Net income		$ 83,784
Earnings per share		$ 8.38

LO5 **Liquidity Ratios**

E 10. The accounts and balances that follow are from the ledger of Fields Corporation. Compute the (1) working capital and (2) current ratio.

Accounts Payable	$ 6,640
Accounts Receivable	4,080
Cash	600
Current Portion of Long-Term Debt	4,000
Long-Term Investments	8,320
Marketable Securities	5,040
Merchandise Inventory	10,160
Notes Payable (90 days)	6,000
Notes Payable (2 years)	16,000
Notes Receivable (90 days)	10,400
Notes Receivable (2 years)	8,000
Prepaid Insurance	160
Property, Plant, and Equipment	48,000
Property Taxes Payable	500
Retained Earnings	22,640
Salaries Payable	340
Supplies	140
Unearned Revenue	300

LO5 **Profitability Ratios**

E 11. The following end-of-year amounts are from the financial statements of Jang's Corporation: total assets, $213,000; total liabilities, $86,000; stockholders' equity, $127,000; net sales, $391,000; cost of goods sold, $233,000; operating expenses, $94,000; income taxes expense, $17,000; and dividends, $20,000. During the past year, total assets increased by $37,500. Total stockholders' equity was affected only by net income and dividends. Compute the (1) profit margin, (2) asset turnover, (3) return on assets, (4) debt to equity ratio, and (5) return on equity.

LO5 **Liquidity and Profitability**

E 12. The simplified balance sheet and income statement for a corporation follow.

Balance Sheet
December 31, 2010

Assets		Liabilities	
Current assets	$ 55,000	Current liabilities	$ 25,000
Investments	10,000	Long-term liabilities	30,000
Property, plant, and equipment	146,500	Total liabilities	$ 55,000
Intangible assets	18,500	**Stockholders' Equity**	
		Common stock	$100,000
		Retained earnings	75,000
		Total stockholders' equity	$175,000
Total assets	$230,000	Total liabilities and stockholders equity	$230,000

Income Statement
For the Year Ended December 31, 2010

Net sales	$415,000
Cost of goods sold	250,000
Gross margin	$165,000
Operating expenses	130,000
Income before income taxes	$ 35,000
Income taxes expense	5,000
Net income	$ 30,000

Total assets and stockholders' equity at the beginning of 2010 were $180,000 and $140,000, respectively.

1. Compute the following liquidity measures: (a) working capital and (b) current ratio.
2. Compute the following profitability measures: (a) profit margin, (b) asset turnover, (c) return on assets, (d) debt to equity ratio, and (e) return on equity.

Problems

LO2 Accounting Conventions

P 1. In each case below, accounting conventions may have been violated.

1. After careful study, Lipski Company, which has offices in 40 states, has determined that its method of depreciating office furniture should be changed. The new method is adopted for the current year, and the change is noted in the financial statements.
2. In the past, Gomez Corporation has recorded operating expenses in general accounts (e.g., Salaries Expense and Utilities Expense). Management has determined that despite the additional recordkeeping costs, the company's income statement should break down each operating expense into its components of selling expense and administrative expense.
3. Param Corporation's auditor discovered that a company official had authorized the payment of a $1,200 bribe to a local official. Management argued that because the item was so small in relation to the size of the company ($1,700,000 in sales), the illegal payment should not be disclosed.
4. K & T Bookstore built a small addition to its main building to house a new computer games section. Because no one could be sure that the computer games section would succeed, the accountant took a conservative approach and recorded the addition as an expense.
5. Since it began operations ten years ago, Chang Company has used the same generally accepted inventory method. The company does not disclose in its financial statements what inventory method it uses.

Required

User insight ▶ In each of these cases, identify the accounting convention that applies, state whether or not the treatment is in accord with the convention and generally accepted accounting principles, and briefly explain why.

LO4 **Forms of the Income Statement**

P 2. The income statements that follow are for Doug's Hardware Corporation.

Doug's Hardware Corporation
Income Statements
For the Years Ended July 31, 2011 and 2010

	2011	2010
Revenues		
Net sales	$464,200	$388,466
Interest income	1,420	750
Total revenues	$465,620	$389,126
Costs and expenses		
Cost of goods sold	$243,880	$198,788
Selling expenses	95,160	55,644
General and administrative expenses	90,840	49,286
Interest expense	5,600	1,100
Total costs and expenses	$435,480	$304,818
Income before income taxes	$ 30,140	$ 84,398
Income taxes expense	8,000	21,250
Net income	$ 22,140	$ 63,148
Earnings per share	$ 2.21	$ 6.31

Required

1. From the information provided, prepare a multistep income statement for 2010 and 2011 showing percentages of net sales for each component.
2. User insight ▶ Did income from operations increase or decrease from 2010 to 2011? Write a short explanation of why this change occurred.
3. User insight ▶ What effect did other revenues and expenses have on the change in income before income taxes? What action by Doug's Hardware's management probably accounted for this change?

LO3 LO5 **Classified Balance Sheet**

P 3. The following information is from the June 30, 2010, post-closing trial balance of Mike's Hardware Corporation.

Account Name	Debit	Credit
Cash	$ 32,000	
Short-Term Investments	33,000	
Notes Receivable	10,000	
Accounts Receivable	276,000	
Merchandise Inventory	145,000	
Prepaid Rent	1,600	
Prepaid Insurance	4,800	
Sales Supplies	1,280	
Office Supplies	440	
Deposit for Future Advertising	3,680	
Building, Not in use	49,600	
Land	23,400	

(*continued*)

Account Name	Debit	Credit
Delivery Equipment	$41,200	
Accumulated Depreciation–Delivery Equipment		$ 28,400
Trademark	4,000	
Accounts Payable		114,600
Salaries Payable		5,200
Interest Payable		1,840
Long-Term Notes Payable		80,000
Common Stock ($1.10 par value)		22,000
Additional Paid-in Capital		160,000
Retained Earnings		213,960

Required

1. From the information provided, prepare a classified balance sheet for Mike's Hardware Corporation.
2. Compute Mike's Hardware's current ratio and debt to equity ratio.

User insight ▶ 3. As a user of the classified balance sheet, why would you want to know the current ratio or the debt to equity ratio?

LO5 **Liquidity and Profitability**

P 4. Arun Products has had poor operating results for the past two years. As the accountant for Arun Products Corporation, you have the following information available to you:

	2010	2009
Current assets	$ 22,500	$ 17,500
Total assets	72,500	55,000
Current liabilities	10,000	5,000
Long-term liabilities	10,000	—
Stockholders' equity	52,500	50,000
Net sales	131,000	100,000
Net income	8,000	5,500

Total assets and stockholders' equity at the beginning of 2009 were $45,000 and $40,000, respectively.

Required

User insight ▶ 1. Compute the following measures of liquidity for 2009 and 2010: (a) working capital and (b) current ratio. Comment on the differences between the years.

User insight ▶ 2. Compute the following measures of profitability for 2009 and 2010: (a) profit margin, (b) asset turnover, (c) return on assets, (d) debt to equity ratio, and (e) return on equity. Comment on the change in performance from 2009 to 2010.

LO3 LO4 LO5 **Classified Financial Statement Preparation and Analysis**

KA KLOOSTER & ALLEN

P 5. Jimenez Corporation sells outdoor sports equipment. At the December 31, 2009, year end, the following financial information was available from the income statement: administrative expenses, $80,800; cost of goods sold, $350,420; income taxes expense, $7,000; interest expense, $22,640; interest income, $2,800; net sales, $714,390; and selling expenses, $220,200.

The following information was available from the balance sheet (after closing entries were made): accounts payable, $32,600; accounts receivable, $104,800; accumulated depreciation–delivery equipment, $17,100; accumulated depreciation–store fixtures, $42,220; cash, $28,400; common stock, $0.50 par value, 20,000 shares authorized, issued, and outstanding, $10,000; delivery equipment, $88,500; inventory, $136,540; investment in securities (long-term), $56,000; investment in U.S. government securities (short-term), $39,600; long-term notes payable, $100,000; additional paid-in capital, $90,000; retained earnings, ending balance, $259,300, beginning balance, $283,170; notes payable (short-term), $50,000; prepaid expenses (short-term), $5,760; and store fixtures, $141,620.

Total assets and total stockholders' equity at December 31, 2008, were $524,400 and $383,170, respectively, and dividends for the year were $60,000.

Required

1. From the information above, prepare (a) an income statement in single-step form, (b) a statement of retained earnings, and (c) a classified balance sheet.

User insight ▶

2. From the statements you have prepared, compute the following measures: (a) working capital and current ratio (for liquidity); and (b) profit margin, asset turnover, return on assets, debt to equity ratio, and return on equity (for profitability).

User insight ▶

3. Using the industry averages for the auto and home supply business in Figures 4-4 through 4-9 in this chapter, determine whether Jimenez Corporation needs to improve its liquidity or its profitability. Explain your answer, making recommendations as to specific areas on which Jimenez Corporation should concentrate.

Alternate Problems

LO2 Accounting Conventions

P 6. In each case below, accounting conventions may have been violated.

1. Rhonda's Manufacturing Company uses the cost method for computing the balance sheet amount of inventory unless the market value of the inventory is less than the cost, in which case the market value is used. At the end of the current year, the market value is $151,000 and the cost is $162,000. Rhonda's uses the $151,000 figure to compute current assets because management believes it is the more cautious approach.
2. Goldman Company has annual sales of $10,000,000. It follows the practice of recording any items costing less than $250 as expenses in the year purchased. During the current year, it purchased several chairs for the executive conference room at $245 each, including freight. Although the chairs were expected to last for at least ten years, they were recorded as an expense in accordance with company policy.
3. Helman Company closed its books on October 31, 2009, before preparing its annual report. On November 3, 2009, a fire destroyed one of the company's two factories. Although the company had fire insurance and would not suffer a loss on the building, a significant decrease in sales in 2009 was expected because of the fire. The fire damage was not reported in the 2009 financial statements because the fire had not affected the company's operations during that year.
4. Cure Drug Company spends a substantial portion of its profits on research and development. The company had been reporting its $6,000,000 expenditure for research and development as a lump sum, but management recently decided to begin classifying the expenditures by project, even though its recordkeeping costs will increase.
5. During the current year, CNC Company changed from one generally accepted method of accounting for inventories to another method.

Required

User insight ▶ For each of these cases, identify the accounting convention that applies, state whether or not the treatment is in accord with the convention and GAAP, and briefly explain why.

LO4 **Forms of the Income Statement**

P 7. Oak Nursery Corporation's single-step income statements for 2010 and 2009 follow.

Oak Nursery Corporation
Income Statements
For the Years Ended April 30, 2010 and 2009

	2010	**2009**
Revenues		
Net sales	$525,932	$475,264
Interest income	1,800	850
Total revenues	$527,732	$476,114
Costs and expenses		
Cost of goods sold	$234,948	$171,850
Selling expenses	161,692	150,700
General and administrative expenses	62,866	42,086
Interest expense	3,600	1,700
Total costs and expenses	$463,106	$366,336
Income before income taxes	$ 64,626	$109,778
Income taxes expense	16,000	28,600
Net income	$ 48,626	$ 81,178
Earnings per share	$ 2.43	$ 4.06

Oak Nursery Corporation had 20,000 shares of common stock outstanding during both 2010 and 2009.

Required

1. From the information provided, prepare multistep income statements for 2009 and 2010 showing percentages of net sales for each component.

User insight ▶ 2. Did income from operations increase or decrease from 2009 to 2010? Write a short explanation of why this change occurred.

User insight ▶ 3. What effect did other revenues and expenses have on the change in income before income taxes? What action by management probably caused this change?

LO5 **Liquidity and Profitability**

P 8. A summary of data from the income statements and balance sheets for Roman Construction Supply, Inc., for 2010 and 2009 appears below.

	2010	2009
Current assets	$ 183,000	$ 155,000
Total assets	1,160,000	870,000
Current liabilities	90,000	60,000
Long-term liabilities	400,000	290,000
Stockholders' equity	670,000	520,000
Net sales	2,300,000	1,740,000
Net income	150,000	102,000

Total assets and stockholders' equity at the beginning of 2009 were $680,000 and $420,000, respectively.

Required

User insight ▶ 1. Compute the following liquidity measures for 2009 and 2010: (a) working capital and (b) current ratio. Comment on the differences between the years.

User insight ▶ 2. Compute the following measures of profitability for 2009 and 2010: (a) profit margin, (b) asset turnover, (c) return on assets, (d) debt to equity ratio, and (e) return on equity. Comment on the change in performance from 2009 to 2010.

LO3 LO5 **Classified Balance Sheet**

P 9. The following information is from the June 30, 2011, post-closing trial balance of Beauty Supplies Corporation.

Account Name	Debit	Credit
Cash	$ 16,000	
Short-Term Investments	16,500	
Notes Receivable	5,000	
Accounts Receivable	138,000	
Merchandise Inventory	72,500	
Prepaid Rent	800	
Prepaid Insurance	2,400	
Sales Supplies	640	
Office Supplies	220	
Deposit for Future Advertising	1,840	
Building, Not in Use	24,800	
Land	11,700	
Delivery Equipment	20,600	
Accumulated Depreciation–Delivery Equipment		$ 14,200
Trademark	2,000	
Accounts Payable		57,300
Salaries Payable		2,600
Interest Payable		920
Long-Term Notes Payable		40,000
Common Stock ($1.10 par value)		11,000
Additional Paid-in Capital		80,000
Retained Earnings		106,980

Required

1. From the information provided, prepare a classified balance sheet for Beauty Supplies Corporation.
2. Compute Beauty Supplies' current ratio and debt to equity ratio.
3. User insight ▶ As a user of the classified balance sheet, why would you want to know the current ratio or the debt to equity ratio?

LO3 LO4 LO5

Classified Financial Statement Preparation and Analysis

P 10. Cubicle Corporation is in the machinery business. At the December 31, 2011, year end, the following financial information was available from the income statement: administrative expenses, $161,600; cost of goods sold, 700,840; income taxes expense, $14,000; interest expense, $45,280; interest income, $5,600; net sales, $1,428,780; and selling expenses, $440,400.

The following information was available from the balance sheet (after closing entries were made): accounts payable, $65,200; accounts receivable, $209,600; accumulated depreciation–delivery equipment, $34,200; accumulated depreciation–store fixtures, $84,440; cash, $56,800; common stock, $1 par value, 20,000 shares authorized, issued, and outstanding, $20,000; delivery equipment, $177,000; inventory, $273,080; investment in securities (long-term), $112,000; investment in U.S. government securities (short-term), $79,200; long-term notes payable, $200,000; additional paid-in capital, $180,000; retained earnings, ending balance, $518,600, beginning balance, $566,340; notes payable (short-term), $100,000; prepaid expenses (short-term), $11,520; and store fixtures, $283,240.

Total assets and total stockholders' equity at December 31, 2010, were $1,048,800 and $766,340, respectively, and dividends for the year were $120,000.

Required

1. From the information above, prepare (a) an income statement in single-step form, (b) a statement of retained earnings, and (c) a classified balance sheet.
2. User insight ▶ From the statements you have prepared, compute the following measures: (a) working capital and current ratio (for liquidity); and (b) profit margin, asset turnover, return on assets, debt to equity ratio, and return on equity (for profitability).
3. User insight ▶ Using the industry averages for the auto and home supply business in Figures 4-4 through 4-9 in this chapter, determine whether Cubicle Corporation needs to improve its liquidity or its profitability. Explain your answer, making recommendations as to specific areas on which Cubicle Corporation should concentrate.

ENHANCING Your Knowledge, Skills, and Critical Thinking

LO2

Consistency and Full Disclosure

C 1. City Parking, which operates a seven-story parking building in downtown Pittsburgh, has a calendar year end. It serves daily and hourly parkers, as well as monthly parkers who pay a fixed monthly rate in advance. The company traditionally has recorded all cash receipts as revenues when received. Most monthly parkers pay in full during the month prior to that in which they have the right to park. The company's auditors have said that beginning in 2009, the company should consider recording the cash receipts from monthly parking on an accrual basis, crediting Unearned Revenues. Total cash receipts for 2009 were $1,250,000, and the cash receipts received in 2009 and applicable to January 2010 were $62,500. Discuss the relevance of the accounting conventions of consistency, full disclosure, and materiality to the decision to record the monthly parking revenues on an accrual basis.

LO2 **Materiality**

C 2. Kubicki, Inc., operates a chain of designer bags and shoes stores in the Houston area. This year the company achieved annual sales of $75 million, on which it earned a net income of $3 million. At the beginning of the year, management implemented a new inventory system that enabled it to track all purchases and sales. At the end of the year, a physical inventory reveals that the actual inventory was $120,000 below what the new system indicated it should be. The inventory loss, which probably resulted from shoplifting, is reflected in a higher cost of goods sold. The problem concerns management but seems to be less important to the company's auditors. What is materiality? Why might the inventory loss concern management more than it does the auditors? Do you think the amount of inventory loss is material?

LO5 **Comparison of Profitability**

C 3. Two of the largest chains of grocery stores in the United States are **Albertson's Inc.** and the **Great Atlantic & Pacific Tea Company (A&P).** Albertson's is now part of **Supervalue, Inc.** In fiscal 2008, Supervalue had a net loss of $2,855 million, and A&P had a net loss of $140 million. It is difficult to judge which company is more profitable from those figures alone because they do not take into account the relative sales, sizes, and investments of the companies. Data (in millions) to complete a financial analysis of the two companies follow:[14]

	Supervalue	A&P
Net sales	$44,564	$9,516
Beginning total assets	21,062	3,644
Ending total assets	17,604	3,546
Beginning total liabilities	15,109	3,226
Ending total liabilities	15,023	3,278
Beginning stockholders' equity	5,953	418
Ending stockholders' equity	2,581	268

1. Determine which company was more profitable by computing profit margin, asset turnover, return on assets, debt to equity ratio, and return on equity for the two companies. Comment on the relative profitability of the two companies.
2. What do the ratios tell you about the factors that go into achieving an adequate return on assets in the grocery industry? For industry data, refer to Figures 4-4 through 4-9 in this chapter.
3. How would you characterize the use of debt financing in the grocery industry and the use of debt by these two companies?

LO5 **Financial Analysis for Loan Decision**

C 4. Krys Ciskowski was recently promoted to loan officer at First Federal Bank. He has authority to issue loans up to $75,000 without approval from a higher bank official. This week two small companies, Zavala Supplies, Inc., and Shoji Fashions, Inc., have each submitted a proposal for a six-month, $75,000 loan. To prepare financial analyses of the two companies, Ciskowski has obtained the following information.

Zavala Supplies, Inc., is a local lumber and home improvement company. Because sales have increased so much during the past two years, Zavala Supplies has had to raise additional working capital, especially as represented by receivables and inventory. The $75,000 loan is needed to assure the company of enough working capital for the next year. Zavala Supplies began the year with total assets of $1,110,000 and stockholders' equity of $390,000. During the past year, the company had a net income of $60,000 on net sales of $1,140,000. Zavala Supplies' unclassified balance sheet as of the current date appears as follows:

Assets		Liabilities and Stockholders' Equity	
Cash	$ 45,000	Accounts payable	$ 300,000
Accounts receivable (net)	225,000	Notes payable (short term)	150,000
Inventory	375,000	Notes payable (long term)	300,000
Land	75,000	Common stock	375,000
Buildings (net)	375,000	Retained earnings	75,000
Equipment (net)	105,000	Total liabilities and stockholders' equity	$1,200,000
Total assets	$1,200,000		

Shoji Fashions, Inc., has for three years been a successful clothing store for young professional women. The leased store is located in the downtown financial district. Shoji's loan proposal asks for $75,000 to pay for stocking a new line of women's suits during the coming season. At the beginning of the year, the company had total assets of $300,000 and total stockholders' equity of $171,000. Over the past year, the company earned a net income of $54,000 on net sales of $720,000. The firm's unclassified balance sheet at the current date is as follows:

Assets		Liabilities and Stockholders' Equity	
Cash	$ 15,000	Accounts payable	$120,000
Accounts receivable (net)	75,000	Accrued liabilities	15,000
Inventory	202,500	Common stock	75,000
Prepaid expenses	7,500	Retained earnings	150,000
Equipment (net)	60,000	Total liabilities and stockholders' equity	$360,000
Total assets	$360,000		

1. Prepare a financial analysis of each company's liquidity before and after receiving the proposed loan. Also compute profitability ratios before and after, as appropriate. Write a brief summary of the effect of the proposed loan on each company's financial position.
2. Assume you are Krys Ciskowski and can make a loan to only one of these companies. Write a memorandum to the bank's vice president outlining your decision and naming the company to which you would lend $75,000. Be sure to state what positive and negative factors could affect each company's ability to pay back the loan in the next year. Also indicate what other information of a financial or nonfinancial nature would be helpful in making a final decision.

LO3 LO4 LO5

Classified Balance Sheet and Multistep Income Statement

C 5. Refer to the **CVS** annual report in the Supplement to Chapter 1 to answer the following questions.

1. Consolidated balance sheets:
   a. Did the amount of working capital increase or decrease from 2007 to 2008? By how much?
   b. Did the current ratio improve from 2007 to 2008?
   c. Does the company have long-term investments or intangible assets?
   d. Did the debt to equity ratio of CVS change from 2007 to 2008?
   e. What is the contributed capital for 2008? How does contributed capital compare with retained earnings?
2. Consolidated statements of operations:
   a. Does CVS use a multistep or single-step income statement?
   b. Is it a comparative statement?
   c. What is the trend of net earnings?
   d. How significant are income taxes for CVS?

LO5

Financial Analysis

C 6. Compare the financial performance of **CVS** and **Southwest Airlines Co.** on the basis of liquidity and profitability for 2008 and 2007. Use the following ratios: working capital, current ratio, debt to equity ratio, profit margin, asset turnover, return on assets, and return on equity. In 2006, total assets and total stockholders' equity for CVS were $20,574.1 million and $9,917.6 million, respectively. Southwest's total assets were $13,460 million, and total stockholders' equity was $6,449 million in 2006. Comment on the relative performance of the two companies. In general, how does Southwest's performance compare to CVS's with respect to liquidity and profitability? What distinguishes Southwest's profitability performance from that of CVS?

LO1

Ethics and Financial Reporting

C 7. Bell Systems, located outside Atlanta, develops computer software and licenses it to financial institutions. The firm uses an aggressive accounting method that records revenues from the software it has developed on a percentage of completion basis. Consequently, revenue for partially completed projects is recognized based on the portion of the project that has been completed. If a project is 50 percent completed, then 50 percent of the contracted revenue is recognized. In 2010, preliminary estimates for a $7 million project are that the project is 75 percent complete. Because the estimate of completion is a matter of judgment, management asks for a new report showing the project to be 90 percent complete. The change will enable senior managers to meet their financial goals for the year and thus receive substantial year-end bonuses. Do you think management's action is ethical? If you were the company controller and were asked to prepare the new report, would you do it? What action would you take?

LO5

Annual Reports and Financial Analysis

C 8. Select a large, well-known company and access its annual report online. In the annual report of the company you have chosen, find the four basic financial statements and the notes to the financial statements. Perform a liquidity analysis, including the calculation of working capital and the current ratio. Perform a profitability analysis, calculating profit margin, asset turnover, return on assets, debt to equity ratio, and return on equity. Be prepared to present your findings in class.

SUPPLEMENT TO CHAPTER

4

The Annual Report Project

Many instructors assign a term project that requires reading and analyzing an annual report. The Annual Report Project described here has been successful in our classes. It may be used with the annual report of any company, including **CVS Caremark Corporation's** annual report and the financial statements from **Southwest Airlines Co.'s** annual report that appear in the Supplement to Chapter 1.

The extent to which financial analysis is required depends on the point in the course at which the Annual Report Project is assigned. Instruction 3E, below, provides several options.

Instructions

1. Choose a company, and obtain its most recent annual report online or through your library or another source.
2. Use the Internet or your library to locate at least two articles about the company and the industry in which it operates. Read the articles, as well as the annual report, and summarize your findings. In addition, access the company's Internet home page directly or through the Needles Accounting Resource Center Website (*www.cengage.com/accounting/needles*). Review the company's products and services and its financial information. Summarize what you have learned.
3. Your analysis should consist of five or six double-spaced pages organized according to the following outline:

A. Introduction

Identify the company by writing a summary that includes the following elements:

- Name of the chief executive officer
- Location of the home office
- Ending date of latest fiscal year
- Description of the company's principal products or services
- Main geographic area of activity
- Name of the company's independent accountants (auditors). In your own words, explain what the accountants said about the company's financial statements.
- The most recent price of the company's stock and its dividend per share. Be sure to provide the date for this information.

B. Industry Situation and Company Plans

Describe the industry and its outlook. Then summarize the company's future plans based on what you learned from the annual report and your other research.

Be sure to include any relevant information from management's letter to the stockholders.

C. Financial Statements

Income Statement: Is the format most like a single-step or multistep format? Determine gross profit, income from operations, and net income for the last two years. Comment on the increases or decreases in these amounts.

Balance Sheet: Show that Assets = Liabilities + Stockholders' Equity for the past two years.

Statement of Cash Flows: Indicate whether the company's cash flows from operations for the past two years were more or less than net income. Also indicate whether the company is expanding through investing activities. Identify the company's most important source of financing. Overall, has cash increased or decreased over the past two years?

D. Accounting Policies

Describe the company's significant accounting policies, if any, relating to revenue recognition, cash, short-term investments, merchandise inventories, and property and equipment. Identify the topics of the notes to the financial statements.

E. Financial Analysis

For the past two years, calculate and discuss the significance of the following ratios:

Option (a): Basic (After Completing Chapter 4)

Liquidity Ratios
- Working capital
- Current ratio

Profitability Ratios
- Profit margin
- Asset turnover
- Return on assets
- Debt to equity ratio
- Return on equity

Option (b): Basic with Enhanced Liquidity Analysis (After Completing Chapter 8)

Liquidity Ratios
- Working capital
- Current ratio
- Receivable turnover
- Days' sales uncollected
- Inventory turnover
- Days' inventory on hand
- Payables turnover
- Days' payable
- Operating cycle
- Financing period

Profitability Ratios
- Profit margin
- Asset turnover
- Return on assets
- Debt to equity ratio
- Return on equity

Option (c): Comprehensive (After Completing Chapter 28)

Liquidity Ratios
- Working capital
- Current ratio
- Receivable turnover
- Days' sales uncollected
- Inventory turnover
- Days' inventory on hand
- Payables turnover
- Days' payable
- Operating cycle
- Financing period

Profitability Ratios
- Profit margin
- Asset turnover
- Return on assets
- Return on equity

Long-Term Solvency Ratios
- Debt to equity ratio
- Interest coverage

Cash Flow Adequacy
- Cash flow yield
- Cash flows to sales
- Cash flows to assets
- Free cash flow

Market Strength Ratios
- Price/earnings per share
- Dividends yield

CHAPTER

5

The Operating Cycle and Merchandising Operations

Focus on Financial Statements

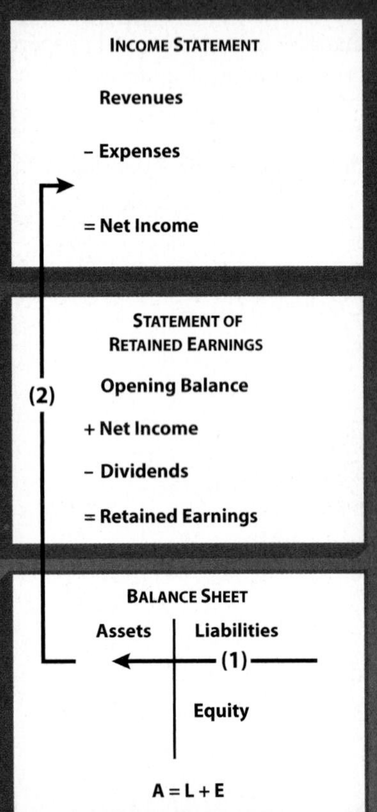

Under the perpetual inventory system, merchandise inventory is updated after every purchase (1) and sale (2).

In the last chapter, we pointed out management's responsibility for ensuring the accuracy and fairness of financial statements. To fulfill that responsibility, management must see that transactions are properly recorded and that the company's assets are protected. That, in turn, requires a system of internal controls. In this chapter, we examine internal controls over the transactions of merchandising companies and the operating cycle in which such transactions take place. The internal controls and other issues that we describe here also apply to manufacturing companies.

LEARNING OBJECTIVES

LO1 Identify the management issues related to merchandising businesses. (pp. 262–267)

LO2 Describe the terms of sale related to merchandising transactions. (pp. 268–270)

LO3 Prepare an income statement and record merchandising transactions under the perpetual inventory system. (pp. 270–274)

LO4 Prepare an income statement and record merchandising transactions under the periodic inventory system. (pp. 274–278)

LO5 Describe the components of internal control, control activities, and limitations on internal control. (pp. 279–281)

LO6 Apply internal control activities to common merchandising transactions. (pp. 281–288)

DECISION POINT ▸ A USER'S FOCUS COSTCO WHOLESALE CORPORATION

- ▸ How can the company efficiently manage its cycle of merchandising operations?
- ▸ How can merchandising transactions be recorded to reflect the company's performance?
- ▸ How can the company maintain control over its merchandising operations?

Costco is a highly successful and fast-growing merchandising company. Like all other merchandisers, Costco has two key decisions to make: the price at which it will sell goods and the level of service it will provide. A department store may set the price of its merchandise at a relatively high level and provide a great deal of service. A discount store, on the other hand, may price its merchandise at a relatively low level and provide limited service. In the type of discount stores that Costco operates, customers buy memberships that allow them to buy in bulk at wholesale prices. Costco purchases merchandise in large quantities from many suppliers, places the goods on racks in its warehouse-like stores, and sells the goods to customers at very low prices, with less personal service.

Costco's large scale, reflected in its Financial Highlights,[1] presents management with many challenges.

COSTCO'S FINANCIAL HIGHLIGHTS
Operating Results (In millions)

Fiscal-Year Ended	August 31, 2008	September 2, 2007	Change
Net revenue	$72,483	$64,400	12.6%
Cost of sales	63,503	56,450	12.5
Gross margin	$ 8,980	$ 7,950	13.0
Operating expenses	7,011	6,342	10.5
Operating income	$ 1,969	$ 1,608	22.5

Managing Merchandising Businesses

LO1 Identify the management issues related to merchandising businesses.

A **merchandising business** earns income by buying and selling goods, which are called **merchandise inventory**. Whether a merchandiser is a wholesaler or a retailer, it uses the same basic accounting methods as a service company. However, the buying and selling of goods adds to the complexity of the business and of the accounting process. To understand the issues involved in accounting for a merchandising business, one must be familiar with the issues involved in managing such a business.

Operating Cycle

Study Note

A company must provide financing for the average days' inventory on hand plus the average number of days to collect credit sales less the average number of days it is allowed to pay its suppliers.

Merchandising businesses engage in a series of transactions called the **operating cycle**. Figure 5-1 shows the transactions that make up this cycle. Some companies buy merchandise for cash and sell it for cash, but these companies are usually small companies like a produce market or a hot dog stand. Most companies buy merchandise on credit and sell it on credit, thereby engaging in the following four transactions:

1. Purchase of merchandise inventory for cash or on credit
2. Payment for purchases made on credit
3. Sales of merchandise inventory for cash or on credit
4. Collection of cash from credit sales

The first three transactions represent the time it takes to purchase inventory, sell it, and collect for it. Merchandisers must be able to do without the cash for this period of time either by relying on cash flows from other sources within the company or by borrowing. If they lack the cash to pay bills when they come due, they can be forced out of business. Thus, managing cash flow is a critical concern.

The suppliers that sold the company the merchandise usually also sell on credit and thus help alleviate the cash flow problem by providing financing for a period of time before they require payment (transaction 4). However, this period is rarely as long as the operating cycle. The period between the time the supplier must be paid and the end of the operating cycle is sometimes referred to as the *cash gap*, and more formally as the *financing period*.

FIGURE 5-1
Cash Flows in the Operating Cycle

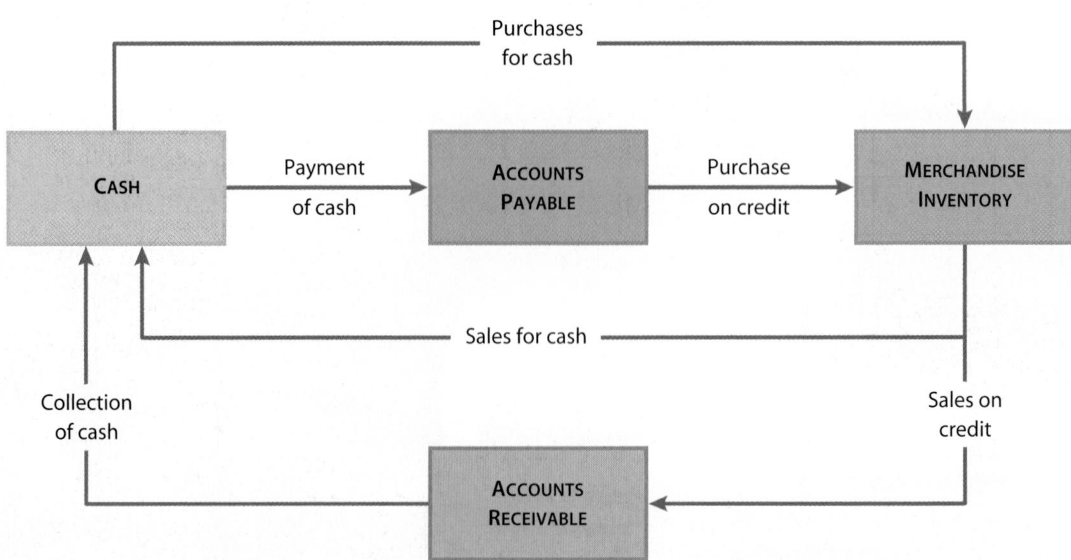

FIGURE 5-2
The Financing Period

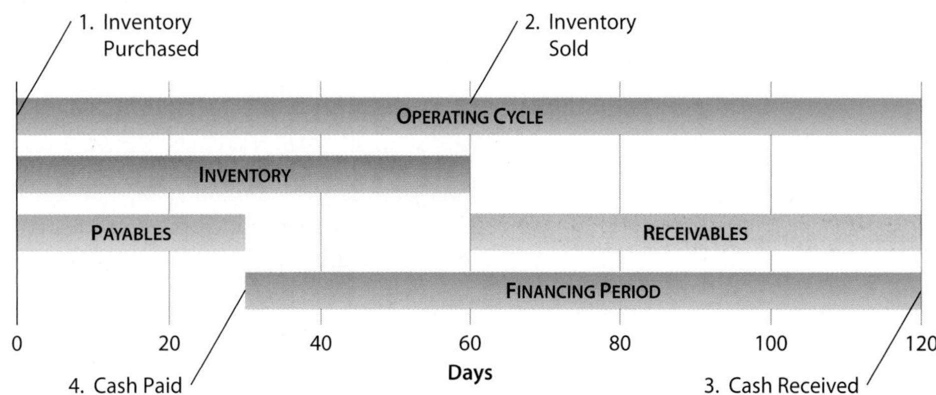

The **financing period**, illustrated in Figure 5-2, is the amount of time from the purchase of inventory until it is sold and payment is collected, less the amount of time creditors give the company to pay for the inventory. Thus, if it takes 60 days to sell the inventory, 60 days to collect for the sale, and creditors' payment terms are 30 days, the financing period is 90 days. During the financing period, the company will be without cash from this series of transactions and will need either to have funds available internally or to borrow from a bank.

The type of merchandising operation in which a company engages can affect the financing period. For example, compare **Costco**'s financing period with that of a traditional discount store chain, **Target Corporation**:

	Target	Costco	Difference
Days' inventory on hand	56 days	29 days	−27 days
Days' receivable	45	4	−41
Less days' payable	−54	−30	−(24)
Financing period	**47 days**	**3 days**	**−44 days**

Costco has an advantage over Target because it holds its inventory for a shorter period before it sells it and collects receivables much faster. Its very short financing period is one of the reasons Costco can charge such low prices. Helpful ratios for calculating the three components of the financing period will be covered in subsequent chapters on inventories, receivables, and current liabilities.

By reducing its financing period, a company can improve its cash flow. Many merchandisers, including Costco, do this by selling as much as possible for cash. Cash sales include sales on bank *credit cards*, such as Visa or MasterCard, and on *debit cards*, which draw directly on the purchaser's bank account. They are considered cash sales because funds from them are available to the merchandiser immediately. Small retail stores may have mostly cash sales and very few credit sales, whereas large wholesale concerns may have almost all credit sales.

Choice of Inventory System

Another issue in managing a merchandising business is the choice of inventory system. Management must choose the system or combination of systems that best achieves the company's goals. The two basic systems of accounting for the many items in merchandise inventory are the perpetual inventory system and the periodic inventory system.

Under the **perpetual inventory system**, continuous records are kept of the quantity and, usually, the cost of individual items as they are bought and sold. Under this system, the cost of each item is recorded in the Merchandise

Study Note

Under the perpetual inventory system, the Merchandise Inventory account and the Cost of Goods Sold account are updated with every sale.

Study Note

The value of ending inventory on the balance sheet is determined by multiplying the quantity of each inventory item by its unit cost.

Inventory account when it is purchased. As merchandise is sold, its cost is transferred from the Merchandise Inventory account to the Cost of Goods Sold account. Thus, at all times the balance of the Merchandise Inventory account equals the cost of goods on hand, and the balance in Cost of Goods Sold equals the cost of merchandise sold to customers.

Managers use the detailed data that the perpetual inventory system provides to respond to customers' inquiries about product availability, to order inventory more effectively and thus avoid running out of stock, and to control the costs associated with investments in inventory.

Under the **periodic inventory system**, the inventory not yet sold, or on hand, is counted periodically. This physical count is usually taken at the end of the accounting period. No detailed records of the inventory on hand are maintained during the accounting period. The figure for inventory on hand is accurate only on the balance sheet date. As soon as any purchases or sales are made, the inventory figure becomes a historical amount, and it remains so until the new ending inventory amount is entered at the end of the next accounting period.

Some retail and wholesale companies use the periodic inventory system because it reduces the amount of clerical work. If a company is fairly small, management can maintain control over its inventory simply through observation or by using an offline system of cards or computer records. However, for larger companies, the lack of detailed records may lead to lost sales or high operating costs.

Because of the difficulty and expense of accounting for the purchase and sale of each item, companies that sell items of low value in high volume have traditionally used the periodic inventory system. Examples of such companies include drugstores, automobile parts stores, department stores, and discount stores. In contrast, companies that sell items that have a high unit value, such as appliances or automobiles, have tended to use the perpetual inventory system.

The distinction between high and low unit value for inventory systems has blurred considerably in recent years. Although the periodic inventory system is still widely used, computerization has led to a large increase in the use of the perpetual inventory system. It is important to note that the perpetual inventory system does not eliminate the need for a physical count of the inventory; one should be taken periodically to ensure that the actual number of goods on hand matches the quantity indicated by the computer records.

Foreign Business Transactions

Most large merchandising and manufacturing firms and even many small ones transact some of their business overseas. For example, a U.S. manufacturer may expand by selling its product to foreign customers, or it may lower its product cost by buying a less expensive part from a source in another country. Such sales and purchase transactions may take place in Japanese yen, British pounds, or some other foreign currency.

When an international transaction involves two different currencies, as most such transactions do, one currency has to be translated into another by using an exchange rate. As we noted earlier in the text, an *exchange rate* is the value of one currency stated in terms of another. We also noted that the values of other currencies in relation to the dollar rise and fall daily according to supply and demand. Thus, if there is a delay between the date of sale or purchase and the date of receipt of payment, the amount of cash involved in an international transaction may differ from the amount originally agreed on.

If the billing of an international sale and the payment for it are both in the domestic currency, no accounting problem arises. For example, if a U.S. maker of precision tools sells $200,000 worth of its products to a British company and bills the British company in dollars, the U.S. company will receive $200,000 when it collects payment. However, if the U.S. company bills the British company in British pounds and accepts payment in pounds, it will incur an **exchange gain or loss** if the exchange rate between dollars and pounds changes between the date of sale and the date of payment.

For example, assume that the U.S. company billed the sale of $200,000 at £125,000, reflecting an exchange rate of 1.6 (that is, $1.60 per pound) on the sale date. Now assume that by the date of payment, the exchange rate has fallen to 1.5. When the U.S. company receives its £125,000, it will be worth only $187,500 (£125,000 × $1.50 = $187,500). It will have incurred an exchange loss of $12,500 because it agreed to accept a fixed number of British pounds in payment for its products, and the value of each pound dropped before the payment was made. Had the value of the pound in relation to the dollar increased, the company would have made an exchange gain.

The same logic applies to purchases as to sales, except that the relationship of exchange gains and losses to changes in exchange rates is reversed. For example, assume that the U.S company purchases products from the British company for $200,000. If the payment is to be made in U.S. dollars, no accounting problem arises. However, if the British company expects to be paid in pounds, the U.S. company will have an exchange gain of $12,500 because it agreed to pay a fixed £125,000, and between the dates of purchase and payment, the exchange value of the pound decreased from $1.60 to $1.50. To make the £125,000 payment, the U.S. company has to expend only $187,500.

Exchange gains and losses are reported on the income statement. Because of their bearing on a company's financial performance, they are of considerable interest to managers and investors. Lack of uniformity in international accounting standards is another matter of which investors must be wary.

The Need for Internal Controls

Buying and selling, the principal transactions of merchandising businesses, involve assets—cash, accounts receivable, and merchandise inventory—that are vulnerable to theft and embezzlement. Cash and inventory can, of course, be fairly easy to steal. The reason the potential for embezzlement exists is that the large number of transactions that are usually involved in a merchandising business (for example, cash receipts, receipts on account, payments for purchases, and receipts and shipments of inventory) makes monitoring the accounting records difficult.

If a merchandising company does not take steps to protect its assets, it can suffer high losses of both cash and inventory. Management's responsibility is to establish an environment, accounting systems, and control procedures that will protect the company's assets. These systems and procedures are called **internal controls**.

Taking a **physical inventory** facilitates control over merchandise inventory. This process involves an actual count of all merchandise on hand. It can be a difficult task because it is easy to accidentally omit items or count them twice. As we noted earlier, a physical inventory must be taken under both the periodic and the perpetual inventory systems.

> **Study Note**
> Inventory shortages can result from honest mistakes, such as accidentally tagging inventory with the wrong number.

A company's merchandise inventory includes all goods intended for sale regardless of where they are located—on shelves, in storerooms, in warehouses, or in trucks between warehouses and stores. It also includes goods in transit from suppliers if title to the goods has passed to the merchandiser. Ending inventory does not include merchandise that a company has sold but not yet delivered to customers. Nor does it include goods that it cannot sell because they are

Merchandise inventory includes all goods intended for sale wherever they are located—on store shelves, in warehouses, on car lots, or in transit from suppliers if title to the goods has passed to the merchandiser. To prevent loss of inventory, a merchandiser must have an effective system of internal control.

Courtesy of Corbis/Jupiter Images.

damaged or obsolete. If damaged or obsolete goods can be sold at a reduced price, however, they should be included in ending inventory at their reduced value.

Merchandisers usually take a physical inventory after the close of business on the last day of their fiscal year. To facilitate the process, they often end the fiscal year in a slow season, when inventories are at relatively low levels. For example, many department stores end their fiscal year in January or February. After hours—at night, on a weekend, or when the store closes for all or part of a day for taking inventory—employees count all items and record the results on numbered inventory tickets or sheets, following procedures to ensure that no items will be missed. Using bar coding to take inventory electronically has greatly facilitated the process in many companies.

Most companies experience losses of merchandise inventory from spoilage, shoplifting, and theft by employees. When such losses occur, the periodic inventory system provides no means of identifying them because the costs are automatically included in the cost of goods sold. For example, suppose a company has lost $1,250 in stolen merchandise during an accounting period. When the physical inventory is taken, the missing items are not in stock, so they cannot be counted. Because the ending inventory does not contain these items, the amount subtracted from the cost of goods available for sale is less than it would be if the goods were in stock. The cost of goods sold, then, is overstated by $1,250. In a sense, the cost of goods sold is inflated by the amount of merchandise that has been lost.

Study Note

An adjustment to the Merchandise Inventory account will be needed if the physical inventory reveals a difference between the actual inventory and the amount in the records.

The perpetual inventory system makes it easier to identify such losses. Because the Merchandise Inventory account is continuously updated for sales, purchases, and returns, the loss will show up as the difference between the inventory records and the physical inventory taken at the end of the accounting period. Once the amount of the loss has been identified, the ending inventory is updated by crediting the Merchandise Inventory account. The offsetting debit is usually an increase in Cost of Goods Sold because the loss is considered a cost that reduces the company's gross margin.

FOCUS ON BUSINESS PRACTICE

Will Sarbanes-Oxley Stop Fraud?

The Sarbanes-Oxley Act has heightened awareness of internal control and requires increased diligence, but it will never stop fraud from occurring. For instance, NBC Universal, the large media company, reported a few years ago that its treasurer had been arrested for theft of $800,000. The theft occurred due to deficiencies in the internal control system, such as giving the treasurer authorization to set up a legal entity, set up a bank account, make purchases, and pay for them. This situation violated a basic rule of internal control in that the treasurer was able to accomplish both the purchase and the payment with no checks by another person.[2]

Management's Responsibility for Internal Control

Management is responsible for establishing a satisfactory system of internal controls. Such a system includes all the policies and procedures needed to ensure the reliability of financial reporting, compliance with laws and regulations, and the effectiveness and efficiency of operations. In other words, management must safeguard the firm's assets, ensure the reliability of its accounting records, and see that its employees comply with all legal requirements and operate the firm to the best advantage of its owners.

Section 404 of the Sarbanes-Oxley act of 2002 requires that the chief executive officer, the chief financial officer, and the auditors of a public company fully document and certify the company's system of internal controls. For example, in its annual report, **Costco**'s management acknowledges its responsibility for internal control as follows:

> [We] are responsible for establishing and maintaining disclosure controls and procedures and internal controls for financial reporting [on behalf of the company].[3]

STOP & APPLY >

The management of SavRite Corporation made the following decisions. Indicate whether each decision pertains primarily to (a) cash flow management, (b) choice of inventory system, or (c) foreign transactions.

1. Decided to decrease the credit terms offered to customers from 30 days to 20 days to speed up collection of accounts.
2. Decided to purchase goods made by a supplier in India.
3. Decided that sales would benefit if sales people knew the amount of each item of inventory that was on hand at any one time.
4. Decided to try to negotiate a longer time to pay suppliers than had been previously granted.

SOLUTION

1. a; 2. c; 3. b; 4. a

Terms of Sale

LO2 Describe the terms of sale related to merchandising transactions.

When goods are sold on credit, both parties should understand the amount and timing of payment as well as other terms of the purchase, such as who pays delivery charges and what warranties or rights of return apply. Sellers quote prices in different ways. Many merchants quote the price at which they expect to sell their goods. Others, particularly manufacturers and wholesalers, quote prices as a percentage (usually 30 percent or more) off their list or catalogue prices. Such a reduction is called a **trade discount**.

Study Note
A trade discount applies to the list or catalogue price. A sales discount applies to the sales price.

For example, if an article is listed at $1,000 with a trade discount of 40 percent, or $400, the seller records the sale at $600, and the buyer records the purchase at $600. The seller may raise or lower the trade discount depending on the quantity purchased. The list or catalogue price and related trade discount are used only to arrive at an agreed-on price; they do not appear in the accounting records.

Sales and Purchases Discounts

The terms of sale are usually printed on the sales invoice and thus constitute part of the sales agreement. Terms differ from industry to industry. In some industries, payment is expected in a short period of time, such as 10 or 30 days. In these cases, the invoice is marked "n/10" ("net 10") or "n/30" ("net 30"), meaning that the amount of the invoice is due either 10 days or 30 days after the invoice date. If the invoice is due 10 days after the end of the month, it is marked "n/10 eom."

Study Note
Early collection also has the advantage of reducing the probability of a customer's defaulting.

In some industries, it is customary to give a discount for early payment. This discount, which is called a **sales discount**, is intended to increase the seller's liquidity by reducing the amount of money tied up in accounts receivable. An invoice that offers a sales discount might be labeled "2/10, n/30," which means that the buyer either can pay the invoice within 10 days of the invoice date and take a 2 percent discount or can wait 30 days and pay the full amount of the invoice. It is often advantageous for a buyer to take the discount because the saving of 2 percent over a period of 20 days (from the 11th day to the 30th day) represents an effective annual rate of 36.5 percent (365 days ÷ 20 days × 2% = 36.5%). Most companies would be better off borrowing money to take the discount. The practice of giving sales discounts has been declining because it is costly to the seller and because, from the buyer's viewpoint, the amount of the discount is usually very small in relation to the price of the purchase.

Because it is not possible to know at the time of a sale whether the customer will pay in time to take advantage of a sales discount, the discounts are recorded only at the time the customer pays. For example, suppose Laboda Sportswear Corporation sells merchandise to a customer on September 20 for $600 on terms of 2/10, n/30. Laboda records the sale on September 20 for the full amount of $600. If the customer takes advantage of the discount by paying on or before September 30, Laboda will receive $588 in cash and will reduce its accounts receivable by $600. The difference of $12 ($600 × 0.02) will be debited to an account called *Sales Discounts.* Sales Discounts is a contra-revenue account with a normal debit balance that is deducted from sales on the income statement.

The same logic applies to **purchases discounts**, which are discounts that a buyer takes for the early payment of merchandise. For example, the buyer in the transaction described above will record the purchase on September 20 at $600. If the buyer pays on or before September 30, it will record cash paid of $588 and reduce its accounts payable by $600. The difference of $12 is recorded as a credit to an account called Purchases Discounts. The *Purchases Discounts* *account* reduces cost of goods sold or purchases depending on the inventory method used.

Transportation Costs

In some industries, the seller usually pays transportation costs and charges a price that includes those costs. In other industries, it is customary for the purchaser to pay transportation charges. Special terms designate whether the seller or the purchaser pays the freight charges.

FOB shipping point means that the seller places the merchandise "free on board" at the point of origin and the buyer bears the shipping costs. The title to the merchandise passes to the buyer at that point. For example, when the sales agreement for the purchase of a car says "FOB factory," the buyer must pay the freight from the factory where the car was made to wherever he or she is located, and the buyer owns the car from the time it leaves the factory.

FOB destination means that the seller bears the transportation costs to the place where the merchandise is delivered. The seller retains title until the merchandise reaches its destination and usually prepays the shipping costs, in which case the buyer makes no accounting entry for freight.

The effects of these special shipping terms are summarized as follows:

Shipping Term	Where Title Passes	Who Pays the Cost of Transportation
FOB shipping point	At origin	Buyer
FOB destination	At destination	Seller

When the buyer pays the transportation charge, it is called **freight-in**, and it is added to the cost of merchandise purchased. Thus, freight-in increases the buyer's cost of merchandise inventory, as well as the cost of goods sold after they are sold. When freight-in is a relatively small amount, most companies include the cost in the cost of goods sold on the income statement rather than going to the trouble of allocating part of it to merchandise inventory.

When the seller pays the transportation charge, it is called **delivery expense**, or *freight-out*. Because the seller incurs this cost to facilitate the sale of its product, the cost is included in selling expenses on the income statement.

Terms of Debit and Credit Card Sales

Many retailers allow customers to use debit or credit cards to charge their purchases. Debit cards deduct directly from a person's bank account, whereas a credit card allows for payment later. Five of the most widely used credit cards are American Express, Discover Card, Diners Club, MasterCard, and Visa. The customer establishes credit with the lender (the credit card issuer) and receives a plastic card to use in making charges. If a seller accepts the card, the customer signs an invoice at the time of the sale. The sale is communicated to the seller's bank, resulting in a cash deposit in the seller's bank account. Thus, the seller does not have to establish the customer's credit, collect from the customer, or tie up money in accounts receivable. As payment, the lender, rather than paying the total amount of the credit card sales, takes a discount of 2 to 6 percent. The discount is a selling expense for the merchandiser. For example, if a restaurant makes sales of $1,000 on Visa credit cards and Visa takes a 4 percent discount on the sales, the restaurant would record Cash in the amount of $960 and Credit Card Expense in the amount of $40.

STOP & APPLY >

A local company sells lawn mowers that it buys from the manufacturer.

a. The manufacturer sets a list or catalogue price of $1,200 for a lawn mower. The manufacturer offers its dealers a 40 percent trade discount.

b. The manufacturer sells the machine under terms of FOB shipping point. The cost of shipping is $60.

c. The manufacturer offers a sales discount of 2/10, n/30. Sales discounts do not apply to shipping costs.

What is the net cost of the lawn mower to the dealer, assuming it is paid for within ten days of purchase?

SOLUTION

a. $1,200 − ($1,200 × 0.40) = $720

b. $720 + $60 = $780

c. $780 − ($720 × 0.02) = $765.60

Perpetual Inventory System

LO3 Prepare an income statement and record merchandising transactions under the perpetual inventory system.

Exhibit 5-1 shows how an income statement appears when a company uses the perpetual inventory system. The focal point of the statement is cost of goods sold, which is deducted from net sales to arrive at gross margin. Under the perpetual inventory system, the Merchandise Inventory and Cost of Goods Sold accounts are continually updated during the accounting period as purchases, sales, and other inventory transactions that affect these accounts occur.

Purchases of Merchandise

Figure 5-3 shows how transactions involving purchases of merchandise are recorded under the perpetual inventory system. As you can see, the focus of these entries is Accounts Payable. In this section, we present a summary of the entries made for merchandise purchases.

EXHIBIT 5-1
Income Statement Under the Perpetual Inventory System

Kloss Motor Corporation
Income Statement
For the Year Ended December 31, 2010

Net sales	$957,300
Cost of goods sold*	525,440
Gross margin	$431,860
Operating expenses	313,936
Income before income taxes	$117,924
Income taxes	20,000
Net income	$ 97,924

*Freight-in has been included in cost of goods sold.

Study Note

On the income statement, freight-in is included as part of cost of goods sold, and delivery expense (freight-out) is included as an operating (selling) expense.

FIGURE 5-3
Recording Purchase Transactions Under the Perpetual Inventory System

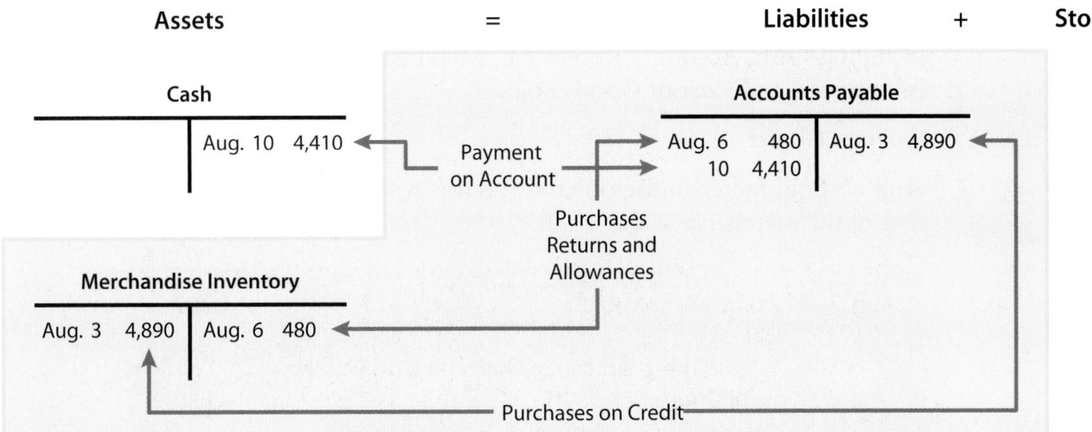

> **Study Note**
> The Merchandise Inventory account increases when a purchase is made.

Purchases on Credit

Aug. 3: Received merchandise purchased on credit, invoice dated Aug. 1, terms n/10, $4,890.

Aug. 3	Merchandise Inventory	4,890	
	Accounts Payable		4,890
	Purchases on credit		

Comment: Under the perpetual inventory system, the cost of merchandise is recorded in the Merchandise Inventory account at the time of purchase. In the transaction described here, payment is due ten days from the invoice date. If an invoice includes a charge for shipping or if shipping is billed separately, it should be debited to Freight-In.

Purchases Returns and Allowances

Aug. 6: Returned part of merchandise received on Aug. 3 for credit, $480.

Aug. 6	Accounts Payable	480	
	Merchandise Inventory		480
	Returned merchandise from purchase		

Comment: Under the perpetual inventory system, when a buyer is allowed to return all or part of a purchase or is given an allowance—a reduction in the amount to be paid, Merchandise Inventory is reduced, as is Accounts Payable.

Payments on Account

Aug. 10: Paid amount in full due for the purchase of Aug. 3, part of which was returned on Aug. 6, $4,410.

Aug. 10	Accounts Payable	4,410	
	Cash		4,410
	Made payment on account		

Comment: Payment is made for the net amount due of $4,410 ($4,890 − $480).

Sales of Merchandise

Study Note

The Cost of Goods Sold account is increased and the Merchandise Inventory account is decreased when a sale is made.

Figure 5-4 shows how transactions involving sales of merchandise are recorded under the perpetual inventory system. These transactions involve several accounts, including Cash, Accounts Receivable, Merchandise Inventory, Sales Returns and Allowances, and Cost of Goods Sold.

Sales on Credit

Aug. 7: Sold merchandise on credit, terms n/30, FOB destination, $1,200; the cost of the merchandise was $720.

Aug. 7	Accounts Receivable	1,200	
	Sales		1,200
	Sold merchandise to Gonzales Distributors		
7	Cost of Goods Sold	720	
	Merchandise Inventory		720
	Transferred the cost of merchandise inventory sold to Cost of Goods Sold		

Comment: Under the perpetual inventory system, sales always require two entries, as shown in Figure 5-4. First, the sale is recorded by increasing Accounts Receivable and Sales. Second, Cost of Goods Sold is updated by a transfer from Merchandise Inventory. In the case of cash sales, Cash rather than Accounts Receivable is debited for the amount of the sale. If the seller pays for the shipping, it should be debited to Delivery Expense.

Sales Returns and Allowances

Aug. 9: Accepted return of part of merchandise sold on Aug. 7 for full credit and returned it to merchandise inventory, $300; the cost of the merchandise was $180.

FIGURE 5-4
Recording Sales Transactions Under the Perpetual Inventory System

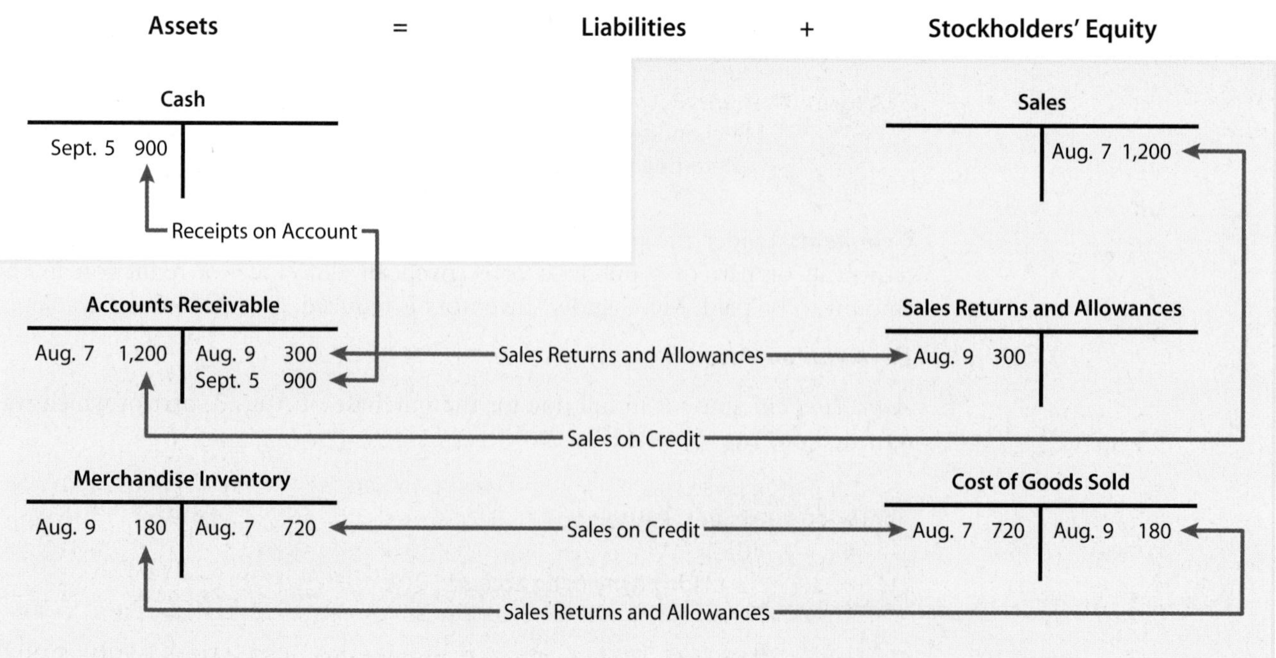

Aug. 9	Sales Returns and Allowances	300	
	Accounts Receivable		300
	Accepted returns of merchandise		
9	Merchandise Inventory	180	
	Cost of Goods Sold		180
	Transferred the cost of merchandise returned to Merchandise Inventory		

Study Note

Because the Sales account is established with a credit, its contra account, Sales Returns and Allowances, is established with a debit.

Comment: Under the perpetual inventory system, when a seller allows the buyer to return all or part of a sale or gives an allowance—a reduction in amount—two entries are again necessary. First, the original sale is reversed by reducing Accounts Receivable and debiting the Sales Returns and Allowances account. The **Sales Returns and Allowances account** gives management a readily available measure of unsatisfactory products and dissatisfied customers. This account is a contra-revenue account with a normal debit balance, and it is deducted from sales on the income statement. Second, the cost of the merchandise must also be transferred from the Cost of Goods Sold account back into the Merchandise Inventory account. If the company makes an allowance instead of accepting a return, or if the merchandise cannot be returned to inventory and resold, this transfer is not made.

Receipts on Account

Sept. 5: Collected in full for sale of merchandise on Aug. 7, less the return on Aug. 9, $900.

Sept. 5	Cash	900	
	Accounts Receivable		900
	Received on account		

Comment: Collection is made for the net amount due of $900 ($1,200 − $300).

STOP & APPLY >

The numbered items below are account titles, and the lettered items are types of merchandising transactions. For each transaction, indicate which accounts are debited or credited by placing the account numbers in the appropriate columns.

1. Cash
2. Accounts Receivable
3. Merchandise Inventory
4. Accounts Payable
5. Sales
6. Sales Returns and Allowances
7. Cost of Goods Sold

	Account Debited	Account Credited		Account Debited	Account Credited
a. Purchase on credit	___	___	e. Sale for cash	___	___
b. Purchase return for credit	___	___	f. Sales return for credit	___	___
c. Purchase for cash	___	___	g. Payment on account	___	___
d. Sale on credit	___	___	h. Receipt on account	___	___

(continued)

SOLUTION

	Account Debited	Account Credited		Account Debited	Account Credited
a. Purchase on credit	3	4	e. Sale for cash	1,7	5,3
b. Purchase return for credit	4	3	f. Sales return for credit	6,3	2,7
c. Purchase for cash	3	1	g. Payment on account	4	1
d. Sale on credit	2,7	5,3	h. Receipt on account	1	2

Periodic Inventory System

LO4 Prepare an income statement and record merchandising transactions under the periodic inventory system.

Exhibit 5-2 shows how an income statement appears when a company uses the periodic inventory system. A major feature of this statement is the computation of cost of goods sold. *Cost of goods sold* must be computed on the income statement because it is not updated for purchases, sales, and other transactions during the accounting period, as it is under the perpetual inventory system. Figure 5-5 illustrates the components of cost of goods sold.

It is important to distinguish between the cost of goods available for sale and the cost of goods sold. **Cost of goods available for sale** is the total cost of merchandise that *could* be sold in the accounting period. Cost of goods sold is the cost of merchandise *actually* sold. The difference between the two numbers is the amount *not* sold, or the ending merchandise inventory. Cost of goods available for sale is the sum of the following two factors:

- The amount of merchandise on hand at the beginning of accounting period or beginning inventory.

EXHIBIT 5-2
Income Statement Under the Periodic Inventory System

Kloss Motor Corporation
Income Statement
For the Year Ended December 31, 2010

Net sales			$957,300
Cost of goods sold			
Merchandise inventory, December 31, 2009		$211,200	
Purchases	$505,600		
Less purchases returns and allowances	31,104		
Net purchases	$474,496		
Freight-in	32,944		
Net cost of purchases		507,440	
Cost of goods available for sale		$718,640	
Less merchandise inventory, December 31, 2010		193,200	
Cost of goods sold			525,440
Gross margin			$431,860
Operating expenses			313,936
Income before income taxes			$117,924
Income taxes			20,000
Net income			$ 97,924

Study Note

Most published financial statements are condensed, eliminating the detail shown here under cost of goods sold.

FIGURE 5-5
The Components of Cost of Goods Sold

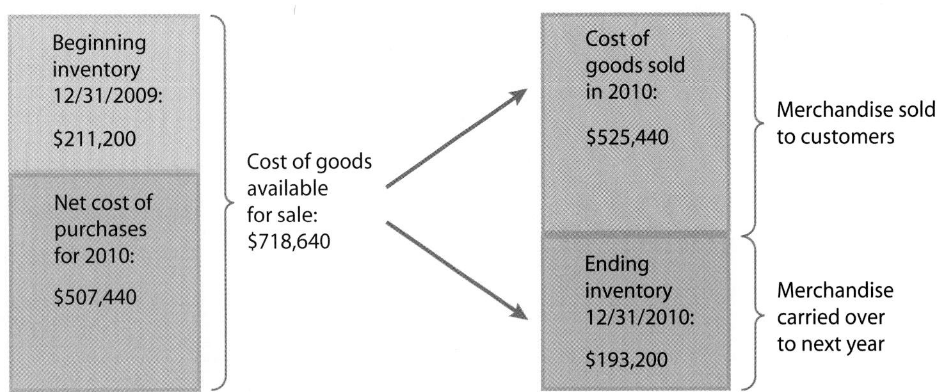

- The net cost of purchases during the period. (Net cost of purchases consist of total purchases less any deductions such as purchases return and allowances, plus freight-in.)

As you can see in Exhibit 5-2, Kloss Motor Corporation has cost of goods available for sale during the period of $718,640 ($211,200 + $507,440). The ending inventory of $193,200 is deducted from this figure to determine the cost of goods sold. Thus, the company's cost of goods sold is $525,440 ($718,640 − $193,200). Figure 5-5 illustrates these relationships.

An important component of the cost of goods sold section is **net cost of purchases**. As you can see in Exhibit 5-2, net cost of purchases is the sum of net purchases and freight-in. **Net purchases** equal total purchases less any deductions, such as purchases returns and allowances and any discounts allowed by suppliers for early payment. Freight-in is added to net purchases because transportation charges are a necessary cost of receiving merchandise for sale.

> **Study Note**
> Purchases accounts and Purchases Returns and Allowances accounts are used only in conjunction with a periodic inventory system.

Purchases of Merchandise

Figure 5-6 shows how transactions involving purchases of merchandise are recorded under the periodic inventory system. A primary difference between the perpetual and periodic inventory systems is that in the perpetual inventory system, the Merchandise Inventory account is adjusted each time a purchase, sale, or other inventory transaction occurs, whereas in the periodic inventory system, the Merchandise Inventory account stays at its beginning balance until the physical inventory is recorded at the end of the period. The periodic system uses a Purchases account to accumulate purchases during an accounting period and a

FIGURE 5-6
Recording Purchases: Under the Perpetual Inventory System

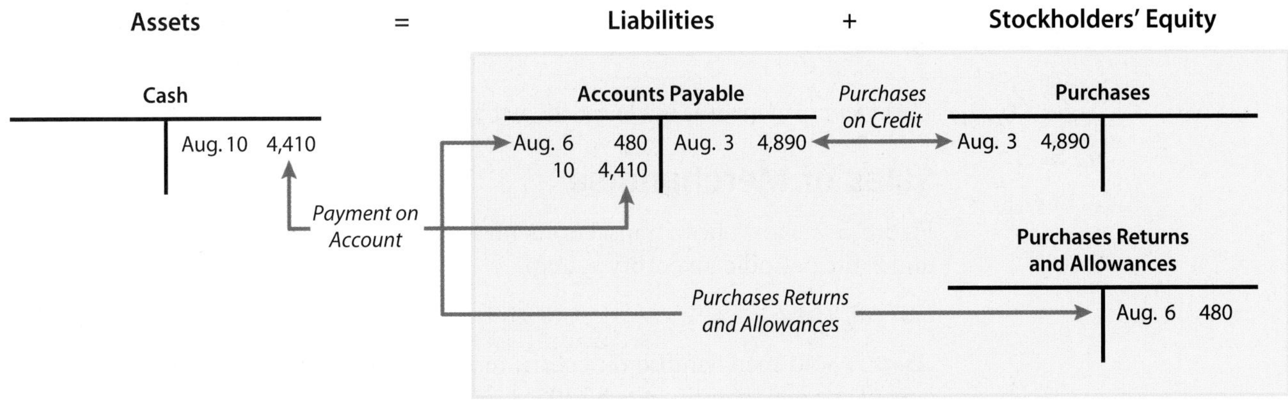

Purchases Returns and Allowances account to accumulate returns of and allowances on purchases.

The following examples illustrate how Kloss Motor Corporation would record purchase transactions under the periodic inventory system.

Purchases on Credit

> **Study Note**
> Under the periodic inventory system, the Purchases account increases when a company makes a purchase.

Aug. 3: Received merchandise purchased on credit, invoice dated Aug. 1, terms n/10, $4,890.

Aug. 3	Purchases	4,890	
	Accounts Payable		4,890
	Purchases on credit		

Comment: Under the periodic inventory system, the cost of merchandise is recorded in the **Purchases account** at the time of purchase. This account is a temporary one used only with the periodic inventory system. Its sole purpose is to accumulate the total cost of merchandise purchased for resale during an accounting period. (Purchases of other assets, such as equipment, are recorded in the appropriate asset account, not in the Purchases account.) The Purchases account does not indicate whether merchandise has been sold or is still on hand.

Purchases Returns and Allowances

Aug. 6: Returned part of merchandise received on Aug. 3 for credit, $480.

Aug. 6	Accounts Payable	480	
	Purchases Returns and Allowances		480
	Returned merchandise from purchase		

> **Study Note**
> Because the Purchases account is established with a debit, its contra account, Purchases Returns and Allowances, is established with a credit.

Comment: Under the periodic inventory system, the amount of a return or allowance is recorded in the **Purchases Returns and Allowances account**. This is a contra-purchases account with a normal credit balance, and it is deducted from purchases on the income statement. Accounts Payable is also reduced.

Payments on Account

Aug. 10: Paid amount in full due for the purchase of Aug. 3, part of which was returned on Aug. 6, $4,410.

Aug. 10	Accounts Payable	4,410	
	Cash		4,410
	Made payment on account		

Comment: Payment is made for the net amount due of $4,410 ($4,890 − $480).

Sales of Merchandise

Figure 5-7 shows how transactions involving sales of merchandise are recorded under the periodic inventory system.

Sales on Credit

Aug. 7: Sold merchandise on credit, terms n/30, FOB destination, $1,200; the cost of the merchandise was $720.

FIGURE 5-7
Recording Sales Transactions Under the Periodic Inventory System

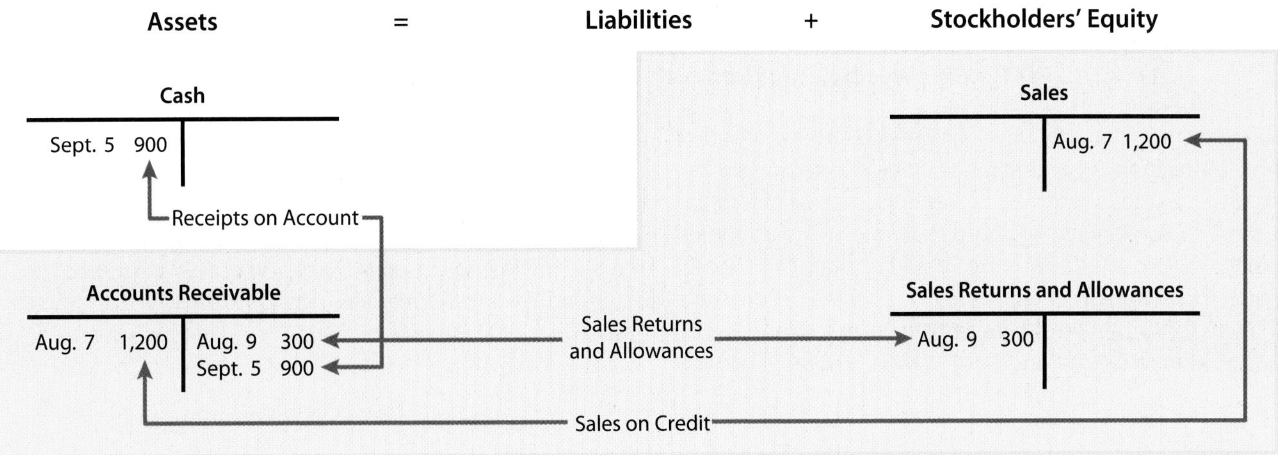

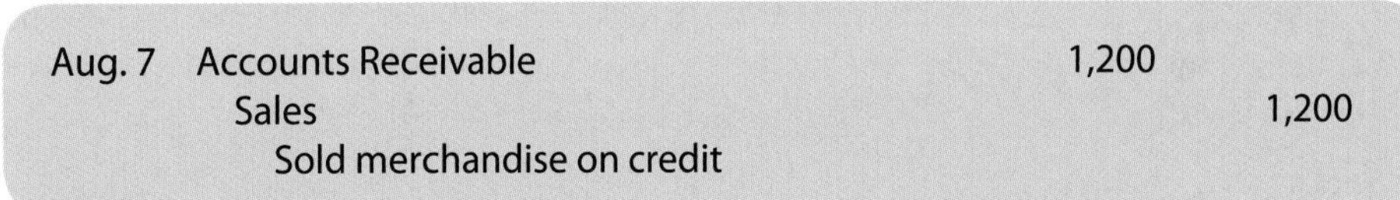

Aug. 7	Accounts Receivable	1,200	
	Sales		1,200
	Sold merchandise on credit		

Comment: As shown in Figure 5-7, under the periodic inventory system, sales require only one entry to increase Sales and Accounts Receivable. In the case of cash sales, Cash rather than Accounts Receivable is debited for the amount of the sale. If the seller pays for the shipping, the amount should be debited to Delivery Expense.

Sales Returns and Allowances

Aug. 9: Accepted return of part of merchandise sold on Aug. 7 for full credit and returned it to merchandise inventory, $300; the cost of the merchandise was $180.

Aug. 9	Sales Returns and Allowances	300	
	Accounts Receivable		300
	Accepted return of merchandise		

Comment: Under the periodic inventory system, when a seller allows the buyer to return all or part of a sale or gives an allowance, only one entry is needed to reduce Accounts Receivable and debit Sales Returns and Allowances. The Sales Returns and Allowances account is a contra-revenue account with a normal debit balance and is deducted from sales on the income statement.

Receipts on Account

Sept. 5: Collected in full for sale of merchandise on Aug. 7, less the return on Aug. 9, $900.

Sept. 5	Cash	900	
	Accounts Receivable		900
	Received on account		

Comment: Collection is made for the net amount due of $900 ($1,200 − $300).

FOCUS ON BUSINESS PRACTICE

Are Sales Returns Worth Accounting For?

Some industries routinely have a high percentage of sales returns. More than 6 percent of all nonfood items sold in stores are eventually returned to vendors. This amounts to over $100 billion a year, or more than the gross national product of two-thirds of the world's nations.[4] Book publishers like **Simon & Schuster** often have returns as high as 30 to 50 percent because to gain the attention of potential buyers, they must distribute large numbers of copies to many outlets. Magazine publishers like **AOL Time Warner** expect to sell no more than 35 to 38 percent of the magazines they send to newsstands and other outlets.[5] In all these businesses, it pays management to scrutinize the Sales Returns and Allowances account for ways to reduce returns and increase profitability.

STOP & APPLY >

The numbered items below are account titles, and the lettered items are types of merchandising transactions. For each transaction, indicate which accounts are debited or credited by placing the account numbers in the appropriate columns.

1. Cash
2. Accounts Receivable
3. Merchandise Inventory
4. Accounts Payable
5. Sales
6. Sales Returns and Allowances
7. Purchases
8. Purchases Returns and Allowances

	Account Debited	Account Credited		Account Debited	Account Credited
a. Purchase on credit	___	___	e. Sale for cash	___	___
b. Purchase return for credit	___	___	f. Sales return for credit	___	___
c. Purchase for cash	___	___	g. Payment on account	___	___
d. Sale on credit	___	___	h. Receipt on account	___	___

SOLUTION

	Account Debited	Account Credited		Account Debited	Account Credited
a. Purchase on credit	7	4	e. Sale for cash	1	5
b. Purchase return for credit	4	8	f. Sales return for credit	6	2
c. Purchase for cash	7	1	g. Payment on account	4	1
d. Sale on credit	2	5	h. Receipt on account	1	2

Internal Control: Components, Activities, and Limitations

LO5 Describe the components of internal control, control activities, and limitations on internal control.

> **Study Note**
> The components of internal control are equally important to manual and computerized accounting systems.

As mentioned earlier, if a merchandising company does not take steps to protect its assets, it can suffer high losses of cash and inventory through embezzlement and theft. To avoid such occurrences, management must set up and maintain a good system of internal control.

Components of Internal Control

An effective system of internal control has five interrelated components.[6] They are as follows:

1. ***Control environment*** The **control environment** is created by management's overall attitude, awareness, and actions. It encompasses a company's ethics, philosophy and operating style, organizational structure, method of assigning authority and responsibility, and personnel policies and practices. Personnel should be qualified to handle responsibilities, which means that they must be trained and informed about what is expected of them. For example, the manager of a retail store should train employees to follow prescribed procedures for handling cash sales, credit card sales, and returns and refunds.
2. ***Risk assessment*** **Risk assessment** involves identifying areas in which risks of loss of assets or inaccuracies in accounting records are high so that adequate controls can be implemented. Among the greater risks in a retail store are that employees may steal cash and customers may steal goods.
3. ***Information and communication*** **Information and communication** pertains to the accounting system established by management—to the way the system gathers and treats information about the company's transactions and to how it communicates individual responsibilities within the system. Employees must understand exactly what their functions are.
4. ***Control activities*** **Control activities** are the policies and procedures management puts in place to see that its directives are carried out. (Control activities are discussed in more detail below.)
5. ***Monitoring*** **Monitoring** involves management's regular assessment of the quality of internal control, including periodic review of compliance with all policies and procedures. Large companies often have a staff of internal auditors who review the company's system of internal control to determine if it is working properly and if procedures are being followed. In smaller businesses, owners and managers conduct these reviews.

Control Activities

Control activities are a very important way of implementing internal control. The goal of these activities is to safeguard a company's assets and ensure the reliability of its accounting records.

Control activities include the following:

1. ***Authorization*** **Authorization** means the approval of certain transactions and activities. In a retail store, for example, cashiers customarily authorize cash sales, but other transactions, such as issuing a refund, may require a manager's approval.
2. ***Recording transactions*** To establish accountability for assets, all transactions should be recorded. For example, if a retail store uses a cash register that records sales, refunds, and other transactions on a paper tape or computer disk, the cashier can be held accountable for the cash received and the merchandise removed during his or her shift.
3. ***Documents and records*** Well-designed documents help ensure that transactions are properly recorded. For example, using prenumbered invoices and other documents is a way of ensuring that all transactions are recorded.

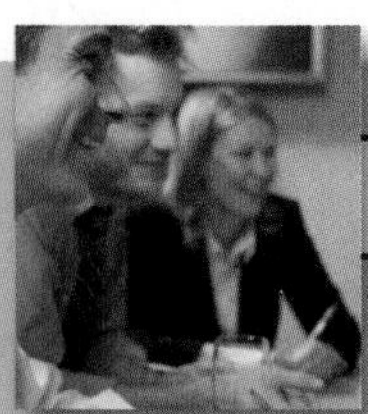

FOCUS ON BUSINESS PRACTICE

Which Frauds Are Most Common?

A survey of 5,000 large U.S. businesses disclosed that 36 percent suffered losses in excess of $1 million (up from 21 percent in 1998) due to fraud or inventory theft. The frauds most commonly cited were credit card fraud, check fraud, false invoices and phantom vendors, and expense account abuse. The most common reasons for the occurrences of these frauds were poor internal controls, management override of internal controls, and collusion. The most common methods of detecting them were notification by an employee, internal controls, internal auditor review, notification by a customer, and accidental discovery.

Companies that are successful in preventing fraud have a good system of internal control, a formal code of ethics, and a program to monitor compliance that includes a system for reporting incidents of fraud. These companies routinely communicate the existence of the program to their employees.[7]

4. ***Physical controls*** **Physical controls** are controls that limit access to assets. For example, in a retail store, only the person responsible for the cash register should have access to it. Other employees should not be able to open the cash drawer when the cashier is not present. Similarly, only authorized personnel should have access to warehouses and storerooms. Access to accounting records, including those stored in company computers, should also be controlled.
5. ***Periodic independent verification*** **Periodic independent verification** means that someone other than the persons responsible for the accounting records and assets should periodically check the records against the assets. For example, at the end of each shift or day in a retail store, the owner or manager should count the cash in the cash drawer and compare the amount with the amount recorded on the tape or computer disk in the cash register. Other examples of independent verification are periodic counts of physical inventory and reconciliations of monthly bank statements.
6. ***Separation of duties*** **Separation of duties** means that no one person should authorize transactions, handle assets, or keep records of assets. For example, in a well-managed electronics store, each employee oversees only a single part of a transaction. A sales employee takes the order and creates an invoice. Another employee receives the customer's cash or credit card payment and issues a receipt. Once the customer has a receipt, and only then, a third employee obtains the item from the warehouse and gives it to the customer. A person in the accounting department subsequently compares all sales recorded on the tape or disk in the cash register with the sales invoices and updates the inventory in the accounting records. The separation of duties means that a mistake, careless or not, cannot be made without being seen by at least one other person.
7. ***Sound personnel practices*** Personnel practices that promote internal control include adequate supervision, rotation of key people among different jobs, insistence that employees take vacations, and bonding of personnel who handle cash or inventory. **Bonding** is the process of carefully checking an employee's background and insuring the company against theft by that person. Bonding does not guarantee against theft, but it does prevent or reduce loss if theft occurs. Prudent personnel practices help ensure that employees know their jobs, are honest, and will find it difficult to carry out and conceal embezzlement over time.

Study Note

No control procedure can guarantee the prevention of theft. However, the more procedures that are in place, the less likely it is that a theft will occur.

Limitations on Internal Control

No system of internal control is without weaknesses. As long as people perform control procedures, an internal control system will be vulnerable to human error.

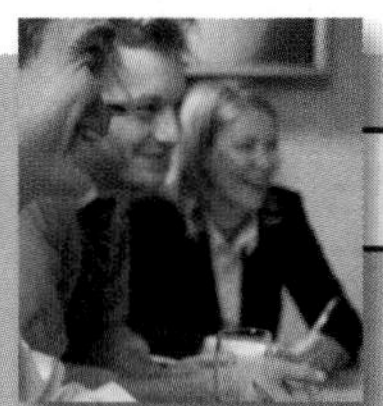

FOCUS ON BUSINESS PRACTICE

Shoplifters: Beware!

With theft from shoplifting approaching $30 billion per year, retailers are increasing their use of physical controls beyond the usual electronic warning if a customer tries to walk out without paying. Companies such as **Macy's** and **Babies 'R' Us** have installed more than 6 million video cameras in stores across the country. Advanced surveillance software can compare a shopper's movements between video images and recognize unusual activity. For instance, removing 10 items from a shelf or opening a drawer that normally is closed would trigger the system to alert a security guard.[8]

Errors can arise from misunderstandings, mistakes in judgment, carelessness, distraction, or fatigue. And separation of duties can be defeated through collusion by employees who secretly agree to deceive a company. In addition, established procedures may be ineffective against employees' errors or dishonesty, and controls that were initially effective may become ineffective when conditions change.

In some cases, the costs of establishing and maintaining elaborate control systems may exceed the benefits. In a small business, for example, active involvement on the part of the owner can be a practical substitute for the separation of some duties.

STOP & APPLY >

Match the internal control components below with the descriptions that follow.

a. Company environment
b. Risk assessment
c. Information and communication
d. Control activities
e. Monitoring

____ 1. Establishes separation of duties
____ 2. Communicates appropriate information to employees
____ 3. Has an internal audit department
____ 4. Periodic independent verification of employees' work
____ 5. Assesses the possibility of losses
____ 6. Instructs and trains employees
____ 7. Has well-designed documents and records
____ 8. Limits physical access to authorized personnel

SOLUTION

1. d; 2. c; 3. e; 4. d; 5. b; 6. a; 7. d; 8. d

Internal Control over Merchandising Transactions

LO6 Apply internal control activities to common merchandising transactions.

Sound internal control activities are needed in all aspects of a business, but particularly when assets are involved. Assets are especially vulnerable when they enter and leave a business. When sales are made, for example, cash or other assets enter the business, and goods or services leave. Controls must be set up to prevent theft during those transactions. Purchases of assets and payments of liabilities must also be controlled; adequate purchasing and payment systems can safeguard most such transactions. In addition, assets on hand, such as cash, investments, inventory, plant, and equipment, must be protected.

In this section of the text, you will see how merchandising companies apply internal control activities to such transactions as cash sales, receipts, purchases, and cash payments. Service and manufacturing businesses use similar procedures.

Internal Control and Management Goals

Study Note

Maintaining internal control is especially difficult for a merchandiser. Management must not only establish controls for cash sales, receipts, purchases, and cash payments but also go to great lengths to manage and protect inventory.

When a system of internal control is applied effectively to merchandising transactions, it can achieve important management goals. As we have noted, it can prevent losses of cash and inventory due to theft or fraud, and it can ensure that records of transactions and account balances are accurate. It can also help managers achieve three broader goals:

1. Keeping enough inventory on hand to sell to customers without overstocking merchandise
2. Keeping sufficient cash on hand to pay for purchases in time to receive discounts
3. Keeping credit losses as low as possible by making credit sales only to customers who are likely to pay on time

One control that managers use to meet these broad goals is the cash budget, which projects future cash receipts and disbursements. By maintaining adequate cash balances, a company is able to take advantage of discounts on purchases, prepare to borrow money when necessary, and avoid the damaging effects of being unable to pay bills when they are due. By investing excess cash, the company can earn interest until the cash is needed.

A more specific control is the separation of duties that involve the handling of cash. Such separation makes theft without detection extremely unlikely unless two or more employees conspire. The separation of duties is easier in large businesses than in small ones, where one person may have to carry out several duties. The effectiveness of internal control over cash varies, based on the size and nature of the company. Most firms, however, should use the following procedures:

1. Separate the functions of authorization, recordkeeping, and custodianship of cash.
2. Limit the number of people who have access to cash, and designate who those people are.
3. Bond all employees who have access to cash.
4. Keep the amount of cash on hand to a minimum by using banking facilities as much as possible.
5. Physically protect cash on hand by using cash registers, cashiers' cages, and safes.
6. Record and deposit all cash receipts promptly, and make payments by check rather than by currency.
7. Have a person who does not handle or record cash make unannounced audits of the cash on hand.
8. Have a person who does not authorize, handle, or record cash transactions reconcile the Cash account each month.

Notice that each of these procedures helps safeguard cash by making it more difficult for any one individual who has access to cash to steal or misuse it without being detected.

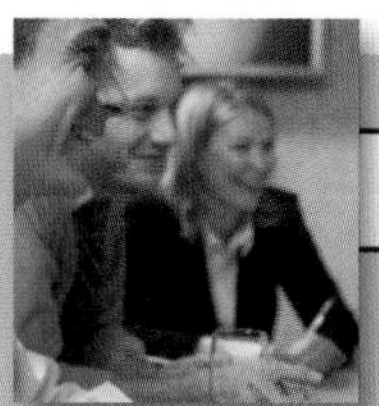

FOCUS ON BUSINESS PRACTICE

How Do Computers Promote Internal Control?

One of the more difficult challenges facing computer programmers is to build good internal controls into accounting programs. Such programs must include controls that prevent unintentional errors, as well as unauthorized access and tampering. They prevent errors through reasonableness checks (such as not allowing any transactions over a specified amount), mathematical checks that verify the arithmetic of transactions, and sequence checks that require documents and transactions to be in proper order. They typically use passwords and questions about randomly selected personal data to prevent unauthorized access to computer records. They may also use firewalls, which are strong electronic barriers to unauthorized access, as well as data encryption. Data encryption is a way of coding data so that if they are stolen, they are useless to the thief.

Control of Cash Receipts

Cash payments for sales of goods and services can be received by mail or over the counter in the form of checks, credit or debit cards, or currency. Whatever the source of the payments, cash should be recorded immediately upon receipt. Such a journal establishes a written record of cash receipts that should prevent errors and make theft more difficult.

Control of Cash Received by Mail Cash received by mail is vulnerable to theft by the employees who handle it. For that reason, companies that deal in mail-order sales generally ask customers to pay by credit card, check, or money order instead of with currency.

When cash is received in the mail, two or more employees should handle it. The employee who opens the mail should make a list in triplicate of the money received. The list should contain each payer's name, the purpose for which the money was sent, and the amount. One copy goes with the cash to the cashier, who deposits the money. The second copy goes to the accounting department for recording. The person who opens the mail keeps the third copy. Errors can be easily caught because the amount deposited by the cashier must agree with the amount received and the amount recorded in the cash receipts journal.

Study Note

The cashier should not be allowed to remove the cash register tape or to record the day's cash receipts.

Control of Cash Received over the Counter Cash registers and prenumbered sales tickets are common tools for controlling cash received over the counter. The amount of a cash sale is rung up on the cash register at the time of the sale. The register should be placed so that the customer can see the amount recorded. Each cash register should have a locked-in tape on which it prints the day's transactions. At the end of the day, the cashier counts the cash in the register and turns it in to the cashier's office. Another employee takes the tape out of the cash register and records the cash receipts for the day in the cash receipts journal. The amount of cash turned in and the amount recorded on the tape should agree; if not, any differences must be explained.

Large retail chains like **Costco** commonly monitor cash receipts by having each cash register tied directly into a computer that records each transaction as it occurs. Whether the elements are performed manually or by computer, separating responsibility for cash receipts, cash deposits, and recordkeeping is necessary to ensure good internal control.

In some stores, internal control is further strengthened by the use of prenumbered sales tickets and a central cash register or cashier's office, where all sales are rung up and collected by a person who does not participate in the sale. The sales person completes a prenumbered sales ticket at the time of the sale, giving one copy to the customer and keeping a copy. At the end of the day, all sales tickets must be accounted for, and the sales total computed from the sales tickets must equal the total sales recorded on the cash register.

Control of Purchases and Cash Disbursements

Cash disbursements are particularly vulnerable to fraud and embezzlement. In one case, the treasurer of one of the nation's largest jewelry retailers was charged with having stolen over $500,000 by systematically overpaying the company's federal income taxes and keeping the refund checks as they came back to the company.

To avoid this type of theft, cash payments should be made only after they have been specifically authorized and supported by documents that establish the validity and amount of the claims. A company should also separate the duties involved in purchasing goods and services and the duties involved in paying for them. The degree of separation that is possible varies, depending on the size of the business.

Figure 5-8 shows how a large company can maximize the separation of duties. Five internal units (the requesting department, the purchasing department, the accounting department, the receiving department, and the treasurer) and two firms outside the company (the vendor and the bank) play a role in this control plan. Notice that business documents are crucial components of the plan.

Figure 5-9 illustrates the typical sequence in which documents are used in a company's internal control plan for purchases and cash disbursements (see pages 286–287).

FIGURE 5-8
Internal Controls in a Large Company: Separation of Duties and Documentation

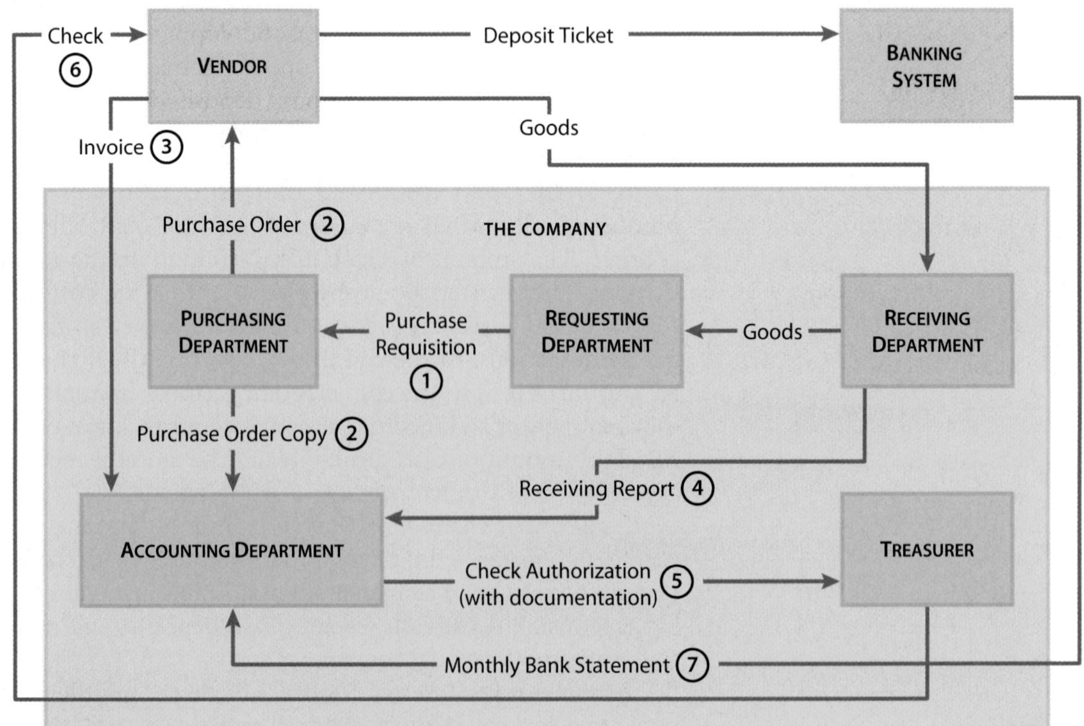

Note: Circled numbers refer to documents in Figure 5-9.

Study Note

A purchase requisition is not the same as a purchase order. A purchase requisition is sent to the purchasing department; a purchase order is sent to the vendor.

Item 1—Purchase Requisition To begin, the credit office (requesting department) of Laboda Sportswear Corporation fills out a formal request for a purchase, or **purchase requisition**, for office supplies. The head of the requesting department approves it and forwards it to the purchasing department.

Item 2—Purchase Order The people in the purchasing department prepare a **purchase order**. The purchase order indicates that Laboda will not pay any bill that does include a purchase order number. The purchase order is addressed to the vendor (seller) and contains a description of the quantity and type of items ordered, the expected price, the shipping date and terms, and other instructions.

Study Note

Invoice is the business term for *bill*. Every business document must have a number for purposes of reference.

Item 3—Invoice After receiving the purchase order, the vendor, Henderson Supply Company, ships the goods and sends an **invoice** to Laboda Sportswear. The invoice shows the quantity of goods delivered, describes what they are, and lists the price and terms of payment. If all the goods cannot be shipped immediately, the invoice indicates the estimated date of shipment for the remainder.

Item 4—Receiving Report When the goods reach Laboda's receiving department, an employee notes the quantity, type of goods, and their condition on a **receiving report**. The receiving department does not receive a copy of the purchase order or the invoice, so its employees don't know what should be received or its value. Thus, they are not tempted to steal any excess that may be delivered.

Study Note

Internal control documents sometimes do not exist in paper form in today's computerized accounting systems, but they do exist internally and are subject to the same separation of duties as in manual systems.

Item 5—Check Authorization The receiving report goes to the accounting department, where it is compared with the purchase order and the invoice. If everything is correct, the accounting department completes a **check authorization** and attaches it to the three supporting documents. The check authorization form shown in Figure 5-9 has a space for each item to be checked off as it is examined. Notice that the accounting department has all the documentary evidence for the transaction but does not have access to the assets purchased. Nor does it write the check for payment. This means that the people doing the accounting cannot conceal fraud by falsifying documents.

Item 6—Check Finally, the treasurer examines all the documents. If the treasurer approves them, he or she signs a check made out to the vendor in the amount of the invoice less any applicable discount. In some systems, the accounting department fills out the check so that all the treasurer has to do is inspect and sign it. The check is then sent to the vendor, with a remittance advice showing what the check is for. A vendor that is not paid the proper amount will complain, of course, thus providing a form of outside control over the payment.

Item 7—Bank Statement The vendor deposits the check in its bank, and the canceled check appears in Laboda Sportswear's next bank statement. If the treasurer has made the check out for the wrong amount (or altered an amount that was already filled in), the problem will show up in the company's bank reconciliation.

As shown in Figure 5-9, every action is documented and verified by at least one other person. Thus, the requesting department cannot work out a kickback scheme to make illegal payments to the vendor because the receiving department independently records receipts and the accounting department verifies prices. The receiving department cannot steal goods because the receiving report must equal the invoice. For the same reason, the vendor cannot bill for more goods than it

FIGURE 5-9
Internal Control Plan for Purchases and Cash Disbursements

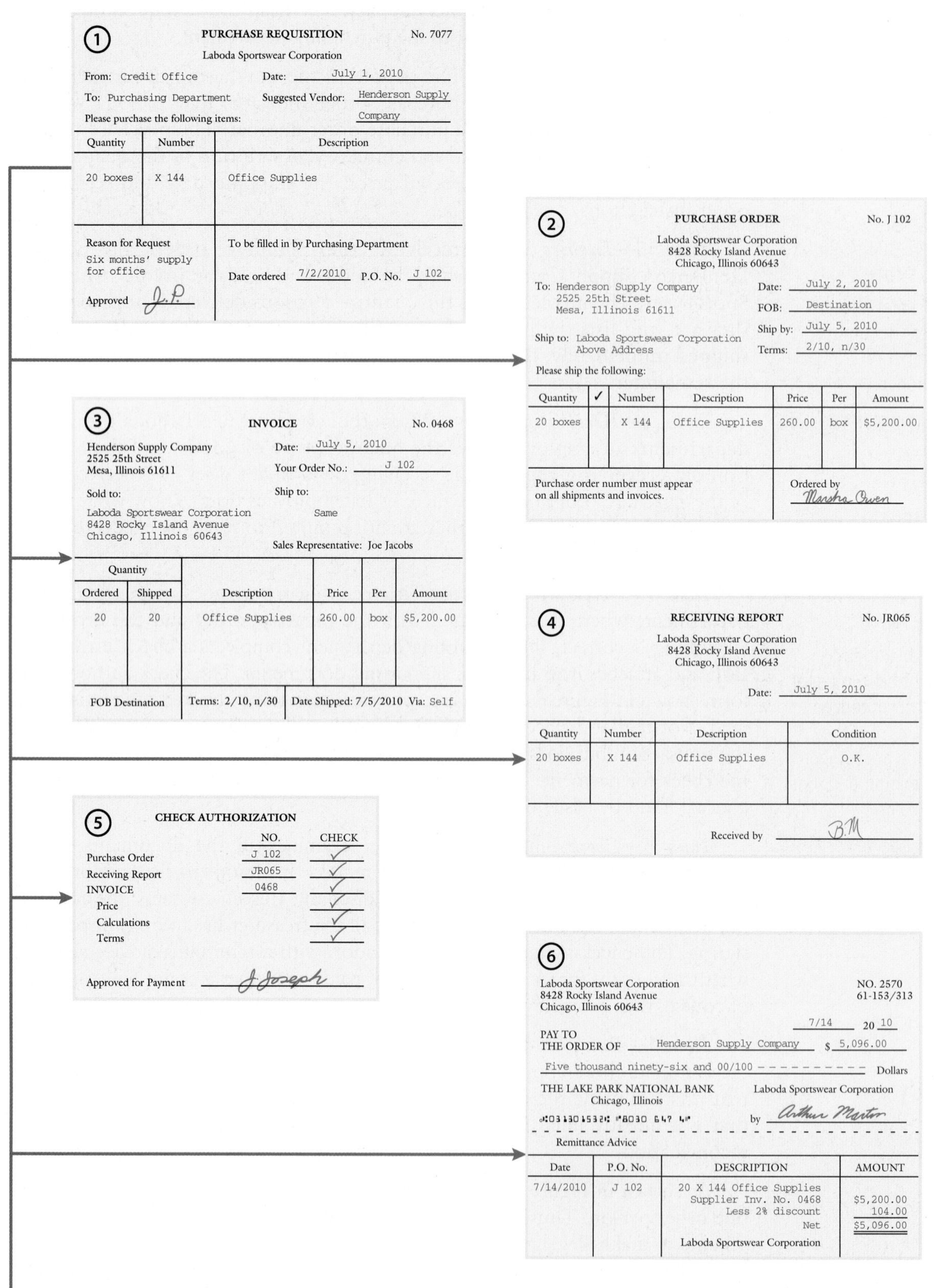

① PURCHASE REQUISITION No. 7077
Laboda Sportswear Corporation
From: Credit Office Date: July 1, 2010
To: Purchasing Department Suggested Vendor: Henderson Supply Company
Please purchase the following items:

Quantity	Number	Description
20 boxes	X 144	Office Supplies

Reason for Request: Six months' supply for office
To be filled in by Purchasing Department
Date ordered 7/2/2010 P.O. No. J 102
Approved J.P.

② PURCHASE ORDER No. J 102
Laboda Sportswear Corporation
8428 Rocky Island Avenue
Chicago, Illinois 60643
To: Henderson Supply Company, 2525 25th Street, Mesa, Illinois 61611
Date: July 2, 2010
FOB: Destination
Ship by: July 5, 2010
Terms: 2/10, n/30
Ship to: Laboda Sportswear Corporation, Above Address
Please ship the following:

Quantity	✓	Number	Description	Price	Per	Amount
20 boxes		X 144	Office Supplies	260.00	box	$5,200.00

Purchase order number must appear on all shipments and invoices.
Ordered by Marsha Owen

③ INVOICE No. 0468
Henderson Supply Company
2525 25th Street
Mesa, Illinois 61611
Date: July 5, 2010
Your Order No.: J 102
Sold to: Laboda Sportswear Corporation, 8428 Rocky Island Avenue, Chicago, Illinois 60643
Ship to: Same
Sales Representative: Joe Jacobs

Quantity Ordered	Quantity Shipped	Description	Price	Per	Amount
20	20	Office Supplies	260.00	box	$5,200.00

FOB Destination | Terms: 2/10, n/30 | Date Shipped: 7/5/2010 Via: Self

④ RECEIVING REPORT No. JR065
Laboda Sportswear Corporation
8428 Rocky Island Avenue
Chicago, Illinois 60643
Date: July 5, 2010

Quantity	Number	Description	Condition
20 boxes	X 144	Office Supplies	O.K.

Received by B.M.

⑤ CHECK AUTHORIZATION

	NO.	CHECK
Purchase Order	J 102	✓
Receiving Report	JR065	✓
INVOICE	0468	✓
Price		✓
Calculations		✓
Terms		✓

Approved for Payment J. Joseph

⑥
Laboda Sportswear Corporation
8428 Rocky Island Avenue
Chicago, Illinois 60643
NO. 2570
61-153/313
7/14 20 10
PAY TO THE ORDER OF Henderson Supply Company $ 5,096.00
Five thousand ninety-six and 00/100 Dollars
THE LAKE PARK NATIONAL BANK, Chicago, Illinois
Laboda Sportswear Corporation
by Arthur Martin

Remittance Advice

Date	P.O. No.	DESCRIPTION	AMOUNT
7/14/2010	J 102	20 X 144 Office Supplies	
		Supplier Inv. No. 0468	$5,200.00
		Less 2% discount	104.00
		Net	$5,096.00
		Laboda Sportswear Corporation	

FIGURE 5-9
Continued

Business Document	Prepared by	Sent to	Verification and Related Procedures
(1) Purchase requisition	Requesting department	Purchasing department	Purchasing verifies authorization.
(2) Purchase order	Purchasing department	Vendor	Vendor sends goods or services in accordance with purchase order.
(3) Invoice	Vendor	Accounting department	Accounting receives invoice from vendor.
(4) Receiving report	Receiving department	Accounting department	Accounting compares invoice, purchase order, and receiving report. Accounting verifies prices.
(5) Check authorization	Accounting department	Treasurer	Accounting attaches check authorization to invoice, purchase order, and receiving report.
(6) Check	Treasurer	Vendor	Treasurer verifies all documents before preparing check.
(7) Bank statement	Buyer's bank	Accounting department	Accounting compares amount and payee's name on returned check with check authorization.

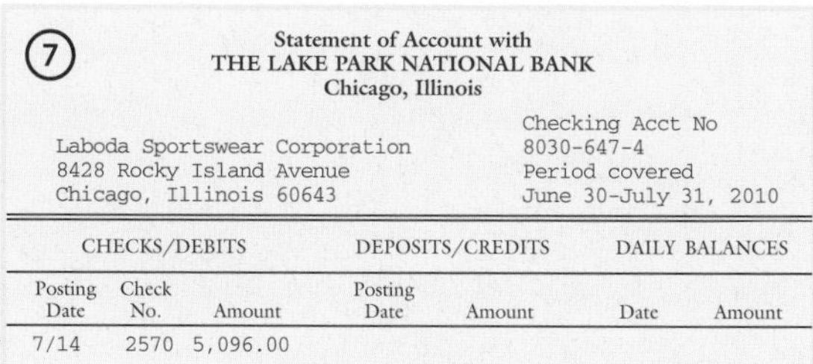
(7)
Statement of Account with
THE LAKE PARK NATIONAL BANK
Chicago, Illinois

Laboda Sportswear Corporation
8428 Rocky Island Avenue
Chicago, Illinois 60643

Checking Acct No
8030-647-4
Period covered
June 30-July 31, 2010

CHECKS/DEBITS			DEPOSITS/CREDITS		DAILY BALANCES	
Posting Date	Check No.	Amount	Posting Date	Amount	Date	Amount
7/14	2570	5,096.00				

ships. The treasurer verifies the accounting department's work, and the accounting department ultimately checks the treasurer's work.

The system we have described is a simple one that provides adequate internal control. There are many variations on it.

STOP & APPLY >

Items **a–e** below are a company's departments. Items **f** and **g** are firms with which the company has transactions:

a. Requesting department
b. Purchasing department
c. Receiving department
d. Accounting department
e. Treasurer
f. Vendor
g. Bank

Use the letter of the department or firm to indicate which one prepares and sends the following business documents:

	Prepared by	Received by		Prepared by	Received by
1. Receiving report	___	___	5. Invoice	___	___
2. Purchase order	___	___	6. Check authorization	___	___
3. Purchase requisition	___	___	7. Bank statement	___	___
4. Check	___	___			

SOLUTION

	Prepared by	Received by		Prepared by	Received by
1. Receiving report	c	d	5. Invoice	f	d
2. Purchase order	b	f	6. Check authorization	d	e
3. Purchase requisition	a	b	7. Bank statement	g	d
4. Check	d, e	f			

A LOOK BACK AT ▸ COSTCO WHOLESALE CORPORATION

In this chapter's Decision Point, we noted that **Costco**'s managers face many challenges. To ensure the company's success, they must address the following questions:

- How can the company efficiently manage its cycle of merchandising operations?
- How can merchandising transactions be recorded to reflect the company's performance?
- How can the company maintain control over its merchandising operations?

Costco is a very efficiently run organization as reflected by its operating cycle. It sells its inventory every 29 days on average and has almost no receivables. The Financial Highlights at the beginning of the chapter also demonstrate operating efficiency. They show that Costco's operating expenses increased by 10.5 percent, an amount that is less than the increase of 12.6 percent in net revenue and 13.0 percent in gross margin. Because operating expenses grew slower than gross margin, Costco's operating income increased by 22.5 percent.

Costco's management states that the sales increase was "driven by an increase in comparable sales in warehouses open at least one year and the opening of 24 new warehouses" and that the increase in operating expenses was caused mostly by "stock-based compensation expense, reserve for litigation settlement, and employee compensation adjustments."[9]

By buying and selling merchandise in bulk, providing very little service, and keeping its financing period to a minimum, Costco is able to offer its customers wholesale prices. A comparison of gross margin with net revenue in 2008 shows that Costco made only 12.4 percent ($8,980 ÷ $72,483) on each dollar of sales.

To sell for less and still make a profit, Costco must have a system of recording sales and purchase transactions that gives a fair view of its financial performance. It must also maintain a system of internal control that will not only ensure that these transactions are properly recorded, but will also protect the company's assets. In his certification of Costco's financial statements, the CEO stated that the company has the "responsibility to provide adequate internal control over financial reporting . . . to provide reasonable assurance regarding the reliability of financial reporting for external purposes."[10]

Review Problem

Merchandising Transactions: Perpetual and Periodic Inventory Systems
LO3 LO4

Fong Company engaged in the following transactions during July:

July 1	Sold merchandise to Pablo Lopez on credit, terms n/30, FOB shipping point, $2,100 (cost, $1,260).
2	Purchased merchandise on credit from Dorothy Company, terms n/30, FOB shipping point, $3,800.
2	Paid Custom Freight $290 for freight charges on merchandise received.
9	Purchased merchandise on credit from MNR Company, terms n/30, FOB shipping point, $3,600, including $200 freight costs paid by MNR Company.
11	Accepted from Pablo Lopez a return of merchandise, which was returned to inventory, $300 (cost, $180).
14	Returned for credit $600 of merchandise purchased on July 2.
16	Sold merchandise for cash, $1,000 (cost, $600).
22	Paid Dorothy Company for purchase of July 2 less return on July 14.
23	Received full payment from Pablo Lopez for his July 1 purchase, less return on July 11.

Required

1. Record these transactions in journal form, assuming Fong Company uses the perpetual inventory system.
2. Record the transactions in journal form, assuming Fong Company uses the periodic inventory system.

Answers to Review Problem

Accounts that differ under the two systems are highlighted.

	A	B	C	D	E	F	G	H	I	J	K	L	M	N
1						**1. Perpetual Inventory System**						**2. Periodic Inventory System**		
2	July	1		Accounts Receivable			2,100			Accounts Receivable			2,100	
3					Sales			2,100			Sales			2,100
4						Sold merchandise on						Sold merchandise on		
5						account to Pablo Lopez,						account to Pablo Lopez,		
6						terms n/30, FOB shipping						terms n/30. FOB shipping		
7						point						point		
8		1		Cost of Goods Sold			1,260							
9					Merchandise Inventory			1,260						
10						Transferred cost of								
11						merchandise sold to Cost								
12						of Goods Sold account								
13		2		Merchandise Inventory			3,800			Purchases			3,800	
14					Accounts Payable			3,800			Accounts Payable			3,800
15						Purchased merchandise						Purchased merchandise		
16						on account from Dorothy						on account from Dorothy		
17						Company, terms n/30, FOB						Company, terms n/30, FOB		
18						shipping point						shipping point		
19		2		Freight-In			290			Freight-In			290	
20					Cash			290			Cash			290
21						Paid freight on previous						Paid freight on previous		
22						purchase						purchase		
23		9		Merchandise Inventory			3,400			Purchases			3,400	
24				Freight-In			200			Freight-In			200	
25					Accounts Payable			3,600			Accounts Payable			3,600
26						Purchased merchandise on						Purchased merchandise on		
27						account from MNR Company,						account from MNR Company,		
28						terms n/30, FOB shipping						terms n/30, FOB shipping		
29						point, freight paid by supplier						point, freight paid by supplier		

(*continued*)

	A	B	C	D	E	F	G	H	I	J	K	L	M	N
1						**1. Perpetual Inventory System**						**2. Periodic Inventory System**		
2	July	11		Sales Returns and Allowances			300			Sales Returns and Allowances			300	
3					Accounts Receivable			300			Accounts Receivable			300
4						Accepted return of						Accepted return of		
5						merchandise from Pablo						merchandise from Pablo		
6						Lopez						Lopez		
7		11		Merchandise Inventory			180							
8					Cost of Goods Sold			180						
9						Transferred cost of								
10						merchandise returned to								
11						Merchandise Inventory								
12						account								
13		14		Accounts Payable			600			Accounts Payable			600	
14					Merchandise Inventory			600			Purchases Returns and Allowances			600
15						Returned portion of						Returned portion of		
16						merchandise purchased						merchandise purchased		
17						from Dorothy Company						from Dorothy Company		
18		16		Cash			1,000			Cash			1,000	
19					Sales			1,000			Sales			1,000
20						Sold merchandise for cash						Sold merchandise for cash		
21		16		Cost of Goods Sold			600							
22					Merchandise Inventory			600						
23						Transferred cost of								
24						merchandise sold to Cost of								
25						Goods Sold account								
26		22		Accounts Payable			3,200			Accounts Payable			3,200	
27					Cash			3,200			Cash			3,200
28						Made payment on account to						Made payment on account to		
29						Dorothy Company						Dorothy Company		
30						\$3,800 – \$600 = \$3,200						\$3,800 – \$600 = \$3,200		
31		23		Cash			1,800			Cash			1,800	
32					Accounts Receivable			1,800			Accounts Receivable			1,800
33						Received payment on						Received payment on		
34						account from Pablo Lopez						account from Pablo Lopez		
35						\$2,100 – \$300 = \$1,800						\$2,100 – \$300 = \$1,800		

& REVIEW >

LO1 Identify the management issues related to merchandising businesses.

Merchandising companies differ from service companies in that they earn income by buying and selling goods. The buying and selling of goods adds to the complexity of the business and raises four issues that management must address. First, the series of transactions in which merchandising companies engage (the operating cycle) requires careful cash flow management. Second, management must choose whether to use the perpetual or the periodic inventory system. Third, if a company has international transactions, it must deal with changing exchange rates. Fourth, management must establish an internal control structure that protects the company's assets—its cash, merchandise inventory, and accounts receivable.

LO2 Describe the terms of sale related to merchandising transactions.

A trade discount is a reduction from the list or catalogue price of a product. A sales discount is a discount given for early payment of a sale on credit. Terms of 2/10, n/30 mean that the buyer can take a 2 percent discount if the invoice is paid within ten days of the invoice date. Otherwise, the buyer is obligated to pay the full amount in 30 days. Discounts on sales are recorded in the Sales Discounts account, and discounts on purchases are recorded in the Purchases Discounts account. FOB shipping point means that the buyer bears the cost of transportation and that title to the goods passes to the buyer at the shipping origin. FOB destination means that the seller bears the cost of transportation and that title does not pass to the buyer until the goods reach their destination. To the seller, debit and credit card sales are similar to cash sales.

LO3 Prepare an income statement and record merchandising transactions under the perpetual inventory system.

Under the perpetual inventory system, the Merchandise Inventory account is continuously adjusted by entering purchases, sales, and other inventory transactions as they occur. Purchases increase the Merchandise Inventory account, and purchases returns decrease it. As goods are sold, their cost is transferred from the Merchandise Inventory account to the Cost of Goods Sold account.

LO4 Prepare an income statement and record merchandising transactions under the periodic inventory system.

When the periodic inventory system is used, the cost of goods sold section of the income statement must include the following elements:

$$\text{Purchases} - \text{Purchases returns and allowances} + \text{Freight-in} = \text{Net cost of purchases}$$

$$\text{Beginning merchandise inventory} + \text{Net cost of purchases} = \text{Cost of goods available for sale}$$

$$\text{Cost of goods available for sale} - \text{Ending merchandise inventory} = \text{Cost of goods sold}$$

Under the periodic inventory system, the Merchandise Inventory account stays at the beginning level until the physical inventory is recorded at the end of the accounting period. A Purchases account is used to accumulate purchases of merchandise during the accounting period, and a Purchases Returns and Allowances account is used to accumulate returns of purchases and allowances on purchases.

LO5 Describe the components of internal control, control activities, and limitations on internal control.

Internal control consists of all the policies and procedures a company uses to ensure the reliability of financial reporting, compliance with laws and regulations, and the effectiveness and efficiency of operations. Internal control has five components: the control environment, risk assessment, information and communication, control activities, and monitoring. Control activities include having managers authorize certain transactions; recording all transactions to establish accountability for assets; using well-designed documents to ensure proper recording of transactions; instituting physical controls; periodically checking records and assets; separating duties; and using sound personnel practices. A system of internal control relies on the people who implement it. Thus, the effectiveness of internal control is limited by the people involved. Human error, collusion, and failure to recognize changed conditions can contribute to a system's failure.

LO6 Apply internal control activities to common merchandising transactions.

To implement internal control over cash sales, receipts, purchases, and disbursements, the functions of authorization, recordkeeping, and custodianship of cash should be kept separate. The people who have access to cash should be specifically designated and their number limited. Employees who have access to cash should be bonded. The control system should also provide for the use of banking services, physical protection of assets, prompt recording and deposit of cash receipts, and payment by check. A person who does not authorize, handle, or record cash transactions should make unannounced audits of the cash on hand, and the Cash account should be reconciled each month.

REVIEW of Concepts and Terminology

The following concepts and terms were introduced in this chapter:

Authorization 279 (LO5)

Bonding 280 (LO5)

Check authorization 285 (LO6)

Control activities 279 (LO5)

Control environment 279 (LO5)

Cost of goods available for sale 274 (LO4)

Delivery expense 269 (LO2)

Exchange gain or loss 265 (LO1)

Financing period 263 (LO1)

FOB destination 269 (LO2)

FOB shipping point 269 (LO2)

Freight-in 269 (LO2)

Information and communication 279 (LO5)

Internal controls 265 (LO1)

Invoice 285 (LO6)

Merchandise inventory 262 (LO1)

Merchandising business 262 (LO1)

Monitoring 279 (LO5)

Net cost of purchases 275 (LO4)

Net purchases 275 (LO4)

Operating cycle 262 (LO1)

Periodic independent verification 280 (LO5)

Periodic inventory system 264 (LO1)

Perpetual inventory system 263 (LO1)

Physical controls 280 (LO5)

Physical inventory 265 (LO1)

Purchase order 285 (LO6)

Purchase requisition 285 (LO6)

Purchases account 276 (LO4)

Purchases discounts 268 (LO2)

Purchases Returns and Allowances account 276 (LO4)

Receiving report 285 (LO6)

Risk assessment 279 (LO5)

Sales discount 268 (LO2)

Sales Returns and Allowances account 273 (LO3)

Separation of duties 280 (LO5)

Trade discount 268 (LO2)

CHAPTER ASSIGNMENTS

BUILDING Your Basic Knowledge and Skills

Short Exercises

LO1 Identification of Management Issues

SE 1. Identify each of the following decisions as most directly related to (a) cash flow management, (b) choice of inventory system, (c) foreign merchandising transactions, or (d) internal controls:

1. Determination of how to protect cash from theft or embezzlement
2. Determination of the effects of changes in exchange rates
3. Determination of policies governing sales of merchandise on credit
4. Determination of whether to use the periodic or the perpetual inventory system

LO1 Operating Cycle

SE 2. On average, Mason Company holds its inventory 40 days before it is sold, waits 25 days for customers' payments, and takes 33 days to pay suppliers. For how many days must it provide financing in its operating cycle?

LO2 Terms of Sale

SE 3. A dealer buys tooling machines from a manufacturer and resells them.

a. The manufacturer sets a list or catalogue price of $12,000 for a machine. The manufacturer offers its dealers a 40 percent trade discount.
b. The manufacturer sells the machine under terms of FOB shipping point. The cost of shipping is $700.
c. The manufacturer offers a sales discount of 2/10, n/30. The sales discount does not apply to shipping costs.

What is the net cost of the tooling machine to the dealer, assuming it is paid for within ten days of purchase?

LO2 Sales and Purchases Discounts

SE 4. On April 15, Meier Company sold merchandise to Curran Company for $5,000 on terms of 2/10, n/30. Assume a return of merchandise on April 20 of $850, and payment in full on April 25. What is the payment by Meier to Curran on April 25?

LO3 Purchases of Merchandise: Perpetual Inventory System

SE 5. Record in T account form each of the following transactions, assuming the perpetual inventory system is used:

Aug. 2 Purchased merchandise on credit from Indio Company, invoice dated August 1, terms n/10, FOB shipping point, $1,150.
3 Received bill from Lee Shipping Company for transportation costs on August 2 shipment, invoice dated August 1, terms n/30, $105.
7 Returned damaged merchandise received from Indio Company on August 2 for credit, $180.
10 Paid in full the amount due to Indio Company for the purchase of August 2, part of which was returned on August 7.

LO4 Purchases of Merchandise: Periodic Inventory System

SE 6. Record in T account form the transactions in **SE 5**, assuming the periodic inventory system is used.

LO4 **Cost of Goods Sold: Periodic Inventory System**

SE 7. Using the following data and assuming cost of goods sold is $273,700, prepare the cost of goods sold section of a merchandising income statement (periodic inventory system). Include the amount of purchases for the month of October.

Freight-in	$13,800
Merchandise inventory, Sept. 30, 2010	37,950
Merchandise inventory, Oct. 31, 2010	50,600
Purchases	?
Purchases returns and allowances	10,350

LO4 **Sales of Merchandise: Periodic Inventory System**

SE 8. Record in T account form the following transactions, assuming the periodic inventory system is used:

Aug. 4 Sold merchandise on credit to Rivera Corporation, terms n/30, FOB destination, $5,040.
5 Paid transportation costs for sale of August 4, $462.
9 Part of the merchandise sold on August 4 was accepted back from Rivera Corporation for full credit and returned to the merchandise inventory, $1,470.
Sept. 3 Received payment in full from Rivera Corporation for merchandise sold on August 4, less the return on August 9.

LO5 LO6 **Internal Control Activities**

SE 9. Match the check-writing policies for a small business described below to the following control activities:

a. Authorization
b. Recording transactions
c. Documents and records
d. Physical controls
e. Periodic independent verification
f. Separation of duties
g. Sound personnel practices

1. The person who writes the checks to pay bills is different from the people who authorize the payments and keep records of the payments.
2. The checks are kept in a locked drawer. The only person who has the key is the person who writes the checks.
3. The person who writes the checks is bonded.
4. Once each month the owner compares and reconciles the amount of money shown in the accounting records with the amount in the bank account.
5. The owner of the business approves each check before it is mailed.
6. Information pertaining to each check is recorded on the check stub.
7. Every day, all checks are recorded in the accounting records, using the information on the check stubs.

LO5 **Limitations of Internal Control**

SE 10. Internal control has several inherent limitations. Indicate whether each of the following situations is an example of (a) human error, (b) collusion among employees, (c) changed conditions, or (d) cost-benefit considerations:

1. Effective separation of duties in a restaurant is impractical because the business is too small.
2. The cashier and the manager of a retail shoe store work together to avoid the internal controls for the purpose of embezzling funds.
3. The cashier in a pizza shop does not understand the procedures for operating the cash register and thus fails to ring up all the sales and count the cash at the end of the day.

4. At a law firm, computer supplies are mistakenly delivered to the reception area instead of the receiving area because the supplier began using a different system of shipment. As a result, the receipt of supplies is not recorded.

Exercises

LO1 LO2

Discussion Questions

E 1. Develop a brief answer to each of the following questions:

1. Can a company have a "negative" financing period?
2. If you sold goods to a company in Europe and the exchange rate for the dollar is declining as it relates to the euro, would you want the eventual payment to be made in dollars or euros?
3. Who has ultimate responsibility for safeguarding a company's assets with a system of internal control?
4. Assume a large shipment of uninsured merchandise to your company is destroyed when the delivery truck has an accident and burns. Would you want the terms to be FOB shipping point or FOB destination?

LO3 LO4 LO5 LO6

Discussion Questions

E 2. Develop a brief answer to each of the following questions:

1. Under the perpetual inventory system, the Merchandise Inventory account is constantly updated. What would cause it to have the wrong balance?
2. Why is a physical inventory needed under both the periodic and perpetual inventory systems?
3. Which of the following accounts would be assigned a higher level of risk: Building or Merchandising Inventory?
4. Why is it important to write down the amount of cash received through the mail or over the counter?

LO1

Management Issues and Decisions

E 3. The decisions that follow were made by the management of Posad Cotton Company. Indicate whether each decision pertains primarily to (a) cash flow management, (b) choice of inventory system, (c) foreign transactions, or (d) control of merchandising operations.

1. Decided to mark each item of inventory with a magnetic tag that sets off an alarm if the tag is removed from the store before being deactivated.
2. Decided to reduce the credit terms offered to customers from 30 days to 20 days to speed up collection of accounts.
3. Decided that the benefits of keeping track of each item of inventory as it is bought and sold would exceed the costs of such a system.
4. Decided to purchase goods made by a Chinese supplier.
5. Decided to purchase a new type of cash register that can be operated only by a person who knows a predetermined code.
6. Decided to switch to a new cleaning service that will provide the same service at a lower cost with payment due in 30 days instead of 20 days.

LO1

Foreign Merchandising Transactions

E 4. Elm Corporation purchased a machine from Ritholz Corporation on credit for €75,000. At the date of purchase, the exchange rate was $1.00 per euro. On the date of the payment, which was made in euros, the value of the euro was $1.25. Did Elm incur an exchange gain or loss? How much was it?

LO2 **Terms of Sale**

E 5. An appliance dealer buys refrigerators from a manufacturer and resells them.

a. The manufacturer sets a list or catalogue price of $2,500 for a refrigerator. The manufacturer offers its dealers a 30 percent trade discount.
b. The manufacturer sells the machine under terms of FOB destination. The cost of shipping is $240.
c. The manufacturer offers a sales discount of 2/10, n/30. Sales discounts do not apply to shipping costs.

What is the net cost of the refrigerator to the dealer, assuming it is paid for within ten days of purchase?

LO2 LO4 **Sales Involving Discounts: Periodic Inventory System**

E 6. Prepare entries in journal form under the periodic inventory system for the transactions of Sanford Company, and determine the total amount received from Penkas Company:

Mar. 1 Sold merchandise on credit to Penkas Company, terms 2/10, n/30, FOB shipping point, $1,000.
3 Accepted a return from Penkas Company for full credit, $400.
10 Received payment from Penkas Company for the sale, less the return and discount.
11 Sold merchandise on credit to Penkas Company, terms 2/10, n/30, FOB shipping point, $1,600.
31 Received payment from Penkas Company for the sale of March 11.

LO2 LO3 **Purchases Involving Discounts: Perpetual Inventory System**

E 7. Lien Company engaged in the following transactions:

July 2 Purchased merchandise on credit from Jonak Company, terms 2/10, n/30, FOB destination, invoice dated July 1, $4,000.
6 Returned some merchandise to Jonak Company for full credit, $500.
11 Paid Jonak Company for purchase of July 2 less return and discount.
14 Purchased merchandise on credit from Jonak Company, terms 2/10, n/30, FOB destination, invoice dated July 12, $4,500.
31 Paid amount owed Jonak Company for purchase of July 14.

Prepare entries in journal form assuming the perpetual inventory system is used and determine the total amount paid to Jonak Company.

LO3 **Preparation of the Income Statement: Perpetual Inventory System**

E 8. Using the selected account balances at December 31, 2010, for Receptions, Etc. that follow, prepare an income statement for the year ended December 31, 2010. Show detail of net sales. The company uses the perpetual inventory system, and Freight-In has not been included in Cost of Goods Sold.

Account Name	Debit	Credit
Sales		$498,000
Sales Returns and Allowances	$ 23,500	
Cost of Goods Sold	284,000	
Freight-In	14,700	
Selling Expenses	43,000	
General and Administrative Expenses	87,000	
Income Taxes	12,000	

LO3 **Recording Purchases: Perpetual Inventory System**

E 9. Give the entries in T account form to record each of the following transactions under the perpetual inventory system:

a. Purchased merchandise on credit, terms n/30, FOB shipping point, $2,500.
b. Paid freight on the shipment in transaction **a**, $135.
c. Purchased merchandise on credit, terms n/30, FOB destination, $1,400.
d. Purchased merchandise on credit, terms n/30, FOB shipping point, $2,600, which includes freight paid by the supplier of $200.
e. Returned part of the merchandise purchased in transaction **c**, $500.
f. Paid the amount owed on the purchase in transaction **a**.
g. Paid the amount owed on the purchase in transaction **d**.
h. Paid the amount owed on the purchase in transaction **c** less the return in **e**.

LO3 **Recording Sales: Perpetual Inventory System**

E 10. On June 15, Palmyra Company sold merchandise for $5,200 on terms of n/30 to Lim Company. On June 20, Lim Company returned some of the merchandise for a credit of $1,200, and on June 25, Lim paid the balance owed. Give Palmyra's entries in T account form to record the sale, return, and receipt of payment under the perpetual inventory system. The cost of the merchandise sold on June 15 was $3,000, and the cost of the merchandise returned to inventory on June 20 was $700.

LO4 **Preparation of the Income Statement: Periodic Inventory System**

E 11. Using the selected year-end account balances at December 31, 2010, for the Morris General Store shown below, prepare a 2010 income statement. Show detail of net sales. The company uses the periodic inventory system. Beginning merchandise inventory was $28,000; ending merchandise inventory is $21,000.

Account Name	Debit	Credit
Sales		$309,000
Sales Returns and Allowances	$ 15,200	
Purchases	114,800	
Purchases Returns and Allowances		7,000
Freight-In	5,600	
Selling Expenses	56,400	
General and Administrative Expenses	37,200	
Income Taxes	18,000	

LO4 **Merchandising Income Statement: Missing Data, Multiple Years**

E 12. Determine the missing data for each letter in the following three income statements for Sampson Paper Company (in thousands):

	2010	2009	2008
Sales	$ p	$ h	$572
Sales returns and allowances	48	38	a
Net sales	q	634	b
Merchandise inventory, beginning	r	i	76
Purchases	384	338	c
Purchases returns and allowances	62	j	34
Freight-in	s	58	44
Net cost of purchases	378	k	d
Cost of goods available for sale	444	424	364
Merchandise inventory, ending	78	l	84
Cost of goods sold	t	358	e
Gross margin	284	m	252
Selling expenses	u	156	f

	2010	2009	2008
General and administrative expenses	$ 78	$ n	$66
Total operating expenses	260	256	g
Income before income taxes	v	o	54
Income taxes	6	4	10
Net income	w	16	44

LO4 Recording Purchases: Periodic Inventory System

E 13. Using the data in **E 9**, give the entries in T-account form to record each of the transactions under the periodic inventory system.

LO4 Recording Sales: Periodic Inventory System

E 14. Using the relevant data in **E 10**, give the entries in T-account form to record each of the transactions under the periodic inventory system.

LO5 Use of Accounting Records in Internal Control

E 15. Careful scrutiny of accounting records and financial statements can lead to the discovery of fraud or embezzlement. Each of the situations that follows may indicate a breakdown in internal control. Indicate the nature of the possible fraud or embezzlement in each of these situations.

1. Wages expense for a branch office was 30 percent higher in 2010 than in 2009, even though the office was authorized to employ only the same four employees and raises were only 5 percent in 2010.
2. Sales returns and allowances increased from 5 percent to 20 percent of sales in the first two months of 2010, after record sales in 2009 resulted in large bonuses for the sales staff.
3. Gross margin decreased from 40 percent of net sales in 2009 to 20 percent in 2010, even though there was no change in pricing. Ending inventory was 50 percent less at the end of 2010 than it was at the beginning of the year. There is no immediate explanation for the decrease in inventory.
4. A review of daily records of cash register receipts shows that one cashier consistently accepts more discount coupons for purchases than do the other cashiers.

LO5 LO6 Control Procedures

E 16. Anna Clapa, who operates a small grocery store, has established the following policies with regard to the checkout cashiers:

1. Each Cashier has his or her own cash drawer, to which no one else has access.
2. Cashiers may accept checks for purchases under $50 with proper identification. For checks over $50, they must receive approval from Clapa.
3. Every sale must be rung up on the cash register and a receipt given to the customer. Each sale is recorded on a tape inside the cash register.
4. At the end of each day, Clapa counts the cash in the drawer and compares it with the amount on the tape inside the cash register.

Match the following conditions for internal control to each of the policies listed above:

a. Transactions are executed in accordance with management's general or specific authorization.
b. Transactions are recorded as necessary to permit preparation of financial statements and maintain accountability for assets.
c. Access to assets is permitted only as allowed by management.
d. At reasonable intervals, the records of assets are compared with the existing assets.

LO5 LO6 **Internal Control Procedures**

E 17. Mega Hits Video Store maintains the following policies with regard to purchases of new videotapes at each of its branch stores:

1. Employees are required to take vacations, and the duties of employees are rotated periodically.
2. Once each month a person from the home office visits each branch store to examine the receiving records and to compare the inventory of videos with the accounting records.
3. Purchases of new videos must be authorized by purchase order in the home office and paid for by the treasurer in the home office. Receiving reports are prepared in each branch and sent to the home office.
4. All new personnel receive one hour of training in how to receive and catalogue new videos.
5. The company maintains a perpetual inventory system that keeps track of all videos purchased, sold, and on hand.

Match the following control procedures to each of the above policies. (Some may have several answers.)

a. Authorization
b. Recording transactions
c. Documents and records
d. Limited access
e. Periodic independent verification
f. Separation of duties
g. Sound personnel policies

Problems

LO1 LO3 **Merchandising Income Statement: Perpetual Inventory System**

P 1. At the end of the fiscal year, June 30, 2010, selected accounts from the adjusted trial balance for Barbara's Video Store, Inc., appeared as shown below.

Barbara's Video Store, Inc.
Partial Adjusted Trial Balance
June 30, 2010

Sales		$870,824
Sales Returns and Allowances	$ 25,500	
Cost of Goods Sold	442,370	
Freight-In	20,156	
Store Salaries Expense	216,700	
Office Salaries Expense	53,000	
Advertising Expense	36,400	
Rent Expense	28,000	
Insurance Expense	5,600	
Utilities Expense	18,320	
Store Supplies Expense	3,328	
Office Supplies Expense	3,628	
Depreciation Expense–Store Equipment	3,600	
Depreciation Expense–Office Equipment	3,700	
Income Taxes	5,000	

Required

1. Prepare a multistep income statement for Barbara's Video Store, Inc. Freight-In should be combined with Cost of Goods Sold. Store Salaries Expense; Advertising Expense; Store Supplies Expense; and Depreciation Expense–Store Equipment are selling expenses. The other expenses are general and administrative expenses. The company uses the perpetual inventory system. Show details of net sales and operating expenses.

User insight ▶ 2. Based on your knowledge at this point in the course, how would you use the income statement for Barbara's Video Store to evaluate the company's profitability? What other financial statement should you consider and why?

LO3 **Merchandising Transactions: Perpetual Inventory System**

P 2. Vargo Company engaged in the following transactions in October 2010:

Oct. 7 Sold merchandise on credit to Ken Smith, terms n/30, FOB shipping point, $3,000 (cost, $1,800).
8 Purchased merchandise on credit from Novak Company, terms n/30, FOB shipping point, $6,000.
9 Paid Smart Company for shipping charges on merchandise purchased on October 8, $254.
10 Purchased merchandise on credit from Mara's Company, terms n/30, FOB shipping point, $9,600, including $600 freight costs paid by Mara's.
14 Sold merchandise on credit to Rose Milito, terms n/30, FOB shipping point, $2,400 (cost, $1,440).
14 Returned damaged merchandise received from Novak Company on October 8 for credit, $600.
17 Received check from Ken Smith for his purchase of October 7.
19 Sold merchandise for cash, $1,800 (cost, $1,080).
20 Paid Mara's Company for purchase of October 10.
21 Paid Novak Company the balance from the transactions of October 8 and October 14.
24 Accepted from Rose Milito a return of merchandise, which was put back in inventory, $200 (cost, $120).

Required

1. Prepare entries in journal form (refer to the Review Problem) to record the transactions, assuming use of the perpetual inventory system.

User insight ▶ 2. Receiving cash rebates from suppliers based on the past year's purchases is a common practice in some industries. If at the end of the year Vargo Company receives rebates in cash from a supplier, should these cash rebates be reported as revenue? Why or why not?

LO1 LO4 **Merchandising Income Statement: Periodic Inventory System**

P 3. Selected accounts from the adjusted trial balance for Louise's Gourmet Shop, Inc., as of March 31, 2010, the end of the fiscal year, are shown below.

Louise's Gourmet Shop, Inc.
Partial Adjusted Trial Balance
March 31, 2010

Sales		$168,700
Sales Returns and Allowances	$ 5,700	
Purchases	70,200	
Purchases Returns and Allowances		2,600
Freight-In	2,300	
Store Salaries Expense	33,125	
Office Salaries Expense	12,875	
Advertising Expense	23,800	
Rent Expense	2,400	
Insurance Expense	1,300	
Utilities Expense	1,560	
Store Supplies Expense	2,880	
Office Supplies Expense	1,075	
Depreciation Expense–Store Equipment	1,050	
Depreciation Expense–Office Equipment	800	
Income Taxes	1,000	

The merchandise inventory for Louise's Gourmet Shop was $38,200 at the beginning of the year and $29,400 at the end of the year.

1. Using the information given, prepare an income statement for Louise's Gourmet Shop, Inc. Store Salaries Expense; Advertising Expense; Store Supplies Expense; and Depreciation Expense–Store Equipment are selling expenses. The other expenses are general and administrative expenses. The company uses the periodic inventory system. Show details of net sales and operating expenses.

User insight ▶ 2. Based on your knowledge at this point in the course, how would you use the income statement for Louise's Gourmet Shop to evaluate the company's profitability? What other financial statements should you consider and why?

LO4 **Merchandising Transactions: Periodic Inventory System**

P 4. Use the data in **P 2** for this problem.

Required

1. Prepare entries in journal form (refer to the Review Problem) to record the transactions, assuming use of the periodic inventory system.

User insight ▶ 2. In their published financial statements most companies call the first line on their income statement "net sales." Other companies simply say "sales." Do you think these terms are equivalent and comparable? What would be the content of "net sales"? What might be the reason a company would use "sales" instead of "net sales"?

LO5 LO6 **Internal Control**

P 5. Handy Andy Company provides maintenance services to factories in the West Bend, Wisconsin, area. The company, which buys a large amount of cleaning supplies, consistently has been over budget in its expenditures for these items. In the past, supplies were left open in the warehouse to be taken each evening as needed by the onsite supervisors. A clerk in the accounting department periodically ordered additional supplies from a long-time supplier. No records were maintained other than to record purchases. Once a year, an inventory of supplies was made for the preparation of the financial statements.

To solve the budgetary problem, management decides to implement a new system for purchasing and controlling supplies. The following actions take place:

1. Management places a supplies clerk in charge of a secured storeroom for cleaning supplies.
2. Supervisors use a purchase requisition to request supplies for the jobs they oversee.
3. Each job receives a predetermined amount of supplies based on a study of each job's needs.
4. In the storeroom, the supplies clerk notes the levels of supplies and completes the purchase requisition when new supplies are needed.
5. The purchase requisition goes to the purchasing clerk, a new position. The purchasing clerk is solely responsible for authorizing purchases and preparing the purchase orders.
6. Supplier prices are monitored constantly by the purchasing clerk to ensure that the lowest price is obtained.
7. When supplies are received, the supplies clerk checks them in and prepares a receiving report. The supplies clerk sends the receiving report to accounting, where each payment to a supplier is documented by the purchase requisition, the purchase order, and the receiving report.
8. The accounting department also maintains a record of supplies inventory, supplies requisitioned by supervisors, and supplies received.
9. Once each month, the warehouse manager takes a physical inventory of cleaning supplies in the storeroom and compares it against the supplies inventory records that the accounting department maintains.

Required

1. Indicate which of the following control activities applies to each of the improvements in the internal control system (more than one may apply):
   a. Authorization
   b. Recording transactions
   c. Documents and records
   d. Physical controls
   e. Periodic independent verification
   f. Separation of duties
   g. Sound personnel practices

User insight ▶ 2. Explain why each new control activity is an improvement over the activities of the old system.

Alternate Problems

LO1 LO3 **Merchandising Income Statement: Perpetual Inventory System**

P 6. At the end of the fiscal year, August 31, 2010, selected accounts from the adjusted trial balance for Pasha's Delivery, Inc., appeared as follows:

Pasha's Delivery, Inc.
Partial Adjusted Trial Balance
August 31, 2010

Sales		$169,000
Sales Returns and Allowances	$ 9,000	
Cost of Goods Sold	61,400	
Freight-In	2,300	
Store Salaries Expense	32,825	
Office Salaries Expense	12,875	
Advertising Expense	24,100	
Rent Expense	2,400	
Insurance Expense	1,200	
Utilities Expense	1,560	
Store Supplies Expense	2,680	
Office Supplies Expense	1,175	
Depreciation Expense–Store Equipment	1,250	
Depreciation Expense–Office Equipment	800	
Income Taxes	2,000	

Required

1. Using the information given, prepare an income statement for Pasha's Delivery, Inc. Store Salaries Expense; Advertising Expense; Stores Supplies Expense; and Depreciation Expense–Store Equipment are selling expenses. The other expenses are general and administrative expenses. The company uses the perpetual inventory system. Show details of net sales and operating expenses.

User insight ▶

2. Based on your knowledge at this point in the course, how would you use the income statement for Pasha's Delivery, Inc. to evaluate the company's profitability? What other financial statement should be considered and why?

LO3 Merchandising Transactions: Perpetual Inventory System

P 7. Sarah Company engaged in the following transactions in July 2010:

July 1 Sold merchandise to Chi Dong on credit, terms n/30, FOB shipping point, $2,100 (cost, $1,260).
3 Purchased merchandise on credit from Angel Company, terms n/30, FOB shipping point, $3,800.
5 Paid Speed Freight for freight charges on merchandise received, $290.
8 Purchased merchandise on credit from Expo Supply Company, terms n/30, FOB shipping point, $3,600, which includes $200 freight costs paid by Expo Supply Company.
12 Returned some of the merchandise purchased on July 3 for credit, $600.
15 Sold merchandise on credit to Tom Kowalski, terms n/30, FOB shipping point, $1,200 (cost, $720).
17 Sold merchandise for cash, $1,000 (cost, $600).
18 Accepted for full credit a return from Chi Dong and returned merchandise to inventory, $200 (cost, $120).
24 Paid Angel Company for purchase of July 3 less return of July 12.
25 Received check from Chi Dong for July 1 purchase less the return on July 18.

Required

1. Prepare entries in journal form (refer to the Review Problem) to record the transactions, assuming use of the perpetual inventory system.

User insight ▶ 2. In their published financial statements, most companies call the first line on their income statement "net sales." Other companies simply say "sales." Do you think these terms are equivalent and comparable? What would be the content of "net sales"? What might be the reason a company would use "sales" instead of "net sales"?

LO1 LO4 **Merchandising Income Statement: Periodic Inventory System**

P 8. The data below are selected accounts from the adjusted trial balance of Daniel's Sports Equipment, Inc., on September 30, 2010, the fiscal year end. The company's beginning merchandise inventory was $81,222 and ending merchandise inventory is $76,664 for the period.

Daniel's Sports Equipment, Inc.
Partial Adjusted Trial Balance
September 30, 2010

Sales		$440,912
Sales Returns and Allowances	$ 18,250	
Purchases	221,185	
Purchases Returns and Allowances		30,238
Freight-In	10,078	
Store Salaries Expense	105,550	
Office Salaries Expense	26,500	
Advertising Expense	20,200	
Rent Expense	15,000	
Insurance Expense	2,200	
Utilities Expense	18,760	
Store Supplies Expense	464	
Office Supplies Expense	814	
Depreciation Expense–Store Equipment	1,800	
Depreciation Expense–Office Equipment	1,850	
Income Taxes	5,000	

Required

1. Prepare a multistep income statement for Daniel's Sports Equipment, Inc. Store Salaries Expense, Advertising Expense, Store Supplies Expense, and Depreciation Expense–Store Equipment are selling expenses. The other expenses are general and administrative expenses. Daniel's Sports Equipment uses the periodic inventory system. Show details of net sales and operating expenses.

User insight ▶ 2. Based on your knowledge at this point in the course, how would you use the income statement for Daniel's Sports Equipment to evaluate the company's profitability? What other financial statements should you consider and why?

LO4 **Merchandising Transactions: Periodic Inventory System**

P 9. Use the data in **P 7** for this problem.

Required

1. Prepare entries in journal form (refer to the Review Problem) to record the transactions, assuming use of the periodic inventory system.
2. Receiving cash rebates from suppliers based on the past year's purchases is common in some industries. If at the end of the year, Sarah Company receives rebates in cash from a supplier, should these cash rebates be reported as revenue? Why or why not?

User insight ▶

LO5 LO6 **Internal Control Activities**

P 10. Fleet's is a retail store with several departments. Its internal control procedures for cash sales and purchases are as follows:

Cash sales. The sales clerk in each department rings up every cash sale on the department's cash register. The cash register produces a sales slip, which the clerk gives to the customer along with the merchandise. A continuous tape locked inside the cash register makes a carbon copy of the sales ticket. At the end of each day, the sales clerk presses a "total" key on the register, and it prints the total sales for the day on the continuous tape. The sales clerk then unlocks the tape, reads the total sales figure, and makes the entry in the accounting records for the day's cash sales. Next, she counts the cash in the drawer, places the $100 change fund back in the drawer, and gives the cash received to the cashier. Finally, she files the cash register tape and is ready for the next day's business.

Purchases. At the request of the various department heads, the purchasing agent orders all goods. When the goods arrive, the receiving clerk prepares a receiving report in triplicate. The receiving clerk keeps one copy; the other two copies go to the purchasing agent and the department head. Invoices are forwarded immediately to the accounting department to ensure payment before the discount period elapses. After payment, the invoice is forwarded to the purchasing agent for comparison with the purchase order, and the receiving report and is then returned to the accounting office for filing.

Required

1. Identify the significant internal control weaknesses in each of the above situations.
2. In each case identified in requirement **1**, recommend changes that would improve the system.

ENHANCING Your Knowledge, Skills, and Critical Thinking

LO1 **Cash Flow Management**

C 1. Jewell Home Source, Inc., has operated in Kansas for 30 years. The company has always prided itself on providing individual attention to its customers. It carries a large inventory so it can offer a good selection and deliver purchases quickly. It accepts credit cards and checks but also provides 90 days credit to reliable customers who have purchased from the company in the past. It maintains good relations with suppliers by paying invoices quickly.

During the past year, the company has been strapped for cash and has had to borrow from the bank to pay its bills. An analysis of its financial statements reveals that, on average, inventory is on hand for 70 days before being sold, and receivables are held for 90 days before being paid. Accounts payable are paid, on average, in 20 days. What are the operating cycle and the financing period? How long are Jewell's operating cycle and financing period? Describe three ways in which Jewell can improve its cash flow management.

LO1 **Periodic Versus Perpetual Inventory Systems**

C 2. Books-For-All is a well-established chain of 20 bookstores in western Ohio. In recent years the company has grown rapidly, adding five new stores in regional malls. The manager of each store selects stock based on the market in his or her region. Managers select items from a master list of available titles that the central office provides. Every six months, a physical inventory is taken, and financial statements are prepared using the periodic inventory system. At that time, books that have not sold well are placed on sale or, whenever possible, returned to the publisher.

Management has found that when selecting books, the new managers are not judging the market as well as the managers of the older, established stores. Thus, management is thinking about implementing a perpetual inventory system and carefully monitoring sales from the central office. Do you think Books-For-All should switch to the perpetual inventory system or stay with the periodic inventory system? Discuss the advantages and disadvantages of each system.

LO3 **Effects of Weak Dollar**

C 3. In 2004, **McDonald's** reported that its sales in Europe exceeded its sales in the United States for the first time. This result has continued in subsequent years. This performance, while reflective of the company's phenomenal success in Europe, was also attributed to the weak dollar in relation to the euro. McDonald's reports its sales wherever they take place in U.S. dollars. Explain why a weak dollar relative to the euro would lead to an increase in McDonald's reported European sales. Why is a weak dollar not relevant to a discussion of McDonald's sales in the United States?

LO5 **Internal Control Lapse**

C 4. Some years ago, **Starbucks Corporation** accused an employee and her husband of embezzling $3.7 million by billing the company for services from a fictitious consulting firm. The couple created a phony company called RAD Services Inc. and charged Starbucks for work they never provided. The employee worked in Starbucks' Information Technology Department. RAD Services Inc. charged Starbucks as much as $492,800 for consulting services in a single week.[11] For such a fraud to have taken place, certain control activities were likely not implemented. Identify and describe these activities.

LO1 LO3 LO4 LO5 **Analysis of Merchandising Income Statement**

C 5. In 2009, Tanika Jones opened a small retail store in a suburban mall. Called Tanika's Jeans Company, the shop sold designer jeans. Tanika Jones worked 14 hours a day and controlled all aspects of the operation. All sales were for cash or bank credit card. Tanika's Jeans Company was such a success that in 2010, Jones decided to open a second store in another mall. Because the new shop needed her attention, she hired a manager to work in the original store with its two existing sales clerks. During 2010, the new store was successful, but the operations of the original store did not match the first year's performance.

Concerned about this turn of events, Jones compared the two years' results for the original store. The figures are as follows:

	2010	2009
Net sales	$325,000	$350,000
Cost of goods sold	225,000	225,000
Gross margin	$100,000	$125,000
Operating expenses	75,000	50,000
Income before income taxes	$ 25,000	$ 75,000

In addition, Jones's analysis revealed that the cost and selling price of jeans were about the same in both years and that the level of operating expenses was roughly the same in both years, except for the new manager's $25,000 salary. Sales returns and allowances were insignificant amounts in both years.

Studying the situation further, Jones discovered the following facts about the cost of goods sold:

	2010	2009
Purchases	$200,000	$271,000
Purchases Returns and allowances	15,000	20,000
Freight-in	19,000	27,000
Physical inventory, end of year	32,000	53,000

Still not satisfied, Jones went through all the individual sales and purchase records for the year. Both sales and purchases were verified. However, the 2010 ending inventory should have been $57,000, given the unit purchases and sales during the year. After puzzling over all this information, Jones comes to you for accounting help.

1. Using Jones's new information, recompute the cost of goods sold for 2009 and 2010, and account for the difference in income before income taxes between 2009 and 2010.
2. Suggest at least two reasons for the discrepancy in the 2010 ending inventory. How might Jones improve the management of the original store?

LO1 Operating Cycle and Financing Period

C 6. Refer to the **CVS** annual report in the Supplement to Chapter 1 and to Figures 5-1 and 5-2 in this chapter. Write a memorandum to your instructor briefly describing CVS's operating cycle and financing period. This memorandum should identify the most common transactions in the operating cycle as it applies to CVS. It should refer to the importance of accounts receivable, accounts payable, and merchandise inventory in the CVS financial statements. Complete the memorandum by explaining why the operating cycle and financing period are favorable to the company.

LO1 Income Statement Analysis

C 7. Refer to the **CVS** annual report in the Supplement to Chapter 1 and to the following data (in millions) for **Walgreens** in 2008: net sales, $59,034; cost of sales, $42,391; total operating expenses, $13,202; and inventories, $7,249. Determine which company—CVS or Walgreens—had more profitable merchandising operations in 2008 by preparing a schedule that compares the companies based on net sales, cost of sales, gross margin, total operating expenses, and income from operations as a percentage of sales. (**Hint:** You should put the income statements in comparable formats.) In addition, for each company, compute inventories as a percentage of the cost of sales. Which company has the highest prices in relation to costs of sales? Which company is more efficient in its operating expenses? Which company manages its inventories better? Overall, on the basis of the income statement, which company is more profitable? Explain your answers.

LO1 LO3 **Barter Transactions**

C 8. Barter transactions in which one company trades goods or services to another company for other goods and services are becoming more common. Broadcasters, for example, often barter advertising air time for goods or services. In such good-faith transactions, the broadcaster will credit revenue for the fair value of on-air advertising while debiting accounts in equal amounts for the nonmonetary goods and services it receives. **Dynergy**, an energy company, and another company agreed to buy and sell power to each other for the same price, terms, and volume. This resulted in no profit for Dynergy but increased its sales for the year, which perhaps helped it meet its sales goals and management's annual incentive bonus plans.[12] Do you think barter transactions that result in little or no profit for either company are ethical? Are they ethical in certain situations but not in others? How could you tell the difference?

LO5 LO6 **Merchandise Inventory and Internal Controls**

C 9. Go to a retail business, such as a bookstore, clothing shop, gift shop, grocery, hardware store, or car dealership in your local shopping area or a shopping mall. Ask to speak to someone who is knowledgeable about the store's inventory methods. Your instructor will assign groups to find the answers to the following questions. Be prepared to discuss your findings in class.

1. *Inventory systems* How is each item of inventory identified? Does the business have a computerized or a manual inventory system? Which inventory system, periodic or perpetual, is used? How often do employees take a physical inventory? What procedures are followed in taking a physical inventory? What kinds of inventory reports are prepared or received?
2. *Internal control structure* How does the company protect itself against inventory theft and loss? What control activities, including authorization, recording transactions, documents and records, physical controls, periodic checks, separation of duties, and sound personnel policies, does the company use? Can you see these control procedures in use?

LO5 LO6 **Internal Control in a Small Company**

C 10. Dan Markus runs a small company called Markus Construction. In the past, Markus's site managers have each purchased construction materials for their jobs. Markus thinks that a centralized purchasing department would help reduce waste and possibly theft. He has asked you, the company's accountant, to write a short memorandum describing such a purchasing system, the accompanying internal controls, and the forms needed to implement it. The company has a central warehouse where material could be received.

CHAPTER

Inventories

Focus on Financial Statements

INCOME STATEMENT
Revenues
– Expenses
= Net Income

STATEMENT OF RETAINED EARNINGS
Opening Balance
+ Net Income
– Dividends
= Retained Earnings

BALANCE SHEET
Assets | Liabilities
Equity
A = L + E

STATEMENT OF CASH FLOWS
Operating activities
+ Investing activities
+ Financing activities
= Change in Cash
+ Starting Balance
= Ending Cash Balance

Valuation of merchandise inventory on the balance sheet is linked to measurement of cost of goods sold on the income statement.

For any company that makes or sells merchandise, inventory is an extremely important asset. Managing this asset is a challenging task. It requires not only protecting goods from theft or loss, but also ensuring that operations are highly efficient. Further, as you will see in this chapter, proper accounting of inventory is essential because misstatements will affect net income in at least two years.

LEARNING OBJECTIVES

LO1 Explain the management decisions related to inventory accounting, evaluation of inventory level, and the effects of inventory misstatements on income measurement. (pp. 312–318)

LO2 Define *inventory cost*, contrast goods flow and cost flow, and explain the lower-of-cost-or-market (LCM) rule. (pp. 318–321)

LO3 Calculate inventory cost under the periodic inventory system using various costing methods. (pp. 321–325)

LO4 Explain the effects of inventory costing methods on income determination and income taxes. (pp. 325–328)

SUPPLEMENTAL OBJECTIVES

SO5 Calculate inventory cost under the perpetual inventory system using various costing methods. (pp. 328–330)

SO6 Use the retail method and gross profit method to estimate the cost of ending inventory. (pp. 330–332)

DECISION POINT ▶ A USER'S FOCUS TOYOTA MOTOR CORPORATION

- What is the impact of inventory decisions on operating results?
- How should inventory be valued?
- How should the level of inventory be evaluated?

Toyota Motor Corporation manufactures and sells automobiles and other vehicles globally. This world-leading Japanese company, which is known for the quality of its products and the efficiency of its operations, is one of the largest employers in the United States. As you can see in Toyota's Financial Highlights,[1] inventory is an important component of the company's total assets.

TOYOTA'S FINANCIAL HIGHLIGHTS
(In millions)

	2008	2007	Change
Product sales	$247,734	$192,038	29.0%
Cost of goods sold	204,135	155,495	31.3
Operating income	22,661	18,964	19.5
Inventories	18,222	15,281	19.2
Total current assets	120,633	99,823	20.8

Managing Inventories

LO1 Explain the management decisions related to inventory accounting, evaluation of inventory level, and the effects of inventory misstatements on income measurement.

Inventory is considered a current asset because a company normally sells it within a year or within its operating cycle. For a merchandising company like **CVS** or **Walgreens**, inventory consists of all goods owned and held for sale in the regular course of business. Because manufacturing companies like **Toyota** are engaged in making products, they have three kinds of inventory:

- Raw materials (goods used in making products)
- Work in process (partially completed products)
- Finished goods ready for sale

In a note to its financial statements, Toyota showed the following breakdown of its inventories (figures are in millions):[2]

Inventories	*2008*	*2007*
Raw materials (includes supplies)	$ 3,734	$ 3,072
Work in process	2,395	2,006
Finished goods	12,093	10,203
Total inventories	$18,222	$15,281

The work in process and the finished goods inventories have three cost components:

- Cost of the raw materials that go into the product
- Cost of the labor used to convert the raw materials to finished goods
- Overhead costs that support the production process

Overhead costs include the costs of indirect materials (such as packing materials), indirect labor (such as the salaries of supervisors), factory rent, depreciation of plant assets, utilities, and insurance.

Inventory Decisions

Study Note
Management considers the behavior of inventory prices over time when selecting inventory costing methods.

The primary objective of inventory accounting is to determine income properly by matching costs of the period against revenues for the period. As you can see in Figure 6-1, in accounting for inventory, management must choose among different processing systems, costing methods, and valuation methods. These different systems and methods usually result in different amounts of reported net income. Thus, management's choices affect investors' and creditors' evaluations of a company, as well as internal evaluations, such as the performance reviews on which bonuses and executive compensation are based.

The consistency convention requires that once a company has decided on the systems and methods it will use in accounting for inventory, it must use them from one accounting period to the next unless management can justify a change. When a change is justifiable, the full disclosure convention requires that the company clearly describe the change and its effects in the notes to its financial statements.

Because the valuation of inventory affects income, it can have a considerable impact on the amount of income taxes a company pays—and the amount of taxes it pays can have a considerable impact on its cash flows. Federal income tax regulations are specific about the valuation methods a company may use. As a result, management is sometimes faced with the dilemma of how to apply GAAP to income determination and still minimize income taxes.

FIGURE 6-1
Management Choices in Accounting for Inventories

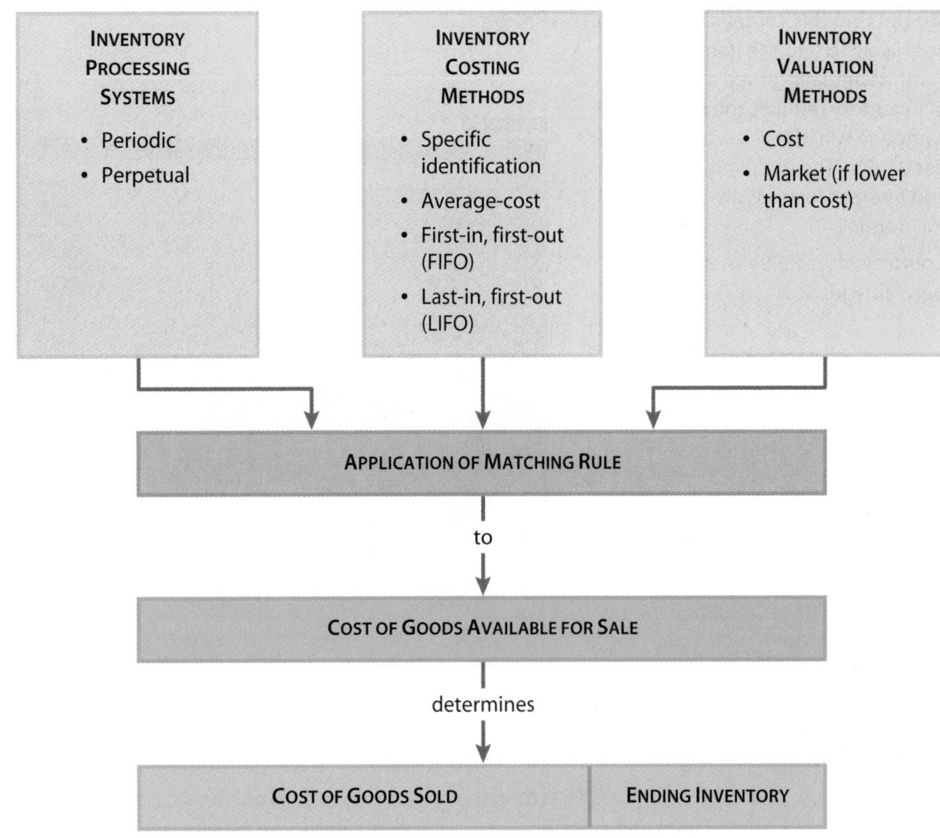

Evaluating the Level of Inventory

Study Note
Some of the costs of carrying inventory are insurance, property taxes, and storage costs. Other costs may result from spoilage and employee theft.

The level of inventory a company maintains has important economic consequences. Ideally, management wants to have a great variety and quantity of goods on hand so that customers have a large choice and do not have to wait for an item to be restocked. But implementing such a policy can be expensive. Handling and storage costs and the interest cost of the funds needed to maintain high inventory levels are usually substantial. On the other hand, low inventory levels can result in disgruntled customers and lost sales.

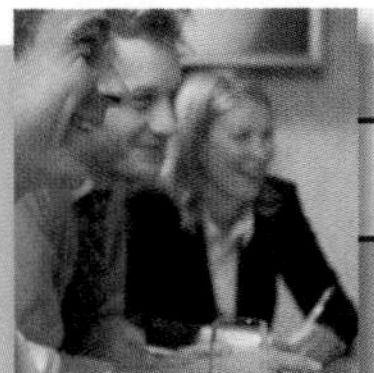

FOCUS ON BUSINESS PRACTICE

A Whirlwind Inventory Turnover—How Does Dell Do It?

Dell Computer Corporation turns its inventory over every five days. How can it do this when other computer companies have inventory on hand for 60 days or even longer? Technology and good inventory management are a big part of the answer.

Dell's speed from order to delivery sets the standard for the computer industry. Consider that a computer ordered by 9 A.M. can be delivered the next day by 9 P.M. How can Dell do this when it does not start ordering components and assembling computers until a customer places an order? First, Dell's suppliers keep components warehoused just minutes from Dell's factories, making efficient, just-in-time operations possible. Another time and money saver is the handling of computer monitors. Monitors are no longer shipped first to Dell and then on to buyers. Dell sends an email message to a shipper, such as **United Parcel Service**, and the shipper picks up a monitor from a supplier and schedules it to arrive with the PC. In addition to contributing to a high inventory turnover, this practice saves Dell about $30 per monitor in freight costs. Dell is showing the world how to run a business in the cyber age by selling more than $1 million worth of computers a day on its website.[3]

Shoppers at this Target store are very likely to find the items they want. Maintaining such a high level of inventory reduces the risk that a company will lose sales, but this policy has a price. The handling, storage, and interest costs involved can be substantial.

Courtesy of Justin Sullivan/ Getty Images.

One measure that managers commonly use to evaluate inventory levels is **inventory turnover**, which is the average number of times a company sells its inventory during an accounting period. It is computed by dividing cost of goods sold by average inventory. For example, using the data presented in this chapter's Decision Point, we can compute **Toyota**'s inventory turnover for 2008 as follows (figures are in millions):

K/R

$$\text{Inventory Turnover} = \frac{\text{Cost of Goods Sold}}{\text{Average Inventory}}$$

$$= \frac{\$204{,}135}{(\$18{,}222 + \$15{,}281) \div 2}$$

$$= \frac{\$204{,}135}{\$16{,}752} = 12.2 \text{ times}$$

Another common measure of inventory levels is **days' inventory on hand**, which is the average number of days it takes a company to sell the inventory it has in stock. For Toyota, it is computed as follows:

K/R

$$\text{Days' Inventory on Hand} = \frac{\text{Number of Days in a Year}}{\text{Inventory Turnover}}$$

$$= \frac{365 \text{ days}}{12.2 \text{ times}} = 29.9 \text{ days}$$

FIGURE 6-2
Inventory Turnover for Selected Industries

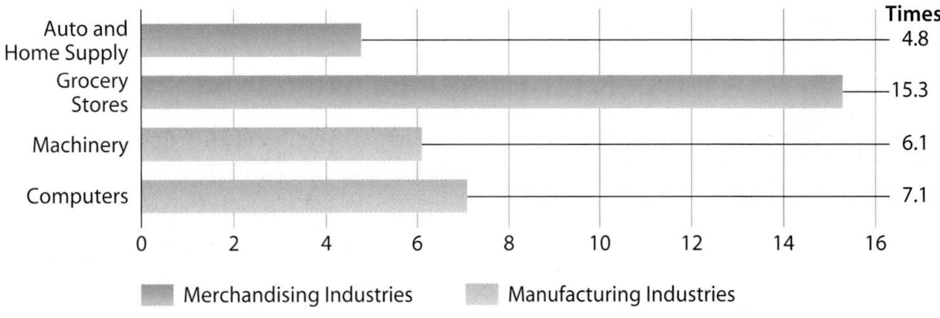

Source: Data from Dun & Bradstreet, *Industry Norms and Key Business Ratios*, 2007–2008

Study Note
Inventory turnover will be systematically higher if year-end inventory levels are low. For example, many merchandisers' year-end is in January when inventories are lower than at any other time of the year.

Toyota turned its inventory over 12.2 times in 2008 or, on average, every 29.9 days. Thus, it had to provide financing for the inventory for a little less than one month before it sold it.

Toyota's great efficiency is demonstrated by the fact that its inventory ratios are much better than the ratios for the machinery and computer industries in Figures 6-2 and 6-3. They are also better than those of other automobile manufacturers whose day's inventory on hand can often exceed 90 days. Although inventory turnover and days' inventory on hand vary by industry, companies like Toyota that maintain their inventories at low levels and still satisfy customers' needs are the most successful.

To reduce their levels of inventory, many merchandisers and manufacturers use supply-chain management in conjunction with a just-in-time operating environment. With **supply-chain management**, a company uses the Internet to order and track goods that it needs immediately. A **just-in-time operating environment** is one in which goods arrive just at the time they are needed.

Toyota uses supply-chain management to increase inventory turnover. It manages its inventory purchases through business-to-business transactions that it conducts over the Internet. Toyota also uses a just-in-time operating environment in which it works closely with suppliers to coordinate and schedule shipments so that the shipments arrive exactly when they are needed. The major benefits of using supply-chain management in a just-in-time operating environment are that Toyota has less money tied up in inventory and its cost of carrying inventory is reduced.

Effects of Inventory Misstatements on Income Measurement

The reason inventory accounting is so important to income measurement is the way income is measured on the income statement. Recall that gross margin is the difference between net sales and cost of goods sold and that cost of goods

FIGURE 6-3
Days' Inventory on Hand for Selected Industries

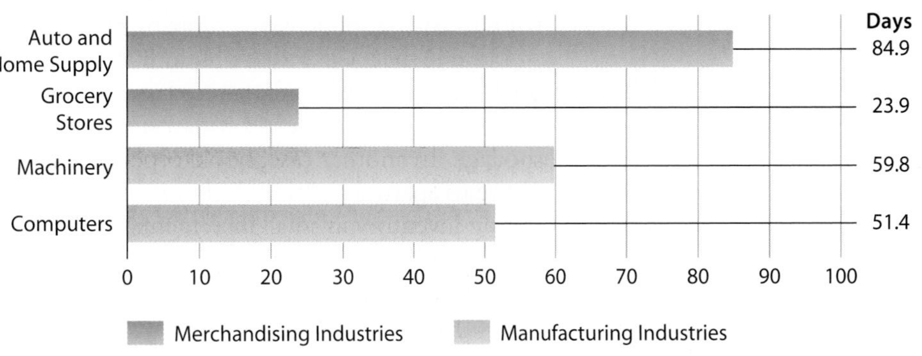

Source: Data from Dun & Bradstreet, *Industry Norms and Key Business Ratios*, 2007–2008

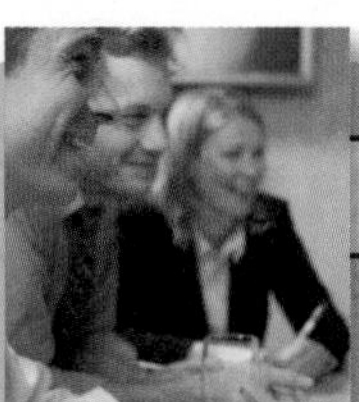

FOCUS ON BUSINESS PRACTICE

What Do You Do to Cure a Bottleneck Headache?

A single seat belt can have as many as 50 parts, and getting the parts from suppliers was once a big problem for **Autoliv, Inc.**, a Swedish maker of auto safety devices. Autoliv's plant in Indianapolis was encountering constant bottlenecks in dealing with 125 different suppliers. To keep the production lines going required high-priced, rush shipments on a daily basis. To solve the problem, the company began using supply-chain management, keeping in touch with suppliers through the Internet rather than through faxes and phone calls. This system allowed suppliers to monitor the inventory at Autoliv and thus to anticipate problems. It also provided information on quantity and time of recent shipments, as well as continuously updated forecasts of parts that would be needed in the next 12 weeks. With supply-chain management, Autoliv reduced inventory by 75 percent and rush freight costs by 95 percent.[4]

sold depends on the portion of cost of goods available for sale assigned to ending inventory. These relationships lead to the following conclusions:

- The higher the value of ending inventory, the lower the cost of goods sold and the higher the gross margin.
- Conversely, the lower the value of ending inventory, the higher the cost of goods sold and the lower the gross margin.

Because the amount of gross margin has a direct effect on net income, the value assigned to ending inventory also affects net income. In effect, the value of ending inventory determines what portion of the cost of goods available for sale is assigned to cost of goods sold and what portion is assigned to the balance sheet as inventory to be carried over into the next accounting period.

The basic issue in separating goods available for sale into two components—goods sold and goods not sold—is to assign a value to the goods not sold, the ending inventory. The portion of the cost of goods available for sale not assigned to the ending inventory is used to determine the cost of goods sold. Because the figures for ending inventory and cost of goods sold are related, a misstatement in the inventory figure at the end of an accounting period will cause an equal misstatement in gross margin and income before income taxes in the income statement. The amount of assets and stockholders' equity on the balance sheet will be misstated by the same amount.

Inventory is particularly susceptible to fraudulent financial reporting. For example, it is easy to overstate or understate inventory by including end-of-the-year purchase and sales transactions in the wrong fiscal year or by simply misstating inventory. A misstatement can occur because of mistakes in the accounting process. It can also occur because of deliberate manipulation of operating results motivated by a desire to enhance the market's perception of the company, obtain bank financing, or achieve compensation incentives.

In one spectacular case of fraudulent financial reporting, **Rite Aid Corporation**, the large drugstore chain, falsified income by manipulating its computerized inventory system to cover losses it had sustained from shoplifting, employee theft, and spoilage. In another case, bookkeepers at **RentWay, Inc.**, a company that rents furniture to apartment dwellers, boosted income artificially over several years by overstating inventory in small increments that were not noticed by top management.

Whatever the causes of an overstatement or understatement of inventory, the three examples that follow illustrate the effects. In each case, beginning inventory, net cost of purchases, and cost of goods available for sale are stated correctly. In

Example 1, ending inventory is correctly stated; in Example 2, it is overstated by $3,000; and in Example 3, it is understated by $3,000.

Example 1. Ending Inventory Correctly Stated at $5,000

Cost of Goods Sold for the Year		*Income Statement for the Year*	
Beginning inventory	$ 6,000	Net sales	$50,000
Net cost of purchases	29,000	Cost of goods sold	30,000
Cost of goods available for sale	$35,000	Gross margin	$20,000
Ending inventory	5,000	Operating expenses	16,000
Cost of goods sold	$30,000	Income before income taxes	$ 4,000

Example 2. Ending Inventory Overstated by $3,000

Cost of Goods Sold for the Year		*Income Statement for the Year*	
Beginning inventory	$ 6,000	Net sales	$50,000
Net cost of purchases	29,000	Cost of goods sold	27,000
Cost of goods available for sale	$35,000	Gross margin	$23,000
Ending inventory	8,000	Operating expenses	16,000
Cost of goods sold	$27,000	Income before income taxes	$ 7,000

Example 3. Ending Inventory Understated by $3,000

Cost of Goods Sold for the Year		*Income Statement for the Year*	
Beginning inventory	$ 6,000	Net sales	$50,000
Net cost of purchases	29,000	Cost of goods sold	33,000
Cost of goods available for sale	$35,000	Gross margin	$17,000
Ending inventory	2,000	Operating expenses	16,000
Cost of goods sold	$33,000	Income before income taxes	$ 1,000

In all three examples, the cost of goods available for sale was $35,000. The difference in income before income taxes resulted from how this $35,000 was divided between ending inventory and cost of goods sold.

Study Note

A misstatement of inventory has the opposite effect in two successive accounting periods.

Because the ending inventory in one period becomes the beginning inventory in the following period, a misstatement in inventory valuation affects not only the current period but the following period as well. Over two periods, the errors in income before income taxes will offset, or counterbalance, each other. For instance, in Example 2, the overstatement of ending inventory will cause a $3,000 overstatement of beginning inventory in the following year, which will result in a $3,000 understatement of income. Because the total income before income taxes for the two periods is the same, it may appear that one need not worry about inventory misstatements. However, the misstatements violate the matching rule. In addition, management, creditors, and investors base many decisions on the accountant's determination of net income. The accountant has an obligation to make the net income figure for each period as useful as possible.

The effects of inventory misstatements on income before income taxes are as follows:

Year 1	Year 2
Ending inventory overstated	**Beginning inventory overstated**
Cost of goods sold understated	Cost of goods sold overstated
Income before income taxes overstated	Income before income taxes understated
Ending inventory understated	**Beginning inventory understated**
Cost of goods sold overstated	Cost of goods sold understated
Income before income taxes understated	Income before income taxes overstated

STOP & APPLY >

During 2010, Max's Sporting Goods had beginning inventory of $500,000, ending inventory of $700,000, and cost of goods sold of $2,100,000. Compute the inventory turnover and days' inventory on hand.

SOLUTION

$$\text{Inventory turnover} = \frac{\text{Cost of Goods Sold}}{\text{Average Inventory}}$$

$$= \frac{\$2{,}100{,}000}{(\$700{,}000 + \$500{,}000) \div 2} = \frac{\$2{,}100{,}000}{\$600{,}000}$$

$$= 3.5 \text{ times}$$

$$\text{Days' inventory on hand} = \frac{\text{Number of Days in a Year}}{\text{Inventory Turnover}}$$

$$= 365 \text{ days}/3.5 \text{ times}$$

$$= 104.3 \text{ days}$$

Inventory Cost and Valuation

LO2 Define *inventory cost*, contrast goods flow and cost flow, and explain the lower-of-cost-or-market (LCM) rule.

The primary basis of accounting for inventories is cost, the price paid to acquire an asset. **Inventory cost** includes the following:

- Invoice price less purchases discounts
- Freight-in, including insurance in transit
- Applicable taxes and tariffs

Other costs—for ordering, receiving, and storing—should in principle be included in inventory cost. In practice, however, it is so difficult to allocate such costs to specific inventory items that they are usually considered expenses of the accounting period rather than inventory costs.

Inventory costing and valuation depend on the prices of the goods in inventory. The prices of most goods vary during the year. A company may have purchased identical lots of merchandise at different prices. Also, when a company deals in identical items, it is often impossible to tell which have been sold and which are still in inventory. When that is the case, it is necessary to make an assumption about the order in which items have been sold. Because the assumed order of sale may or may not be the same as the actual order of sale, the assumption is really about the *flow of costs* rather than the *flow of physical inventory*.

Goods Flows and Cost Flows

> **Study Note**
> The assumed flow of inventory costs does not have to correspond to the physical flow of goods.

Goods flow refers to the actual physical movement of goods in the operations of a company. **Cost flow** refers to the association of costs with their *assumed* flow in the operations of a company. The assumed cost flow may or may not be the same as the actual goods flow. The possibility of a difference between cost flow and goods flow may seem strange at first, but it arises because several choices of assumed cost flow are available under generally accepted accounting principles. In fact, it is sometimes preferable to use an assumed cost flow that bears no relationship to goods flow because it gives a better estimate of income, which is the main goal of inventory valuation.

Merchandise in Transit Because merchandise inventory includes all items that a company owns and holds for sale, the status of any merchandise in transit, whether the company is selling it or buying it, must be evaluated to see if the merchandise should be included in the inventory count. Neither the seller nor the buyer has *physical* possession of merchandise in transit. As Figure 6-4 shows, ownership is determined by the terms of the shipping agreement, which indicate when title passes. Outgoing goods shipped FOB (free on board) destination are included in the seller's merchandise inventory, whereas those shipped FOB shipping point are not. Conversely, incoming goods shipped FOB shipping point are included in the buyer's merchandise inventory, but those shipped FOB destination are not.

Merchandise on Hand Not Included in Inventory At the time a company takes a physical inventory, it may have merchandise on hand to which it does not hold title. For example, it may have sold goods but not yet delivered them to the buyer, but because the sale has been completed, title has passed to the buyer. Thus, the merchandise should be included in the buyer's inventory, not the seller's. Goods held on consignment also fall into this category.

FIGURE 6-4
Merchandise in Transit

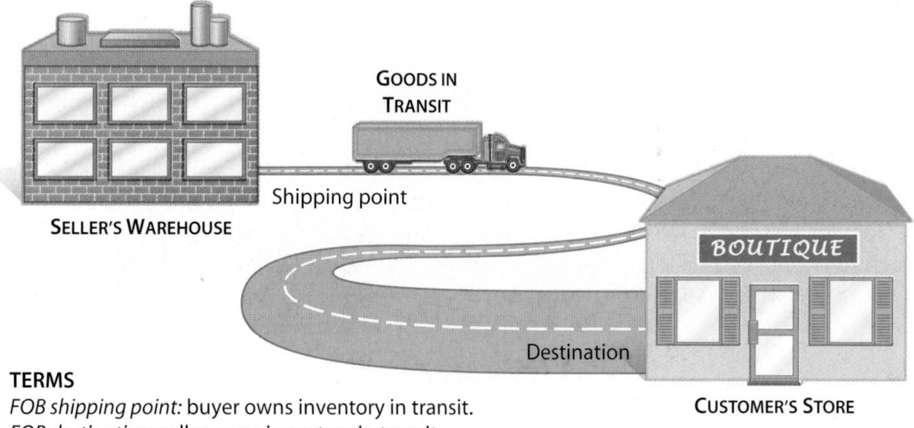

A **consignment** is merchandise that its owner (the consignor) places on the premises of another company (the consignee) with the understanding that payment is expected only when the merchandise is sold and that unsold items may be returned to the consignor. Title to consigned goods remains with the consignor until the consignee sells the goods. Consigned goods should not be included in the consignee's physical inventory because they still belong to the consignor.

Lower-of-Cost-or-Market (LCM) Rule

Study Note

Cost must be determined by one of the inventory costing methods before it can be compared with the market value.

Although cost is usually the most appropriate basis for valuation of inventory, inventory may at times be properly shown in the financial statements at less than its historical, or original, cost. If the market value of inventory falls below its historical cost because of physical deterioration, obsolescence, or decline in price level, a loss has occurred. This loss is recognized by writing the inventory down to **market**—that is, to its current replacement cost. For a merchandising company, market is the amount that it would pay at the present time for the same goods, purchased from the usual suppliers and in the usual quantities.

When the replacement cost of inventory falls below its historical cost (as determined by an inventory costing method), the **lower-of-cost-or-market (LCM) rule** requires that the inventory be written down to the lower value and that a loss be recorded. This rule is an example of the application of the conservatism convention because the loss is recognized before an actual transaction takes place. Under historical cost accounting, the inventory would remain at cost until it is sold. According to an AICPA survey, approximately 80 percent of 600 large companies apply the LCM rule to their inventories for financial reporting.[5]

Disclosure of Inventory Methods

The full disclosure convention requires that companies disclose their inventory methods, including the use of LCM, in the notes to their financial statements, and users should pay close attention to them. For example, Toyota discloses that it uses the lower-of-cost-or-market method in this note to its financial statements:

> Inventories are valued at cost, not in excess of market, cost being determined on the "average cost" basis, . . .[6]

FOCUS ON BUSINESS PRACTICE

Lower of Cost or Market Can Be Costly

When the lower-of-cost-or-market rule comes into play, it can be an indication of how bad things are for a company. When the market for Internet and telecommunications equipment had soured, **Cisco Systems**, a large Internet supplier, found itself faced with probably the largest inventory loss in history. It had to write down to zero almost two-thirds of its $2.5 billion inventory, 80 percent of which consisted of raw materials that would never be made into final products.[7] In another case, through poor management, a downturn in the economy, and underperforming stores, **Kmart**, the discount department store, found itself with a huge amount of excess merchandise, including more than 5,000 truckloads of goods stored in parking lots, which it could not sell except at drastically reduced prices. The company had to mark down its inventory by $1 billion in order to sell it, which resulted in a debilitating loss.[8]

STOP & APPLY >

Match the letter of each item below with the numbers of the related items:

a. An inventory cost
b. An assumption used in the valuation of inventory
c. Full disclosure convention
d. Conservatism convention
e. Consistency convention
f. Not an inventory cost

1. Cost of consigned goods
2. A note to the financial statements explaining inventory policies
3. Application of the LCM rule
4. Goods flow
5. Transportation charge for purchased merchandise shipped FOB shipping point
6. Cost flow
7. Choosing a method and sticking with it
8. Transportation charge for purchased merchandise shipped FOB destination

SOLUTION

1. f; 2. c; 3. d; 4. b; 5. a; 6. f; 7. e; 8. f

Inventory Cost Under the Periodic Inventory System

LO3 Calculate inventory cost under the periodic inventory system using various costing methods.

The value assigned to ending inventory is the result of two measurements: quantity and cost. Under the periodic inventory system, quantity is determined by taking a physical inventory; under the perpetual inventory system, quantities are updated as purchases and sales take place. Cost is determined by using one of the following methods, each based on a different assumption of cost flow:

1. Specific identification method
2. Average-cost method
3. First-in, first-out (FIFO) method
4. Last-in, first-out (LIFO) method

The choice of method depends on the nature of the business, the financial effects of the method, and the cost of implementing the method.

To illustrate how each method is used under the periodic inventory system, we use the following data for April, a month in which prices were rising:

April 1	Inventory	160 units @ $10.00	$ 1,600
6	Purchase	440 units @ $12.50	5,500
25	Purchase	400 units @ $14.00	5,600
Goods available for sale		1,000 units	$12,700
On hand April 30		440 units	
Sales		560 units	

The problem of inventory costing is to divide the cost of the goods available for sale ($12,700) between the 560 units sold and the 440 units on hand.

Study Note

If the prices of merchandise purchased never changed, there would be no need for inventory methods. It is price changes that make some assumption about the order in which goods are sold necessary.

Specific Identification Method

The **specific identification method** identifies the cost of each item in ending inventory. It can be used only when it is possible to identify the units in ending inventory as coming from specific purchases. For instance, if the April 30 inventory consisted of 100 units from the April 1 inventory, 200 units from the April 6 purchase, and 140 units from the April 25 purchase, the specific identification method would assign the costs as follows:

Periodic Inventory System—Specific Identification Method

100 units @ $10.00	$1,000	Cost of goods available for sale	$12,700
200 units @ $12.50	2,500		
140 units @ $14.00	1,960	Less April 30 inventory	5,460
440 units at a cost of	$5,460	Cost of goods sold	$ 7,240

Although the specific identification method may appear logical, most companies do not use it for the following reasons:

1. It is usually impractical, if not impossible, to keep track of the purchase and sale of individual items.
2. When a company deals in items that are identical but that it bought at different prices, deciding which items were sold becomes arbitrary. If the company were to use the specific identification method, it could raise or lower income by choosing the lower- or higher-priced items.

Average-Cost Method

Under the **average-cost method**, inventory is priced at the average cost of the goods available for sale during the accounting period. Average cost is computed by dividing the total cost of goods available for sale by the total units available for sale. This gives an average unit cost that is applied to the units in ending inventory.

In our illustration, the ending inventory would be $5,588, or $12.70 per unit, determined as follows:

Periodic Inventory System—Average-Cost Method

Cost of Goods Available for Sale ÷ Units Available for Sale = Average Unit Cost
$12,700 ÷ 1,000 units = $12.70

Ending inventory: 440 units @ $12.70	= $ 5,588
Cost of goods available for sale	$12,700
Less April 30 inventory	5,588
Cost of goods sold	$ 7,112

The average-cost method tends to level out the effects of cost increases and decreases because the cost of the ending inventory is influenced by all the prices paid during the year and by the cost of beginning inventory. Some analysts, however, criticize this method because they believe recent costs are more relevant for income measurement and decision making.

First-In, First-Out (FIFO) Method

The **first-in, first-out (FIFO) method** assumes that the costs of the first items acquired should be assigned to the first items sold. The costs of the goods on hand at the end of a period are assumed to be from the most recent purchases,

Study Note

Because of their perishable nature, some products, such as milk, require a physical flow of first-in, first-out. However, the inventory method used to account for them can be based on an assumed cost flow that differs from FIFO, such as average-cost or LIFO.

and the costs assigned to goods that have been sold are assumed to be from the earliest purchases. Any business, regardless of its goods flow, can use the FIFO method because the assumption underlying it is based on the flow of costs, not the flow of goods. In our illustration, the FIFO method would result in an ending inventory of $6,100, computed as follows:

Periodic Inventory System—FIFO Method

400 units @ $14.00 from purchase of April 25	$ 5,600
40 units @ $12.50 from purchase of April 6	500
440 units at a cost of	$ 6,100
Cost of goods available for sale	$12,700
Less April 30 inventory	6,100
Cost of goods sold	$ 6,600

Thus, the FIFO method values ending inventory at the most recent costs and includes earlier costs in cost of goods sold. During periods of rising prices, FIFO yields the highest possible amount of net income because cost of goods sold shows the earliest costs incurred, which are lower during periods of inflation. Another reason for this is that businesses tend to raise selling prices as costs increase, even when they purchased the goods before the cost increase. In periods of declining prices, FIFO tends to charge the older and higher prices against revenues, thus reducing income. Consequently, a major criticism of FIFO is that it magnifies the effects of the business cycle on income.

Last-In, First-Out (LIFO) Method

Study Note

Physical flow under LIFO can be likened to the changes in a gravel pile as the gravel is sold. As the gravel on top leaves the pile, more is purchased and added to the top. The gravel on the bottom may never be sold. Although the physical flow is last-in, first-out, any acceptable cost flow assumption can be made.

The **last-in, first-out (LIFO) method** of costing inventories assumes that the costs of the last items purchased should be assigned to the first items sold and that the cost of ending inventory should reflect the cost of the goods purchased earliest. Under LIFO, the April 30 inventory would be $5,100:

Periodic Inventory System—LIFO Method

160 units @ $10.00 from April 1 inventory	$ 1,600
280 units @ $12.50 from purchase of April 6	3,500
440 units at a cost of	$ 5,100
Cost of goods available for sale	$12,700
Less April 30 inventory	5,100
Cost of goods sold	$ 7,600

FOCUS ON BUSINESS PRACTICE

IFRS

How Widespread Is LIFO?

Achieving convergence in inventory methods between U.S. and international accounting standards will be very difficult. As may be seen in Figure 6-6 (on page 326), LIFO is the second most popular inventory method in the United States. However, outside the United States, hardly any companies use LIFO because it is not allowed under international financial reporting standards (IFRS). Further, U.S. companies may use different inventory methods for different portions of their inventory as long as there is proper disclosure. International standards only allow this practice in very limited cases. Also, U.S. and international standards have different ways of measuring "market" value of inventories. Because these obstacles are so significant, there is no current effort to resolve them.[9]

FOCUS ON BUSINESS PRACTICE

IFRS

Is "Market" the Same as Fair Value?

When the lower-of-cost-or-market rule is used, what does "market" mean? Under International Financial Reporting Standards (IFRS), market is determined to be fair value, which is understood to be the amount at which an asset can be sold. However, under U.S. standards, market in valuing inventory is normally considered to be replacement cost or the amount at which the asset can be purchased. The two "market" values, selling price and purchasing price, can often be quite different for the same asset. This is an issue that will have to be addressed if the U.S. and international standards are to achieve convergence.

The effect of LIFO is to value inventory at the earliest prices and to include the cost of the most recently purchased goods in the cost of goods sold. This assumption, of course, does not agree with the actual physical movement of goods.

There is, however, a strong logical argument to support LIFO. A certain size of inventory is necessary in a going concern—when inventory is sold, it must be replaced with more goods. The supporters of LIFO reason that the fairest determination of income occurs if the current costs of merchandise are matched against current sales prices, regardless of which physical units of merchandise are sold. When prices are moving either up or down, the cost of goods sold will, under LIFO, show costs closer to the price level at the time the goods are sold. Thus, the LIFO method tends to show a smaller net income during inflationary times and a larger net income during deflationary times than other methods of inventory valuation. The peaks and valleys of the business cycle tend to be smoothed out.

Study Note

In inventory valuation, the flow of costs—and hence income determination—is more important than the physical movement of goods and balance sheet valuation.

An argument can also be made against LIFO. Because the inventory valuation on the balance sheet reflects earlier prices, it often gives an unrealistic picture of the inventory's current value. Balance sheet measures like working capital and current ratio may be distorted and must be interpreted carefully.

Summary of Inventory Costing Methods

Figure 6-5 summarizes how the four inventory costing methods affect the cost of goods sold on the income statement and inventory on the balance sheet when

FIGURE 6-5
The Impact of Costing Methods on the Income Statement and Balance Sheet Under the Periodic Inventory System

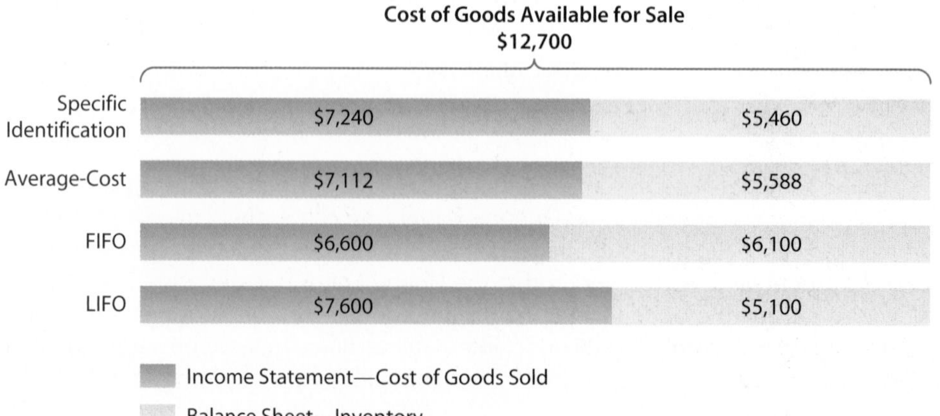

a company uses the periodic inventory system. In periods of rising prices, FIFO yields the highest inventory valuation, the lowest cost of goods sold, and hence a higher net income; LIFO yields the lowest inventory valuation, the highest cost of goods sold, and thus a lower net income.

STOP & APPLY >

Match the following inventory costing methods to the statements to which they apply.
(a) average cost, (b) FIFO, or (c) LIFO

1. In periods of rising prices, this method results in the highest cost of goods sold.
2. In periods of rising prices, this method results in the highest income.
3. In periods of rising prices, this method results in the lowest ending inventory cost.
4. In periods of decreasing prices, this method results in the neither the highest inventory cost or the lowest income.
5. In periods of decreasing prices, this method results in the lowest income.
6. In periods of decreasing prices, this method results in the highest cost of goods sold.

SOLUTION
1. c; 2. b; 3. c; 4. a; 5. b; 6. b

Impact of Inventory Decisions

LO4 Explain the effects of inventory costing methods on income determination and income taxes.

Table 6-1 shows how the specific identification, average-cost, FIFO, and LIFO methods of pricing inventory affect gross margin. The table uses the same data as in the previous section and assumes April sales of $10,000.

Keeping in mind that April was a period of rising prices, you can see in Table 6-1 that LIFO, which charges the most recent—and, in this case, the highest—prices to cost of goods sold, resulted in the lowest gross margin. Conversely, FIFO, which charges the earliest—and, in this case, the lowest—prices to cost of goods sold, produced the highest gross margin. The gross margin under the average-cost method falls between the gross margins produced by LIFO and FIFO, so this method clearly has a less pronounced effect.

TABLE 6-1
Effects of Inventory Costing Methods on Gross Margin

	Specific Identification Method	Average-Cost Method	FIFO Method	LIFO Method
Sales	$10,000	$10,000	$10,000	$10,000
Cost of goods sold				
Beginning inventory	$ 1,600	$ 1,600	$ 1,600	$ 1,600
Purchases	11,100	11,100	11,100	11,100
Cost of goods available for sale	$12,700	$12,700	$12,700	$12,700
Less ending inventory	5,460	5,588	6,100	5,100
Cost of goods sold	$ 7,240	$ 7,112	$ 6,600	$ 7,600
Gross margin	$ 2,760	$ 2,888	$ 3,400	$ 2,400

FIGURE 6-6
Inventory Costing Methods Used by 600 Large Companies

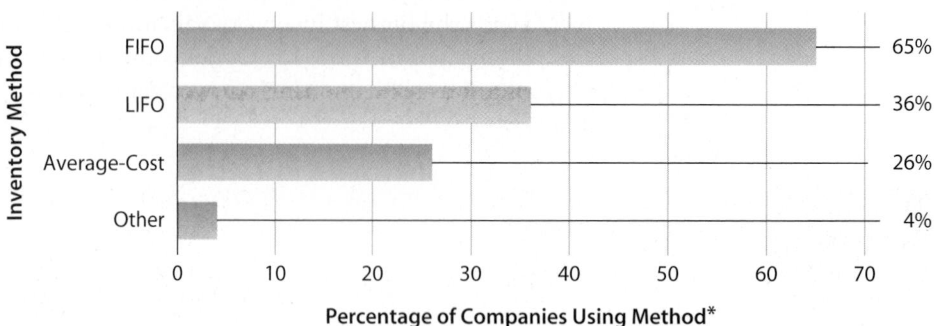

** Totals more than 100% due to use of more than one method.*
Source: "Industry Costing Methods Used by 600 Large Companies." Copyright © 2008 by AICPA. Reproduced with permission.

During a period of declining prices, the LIFO method would produce a higher gross margin than the FIFO method. It is apparent that both these methods have the greatest impact on gross margin during prolonged periods of price changes, whether up or down. Because the specific identification method depends on the particular items sold, no generalization can be made about the effect of changing prices on gross margin.

Effects on the Financial Statements

As Figure 6-6 shows, the FIFO, LIFO, and average-cost methods of inventory costing are widely used. Each method has its advantages and disadvantages—none is perfect. Among the factors managers should consider in choosing an inventory costing method are the trend of prices and the effects of each method on financial statements, income taxes, and cash flows.

As we have pointed out, inventory costing methods have different effects on the income statement and balance sheet. The LIFO method is best suited for the income statement because it matches revenues and cost of goods sold. But it is not the best method for valuation of inventory on the balance sheet, particularly during a prolonged period of price increases or decreases. FIFO, on the other hand, is well suited to the balance sheet because the ending inventory is closest to current values and thus gives a more realistic view of a company's current assets. Readers of financial statements must be alert to the inventory methods a company uses and be able to assess their effects.

Effects on Income Taxes

The Internal Revenue Service governs how inventories must be valued for federal income tax purposes. IRS regulations give companies a wide choice of inventory costing methods, including specific identification, average-cost, FIFO, and LIFO, and, except when the LIFO method is used, it allows them to apply the lower-of-cost-or-market rule. However, if a company wants to change the valuation method it uses for income tax purposes, it must have advance approval from the IRS.* This requirement conforms to the consistency convention. A company should change its inventory method only if there is a good reason to do so. The company must show the nature and effect of the change in its financial statements.

*A single exception to this rule is that when companies change to LIFO from another method, they do not need advance approval from the IRS.

Many accountants believe that using the FIFO and average-cost methods in periods of rising prices causes businesses to report more than their actual profit, resulting in excess payment of income tax. Profit is overstated because cost of goods sold is understated relative to current prices. Thus, the company must buy replacement inventory at higher prices, while additional funds are needed to pay income taxes. During periods of rapid inflation, billions of dollars reported as profits and paid in income taxes were believed to be the result of poor matching of current costs and revenues under the FIFO and average-cost methods. Consequently, many companies, believing that prices would continue to rise, switched to the LIFO inventory method.

Study Note

In periods of rising prices, LIFO results in lower net income and thus lower taxes.

When a company uses the LIFO method to report income for tax purposes, the IRS requires that it use the same method in its accounting records, and, as we have noted, it disallows use of the LCM rule. The company may, however, use the LCM rule for financial reporting purposes.

Over a period of rising prices, a business that uses the LIFO method may find that for balance sheet purposes, its inventory is valued at a figure far below what it currently pays for the same items. Management must monitor such a situation carefully, because if it lets the inventory quantity at year end fall below the level at the beginning of the year, the company will find itself paying higher income taxes. Higher income before taxes results because the company expenses the historical costs of inventory, which are below current costs. When sales have reduced inventories below the levels set in prior years, it is called a **LIFO liquidation**—that is, units sold exceed units purchased for the period.

Managers can prevent a LIFO liquidation by making enough purchases before the end of the year to restore the desired inventory level. Sometimes, however, a LIFO liquidation cannot be avoided because products are discontinued or supplies are interrupted, as in the case of a strike. In 2006, 18 out of 600 large companies reported a LIFO liquidation in which their net income increased due to the matching of historical costs with present sales dollars.[10]

Effects on Cash Flows

Generally speaking, the choice of accounting methods does not affect cash flows. For example, a company's choice of average cost, FIFO, or LIFO does not affect what it pays for goods or the price at which it sells them. However, the fact that income tax law requires a company to use the same method for income tax purposes and financial reporting means that the choice of inventory method will affect the amount of income tax paid. Therefore, choosing a method that results in lower income will result in lower income taxes due. In most other cases where there is a choice of accounting method, a company may choose different methods for income tax computations and financial reporting.

STOP & APPLY >

Match the inventory costing methods below to the descriptions that follow.

a. Specific identification
b. Average-cost
c. First-in, first-out (FIFO)
d. Last-in, first-out (LIFO)

1. Matches recent costs with recent revenues
2. Assumes that each item of inventory is identifiable
3. Results in the most realistic balance sheet valuation
4. Results in the lowest net income in periods of deflation
5. Results in the lowest net income in periods of inflation

(continued)

6. Matches the oldest costs with recent revenues
7. Results in the highest net income in periods of inflation
8. Results in the highest net income in periods of deflation
9. Tends to level out the effects of inflation
10. Is unpredictable as to the effects of inflation

SOLUTION

1. d; 2. a; 3. c; 4. c; 5. d; 6. c; 7. c; 8. d; 9. b; 10. a

Inventory Cost Under the Perpetual Inventory System

SO5 Calculate inventory cost under the perpetual inventory system using various costing methods.

Study Note

The costs of an automated perpetual system are considerable. They include the costs of automating the system, maintaining the system, and taking a physical inventory.

Under the perpetual inventory system, cost of goods sold is accumulated as sales are made and costs are transferred from the Inventory account to the Cost of Goods Sold account. The cost of the ending inventory is the balance of the Inventory account. To illustrate costing methods under the perpetual inventory system, we use the following data:

Inventory Data—April 30

April	1	Inventory	160 units @ $10.00
	6	Purchase	440 units @ $12.50
	10	Sale	560 units
	25	Purchase	400 units @ $14.00
	30	Inventory	440 units

The specific identification method produces the same inventory cost and cost of goods sold under the perpetual system as under the periodic system because cost of goods sold and ending inventory are based on the cost of the identified items sold and on hand. The detailed records of purchases and sales maintained under the perpetual system facilitate the use of the specific identification method.

The average-cost method uses a different approach under the perpetual and periodic systems, and it produces different results. Under the periodic system, the average cost is computed for all goods available for sale during the period. Under the perpetual system, an average is computed after each purchase or series of purchases, as follows:

Perpetual Inventory System—Average-Cost Method

April	1	Inventory	160 units @ $10.00	$1,600
	6	Purchase	440 units @ $12.50	5,500
	6	Balance	600 units @ $11.83*	$7,100
				(new average computed)
	10	Sale	560 units @ $11.83*	(6,625*)
	10	Balance	40 units @ $11.83*	$ 475
	25	Purchase	400 units @ $14.00	5,600
	30	Inventory	440 units @ $13.80*	$6,075
				(new average computed)
Cost of goods sold				$6,625

The costs applied to sales become the cost of goods sold, $6,625. The ending inventory is the balance, $6,075.

*Rounded.

When costing inventory with the FIFO and LIFO methods, it is necessary to keep track of the components of inventory at each step of the way because as sales are made, the costs must be assigned in the proper order. The FIFO method is applied as follows:

Perpetual Inventory System—FIFO Method

April	1	Inventory	160 units @ $10.00		$1,600
	6	Purchase	440 units @ $12.50		5,500
	10	Sale	160 units @ $10.00	($1,600)	
			400 units @ $12.50	(5,000)	(6,600)
	10	Balance	40 units @ $12.50		$ 500
	25	Purchase	400 units @ $14.00		5,600
	30	Inventory	40 units @ $12.50	$ 500	
			400 units @ $14.00	5,600	$6,100
Cost of goods sold					$6,600

Note that the ending inventory of $6,100 and the cost of goods sold of $6,600 are the same as the figures computed earlier under the periodic inventory system. This will always occur because the ending inventory under both systems consists of the last items purchased—in this case, the entire purchase of April 25 and 40 units from the purchase of April 6.

The LIFO method is applied as follows:

Perpetual Inventory System—LIFO Method

April	1	Inventory	160 units @ $10.00		$1,600
	6	Purchase	440 units @ $12.50		5,500
	10	Sale	440 units @ $12.50	($5,500)	
			120 units @ $10.00	(1,200)	(6,700)
	10	Balance	40 units @ $10.00		$ 400
	25	Purchase	400 units @ $14.00		5,600
	30	Inventory	40 units @ $10.00	$ 400	
			400 units @ $14.00	5,600	$6,000
Cost of goods sold					$6,700

Notice that the ending inventory of $6,000 includes 40 units from the beginning inventory and 400 units from the April 25 purchase.

Figure 6-7 compares the average-cost, FIFO, and LIFO methods under the perpetual inventory system. The rank of the results is the same as under the periodic inventory system, but some amounts have changed. For example, LIFO has

FIGURE 6-7
The Impact of Costing Methods on the Income Statement and Balance Sheet Under the Perpetual Inventory System

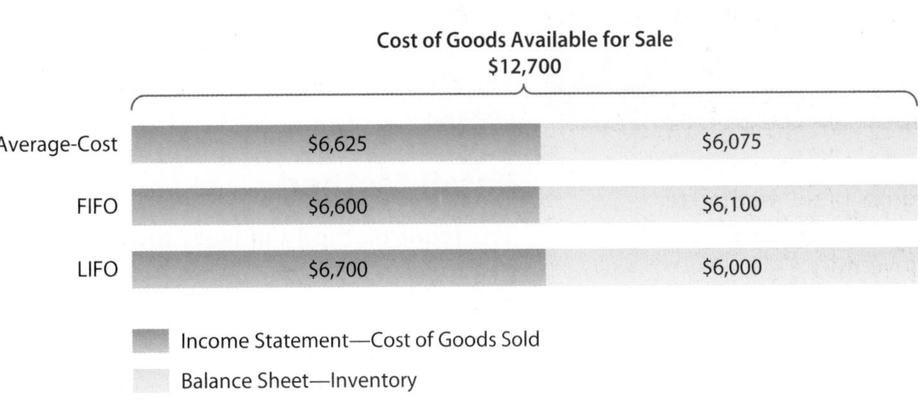

FOCUS ON BUSINESS PRACTICE

More Companies Enjoy LIFO!

The availability of better technology may partially account for the increasing use of LIFO in the United States. Using the LIFO method under the perpetual inventory system has always been a tedious process, especially if done manually. The development of faster and less expensive computer systems has made it easier for companies that use the perpetual inventory system to switch to LIFO and enjoy that method's economic benefits.

the lowest balance sheet inventory valuation regardless of the inventory system used, but the amount is $6,000 using the perpetual system versus $5,100 using the periodic system.

STOP & APPLY >

Make the calculations asked for below given the following data:

Inventory Data—May

May 1	Inventory	100 units @ $4.00
5	Purchase	200 units @ $5.00
6	Sale	250 units

Using the perpetual inventory system, determine the cost of goods sold associated with the sale on May 6 under the following methods: (a) average-cost, (b) FIFO, and (c) LIFO

SOLUTION

a. Average-cost method:

100 units × $4.00	$ 400
200 units × $5.00	1,000
300 units	$1,400

$1,400/300 units = $4.67 per unit

Cost of good sold = 250 units × $4.67 = $1,168*

b. FIFO method:

100 units × $4.00	$ 400
150 units × $5.00	750
Cost of goods sold	$1,150

c. LIFO method:

200 units × $5.00	$1,000
50 units × $4.00	200
Cost of goods sold	$1,200

*Rounded.

Valuing Inventory by Estimation

SO6 Use the retail method and gross profit method to estimate the cost of ending inventory.

It is sometimes necessary or desirable to estimate the value of ending inventory. The retail method and gross profit method are most commonly used for this purpose.

Retail Method

The **retail method** estimates the cost of ending inventory by using the ratio of cost to retail price. Retail merchandising businesses use this method for two main reasons:

1. To prepare financial statements for each accounting period, one must know the cost of inventory; the retail method can be used to estimate the cost

TABLE 6-2
Retail Method of Inventory Estimation

	Cost	Retail
Beginning inventory	$ 80,000	$110,000
Net purchases for the period (excluding freight-in)	214,000	290,000
Freight-in	6,000	
Goods available for sale	$300,000	$400,000
Ratio of cost to retail price: $\frac{\$300,000}{\$400,000} = 75\%$		
Net sales during the period		320,000
Estimated ending inventory at retail		$ 80,000
Ratio of cost to retail	75%	
Estimated cost of ending inventory	$ 60,000	

Study Note

Freight-in does not appear in the Retail column because retailers automatically price their goods high enough to cover freight charges.

without taking the time or going to the expense of determining the cost of each item in the inventory.

2. Because items in a retail store normally have a price tag or a universal product code, it is common practice to take the physical inventory at retail from these price tags or codes and to reduce the total value to cost by using the retail method. The term *at retail* means the amount of the inventory at the marked selling prices of the inventory items.

When the retail method is used to estimate ending inventory, the records must show the beginning inventory at cost and at retail. They must also show the amount of goods purchased during the period at cost and at retail. The net sales at retail is the balance of the Sales account less returns and allowances. A simple example of the retail method is shown in Table 6-2.

Study Note

When estimating inventory by the retail method, the inventory need not be counted.

Goods available for sale is determined at cost and at retail by listing beginning inventory and net purchases for the period at cost and at their expected selling price, adding freight-in to the cost column, and totaling. The ratio of these two amounts (cost to retail price) provides an estimate of the cost of each dollar of retail sales value. The estimated ending inventory at retail is then determined by deducting sales for the period from the retail price of the goods that were available for sale during the period. The inventory at retail is then converted to cost on the basis of the ratio of cost to retail.

The cost of ending inventory can also be estimated by applying the ratio of cost to retail price to the total retail value of the physical count of the ending inventory. Applying the retail method in practice is often more difficult than this simple example because of such complications as changes in retail price during the period, different markups on different types of merchandise, and varying volumes of sales for different types of merchandise.

Gross Profit Method

The **gross profit method** (also known as the *gross margin method*) assumes that the ratio of gross margin for a business remains relatively stable from year to year. The gross profit method is used in place of the retail method when records of the retail prices of beginning inventory and purchases are not available. It is a useful way of estimating the amount of inventory lost or destroyed by theft, fire, or other hazards; insurance companies often use it to verify loss claims. The gross profit method is acceptable for estimating the cost of inventory for interim reports, but it is not acceptable for valuing inventory in the annual financial statements.

TABLE 6-3
Gross Profit Method of Inventory Estimation

1. Beginning inventory at cost		$100,000
Purchases at cost (including freight-in)		580,000
Cost of goods available for sale		$680,000
2. Less estimated cost of goods sold		
Sales at selling price	$800,000	
Less estimated gross margin ($800,000 × 30%)	240,000	
Estimated cost of goods sold		560,000
3. Estimated cost of ending inventory		$120,000

As Table 6-3 shows, the gross profit method is simple to use. First, figure the cost of goods available for sale in the usual way (add purchases to beginning inventory). Second, estimate the cost of goods sold by deducting the estimated gross margin of 30 percent from sales. Finally, deduct the estimated cost of goods sold from the cost of goods available for sale to arrive at the estimated cost of ending inventory.

STOP & APPLY >

Campus Jeans Shop had net retail sales of $195,000 during the current year. The following additional information was obtained from the company's accounting records:

	At Cost	At Retail
Beginning inventory	$ 40,000	$ 60,000
Net purchases (excluding freight-in)	130,000	210,000
Freight-in	10,000	

Using the retail method, estimate the company's ending inventory at cost. Assuming that a physical inventory taken at year end revealed an inventory on hand of $66,000 at retail value, what is the estimated amount of inventory shrinkage (loss due to theft, damage, etc.) at cost using the retail method?

SOLUTION

	Cost	Retail
Beginning inventory	$ 40,000	$ 60,000
Net purchases for the period (excluding freight-in)	130,000	210,000
Freight-in	10,000	
Goods available for sale	$180,000	$270,000
Ratio of cost to retail price: $180,000 / $270,000 = 66.7%*		
Net sales during the period		195,000
Estimated ending inventory at retail		$ 75,000
Ratio of cost to retail	66.7%	
Estimated cost of ending inventory	$ 50,000	

Estimated inventory loss = Estimated cost − (Retail inventory count × 66.7)
= $50,000 − ($66,000 × 66.7) = $50,000 − $44,000
= $6,000

*Rounded.

A LOOK BACK AT ▸ TOYOTA MOTOR CORPORATION

In this chapter's Decision Point, we posed the following questions:

- What is the impact of inventory decisions on operating results?
- How should inventory be valued?
- How should the level of inventory be evaluated?

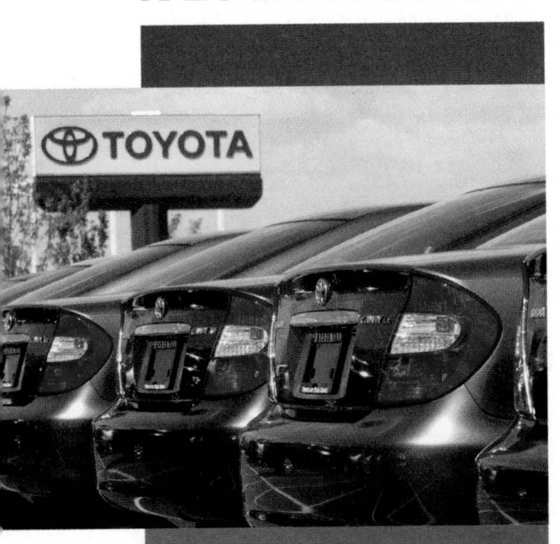

As we pointed out in the chapter, Toyota uses supply-chain management and a just-in-time operating environment to manage its inventory. By doing so, it reduces its operating costs. We also pointed out that a note in Toyota's annual report disclosed that the company used the average costing method and applied the lower-of-cost-or-market rule to its inventories. Toyota's approach to valuation adheres to the conservatism convention because it may recognize losses in value before the products are sold if their value decreases.

Using data from Toyota's Financial Highlights, we can evaluate the company's success in managing its inventories by comparing its inventory turnover ratio and days' inventory on hand in 2008 and 2007 (dollar amounts are in millions; inventory in 2006 was $13,799):

	2008	2007
Cost of Goods Sold / Average Inventory	$204,135 / ($18,222 + $15,281) ÷ 2	$155,495 / ($15,281 + $13,799) ÷ 2
	$204,135 / $16,752	$155,495 / $14,540
Inventory Turnover:	12.2 times*	10.7 times*
Number of Days in a Year / Inventory Turnover	365 days / 12.2 times	365 days / 10.7 times
Days' Inventory on Hand:	29.9 days*	34.1 days*

*Rounded.

Thus, in 2008, Toyota experienced an improvement in its inventory turnover, as well as a reduction in the number of days it had inventory on hand. This is a very good performance, especially in light of the decline in the economy in the latter part of 2007.

Review Problem

Periodic and Perpetual Inventory Systems

LO1 LO3

The following table summarizes the beginning inventory, purchases, and sales of Zeta Company's single product during May:

	A	B	C	D	E	F	G	H
1					Beginning Inventory and Purchases			
2	Date				Units	Cost	Total	Sales Units
3	May	1		Inventory	2,800	$20	$ 56,000	
4		8		Purchase	1,200	22	26,400	
5		10		Sale				3,200
6		24		Purchase	1,600	24	38,400	
7								
8	Totals				5,600		$120,800	3,200
9								

Required

1. Assuming that the company uses the periodic inventory system, compute the cost that should be assigned to ending inventory and to cost of goods sold using (a) the average-cost method, (b) the FIFO method, and (c) the LIFO method.
2. Assuming that the company uses the perpetual inventory system, compute the cost that should be assigned to ending inventory and to cost of goods sold using (a) the average-cost method, (b) the FIFO method, and (c) the LIFO method.
3. Compute inventory turnover and days' inventory on hand under each of the inventory cost flow assumptions in requirement **1**. What conclusion can you draw from this comparison?

Answers to Review Problem

	Units	Amount
Beginning inventory	2,800	$ 56,000
Purchases	2,800	64,800
Goods available for sale	5,600	$120,800
Sales	3,200	
Ending inventory	2,400	

1. Periodic inventory system:
   a. Average-cost method

Cost of goods available for sale	$120,800
Less ending inventory consisting of 2,400 units at $21.57*	51,768
Cost of goods sold	$ 69,032

*$120,800 ÷ 5,600 units = $21.57 (rounded)

b. FIFO method

Cost of goods available for sale		$120,800
Less ending inventory consisting of		
May 24 purchase (1,600 × $24)	$38,400	
May 8 purchase (800 × $22)	17,600	56,000
Cost of goods sold		$ 64,800

c. LIFO method

Cost of goods available for sale	$120,800
Less ending inventory consisting of	
beginning inventory (2,400 × $20)	48,000
Cost of goods sold	$ 72,800

2. Perpetual inventory system:

a. Average-cost method

Date			Units	Cost	Amount
May	1	Inventory	2,800	$20.00	$56,000
	8	Purchase	1,200	22.00	26,400
	8	Balance	4,000	20.60	$82,400
	10	Sale	(3,200)	20.60	(65,920)
	10	Balance	800	20.60	$16,480
	24	Purchase	1,600	24.00	38,400
	31	Inventory	2,400	22.87*	$54,880
Cost of goods sold					$65,920

*Rounded.

b. FIFO method

Date			Units	Cost	Amount
May	1	Inventory	2,800	$20	$56,000
	8	Purchase	1,200	22	26,400
	8	Balance	2,800	20	
			1,200	22	$82,400
	10	Sale	(2,800)	20	
			(400)	22	(64,800)
	10	Balance	800	22	$17,600
	24	Purchase	1,600	24	38,400
	31	Inventory	800	22	
			1,600	24	$56,000
Cost of goods sold					$64,800

c. LIFO method

Date			Units	Cost	Amount
May	1	Inventory	2,800	$20	$56,000
	8	Purchase	1,200	22	26,400
	8	Balance	2,800	20	
			1,200	22	$82,400
	10	Sale	(1,200)	22	
			(2,000)	20	(66,400)
	10	Balance	800	20	$16,000
	24	Purchase	1,600	24	38,400
	31	Inventory	800	20	
			1,600	24	$54,400
Cost of goods sold					$66,400

3. Ratios computed:

	Average-Cost	FIFO	LIFO
$\frac{\text{Cost of Goods Sold}}{\text{Average Inventory}}$	$\frac{\$69{,}032}{(\$51{,}768 + \$56{,}000) \div 2} =$	$\frac{\$64{,}800}{(\$56{,}000 + \$56{,}000) \div 2} =$	$\frac{\$72{,}800}{(\$48{,}000 + \$56{,}000) \div 2} =$
	$\frac{\$69{,}032}{\$53{,}884} = 1.3$ times	$\frac{\$64{,}800}{\$56{,}000} = 1.2$ times	$\frac{\$72{,}800}{\$52{,}000} = 1.4$ times
Inventory Turnover:	1.3 times	1.2 times	1.4 times
Days' Inventory on Hand:	(365 days ÷ 1.3 times) 280.8 days*	(365 days ÷ 1.2 times) 304.2 days*	(365 days ÷ 1.4 times) 260.7 days*

In periods of rising prices, the LIFO method will always result in a higher inventory turnover and lower days' inventory on hand than the other costing methods. When comparing inventory ratios for two or more companies, their inventory methods should be considered.

*Rounded.

LO1 Explain the management decisions related to inventory accounting, evaluation of inventory level, and the effects of inventory misstatements on income measurement.

The objective of inventory accounting is the proper determination of income through the matching of costs and revenues. In accounting for inventories, management must choose the type of processing system, costing method, and valuation method the company will use. Because the value of inventory affects a company's net income, management's choices will affect not only external and internal evaluations of the company, but also the amount of income taxes the company pays and its cash flows.

The level of inventory a company maintains has important economic consequences. To evaluate inventory levels, managers commonly use inventory turnover and its related measure, days' inventory on hand. Supply-chain management and a just-in-time operating environment are a means of increasing inventory turnover and reducing inventory carrying costs. If the value of ending inventory is understated or overstated, a corresponding error—dollar for dollar—will be made in income before income taxes. Furthermore, because the ending inventory of one period is the beginning inventory of the next, the misstatement affects two accounting periods, although the effects are opposite.

LO2 Define *inventory cost*, contrast goods flow and cost flow, and explain the lower-of-cost-or-market (LCM) rule.

Inventory cost includes the invoice price less purchases discounts; freight-in, including insurance in transit; and applicable taxes and tariffs. Goods flow refers to the actual physical flow of merchandise in a business, whereas cost flow refers to the assumed flow of costs. The lower-of-cost-or-market rule states that if the replacement cost (market cost) of the inventory is lower than the original cost, the lower figure should be used.

LO3 Calculate inventory cost under the periodic inventory system using various costing methods.

The value assigned to ending inventory is the result of two measurements: quantity and cost. Quantity is determined by taking a physical inventory. Cost is determined by using one of four inventory methods, each based on a different assumption of cost flow. Under the periodic inventory system, the specific identification method identifies the actual cost of each item in inventory. The average-cost method assumes that the cost of inventory is the average cost of goods available for sale during the period. The first-in, first-out (FIFO) method assumes that the costs of the first items acquired should be assigned to the first items sold. The last-in, first-out (LIFO) method assumes that the costs of the last items acquired should be assigned to the first items sold.

LO4 Explain the effects of inventory costing methods on income determination and income taxes.

During periods of rising prices, the LIFO method will show the lowest net income; FIFO, the highest; and average-cost, in between. LIFO and FIFO have the opposite effects in periods of falling prices. No generalization can be made regarding the specific identification method. The Internal Revenue Service requires that if LIFO is used for tax purposes, it must be used for financial statements; it also does not allow the lower-of-cost-or-market rule to be applied to the LIFO method.

Supplemental Objectives

SO5 Calculate inventory cost under the perpetual inventory system using various costing methods.

Under the perpetual inventory system, cost of goods sold is accumulated as sales are made and costs are transferred from the Inventory account to the Cost of Goods Sold account. The cost of the ending inventory is the balance of the Inventory account. The specific identification method and the FIFO method produce the same results under both the perpetual and periodic inventory systems. The results differ for the average-cost method because an average is calculated after each sale rather than at the end of the accounting period. Results also differ for the LIFO method because the cost components of inventory change constantly as goods are bought and sold.

SO6 Use the retail method and gross profit method to estimate the cost of ending inventory.

Two methods of estimating the value of inventory are the retail method and the gross profit method. Under the retail method, inventory is determined at retail prices and is then reduced to estimated cost by applying a ratio of cost to retail price. Under the gross profit method, cost of goods sold is estimated by reducing sales by estimated gross margin. The estimated cost of goods sold is then deducted from the cost of goods available for sale to estimate the cost of ending inventory.

REVIEW of Concepts and Terminology

The following concepts and terms were introduced in this chapter:

Average-cost method 322 (LO3)

Consignment 320 (LO2)

Cost flow 319 (LO2)

First-in, first-out (FIFO) method 322 (LO3)

Goods flow 319 (LO2)

Gross profit method 331 (SO6)

Inventory cost 318 (LO2)

Just-in-time operating environment 315 (LO1)

Last-in, first-out (LIFO) method 323 (LO3)

LIFO liquidation 327 (LO4)

Lower-of-cost-or-market (LCM) rule 320 (LO2)

Market 320 (LO2)

Retail method 330 (SO6)

Specific identification method 322 (LO3)

Supply-chain management 315 (LO1)

Key Ratios

Days' inventory on hand 314 (LO1)

Inventory turnover 314 (LO1)

CHAPTER ASSIGNMENTS

BUILDING Your Basic Knowledge and Skills

Short Exercises

LO1 **Management Issues**

SE 1. Indicate whether each of the following items is associated with (a) allocating the cost of inventories in accordance with the matching rule, (b) assessing the impact of inventory decisions, (c) evaluating the level of inventory, or (d) engaging in an unethical practice.

1. Calculating days' inventory on hand
2. Ordering a supply of inventory to satisfy customer needs
3. Valuing inventory at an amount to achieve a specific profit objective
4. Calculating the income tax effect of an inventory method
5. Deciding the cost to place on ending inventory

LO1 **Inventory Turnover and Days' Inventory on Hand**

SE 2. During 2009, Gabriella's Fashion had beginning inventory of $960,000, ending inventory of $1,120,000, and cost of goods sold of $4,400,000. Compute the inventory turnover and days' inventory on hand.

LO3 **Specific Identification Method**

SE 3. Assume the following data with regard to inventory for Caciato Company:

Aug. 1 Inventory	40 units @ $10 per unit	$ 400
8 Purchase	50 units @ $11 per unit	550
22 Purchase	35 units @ $12 per unit	420
Goods available for sale	125 units	$1,370
Aug. 15 Sale	45 units	
28 Sale	25 units	
Inventory, Aug. 31	55 units	

Assuming that the inventory consists of 30 units from the August 8 purchase and 25 units from the purchase of August 22, calculate the cost of ending inventory and cost of goods sold.

LO3 **Average-Cost Method: Periodic Inventory System**

SE 4. Using the data in **SE 3**, calculate the cost of ending inventory and cost of goods sold according to the average-cost method under the periodic inventory system.

LO3 **FIFO Method: Periodic Inventory System**

SE 5. Using the data in **SE 3**, calculate the cost of ending inventory and cost of goods sold according to the FIFO method under the periodic inventory system.

LO3 **LIFO Method: Periodic Inventory System**

SE 6. Using the data in **SE 3**, calculate the cost of ending inventory and cost of goods sold according to the LIFO method under the periodic inventory system.

LO4 **Effects of Inventory Costing Methods and Changing Prices**

SE 7. Using Table 6-1 as an example, prepare a table with four columns that shows the ending inventory and cost of goods sold for each of the results from your calculations in **SE 3** through **SE 6**, including the effects of the different prices at which the merchandise was purchased. Which method(s) would result in the lowest income taxes?

SO5 **Average-Cost Method: Perpetual Inventory System**

SE 8. Using the data in **SE 3**, calculate the cost of ending inventory and cost of goods sold according to the average-cost method under the perpetual inventory system.

SO5 **FIFO Method: Perpetual Inventory System**

SE 9. Using the data in **SE 3**, calculate the cost of ending inventory and cost of goods sold according to the FIFO method under the perpetual inventory system.

SO5 **LIFO Method: Perpetual Inventory System**

SE 10. Using the data in **SE 3**, calculate the cost of ending inventory and cost of goods sold according to the LIFO method under the perpetual inventory system.

Exercises

LO1 LO2 **Discussion Questions**

E 1. Develop a brief answer to each of the following questions:

1. Is it good or bad for a retail store to have a large inventory?
2. Which is more important from the standpoint of inventory costing: the flow of goods or the flow of costs?
3. Why is misstatement of inventory one of the most common means of financial statement fraud?
4. Given that the LCM rule is an application of the conservatism convention in the current accounting period, is the effect of this application also conservative in the next period?

LO4 SO5 SO6 **Discussion Questions**

E 2. Develop a brief answer to each of the following questions:

1. Under what condition would all four methods of inventory pricing produce exactly the same results?
2. Under the perpetual inventory system, why is the cost of goods sold not determined by deducting the ending inventory from the cost of goods available for sale, as it is under the periodic inventory method?
3. Which of the following methods do not require a physical inventory: periodic inventory system, perpetual inventory method, retail method, or gross profit method?

LO1 **Management Issues**

E 3. Indicate whether each of the following items is associated with (a) allocating the cost of inventories in accordance with the matching rule, (b) assessing the impact of inventory decisions, (c) evaluating the level of inventory, or (d) engaging in an unethical action.

1. Computing inventory turnover
2. Valuing inventory at an amount to meet management's targeted net income
3. Application of the just-in-time operating environment
4. Determining the effects of inventory decisions on cash flows

5. Apportioning the cost of goods available for sale to ending inventory and cost of goods sold
6. Determining the effects of inventory methods on income taxes
7. Determining the assumption about the flow of costs into and out of the company

LO1 **Inventory Ratios**

E 4. Just a Buck Discount Stores is assessing its levels of inventory for 2009 and 2010 and has gathered the following data:

	2010	2009	2008
Ending inventory	$ 96,000	$ 81,000	$69,000
Cost of goods sold	480,000	450,000	

Compute the inventory turnover and days' inventory on hand for 2009 and 2010 and comment on the results.

LO1 **Effects of Inventory Errors**

E 5. Condensed income statements for Ken-Du Company for two years are shown below.

	2010	2009
Sales	$504,000	$420,000
Cost of goods sold	300,000	216,000
Gross margin	$204,000	$204,000
Operating expenses	120,000	120,000
Income before income taxes	$ 84,000	$ 84,000

After the end of 2010, the company discovered that an error had resulted in a $36,000 understatement of the 2009 ending inventory.

Compute the corrected income before income taxes for 2009 and 2010. What effect will the error have on income before income taxes and stockholders' equity for 2011?

LO1 LO2 LO3 **Accounting Conventions and Inventory Valuation**

E 6. Turnbow Company, a telecommunications equipment company, has used the LIFO method adjusted for lower of cost or market for a number of years. Due to falling prices of its equipment, it has had to adjust (reduce) the cost of inventory to market each year for two years. The company is considering changing its method to FIFO adjusted for lower of cost or market in the future.

Explain how the accounting conventions of consistency, full disclosure, and conservatism apply to this decision. If the change were made, why would management expect fewer adjustments to market in the future?

LO3 **Periodic Inventory System and Inventory Costing Methods**

E 7. Gary's Parts Shop recorded the following purchases and sales during the past year:

Jan. 1 Beginning inventory	125 cases @ $46	$ 5,750
Feb. 25 Purchase	100 cases @ $52	5,200
June 15 Purchase	200 cases @ $56	11,200
Oct. 15 Purchase	150 cases @ $56	8,400
Dec. 15 Purchase	100 cases @ $60	6,000
Goods available for sale	675 cases	$36,550
Total sales	500 cases	
Dec. 31 Ending inventory	175 cases	

Assume that Gary's Parts Shop sold all of the June 15 purchase and 100 cases each from the January 1 beginning inventory, the October 15 purchase, and the December 15 purchase.

Determine the costs that should be assigned to ending inventory and cost of goods sold under each of the following assumptions: (1) costs are assigned by the specific identification method; (2) costs are assigned by the average-cost method; (3) costs are assigned by the FIFO method; (4) costs are assigned by the LIFO method. What conclusions can be drawn about the effect of each method on the income statement and the balance sheet of Gary's Parts Shop? Round your answers to the nearest whole number and assume that the company uses the periodic inventory system.

LO3 Periodic Inventory System and Inventory Costing Methods

E 8. During its first year of operation, Deja Vu Company purchased 5,600 units of a product at $21 per unit. During the second year, it purchased 6,000 units of the same product at $24 per unit. During the third year, it purchased 5,000 units at $30 per unit. Deja Vu Company managed to have an ending inventory each year of 1,000 units. The company uses the periodic inventory system.

Prepare cost of goods sold statements that compare the value of ending inventory and the cost of goods sold for each of the three years using (1) the FIFO inventory costing method and (2) the LIFO method. From the resulting data, what conclusions can you draw about the relationships between the changes in unit price and the changes in the value of ending inventory?

LO3 Periodic Inventory System and Inventory Costing Methods

E 9. In chronological order, the inventory, purchases, and sales of a single product for a recent month are as follows:

			Units	Amount per Unit
June	1	Beginning inventory	150	$ 60
	4	Purchase	400	66
	12	Purchase	800	72
	16	Sale	1,300	120
	24	Purchase	300	78

Using the periodic inventory system, compute the cost of ending inventory, cost of goods sold, and gross margin. Use the following inventory costing methods: average-cost, FIFO, and LIFO. Explain the differences in gross margin produced by the three methods, and round the unit costs to cents and the totals to dollars.

LO4 Effects of Inventory Costing Methods on Cash Flows

E 10. Infinite Products, Inc., sold 120,000 cases of glue at $40 per case during 2010. Its beginning inventory consisted of 20,000 cases at a cost of $24 per case. During 2010, it purchased 60,000 cases at $28 per case and later 50,000 cases at $30 per case. Operating expenses were $1,100,000, and the applicable income tax rate was 30 percent.

Using the periodic inventory system, compute net income using the FIFO method and the LIFO method for costing inventory. Which alternative produces the larger cash flow?

The company is considering a purchase of 10,000 cases at $30 per case just before the year end. What effect on net income and on cash flow will this proposed purchase have under each method? (**Hint:** What are the income tax consequences?)

SO5 **Perpetual Inventory System and Inventory Costing Methods**

E 11. Referring to the data provided in E 9 and using the perpetual inventory system, compute the cost of ending inventory, cost of goods sold, and gross margin. Use the average-cost, FIFO, and LIFO inventory costing methods. Explain the reasons for the differences in gross margin produced by the three methods. Round unit costs to cents and totals to dollars.

LO3 SO5 **Periodic and Perpetual Systems and Inventory Costing Methods**

E 12. During July 2010, Tricoci, Inc., sold 250 units of its product Empire for $4,000. The following units were available:

	Units	Cost
Beginning inventory	100	$ 2
Purchase 1	40	4
Purchase 2	60	6
Purchase 3	150	9
Purchase 4	90	12

A sale of 250 units was made after purchase 3. Of the units sold, 100 came from beginning inventory and 150 came from purchase 3.

Determine the goods available for sale in units and in dollars and ending inventory in units. Then determine the costs that should be assigned to cost of goods sold and ending inventory under each of the following assumptions: (1) Costs are assigned under the periodic inventory system using (a) the specific identification method, (b) the average-cost method, (c) the FIFO method, and (d) the LIFO method. (2) Costs are assigned under the perpetual inventory system using (a) the average-cost method, (b) the FIFO method, and (c) the LIFO method. For each alternative, show the gross margin. Round unit costs to cents and totals to dollars.

SO6 **Retail Method**

E 13. Olivia's Dress Shop had net retail sales of $125,000 during the current year. The following additional information was obtained from the company's accounting records:

	At Cost	At Retail
Beginning inventory	$20,000	$ 30,000
Net purchases (excluding freight-in)	70,000	110,000
Freight-in	5,200	

1. Using the retail method, estimate the company's ending inventory at cost.
2. Assume that a physical inventory taken at year end revealed an inventory on hand of $9,000 at retail value. What is the estimated amount of inventory shrinkage (loss due to theft, damage, etc.) at cost using the retail method?

SO6 **Gross Profit Method**

E 14. Chen Mo-Wan was at home when he received a call from the fire department telling him his store had burned. His business was a total loss. The insurance company asked him to prove his inventory loss. For the year, until the date of the fire, Chen's company had sales of $900,000 and purchases of $560,000. Freight-in amounted to $27,400, and beginning inventory was $90,000. Chen always priced his goods to achieve a gross margin of 40 percent.

Compute Chen's estimated inventory loss.

Problems

LO1 LO3 **Periodic Inventory System and Inventory Costing Methods**

P 1. El Faro Company merchandises a single product called Smart. The following data represent beginning inventory and purchases of Smart during the past year: January 1 inventory, 34,000 units at $11.00; February purchases, 40,000 units at $12.00; March purchases, 80,000 units at $12.40; May purchases, 60,000 units at $12.60; July purchases, 100,000 units at $12.80; September purchases, 80,000 units at $12.60; and November purchases, 30,000 units at $13.00. Sales of Smart totaled 393,000 units at $20.00 per unit. Selling and administrative expenses totaled $2,551,000 for the year. El Faro Company uses the periodic inventory system.

Required

1. Prepare a schedule to compute the cost of goods available for sale.
2. Compute income before income taxes under each of the following inventory cost flow methods: (a) the average-cost method; (b) the FIFO method; and (c) the LIFO method.

User insight ▶

3. Compute inventory turnover and days' inventory on hand under each of the inventory cost flow assumptions listed in requirement **2**. What conclusion can you draw?

LO1 LO3 **Periodic Inventory System and Inventory Costing Methods**

P 2. The inventory of Product PIT and data on purchases and sales for a two-month period follow. The company closes its books at the end of each month. It uses the periodic inventory system.

Apr.	1	Beginning inventory	50 units @ $204
	10	Purchase	100 units @ $220
	17	Sale	90 units
	30	Ending inventory	60 units
May	2	Purchase	100 units @ $216
	14	Purchase	50 units @ $224
	22	Purchase	60 units @ $234
	30	Sale	200 units
	31	Ending inventory	70 units

Required

1. Compute the cost of ending inventory of Product PIT on April 30 and May 31 using the average-cost method. In addition, determine cost of goods sold for April and May. Round unit costs to cents and totals to dollars.
2. Compute the cost of the ending inventory on April 30 and May 31 using the FIFO method. In addition, determine cost of goods sold for April and May.
3. Compute the cost of the ending inventory on April 30 and May 31 using the LIFO method. In addition, determine cost of goods sold for April and May.

User insight ▶

4. Do the cash flows from operations for April and May differ depending on which inventory costing method is used? Explain.

LO1 SO5 **Perpetual Inventory System and Inventory Costing Methods**

P 3. Use the data provided in **P 2**, but assume that the company uses the perpetual inventory system. (**Hint**: In preparing the solutions required below, it is helpful to determine the balance of inventory after each transaction, as shown in the Review Problem in this chapter.)

Required

1. Determine the cost of ending inventory and cost of goods sold for April and May using the average-cost method. Round unit costs to cents and totals to dollars.
2. Determine the cost of ending inventory and cost of goods sold for April and May using the FIFO method.
3. Determine the cost of ending inventory and cost of goods sold for April and May using the LIFO method.

User insight ▶ 4. Assume that this company grows for many years in a long period of rising prices. How realistic do you think the balance sheet value for inventory would be and what effect would it have on the inventory turnover ratio?

SO6 Retail Method

P 4. Ptak Company operates a large discount store and uses the retail method to estimate the cost of ending inventory. Management suspects that in recent weeks there have been unusually heavy losses from shoplifting or employee pilferage. To estimate the amount of the loss, the company has taken a physical inventory and will compare the results with the estimated cost of inventory. Data from the accounting records of Ptak Company are as follows:

	At Cost	At Retail
October 1 beginning inventory	$102,976	$148,600
Purchases	143,466	217,000
Purchases returns and allowances	(4,086)	(6,400)
Freight-in	1,900	
Sales		218,366
Sales returns and allowances		(1,866)
October 31 physical inventory at retail		124,900

Required

1. Using the retail method, prepare a schedule to estimate the dollar amount of the store's month-end inventory at cost.
2. Use the store's cost to retail ratio to reduce the retail value of the physical inventory to cost.
3. Calculate the estimated amount of inventory shortage at cost and at retail.

User insight ▶ 4. Many retail chains use the retail method because it is efficient. Why do you think using this method is an efficient way for these companies to operate?

SO6 Gross Profit Method

P 5. Rudy Brothers is a large retail furniture company that operates in two adjacent warehouses. One warehouse is a showroom, and the other is used to store merchandise. On the night of April 22, 2010, a fire broke out in the storage warehouse and destroyed the merchandise stored there. Fortunately, the fire did not reach the showroom, so all the merchandise on display was saved.

Although the company maintained a perpetual inventory system, its records were rather haphazard, and the last reliable physical inventory had been taken on December 31. In addition, there was no control of the flow of goods between the showroom and the warehouse. Thus, it was impossible to tell what goods would have been in either place. As a result, the insurance company required an independent estimate of the amount of loss. The insurance company examiners were satisfied when they received the following information:

Merchandise inventory on December 31, 2009	$363,700.00
Purchases, January 1 to April 22, 2010	603,050.00
Purchases returns, January 1 to April 22, 2010	(2,676.50)
Freight-in, January 1 to April 22, 2010	13,275.00

Sales, January 1 to April 22, 2010	$989,762.50
Sales returns, January 1 to April 22, 2010	(7,450.00)
Merchandise inventory in showroom on April 22, 2010	100,740.00
Average gross margin	44%

Required

1. Prepare a schedule that estimates the amount of the inventory loss that Rudy Brothers suffered in the fire.

User insight ▶ 2. What are some other reasons management might need to estimate the amount of inventory?

Alternate Problems

LO1 LO3 **Periodic Inventory System and Inventory Costing Methods**

P 6. The Jarmen Cabinet Company sold 2,200 cabinets during 2010 at $80 per cabinet. Its beginning inventory on January 1 was 130 cabinets at $28. Purchases made during the year were as follows:

February	225 cabinets @ $31.00
April	350 cabinets @ $32.50
June	700 cabinets @ $35.00
August	300 cabinets @ $33.00
October	400 cabinets @ $34.00
November	250 cabinets @ $36.00

The company's selling and administrative expenses for the year were $50,500. The company uses the periodic inventory system.

Required

1. Prepare a schedule to compute the cost of goods available for sale.
2. Compute income before income taxes under each of the following inventory cost flow assumptions: (a) the average-cost method, (b) the FIFO method, and (c) the LIFO method.

User insight ▶ 3. Compute inventory turnover and days' inventory on hand under each of the inventory cost flow assumptions in requirement 2. What conclusion can you draw from this comparison?

LO1 LO3 **Periodic Inventory System and Inventory Costing Methods**

P 7. The inventory, purchases, and sales of Product CAT for March and April are listed below. The company closes its books at the end of each month. It uses the periodic inventory system.

Mar.	1	Beginning inventory	60 units @ $98
	10	Purchase	100 units @ $104
	19	Sale	90 units
	31	Ending inventory	70 units
Apr.	4	Purchase	120 units @ $106
	15	Purchase	50 units @ $108
	23	Sale	200 units
	25	Purchase	100 units @ $110
	30	Ending inventory	140 units

Required

1. Compute the cost of the ending inventory on March 31 and April 30 using the average-cost method. In addition, determine cost of goods sold for March and April. Round unit costs to cents and totals to dollars.

2. Compute the cost of the ending inventory on March 31 and April 30 using the FIFO method. Also determine cost of goods sold for March and April.
3. Compute the cost of the ending inventory on March 31 and April 30 using the LIFO method. Also determine cost of goods sold for March and April.

User insight ▶ 4. Do the cash flows from operations for March and April differ depending on which inventory costing method is used—average-cost, FIFO, or LIFO? Explain.

LO1 SO5 **Perpetual Inventory System and Inventory Costing Methods**

P 8. Use the data provided in **P** 7, but assume that the company uses the perpetual inventory system. (**Hint**: In preparing the solutions required below, it is helpful to determine the balance of inventory after each transaction, as shown in the Review Problem in this chapter.)

Required

1. Determine the cost of ending inventory and cost of goods sold for March and April using the average-cost method. Round unit costs to cents and totals to dollars.
2. Determine the cost of ending inventory and cost of goods sold for March and April using the FIFO method.
3. Determine the cost of ending inventory and cost of goods sold for March and April using the LIFO method.

User insight ▶ 4. Assume that this company grows for many years in a long period of rising prices. How realistic do you think the balance sheet value for inventory would be and what effect would it have on the inventory turnover ratio?

SO6 **Retail Method**

P 9. Decent Company operates a large discount store and uses the retail method to estimate the cost of ending inventory. Management suspects that in recent weeks there have been unusually heavy losses from shoplifting or employee pilferage. To estimate the amount of the loss, the company has taken a physical inventory and will compare the results with the estimated cost of inventory. Data from the accounting records of Decent Company are as follows:

	At Cost	At Retail
August 1 beginning inventory	$51,488	$ 74,300
Purchases	71,733	108,500
Purchases returns and allowances	(2,043)	(3,200)
Freight-in	950	
Sales		109,183
Sales returns and allowances		(933)
August 31 physical inventory at retail		62,450

Required

1. Using the retail method, prepare a schedule to estimate the dollar amount of the store's month-end inventory at cost.
2. Use the store's cost to retail ratio to reduce the retail value of the physical inventory to cost.
3. Calculate the estimated amount of inventory shortage at cost and at retail.

User insight ▶ 4. Many retail chains use the retail method because it is efficient. Why do you think using this method is an efficient way for these companies to operate?

SO6 **Gross Profit Method**

P 10. Pearly Tooth Corporation is a large retailer of medical equipment. It operates in two adjacent warehouses. One warehouse is a showroom, and the other is used to store merchandise. On the night of May 5, 2009, a fire broke out in the storage warehouse and destroyed the merchandise stored there. Fortunately, the fire did not reach the showroom, so all the merchandise on display was saved.

Although the company maintained a perpetual inventory system, its records were rather haphazard, and the last reliable physical inventory had been taken on December 31. In addition, there was no control of the flow of goods between the showroom and the warehouse. Thus, it was impossible to tell what goods would have been in either place. As a result, the insurance company required an independent estimate of the amount of loss. The insurance company examiners were satisfied when they received the following information:

Merchandise inventory on December 31, 2008	$ 727,400
Purchases, January 1 to May 5, 2009	1,206,100
Purchases returns, January 1 to May 5, 2009	(5,353)
Freight-in, January 1 to May 5, 2009	26,550
Sales, January 1 to May 5, 2009	1,979,525
Sales returns, January 1 to May 5, 2009	(14,900)
Merchandise inventory in showroom on May 5, 2009	201,480
Average gross margin	48%

Required

1. Prepare a schedule that estimates the amount of the inventory lost in the fire.

User insight ▶ 2. What are some other reasons management might need to estimate the amount of inventory?

ENHANCING Your Knowledge, Skills, and Critical Thinking

LO1 **Evaluation of Inventory Levels**

C 1. J. C. Penney, a large retail company, has an inventory turnover of 3.4 times. **Dell Computer Corporation**, a well-known computer manufacturer, has an inventory turnover of 75.0. Dell achieves its high turnover through supply-chain management in a just-in-time operating environment. Why is inventory turnover important to companies like J. C. Penney and Dell? Why are comparisons among companies important? Are J. C. Penney and Dell a good match for comparison? Describe supply-chain management and a just-in-time operating environment. Why are they important to achieving a favorable inventory turnover?

LO1 **Misstatement of Inventory**

C 2. Crazy Eddie, Inc., a discount consumer electronics chain, seemed to be missing $52 million in merchandise inventory. "It was a shock," the new management was quoted as saying. It was also one of the nation's largest swindles. Investors lost $145.6 million when the company declared bankruptcy. A count turned up only $75 million in inventory, compared with $126.7 million reported by former management. Net sales could account for only $6.7 million of the difference. At the time, it was not clear whether bookkeeping errors in prior years or an actual physical loss created the shortfall, although at least one store manager felt it was a bookkeeping error because security was strong. "It would be hard for someone to steal anything," he said. Former management was eventually fined \$72.7 million.[11]

1. What was the effect of the misstatement of inventory on Crazy Eddie's reported earnings in prior accounting periods?
2. Is this a situation you would expect in a company that is experiencing financial difficulty? Explain.

LO4 **LIFO Inventory Method**

C 3. Sixty-nine percent of chemical companies use the LIFO inventory method for the costing of inventories, whereas only 10 percent of computer equipment companies use LIFO.[12]

Describe the LIFO inventory method. What effects does it have on reported income, cash flows, and income taxes during periods of price changes? Why do you think so many chemical companies use LIFO while most companies in the computer industry do not?

LO2 **LCM and Conservatism**

C 4. **ExxonMobil Corporation**, the world's largest company, uses the LIFO inventory method for most of its inventories. Its inventory costs are heavily dependent on the cost of oil. In a recent year when the price of oil was down, **ExxonMobil**, following the lower-of-cost-or-market (LCM) rule, wrote down its inventory by \$325 million. In the next year, when the price of oil recovered, the company reported that market price exceeded the LIFO carrying values by \$6.8 billion.[13] Explain why the LCM rule resulted in a write-down in the first year. What is the inconsistency between the first- and second-year treatments of the change in the price of oil? How does the accounting convention of conservatism explain the inconsistency? If the price of oil declined substantially in a third year, what would be the likely consequence?

LO1 LO4 **FIFO and LIFO**

C 5. **ExxonMobil Corporation** had net income of \$45.2 billion in 2008. Inventories under the LIFO method used by the company were \$9.3 billion in 2008. Inventory would have been \$10.0 billion higher if the company had used FIFO.[14] Why do you suppose **ExxonMobil**'s management chooses to use the LIFO inventory method? On what economic conditions, if any, do those reasons depend?

LO3 LO4 **FIFO versus LIFO Analysis**

C 6. Semi Truck Sales Company (STS Company) buys large trucks from the manufacturer and sells them to companies and independent truckers who haul goods over long distances. STS has been successful in this niche of the industry. Because of the high cost of the trucks and of financing inventory, STS tries to maintain as small an inventory as possible. In fact, at the beginning of July the company had no inventory or liabilities, as shown on the balance sheet on the next page.

On July 9, STS took delivery of a truck at a price of \$150,000. On July 19, an identical truck was delivered to the company at a price of \$160,000. On July 28, the company sold one of the trucks for \$195,000. During July, expenses totaled \$15,000. All transactions were paid in cash.

STS Company
Balance Sheet
July 1, 2010

Assets		Stockholders' Equity	
Cash	$400,000	Common stock	$400,000
Total assets	$400,000	Total stockholders' equity	$400,000

1. Prepare income statements and balance sheets for STS on July 31 using (a) the FIFO method of inventory valuation and (b) the LIFO method of inventory valuation. Assume an income tax rate of 40 percent. Explain the effects of each method on the financial statements.
2. Assume that the management of STS Company has a policy of declaring a cash dividend each period that is exactly equal to net income. What effects does this action have on each balance sheet prepared in requirement **1**? How do the resulting balance sheets compare with the balance sheet at the beginning of the month? Which inventory method, if either, do you feel is more realistic in representing STS's income?
3. Assume that STS receives notice of another price increase of $10,000 on trucks, to take effect on August 1. How does this information relate to management's dividend policy, and how will it affect next month's operations?

LO1 LO4 SO5 SO6 **Inventory Costing Methods and Ratios**

C 7. Refer to the note related to inventories in the **CVS** annual report in the Supplement to Chapter 1 to answer the following questions: What inventory method(s) does CVS use? If LIFO inventories had been valued at FIFO, why would there be no difference? Do you think many of the company's inventories are valued at market? Why or why not? Few companies use the retail method, so why do you think CVS uses it? Compute and compare the inventory turnover and days' inventory on hand for CVS for 2008 and 2007. Ending 2006 inventories were $7,108.9 million.

LO1 **Inventory Efficiency**

C 8. Refer to **CVS**'s annual report in the Supplement to Chapter 1 and to the following data (in millions) for **Walgreens**: cost of goods sold, $42,391 and $38,518.1 for 2008 and 2007, respectively; inventories, $7,249, $6,790, and $6,050.4 for 2008, 2007, and 2006, respectively. Ending inventories for 2006 for CVS were $7,108.9 million.

Calculate inventory turnover and days' inventory on hand for 2008 and 2007. If you did **C 7**, refer to your answer there for CVS. Has either company improved its performance over the past two years? What advantage does the superior company's performance provide to it? Which company appears to make the most efficient use of inventories? Explain your answers.

LO1 LO4 **Inventories, Income Determination, and Ethics**

C 9. Jazz, Inc., which has a December 31 year end, designs and sells fashions for young professional women. Lyla Hilton, president of the company, fears that the forecasted 2010 profitability goals will not be reached. She is pleased when Jazz receives a large order on December 30 from The Executive Woman, a retail chain of upscale stores for businesswomen. Hilton immediately directs the controller to record the sale, which represents 13 percent of Jazz's annual sales. At the same time, she directs the inventory control department not to separate the goods for shipment until after January 1. Separated goods are not included in inventory because they have been sold.

On December 31, the company's auditors arrive to observe the year-end taking of the physical inventory under the periodic inventory system. How will Hilton's actions affect Jazz's 2010 profitability? How will they affect Jazz's 2011 profitability? Were Hilton's actions ethical? Why or why not?

LO2 LO4 **Retail Business Inventories**

C 10. Assign teams to various types of stores in your community—a grocery, clothing, book, music, or appliance store. Make an appointment to interview the manager for 30 minutes to discuss the company's inventory accounting system. The store may be a branch of a larger company. Ask the following questions, summarize your findings in a paper, and be prepared to discuss your results in class:

1. What is the physical flow of merchandise into the store, and what documents are used in connection with this flow?
2. What documents are prepared when merchandise is sold?
3. Does the store keep perpetual inventory records? If so, does it keep the records in units only, or does it keep track of cost as well? If not, what system does the store use?
4. How often does the company take a physical inventory?
5. How are financial statements generated for the store?
6. What inventory method does the company use to cost its inventory for financial statements?

LO1 LO2 **Inventory Ratio Analysis**

LO3

C 11. Yamaha Corporation and **Pioneer Corporation** are two large, diversified Japanese electronics companies. Both use the average-cost method and the lower-of-cost-or-market rule to account for inventories. The following data are for their 2008 fiscal years (in millions of yen):[15]

	Yamaha	Pioneer
Beginning inventory	¥ 76,304	¥104,876
Ending inventory	80,694	84,886
Cost of goods sold	290,381	477,965

Assume you have been asked to analyze the inventory efficiency of the two companies. Prepare a memorandum to your boss that compares the inventory efficiency of Yamaha and Pioneer by computing the inventory turnover and days' inventory on hand for both companies in 2009. Show and comment on the relative efficiency of the two companies. Also comment on how the inventory method would affect your evaluation if you were to compare Yamaha and Pioneer to each other and to a U.S. company given the fact that most companies in the United States use the LIFO inventory method. Mention what could be done to make the results comparable.

CHAPTER 7

Cash and Receivables

Focus on Financial Statements

INCOME STATEMENT

Revenues
– Expenses
= Net Income

STATEMENT OF RETAINED EARNINGS

Opening Balance
+ Net Income
– Dividends
= Retained Earnings

BALANCE SHEET

Assets | Liabilities
Equity

A = L + E

STATEMENT OF CASH FLOWS

Operating activities
+ Investing activities
+ Financing activities
= Change in Cash
+ Starting Balance
= Ending Cash Balance

Valuation of accounts receivable on the balance sheet is linked to measurement of uncollectible accounts expense on the income statement.

Cash and receivables require careful oversight to ensure that they are ethically handled. If cash is mismanaged or stolen, it can bring about the downfall of a business. Because accounts receivable and notes receivable require estimates of future losses, they can be easily manipulated to show improvement in reported earnings. Improved earnings can, of course, enhance a company's stock price, as well as the bonuses of its executives. In this chapter, we address the management of cash and demonstrate the importance of estimates in accounting for receivables.

LEARNING OBJECTIVES

LO1 **Identify and explain the management and ethical issues related to cash and receivables.** (pp. 354–360)

LO2 **Define *cash equivalents*, and explain methods of controlling cash, including bank reconciliations.** (pp. 361–365)

LO3 **Apply the allowance method of accounting for uncollectible accounts.** (pp. 365–372)

LO4 **Define *promissory note*, and make common calculations for promissory notes receivable.** (pp. 372–376)

DECISION POINT ▸ A USER'S FOCUS NIKE, INC.

- How can the company control its cash needs?
- How can the company evaluate credit policies and the level of its receivables?
- How should the company estimate the value of its receivables?

Nike, one of the world's largest and best-known athletic sportswear companies, must give the retail stores that buy its products time to pay for their purchases. At the same time, however, Nike must have enough cash on hand to pay its suppliers. As you can see in Nike's Financial Highlights, cash and accounts receivable have made up over 50 percent of its current assets in recent years.[1] The company must therefore plan and control its cash flows very carefully.

NIKE'S FINANCIAL HIGHLIGHTS
(In millions)

	2009	2008	2007
Cash	$ 2,291.1	$ 2,133.9	$ 1,856.7
Accounts receivable, net	2,883.9	2,795.3	2,494.7
Total current assets	9,734.0	8,839.3	8,076.5
Net sales	19,176.1	18,627.0	16,325.9

Management Issues Related to Cash and Receivables

LO1 Identify and explain the management and ethical issues related to cash and receivables.

The management of cash and accounts and notes receivable is critical to maintaining adequate liquidity. These assets are important components of the operating cycle, which also includes inventories and accounts payable. In dealing with cash and receivables, management must address five key issues: managing cash needs, setting credit policies, evaluating the level of accounts receivable, financing receivables, and making ethical estimates of credit losses.

Cash Management

On the balance sheet, **cash** usually consists of currency and coins on hand, checks and money orders from customers, and deposits in checking and savings accounts. Cash is the most liquid of all assets and the most readily available to pay debts. It is central to the operating cycle because all operating transactions eventually use or generate cash.

Cash may include a *compensating balance*, an amount that is not entirely free to be spent. A **compensating balance** is a minimum amount that a bank requires a company to keep in its bank account as part of a credit-granting arrangement. Such an arrangement restricts cash; in effect, it increases the interest on the loan and reduces a company's liquidity. The Securities and Exchange Commission therefore requires companies that have compensating balances to disclose the amounts involved.

Most companies experience seasonal cycles of business activity during the year. During some periods, sales are weak; during others, they are strong. There are also periods when expenditures are high, and periods when they are low. For toy companies, college textbook publishers, amusement parks, construction companies, and manufacturers of sports equipment, the cycles are dramatic, but all companies experience them to some degree.

Seasonal cycles require careful planning of cash inflows, cash outflows, borrowing, and investing. Figure 7-1 shows the seasonal cycles typical of an athletic sportswear company like **Nike**. As you can see, cash receipts from sales are highest in the late spring, summer, and fall because that is when most people engage in outdoor sports. Sales are relatively low in the winter months. On the other hand, cash expenditures are highest in late winter and spring as the company builds up inventory for spring and summer selling. During the late summer, fall, and winter, the company has excess cash on hand that it needs to invest in a way

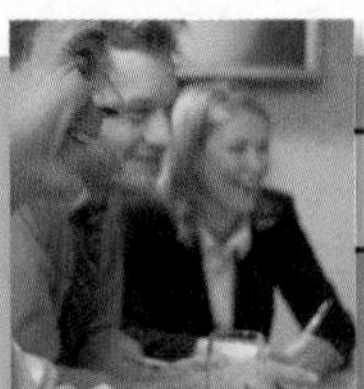

FOCUS ON BUSINESS PRACTICE

How Do Good Companies Deal with Bad Times?

Good companies manage their cash well even in bad times. When a slump in the technology market caused **Texas Instrument's** sales to decline by more than 40 percent, resulting in a loss of nearly $120 million, this large electronics firm actually increased its cash by acting quickly to cut its purchases of plant assets by two-thirds. It also reduced its payroll and lowered the average number of days it had inventory on hand from 71 to 58.[2]

In similar circumstances, some companies have not reacted as quickly as Texas Instruments. For example, before 9/11, the Big Three automakers—**General Motors**, **Ford**, and **DaimlerChrysler**—were awash in cash. However, in little over a year, the three companies went through $28 billion in cash through various purchases, losses, dividends, and share buybacks. Then, with increasing losses from rising costs, big rebates, and zero percent financing, they were suddenly faced with a shortage of cash. As a result, Standard & Poor's lowered their credit ratings, which raises the interest cost of borrowing money. Perhaps the Big Three should have held on to some of that cash.[3]

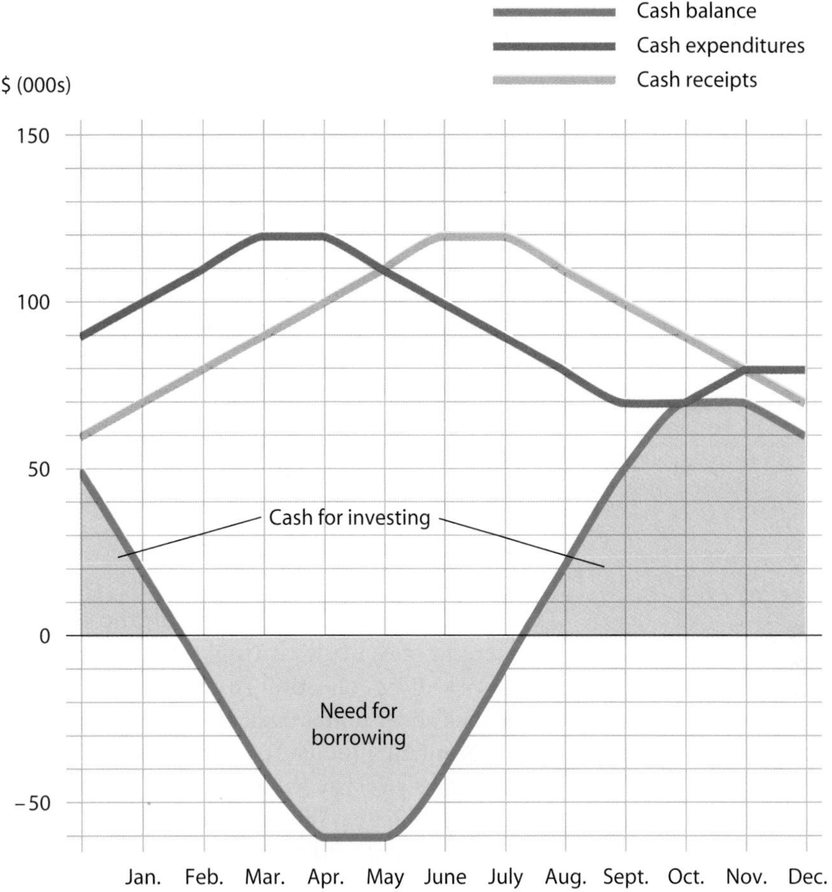

FIGURE 7-1
Seasonal Cycles and Cash Requirements for an Athletic Sportswear Company

that will earn a return but still permit access to cash as needed. During late spring and early summer, the company needs to plan for short-term borrowing to tide it over until cash receipts pick up later in the year.

Accounts Receivable and Credit Policies

Like cash, accounts receivable and notes receivable are major types of **short-term financial assets**. Both kinds of receivables result from extending credit to individual customers or to other companies. Retailers like **Sears** (now merged with **Kmart**) have made credit available to nearly every responsible person in the United States. Every field of retail trade has expanded by allowing customers to make payments a month or more after the date of sale. What is not so apparent is that credit has expanded even more among wholesalers and manufacturers like **Nike** than at the retail level. Figure 7-2 shows the levels of accounts receivable in selected industries.

As we have indicated, **accounts receivable** are the short-term financial assets of a wholesaler or retailer that arise from sales on credit. This type of credit is often called **trade credit**. Terms of trade credit usually range from 5 to 60 days, depending on industry practice. For some companies that sell to consumers, **installment accounts receivable**, which allow the buyer to make a series of time payments, constitute a significant portion of accounts receivable. Department stores, appliance stores, furniture stores, used car dealers, and other retail businesses often offer installment credit. The installment accounts receivable of retailers like **Sears** and **J.C. Penney** can amount to millions of dollars. Although the payment period may be 24 months or more, installment accounts receivable are classified as current assets if such credit policies are customary in the industry.

FIGURE 7-2
Accounts Receivable as a Percentage of Total Assets for Selected Industries

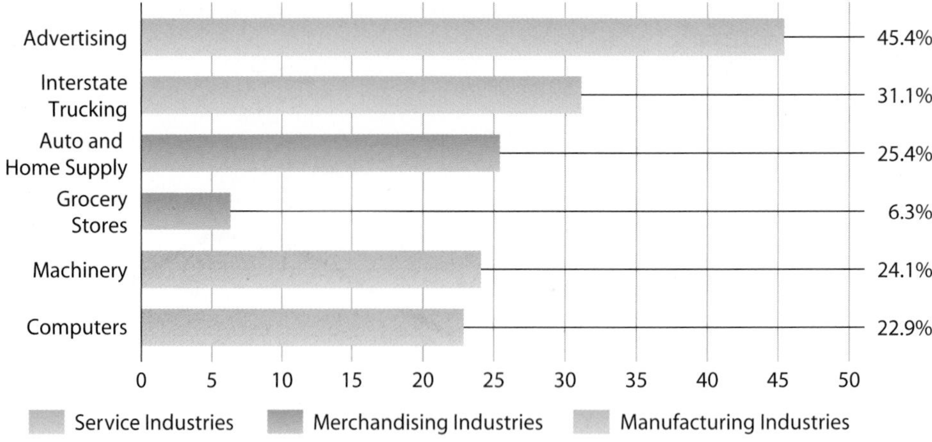

Source: Data from Dun & Bradstreet, *Industry Norms and Key Business Ratios,* 2007–2008.

On the balance sheet, *accounts receivable* designates amounts arising from credit sales made to customers in the ordinary course of business. Because loans or credit sales made to employees, officers, or owners of the corporation increase the risk of uncollectibility and conflict of interest, they appear separately on the balance sheet under asset titles like *receivables from employees.*

Normally, individual accounts receivable have debit balances, but sometimes customers overpay their accounts either by mistake or in anticipation of making future purchases. When these accounts show credit balances, the company should show the total credits on its balance sheet as a current liability. The reason for this is that if the customers make no future purchases, the company will have to grant them refunds.

Companies that sell on credit do so to be competitive and to increase sales. In setting credit terms, a company must keep in mind the credit terms of its competitors and the needs of its customers. Obviously, any company that sells on credit wants customers who will pay their bills on time. To increase the likelihood of selling only to customers who will pay on time, most companies develop control procedures and maintain a credit department. The credit department's responsibilities include examining each person or company that applies for credit and approving or rejecting a credit sale to that customer. Typically, the credit department asks for information about the customer's financial resources and debts. It may also check personal references and credit bureaus for further information. Then, based on the information it has gathered, it decides whether to extend credit to the customer.

Companies that are too lenient in granting credit can run into difficulties when customers don't pay. For example, **Sprint**, one of the weaker companies in the highly competitive cell phone industry, targeted customers with poor credit histories. It attracted so many who failed to pay their bills that its stock dropped by 50 percent to $2.50 because of the losses that resulted.[4]

Evaluating the Level of Accounts Receivable

Two common measures of the effect of a company's credit policies are receivable turnover and days' sales uncollected. The **receivable turnover** shows how many times, on average, a company turned its receivables into cash during an accounting period. This measure reflects the relative size of a company's accounts receivable and the success of its credit and collection policies. It may also be affected by external factors, such as seasonal conditions and interest rates. **Days' sales uncollected** is a related measure that shows, on average, how long it takes to collect accounts receivable.

The receivable turnover is computed by dividing net sales by average accounts receivable (net of allowances). Theoretically, the numerator should be net credit sales, but the amount of net credit sales is rarely available in public reports, so investors use total net sales. Using data from **Nike**'s Financial Highlights at the beginning of the chapter, we can compute the company's receivable turnover as follows (dollar amounts are in millions):

K/R

$$\text{Receivable Turnover} = \frac{\text{Net Sales}}{\text{Average Accounts Receivable}}$$

$$= \frac{\$19{,}176.1}{(\$2{,}883.9 + \$2{,}795.3 \div 2)}$$

$$= \frac{\$19{,}176.1}{\$2{,}839.6} = 6.8 \text{ times}$$

To find days' sales uncollected, the number of days in a year is divided by the receivable turnover, as follows:

K/R

$$\text{Days' Sales Uncollected} = \frac{365 \text{ days}}{\text{Receivable Turnover}} = \frac{365 \text{ days}}{6.8 \text{ times}} = 53.7 \text{ days}$$

Study Note

For many businesses with seasonal sales activity, such as **Nordstrom, Dillard's, Marshall Field's**, and **Macy's**, the fourth quarter produces more than 25 percent of annual sales. For these businesses, receivables are highest at the balance sheet date, resulting in an artificially low receivable turnover and high days' sales uncollected.

Thus, Nike turned its receivables 6.8 times a year, or an average of every 53.7 days. A turnover period of this length is not unusual among apparel companies because their credit terms allow retail outlets time to sell products before paying for them. However, it is longer than the turnover period of many companies in other industries. To interpret a company's ratios, you must take into consideration the norms of the industry in which it operates.

As Figure 7-3 shows, the receivable turnover ratio varies substantially from industry to industry. Because grocery stores have few receivables, they have a very quick turnover. The turnover in interstate trucking is 9.3 times because the typical credit terms in that industry are 30 days. The turnover in the machinery and computer industries is lower because those industries tend to have longer credit terms.

Figure 7-4 shows the days' sales uncollected for the industries listed in Figure 7-3. Grocery stores, which have the lowest ratio (4.8 days) require the least amount of receivables financing; the computer industry, with days' sales uncollected of 89.0 days, requires the most.

FIGURE 7-3
Receivable Turnover for Selected Industries

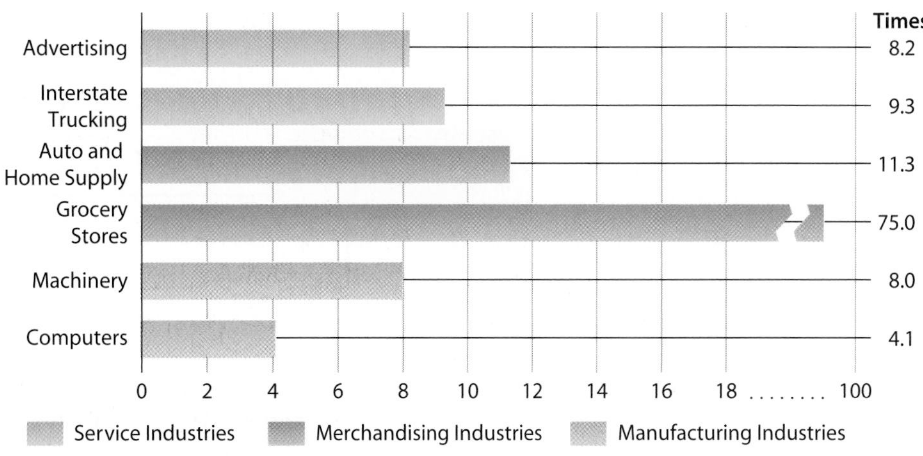

Source: Data from Dun & Bradstreet, *Industry Norms and Key Business Ratios*, 2007–2008.

FIGURE 7-4
Days' Sales Uncollected for Selected Industries

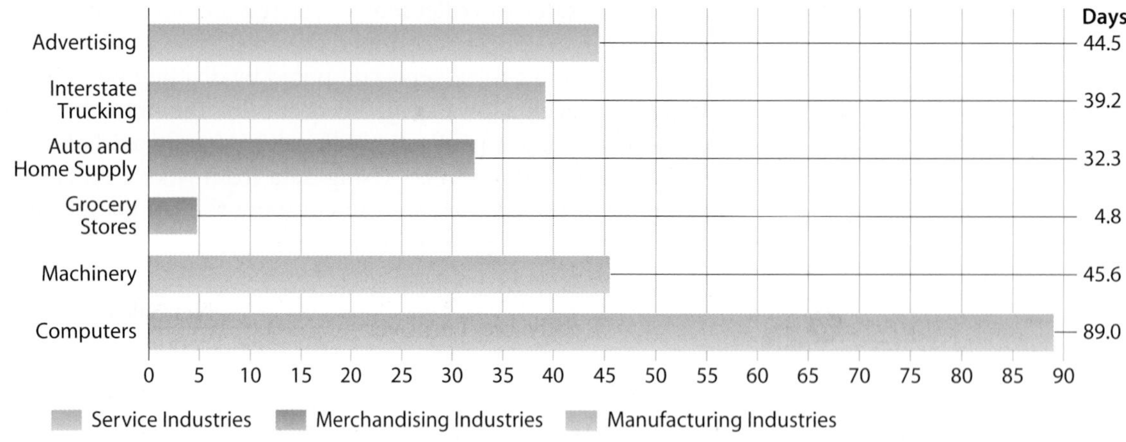

Source: Data from Dun & Bradstreet, *Industry Norms and Key Business Ratios,* 2007–2008.

Financing Receivables

Financial flexibility is important to most companies. Companies that have significant amounts of assets tied up in accounts receivable may be unwilling or unable to wait until they collect cash from their receivables. Many corporations have set up finance companies to help their customers pay for the purchase of their products. For example, **Ford** has set up Ford Motor Credit Company (FMCC) and **Sears** has set up Sears Roebuck Acceptance Corporation (SRAC). Other companies borrow funds by pledging their accounts receivable as collateral. If a company does not pay back its loan, the creditor can take the collateral (in this case, the accounts receivable) and convert it to cash to satisfy the loan.

Study Note

A company that factors its receivables will have a better receivable turnover and days' sales uncollected than a company that does not factor them.

Companies can also raise funds by selling or transferring accounts receivable to another entity, called a **factor**, as illustrated in Figure 7-5. The sale or transfer of accounts receivable, called **factoring**, can be done with or without recourse. *With recourse* means that the seller of the receivables is liable to the factor (i.e., the purchaser) if a receivable cannot be collected. *Without recourse* means that the factor bears any losses from unpaid accounts. A company's acceptance of credit cards like Visa, MasterCard, or American Express is an example of factoring without recourse because the issuers of the cards accept the risk of nonpayment.

The factor, of course, charges a fee for its service. The fee for sales with recourse is usually about 2 percent of the accounts receivable. The fee is higher for sales without recourse because the factor's risk is greater. In accounting terminology, a seller of receivables with recourse is said to be contingently liable. A **contingent liability** is a potential liability that can develop into a real liability

FIGURE 7-5
How Factoring Works

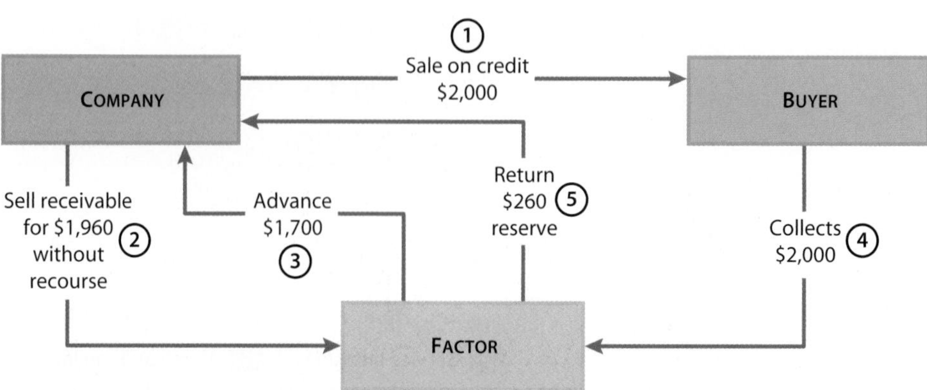

Note: Factor will keep $260 reserve if buyer does not pay.

FOCUS ON BUSINESS PRACTICE

Why Are Subprime Loans Bad?

Although subprime loans (home loans to individuals with poor credit ratings and low incomes) represent only a small portion of the mortgage loan market, they have caused huge problems in the real estate market in recent years. These loans are a form of securitization in that they are batched together and sold in units as safe investments, when in fact they are quite risky. As just one of many examples, when people by the thousands were unable to keep up with their mortgage payments, the investments were marked down to their fair value. This loss of value led to the demise of such venerable firms as Lehman Brothers, the sale of Merrill Lynch, and ultimately to a massive government bailout.[5]

if a particular event occurs. In this case, the event would be a customer's nonpayment of a receivable. A contingent liability generally requires disclosure in the notes to the financial statements.

Another way for a company to generate cash from its receivables is through a process called securitization. Under **securitization**, a company groups its receivables in batches and sells them at a discount to companies and investors. When the receivables are paid, the buyers get the full amount; their profit depends on the amount of the discount. **Circuit City** tried to avoid bankruptcy by selling all its receivables without recourse, which means that after selling them, it had no further liability, even if no customers were to pay. If Circuit City sold its receivables with recourse and a customer did not pay, it would have had to make good on the debt.[6] However, by selling without recourse, it had to accept a lower price for its receivables. This strategy did not prevent it from going bankrupt.

Another method of financing receivables is to sell promissory notes held as notes receivable to a financial lender, usually a bank. This practice is called **discounting** because the bank derives its profit by deducting the interest from the maturity value of the note. The holder of the note (usually the payee) endorses the note and turns it over it to the bank. The bank expects to collect the maturity value of the note (principal plus interest) on the maturity date, but it also has recourse against the note's endorser.

For example, if Company X holds a $20,000 note from Company Z and the note will pay $1,200 in interest, a bank may be willing to buy the note for $19,200. If Company Z pays, the bank will receive $21,200 at maturity and realize a $2,000 profit. If it fails to pay, Company X is liable to the bank for payment. In the meantime, Company X has a contingent liability in the amount of the discounted note plus interest that it must disclose in the notes to its financial statements.

Ethics and Estimates in Accounting for Receivables

As we have noted, companies extend credit to customers because they expect it will increase their sales and earnings, but they know they will always have some credit customers who cannot or will not pay. The accounts of such customers are called **uncollectible accounts**, or *bad debts*, and they are expenses of selling on credit. To match these expenses, or losses, to the revenues they help generate, they should be recognized at the time credit sales are made.

Of course, at the time a company makes credit sales, it cannot identify which customers will not pay their bills, nor can it predict the exact amount of money it will lose. Therefore, to adhere to the matching rule, it must estimate losses from uncollectible accounts. The estimate becomes an expense in the fiscal year in which the sales are made.

Because the amount of uncollectible accounts can only be estimated and the exact amount will not be known until later, a company's earnings can be easily manipulated. Earnings can be overstated by underestimating the amount of losses from uncollectible accounts and understated by overestimating the amount of the losses. Misstatements of earnings can occur simply because of a bad estimate. But, as we have noted, they can be deliberately made to meet analysts' estimates of earnings, reduce income taxes, or meet benchmarks for bonuses.

Among the many examples of unethical or questionable practices in dealing with uncollectible accounts are the following:

- **WorldCom** (now **MCI**) increased revenues and hid losses by continuing to bill customers for service for years after the customers had quit paying.
- The policy of **Household International**, a large personal finance company, seems to be flexible about when to declare loans delinquent. As a result, the company can vary its estimates of uncollectible accounts from year to year.[7]
- By making large allowances for estimated uncollectible accounts and then gradually reducing them, **Bank One** improved its earnings over several years.[8]
- **HealthSouth** manipulated its income by varying its estimates of the difference between what it charged patients and what it could collect from insurance companies.[9]

Companies with high ethical standards try to be accurate in their estimates of uncollectible accounts, and they disclose the basis of their estimates. For example, **Nike**'s management describes its estimates as follows:

> We make ongoing estimates relating to the collectibility of our accounts receivables and maintain an allowance for estimated losses resulting from the inability of our customers to make required payments. In determining the amount of the allowance, we consider our historical level of credit losses and make judgments about the creditworthiness of significant customers based on ongoing credit evaluations. Since we cannot predict future changes in the financial stability of our customers, actual future losses from uncollectible accounts may differ from our estimates.[10]

& APPLY >

Santorini Company has cash of \$20,000, net accounts receivable of \$60,000, and net sales of \$500,000. Last year's net accounts receivable were \$40,000. Compute the following ratios: receivable turnover and days' sales uncollected.

SOLUTION

$$\text{Receivable turnover} = \frac{\text{Net Sales}}{\text{Average Accounts Receivable}}$$

$$= \frac{\$500{,}000}{(\$60{,}000 + \$40{,}000) \div 2} = \frac{\$500{,}000}{\$50{,}000} = 10.0 \text{ times}$$

$$\text{Days' sales uncollected} = \frac{\text{365 days}}{\text{Receivable Turnover}}$$

$$= \frac{\text{365 days}}{\text{10.0 times}} = 36.5 \text{ days}$$

Cash Equivalents and Cash Control

LO2 Define *cash equivalents*, and explain methods of controlling cash, including bank reconciliations.

Study Note

The statement of cash flows explains the change in the balance of cash and cash equivalents from one accounting period to the next.

Cash Equivalents

As we noted earlier, cash is the asset most readily available to pay debts, but at times a company may have more cash on hand than it needs to pay its debts. Excess cash should not remain idle, especially during periods of high interest rates. Management may decide to invest the excess cash in short-term interest-bearing accounts or certificates of deposit (CDs) at banks and other financial institutions, in government securities (such as U.S. Treasury notes), or in other securities. If these investments have a term of 90 days or less when they are purchased, they are called **cash equivalents** because the funds revert to cash so quickly they are treated as cash on the balance sheet.

Nike describes its treatment of cash and cash equivalents as follows:

> Cash and equivalents represent cash and short-term, highly liquid investments with maturities of three months or less at date of purchase. The carrying amounts reflected in the consolidated balance sheet for cash and equivalents approximate fair value.[11]

According to a survey of 600 large U.S. corporations, 6 percent use the term *cash* as the balance sheet caption, and 89 percent use either *cash and cash equivalents* or *cash and equivalents*. The rest either combine cash with marketable securities or have no cash.[12]

Fair Value of Cash and Cash Equivalents

Cash and cash equivalents are financial instruments that are valued at fair value. In most cases the amount recorded in the records approximates fair value, and most businesses and other entities consider cash equivalents to be very safe investments. Companies often invest these funds in money market funds to earn interest with cash when they don't need cash for current operations. Money market funds usually invest in very safe securities, such as commercial paper, which is short-term debt of other entities. Although money market funds are not guaranteed, investors do not expect losses on these investments. However, in recent years a few of these funds invested in batches of subprime mortgages in an attempt to earn a little higher interest rate. The result has been traumatic for all parties. **Bank of America**, for instance, shut down its $34 billion Columbia Strategic Cash Portfolio money market fund when investors pulled out $21 billion because the fund was losing so much money from investing in subprime loans.[13]

Cash Control Methods

In an earlier chapter, we discussed the concept of internal control and how it applies to cash transactions. Here, we address three additional ways of controlling cash: imprest systems; banking services, including electronic funds transfer; and bank reconciliations.

Imprest Systems Most companies need to keep some currency and coins on hand. Currency and coins are needed for cash registers, for paying expenses that are impractical to pay by check, and for situations that require cash advances—for example, when sales representatives need cash for travel expenses. One way to control a cash fund and cash advances is by using an **imprest systems**.

A common form of imprest system is a petty cash fund, which is established at a fixed amount. A receipt documents each cash payment made from the fund. The fund is periodically reimbursed, based on the documented expenditures, by the exact amount necessary to restore its original cash balance. The person responsible for the petty cash fund must always be able to account for its contents by showing that total cash and receipts equal the original fixed amount.

Banking Services All businesses rely on banks to control cash receipts and cash disbursements. Banks serve as safe depositories for cash, negotiable instruments, and other valuable business documents, such as stocks and bonds. The checking accounts that banks provide improve control by minimizing the amount of currency a company needs to keep on hand and by supplying permanent records of all cash payments. Banks also serve as agents in a variety of transactions, such as the collection and payment of certain kinds of debts and the exchange of foreign currencies.

> **Study Note**
> Periodically, banks detect individuals who are *kiting*. Kiting is the illegal issuing of checks when there is insufficient money to cover them. Before one kited check clears the bank, a kited check from another account is deposited to cover it, making an endless circle.

Electronic funds transfer (EFT) is a method of conducting business transactions that does not involve the actual transfer of cash. With EFT, a company electronically transfers cash from its bank to another company's bank. For the banks, the electronic transfer is simply a bookkeeping entry. Companies today rely heavily on this method of payment. **Wal-Mart**, for example, makes 75 percent of its payments to suppliers through EFT.

Because of EFT and other electronic banking services, we are rapidly becoming a cashless society. Automated teller machines (ATMs) allow bank customers to make deposits, withdraw cash, transfer funds among accounts, and pay bills. Large consumer banks like **Citibank**, **Chase**, and **Bank of America** process hundreds of thousands of ATM transactions each week. Many banks also give customers the option of paying bills over the telephone and with *debit cards*. In 2009, debit cards accounted for more than $1.5 trillion in transactions.[14] When a customer makes a retail purchase using a debit card, the amount of the purchase is deducted directly from the buyer's bank account. The bank usually documents debit card transactions for the retailer, but the retailer must develop new internal controls to ensure that the transactions are recorded properly and that unauthorized transfers do not occur. It is expected that within a few years, a majority of all retail activity will be handled electronically.

> **Study Note**
> The ending balance on a company's bank statement does not represent the amount of cash that should appear on its balance sheet. At the balance sheet date, deposits may be in transit to the bank, and some checks may be outstanding. That is why companies must prepare a bank reconciliation.

Bank Reconciliations Rarely does the balance of a company's Cash account exactly equal the cash balance on its bank statement. The bank may not yet have recorded certain transactions that appear in the company's records, and the company may not yet have recorded certain bank transactions. A bank reconciliation is therefore a necessary step in internal control. A **bank reconciliation** is the process of accounting for the difference between the balance on a company's bank statement and the balance in its Cash account. This process involves making additions to and subtractions from both balances to arrive at the adjusted cash balance.

The following are the transactions that most commonly appear in a company's records but not on its bank statement:

1. *Outstanding checks:* These are checks that a company has issued and recorded but that do not yet appear on its bank statement.
2. *Deposits in transit:* These are deposits a company has sent to its bank but that the bank did not receive in time to enter on the bank statement.

Transactions that may appear on the bank statement but not in the company's records include the following:

1. *Service charges* (SC): Banks often charge a fee, or service charge, for the use of a checking account. Many banks base the service charge on a number of factors, such as the average balance of the account during the month or the number of checks drawn.

> **Study Note**
> Bank reconciliations perform an important function in internal control. If carried out by someone who does not have access to the bank account, they provide an independent check on the person or persons who do have that access.

2. NSF *(nonsufficient funds) checks*: An NSF check is a check that a company has deposited but that is not paid when the bank presents it to the issuer's bank. The bank charges the company's account and returns the check so that the company can try to collect the amount due. If the bank has deducted the NSF check on the bank statement but the company has not deducted it from its book balance, an adjustment must be made in the bank reconciliation. The company usually reclassifies the NSF check from Cash to Accounts Receivable because it must now collect from the person or company that wrote the check.
3. *Miscellaneous debits and credits*: Banks also charge for other services, such as stopping payment on checks and printing checks. The bank notifies the depositor of each deduction by including a debit memorandum with the monthly statement. A bank also sometimes serves as an agent in collecting on promissory notes for the depositor. When it does, it includes a credit memorandum in the bank statement, along with a debit memorandum for the service charge.

> **Study Note**
> A credit memorandum means that an amount was *added* to the bank balance; a debit memorandum means that an amount was *deducted.*

4. *Interest income*: Banks commonly pay interest on a company's average balance. Accounts that pay interest are sometimes called NOW or money market accounts.

An error by either the bank or the depositor will, of course, require immediate correction.

To illustrate the preparation of a bank reconciliation, suppose that Terry Services Company's bank statement for August shows a balance of $1,735.53 on August 31 and that on the same date, the company's records show a cash balance of $1,207.95. The purpose of a bank reconciliation is to identify the items that make up the difference between these amounts and to determine the correct cash balance. Exhibit 7-1 shows Terry Services Company's bank reconciliation for August. The circled numbers in the exhibit refer to the following:

1. The bank has not recorded a deposit in the amount of $138.00 that the company mailed to the bank on August 31.
2. The bank has not paid the five checks that the company issued in July and August. Even though the July 14 check was deducted in the July 30 reconciliation, it must be deducted again in each subsequent month in which it remains outstanding.
3. The company incorrectly recorded a $150 deposit from cash sales as $165.00. On August 6, the bank received the deposit and corrected the amount.
4. Among the returned checks was a credit memorandum showing that the bank had collected a promissory note from K. Diaz in the amount of $140.00, plus $10.00 in interest on the note. A debit memorandum was also enclosed for the $2.50 collection fee. The company had not entered these amounts in its records.
5. Also returned with the bank statement was an NSF check for $64.07 that the company had received from a customer named Austin Chase. The NSF check was not reflected in the company's records.
6. A debit memorandum was enclosed for the regular monthly service charge of $6.25. The company had not yet recorded this charge.
7. Interest earned on the company's average balance was $7.81.

EXHIBIT 7-1
Bank Reconciliation

Terry Services Company
Bank Reconciliation
August 31, 2010

Balance per bank, August 31		$ 1,735.53
① Add deposit of August 31 in transit		138.00
		$ 1,873.53
② Less outstanding checks:		
No. 551, issued on July 14	$ 75.00	
No. 576, issued on Aug. 30	20.34	
No. 578, issued on Aug. 31	250.00	
No. 579, issued on Aug. 31	185.00	
No. 580, issued on Aug. 31	65.25	595.59
Adjusted bank balance, August 31		**$1,277.94**
Balance per books, August 31		$ 1,207.95
Add:		
④ Note receivable collected by bank	$140.00	
④ Interest income on note	10.00	
⑦ Interest income	7.81	157.81
		$ 1,365.76
Less:		
③ Overstatement of deposit of August 6	$ 15.00	
④ Collection fee	2.50	
⑤ NSF check of Austin Chase	64.07	
⑥ Service charge	6.25	87.82
Adjusted book balance, August 31		**$1,277.94**

Study Note

It is possible to place an item in the wrong section of a bank reconciliation and still have it balance. The *correct* adjusted balance must be obtained.

As you can see in Exhibit 7-1, starting from their separate balances, both the bank and book amounts are adjusted to the amount of $1,277.94. This adjusted balance is the amount of cash the company owns on August 31 and thus is the amount that should appear on its August 31 balance sheet.

When outstanding checks are presented to the bank for payment and the bank receives and records the deposit in transit, the bank balance will automatically become correct. However, the company must update its book balance by recording all the items reported by the bank. Thus, Terry Services Company would record an increase (debit) in Cash with the following items:

- Decrease (credit) in Notes Receivable, $140.00
- Increase (credit) in Interest Income, $10.00 (interest on note)
- Increase (credit) in Interest Income, $7.81 (interest on average bank balance)

The company would record a reduction (credit) in Cash with the following items:

- Decrease (debit) in Sales, $15.00 (error in recording deposit)
- Increase (debit) in Accounts Receivable, $64.07 (return of NSF check)
- Increase (debit) in Bank Service Charges, $8.75 ($6.25 + $2.50)

As the use of electronic funds transfer, automatic payments, and debit cards increases, the items that most businesses will have to deal with in their bank reconciliations will undoubtedly grow.

STOP & APPLY >

At year end, Sunjin Company had currency and coins in cash registers of $1,100, money orders from customers of $2,000, deposits in checking accounts of $12,000, U.S. Treasury bills due in 80 days of $50,000, certificates of deposit at the bank that mature in six months of $200,000, and U.S. Treasury bonds due in one year of $100,000. Calculate the amount of cash and cash equivalents that will be shown on the company's year-end balance sheet.

SOLUTION

Currency and coins	$ 1,100
Money orders	2,000
Checking accounts	12,000
U.S. Treasury bills (due in 80 days)	50,000
Cash and Cash equivalents	$65,100

The certificates of deposit and U.S. Treasury Bonds mature in more than 90 days and thus are not cash equivalents.

Uncollectible Accounts

LO3 Apply the allowance method of accounting for uncollectible accounts.

Some companies recognize a loss at the time they determine that an account is uncollectible by reducing Accounts Receivable and increasing Uncollectible Accounts Expense. Federal regulations require companies to use this method of recognizing a loss—called the **direct charge-off method**—in computing taxable income. Although small companies may use this method for all purposes, companies that follow generally accepted accounting principles do not use it in their financial statements. The reason they do not is that a direct charge-off is usually recorded in a different accounting period from the one in which the sale takes place, and the method therefore does not conform to the matching rule. Companies that follow GAAP prefer the allowance method.

> **Study Note**
> The direct charge-off method does not conform to the matching rule.

The Allowance Method

Under the **allowance method**, losses from bad debts are matched against the sales they help to produce. As mentioned earlier, when management extends credit to increase sales, it knows it will incur some losses from uncollectible accounts. Losses from credit sales should be recognized at the time the sales are made so that they are matched to the revenues they help generate. Of course, at the time a company makes credit sales, management cannot identify which customers will not pay their debts, nor can it predict the exact amount of money the company will lose. Therefore, to observe the matching rule, losses from uncollectible accounts must be estimated, and the estimate becomes an expense in the period in which the sales are made.

> **Study Note**
> The allowance method relies on an estimate of uncollectible accounts but is in accord with the matching rule.

For example, suppose that Sharon Sales Company made most of its sales on credit during its first year of operation, 2010. At the end of the year, accounts receivable amounted to $200,000. On December 31, 2010, management reviewed the collectible status of the accounts receivable. Approximately $12,000 of the $200,000 of accounts receivable were estimated to be uncollectible. This adjusting entry would be made on December 31 of that year:

A	= L +	SE
−12,000		−12,000

2010			
Dec. 31	Uncollectible Accounts Expense	12,000	
	Allowance for Uncollectible Accounts		12,000
	To record the estimated uncollectible accounts expense for the year		

Disclosure of Uncollectible Accounts

Study Note

Allowance for Uncollectible Accounts reduces the gross accounts receivable to the amount estimated to be collectible (net realizable value). The purpose of another contra account, Accumulated Depreciation, is *not* to reduce the gross plant and equipment accounts to realizable value. Rather, its purpose is to show how much of the cost of the plant and equipment has been allocated as an expense to previous accounting periods.

Uncollectible Accounts Expense appears on the income statement as an operating expense. **Allowance for Uncollectible Accounts** appears on the balance sheet as a contra account that is deducted from accounts receivable. It reduces the accounts receivable to the amount expected to be collected in cash, as follows:

Current assets:		
Cash		$ 20,000
Short-term investments		30,000
Accounts receivable	$200,000	
Less allowance for uncollectible accounts	12,000	188,000
Inventory		112,000
Total current assets		$350,000

Accounts receivable may also be shown on the balance sheet as follows:

Accounts receivable (net of allowance for uncollectible accounts of $12,000)	$188,000

Study Note

The allowance account is necessary because the specific uncollectible accounts will not be identified until later.

Accounts receivable may also be shown at "net," with the amount of the allowance for uncollectible accounts identified in a note to the financial statements. For most companies, the "net" amount of accounts receivable approximates fair value. Fair value disclosures are not required for accounts receivable but 341 of 600 large companies made this disclosure voluntarily. Of those, 325, or 95 percent, indicated that the net accounts receivable approximated fair value.[15]

The allowance account often has other titles, such as *Allowance for Doubtful Accounts* and *Allowance for Bad Debts.* Once in a while, the older phrase *Reserve for Bad Debts* will be seen, but in modern practice it should not be used. *Bad Debts Expense* is a title often used for Uncollectible Accounts Expense.

Estimating Uncollectible Accounts Expense

Study Note

The accountant looks at both local and national economic conditions in determining the estimated uncollectible accounts expense.

As noted, expected losses from uncollectible accounts must be estimated. Of course, estimates can vary widely. If management takes an optimistic view and projects a small loss from uncollectible accounts, the resulting net accounts receivable will be larger than if management takes a pessimistic view. The net income will also be larger under the optimistic view because the estimated expense will be smaller. The company's accountant makes an estimate based on past experience and current economic conditions. For example, losses from uncollectible accounts are normally expected to be greater in a recession than during a period of economic growth. The final decision, made by management, on the amount of the expense will depend on objective information, such as the accountant's analyses, and on certain qualitative factors, such as how investors,

FOCUS ON BUSINESS PRACTICE

Cash Collections Can Be Hard to Estimate

Companies must not only sell goods and services; they must also generate cash flows by collecting on those sales. When there are changes in the economy, some companies make big mistakes in estimating the amount of accounts they will collect. For example, when the dot-com bubble burst in the early 2000s, companies like **Nortel Networks**, **Cisco Systems**, and **Lucent Technologies** increased their estimates of allowances for uncollectible accounts—actions that eliminated previously reported earnings and caused the companies' stock prices to fall.[16] However, it turned out that these companies had overestimated how bad the losses would be. In later years, they reduced their allowances for credit losses, thereby increasing their reported earnings.[17]

bankers, creditors, and others view the performance of the debtor company. Regardless of the qualitative considerations, the estimated losses from uncollectible accounts should be realistic.

Two common methods of estimating uncollectible accounts expense are the percentage of net sales method and the accounts receivable aging method.

> **Study Note**
> Unlike the direct charge-off method, the percentage of net sales method matches revenues with expenses.

Percentage of Net Sales Method The **percentage of net sales method** asks the question, How much of this year's *net sales* will not be collected? The answer determines the amount of uncollectible accounts expense for the year. For example, the following balances represent Shivar Company's ending figures for 2012:

Sales			
		Dec. 31	322,500

Sales Returns and Allowances			
Dec. 31	20,000		

Sales Discounts			
Dec. 31	2,500		

Allowance for Uncollectible Accounts			
		Dec. 31	1,800

The following are Shivar's actual losses from uncollectible accounts for the past three years:

Year	*Net Sales*	*Losses from Uncollectible Accounts*	*Percentage*
2009	$260,000	$ 5,100	1.96
2010	297,500	6,950	2.34
2011	292,500	4,950	1.69
Total	$850,000	$17,000	2.00

Credit sales often constitute most of a company's sales. If a company has substantial cash sales, it should use only its net credit sales in estimating uncollectible accounts.

Shivar's management believes that its uncollectible accounts will continue to average about 2 percent of net sales. The uncollectible accounts expense for the year 2012 is therefore estimated as follows:

$$0.02 \times (\$322,500 - \$20,000 - \$2,500) = 0.02 \times \$300,000 = \$6,000$$

The following entry would be made to record the estimate:

A	= L +	SE
−6,000		−6,000

2012			
Dec. 31	Uncollectible Accounts Expense	6000	
	Allowance for Uncollectible Accounts		6000
	To record uncollectible accounts expense at 2 percent of $300,000 net sales		

Allowance for Uncollectible Accounts will now have a balance of $7,800:

ALLOWANCE FOR UNCOLLECTIBLE ACCOUNTS			
	Dec. 31		1,800
	Dec. 31	Adj.	6,000
	Dec. 31	**Bal.**	**7,800**

The balance consists of the $6,000 estimated uncollectible accounts receivable from 2012 sales and the $1,800 estimated uncollectible accounts receivable from previous years.

Accounts Receivable Aging Method The **accounts receivable aging method** asks the question, How much of the *ending balance of accounts receivable* will not be collected? With this method, the ending balance of Allowance for Uncollectible Accounts is determined directly through an analysis of accounts receivable. The difference between the amount determined to be uncollectible and the actual balance of Allowance for Uncollectible Accounts is the expense for the period. In theory, this method should produce the same result as the percentage of net sales method, but in practice it rarely does.

The **aging of accounts receivable** is the process of listing each customer's receivable account according to the due date of the account. If the customer's account is past due, there is a possibility that the account will not be paid. And that possibility increases as the account extends further beyond the due date. The aging of accounts receivable helps management evaluate its credit and collection policies and alerts it to possible problems.

Study Note

An aging of accounts receivable is an important tool in cash management because it helps to determine what amounts are likely to be collected in the months ahead.

Exhibit 7-2 illustrates the aging of accounts receivable for Gomez Company. Each account receivable is classified as being not yet due or as being 1–30 days, 31–60 days, 61–90 days, or over 90 days past due. Based on past experience, the estimated percentage for each category is determined and multiplied by the amount in each category to determine the estimated, or target, balance of Allowance for Uncollectible Accounts. In total, it is estimated that $4,918 of the $88,800 in accounts receivable will not be collected.

Study Note

When the write-offs in an accounting period exceed the amount of the allowance, a debit balance in the allowance for uncollectible accounts account results.

Once the target balance for Allowance for Uncollectible Accounts has been found, it is necessary to determine the amount of the adjustment. The amount depends on the current balance of the allowance account. Let us assume two cases for the December 31 balance of Gomez Company's Allowance for Uncollectible Accounts: (1) a credit balance of $1,600 and (2) a debit balance of $1,600.

In the first case, an adjustment of $3,318 is needed to bring the balance of the allowance account to a $4,918 credit balance:

Targeted balance for allowance for uncollectible accounts	$4,918
Less current credit balance of allowance for uncollectible accounts	1,600
Uncollectible accounts expense	$3,318

EXHIBIT 7-2 Analysis of Accounts Receivable by Age

Gomez Company
Analysis of Accounts Receivable by Age
December 31, 2010

Customer	Total	Not Yet Due	1–30 Days Past Due	31–60 Days Past Due	61–90 Days Past Due	Over 90 Days Past Due
K. Wu	$ 300		$ 300			
R. List	800			$ 800		
B. Smith	2,000	$ 1,800	200			
T. Vigo	500				$ 500	
Others	85,200	42,200	28,000	7,600	4,400	$3,200
Totals	$88,800	$43,800	$28,500	$8,400	$4,900	$3,200
Estimated percentage uncollectible		1.0	2.0	10.0	30.0	50.0
Allowance for Uncollectible Accounts	$ 4,918	$ 438	$ 570	$ 840	$1,470	$1,600

The uncollectible accounts expense is recorded as follows:

A	= L +	SE
−3,318		−3,318

2010			
Dec. 31	Uncollectible Accounts Expense	3,318	
	Allowance for Uncollectible Accounts		3,318
	To bring the allowance for uncollectible accounts to the level of estimated losses		

The resulting balance of Allowance for Uncollectible Accounts is $4,918:

ALLOWANCE FOR UNCOLLECTIBLE ACCOUNTS		
	Dec. 31	1,600
	31 Adj.	3,318
	Dec. 31 Bal.	**4,918**

In the second case, because Allowance for Uncollectible Accounts has a debit balance of $1,600, the estimated uncollectible accounts expense for the year will have to be $6,518 to reach the targeted balance of $4,918. This calculation is as follows:

Targeted balance for allowance for uncollectible accounts	$4,918
Plus current debit balance of allowance for uncollectible accounts	1,600
Uncollectible accounts expense	$6,518

The uncollectible accounts expense is recorded as follows:

A	= L +	SE
−6,518		−6,518

2010			
Dec. 31	Uncollectible Accounts Expense	6,518	
	Allowance for Uncollectible Accounts		6,518
	To bring the allowance for uncollectible accounts to the level of estimated losses		

FIGURE 7-6
Two Methods of Estimating Uncollectible Accounts

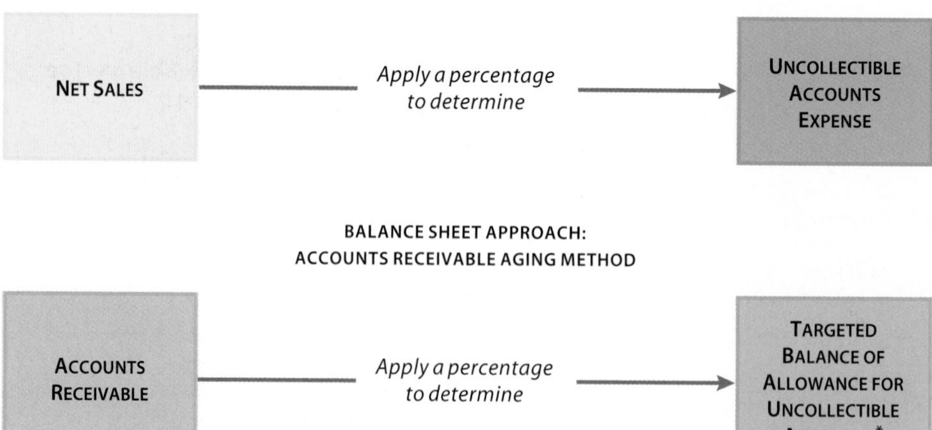

**Add current debit balance or subtract current credit balance to determine uncollectible accounts expense.*

After this entry, Allowance for Uncollectible Accounts has a credit balance of $4,918:

Allowance for Uncollectible Accounts			
Dec. 31	1,600	Dec. 31 Adj.	6,518
		Dec. 31 Bal.	**4,918**

> **Study Note**
> Describing the aging method as the balance sheet method emphasizes that the computation is based on ending accounts receivable rather than on net sales for the period.

Comparison of the Two Methods Both the percentage of net sales method and the accounts receivable aging method estimate the uncollectible accounts expense in accordance with the matching rule, but as shown in Figure 7-6, they do so in different ways. The percentage of net sales method is an income statement approach. It assumes that a certain proportion of sales will not be collected, and this proportion is the *amount of Uncollectible Accounts Expense* for the period. The accounts receivable aging method is a balance sheet approach. It assumes that a certain proportion of accounts receivable outstanding will not be collected. This proportion is the *targeted balance of the Allowance for Uncollectible Accounts account.* The expense for the accounting period is the difference between the targeted balance and the current balance of the allowance account.

Writing Off Uncollectible Accounts

Regardless of the method used to estimate uncollectible accounts, the total of accounts receivable written off in an accounting period will rarely equal the estimated uncollectible amount. The allowance account will show a credit balance when the total of accounts written off is less than the estimated uncollectible amount. It will show a debit balance when the total of accounts written off is greater than the estimated uncollectible amount.

> **Study Note**
> When writing off an individual account, debit Allowance for Uncollectible Accounts, not Uncollectible Accounts Expense.

When it becomes clear that a specific account receivable will not be collected, the amount should be written off to Allowance for Uncollectible Accounts. Remember that the uncollectible amount was already accounted for as an expense when the allowance was established. For example, assume that on January 15, 2011, T. Vigo, who owes Gomez Company $500, is declared bankrupt by a federal court. The entry in journal form to *write off* this account is as follows:

A	= L +	SE
+500		
−500		

2011			
Jan. 15	Allowance for Uncollectible Accounts	500	
	Accounts Receivable		500
	To write off receivable from T. Vigo as uncollectible because of his bankruptcy		

Although the write-off removes the uncollectible amount from Accounts Receivable, it does not affect the estimated net realizable value of accounts receivable. It simply reduces T. Vigo's account to zero and reduces Allowance for Uncollectible Accounts by $500, as follows:

	Balances Before Write-off	*Balances After Write-off*
Accounts receivable	$88,800	$88,300
Less allowance for uncollectible accounts	4,918	4,418
Estimated net realizable value of accounts receivable	$83,882	$83,882

Occasionally, a customer whose account has been written off as uncollectible will later be able to pay some or all of the amount owed. When that happens, two entries must be made: one to reverse the earlier write-off (which is now incorrect) and another to show the collection of the account.

STOP & APPLY >

Jazz Instruments, Inc., sells its merchandise on credit. In the company's last fiscal year, which ended July 31, it had net sales of $7,000,000. At the end of the fiscal year, it had Accounts Receivable of $1,800,000 and a credit balance in Allowance for Uncollectible Accounts of $11,200. In the past, the company has been unable to collect on approximately 1 percent of its net sales. An aging analysis of accounts receivable has indicated that $80,000 of current receivables are uncollectible.

1. Calculate the amount of uncollectible accounts expense, and use T accounts to determine the resulting balance of Allowance for Uncollectible Accounts under the percentage of net sales method and the accounts receivable aging method.
2. How would your answers change if Allowance for Uncollectible Accounts had a debit balance of $11,200 instead of a credit balance?

(continued)

SOLUTION

1. Percentage of net sales method:

Allowance for Uncollectible Accounts

	July 31		11,200
	31	UA Exp.	70,000*
	July 31	**Bal.**	81,200

*Uncollectible Accounts Expense = $7,000,000 × 0.01

Aging Method:

Allowance for Uncollectible Accounts

	July 31		11,200
	31	UA Exp.	68,800*
	July 31	**Bal.**	80,000

*Uncollectible Accounts Expense = $80,000 − $11,200

2. Under the percentage of net sales method, the amount of the expense is the same in **1** and **2** but the ending balance will be $58,800 ($70,000 − $11,200). Under the aging method, the ending balance is the same, but the amount of the expense will be $91,200 ($80,000 + $11,200).

Notes Receivable

LO4 Define *promissory note,* and make common calculations for promissory notes receivable.

A **promissory note** is an unconditional promise to pay a definite sum of money on demand or at a future date. The person or company that signs the note and thereby promises to pay is the *maker* of the note. The entity to whom payment is to be made is the *payee.* The promissory note shown in Figure 7-7 is an unconditional promise by the maker, Samuel Mason, to pay a definite sum—or principal ($1,000)—to the payee, Cook County Bank & Trust, on August 18, 2010. As

FIGURE 7-7
A Promissory Note

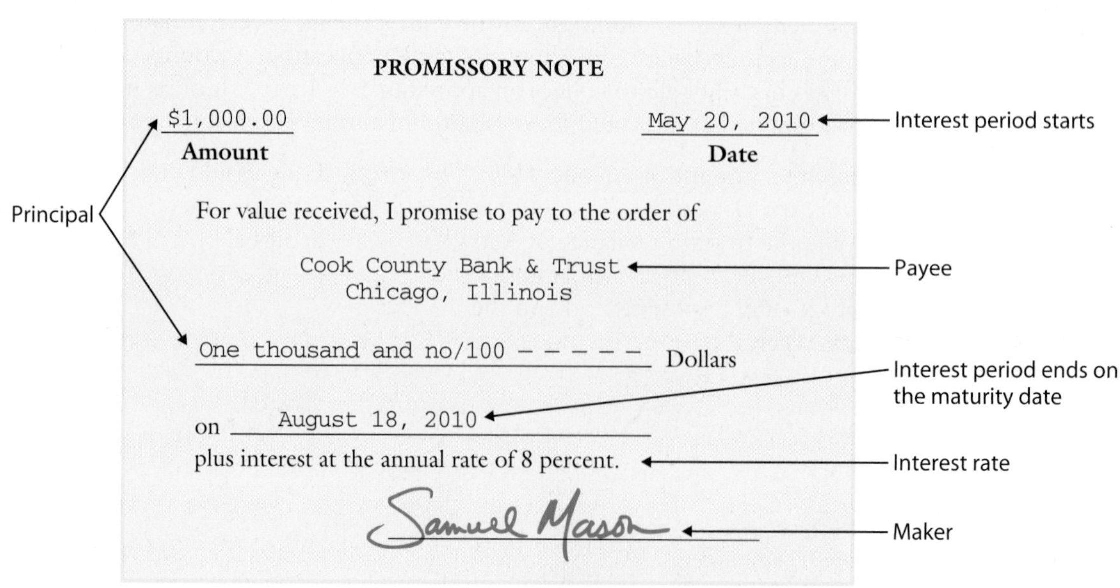

Automobile manufacturers like Toyota, whose assembly line is pictured here, often accept promissory notes, which are unconditional promises to pay a definite sum of money on demand or at a future date. These notes produce interest income and represent a stronger legal claim against a debtor than do accounts receivable. In addition, firms commonly raise money by selling—or discounting—promissory notes to banks.

Courtesy of Ricardo Azoury/iStockphoto.com.

you can see, this promissory note is dated May 20, 2010, and bears an interest rate of 8 percent.

Study Note

Notes receivable and notes payable are distinguished from accounts receivable and accounts payable because the latter were not created by a formal promissory note.

A payee includes all the promissory notes it holds that are due in less than one year in **notes receivable** in the current assets section of its balance sheet. A maker includes them in **notes payable** in the current liabilities section of its balance sheet. Since notes receivable and notes payable are financial instruments, companies may voluntarily disclose their fair value. In most cases, fair value approximates the amount in the account records, but sometimes the adjustments to fair value are significant, such as in the recent cases of subprime loans gone bad.

The nature of a company's business generally determines how frequently it receives promissory notes from customers. Firms that sell durable goods of high value, such as farm machinery and automobiles, often accept promissory notes. Among the advantages of these notes are that they produce interest income and represent a stronger legal claim against a debtor than do accounts receivable. In addition, selling—or discounting—promissory notes to banks is a common financing method. Almost all companies occasionally accept promissory notes, and many companies obtain them in settlement of past-due accounts.

Maturity Date

The **maturity date** is the date on which a promissory note must be paid. This date must be stated on the note or be determinable from the facts stated on the note. The following are among the most common statements of maturity date:

1. A specific date, such as "November 14, 2010"
2. A specific number of months after the date of the note, such as "three months after November 14, 2010"
3. A specific number of days after the date of the note, such as "60 days after November 14, 2010"

The maturity date is obvious when a specific date is stated. And when the maturity date is a number of months from the date of the note, one simply uses the same day in the appropriate future month. For example, a note dated January 20 that is due in two months would be due on March 20.

When the maturity date is a specific number of days from the date of the note, however, the exact maturity date must be determined. In computing the maturity date, it is important to exclude the date of the note. For example, a note dated May 20 and due in 90 days would be due on August 18, determined as follows:

Days remaining in May (31 − 20)	11
Days in June	30
Days in July	31
Days in August	18
Total days	90

Duration of a Note

Study Note

Another way to compute the duration of notes is to begin with the interest period, as in this example:

90	Interest period
−11	days remaining in May (31 − 20)
79	
−30	days in June
49	
−31	days in July
18	due date in August

The **duration of a note** is the time between a promissory note's issue date and its maturity date. Knowing the exact number of days in the duration of a note is important because interest is calculated on that basis. Identifying the duration is easy when the maturity date is stated as a specific number of days from the date of the note because the two numbers are the same. However, when the maturity date is stated as a specific date, the exact number of days must be determined. Assume that a note issued on May 10 matures on August 10. The duration of the note is 92 days:

Days remaining in May (31 − 10)	21
Days in June	30
Days in July	31
Days in August	10
Total days	92

Interest and Interest Rate

Interest is the cost of borrowing money or the return on lending money, depending on whether one is the borrower or the lender. The amount of interest is based on three factors: the principal (the amount of money borrowed or lent), the rate of interest, and the loan's length of time. The formula used in computing interest is as follows:

$$\text{Principal} \times \text{Rate of Interest} \times \text{Time} = \text{Interest}$$

Interest rates are usually stated on an annual basis. For example, the interest on a one-year, 8 percent, \$1,000 note would be \$80 ($\$1,000 \times 8/100 \times 1 = \$80$). If the term, or time period, of the note is three months instead of a year, the interest charge would be \$20 ($\$1,000 \times 8/100 \times 3/12 = \$20$).

When the term of a note is expressed in days, the exact number of days must be used in computing the interest. Thus, if the term of the note described above was 45 days, the interest would be \$9.86, computed as follows: $\$1,000 \times 8/100 \times 45/365 = \$9.86$.

Maturity Value

The **maturity value** is the total proceeds of a promissory note—face value plus interest—at the maturity date. The maturity value of a 90-day, 8 percent, $1,000 note is computed as follows:

$$\begin{aligned} \text{Maturity Value} &= \text{Principal} + \text{Interest} \\ &= \$1{,}000 + (\$1{,}000 \times 8/100 \times 90/365) \\ &= \$1{,}000 + \$19.73 \\ &= \$1{,}019.73 \end{aligned}$$

There are also so-called non-interest-bearing notes. The maturity value is the face value, or principal amount. In this case, the principal includes an implied interest cost.

Accrued Interest

A promissory note received in one accounting period may not be due until a later period. The interest on a note accrues by a small amount each day of the note's duration. As we described in an earlier chapter, the matching rule requires that the accrued interest be apportioned to the periods in which it belongs. For example, assume that the $1,000, 90-day, 8 percent note discussed above was received on August 31 and that the fiscal year ended on September 30. In this case, 30 days interest, or $6.58 ($\$1{,}000 \times 8/100 \times 30/365 = \$6.58$), would be earned in the fiscal year that ends on September 30. An adjusting entry would be made to record the interest receivable as an asset and the interest income as revenue. The remainder of the interest income, $13.15 ($\$1{,}000 \times 8/100 \times 60/365$), would be recorded as income, and the interest receivable ($6.58) would be shown as received when the note is paid. Note that all the cash for the interest is received when the note is paid, but the interest income is apportioned to two fiscal years.

Dishonored Note

When the maker of a note does not pay the note at maturity, it is said to be a **dishonored note**. The holder, or payee, of a dishonored note should make an entry to transfer the total amount due (including interest income) from Notes Receivable to an account receivable from the debtor. Two objectives are accomplished by transferring a dishonored note into an Accounts Receivable account. First, it leaves only notes that have not matured and are presumably negotiable and collectible in the Notes Receivable account. Second, it establishes a record in the borrower's accounts receivable account that the customer has dishonored a note receivable. Such information may be helpful in deciding whether to extend credit to the customer in the future.

STOP & APPLY >

Assume that on December 1, 2011, a company receives a 90-day, 8 percent, $5,000 note and that the company prepares financial statements monthly.

1. What is the maturity date of the note?
2. How much interest will be earned on the note if it is paid when due?
3. What is the maturity value of the note?
4. If the company's fiscal year ends on December 31, describe the adjusting entry that would be made, including the amount.
5. How much interest will be earned on this note in 2012?

SOLUTION

1. Maturity date is March 1, 2012, determined as follows:

Days remaining in December (31 − 1)	30
Days in January	31
Days in February	28
Days in March	1
Total days	90

2. Interest: $\$5{,}000 \times 8/100 \times 90/365 = \$98.63$
3. Maturity value: $\$5{,}000.00 + \$98.63 = \$5{,}098.63$
4. An adjusting entry to accrue 30 days of interest income in the amount of $32.88 ($\$5{,}000 \times 8/100 \times 30/365$) would be needed.
5. Interest earned in 2012: $65.75 ($98.63 − $32.88)

A LOOK BACK AT ▸ NIKE, INC.

In this chapter's Decision Point, we noted that **Nike** must give the retailers that buy its products time to pay for their purchases, but at the same time, Nike must have enough cash on hand to pay its suppliers. To plan the company's cash flows, Nike's management must address the following questions:

- How can the company control its cash needs?
- How can the company evaluate credit policies and the level of its receivables?
- How should the company estimate the value of its receivables?

As you saw in Figure 7-1, companies like Nike go through seasonal cycles that affect their cash flows. At times, Nike may have excess cash available that it can invest in a way that earns a return but still permits ready access to cash. At other times, it may have to borrow funds. To ensure that it can borrow funds when it needs to, Nike maintains good relations with its banks.

To evaluate the company's credit policies and the level of its accounts receivable, management can compare the current year's receivable turnover and days' sales uncollected with those ratios in previous years. Using data from Nike's Financial Highlights, we can compute these ratios for 2009 and 2008 as follows (dollars are in millions):

		2009	2008
Receivable Turnover: K/R	$\frac{\text{Net Sales}}{\text{Average Accounts Receivable}}$	$\frac{\$19{,}176.1}{(\$2{,}883.9 + \$2{,}795.3) \div 2}$	$\frac{\$18{,}627.0}{(\$2{,}795.3 + \$2{,}494.7) \div 2}$
		$\frac{\$19{,}176.1}{\$2{,}839.6}$	$\frac{\$18{,}627}{\$2{,}645}$
		6.8 times	7.0 times
Days' Sales Uncollected: K/R	$\frac{\text{Number of Days in a Year}}{\text{Receivable Turnover}}$	$\frac{365 \text{ days}}{6.8 \text{ times}}$	$\frac{365 \text{ days}}{7.0 \text{ times}}$
		53.7 days	52.1 days

Thus, in 2009, Nike had a decrease in its receivable turnover. It also increased the number of days it takes to collect accounts receivable. An increase of 1.6 days may not seem like much, but it represents about $84 million in cash.

Review Problem

Estimating Uncollectible Accounts and Receivables Analysis

LO1 LO3

Pente Metal Corporation sells merchandise on credit and also accepts notes as payment. During the year ended June 30, the company had net sales of $2,400,000. At the end of the year, it had Accounts Receivable of $800,000 and a debit balance in Allowance for Uncollectible Accounts of $4,200. In the past, approximately 1.5 percent of net sales has been uncollectible. Also, an aging analysis of accounts receivable reveals that $34,000 in accounts receivable appears to be uncollectible.

Required

1. Compute Uncollectible Accounts Expense, and determine the ending balance of Allowance for Uncollectible Accounts and Accounts Receivable, Net, under (a) the percentage of net sales method and (b) the accounts receivable aging method.
2. Compute the receivable turnover and days' sales uncollected using the data from the accounts receivable aging method in requirement **1** and assuming that the prior year's net accounts receivable were $706,000.

Answers to Review Problem

1. Uncollectible Accounts Expense and ending account balances

   a. Percentage of net sales method:

   Uncollectible Accounts Expense = 1.5 percent × $2,400,000 = $36,000

   Allowance for Uncollectible Accounts = $36,000 − $4,200 = $31,800

   Accounts Receivable, Net = $800,000 − $31,800 = $768,200

   b. Accounts receivable aging method:

   Uncollectible Accounts Expense = $4,200 + $34,000 = $38,200

   Allowance for Uncollectible Accounts = $34,000

   Accounts Receivable, Net = $800,000 − $34,000 = $766,000

2. Receivable turnover and days' sales uncollected

$$\text{Receivable Turnover} = \frac{\$2{,}400{,}000}{(\$766{,}000 + \$706{,}000) \div 2} = 3.3 \text{ times}$$

$$\text{Days' Sales Uncollected} = \frac{365 \text{ days}}{3.3 \text{ times}} = 110.6 \text{ days}$$

LO1 Identify and explain the management and ethical issues related to cash and receivables.

The management of cash and receivables is critical to maintaining adequate liquidity. In dealing with these assets, management must (1) consider the need for short-term investing and borrowing as the business's balance of cash fluctuates during seasonal cycles, (2) establish credit policies that balance the need for sales with the ability to collect, (3) evaluate the level of receivables using receivable turnover and days' sales uncollected, (4) assess the need to increase cash flows through the financing of receivables, and (5) understand the importance of ethics in estimating credit losses.

LO2 Define *cash equivalents*, and explain methods of controlling cash, including bank reconciliations.

Cash equivalents are investments that have a term of 90 days or less. Cash and cash equivalents are financial instruments that are valued at fair value. Methods of controlling cash include imprest systems; banking services, including electronic funds transfer; and bank reconciliations. A bank reconciliation accounts for the difference between the balance on a company's bank statement and the balance in its Cash account. It involves adjusting for outstanding checks, deposits in transit, service charges, NSF checks, miscellaneous debits and credits, and interest income.

LO3 Apply the allowance method of accounting for uncollectible accounts.

Because of the time lag between credit sales and the time accounts are judged uncollectible, the allowance method is used to match the amount of uncollectible accounts against revenues in any given period. Uncollectible accounts expense is estimated by using either the percentage of net sales method or the accounts receivable aging method. When the first method is used, bad debts are judged to be a certain percentage of sales during the period. When the second method is used, certain percentages are applied to groups of accounts receivable that have been arranged by due dates.

Allowance for Uncollectible Accounts is a contra-asset account to Accounts Receivable. The estimate of uncollectible accounts is debited to Uncollectible Accounts Expense and credited to the allowance account. When an individual account is determined to be uncollectible, it is removed from Accounts Receivable by debiting the allowance account and crediting Accounts Receivable. If the written-off account is later collected, the earlier entry is reversed and the collection is recorded in the normal way.

LO4 Define *promissory note*, and make common calculations for promissory notes receivable.

A promissory note is an unconditional promise to pay a definite sum of money on demand or at a future date. Companies that sell durable goods of high value, such as farm machinery and automobiles, often accept promissory notes. Selling these notes to banks is a common financing method. In accounting for promissory notes, it is important to know how to calculate the maturity date, duration of a note, interest and interest rate, and maturity value.

REVIEW of Concepts and Terminology

The following concepts and terms were introduced in this chapter:

Accounts receivable 355 (LO1)

Accounts receivable aging method 368 (LO3)

Aging of accounts receivable 368 (LO3)

Allowance for Uncollectible Accounts 366 (LO3)

Allowance method 365 (LO3)

Bank reconciliation 362 (LO2)

Cash 354 (LO1)

Cash equivalents 361 (LO2)

Compensating balance 354 (LO1)

Contingent liability 358 (LO1)

Direct charge-off method 365 (LO3)

Discounting 359 (LO1)

Dishonored note 375 (LO4)

Duration of a note 374 (LO4)

Electronic funds transfer (EFT) 362 (LO2)

Factor 358 (LO1)

Factoring 358 (LO1)

Imprest systems 361 (LO2)

Installment accounts receivable 355 (LO1)

Interest 374 (LO4)

Maturity date 373 (LO4)

Maturity value 375 (LO4)

Notes payable 373 (LO4)

Notes receivable 373 (LO4)

Percentage of net sales method 367 (LO3)

Promissory note 372 (LO4)

Securitization 359 (LO1)

Short-term financial assets 355 (LO1)

Trade credit 355 (LO1)

Uncollectible accounts 359 (LO1)

Key Ratios

Days' sales uncollected 357 (LO1)

Receivable turnover 356 (LO1)

CHAPTER ASSIGNMENTS

BUILDING Your Basic Knowledge and Skills

Short Exercises

LO1 **Management Issues**

SE 1. Indicate whether each of the following actions is related to (a) managing cash needs, (b) setting credit policies, (c) financing receivables, or (d) ethically reporting receivables:

1. Selling accounts receivable to a factor
2. Borrowing funds for short-term needs during slow periods
3. Conducting thorough checks of new customers' ability to pay
4. Making every effort to reflect possible future losses accurately

LO1 **Short-Term Liquidity Ratios**

SE 2. Graff Company has cash of $40,000, net accounts receivable of $90,000, and net sales of $720,000. Last year's net accounts receivable were $70,000. Compute the following ratios: (a) receivable turnover and (b) days' sales uncollected.

LO2 **Cash and Cash Equivalents**

SE 3. Compute the amount of cash and cash equivalents on Car Wash Company's balance sheet if, on the balance sheet date, it has currency and coins on hand of $125, deposits in checking accounts of $750, U.S. Treasury bills due in 80 days of $7,500, and U.S. Treasury bonds due in 200 days of $12,500.

LO2 **Bank Reconciliation**

SE 4. Prepare a bank reconciliation from the following information:

a. Balance per bank statement as of June 30, $4,862.77
b. Balance per books as of June 30, $2,479.48
c. Deposits in transit, $654.24
d. Outstanding checks, $3,028.89
e. Interest on average balance, $8.64

LO3 **Percentage of Net Sales Method**

SE 5. At the end of October, Zion Company's management estimates the uncollectible accounts expense to be 1 percent of net sales of $1,500,000. Prepare the entry in journal form to record the uncollectible accounts expense, assuming the Allowance for Uncollectible Accounts has a debit balance of $7,000.

LO3 **Accounts Receivable Aging Method**

SE 6. An aging analysis on June 30 of the accounts receivable of Sung Corporation indicates that uncollectible accounts amount to $86,000. Prepare the entry in journal form to record uncollectible accounts expense under each of the following independent assumptions:

a. Allowance for Uncollectible Accounts has a credit balance of $18,000 before adjustment.
b. Allowance for Uncollectible Accounts has a debit balance of $14,000 before adjustment.

LO3 **Write-off of Accounts Receivable**

SE 7. Windy Corporation, which uses the allowance method, has accounts receivable of $50,800 and an allowance for uncollectible accounts of $9,800. An account receivable from Tom Novak of $4,400 is deemed to be uncollectible and is written off. What is the amount of net accounts receivable before and after the write-off?

LO4 **Notes Receivable Calculations**

SE 8. On August 25, Champion Company received a 90-day, 9 percent note in settlement of an account receivable in the amount of $20,000. Determine the maturity date, amount of interest on the note, and maturity value.

Exercises

LO1 LO2 **Discussion Questions**

E 1. Develop a brief answer to each of the following questions:

1. Name some businesses whose needs for cash fluctuate during the year. Name some whose needs for cash are relatively stable over the year.
2. Why is it advantageous for a company to finance its receivables?
3. To increase its sales, a company decides to increase its credit terms from 15 to 30 days. What effect will this change in policy have on receivable turnover and days' sales uncollected?
4. How might the receivable turnover and days' sales uncollected reveal that management is consistently underestimating the amount of losses from uncollectible accounts? Is this action ethical?

LO3 LO4 **Discussion Questions**

E 2. Develop a brief answer to each of the following questions:

1. What accounting rule is violated by the direct charge-off method of recognizing uncollectible accounts? Why?
2. In what ways is Allowance for Uncollectible Accounts similar to Accumulated Depreciation? In what ways is it different?
3. Under what circumstances would an accrual of interest income on an interest-bearing note receivable not be required at the end of an accounting period?

LO1 **Management Issues**

E 3. Indicate whether each of the following actions is primarily related to (a) managing cash needs, (b) setting credit policies, (c) financing receivables, or (d) ethically reporting accounts receivable:

1. Buying a U.S. Treasury bill with cash that is not needed for a few months
2. Comparing receivable turnovers for two years
3. Setting a policy that allows customers to buy on credit
4. Selling notes receivable to a financing company
5. Making careful estimates of losses from uncollectible accounts
6. Borrowing funds for short-term needs in a period when sales are low
7. Changing the terms for credit sales in an effort to reduce the days' sales uncollected
8. Revising estimated credit losses in a timely manner when economic conditions change
9. Establishing a department whose responsibility is to approve customers' credit

LO1 **Short-Term Liquidity Ratios**

E 4. Using the following data from Lopez Corporation's financial statements, compute the receivable turnover and the days' sales uncollected:

Current assets	
Cash	$ 35,000
Short-term investments	85,000
Notes receivable	120,000
Accounts receivable, net	200,000
Inventory	250,000
Prepaid assets	25,000
Total current assets	$ 715,000
Current liabilities	
Notes payable	$ 300,000
Accounts payable	75,000
Accrued liabilities	10,000
Total current liabilities	$ 385,000
Net sales	$1,600,000
Last accounts receivable, net	$ 180,000

LO2 **Cash and Cash Equivalents**

E 5. At year end, Lam Company had currency and coins in cash registers of $2,800, money orders from customers of $5,000, deposits in checking accounts of $32,000, U.S. Treasury bills due in 80 days of $90,000, certificates of deposit at the bank that mature in six months of $100,000, and U.S. Treasury bonds due in one year of $50,000. Calculate the amount of cash and cash equivalents that will be shown on the company's year-end balance sheet.

LO2 **Bank Reconciliation**

E 6. Prepare a bank reconciliation from the following information:

a. Balance per bank statement as of May 31, $17,755.44
b. Balance per books as of May 31, $12,211.94
c. Deposits in transit, $2,254.81
d. Outstanding checks, $7,818.16
e. Bank service charge, $19.85

LO3 **Percentage of Net Sales Method**

E 7. At the end of the year, Emil Enterprises estimates the uncollectible accounts expense to be 0.8 percent of net sales of $7,575,000. The current credit balance of Allowance for Uncollectible Accounts is $12,900. Prepare the entry in journal form to record the uncollectible accounts expense. What is the balance of Allowance for Uncollectible Accounts after this adjustment?

LO3 **Accounts Receivable Aging Method**

E 8. The Accounts Receivable account of Samson Company shows a debit balance of $52,000 at the end of the year. An aging analysis of the individual accounts indicates estimated uncollectible accounts to be $3,350.

Prepare the entry in journal form to record the uncollectible accounts expense under each of the following independent assumptions: (a) Allowance for Uncollectible Accounts has a credit balance of $400 before adjustment, and (b) Allowance for Uncollectible Accounts has a debit balance of $400 before adjustment. What is the balance of Allowance for Uncollectible Accounts after each of these adjustments?

LO3 **Aging Method and Net Sales Method Contrasted**

E 9. At the beginning of 2010, the balances for Accounts Receivable and Allowance for Uncollectible Accounts were $430,000 and $31,400 (credit), respectively.

During the year, credit sales were $3,200,000, and collections on account were $2,950,000. In addition, $35,000 in uncollectible accounts was written off.

Using T accounts, determine the year-end balances of Accounts Receivable and Allowance for Uncollectible Accounts. Then prepare the year-end adjusting entry to record the uncollectible accounts expense under each of the following conditions. Also show the year-end balance sheet presentation of accounts receivable and allowance for uncollectible accounts.

a. Management estimates the percentage of uncollectible credit sales to be 1.4 percent of total credit sales.
b. Based on an aging of accounts receivable, management estimates the end-of-year uncollectible accounts receivable to be $38,700.

Post the results of each of the entries to the T account for Allowance for Uncollectible Accounts.

LO3 Aging Method and Net Sales Method Contrasted

E 10. During 2010, Omega Company had net sales of $11,400,000. Most of the sales were on credit. At the end of 2010, the balance of Accounts Receivable was $1,400,000, and Allowance for Uncollectible Accounts had a debit balance of $48,000.

Omega Company's management uses two methods of estimating uncollectible accounts expense: the percentage of net sales method and the accounts receivable aging method. The percentage of uncollectible sales is 1.5 percent of net sales, and based on an aging of accounts receivable, the end-of-year uncollectible accounts total $140,000.

Prepare the end-of-year adjusting entry to record the uncollectible accounts expense under each method. What will the balance of Allowance for Uncollectible Accounts be after each adjustment? Why are the results different? Which method is likely to be more reliable? Why?

LO3 Aging Method and Net Sales Method Contrasted

E 11. The First Fence Company sells merchandise on credit. During the fiscal year ended July 31, the company had net sales of $1,150,000. At the end of the year, it had Accounts Receivable of $300,000 and a debit balance in Allowance for Uncollectible Accounts of $1,700. In the past, approximately 1.4 percent of net sales have proved to be uncollectible. Also, an aging analysis of accounts receivable reveals that $15,000 of the receivables appears to be uncollectible.

Prepare entries in journal form to record uncollectible accounts expense using (a) the percentage of net sales method and (b) the accounts receivable aging method. What is the resulting balance of Allowance for Uncollectible Accounts under each method? How would your answers under each method change if Allowance for Uncollectible Accounts had a credit balance of $1,700 instead of a debit balance? Why do the methods result in different balances?

LO3 Write-off of Accounts Receivable

E 12. Colby Company, which uses the allowance method, has Accounts Receivable of $65,000 and an allowance for uncollectible accounts of $6,400 (credit). The company sold merchandise to Irma Hegerman for $7,200 and later received $2,400 from Hegerman. The rest of the amount due from Hegerman had to be written off as uncollectible. Using T accounts, show the beginning balances and the effects of the Hegerman transactions on Accounts Receivable and Allowance for Uncollectible Accounts. What is the amount of net accounts receivable before and after the write-off?

LO4 **Interest Computations**

E 13. Determine the interest on the following notes:

a. $77,520 at 10 percent for 90 days
b. $54,400 at 12 percent for 60 days
c. $61,200 at 9 percent for 30 days
d. $102,000 at 15 percent for 120 days
e. $36,720 at 6 percent for 60 days

LO4 **Notes Receivable Calculations**

E 14. Determine the maturity date, interest at maturity, and maturity value for a 90-day, 10 percent, $36,000 note from Archer Corporation dated February 15.

LO4 **Notes Receivable Calculations**

E 15. Determine the maturity date, interest in 2010 and 2011, and maturity value for a 90-day, 12 percent, $30,000 note from a customer dated December 1, 2010, assuming a December 31 year-end.

LO4 **Notes Receivable Calculations**

E 16. Determine the maturity date, interest at maturity, and maturity value for each of the following notes:

a. A 60-day, 10 percent, $4,800 note dated January 5 received from A. Gal for granting a time extension on a past-due account.
b. A 60-day, 12 percent, $3,000 note dated March 9 received from T. Kawa for granting a time extension on a past-due account.

Problems

LO2 **Bank Reconciliation**

P 1. The following information is available for Unique Globe, Inc., as of May 31, 2010:

a. Cash on the books as of May 31 amounted to $43,784.16. Cash on the bank statement for the same date was $53,451.46.
b. A deposit of $5,220.94, representing cash receipts of May 31, did not appear on the bank statement.
c. Outstanding checks totaled $3,936.80.
d. A check for $1,920.00 returned with the statement was recorded incorrectly in the check register as $1,380.00. The check was for a cash purchase of merchandise.
e. The bank service charge for May amounted to $30.
f. The bank collected $12,200.00 for Unique Globe, Inc., on a note. The face value of the note was $12,000.00.
g. An NSF check for $178.56 from a customer, Eve Lay, was returned with the statement.
h. The bank mistakenly charged to the company account a check for $750.00 drawn by another company.
i. The bank reported that it had credited the account for $250.00 in interest on the average balance for May.

Required

1. Prepare a bank reconciliation for Unique Globe, Inc., as of May 31, 2010.
2. Prepare the entries in journal form necessary to adjust the accounts.
3. What amount of cash should appear on Unique Globe, Inc.'s balance sheet as of May 31?

User insight ▶ 4. Why is a bank reconciliation considered an important control over cash?

LO1 LO3

Methods of Estimating Uncollectible Accounts and Receivables Analysis

P 2. Moore Company had an Accounts Receivable balance of $640,000 and a credit balance in Allowance for Uncollectible Accounts of $33,400 at January 1, 2010. During the year, the company recorded the following transactions:

a. Sales on account, $2,104,000
b. Sales returns and allowances by credit customers, $106,800
c. Collections from customers, $1,986,000
d. Worthless accounts written off, $39,600

The company's past history indicates that 2.5 percent of its net credit sales will not be collected.

Required

1. Prepare T accounts for Accounts Receivable and Allowance for Uncollectible Accounts. Enter the beginning balances, and show the effects on these accounts of the items listed above, summarizing the year's activity. Determine the ending balance of each account.
2. Compute Uncollectible Accounts Expense and determine the ending balance of Allowance for Uncollectible Accounts under (a) the percentage of net sales method and (b) the accounts receivable aging method, assuming an aging of the accounts receivable shows that $48,000 may be uncollectible.
3. Compute the receivable turnover and days' sales uncollected, using the data from the accounts receivable aging method in requirement **2**.

User insight ▶

4. How do you explain that the two methods used in requirement **2** result in different amounts for Uncollectible Accounts Expense? What rationale underlies each method?

LO3

Accounts Receivable Aging Method

P 3. The Ciao Style Store uses the accounts receivable aging method to estimate uncollectible accounts. On February 1, 2010, the balance of the Accounts Receivable account was a debit of $442,341, and the balance of Allowance for Uncollectible Accounts was a credit of $43,700. During the year, the store had sales on account of $3,722,000, sales returns and allowances of $60,000, worthless accounts written off of $44,300, and collections from customers of $3,211,000. As part of the end-of-year (January 31, 2011) procedures, an aging analysis of accounts receivable is prepared. The analysis, which is partially complete, is as follows:

Customer Account	Total	Not Yet Due	1–30 Days Past Due	31–60 Days Past Due	61–90 Days Past Due	Over 90 Days Past Due
Balance Forward	$793,791	$438,933	$149,614	$106,400	$57,442	$41,402

To finish the analysis, the following accounts need to be classified:

Account	Amount	Due Date
J. Kras	$11,077	Jan. 15
T. Lopez	9,314	Feb. 15 (next fiscal year)
L. Zapal	8,664	Dec. 20
R. Caputo	780	Oct. 1
E. Rago	14,710	Jan. 4
S. Smith	6,316	Nov. 15
A. Quinn	4,389	Mar. 1 (next fiscal year)
	$55,250	

From past experience, the company has found that the following rates are realistic for estimating uncollectible accounts:

Time	Percentage Considered Uncollectible
Not yet due	2
1–30 days past due	5
31–60 days past due	15
61–90 days past due	25
Over 90 days past due	50

Required

1. Complete the aging analysis of accounts receivable.
2. Compute the end-of-year balances (before adjustments) of Accounts Receivable and Allowance for Uncollectible Accounts.
3. Prepare an analysis computing the estimated uncollectible accounts.
4. How much is Ciao Style Store's estimated uncollectible accounts expense for the year? (Round the adjustment to the nearest whole dollar.)

User insight ▶

5. What role do estimates play in applying the aging analysis? What factors might affect these estimates?

LO4 **Notes Receivable Calculations**

P 4. Rich Importing Company engaged in the following transactions involving promissory notes:

May 3 Sold engines to Kabel Company for $30,000 in exchange for a 90-day, 12 percent promissory note.

16 Sold engines to Vu Company for $16,000 in exchange for a 60-day, 13 percent note.

31 Sold engines to Vu Company for $15,000 in exchange for a 90-day, 11 percent note.

Required

1. For each of the notes, determine the (a) maturity date, (b) interest on the note, and (c) maturity value.
2. Assume that the fiscal year for Rich Importing Company ends on June 30. How much interest income should be recorded on that date?

User insight ▶

3. What are the effects of the transactions in May on cash flows for the year ended June 30?

Alternate Problems

LO2 **Bank Reconciliation**

P 5. The following information is available for Prime Corporation as of April 30, 2010:

a. Cash on the books as of April 30 amounted to $113,175.28. Cash on the bank statement for the same date was $140,717.08.

b. A deposit of $14,349.84, representing cash receipts of April 30, did not appear on the bank statement.

c. Outstanding checks totaled $7,302.64.

d. A check for $2,420.00 returned with the statement was recorded as $2,024.00. The check was for advertising.

e. The bank service charge for April amounted to $35.00.

f. The bank collected $36,300.00 for Prime Corporation on a note. The face value of the note was $36,000.00.

g. An NSF check for $1,140.00 from a customer, Tom Jones, was returned with the statement.
h. The bank mistakenly deducted a check for $700.00 that was drawn by Tiger Corporation.
i. The bank reported a credit of $560.00 for interest on the average balance.

Required

1. Prepare a bank reconciliation for Prime Corporation as of April 30, 2010.
2. Prepare the necessary entries in journal form from the reconciliation.
3. State the amount of cash that should appear on Prime Corporation's balance sheet as of April 30.
4. User insight ▶ Why is a bank reconciliation a necessary internal control?

LO1 LO3 **Methods of Estimating Uncollectible Accounts and Receivables Analysis**

P 6. On December 31 of last year, the balance sheet of Korab Company had Accounts Receivable of $149,000 and a credit balance in Allowance for Uncollectible Accounts of $10,150. During the current year, Korab Company's financial records included the following selected activities: (a) sales on account, $597,500; (b) sales returns and allowances, $36,500; (c) collections from customers, $575,000; and (d) accounts written off as worthless, $8,000. In the past, 1.6 percent of Korab Company's net sales have been uncollectible.

Required

1. Prepare T accounts for Accounts Receivable and Allowance for Uncollectible Accounts. Enter the beginning balances, and show the effects on these accounts of the items listed above, summarizing the year's activity. Determine the ending balance of each account.
2. Compute Uncollectible Accounts Expense and determine the ending balance of Allowance for Uncollectible Accounts under (a) the percentage of net sales method and (b) the accounts receivable aging method. Assume that an aging of the accounts receivable shows that $10,000 may be uncollectible.
3. Compute the receivable turnover and days' sales uncollected, using the data from the accounts receivable aging method in requirement **2**.
4. User insight ▶ How do you explain that the two methods used in requirement **2** result in different amounts for Uncollectible Accounts Expense? What rationale underlies each method?

LO3 **Accounts Receivable Aging Method**

P 7. Garcia Company uses the accounts receivable aging method to estimate uncollectible accounts. At the beginning of the year, the balance of the Accounts Receivable account was a debit of $90,430, and the balance of Allowance for Uncollectible Accounts was a credit of $8,100. During the year, the store had sales on account of $475,000, sales returns and allowances of $6,200, worthless accounts written off of $8,800, and collections from customers of $452,730. At the end of year (December 31, 2010), a junior accountant for Garcia Company was preparing an aging analysis of accounts receivable. At the top of page 6 of the report, the following totals appeared:

Customer Account	Total	Not Yet Due	1–30 Days Past Due	31–60 Days Past Due	61–90 Days Past Due	Over 90 Days Past Due
Balance Forward	$89,640	$49,030	$24,110	$9,210	$3,990	$3,300

To finish the analysis, the following accounts need to be classified:

Account	Amount	Due Date
B. Smith	$ 930	Jan. 14 (next year)
L. Wing	645	Dec. 24
A. Rak	1,850	Sept. 28
T. Cat	2,205	Aug. 16
M. Nut	350	Dec. 14
S. Prince	1,785	Jan. 23 (next year)
J. Wind	295	Nov. 5
	$8,060	

From past experience, the company has found that the following rates are realistic for estimating uncollectible accounts:

Time	Percentage Considered Uncollectible
Not yet due	2
1–30 days past due	5
31–60 days past due	15
61–90 days past due	25
Over 90 days past due	50

Required

1. Complete the aging analysis of accounts receivable.
2. Compute the end-of-year balances (before adjustments) of Accounts Receivable and Allowance for Uncollectible Accounts.
3. Prepare an analysis computing the estimated uncollectible accounts.
4. Calculate Garcia Company's estimated uncollectible accounts expense for the year (round the amount to the nearest whole dollar).

User insight ▶ 5. What role do estimates play in applying the aging analysis? What factors might affect these estimates?

LO4 Notes Receivable Calculations

P 8. Abraham Motor Company performed the following transactions involving promissory notes:

March	3	Sold machines to Anton Company for $60,000 in exchange for a 90-day, 10 percent promissory note.
	16	Sold machines to Yu Company for $32,000 in exchange for a 60-day, 11 percent note.
	31	Sold machines to Yu Company for $30,000 in exchange for a 90-day, 9 percent note.

Required

1. For each of the notes, determine the (a) maturity date, (b) interest on the note, and (c) maturity value.
2. Assume that the fiscal year for Abraham Motor Company ends on April 30. How much interest income should be recorded on that date?

User insight ▶ 3. What are the effects of the transactions in March on cash flows for the year ended April 30?

ENHANCING Your Knowledge, Skills, and Critical Thinking

LO1 **Role of Credit Sales**

C 1. Mitsubishi Corp., a broadly diversified Japanese corporation, instituted a credit plan called Three Diamonds for customers who buy its major electronic products, such as large-screen televisions and videotape recorders, from specified retail dealers.[18] Under the plan, approved customers who make purchases in July of one year do not have to make any payments until September of the next year. Nor do they have to pay interest during the intervening months. Mitsubishi pays the dealer the full amount less a small fee, sends the customer a Mitsubishi credit card, and collects from the customer at the specified time.

What was Mitsubishi's motivation for establishing such generous credit terms? What costs are involved? What are the accounting implications?

LO1 LO3 **Role of Estimates in Accounting for Receivables**

C 2. CompuCredit is a credit card issuer in Atlanta. It prides itself on making credit cards available to almost anybody in a matter of seconds over the Internet. The cost to the consumer is an interest rate of 28 percent, about double that of companies that provide cards only to customers with good credit. Despite its high interest rate, CompuCredit has been successful, reporting 1.9 million accounts and an income of approximately $100 million in a recent year. To calculate its income, the company estimates that 10 percent of its $1.3 billion in accounts receivable will not be paid; the industry average is 7 percent. Some analysts have been critical of CompuCredit for being too optimistic in its projections of losses.[19]

Why are estimates necessary in accounting for receivables? If CompuCredit were to use the same estimate of losses as other companies in its industry, what would its income have been for the year? How would one determine if CompuCredit's estimate of losses is reasonable?

LO1 **Receivables Financing**

C 3. Bernhardt Appliances, Inc., located in central Ohio, is a small manufacturer of washing machines and dryers. Bernhardt sells most of its appliances to large, established discount retail companies that market the appliances under their own names. Bernhardt sells the appliances on trade credit terms of n/60. If a customer wants a longer term, however, Bernhardt will accept a note with a term of up to nine months. At present, the company is having cash flow troubles and needs $10 million immediately. Its cash balance is $400,000, its accounts receivable balance is $4.6 million, and its notes receivable balance is $7.4 million.

How might Bernhardt Appliance's management use its accounts receivable and notes receivable to raise the cash it needs? What are the company's prospects for raising the needed cash?

LO1 **Comparison and Interpretation of Ratios**

C 4. Fosters Group Limited and **Heineken N.V.** are two well-known beer companies. Fosters is an Australian company, and Heineken is Dutch. Fosters is about half the size of Heineken.

Ratios can help in comparing and understanding companies that are different in size and that use different currencies. For example, the receivable turnovers for Fosters and Heineken in 2008 and 2007 were as follows:[20]

	2008	2007
Fosters	3.8 times	4.3 times
Heineken	6.7 times	6.3 times

What do the ratios tell you about the credit policies of the two companies? How long does it take each, on average, to collect a receivable? What do the ratios tell you about the companies' relative needs for capital to finance receivables? Which company is improving? Can you tell which company has a better credit policy? Explain your answers.

LO1 LO3 **Accounting for Accounts Receivable**

C 5. Makay Products Co. is a major consumer goods company that sells over 3,000 products in 135 countries. The company's annual report to the Securities and Exchange Commission presented the following data (in thousands) pertaining to net sales and accounts related to accounts receivable for 2008, 2009, and 2010.

	2010	2009	2008
Net sales	$9,820,000	$9,730,000	$9,888,000
Accounts receivable	1,046,000	1,048,000	1,008,000
Allowance for uncollectible accounts	37,200	42,400	49,000
Uncollectible accounts expense	30,000	33,400	31,600
Uncollectible accounts written off	38,600	40,200	35,400
Recoveries of accounts previously written off	3,400	200	2,000

1. Compute the ratio of uncollectible accounts expense to net sales and to accounts receivable, and the ratio of allowance for uncollectible accounts to accounts receivable for 2008, 2009, and 2010.
2. Compute the receivable turnover and days' sales uncollected for each year, assuming 2007 net accounts receivable were $930,000,000.
3. What is your interpretation of the ratios? Describe management's attitude toward the collectibility of accounts receivable over the three-year period.

LO1 LO2 LO3 **Cash and Receivables**

C 6. Refer to the **CVS** annual report in the Supplement to Chapter 1 to answer the following questions:

1. What amount of cash and cash equivalents did CVS have in 2008? Do you suppose most of that amount is cash in the bank or cash equivalents?
2. What customers represent the main source of CVS's accounts receivable, and how much is CVS's allowance for uncollectible accounts?
3. What do you think CVS's seasonal needs for cash are? Where in CVS's financial statements is the seasonality of sales discussed?

LO1 **Accounts Receivable Analysis**

C 7. Refer to the **CVS** annual report in the Supplement to Chapter 1 and to the following data (in millions) for **Walgreens**: net sales, $59,034.0, and $53,762.0 for 2008 and 2007, respectively; accounts receivable, net, $2,527.0 and $2,237.0 for 2008 and 2007, respectively.

1. Compute receivable turnover and days' sales uncollected for 2008 and 2007 for CVS and Walgreens. Accounts Receivable in 2006 were $2,377.4 million for CVS and $2,062.7 million for Walgreens.
2. Do you discern any differences in the two companies' credit policies? Explain your answer.

LO1 LO3 **Ethics and Uncollectible Accounts**

C 8. Caldwell Interiors, a successful retail furniture company, is located in an affluent suburb where a major insurance company has just announced a restructuring that will lay off 4,000 employees. Caldwell Interiors sells quality furniture, usually on credit. Accounts Receivable is one of its major assets. Although the company's annual uncollectible accounts losses are not out of line, they represent a sizable amount. The company depends on bank loans for its financing. Sales and net income have declined in the past year, and some customers are falling behind in paying their accounts.

Abby Caldwell, the owner of the business, knows that the bank's loan officer likes to see a steady performance. She has therefore instructed the company's controller to underestimate the uncollectible accounts this year to show a small growth in earnings. Caldwell believes this action is justified because earnings in future years will average out the losses, and since the company has a history of success, she believes the adjustments are meaningless accounting measures anyway.

Are Caldwell's actions ethical? Would any parties be harmed by her actions? How important is it to try to be accurate in estimating losses from uncollectible accounts?

LO1 LO3 **Comparison of J.C. Penney, Inc., and Dillard's, Inc.**

C 9. Access the annual reports of **J.C. Penney** and **Dillard's**. Find the accounts receivable on each company's balance sheet and the notes to the financial statements that are related to those accounts. Which company has the most accounts receivable as a percentage of total assets? What is the percentage of the allowance account to gross accounts receivable for each company? Which company experienced the highest loss rate on its receivables? Why do you think there is a difference? Do the companies finance their receivables? Be prepared to discuss your findings in class.

LO1 **Effects of Credit Policies**

C 10. **Tenet Healthcare Corp.**, a major publicly traded hospital chain in the United States, had a large amount of uncollectible accounts expense because so many patients were unable to pay their medical bills. Its uncollectible accounts expense amounted to about 11 percent of its revenues. After managers analyzed the problem, they found that 70 percent of the losses came from uninsured patients and 30 percent from those who had insurance. The company realized that many of the uninsured could not be expected to pay and that the large amount of the bills simply discouraged patients from seeking health care. The company decided to start charging these patients less, hoping it could eliminate 40 to 60 percent of its bad debts loss. The company's chief financial officer said, "A significant amount of the revenue will never be recorded in the first place due to this pricing, so that it will not have to be written off as bad debt."[21]

In informal groups in class, discuss and report on the following questions: What effect will the new pricing policy have on the company's reported earnings? Why would the company want to show lower uncollectible accounts expense? Do you think the new policy has ethical ramifications?

CHAPTER 8

Current Liabilities and Fair Value Accounting

Focus on Financial Statements

INCOME STATEMENT

Revenues

− Expenses

= Net Income

STATEMENT OF RETAINED EARNINGS

Opening Balance

+ Net Income

− Dividends

= Retained Earnings

BALANCE SHEET

Assets | Liabilities

Equity

A = L + E

STATEMENT OF CASH FLOWS

Operating activities

+ Investing activities

+ Financing activities

= Change in Cash

+ Starting Balance

= Ending Cash Balance

Valuation of unearned revenues and accrued liabilities on the balance sheet is linked to measurement of revenues and expenses on the income statement.

Although some current liabilities, such as accounts payable, are recorded when a company makes a purchase, others accrue during an accounting period and are not recorded until adjusting entries are made at the end of the period. In addition, the value of some accruals must be estimated. If accrued liabilities are not recognized and valued properly, both liabilities and expenses will be understated on the financial statements, making the company's performance look better than it actually is.

LEARNING OBJECTIVES

LO1 Identify the management issues related to current liabilities. (pp. 394–398)

LO2 Identify, compute, and record definitely determinable and estimated current liabilities. (pp. 398–407)

LO3 Distinguish *contingent liabilities* from *commitments*. (pp. 408)

LO4 Identify the valuation approaches to fair value accounting, and define *time value of money* and *interest* and apply them to present values. (pp. 409–413)

LO5 Apply present value to simple valuation situations. (pp. 414–416)

DECISION POINT ▸ A USER'S FOCUS MICROSOFT

Microsoft is the world's leading computer software company. It earns revenue by developing, manufacturing, licensing, and supporting a wide range of software products, including its new Windows 7, and Xbox360. As you can see in Microsoft's Financial Highlights, its total current liabilities in 2009 were over $27.0 billion, or about 68.3 percent of its stockholders' equity of $39.6 billion.[1]

Managing liabilities is obviously important to achieving profitability and liquidity. If a company has too few liabilities, it may not be earning up to its potential. If it has too many liabilities, it may be incurring excessive risks. A company that does not manage its debt carefully is vulnerable to failure.

MICROSOFT'S FINANCIAL HIGHLIGHTS (In millions)

Current Liabilities	2009	2008
Accounts payable	$ 3,324	$ 4,034
Short-term debt	2,000	—
Accrued compensation	3,156	2,934
Income taxes payable	725	3,248
Short-term unearned revenue	13,003	13,397
Securities lending payable and other	4,826	6,273
Total current liabilities	$27,034	$29,886
Long-term debt	3,746	—
Long-term debt unearned revenue and other long-term liabilities	7,550	6,621
Total liabilities	$38,330	$36,507

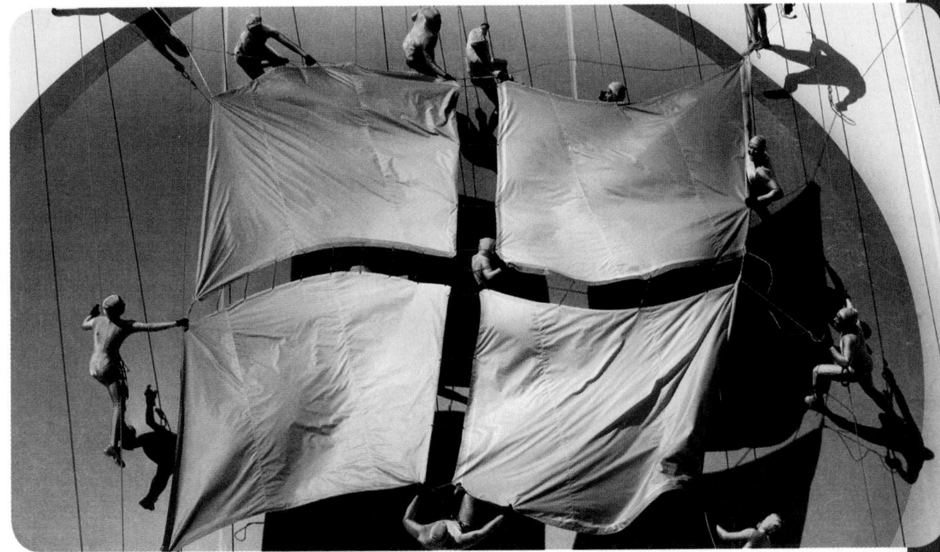

- ▸ How does Microsoft's decision to incur heavy debt relate to the goals of the business?
- ▸ Is the level of accounts payable in the operating cycle satisfactory?
- ▸ Has the company properly identified and accounted for all its current liabilities?

Management Issues Related to Current Liabilities

Current liabilities require not only careful management of liquidity and cash flows, but close monitoring of accounts payable as well. In reporting on current liabilities, managers must understand how they should be recognized, valued, classified, and disclosed.

LO1 Identify the management issues related to current liabilities.

Managing Liquidity and Cash Flows

The primary reason a company incurs current liabilities is to meet its needs for cash during the operating cycle. As explained in Chapter 5, the operating cycle is the length of time it takes to purchase inventory, sell the inventory, and collect the resulting receivable. Most current liabilities arise in support of this cycle, as when accounts payable arise from purchases of inventory, accrued expenses arise from operating costs, and unearned revenues arise from customers' advance payments. Companies incur short-term debt to raise cash during periods of inventory build-up or while waiting for collection of receivables. They use the cash to pay the portion of long-term debt that is currently due and to pay liabilities arising from operations.

Failure to manage the cash flows related to current liabilities can have serious consequences for a business. For instance, if suppliers are not paid on time, they may withhold shipments that are vital to a company's operations. Continued failure to pay current liabilities can lead to bankruptcy. To evaluate a company's ability to pay its current liabilities, analysts often use two measures of liquidity—working capital and the current ratio, both of which we defined in an earlier chapter. Current liabilities are a key component of both these measures. They typically equal from 25 to 50 percent of total assets.

As shown below (in millions), **Microsoft**'s short-term liquidity as measured by working capital and the current ratio was positive in 2008 and declined somewhat in 2009.

	Current Assets	–	Current Liabilities	=	Working Capital	Current Ratio*
2008	$49,280	–	$27,034	=	$22,246	1.82
2009	$43,242	–	$29,886	=	$13,356	1.45

The decline in Microsoft's working capital and current ratio stemmed primarily from Microsoft's use of cash to purchase its own stock. Overall, Microsoft is in a strong current situation and exercises very good management of its cash flow. Note the large amounts of both short-term and long-term unearned revenue. These are fees for licenses and services that customers pay in advance, thus helping cash flow. Microsoft will, of course, have to perform the services to earn the revenues.

Evaluating Accounts Payable

Another consideration in managing liquidity and cash flows is the time suppliers give a company to pay for purchases. Measures commonly used to assess a company's ability to pay within a certain time frame are **payables turnover** and **days' payables**. Payables turnover is the number of times, on average, that a company pays its accounts payable in an accounting period. Days' payable shows how long, on average, a company takes to pay its accounts payables.

*Current assets divided by current liabilities

FOCUS ON BUSINESS PRACTICE

Debt Problems Can Plague Even Well-Known Companies

In a Wall Street horror story that illustrates the importance of managing current liabilities, **Xerox Corporation**, one of the most storied names in American business, found itself combating rumors that it was facing bankruptcy. Following a statement by Xerox's CEO that the company's financial model was "unsustainable," management was forced to defend the company's liquidity by saying it had adequate funds to continue operations. But in a report filed with the SEC, management acknowledged that it had tapped into its $7 billion line of bank credit for more than $3 billion to pay off short-term debt that was coming due. Unable to secure more money from any other source to pay these debts, Xerox had no choice but to turn to the line of credit from its bank. Had it run out, the company might well have gone bankrupt.[2] Fortunately, Xerox was able to restructure its line of credit to stay in business.

To measure payables turnover for **Microsoft**, we must first calculate purchases by adjusting cost of goods sold for the change in inventory. An increase in inventory means purchases were more than cost of goods sold; a decrease means purchases were less than cost of goods sold. Microsoft's cost of goods sold in 2009 was $12,155 million, and its inventory decreased by $268 million. Much of its inventory consists of its new consumer product, Xbox360. Its payables turnover is computed as follows (in millions):

K/R

$$\text{Payables Turnover} = \frac{\text{Cost of Goods Sold} \pm \text{Change in Merchandise Inventory}}{\text{Average Accounts Payable}}$$

$$= \frac{\$12{,}155 - \$268}{(\$3{,}324 + \$4{,}034) \div 2}$$

$$= \frac{\$11{,}887}{\$3{,}679} = 3.2 \text{ times}$$

To find the day's payable, the number of days in a year is divided by the payable turnover:

K/R

$$\text{Days' Payable} = \frac{365 \text{ Days}}{\text{Payables Turnover}} = \frac{365 \text{ days}}{3.2 \text{ times}} = 114.1 \text{ days}$$

The payables turnover of 3.2 times and days' payable of 114.1 days indicate that the credit terms Microsoft receives from its suppliers are excellent. These results also stem partly from the fact that some product costs are small relative to sales price. After development, some software is not costly to produce, because products like Windows 7 can be licensed to businesses and sold and delivered online. In other industries, credit terms and product costs are not nearly as favorable. As you can see in Figures 8-1 and 8-2, companies in other industries have higher payables turnover and lower days' payable than Microsoft. These key ratios have been a major factor in Microsoft's ability to maintain adequate liquidity. To get a full picture of a company's operating cycle and liquidity, analysts also consider

FIGURE 8-1
Payables Turnover for Selected Industries

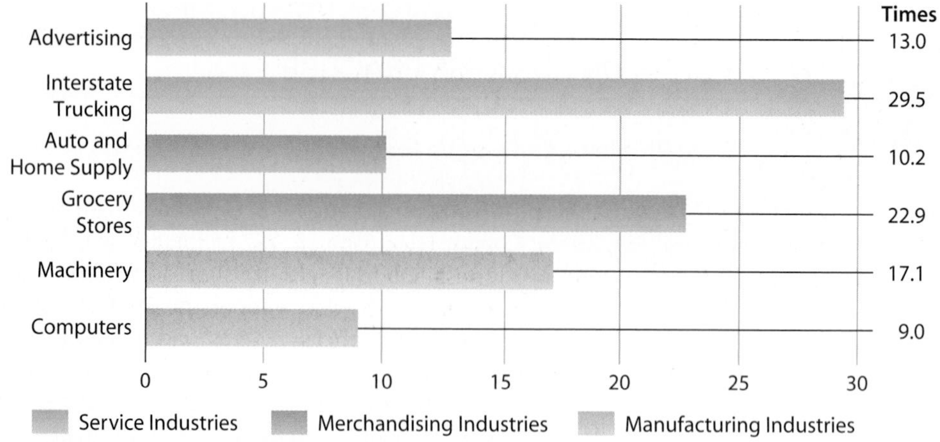

Source: Data from Dun & Bradstreet, *Industry Norms and Key Business Ratios*, 2007–2008.

payables turnover and days' payable in relation to the other components of the operating cycle: inventory and receivable turnovers and their related number of days' ratios.

Reporting Liabilities

In deciding whether to buy stock in a company or lend money to it, investors and creditors must evaluate not only the company's current liabilities, but its future obligations as well. In doing so, they have to rely on the integrity of the company's financial statements.

Ethical reporting of liabilities requires that they be properly recognized, valued, classified, and disclosed. In one notable case involving unethical reporting of liabilities, the CEO and other employees of **Nortel Networks Corporation**, a Canadian manufacturer of telecommunications equipment, understated accrued liabilities (and corresponding expenses) in order to report a profit and obtain salary bonuses. After all accrued liabilities had been identified, it was evident that the company was in fact losing money. The board of directors of the corporation fired all who had been involved.[3]

FIGURE 8-2
Days' Payable for Selected Industries

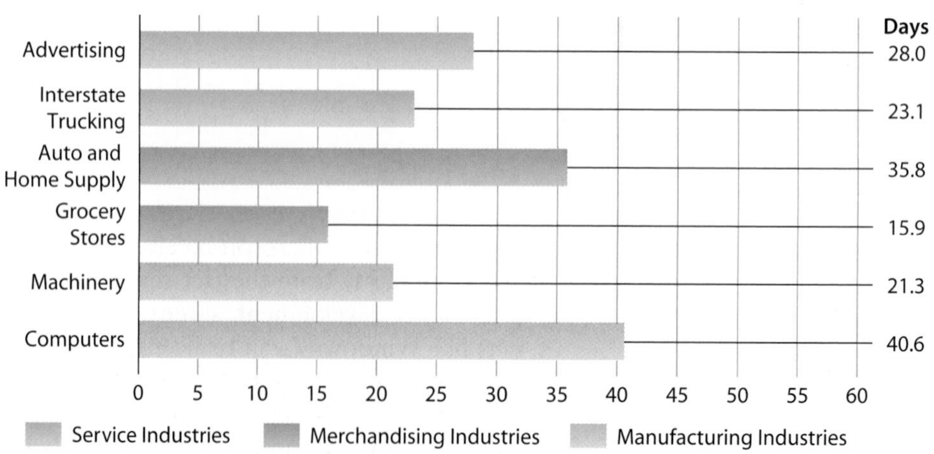

Source: Data from Dun & Bradstreet, *Industry Norms and Key Business Ratios*, 2007–2008.

Recognition Timing is important in the recognition of liabilities. Failure to record a liability in an accounting period very often goes along with failure to record an expense. The two errors lead to an understatement of expense and an overstatement of income.

Generally accepted accounting principles require that a liability be recorded when an obligation occurs. This rule is harder to apply than it might appear. When a transaction obligates a company to make future payments, a liability arises and is recognized, as when goods are bought on credit. However, some current liabilities are not the result of direct transactions. One of the key reasons for making adjusting entries at the end of an accounting period is to recognize unrecorded liabilities that accrue during the period. Accrued liabilities include salaries payable and interest payable. Other liabilities that can only be estimated, such as taxes payable, must also be recognized through adjusting entries.

Agreements for future transactions do not have to be recognized. For instance, **Microsoft** might agree to pay an executive $250,000 a year for a period of three years, or it might agree to buy an unspecified amount of advertising at a certain price over the next five years. Such contracts, though they are definite commitments, are not considered liabilities because they are for future—not past—transactions. Because there is no current obligation, no liability is recognized, but they would be mentioned in the notes to the financial statements and SEC filings if material.

Valuation On the balance sheet, a liability is generally valued at the amount of money needed to pay the debt or at the fair market value of the goods or services to be delivered.

Study Note

Disclosure of the fair value and the bases for estimating the fair value of short-term notes payable, loans payable, and other short-term debt are required unless it is not practical to estimate the value. Guidance for determining fair value is covered later in this chapter.

The amount of most liabilities is definitely known. For example, **Amazon.com** sells a large number of gift certificates that are redeemable in the future. The amount of the liability (unearned revenue) is known, but the exact timing is not known.

Some companies, however, must estimate future liabilities. For example, an automobile dealer that sells a car with a one-year warranty must provide parts and service during the year. The obligation is definite because the sale has occurred, but the amount of the obligation can only be estimated. Such estimates are usually based on past experience and anticipated changes in the business environment.

Classification As you may recall from our discussion of classified balance sheets in an earlier chapter, **current liabilities** are debts and obligations that a company expects to satisfy within one year or within its normal operating cycle, whichever is longer. These liabilities are normally paid out of current assets or with cash generated by operations. **Long-term liabilities** are liabilities due beyond one year or beyond the normal operating cycle. For example, Microsoft incurs long-term liabilities to finance its software development among other objectives. The distinction between current and long-term liabilities is important because it affects the evaluation of a company's liquidity. Microsoft carefully distinguishes between short-term unearned revenues, which represent services to be performed in the next year, and long-term unearned revenues, which represent services that will be performed in future years.

Disclosure A company may have to include additional explanation of some liability accounts in the notes to its financial statements. For example, if a company's Notes Payable account is large, it should disclose the balances, maturity dates, interest rates, and other features of the debts in an explanatory note. Any special credit arrangements should also be disclosed. For instance, in a note to its

2008 financial statements, **Hershey Foods Corporation**, the famous candy company, discloses the nature of its credit arrangements:

> **Short-Term Debt and Financing Arrangements**
>
> As a source of short-term financing, we utilize commercial paper, or bank loans with an original maturity of three months or less . . . in addition, we maintain line of credit with domestic and international commercial banks.[4]

Unused lines of credit allow a company to borrow on short notice up to the credit limit, with little or no negotiation. Thus, the type of disclosure in Hershey's note is helpful in assessing whether a company has additional borrowing power.

STOP & APPLY >

Jackie's Cookie Company has current assets of $30,000 and current liabilities of $20,000, of which accounts payable are $15,000. Jackie's cost of goods sold is $125,000, its merchandise inventory increased by $5,000, and accounts payable were $11,000 the prior year. Calculate Jackie's current ratio, payables turnover, and days' payable.

SOLUTION

Current Ratio = Current Assets ÷ Current Liabilities
= $30,000 ÷ $20,000
= 1.5 times

$$\text{Payables Turnover} = \frac{\text{Cost of Goods Sold} \pm \text{Change in Inventory}}{\text{Average Accounts Payable}}$$

$$= \frac{\$125{,}000 + \$5{,}000}{(\$15{,}000 + \$11{,}000) \div 2} = \frac{\$130{,}000}{\$13{,}000}$$

= 10 times

Days' Payable = 365 Days ÷ Payables Turnover

$$= \frac{365 \text{ days}}{10 \text{ times}} = 36.5 \text{ days}$$

Common Types of Current Liabilities

LO2 Identify, compute, and record definitely determinable and estimated current liabilities.

As noted earlier, a company incurs current liabilities to meet its needs for cash during the operating cycle. These liabilities fall into two major groups: definitely determinable liabilities and estimated liabilities.

Definitely Determinable Liabilities

Current liabilities that are set by contract or statute and that can be measured exactly are called **definitely determinable liabilities**. The problems in accounting for these liabilities are to determine their existence and amount and to see that they are recorded properly. The most common definitely determinable liabilities are described at the top of the next page.

Study Note

On the balance sheet, the order of presentation for current liabilities is not as strict as for current assets. Generally, accounts payable or notes payable appear first, and the rest of current liabilities follow.

Accounts Payable Accounts payable (sometimes called *trade accounts payable*) are short-term obligations to suppliers for goods and services. The amount in the Accounts Payable account is generally supported by an accounts payable subsidiary ledger, which contains an individual account for each person or company to which money is owed. As shown in the Financial Highlights at the beginning of the chapter, accounts payable make up more than 12 percent of **Microsoft**'s current liabilities in 2009.

Bank Loans and Commercial Paper Management often establishes a **line of credit** with a bank. This arrangement allows the company to borrow funds when they are needed to finance current operations. In a note to its financial statements, **Goodyear Tire & Rubber Company** describes its lines of credit as follows: "In aggregate, we had credit arrangements of $7,127 million available at December 31, 2008, of which $1,677 million were unused."[5]

Although a company signs a promissory note for the full amount of a line of credit, it has great flexibility in using the available funds. It can increase its borrowing up to the limit when it needs cash and reduce the amount borrowed when it generates enough cash of its own. Both the amount borrowed and the interest rate charged by the bank may change daily. The bank may require the company to meet certain financial goals (such as maintaining specific profit margins, current ratios, or debt to equity ratios) to retain its line of credit.

Companies with excellent credit ratings can borrow short-term funds by issuing **commercial paper**. *Commercial paper* refers to unsecured loans (i.e., loans not backed up by any specific assets) that are sold to the public, usually through professionally managed investment firms. Highly rated companies rely heavily on commercial paper to raise short-term funds, but they can quickly lose access to this means of borrowing if their credit rating drops. Because of disappointing operating results in recent years, well-known companies like **DaimlerChrysler**, **Lucent Technologies**, and **Motorola** have lost some or all of their ability to issue commercial paper.

Study Note

Only the used portion of a line of credit is recognized as a liability in the financial statements.

The portion of a line of credit currently borrowed and the amount of commercial paper issued are usually combined with notes payable in the current liabilities section of the balance sheet. Details are disclosed in a note to the financial statements.

Notes Payable Short-term notes payable are obligations represented by promissory notes. A company may sign promissory notes to obtain bank loans, pay suppliers for goods and services, or secure credit from other sources.

Interest is usually stated separately on the face of the note, as shown in Figure 8-3. The entries in journal form to record the note in Figure 8-3 are as follows:

ISSUANCE

A	=	L	+	SE
+10,000.00		+10,000.00		

Aug. 31	Cash	10,000.00	
	Notes Payable		10,000.00
	Issued 60-day, 12% promissory note		

PAYMENT

A	=	L	+	SE
−10,197.26		−10,000.00		−197.26

Oct. 30	Notes Payable	10,000.00	
	Interest Expense	197.26	
	Cash		10,197.26
	Payment of promissory note with interest		
	$\$10,000 \times \frac{12}{100} \times \frac{60}{365} = \$197.26^*$		

*Rounded.

FIGURE 8-3
Promissory Note

Chicago, Illinois August 31, 2010

Sixty days after date I promise to pay First Federal Bank the sum of $10,000 with interest at the rate of 12% per annum.

Sandra Caron
Caron Corporation

Accrued Liabilities As we noted earlier, a key reason for making adjusting entries at the end of an accounting period is to recognize liabilities that are not already in the accounting records. This practice applies to any type of liability. As you will see, accrued liabilities (also called *accrued expenses*) can include estimated liabilities. For example, as can be seen in **Microsoft**'s Financial Highlights, the company had accrued compensation of $3,156 million in 2009.

Here, we focus on interest payable, a definitely determinable liability. Interest accrues daily on interest-bearing notes. In accordance with the matching rule, an adjusting entry is made at the end of each accounting period to record the interest obligation up to that point. For example, if the accounting period of the maker of the note in Figure 8-3 ends on September 30, or 30 days after the issuance of the 60-day note, the adjusting entry would be as follows:

A	=	L	+	SE
		+98.63		−98.63

Sept. 30	Interest Expense	98.63	
	Interest Payable		98.63
	To record 30 days' interest expense on promissory note		
	$\$10{,}000 \times \frac{12}{100} \times \frac{60}{365} = \$98.63^*$		

*Rounded.

Dividends Payable As you know, cash dividends are a distribution of earnings to a corporation's stockholders, and a corporation's board of directors has the sole authority to declare them. The corporation has no liability for dividends until the date of declaration. The time between that date and the date of payment of dividends is usually short. During this brief interval, the dividends declared are considered current liabilities of the corporation.

Sales and Excise Taxes Payable Most states and many cities levy a sales tax on retail transactions, and the federal government imposes an excise tax on some products, such as gasoline. A merchant that sells goods subject to these taxes must collect the taxes and forward them periodically to the appropriate government agency. Until the merchant remits the amount it has collected to the government, that amount represents a current liability.

For example, suppose a merchant makes a $200 sale that is subject to a 5 percent sales tax and a 10 percent excise tax. If the sale takes place on June 1, the entry in journal form to record it is as follows:

A	=	L	+	SE
+230		+10		+200
		+20		

June 1	Cash	230	
	Sales		200
	Sales Tax Payable		10
	Excise Tax Payable		20
	Sale of merchandise and collection of sales and excise tax		

FOCUS ON BUSINESS PRACTICE

Small Businesses Offer Benefits, Too

A survey of small business in the Midwest focused on the employee benefits that these companies offer. The graph at the right presents the results. As you can see, 40 percent of respondents provided paid vacation, 38 percent provided health/medical benefits, and 8 percent even offered their employees tuition reimbursement.[6]

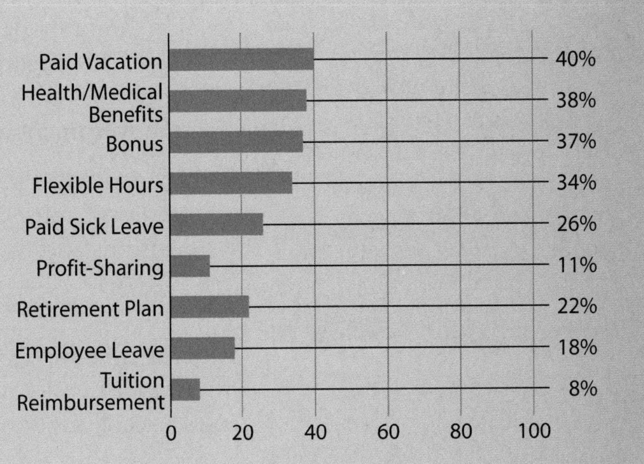

The sale is properly recorded at $200, and the taxes collected are recorded as liabilities to be remitted to the appropriate government agencies.

Companies that have a physical presence in many cities and states require a complex accounting system for sales taxes because the rates vary from state to state and city to city. For Internet companies, the sales tax situation is simpler. For example, **Amazon.com** is an Internet company without a physical presence in most states and thus does not always have to collect sales tax from its customers. This situation may change in the future, but so far Congress has exempted most Internet sales from sales tax.

Current Portion of Long-Term Debt If a portion of long-term debt is due within the next year and is to be paid from current assets, that portion is classified as a current liability. It is common for companies to have portions of long-term debt, such as notes or mortgages, due in the next year. No entry is necessary when this is the case. The total debt is simply reclassified or divided into two categories—short-term and long-term—when the company prepares its balance sheet and other financial statements.

Payroll Liabilities For most organizations, the cost of labor and payroll taxes is a major expense. In the banking and airlines industries, payroll costs represent more than half of all operating costs. Payroll accounting is important because complex laws and significant liabilities are involved. The employer is liable to employees for wages and salaries and to various agencies for amounts withheld from wages and salaries and for related taxes. **Wages** are compensation of employees at an hourly rate; **salaries** are compensation of employees at a monthly or yearly rate.

Because payroll accounting applies only to an organization's employees, it is important to distinguish between employees and independent contractors. Employees are paid a wage or salary by the organization and are under its direct supervision and control. Independent contractors are not employees of the organization and so are not accounted for under the payroll system. They offer services to the organization for a fee, but they are not under its direct control or supervision. Certified public accountants, advertising agencies, and lawyers, for example, often act as independent contractors.

Study Note

In many organizations, a large portion of the cost of labor is not reflected in employees' regular paychecks. Vacation pay, sick pay, personal days, health insurance, life insurance, and pensions are some of the additional cost that may be negotiated between employers and employees.

Figure 8-4 shows how payroll liabilities relate to employee earnings and employer taxes and other costs. When accounting for payroll liabilities, it is important to keep the following in mind:

- The amount payable to employees is less than the amount of their earnings. This occurs because employers are required by law or are requested by employees to withhold certain amounts from wages and send them directly to government agencies or other organizations.
- An employer's total liabilities exceed employees' earnings because the employer must pay additional taxes and make other contributions (e.g., for pensions and medical care) that increase the cost and liabilities.

The most common withholdings, taxes, and other payroll costs are described below.

Study Note

The employee pays all federal, state, and local taxes on income. The employer and employee share FICA and Medicare taxes. The employer bears FUTA and state unemployment taxes.

Federal Income Taxes Employers are required to withhold federal income taxes from employees' paychecks and pay them to the United States Treasury. These taxes are collected each time an employee is paid.

State and Local Income Taxes Most states and some local governments levy income taxes. In most cases, the procedures for withholding are similar to those for federal income taxes.

Social Security (FICA) Tax The social security program (the Federal Insurance Contribution Act) provides retirement and disability benefits and survivor's benefits. About 90 percent of the people working in the United States fall under the provisions of this program. The 2010 social security tax rate of 6.2 percent was paid by *both* employee and employer on the first $106,800 earned by an employee during the calendar year. Both the rate and the base to which it applies are subject to change in future years.

Medicare Tax A major extension of the social security program is Medicare, which provides hospitalization and medical insurance for persons over age 65. In 2010, the Medicare tax rate was 1.45 percent of gross income, with no limit, paid by *both* employee and employer.

Medical Insurance Many organizations provide medical benefits to employees. Often, the employee contributes a portion of the cost through withholdings from income and the employer pays the rest—usually a greater amount—to the insurance company.

Pension Contributions Many organizations also provide pension benefits to employees. A portion of the pension contribution is withheld from the employee's income, and the organization pays the rest of the amount into the pension fund.

Federal Unemployment Insurance (FUTA) Tax This tax pays for programs for unemployed workers. It is paid *only* by employers and recently was 6.2 percent of the first $7,000 earned by each employee (this amount may vary from state to state). The employer is allowed a credit for unemployment taxes it pays to the state. The maximum credit is 5.4 percent of the first $7,000 earned by each employee. Most states set their rate at this maximum. Thus, the FUTA tax most often paid is 0.8 percent (6.2 percent − 5.4 percent) of the taxable wages.

State Unemployment Insurance Tax State unemployment programs provide compensation to eligible unemployed workers. The compensation is paid out of the fund provided by the 5.4 percent of the first $7,000 (or the amount the state sets) earned by each employee. In some states, employers with favorable employment records may be entitled to pay less than 5.4 percent.

To illustrate the recording of a payroll, suppose that on February 15, a company's wages for employees are $65,000 and withholdings for employees are as follows: $10,800 for federal income taxes, $2,400 for state income taxes,

FIGURE 8-4
Illustration of Payroll Costs

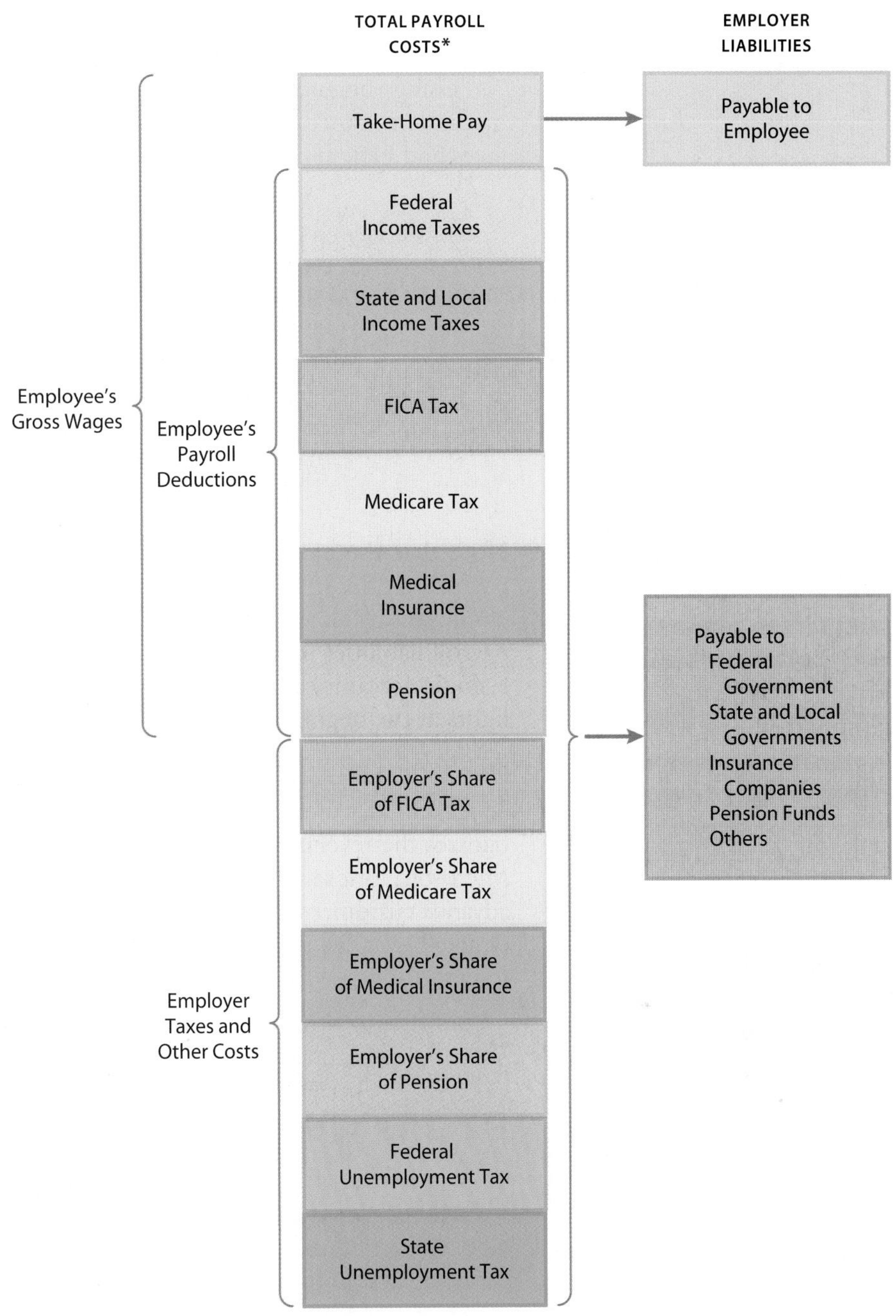

Boxes are not proportional to amounts.

$4,030 for social security tax, $942 for Medicare tax, $1,800 for medical insurance, and $2,600 for pension contributions. The entry in journal form to record this payroll is:

A	=	L	+	SE
		+10,800		−65,000
		+2,400		
		+4,030		
		+942		
		+1,800		
		+2,600		
		+42,428		

Feb. 15	Wages Expense	65,000	
	Employees' Federal Income Taxes Payable		10,800
	Employees' State Income Taxes Payable		2,400
	Social Security Tax Payable		4,030
	Medicare Tax Payable		942
	Medical Insurance Premiums Payable		1,800
	Pension Contributions Payable		2,600
	Wages Payable		42,428
	To record the payroll		

Note that although the employees earned $65,000, their take-home pay was only $42,428.

Using the same data but assuming that the employer pays 80 percent of the medical insurance premiums and half of the pension contributions, the employer's taxes and benefit costs would be recorded as follows:

A	=	L	+	SE
		+4,030		−18,802
		+942		
		+7,200		
		+2,600		
		+520		
		+3,510		

Feb. 15	Payroll Taxes and Benefits Expense	18,802	
	Social Security Tax Payable		4,030
	Medicare Tax Payable		942
	Medical Insurance Premiums Payable		7,200
	Pension Contributions Payable		2,600
	Federal Unemployment Tax Payable		520
	State Unemployment Tax Payable		3,510
	To record payroll taxes and other costs		

Note that the payroll taxes and benefits expense increase the total cost of the payroll to $83,802 ($18,802 + $65,000), which exceeds the amount earned by employees by almost 29 percent. This is a typical situation. **Microsoft** has all these payroll liabilities in its internal records, but for simplicity combines them all into a single account called Accrued Compensation, as shown in the Financial Highlights at the beginning of this chapter.

Unearned Revenues **Unearned revenues** are advance payments for goods or services that a company must provide in a future accounting period. It then recognizes the revenue over the period in which it provides the products or services. Microsoft, for example, states in its annual report that unearned revenue represents advance customer billings, which it accounts for as subscriptions with revenue recognized over the period covered by the billing. Assume that Microsoft bills a customer in advance for a one-year subscription. The following entry would be made:

A	=	L	+	SE
+3,600		+3,600		

Accounts Receivable	3,600	
Unearned Revenue		3,600
Subscriptions billed in advance		

Microsoft will soon receive cash in the amount of $3,600, but it also has a liability of $3,600 that will slowly be reduced over the year as it provides the service. After the first month, the company records the recognition of revenue as follows:

A	=	L	+	SE
		−300		+300

Unearned Revenue	300	
Revenue		300
Recognition of revenue for services provided		

Study Note

Estimated liabilities are recorded and presented in the financial statements in the same way as definitely determinable liabilities. The only difference is that the computation of estimated liabilities involves some uncertainty.

Many businesses, including repair companies, construction companies, and special-order firms, ask for a deposit before they will begin work. Until they deliver the goods or services, these deposits are current liabilities.

Estimated Liabilities

Estimated liabilities are definite debts or obligations whose exact dollar amount cannot be known until a later date. Because there is no doubt that a legal obligation exists, the primary accounting problem is to estimate and record the amount of the liability. The following are examples of estimated liabilities.

FOCUS ON BUSINESS PRACTICE

Those Little Coupons Can Add Up

Many companies promote their products by issuing coupons that offer "cents off" or other enticements. Because four out of five shoppers use coupons, companies are forced by competition to distribute them. The total value of unredeemed coupons, each of which represents a potential liability for the issuing company, is staggering. In 2006, marketers distributed almost 300 billion coupons, of which about 700 million were internet coupons. In total the coupons were worth about $330 billion, but consumers redeemed only 2.6 billion coupons worth just over $2.6 billion. Thus, a big advertiser can issue millions of coupons and expect less than one percent to be redeemed.[7]

Income Taxes Payable The federal government, most state governments, and some cities and towns levy a tax on a corporation's income. The amount of the liability depends on the results of a corporation's operations, which are often not known until after the end of the corporation's fiscal year. However, because income taxes are an expense in the year in which income is earned, an adjusting entry is necessary to record the estimated tax liability. **Microsoft**, for example, has income taxes payable in 2009 of $725 million, as shown in the Financial Highlights at the beginning of this chapter.

Sole proprietorships and partnerships do *not* pay income taxes. However, their owners must report their share of the firm's income on their individual tax returns.

Property Taxes Payable Property taxes are a main source of revenue for local governments. They are levied annually on real property, such as land and buildings, and on personal property, such as inventory and equipment. Because the fiscal years of local governments rarely correspond to a company's fiscal year, it is necessary to estimate the amount of property taxes that applies to each month of the year.

Promotional Costs You are no doubt familiar with the coupons and rebates that are part of many companies' marketing programs and with the frequent flyer programs that airlines have been offering for more than 20 years. Companies usually record the costs of these programs as a reduction in sales (a contra-sales account) rather than as an expense with a corresponding current liability. As

FOCUS ON BUSINESS PRACTICE

What Is the Cost of Frequent Flyer Miles?

In the early 1980s, **American Airlines** developed a frequent flyer program that awards free trips and other bonuses to customers based on the number of miles they fly on the airline. Since then, many other airlines have instituted similar programs, and it is estimated that 180 million people now participate in them. Today, U.S. airlines have more than 10 trillion "free miles" outstanding, and 8 percent of passengers travel on "free" tickets. Estimated liabilities for these tickets have become an important consideration in evaluating an airline's financial position. Complicating the estimate is that almost half the miles have been earned through purchases from hotels, car rental and telephone companies, Internet service providers like **AOL**, and bank credit cards.[8]

Hershey Foods Corporation acknowledges in its annual report, promotional costs are hard to estimate:

> Accrued liabilities requiring the most difficult or subjective judgments include liabilities associated with marketing promotion programs.... We recognize the costs of marketing programs as a reduction to net sales along with a corresponding accrued liability based on estimates at the time of revenue recognition.... We determine the amount of the accrued liability by analysis of programs offered, historical trends, expectations regarding customer and consumer participation, sales and payment trends and experience... with previously offered programs.[9]

Hershey accrues over $760 million in promotional costs each year and reports that its estimates are usually accurate within about 4 percent, or $30.4 million.

Study Note

Recording a product warranty expense in the period of the sale is an application of the matching rule.

Product Warranty Liability When a firm sells a product or service with a warranty, it has a liability for the length of the warranty. The warranty is a feature of the product and is included in the selling price; its cost should therefore be debited to an expense account in the period of the sale. Based on past experience, it should be possible to estimate the amount the warranty will cost in the future. Some products will require little warranty service; others may require much. Thus, there will be an average cost per product.

For example, suppose a muffler company like **Midas** guarantees that it will replace free of charge any muffler it sells that fails during the time the buyer owns the car. The company charges a small service fee for replacing the muffler. In the past, 6 percent of the mufflers sold have been returned for replacement under the warranty. The average cost of a muffler is $50. If the company sold 700 mufflers during July, the accrued liability would be recorded as an adjustment at the end of July, as shown in the following entry in journal form:

A	=	L	+	SE
		+2,100		−2,100

July 31	Product Warranty Expense	2,100	
	Estimated Product Warranty Liability		2,100
	To record estimated product warranty expense:		
	Number of units sold	700	
	Rate of replacement under warranty	× 0.06	
	Estimated units to be replaced	42	
	Estimated cost per unit	× $50	
	Estimated liability for product warranty	$2,100	

When a muffler is returned for replacement under the warranty, the cost of the muffler is charged against the Estimated Product Warranty Liability account. For example, suppose that on December 5, a customer returns a defective muffler, which cost $60, and pays a $30 service fee to have it replaced. The entry in journal form is:

A	=	L	+	SE
+30		−60		+30
−60				

Dec. 5	Cash	30	
	Estimated Product Warranty Liability	60	
	Service Revenue		30
	Merchandise Inventory		60
	Replacement of muffler under warranty		

Vacation Pay Liability In most companies, employees accrue paid vacation as they work during the year. For example, an employee may earn two weeks of paid vacation for each 50 weeks of work. Thus, the person is paid 52 weeks' salary for 50 weeks' work. The cost of the two weeks' vacation should be allocated as an expense over the whole year so that month-to-month costs will not be distorted. The vacation pay represents 4 percent (two weeks' vacation divided by 50 weeks) of a worker's pay. Every week worked earns the employee a small fraction (2 percent) of vacation pay, which is 4 percent of total annual salary.

Vacation pay liability can represent a substantial amount of money. As an example, in the 10-K form that **US Airways** submitted to the SEC for 2008, the airline reported accrued salaries, wages, and vacation liabilities of $158 million.

Suppose that a company with a vacation policy of two weeks of paid vacation for each 50 weeks of work has a payroll of $42,000 and that it paid $2,000 of that amount to employees on vacation for the week ended April 20. Because of turnover and rules regarding term of employment, the company assumes that only 75 percent of employees will ultimately collect vacation pay. The computation of vacation pay expense based on the payroll of employees not on vacation ($42,000 − $2,000) is as follows: $40,000 × 4 percent × 75 percent = $1,200. The company would make the following entry in journal form to record vacation pay expense for the week ended April 20:

A	=	L	+	SE
		+1,200		−1,200

Apr. 20	Vacation Pay Expense	1,200	
	Estimated Liability for Vacation Pay		1,200
	Estimated vacation pay expense		

At the time employees receive their vacation pay, an entry is made debiting Estimated Liability for Vacation Pay and crediting Cash or Wages Payable. The following entry records the $2,000 paid to employees on vacation during the month of August:

A*	=	L	+	SE
−2,000		−2,000		

*Assumes cash paid.

Aug. 31	Estimated Liability for Vacation Pay	2,000	
	Cash (or Wages Payable)		2,000
	Wages of employees on vacation		

The treatment of vacation pay presented here can also be applied to other payroll costs, such as bonus plans and contributions to pension plans.

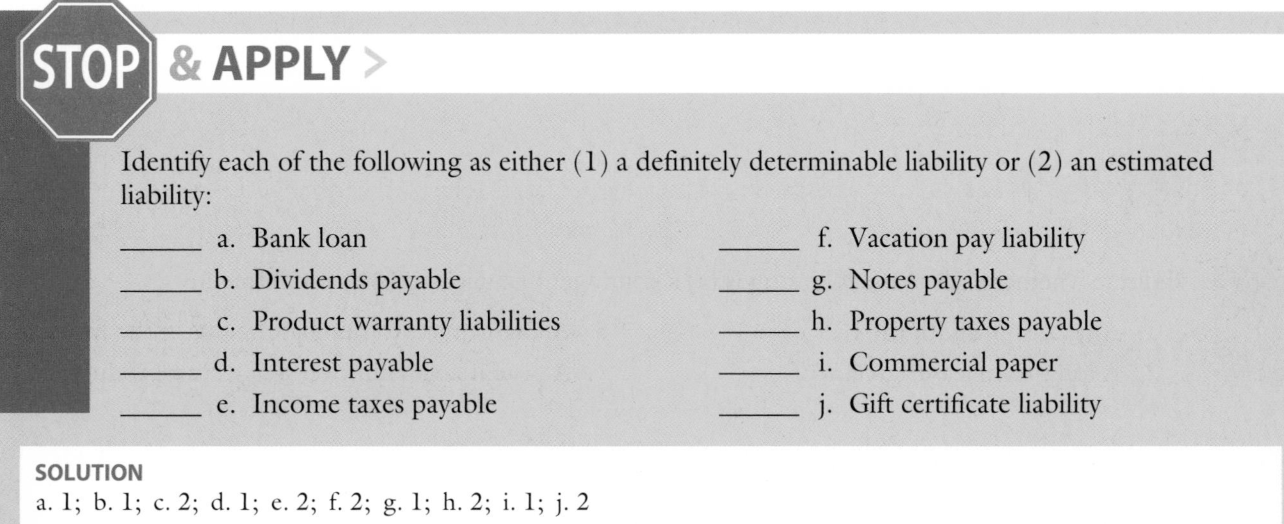

STOP & APPLY >

Identify each of the following as either (1) a definitely determinable liability or (2) an estimated liability:

______	a. Bank loan	______	f. Vacation pay liability
______	b. Dividends payable	______	g. Notes payable
______	c. Product warranty liabilities	______	h. Property taxes payable
______	d. Interest payable	______	i. Commercial paper
______	e. Income taxes payable	______	j. Gift certificate liability

SOLUTION

a. 1; b. 1; c. 2; d. 1; e. 2; f. 2; g. 1; h. 2; i. 1; j. 2

Contingent Liabilities and Commitments

LO3 Distinguish *contingent liabilities* from *commitments.*

The FASB requires companies to disclose in a note to their financial statements any contingent liabilities and commitments they may have. A **contingent liability** is not an *existing* obligation. Rather, it is a *potential* liability because it depends on a future event arising out of a past transaction. Contingent liabilities often involve lawsuits, income tax disputes, discounted notes receivable, guarantees of debt, and failure to follow government regulations. For instance, a construction company that built a bridge may have been sued by the state for using poor materials. The past transaction is the building of the bridge under contract. The future event is the outcome of the lawsuit, which is not yet known.

The FASB has established two conditions for determining when a contingency should be entered in the accounting records:

1. The liability must be probable.
2. The liability can be reasonably estimated.[10]

Study Note

Contingencies are recorded when they are probable and can be reasonably estimated.

Estimated liabilities like the income tax, warranty, and vacation pay liabilities that we have described meet those conditions. They are therefore accrued in the accounting records.

In a survey of 600 large companies, the most common types of contingencies reported were litigation, which can involve many different issues, and environmental concerns, such as toxic waste cleanup.[11] In a note to its financial statements, **Microsoft** describes contingent liabilities in the area of lawsuits involving potential infringement of European competition law, antitrust and overcharge actions, patent and intellectual property claims, and others. Microsoft's management states:

> While we intend to vigorously defend these matters, there exists the possibility of adverse outcomes that we estimate could be up to $4.15 billion in aggregate beyond recorded amounts.[12]

A **commitment** is a legal obligation that does not meet the technical requirements for recognition as a liability and so is not recorded. The most common examples are purchase agreements and leases.[13]

For example, Microsoft also reports in its notes to the financial statements construction commitments in the amount of $821 million and purchase commitments in the amount of $3,672 million. Knowledge of these amounts is very important for planning cash flows in the coming year.

STOP & APPLY >

Indicate whether each of the following is (a) a contingent liability or (b) a commitment:

1. A tax dispute with the IRS
2. A long-term lease agreement
3. An agreement to purchase goods in the future
4. A potential lawsuit over a defective product

SOLUTION

1. a; 2. b; 3. b; 4. a

Valuation Approaches to Fair Value Accounting

LO4 Identify the valuation approaches to fair value accounting, and define *time value of money* and *interest* and apply them to present values.

Recall that fair value is the price for which an asset or liability could be sold, or exit the company, as opposed to the price the company could buy the asset or liability. As pointed out previously, the concept of fair value applies to financial assets, such as cash equivalents, accounts receivable, and investments, and to liabilities, such as accounts payable and short-term loans. Fair value is also applicable to determining whether tangible assets such as inventories and long-term assets have sustained a permanent decline in value below their cost. The FASB identifies three levels or approaches to measurement of fair value:[14]

- ***Market approach (level 1).*** When available, external market transactions involving identical or comparable assets or liabilities are ideal. For example, the market approach is good for valuing investments and liabilities for which there is a ready market. However, a ready market is not always available. For example, there may not be a market for special-purpose equipment. In these cases, other approaches must be used.
- ***Income (or cash flow) approach (level 2).*** The income approach, as defined by the FASB, converts future cash flows to a single present value. This approach is based on management's best determination of the future cash amounts generated by an asset or payments that will be made for a liability. It is based on internally generated information, which should be reasonable for the circumstances.
- ***Cost (or comparables) approach (level 3).*** The cost or comparables approach is based on the amount that currently would be required to replace an asset with the same or comparable asset. For example, inventory is usually valued at lower of cost or market, where market is the replacement cost. For a plant asset, the replacement cost of a new asset must be adjusted to take into account the asset's age, condition, depreciation, and obsolescence.

Complicating factors may arise in applying the market and cost approaches, but conceptually they are relatively straightforward. The income or cash flow approach requires knowledge of interest and the time value of money, and present value techniques, as presented in the following sections.

Interest and the Time Value of Money

"Time is money" is a common expression. It derives from the concept of the **time value of money**, which refers to the costs or benefits derived from holding or not holding money over time. **Interest** is the cost of using money for a specific period.

The interest associated with the time value of money is an important consideration in any kind of business decision. For example, if you sell a bicycle for $100 and hold that amount for one year without putting it in a savings account, you have forgone the interest that the money would have earned. However, if you accept a note payable instead of cash and add the interest to the price of the bicycle, you will not forgo the interest that the cash could have earned.

Simple interest is the interest cost for one or more periods when the principal sum—the amount on which interest is computed—stays the same from period to period. **Compound interest** is the interest cost for two or more periods when after each period, the interest earned in that period is added to the amount on which interest is computed in future periods. In other words, the principal sum is increased at the end of each period by the interest earned in that period. The following two examples illustrate these concepts:

> **Study Note**
> In business, compound interest is the most useful concept of interest because it helps decision makers choose among alternative courses of action.

Example of Simple Interest Willy Wang accepts an 8 percent, $15,000 note due in 90 days. How much will he receive at that time? The interest is calculated as follows:

$$\begin{aligned}\text{Interest} &= \text{Principal} \times \text{Rate} \times \text{Time}\\ &= \$15{,}000 \times 8/100 \times 90/365\\ &= \$295.89^*\end{aligned}$$

*Rounded.

Therefore, the total that Wang will receive is $15,295.89, calculated as follows:

$$\begin{aligned}\text{Total} &= \text{Principal} + \text{Interest}\\ &= \$15{,}000.00 + \$295.89\\ &= \$15{,}295.89\end{aligned}$$

Example of Compound Interest Terry Soma deposits $10,000 in an account that pays 6 percent interest. She expects to leave the principal and accumulated interest in the account for three years. How much will the account total at the end of three years? Assume that the interest is paid at the end of the year and is added to the principal at that time, and that this total in turn earns interest. The amount at the end of three years is computed as follows:

(1)	(2)	(3)	(4)
Year	*Principal Amount at Beginning of Year*	*Annual Amount of Interest (Col. 2 × 6%)*	*Accumulated Amount at End of Year (Col. 2 + Col. 3)*
1	$10,000.00	$600.00	$10,600.00
2	10,600.00	636.00	11,236.00
3	11,236.00	674.16	11,910.16

At the end of three years, Soma will have $11,910.16 in her account. Note that the amount of interest increases each year by the interest rate times the interest of the previous year. For example, between year 1 and year 2, the interest increased by $36, which equals 6 percent times $600. The final amount of $11,910.16 is referred to as the **future value**, which is the amount an investment ($10,000 in this case), will be worth at a future date if invested at compound interest.

Calculating Present Value

Study Note

Present value is a method of valuing future cash flows. Financial analysts commonly compute present value to determine the value of potential investments.

Suppose you had the choice of receiving $100 today or one year from today. No doubt, you would choose to receive it today. Why? If you have the money today, you can put it in a savings account to earn interest so you will have more than $100 a year from today. In other words, an amount to be received in the future (future value) is not worth as much today as an amount received today (present value). **Present value** is the amount that must be invested today at a given rate of interest to produce a given future value. Thus, present value and future value are closely related.

For example, suppose Kelly Fontaine needs $10,000 one year from now. How much does she have to invest today to achieve that goal if the interest rate is 5 percent? From earlier examples, we can establish the following equation:

$$\begin{aligned}\text{Present Value} \times (1.0 + \text{Interest Rate}) &= \text{Future Value}\\ \text{Present Value} \times 1.05 &= \$10{,}000.00\\ \text{Present Value} &= \$10{,}000.00 \div 1.05\\ \text{Present Value} &= \$9{,}523.81^*\end{aligned}$$

*Rounded.

To achieve a future value of $10,000, Fontaine must invest a present value of $9,523.81. Interest of 5 percent on $9,523.81 for one year equals $476.19, and these two amounts added together equal $10,000.

Present Value of a Single Sum Due in the Future When more than one period is involved, the calculation of present value is more complicated. For example, suppose Ron More wants to be sure of having $8,000 at the end of three years. How much must he invest today in a 5 percent savings account to achieve this goal? We can compute the present value of $8,000 at compound interest of 5 percent for three years by adapting the above equation:

Year	*Amount at End of Year*		*Divide by*		*Present Value at Beginning of Year*
3	$8,000.00	÷	1.05	=	$7,619.05
2	7,619.05	÷	1.05	=	7,256.24
1	7,256.24	÷	1.05	=	6,910.70

Ron More must invest $6,910.70 today to achieve a value of $8,000 in three years.

We can simplify the calculation by using a table of present values. In Table 8-1, the point at which the 5 percent column and the row for period 3 intersect shows a factor of 0.864. This factor, when multiplied by $1, gives the present value of $1 to be received three years from now at 5 percent interest. Thus, we solve the problem as follows:

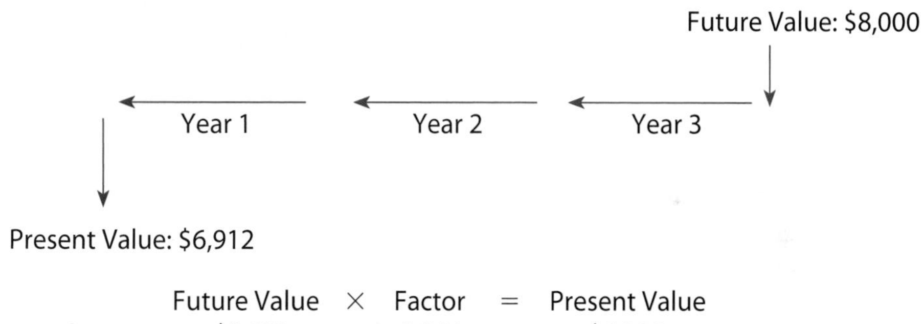

Future Value	×	Factor	=	Present Value
$8,000	×	0.864	=	$6,912

Except for a rounding difference of $1.30, this result is the same as our earlier one.

Present Value of an Ordinary Annuity It is often necessary to compute the present value of a series of receipts or payments equally spaced over time—in other words, the present value of an **ordinary annuity**. For example, suppose Vickie Long has sold a piece of property and is to receive $18,000 in three equal annual payments of $6,000 beginning one year from today. What is the present value of this sale if the current interest rate is 5 percent?

Using Table 8-1, we can compute the present value by calculating a separate value for each of the three payments and summing the results, as follows:

Future Receipts (Annuity)				*Present Value Factor at 5%*		
Year 1	*Year 2*	*Year 3*		*(from Table 8-1)*		*Present Value*
$6,000			×	0.952	=	$ 5,712
	$6,000		×	0.907	=	5,442
		$6,000	×	0.864	=	5,184
Total Present Value						$16,338

TABLE 8-1 Present Value of $1 to Be Received at the End of a Given Number of Periods

Period	1%	2%	3%	4%	5%	6%	7%	8%	9%	10%
1	0.990	0.980	0.971	0.962	0.952	0.943	0.935	0.926	0.917	0.909
2	0.980	0.961	0.943	0.925	0.907	0.890	0.873	0.857	0.842	0.826
3	0.971	0.942	0.915	0.889	0.864	0.840	0.816	0.794	0.772	0.751
4	0.961	0.924	0.888	0.855	0.823	0.792	0.763	0.735	0.708	0.683
5	0.951	0.906	0.863	0.822	0.784	0.747	0.713	0.681	0.650	0.621
6	0.942	0.888	0.837	0.790	0.746	0.705	0.666	0.630	0.596	0.564
7	0.933	0.871	0.813	0.760	0.711	0.665	0.623	0.583	0.547	0.513
8	0.923	0.853	0.789	0.731	0.677	0.627	0.582	0.540	0.502	0.467
9	0.914	0.837	0.766	0.703	0.645	0.592	0.544	0.500	0.460	0.424
10	0.905	0.820	0.744	0.676	0.614	0.558	0.508	0.463	0.422	0.386

The present value of the sale is $16,338. Thus, there is an implied interest cost (given the 5 percent rate) of $1,662 associated with the payment plan that allows the purchaser to pay in three installments.

We can make this calculation more easily by using Table 8-2. The point at which the 5 percent column intersects the row for period 3 shows a factor of 2.723. When multiplied by $1, this factor gives the present value of a series of three $1 payments (spaced one year apart) at compound interest of 5 percent. Thus, we solve the problem as follows:

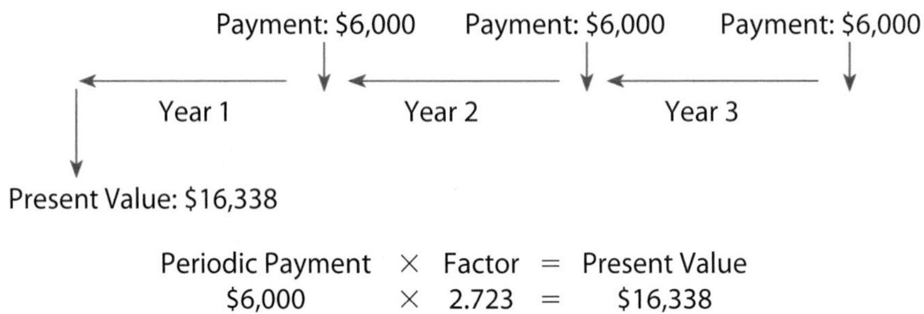

Periodic Payment	×	Factor	=	Present Value
$6,000	×	2.723	=	$16,338

This result is the same as the one we computed earlier.

Study Note

The interest rate used when compounding interest for less than one year is the annual rate divided by the number of periods in a year.

Time Periods As in all our examples, the compounding period is in most cases one year, and the interest rate is stated on an annual basis. However, the left-hand column in Tables 8-1 and 8-2 refers not to years but rather to periods. This wording accommodates compounding periods of less than one year. Savings accounts that record interest quarterly and bonds that pay interest semiannually are cases in which the compounding period is less than one year. To use the tables in these cases, it is necessary to (1) divide the annual interest rate by the number of periods in the year, and (2) multiply the number of periods in one year by the number of years.

For example, suppose we want to compute the present value of a $6,000 payment that is to be received in two years, assuming an annual interest rate of 8 percent. The compounding period is semiannual. Before using Table 8-1 in this

TABLE 8-2 Present Value of an Ordinary $1 Annuity Received in Each Period for a Given Number of Periods

Period	1%	2%	3%	4%	5%	6%	7%	8%	9%	10%
1	0.990	0.980	0.971	0.962	0.952	0.943	0.935	0.926	0.917	0.909
2	1.970	1.942	1.913	1.886	1.859	1.833	1.808	1.783	1.759	1.736
3	2.941	2.884	2.829	2.775	2.723	2.673	2.624	2.577	2.531	2.487
4	3.902	3.808	3.717	3.630	3.546	3.465	3.387	3.312	3.240	3.170
5	4.853	4.713	4.580	4.452	4.329	4.212	4.100	3.993	3.890	3.791
6	5.795	5.601	5.417	5.242	5.076	4.917	4.767	4.623	4.486	4.355
7	6.728	6.472	6.230	6.002	5.786	5.582	5.389	5.206	5.033	4.868
8	7.652	7.325	7.020	6.733	6.463	6.210	5.971	5.747	5.535	5.335
9	8.566	8.162	7.786	7.435	7.108	6.802	6.515	6.247	5.995	5.759
10	9.471	8.983	8.530	8.111	7.722	7.360	7.024	6.710	6.418	6.145

computation, we must compute the interest rate that applies to each compounding period and the total number of compounding periods. First, the interest rate to use is 4 percent (8% annual rate ÷ 2 periods per year). Second, the total number of compounding periods is 4 (2 periods per year × 2 years). From Table 8-1, therefore, the present value of the payment is computed as follows:

Principal	×	Factor	=	Present Value
$6,000	×	0.855	=	$5,130

The present value of the payment is $5,130. This procedure is used anytime the corresponding period is less than one year. For example, a monthly compounding requires dividing the annual interest rate by 12 and multiplying the number of years by 12 to use the tables.

This method of determining the interest rate and the number of periods when the compounding period is less than one year can be used with Tables 8-1 and 8-2.

& APPLY >

Use Tables 8-1 and 8-2 to determine the present value of (1) a single payment of $10,000 at 5 percent for 10 years, (2) 10 annual payments of $1,000 at 5 percent, (3) a single payment of $10,000 at 7 percent for five years, and (4) ten annual payments of $1,000 at 9 percent.

SOLUTION

1. From Table 8-1: $10,000 × 0.614 = $6,140
2. From Table 8-2: $1,000 × 7.722 = $7,722
3. From Table 8-1: $10,000 × 0.713 = $7,130
4. From Table 8-2: $1,000 × 6.418 = $6,418

Applications Using Present Value

LO5 Apply present value to simple valuation situations.

The concept of present value is widely used in business decision making and financial reporting. As mentioned above, the FASB has made it the foundation of its approach in determining the fair value of assets and liabilities when a ready market price is not available. For example, the value of a long-term note receivable or payable can be determined by calculating the present value of the future interest payments.

The Office of the Chief Accountant of the SEC has issued guidance on how to apply fair value accounting.[15] For instance, it says that management's internal assumptions about expected cash flows may be used to measure fair value and that market quotes may be used when they are from an orderly, active market as opposed to a distressed, inactive market. Thus, **Microsoft** may determine the expected present value of the future cash flows of an investment by using its internal cash flow projections and a market rate of interest. By comparing the result to the current value of the investment, Microsoft can determine if an adjustment needs to be made to record a gain or loss.

In the sections that follow, we illustrate two simple, useful applications of present value, which will be helpful in understanding the uses of present value in subsequent chapters.

Valuing an Asset

An asset is something that will provide future benefits to the company that owns it. Usually, the purchase price of an asset represents the present value of those future benefits. It is possible to evaluate a proposed purchase price by comparing it with the present value of the asset to the company.

For example, Mike Yeboah is thinking of buying a new machine that will reduce his annual labor cost by $1,400 per year. The machine will last eight years. The interest rate that Yeboah assumes for making managerial decisions is 10 percent. What is the maximum amount (present value) that Yeboah should pay for the machine?

The present value of the machine to Yeboah is equal to the present value of an ordinary annuity of $1,400 per year for eight years at compound interest of 10 percent. Using the factor from Table 8-2, we compute the value as follows:

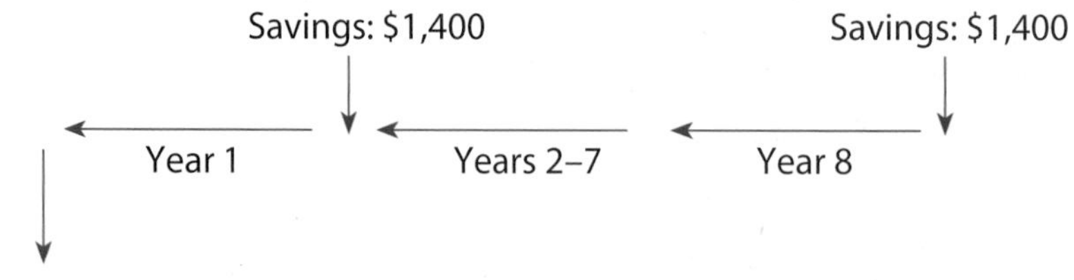

Periodic Savings	×	Factor	=	Present Value
$1,400	×	5.335	=	$7,469

Yeboah should not pay more than $7,469 for the machine because this amount equals the present value of the benefits he would receive from owning it.

Deferred Payment

To encourage buyers to make a purchase, sellers sometimes agree to defer payment for a sale. This practice is common among companies that sell agricultural equipment; to accommodate farmers who often need new equipment in the

Companies that sell agricultural equipment like these combine harvesters often agree to defer payment for a sale. This practice is common because farmers often need new equipment in the spring but cannot pay for it until they sell their crops in the fall. Deferred payment is a useful application of the time value of money.

Courtesy of istockphoto.com.

spring but cannot pay for it until they sell their crops in the fall, these companies are willing to defer payment.

Suppose Field Helpers Corporation sells a tractor to Sasha Ptak for $100,000 on February 1 and agrees to take payment ten months later, on December 1. When such an agreement is made, the future payment includes not only the selling price, but also an implied (imputed) interest cost. If the prevailing annual interest rate for such transactions is 12 percent compounded monthly, the actual price of the tractor would be the present value of the future payment, computed using the factor from Table 8-1 [10 periods, 1 percent (12 percent divided by 12 months)], as follows:

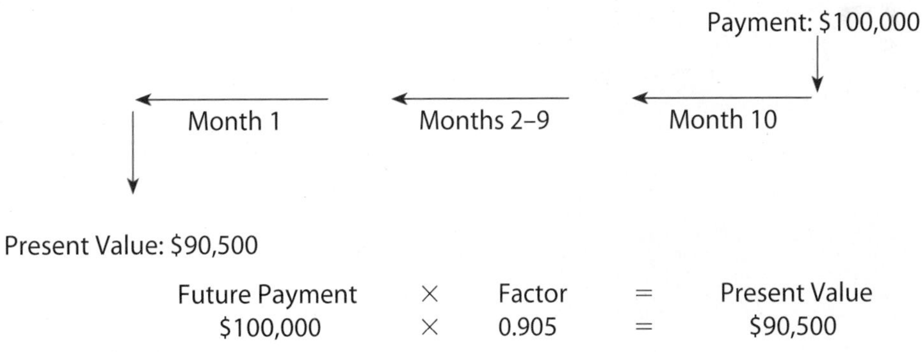

Future Payment	×	Factor	=	Present Value
$100,000	×	0.905	=	$90,500

Ptak records the present value, $90,500, in his purchase records, and Field Helpers Corporation records it in its sales records. The balance consists of interest expense or interest income.

Other Applications

There are many other applications of present value in accounting, including computing imputed interest on non-interest-bearing notes, accounting for installment notes, valuing a bond, and recording lease obligations. Present value is also applied in accounting for pension obligations; valuing debt; depreciating property, plant, and equipment; making capital expenditure decisions; and generally in accounting for any item in which time is a factor.

STOP & APPLY >

Jerry owns a restaurant and has the opportunity to buy a high-quality espresso coffee machine for $5,000. After carefully studying projected costs and revenues, Jerry estimates that the machine will produce a net cash flow of $1,600 annually and will last for five years. He determines that an interest rate of 10 percent is an adequate return on investment for his business.

Calculate the present value of the machine to Jerry. Based on your calculation, do you think a decision to purchase the machine would be wise?

SOLUTION

Calculation of the present value:

Annual cash flow	$ 1,600.00
Factor from Table 8-2 (5 years at 10%)	× 3.791
Present value of net cash flows	$ 6,065.60
Less purchase price	− 5,000.00
Net present value	$ 1,065.60

The present value of the net cash flows from the machine exceeds the purchase price. Thus, the investment will return more than 10 percent to Jerry's business. A decision to purchase the machine would therefore be wise.

A LOOK BACK AT ▸ MICROSOFT

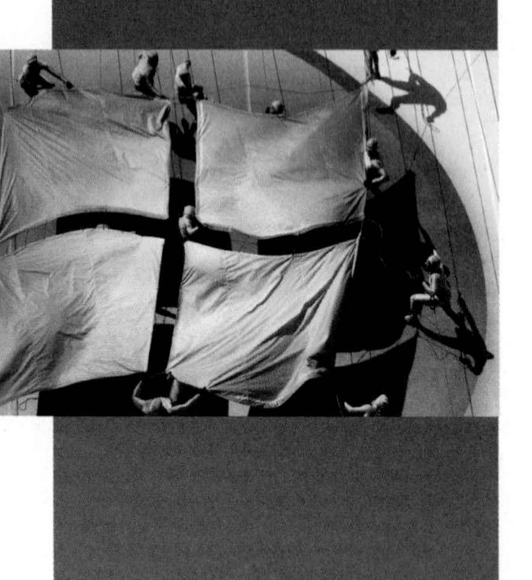

At the beginning of the chapter, we noted that Microsoft is the market leader in software. To stay a leader Microsoft must continue to develop new products and services. To accomplish this, the company has to provide investors and creditors with satisfactory answers to these questions:

- How does Microsoft's decision to incur debt relate to the goals of the business?
- Is the level of accounts payable in the operating cycle satisfactory?
- Has the company properly identified and accounted for all its current liabilities?

The development of new products and services requires a lot of capital, much of which the company raises by borrowing money. Management has committed $9.01 billion to research and development. It has analyzed its future cash flows in terms of present value and carefully planned its cash needs by making very good use of the operating cycle. By using advance billings, keeping inventories low, and making maximum use of credit from its suppliers, it has been able to keep its cash needs to a minimum. This is particularly evident when we compare its payables turnover and days' payable for 2008 and 2009 (dollar amounts are in millions). Microsoft's Merchandise Inventory in 2007 was $1,127 million and Accounts Payable in 2007 were $3,247 million.

		2009	2008
(Cost of Goods Sold ± Change in Merchandise Inventory) / Average Accounts Payable	=	($12,155 − $268) / (($3,324 + $4,034) ÷ 2)	($11,598 − $142) / ($4,034 − $3,247 ÷ 2)
	=	$11,887 / $3,679	$11,456 / $3,641*

*Rounded.

Payables Turnover	=	3.2 times*	3.1 times*
$\frac{\text{365 days}}{\text{Payables Turnover}}$	=	$\frac{\text{365 days}}{\text{3.2 times}}$	$\frac{\text{365 days}}{\text{3.1 times}}$
Days' Payable	=	114.1 days*	117.7 days*

*Rounded.

Clearly, Microsoft maintained a favorable payables turnover and days' payable ratio over the two-year period. The list of current liabilities that it presents in its 2009 annual report gives readers a clear picture of the company's short-term obligations.

Review Problem

Identification and Evaluation of Current Liabilities

LO1

Maggie Lee started a fitness business, Maggie's Fitness Center, last year. In addition to offering exercise classes, she sells nutritional supplements. She has not yet filed any tax reports for her business and therefore owes taxes. Because she has limited experience in running a business, she has brought you all her business records—a checkbook, canceled checks, deposit slips, suppliers' invoices, a notice of annual property taxes of $3,600 due to the city, and a promissory note to her bank for $16,000. She wants you to determine what her business owes the government and other parties.

You analyze all her records and determine the following as of December 31, 2010:

Unpaid invoices for nutritional supplements	$12,000
Sales of nutritional supplements (excluding sales tax)	57,000
Cost of supplements sold	33,600
Exercise instructors' salaries	22,800
Exercise revenues	81,400
Current assets	40,000
Supplements inventory (12/31/10)	27,000
Supplements inventory (12/31/09)	21,000

You learn that the company has sold gift certificates in the amount of $700 that have not been redeemed and that it has deducted $1,374 from its two employees' salaries for federal income taxes owed to the government. The current social security tax is 6.2 percent on maximum earnings of $102,000 for each employee, and the current Medicare tax is 1.45 percent (no maximum earnings). The FUTA tax is 5.4 percent to the state and 0.8 percent to the federal government on the first $7,000 earned by each employee; both employees earned more than $7,000. Lee has not filed a sales tax report to the state (6 percent of supplements sales).

Required

1. Given these facts, determine the company's current liabilities as of December 31, 2010.
2. ***User insight:*** Your analysis of the company's current liabilities has been based on documents that the owner showed you. What liabilities may be missing from your analysis?
3. ***User insight:*** Evaluate the company's liquidity by calculating working capital, payables turnover, and days' payable. Comment on the results. (Assume average accounts payable were the same as year-end accounts payable.)

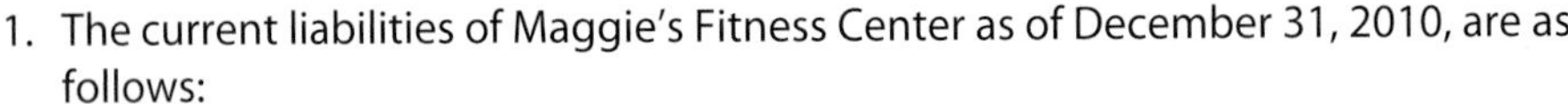

Answers to Review Problem

1. The current liabilities of Maggie's Fitness Center as of December 31, 2010, are as follows:

	A	B	C	D	E	F	G
1	Accounts payable						$12,000.00
2	Notes payable						16,000.00
3	Property taxes payable						3,600.00
4	Sales tax payable	(	$57,000	x	0.06	)	3,420.00
5	Social security tax payable	(	$22,800	x	0.062	)	1,413.60
6	Medicare tax payable	(	$22,800	x	0.0145	)	330.60
7	State unemployment tax payable	(	$22,800	x	0.054	)	1,231.20
8	Federal unemployment tax payable	(	$22,800	x	0.008	)	182.40
9	Employees' federal income taxes payable						1,374.00
10	Unearned revenues						700.00
11	Total current liabilities						$40,251.80

2. The company may have current liabilities for which you have not seen any documentary evidence. For instance, invoices for accounts payable could be missing. In addition, the company may have accrued liabilities, such as vacation pay for its two employees, which would require establishing an estimated liability. If the promissory note to Lee's bank is interest-bearing, it also would require an adjustment to accrue interest payable, and the company could have other loans outstanding for which you have not seen documentary evidence. Moreover, it may have to pay penalties and interest to the federal and state governments because of its failure to remit tax payments on a timely basis. City and state income tax withholding for the employees could be another overlooked liability.

3. Liquidity ratios computed and evaluated:

	A	B	C	D	E	F	G
1	Working Capital	=	Current Assets		–	Current Liabilities	
2		=	$40,000.00		–	$40,251.80	
3		=	($251.80)				
4							
5	Payables Turnover	=	Cost of Goods Sold +/– Change in Merchandise Inventory				
6			Accounts Payable				
7							
8		=	$33,600		+	$6,000	
9			$12,000				
10							
11		=	$39,600				
12			$12,000				
13							
14		=	3.3	times			
15							
16	Days' Payable	=	365	Days			
17			Payables Turnover				
18							
19		=	365	days			
20			3.3	times			
21							
22		=	110.6	days*			
23							

Maggie's Fitness Center has a negative working capital of $251.80, its payables turnover is only 3.3 times, and it takes an average of 110.6 days to pay its accounts payable. Its liquidity is therefore highly questionable. Many of its current assets are inventory, which it must sell to generate cash, and it must pay most of its current liabilities sooner than the 110.6 days would indicate.

*Rounded.

LO1 Identify the management issues related to current liabilities.

Current liabilities are an important consideration in managing a company's liquidity and cash flows. Key measures of liquidity are working capital, payables turnover, and days' payable. Liabilities result from past transactions and should be recognized at the time a transaction obligates a company to make future payments. They are valued at the amount of money necessary to satisfy the obligation or at the fair value of the goods or services to be delivered. Liabilities are classified as current or long term. Companies are required to provide supplemental disclosure when the nature or details of the obligations would help in understanding the liability.

LO2 Identify, compute, and record definitely determinable and estimated current liabilities.

The two major categories of current liabilities are definitely determinable liabilities and estimated liabilities. Definitely determinable liabilities can be measured exactly. These liabilities include accounts payable, bank loans and commercial paper, notes payable, accrued liabilities, dividends payable, sales and excise taxes payable, the current portion of long-term debt, payroll liabilities, and unearned revenues.

Estimated liabilities definitely exist, but their amounts are uncertain and must be estimated. They include liabilities for income taxes, property taxes, promotional costs, product warranties, and vacation pay.

LO3 Distinguish *contingent liabilities* from *commitments*.

A contingent liability is a potential liability that arises from a past transaction and is dependent on a future event. Contingent liabilities often involve lawsuits, income tax disputes, discounted notes receivable, guarantees of debt, and failure to follow government regulations. A commitment is a legal obligation, such as a purchase agreement, that is not recorded as a liability.

LO4 Identify the valuation approaches to fair value accounting, and define *time value of money* and *interest* and apply them to present values.

Three approaches to measurement of fair value are market, income (or cash flow), and cost. The time value of money refers to the costs or benefits derived from holding or not holding money over time.

Interest is the cost of using money for a specific period. In the computation of simple interest, the amount on which the interest is computed stays the same from period to period. In the computation of compound interest, the interest for a period is added to the principal amount before the interest for the next period is computed.

Future value is the amount an investment will be worth at a future date if invested at compound interest. Present value is the amount that must be invested today at a given rate of interest to produce a given future value.

An ordinary annuity is a series of equal payments made at the end of equal intervals of time, with compound interest on the payments. The present value of an ordinary annuity is the present value of a series of payments. Calculations of present values are simplified by using the appropriate tables, which appear in an appendix to the book.

LO5 Apply present value to simple valuation situations.

Present value is commonly used in determining fair value and may be used in determining the value of an asset, in computing the present value of deferred payments, in establishing a fund for loan repayment, and in numerous other accounting situations in which time is a factor.

REVIEW of Concepts and Terminology

The following concepts and terms were introduced in this chapter:

Commercial paper 399 (LO2)

Commitment 408 (LO3)

Compound interest 409 (LO4)

Contingent liability 408 (LO3)

Current liabilities 397 (LO1)

Definitely determinable liabilities 398 (LO2)

Estimated liabilities 404 (LO2)

Future value 410 (LO4)

Interest 409 (LO4)

Line of credit 399 (LO2)

Long-term liabilities 397 (LO1)

Ordinary annuity 411 (LO4)

Present value 410 (LO4)

Salaries 401 (LO2)

Simple interest 409 (LO4)

Time value of money 409 (LO4)

Unearned revenues 404 (LO2)

Wages 401 (LO2)

Key Ratios

Days' payable 394 (LO1)

Payables turnover 394 (LO1)

CHAPTER ASSIGNMENTS

BUILDING Your Basic Knowledge and Skills

Short Exercises

LO1 **Issues in Accounting for Liabilities**

SE 1. Indicate whether each of the following actions relates to (a) managing liquidity and cash flow, (b) recognition of liabilities, (c) valuation of liabilities, (d) classification of liabilities, or (e) disclosure of liabilities:

1. Determining that a liability will be paid in less than one year
2. Estimating the amount of a liability
3. Providing information about when liabilities are due and their interest rates
4. Determining when a liability arises
5. Assessing working capital and payables turnover

LO1 **Measuring Short-Term Liquidity**

SE 2. Robinson Company has current assets of $65,000 and current liabilities of $40,000, of which accounts payable are $35,000. Robinson's cost of goods sold is $230,000, its merchandise inventory increased by $10,000, and accounts payable were $25,000 the prior year. Calculate Robinson's working capital, payables turnover, and days' payable.

LO2 LO3 **Types of Liabilities**

SE 3. Indicate whether each of the following is (a) a definitely determinable liability, (b) an estimated liability, (c) a commitment, or (d) a contingent liability:

1. Dividends payable
2. Pending litigation
3. Income taxes payable
4. Current portion of long-term debt
5. Vacation pay liability
6. Guaranteed loans of another company
7. Purchase agreement

LO2 **Interest Expense on Note Payable**

SE 4. On the last day of August, Avenue Company borrowed $240,000 on a bank note for 60 days at 12 percent interest. Assume that interest is stated separately. Prepare the following entries in journal form: (1) August 31, recording of note; and (2) October 30, payment of note plus interest.

LO2 **Payroll Expenses**

SE 5. The following payroll totals for the month of April are from the payroll register of Young Corporation: salaries, $223,000; federal income taxes withheld, $31,440; social security tax withheld, $13,826; Medicare tax withheld, $3,234; medical insurance deductions, $6,580; and salaries subject to unemployment taxes, $156,600.

Determine the total and components of (1) the monthly payroll and (2) employer's payroll expense, assuming social security and Medicare taxes equal to the amounts for employees, a federal unemployment insurance tax of 0.8 percent, a state unemployment tax of 5.4 percent, and medical insurance premiums for which the employer pays 80 percent of the cost.

LO2 **Product Warranty Liability**

SE 6. Harper Corp. manufactures and sells travel clocks. Each clock costs $12.50 to produce and sells for $25. In addition, each clock carries a warranty that provides for free replacement if it fails during the two years following the sale. In the past, 5 percent of the clocks sold have had to be replaced under the warranty. During October, Harper sold 52,000 clocks, and 2,800 clocks were replaced under the warranty. Prepare entries in journal form to record the estimated liability for product warranties during the month and the clocks replaced under warranty during the month.

Note: Tables 1 and 2 in the appendix on present value tables may be used where appropriate to solve **SE 7** through **SE 9**.

LO4 **Simple and Compound Interest**

SE 7. Ursus Motors, Inc., receives a one-year note that carries a 12 percent annual interest rate on $6,000 for the sale of a used car. Compute the maturity value under each of the following assumptions: (1) Simple interest is charged. (2) The interest is compounded semiannually. (3) The interest is compounded quarterly. (4) The interest is compounded monthly.

LO4 **Present Value Calculations**

SE 8. Find the present value of (1) a single payment of $24,000 at 6 percent for 12 years, (2) 12 annual payments of $2,000 at 6 percent, (3) a single payment of $5,000 at 9 percent for five years, and (4) five annual payments of $5,000 at 9 percent.

LO5 **Valuing an Asset for the Purpose of Making a Purchasing Decision**

SE 9. Hogan Whitner owns a machine shop and has the opportunity to purchase a new machine for $30,000. After carefully studying projected costs and revenues, Whitner estimates that the new machine will produce a net cash flow of $7,200 annually and will last for eight years. Whitner believes that an interest rate of 10 percent is adequate for his business.

Calculate the present value of the machine to Whitner. Does the purchase appear to be a smart business decision?

Exercises

LO1 LO2 LO3 **Discussion Questions**

E 1. Develop a brief answer to each of the following questions:

1. Nimish Banks, a star college basketball player, received a contract from the Midwest Blazers to play professional basketball. The contract calls for a salary of $420,000 a year for four years, dependent on his making the team in each of those years. Should this contract be considered a liability and recorded on the books of the basketball team? Why or why not?
2. Is an increasing payables turnover good or bad for a company? Why or why not?
3. Do adjusting entries involving estimated liabilities and accruals ever affect cash flows?
4. When would a commitment be recognized in the accounting records?

LO4 **Discussion Questions**

E 2. Develop a brief answer to each of the following questions:

1. Is a friend who borrows money from you for three years and agrees to pay you interest after each year paying you simple or compound interest?

2. Ordinary annuities assume that the first payment is made at the end of each year. In a transaction, who is better off in this arrangement, the payer or the receiver? Why?
3. Why is present value one of the most useful concepts in making business decisions?

LO1 Issues in Accounting for Liabilities

E 3. Indicate whether each of the following actions relates to (a) managing liquidity and cash flows, (b) recognition of liabilities, (c) valuation of liabilities, (d) classification of liabilities, or (e) disclosure of liabilities:

1. Setting a liability at the fair market value of goods to be delivered
2. Relating the payment date of a liability to the length of the operating cycle
3. Recording a liability in accordance with the matching rule
4. Providing information about financial instruments on the balance sheet
5. Estimating the amount of "cents-off" coupons that will be redeemed
6. Categorizing a liability as long-term debt
7. Measuring working capital
8. Compare this year's days' payable with last year's

LO1 Measuring Short-Term Liquidity

E 4. In 2010, Hagler Company had current assets of $310,000 and current liabilities of $200,000, of which accounts payable were $130,000. Cost of goods sold was $850,000, merchandise inventory increased by $80,000, and accounts payable were $110,000 in the prior year. In 2011, Hagler had current assets of $420,000 and current liabilities of $320,000, of which accounts payable were $150,000. Cost of goods sold was $950,000, and merchandise inventory decreased by $30,000. Calculate Hagler's working capital, payables turnover, and days' payable for 2010 and 2011. Assess Hagler's liquidity and cash flows in relation to the change in the payables turnover from 2010 to 2011.

LO2 Interest Expense on Note Payable

E 5. On the last day of October, Wicker Company borrows $120,000 on a bank note for 60 days at 11 percent interest. Interest is not included in the face amount. Prepare the following entries in journal form: (1) October 31, recording of note; (2) November 30, accrual of interest expense; and (3) December 30, payment of note plus interest.

LO2 Sales and Excise Taxes

E 6. Web Design Services billed its customers a total of $490,200 for the month of August, including 9 percent federal excise tax and 5 percent sales tax.

1. Determine the proper amount of service revenue to report for the month.
2. Prepare an entry in journal form to record the revenue and related liabilities for the month.

LO2 Payroll Expenses

E 7. At the end of October, the payroll register for Global Tool Corporation contained the following totals: wages, $742,000; federal income taxes withheld, $189,768; state income taxes withheld, $31,272; social security tax withheld, $46,004; Medicare tax withheld, $10,759; medical insurance deductions, $25,740; and wages subject to unemployment taxes, $114,480.

Determine the total and components of the (1) monthly payroll and (2) employer payroll expenses, assuming social security and Medicare taxes equal to the amount for employees, a federal unemployment insurance tax of 0.8 percent, a state unemployment tax of 5.4 percent, and medical insurance premiums for which the employer pays 80 percent of the cost.

LO2 Product Warranty Liability

E 8. Sanchez Company manufactures and sells electronic games. Each game costs $50 to produce, sells for $90, and carries a warranty that provides for free replacement if it fails during the two years following the sale. In the past, 7 percent of the games sold had to be replaced under the warranty. During July, Sanchez sold 6,500 games, and 700 games were replaced under the warranty.

1. Prepare an entry in journal form to record the estimated liability for product warranties during the month.
2. Prepare an entry in journal form to record the games replaced under warranty during the month.

LO2 Vacation Pay Liability

E 9. Angel Corporation gives three weeks' paid vacation to each employee who has worked at the company for one year. Based on studies of employee turnover and previous experience, management estimates that 65 percent of the employees will qualify for vacation pay this year.

1. Assume that Angel's July payroll is $150,000, of which $10,000 is paid to employees on vacation. Figure the estimated employee vacation benefit for the month.
2. Prepare an entry in journal form to record the employee benefit for July.
3. Prepare an entry in journal form to record the pay to employees on vacation.

Note: Tables 1 and 2 in the appendix on present value tables may be used where appropriate to solve **E10** through **E16**.

LO4 LO5 Determining an Advance Payment

E 10. Tracy Collins is contemplating paying five years' rent in advance. Her annual rent is $25,200. Calculate the single sum that would have to be paid now for the advance rent if we assume compound interest of 8 percent.

LO4 Present Value Calculations

E 11. Find the present value of (1) a single payment of $12,000 at 6 percent for 12 years, (2) 12 annual payments of $1,000 at 6 percent, (3) a single payment of $2,500 at 9 percent for five years, and (4) five annual payments of $2,500 at 9 percent.

LO4 LO5 Present Value of a Lump-Sum Contract

E 12. A contract calls for a lump-sum payment of $15,000. Find the present value of the contract, assuming that (1) the payment is due in five years, and the current interest rate is 9 percent; (2) the payment is due in ten years, and the current interest rate is 9 percent; (3) the payment is due in five years, and the current interest rate is 5 percent; and (4) the payment is due in ten years, and the current interest rate is 5 percent.

LO4 LO5 **Present Value of an Annuity Contract**

E 13. A contract calls for annual payments of $1,200. Find the present value of the contract, assuming that (1) the number of payments is seven, and the current interest rate is 6 percent; (2) the number of payments is 14, and the current interest rate is 6 percent; (3) the number of payments is seven, and the current interest rate is 8 percent; and (4) the number of payments is 14, and the current interest rate is 8 percent.

LO4 LO5 **Valuing an Asset for the Purpose of Making a Purchasing Decision**

E 14. Robert Baka owns a service station and has the opportunity to purchase a car wash machine for $30,000. After carefully studying projected costs and revenues, Baka estimates that the car wash machine will produce a net cash flow of $5,200 annually and will last for eight years. He determines that an interest rate of 14 percent is adequate for his business. Calculate the present value of the machine to Baka. Does the purchase appear to be a smart business decision?

LO4 LO5 **Deferred Payment**

E 15. Larson Equipment Corporation sold a precision tool machine with computer controls to Bondie Corporation for $200,000 on January 2 and agreed to take payment nine months later on October 2. Assuming that the prevailing annual interest rate for such a transaction is 16 percent compounded quarterly, what is the actual sale (purchase) price of the machine tool?

LO4 LO5 **Negotiating the Sale of a Business**

E 16. Eva Prokop is attempting to sell her business to Joseph Kahn. The company has assets of $3,600,000, liabilities of $3,200,000, and stockholders' equity of $400,000. Both parties agree that the proper rate of return to expect is 12 percent; however, they differ on other assumptions. Prokop believes that the business will generate at least $400,000 per year of cash flows for 20 years. Kahn thinks that $320,000 in cash flows per year is more reasonable and that only ten years in the future should be considered. Using Table 2 in the appendix on present value tables, determine the range for negotiation by computing the present value of Prokop's offer to sell and of Kahn's offer to buy.

Problems

LO1 LO2 LO3 **Identification of Current Liabilities, Contingencies, and Commitments**

P 1. Listed below are common types of current liabilities, contingencies, and commitments:

a. Accounts payable
b. Bank loans and commercial paper
c. Notes payable
d. Dividends payable
e. Sales and excise taxes payable
f. Current portion of long-term debt
g. Payroll liabilities
h. Unearned revenues
i. Income taxes payable
j. Property taxes payable
k. Promotional costs
l. Product warranty liability
m. Vacation pay liability
n. Contingent liability
o. Commitment

Required

1. For each of the following statements, identify the category above to which it gives rise or with which it is most closely associated:

    1. A company agrees to replace parts of a product if they fail.
    2. An employee earns one day off for each month worked.
    3. A company signs a contract to lease a building for five years.
    4. A company puts discount coupons in the newspaper.
    5. A company agrees to pay insurance costs for employees.
    6. A portion of a mortgage on a building is due this year.
    7. The board of directors declares a dividend.
    8. A company has trade payables.
    9. A company has a lawsuit pending against it.
    10. A company arranges for a line of credit.
    11. A company signs a note due in 60 days.
    12. A company operates in a state that has a sales tax.
    13. A company earns a profit that is taxable.
    14. A company owns buildings that are subject to property taxes.

User insight ▶ 2. Of the items listed from **a** to **o** above, which ones would you not expect to see listed on the balance sheet with a dollar amount? Of those items that would be listed on the balance sheet with a dollar amount, which ones would you consider to involve the most judgment or discretion on the part of management?

LO2 Notes Payable and Wages Payable

P 2. Part A: State Mill Company, whose fiscal year ends December 31, completed the following transactions involving notes payable:

2010		
Nov.	25	Purchased a new loading cart by issuing a 60-day, 10 percent note for $86,400.
Dec.	31	Made the end-of-year adjusting entry to accrue interest expense.
2011		
Jan.	24	Paid off the loading cart note.

Required

1. Prepare entries in journal form for State Mill's notes payable transactions.

User insight ▶ 2. When notes payable appears on the balance sheet, what other current liability would you look for to be associated with the notes? What would it mean if this other current liability did not appear?

Part B: At the end of October 2011, the payroll register for State Mill Company contained the following totals: wages, $185,500; federal income taxes withheld, $47,442; state income taxes withheld, $7,818; social security tax withheld, $11,501; Medicare tax withheld, $2,690; medical insurance deductions, $6,400; and wages subject to unemployment taxes, $114,480.

Required

Prepare entries to record the (1) monthly payroll and (2) employer payroll expenses, assuming social security and Medicare taxes equal to the amount for employees, a federal unemployment insurance tax of 0.8 percent, a state unemployment tax of 5.4 percent, and medical insurance premiums for which the employer pays 80 percent of the cost.

LO2 **Product Warranty Liability**

P 3. The Smart Way Products Company manufactures and sells wireless video cell phones, which it guarantees for five years. If a cell phone fails, it is replaced free, but the customer is charged a service fee for handling. In the past, management has found that only 3 percent of the cell phones sold required replacement under the warranty. The average cell phone costs the company $120. At the beginning of September, the account for estimated liability for product warranties had a credit balance of $104,000. During September, 250 cell phones were returned under the warranty. The company collected $4,930 of service fees for handling. During the month, the company sold 2,800 cell phones.

Required

1. Prepare entries in journal form to record (a) the cost of cell phones replaced under warranty and (b) the estimated liability for product warranties for cell phones sold during the month.
2. Compute the balance of the Estimated Product Warranty Liability account at the end of the month.
3. User insight ▶ If the company's product warranty liability is underestimated, what are the effects on current and future years' income?

LO1 **Identification and Evaluation of Current Liabilities**

P 4. Tony Garcia opened a small motorcycle repair shop, Garcia Cycle Repair, on January 2, 2009. The shop also sells a limited number of motorcycle parts. In January 2010, Garcia realized he had never filed any tax reports for his business and therefore probably owes a considerable amount of taxes. Since he has limited experience in running a business, he has brought you all his business records, including a checkbook, canceled checks, deposit slips, suppliers' invoices, a notice of annual property taxes of $2,310 due to the city, and a promissory note to his father-in-law for $2,500. He wants you to determine what his business owes the government and other parties.

You analyze all his records and determine the following as of December 31, 2009:

Unpaid invoices for motorcycle parts	$ 9,000
Parts sales (excluding sales tax)	44,270
Cost of Parts Sold	31,125
Workers' salaries	18,200
Repair revenues	60,300
Current assets	16,300
Motorcycle parts inventory	11,750

You learn that the company has deducted $476 from the two employees' salaries for federal income taxes owed to the government. The current social security tax is 6.2 percent on maximum earnings of $102,000 for each employee, and the current Medicare tax is 1.45 percent (no maximum earnings). The FUTA tax is 5.4 percent to the state and 0.8 percent to the federal government on the first $7,000 earned by each employee, and both employees earned more than $7,000. Garcia has not filed a sales tax report to the state (5 percent of sales).

Required

1. Given these limited facts, determine Garcia Cycle Repair's current liabilities as of December 31, 2009.
2. User insight ▶ What additional information would you want from Garcia to satisfy yourself that all current liabilities have been identified?

User insight ▶ 3. Evaluate Garcia's liquidity by calculating working capital, payables turnover, and days' payable. Comment on the results. (Assume average accounts payable were the same as year-end accounts payable.)

LO4 LO5 **Applications of Present Value**

P 5. Andy Corporation's management took the following actions, which went into effect on January 2, 2010. Each action involved an application of present value.

a. Andy Corporation enters into a purchase agreement that calls for a payment of $500,000 three years from now.
b. Bought out the contract of a member of top management for a payment of $50,000 per year for four years beginning January 2, 2011.

Required

1. Assuming an annual interest rate of 10 percent and using Tables 8-1 and 8-2, answer the following questions:
   a. In action **a**, what is the present value of the liability for the purchase agreement?
   b. In action **b**, what is the cost (present value) of the buyout?

User insight ▶ 2. Many businesses analyze present value extensively when making decisions about investing in long-term assets. Why is this type of analysis particularly appropriate for such decisions?

Alternate Problems

LO2 **Notes Payable and Wages Payable**

P 6. Part A: Nazir Corporation, whose fiscal year ended June 30, 2010, completed the following transactions involving notes payable:

May	21	Obtained a 60-day extension on an $18,000 trade account payable owed to a supplier by signing a 60-day, $18,000 note. Interest is in addition to the face value, at the rate of 14 percent.
June	30	Made the end-of-year adjusting entry to accrue interest expense.
July	20	Paid off the note plus interest due the supplier.

Required

1. Prepare entries in journal form for the notes payable transactions.

User insight ▶ 2. When notes payable appears on the balance sheet, what other current liability would you look for to be associated with the notes? What would it mean if this other current liability did not appear?

Part B: The payroll register for Nazir Corporation contained the following totals at the end of July 2010: wages, $139,125; federal income taxes withheld, $35,582; state income taxes withheld, $5,863; social security tax withheld, $8,626; Medicare tax withheld, $2,017; medical insurance deductions, $4,800; and wages subject to unemployment taxes, $85,860.

Required

Prepare entries in journal form to record the (1) monthly payroll and (2) employer payroll expenses, assuming social security and Medicare taxes equal to the amount for employees, a federal unemployment insurance tax of 0.8 percent, a state unemployment tax of 5.4 percent, and medical insurance premiums for which the employer pays 80 percent of the cost.

LO2 **Product Warranty Liability**

P 7. Telemix Company is engaged in the retail sale of high-definition televisions (HDTVs). Each HDTV has a 24-month warranty on parts. If a repair under warranty is required, a charge for the labor is made. Management has found that 20 percent of the HDTVs sold require some work before the warranty expires. Furthermore, the average cost of replacement parts has been $60 per repair. At the beginning of January, the account for the estimated liability for product warranties had a credit balance of $14,300. During January, 112 HDTVs were returned under the warranty. The cost of the parts used in repairing the HDTVs was $8,765, and $9,442 was collected as service revenue for the labor involved. During January, the month before the Super Bowl, Telemix Company sold 450 new HDTVs.

Required

1. Prepare entries in journal form to record each of the following: (a) the warranty work completed during the month, including related revenue; (b) the estimated liability for product warranties for HDTVs sold during the month.
2. Compute the balance of the Estimated Product Warranty Liability account at the end of the month.
3. User insight ▶ If the company's product warranty liability is overestimated, what are the effects on current and future years' income?

LO1 **Identification and Evaluation of Current Liabilities**

P 8. Linda Lopez opened a beauty studio, Linda's Salon, on January 2, 2010. The salon also sells beauty supplies. In January 2011, Lopez realized she had never filed any tax reports for her business and therefore probably owes a considerable amount of taxes. Since she has limited experience in running a business, she has brought you all her business records, including a checkbook, canceled checks, deposit slips, suppliers' invoices, a notice of annual property taxes of $1,970 due to the city, and a promissory note to her father-in-law for $3,000. She wants you to determine what her business owes the government and other parties.

You analyze all her records and determine the following as of December 31, 2010:

Unpaid invoices for beauty supplies	$ 7,500
Beauty supplies sales (excluding sales tax)	39,430
Cost of beauty supplies sold	27,631
Workers' salaries	17,750
Service revenues	51,900
Current assets	15,800
Beauty supplies inventory	9,980

You learn that the company has deducted $516 from the two employees' salaries for federal income taxes owed to the government. The current social security tax is 6.2 percent on maximum earnings of $102,000 for each employee, and the current Medicare tax is 1.45 percent (no maximum earnings). The FUTA tax is 5.4 percent to the state and 0.8 percent to the federal government on the first $7,000 earned by each employee, and both employees earned more than $7,000. Lopez has not filed a sales tax report to the state (5 percent of sales).

Required

1. Given these limited facts, determine Linda's Salon current liabilities as of December 31, 2010.
2. User insight ▶ What additional information would you want from Lopez to satisfy yourself that all current liabilities have been identified?

User insight ▶ 3. Evaluate Lopez's liquidity by calculating working capital, payables turnover, and days' payable. Comment on the results. (Assume average accounts payable were the same as year-end accounts payable.)

LO4 LO5 **Applications of Present Value**

P 9. Kowalski Corporation's management took the following actions, which went into effect on January 2, 2009. Each action involved an application of present value.

a. Kowalski Corporation enters into a purchase agreement that calls for a payment of $650,000 six years from now.
b. Bought out the contract of a member of top management for a payment of $70,000 per year for five years beginning January 2, 2010.

Required

1. Assuming an annual interest rate of 10 percent and using Tables 8-1 and 8-2, answer the following questions:
   a. In action **a**, what is the present value of the liability for the purchase agreement?
   b. In action **b**, what is the cost (present value) of the buyout?

User insight ▶ 2. Many businesses analyze present value extensively when making decisions about investing in long-term assets. Why is this type of analysis particularly appropriate for such decisions?

ENHANCING Your Knowledge, Skills, and Critical Thinking

LO2 **Frequent Flyer Plan**

C 1. JetGreen Airways instituted a frequent flyer program in which passengers accumulate points toward a free flight based on the number of miles they fly on the airline. One point was awarded for each mile flown, with a minimum of 750 miles being given for any flight. Because of competition in 2010, the company began a bonus plan in which passengers receive triple the normal mileage points. In the past, about 1.5 percent of passenger miles were flown by passengers who had converted points to free flights. With the triple mileage program, JetGreen expects that a 2.5 percent rate will be more appropriate for future years.

During 2010, the company had passenger revenues of $966.3 million and passenger transportation operating expenses of $802.8 million before depreciation and amortization. Operating income was $86.1 million. What is the appropriate rate to use to estimate free miles? What would be the effect of the estimated liability for free travel by frequent flyers on 2010 net income? Describe several ways to estimate the amount of this liability. Be prepared to discuss the arguments for and against recognizing this liability.

LO3 **Lawsuits and Contingent Liabilities**

C 2. When faced with lawsuits, many companies recognize a loss and therefore credit a liability or reserve account for any future losses that may result. For instance, in the famous **WorldCom** case, **Citibank**, the world's largest financial services firm, announced it was setting up reserves or liabilities of $5.6 billion in connection with pending lawsuits related to its relationship with WorldCom.[16] Are these lawsuits contingent liabilities? Using the two criteria established by the FASB for recording a contingency, what conditions must exist for Citibank to record these lawsuits when they have not yet been heard in court?

LO4 LO5 **Present Value**

C 3. In its "Year-End Countdown Sale," a local **Cadillac** auto dealer advertised "0% interest for 60 months!"[17] What role does the time value of money play in this promotion? Assuming that Cadillac is able to borrow funds at 8 percent interest, what is the cost to Cadillac of every customer who takes advantage of this offer? If you were able to borrow to pay cash for this car, which rate would be more relevant in determining how much you might offer for the car—the rate at which you borrow money or the rate Cadillac borrows money?

LO1 **Comparison of Two Companies' Ratios with Industry Ratios**

C 4. Both **Sun Microsystems Inc.** and **Cisco Systems** are in the computer industry. These data (in millions) are for their fiscal year ends:[18]

	Sun	Cisco
Accounts payable	$1,027	$ 675
Cost of goods sold	6,718	13,023
Increase (decrease) in inventory	(114)	(161)

Compare the payables turnover ratio and days' payable for both companies. How are cash flows affected by days' payable? How do Sun Microsystems' and Cisco Systems' ratios compare with the computer industry ratios shown in Figures 8-1 and 8-2? (Use year-end amounts for ratios.)

LO2 **Nature and Recognition of an Estimated Liability**

C 5. The decision to recognize and record a liability is sometimes a matter of judgment. People who use **General Motors** credit cards earn rebates toward the purchase or lease of GM vehicles in relation to the amount of purchases they make with their cards. General Motors chooses to treat these outstanding rebates as a commitment in the notes to its financial statements:

> GM sponsors a credit card program... which offers rebates that can be applied primarily against the purchase or lease of GM vehicles. The amount of rebates available to qualified cardholders (net of deferred program income) was $3.4 billion and $3.9 billion at December 31, 2008, and 2007, respectively.[19]

Using the two criteria established by the FASB for recording a contingency, explain GM's reasoning in treating this liability as a commitment in the notes, where it will likely receive less attention by analysts, rather than including it on the income statement as an expense and on the balance sheet as an estimated liability. Do you agree with this position? (**Hint**: Apply the matching rule.)

LO4 LO5 **Baseball Contract**

C 6. The Houston Texans' fifth-year pitcher Juan Alvarez made the All-Star team in 2010. Alvarez has three years left on a contract that is to pay him $2.4 million a year. He wants to renegotiate his contract because other players who have equally outstanding records (although they also have more experience) are receiving as much as $10.5 million per year for five years. Management has a policy of never renegotiating a current contract but is willing to consider extending the contract to additional years. In fact, the Texans have offered Alvarez an additional three years at $6.0 million, $9.0 million, and $12.0 million, respectively. In addition, they have added an option year at $15.0 million. Management points out that this package is worth $42.0 million, or $10.5 million per year on average. Alvarez is considering this offer and is also considering asking for a bonus to be paid upon signing the contract. Write a memorandum to Alvarez that comments on management's position and evaluates the offer, assuming a current interest rate of 10 percent. (**Hint**: Use present values.) Propose a range for the signing bonus. Finally, include other considerations that may affect the value of the offer.

LO1 LO3 **Short-Term Liabilities and Seasonality; Commitments and Contingencies**

C 7. Refer to the quarterly financial report near the end of the notes to the financial statements in **CVS**'s annual report. Is CVS a seasonal business? Would you expect short-term borrowings and accounts payable to be unusually high or unusually low at the balance sheet date of December 31, 2008?

Read CVS's note on commitments and contingencies. What commitments and contingencies does the company have? Why is it important to consider this information in connection with payables analysis?

LO1 **Payables Analysis**

C 8. Refer to **CVS**'s financial statements in the Supplement to Chapter 1 and to the following data for **Walgreens**:

	2008	2007	2006
Cost of goods sold	$42,391	$38,518	
Accounts payable	4,289	3,734	$4,039
Increase in merchandise inventory	459	740	

Compute the payables turnover and days' payable for CVS and Walgreens for the past two years. In 2006, CVS had accounts payable of $2,521.5 million, and its merchandise inventory increased by $899.3 in 2007. Which company do you think makes the most use of creditors for financing the needs of the operating cycle? Has the trend changed?

LO2 **Known Legal Violations**

C 9. Harbor Restaurant is a large steak restaurant in the suburbs of Detroit. Jake Takas, an accounting student at a nearby college, recently secured a full-time accounting job at the restaurant. He felt fortunate to have a good job that accommodated his class schedule because the local economy was very bad. After a few weeks on the job, Takas realized that his boss, the owner of the business, was paying the kitchen workers in cash and was not withholding federal and state income taxes or social security and Medicare taxes. Takas understands that federal and state laws require these taxes to be withheld and paid to the appropriate agency in a timely manner. He also realizes that if he raises this issue, he could lose his job. What alternatives are available to Takas? What action would you take if you were in his position? Why did you make this choice?

LO2 LO3 **Pain in the Drug Industry**

C 10. Pain medications have been in the news. The big drug company **Merck** had to withdraw its pain killer Vioxx from the market when it became known that the drug increased the risk of heart attacks. Other drugs are under scrutiny, like Celebrex from **Pfizer**. Do an Internet search on these drugs and companies. Find out if any lawsuits have been initiated and how these companies are reacting. Access their annual reports and find out what they report under contingent liabilities in the notes to the financial statements and elsewhere. Have they set aside any reserves for liabilities? What are the criteria for recognizing potential liabilities in the accounting records?

LO2 LO5 Nature and Recognition of an Estimated Liability

C 11. Assume that you work for Theater-At-Home, Inc., a retail company that sells basement movie projection systems for $10,000. Your boss is considering two types of promotions:

1. Offering customers a $1,000 coupon that they can apply to future purchases, including the purchase of annual maintenance.
2. Offering credit terms that allow payments of $2,000 down and $2,000 per year for four years starting one year after the purchase. Theater-At-Home would have to borrow money at 7 percent interest to finance these credit arrangements.

Your instructor will divide the class into groups. After discussing the relative merits of these two plans, including their implications for accounting and the time value of money, each group should decide on the best alternative. The groups may recommend changes in the plans. A representative of each group should report the group's findings to the class.

LO5 Evaluation of an Auto Lease

C 12. **Ford Credit** ran an advertisement offering three alternatives for a 24-month lease on a new Lincoln automobile. The three alternatives were zero dollars down and $587 per month for 24 months, $1,975 down and $499 per month for 24 months, or $12,283 down and no monthly payments.[20] Your boss asks you to prepare an analysis of the three alternatives assuming a 12 percent annual return compounded monthly is the relevant interest rate for the company. Present your analysis and make a recommendation to your boss in a one-page business memorandum. Use Table 2 in the appendix on present value tables to determine which is the best deal. How would your recommendation change if the interest rate were higher? If it were lower?

CHAPTER

Long-Term Assets

Focus on Financial Statements

INCOME STATEMENT
Revenues
− Expenses
= Net Income

STATEMENT OF RETAINED EARNINGS
Opening Balance
+ Net Income
− Dividends
= Retained Earnings

BALANCE SHEET
Assets | Liabilities
Equity
A = L + E

STATEMENT OF CASH FLOWS
Operating activities
+ Investing activities
+ Financing activities
= Change in Cash
+ Starting Balance
= Ending Cash Balance

Allocating cost of long-term assets on balance sheet affects income statement. Buying/disposing of long-term assets affects statement of cash flows.

Long-term assets include tangible assets, such as land, buildings, and equipment; natural resources, such as timberland and oil fields; and intangible assets, such as patents and copyrights. These assets represent a company's strategic commitments well into the future. The judgments related to their acquisition, operation, and disposal and to the allocation of their costs will affect a company's performance for years to come. Investors and creditors rely on accurate and full reporting of the assumptions and judgments that underlie the measurement of long-term assets.

LEARNING OBJECTIVES

LO1 Define *long-term assets*, and explain the management issues related to them. (pp. 436–441)

LO2 Distinguish between *capital expenditures* and *revenue expenditures*, and account for the cost of property, plant, and equipment. (pp. 441–445)

LO3 Compute depreciation under the straight-line, production, and declining-balance methods. (pp. 445–452)

LO4 Account for the disposal of depreciable assets. (pp. 452–454)

LO5 Identify the issues related to accounting for natural resources, and compute depletion. (pp. 455–457)

LO6 Identify the issues related to accounting for intangible assets, including research and development costs and goodwill. (pp. 458–462)

DECISION POINT ▸ A USER'S FOCUS APPLE COMPUTER, INC.

- ▸ What are Apple's long-term assets?
- ▸ What are its policies in accounting for long-term assets?
- ▸ Does the company generate enough cash flow to finance its continued growth?

Long known for its innovative technology and design of computers, **Apple** revolutionized the music industry with its digital iPod music player. The company's success stems from its willingness to invest in research and development and long-term assets to create new products. Each year, it spends almost $1,109 million on research and development and about $1,091 million on new long-term assets. About 12 percent of its assets are long term. You can get an idea of the extent and importance of Apple's long-term assets by looking at the Financial Highlights from its balance sheet.[1]

Apple Computer's Financial Highlights (In millions)

	2008	2007
Property, Plant, and Equipment:		
Land and buildings	$ 810	$ 762
Machinery, equipment, and internal-use software	1,491	954
Office furniture and equipment	122	106
Leasehold improvements	1,324	1,019
	3,747	2,841
Less accumulated depreciation and amortization	1,292	1,009
Total property, plant, and equipment, net	$2,455	$1,832
Other Noncurrent Assets:		
Goodwill	$ 207	$ 38
Acquired intangible assets	285	299
Capitalized software development costs	67	83
Other noncurrent assets	1,868	1,139
Total other noncurrent assets	$2,427	$1,559

Management Issues Related to Long-Term Assets

LO1 Define *long-term assets,* and explain the management issues related to them.

Long-term assets were once called fixed assets, but this term has fallen out of favor because it implies that the assets last forever, which they do not. Long-term assets have the following characteristics:

- **They have a useful life of more than one year.** This distinguishes them from current assets, which a company expects to use up or convert to cash within one year or during its operating cycle, whichever is longer. They also differ from current assets in that they support the operating cycle, rather than being part of it. Although there is no strict rule for defining the useful life of a long-term asset, the most common criterion is that the asset be capable of repeated use for at least a year. Included in this category is equipment used only in peak or emergency periods, such as electric generators.
- **They are used in the operation of a business.** Assets not used in the normal course of business, such as land held for speculative reasons or buildings no longer used in ordinary business operations, should be classified as long-term investments, not as long-term assets.
- **They are not intended for resale to customers.** An asset that a company intends to resell to customers should be classified as inventory—not as a long-term asset—no matter how durable it is. For example, a printing press that a manufacturer offers for sale is part of the manufacturer's inventory, but it is a long-term asset for a printing company that buys it to use in its operations.

Study Note

To be classified as property, plant, and equipment, an assest must be "put in use," which means it is available for its intended purpose. An emergency generator is "put in use" when it is available for emergencies, even if it is never used.

Figure 9-1 shows the relative importance of long-term assets in various industries. Figure 9-2 shows how long-term assets are classified and defines the methods of accounting for them. Plant assets, which are **tangible assets**, are accounted for through **depreciation**, the periodic allocation of the cost of a tangible long-lived asset over its estimated useful life. (Although land is a tangible asset, it is not depreciated because it has an unlimited life.) **Natural resources**, which are also tangible assets, are accounted for through **depletion**, the proportional allocation of the cost of a natural resource to the units extracted. Most **intangible assets** are accounted for through **amortization**, the periodic allocation of the cost of the asset to the periods it benefits. However, some intangible assets, including goodwill, are not subject to amortization if their fair value is below the carrying value.

Study Note

A computer that a company uses in an office is a long-term plant asset. An identical computer that a company sells to customers is considered inventory.

Carrying value (also called *book value*) is the unexpired part of an asset's cost (see Figure 9-3). Long-term assets are generally reported at carrying value. If a

FIGURE 9-1
Long-Term Assets as a Percentage of Total Assets for Selected Industries

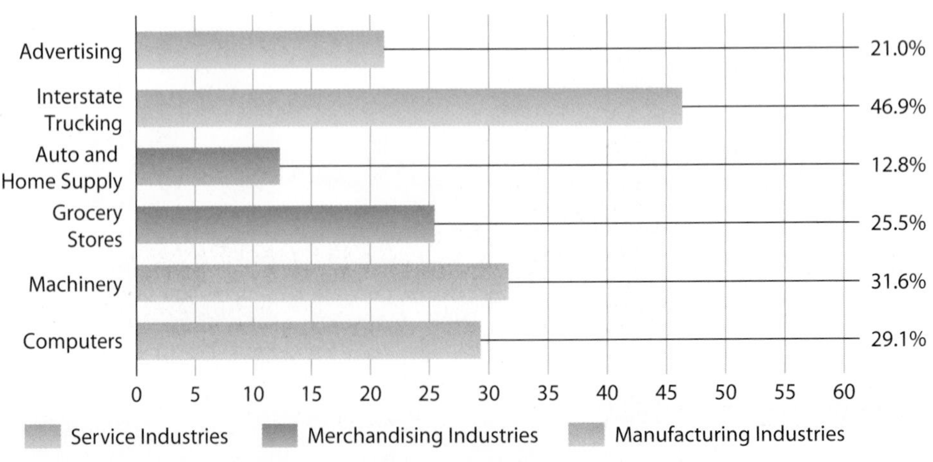

Source: Data from Dun & Bradstreet, *Industry Norms and Key Business Ratios*, 2007–2008.

FIGURE 9-2 Classification of Long-Term Assets and Methods of Accounting for Them

BALANCE SHEET **Long-Term Assets**	INCOME STATEMENT **Expenses**
 **Tangible Assets:** long-term assets that have physical substance Land Plant, Buildings, Equipment (plant assets)	Land is not expensed because it has an unlimited life. **Depreciation:** periodic allocation of the cost of a tangible long-lived asset (other than land and natural resources) over its estimated useful life
 **Natural Resources:** long-term assets purchased for the economic value that can be taken from the land and used up, as with ore, lumber, oil, and gas or other resources contained in the land Mines Timberland Oil and Gas Fields	**Depletion:** exhaustion of a natural resource through mining, cutting, pumping, or other extraction, and the way in which the cost is allocated
Intangible Assets: long-term assets that have no physical substance but have a value based on rights or advantages accruing to the owner Patents, Copyrights, Software, Trademarks, Licenses, Brands, Franchises, Leaseholds, Noncompete Covenants, Customer Lists, Goodwill	**Amortization:** periodic allocation of the cost of an intangible asset to the periods it benefits

long-term asset loses any of its potential to generate revenue before the end of its useful life, it is deemed *impaired*, and its carrying value is reduced.

All long-term assets, including intangible assets that are not subject to amortization, are subject to an annual impairment evaluation. **Asset impairment** occurs when the carrying value of a long-term asset exceeds its fair value.[2] *Fair value* is the amount for which the asset could be bought or sold in a current transaction. For example, if the sum of the expected cash flows from an asset is less than its carrying value, the asset would be impaired. Reducing carrying value to fair value, as measured by the present value of future cash flows, is an application of conservatism. A reduction in carrying value as the result of impairment is recorded as a loss. When the market prices used to establish fair value are not available, the amount of an impairment must be estimated from the best available information.

Study Note

To be classified as intangible, an asset must lack physical substance, be long term, and represent a legal right or advantage.

FIGURE 9-3 Carrying Value of Long-Term Assets on the Balance Sheet

Plant Assets	Natural Resources	Intangible Assets
Less Accumulated Depreciation	Less Accumulated Depletion	Less Accumulated Amortization
Carrying Value	Carrying Value	Carrying Value

In 2004, **Apple** recognized losses of $5.5 million in asset impairments, but it recognized none in subsequent years. A few years earlier, in the midst of an economic slowdown in the telecommunications industry, **WorldCom** recorded asset impairments that totaled $79.8 billion, the largest impairment write-down in history. Since then, other telecommunications companies, including **AT&T** and **Qwest Communications**, have taken large impairment write-downs. Due to these companies' declining revenues, the carrying value of some of their long-term assets no longer exceeded the cash flows that they were meant to help generate.[3] Because of the write-downs, these companies reported large operating losses.

Taking a large write-down in a bad year is often called "taking a big bath" because it "cleans" future years of the bad year's costs and thus can help a company return to a profitable status. In other words, by taking the largest possible loss on a long-term asset in a bad year, companies hope to reduce the costs of depreciation or amortization on the asset in subsequent years.[4]

In the next few pages, we discuss the management issues related to long-term assets—how management decides whether it will acquire them, how it will finance them, and how it will account for them.

Acquiring Long-Term Assets

The decision to acquire a long-term asset is a complex process. For example, **Apple**'s decision to invest capital in establishing its own retail stores throughout the country required very careful analysis. Methods of evaluating data to make rational decisions about acquiring long-term assets are grouped under a topic called capital budgeting, which is a managerial accounting topic covered in a later chapter. However, an awareness of the general nature of the problem is helpful in understanding the management issues related to long-term assets.

To illustrate an acquisition decision, suppose that Apple's management is considering the purchase of a $100,000 customer-relations software package. Management estimates that the new software will save net cash flows of $40,000 per year for four years, the usual life of new software, and that the software will be worth $20,000 at the end of that period. These data are shown in Table 9-1.

To put the cash flows on a comparable basis, it is helpful to use present value tables, such as Tables 1 and 2 in the appendix on present value tables. If the interest rate set by management as a desirable return is 10 percent compounded annually, the purchase decision would be evaluated as follows:

		Present Value
Acquisition cost	Present value factor = 1.000 1.000 × $100,000	($100,000)
Net annual savings in cash flows	Present value factor = 3.170 (Table 2: 4 periods, 10%) 3.170 × $40,000	126,800
Disposal value	Present value factor = 0.683 (Table 1: 4 periods, 10%) 0.683 × $20,000	13,660
Net present value		$ 40,460

As long as the net present value is positive, Apple will earn at least 10 percent on the investment. In this case, the return is greater than 10 percent because

TABLE 9-1
Illustration of an Acquisition Decision

	Year 1	Year 2	Year 3	Year 4
Acquisition cost	($100,000)			
Net annual savings in cash flows	40,000	$40,000	$40,000	$40,000
Disposal price				20,000
Net cash flows	($ 60,000)	$40,000	$40,000	$60,000

the net present value is a positive $40,460. Moreover, the net present value is large relative to the investment. Based on this analysis, it appears that Apple's management should make the decision to purchase. However, in making its decision, it should take other important considerations into account, including the costs of training personnel to use the software. It should also allow for the possibility that because of unforeseen circumstances, the savings may not be as great as expected.

Information about acquisitions of long-term assets appears in the investing activities section of the statement of cash flows. In referring to this section of its 2008 annual report, Apple's management makes the following statement:

> The Company's cash payments for capital asset purchases were $1.1 billion during [fiscal] 2008. . . . The Company anticipates utilizing approximately $1.5 billion for capital asset purchases during 2009, including approximately $400 million for Retail facilities and approximately $1.1 billion for corporate facilities and infrastructure.

Financing Long-Term Assets

When management decides to acquire a long-term asset, it must also decide how to finance the purchase. Many financing arrangements are based on the life of the asset. For example, an automobile loan generally spans 4 or 5 years, whereas a mortgage on a house may span 30 years. For a major long-term acquisition, a company may issue stock, long-term notes, or bonds. Some companies are profitable enough to pay for long-term assets out of cash flows from operations. A good place to study a company's investing and financing activities is its statement of cash flows, and a good measure of its ability to finance long-term assets is free cash flow.

Free cash flow is the amount of cash that remains after deducting the funds a company must commit to continue operating at its planned level. The commitments to be covered include current or continuing operations, interest, income taxes, dividends, and net capital expenditures (purchases of plant assets minus sales of plant assets). If a company fails to pay for current or continuing operations, interest, and income taxes, its creditors and the government can take legal action. Although the payment of dividends is not strictly required, dividends normally represent a commitment to stockholders. If they are reduced or eliminated, stockholders will be unhappy, and the price of the company's stock will fall. Net capital expenditures represent management's plans for the future.

A positive free cash flow means that a company has met all its cash commitments and has cash available to reduce debt or to expand its operations. A negative free cash flow means that it will have to sell investments, borrow money, or issue stock in the short term to continue at its planned level. If free cash flow remains negative for several years, a company may not be able to raise cash by issuing stock or bonds.

Using data from **Apple**'s statement of cash flows in its 2008 annual report, we can compute the company's free cash flow as follows (in millions):

$$\begin{aligned}\text{Free Cash Flow} &= \text{Net Cash Flows from Operating Activities} - \text{Dividends} \\ &\quad - \text{Purchases of Plant Assets} + \text{Sales of Plant Assets} \\ &= \$9{,}596 - \$0 - \$1{,}091 + \$0 \\ &= \$8{,}505\end{aligned}$$

This analysis confirms Apple's strong financial position. Its cash flow from operating activities far exceeds its net capital expenditures of $1,091 million. A factor that contributes to its positive free cash flow of $8,505 million is that the company pays no dividends. The financing activities section of Apple's statement of cash flows also indicates that the company, rather than incurring debt for expansion, actually made net investments of $6,760 million.

Applying the Matching Rule

When a company records an expenditure as a long-term asset, it is deferring an expense until a later period. Thus, the current period's profitability looks better than it would if the expenditure had been expensed immediately. Management has considerable latitude in making the judgments and estimates necessary to account for all types and aspects of long-term assets. Sometimes, this latitude is used unwisely and unethically. For example, in the infamous **WorldCom** accounting fraud, management ordered that certain expenditures that should have been recorded as operating expenses be capitalized as long-term assets and written off over several years. The result was an overstatement of income by about $10 billion, which ultimately led to the largest bankruptcy in the history of U.S. business.

To avoid fraudulent reporting of long-term assets, a company's management must apply the matching rule in resolving two important issues. The first is how much of the total cost of a long-term asset to allocate to expense in the current accounting period. The second is how much to retain on the balance sheet as an asset that will benefit future periods. To resolve these issues, management must answer four important questions about the acquisition, use, and disposal of each long-term asset (see Figure 9-4):

FIGURE 9-4
Issues in Accounting for Long-Term Assets

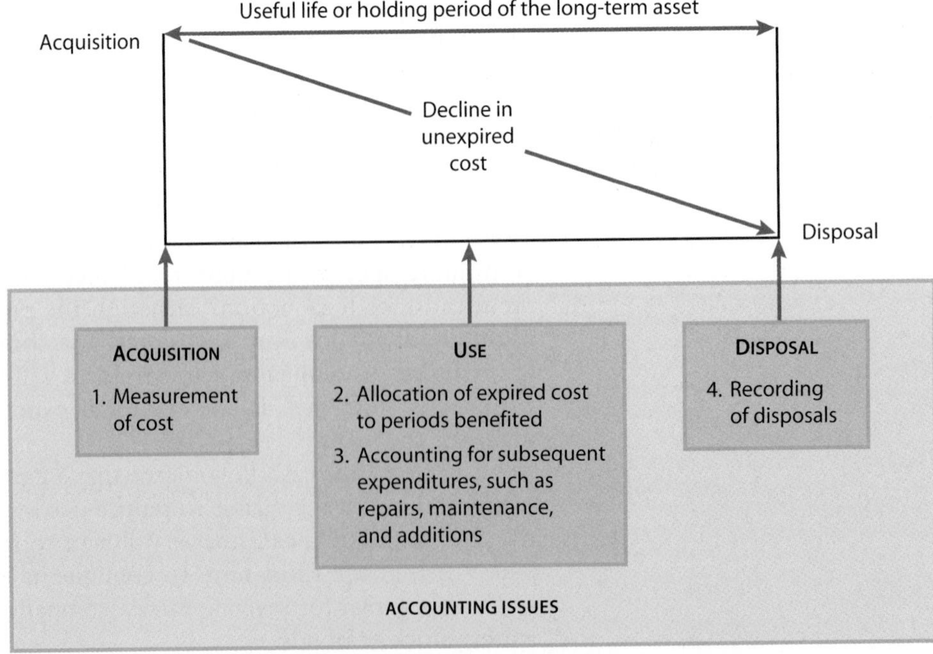

1. How is the cost of the long-term asset determined?
2. How should the expired portion of the cost of the long-term asset be allocated against revenues over time?
3. How should subsequent expenditures, such as repairs and additions, be treated?
4. How should disposal of the long-term asset be recorded?

Management's answers to these questions can be found in the company's annual report under management's discussion and analysis and in the notes to the financial statements.

STOP & APPLY >

Corus Company had cash flows from operating activities during the past year of $133,000. During the year, the company expended $61,000 for property, plant, and equipment; sold property, plant, and equipment for $14,000; and paid dividends of $20,000. Calculate the company's free cash flow. What does the result tell you about the company?

SOLUTION

Net cash flows from operating activities	$133,000
Purchases of property, plant, and equipment	(61,000)
Sales of property, plant, and equipment	14,000
Dividends	(20,000)
Free cash flow	$ 66,000

Corus's operations provide sufficient cash flows to fund its current expansion and dividends without raising additional capital through borrowing or owner investments.

Acquisition Cost of Property, Plant, and Equipment

LO2 Distinguish between *capital expenditures* and *revenue expenditures*, and account for the cost of property, plant, and equipment.

Expenditure refers to a payment or an obligation to make a future payment for an asset, such as a truck, or for a service, such as a repair. Expenditures are classified as capital expenditures or revenue expenditures.

- A **capital expenditure** is an expenditure for the purchase or expansion of a long-term asset. Capital expenditures are recorded in asset accounts because they benefit several future accounting periods.
- A **revenue expenditure** is an expenditure made for the ordinary repairs and maintenance needed to keep a long-term asset in good operating condition. For example, trucks, machines, and other equipment require periodic tune-ups and routine repairs. Expenditures of this type are recorded in expense accounts because their benefits are realized in the current period.

Capital expenditures include outlays for plant assets, natural resources, and intangible assets. They also include expenditures for the following:

- **Additions**, which are enlargements to the physical layout of a plant asset. For example, if a new wing is added to a building, the benefits from the expenditure will be received over several years, and the amount paid should be debited to an asset account.

- **Betterments**, which are improvements to a plant asset but that do not add to the plant's physical layout. Installation of an air-conditioning system is an example. Because betterments provide benefits over a period of years, their costs should be debited to an asset account.
- **Extraordinary repairs**, which are repairs that significantly enhance a plant asset's estimated useful life or residual value. For example, a complete overhaul of a building's heating and cooling system may extend the system's useful life by five years. Extraordinary repairs are typically recorded by reducing the Accumulated Depreciation account; the assumption in doing so is that some of the depreciation previously recorded on the asset has now been eliminated. The effect of the reduction is to increase the asset's carrying value by the cost of the extraordinary repair. The new carrying value should be depreciated over the asset's new estimated useful life.

The distinction between capital and revenue expenditures is important in applying the matching rule. For example, if the purchase of a machine that will benefit a company for several years is mistakenly recorded as a revenue expenditure, the total cost of the machine becomes an expense on the income statement in the current period. As a result, current net income will be reported at a lower amount (understated), and in future periods, net income will be reported at a higher amount (overstated). If, on the other hand, a revenue expenditure, such as the routine overhaul of a piece of machinery, is charged to an asset account, the expense of the current period will be understated. Current net income will be overstated by the same amount, and the net income of future periods will be understated.

General Approach to Acquisition Costs

Study Note

Expenditures necessary to prepare an asset for its intended use are a cost of the asset.

The acquisition cost of property, plant, and equipment includes all expenditures reasonable and necessary to get an asset in place and ready for use. For example, the cost of installing and testing a machine is a legitimate cost of acquiring the machine. However, if the machine is damaged during installation, the cost of repairs is an operating expense, not an acquisition cost.

Acquisition cost is easiest to determine when a purchase is made for cash. In that case, the cost of the asset is equal to the cash paid for it plus expenditures for freight, insurance while in transit, installation, and other necessary related costs. Expenditures for freight, insurance while in transit, and installation are included in the cost of the asset because they are necessary if the asset is to function. In accordance with the matching rule, these expenditures are allocated over the asset's useful life rather than charged as expenses in the current period.

Any interest charges incurred in purchasing an asset are not a cost of the asset; they are a cost of borrowing the money to buy the asset and are therefore an operating expense. An exception to this rule is that interest costs incurred during the construction of an asset are properly included as a cost of the asset.[5]

As a matter of practicality, many companies establish policies that define when an expenditure should be recorded as an expense or as an asset. For example, small expenditures for items that qualify as long-term assets may be treated as expenses because the amounts involved are not material in relation to net income. Thus, although a wastebasket may last for years, it would be recorded as supplies expense rather than as a depreciable asset.

Specific Applications

In the sections that follow, we discuss some of the problems of determining the cost of long-term plant assets.

Study Note

Many costs may be incurred to prepare land for its intended use. All such costs are a cost of the land.

Study Note

The costs of tearing down buildings can be major. Companies may spend millions of dollars imploding buildings so they can remove them and build new ones.

Land The purchase price of land should be debited to the Land account. Other expenditures that should be debited to the Land account include commissions to real estate agents; lawyers' fees; accrued taxes paid by the purchaser; costs of preparing the land to build on, such as the costs of tearing down old buildings and grading the land; and assessments for local improvements, such as putting in streets and sewage systems. The cost of landscaping is usually debited to the Land account because such improvements are relatively permanent. Land is not subject to depreciation because it has an unlimited useful life.

Let us assume that a company buys land for a new retail operation. The net purchase price is $340,000. The company also pays brokerage fees of $12,000, legal fees of $4,000, $20,000 to have an old building on the site torn down, and $2,000 to have the site graded. It receives $8,000 in salvage from the old building. The cost of the land is $370,000, calculated as follows:

Net purchase price		$340,000
Brokerage fees		12,000
Legal fees		4,000
Tearing down old building	$20,000	
Less salvage	8,000	12,000
Grading		2,000
Total cost		$370,000

Land Improvements Some improvements to real estate, such as driveways, parking lots, and fences, have a limited life and thus are subject to depreciation. They should be recorded in an account called Land Improvements rather than in the Land account.

Buildings When a company buys a building, the cost includes the purchase price of the building and all repairs and other expenditures required to put the

Like other costs involved in preparing land for use, the cost of implosion is debited to the Land account. Other expenditures debited to the Land account include the purchase price of the land, brokerage and legal fees involved in the purchase, taxes paid by the purchaser, and landscaping.

Courtesy of Ariel Bravy, 2009/Used under license from shutterstock.com.

building in usable condition. When a company uses a contractor to construct a building, the cost includes the net contract price plus other expenditures necessary to put the building in usable condition. When a company constructs its own building, the cost includes all reasonable and necessary expenditures. Reasonable and necessary expenditures include the costs of materials, labor, part of the overhead and other indirect costs, architects' fees, insurance during construction, interest on construction loans during the period of construction, lawyers' fees, and building permits. Because buildings have a limited useful life, they are subject to depreciation.

Leasehold Improvements Improvements to leased property that become the property of the lessor (the owner of the property) at the end of the lease are called **leasehold improvements**.

For example, a tenant's installation of light fixtures, carpets, or walls would be considered a leasehold improvement. These improvements are usually classified as tangible assets in the property, plant, and equipment section of the balance sheet. Sometimes, they are included in the intangible assets section; the theory in reporting them as intangibles is that because they revert to the lessor at the end of the lease, they are more of a right than a tangible asset. The cost of a leasehold improvement is depreciated or amortized over the remaining term of the lease or the useful life of the improvement, whichever is shorter.

Leasehold improvements are fairly common in large businesses. A study of large companies showed that 22 percent report leasehold improvements. The percentage is likely to be much higher for small businesses because they generally operate in leased premises.[6]

Study Note

The wiring and plumbing of a dental chair are included in the cost of the asset because they are a necessary cost of preparing the asset for use.

Equipment The cost of equipment includes all expenditures connected with purchasing the equipment and preparing it for use. Among these expenditures are the invoice price less cash discounts; freight, including insurance; excise taxes and tariffs; buying expenses; installation costs; and test runs to ready the equipment for operation. Equipment is subject to depreciation.

Group Purchases Companies sometimes purchase land and other assets for a lump sum. Because land has an unlimited life and is a nondepreciable asset, it must have a separate ledger account, and the lump-sum purchase price must be apportioned between the land and the other assets.

For example, suppose a company buys a building and the land on which it is situated for a lump sum of $170,000. The company can apportion the costs by determining what it would have paid for the building and for the land if it had purchased them separately and applying the appropriate percentages to the lump-sum price. Assume that appraisals yield estimates of $20,000 for the land and $180,000 for the building if purchased separately. In that case, 10 percent of the lump-sum price, or $17,000, would be allocated to the land, and 90 percent, or $153,000, would be allocated to the building.

The allocation would be as follows:

	Appraisal	*Percentage*		*Apportionment*	
Land	$ 20,000	10%	($20,000 ÷ $200,000)	$ 17,000	($170,000 × 10%)
Building	180,000	90%	($180,000 ÷ $200,000)	153,000	($170,000 × 90%)
Totals	$200,000	100%		$170,000	

STOP & APPLY >

Match each term below with the corresponding action in the list that follows by writing the appropriate numbers in the blanks:

1. Addition
2. Betterment
3. Extraordinary repair
4. Land
5. Land improvement
6. Leasehold improvement
7. Buildings
8. Equipment
9. Not a capital expenditure

____ a. Purchase of a computer
____ b. Purchase of a lighting system for a parking lot
____ c. Repainting of an existing building
____ d. Installation of a new roof that extends an existing building's useful life
____ e. Construction of a foundation for a new building
____ f. Erection of a new storage facility at the back of an existing building
____ g. Installation of partitions and shelves in a leased space
____ h. Clearing of land in preparation for construction of a new building
____ i. Installation of a new heating system in an existing building

SOLUTION
a. 8; b. 5; c. 9; d. 3; e. 7; f. 1; g. 6; h. 4; i. 2

Depreciation

LO3 Compute depreciation under the straight-line, production, and declining-balance methods.

As we noted earlier, *depreciation* is the periodic allocation of the cost of a tangible asset (other than land and natural resources) over the asset's estimated useful life. In accounting for depreciation, it is important to keep the following points in mind:

- ***All tangible assets except for land have a limited useful life, and the costs of these assets must be distributed as expenses over the years they benefit.*** Physical deterioration and obsolescence are the major factors in limiting a depreciable asset's useful life.
  - **Physical deterioration** results from use and from exposure to the elements, such as wind and sun. Periodic repairs and a sound maintenance policy may keep buildings and equipment in good operating order and prolong their useful lives, but every machine or building must at some point be discarded. Repairs do not eliminate the need for depreciation.
  - **Obsolescence** refers to the process of going out of date. Because of fast-changing technology and fast-changing demands, machinery and even buildings often become obsolete before they wear out.

  Accountants do not distinguish between physical deterioration and obsolescence because they are interested in the length of an asset's useful life, not in what limits its useful life.

- ***Depreciation refers to the allocation of the cost of a plant asset to the periods that benefit from the asset, not to the asset's physical deterioration or decrease***

Study Note

A computer may be functioning as well as it did on the day it was purchased four years ago, but because much faster, more efficient computers have become available, the old computer is now obsolete.

Study Note

Depreciation is the allocation of the acquisition cost of a plant asset, and any similarity between undepreciated cost and current market value is pure coincidence.

in market value. The term *depreciation* describes the gradual conversion of the cost of the asset into an expense.

- ***Depreciation is not a process of valuation.*** Accounting records are not indicators of changing price levels; they are kept in accordance with the cost principle. Because of an advantageous purchase price and market conditions, the value of a building may increase. Nevertheless, because depreciation is a process of allocation, not valuation, depreciation on the building must continue to be recorded. Eventually, the building will wear out or become obsolete regardless of interim fluctuations in market value.

Factors in Computing Depreciation

Four factors affect the computation of depreciation:

1. ***Cost.*** As explained earlier, cost is the net purchase price of an asset plus all reasonable and necessary expenditures to get it in place and ready for use.
2. ***Residual value.*** **Residual value** is the portion of an asset's acquisition cost that a company expects to recover when it disposes of the asset. Other terms used to describe residual value are *salvage value, disposal value*, and *trade-in value*.
3. ***Depreciable cost.*** **Depreciable cost** is an asset's cost less its residual value. For example, a truck that cost $24,000 and that has a residual value of $6,000 would have a depreciable cost of $18,000. Depreciable cost must be allocated over the useful life of the asset.
4. ***Estimated useful life.*** **Estimated useful life** is the total number of service units expected from a long-term asset. Service units may be measured in terms of the years an asset is expected to be used, the units it is expected to produce, the miles it is expected to be driven, or similar measures. In computing an asset's estimated useful life, an accountant should consider all relevant information, including past experience with similar assets, the asset's present condition, the company's repair and maintenance policy, and current technological and industry trends.

Study Note

It is depreciable cost, not acquisition cost, that is allocated over a plant asset's useful life.

Study Note

Residual value and useful life are, at best, educated guesses.

Depreciation is recorded at the end of an accounting period with an adjusting entry that takes the following form:

A	= L +	SE
−XXX		−XXX

Depreciation Expense—Asset Name	XXX	
Accumulated Depreciation—Asset Name		XXX
To record depreciation for the period		

Methods of Computing Depreciation

Many methods are used to allocate the cost of plant assets to accounting periods through depreciation. Each is appropriate in certain circumstances. The most common methods are the straight-line method, the production method, and an accelerated method known as the declining-balance method.

Straight-Line Method When the **straight-line method** is used to calculate depreciation, the asset's depreciable cost is spread evenly over the estimated useful life of the asset. The straight-line method is based on the assumption that depreciation depends only on the passage of time. The depreciation expense for each

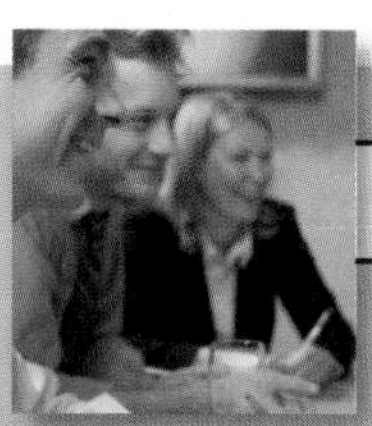

FOCUS ON BUSINESS PRACTICE

How Long Is the Useful Life of an Airplane?

Most airlines depreciate their planes over an estimated useful life of 10 to 20 years. But how long will a properly maintained plane really last? Western Airlines paid $3.3 million for a new Boeing 737 in July 1968. More than 78,000 flights and 30 years later, this aircraft was still flying for Vanguard Airlines, a no-frills airline. Among the other airlines that have owned this plane are **Piedmont**, **Delta**, and **US Airways**. Virtually every part of the plane has been replaced over the years. **Boeing** believes the plane could theoretically make double the number of flights before it is retired.

The useful lives of many types of assets can be extended indefinitely if the assets are correctly maintained, but proper accounting in accordance with the matching rule requires depreciation over a "reasonable" useful life. Each airline that owned the plane would have accounted for the plane in this way.

period is computed by dividing the depreciable cost (the cost of the depreciating asset less its estimated residual value) by the number of accounting periods in the asset's estimated useful life. The rate of depreciation is the same in each year.

Suppose, for example, that a delivery truck cost $20,000 and has an estimated residual value of $2,000 at the end of its estimated useful life of five years. Under the straight-line method, the annual depreciation would be $3,600, calculated as follows:

$$\frac{\text{Cost} - \text{Residual Value}}{\text{Estimated Useful Life}} = \frac{\$20{,}000 - \$2{,}000}{5 \text{ years}} = \$3{,}600 \text{ per year}$$

Table 9-2 shows the depreciation schedule for the five years. Note that in addition to annual depreciation's being the same each year, the accumulated depreciation increases uniformly, and the carrying value decreases uniformly until it reaches the estimated residual value.

Study Note

The production method is appropriate when a company has widely fluctuating rates of production. For example, carpet mills often close during the first two weeks in July but may run double shifts in September. With the production method, depreciation would be in direct relation to a mill's units of output.

Production Method The **production method** is based on the assumption that depreciation is solely the result of use and that the passage of time plays no role in the process. If we assume that the delivery truck in the previous example has an estimated useful life of 90,000 miles, the depreciation cost per mile would be determined as follows:

$$\frac{\text{Cost} - \text{Residual Value}}{\text{Estimated Units of Useful Life}} = \frac{\$20{,}000 - \$2{,}000}{90{,}000} = \$0.20 \text{ per mile}$$

TABLE 9-2
Depreciation Schedule, Straight-Line Method

	Cost	Annual Depreciation	Accumulated Depreciation	Carrying Value
Date of purchase	$20,000	—	—	$20,000
End of first year	20,000	$3,600	$ 3,600	16,400
End of second year	20,000	3,600	7,200	12,800
End of third year	20,000	3,600	10,800	9,200
End of fourth year	20,000	3,600	14,400	5,600
End of fifth year	20,000	3,600	18,000	2,000

TABLE 9-3
Depreciation Schedule, Production Method

	Cost	Miles	Annual Depreciation	Accumulated Depreciation	Carrying Value
Date of purchase	$20,000	—	—	—	$20,000
End of first year	20,000	20,000	$4,000	$ 4,000	16,000
End of second year	20,000	30,000	6,000	10,000	10,000
End of third year	20,000	10,000	2,000	12,000	8,000
End of fourth year	20,000	20,000	4,000	16,000	4,000
End of fifth year	20,000	10,000	2,000	18,000	2,000

If the truck were driven 20,000 miles in the first year, 30,000 miles in the second, 10,000 miles in the third, 20,000 miles in the fourth, and 10,000 miles in the fifth, the depreciation schedule for the truck would be as shown in Table 9-3.

As you can see, the amount of depreciation each year is directly related to the units of use. The accumulated depreciation increases annually in direct relation to these units, and the carrying value decreases each year until it reaches the estimated residual value.

The production method should be used only when the output of an asset over its useful life can be estimated with reasonable accuracy. In addition, the unit used to measure the estimated useful life of an asset should be appropriate for the asset. For example, the number of items produced may be an appropriate measure for one machine, but the number of hours of use may be a better measure for another.

> **Study Note**
> Accelerated depreciation is appropriate for assets that provide the greatest benefits in their early years. Under an accelerated method, depreciation charges will be highest in years when revenue generation from the asset is highest.

Declining-Balance Method An **accelerated method** of depreciation results in relatively large amounts of depreciation in the early years of an asset's life and smaller amounts in later years. This type of method, which is based on the passage of time, assumes that many plant assets are most efficient when new and so provide the greatest benefits in their first years. It is consistent with the matching rule to allocate more depreciation to an asset in its earlier years than to later ones if the benefits it provides in its early years are greater than those it provides later on.

Fast-changing technologies often cause equipment to become obsolescent and lose service value rapidly. In such cases, using an accelerated method is appropriate because it allocates more depreciation to earlier years than to later ones. Another argument in favor of using an accelerated method is that repair expense is likely to increase as an asset ages. Thus, the total of repair and depreciation expense will remain fairly constant over the years. This result naturally assumes that the services received from the asset are roughly equal from year to year.

The **declining-balance method** is the most common accelerated method of depreciation. With this method, depreciation is computed by applying a fixed rate to the carrying value (the declining balance) of a tangible long-term asset. It therefore results in higher depreciation charges in the early years of the asset's life. Though any fixed rate can be used, the most common rate is a percentage equal to twice the straight-line depreciation percentage. When twice the straight-line rate is used, the method is usually called the **double-declining-balance method**.

> **Study Note**
> The double-declining-balance method is the only method presented here in which the residual value is not deducted before beginning the depreciation calculation.

In our example of the straight-line method, the delivery truck had an estimated useful life of five years, and the annual depreciation rate for the truck was therefore 20 percent (100 percent ÷ 5 years). Under the double-declining-balance method, the fixed rate would be 40 percent (2 × 20 percent). This fixed rate is applied to the carrying value that remains at the end of each year. With this method, the depreciation schedule would be as shown in Table 9-4.

TABLE 9-4
Depreciation Schedule, Double-Declining-Balance Method

	Cost	Annual Depreciation	Accumulated Depreciation	Carrying Value
Date of purchase	$20,000	—	—	$20,000
End of first year	20,000	(40% × $20,000) = $8,000	$ 8,000	12,000
End of second year	20,000	(40% × $12,000) = 4,800	12,800	7,200
End of third year	20,000	(40% × $ 7,200) = 2,880	15,680	4,320
End of fourth year	20,000	(40% × $ 4,320) = 1,728	17,408	2,592
End of fifth year	20,000	592*	18,000	2,000

*Depreciation is limited to the amount necessary to reduce carrying value to residual value: $2,592 (previous carrying value) − $2,000 (residual value) = $592.

Note that the fixed rate is always applied to the carrying value at the end of the previous year. Depreciation is greatest in the first year and declines each year after that. The depreciation in the last year is limited to the amount necessary to reduce carrying value to residual value.

Comparison of the Three Methods Figure 9-5 compares yearly depreciation and carrying value under the three methods. The graph on the left shows yearly depreciation. As you can see, straight-line depreciation is uniform at $3,600 per year over the five-year period. The double-declining-balance method begins at $8,000 and decreases each year to amounts that are less than straight-line (ultimately, $592). The production method does not generate a regular pattern because of the random fluctuation of the depreciation from year to year.

The graph on the right side of Figure 9-5 shows the carrying value under the three methods. Each method starts in the same place (cost of $20,000) and ends at the same place (residual value of $2,000). However, the patterns of carrying value during the asset's useful life differ. For instance, the carrying value under the straight-line method is always greater than under the double-declining-balance method, except at the beginning and end of the asset's useful life.

FIGURE 9-5
Graphic Comparison of Three Methods of Determining Depreciation

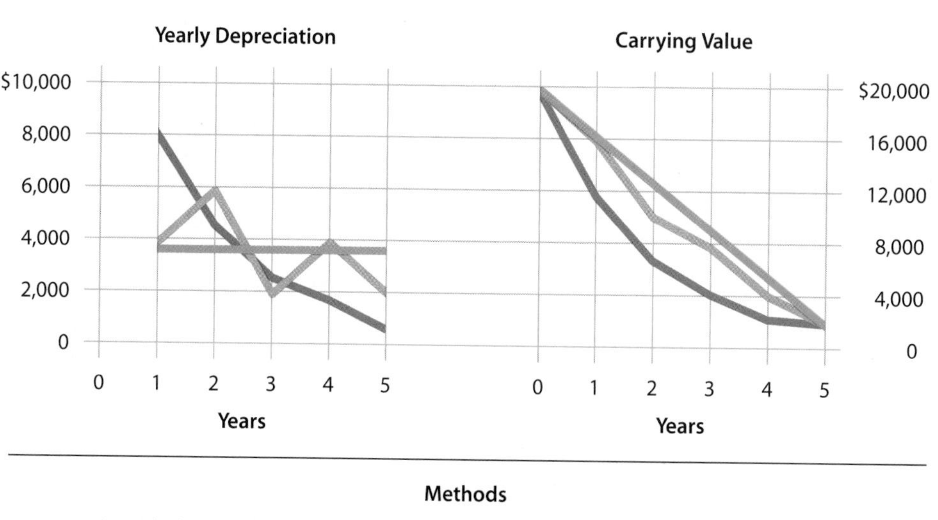

FOCUS ON BUSINESS PRACTICE

Accelerated Methods Save Money!

As shown in the figure below, an AICPA study of 600 large companies found that the overwhelming majority used the straight-line method of depreciation for financial reporting. Only about 7 percent used some type of accelerated method, and 3 percent used the production method. These figures tend to be misleading about the importance of accelerated depreciation methods, however, especially when it comes to income taxes. Federal income tax laws allow either the straight-line method or an accelerated method, and for tax purposes, about 75 percent of the 600 companies studied preferred an accelerated method.

Companies use different methods of depreciation for good reason. The straight-line method can be advantageous for financial reporting because it can produce the highest net income, and an accelerated method can be beneficial for tax purposes because it can result in lower income taxes.

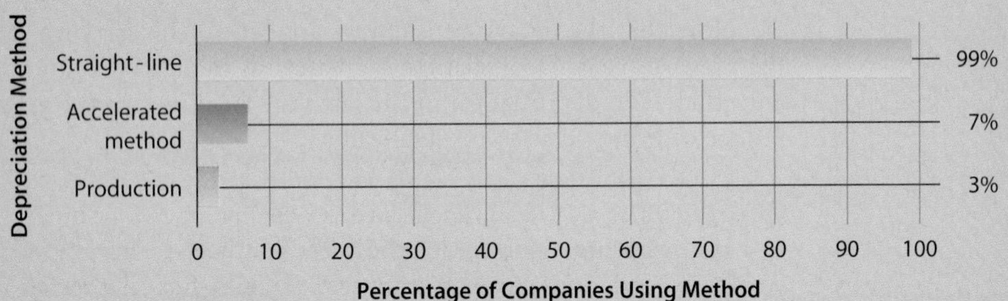

Note: Total percentage exceeds 100 because some companies used different methods for different types of depreciable assets.
Source: "Depreciation Methods Used by 600 Large Companies." Copyright © 2008 by AICPA. Reproduced with permission.

Special Issues in Depreciation

Other issues in depreciating assets include group depreciation, depreciation for partial years, revision of depreciation rates, and accelerated cost recovery for tax purposes.

Group Depreciation The estimated useful life of an asset is the average length of time assets of the same type are expected to last. For example, the average useful life of a particular type of machine may be six years, but some machines in this category may last only two or three years, while others may last eight or nine years or longer. For this reason, and for convenience, large companies group similar assets, such as machines, trucks, and pieces of office equipment, to calculate depreciation. This method, called **group depreciation**, is widely used in all fields of industry and business. A survey of large businesses indicated that 65 percent used group depreciation for all or part of their plant assets.[7]

Depreciation for Partial Years To simplify our examples of depreciation, we have assumed that plant assets were purchased at the beginning or end of an accounting period. Usually, however, businesses buy assets when they are needed and sell or discard them when they are no longer needed or useful. The time of year is normally not a factor in the decision. Thus, it is often necessary to calculate depreciation for partial years. Some companies compute depreciation to the nearest month. Others use the half-year convention, in which one-half year of depreciation is taken in the year the asset is purchased and one-half year is taken in the year the asset is sold.

Revision of Depreciation Rates Because a depreciation rate is based on an estimate of an asset's useful life, the periodic depreciation charge is seldom precise. It is sometimes very inadequate or excessive. Such a situation may result from an underestimate or overestimate of the asset's useful life or from a wrong estimate of its residual value. What should a company do when it discovers that a piece of equipment that it has used for several years will last a shorter—or longer—time than originally estimated? Sometimes, it is necessary to revise the estimate of useful life so that the periodic depreciation expense increases or decreases. Then, to reflect the revised situation, the remaining depreciable cost of the asset is spread over the remaining years of useful life.

With this technique, the annual depreciation expense is increased or decreased to reduce the asset's carrying value to its residual value at the end of its remaining useful life. For example, suppose a delivery truck cost $14,000 and has a residual value of $2,000. At the time of the purchase, the truck was expected to last six years, and it was depreciated on the straight-line basis. However, after two years of intensive use, it is determined that the truck will last only two more years, but its residual value at the end of the two years will still be $2,000. In other words, at the end of the second year, the truck's estimated useful life is reduced from six years to four years. At that time, the asset account and its related accumulated depreciation account would be as follows:

Delivery Truck				Accumulated Depreciation—Delivery Truck			
Cost	14,000					Depreciation, Year 1	2,000
						Depreciation, Year 2	2,000

The remaining depreciable cost is computed as follows:

Cost	−	Depreciation Already Taken	−	Residual Value	
$14,000	−	$4,000	−	$2,000	= $8,000

The new annual periodic depreciation charge is computed by dividing the remaining depreciable cost of $8,000 by the remaining useful life of two years. Therefore, the new periodic depreciation charge is $4,000. This method of revising depreciation is used widely in industry. It is also supported by *Opinion No. 9* and *Opinion No. 20* of the Accounting Principles Board of the AICPA.

Study Note

For financial reporting purposes, the objective is to measure performance accurately. For tax purposes, the objective is to minimize tax liability.

Special Rules for Tax Purposes Over the years, to encourage businesses to invest in new plant and equipment, Congress has revised the federal income tax law to provide an economic stimulus to the economy. For instance, for tax purposes the law allows rapid write-offs of plant assets through accelerated depreciation, which differs considerably from the depreciation methods most companies use for financial reporting. Tax methods of depreciation are usually not acceptable for financial reporting because the periods over which deductions may be taken are often shorter than the assets' estimated useful lives. The most recent changes in the federal income tax law—the **Economic Stimulus Act of 2008**—allows a small company to expense the first $250,000 of equipment expenditures rather than recording them as assets and depreciating them over their useful lives. Also, for assets that are subject to depreciation, there is a bonus first-year deduction. These laws are quite complex and are the subject of more advanced courses.

STOP & APPLY >

On January 13, 2010, Chen Company purchased a company car for $47,500. Chen expects the car to last five years or 120,000 miles, with an estimated residual value of $7,500 at the end of that time. During 2011, the car is driven 24,000 miles. Chen's year-end is December 31. Compute the depreciation for 2011 under each of the following methods: (1) straight-line, (2) production, and (3) double-declining-balance. Using the amount computed in (3), prepare the entry in journal form to record depreciation expense for the second year, and show how the Company Car account would appear on the balance sheet.

SOLUTION

Depreciation computed:

Straight-line method: ($47,500 − $7,500) ÷ 5 years = $8,000

Production method: ($47,500 − $7,500) ÷ 120,000 miles = $0.33 1/3 per mile

24,000 miles × $0.33 1/3 = $8,000

Double-declining-balance method: 1/5 × 2 = 0.40

Year 1: $47,500 × 0.40 = $19,000

Year 2: ($47,500 − $19,000) × 0.40 = $11,400

Entry in journal form:

Depreciation Expense	$11,400	
Accumulated Depreciation		$11,400

Balance sheet presentation:

Company car	$47,500	
Less accumulated depreciation	30,400	$17,100

Disposal of Depreciable Assets

LO4 Account for the disposal of depreciable assets.

When plant assets are no longer useful because they have physically deteriorated or become obsolete, a company can dispose of them by discarding them, selling them for cash, or trading them in on the purchase of a new asset. Regardless of how a company disposes of a plant asset, it must record depreciation expense for the partial year up to the date of disposal. This step is required because the company used the asset until that date and, under the matching rule, the accounting period should receive the proper allocation of depreciation expense.

In the next sections, we show how to record each type of disposal. As our example, we assume that KOT Company buys a machine on January 2, 2009, for $13,000 and plans to depreciate it on a straight-line basis over an estimated useful life of eight years. The machine's residual value at the end of eight years is estimated to be $600. On December 31, 2014, the balances of the relevant accounts are as shown below, and on January 2, 2015, management disposes of the asset.

Study Note

When it disposes of an asset, a company must bring the depreciation up to date and remove all evidence of ownership of the asset, including the contra account Accumulated Depreciation.

Machinery		Accumulated Depreciation—Machinery	
13,000			9,300

Discarded Plant Assets

A plant asset rarely lasts exactly as long as its estimated life. If it lasts longer, it is not depreciated past the point at which its carrying value equals its residual value. The purpose of depreciation is to spread the depreciable cost of an asset over its estimated life. Thus, the total accumulated depreciation should never exceed the total depreciable cost. If an asset remains in use beyond the end of its estimated life, its cost and accumulated depreciation remain in the ledger accounts. Proper records will thus be available for maintaining control over plant assets. If the residual value is zero, the carrying value of a fully depreciated asset is zero until the asset is disposed of. If such an asset is discarded, no gain or loss results. In our example, however, the discarded equipment has a carrying value of $3,700 at the time of its disposal. The carrying value is computed from the T accounts as machinery of $13,000 less accumulated depreciation of $9,300. A loss equal to the carrying value should be recorded when the machine is discarded, as follows:

A	= L +	SE
+ 9,300		−3,700
−13,000		

2015			
Jan. 2	Accumulated Depreciation–Machinery	9,300	
	Loss on Disposal of Machinery	3,700	
	Machinery		13,000
	Disposal of machine no longer in use		

Gains and losses on disposals of plant assets are classified as other revenues and expenses on the income statement.

Study Note

When an asset is discarded or sold for cash, the gain or loss equals cash received minus the carrying value.

Plant Assets Sold for Cash

The entry to record a plant asset sold for cash is similar to the one just illustrated, except that the receipt of cash should also be recorded. The following entries in journal form show how to record the sale of a machine under three assumptions about the selling price. In the first case, the $3,700 cash received is exactly equal to the $3,700 carrying value of the machine; therefore, no gain or loss occurs:

A	= L +	SE
+ 3,700		
+ 9,300		
−13,000		

2015			
Jan. 2	Cash	3,700	
	Accumulated Depreciation–Machinery	9,300	
	Machinery		13,000
	Sale of machine for carrying value; no gain or loss		

In the second case, the $2,000 cash received is less than the carrying value of 3,700, so a loss of $1,700 is recorded:

A	= L +	SE
+ 2,000		−1,700
+ 9,300		
−13,000		

2015			
Jan. 2	Cash	2,000	
	Accumulated Depreciation–Machinery	9,300	
	Loss on Sale of Machinery	1,700	
	Machinery		13,000
	Sale of machine at less than carrying value; loss of $1,700 ($3,700 − $2,000) recorded		

In the third case, the $4,000 cash received exceeds the carrying value of $3,700, so a gain of $300 is recorded:

A	= L +	SE
+ 4,000		+300
+ 9,300		
−13,000		

2015			
Jan. 2	Cash	4,000	
	Accumulated Depreciation–Machinery	9,300	
	Machinery		13,000
	Gain on Sale of Machinery		300
	Sale of machine at more than the carrying value; gain of $300 ($4,000 − $3,700) recorded		

Exchanges of Plant Assets

As we have noted, businesses can dispose of plant assets by trading them in on the purchase of other plant assets. Exchanges may involve similar assets, such as an old machine traded in on a newer model, or dissimilar assets, such as a cement mixer traded in on a truck. In either case, the purchase price is reduced by the amount of the trade-in allowance.

Basically, accounting for exchanges of plant assets is similar to accounting for sales of plant assets for cash. If the trade-in allowance is greater than the asset's carrying value, the company realizes a gain. If the allowance is less, it suffers a loss. (Some special rules apply and are addressed in more advanced courses.)

& APPLY >

Chen Company sold a company car that cost $47,500 and on which $30,400 of accumulated depreciation had been recorded on January 2, the first day of business of the current year. For each of the following assumptions, prepare the entry in journal form (without explanation) for the disposal. (1) The car was sold for $17,100 cash. (2) The car was sold for $15,000 cash. (3) The car was sold for $20,000 cash.

SOLUTION

(1) Cash	17,100	
Company Car	30,400	
Accumulated Depreciation–Company Car		47,500
(2) Cash	15,000	
Company Car	30,400	
Loss on Sale of Company Car	2,100	
Accumulated Depreciation–Company Car		47,500
(3) Cash	20,000	
Company Car	30,400	
Accumulated Depreciation–Company Car		47,500
Gain on Sale of Company Car		2,900

Natural Resources

LO5 Identify the issues related to accounting for natural resources, and compute depletion.

Natural resources are long-term assets that appear on a balance sheet with descriptive titles like Timberlands, Oil and Gas Reserves, and Mineral Deposits. The distinguishing characteristic of these assets is that they are converted to inventory by cutting, pumping, mining, or other extraction methods.

Natural resources are recorded at acquisition cost, which may include some costs of development. As a natural resource is extracted and converted to inventory, its asset account must be proportionally reduced. For example, the carrying value of oil reserves on the balance sheet is reduced by the proportional cost of the barrels pumped during the period. As a result, the original cost of the oil reserves is gradually reduced, and depletion is recognized in the amount of the decrease.

Depletion

Depletion refers not only to the exhaustion of a natural resource, but also to the proportional allocation of the cost of a natural resource to the units extracted. The way in which the cost of a natural resource is allocated closely resembles the production method of calculating depreciation. When a natural resource is purchased or developed, the total units that will be available, such as barrels of oil, tons of coal, or board-feet of lumber, must be estimated. The depletion cost per unit is determined by dividing the cost of the natural resource (less residual value, if any) by the estimated number of units available. The amount of the depletion cost for each accounting period is then computed by multiplying the depletion cost per unit by the number of units extracted and sold.

For example, suppose a mine was purchased for \$3,600,000 and that it has an estimated residual value of \$600,000 and contains an estimated 3,000,000 tons of coal. The depletion charge per ton of coal is \$1, calculated as follows:

$$\frac{\$3,600,000 - \$600,000}{3,000,000 \text{ tons}} = \$1 \text{ per ton}$$

When you season your food with salt, you probably don't think of it as using a natural resource, but that is what salt is. Table salt is produced by evaporation methods; rock salt, which is used for highway maintenance, is mined. Natural resources are considered components of property, plant, and equipment. These long-term assets are recorded at acquisition cost, which may include some costs of development.

Courtesy of AP Images/The WIchita Eagle, Brian Com.

Thus, if 230,000 tons of coal are mined and sold during the first year, the depletion charge for the year is $230,000. This charge would be recorded as follows:

A	= L +	SE
−230,000		−230,000

		Dr.	Cr.
Dec. 31	Depletion Expense–Coal Deposits	230,000	
	Accumulated Depletion–Coal Deposits		230,000
	To record depletion of coal mine: $1 per ton for 230,000 tons mined and sold		

On the balance sheet, data for the mine would be presented as follows:

Coal deposits	$3,600,000	
Less accumulated depletion	230,000	$3,370,000

Sometimes, a natural resource is not sold in the year it is extracted. It is important to note that it would then be recorded as a depletion *expense* in the year it is *sold*. The part not sold is considered inventory.

Depreciation of Related Plant Assets

The extraction of natural resources generally requires special on-site buildings and equipment (e.g., conveyors, drills, and pumps). The useful life of these plant assets may be longer than the estimated time it will take to deplete the resources. However, a company may plan to abandon these assets after all the resources have been extracted because they no longer serve a useful purpose. In this case, they should be depreciated on the same basis as the depletion.

> **Study Note**
> A company may abandon equipment that is still in good working condition because of the expense involved in dismantling the equipment and moving it to another site.

For example, if machinery with a useful life of ten years is installed on an oil field that is expected to be depleted in eight years, the machinery should be depreciated over the eight-year period, using the production method. That way, each year's depreciation will be proportional to the year's depletion. If one-sixth of the oil field's total reserves is pumped in one year, then the depreciation should be one-sixth of the machinery's cost minus the residual value.

If the useful life of a long-term plant asset is less than the expected life of the resource, the shorter life should be used to compute depreciation. In such cases, or when an asset will not be abandoned after all reserves have been depleted, other depreciation methods, such as straight-line or declining-balance, are appropriate.

Development and Exploration Costs in the Oil and Gas Industry

The costs of exploring and developing oil and gas resources can be accounted for under one of two methods. Under **successful efforts accounting**, the cost of successful exploration—for example, producing an oil well—is a cost of the resource. It should be recorded as an asset and depleted over the estimated life of the resource. The cost of an unsuccessful exploration—such as the cost of a dry well—is written off immediately as a loss. Because of these immediate write-offs, successful efforts accounting is considered the more conservative method and is used by most large oil companies.

On the other hand, smaller, independent oil companies argue that the cost of dry wells is part of the overall cost of the systematic development of an oil field and is thus a part of the cost of producing wells. Under the **full-costing method**,

FOCUS ON BUSINESS PRACTICE

How Do You Measure What's Underground? With a Good Guess.

Accounting standards require publicly traded energy companies to disclose in their annual reports their production activities, estimates of their proven oil and gas reserves, and estimates of the present value of the future cash flows those reserves are expected to generate. The figures are not easy to estimate. After all, the reserves are often miles underground or beneath deep water. These figures are therefore considered "supplementary" and not reliable enough to be audited independently. As a result, some companies have overestimated their reserves and thus overestimated their future prospects. Apparently, some managers at **Royal Dutch/Shell Group** were receiving bonuses based on the amount of new reserves added to the annual report. When the company announced that it was reducing its reported reserves by 20 percent, the price of its stock dropped.[8]

all costs, including the cost of dry wells, are recorded as assets and depleted over the estimated life of the producing resources. This method tends to improve a company's earnings performance in its early years.

The Financial Accounting Standards Board permits the use of either method.[9]

STOP & APPLY >

Ouyang Mining Company paid $8,800,000 for land containing an estimated 40 million tons of ore. The land without the ore is estimated to be worth $2,000,000. The company spent $1,380,000 to erect buildings on the site and $2,400,000 on installing equipment. The buildings have an estimated useful life of 30 years, and the equipment has an estimated useful life of 10 years. Because of the remote location, neither the buildings nor the equipment has a residual value. The company expects that it can mine all the usable ore in 10 years. During its first year of operation, it mined and sold 2,800,000 tons of ore.

1. Compute the depletion charge per ton.
2. Compute the depletion expense that Ouyang Mining should record for its first year of operation.
3. Determine the depreciation expense for the year for the buildings, making it proportional to the depletion.
4. Determine the depreciation expense for the year for the equipment under two alternatives: (a) making the expense proportional to the depletion, and (b) using the straight-line method.

SOLUTION

1. $\dfrac{\$8{,}800{,}000 - \$2{,}000{,}000}{40{,}000{,}000 \text{ tons}} = \$0.17 \text{ per ton}$

2. 2,800,000 tons × $0.17 per ton = $476,000

3. $\dfrac{2{,}800{,}000 \text{ tons}}{40{,}000{,}000 \text{ tons}} \times \$1{,}380{,}000 = \$96{,}600$

4. a. $\dfrac{2{,}800{,}000 \text{ tons}}{40{,}000{,}000 \text{ tons}} \times \$2{,}400{,}000 = \$168{,}000$

   b. $\dfrac{\$2{,}400{,}000}{10 \text{ years}} \times 1 \text{ year} = \$240{,}000$

Intangible Assets

LO6 Identify the issues related to accounting for intangible assets, including research and development costs and goodwill.

An intangible asset is both long term and nonphysical. Its value comes from the long-term rights or advantages it affords its owner. Table 9-5 describes the most common types of intangible assets—goodwill, trademarks and brand names, copyrights, patents, franchises and licenses, leaseholds, software, noncompete covenants, and customer lists—and their accounting treatment. Like intangible assets, some current assets—for example, accounts receivable and certain prepaid expenses—have no physical substance, but because current assets are short term, they are not classified as intangible assets.

TABLE 9-5 Accounting for Intangible Assets

Type	Description	Usual Accounting Treatment
	Subject to Amortization and Annual Impairment Test	
Copyright	An exclusive right granted by the federal government to reproduce and sell literary, musical, and other artistic materials and computer programs for a period of the author's life plus 70 years	Record at acquisition cost, and amortize over the asset's useful life, which is often much shorter than its legal life. For example, the cost of paperback rights to a popular novel would typically be amortized over a useful life of two to four years.
Patent	An exclusive right granted by the federal government for a period of 20 years to make a particular product or use a specific process. A design may be granted a patent for 14 years.	The cost of successfully defending a patent in a patent infringement suit is added to the acquisition cost of the patent. Amortize over the asset's useful life, which may be less than its legal life.
Leasehold	A right to occupy land or buildings under a long-term rental contract. For example, if Company A sells or subleases its right to use a retail location to Company B for ten years in return for one or more rental payments, Company B has purchased a leasehold.	The lessor (Company A) debits Leasehold for the amount of the rental payment and amortizes it over the remaining life of the lease. The lessee (Company B) debits payments to Lease Expense.
Software	Capitalized costs of computer programs developed for sale, lease, or internal use	Record the amount of capitalizable production costs, and amortize over the estimated economic life of the product.
Noncompete covenant	A contract limiting the rights of others to compete in a specific industry or line of business for a specified period	Record at acquisition cost, and amortize over the contract period.
Customer list	A list of customers or subscribers	Debit Customer Lists for amount paid, and amortize over the asset's expected life.
	Subject to Annual Impairment Test Only	
Goodwill	The excess of the amount paid for a business over the fair market value of the business's net assets	Debit Goodwill for the acquisition cost, and review impairment annually.
Trademark, Brand name	A registered symbol or name that can be used only by its owner to identify a product or service	Debit Trademark or Brand Name for the acquisition cost, and amortize it over a reasonable life.
Franchise, License	A right to an exclusive territory or market, or the right to use a formula, technique, process, or design	Debit Franchise or License for the acquisition cost, and amortize it over a reasonable life, not to exceed 40 years.

FIGURE 9-6
Intangible Assets Reported by 600 Large Companies

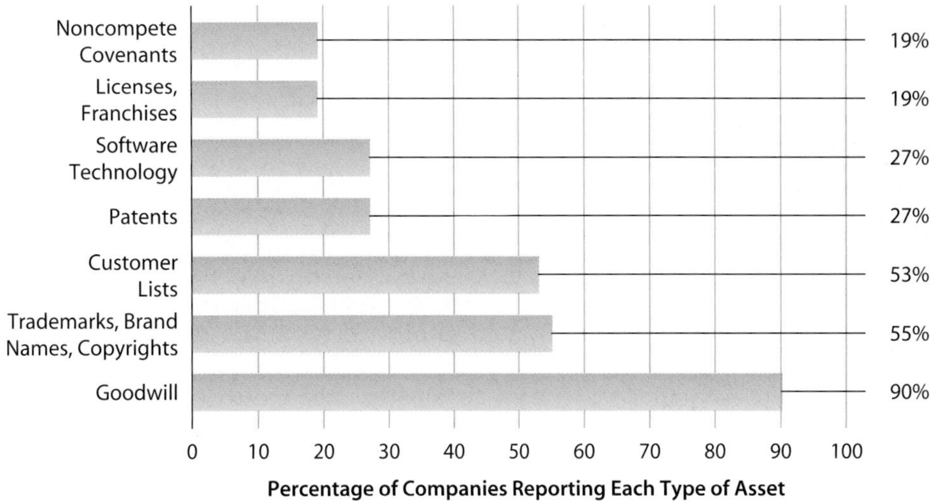

Source: Data from American Institute of Certified Public Accountants, *Accounting Trends & Techniques* (New York: AICPA, 2008).

Figure 9-6 shows the percentage of companies (out of 600 companies surveyed) that report the various types of intangible assets. For some companies, intangible assets make up a substantial portion of total assets. As was noted in the Decision Point, **Apple Computer**'s goodwill, other acquired intangible assets, and capitalized software costs amounted to $559 million in 2008. How these assets are accounted for has a major effect on Apple's performance.

The purchase of an intangible asset is a special kind of capital expenditure. Such assets are accounted for at acquisition cost—that is, the amount that a company paid for them. Some intangible assets, such as goodwill and trademarks, may be acquired at little or no cost. Even though these assets may have great value and be needed for profitable operations, a company should include them on its balance sheet only if it purchased them from another party at a price established in the marketplace. When a company develops its own intangible assets, it should record the costs of development as expenses. An exception to this is the cost of internally developed computer software after a working prototype of the software has been developed.

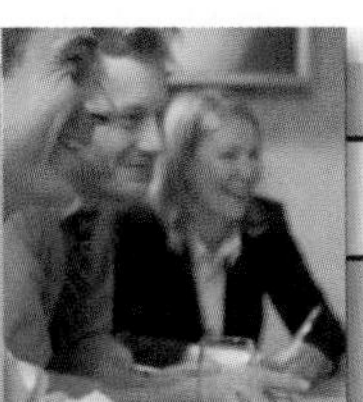

FOCUS ON BUSINESS PRACTICE

Who's Number One in Brands?

Brands are intangible assets that often do not appear on a company's balance sheet because rather than purchasing them, the company has developed them over time. A recent report attempted to value brands by the discounted present value of future cash flows.[11] According to the report, the ten most valuable brands in the world were as follows:

Coca-Cola
IBM
Microsoft
GE
Nokia
Toyota
Intel
McDonald's
Disney
Google

Coca-Cola's brand was valued at almost $6.7 billion, whereas Google's brand was valued at $5.6 billion. Where did **Apple Computer** stand? It was number 24 at $13.7 billion, up from number 39 one year before, which reflects the increased brand power from the great success of the iPod and iPhone.

FOCUS ON BUSINESS PRACTICE

Should a Customer List Be Amortized?

One of the most valuable intangible assets some companies have is a list of customers. The Internal Revenue Service has argued that a customer list has an *indefinite useful life* and therefore cannot be used to provide tax deductions through amortization. However, the U.S. Supreme Court has upheld the right to amortize the value of a customer list, arguing that it has a *limited useful life*. This ruling has benefited numerous businesses. For example, **The New York Times Company**, a major newspaper, has spent $28 million on subscriber lists and amortized them to the extent of $17 million, leaving a carrying value of $11 million.[12]

Purchased intangible assets are recorded at cost, or at fair value when purchased as part of a group of assets. The useful life of an intangible asset is the period over which the asset is expected to contribute to future cash flows of the entity. The useful life may be definite or indefinite:[10]

- Definite useful life: A definite useful life means the useful life is subject to a legal limit or can be reasonably estimated. Examples include patents, copyrights, and leaseholds. Often the estimated useful lives of these assets are less than their legal limits. The cost of an intangible asset with a definite useful life should be allocated to expense through periodic amortization over the asset's useful life in much the same way that a building is depreciated.
- Indefinite useful life: An indefinite useful life means that the useful life of the asset is not limited by legal, regulatory, contractual, competitive, economic, or other factors. This definition does not imply that these assets last forever. Examples can include trademarks and brands. The costs of intangible assets with an indefinite life are not amortized as long as circumstances continue to support an indefinite life.

Study Note

The cost of a customer list may be recorded as an asset because it will be used over and over and will benefit future accounting periods.

All intangible assets, whether they have a definite or indefinite life, are subject to an annual impairment test to determine if the assets justify their value on the balance sheet. If it is determined that they have lost some or all of their value in producing future cash flows, they should be written down to their fair value or to zero if they have no fair value. The amount of the write-down is shown on the income statement as an impairment charge (deduction) in income from operations.

To illustrate these procedures, suppose WATER Bottling Company purchases a patent on a unique bottle cap for $36,000. The purchase would be recorded with an entry of $36,000 in the asset account Patents. (Note that if the company developed the bottle cap internally instead of purchasing the patent, the costs of developing the cap—such as researchers' salaries and the costs of supplies and equipment used in testing—would be expensed as incurred.) Although the patent for the bottle cap will last for 20 years, WATER determines that it will sell the product that uses the cap for only six years.

The entry to record the annual amortization expense is for $6,000 ($36,000 ÷ 6 years). The Patents account is reduced directly by the amortization expense in contrast to the treatment of other long-term asset accounts, for which depreciation or depletion is accumulated in separate contra accounts.

If the patent becomes worthless before it is fully amortized, the remaining carrying value is written off as a loss by removing it from the Patents account.

Research and Development Costs

Most successful companies carry out research and development (R&D) activities, often within a separate department. Among these activities are development of new products, testing of existing and proposed products, and pure research. The costs of these activities are substantial for many companies. In a recent year, **General Motors** spent $8.0 billion, or about 5.4 percent of its revenues, on R&D.[13] R&D costs can be even greater in high-tech fields like pharmaceuticals. For example, **Abbott Laboratories** recently spent $2.7 billion, or 9.2 percent of its revenues, on R&D.[14]

The Financial Accounting Standards Board requires that all R&D costs be treated as revenue expenditures and charged to expense in the period in which they are incurred.[15] The reasoning behind this requirement is that it is too hard to trace specific costs to specific profitable developments. Also, the costs of research and development are continuous and necessary for the success of a business and so should be treated as current expenses. To support this conclusion, the FASB cited studies showing that 30 to 90 percent of all new products fail and that 75 percent of new-product expenses go to unsuccessful products. Thus, their costs do not represent future benefits.

Computer Software Costs

The costs that companies incur in developing computer software for sale or lease or for their own internal use are considered research and development costs until the product has proved technologically feasible. Thus, costs incurred before that point should be charged to expense as they are incurred. A product is deemed technologically feasible when a detailed working program has been designed. Once that occurs, all software production costs are recorded as assets and are amortized over the software's estimated economic life using the straight-line method. Capitalized software costs are becoming more prevalent and as shown in Figure 9-6 appear on 27 percent of 600 large companies' balance sheets, including $67 million for Apple (see Decision Point at the beginning of the chapter). If at any time a company cannot expect to realize from the software the amount of the unamortized costs on the balance sheet, the asset should be written down to the amount expected to be realized.[16]

Goodwill

Goodwill means different things to different people. Generally, it refers to a company's good reputation. From an accounting standpoint, goodwill exists when a purchaser pays more for a business than the fair market value of the business's net assets. In other words, the purchaser would pay less if it bought the assets separately. Most businesses are worth more as going concerns than as collections of assets.

When the purchase price of a business is more than the fair market value of its physical assets, the business must have intangible assets. If it does not have patents, copyrights, trademarks, or other identifiable intangible assets of value, the excess payment is assumed to be for goodwill. Goodwill reflects all the factors that allow a company to earn a higher-than-market rate of return on its assets, including customer satisfaction, good management, manufacturing efficiency, the advantages of having a monopoly, good locations, and good employee relations. The payment above and beyond the fair market value of the tangible assets and other specific intangible assets is properly recorded in the Goodwill account.

The FASB requires that purchased goodwill be reported as a separate line item on the balance sheet and that it be reviewed annually for impairment. If the

FOCUS ON BUSINESS PRACTICE

Wake up, Goodwill Is Growing!

As Figure 9-6 shows, 90 percent of 600 large companies separately report goodwill as an asset. Because much of the growth of these companies has come through purchasing other companies, goodwill as a percentage of total assets has also grown. As the table at the right shows, the amount of goodwill can be material.[17]

	Goodwill (In billions)	Percentage of Total Assets
General Mills	$6,663	37%
Heinz	$2,688	28%
Cisco Systems	$12,925	19%

fair value of goodwill is less than its carrying value on the balance sheet, goodwill is considered impaired. In that case, goodwill is reduced to its fair value, and the impairment charge is reported on the income statement. A company can perform the fair value measurement for each reporting unit at any time as long as the measurement date is consistent from year to year.[18]

A company should record goodwill only when it acquires a controlling interest in another business. The amount to be recorded as goodwill can be determined by writing the identifiable net assets up to their fair market values at the time of purchase and subtracting the total from the purchase price. For example, suppose a company pays $11,400,000 to purchase another business. If the net assets of the business (total assets − total liabilities) are fairly valued at $10,000,000, then the amount of the goodwill is $1,400,000 ($11,400,000 − $10,000,000). If the fair market value of the net assets is more or less than $10,000,000, an entry is made in the accounting records to adjust the assets to the fair market value. The goodwill would then represent the difference between the adjusted net assets and the purchase price of $11,400,000.

STOP & APPLY >

For each of the following intangible assets, indicate (a) if the asset is to be amortized over its useful life or (b) if the asset is not amortized but only subject to annual impairment test:

1. Goodwill
2. Copyright
3. Brand
4. Patent
5. Trademark

SOLUTION

1. b; 2. a; 3. b; 4. a; 5. b

A LOOK BACK AT

▶ APPLE COMPUTER, INC.

We began the chapter by emphasizing that **Apple's** success as an innovator and marketer comes from wise and steady investments in long-term assets and related expenditures like research and development. In evaluating Apple's performance, investors and creditors look for answers to the following questions:

- What are Apple's long-term assets?
- What are its policies in accounting for long-term assets?
- Does the company generate enough cash flows to finance its continued growth?

Apple's tangible long-term assets include land, manufacturing facilities, office buildings, machinery, equipment, and leasehold improvements to its retail stores. Its balance sheet also includes goodwill and intangible assets that it acquired through acquisitions. Because internally developed intangible assets are not recorded as assets, the value of Apple's own brand name is not reflected on the balance sheet. Clearly, however, it far exceeds the value of the intangible assets that are listed.

In accordance with GAAP, Apple's accounting policies include using the straight-line depreciation method for tangible assets, amortizing intangible assets over a reasonable useful life, and expensing research and development costs. In addition, it evaluates its long-term assets for impairment each year to ensure that it is not carrying assets on its balance sheet at amounts that exceed their value.

A good measure of the funds that Apple has available for growth is its free cash flow:

Free Cash Flow = Net Cash Flows from Operating Activities − Dividends − Purchases of Plant Assets + Sales of Plant Assets

CASH FLOW

		2008		2007
Free Cash Flow	=	\$9,596 − \$0 − \$1,091 + \$0		\$5,470 − \$0 − \$735 + \$0
	=	\$8,505	=	\$4,735

This two-year view of Apple's free cash flow shows great improvement in 2008 due to the phenomenal success of the iPod and iPhone. The company obviously generated enough cash to finance its continued growth. Its policy of not paying dividends contributes to the amount of cash it has available for this purpose. Although Apple may have sold some plant assets, the amounts were sufficiently immaterial that it did not report them separately.

Review Problem

Comparison of Depreciation Methods

LO3

Peter Construction Company purchased a cement mixer on January 2, 2010, for \$29,000. The mixer was expected to have a useful life of five years and a residual value of \$2,000. The company's engineers estimated that the mixer would have a useful life of 15,000 hours. It was used for 3,000 hours in 2010, 5,250 hours in 2011, 4,500 hours in 2012, 1,500 hours in 2013, and 750 hours in 2014. The company's fiscal year ends on December 31.

Required

1. Compute the depreciation expense and carrying value for 2010 to 2014, using the following methods: (a) straight-line, (b) production, and (c) double-declining-balance.
2. Show the balance sheet presentation for the cement mixer on December 31, 2010. Assume the straight-line method.
3. What conclusions can you draw from the patterns of yearly depreciation?

Answers to Review Problem

1. Depreciation computed:

Depreciation Method	Year	Computation			Depreciation	Carrying Value
a. Straight-line	2010	$27,000*	÷	5	$ 5,400	$23,600
	2011	27,000	÷	5	5,400	18,200
	2012	27,000	÷	5	5,400	12,800
	2013	27,000	÷	5	5,400	7,400
	2014	27,000	÷	5	5,400	2,000
b. Production	2010	$27,000*	x	3,000 / 15,000	$ 5,400	$23,600
	2011	27,000	x	5,250 / 15,000	9,450	14,150
	2012	27,000	x	4,500 / 15,000	8,100	6,050
	2013	27,000	x	1,500 / 15,000	2,700	3,350
	2014	27,000	x	750 / 15,000	1,350	2,000
c. Double-declining-balance	2010	$29,000	x	0.40	$11,600	$17,400
	2011	17,400	x	0.40	6,960	10,440
	2012	10,440	x	0.40	4,176	6,264
	2013	6,264	x	0.40	2,506***	3,758
	2014	3,758	–	2,000	1,758**	2,000

* ($29,000 – $2,000 = $27,000)

** Remaining depreciation to reduce carrying value to residual value ($3,758 – $2,000).

***Rounded.

2. Balance sheet presentation on December 31, 2010:

Property, plant, and equipment	
Cement mixer	$29,000
Less accumulated depreciation	5,400
	$23,600

3. The pattern of depreciation for the straight-line method differs significantly from the pattern for the double-declining-balance method. In the earlier years, the amount of depreciation under the double-declining-balance method is significantly greater than the amount under the straight-line method. In the later years, the opposite is true. The carrying value under the straight-line method is greater than under the double-declining-balance method at the end of all years except the fifth year. Depreciation under the production method differs from depreciation under the other methods in that it follows no regular pattern. It varies with the amount of use. Consequently, depreciation is greatest in 2011 and 2012, which are the years of greatest use. Use declined significantly in the last two years.

LO1 Define *long-term assets*, and explain the management issues related to them.

Long-term assets have a useful life of more than one year, are used in the operation of a business, and are not intended for resale. They can be tangible or intangible. In the former category are land, plant assets, and natural resources. In the latter are patents, trademarks, franchises, and other rights, as well as goodwill. The management issues related to long-term assets include decisions about whether to acquire the assets, how to finance them, and how to account for them.

LO2 Distinguish between *capital expenditures* and *revenue expenditures*, and account for the cost of property, plant, and equipment.

Capital expenditures are recorded as assets, whereas revenue expenditures are recorded as expenses of the current period. Capital expenditures include not only outlays for plant assets, natural resources, and intangible assets, but also expenditures for additions, betterments, and extraordinary repairs that increase an asset's residual value or extend its useful life. Revenue expenditures are made for ordinary repairs and maintenance. The error of classifying a capital expenditure as a revenue expenditure, or vice versa, has an important effect on net income.

The acquisition cost of property, plant, and equipment includes all expenditures reasonable and necessary to get the asset in place and ready for use. Among these expenditures are purchase price, installation cost, freight charges, and insurance during transit. The acquisition cost of a plant asset is allocated over the asset's useful life.

LO3 Compute depreciation under the straight-line, production, and declining-balance methods.

Depreciation—the periodic allocation of the cost of a plant asset over its estimated useful life—is commonly computed by using the straight-line method, the production method, or an accelerated method. The straight-line method is related directly to the passage of time, whereas the production method is related directly to use or output. An accelerated method, which results in relatively large amounts of depreciation in earlier years and reduced amounts in later years, is based on the assumption that plant assets provide greater economic benefits in their earlier years than in later ones. The most common accelerated method is the declining-balance method.

LO4 Account for the disposal of depreciable assets.

A company can dispose of a long-term plant asset by discarding or selling it or exchanging it for another asset. Regardless of the way in which a company disposes of such an asset, it must record depreciation up to the date of disposal. To do so, it must remove the carrying value from the asset account and the depreciation to date from the accumulated depreciation account. When a company sells a depreciable long-term asset at a price that differs from its carrying value, it should report the gain or loss on its income statement. In recording exchanges of similar plant assets, a gain or loss may arise.

LO5 Identify the issues related to accounting for natural resources, and compute depletion.

Natural resources are depletable assets that are converted to inventory by cutting, pumping, mining, or other forms of extraction. They are recorded at cost as long-term assets. As natural resources are sold, their costs are allocated as expenses through depletion charges. The depletion charge is based on the ratio of the resource extracted to the total estimated resource. A major issue related to this subject is accounting for oil and gas reserves.

LO6 Identify the issues related to accounting for intangible assets, including research and development costs and goodwill.

The purchase of an intangible asset should be treated as a capital expenditure and recorded at acquisition cost. All intangible assets are subject to annual tests for impairment of value. Intangible assets with a definite life are also amortized annually. The FASB requires that research and development costs be treated as revenue expenditures and charged as expenses in the periods of expenditure. Software costs are treated as research and development costs and expensed until a feasible working program is developed, after which time the costs may be capitalized and amortized over a reasonable estimated life. Goodwill is the excess of the amount paid for a business over the fair market value of the net assets and is usually related to the business's superior earning potential. It should be recorded only when a company purchases an entire business, and it should be reviewed annually for possible impairment.

REVIEW of Concepts and Terminology

The following concepts and terms were introduced in this chapter:

Accelerated method 448 (LO3)

Additions 441 (LO2)

Amortization 436 (LO1)

Asset impairment 437 (LO1)

Betterments 442 (LO2)

Brand name 458 (LO6)

Capital expenditure 441 (LO2)

Carrying value 436 (LO1)

Copyright 458 (LO6)

Customer list 458 (LO6)

Declining-balance method 448 (LO3)

Depletion 436 (LO1)

Depreciable cost 446 (LO3)

Depreciation 436 (LO1)

Double-declining-balance method 448 (LO3)

Economic Stimulus Act of 2008 451 (LO3)

Estimated useful life 446 (LO3)

Expenditure 441 (LO2)

Extraordinary repairs 442 (LO2)

Franchise 458 (LO6)

Free cash flow 439 (LO1)

Full-costing method 456 (LO5)

Goodwill 458 (LO6)

Group depreciation 450 (LO3)

Intangible assets 436 (LO1)

Leasehold 458 (LO6)

Leasehold improvements 444 (LO2)

License 458 (LO6)

Long-term assets 436 (LO1)

Natural resources 436 (LO1)

Noncompete covenant 458 (LO6)

Obsolescence 445 (LO3)

Patent 458 (LO6)

Physical deterioration 445 (LO3)

Production method 447 (LO3)

Residual value 446 (LO3)

Revenue expenditure 441 (LO2)

Software 458 (LO6)

Straight-line method 446 (LO3)

Successful efforts accounting 456 (LO5)

Tangible assets 436 (LO1)

Trademark 458 (LO6)

CHAPTER ASSIGNMENTS

BUILDING Your Basic Knowledge and Skills

Short Exercises

LO1 **Management Issues**

SE 1. Indicate whether each of the following actions is primarily related to (a) acquisition of long-term assets, (b) evaluating the adequacy of financing of long-term assets, or (c) applying the matching rule to long-term assets.

1. Deciding between common stock and long-term notes for the raising of funds
2. Relating the acquisition cost of a long-term asset to the cash flows generated by the asset
3. Determining how long an asset will benefit the company
4. Deciding to use cash flows from operations to purchase long-term assets
5. Determining how much an asset will sell for when it is no longer useful to the company
6. Calculating free cash flow

LO1 **Free Cash Flow**

SE 2. Rak Corporation had cash flows from operating activities during the past year of $97,000. During the year, the company expended $12,500 for dividends; expended $79,000 for property, plant, and equipment; and sold property, plant, and equipment for $6,000. Calculate the company's free cash flow. What does the result tell you about the company?

LO2 **Determining Cost of Long-Term Assets**

SE 3. Smith Auto purchased a neighboring lot for a new building and parking lot. Indicate whether each of the following expenditures is properly charged to (a) Land, (b) Land Improvements, or (c) Buildings.

1. Paving costs
2. Architects' fee for building design
3. Cost of clearing the property
4. Cost of the property
5. Building construction costs
6. Lights around the property
7. Building permit
8. Interest on the construction loan

LO2 **Group Purchase**

SE 4. Lian Company purchased property with a warehouse and parking lot for $1,500,000. An appraiser valued the components of the property if purchased separately as follows:

Land	$ 400,000
Land improvements	200,000
Building	1,000,000
Total	$1,600,000

Determine the cost to be assigned to each component.

LO3 **Straight-Line Method**

SE 5. Kelly's Fitness Center purchased a new step machine for $16,500. The apparatus is expected to last four years and have a residual value of $1,500. What will the depreciation expense be for each year under the straight-line method?

LO3 **Production Method**

SE 6. Assume that the step machine in **SE 5** has an estimated useful life of 8,000 hours and was used for 2,400 hours in year 1, 2,000 hours in year 2, 2,200 hours in year 3, and 1,400 hours in year 4. How much would depreciation expense be in each year?

LO3 **Double-Declining-Balance Method**

SE 7. Assume that the step machine in **SE 5** is depreciated using the double-declining-balance method. How much would depreciation expense be in each year?

LO4 **Disposal of Plant Assets: No Trade-In**

SE 8. Alarico Printing owned a piece of equipment that cost $16,200 and on which it had recorded $9,000 of accumulated depreciation. The company disposed of the equipment on January 2, the first day of business of the current year.

1. Calculate the carrying value of the equipment.
2. Calculate the gain or loss on the disposal under each of the following assumptions:
   a. The equipment was discarded as having no value.
   b. The equipment was sold for $3,000 cash.
   c. The equipment was sold for $8,000 cash.

LO5 **Natural Resources**

SE 9. Narda Company purchased land containing an estimated 4,000,000 tons of ore for $16,000,000. The land will be worth $2,400,000 without the ore after eight years of active mining. Although the equipment needed for the mining will have a useful life of 20 years, it is not expected to be usable and will have no value after the mining on this site is complete. Compute the depletion charge per ton and the amount of depletion expense for the first year of operation, assuming that 600,000 tons of ore are mined and sold. Also, compute the first-year depreciation on the mining equipment using the production method, assuming a cost of $19,200,000 with no residual value.

LO6 **Intangible Assets: Computer Software**

SE 10. Danya Company has created a new software application for PCs. Its costs during research and development were $250,000. Its costs after the working program was developed were $175,000. Although the company's copyright may be amortized over 40 years, management believes that the product will be viable for only five years. How should the costs be accounted for? At what value will the software appear on the balance sheet after one year?

Exercises

LO1 LO2 LO3 **Discussion Questions**

E 1. Develop a brief answer for each of the following questions:

1. Is carrying value ever the same as market value?
2. What major advantage does a company that has positive free cash flow have over a company that has negative free cash flow?
3. What incentive does a company have to allocate more of a group purchase price to land than to building?
4. Which depreciation method would best reflect the risk of obsolescence from rapid technological changes?

LO4 LO5 LO6 **Discussion Questions**

E 2. Develop a brief answer for each of the following questions:

1. When would the disposal of a long-term asset result in no gain or loss?

2. When would annual depletion not equal depletion expense?
3. Why would a firm amortize a patent over fewer years than the patent's life?
4. Why would a company spend millions of dollars on goodwill?

LO1 **Management Issues**

E 3. Indicate whether each of the following actions is primarily related to (a) acquisition of long-term assets, (b) evaluating the financing of long-term assets, or (c) applying the matching rule to long-term assets.

1. Deciding to use the production method of depreciation
2. Allocating costs on a group purchase
3. Determining the total units a machine will produce
4. Deciding to borrow funds to purchase equipment
5. Estimating the savings a new machine will produce and comparing that amount to cost
6. Examining the trend of free cash flow over several years
7. Deciding whether to rent or buy a piece of equipment

LO1 **Purchase Decision—Present Value Analysis**

E 4. Management is considering the purchase of a new machine for a cost of \$12,000. It is estimated that the machine will generate positive net cash flows of \$3,000 per year for five years and will have a disposal price at the end of that time of \$1,000. Assuming an interest rate of 9 percent, determine if management should purchase the machine. Use Tables 1 and 2 in the appendix on present value tables to determine the net present value of the new machine.

LO1 **Free Cash Flow**

E 5. Zedek Corporation had cash flows from operating activities during the past year of \$216,000. During the year, the company expended \$462,000 for property, plant, and equipment; sold property, plant, and equipment for \$54,000; and paid dividends of \$50,000. Calculate the company's free cash flow. What does the result tell you about the company?

LO2 **Special Types of Capital Expenditures**

E 6. Tell whether each of the following transactions related to an office building is a revenue expenditure (RE) or a capital expenditure (CE). In addition, indicate whether each transaction is an ordinary repair (OR), an extraordinary repair (ER), an addition (A), a betterment (B), or none of these (N).

1. The hallways and ceilings in the building are repainted at a cost of \$6,250.
2. The hallways, which have tile floors, are carpeted at a cost of \$28,000.
3. A new wing is added to the building at a cost of \$105,470.
4. Furniture is purchased for the entrance to the building at a cost of \$13,250.
5. The air-conditioning system is overhauled at a cost of \$21,153. The overhaul extends the useful life of the air-conditioning system by ten years.
6. A cleaning firm is paid \$150 per week to clean the newly installed carpets.

LO2 **Determining Cost of Long-Term Assets**

E 7. Colletta Manufacturing purchased land next to its factory to be used as a parking lot. The expenditures incurred by the company were as follows: purchase price, \$600,000; broker's fees, \$48,000; title search and other fees, \$4,400; demolition of a cottage on the property, \$16,000; general grading of property, \$8,400; paving parking lots, \$80,000; lighting for parking lots, \$64,000; and signs for parking lots, \$12,800. Determine the amounts that should be debited to the Land account and the Land Improvements account.

LO2 Group Purchase

E 8. Joanna Mak purchased a car wash for $480,000. If purchased separately, the land would have cost $120,000, the building $270,000, and the equipment $210,000. Determine the amount that should be recorded in the new business's records for land, building, and equipment.

LO2 LO3 Cost of Long-Term Asset and Depreciation

E 9. Nick Santiago purchased a used tractor for $35,000. Before the tractor could be used, it required new tires, which cost $2,200, and an overhaul, which cost $2,800. Its first tank of fuel cost $150. The tractor is expected to last six years and have a residual value of $4,000. Determine the cost and depreciable cost of the tractor and calculate the first year's depreciation under the straight-line method.

LO3 Depreciation Methods

E 10. On January 13, 2010, Silverio Oil Company purchased a drilling truck for $45,000. Silverio expects the truck to last five years or 200,000 miles, with an estimated residual value of $7,500 at the end of that time. During 2011, the truck is driven 48,000 miles. Silverio's year end is December 31. Compute the depreciation for 2011 under each of the following methods: (1) straight-line, (2) production, and (3) double-declining-balance. Using the amount computed in (3), prepare the entry in journal form to record depreciation expense for the second year, and show how the Drilling Truck account would appear on the balance sheet.

LO3 Double-Declining-Balance Method

E 11. Stop Burglar Alarm Systems Company purchased a computer for $2,240. It has an estimated useful life of four years and an estimated residual value of $240. Compute the depreciation charge for each of the four years using the double-declining-balance method.

LO3 Revision of Depreciation Rates

E 12. Hope Hospital purchased a special x-ray machine. The machine, which cost $311,560, was expected to last ten years, with an estimated residual value of $31,560. After two years of operation (and depreciation charges using the straight-line method), it became evident that the x-ray machine would last a total of only seven years. The estimated residual value, however, would remain the same. Given this information, determine the new depreciation charge for the third year on the basis of the revised estimated useful life.

LO4 Disposal of Plant Assets

E 13. A piece of equipment that cost $32,400 and on which $18,000 of accumulated depreciation had been recorded was disposed of on January 2, the first day of business of the current year. For each of the following assumptions, compute the gain or loss on the disposal.

1. The equipment was discarded as having no value.
2. The equipment was sold for $6,000 cash.
3. The equipment was sold for $18,000 cash.

LO4 Disposal of Plant Assets

E 14. Samson Company purchased a computer on January 2, 2009, at a cost of $1,250. The computer is expected to have a useful life of five years and a residual value of $125. Assume that the computer is disposed of on July 1, 2012. Record the depreciation expense for half a year and the disposal under each of the following assumptions:

1. The computer is discarded.
2. The computer is sold for $200.
3. The computer is sold for $550.

LO5 Natural Resource Depletion and Depreciation of Related Plant Assets

E 15. Nelson Company purchased land containing an estimated 2.5 million tons of ore for a cost of $4,400,000. The land without the ore is estimated to be worth $250,000. During its first year of operation, the company mined and sold 375,000 tons of ore. Compute the depletion charge per ton. Compute the depletion expense that Nelson should record for the year.

LO6 Copyrights and Trademarks

E 16. The following exercise is about amortizing copyrights and trademarks.

1. Fulton Publishing Company purchased the copyright to a basic computer textbook for $80,000. The usual life of a textbook is about four years. However, the copyright will remain in effect for another 50 years. Calculate the annual amortization of the copyright.
2. Sloan Company purchased a trademark from a well-known supermarket for $640,000. The management of the company argued that the trademark's useful life was indefinite. Explain how the cost should be accounted for.

LO6 Accounting for a Patent

E 17. At the beginning of the fiscal year, Andy Company purchased for $2,060,000 a patent that applies to the manufacture of a unique tamper-proof lid for medicine bottles. Andy incurred legal costs of $900,000 in successfully defending use of the lid by a competitor. Andy estimated that the patent would be valuable for at least ten years. During the first two years of operations, Andy successfully marketed the lid. At the beginning of the third year, a study appeared in a consumer magazine showing that children could in fact remove the lid. As a result, all orders for the lids were canceled, and the patent was rendered worthless.

Prepare entries in journal form to record the following: (a) purchase of the patent; (b) successful defense of the patent; (c) amortization expense for the first year; and (d) write-off of the patent as worthless.

Problems

LO1 LO2 Identification of Long-Term Assets Terminology

P 1. Listed below are common terms associated with long-term assets:

a. Tangible assets
b. Natural resources
c. Intangible assets
d. Additions
e. Betterments
f. Extraordinary repair
g. Depreciation
h. Depletion
i. Amortization
j. Revenue expenditure
k. Free cash flow

Required

1. For each of the following statements, identify the term listed above with which it is associated. (If two terms apply, choose the one that is most closely associated.)

1. Periodic cost associated with intangible assets
2. Cost of constructing a new wing on a building
3. A measure of funds available for expansion
4. A group of assets encompassing property, plant, and equipment
5. Cost associated with enhancing a building but not expanding it
6. Periodic cost associated with tangible assets
7. A group of assets that gain their value from contracts or rights
8. Cost of normal repairs to a building
9. Assets whose value derives from what can be extracted from them
10. Periodic cost associated with natural resources
11. Cost of a repair that extends the useful life of a building

User insight ▶ 2. Assuming the company uses cash for all its expenditures, which of the items listed above would you expect to see on the income statement? Which ones would not result in an outlay of cash?

LO2 **Determining Cost of Assets**

P 2. Siber Computers constructed a new training center in 2010. You have been hired to manage the training center. A review of the accounting records shows the following expenditures debited to an asset account called Training Center:

Attorney's fee, land acquisition	$ 35,200
Cost of land	597,000
Architect's fee, building design	102,000
Building	1,025,000
Parking lot and sidewalk	135,600
Electrical wiring, building	168,000
Landscaping	55,000
Cost of surveying land	8,900
Training equipment, tables, and chairs	136,400
Installation of training equipment	65,600
Cost of grading the land	14,000
Cost of changes in building to soundproof rooms	58,700
Total account balance	$2,401,400

An employee of Siber Computers worked full time overseeing the construction project. He spent two months on the purchase and preparation of the site, six months on the construction, one month on land improvements, and one month on equipment installation and training room furniture purchase and setup. His salary of $72,000 during these ten months was charged to Administrative Expense. The training center was placed in operation on November 1.

Required

1. Prepare a schedule with the following four column (account) headings: Land, Land Improvements, Building, and Equipment. Place each of the above expenditures in the appropriate column. Total the columns.

User insight ▶ 2. What impact does the classification of the items among several accounts have on evaluating the profitability performance of the company?

LO3 LO4 **Comparison of Depreciation Methods**

P 3. Ivan Manufacturing Company purchased a robot for $360,000 at the beginning of year 1. The robot has an estimated useful life of four years and an estimated residual value of $30,000. The robot, which should last 20,000 hours, was operated 6,000 hours in year 1; 8,000 hours in year 2; 4,000 hours in year 3; and 2,000 hours in year 4.

Required

1. Compute the annual depreciation and carrying value for the robot for each year assuming the following depreciation methods: (a) straight-line, (b) production, and (c) double-declining-balance.
2. If the robot is sold for $375,000 after year 2, what would be the amount of gain or loss under each method?

User insight ▶

3. What conclusions can you draw from the patterns of yearly depreciation and carrying value in requirement **1**? Do the three methods differ in their effect on the company's profitability? Do they differ in their effect on the company's operating cash flows? Explain.

LO3 LO4

Comparison of Depreciation Methods

P 4. Roman's Construction Company purchased a new crane for $721,000 at the beginning of year 1. The crane has an estimated residual value of $70,000 and an estimated useful life of six years. The crane is expected to last 10,000 hours. It was used 1,800 hours in year 1; 2,000 in year 2; 2,500 in year 3; 1,500 in year 4; 1,200 in year 5; and 1,000 in year 6.

Required

1. Compute the annual depreciation and carrying value for the new crane for each of the six years (round to the nearest dollar where necessary) under each of the following methods: (a) straight-line, (b) production, and (c) double-declining-balance.
2. If the crane is sold for $500,000 after year 3, what would be the amount of gain or loss under each method?

User insight ▶

3. Do the three methods differ in their effect on the company's profitability? Do they differ in their effect on the company's operating cash flows? Explain.

LO5

Natural Resource Depletion and Depreciation of Related Plant Assets

P 5. Kulig Company purchased land containing an estimated 10 million tons of ore for a cost of $3,300,000. The land without the ore is estimated to be worth $600,000. The company expects that all the usable ore can be mined in 10 years. Buildings costing $300,000 with an estimated useful life of 20 years were erected on the site. Equipment costing $360,000 with an estimated useful life of 10 years was installed. Because of the remote location, neither the buildings nor the equipment has an estimated residual value. During its first year of operation, the company mined and sold 450,000 tons of ore.

Required

1. Compute the depletion charge per ton.
2. Compute the depletion expense that Kulig should record for the year.
3. Determine the depreciation expense for the year for the buildings, making it proportional to the depletion.
4. Determine the depreciation expense for the year for the equipment under two alternatives: (a) making the expense proportional to the depletion and (b) using the straight-line method.

User insight ▶

5. Suppose the company mined and sold 250,000 tons of ore (instead of 450,000) during the first year. Would the change in the results in requirement **2** or **3** affect earnings or cash flows? Explain.

Alternate Problems

LO2 **Determining Cost of Assets**

P 6. Global Company was formed on January 1, 2010, and began constructing a new plant. At the end of 2010, its auditor discovered that all expenditures involving long-term assets had been debited to an account called Fixed Assets. An analysis of the Fixed Assets account, which had a year-end balance of $2,659,732, disclosed that it contained the following items:

Cost of land	$ 320,600
Surveying costs	4,100
Transfer of title and other fees required by the county	920
Broker's fees for land	21,144
Attorney's fees associated with land acquisition	7,048
Cost of removing timber from land	49,600
Cost of grading land	4,200
Cost of digging building foundation	35,100
Architect's fee for building and land improvements (80 percent building)	67,200
Cost of building construction	715,000
Cost of sidewalks	11,400
Cost of parking lots	54,400
Cost of lighting for grounds	80,300
Cost of landscaping	11,800
Cost of machinery	993,000
Shipping cost on machinery	55,300
Cost of installing machinery	176,200
Cost of testing machinery	21,600
Cost of changes in building to comply with safety regulations pertaining to machinery	12,540
Cost of repairing building that was damaged in the installation of machinery	8,900
Cost of medical bill for injury received by employee while installing machinery	2,560
Cost of water damage to building during heavy rains prior to opening the plant for operation	6,820
Account balance	$2,659,732

Global Company sold the timber it cleared from the land to a firewood dealer for $7,000. This amount was credited to Miscellaneous Income.

During the construction period, two of Global's supervisors devoted full time to the construction project. Their annual salaries were $51,000 and $39,000, respectively. They spent two months on the purchase and preparation of the land, six months on the construction of the building (approximately one-sixth of which was devoted to improvements on the grounds), and one month on machinery installation. When the plant began operation on October 1, the supervisors returned to their regular duties. Their salaries were debited to Factory Salaries Expense.

Required

1. Prepare a schedule with the following column headings: Land, Land Improvements, Buildings, Machinery, and Expense. Place each of the above expenditures in the appropriate column. Negative amounts should be shown in parentheses. Total the columns.

User insight ▶ 2. What impact does the classification of the items among several accounts have on evaluating the profitability performance of the company?

LO3 LO4 **Comparison of Depreciation Methods**

P 7. Relax Designs, Inc., purchased a computerized blueprint printer that will assist in the design and display of plans for factory layouts. The cost of the printer was $45,000, and its expected useful life is four years. The company can probably sell the printer for $5,000 at the end of four years. The printer is expected to last 6,000 hours. It was used 1,200 hours in year 1; 1,800 hours in year 2; 2,400 hours in year 3; and 600 hours in year 4.

Required

1. Compute the annual depreciation and carrying value for the new blueprint printer for each of the four years (round to the nearest dollar where necessary) under each of the following methods: (a) straight-line, (b) production, and (c) double-declining-balance.
2. If the printer is sold for $24,000 after year 2, what would be the gain or loss under each method?

User insight ▶

3. What conclusions can you draw from the patterns of yearly depreciation and carrying value in requirement **1**? Do the three methods differ in their impact on profitability? Do they differ in their effect on the company's operating cash flows? Explain.

LO5 **Natural Resource Depletion and Depreciation of Related Plant Assets**

P 8. Fuentez Mining Company purchased land containing an estimated 20 million tons of ore for a cost of $8,800,000. The land without the ore is estimated to be worth $1,600,000. The company expects that all the usable ore can be mined in 10 years. Buildings costing $800,000 with an estimated useful life of 30 years were erected on the site. Equipment costing $960,000 with an estimated useful life of 10 years was installed. Because of the remote location, neither the buildings nor the equipment has an estimated residual value. During its first year of operation, the company mined and sold 1,600,000 tons of ore.

Required

1. Compute the depletion charge per ton.
2. Compute the depletion expense that should be recorded for the year.
3. Determine the depreciation expense for the year for the buildings, making it proportional to the depletion.
4. Determine the depreciation expense for the year for the equipment under two alternatives: (a) making the expense proportional to the depletion and (b) using the straight-line method.

User insight ▶

5. Suppose the company mined and sold 2,000,000 tons of ore (instead of 1,600,000) during the first year. Would the change in the results in requirements **2** or **3** affect earnings or cash flows? Explain.

LO3 LO4 **Comparison of Depreciation Methods**

P 9. Diego Corporation purchased a new truck for $515,000 at the beginning of year 1. The truck has an estimated residual value of $50,000 and an estimated useful life of five years. The truck is expected to last 18,000 hours. It was used 3,600 hours in year 1; 4,000 in year 2; 5,000 in year 3; 3,000 in year 4; and 2,400 in year 5.

Required

1. Compute the annual depreciation and carrying value for the new truck for each of the five years (round to the nearest dollar where necessary) under each of the following methods: (a) straight-line, (b) production, and (c) double-declining-balance.

2. If the truck is sold for $300,000 after year 3, what would be the amount of gain or loss under each method?

User insight ▶ 3. Do the three methods differ in their effect on the company's profitability? Do they differ in their effect on the company's operating cash flows? Explain.

ENHANCING Your Knowledge, Skills, and Critical Thinking

LO1 **Effect of Change in Estimates**

C 1. The airline industry was hit particularly hard after the 9/11 attacks on the World Trade Center in 2001. In 2002, **Southwest Airlines**, one of the healthier airlines companies, made a decision to lengthen the useful lives of its aircraft from 22 to 27 years. Shortly thereafter, following Southwest's leadership, other airlines made the same move.[19] What advantage, if any, can the airlines gain by making this change in estimate? Will it change earnings or cash flows and, if it does, will the change be favorable or negative?

Some people argue that the useful lives and depreciation of airplanes are irrelevant. They claim that because of the extensive maintenance and testing that airline companies are required by law to perform, the planes theoretically can be in service for an indefinite future period. What is wrong with this argument?

LO1 **Impairment Test**

C 2. The annual report for **Costco Wholesale Corporation**, the large discount company, contains the following statement:

> The Company periodically evaluates the realizability of long-lived assets for impairment when [circumstances] may indicate the carrying amount of the asset group . . . may not be fully recoverable.[20]

What does the concept of impairment mean in accounting? What effect does impairment have on profitability and cash flows? Why would the concept of impairment be referred to as a conservative accounting approach?

LO3 **Accounting Policies**

C 3. **IBM**, the large computer equipment and services company, states in its annual report that "plant, rental machines and other property are carried at cost and depreciated over their estimated useful lives using the straight-line method."[21] What estimates are necessary to carry out this policy? What factors should be considered in making each of the estimates?

LO6 **Brands**

C 4. **Hilton Hotels Corporation** and **Marriott International** provide hospitality services. Hilton Hotels' well-known brands include Hilton, Doubletree, Hampton Inn, Embassy Suites, Red Lion Hotels and Inns, and Homewood Suites. Marriott also owns or manages properties with recognizable brand names, such as Marriott Hotels, Resorts and Suites; Ritz-Carlton; Renaissance Hotels; Residence Inn; Courtyard; and Fairfield Inn.

On its balance sheet, Hilton Hotels Corporation includes brands of $2.8 billion, or 17 percent of total assets. Marriott International, however, does not list brands among its intangible assets.[22] What principles of accounting for intangibles would cause Hilton to record brands as an asset while Marriott does not? How will these differences in accounting for brands generally affect the net income and return on assets of these two competitors?

LO3 Effects of Change in Accounting Method

C 5. Depreciation expense is a significant cost for companies in which plant assets are a high proportion of assets. The amount of depreciation expense in a given year is affected by estimates of useful life and choice of depreciation method. In 2010, Century Steelworks Company, a major integrated steel producer, changed the estimated useful lives for its major production assets. It also changed the method of depreciation for other steel-making assets from straight-line to the production method.

In its 2010 annual report, Century Steelworks makes the following statement:

> A recent study conducted by management shows that actual years-in-service figures for our major production equipment and machinery are, in most cases, higher than the estimated useful lives assigned to these assets. We have recast the depreciable lives of such assets so that equipment previously assigned a useful life of 8 to 26 years now has an extended depreciable life of 10 to 32 years.

The report goes on to explain the new production method of depreciation, as follows:

> [The method] recognizes that depreciation of production equipment and machinery correlates directly to both physical wear and tear and the passage of time. The production method of depreciation, which we have now initiated, more closely allocates the cost of these assets to the periods in which products are manufactured.

The report summarizes the effects of the changes in estimated useful lives and depreciation method on the year 2010 as shown in the following table:

Incremental Increase in Net Income	In Millions	Per Share
Lengthened lives	$11.0	$0.80
Production method		
Current year	7.3	0.53
Prior years	2.8	0.20
Total increase	$21.1	$1.53

During 2010, Century Steelworks reported a net loss of $83,156,500 ($6.03 per share). Depreciation expense for 2010 was $87,707,200.

In explaining the changes the company has made, the controller of Century Steelworks was quoted in an article in *Business Journal* as follows: "There is no reason for Century Steelworks to continue to depreciate our assets more conservatively than our competitors do." But the article also quotes an industry analyst who argues that by slowing its method of depreciation, Century Steelworks could be viewed as reporting lower-quality earnings.

1. Explain the accounting treatment when there is a change in the estimated lives of depreciable assets. What circumstances must exist for the production method to produce the effect it did in relation to the straight-line method? What would Century Steelworks' net income or loss have been if the changes had not been made? What might have motivated management to make the changes?
2. What does the controller of Century Steelworks mean when he says that Century had been depreciating "more conservatively than our competitors do"? Why might the changes at Century Steelworks indicate, as the analyst asserts, "lower-quality earnings"? What risks might Century face as a result of its decision to use the production method of depreciation?

LO1 **Purchase Decision and Time Value of Money**

C 6. Page Machine Works has obtained a subcontract from the government to manufacture special parts for a new military aircraft. The parts are to be delivered over the next five years, and the company will be paid as the parts are delivered.

To make the parts, Page Machine Works will have to purchase new equipment. Two types are available. Type A is conventional equipment that can be put into service immediately; Type B requires one year to be put into service but is more efficient than Type A. Type A requires an immediate cash investment of $1,000,000 and will produce enough parts to provide net cash receipts of $340,000 each year for the five years. Type B may be purchased by signing a two-year non-interest-bearing note for $1,346,000. It is projected that Type B will produce net cash receipts of zero in year 1, $500,000 in year 2, $600,000 in year 3, $600,000 in year 4, and $200,000 in year 5. Neither type of equipment can be used on other contracts, and neither type will have any useful life remaining at the end of the contract. Page currently pays an interest rate of 16 percent to borrow money.

1. What is the present value of the investment required for each type of equipment? (Use Table 1 in the appendix on present value tables.)
2. Compute the net present value of each type of equipment based on your answer in **1** and the present value of the net cash receipts projected to be received. (Use Tables 1 and 2 in the appendix on present value tables.)
3. Write a memorandum to the board of directors recommending the best option for Page. Explain your reasoning and include **1** and **2** as attachments.

LO1 LO2 LO3 LO6 **Long-Term Assets**

C 7. To answer the following questions, refer to the **CVS** annual report in the Supplement to Chapter 1. Examine the balance sheets and the summary of significant accounting policies on property and equipment in the notes to the financial statements.

1. What percentage of total assets in the most recent year was property and equipment, net? Identify the major categories of CVS's property and equipment. Which is the most significant type of property and equipment? What are leasehold improvements? How significant are these items, and what are their effects on the earnings of the company?
2. Continue with the summary of significant accounting policies item on property and equipment in the CVS annual report. What method of depreciation does CVS use? How long does management estimate its buildings will last as compared with furniture and equipment? What does this say about the company's need to remodel its stores?
3. Refer to the note on impairment of long-lived assets in the summary of significant accounting policies in CVS Corporation's annual report. How does the company determine if it has impaired assets?

LO1 **Long-Term Assets and Free Cash Flows**

C 8. Refer to the **CVS** annual report and to the financial statements of **Southwest Airlines Co.** in the Supplement to Chapter 1 to answer the questions below.

1. Prepare a table that shows the net amount each company spent on property and equipment (from the statement of cash flows), the total property and equipment (from the balance sheet), and the percentage of the first figure to the second for each of the past two years. Which company grew its property and equipment at a faster rate?

2. Calculate free cash flow for each company for the past two years. What conclusions can you draw about the need for each company to raise funds from debt and equity and the ability of each company to grow?

LO2 **Ethics and Allocation of Acquisition Costs**

C 9. Raintree Company has purchased land and a warehouse for \$18,000,000. The warehouse is expected to last 20 years and to have a residual value equal to 10 percent of its cost. The chief financial officer (CFO) and the controller are discussing the allocation of the purchase price. The CFO believes that the largest amount possible should be assigned to the land because this action will improve reported net income in the future. Depreciation expense will be lower because land is not depreciated. He suggests allocating one-third, or \$6,000,000, of the cost to the land. This results in depreciation expense each year of \$540,000 [(\$12,000,000 − \$1,200,000) ÷ 20 years].

The controller disagrees. She argues that the smallest amount possible, say one-fifth of the purchase price, should be allocated to the land, thereby saving income taxes, since the depreciation, which is tax-deductible, will be greater. Under this plan, annual depreciation would be \$648,000 [(\$14,400,000 − \$1,440,000) ÷ 20 years]. The annual tax savings at a 30 percent tax rate is \$32,400 [(\$648,000 − \$540,000) × 0.30]. How would each decision affect the company's cash flows? Ethically, how should the purchase cost be allocated? Who will be affected by the decision?

LO2 LO6 **Ethics of Aggressive Accounting Policies**

C 10. Is it ethical to choose aggressive accounting practices to advance a company's business? During the 1990s, **America Online (AOL)**, the largest Internet service provider in the United States, was one of the hottest stocks on Wall Street. After its initial stock offering in 1992, AOL's stock price shot up by several thousand percent.

Accounting is very important to a company like AOL because earnings enable it to sell shares of stock and raise more cash to fund its growth. In its early years, AOL was one of the most aggressive companies in its choice of accounting principles. AOL's strategy called for building the largest customer base in the industry. Consequently, it spent many millions of dollars each year marketing its services to new customers. Such costs are usually recognized as operating expenses in the year in which they are incurred. However, AOL treated these costs as long-term assets, called "deferred subscriber acquisition costs," and expensed them over several years, because it said the average customer was going to stay with the company for three years or more. The company also recorded research and development costs as "product development costs" and amortized them over five years.

Both of these practices are justifiable theoretically, but they are not common practice. If the standard, more conservative practice had been followed, the company would have had a net loss in every year it has been in business.[23] This result would have greatly limited AOL's ability to raise money and grow.

Form groups to discuss this case. Determine whether your group thinks AOL was justified in adopting the "aggressive" accounting techniques. What was "aggressive" about these techniques? What was management's rationale for adopting the accounting policies that it did? What could go wrong with such a plan? How would you evaluate the ethics of AOL's actions? Who benefits from the actions? Who is harmed by these actions? Be prepared to support your conclusions in class.

CHAPTER

10 Long-Term Liabilities

Focus on Financial Statements

INCOME STATEMENT

Revenues

– Expenses

= Net Income

STATEMENT OF RETAINED EARNINGS

Opening Balance

+ Net Income

– Dividends

= Retained Earnings

BALANCE SHEET

Assets	Liabilities
	Equity

A = L + E

STATEMENT OF CASH FLOWS

Operating activities

+ Investing activities

+ Financing activities

= Change in Cash

+ Starting Balance

= Ending Cash Balance

Interest on long-term liabilities on balance sheet is an expense on income statement. Borrowing/repaying long-term liabilities affects statement of cash flows.

Long-term liabilities can be an attractive means of financing the expansion of a business. By incurring long-term debt to fund growth, a company may be able to earn a return that exceeds the interest it pays on the debt. When it does, it increases earnings for stockholders—that is, return on equity. Many companies reward top managers with bonuses for improving return on equity. This incentive provides a temptation to incur too much debt, which increases a company's financial risk. Thus, in deciding on an appropriate level of debt, as in so many other management issues, ethics is a major concern.

LEARNING OBJECTIVES

LO1 Identify the management issues related to long-term debt. (pp. 482–490)

LO2 Describe the features of a bond issue and the major characteristics of bonds. (pp. 490–493)

LO3 Record bonds issued at face value and at a discount or premium. (pp. 493–496)

LO4 Use present values to determine the value of bonds. (pp. 497–498)

LO5 Amortize bond discounts and bond premiums using the straight-line and effective interest methods. (pp. 499–507)

SUPPLEMENTAL OBJECTIVES

SO6 Account for the retirement of bonds and the conversion of bonds into stock. (pp. 507–508)

SO7 Record bonds issued between interest dates and year-end adjustments. (pp. 509–511)

DECISION POINT ▸ USER'S FOCUS McDONALD'S CORPORATION

McDonald's, the world's largest restaurant chain, passed a milestone when it earned more revenues in Europe than in the United States. To finance its continued global expansion, the company raises funds by issuing both debt and capital stock. As you can see in its Financial Highlights, McDonald's relies heavily on debt financing. In 2007, its long-term liabilities were 63 percent of total stockholders' equity, and, together with current liabilities, they were over 92 percent of stockholders' equity. In 2008, its long-term liabilities were 94 percent of total stockholders' equity and its total current and long-term liabilities amounted to almost 113 percent of stockholders' equity. McDonald's long-term obligations also include numerous leases on real estate, as well as employee pension and health plans.[1]

- ▸ What are McDonald's most important long-term debts?
- ▸ What are its considerations in deciding to issue long-term debt?
- ▸ How does one evaluate whether a company has too much debt?

MCDONALD'S FINANCIAL HIGHLIGHTS (In millions)

	2008	2007
Total current liabilities	$ 2,537.9	$ 4,498.5
Long-term debt	$10,186.0	$ 7,310.0
Other long-term liabilities	1,410.1	1,342.5
Deferred income taxes	944.9	960.9
Total long-term liabilities	$12,541.0	$ 9,613.4
Total stockholders' equity	$13,382.6	$15,279.8
Total liabilities and stockholders' equity	$28,461.5	$29,391.7

Management Issues Related to Issuing Long-Term Debt

LO1 Identify the management issues related to long-term debt.

Profitable operations and short-term credit seldom provide sufficient cash for a growing business. Growth usually requires investment in long-term assets and in research and development and other activities that will produce income in future years. To finance these assets and activities, a company needs funds that will be available for long periods. Two key sources of long-term funds are the issuance of capital stock and the issuance of long-term debt. The management issues related to long-term debt financing are whether to take on long-term debt, how much long-term debt to carry, and what types of long-term debt to incur.

Deciding to Issue Long-Term Debt

A key decision for management is whether to rely solely on stockholders' equity—capital stock issued and retained earnings—for long-term funds or to rely partially on long-term debt. Some companies, such as **Microsoft** and **Apple Computer**, do not issue long-term debt, but like **McDonald's**, most companies find it useful to do so.

Because long-term debt must be paid at maturity and because it usually requires periodic payments of interest, issuing common stock has two advantages over issuing long-term debt: (1) it does not have to be paid back, and (2) a company normally pays dividends on common stock only if it earns sufficient income. Issuing long-term debt, however, has the following advantages over issuing common stock:

- **No loss of stockholder control.** When a corporation issues long-term debt, common stockholders do not relinquish any of their control over the company because bondholders and other creditors do not have voting rights. But when a corporation issues additional shares of common stock, the votes of the new stockholders may force current stockholders and management to give up some control.
- **Tax effects.** The interest on debt is tax-deductible, whereas dividends on common stock are not. For example, if a corporation pays $100,000 in interest and its income tax rate is 30 percent, its net cost will be $70,000 because it will save $30,000 on income taxes. To pay $100,000 in dividends on common stock, the corporation would have to earn $142,857 before income taxes [($100,000 ÷ (1 − 0.30)].
- **Financial leverage.** If a corporation earns more from the funds it raises by incurring long-term debt than it pays in interest on the debt, the excess will increase its earnings for the stockholders. This concept is called **financial leverage**, or *trading on equity*. For example, if a company earns 12 percent on a $1,000,000 investment financed by long-term 10 percent notes, it will earn $20,000 before income taxes ($120,000 − $100,000). The debt to equity ratio is considered an overall measure of a company's financial leverage.

Despite these advantages, debt financing is not always in a company's best interest. It may entail the following:

- **Financial risk.** A high level of debt exposes a company to financial risk. A company whose plans for earnings do not pan out, whose operations are subject to the ups and downs of the economy, or whose cash flow is weak may be unable to pay the principal amount of its debt at the maturity date or even to make periodic interest payments. Creditors can then force the company into bankruptcy—something that has occurred often in the heavily debt-financed airline industry. **TWA**, **Continental Airlines**, and **United Airlines** filed for bankruptcy protection because they could not make payments on their long-term debt and other liabilities. (While in bankruptcy, they restructured their debt and interest payments: TWA sold off its assets, Continental survived, and United is still trying to come out of bankruptcy.)

- **Negative financial leverage.** Financial leverage can work against a company if the earnings from its investments do not exceed its interest payments. For example, many small Internet companies failed in recent years because they relied too heavily on debt financing before developing sufficient resources to ensure their survival.

Evaluating Long-Term Debt

The amount of long-term debt that companies carry varies widely. For many companies, it is less than 100 percent of stockholders' equity. However, as Figure 10-1 shows, the average debt to equity for selected industries often exceeds 100 percent of stockholders' equity. The range is from 75.4 percent to 198.8 percent of equity. To assess how much debt to carry, managers compute the debt to equity ratio. Using data from **McDonald's** Financial Highlights, we can compute its debt to equity ratio in 2008 as follows (in millions):

K/R

$$\text{Debt to Equity} = \frac{\text{Total Liabilities}}{\text{Total Stockholders' Equity}}$$

$$= \frac{\$2,537.9 + \$12,541.0}{\$13,382.6} = \frac{\$15,078.9}{\$13,382.6} = 1.13 \text{ times}$$

A debt to equity ratio of 1.13 is relatively large, but it does not tell the whole story. McDonald's also has long-term leases on property at about 13,620 locations. McDonald's structures these leases in such a way that they do not appear as liabilities on its balance sheet. This practice is called **off-balance-sheet financing** and, as used by McDonald's, is entirely legal. The leases are, however, long-term commitments of cash payments and so have the effect of long-term liabilities. McDonald's total commitment for its leases, which are generally for 20 years, is $10,078 million.[2] If we add the discounted present value of these lease obligations to McDonald's balance sheet debt, it brings the total debt to about $20,000 million.

Financial leverage—using long-term debt to fund investments or operations that increase return on equity—is advantageous as long as a company is able to

FIGURE 10-1
Average Debt to Equity for Selected Industries

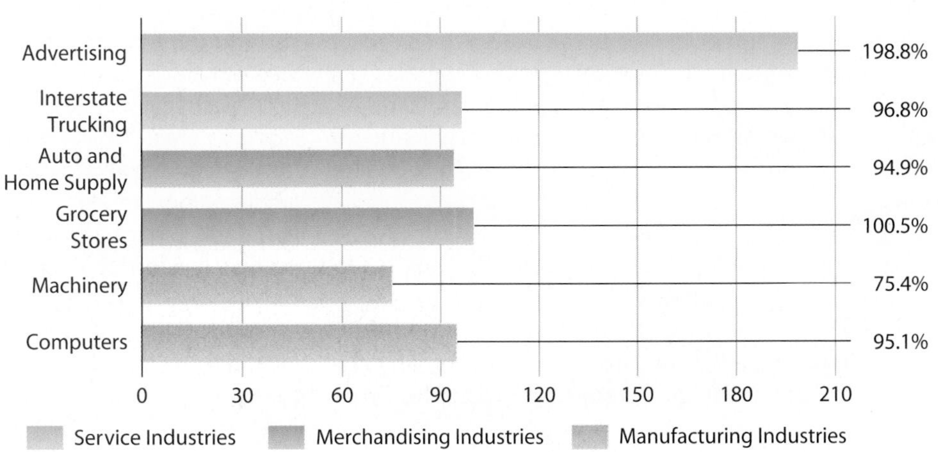

Source: Data from Dun & Bradstreet, *Industry Norms and Key Business Ratios,* 2007–2008.

make timely interest payments and repay the debt at maturity. Because failure to do so can force a company into bankruptcy, companies must assess the financial risk involved. A common measure of how much risk a company undertakes by assuming long-term debt is the **interest coverage ratio**. It measures the degree of protection a company has from default on interest payments. Most analysts want to see an interest coverage ratio of at least 3 or 4 times. Lower interest coverage would mean the company is at risk from a downturn in the economy.

McDonald's 2008 annual report shows that the company had income before taxes of $6,158.0 million and interest expense of $522.6 million. Using these figures, we can compute McDonald's interest coverage ratio as follows:

K/R

$$\text{Interest Coverage Ratio} = \frac{\text{Income Before Income Taxes} + \text{Interest Expense}}{\text{Interest Expense}}$$

$$= \frac{\$6{,}158.0 + \$522.6}{\$522.6}$$

$$= \frac{\$6{,}680.6}{\$522.6}$$

$$= 12.8 \text{ times}$$

McDonald's strong interest coverage ratio of 12.8 times shows that it was in no danger of being unable to make interest payments. However, in computing this ratio, management will add the company's off-balance-sheet rent expense of $1,230.3 to its interest expense. This procedure decreases the coverage ratio to 4.5 times. Although still adequate to cover interest payments, the adjusted coverage ratio is far less robust, which shows the significant effect that off-balance-sheet financing for leases can have on a company's financial situation.

Types of Long-Term Debt

To structure long-term financing to the best advantage of their companies, managers must know the characteristics of the various types of long-term debt.

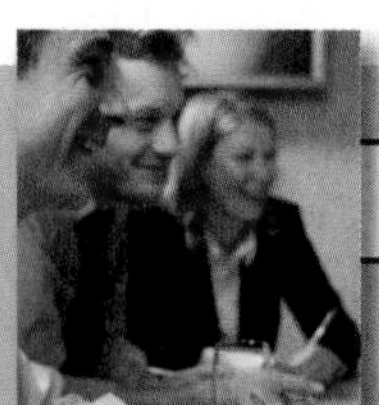

FOCUS ON BUSINESS PRACTICE

How Does Debt Affect a Company's Ability to Borrow?

Credit ratings by agencies like Standard & Poor's reflect the fact that the greater a company's debt, the greater its financial risk. Standard & Poor's rates companies from AAA (best) to CCC (worst) based on various factors, including a company's debt to equity ratio, as shown in the table below.

Rating	AAA	AA	A	BBB	BB	B	CCC
Debt/Equity Ratio*	4.5	34.1	42.9	47.9	59.8	76.0	75.7

These ratings affect not only how much a company can borrow, but also what the interest will cost. The lower its rating, the more a company must pay in interest, and vice versa.

In the heavily debt-laden auto industry, a change in debt rating can mean millions of dollars. For instance, when S & P lowered **General Motors'** and **Ford Motor Company's** credit ratings to "junk status"—BB—it meant that these companies might have to pay 1 or more percentage points in additional interest, which on a debt of $291 billion for GM and $161 billion for Ford would amount to about $2–3 billion.[3] Thus, companies must pay close attention to their financial risk as expressed by the debt to equity ratio. **McDonald's** solid credit is reflected in an A rating.

*Averages of companies with similar ratings.

The most common are bonds payable, notes payable, mortgages payable, long-term leases, pension liabilities, other postretirement benefits, and deferred income taxes.

Bonds Payable Long-term bonds are the most common type of long-term debt. They can have many different characteristics, including the amount of interest, whether the company can elect to repay them before their maturity date, and whether they can be converted to common stock. We cover bonds in detail in later sections of this chapter.

Notes Payable Long-term notes payable, those that come due in more than one year, are also very common. They differ from bonds mainly in the way the contract with the creditor is structured. A long-term note is a promissory note that represents a loan from a bank or other creditor, whereas a bond is a more complex financial instrument that usually involves debt to many creditors. Analysts often do not distinguish between long-term notes and bonds because they have similar effects on the financial statements. Recently, in one of the largest debt offerings in history, **Deutsche Telekom International Finance** raised $14.6 billion by issuing a series of long-term notes denominated in dollars, Euros, pounds, and yen. Some notes were due in 2005, 2010, and 2030.[4]

Mortgages Payable A **mortgage** is a long-term debt secured by real property. It is usually paid in equal monthly installments. Each monthly payment includes interest on the debt and a reduction in the debt. Table 10-1 shows the first three monthly payments on a $100,000, 12 percent mortgage. The mortgage was obtained on June 1, and the monthly payments are $1,600. The entry in journal form to record the July 1 payment would be as follows:

A	=	L	+	SE
−1,600		−600		−1,000

July 1	Mortgage Payable	600	
	Mortgage Interest Expense	1,000	
	Cash		1,600
	Made monthly mortgage payment		

Notice from the entry and from Table 10-1 that the July 1 payment represents interest expense of $1,000 ($\$100{,}000 \times 0.12 \times 1/12$) and a reduction in the debt of $600 ($\$1{,}600 - \$1{,}000$). Therefore, the July payment reduces the unpaid balance to $99,400. August's interest expense is slightly less than July's because of the decrease in the debt.

TABLE 10-1
Monthly Payment Schedule on a $100,000, 12 Percent Mortgage

Payment Date	A Unpaid Balance at Beginning of Period	B Monthly Payment	C Interest for 1 Month at 1% on Unpaid Balance* (1% × A)	D Reduction in Debt (B − C)	E Unpaid Balance at End of Period (A − D)
June 1					$100,000
July 1	$100,000	$1,600	$1,000	$600	99,400
Aug. 1	99,400	1,600	994	606	98,794
Sept. 1	98,794	1,600	988	612	98,182

*Rounded to the nearest dollar.

Long-Term Leases A company can obtain an operating asset in three ways:

1. By borrowing money and buying the asset
2. By renting the asset on a short-term lease
3. By obtaining the asset on a long-term lease

The first two methods do not create accounting problems. When a company uses the first method, it records the asset and liability at the amount paid, and the asset is subject to periodic depreciation.

When a company uses the second method, the lease is short in relation to the useful life of the asset, and the risks of ownership remain with the lessor. This type of agreement is called an **operating lease**. Payments on operating leases are properly treated as rent expense.

The third method is one of the fastest-growing ways of financing plant assets in the United States today. A long-term lease on a plant asset has several advantages. It requires no immediate cash payment, the rental payment is deducted in full for tax purposes, and it costs less than a short-term lease. Acquiring the use of plant assets under long-term leases does create several accounting challenges, however.

Long-term leases may be carefully structured, as they are by **McDonald's**, so that they can be accounted for as operating leases. Accounting standards require, however, that a long-term lease be treated as a **capital lease** when it meets the following conditions:

> **Study Note**
> Under a capital lease, the lessee should record depreciation, using any allowable method.

- It cannot be canceled.
- Its duration is about the same as the useful life of the asset.
- It stipulates that the lessee has the option to buy the asset at a nominal price at the end of the lease.

> **Study Note**
> A capital lease is in substance an installment purchase, and the leased asset and related liability must be recognized at their present value.

A capital lease is thus more like a purchase or sale on installment than a rental. The lessee in a capital lease should record an asset, depreciation on the asset, and a long-term liability equal to the present value of the total lease payments during the lease term.[5] Much like a mortgage payment, each lease payment consists partly of interest expense and partly of repayment of debt.

Suppose, for example, that Polany Manufacturing Company enters into a long-term lease for a machine. The lease terms call for an annual payment of $8,000 for six years, which approximates the useful life of the machine. At the end of the lease period, the title to the machine passes to Polany. This lease is clearly a capital lease and should be recorded as an asset and a liability.

Present value techniques can be used to place a value on the asset and on the corresponding liability in a capital lease. Suppose Polany's interest cost on the unpaid part of its obligation is 16 percent. Using the factor for 16 percent and six periods in Table 2 in the appendix on present values tables, we can compute the present value of the lease payments as follows:

$$\text{Periodic Payment} \times \text{Factor} = \text{Present Value}$$
$$\$8{,}000 \times 3.685 = \$29{,}480$$

The entry in journal form to record the lease is as follows:

A	=	L	+ SE
+29,480		+29,480	

	Debit	Credit
Capital Lease Equipment	29,480	
Capital Lease Obligations		29,480
To record capital lease on machinery		

TABLE 10-2
Payment Schedule on a 16 Percent Capital Lease

Year	A Lease Payment	B Interest (16%) on Unpaid Obligation* (D × 16%)	C Reduction of Lease Obligation (A − B)	D Balance of Lease Obligation (D − C)
Beginning				$29,480
1	$ 8,000	$ 4,717	$ 3,283	26,197
2	8,000	4,192	3,808	22,389
3	8,000	3,582	4,418	17,971
4	8,000	2,875	5,125	12,846
5	8,000	2,055	5,945	6,901
6	8,000	1,099†	6,901	—
	$48,000	$18,520	$29,480	

*Rounded to the nearest dollar.

†The last year's interest equals $1,099 ($8,000 − $6,901); it does not exactly equal $1,104 ($6,901 × $\frac{16}{100}$ × 1) because of the cumulative effect of rounding.

Capital Lease Equipment is classified as a long-term asset. Capital Lease Obligations is classified as a long-term liability.

Each year, Polany must record depreciation on the leased asset. Using straight-line depreciation, a six-year life, and no residual value, the following entry would record the depreciation:

A	= L +	SE
−4,913		−4,913

	Dr.	Cr.
Depreciation Expense, Capital Lease Equipment	4,913	
Accumulated Depreciation, Capital Lease Equipment		4,913
To record depreciation expense on capital lease		

The interest expense for each year is computed by multiplying the interest rate (16 percent) by the amount of the remaining lease obligation. Table 10-2 shows these calculations. Using the data in the table, the first lease payment would be recorded as follows:

A	=	L	+	SE
−8,000		−3,283		−4,717

	Dr.	Cr.
Interest Expense (Column B)	4,717	
Capital Lease Obligations (Column C)	3,283	
Cash (Column A)		8,000
Made payment on capital lease		

This example suggests why companies are motivated to engage in off-balance-sheet financing for leases. By structuring long-term leases so that they can be accounted for as operating leases, companies avoid recording them on the balance sheet as long-term assets and liabilities. This practice, which, as we have noted, is legal and which **McDonald's** uses with skill, not only improves the debt to equity ratio by showing less debt on the balance sheet; it also improves the return on assets by reducing the total assets.

Pension Liabilities Most employees of medium-sized and large companies are covered by a **pension plan**, a contract that requires a company to pay benefits to its employees after they retire. Some companies pay the full cost of the pension plan, but in many companies, employees share the cost by contributing part of their salaries or wages. The contributions from employer and employees are usually paid into a **pension fund**, which is invested on behalf of the employees and from which benefits are paid to retirees. Pension benefits typically consist of monthly payments to retired employees and other payments upon disability or death.

Employers whose pension plans do not have sufficient assets to cover the present value of their pension obligations must record the amount of the shortfall as a liability on their balance sheets. If a pension plan has sufficient assets to cover its obligations, no balance sheet reporting is required or permitted.

There are two kinds of pension plans:

Study Note

Companies prefer defined contribution plans because the employees assume the risk that their pension assets will earn a sufficient return to meet their retirement needs.

- ***Defined contribution plan.*** Under a defined contribution plan, the employer makes a fixed annual contribution, usually a percentage of the employee's gross pay; the amount of the contribution is specified in an agreement between the company and the employees. Retirement payments vary depending on how much the employee's retirement account earns. Employees usually control their own investment accounts, can make additional contributions of their own, and can transfer the funds if they leave the company. Examples of defined contribution plans include 401(k) plans, profit-sharing plans, and employee stock ownership plans (ESOPs).

Study Note

Accounting for a defined benefit plan is far more complex than accounting for a defined contribution plan. Fortunately, accountants can rely on the calculations of professional actuaries, whose expertise includes the mathematics of pension plans.

- ***Defined benefit plan.*** Under a defined benefit plan, the employer contributes an amount annually required to fund estimated future pension liability arising from employment in the current year. The exact amount of the liability will not be known until the retirement and death of the current employees. Although the amount of future benefits is fixed, the annual contributions vary depending on assumptions about how much the pension fund will earn.

Annual pension expense under a defined contribution plan is simple and predictable. Pension expense equals the fixed amount of the annual contribution. In contrast, annual expense under a defined benefit plan is one of the most complex topics in accounting. The intricacies are reserved for advanced courses, but in concept, the procedure is simple. Computation of the annual expense takes into account the estimation of many factors, such as the average remaining service life of active employees, the long-run return on pension plan assets, and future salary increases. A new accounting standard requires companies and other entities with defined benefit plans not backed by a fund sufficient to pay them to record the unfunded portion as a liability.[6] For many companies this can amount to millions or even billions of dollars. **General Motors Corporation**, for example, has a pension liability of $25.2 billion.[7]

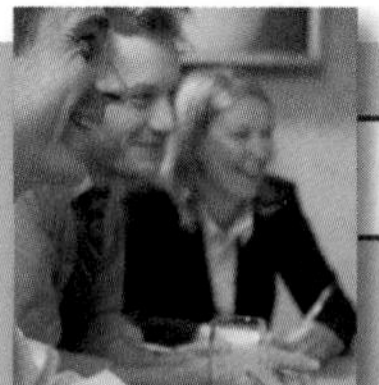

FOCUS ON BUSINESS PRACTICE

Postretirement Liabilities Affect Everyone

The rule requiring recognition of unfunded pension plans as liabilities impacts even government entities. Most government entities have defined benefit pension plans and provide postretirement medical benefits. As a result, states, school districts, and municipalities are all encountering previously ignored pension and health care liabilities. For example, a series of evasive tactics in San Diego led to a $1.1 billion shortfall, which almost caused the city to declare bankruptcy.[8] The state of New Jersey actually stopped setting aside funds to pay for health care in order to give a tax cut. No one added up the cost until the new accounting rule required it. The estimated cost to provide the health care promised to New Jersey's current and future retirees is $58 billion, or twice the state's annual budget.[9] These cases, while extreme, are not unusual. Citizens across the country will face tax increases to pay for these liabilities.

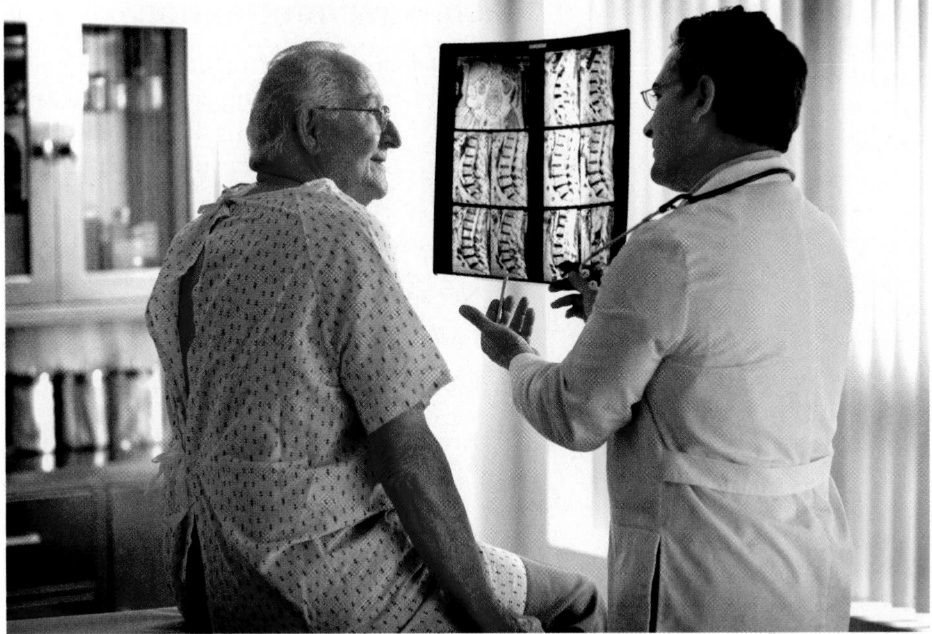

Postretirement benefits, such as health care, are a type of long-term debt for the company that provides them. Recent accounting standards hold that employees earn these benefits during their employment and that the benefits should therefore be estimated and accrued while the employee is working.

Courtesy of Steve Cole/iStockphoto .com.

Because pension expense under a defined benefit plan is not predictable and can vary from year to year, many companies are adopting the more predictable defined contribution plans. For example, in its 2008 annual report, **McDonald's** states that its plan "includes profit sharing, 401(k) and . . . ESOP features."

Study Note

Other postretirement benefits should be expensed as the employee earns them, not when they are paid after the employee retires. This practice conforms to the matching rule.

Other Postretirement Benefits Many companies provide retired employees not only with pensions, but also with health care and other benefits. In the past, these **other postretirement benefits** were accounted for on a cash basis—that is, they were expensed when the benefits were paid, after an employee had retired. More recent accounting standards hold that employees earn these benefits during their employment and that, in accordance with the matching rule, they should be estimated and accrued during the time the employee is working.[10]

The estimates must take into account assumptions about retirement age, mortality, and, most significantly, future trends in health care benefits. Like pension benefits, such future benefits should be discounted to the current period. A field test conducted by the Financial Executives Research Foundation determined that the change to accrual accounting increased postretirement benefits by two to seven times the amount recognized on a cash basis. **General Motors**, the nation's largest private purchaser of health care, recently reported that its future health care liabilities for retirees were almost $29 billion.[11]

Deferred Income Taxes Among the long-term liabilities on the balance sheets of many companies, including **McDonald's**, is an account called **Deferred Income Taxes**. Deferred income taxes are the result of using different accounting methods to calculate income taxes on the income statement and income tax liability on the income tax return. For instance, companies often use straight-line depreciation for financial reporting and an accelerated method to calculate income tax liability. Because straight-line depreciation is less than accelerated depreciation in the early years of an asset's life, the presumption is that the income taxes will eventually have to be paid. Thus, the difference is listed as a long-term liability, deferred income taxes. Because companies try to manage their affairs to minimize income taxes paid, deferred income taxes can become quite large. In McDonald's case, as shown in the company's Financial Highlights, they amounted to almost $1 billion in 2008. We cover deferred income taxes in greater detail in a later chapter.

Cash Flow Information

The best source of information concerning cash flows about short-term and long-term debt is the financing activities section of the statement of cash flows. For instance, McDonald's cash flows from these activities are clearly revealed in this partial section of the company's statement of cash flows (in millions):

	2008	*2007*	*2006*
Financing Activities			
Net short-term borrowings	$ 266.7	$ 101.3	$ 34.5
Long-term financing issuances	3,477.5	2,116.8	1.9
Long-term financing repayments	(2,698.5)	(1,645.5)	(2,301.1)

Note that McDonald's has little short-term borrowing and that the company's cash outflows for long-term borrowing for the three years exceeded cash inflows by $1,048.9 million.

STOP & APPLY >

Each type of long-term liability below is closely related to one of the statements in the list that follows. Write the number of the liability next to the statement to which it applies.

1. Bonds payable
2. Long-term notes payable
3. Mortgage payable
4. Long-term lease
5. Pension liabilities
6. Other postretirement benefits
7. Deferred income taxes

____ a. Cost of health care after employees' retirement

____ b. The most common type of long-term debt

____ c. The result of differences between accounting income and taxable income

____ d. Debt that is secured by real estate

____ e. Promissory note that is due in more than one year

____ f. May be based on a percentage of employees' wages or on future benefits

____ g. Can be similar in form to an installment purchase

SOLUTION

a. 6; b. 1; c. 7; d. 3; e. 2; f. 5; g. 4

The Nature of Bonds

LO2 Describe the features of a bond issue and the major characteristics of bonds.

A **bond** is a security, usually long term, representing money that a corporation borrows from the investing public. (The federal, state, and local governments also issue bonds to raise money, as do foreign countries.) A bond entails a promise to repay the amount borrowed, called the ***principal***, on a specified date and to pay interest at a specified rate at specified times—usually semiannually. In contrast to stockholders, who are the owners of a corporation, bondholders are a corporation's creditors.

When a public corporation decides to issue bonds, it must submit the appropriate legal documents to the Securities and Exchange Commission for permission to borrow the funds. The SEC reviews the corporation's financial health and the specific terms of the **bond indenture**, which is a contract that defines the

Study Note

An investor who purchases debt securities, such as bonds or notes, is a creditor of the organization, not an owner.

rights, privileges, and limitations of the bondholders. The bond indenture generally describes such things as the maturity date of the bonds, interest payment dates, and the interest rate. It may also cover repayment plans and restrictions. Once the bond issue is approved, the corporation has a limited time in which to issue the authorized bonds. As evidence of its debt to the bondholders, the corporation provides each of them with a **bond certificate**.

Bond Issue: Prices and Interest Rates

Study Note

When bonds with an interest rate different from the market rate are issued, they sell at a discount or premium. The discount or premium acts as an equalizing factor.

A **bond issue** is the total value of bonds issued at one time. For example, a $1,000,000 bond issue could consist of a thousand $1,000 bonds. The prices of bonds are stated in terms of a percentage of the face value, or principal, of the bonds. A bond issue quoted at 103½ means that a $1,000 bond costs $1,035 ($1,000 × 1.035). When a bond sells at exactly 100, it is said to sell at face (or par) value. When it sells below 100, it is said to sell at a discount; above 100, at a premium. For instance, a $1,000 bond quoted at 87.62 would be selling at a discount and would cost the buyer $876.20.

Face Interest Rate and Market Interest Rate Two interest rates relevant to bond prices are the face interest rate and market interest rate:

Study Note

A bond sells at face value when the face interest rate of the bond is identical to the market interest rate for similar bonds on the date of issue.

- The **face interest rate** is the fixed rate of interest paid to bondholders based on the face value of the bonds. The rate and amount are fixed over the life of the bond. To allow time to file with the SEC, publicize the bond issue, and print the bond certificates, a company must decide in advance what the face interest rate will be. Most companies try to set the face interest rate as close as possible to the market interest rate.
- The **market interest rate** is the rate of interest paid in the market on bonds of similar risk.* It is also called the *effective interest rate.* The market interest rate fluctuates daily. Because a company has no control over it, the market interest rate often differs from the face interest rate on the issue date.

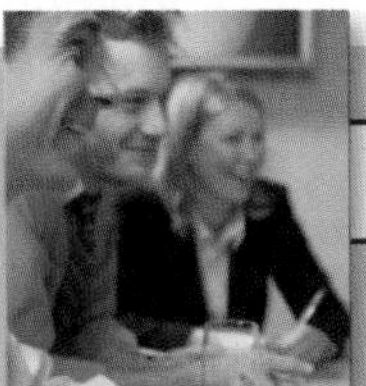

FOCUS ON BUSINESS PRACTICE

Check Out Those Bond Prices!

The price of many bonds can be found daily in business publications like *The Wall Street Journal*. For instance, shown below are quotations for the bonds of Ford Motor Company and Abbott Laboratories, two very active corporate bond traders:[12]

	Face Rate	Maturity	Last Price	Last Yield
Ford Motor	9.980	2/47	82.500	12.112
Abbott	5.150	11/02	102.106	4.666

Abbott is one of the strongest companies financially, while Ford Motor is one of the weaker ones. Note that the face rate on Abbott's bond is lower than the face rate on Ford Motor's (5.150 percent versus 9.980 percent). In addition, the last price on Ford Motor's bond is less than 100 (82.500); thus, the market rate of interest on the bond (last yield of 12.112 percent) is greater than the face rate. This means that investors are not willing to settle for the 9.980 percent face rate and are demanding a higher rate by paying less than 100. Conversely, Abbott's bond sells for more than 100 (102.106), which means that investors are willing to accept a market rate (4.666 percent) that is even less than the bond's face rate. The prices of bonds vary daily as companies' fortunes and interest rates change.

*At the time this chapter was written, the market interest rates on corporate bonds were volatile. Therefore, we use a variety of interest rates in our examples.

Discounts and Premiums If the market interest rate fluctuates from the face interest rate before the issue date, the issue price of bonds will not equal their face value. This fluctuation in market interest rate causes the bonds to sell at either a discount or premium:

- A **discount** equals the excess of the face value over the issue price. The issue price will be less than the face value when the market interest rate is higher than the face interest rate.
- A **premium** equals the excess of the issue price over the face value. The issue price will be more than the face value when the market interest rate is lower than the face interest rate.

Discounts or premiums are contra-accounts that are subtracted from or added to bonds payable on the balance sheet.

Characteristics of Bonds

A bond indenture can be written to fit an organization's financing needs. As a result, the bonds issued in today's financial markets have many different features. We describe several of the more important features of bonds in the following paragraphs.

> **Study Note**
> Do not confuse the terms *indenture* and *debenture*. They sound alike, but an indenture is a bond contract, whereas a debenture is an unsecured bond. A debenture bond of a stable company actually might be a less risky investment than a secured bond of an unstable company.

Unsecured and Secured Bonds Bonds can be either unsecured or secured. **Unsecured bonds** (also called *debenture bonds*) are issued on the basis of a corporation's general credit. **Secured bonds** carry a pledge of certain corporate assets as a guarantee of repayment. A pledged asset may be a specific asset, such as a truck, or a general category of asset, such as property, plant, or equipment.

Term and Serial Bonds When all the bonds of an issue mature at the same time, they are called **term bonds**. For instance, a company may decide to issue $1,000,000 worth of bonds, all due 20 years from the date of issue.

When the bonds of an issue mature on different dates, they are called **serial bonds**. For example, suppose a $1,000,000 bond issue calls for paying $200,000 of the principal every five years. This arrangement means that after the first $200,000 payment is made, $800,000 of the bonds would remain outstanding for the next five years, $600,000 for the next five years, and so on. A company may issue serial bonds to ease the task of retiring its debt—that is, paying off what it owes on the bonds.

> **Study Note**
> An advantage of issuing serial bonds is that the organization retires the bonds over a period of years, rather than all at once.

Callable and Convertible Bonds When bonds are callable and convertible, a company may be able to retire them before their maturity dates. When a company does retire a bond issue before its maturity date, it is called **early extinguishment of debt**. Doing so can be to a company's advantage.

Callable bonds give the issuer the right to buy back and retire the bonds before maturity at a specified **call price**, which is usually above face value. Callable bonds give a company flexibility in financing its operations. For example, if bond interest rates drop, the company can call the bonds and reissue debt at a lower interest rate. A company might also call its bonds if it has earned enough to pay off the debt, if the reason for having the debt no longer exists, or if it wants to restructure its debt to equity ratio. The bond indenture states the time period and the prices at which the bonds can be redeemed.

Convertible bonds allow the bondholder to exchange a bond for a specified number of shares of common stock. The face value of a convertible bond when issued is greater than the market value of the shares to which it can be converted.

However, if the market price of the common stock rises above a certain level, the value of the bond rises in relation to the value of the common stock. Even if the stock price does not rise, the investor still holds the bond and receives both the periodic interest payments and the face value at the maturity date.

One advantage of issuing convertible bonds is that the interest rate is usually lower because investors are willing to give up some current interest in the hope that the value of the stock will increase and the value of the bonds will therefore also increase. In addition, if the bonds are both callable and convertible and the market value of the stock rises to a level at which the bond is worth more than face value, management can avoid repaying the bonds by calling them for redemption, thereby forcing the bondholders to convert their bonds into common stock. The bondholders will agree to convert because no gain or loss results from the transaction.

Registered and Coupon Bonds **Registered bonds** are issued in the names of the bondholders. The issuing organization keeps a record of the bondholders' names and addresses and pays them interest by check on the interest payment date. Most bonds today are registered.

Coupon bonds are not registered with the organization. Instead, they bear coupons stating the amount of interest due and the payment date. The bondholder removes the coupons from the bonds on the interest payment dates and presents them at a bank for collection.

STOP & APPLY >

Each term related to bonds below is the opposite to one of the terms in the list that follows. Write the number of the term in the first list next to the term to which it opposes.

1. Face interest rate	____ a. Secured
2. Discount	____ b. Coupon
3. Unsecured	____ c. Convertible
4. Term	____ d. Premium
5. Registered	____ e. Market interest rate
6. Callable	____ f. Serial
7. Deferred income taxes	

SOLUTION

a. 3; b. 5; c. 6; d. 2; e. 1; f. 4

Accounting for the Issuance of Bonds

LO3 Record bonds issued at face value and at a discount or premium.

When the board of directors of a public corporation decides to issue bonds, the company must submit the appropriate legal documents to the Securities and Exchange Commission for authorization to borrow the funds. It is not necessary to make a journal entry to record the authorization of a bond issue. However, most companies disclose the authorization in the notes to their financial statements. The note lists the number and value of bonds authorized, the interest rate, the interest payment dates, and the life of the bonds.

In sections that follow, we show how to record bonds issued at face value, at a discount, and at a premium.

Bonds Issued at Face Value

Suppose Bharath Corporation issues $200,000 of 9 percent, five-year bonds on January 1, 2010, and sells them on the same date for their face value. The bond indenture states that interest is to be paid on January 1 and July 1 of each year. The entry in journal form to record the bond issue is as follows:

A	=	L	+	SE
+200,000		+200,000		

		Debit	Credit
2010			
Jan. 1	Cash	200,000	
	Bonds Payable		200,000
	Sold $200,000 of 9%, 5-year bonds at face value		

Study Note
When calculating semiannual interest, do not use the annual rate (9 percent in this case). Rather, use half the annual rate.

Once a corporation issues bonds, it must pay interest to the bondholders over the life of the bonds, usually semiannually, and the principal of the bonds at maturity. In this example, interest is paid on January 1 and July 1 of each year. Thus, Bharath Corporation would owe the bondholders $9,000 interest on July 1, 2010:

$$
\begin{aligned}
\text{Interest} &= \text{Principal} \times \text{Rate} \times \text{Time} \\
&= \$200{,}000 \times \frac{9}{100} \times 6/12 \text{ year} \\
&= \$9{,}000
\end{aligned}
$$

Bharath would record the interest paid to the bondholders on each semiannual interest payment date (January 1 or July 1) as follows:

A*	=	L	+	SE
−9,000				−9,000

*Assumes cash paid.

	Debit	Credit
Bond Interest Expense	9,000	
Cash (or Interest Payable)		9,000
Paid (or accrued) semiannual interest to bondholders of 9%, 5-year bonds		

Bonds Issued at a Discount

Suppose Bharath Corporation issues $200,000 of 9 percent, five-year bonds at 96.149 on January 1, 2010, when the market interest rate is 10 percent. In this case, the bonds are being issued at a discount because the market interest rate exceeds the face interest rate. The following entry in journal form records the issuance of the bonds at a discount:

A	=	L	+	SE
+192,298		−7,702		
		+200,000		

			Debit	Credit
2010				
Jan. 1	Cash		192,298	
	Unamortized Bond Discount		7,702	
	Bonds Payable			200,000
	Sold $200,000 of 9%, 5-year bonds at 96.149			
	Face amount of bonds	$200,000		
	Less purchase price of bonds ($200,000 × 0.96149)	192,298		
	Unamortized bond discount	$ 7,702		

In this entry, Cash is debited for the amount received ($192,298), Bonds Payable is credited for the face amount ($200,000) of the bond liability, and the

FOCUS ON BUSINESS PRACTICE

100-Year Bonds Are Not for Everyone

In 1993, interest rates on long-term debt were at historically low levels, which induced some companies to attempt to lock in those low costs for long periods. One of the most aggressive companies in that regard was **The Walt Disney Company**, which issued $150 million of 100-year bonds at a yield of only 7.5 percent. It was the first time since 1954 that 100-year bonds had been issued. Among the others that followed Walt Disney's lead by issuing 100-year bonds were the **Coca-Cola Company**, **Columbia HCA Healthcare**, **Bell South**, **IBM**, and even the People's Republic of China. Some analysts wondered if even Mickey Mouse could survive 100 years. Investors who purchase such bonds take a financial risk because if interest rates rise, which is always likely, the market value of the bonds will decrease.[13]

difference ($7,702) is debited to Unamortized Bond Discount. If a balance sheet is prepared right after the bonds are issued at a discount, the liability for bonds payable is reported as follows:

Long-term liabilities		
9% bonds payable, due 1/1/2015	$200,000	
Less unamortized bond discount	7,702	$192,298

Unamortized Bond Discount is a contra-liability account. Its balance is deducted from the face amount of the bonds to arrive at the carrying value, or present value, of the bonds. The bond discount is described as unamortized because it will be amortized (written off) over the life of the bonds.

Bonds Issued at a Premium

When bonds have a face interest rate above the market rate for similar investments, they are issued at a price above the face value, or at a premium. For example, suppose Bharath Corporation issues $200,000 of 9 percent, five-year bonds

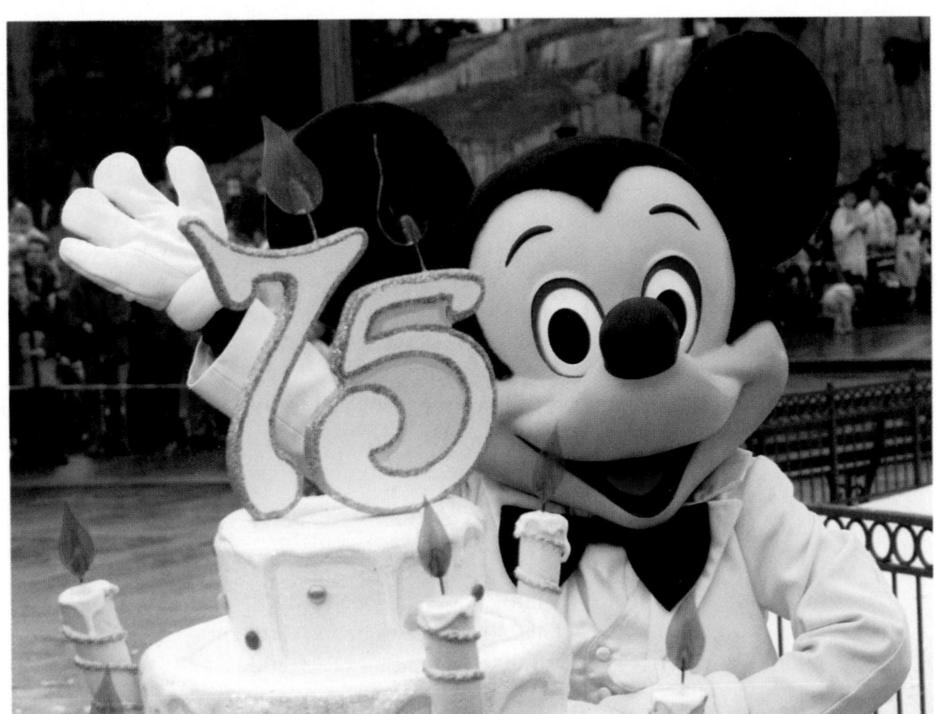

In 1993, the Walt Disney Company issued $150 million of 100-year bonds at a yield of 7.5 percent. At the time, some analysts wondered if even Mickey Mouse could survive 100 years. However, Mickey, who first appeared in 1928 in the animated short film *Steamboat Willie*, goes on. In 2003, he celebrated his 75th birthday. The bonds must be paid by 2093, but Disney has the option of repaying the bonds beginning in 2023.

Courtesy of Mehdi Fedouach/AFP/Getty Images.

for $208,200 on January 1, 2010, when the market interest rate is 8 percent. This means that investors will purchase the bonds at 104.1 percent of their face value. The issuance would be recorded as follows:

A	=	L	+	SE
+208,200		+8,200		
		+200,000		

2010			
Jan. 1	Cash	208,200	
	Unamortized Bond Premium		8,200
	Bonds Payable		200,000
	Sold $200,000 of 9%, 5-year bonds at 104.1 ($200,000 × 1.041)		

Study Note

The carrying amount is always the face value of the bonds less the unamortized discount or plus the unamortized premium. The carrying amount always approaches the face value over the life of the bond.

Right after this entry is made, bonds payable would be presented on the balance sheet as follows:

Long-term liabilities		
9% bonds payable, due 1/1/2015	$200,000	
Unamortized bond premium	8,200	$208,200

The carrying value of the bonds payable is $208,200, which equals the face value of the bonds plus the unamortized bond premium. The cash received from the bond issue is also $208,200. This means that the purchasers were willing to pay a premium of $8,200 to buy these bonds because their face interest rate was higher than the market interest rate.

Bond Issue Costs

The costs of issuing bonds can amount to as much as 5 percent of a bond issue. These costs often include the fees of underwriters, whom corporations hire to take care of the details of marketing a bond issue. Because the issue costs benefit the whole life of a bond issue, it makes sense to spread them over that period. It is generally accepted practice to establish a separate account for these costs and to amortize them over the life of the bonds.

Because issue costs decrease the amount of money a company receives from a bond issue, they have the effect of raising the discount or lowering the premium on the issue. Thus, bond issue costs can be spread over the life of the bonds through the amortization of a discount or premium. This method simplifies recordkeeping. In the rest of our discussion, we assume that all bond issue costs increase the discounts or decrease the premiums on bond issues.

STOP & APPLY >

Gill Foods is planning to issue $1,000,000 in long-term bonds. Depending on market conditions, Gill's CPA advises that the bonds could be issued at (a) 99, (b) 100, or (c) 101. Calculate the amount that Gill would receive under each alternative and indicate whether it is at face value, a discount or a premium and the amount of each.

SOLUTION

(a) $1,000,000 × 0.99 = $990,000; a discount of $10,000
(b) $1,000,000 × 1.00 = $1,000,000; at face value; no discount or premium
(c) $1,000,000 × 1.01 = $1,010,000; a premium of $10,000

Using Present Value to Value a Bond

LO4 Use present values to determine the value of bonds.

A bond's value is based on the present value of two components of cash flow: a series of fixed interest payments, and a single payment at maturity. The amount of interest a bond pays is fixed over its life, but the market interest rate varies from day to day. Thus, the amount investors are willing to pay for a bond varies as well.

Case 1: Market Rate Above Face Rate

Suppose a bond has a face value of $20,000 and pays fixed interest of $900 every six months (a 9 percent annual rate). The bond is due in five years. If the market interest rate today is 12 percent, what is the present value of the bond?

To answer this question, we use Table 2 in the appendix on present value tables to calculate the present value of the periodic interest payments of $900, and we use Table 1 in the same appendix to calculate the present value of the single payment of $20,000 at maturity. Because interest payments are made every six months, the compounding period is half a year. Thus, we have to convert the annual rate to a semiannual rate of 6 percent (12 percent divided by two six-month periods per year) and use ten periods (five years multiplied by two six-month periods per year). With this information, we can compute the present value of the bond as follows:

Present value of 10 periodic payments at 6%: $900 × 7.360 (from Table 2 in the appendix)	$ 6,624
Present value of a single payment at the end of 10 periods at 6%: $20,000 × 0.558 (from Table 1 in the appendix):	11,160
Present value of $20,000 bond	$17,784

The market interest rate has increased so much since the bond was issued—from 9 percent to 12 percent—that the value of the bond today is only $17,784. That amount is all investors would be willing to pay at this time for a bond that provides income of $900 every six months and a return of the $20,000 principal in five years.

Case 2: Market Rate Below Face Rate

As Figure 10-2 shows, if the market interest rate on the bond described above falls below the face interest rate, say to 8 percent (4 percent semiannually), the present value of the bond will be greater than the face value of $20,000:

Present value of 10 periodic payments at 4%: $900 × 8.111 (from Table 2 in the appendix)	$ 7,300
Present value of a single payment at the end of 10 periods at 4%: $20,000 × 0.676 (from Table 1 in the appendix)	13,520
Present value of $20,000 bond	$20,820

FIGURE 10-2
Using Present Value to Value a $20,000, 9 Percent, Five-Year Bond

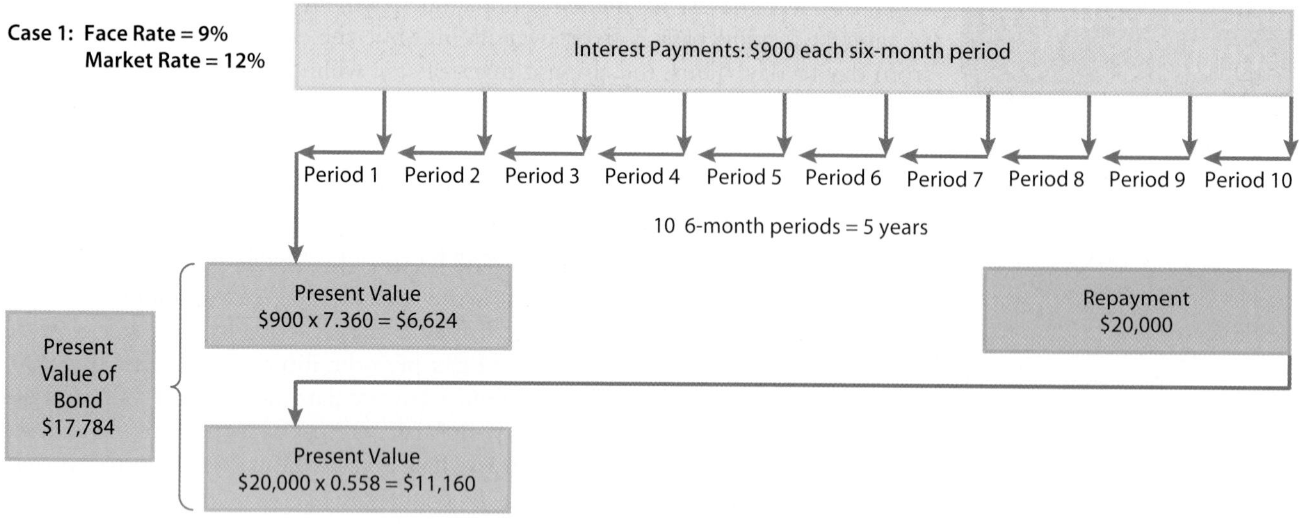

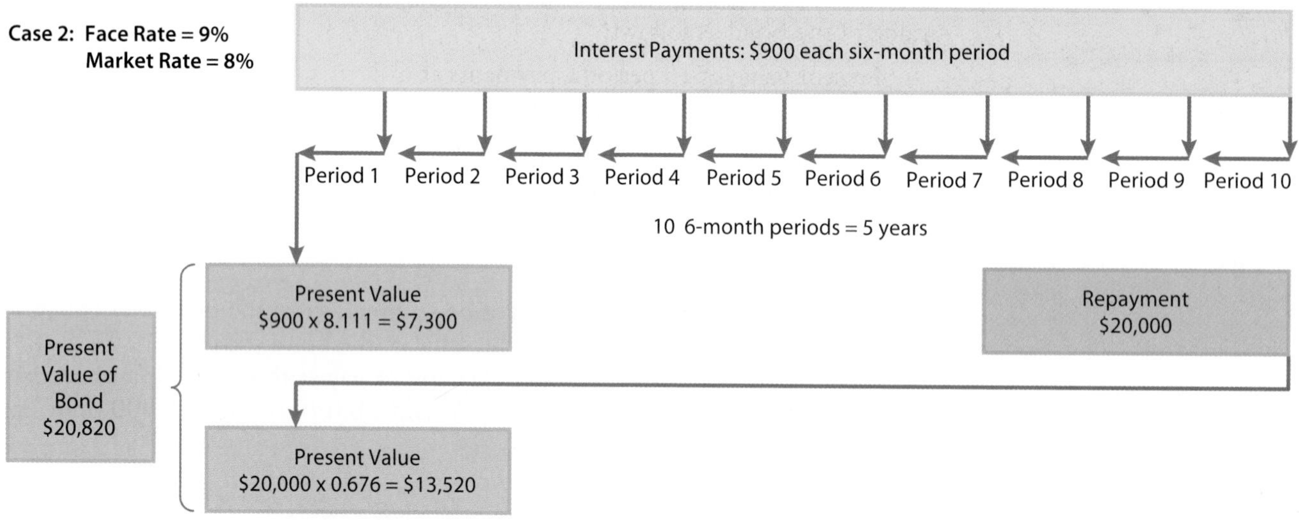

STOP & APPLY >

Tyler Company's $500,000 bond issue pays semiannual interest of $16,000 and is due in 20 years. Assume that the market interest rate is 6 percent. Calculate the amount that Tyler Company will pay at maturity. (Calculate the present value of each bond issue and sum.)

SOLUTION

Present value of 40 periodic payments of 3% (From Table 2*):
$16,000 × 23.115* = $369,840

Present value of a single payment at the end of 40 years at 3% (From Table 1†):
$500,000 × 0.307† = $153,500
Total value of the bond issue $523,340

*From Table 2 in appendix on present value tables
†From Table 1 in appendix on present value tables

Amortization of Bond Discounts and Premiums

LO5 Amortize bond discounts and bond premiums using the straight-line and effective interest methods.

A bond discount or premium represents the amount by which the total interest cost is higher or lower than the total interest payments. To record interest expense properly and ensure that the carrying value of bonds payable at maturity equals face value, it is necessary to systematically reduce the bond discount or premium—that is, to amortize them—over the life of the bonds. This can be accomplished by using either the straight-line method or the effective interest method.

Amortizing a Bond Discount

In one of our earlier examples, Bharath Corporation issued $200,000 of five-year bonds at a time when the market interest rate of 10 percent exceeded the face interest rate of 9 percent. The bonds sold for $192,298, resulting in an unamortized bond discount of $7,702.

Because a bond discount affects interest expense in each year of a bond issue, the bond discount should be amortized over the life of the bond issue. In this way, the unamortized bond discount will decrease gradually over time, and the carrying value of the bond issue (face value less unamortized discount) will gradually increase. By the maturity date, the carrying value of the bond issue will equal its face value, and the unamortized bond discount will be zero.

In the following sections, we calculate Bharath Corporation's total interest cost and amortize its bond discount using the straight-line and the effective interest methods.

Study Note

A bond discount is a component of interest cost because it represents the amount in excess of the issue price that a corporation must pay on the maturity date.

Calculating Total Interest Cost When a corporation issues bonds at a discount, the market (or effective) interest rate that it pays is greater than the face interest rate on the bonds. The reason is that the interest cost is the stated interest payments *plus* the amount of the bond discount. That is, although the company does not receive the full face value of the bonds on issue, it still must pay back the full face value at maturity. The difference between the issue price and the face value must be added to the total interest payments to arrive at the actual interest expense.

The full cost to Bharath of issuing its bonds at a discount is as follows:

Cash to be paid to bondholders	
Face value at maturity	$200,000
Interest payments ($200,000 × 0.09 × 5 years)	90,000
Total cash paid to bondholders	$290,000
Less cash received from bondholders	192,298
Total interest cost	$ 97,702

Or, alternatively:

Interest payments ($200,000 × 0.09 × 5 years)	$ 90,000
Bond discount	7,702
Total interest cost	$ 97,702

The total interest cost of $97,702 is made up of $90,000 in interest payments and the $7,702 bond discount. Thus, the bond discount increases the interest paid on the bonds from the face interest rate to the market interest rate. The market (or effective) interest rate is the real interest cost of the bond over its life.

To have each year's interest expense reflect the market interest rate, the discount must be allocated over the remaining life of the bonds as an increase in the interest expense each period. Thus, the interest expense for each period will exceed the actual payment of interest by the amount of the bond discount that is amortized over the period. This process of allocation is called *amortization of the bond discount*.

Study Note

The discount on a zero coupon bond represents the interest that will be paid (in its entirety) on the maturity date.

Some bonds do not require periodic interest payments. These bonds, called **zero coupon bonds**, are simply a promise to pay a fixed amount at the maturity date. They are issued at a large discount because the only interest that the buyer earns or the issuer pays is the discount. For example, a five-year, $200,000 zero coupon bond issued when the market rate is 14 percent, compounded semiannually, would sell for only $101,600. That amount is the present value of a single payment of $200,000 at the end of five years. The discount of $98,400 ($200,000 − $101,600) is the total interest cost, which is amortized over the life of the bond.

Straight-Line Method The **straight-line method** equalizes amortization of a bond discount for each interest period. Using our example of Bharath Corporation, the interest payment dates of the bond issue are January 1 and July 1 of each year, and the bonds mature in five years. With the straight-line method, the amount of the bond discount amortized and the interest expense for each semiannual period are calculated in four steps:

1. Total Interest Payments = Interest Payments per Year × Life of Bonds
   = 2 × 5 = 10
2. Amortization of Bond Discount per Interest Period = $\frac{\text{Bond Discount}}{\text{Total Interest Payments}}$
   = $\frac{\$7{,}702}{10}$
   = $770*
3. Cash Interest Payment = Face Value × Face Interest Rate × Time
   = $200,000 × 0.09 × 6/12 = $9,000
4. Interest Expense per Interest Period = Interest Payment + Amortization of Bond Discount
   = $9,000 + $770 = $9,770

On July 1, 2010, the first semiannual interest date, the entry in journal form would be:

A*	=	L	+	SE
−9,000		+770		−9,770

*Assumes cash paid.

		Dr.	Cr.
2010			
July 1	Bond Interest Expense	9,770	
	Unamortized Bond Discount		770
	Cash (or Interest Payable)		9,000
	Paid (or accrued) semiannual interest to bondholders and amortized the discount on 9%, 5-year bonds		

Notice that the bond interest expense is $9,770, but the amount paid to the bondholders is the $9,000 face interest payment. The difference of $770 is the credit to Unamortized Bond Discount. This lowers the debit balance of Unamortized Bond Discount and raises the carrying value of the bonds payable by $770 each interest period. If no changes occur in the bond issue, this entry will be made every six months for the life of the bonds. When the bond issue matures, the Unamortized Bond Discount account will have a zero balance, and the carrying value of the bonds will be $200,000—exactly equal to the amount due the bondholders.

*Rounded.

Although the straight-line method has long been used, it has a certain weakness. When it is used to amortize a discount, the carrying value goes up each period, but the bond interest expense stays the same; thus, the rate of interest falls over time. Conversely, when this method is used to amortize a premium, the rate of interest rises over time. The Accounting Principles Board therefore holds that the straight-line method should be used only when it does not lead to a material difference from the effective interest method.[14] A material difference is one that affects the evaluation of a company.

Effective Interest Method When the **effective interest method** is used to compute the interest and amortization of a bond discount, a constant interest rate is applied to the carrying value of the bonds at the beginning of each interest period. This constant rate is the market rate (i.e., the effective rate) at the time the bonds were issued. The amount amortized each period is the difference between the interest computed by using the market rate and the actual interest paid to bondholders.

As an example, we use the same facts we used earlier—a $200,000 bond issue at 9 percent, with a five-year maturity and interest to be paid twice a year. The market rate at the time the bonds were issued was 10 percent, so the bonds sold for $192,298, a discount of $7,702. Table 10-3 shows the interest and amortization of the bond discount.

Study Note

Whether a bond is sold at a discount or a premium, its carrying value will equal its face value on the maturity date.

The amounts in the table for period 1 were computed as follows:

Column A: The carrying value of the bonds is their face value less the unamortized bond discount ($200,000 − $7,702 = $192,298).

TABLE 10-3 Interest and Amortization of a Bond Discount: Effective Interest Method

	A	B	C	D	E	F
Semiannual Interest Period	Carrying Value at Beginning of Period	Semiannual Interest Expense at 10% to Be Recorded* (5% × A)	Semiannual Interest Payment to Bondholders (4½% × $200,000)	Amortization of Bond Discount (B − C)	Unamortized Bond Discount at End of Period (E − D)	Carrying Value at End of Period (A + D)
0					$7,702	$192,298
1	$192,298	$9,615	$9,000	$615	7,087	192,913
2	192,913	9,646	9,000	646	6,441	193,559
3	193,559	9,678	9,000	678	5,763	194,237
4	194,237	9,712	9,000	712	5,051	194,949
5	194,949	9,747	9,000	747	4,304	195,696
6	195,696	9,785	9,000	785	3,519	196,481
7	196,481	9,824	9,000	824	2,695	197,305
8	197,305	9,865	9,000	865	1,830	198,170
9	198,170	9,908	9,000	908	922	199,078
10	199,078	9,922†	9,000	922	—	200,000

*Rounded to the nearest dollar.
†Last period's interest expense equals $9,922 ($9,000 + $922); it does not equal $9,954 ($199,078 × 0.05) because of the cumulative effect of rounding.

Column B: The interest expense to be recorded is the effective interest. It is found by multiplying the carrying value of the bonds by the market interest rate for one-half year ($192,298 × 0.10 × 6/12 = $9,615).

Column C: The interest paid in the period is a constant amount computed by multiplying the face value of the bonds by their face interest rate by the interest time period ($200,000 × 0.09 × 6/12 = $9,000).

Column D: The discount amortized is the difference between the effective interest expense to be recorded and the interest to be paid on the interest payment date ($9,615 − $9,000 = $615).

Column E: The unamortized bond discount is the balance of the bond discount at the beginning of the period less the current period amortization of the discount ($7,702 − $615 = $7,087). The unamortized discount decreases in each interest payment period because it is amortized as a portion of interest expense.

Column F: The carrying value of the bonds at the end of the period is the carrying value at the beginning of the period plus the amortization during the period ($192,298 + $615 = $192,913). Notice that the sum of the carrying value and the unamortized discount (Column F + Column E) always equals the face value of the bonds ($192,913 + $7,087 = $200,000).

The entry to record the interest expense is exactly like the one when the straight-line method is used. However, the amounts debited and credited to the various accounts are different. Using the effective interest method, the entry in journal form for July 1, 2010, would be as follows:

A*	=	L	+	SE
−9,000		+615		−9,615

*Assumes cash paid.

2010			
July 1	Bond Interest Expense	9,615	
	Unamortized Bond Discount		615
	Cash (or Interest Payable)		9,000
	Paid (or accrued) semiannual interest to bondholders and amortized the discount on 9%, 5-year bonds		

Study Note

The bond interest expense recorded exceeds the amount of interest paid because of the amortization of the bond discount. The matching rule dictates that the discount be amortized over the life of the bond.

Although an interest and amortization table is useful because it can be prepared in advance for all periods, it is not necessary to have one to determine the amortization of a discount for any one interest payment period. It is necessary only to multiply the carrying value by the effective interest rate and subtract the interest payment from the result. For example, the amount of discount to be amortized in the seventh interest payment period is $824, calculated as follows: ($196,481 × 0.05) − $9,000.

Figure 10-3, which is based on the data in Table 10-3, shows how the effective interest method affects the amortization of a bond discount. Notice that the carrying value (the issue price) is initially less than the face value, but that it gradually increases toward face value over the life of the bond issue. Notice also that interest expense exceeds interest payments by the amount of the bond discount amortized. Interest expense increases gradually over the life of the bond because it is based on the gradually increasing carrying value (multiplied by the market interest rate).

Study Note

The bond interest increases each period because the carrying value of the bonds (the principal on which the interest is calculated) increases each period.

Amortizing a Bond Premium

In our earlier example of bonds issued at a premium, Bharath Corporation issued $200,000 of five-year bonds at a time when the market interest rate was 8 percent

FIGURE 10-3
Carrying Value and Interest Expense—Bonds Issued at a Discount

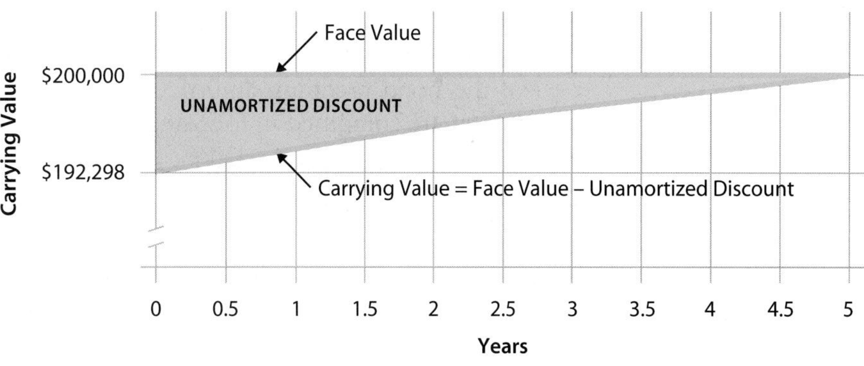

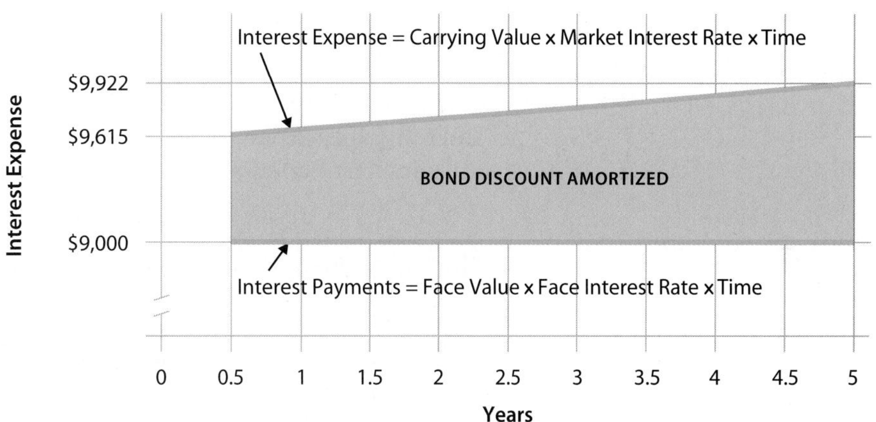

and the face interest rate was 9 percent. The bonds sold for $208,200, which resulted in an unamortized bond premium of $8,200. Like a discount, a premium must be amortized over the life of the bonds so that it can be matched to its effects on interest expense during that period.

In the following sections, we calculate Bharath Corporation's total interest cost and amortize its bond premium using the straight-line and effective interest methods.

> **Study Note**
> A bond premium is deducted from interest payments in calculating total interest cost because a bond premium represents an amount over the face value of a bond that the corporation never has to return to the bondholders. In effect, it reduces the higher-than-market interest the corporation is paying on the bond.

Calculation of Total Interest Cost Because the bondholders paid more than face value for the bonds, the premium of $8,200 ($208,200 − $200,000) represents an amount that the bondholders will not receive at maturity. The premium is in effect a reduction, in advance, of the total interest paid on the bonds over the life of the bond issue. The total interest cost over the issue's life can be computed as follows:

Cash to be paid to bondholders	
Face value at maturity	$200,000
Interest payments ($200,000 × 0.09 × 5 years)	90,000
Total cash paid to bondholders	$290,000
Less cash received from bondholders	208,200
Total interest cost	$ 81,800

Alternatively, the total interest cost can be computed as follows:

Interest payments ($200,000 × 0.09 × 5 years)	$90,000
Less bond premium	8,200
Total interest cost	$81,800

Notice that the total interest payments of $90,000 exceed the total interest cost of $81,800 by $8,200, the amount of the bond premium.

Straight-Line Method Under the straight-line method, the bond premium is spread evenly over the life of the bond issue. As with bond discounts, the amount of the bond premium amortized and the interest expense for each semiannual period are computed in four steps:

1. Total Interest Payments = Interest Payments per Year × Life of Bonds

$$= 2 \times 5 = 10$$

2. Amortization of Bond Premium per Interest Period $= \dfrac{\text{Bond Premium}}{\text{Total Interest Payments}}$

$$= \frac{\$8{,}200}{10}$$

$$= \$820$$

3. Cash Interest Payment = Face Value × Face Interest Rate × Time

$$= \$200{,}000 \times 0.09 \times 6/12 = \$9{,}000$$

4. Interest Expense per Interest Period = Interest Payment − Amortization of Bond Premium

$$= \$9{,}000 - \$820 = \$8{,}180$$

On July 1, 2010, the first semiannual interest date, the entry in journal form would be like this:

A*	=	L	+	SE
−9,000		−820		−8,180

*Assumes cash paid.

2010			
July 1	Bond Interest Expense	8,180	
	Unamortized Bond Premium	820	
	Cash (or Interest Payable)		9,000
	Paid (or accrued) semiannual interest to bondholders and amortized the premium on 9%, 5-year bonds		

Study Note

The bond interest expense recorded is less than the amount of interest paid because of the amortization of the bond premium. The matching rule dictates that the premium be amortized over the life of the bond.

Note that the bond interest expense is $8,180, but the amount that bondholders receive is the $9,000 face interest payment. The difference of $820 is the debit to Unamortized Bond Premium. This lowers the credit balance of the Unamortized Bond Premium account and the carrying value of the bonds payable by $820 each interest period. If the bond issue remains unchanged, the same entry will be made on every semiannual interest date over the life of the bond issue. When the bond issue matures, the balance in the Unamortized Bond Premium account will be zero, and the carrying value of the bonds payable will be $200,000—exactly equal to the amount due the bondholders.

As noted earlier, the straight-line method should be used only when it does not lead to a material difference from the effective interest method.

Effective Interest Method Under the straight-line method, the effective interest rate changes constantly, even though the interest expense is fixed, because the effective interest rate is determined by comparing the fixed interest expense with a carrying value that changes as a result of amortizing the discount or premium. To apply a fixed interest rate over the life of the bonds based on the actual market rate at the time of the bond issue, one must use the effective interest method. With this method, the interest expense decreases slightly each period (see Table 10-4, Column B) because the amount of the bond premium amortized

TABLE 10-4 Interest and Amortization of a Bond Premium: Effective Interest Method

	A	B	C	D	E	F
Semiannual Interest Period	Carrying Value at Beginning of Period	Semiannual Interest Expense at 8% to Be Recorded* (4% × A)	Semiannual Interest Payment to Bondholders (4½% × $200,000)	Amortization of Bond Premium (C − B)	Unamortized Bond Premium at End of Period (E − D)	Carrying Value at End of Period (A − D)
0					$8,200	$208,200
1	$208,200	$8,328	$9,000	$672	7,528	207,528
2	207,528	8,301	9,000	699	6,829	206,829
3	206,829	8,273	9,000	727	6,102	206,102
4	206,102	8,244	9,000	756	5,346	205,346
5	205,346	8,214	9,000	786	4,560	204,560
6	204,560	8,182	9,000	818	3,742	203,742
7	203,742	8,150	9,000	850	2,892	202,892
8	202,892	8,116	9,000	884	2,008	202,008
9	202,008	8,080	9,000	920	1,088	201,088
10	201,088	7,912†	9,000	1,088	—	200,000

*Rounded to the nearest dollar.
†Last period's interest expense equals $7,912 ($9,000 − $1,088); it does not equal $8,044 ($201,088 × 0.04) because of the cumulative effect of rounding.

increases slightly (Column D). This occurs because a fixed rate is applied each period to the gradually decreasing carrying value (Column A). The first interest payment is recorded as follows:

A*	=	L	+	SE
−9,000		−672		−8,328

*Assumes cash paid.

2010			
July 1	Bond Interest Expense	8,328	
	Unamortized Bond Premium	672	
	Cash (or Interest Payable)		9,000
	Paid (or accrued) semiannual interest to bondholders and amortized the premium on 9%, 5-year bonds		

Note that the unamortized bond premium (Column E) decreases gradually to zero as the carrying value decreases to the face value (Column F). To find the amount of premium amortized in any one interest payment period, subtract the effective interest expense (the carrying value times the effective interest rate, Column B) from the interest payment (Column C). In semiannual interest period 5, for example, the amortization of premium is $786, which is calculated in the following manner: $9,000 − ($205,346 × 0.04).

Figure 10-4, which is based on the data in Table 10-4, shows how the effective interest method affects the amortization of a bond premium. Note that the carrying value (issue price) is initially greater than the face value, but it gradually decreases toward the face value over the bond issue's life. Note also that interest payments exceed interest expense by the amount of the premium amortized. Interest expense decreases gradually over the life of the bond because it is based on the gradually decreasing carrying value (multiplied by the market interest rate).

FIGURE 10-4
Carrying Value and Interest Expense—Bonds Issued at a Premium

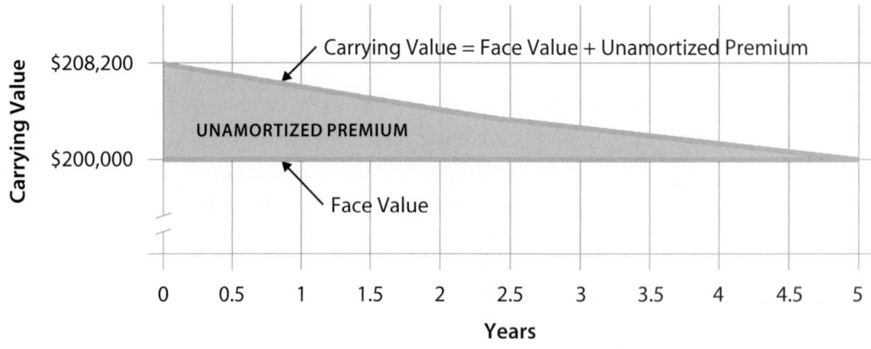

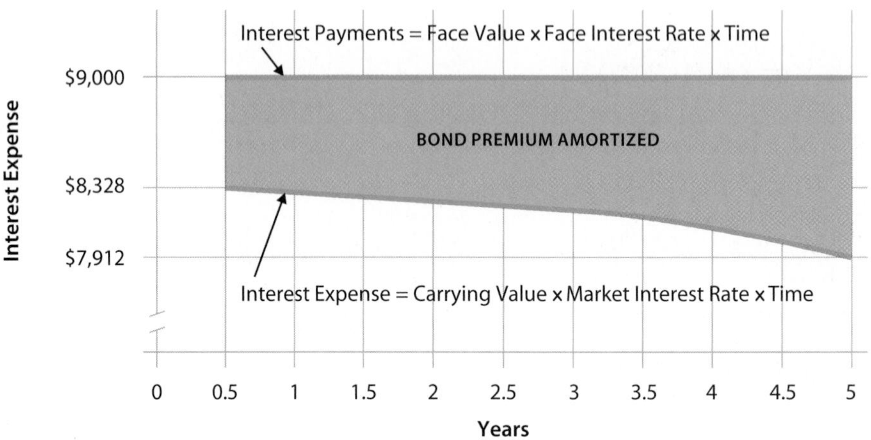

STOP & APPLY >

On June 1, Lazo Corporation issues $4,000,000 of 8 percent, 20-year bonds at 97. Interest is payable semiannually, on May 31 and November 30. Lazo's fiscal year ends on November 30.

1. Using the straight-line method of amortization, prepare entries in journal form for June 1 and November 30.
2. Using the effective interest method and assuming the same facts as above except that the market rate of interest is 8.5 percent, prepare the entry in journal form for November 30.

SOLUTION

1. Straight-line method

June 1	Cash	3,880,000	
	Unamortized Bond Discount	120,000	
	Bonds Payable		4,000,000
	Issue of $4,000,000 of 8%, 20-year bonds at 97 $4,000,000 × 0.97 = $3,880,000		
Nov. 30	Bond Interest Expense	163,000	
	Unamortized Bond Discount		3,000
	Cash		160,000
	Paid bondholders semiannual interest and amortized the discount on 8%, 20-year bonds $120,000 ÷ 40 periods = $3,000 $4,000,000 × 0.04 = $160,000		

2. Effective interest method

Nov. 30	Bond Interest Expense	164,900	
	Unamortized Bond Discount		4,900
	Cash		160,000
	Paid bondholders semiannual interest and amortized the discount on 8%, 20-year bonds		
	$3,880,000 × 0.0425 = $164,900		
	$4,000,000 × 0.04 = $160,000		

Retirement of Bonds

SO6 Account for the retirement of bonds and the conversion of bonds into stock.

Usually, companies pay bonds when they are due—on the maturity date. However, as noted in our discussion of callable and convertible bonds, retiring a bond issue before its maturity date can be to a company's advantage. For example, when interest rates drop, many companies refinance their bonds at the lower rate, much like homeowners who refinance their mortgage loans when interest rates go down. Although companies usually pay a premium for early extinguishment of bond debt, what they save on interest can make the refinancing cost-effective.

Calling Bonds

Suppose Bharath Corporation can call, or retire, at 105 the $200,000 of bonds it issued at a premium (104.1) on January 1, 2010, and it decides to do so on July 1, 2013. The retirement thus takes place on the seventh interest payment date. Assume the entry for the required interest payment and the amortization of the premium has been made. The entry in journal form to record the retirement of the bonds is:

A*	=	L	+	SE
−210,000		−200,000		−7,108
		−2,892		

*Assumes cash paid.

2013			
July 1	Bonds Payable	200,000	
	Unamortized Bond Premium	2,892	
	Loss on Retirement of Bonds	7,108	
	Cash		210,000
	Retired 9% bonds at 105		

In this entry, the cash paid is the face value times the call price ($200,000 × 1.05 = $210,000). The unamortized bond premium can be found in Column E of Table 10-4. The loss on retirement of bonds occurs because the call price of the bonds is greater than the carrying value ($210,000 − $202,892 = $7,108).

Sometimes, a rise in the market interest rate can cause the market value of bonds to fall considerably below their face value. If it has the cash to do so, the company may find it advantageous to purchase the bonds on the open market and retire them, rather than wait and pay them off at face value. A gain is recognized for the difference between the purchase price of the bonds and the carrying value of the retired bonds.

For example, suppose that because of a rise in interest rates, Bharath Corporation is able to purchase the $200,000 bond issue on the open market at 85. The entry would be as follows:

A	=	L	+	SE
−170,000		−200,000		+32,892
		−2,892		

2013			
July 1	Bonds Payable	200,000	
	Unamortized Bond Premium	2,892	
	Cash		170,000
	Gain on Retirement of Bonds		32,892
	Retired 9% bonds at 85		

Converting Bonds

When a bondholder converts bonds to common stock, the company records the common stock at the carrying value of the bonds. The bond liability and the unamortized discount or premium are written off the books. For this reason, no gain or loss on the transaction is recorded. For example, suppose Bharath Corporation does not call its bonds on July 1, 2013. Instead, the corporation's bondholders decide to convert all their bonds to $8 par value common stock under a convertible provision of 40 shares of common stock for each $1,000 bond. The entry would be as follows:

A	=	L	+	SE
		−200,000		+64,000
		−2,892		+138,892

2013			
July 1	Bonds Payable	200,000	
	Unamortized Bond Premium	2,892	
	Common Stock		64,000
	Additional Paid-in Capital		138,892
	Converted 9% bonds payable into $8 par value common stock at a rate of 40 shares for each $1,000 bond		

The unamortized bond premium is found in Column E of Table 10-4. At a rate of 40 shares for each $1,000 bond, 8,000 shares will be issued, with a total par value of $64,000 (8,000 × $8). The Common Stock account is credited for the amount of the par value of the stock issued. In addition, Additional Paid-in Capital is credited for the difference between the carrying value of the bonds and the par value of the stock issued ($202,892 − $64,000 = $138,892). No gain or loss is recorded.

STOP & APPLY >

Schiff Stores has outstanding $100,000 of 7 percent bonds callable at 103. On July 1, immediately after recording the payment of the semiannual interest and the amortization of the premium, the unamortized bond premium equaled $2,500. On that date, all of the bonds were called and retired.

a. How much cash must be paid to retire the bonds?

b. Is there a gain or loss on retirement, and if so, how much is it?

SOLUTION

a. Amount paid: $100,000 × 1.03 = $103,000

b. There is a loss on retirement of $500, computed as follows:

Cash paid – Book value: $103,000 − ($100,000 + 2,500) = $500

Other Bonds Payable Issues

Among the other issues involved in accounting for bonds payable are the sale of bonds between interest payment dates and the year-end accrual of bond interest expense.

SO7 Record bonds issued between interest dates and year-end adjustments.

Sale of Bonds Between Interest Dates

Although corporations may issue bonds on an interest payment date, as in our previous examples, they often issue them between interest payment dates. When that is the case, they generally collect from the investors the interest that would have accrued for the partial period preceding the issue date, and at the end of the first interest period, they pay the interest for the entire period. In other words, the interest collected when bonds are sold is returned to investors on the next interest payment date.

There are two reasons for following this procedure:

1. From a practical standpoint, if a company issued bonds on several different days and did not collect the accrued interest, records would have to be maintained for each bondholder and date of purchase. The interest due each bondholder would therefore have to be computed for a different time period. Clearly, this procedure would involve large bookkeeping costs. On the other hand, if accrued interest is collected when the bonds are sold, the corporation can pay the interest due for the entire period on the interest payment date, thereby eliminating the extra computations and costs.
2. When accrued interest is collected in advance, the amount is subtracted from the full interest paid on the interest payment date. Thus, the resulting interest expense represents the amount for the time the money was borrowed.

For example, suppose Bharath Corporation sold $200,000 of 9 percent, five-year bonds for face value on May 1, 2010, rather than on January 1, 2010. The entry in journal form to record the sale of the bonds is as follows:

A	=	L	+	SE
+206,000		+200,000		+6,000

2010			
May 1	Cash	206,000	
	Bond Interest Expense		6,000
	Bonds Payable		200,000
	Sold 9%, 5-year bonds at face value plus 4 months' accrued interest $200,000 × 0.09 × 4/12 = $6,000		

Cash is debited for the amount received, $206,000 (the face value of $200,000 plus four months' accrued interest of $6,000). Bond Interest Expense is credited for the $6,000 of accrued interest, and Bonds Payable is credited for the face value of $200,000.

When the first semiannual interest payment date arrives, the following entry is made:

A*	=	L	+	SE
−9,000				−9,000

*Assumes cash paid.

2010			
July 1	Bond Interest Expense	9,000	
	Cash (or Interest Payable)		9,000
	Paid (or accrued) semiannual interest $200,000 × 0.09 × 6/12 = $9,000		

FIGURE 10-5
Interest Expense When Bonds Are Issued Between Interest Dates

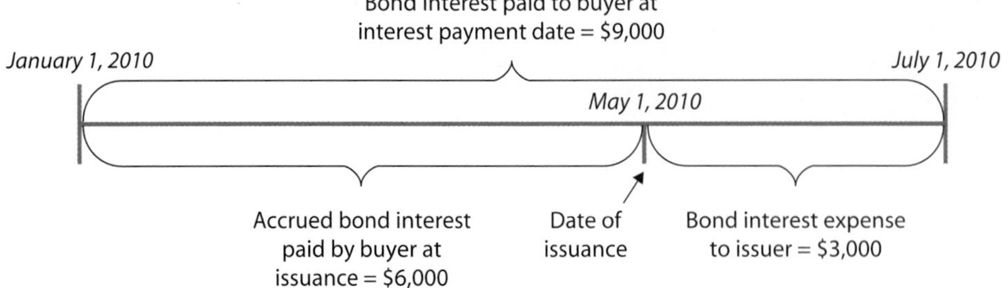

Notice that the entire half-year interest is debited to Bond Interest Expense and credited to Cash because the corporation pays bond interest every six months, in full six-month amounts. Figure 10-5 illustrates this process. The actual interest expense for the two months that the bonds were outstanding is $3,000. This amount is the net balance of the $9,000 debit to Bond Interest Expense on July 1 less the $6,000 credit to Bond Interest Expense on May 1. You can see these steps clearly in the following T account:

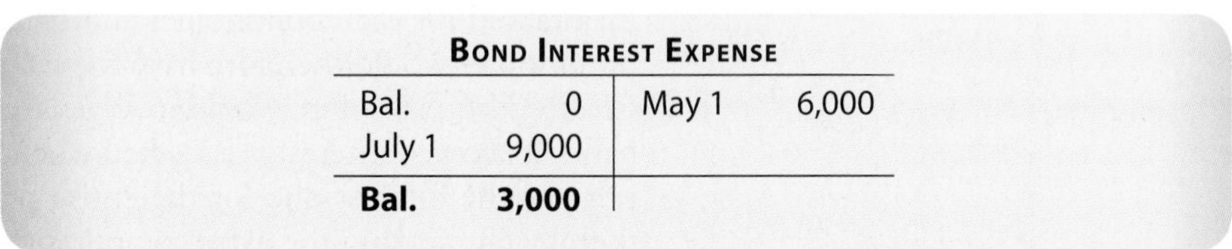

Bond Interest Expense

Bal.	0	May 1	6,000
July 1	9,000		
Bal.	**3,000**		

Year-End Accrual of Bond Interest Expense

Study Note
Remember that adjusting entries never affect cash.

Bond interest payment dates rarely correspond with a company's fiscal year. Therefore, an adjustment must be made to accrue the interest expense on the bonds from the last interest payment date to the end of the fiscal year. In addition, any discount or premium on the bonds must be amortized for the partial period.

In our example of bonds issued at a premium, Bharath Corporation issued $200,000 of bonds on January 1, 2010, at 104.1 percent of face value. Suppose Bharath's fiscal year ends on September 30, 2010. In the period since the interest payment and amortization of the premium on July 1, three months' worth of interest has accrued. Under the effective interest method, the following adjusting entry would be made:

A	=	L	+	SE
		−349.50		−4,150.50
		+4,500.00		

2010			
Sept. 30	Bond Interest Expense	4,150.50	
	Unamortized Bond Premium	349.50	
	Bond Interest Payable		4,500.00
	To record accrual of interest on 9% bonds payable for 3 months and amortization of one-half of the premium for the second interest payment period		

This entry covers one-half of the second interest period. Unamortized Bond Premium is debited for $349.50, which is one-half of $699, the amortization of the premium for the second period from Table 10-4. Bond Interest Payable is credited for $4,500, three months' interest on the face value of the bonds ($200,000 × 0.09 × 3/12). The net debit figure of $4,150.50 ($4,500.00 − $349.50) is the bond interest expense for the three-month period.

On the interest payment date of January 1, 2011, the entry to pay the bondholders and amortize the premium is as follows:

A	=	L	+	SE
−9,000.00		−4,500.00		−4,150.00
		−349.50		

2011			
Jan. 1	Bond Interest Expense	4,150.50	
	Bond Interest Payable	4,500.00	
	Unamortized Bond Premium	349.50	
	Cash		9,000.00
	Paid semiannual interest, including interest previously accrued, and amortized the premium for the period since the end of the fiscal year		

Study Note

The matching rule dictates that both the accrued interest and the amortization of a premium or discount be recorded at year end.

One-half ($4,500) of the amount paid ($9,000) was accrued on September 30. Unamortized Bond Premium is debited for $349.50, the remaining amount to be amortized for the period ($699.00 − $349.50). The resulting bond interest expense is the amount that applies to the three-month period from October 1 to December 31.

Bond discounts are recorded at year end in the same way as bond premiums. The difference is that the amortization of a bond discount increases interest expense instead of decreasing it.

STOP & APPLY >

Hardin Associates is authorized to issue $1,000,000 in bonds on January 1. The bonds carry a face interest rate of 8 percent, which is to be paid on January 1 and July 1. Prepare entries in journal form for (a) the issue of the bonds on April 1 at 100 and (b) the interest payment on July 1. (c) How much was the total interest expense for the first six months of the year?

SOLUTION

(a) April 1	Cash	1,020,000	
	Bonds Payable		1,000,000
	Bond Interest Expense		20,000
	Issuance of 8 percent bonds plus accrued interest		
(b) July 1	Bond Interest Expense	40,000	
	Cash		40,000
	Payment of interest		

(c) Total interest expense: $40,000 − $20,000 = $20,000.

A LOOK BACK AT ▸ McDONALD'S CORPORATION

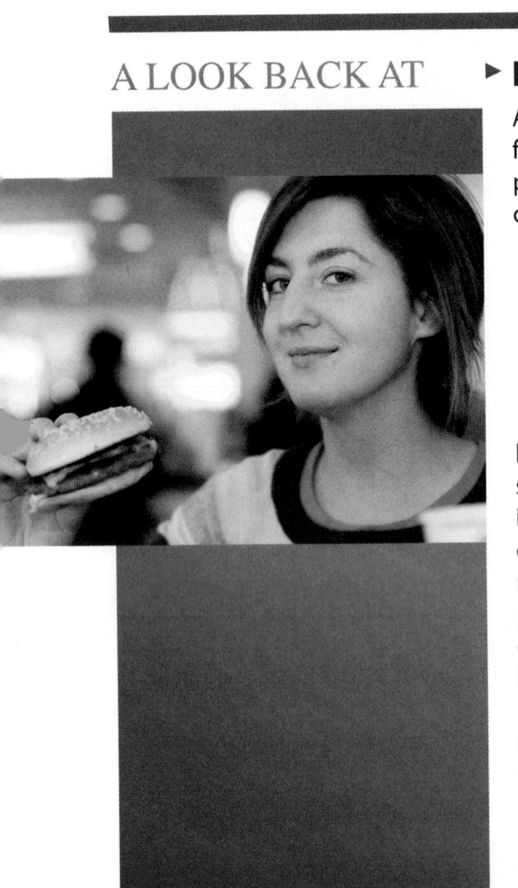

As we noted in this chapter's Decision Point, McDonald's relies on both debt and equity financing to support its continued global expansion. Because of the extent of the company's long-term debt, potential investors and creditors need to address the following questions:

- What are McDonald's most important long-term debts?
- What are its considerations in deciding to issue long-term debt?
- How does one evaluate whether a company has too much debt?

In addition to bonds, notes, and mortgages, McDonald's long-term debt includes leases on numerous properties. The company also has deferred income taxes and pension and health plans. Its purpose in taking on long-term debt is to foster growth and increase earnings. By using financial leverage in this way, McDonald's, like any other company, assumes financial risk. In McDonald's case, the risk is partially offset because much of its long-term debt relates to leases on real estate, an area in which the company has long experience and great expertise. McDonald's management commits the company to long-term leases not only because it believes the company will stay in the leased locations for a long time, but also because it is a way of financing expansion.

McDonald's 2008 annual report includes a detailed description of management's approach to debt financing. It points out that Standard & Poor's gives the company an "A" credit rating and that management carefully monitors key credit ratios that "incorporate capitalized operating leases to estimate total adjusted debt."

We can evaluate whether McDonald's maintains an appropriate level of debt by computing its interest coverage ratio over a two-year period, as follows:

$$\text{Interest Coverage Ratio} = \frac{\text{Income Before Income Taxes} + \text{Interest Expense}}{\text{Interest Expense}}$$

K/R

	2008	2007
Interest Coverage Ratio =	$\frac{\$6,158.0 + \$522.6}{\$522.6}$	$\frac{\$3,572.1 + \$410.1}{\$410.1}$
=	$\frac{\$6,680.6}{\$522.6}$	$\frac{\$3,982.2}{\$410.1}$
=	12.8 times	9.7 times

This analysis shows that McDonald's can easily cover its interest payments. There is plenty of cushion in this ratio to cover all of McDonald's balance sheet commitments, including long-term leases.

Review Problem

Accounting for a Bond Discount, Bond Retirement, and Bond Conversion

LO3 LO5 SO6

When Wilson Manufacturing Company wanted to expand its metal window division, it did not have enough capital to finance the project. To fund it, management sought and received approval from the board of directors to issue bonds. The bond indenture stated that the company would issue $2,500,000 of 8 percent, five-year bonds on January 1, 2009, and would pay interest semiannually, on June 30 and December 31 of each of the five years. It also stated that the bonds would be callable at 104 and that each $1,000 bond would be convertible to 30 shares of $10 par value common stock. Wilson sold the bonds on January 1, 2009, at 96 because the market rate of interest for similar investments was 9 percent. It decided to amortize the bond discount by using the effective interest method. On July 1, 2011, management called and retired half the bonds, and investors converted the other half to common stock.

Required

1. Prepare an interest and amortization schedule for the first five interest periods.
2. Prepare entries in journal form to record the sale of the bonds, the first two interest payments, the bond retirement, and the bond conversion.

Answers to Review Problem

1. Schedule for the first five interest periods:

	Interest and Amortization of Bond Discount						
2–3	Semiannual Interest Payment Date	Carrying Value at Beginning of Period	Seminannual Interest Expense* (9% x 1/2)	Seminannual Interest Expense (8% x 1/2)	Amortization of Discount	Unamortized Bond Discount at End of Period	Carrying Value at End of Period
4	Jan. 1, 2009					$100,000	$2,400,000
5	June 30, 2009	$2,400,000	$108,000	$100,000	$8,000	92,000	2,408,000
6	Dec. 31, 2009	2,408,000	108,360	100,000	8,360	83,640	2,416,360
7	June 30, 2010	2,416,360	108,736	100,000	8,736	74,904	2,425,096
8	Dec. 31, 2010	2,425,096	109,129	100,000	9,129	65,775	2,434,225
9	June 30, 2011	2,434,225	109,540	100,000	9,540	56,235	2,443,765
10							
11	*Rounded to the nearest dollar.						
12							

2. Entries in journal form:

	A	B	C	D	E	F	G
1	2009						
2	Jan.	1	Cash			2,400,000	
3			Unamortized Bond Discount			100,000	
4				Bonds Payable			2,500,000
5					Sold $2,500,000 of 8%, 5-year bonds at 96		
6	June	30	Bond Interest Expense			108,000	
7				Unamortized Bond Discount			8,000
8				Cash			100,000
9					Paid semiannual interest and amortized		
10					the discount on 8%, 5-year bonds		
11	2009						
12	Dec.	31	Bond Interest Expense			108,360	
13				Unamortized Bond Discount			8,360
14				Cash			100,000
15					To record accrued semiannual interest and		
16					amortize the discount on 8%, 5-year bonds		
17	2011						
18	July	1	Bonds Payable			1,250,000	
19			Loss on Retirement of Bonds			78,118	
20				Unamortized Bond Discount			28,118
21				Cash			1,300,000
22					Called $1,250,000 of 8% bonds and retired		
23					them at 104 ($56,235 x 1/2 = $28,118*)		
24			Bonds Payable			1,250,000	
25				Unamortized Bond Discount			28,117
26				Common Stock			375,000
27				Additional Paid-in Capital			846,883
28					Converted $1,250,000 of 8% bonds into		
29					common stock		
30					1,250 x 30 shares = 37,500 shares		
31					37,500 shares x $10 = $375,000		
32					$56,235 – $28,118 = $28,117		
33					$1,250,000 – ($28,117 + $375,000)		
					= $846,883		

LO1 Identify the management issues related to long-term debt.

Long-term debt is used to finance assets and business activities, such as research and development, that will produce income in future years. The management issues related to long-term debt are whether to take on long-term debt, how much debt to carry, and what types of debt to incur. The advantages of issuing long-term debt are that common stockholders do not relinquish any control, interest on debt is tax-deductible, and financial leverage can increase earnings. The disadvantages are that interest and principal must be paid on time and financial leverage can work against a company if an investment is not successful. The level of debt can be evaluated using the debt to equity ratio and the interest coverage ratio. Common types of long-term debt are bonds, notes, mortgages, long-term leases, pension liabilities, other postretirement benefits, and deferred income taxes.

LO2 Describe the features of a bond issue and the major characteristics of bonds.

A bond is a security that represents money borrowed from the investing public. When a corporation issues bonds, it enters into a contract, called a bond indenture, with the bondholders. The bond indenture defines the terms of the bond issue. A bond issue is the total value of bonds issued at one time. The prices of bonds are stated in terms of a percentage of the face value, or principal, of the bonds. The face interest rate is the fixed rate of interest paid to bondholders based on the face value. The market interest rate is the rate of interest paid in the market on bonds of similar risk. If the market rate fluctuates from the face interest rate before the bond issue date, the bonds will sell at either a discount or a premium.

A corporation can issue several types of bonds, each having different characteristics. For example, a bond issue may or may not require security (secured versus unsecured bonds). It may be payable at a single time (term bonds) or at several times (serial bonds). And the holder may receive interest automatically (registered bonds) or may have to return coupons to receive interest payable (coupon bonds). Bonds may also be callable and convertible.

LO3 Record bonds issued at face value and at a discount or premium.

Bondholders pay face value for bonds when the interest rate on the bonds approximates the market rate for similar investments. The issuing corporation records the bond issue at face value as a long-term liability in the Bonds Payable account. Bonds are issued at a discount when their face interest rate is lower than the market rate for similar investments. The difference between the face value and the issue price is debited to Unamortized Bond Discount. Bonds are issued at a premium when their face interest rate is greater than the market interest rate on similar investments. The difference between the issue price and the face value is credited to Unamortized Bond Premium.

LO4 Use present values to determine the value of bonds.

The value of a bond is determined by summing the present values of (1) the series of fixed interest payments of the bond issue and (2) the single payment of the face value at maturity. Tables 1 and 2 in the appendix on present value tables should be used in making these computations.

LO5 Amortize bond discounts and bond premiums using the straight-line and effective interest methods.

The straight-line method allocates a fixed portion of a bond discount or premium each interest period to adjust the interest payment to interest expense. The effective interest method, which is used when the effects of amortization are material, applies a constant rate of interest to the carrying value of the bonds. To find interest and the amortization of discounts or premiums, the effective interest rate is applied to the carrying value of the bonds (face value minus the discount or plus the premium) at the beginning of the interest period. The amount of the discount or premium to be amortized is the difference between the interest figured by using the effective rate and that obtained by using the face rate. The results of using the effective interest method on bonds issued at a discount or a premium are summarized below and compared with issuance at face value:

	Bonds Issued at		
	Face Value	**Discount**	**Premium**
Trend in carrying value over bond term	Constant	Increasing	Decreasing
Trend in interest expense over bond term	Constant	Increasing	Decreasing
Interest expense versus interest payments	Interest expense = interest payments	Interest expense > interest payments	Interest expense < interest payments
Classification of bond discount or premium	Not applicable	Contra-liability (deducted from Bonds Payable)	Adjunct-liability (added to Bonds Payable)

Supplemental Objectives

SO6 Account for the retirement of bonds and the conversion of bonds into stock.

Callable bonds can be retired before maturity at the option of the issuing corporation. The call price is usually an amount greater than the face value of the bonds, in which case the corporation recognizes a loss on the retirement of the bonds. Sometimes, a rise in the market interest rate causes the market value of the bonds to fall below face value. If a company purchases its bonds on the open market at a price below carrying value, it recognizes a gain on the transaction.

Convertible bonds allow the bondholder to convert bonds to the issuing corporation's common stock. When bondholders exercise this option, the common stock issued is recorded at the carrying value of the bonds being converted. No gain or loss is recognized.

SO7 Record bonds issued between interest dates and year-end adjustments.

When bonds are sold between the interest payment dates, the issuing corporation collects from investors the interest that has accrued since the last interest payment date. When the next interest payment date arrives, the corporation pays the bondholders interest for the entire interest period.

When the end of a corporation's fiscal year does not fall on an interest payment date, the corporation must accrue bond interest expense from the last interest payment date to the end of its fiscal year. This accrual results in the inclusion of the interest expense in the year it is incurred.

REVIEW of Concepts and Terminology

The following concepts and terms were introduced in this chapter:

Bond 490 (LO2)

Bond certificate 491 (LO2)

Bond indenture 490 (LO2)

Bond issue 491 (LO2)

Callable bonds 492 (LO2)

Call price 492 (LO2)

Capital lease 486 (LO1)

Convertible bonds 492 (LO2)

Coupon bonds 493 (LO2)

Deferred income taxes 489 (LO1)

Discount 492 (LO2)

Early extinguishment of debt 492 (LO2)

Effective interest method 501 (LO5)

Face interest rate 491 (LO2)

Financial leverage 482 (LO1)

Market interest rate 491 (LO2)

Mortgage 485 (LO1)

Off-balance-sheet financing 483 (LO1)

Operating lease 486 (LO1)

Other postretirement benefits 489 (LO1)

Pension fund 488 (LO1)

Pension plan 487 (LO1)

Premium 492 (LO2)

Registered bonds 493 (LO2)

Secured bonds 492 (LO2)

Serial bonds 492 (LO2)

Straight-line method 500 (LO5)

Term bonds 492 (LO2)

Unsecured bonds 492 (LO2)

Zero coupon bonds 500 (LO5)

Key Ratio

Interest coverage ratio 484 (LO1)

CHAPTER ASSIGNMENTS

BUILDING Your Basic Knowledge and Skills

Short Exercises

LO1 **Bond Versus Common Stock Financing**

SE 1. Indicate whether each of the following is an advantage or a disadvantage of using long-term bond financing rather than issuing common stock.

1. Interest paid on bonds is tax-deductible.
2. Investments are sometimes not as successful as planned.
3. Financial leverage can have a negative effect when investments do not earn as much as the interest payments on the related debt.
4. Bondholders do not have voting rights in a corporation.
5. Positive financial leverage may be achieved.

LO1 **Types of Long-Term Liabilities**

SE 2. Place the number of the liability next to the statement to which it applies.

1. Bonds payable	___ a. May result in a capital lease
2. Long-term notes payable	___ b. Differences in income taxes on accounting income and taxable income
3. Mortgage payable	___ c. The most popular form of long-term financing
4. Long-term lease	___ d. Often used to purchase land and buildings
5. Pension liabilities	___ e. Often used interchangeably with bonds payable
6. Other postretirement benefits	___ f. Future health care costs are a major component
7. Deferred income taxe	___ g. May include 401(k), ESOPs, or profit-sharing

LO1 **Mortgage Payable**

SE 3. Karib Corporation purchased a building by signing a $150,000 long-term mortgage with monthly payments of $1,200. The mortgage carries an interest rate of 8 percent. Prepare a monthly payment schedule showing the monthly payment, the interest for the month, the reduction in debt, and the unpaid balance for the first three months. (Round to the nearest dollar.)

LO4 **Valuing Bonds Using Present Value**

SE 4. Rogers Paints, Inc., is considering the sale of two bond issues. Choice A is a $600,000 bond issue that pays semiannual interest of $32,000 and is due in 20 years. Choice B is a $600,000 bond issue that pays semiannual interest of $30,000 and is due in 15 years. Assume that the market interest rate for each bond is 12 percent. Calculate the amount that Rogers Paints will receive if both bond issues occur. (Calculate the present value of each bond issue and sum.)

LO3 LO5 **Straight-Line Method**

SE 5. On April 1, 2009, Morimoto Corporation issued $8,000,000 in 8.5 percent, five-year bonds at 98. The semiannual interest payment dates are April 1 and October 1. Prepare entries in journal form for the issue of the bonds by Morimoto on April 1, 2009, and the first two interest payments on October 1, 2009, and April 1, 2010. Use the straight-line method and ignore year-end accruals.

LO3 LO5 SO7

Effective Interest Method

SE 6. On March 1, 2010, Fast Freight Company sold $400,000 of its 9.5 percent, 20-year bonds at 106. The semiannual interest payment dates are March 1 and September 1. The market interest rate is 8.9 percent. The firm's fiscal year ends August 31. Prepare entries in journal form to record the sale of the bonds on March 1, the accrual of interest and amortization of premium on August 31, and the first interest payment on September 1. Use the effective interest method to amortize the premium.

SO6

Bond Retirement

SE 7. The Silk Corporation has outstanding $200,000 of 8 percent bonds callable at 104. On December 1, immediately after the payment of the semiannual interest and the amortization of the bond discount were recorded, the unamortized bond discount equaled $5,250. On that date, $120,000 of the bonds were called and retired. Prepare the entry in journal form to record the retirement of the bonds on December 1.

SO6

Bond Conversion

SE 8. The Tramot Corporation has $2,000,000 of 6 percent bonds outstanding. There is $40,000 of unamortized discount remaining on the bonds after the March 1, 2009, semiannual interest payment. The bonds are convertible at the rate of 20 shares of $10 par value common stock for each $1,000 bond. On March 1, 2009, bondholders presented $1,200,000 of the bonds for conversion. Prepare the entry in journal form to record the conversion of the bonds.

SO7

Bond Issue Between Interest Dates

SE 9. Downey Corporation sold $400,000 of 9 percent, ten-year bonds for face value on September 1, 2010. The issue date of the bonds was May 1, 2010. The company's fiscal year ends on December 31, and this is its only bond issue. Record the sale of the bonds on September 1 and the first semiannual interest payment on November 1, 2010. What is the bond interest expense for the year ended December 31, 2010?

LO3 LO5 SO7

Year-End Accrual of Bond Interest

SE 10. On October 1, 2010, Tender Corporation issued $500,000 of 9 percent bonds at 96. The bonds are dated October 1 and pay interest semiannually. The market rate of interest is 10 percent, and the company's year end is December 31. Prepare the entries in journal form to record the issuance of the bonds, the accrual of the interest on December 31, 2010, and the payment of the first semiannual interest on April 1, 2011. Assume the company uses the effective interest method to amortize the bond discount.

Exercises

LO1 LO2 SO6

Discussion Questions

E 1. Develop brief answers to each of the following questions:

1. How does a lender assess the risk that a borrower may default—that is, not pay interest and principal when due?
2. If a company with a high debt to equity ratio wants to increase its debt when the economy is weak, what kind of bond might it issue?
3. Why might a company lease a long-term asset rather than buy it and issue long-term bonds?
4. Why are callable and convertible bonds considered to add to management's future flexibility in financing a business?

LO3 LO4 **Discussion Questions**

LO5 SO7 **E 2.** Develop brief answers to each of the following questions:

1. What determines whether bonds are issued at a discount, premium, or face value?
2. Why does the market price of a bond vary over time?
3. When is it acceptable to use the straight-line method to amortize a bond discount or premium?
4. Why must the accrual of bond interest be recorded at the end of an accounting period?

LO1 **Interest Coverage Ratio**

E 3. Compute the interest coverage ratios for 2010 and 2011 from the partial income statements of Chimney Company that appear below. State whether the ratio improved or worsened over time.

	2011	2010
Income from operations	$23,890	$18,460
Interest expense	5,800	3,300
Income before income taxes	$18,090	$15,160
Income taxes	5,400	4,500
Net income	$12,690	$10,660

LO1 **Mortgage Payable**

E 4. Victory Corporation purchased a building by signing a $150,000 long-term mortgage with monthly payments of $2,000. The mortgage carries an interest rate of 12 percent.

1. Prepare a monthly payment schedule showing the monthly payment, the interest for the month, the reduction in debt, and the unpaid balance for the first three months. (Round to the nearest dollar.)
2. Prepare entries in journal form to record the purchase and the first two monthly payments.

LO1 **Recording Lease Obligations**

E 5. Tapas Corporation has leased a piece of equipment that has a useful life of 12 years. The terms of the lease are payments of $43,000 per year for 12 years. Tapas currently is able to borrow money at a long-term interest rate of 15 percent. (Round answers to the nearest dollar.)

1. Calculate the present value of the lease.
2. Prepare the entry in journal form to record the lease agreement.
3. Prepare the entry in journal form to record depreciation of the equipment for the first year using the straight-line method.
4. Prepare the entries in journal form to record the lease payments for the first two years.

LO4 **Valuing Bonds Using Present Value**

E 6. Avanti, Inc., is considering the sale of two bond issues. Choice A is an $800,000 bond issue that pays semiannual interest of $64,000 and is due in 20 years. Choice B is an $800,000 bond issue that pays semiannual interest of $60,000 and is due in 15 years. Assume that the market interest rate for each bond is 12 percent. Calculate the amount that Avanti, Inc., will receive if both bond issues are made. (**Hint**: Calculate the present value of each bond issue and sum.)

LO4 Valuing Bonds Using Present Value

E 7. Use Tables 1 and 2 in the appendix on present value tables to calculate the issue price of a $300,000 bond issue in each of the following independent cases. Assume interest is paid semiannually.

a. A 10-year, 8 percent bond issue; the market interest rate is 10 percent.
b. A 10-year, 8 percent bond issue; the market interest rate is 6 percent.
c. A 10-year, 10 percent bond issue; the market interest rate is 8 percent.
d. A 20-year, 10 percent bond issue; the market interest rate is 12 percent.
e. A 20-year, 10 percent bond issue; the market interest rate is 6 percent.

LO4 Zero Coupon Bonds

E 8. The state of Ohio needs to raise $25,000,000 for highway repairs. Officials are considering issuing zero coupon bonds, which do not require periodic interest payments. The current market interest rate for the bonds is 10 percent. What face value of bonds must be issued to raise the needed funds, assuming the bonds will be due in 30 years and compounded annually? How would your answer change if the bonds were due in 50 years? How would both answers change if the market interest rate were 8 percent instead of 10 percent?

LO3 LO5 Straight-Line Method

E 9. DNA Corporation issued $4,000,000 in 10.5 percent, ten-year bonds on February 1, 2010, at 104. Semiannual interest payment dates are January 31 and July 31. Use the straight-line method and ignore year-end accruals.

1. With regard to the bond issue on February 1, 2010:
   a. How much cash is received?
   b. How much is Bonds Payable?
   c. What is the difference between **a** and **b** called and how much is it?
2. With regard to the bond interest payment on July 31, 2010:
   a. How much cash is paid in interest?
   b. How much is the amortization?
   c. How much is interest expense?
3. With regard to the bond interest payment on January 31, 2011:
   a. How much cash is paid in interest?
   b. How much is the amortization?
   c. How much is interest expense?

LO3 LO5 Straight-Line Method

E 10. Nina Corporation issued $8,000,000 in 8.5 percent, five-year bonds on March 1, 2010, at 96. The semiannual interest payment dates are September 1 and March 1. Prepare entries in journal form for the issue of the bonds by Nina on March 1, 2010, and the first two interest payments on September 1, 2010, and March 1, 2011. Use the straight-line method and ignore year-end accruals.

LO3 LO5 Effective Interest Method

E 11. Smart Toy Company sold $500,000 of 9.5 percent, 20-year bonds on April 1, 2009, at 106. The semiannual interest payment dates are March 31 and September 30. The market interest rate is 8.9 percent. The company's fiscal year ends September 30. Use the effective interest method to calculate the amortization.

1. With regard to the bond issue on April 1, 2009:
   a. How much cash is received?
   b. How much is Bonds Payable?
   c. What is the difference between **a** and **b** called and how much is it?
2. With regard to the bond interest payment on September 30, 2009:
   a. How much cash is paid in interest?
   b. How much is the amortization?
   c. How much is interest expense?
3. With regard to the bond interest payment on March 31, 2010:
   a. How much cash is paid in interest?
   b. How much is the amortization?
   c. How much is interest expense?

LO3 LO5 **Effective Interest Method**

E 12. On March 1, 2010, Knap Corporation issued $1,200,000 of 10 percent, five-year bonds. The semiannual interest payment dates are February 28 and August 31. Because the market rate for similar investments was 11 percent, the bonds had to be issued at a discount. The discount on the issuance of the bonds was $48,670. The company's fiscal year ends February 28. Prepare entries in journal form to record the bond issue on March 1, 2010, the payment of interest, and the amortization of the discount on August 31, 2010 and on February 28, 2011. Use the effective interest method. (Round answers to the nearest dollar.)

SO6 **Bond Retirement**

E 13. The Rondo Corporation has outstanding $400,000 of 8 percent bonds callable at 104. On September 1, immediately after recording the payment of the semiannual interest and the amortization of the discount, the unamortized bond discount equaled $10,500. On that date, $240,000 of the bonds was called and retired.

1. How much cash must be paid to retire the bonds?
2. Is there a gain or loss on retirement, and if so, how much is it?

SO6 **Bond Conversion**

E 14. The Jolly Corporation has $400,000 of 6 percent bonds outstanding. There is $20,000 of unamortized discount remaining on these bonds after the July 1, 2011, semiannual interest payment. The bonds are convertible at the rate of 20 shares of $5 par value common stock for each $1,000 bond. On July 1, 2011, bondholders presented $300,000 of the bonds for conversion.

1. Is there a gain or loss on conversion, and if so, how much is it?
2. How many shares of common stock are issued in exchange for the bonds?
3. In dollar amounts, how does this transaction affect the total liabilities and the total stockholders' equity of the company? In your answer, show the effects on four accounts.

LO5 SO7 **Effective Interest Method and Interest Accrual**

E 15. The long-term debt section of the Midwest Corporation's balance sheet at the end of its fiscal year, December 31, 2009, is as follows:

Long-term liabilities		
Bonds payable—8%, interest payable 1/1 and 7/1, due 12/31/16	$250,000	
Less unamortized bond discount	20,000	$230,000

Prepare entries in journal form relevant to the interest payments on July 1, 2010, December 31, 2010, and January 1, 2011. Assume a market interest rate of 10 percent.

LO4 SO6 **Time Value of Money and Early Extinguishment of Debt**

E 16. Anna's, Inc., has a $350,000, 8 percent bond issue that was issued a number of years ago at face value. There are now ten years left on the bond issue, and the market interest rate is 16 percent. Interest is paid semi-annually. The company purchases the bonds on the open market at the calculated current market value and retires the bonds.

1. Using present value tables, calculate the current market value of the bond issue.
2. Is there a gain or loss on retirement of bonds, and if so, how much is it?

LO3 SO7 **Bond Issue On and Between Interest Dates**

E 17. Jigar Tech, Inc., is authorized to issue $1,800,000 in bonds on June 1. The bonds carry a face interest rate of 9 percent, which is to be paid on June 1 and December 1. Prepare entries in journal form for the issue of the bonds by Jigar Tech, Inc., under the assumptions that (a) the bonds are issued on September 1 at 100 and (b) the bonds are issued on June 1 at 105.

SO7 **Bond Issue Between Interest Dates**

E 18. Arif Corporation sold $400,000 of 12 percent, ten-year bonds at face value on September 1, 2010. The issue date of the bonds was May 1, 2010.

1. Record the sale of the bonds on September 1 and the first semiannual interest payment on November 1, 2010.
2. Arif's fiscal year ends on December 31, and this is its only bond issue. What is the bond interest expense for the year ended December 31, 2010?

LO3 LO5 SO7 **Year-End Accrual of Bond Interest**

E 19. Hinali Corporation issued $1,000,000 of 9 percent bonds on October 1, 2010, at 96. The bonds are dated October 1 and pay interest semiannually. The market interest rate is 10 percent, and Hinali's fiscal year ends on December 31. Prepare the entries in journal form to record the issuance of the bonds, the accrual of the interest on December 31, 2010, and the first semiannual interest payment on April 1, 2011. Assume the company uses the effective interest method to amortize the bond discount.

Problems

LO1 **Lease Versus Purchase**

P 1. Shen Corporation can either lease or buy a small garage next to its business that will provide parking for its customers. The company can lease the building for a period of 12 years, which approximates the useful life of the facility and thus qualifies as a capital lease. The terms of the lease are payments of $12,000 per year for 12 years. Shen currently is able to borrow money at a long-term interest rate of 9 percent. The company can purchase the building by signing an $80,000 long-term mortgage with monthly payments of $1,000. The mortgage also carries an interest rate of 9 percent.

Required

1. With regard to the lease option,
   a. Calculate the present value of the lease. (Round answers to the nearest dollar.)
   b. Prepare the entry in journal form to record the lease agreement.
   c. Prepare the entry in journal form to record depreciation of the equipment for the first year using the straight-line method.
   d. Prepare the entries in journal form to record the lease payments for the first two years.
2. With regard to the purchase option,
   a. Prepare a monthly payment schedule showing the monthly payment, the interest for the month, the reduction in debt, and the unpaid balance for the first three months. (Round to the nearest dollar.)
   b. Prepare entries in journal form to record the purchase and the first two monthly payments.

User insight ▶ 3. Based on your calculations, which option seems to be best? Aside from cost, name an advantage and a disadvantage of each option.

LO1 LO2 LO3

Bond Terminology

P 2. Listed below are common terms associated with bonds:

a. Bond certificate
b. Bond issue
c. Bond indenture
d. Unsecured bonds
e. Debenture bonds
f. Secured bonds
g. Term bonds
h. Serial bonds
i. Registered bonds
j. Coupon bonds
k. Callable bonds
l. Convertible bonds
m. Face interest rate
n. Market interest rate
o. Effective interest rate
p. Bond premium
q. Bond discount

Required

1. For each of the following statements, identify the term with which it is associated. (If more than one statement applies, choose the term with which it is most closely associated.)
   1. Occurs when bonds are sold at more than face value
   2. Rate of interest that will vary depending on economic conditions
   3. Bonds that may be exchanged for common stock
   4. Bonds that are not registered
   5. A bond issue in which all bonds are due on the same date
   6. Occurs when bonds are sold at less than face value
   7. Rate of interest that will be paid regardless of market conditions
   8. Bonds that may be retired at management's option
   9. A document that is evidence of a company's debt
   10. Same as market rate of interest
   11. Bonds for which the company knows who owns them
   12. A bond issue for which bonds are due at different dates
   13. The total value of bonds issued at one time
   14. Bonds whose payment involves a pledge of certain assets
   15. Same as debenture bonds
   16. Contains the terms of the bond issue
   17. Bonds issued on the general credit of the company

User insight ▶ 2. What effect will a decrease in interest rates below the face interest rate and before a bond is issued have on the cash received from the bond issue? What effect will the decrease have on interest expense? What effect will the decrease have on the amount of cash paid for interest?

LO3 LO5 SO6

Bond Basics—Straight-Line Method, Retirement and Conversion

P 3. Murcia Corporation has $4,000,000 of 9.5 percent, 25-year bonds dated May 1, 2009, with interest payable on April 30 and October 31. The company's fiscal year ends on December 31, and it uses the straight-line method to amortize bond premiums or discounts. The bonds are callable after ten years at 103 or convertible into 40 shares of $10 par value common stock.

Required

1. Assume the bonds are issued at 103.5 on May 1, 2009.
   a. How much cash is received?
   b. How much is Bonds Payable?
   c. What is the difference between **a** and **b** called and how much is it?
   d. With regard to the bond interest payment on October 31, 2009:
      (1) How much cash is paid in interest?
      (2) How much is the amortization?
      (3) How much is interest expense?
2. Assume the bonds are issued at 96.5 on May 1, 2009.
   a. How much cash is received?
   b. How much is Bonds Payable?
   c. What is the difference between **a** and **b** called and how much is it?
   d. With regard to the bond interest payment on October 31, 2009:
      (1) How much cash is paid in interest?
      (2) How much is the amortization?
      (3) How much is interest expense?
3. Assume the issue price in requirement **1** and that the bonds are called and retired ten years later.
   a. How much cash will have to be paid to retire the bonds?
   b. Is there a gain or loss on the retirement? If there is a gain or loss, how much is it?
4. Assume the issue price in requirement **2** and that the bonds are converted to common stock ten years later.
   a. Is there a gain or loss on conversion, and if so, how much is it?
   b. How many shares of common stock are issued in exchange for the bonds?
   c. In dollar amounts, how does this transaction affect the total liabilities and the total stockholders' equity of the company? In your answer, show the effects on four accounts.

User insight ▶

5. Assume that after ten years market interest rates have dropped significantly and that the price of the company's common stock has risen significantly. Also assume that management wants to improve its credit rating by reducing its debt to equity ratio and that it needs what cash it currently has for expansion. Would management prefer the approach and result in requirement **3** or **4**? Explain your answer. What would be a disadvantage of the approach you chose?

LO3 LO5 **Bond Transactions—Effective Interest Method**

P 4. Dygat Corporation has $10,000,000 of 10.5 percent, 20-year bonds dated June 1, 2010 with interest payment dates of May 31 and November 30. The company's fiscal year ends November 30. It uses the effective interest method to amortize bond premiums or discounts.

Required

1. Assume the bonds are issued at 103 on June 1 to yield an effective interest rate of 10.1 percent. Prepare entries in journal form for June 1, 2010, November 30, 2010, and May 31, 2011. (Round amounts to the nearest dollar.)
2. Assume the bonds are issued at 97 on June 1 to yield an effective interest rate of 10.9 percent. Prepare entries in journal form for June 1, 2010, November 30, 2010, and May 31, 2011. (Round amounts to the nearest dollar.)

User insight ▶

3. Explain the role that market interest rates play in causing a premium in requirement **1** and a discount in requirement **2**.

LO3 LO5 SO7 **Bonds Issued at a Discount and a Premium—Effective Interest Method**

P 5. Johnson Corporation issued bonds twice during 2010. The transactions were as follows:

2010

Jan. 1 Issued $1,000,000 of 9.2 percent, ten-year bonds dated January 1, 2010, with interest payable on June 30 and December 31. The bonds were sold at 98.1, resulting in an effective interest rate of 9.5 percent.

Apr. 1 Issued $2,000,000 of 9.8 percent, ten-year bonds dated April 1, 2010, with interest payable on March 31 and September 30. The bonds were sold at 101, resulting in an effective interest rate of 9.5 percent.

June 30 Paid semiannual interest on the January 1 issue and amortized the discount, using the effective interest method.

Sept. 30 Paid semiannual interest on the April 1 issue and amortized the premium, using the effective interest method.

Dec. 31 Paid semiannual interest on the January 1 issue and amortized the discount, using the effective interest method.

31 Made an end-of-year adjusting entry to accrue interest on the April 1 issue and to amortize half the premium applicable to the second interest period.

2011

Mar. 31 Paid semiannual interest on the April 1 issue and amortized the premium applicable to the second half of the second interest period.

Required

1. Prepare entries in journal form to record the bond transactions. (Round amounts to the nearest dollar.)

User insight ▶

2. Describe the effect of the above transactions on profitability and liquidity by answering the following questions.
   a. What is the total interest expense in 2010 for each of the bond issues?
   b. What is the total cash paid in 2010 for each of the bond issues?
   c. What differences, if any, do you observe and how do you explain them?

Alternate Problems

LO3 LO5 SO6

Bond Basics—Straight-line Method, Retirement, and Conversion

P 6. Golden Corporation has $20,000,000 of 10.5 percent, 20-year bonds dated June 1, 2010, with interest payment dates of May 31 and November 30. After ten years the bonds are callable at 104, and each $1,000 bond is convertible into 25 shares of $20 par value common stock. The company's fiscal year ends on December 31. It uses the straight-line method to amortize bond premiums or discounts.

Required

1. Assume the bonds are issued at 103 on June 1, 2010.
   a. How much cash is received?
   b. How much is Bonds Payable?
   c. What is the difference between **a** and **b** called and how much is it?
   d. With regard to the bond interest payment on November 30, 2010:
      (1) How much cash is paid in interest?
      (2) How much is the amortization?
      (3) How much is interest expense?
2. Assume the bonds are issued at 97 on June 1, 2010.
   a. How much cash is received?
   b. How much is Bonds Payable?
   c. What is the difference between **a** and **b** called and how much is it?
   d. With regard to the bond interest payment on November 30, 2010:
      (1) How much cash is paid in interest?
      (2) How much is the amortization?
      (3) How much is interest expense?
3. Assume the issue price in requirement **1** and that the bonds are called and retired ten years later.
   a. How much cash will have to be paid to retire the bonds?
   b. Is there a gain or loss on the retirement, and if so, how much is it?
4. Assume the issue price in requirement **2** and that the bonds are converted to common stock ten years later.
   a. Is there a gain or loss on the conversion, and if so, how much is it?
   b. How many shares of common stock are issued in exchange for the bonds?
   c. In dollar amounts, how does this transaction affect the total liabilities and the total stockholders' equity of the company? In your answer, show the effects on four accounts.

User insight ▶

5. Assume that after ten years, market interest rates have dropped significantly and that the price of the company's common stock has risen significantly. Also assume that management wants to improve its credit rating by reducing its debt to equity ratio and that it needs what cash it has for expansion. Which approach would management prefer—the approach and result in requirement **3** or **4**? Explain your answer. What would be a disadvantage of the approach you chose?

LO3 LO5

Effective Interest Method

P 7. Jose Corporation has $4,000,000 of 9.5 percent, 25-year bonds dated March 1, 2010, with interest payable on February 28 and August 31. The company's fiscal year end is February 28. It uses the effective interest method to amortize bond premiums or discounts. (Round amounts to the nearest dollar.)

Required

1. Assume the bonds are issued at 102.5 on March 1, 2010, to yield an effective interest rate of 9.2 percent. Prepare entries in journal form for March 1, 2010, August 31, 2010, and February 28, 2011.
2. Assume the bonds are issued at 97.5 on March 1, 2010, to yield an effective interest rate of 9.8 percent. Prepare entries in journal form for March 1, 2010, August 31, 2010, and February 28, 2011.

User insight ▶ 3. Explain the role that market interest rates play in causing a premium in requirement **1** and a discount in requirement **2**.

LO3 LO5 SO7

Bonds Issued at a Discount and a Premium—Effective Interest Method

P 8. Rago Corporation issued bonds twice during 2010. A summary of the transactions involving the bonds follows.

2010

Jan. 1	Issued $3,000,000 of 9.9 percent, ten-year bonds dated January 1, 2010, with interest payable on June 30 and December 31. The bonds were sold at 102.6, resulting in an effective interest rate of 9.4 percent.
Mar. 1	Issued $2,000,000 of 9.2 percent, ten-year bonds dated March 1, 2010, with interest payable March 1 and September 1. The bonds were sold at 98.2, resulting in an effective interest rate of 9.5 percent.
June 30	Paid semiannual interest on the January 1 issue and amortized the premium, using the effective interest method.
Sept. 1	Paid semiannual interest on the March 1 issue and amortized the discount, using the effective interest method.
Dec. 31	Paid semiannual interest on the January 1 issue and amortized the premium, using the effective interest method.
31	Made an end-of-year adjusting entry to accrue interest on the March 1 issue and to amortize two-thirds of the discount applicable to the second interest period.

2011

Mar. 1	Paid semiannual interest on the March 1 issue and amortized the remainder of the discount applicable to the second interest period.

Required

1. Prepare entries in journal form to record the bond transactions. (Round amounts to the nearest dollar.)

User insight ▶ 2. Describe the effect on profitability and liquidity by answering the following questions.
   a. What is the total interest expense in 2010 for each of the bond issues?
   b. What is the total cash paid in 2010 for each of the bond issues?
   c. What differences, if any, do you observe and how do you explain these differences?

ENHANCING Your Knowledge, Skills, and Critical Thinking

LO1 Effect of Long-Term Leases

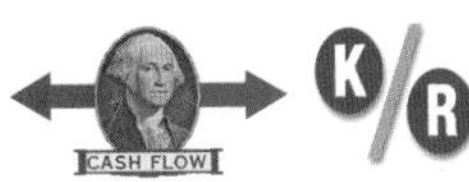

C 1. Many companies use long-term leases to finance long-term assets. Although these leases are similar to mortgage payments, they are structured in such a way that they qualify as operating leases. As a result, the lease commitments do not appear on the companies' balance sheets.

In a recent year, **Continental Airlines** had almost $15 billion in total operating lease commitments, of which $1.5 billion was due in the current year. Further, the airline had total assets of $12.7 billion and total liabilities of $12.6 billion. Because of heavy losses in previous years, its stockholders' equity was only $0.1 billion.[15]

What effect do these types of leases have on the balance sheet? Why would the use of these long-term leases make a company's debt to equity ratio, interest coverage ratio, and free cash flow look better than they really are? What is a capital lease? How does the application of capital lease accounting provide insight into a company's financial health?

LO2 LO6 Bond Issue

C 2. **Eastman Kodak**, the photography company, issued a $1 billion bond issue. Even though the company's credit rating was low, the bond issue was well received by the investment community because the company offered attractive terms. The offering comprised $500 million of 10-year unsecured notes and $500 million of 30-year convertible bonds. The convertibles were callable after seven years and would be convertible into common stock about 40 to 45 percent higher than the current price.[16]

What are unsecured notes? Why would they carry a relatively high interest rate? What are convertible securities? Why are they good for the investor and for the company? Why would they carry a relatively low interest rate? What does *callable* mean? What advantage does this feature give the company?

LO2 LO3 Bond Interest Rates and Market Prices

C 3. **Dow Chemical** is one of the largest chemical companies in the world. Among its long-term liabilities was a bond due in 2011 that carried a face interest rate of 6.125 percent.[17] Recently, this bond sold on the New York Stock Exchange at $104\frac{5}{8}$.

Did this bond sell at a discount or a premium? Assuming the bond was originally issued at face value, did interest rates rise or decline after the date of issue? Would you have expected the market rate of interest on this bond to be more or less than 6.125 percent? Did the current market price affect either the amount that the company paid in semiannual interest or the amount of interest expense for the same period? Explain your answers.

LO1 Leverage, Debt to Equity and Financial Risk

C 4. *The Wall Street Journal* reported recently that many public companies are "loading up on debt to improve returns for the shareholders. . . . **Domino's Pizza Inc.**, **Health Management Associates, Inc.**, and **Dean Foods Co.** unveiled plans to take on significant debt and distribute much of their cash to shareholders through dividends or one-time share buybacks. This is resulting in higher leverage [and] making the per-share earnings they report look better."[18] With higher earnings per share, the price of the companies' stock should go up.

What is leverage? Why does this plan result in higher leverage and what ratio reflects the higher leverage? Will the companies have more or less financial risk after these transactions? Why will this plan make earnings per share look better?

LO2 Characteristics of Convertible Debt

C 5. **Amazon.com, Inc.**, gained fame as an online marketplace for books, records, and other products. Although the increase in its stock price was initially meteoric, only recently has the company begun to earn a profit. To support its enormous growth, Amazon.com issued $500,000,000 in 6.875 percent convertible notes due in 2010 at face value. Interest is payable on February 1 and August 1. The notes are convertible into common stock at a price of $112 per share, which at the time of issue was above the market price. The market value of Amazon.com's common stock has been quite volatile, from $35 to $96 in 2008.[19]

What reasons can you suggest for Amazon.com's management choosing notes that are convertible into common stock rather than simply issuing nonconvertible notes or issuing common stock directly? Are there any disadvantages to this approach? If the price of the company's common stock goes to $100 per share, what would be the total theoretical value of the notes? If the holders of the notes were to elect to convert the notes into common stock, what would be the effect on the company's debt to equity ratio, and what would be the effect on the percentage ownership of the company by other stockholders?

LO1 LO2 Issuance of Long-Term Bonds Versus Leasing

C 6. The Fertile Corporation plans to build or lease a new plant that will produce liquid fertilizer for the agricultural market. The plant is expected to cost $800,000,000 and will be located in the southwestern United States. The company's chief financial officer, Sharon Weiss, has spent the last several weeks studying different means of financing the plant. Following her talks with bankers and other financiers, she has decided that there are two basic choices: the plant can be financed through the issuance of a long-term bond or through a long-term lease. Details for the two options are as follows:

1. Issue $800,000,000 of 25-year, 16 percent bonds secured by the new plant. Interest on the bonds would be payable semiannually.
2. Sign a 25-year lease for an existing plant calling for lease payments of $65,400,000 on a semiannual basis.

Weiss wants to know what effect each choice would have on the company's financial statements. She estimates that the useful life of the plant is 25 years, at which time the plant is expected to have an estimated residual value of $80,000,000.

Weiss is planning a meeting to discuss the alternatives. Write a short memorandum to her identifying the issues that should be considered at this meeting. (**Note**: You are not asked to make any calculations, discuss the factors, or recommend an action.)

LO1 Business Practice, Long-Term Debt, Leases, and Pensions

C 7. To answer the following questions, refer to the financial statements and the notes to the financial statements in the **CVS** annual report in the Supplement to Chapter 1:

1. Is it the practice of CVS to own or lease most of its buildings?
2. Does CVS lease property predominantly under capital leases or under operating leases? How much was rental expense for operating leases in 2008?
3. Does CVS have a defined benefit pension plan? Does it offer postretirement benefits?

LO1 **Use of Debt Financing**

C 8. Refer to the **CVS** annual report and the financial statements of **Southwest Airlines Co.** in the Supplement to Chapter 1. Calculate the debt to equity ratio and the interest coverage ratio for both companies' two most recent years. Find the note to the financial statements that contains information on leases and lease commitments by CVS. Southwest's lease expenses were $527 million and $469 million in 2007 and 2008, respectively, and total lease commitments for future years were $2,032 million. What effect do the total lease commitments and lease expense have on your assessment of the ratios you calculated? Evaluate and comment on the relative performance of the two companies with regard to debt financing. Which company has more risk of not being able to meet its interest obligations? How does leasing affect the analysis? Explain.

LO2 **Bond Indenture and Ethical Reporting**

C 9. Bio-Phar Technology, Inc., a biotech company, has a $24,000,000 bond issue outstanding. The bond indenture has several restrictive provisions, including requirements that current assets exceed current liabilities by a ratio of 2 to 1 and that income before income taxes exceed the annual interest on the bonds by a ratio of 3 to 1. If those requirements are not met, the bondholders can force the company into bankruptcy. The company is still awaiting Food and Drug Administration (FDA) approval of its new product, CMZ-12, a cancer treatment drug. Management has been counting on sales of CMZ-12 this year to meet the provisions of the bond indenture. As the end of the fiscal year approaches, the company does not have sufficient current assets or income before income taxes to meet the requirements.

Joan Miller, the chief financial officer, proposes, "Since we can assume that FDA approval will occur early next year, I suggest we book sales and receivables from our major customers now in anticipation of next year's sales. This action will increase our current assets and our income before income taxes. It is essential that we do this to save the company. Look at all the people who will be hurt if we don't do it."

Is Miller's proposal acceptable accounting? Is it ethical? Who could be harmed by it? What steps might management take?

LO2 **Bond Rating Changes**

C 10. During economic or industry recessions, it is common to see downward revisions of bond ratings. Access Standard & Poor's list of companies with lowered bond ratings and identify three whose names you recognize. Based on your general knowledge of these companies, give reasons that you believe contributed to the downgrade of the ratings.

CHAPTER

11 Contributed Capital

Focus on Financial Statements

INCOME STATEMENT

Revenues

− Expenses

= Net Income

STATEMENT OF RETAINED EARNINGS

Opening Balance

+ Net Income

− Dividends

= Retained Earnings

BALANCE SHEET

Assets	Liabilities
	Equity

A = L + E

STATEMENT OF CASH FLOWS

Operating activities
+ Investing activities
+ Financing activities
= Change in Cash
+ Starting Balance
= Ending Cash Balance

Sale/repurchase of capital stock and payment of cash dividends on the balance sheet are financing activities on the statement of cash flows.

In the last chapter, we focused on long-term *debt* financing. Here, we focus on long-term *equity* financing—that is, on the capital that stockholders contribute to a corporation. The issues involved in equity financing—including the type of stock a corporation issues, the dividends that it pays, and the treasury stock that it purchases—can significantly affect return on equity and other measures of profitability on which management's compensation is based. Thus, as with the management issues involved in long-term debt financing, ethics is a major concern. Management's decisions must be based not on personal gain, but on the value created for the corporation's owners.

LEARNING OBJECTIVES

LO1 Identify and explain the management issues related to contributed capital. (pp. 534–542)

LO2 Identify the components of stockholders' equity. (pp. 543–545)

LO3 Identify the characteristics of preferred stock. (pp. 546–549)

LO4 Account for the issuance of stock for cash and other assets. (pp. 549–552)

LO5 Account for treasury stock. (pp. 553–556)

DECISION POINT ▸ A USER'S FOCUS GOOGLE, INC.

When a company issues stock to the public for the first time, it is called an **initial public offering (IPO)**. There are many initial public offerings in any given year, but when **Google**, the popular Internet search engine company, went to market with its IPO in August 2004, it created a national sensation for two reasons. First, it was the largest IPO by an Internet company after the tech-bust in 2001 and 2002. Second, Google provides a very well known and widely used search service. Those who were fortunate enough to get shares saw the price per share soar to $135 in a few days and reach $700 per share in 2008 before dropping to below $300 (before recovering to almost $600 by the beginning of 2010). Google's Financial Highlights show the components of Google's stockholders' equity.[1]

GOOGLE'S FINANCIAL HIGHLIGHTS (In thousands)

	Dec. 31 2008	Dec. 31 2007
Stockholders' equity		
Preferred stock	$ —	$ —
Common stock	315	313
Additional paid-in capital	14,450,338	13,241,221
Retained earnings	13,561,630	9,334,772
Accumulated other comprehensive income	226,579	113,373
Total stockholders' equity	$28,238,862	$22,689,679
Total assets	$31,767,575	$25,335,806

- ▸ Why did Google's management choose to issue common stock to satisfy its needs for new capital?
- ▸ What are some of the advantages and disadvantages of this approach to financing a business?
- ▸ What measures should an investor use in evaluating management's performance?

Management Issues Related to Contributed Capital

LO1 Identify and explain the management issues related to contributed capital.

In Chapter 1, we defined a *corporation* as a business unit chartered by the state and legally separate from its owners—that is, its stockholders. *Contributed capital*, which refers to stockholders' investments in a corporation, is a major means of financing a corporation. Managing contributed capital requires an understanding of the advantages and disadvantages of the corporate form of business and of the issues involved in equity financing. It also requires familiarity with dividend policies, with how to use return on equity to evaluate performance, and with stock option plans.

The Corporate Form of Business

The corporate form of business is well suited to today's trends toward large organizations, international trade, and professional management. Although fewer in number than sole proprietorships and partnerships, corporations dominate the U.S. economy in part because of their ability to raise large amounts of capital. Figure 11-1 shows the amount and sources of capital that corporations have raised in recent years. As you can see, the total funds raised by U.S. corporations increased in most years during the last decade, but dropped during the financial crisis of 2008. Nevertheless, nearly $1 trillion was raised. Of this amount, $748 billion, or about 75.5 percent, was from bond issues; $164.9 billion, or 16.7 percent, from common stock; and 77.9 billion, or 7.9 percent, from preferred stock.

Advantages of Incorporation Managers of a corporation must be familiar with the advantages and disadvantages of this form of business. Some of the advantages are as follows:

- **Separate Legal Entity** As a separate legal entity, a corporation can buy and sell property, sue other parties, enter into contracts, hire and fire employees, and be taxed.
- **Limited Liability** Because a corporation is a legal entity, separate from its owners, its creditors can satisfy their claims only against the assets of the corporation, not against the personal property of the corporation's owners. Because the owners are not responsible for the corporation's debts, their liability is limited to the amount of their investment. In contrast, the personal property of sole proprietors and partners generally is available to creditors.
- **Ease of Capital Generation** It is fairly easy for a corporation to raise capital because shares of ownership in the business are available to a great number of potential investors for a small amount of money. As a result, a single corporation can have many owners.
- **Ease of Transfer of Ownership** A **share of stock**, a unit of ownership in a corporation, is easily transferable. A stockholder can normally buy and sell shares without affecting the corporation's activities or needing the approval of other owners.
- **Lack of Mutual Agency** Mutual agency is not a characteristic of the corporate form of business. If a stockholder tries to enter into a contract for the corporation, the corporation is not bound by the contract. But in a partnership, because of mutual agency, all the partners can be bound by one partner's actions.
- **Continuous Existence** Because a corporation is a separate legal entity, an owner's death, incapacity, or withdrawal does not affect the life of the corporation. A corporation's life is set by its charter and regulated by state laws.

FIGURE 11-1
Sources of Capital Raised by Corporations in the United States

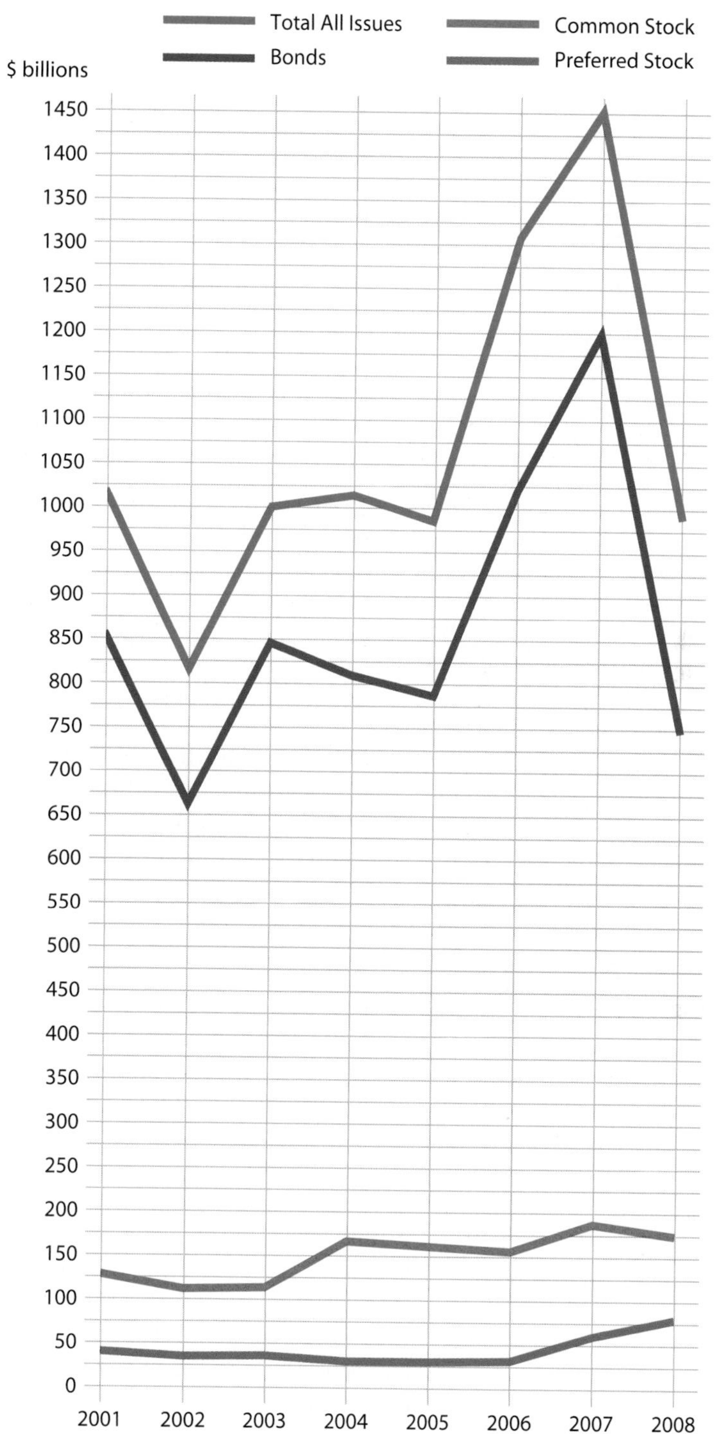

Source: "US Key Stats," Securities Industry and Financial Markets Association.

Centralized Authority and Responsibility The board of directors represents the stockholders and delegates the responsibility and authority for the day-to-day operation of the corporation to a single person, usually the president. Operating power is not divided among the many owners of the business. The president may delegate authority over certain segments of the business to others, but he or she is held accountable to the board of directors. If the board is dissatisfied with the performance of the president, it can replace that person.

- **Professional Management** Large corporations have many owners, the vast majority of whom are unequipped to make timely decisions about business operations. So, in most cases, management and ownership are separate. This allows a corporation to hire the best talent available to manage the business.

Disadvantages of Incorporation The disadvantages of corporations include the following:

- **Government Regulation** Corporations must meet the requirements of state laws. As "creatures of the state," they are subject to greater state control and regulation than are other forms of business. They must file many reports with the state in which they are chartered. Publicly held corporations must also file reports with the Securities and Exchange Commission and with the stock exchanges on which they are listed. Meeting these requirements is very costly.
- **Taxation** A major disadvantage of the corporate form of business is **double taxation**. Because a corporation is a separate legal entity, its earnings are subject to federal and state income taxes, which may be as much as 35 percent of corporate earnings. If any of the corporation's after-tax earnings are paid out as dividends, the earnings are taxed again as income to the stockholders. In contrast, the earnings of sole proprietorships and partnerships are taxed only once, as personal income to the owners.
- **Limited Liability** Although limited liability is an advantage of incorporation, it can also be a disadvantage. Limited liability restricts the ability of a small corporation to borrow money. Because creditors can lay claim only to the assets of a corporation, they may limit their loans to the level secured by those assets or require stockholders to guarantee the loans personally.
- **Separation of Ownership and Control** Just as limited liability can be a drawback, so can the separation of ownership and control. Management sometimes makes decisions that are not good for the corporation as a whole. Poor communication can also make it hard for stockholders to exercise control over the corporation or even to recognize that management's decisions are harmful.

Study Note

Among the agencies that regulate corporations are the Public Company Accounting Oversight Board (PCAOB), Securities and Exchange Commission (SEC), the Occupational Safety and Health Administration (OSHA), the Federal Trade Commission (FTC), the Environmental Protection Agency (EPA), the Nuclear Regulatory Commission (NRC), the Equal Employment Opportunity Commission (EEOC), the Interstate Commerce Commission (ICC), the National Transportation Safety Board (NTSB), the Federal Aviation Administration (FAA), and the Federal Communications Commission (FCC).

Study Note

Lenders to a small corporation may require the corporation's officers to sign a promissory note, which makes them personally liable for the debt.

Equity Financing

Equity financing is accomplished through the issuance of stock to investors in exchange for assets, usually cash. Once the stock has been issued to them, the stockholders can transfer their ownership at will. When they do, they must sign their **stock certificates**, documents showing the number of shares that they own, and send them to the corporation's secretary. In large corporations that are listed on the stock exchanges, stockholders' records are hard to maintain. Such companies can have millions of shares of stock, thousands of which change ownership every day. Therefore, they often appoint independent registrars and transfer agents (usually banks and trust companies) to help perform the secretary's duties. The outside agents are responsible for transferring the corporation's stock, maintaining stockholders' records, preparing a list of stockholders for stockholders' meetings, and paying dividends.

Par value and *legal capital* are important terms in equity financing:

- **Par value** is an arbitrary amount assigned to each share of stock. It must be recorded in the capital stock accounts, and it constitutes a corporation's legal capital.

- **Legal capital** is the number of shares issued times the par value. It is the minimum amount that a corporation can report as contributed capital.

Par value usually bears little if any relationship to the market value or book value of the shares. For example, although **Google**'s stock initially sold for $85 per share and the market value is now much higher, its par value per share is only $0.001. Google's legal capital is only about $315,000 (315 million shares × $0.001) even though the total market value of its shares exceeds $150 billion.

To help with its initial public offering (IPO), a corporation often uses an **underwriter**—an intermediary between the corporation and the investing public. For a fee—usually less than 1 percent of the selling price—the underwriter guarantees the sale of the stock. The corporation records the amount of the net proceeds of the offering—what the public paid less the underwriter's fees, legal and printing expenses, and any other direct costs of the offering—in its capital stock and additional paid-in capital accounts. Because of the size of its IPO, Google used a group of investment banks headed by two well-known investment bankers, **Morgan Stanley** and **Credit Suisse First Boston.**

The costs of forming a corporation are called **start-up and organization costs**. These costs, which are incurred before a corporation begins operations, include state incorporation fees and attorneys' fees for drawing up the articles of incorporation. They also include the cost of printing stock certificates, accountants' fees for registering the firm's initial stock, and other expenditures necessary for the formation of the corporation. Because Google's IPO was so large, the fees of the lawyers, accountants, and underwriters who helped arrange the IPO amounted to millions of dollars.

Study Note

Start-up and organization costs are expensed when incurred.

Theoretically, start-up and organization costs benefit the entire life of a corporation. For that reason, a case can be made for recording them as intangible assets and amortizing them over the life of the corporation. However, a corporation's life normally is not known, so accountants expense start-up and organization costs as they are incurred.

Advantages of Equity Financing Financing a business by issuing common stock has several advantages:

- It is less risky than financing with bonds because a company does not pay dividends on common stock unless the board of directors decides to pay them. In contrast, if a company does not pay interest on bonds, it can be forced into bankruptcy.
- When a company does not pay a cash dividend, it can plow the cash generated by profitable operations back into the company's operations. **Google**, for instance, does not currently pay any dividends, and its issuance of common stock provides it with funds for expansion.
- A company can use the proceeds of a common stock issue to maintain or improve its debt to equity ratio.

Disadvantages of Equity Financing Issuing common stock also has certain disadvantages:

- Unlike interest on bonds, dividends paid on stock are not tax-deductible.
- When a corporation issues more stock, it dilutes its ownership. Thus, the current stockholders must yield some control to the new stockholders.

Dividend Policies

A **dividend** is a distribution among stockholders of the assets that a corporation's earnings have generated. Stockholders receive these assets, usually cash, in proportion to the number of shares they own. A corporation's board of directors has sole authority to declare dividends, but senior managers, who usually serve as members of the board, influence dividend policies. Receiving dividends is one of two ways in which stockholders can earn a return on their investment in a corporation. The other way is to sell their shares for more than they paid for them.

Although a corporation may have sufficient cash and retained earnings to pay a dividend, its board of directors may not declare one for several reasons. The corporation may need the cash for expansion; it may want to improve its overall financial position by liquidating debt; or it may be facing major uncertainties, such as a pending lawsuit or strike or a projected decline in the economy, which makes it prudent to preserve resources.

A corporation pays dividends quarterly, semiannually, annually, or at other times declared by its board of directors. Most states do not allow a corporation to declare a dividend that exceeds its retained earnings. When a corporation does declare a dividend that exceeds retained earnings, it is, in essence, returning to the stockholders part of their contributed capital. This is called a **liquidating dividend**. A corporation usually pays a liquidating dividend only when it is going out of business or reducing its operations.

Having sufficient retained earnings in itself does not justify the declaration of a dividend. If a corporation does not have cash or other assets readily available for distribution, it might have to borrow money to pay the dividend—an action most boards of directors want to avoid.

> Study Note
>
> Entries for dividends are made only on the declaration date and the payment date.

Dividend Dates Three important dates are associated with dividends:

- The **declaration date** is the date on which the board of directors formally declares that the corporation is going to pay a dividend. Because the legal obligation to pay the dividend arises at this time, a liability for Dividends Payable is recorded and the Dividends account is debited on this date. In the accounting process, Retained Earnings will be reduced by the total dividends declared during the period.
- The **record date** is the date on which ownership of stock, and therefore the right to receive a dividend, is determined. Persons who own the stock on the record date will receive the dividend. No entry is made on this date. Between the record date and the date of payment, the stock is said to be **ex-dividend**. If the owner on the date of record sells the shares of stock before the date of payment, the right to the dividend remains with that person; it does not transfer with the shares to the second owner.
- The **payment date** is the date on which the dividend is paid to the stockholders of record. On this date, the Dividends Payable account is eliminated, and the Cash account is reduced.

Because an accounting period may end between the record date and the payment date, dividends declared during the period may exceed the amount paid for dividends. For example, in Figure 11-2, the accounting period ends on December 31. The declaration date for the dividends is December 21, the record date is December 31, and the payment date is January 11. In this case, the statement of retained earnings for the accounting period will show a decrease in the amount of the dividends declared, but the statement of cash flows will not show the dividends because the cash has not yet been paid out.

FIGURE 11-2
Dividend Dates

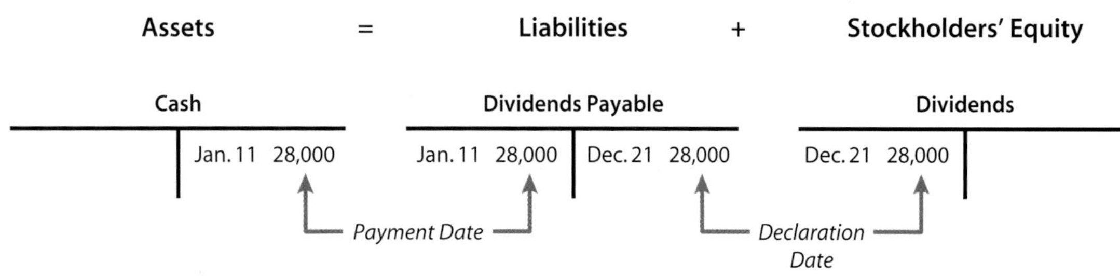

Note: No entry necessary on Dec. 31 record date

Evaluating Dividend Policies To evaluate the amount of dividends they receive, investors use the **dividends yield** ratio. Dividends yield is computed by dividing the dividends per share by the market price per share. **Microsoft**'s history of dividend payments provides an interesting example. Having built up a large cash balance through its years of profitable operations, Microsoft increased its annual dividend to $4.5 billion ($0.52 per share) in 2009.[2] Using Microsoft's regular annual dividend as a more realistic measure of what investors can expect in the future, its dividends yield is computed as follows:

$$\text{Dividends Yield} = \frac{\text{Dividends per Share}}{\text{Market Price per Share}} = \frac{\$0.52}{\$28.22} = 1.8\%$$

Figure 11-3 shows how Microsoft's dividends yield and last price are quoted on NASDAQ. Because the yield on corporate bonds exceeds 7 percent, Microsoft shareholders must expect some of their return to come from increases in the price of the shares.

Companies usually pay dividends only when they have had profitable operations. For example, **Apple Computer** began paying dividends in 1987, but it stopped those payments in 1996 to conserve cash after it suffered large operating losses in 1995. Now that Apple is profitable again, it may resume paying dividends. However, factors other than earnings affect the decision to pay dividends. Among them are the following:

FIGURE 11-3
Stock Quotations on NASDAQ

NASDAQ GLOBAL MARKET

YTD % CHG	STOCK	SYM	YLD	DIV	PE	LAST	NET CHG
64.4	♦ Micros Systems	MCRS	...	...	22	26.83	0.53
12.5	Microsemi Corp.i	MSCC	...	...	178	14.22	0.42
45.2	♦ Microsoft Corp.	MSFT	1.8	0.52	18	28.22	0.20
97.8	MicroStrategy Inc.	MSTR	...	...	21	73.44	−0.46
−14.7	Microtune Inc.	TUNE	...	...	dd	1.74	−0.06
▼ 138.1	MicroVision Inc.	MVIS	...	...	dd	4.00	0.23
4.9	Micrus Endovascular Corp.	MEND	...	...	dd	12.18	0.27
−33.3	MiddleBrook Pharmaceuticals Inc.	MBRK	...	...	dd	1.00	0.07
72.7	Middleby Corp.	MIDD	...	...	13	47.09	0.81
▼ −10.1	Middlesex Water Co.	MSEX	4.6	0.72f	20	15.49	0.18
−64.3	Midwest Banc Holdings Inc.	MBHI	...	...	dd	0.50	−0.06
−15.7	Midwest Financial Group Inc.	MOFG	2.4	0.20	dd	8.35	0.05
20.9	Miller (Herman) Inc.	MLHR	0.6	0.09	13	15.75	0.44
45.8	Millicom International Cellular S.A.	MICC	...	...	...	65.46	2.23

Source: Stock quotes on the NASDAQ from *The Wall Street Journal*, October 29, 2009. Copyright © 2009 Dow Jones & Co., Inc. Reprinted by permission of Dow Jones & Company via Copyright Clearance Center.

- **Industry policies** A company may change its dividend policy to bring it into line with the prevailing policy in its industry. For example, despite positive earnings, **AT&T Corporation** slashed its dividends by 83 percent. This action put AT&T's policy more in line with the policies of its peers in the telecommunications industry, most of which do not pay dividends.[3]
- **Volatility of earnings** If a company has years of good earnings followed by years of poor earnings, it may want to keep dividends low to avoid giving a false impression of sustained high earnings. For example, for years, **General Motors** paid a fairly low but stable dividend but declared a bonus dividend in especially good years.

- **Effect on cash flows** A company may not pay dividends because its operations do not generate enough cash to do so or because it wants to invest cash in future operations. **Abbott Laboratories** increases its dividends per share each year to reward its stockholders but also keeps back a portion of its earnings to spend for other purposes, such as researching and developing new drugs that will generate revenue in the future. In a recent year, for example, the company paid $1.44 per share dividend on earnings per share of $3.16.[4]

In recent years, because of a 15 percent reduction in the tax rate on dividends, attitudes toward dividends have changed. Many companies have either increased their dividends or started to pay dividends for the first time. The special dividend by Microsoft mentioned above is a good example of this effect.

Using Return on Equity to Measure Performance

Return on equity is the most important ratio associated with stockholders' equity. It is also a common measure of management's performance. For instance, when *BusinessWeek* and *Forbes* rate companies on their success, return on equity is the major basis of their evaluations. In addition, the compensation of top executives is often tied to return on equity benchmarks.

Google's return on equity in 2008 is computed as follows:[5]

K/R

$$\text{Return on Equity} = \frac{\text{Net Income}}{\text{Average Stockholders' Equity}}$$

$$= \frac{\$4,226,858}{(\$28,238,862 + \$22,689,679) \div 2}$$

$$= \frac{\$\ 4,226,858}{\$25,464,270.5}$$

$$= 16.6\%$$

Google's healthy return on equity of 16.6 percent depends, of course, on the amount of net income the company earns. However, it also depends on the level of stockholders' equity, which in turn depends on management decisions about the amount of stock the company sells to the public. As the company sells more shares, stockholders' equity increases, and as a result, return on equity decreases. Management can keep stockholders' equity at a minimum by financing the business with cash flows from operations and by issuing debt instead of stock. However, as we have pointed out, issuing bonds and other types of debt increases a company's risk because the interest and principal of the debt must be paid in a timely manner.

Management can also reduce the number of shares in the hands of the public by buying back the company's shares on the open market. The cost of these shares, which are called **treasury stock**, has the effect of reducing stockholders' equity and thereby increasing return on equity. Many companies follow this practice instead of paying or increasing dividends. Their reason for doing so is that it puts money into the hands of stockholders in the form of market price appreciation without creating a commitment to higher dividends in the future. For instance, in 2008, **Microsoft** purchased $9.4 billion of its common stock on the open market.[6] Microsoft's stock repurchases will improve the company's return on equity, increase its earnings per share, and lower its price/earnings ratio.

The **price/earnings (P/E) ratio** is a measure of investors' confidence in a company's future. It is calculated by dividing the market price per share by the earnings per share. The price/earnings ratio will vary as market price per share fluctuates daily and the amount of earnings per share changes. If you look back at Figure 11-3, you will see that it shows a P/E ratio of 18 (Rounded up) for Microsoft. It was computed using the annual earnings per share from Microsoft's most recent income statement, as follows:

K/R

$$\frac{\text{Price/Earnings}}{\text{(P/E) Ratio}} = \frac{\text{Market Price per Share}}{\text{Earnings per Share}} = \frac{\$28.22}{\$1.62} = 17.4 \text{ times}$$

Because the market price is 17.4 times earnings, investors are paying a good price in relation to earnings. They do so in the expectation that this software company will continue to be successful.

Stock Options as Compensation

More than 97 percent of public companies encourage employees to invest in their common stock through **stock option plans**.[7] Most such plans give employees the right to purchase stock in the future at a fixed price. Some companies offer stock option plans only to management personnel, but others, including **Google**, make them available to all employees. Because the market value of a company's stock is tied to a company's performance, these plans are a means of both motivating and compensating employees. As the market value of the stock goes up, the difference between the option price and the market price grows, which increases the amount of compensation. Another key benefit of stock option plans is that compensation expense is tax-deductible.

On the date stock options are granted, the fair value of the options must be estimated. The amount in excess of the exercise price is recorded as compensation expense over the grant period.[8]

For example, suppose that on July 1, 2010, a company grants its top executives the option to purchase 50,000 shares of $10 par value common stock at its current market value of $15 per share. The fair value of the option must be estimated on that date to determine compensation expense. Any one of several methods of estimating the fair value of options at the grant date may be used; they are dealt with in more advanced courses. Later, when the market price is $25 per share, one of the firm's vice presidents exercises her option and purchases 2,000 shares. Although the vice president has a gain of $20,000 (the $50,000 market value less the $30,000 option price), no compensation expense is recorded. The company receives only the option price, not the current market value.

In one example of how firms value stock options, **Google** recognized $1,119,766 of stock-based compensation expense in 2008. This amount represented about 7.4 percent of the company's total expenses and almost 26.5 percent of the net income. Management used a well-known statistical method to estimate the option values.[9]

FOCUS ON BUSINESS PRACTICE

Politics and Accounting Don't Mix

The FASB has long held that stock options should be treated as an expense, but in trying to pass this rule, it has encountered heavy opposition from the technology industry, which is the largest user of stock options. Leaders of the technology industry have maintained that expensing stock options would hurt their companies' profits and growth. The FASB argued that stock options are a form of compensation and therefore have value. The U.S. Congress got involved and pressured the FASB to back down, using the companies' reasoning that stock options essentially have no value and thus are not an expense on the income statement, although they should be mentioned in a note to the financial statements. What was happening was that many stock options were granted, and companies granting them were very loose in how they accounted for them. Many of the stock transactions were back-dated so that the exercise price would be most advantageous to the executives who were benefiting. The SEC has more than 100 ongoing criminal investigations of backdating practices. Estimates are that between 1994 and 2005, when the FASB finally ruled that all publicly traded companies must expense stock options, $246 billion of options compensation expense had been ignored, overstating reported earnings by 7 percent.[10]

Cash Flow Information

The best source of information concerning cash flows related to stock transactions and dividends is the financing activities section of the statement of cash flows. For instance, **Microsoft**'s cash flows from these activities are clearly revealed in this partial section of the company's statement of cash flows (in millions):

	2009	2008	2007
Financing Activities			
Common stock issued	$ 579	$ 3,494	$ 6,782
Common stock repurchased	(9,353)	(12,533)	(27,575)
Common stock cash dividend	(4,468)	(4,015)	(3,805)

Note the decreasing amounts of common stock repurchased (treasury stock) and the small amount of new common stock issued by the company in the 2009 fiscal year. Both actions are a reflection of the company's success.

STOP & APPLY >

Indicate whether each of the following is related to (a) advantages of the corporate form of business, (b) disadvantages of corporations, (c) dividend policies, (d) performance evaluation, or (e) stock options:

1. U.S. tax policies
2. Return on equity
3. Separate legal entity
4. Employee's right to purchase shares at a given price
5. Ease of ownership transfer
6. Distributing cash to stockholders
7. Need to deal with government regulation

SOLUTION

1. b; 2. d; 3. a; 4. e; 5. a; 6. c; 7. b

Components of Stockholders' Equity

LO2 Identify the components of stockholders' equity.

In a corporation's balance sheet, the owners' claims to the business are called *stockholders' equity*. As shown in Exhibit 11-1, this section of a corporate balance sheet usually has at least three components.

- **Contributed capital**—the stockholders' investments in the corporation
- **Retained earnings**—the earnings of the corporation since its inception, less any losses, dividends, or transfers to contributed capital. Retained earnings are reinvested in the business. They are not a pool of funds to be distributed to the stockholders; instead, they represent the stockholders' claim to assets resulting from profitable operations.
- **Treasury stock**—shares of its own stock that the corporation has bought back on the open market. The cost of these shares is treated not as an investment, but as a reduction in stockholders' equity. By buying back the shares, the corporation reduces the ownership of the business.

As you can see in **Google**'s Financial Highlights at the beginning of the chapter, "other items" may also appear in the stockholders' equity section. We discuss these items in a later chapter.

A corporation can issue two types of stock:

- **Common stock** is the basic form of stock that a corporation issues; that is, if a corporation issues only one type of stock, it is common stock. Because shares of common stock carry voting rights, they generally provide their owners with the means of controlling the corporation. Common stock is also called **residual equity**, which means that if the corporation is liquidated, the claims of all creditors and usually those of preferred stockholders rank ahead of the claims of common stockholders.
- To attract investors whose goals differ from those of common stockholders, a corporation may also issue **preferred stock**. Preferred stock gives its owners preference over common stockholders, usually in terms of receiving dividends and in terms of claims to assets if the corporation is liquidated. (We describe these preferences in more detail later in the chapter.)

In keeping with the convention of full disclosure, the stockholders' equity section of a corporate balance sheet gives a great deal of information about the corporation's stock. Under contributed capital, it lists the kinds of stock; their par value; and the number of shares authorized, issued, and outstanding.

EXHIBIT 11-1
Stockholders' Equity Section of a Balance Sheet

Stockholders' Equity		
Contributed capital		
Preferred stock, $50 par value, 2,000 shares authorized, issued, and outstanding		$100,000
Common stock, $5 par value, 60,000 shares authorized, 40,000 shares issued, 36,000 shares outstanding	$200,000	
Additional paid-in capital	100,000	300,000
Total contributed capital		$400,000
Retained earnings		120,000
Total contributed capital and retained earnings		$520,000
Less treasury stock, common (4,000 shares at cost)		40,000
Total stockholders' equity		$480,000

FOCUS ON BUSINESS PRACTICE

Are You a First-Class or Second-Class Stockholder?

When companies go public, insiders—usually the founders of the company or top management—often get first-class shares with extra votes, while outsiders get second-class shares with fewer votes. The class A and class B shares of **Adolph Coors Company**, the large brewing firm, are an extreme example. The company's class B shares, owned by the public, have no votes except in the case of a merger. Its class A shares, held by the Coors family trust, have all the votes on other issues.

Google also has two classes of common shares. Both classes are identical except that each class B share is entitled to ten votes and each class A share is entitled to only one vote. Class A shares are the ones that Google offered to the public in its IPO. As a result, Class B holders controls 78 percent of the company.[11]

Shareholder advocates denounce the class division of shares as undemocratic. They maintain that this practice gives a privileged few shareholders all or most of the control of a company and that it denies other shareholders voting power consistent with the risk they are taking. Defenders of the practice argue that it shields top executives from the market's obsession with short-term results and allows them to make better long-term decisions. They also point out that many investors don't care about voting rights as long as the stock performs well.

- **Authorized shares** are the maximum number of shares that a corporation's state charter allows it to issue. Most corporations are authorized to issue more shares than they need to issue at the time they are formed. Thus, they are able to raise more capital in the future by issuing additional shares. When a corporation issues all of its authorized shares, it cannot issue more without a change in its state charter.
- **Issued shares** are those that a corporation sells or otherwise transfers to stockholders. The owners of a corporation's issued shares own 100 percent of the business. Unissued shares have no rights or privileges until they are issued.
- **Outstanding shares** are shares that a corporation has issued and that are still in circulation. Treasury stock is not outstanding because it consists of shares that a corporation has issued but that it has bought back and thereby put out

Larry Page (left) and Sergey Brin, who founded Google, Inc., in 1998, have a lot to look happy about. In its IPO in August 2004, Google issued about 22.5 million shares at $85 per share for a total of $1.9 billion. The price per share soared to $135 in a few days and reached $300 in 2005 and $700 in 2008. The ability to raise large amounts of capital by issuing stocks and bonds is part of the reason corporations dominate the U.S. economy.

Courtesy of Kim Kulish/Corbis News/Corbis.

FIGURE 11-4
Relationship of Authorized Shares to Unissued, Issued, Outstanding, and Treasury Shares

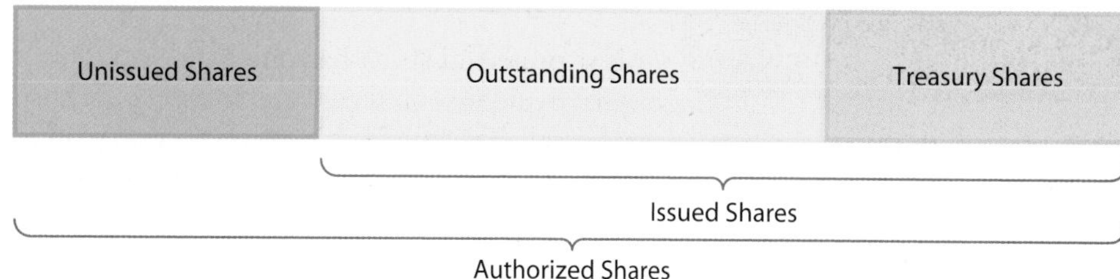

of circulation. Thus, a corporation can have more shares issued than are currently outstanding.

Figure 11-4 shows the relationship of authorized shares to issued, unissued, outstanding, and treasury shares. In this regard, Google is an interesting example. The company has 9 billion authorized shares of stock and only about 309 million shares issued. With its excess of authorized issues, Google obviously has plenty of flexibility for future stock transactions.

The following data are from the records of Garcia Corporation on December 31, 2010:

	Balance
Preferred stock, $100 par value, 6 percent noncumulative, 5,000 shares authorized, issued, and outstanding	$500,000
Common stock, $2 par value, 100,000 shares authorized, 90,000 shares issued, and 85,000 shares outstanding	180,000
Additional paid-in capital	489,000
Retained earnings	172,500
Treasury stock, common (5,000 shares, at cost)	110,000

Prepare a stockholders' equity section for Garcia Corporation's balance sheet.

SOLUTION

Garcia Corporation
Balance Sheet
December 31, 2010
Stockholders' Equity

Contributed capital		
Preferred stock, $100 par value, 6 percent noncumulative, 5,000 shares authorized, issued, and outstanding		$ 500,000
Common stock, $2 par value, 100,000 shares authorized, 90,000 shares issued, and 85,000 shares outstanding	$180,000	
Additional paid-in capital	489,000	669,000
Total contributed capital		$1,169,000
Retained earnings		172,500
Total contributed capital and retained earnings		$1,341,500
Less treasury stock, common (5,000 shares at cost)		110,000
Total stockholders' equity		$1,231,500

Preferred Stock

LO3 Identify the characteristics of preferred stock.

Most preferred stock has one or more of the following characteristics: preference as to dividends, preference as to assets if a corporation is liquidated, convertibility, and a callable option. A corporation may offer several different classes of preferred stock, each with distinctive characteristics to attract different investors.

> **Study Note**
> Preferred stock has many different characteristics. They are rarely exactly the same from company to company.

Preference as to Dividends

Preferred stockholders ordinarily must receive a certain amount of dividends before common stockholders receive anything. The amount that preferred stockholders must be paid before common stockholders can be paid is usually stated in dollars per share or as a percentage of the par value of the preferred shares. For example, a company might pay an annual dividend of $4 per share on preferred stock, or it might issue preferred stock at $50 par value and pay an annual dividend of 8 percent of par value, which would also be $4 per share.

Preferred stockholders have no guarantee of ever receiving dividends. A company must have earnings and its board of directors must declare dividends on preferred stock before any liability arises. The consequences of not granting an annual dividend on preferred stock vary according to whether the stock is noncumulative or cumulative:

- If the stock is **noncumulative preferred stock** and the board of directors fails to declare a dividend on it in any given year, the company is under no obligation to make up the missed dividend in future years.
- If the stock is **cumulative preferred stock**, the dividend amount per share accumulates from year to year, and the company must pay the whole amount before it pays any dividends on common stock.

Dividends not paid in the year they are due are called **dividends in arrears**. For example, suppose that a corporation has 20,000 shares of $100 par value, 5 percent cumulative preferred stock outstanding. If the corporation pays no dividends in 2011, preferred dividends in arrears at the end of the year would amount to $100,000 (20,000 shares × $100 × 0.05 = $100,000). If the corporation's board declares dividends in 2012, the corporation must pay preferred stockholders the dividends in arrears plus their current year's dividends before paying any dividends on common stock.

Dividends in arrears are not recognized as liabilities because no liability exists until the board of directors declares a dividend. A corporation cannot be sure it is going to make a profit, so, of course, it cannot promise dividends to stockholders. However, if it has dividends in arrears, it should report the amount either in the body of its financial statements or in a note to its financial statements.

The following note is typical of one that might appear in a company's annual report:

> On December 31, 2010, the company was in arrears by $37,851,000 ($1.25 per share) on dividends to its preferred stockholders. The company must pay all dividends in arrears to preferred stockholders before paying any dividends to common stockholders.

Suppose that on January 1, 2011, a corporation issued 20,000 shares of $10 par value, 6 percent cumulative preferred stock and 100,000 shares of common stock. Operations in 2011 produced income of only $8,000. However, in the same year, the corporation's board of directors declared a $6,000 cash dividend to the preferred stockholders. Thus, the dividend picture at the end of 2011 was as follows:

2011 dividends due preferred stockholders ($200,000 × 0.06)	$12,000
Less 2011 dividends declared to preferred stockholders	6,000
2011 preferred stock dividends in arrears	$ 6,000

Now suppose that in 2012, the corporation earns income of $60,000 and wants to pay dividends to both the preferred and the common stockholders. Because the preferred stock is cumulative, the corporation must pay the $6,000 in arrears on the preferred stock, plus the current year's dividends on the preferred stock, before it can distribute a dividend to the common stockholders. If the corporation's board of directors now declares a $24,000 dividend to be distributed to preferred and common stockholders, the distribution would be as follows:

2012 declaration of dividends	$24,000
Less 2011 preferred stock dividends in arrears	6,000
Amount available for 2012 dividends	$18,000
Less 2012 dividends due preferred stockholders ($200,000 × 0.06)	12,000
Remainder available to common stockholders	$ 6,000

Preference as to Assets

Preferred stockholders often have preference in terms of their claims to a corporation's assets if the corporation is liquidated. If a corporation does go out of business, these preferred stockholders have a right to receive the par value of their stock or a larger stated liquidation value per share before the common stockholders receive any share of the corporation's assets. This preference can also extend to any dividends in arrears owed to the preferred stockholders.

Convertible Preferred Stock

Study Note

When preferred stockholders convert their shares to common stock, they gain voting rights but lose the dividend and liquidation preference. Conversion back to preferred stock is not an option.

Like all preferred stockholders, owners of **convertible preferred stock** are more likely than common stockholders to receive regular dividends. In addition, they can exchange their shares of preferred stock for shares of common stock at a ratio stated in the company's preferred stock contract. If the market value of the company's common stock increases, the conversion feature allows these stockholders to share in the increase by converting their stock to common stock. For example, if you look back at **Google**'s Financial Highlights at the beginning of the chapter, you will see that Google has preferred stock but none is issued. The reason is that the initial investors in the company received convertible preferred stock. These stockholders took advantage of the steep increase in the price of the common stock by converting their shares to common stock. Thus, by including the conversion feature, Google was able to make its preferred stock more attractive to investors. The stock is still authorized, and the company may decide to issue it again in the future.

Suppose, for instance, that a company issues 1,000 shares of 8 percent, $100 par value convertible preferred stock for $100 per share. Each share of stock can be converted to five shares of the company's common stock at any time. The

FOCUS ON BUSINESS PRACTICE

How Does a Stock Become a Debt?

Some companies have used the flexibility of preferred stocks to create a type of stock that is similar to debt. Usually, stocks do not have maturity dates, and companies do not buy them back except at the option of management. However, **CMS Energy**, **Time Warner**, **Xerox**, and other companies have issued preferred stock that is "mandatorily redeemable." This means that the issuing companies are required to buy back the stock at fixed future dates or under predetermined conditions. Thus, these special preferred stocks are similar to bonds in that they have a fixed maturity date. In addition, in much the same way as bonds require periodic interest payments at a fixed rate, these stocks require an annual dividend payment, also at a fixed rate. Even though companies list these stocks in the stockholders' equity section of their balance sheets, the astute analyst will treat them as debt when calculating a company's debt to equity ratio.[12] The FASB is considering a proposal that would require these special preferred stocks to be classified as a liability on the balance sheet.[13]

market value of the common stock at the time the company issues the convertible preferred stock is $15 per share. In the past, an owner of the common stock could expect dividends of about $1 per share per year. The owner of one share of preferred stock, on the other hand, now holds an investment that has a market value of about $75 and is also more likely than a common stockholder to receive dividends.

Now suppose that in the next several years, the corporation's earnings increase, the dividends paid to common stockholders increase to $3 per share, and the market value of a share of common stock increases from $15 to $30. Preferred stockholders can convert each of their preferred shares to five common shares, thereby increasing their dividends from $8 on each preferred share to $15 ($3 on each of five common shares). Moreover, the market value of each share of preferred stock will be close to the $150 value of the five shares of common stock because each share can be converted to five shares of common stock.

Callable Preferred Stock

Most preferred stock is **callable preferred stock**—that is, the issuing corporation can redeem or retire it at a price stated in the preferred stock contract. An owner of nonconvertible preferred stock must surrender it to the issuing corporation when asked to do so. If the preferred stock is convertible, the stockholder can either surrender the stock to the corporation or convert it to common stock when the corporation calls the stock. The *call price*, or redemption price, is usually higher than the stock's par value. For example, preferred stock that has a $100 par value might be callable at $103 per share.

When preferred stock is called and surrendered, the stockholder is entitled to the following:

- The par value of the stock
- The call premium
- Any dividends in arrears
- The current period's dividend prorated by the proportion of the year to the call date

A corporation may decide to call its preferred stock for any of the following reasons:

- It may want to force conversion of the preferred stock to common stock because the dividend that it pays on preferred shares is higher than the dividend that it pays on the equivalent number of common shares.
- It may be able to replace the outstanding preferred stock with a preferred stock at a lower dividend rate or with long-term debt, which can have a lower after-tax cost.
- It may simply be profitable enough to retire the preferred stock.

& APPLY >

Sung Corporation has 2,000 shares of $100 par value, 7 percent cumulative preferred stock outstanding and 200,000 shares of $1 par value common stock outstanding. In the corporation's first three years of operation, its board of directors declared cash dividends as follows:

2010: none
2011: $20,000
2012: $30,000

Determine the total cash dividends paid to the preferred and common stockholders during each of the three years.

SOLUTION

2010:	None	
2011:	Preferred dividends in arrears (2,000 shares × $100 × 0.07)	$14,000
	Current year remainder to preferred ($20,000 − $14,000)	6,000
	Total to preferred stockholders	$20,000
2012:	Preferred dividends in arrears ($14,000 − $6,000)	$ 8,000
	Current year to preferred (2,000 shares × $100 × 0.07)	14,000
	Total to preferred stockholders	$22,000
	Total to common stockholders ($30,000 − $22,000)	8,000
	Total dividends in 2012	$30,000

Issuance of Common Stock

LO4 Account for the issuance of stock for cash and other assets.

A share of capital stock may be either par or no-par. The value of par stock is stated in the corporate charter and must be printed on each stock certificate. It can be $0.01, $1, $5, $100, or any other amount established by the organizers of the corporation. For instance, the par value of **Google**'s common stock is $0.001. The par values of common stocks tend to be lower than those of preferred stocks.

As noted earlier, par value is the amount per share that is recorded in a corporation's capital stock accounts, and it constitutes a corporation's legal capital. A corporation cannot declare a dividend that would cause stockholders' equity to fall below the firm's legal capital. Par value is thus a minimum cushion of capital that protects a corporation's creditors. Any amount in excess of par value that

Study Note

Legal capital is the minimum amount a corporation can report as contributed capital. To protect creditors, a corporation cannot declare a dividend that would reduce capital below the amount of legal capital.

a corporation receives from a stock issue is recorded in its Additional Paid-in Capital account and represents a portion of its contributed capital.

No-par stock is capital stock that does not have a par value. A corporation may issue stock without a par value for several reasons. For one thing, rather than recognizing par value as an arbitrary figure, investors may confuse it with the stock's market value. For another, most states do not allow a stock issue below par value, and this limits a corporation's flexibility in obtaining capital.

State laws often require corporations to place a **stated value** on each share of stock that they issue, but even when this is not required, a corporation's board of directors may do so as a matter of convenience. The stated value can be any value set by the board unless the state specifies a minimum amount, which is sometimes the case. The stated value can be set before or after the shares are issued if the state law is not specific.

Par Value Stock

When a corporation issues par value stock, the appropriate capital stock account (usually Common Stock or Preferred Stock) is credited for the par value regardless of whether the proceeds are more or less than the par value.

When a corporation issues stock at a price greater than par value, as is usually the case, the proceeds in excess of par are credited to an account called Additional Paid-in Capital. For example, suppose Nocek Corporation is authorized to issue 10,000 shares of $10 par value common stock and that it issues 5,000 shares at $12 each on January 1, 2010. The entry in journal form to record the issuance of the stock at the price in excess of par value would be as follows:

A	= L +	SE
+60,000		+50,000
		+10,000

		Debit	Credit
Jan. 1	Cash	60,000	
	Common Stock		50,000
	Additional Paid-in Capital		10,000
	Issued 5,000 shares of $10 par value common stock for $12 per share		

Cash is debited for the proceeds of $60,000 (5,000 shares × $12), and Common Stock is credited for the total par value of $50,000 (5,000 shares × $10). Additional Paid-in Capital is credited for the difference of $10,000 (5,000 shares × $2).

The amount in excess of par value is part of Nocek Corporation's contributed capital and will be included in the stockholders' equity section of its balance sheet. Immediately after the stock issue, this section of Nocek's balance sheet would appear as follows:

Contributed capital	
Common stock, $10 par value, 10,000 shares authorized, 5,000 shares issued and outstanding	$50,000
Additional paid-in capital	10,000
Total contributed capital	$60,000
Retained earnings	—
Total stockholders' equity	$60,000

If a corporation issues stock for less than par value, an account called Discount on Capital Stock is debited for the difference. The issuance of stock at a discount rarely occurs; it is illegal in many states.

No-Par Stock

> **Study Note**
> When no-par stock has a stated value, the stated value serves the same purpose as par value in that it represents the minimum legal capital.

Most states require that all or part of the proceeds from a corporation's issuance of no-par stock be designated as legal capital, which cannot be used unless the corporation is liquidated. The purpose of this requirement is to protect the corporation's assets for creditors.

Suppose that on January 1, 2010, Nocek Corporation issues 5,000 shares of no-par common stock at $15 per share. The $75,000 (5,000 shares × $15) in proceeds would be recorded as follows:

A	= L +	SE
+75,000		+75,000

Jan. 1	Cash	75,000	
	Common Stock		75,000
	Issued 5,000 shares of no-par common stock for $15 per share		

Because the stock does not have a stated or par value, all proceeds of the issue are credited to Common Stock and are part of the company's legal capital.

As noted earlier, state laws may require corporations to put a stated value on each share of stock that they issue. Assuming the same facts as above except that Nocek puts a $10 stated value on each share of its no-par stock, the entry in journal form would be as follows:

A	= L +	SE
+75,000		+50,000
		+25,000

Jan. 1	Cash	75,000	
	Common Stock		50,000
	Additional Paid-in Capital		25,000
	Issued 5,000 shares of no-par common stock with $10 stated value for $15 per share		

Notice that the legal capital credited to Common Stock is the stated value decided by Nocek's board of directors. Also note that the Additional Paid-in Capital account is credited for $25,000, which is the difference between the proceeds ($75,000) and the total stated value ($50,000).

Issuance of Stock for Noncash Assets

A corporation may issue stock in return for assets or services other than cash. Transactions of this kind usually involve a corporation's exchange of stock for land or buildings or for the services of attorneys and others who help organize the corporation. In such cases, the problem is to determine the dollar amount at which the exchange should be recorded.

> **Study Note**
> In establishing the fair market value of property that a corporation exchanges for stock, a board of directors cannot be arbitrary; it must use all the information at its disposal.

A corporation's board of directors has the right to determine the fair market value of the assets or services that the corporation receives in exchange for its stock. Generally, this kind of transaction is recorded at the fair market value of the stock that the corporation is giving up. If the stock's fair market value cannot be determined, the fair market value of the assets or services received can be used.

For example, suppose that when Nocek Corporation was formed on January 1, 2010, its attorney agreed to accept 200 shares of its $10 par value common stock for services rendered. At that time, the market value of the stock could not be determined. However, for similar services, the attorney would have charged Nocek $3,000. The entry in journal form to record this noncash transaction is as follows:

A	= L +	SE
		−3,000
		+2,000
		+1,000

Jan. 1	Start-up and Organization Costs	3,000	
	Common Stock		2,000
	Additional Paid-in Capital		1,000
	Issued 200 shares of $10 par value common stock for attorney's services		

Now suppose that two years later, Nocek Corporation exchanged 500 shares of its $10 par value common stock for a piece of land. At the time of the exchange, Nocek's stock was selling on the market for $16 per share. The following entry in journal form records this exchange:

A	= L +	SE
+8,000		+5,000
		+3,000

Jan. 1	Land	8,000	
	Common Stock		5,000
	Additional Paid-in Capital		3,000
	Issued 500 shares of $10 par value common stock with a market value of $16 per share for a piece of land		

Arena Company is authorized to issue 10,000 shares of common stock. The company sold 1,000 shares at $10 per share. Prepare entries in journal form to record the sale of stock for cash under each of the following independent alternatives: (1) The stock has a par value of $2, and (2) the stock has no-par value but a stated value of $1 per share.

SOLUTION

1. The stock has a par value of $2.

Cash	10,000	
Common Stock		2,000
Additional Paid-in Capital		8,000
Issued $5 par value common stock at $10 per share		

2. The stock has a no-par value but has a stated value of $1.

Cash	10,000	
Common Stock		1,000
Additional Paid-in Capital		9,000
Issued no-par value common stock with a stated value of $1 at $10 per share		

Accounting for Treasury Stock

LO5 Account for treasury stock.

As we noted earlier, treasury stock is stock that the issuing company has reacquired, usually by purchasing shares on the open market. Although repurchasing its own stock can be a severe drain on a corporation's cash, it is common practice. In a recent year, 386, or 64 percent, of 600 large companies held treasury stock.[14]

Among the reasons a company may want to buy back its own stock are the following:

- It may want stock to distribute to employees through stock option plans.
- It may be trying to maintain a favorable market for its stock.
- It may want to increase its earnings per share or stock price per share.
- It may want to have additional shares of stock available for purchasing other companies.
- It may want to prevent a hostile takeover.

Study Note

Treasury stock is not the same as unissued stock. Treasury stock represents shares that have been issued but are no longer outstanding. Unissued shares, on the other hand, have never been in circulation.

A purchase of treasury stock reduces a company's assets and stockholders' equity. It is not considered a purchase of assets, as the purchase of shares in another company would be. A company can hold treasury shares for an indefinite period or reissue or retire them. Treasury shares have no rights until they are reissued. Like unissued shares, they do not have voting rights, rights to dividends, or rights to assets during liquidation of the company. However, there is one major difference between unissued shares and treasury shares. A share of stock issued at par value or greater and that was reacquired as treasury stock can be reissued at less than par value without negative results.

Purchase of Treasury Stock

When treasury stock is purchased, it is recorded at cost. The par value, stated value, or original issue price of the stock is ignored. As noted above, the purchase reduces both a firm's assets and its stockholders' equity. For example, suppose that on September 15, Amber Corporation purchases 2,000 shares of its

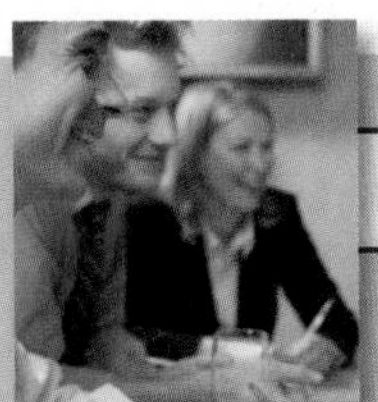

FOCUS ON BUSINESS PRACTICE

Are Share Buybacks Really Good?

Corporate America sets new records for share buybacks every year: $10 billion in 1991, $123 billion in 2000; $197 billion in 2004; and an estimated $500 billion in 2007. **Home Depot, Inc, Wal-Mart, Inc, General Electric, Johnson & Johnson** and **Microsoft**, along with many other companies, spent billions to boost their stock prices—but to no avail. The stated aim is to boost stock prices and earnings per share by reducing the supply of stock in public hands.

According to renowned investor Warren Buffett and others, share buybacks are ill-advised. Many of the purchases in 2007, for example, occurred when the market was experiencing record highs. Also, what is often not stated publicly is that many shares do not stay out of public hands because the companies recycle the stock into generous stock options for management and thus do not achieve the stated goal of reducing outstanding shares. Estimates are that perhaps half of the stock purchased is little more than a "backdoor compensation" for employees. Furthermore, many companies have borrowed money to repurchase stock, thereby increasing their debt to equity ratios. These companies later suffered reductions in their credit ratings and severe declines in their stock prices.[15]

common stock on the market at a price of $50 per share. The purchase would be recorded as follows:

A	= L +	SE
−100,000		−100,000

Sept. 15	Treasury Stock, Common	100,000	
	Cash		100,000
	Acquired 2,000 shares of the company's common stock for $50 per share		

Study Note

Because treasury stock reduces stockholder's equity—the denominator of the return on equity ratio—the return on equity will increase when treasury shares are purchased even though there is no increase in earnings.

The stockholders' equity section of Amber's balance sheet shows the cost of the treasury stock as a deduction from the total of contributed capital and retained earnings:

Contributed capital	
Common stock, $5 par value, 200,000 shares authorized, 60,000 shares issued, 58,000 shares outstanding	$ 300,000
Additional paid-in capital	60,000
Total contributed capital	$ 360,000
Retained earnings	1,800,000
Total contributed capital and retained earnings	$2,160,000
Less treasury stock, common (2,000 shares at cost)	100,000
Total stockholders' equity	$2,060,000

Notice that the number of shares issued, and therefore the legal capital, has not changed. However, the number of shares outstanding has decreased as a result of the transaction.

Sale of Treasury Stock

Treasury shares can be sold at cost, above cost, or below cost. For example, suppose that on November 15, Amber Corporation sells its 2,000 treasury shares for $50 per share. The following entry in journal form records the transaction:

A	= L +	SE
+100,000		+100,000

Nov. 15	Cash	100,000	
	Treasury Stock, Common		100,000
	Reissued 2,000 shares of treasury stock for $50 per share		

When treasury shares are sold for an amount greater than their cost, the excess of the sales price over cost should be credited to Paid-in Capital, Treasury Stock. No gain should be recorded.

For instance, suppose that on November 15, Amber Corporation sells its 2,000 treasury shares for $60 per share. This entry would record the reissue:

A	= L +	SE
+120,000		+100,000
		+20,000

Nov. 15	Cash	120,000	
	Treasury Stock, Common		100,000
	Paid-in Capital, Treasury Stock		20,000
	Sold 2,000 shares of treasury stock for $60 per share; cost was $50 per share		

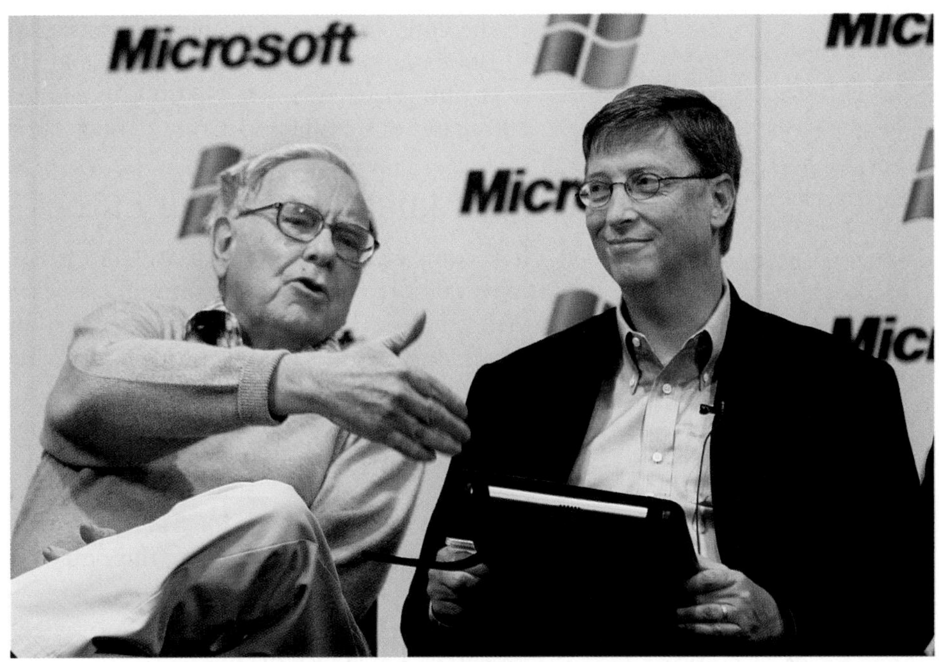

In 2004, Microsoft's board approved a plan to buy back $30 billion of the company's common stock over the next four years. By 2007, the company had repurchased more than $60 billion of its own stock. When are share buybacks not a good idea? According to investor Warren Buffett, shown here offering his hand to Microsoft's Bill Gates, buybacks are ill-advised when a company buys high and sells low and when it borrows money to finance a buyback.

Courtesy of Reuters/ Anthony P. Bolante/Corbis.

Study Note

Gains and losses on the reissue of treasury stock are never recognized as such. Instead, the Retained Earnings and Paid-in Capital, Treasury Stock accounts are used.

When treasury shares are sold below their cost, the difference is deducted from Paid-in Capital, Treasury Stock. If this account does not exist or if its balance is insufficient to cover the excess of cost over the reissue price, Retained Earnings absorbs the excess. No loss is recorded.

For example, suppose that on September 15, Amber bought 2,000 shares of its common stock on the market at a price of $50 per share. On October 15, the company sold 800 shares for $60 per share, and on December 15, it sold the remaining 1,200 shares for $42 per share.

The entries in journal form for these three transactions are as follows:

A	= L +	SE
−100,000		−100,000

Sept. 15	Treasury Stock, Common	100,000	
	Cash		100,000
	Purchased 2,000 shares of treasury stock at $50 per share		

A	= L +	SE
+48,000		+40,000
		+8,000

Oct. 15	Cash	48,000	
	Treasury Stock, Common		40,000
	Paid-in Capital, Treasury Stock		8,000
	Sold 800 shares of treasury stock for $60 per share; cost was $50 per share		

A	= L +	SE
+50,400		−8,000
		−1,600
		+60,000

Dec. 15	Cash	50,400	
	Paid-in Capital, Treasury Stock	8,000	
	Retained Earnings	1,600	
	Treasury Stock, Common		60,000
	Sold 1,200 shares of treasury stock for $42 per share; cost was $50 per share		

Study Note

Retained Earnings is debited only when the Paid-in Capital, Treasury Stock account has been depleted. In this case, the credit balance of $8,000 is completely exhausted before Retained Earnings absorbs the excess.

In the entry for the December 15 transaction, Retained Earnings is debited for $1,600 because the 1,200 shares were sold for $9,600 less than cost. That amount is $1,600 greater than the $8,000 of paid-in capital generated by the sale of the 800 shares of treasury stock on October 15.

Retirement of Treasury Stock

If a company decides that it will not reissue treasury stock, it can, with the approval of its stockholders, retire the stock. All items related to those shares are then removed from the associated capital accounts. If the cost of buying back the treasury stock is less than the company received when it issued the stock, the difference is recorded in Paid-in Capital, Retirement of Stock. If the cost is more than was received when the stock was first issued, the difference is a reduction in stockholders' equity and is debited to Retained Earnings. For instance, suppose that on November 15, Amber Corporation decides to retire the 2,000 shares of stock that it bought back for $100,000. If the $5 par value common stock was originally issued at $6 per share, this entry would record the retirement:

A	=	L +	SE
			−10,000
			−2,000
			−88,000
			+100,000

Date	Account	Debit	Credit
Nov. 15	Common Stock	10,000	
	Additional Paid-in Capital	2,000	
	Retained Earnings	88,000	
	Treasury Stock, Common		100,000
	Retired 2,000 shares that cost $50 per share and were issued originally at $6 per share		

STOP & APPLY >

Prepare in journal form the entries necessary to record the following stock transactions of the Paulo Company during 2011:

May 1 Purchased 5,000 shares of its own $1 par value common stock for $10 per share, the current market price.

17 Sold 1,000 shares of treasury stock purchased on May 1 for $11 per share.

SOLUTION

Date	Account	Debit	Credit
May 1	Treasury Stock	50,000	
	Cash		50,000
	Purchased 5,000 shares of Paulo Company's common stock at $10 per share		
17	Cash	11,000	
	Treasury Stock		10,000
	Paid-in Capital, Treasury Stock		1,000
	Sold 1,000 shares of treasury stock for $11 per share		

A LOOK BACK AT ▸ GOOGLE, INC.

This chapter's Decision Point focused on one of the most exciting financing events of recent history, **Google's** IPO. In evaluating Google's performance since its IPO, those who invested in its stock should consider the following questions:

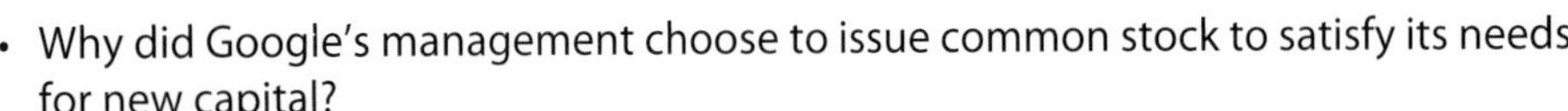

- Why did Google's management choose to issue common stock to satisfy its needs for new capital?
- What are some of the advantages and disadvantages of this approach to financing a business?
- What measures should an investor use in evaluating management's performance?

As a relatively new company, Google needed to raise capital so that it could expand its operations. The company's management decided to do so by issuing common stock. This approach to financing does not burden a company with debt or interest payments. In addition, the company has the option of paying or not paying dividends. Because Google currently does not pay dividends, it can invest cash from its earnings in expanding the company. Issuing stock does, however, dilute the ownership of a company's current owners, and if the company pays dividends, they are not tax-deductible, as interest on debt is.

Return on equity is, of course, a key measure of management's performance. Using the data from Google's Financial Highlights, 2007 net income of \$4,203,720 thousand, 2008 net income of \$4,226,858 thousand, and 2006 stockholders' equity of \$17,039,840 thousand, we can compute the company's return on equity for 2008 and 2007 as follows (in thousands):

$$\text{Return on Equity} = \frac{\text{Net Income}}{\text{Average Stockholders' Equity}}$$

	2008	**2007**
Return on Equity =	$\frac{\$4,226,858}{(\$28,238,862 + \$22,689,679) \div 2}$	$\frac{\$4,203,720}{(\$22,689,679 + \$17,039,840) \div 2}$
	= 16.6%	= 21.2%

Google's return on equity declined from 21.2 percent to 16.6 percent but still remains at a very good level.

At the time of the IPO, when Google's stock sold for \$85 per share, its P/E ratio was 74.6 times. During the last two years its ratios have been as follows:

$$\text{P/E Ratio} = \frac{\text{Market Price per Share}}{\text{Earnings per Share}}$$

	2008	**2007**
P/E Ratio =	$\frac{\$332}{\$13.31}$ = 24.9 times	$\frac{\$658}{\$13.29}$ = 49.5 times

Even with the drop in stock price in 2008, these are very high P/E ratios. Further, at the beginning of 2010, Google's stock price recovered to near the \$600 level, and the average P/E ratio for S&P 500 stocks was only about 17. Evidently, despite Google's not paying dividends, investors are rewarding the company's high return on equity and think the company's future is very bright.

Review Problem

Recording Stock Issues and Calculating Related Ratios
LO1 LO2 LO3 LO4 LO5

Fisher Corporation was organized in 2010 in Arizona. Its state charter authorized it to issue 2 million shares of $1 par value common stock and 50,000 shares of 4 percent, $20 par value cumulative and convertible preferred stock. Fisher's stock transactions during 2010 were as follows:

Feb.	1	Issued 200,000 shares of common stock for $250,000.
	15	Issued 6,000 shares of common stock for accounting and legal services. The bills for these services totaled $7,200.
Mar.	15	Issued 240,000 shares of common stock to Tom Lee in exchange for a building and land appraised at $200,000 and $50,000, respectively.
Apr.	2	Purchased 40,000 shares of common stock for the treasury at $1.25 per share from a person who changed her mind about investing in the company.
July	1	Issued 50,000 shares of preferred stock for $1,000,000.
Sept.	30	Sold 20,000 of the shares in the treasury for $1.50 per share.
Dec.	31	Fisher's board of directors declared dividends of $49,820 payable on January 15, 2011, to stockholders of record on January 7. Dividends included preferred stock dividends of $20,000 for one-half year.

For the period ended December 31, 2010, Fisher reported net income of $80,000 and earnings per common share of $0.14. At December 31, the market price per common share was $1.60.

Required

1. Record Fisher's stock transactions in T accounts.
2. Prepare the stockholders' equity section of Fisher's balance sheet as of December 31, 2010. (**Hint**: Use net income and dividends to calculate retained earnings.)
3. Calculate Fisher's dividends yield on common stock, price/earnings ratio of common stock, and return on equity.

Answers to Review Problem

1. Entries in T accounts:

Assets = Liabilities + Stockholders' Equity

Assets

Cash

Feb.	1	250,000	Apr.	2	50,000
July	1	1,000,000			
Sept.	30	30,000			

Building

Mar.	15	200,000			

Land

Mar.	15	50,000			

Liabilities

Dividends Payable

			Dec.	31	49,820

Stockholders' Equity

Preferred Stock

			July	1	1,000,000

Common Stock

			Feb.	1	200,000
				15	6,000
			Mar.	15	240,000
			Bal.		446,000

Additional Paid-in Capital

			Feb.	1	50,000
				15	1,200
			Mar.	15	10,000
			Bal.		61,200

Paid-in Capital, Treasury Stock

			Sept.	30	5,000

Dividends

Dec.	31	49,820			

Treasury Stock

Apr.	2	50,000	Sept.	30	25,000
Bal.		25,000			

Start-up and Organization Costs

Feb.	15	7,200			

2. Stockholders' equity section of the balance sheet:

Fisher Corporation
Balance Sheet
December 31, 2010

Stockholders' Equity

Contributed capital		
Preferred stock, 4 percent cumulative, convertible, $20 par value, 50,000 shares authorized, issued, and outstanding		$1,000,000
Common stock, $1 par value, 2,000,000 shares authorized, 446,000 shares issued, and 426,000 shares outstanding		446,000
Additional paid-in capital		61,200
Paid-in capital, treasury stock		5,000
Total contributed capital		$1,512,200
Retained earnings		30,180 *
Total contributed capital and retained earnings		$1,542,380
Less treasury stock (20,000 shares, at cost)		25,000
Total stockholders' equity		$1,517,380

* Retained Earnings = Net Income − Cash Dividends Declared
Retained Earnings = $80,000 − $49,820 = $30,180

3. Dividends yield on common stock, price/earnings ratio of common stock, and return on equity:

$$\text{Dividends per Share} = \frac{\text{Common Stock Dividend}}{\text{Common Shares Outstanding}} = \frac{\$29{,}820}{426{,}000} = \$0.07$$

$$\text{Dividends Yield} = \frac{\text{Dividends per Share}}{\text{Market Price per Share}} = \frac{\$0.07}{\$1.60} = 4.4\%$$

$$\text{Price/Earnings Ratio} = \frac{\text{Market Price per Share}}{\text{Earnings per Share}} = \frac{\$1.60}{\$0.14} = 11.4 \text{ times}$$

The opening balance of stockholders' equity on February 1, 2010, was $250,000.

$$\text{Return on Equity} = \frac{\text{Net Income}}{\text{Average Stockholders' Equity}}$$

$$= \frac{\$80{,}000}{(\$1{,}517{,}380 + \$250{,}000) \div 2}$$

$$= \frac{\$80{,}000}{\$883{,}690}$$

$$= 9.1\%$$

LO1 Identify and explain the management issues related to contributed capital.

Contributed capital is a critical component in corporate financing. Managing contributed capital requires an understanding of the advantages and disadvantages of the corporate form of business and of the issues involved in using equity financing. Managers must also know how to determine dividend policies and how to evaluate these policies using dividends yield, return on equity, and the price/earnings ratio. The liability for payment of dividends arises on the date the board of directors declares a dividend. The declaration is recorded with a debit to Dividends and a credit to Dividends Payable. The record date—the date on which ownership of the stock, and thus of the right to receive a dividend, is determined—requires no entry. On the payment date, the Dividends Payable account is eliminated, and the Cash account is reduced. Another issue involved in managing contributed capital is using stock options as compensation.

LO2 Identify the components of stockholders' equity.

The stockholders' equity section of a corporate balance sheet usually has at least three components: contributed capital, retained earnings, and treasury stock. Contributed capital consists of money raised through stock issues. A corporation can issue two types of stock: common stock and preferred stock. Common stockholders have voting rights; they also share in the corporation's earnings. Preferred stockholders usually have preference over common stockholders in one or more areas. Retained earnings are reinvested in the corporation; they represent stockholders' claims to assets resulting from profitable operations. Treasury stock is stock that the issuing corporation has reacquired. It is treated as a deduction from stockholders' equity.

LO3 Identify the characteristics of preferred stock.

Preferred stock generally gives its owners first right to dividend payments. Only after these stockholders have been paid can common stockholders receive any portion of a dividend. If the preferred stock is cumulative and dividends are in arrears, a corporation must pay the amount in arrears to preferred stockholders before it pays any dividends to common stockholders. Preferred stockholders also usually have preference over common stockholders in terms of their claims to corporate assets if the corporation is liquidated. In addition, preferred stock may be convertible to common stock, and it is often callable at the option of the corporation.

LO4 Account for the issuance of stock for cash and other assets.

Corporations normally issue their stock in exchange for cash or other assets. Most states require corporations to issue stock at a minimum value called *legal capital.* Legal capital is represented by the stock's par or stated value.

When stock is issued for cash at par or stated value, Cash is debited and Common Stock or Preferred Stock is credited. When stock is sold at an amount greater than par or stated value, the excess is recorded in Additional Paid-in Capital.

When stock is issued for noncash assets, the general rule is to record the stock at its market value. If this value cannot be determined, the fair market value of the asset received is used to record the transaction.

LO5 Account for treasury stock.

Treasury stock is stock that the issuing company has reacquired. A company may buy back its own stock for several reasons, including a desire to create stock option plans, maintain a favorable market for the stock, increase earnings per share, or purchase other companies. Treasury stock is recorded at cost and is deducted from stockholders' equity. It can be reissued or retired. It is similar to unissued stock in that it does not have rights until it is reissued.

REVIEW of Concepts and Terminology

The following concepts and terms were introduced in this chapter:

Authorized shares 544 (LO2)

Callable preferred stock 548 (LO3)

Common stock 543 (LO2)

Convertible preferred stock 547 (LO3)

Cumulative preferred stock 546 (LO3)

Declaration date 538 (LO1)

Dividend 538 (LO1)

Dividends in arrears 546 (LO3)

Double taxation 536 (LO1)

Ex-dividend 538 (LO1)

Initial public offering (IPO) 533 (Decision Point)

Issued shares 544 (LO2)

Legal capital 537 (LO1)

Liquidating dividend 538 (LO1)

Noncumulative preferred stock 546 (LO3)

No-par stock 550 (LO4)

Outstanding shares 544 (LO2)

Par value 536 (LO1)

Payment date 538 (LO1)

Preferred stock 543 (LO2)

Record date 538 (LO1)

Residual equity 543 (LO2)

Share of stock 534 (LO1)

Start-up and organization costs 537 (LO1)

Stated value 550 (LO4)

Stock certificates 536 (LO1)

Stock option plans 541 (LO1)

Treasury stock 541 (LO1)

Underwriter 537 (LO1)

Key Ratios

Dividends yield 539 (LO1)

Price/earnings (P/E) ratio 541 (LO1)

Return on equity 540 (LO1)

CHAPTER ASSIGNMENTS

BUILDING Your Basic Knowledge and Skills

Short Exercises

LO1 **Management Issues**

SE 1. Indicate whether each of the following actions is related to (a) managing under the corporate form of business, (b) using equity financing, (c) determining dividend policies, (d) evaluating performance using return on equity, or (e) issuing stock options:

1. Considering whether to make a distribution to stockholders
2. Controlling day-to-day operations
3. Determining whether to issue preferred or common stock
4. Compensating management based on the company's meeting or exceeding the targeted return on equity
5. Compensating employees by giving them the right to purchase shares at a given price
6. Transferring shares without the approval of other owners

LO1 **Advantages and Disadvantages of a Corporation**

SE 2. Identify whether each of the following characteristics is an advantage or a disadvantage of the corporate form of business:

1. Ease of transfer of ownership
2. Taxation
3. Separate legal entity
4. Lack of mutual agency
5. Government regulation
6. Continuous existence

LO2 **Effect of Start-up and Organization Costs**

SE 3. At the beginning of 2009, Patel Company incurred the following start-up and organization costs: (1) attorneys' fees with a market value of $20,000, paid with 12,000 shares of $1 par value common stock, and (2) incorporation fees of $12,000. Calculate total start-up and organization costs. What will be the effect of these costs on the income statement and balance sheet?

LO1 **Exercise of Stock Options**

SE 4. On June 6, Aretha Dafoe received an option to purchase 20,000 shares of Shalom Company $1 par value common stock at an option price of $8 per share, which is equal to the market price on that date. The market price of the common stock on the date Dafoe exercises the option is $25 per share. (1) What value must be estimated to determine the expense of the option on June 6? (2) What relevance does the market price per share have when Dafoe later exercises the option?

LO2 **Stockholders' Equity**

SE 5. Prepare the stockholders' equity section of Fina Corporation's balance sheet from the following accounts and balances on December 31, 2010:

Common Stock, $10 par value, 30,000 shares authorized, 20,000 shares issued, and 19,500 shares outstanding	$200,000
Additional Paid-in Capital	100,000
Retained Earnings	15,000
Treasury Stock, Common (500 shares, at cost)	7,500

LO1 Cash Dividends

SE 6. Tone Corporation has authorized 200,000 shares of $1 par value common stock, of which 160,000 are issued and 140,000 are outstanding. On May 15, the board of directors declared a cash dividend of $.20 per share, payable on June 15 to stockholders of record on June 1. Prepare the entries in T accounts, as necessary, for each of the three dates.

LO3 Preferred Stock Dividends with Dividends in Arrears

SE 7. The Ferris Corporation has 2,000 shares of $100, 8 percent cumulative preferred stock outstanding and 40,000 shares of $1 par value common stock outstanding. In the company's first three years of operation, its board of directors paid cash dividends as follows: 2009, none; 2010, $40,000; and 2011, $80,000. Determine the total cash dividends and dividends per share paid to the preferred and common stockholders during each of the three years.

LO4 Issuance of Stock

SE 8. Rattich Company is authorized to issue 50,000 shares of common stock. The company sold 2,500 shares at $12 per share. Prepare entries in journal form to record the sale of stock for cash under each of the following independent alternatives: (1) The stock has a par value of $5, and (2) the stock has no par value but a stated value of $1 per share.

LO4 Issuance of Stock for Noncash Assets

SE 9. Embossing Corporation issued 32,000 shares of its $1 par value common stock in exchange for land that had a fair market value of $200,000. Prepare in journal form the entries necessary to record the issuance of the stock for the land under each of these conditions: (1) The stock was selling for $7 per share on the day of the transaction; (2) management attempted to place a value on the common stock but could not do so.

LO5 Treasury Stock Transactions

SE 10. Prepare in journal form the entries necessary to record the following stock transactions of the Seoul Company during 2010:

Oct.	1	Purchased 2,000 shares of its own $2 par value common stock for $20 per share, the current market price.
	17	Sold 500 shares of treasury stock purchased on October 1 for $25 per share.

LO5 Retirement of Treasury Stock

SE 11. On October 28, 2010, the Seoul Company (**SE 10**) retired the remaining 1,500 shares of treasury stock. The shares were originally issued at $5 per share. Prepare the necessary entry in journal form.

Exercises

LO1 LO2 Discussion Questions

E 1. Develop brief answers to each of the following questions:

1. Why are most large companies established as corporations rather than as partnerships?
2. Why do many companies like to give stock options as compensation?
3. If an investor sells shares after the declaration date but before the date of record, does the seller still receive the dividend?
4. Why does a company usually not want to issue all its authorized shares?

LO3 LO4 LO5
Discussion Questions

E 2. Develop brief answers to each of the following questions:

1. Why would a company want to issue callable preferred stock?
2. What arguments can you give for treating preferred stock as debt rather than equity when carrying out financial analysis?
3. What relevance does par value or stated value have to a financial ratio, such as return on equity or debit to equity?
4. Why is treasury stock not considered an investment or an asset?

LO1
Dividends Yield and Price/Earnings Ratio

E 3. In 2011, Rainbow Corporation earned $8.80 per share and paid a dividend of $4.00 per share. At year end, the price of its stock was $132.00 per share. Calculate the dividends yield and the price/earnings ratio.

LO2
Stockholders' Equity

E 4. The following accounts and balances are from the records of Stuard Corporation on December 31, 2010:

Preferred Stock, $100 par value, 9 percent cumulative, 10,000 shares authorized, 3,000 shares issued and outstanding	$300,000
Common Stock, $12 par value, 45,000 shares authorized, 15,000 shares issued, and 14,250 shares outstanding	180,000
Additional Paid-in Capital	97,000
Retained Earnings	11,500
Treasury Stock, Common (750 shares, at cost)	15,000

Prepare the stockholders' equity section for Stuard Corporation's balance sheet as of December 31, 2010.

LO2 LO3
Characteristics of Common and Preferred Stock

E 5. Indicate whether each of the following characteristics is more closely associated with common stock (C) or preferred stock (P):

1. Often receives dividends at a set rate
2. Is considered the residual equity of a company
3. Can be callable
4. Can be convertible
5. More likely to have dividends that vary in amount from year to year
6. Can be entitled to receive dividends not paid in past years
7. Likely to have full voting rights
8. Receives assets first in liquidation
9. Generally receives dividends before other classes of stock

LO2 LO4
Stock Entries Using T Accounts; Stockholders' Equity

E 6. Shark School Supply Corporation was organized in 2010. It was authorized to issue 200,000 shares of no-par common stock with a stated value of $5 per share, and 40,000 shares of $100 par value, 6 percent noncumulative preferred stock. On March 1, the company issued 60,000 shares of its common stock for $15 per share and 8,000 shares of its preferred stock for $100 per share.

1. Record the issuance of the stock in T accounts.
2. Prepare the stockholders' equity section of Shark School Supply Corporation's balance sheet as it would appear immediately after the company issued the common and preferred stock.

LO1 **Cash Dividends**

E 7. Pine Corporation secured authorization from the state for 100,000 shares of $10 par value common stock. It has 40,000 shares issued and 35,000 shares outstanding. On June 5, the board of directors declared a $0.25 per share cash dividend to be paid on June 25 to stockholders of record on June 15. Prepare entries in T accounts to record these events.

LO1 LO5 **Cash Dividends**

E 8. Avena Corporation has 250,000 authorized shares of $1 par value common stock, of which 100,000 are issued, including 10,000 shares of treasury stock. On October 15, the corporation's board of directors declared a cash dividend of $0.50 per share payable on November 15 to stockholders of record on November 1. Prepare entries in T accounts for each of the three dates.

LO3 **Cash Dividends with Dividends in Arrears**

E 9. Ghana Corporation has 10,000 shares of its $100 par value, 7 percent cumulative preferred stock outstanding, and 50,000 shares of its $1 par value common stock outstanding. In Ghana's first four years of operation, its board of directors paid cash dividends as follows: 2009, none; 2010, $120,000; 2011, $140,000; 2012, $140,000. Determine the dividends per share and total cash dividends paid to the preferred and common stockholders during each of the four years.

LO3 **Cash Dividends on Preferred and Common Stock**

E 10. Dylan Corporation pays dividends at the end of each year. The dividends that it paid for 2009, 2010, and 2011 were $80,000, $60,000, and $180,000, respectively. Calculate the total amount of dividends Dylan Corporation paid in each of these years to its common and preferred stockholders under both of the following capital structures: (1) 20,000 shares of $100 par, 6 percent noncumulative preferred stock and 60,000 shares of $10 par common stock; (2) 10,000 shares of $100 par, 7 percent cumulative preferred stock and 60,000 shares of $10 par common stock. Dylan Corporation had no dividends in arrears at the beginning of 2009.

LO4 **Issuance of Stock**

E 11. Power Net Company is authorized to issue 50,000 shares of common stock. On August 1, the company issued 2,500 shares at $25 per share. Prepare entries in journal form to record the issuance of stock for cash under each of the following alternatives:

1. The stock has a par value of $25.
2. The stock has a par value of $10.
3. The stock has no par value.
4. The stock has a stated value of $1 per share.

LO4 **Issuance of Stock for Noncash Assets**

E 12. On July 1, 2010, Kosa, a new corporation, issued 20,000 shares of its common stock to finance a corporate headquarters building. The building has a fair market value of $600,000 and a book value of $400,000. Because Kosa is a new corporation, it is not possible to establish a market value for its common stock. Record the issuance of stock for the building, assuming the following conditions:

(1) the par value of the stock is $10 per share; (2) the stock is no-par stock; and (3) the stock has a stated value of $4 per share.

LO5 **Treasury Stock Transactions**

E 13. Record in T accounts the following stock transactions of Pigua Company, which represent all of the company's treasury stock transactions during 2010:

May	5	Purchased 1,600 shares of its own $2 par value common stock for $40 per share, the current market price.
	17	Sold 600 shares of treasury stock purchased on May 5 for $44 per share.
	21	Sold 400 shares of treasury stock purchased on May 5 for $40 per share.
	28	Sold the remaining 600 shares of treasury stock purchased on May 5 for $38 per share.

LO5 **Treasury Stock Transactions Including Retirement**

E 14. Record in T accounts the following stock transactions of Lopez Corporation, which represent all its treasury stock transactions for the year:

June	1	Purchased 2,000 shares of its own $15 par value common stock for $35 per share, the current market price.
	10	Sold 500 shares of treasury stock purchased on June 1 for $40 per share.
	20	Sold 700 shares of treasury stock purchased on June 1 for $29 per share.
	30	Retired the remaining shares purchased on June 1. The original issue price was $21 per share.

Problems

LO1 LO2 LO4 **Common Stock Transactions and Stockholders' Equity**

P 1. On March 1, 2010, Dora Corporation began operations with a charter it received from the state that authorized 50,000 shares of $4 par value common stock. Over the next quarter, the company engaged in the transactions that follow.

Mar.	1	Issued 15,000 shares of common stock, $100,000.
	2	Paid fees associated with obtaining the charter and starting up and organizing the corporation, $12,000.
Apr.	10	Issued 6,500 shares of common stock, $65,000.
	15	Purchased 2,500 shares of common stock, $25,000
May	31	The board of directors declared a $0.20 per share cash dividend to be paid on June 15 to shareholders of record on June 10.

Required

1. Record the above transactions in T accounts.
2. Prepare the stockholders' equity section of Dora Corporation's balance sheet on May 31, 2010. Net income earned during the first quarter was $15,000.

User insight ▶
3. What effect, if any, will the cash dividend declaration on May 31 have on Dora Corporation's net income, retained earnings, and cash flows?

LO1 LO3 **Preferred and Common Stock Dividends and Dividends Yield**

P 2. The Rago Corporation had the following stock outstanding from 2009 through 2012:

Preferred stock: $100 par value, 8 percent cumulative, 5,000 shares authorized, issued, and outstanding

Common stock: $10 par value, 100,000 shares authorized, issued, and outstanding

The company paid $30,000, $30,000, $94,000, and $130,000 in dividends during 2009, 2010, 2011, and 2012, respectively. The market price per common share was $7.25 and $8.00 per share at the end of years 2011 and 2012, respectively.

Required

1. Determine the dividends per share and the total dividends paid to common stockholders and preferred stockholders in the years 2009, 2010, 2011, and 2012.
2. Perform the same computations, with the assumption that the preferred stock was noncumulative.
3. Calculate the 2011 and 2012 dividends yield for common stock, using the dividends per share computed in requirement **2**.

User insight ▶

4. How are cumulative preferred stock and noncumulative preferred stock similar to long-term bonds? How do they differ from long-term bonds?

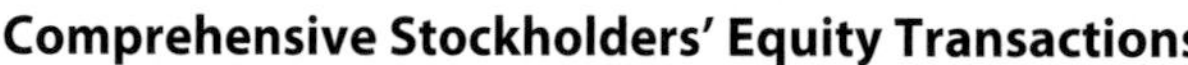

LO1 LO2 LO3 LO4 LO5 **Comprehensive Stockholders' Equity Transactions**

P 3. In January 2010, the Janas Corporation was organized and authorized to issue 1,000,000 shares of no-par common stock and 25,000 shares of 5 percent, $50 par value, noncumulative preferred stock.

The stock-related transactions for the first year's operations are listed below and on the following page.

			Account	
			Debited	Credited
Jan.	19	Sold 7,500 shares of common stock for $15,750. State law requires a minimum of $1 stated value per share.	110 ($15,750)	310 ($7,500) 312 ($8,250)
	21	Issued 2,500 shares of common stock to attorneys and accountants for services valued at $5,500 and provided during the organization of the corporation.	______	______
Feb.	7	Issued 15,000 shares of common stock for a building that had an appraised value of $39,000.	______	______
Mar.	22	Purchased 5,000 shares of its common stock at $3 per share.	______	______

		Account Debited	Account Credited
July 15	Issued 2,500 shares of common stock to employees under a stock option plan that allows any employee to buy shares at the current market price, which is now $3 per share.	______	______
Aug. 1	Sold 1,250 shares of treasury stock for $4 per share.	______	______
Sept. 1	Declared a cash dividend of $0.15 per common share to be paid on September 25 to stockholders of record on September 15.	______	______
15	Date of record for cash dividends.	______	______
25	Paid cash dividends to stockholders of record on September 15.	______	______
Oct. 30	Issued 2,000 shares of common stock for a piece of land. The stock was selling for $3 per share, and the land had a fair market value of $6,000.	______	______
Dec. 15	Issued 1,100 shares of preferred stock for $50 per share.	______	______

Required

1. For each of the above transactions, enter in the blanks provided the account numbers and dollar amounts (as shown in the example) for the account(s) debited and credited. The account numbers are listed below.

110 Cash	312 Additional Paid-in Capital
120 Land	313 Paid-in Capital, Treasury Stock
121 Building	340 Retained Earnings
220 Dividends Payable	341 Dividends
305 Preferred Stock	350 Treasury Stock, Common
310 Common Stock	510 Start-up and Organization Costs

User insight ▶ 2. Why is the stockholders' equity section of the balance sheet an important consideration in analyzing the performance of a company?

LO1 LO2 LO3 LO4 LO5

Comprehensive Stockholders' Equity Transactions and Stockholders' Equity

P 4. Kras, Inc., was organized and authorized to issue 5,000 shares of $100 par value, 9 percent preferred stock and 50,000 shares of no-par, $5 stated value common stock on July 1, 2010. Stock-related transactions for Kras are as follows:

July	1	Issued 10,000 shares of common stock at $11 per share.
	1	Issued 500 shares of common stock at $11 per share for services rendered in connection with the organization of the company.
	2	Issued 1,000 shares of preferred stock at par value for cash.
	10	Issued 2,500 shares of common stock for land on which the asking price was $70,000. Market value of the stock was $12. Management wishes to record the land at full market value of the stock.
Aug.	2	Purchased 1,500 shares of its common stock at $13 per share.
	10	Declared a cash dividend for one month on the outstanding preferred stock and $.02 per share on common stock outstanding, payable on August 22 to stockholders of record on August 12.
	12	Date of record for cash dividends.
	22	Paid cash dividends.

Required

1. Record the transactions in journal form.
2. Prepare the stockholders' equity section of the balance sheet as it would appear on August 31, 2010. The Company's net income for July and August was $11,500.
3. User insight ▶ Calculate dividends yield, price/earnings ratio, and return on equity. Assume earnings per common share are $1.00 and market price per common share is $20. For beginning stockholders' equity, use the balance after the July transactions.
4. User insight ▶ Discuss the results in requirement **3**, including the effect on investors' returns and the company's profitability as it relates to stockholders' equity.

LO1 LO5

Treasury Stock

P 5. The Rolek Company was involved in the following treasury stock transactions during 2010:

a. Purchased 40,000 shares of its $1 par value common stock on the market for $2.50 per share.
b. Purchased 8,000 shares of its $1 par value common stock on the market for $2.80 per share.
c. Sold 22,000 shares purchased in **a** for $65,500.
d. Sold the other 18,000 shares purchased in **a** for $36,000.
e. Sold 3,000 of the remaining shares of treasury stock for $1.60 per share.
f. Retired all the remaining shares of treasury stock. All shares originally were issued at $1.50 per share.

Required

1. Record the treasury stock transactions in T accounts.
2. User insight ▶ What do you think is the reasoning behind treating the purchase of treasury stock as a reduction in stockholders' equity as opposed to treating it as an investment asset?

Alternate Problems

LO1 LO2 LO4 LO5

Common Stock Transactions and Stockholders' Equity

P 6. Glass Corporation began operations on September 1, 2010. The corporation's charter authorized 150,000 shares of $8 par value common stock. Glass Corporation engaged in the following transactions during its first quarter:

Sept.	1	Issued 25,000 shares of common stock, $250,000.
	1	Paid an attorney $16,000 to help start up and organize the corporation and obtain a corporate charter from the state.
Oct.	2	Issued 40,000 shares of common stock, $480,000.
	15	Purchased 5,000 shares of common stock for $75,000.
Nov.	30	Declared a cash dividend of $0.40 per share to be paid on December 15 to stockholders of record on December 10.

Required

1. Prepare entries in T accounts to record the transactions on the previous page.
2. Prepare the stockholders' equity section of Glass Corporation's balance sheet on November 30, 2010. Net income for the quarter was $40,000.
3. What effect, if any, will the cash dividend declaration on November 30 have on net income, retained earnings, and cash flows? (User insight ▶)

LO1 LO3

Preferred and Common Stock Dividends and Dividend Yield

P 7. The Vegas Corporation had both common stock and preferred stock outstanding from 2009 through 2011. Information about each stock for the three years is as follows:

Type	Par Value	Shares Outstanding	Other
Preferred	$100	20,000	7% cumulative
Common	20	300,000	

The company paid $70,000, $400,000, and $550,000 in dividends for 2009 through 2011, respectively. The market price per common share was $15 and $17 per share at the end of years 2010 and 2011, respectively.

Required

1. Determine the dividends per share and total dividends paid to the common and preferred stockholders each year.
2. Assuming that the preferred stock was noncumulative, repeat the computations performed in requirement **1**.
3. Calculate the 2010 and 2011 dividends yield for common stock using dividends per share computed in requirement **2**.
4. How are cumulative preferred stock and noncumulative preferred stock similar to long-term bonds? How do they differ from long-term bonds? (User insight ▶)

LO1 LO2 LO3 LO4 LO5

Comprehensive Stockholders' Equity Transactions and Financial Ratios

P 8. Stavski Plastics Corporation was chartered in the state of Massachusetts. The company was authorized to issue 10,000 shares of $100 par value, 6 percent preferred stock and 50,000 shares of no-par common stock. The common stock has a $2 stated value. The stock-related transactions for the quarter ended October 31, 2010, were as follows:

Aug.	3	Issued 10,000 shares of common stock at $22 per share.
	15	Issued 8,000 shares of common stock for land. Asking price for the land was $100,000. Common stock's market value was $12 per share.
	22	Issued 5,000 shares of preferred stock for $500,000.

Oct. 4 Issued 5,000 shares of common stock for $60,000.
10 Purchased 2,500 shares of common stock for the treasury for $6,500.
15 Declared a quarterly cash dividend on the outstanding preferred stock and $.10 per share on common stock outstanding, payable on October 31 to stockholders of record on October 25.
25 Date of record for cash dividends.
31 Paid cash dividends.

Required

1. Record transactions for the quarter ended October 31, 2010, in T accounts.
2. Prepare the stockholders' equity section of the balance sheet as of October 31, 2010. Net income for the quarter was $23,000.

User insight ▶ 3. Calculate dividends yield, price/earnings ratio, and return on equity. Assume earnings per common share are $1.97 and market price per common share is $25. For beginning stockholders' equity, use the balance after the August transactions.

User insight ▶ 4. Discuss the results in requirement **3**, including the effect on investors' returns and the firm's profitability as it relates to stockholders' equity.

LO1 LO2 LO3 LO4 LO5

Comprehensive Stockholders' Equity Transactions

P 9. In January 2011, the Delgado Corporation was organized and authorized to issue 2,000,000 shares of no-par common stock and 50,000 shares of 5 percent, $50 par value, noncumulative preferred stock. The stock-related transactions for the first year's operations were as follows:

		Account			
		Debited		Credited	
		Account Number	Dollar Amount	Account Number	Dollar Amount
Jan. 19	Sold 15,000 shares of common stock for $31,500. State law requires a minimum of $1 stated value per share.	110	$31,500	310 312	$15,000 $16,500
21	Issued 5,000 shares of common stock to attorneys and accountants for services valued at $11,000 and provided during the organization of the corporation.				
Feb. 7	Issued 30,000 shares of common stock for a building that had an appraised value of $78,000.				
Mar. 22	Purchased 10,000 shares of its common stock at $3 per share.				

		Account			
		Debited		Credited	
		Account Number	Dollar Amount	Account Number	Dollar Amount
July 15	Issued 5,000 shares of common stock to employees under a stock option plan that allows any employee to buy shares at the current market price, which is now $3 per share.				
Aug. 1	Sold 2,500 shares of treasury stock for $4 per share.				
Sept. 1	Declared a cash dividend of $0.15 per common share to be paid on September 25 to stockholders of record on September 15.				
15	Date of record for cash dividends.				
25	Paid cash dividends to stockholders of record on September 15.				
Oct. 30	Issued 4,000 shares of common stock for a piece of land. The stock was selling for $3 per share, and the land had a fair market value of $12,000.				
Dec. 15	Issued 2,200 shares of preferred stock for $50 per share.				

Required

1. For each of the above transactions, enter in the blanks provided the account numbers and dollar amounts (as shown in the example) for the account(s) debited and credited. The account numbers are listed below.

110 Cash	312 Additional Paid-in Capital
120 Land	313 Paid-in Capital, Treasury Stock
121 Building	340 Retained Earnings
220 Dividends Payable	341 Dividends
305 Preferred Stock	350 Treasury Stock, Common
310 Common Stock	510 Start-up and Organization Costs

User insight ▶ 2. Why is the stockholders' equity section of the balance sheet an important consideration in analyzing the performance of a company?

LO1 LO5 **Treasury Stock**

P 10. The Murphy Corporation had the following treasury stock transactions during 2011:

a. Purchased 80,000 shares of its $1 par value common stock on the market for $2.50 per share.
b. Purchased 16,000 shares of its $1 par value common stock on the market for $2.80 per share.
c. Sold 44,000 shares purchased in **a** for $131,000.
d. Sold the other 36,000 shares purchased in **a** for $72,000.
e. Sold 6,000 of the remaining shares of treasury stock for $1.60 per share.
f. Retired all the remaining shares of treasury stock. All shares originally were issued at $1.50 per share.

Required

1. Record the treasury stock transactions in T accounts.

User insight ▶

2. What is the reasoning behind treating the purchase of treasury stock as a reduction in stockholders' equity as opposed to treating it as an investment asset?

ENHANCING Your Knowledge, Skills, and Critical Thinking

LO1 **Reasons for Issuing Common Stock**

C 1. DreamWorks Animation, led by billionaire Microsoft founder Paul Allen, went public in a recent year with its class A common stock at $28 per share, raising $650 million. By the end of the first day, it was up 27 percent to $38 per share, giving the company a value of almost $1 billion.[16] This initial enthusiasm did not last. By the end of 2007, the price was only around $33 per share. As a growing company that has produced such animated hits as *Shrek* and *Shrek II*, DreamWorks could have borrowed significant funds by issuing long-term debt. What are some advantages of issuing common stock as opposed to bonds? What are some disadvantages?

LO3 **Reasons for Issuing Preferred Stock**

C 2. Preferred stock is a hybrid security; it has some of the characteristics of stock and some of the characteristics of bonds. Historically, preferred stock has not been a popular means of financing. In the past few years, however, it has become more attractive to companies and individual investors alike, and investors are buying large amounts because of high yields. Large preferred stock issues have been made by such banks as **Chase**, **Citibank**, **HSBC Bank USA**, and **Wells Fargo**, as well as by other companies. The dividends yields on these stocks are over 9 percent, higher than the interest rates on bonds of comparable risk.[17] Especially popular are preferred equity redemption convertible stocks, or PERCs, which are automatically convertible into common stock after three years if the company does not call them first and retire them. What reasons can you give for the popularity of preferred stock, and of PERCs in particular, when the tax-deductible interest on bonds is lower? Discuss from both the company's and the investor's standpoint.

LO5 **Purposes of Treasury Stock**

C 3. Many companies in recent years have bought back their common stock. For example, **IBM**, with large cash holdings, spent almost $37.5 billion over three years repurchasing its stock.[18] What are the reasons companies buy back their own shares? What is the effect of common stock buybacks on earnings per share, return on equity, return on assets, debt to equity, and the current ratio?

LO4 **Effect of Stock Issue**

C 4. When **Google, Inc.** went public with an IPO, it used an auction system that allowed everyone to participate rather than allocating shares of stock to a few insiders. As mentioned in the Decision Point at the beginning of this chapter, the company's IPO drew widespread attention. Announcements of the IPO would have been similar to the following:

22,500,000 Shares
GOOGLE, INC.
$0.001 Par Value Common Stock
Price $85 a share

The gross proceeds of the IPO before issue costs were $1.9 billion.

Shown below is a portion of the stockholders' equity section of the balance sheet adapted from Google's annual report, which was issued prior to this stock offering:

Stockholders' Equity
(in thousands)

Common Stock, $0.001 par value, 700,000,000 shares authorized; 161,000,000 shares issued and outstanding	$ 161
Additional paid-in capital	725,219
Retained earnings	191,352

1. Assume that the net proceeds to Google after issue costs were $1.8 billion. Record the stock issuance on Google's accounting records in journal form.
2. Prepare the portion of the stockholders' equity section of the balance sheet shown above after the issue of the common stock, based on the information given. Round all answers to the nearest thousand.
3. Based on your answer in **2**, did Google have to increase its authorized shares to undertake this stock issue?
4. What amount per share did Google receive and how much did Google's underwriters receive to help in issuing the stock? What do underwriters do to earn their fee?

LO3 **Effect of Deferring Preferred Dividends**

C 5. US Airways had indefinitely deferred the quarterly dividend on its $358 million of cumulative convertible 91¼ percent preferred stock.[19] According to a US Airways spokesperson, the company did not want to "continue to pay a dividend while the company is losing money." Others interpreted the action as "an indication of a cash crisis situation."

At the time, **Berkshire Hathaway**, the large company run by Warren Buffett and the owner of the preferred stock, was not happy. However, US Airways was able to turn around, become profitable, and return to paying its cumulative dividends on preferred stock. Berkshire Hathaway was able to convert the preferred stock into 9.24 million common shares of US Airways' common stock at $38.74 per share at a time when the market value had risen to $62.[20]

What is cumulative convertible preferred stock? Why is deferring dividends on those shares a drastic action? What is the impact on profitability and liquidity? Why did using preferred stock instead of long-term bonds as a financing method probably save the company from bankruptcy? What was Berkshire Hathaway's gain on its investment at the time of the conversion?

LO1 LO2 **Stockholders' Equity**

C 6. Refer to the **CVS** annual report in the Supplement to Chapter 1 to answer the following questions:

1. What type of capital stock does CVS have? What is the par value? How many shares were authorized, issued, and outstanding at the end of fiscal 2008?
2. What is the dividends yield (use average price of stock in last quarter) for CVS and its relationship to the investors' total return? Does the company rely mostly on stock or on earnings for its stockholders' equity?
3. Does the company have a stock option plan? To whom do the stock options apply? Do employees have significant stock options? Given the market price of the stock shown in the report, do these options represent significant value to the employees?

LO1 LO5 **Return on Equity, Treasury Stock, and Dividends Policy**

C 7. Refer to the **CVS** annual report and the financial statements of **Southwest Airlines Co.** in the Supplement to Chapter 1.

1. Compute the return on equity for both companies for fiscal 2008 and 2007. Total stockholders' equity for CVS and Southwest in 2006 was $9,917.6 million and $6,449 million, respectively.
2. Did either company purchase treasury stock during these years? How will the purchase of treasury stock affect return on equity and earnings per share?
3. Did either company issue stock during these years? What are the details?
4. Compare the dividend policy of the two companies.

LO1 LO5 **Ethics, Management Compensation, and Treasury Stock**

C 8. Compensation of senior management is often tied to earnings per share or return on equity. Treasury stock purchases have a favorable impact on both these measures. In the recent buyback boom, many companies borrowed money to purchase treasury shares. In some cases, the motivation for the borrowing and repurchase of shares was the desire of executives to secure their year-end cash bonuses. Did these executives act ethically? Were their actions in the best interests of stockholders? Why or why not? How might such behavior be avoided in the future?

LO1 LO2 LO3 LO4 LO5 **Comprehensive Analysis of Stockholders' Equity**

C 9. Many Internet companies have gone public in recent years. These companies are generally unprofitable in their start-up years and require a great deal of cash to finance expansion. They also reward their employees with stock options. Choose any one of the following Internet companies: **Amazon.com**, **Yahoo!**, or **eBay**. Go to the website of the company you have selected. In the company's latest annual report, look at the financing section of the statement of cash flows for the last three years. How has the company financed its business? Has it issued stock or long-term debt? Has it purchased treasury stock, paid dividends, or issued stock under stock option plans? Is the company profitable (see net income or earnings at the top of the statement)? Are your findings in line with your expectations about Internet companies? Find the company's stock price, either on its website or in a newspaper, and compare it with the average issue price of the company's past stock issues. Summarize your findings and conclusions.

LO1 LO5 **Treasury Stock or Dividends?**

C 10. In your class, divide into small groups. Assume the president of a small company that has been profitable for several years but has not paid a dividend has hired your group. The company has built up a cash reserve. It has 20 stockholders, but the president owns 40 percent of the company's shares. Several of the stockholders with smaller numbers of shares would like to sell their shares, but there is no ready market. The president of the company has asked your group to determine whether it would be better to recommend to the board of directors that they pay a dividend to all stockholders or whether they should buy out the smaller stockholders to hold in the treasury shares and possibly retire them. In your group, decide which recommendation you will make to the president. Develop a series of points to support your argument. Participate in a class debate among teams who have chosen opposing positions.

LO1 **Debt or Equity Financing**

K/R

C 11. As noted in Case 4, **Google, Inc.**, announced a common stock issue:

2,500,000 Shares
$0.001 Par Value Common Stock
Price $85 a share

The net proceeds before issue costs were approximately $1.9 billion.

Given Google's successful track record as a start-up company, it is likely the company could have borrowed over $1.9 billion in debt financing rather than issue common stock. Write a one-page business memorandum that takes either the position that (1) Google should have issued debt at an interest rate of 8 percent or (2) Google is correct in issuing common stock. Be sure to include in your presentation the effect of your alternative on the debt to equity ratio and return on equity.

CHAPTER

12 Investments

Focus on Financial Statements

INCOME STATEMENT

Revenues

− Expenses

= Net Income

STATEMENT OF RETAINED EARNINGS

Opening Balance

+ Net Income

− Dividends

= Retained Earnings

BALANCE SHEET

Assets	Liabilities
	Equity

A = L + E

STATEMENT OF CASH FLOWS

Operating activities

+ Investing activities

+ Financing activities

= Change in Cash

+ Starting Balance

= Ending Cash Balance

Sales of investments for cash, a financing activity on cash flow statement, may result in gain/loss on income statement and affect operating activities on cash flow statement.

Many companies invest in the stock or debt securities of other firms. They may do so for several reasons. A company may temporarily have excess funds on which it can earn a return, or investments may be an integral part of its business, as in the case of a bank. A company may also invest in other firms for the purpose of partnering with or controlling them. This chapter presents an overview of both short-term and long-term investments, including the importance of avoiding unethical trading in securities.

LEARNING OBJECTIVES

LO1 Identify and explain the management issues related to investments. (pp. 580–584)

LO2 Explain the financial reporting implications of short-term investments. (pp. 584–587)

LO3 Explain the financial reporting implications of long-term investments in stock and the cost-adjusted-to-market and equity methods used to account for them. (pp. 588–592)

LO4 Explain the financial reporting implications of consolidated financial statements. (pp. 593–600)

LO5 Explain the financial reporting implications of debt investments. (pp. 600–602)

DECISION POINT ▸ A USER'S FOCUS EBAY, INC.

- What are the effects of eBay's investments on its financial performance?
- How does eBay's acquisition of other companies affect its financial performance?

eBay, the world's largest online trading company, enables a global community of buyers and sellers to interact and trade with one another. Since the company went public in 1998, it has grown very rapidly. In addition to having expanded its core business, it has grown by investing in and acquiring other companies. It has also invested cash in the debt securities of other companies. As you can see in eBay's Financial Highlights, these investments and the related accounts are important components of its financial statements.[1]

EBAY'S FINANCIAL HIGHLIGHTS (In millions)

	2008	**2007**
Balance Sheet		
Short-term investments	$ 164	$ 676
Long-term investments	106	138
Goodwill	7,025	6,257
Total assets	15,592	15,366
Income Statement		
Interest and other income, net	$ 116	$ 154
Impairment of goodwill	—	1,391
Income from operations	2,076	613
Statement of Cash Flows		
Cash flows from investing activities		
Purchases of investments	($ 108)	($ 271)
Sales of investments	136	889
Acquisitions, net of cash required	(1,360)	(864)

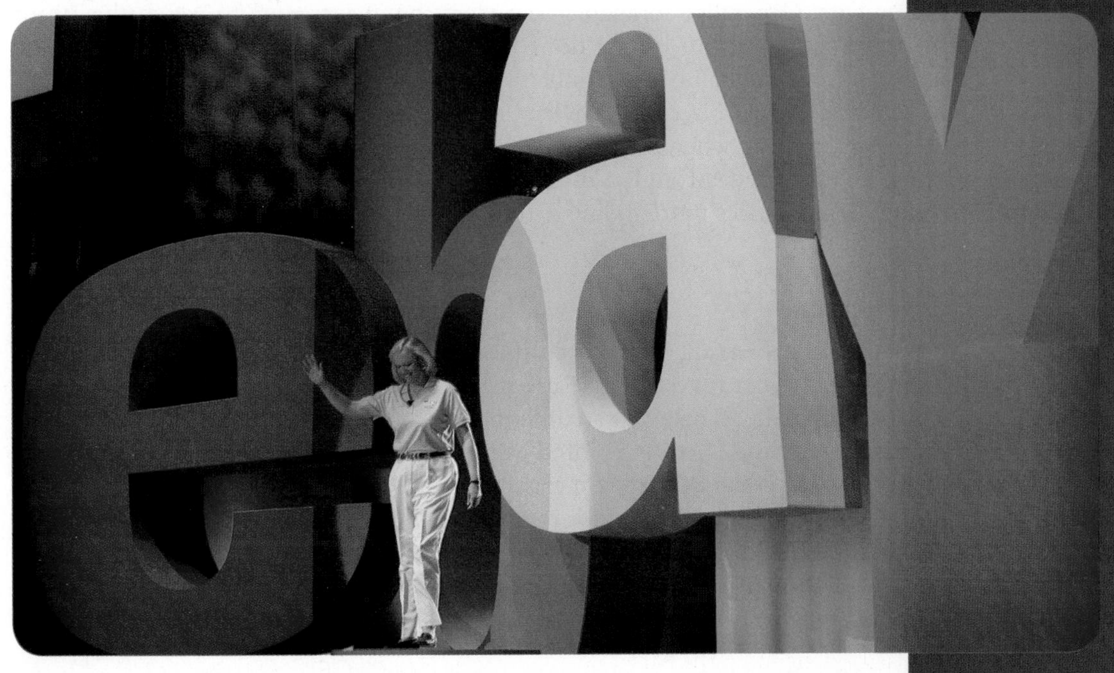

Management Issues Related to Investments

LO1 Identify and explain the management issues related to investments.

In making investments, **eBay**'s management, like the management of any company, must understand issues related to the recognition, valuation, classification, disclosure, and ethics of investments.

Recognition

Recognition of investments as assets follows the general rule for recording transactions that we described earlier in the text. Purchases of investments are recorded on the date on which they are made, and sales of investments are reported on the date of sale. At the time of the transaction, there is either a transfer of funds or a definite obligation to pay. Income from investments is reported as other income on the income statement. Any gains or losses on investments are also reported on the income statement. Gains and losses appear as adjustments in the operating activities section of the statement of cash flows. The cash amounts of purchases and sales of investments appear in the investing activities section of the statement of cash flows.

Valuation

Like other purchase transactions, investments are valued according to the *cost principle*—that is, they are valued in terms of their cost at the time they are purchased. The cost, or purchase price, includes any commissions or fees. However, after the purchase, the value of investments on the balance sheet is adjusted to reflect subsequent conditions. These conditions may reflect changes in the market value or fair value of the investments, changes caused by the passage of time (as in amortization), or changes in the operations of the investee companies. Long-term investments must be evaluated annually for any impairment or decline in value that is more than temporary. If such an impairment exists, a loss on the investment must be recorded.

Under a new accounting standard, companies may elect to measure investments at fair value. Recall that **fair value** is defined as the *exchange price* associated with an actual or potential business transaction between market participants. This option applies to all investments discussed in this chapter, except in the case of an investment in a subsidiary that is consolidated with the parent's financial statements. Generally, companies can elect the investments to which they want to apply fair value, but having done so, they cannot change the use of fair value in the future. Fair value is not difficult to determine when there is a ready market in which there are buyers and sellers for an asset, but its determination becomes more problematic when there is no ready market. In the latter case, the fair value must be estimated through a method such as net present value.[2] The goal is to bring U.S. practices more in line with international financial reporting standards.

Classification

Investments in debt and equity securities are classified as either short-term or long-term. **Short-term investments**, also called **marketable securities**, have a maturity of more than 90 days but are intended to be held only until cash is needed for current operations. (As we pointed out in an earlier chapter, investments with a maturity of *less* than 90 days are classified as cash equivalents.) *Long-term investments* are intended to be held for more than one year. Long-term investments are reported in the investments section of the balance sheet, not in the current assets section. Although long-term investments may be just as marketable as short-term assets, management intends to hold them for an indefinite time.

FOCUS ON BUSINESS PRACTICE

What Role Did Accounting Play in the Subprime Mortgage Collapse?

Investment banks and brokers have been in the news as they have experienced spectacular losses related to subprime mortgage securities. **UBS**, the large Swiss bank, had write-offs of $18.4 billion. **Bear Stearns**, the large U.S. brokerage company, saw its stock drop from more than $90 per share to $2 per share in less than a week when it was bailed out by the Federal Reserve and **J.P. Morgan**. What is going on? When interest rates rose and home prices fell, the fair value of the mortgages that backed up securities held by these companies dropped. Under accounting standards, the companies were required to write down the securities to their fair value, which was now substantially below the carrying value. The accounting rules that brought these losses to light are challenged in an editorial in *The Wall Street Journal*, which called fair value accounting a "fabulous failure" and predicts substantial write-ups once the crisis is over.[3] The supporters of fair value argue that the write-offs are not caused by accounting but reflect a real decline in value and that investors should have been able to act on this information as soon as possible.

Short-term and long-term investments must be further classified as trading securities, available-for-sale securities, or held-to-maturity securities.[4]

- **Trading securities** are debt or equity securities bought and held principally for the purpose of being sold in the near term.
- **Available-for-sale securities** are debt or equity securities that do not meet the criteria for either trading or held-to-maturity securities. They may be short-term or long-term depending on what management intends to do with them.
- **Held-to-maturity securities** are debt securities that management intends to hold until their maturity date.

Figure 12-1 illustrates the classification of short-term and long-term investments. Table 12-1 shows the relationship between the percentage of ownership in a company's stock and the investing company's level of control, as well as the classifications and accounting treatments of these stock investments. These classifications are important because each one requires a different accounting treatment. We discuss the accounting treatments later in this chapter.

FIGURE 12-1
Classification of Investments

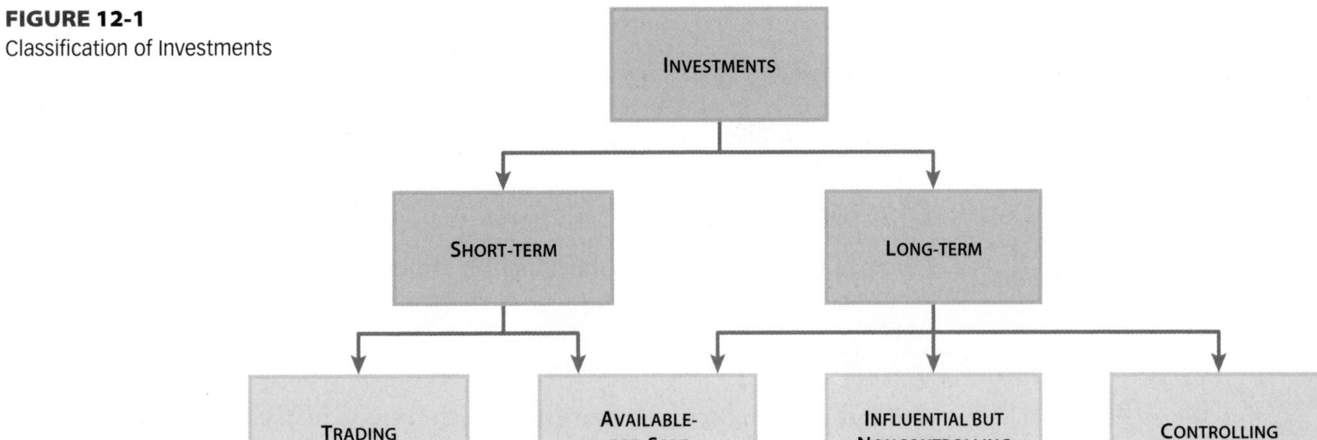

TABLE 12-1
Accounting for Equity Investments

Level of Control	Percentage of Ownership	Classification	Accounting Treatment
Noninfluential and noncontrolling	Less than 20%	Short-term investments—trading securities	Recorded at cost initially; cost adjusted after purchase for changes in market value; unrealized gains and losses reported on income statement
		Short-term or long-term investments—available-for-sale securities	Recorded at cost initially; cost adjusted for changes in market value with unrealized gains and losses to stockholders' equity
Influential but noncontrolling	Between 20% and 50%	Long-term investments	Equity method: recorded at cost initially; cost subsequently adjusted for investor's share of net income or loss and for dividends received
Controlling	More than 50%	Long-term investments	Financial statements consolidated

In general, the percentage of ownership in another company's stock has the following effects:

- ***Noninfluential and noncontrolling investment*:** A firm that owns less than 20 percent of the stock of another company has no influence on the other company's operations.
- ***Influential but noncontrolling investment*:** A firm that owns between 20 to 50 percent of another company's stock can exercise **significant influence** over that company's operating and financial policies, even though it holds 50 percent or less of the voting stock. Indications of significant influence include representation on the board of directors, participation in policy-making, exchange of managerial personnel, and technological dependency between the two companies.
- ***Controlling investment*:** A firm that owns more than 50 percent of another company's stock can exercise **control** over that company's operating and financial policies.

Study Note
Influence and control are related specifically to equity holdings, not debt holdings.

Disclosure

Companies provide detailed information about their investments and how they account for them in the notes to their financial statements. For instance, in 2008, in a note summarizing its significant accounting policies, **eBay** made this disclosure:

> Short and long-term investments, which include marketable equity securities, and government and corporate bonds, are classified as available for sale and reported at fair value. . . .[5]

FOCUS ON BUSINESS PRACTICE

What Are Special-Purpose Entities?

When **Enron** imploded in 2001 and its use of special purpose entities (SPEs) was widely reported, many accountants were unaware of the intricacies of accounting for these entities. SPEs are firms with limited lives that are created to achieve a specific objective (or objectives) of the parent company. They may take the form of a partnership, corporation, trust, or joint venture. SPEs have been around since the 1970s and have been used primarily by banks and other financial institutions as a way of raising funds by bundling together receivables and other loans into packages that can be sold to investors or used to borrow funds. Enron turned this use of SPEs on its head. It used its SPEs to transfer assets and any related debt off its balance sheet, conceal its losses and borrow money, and generally make its financial statements look far better than they actually were. By setting up the SPEs as partnerships and using the arcane accounting rules for SPEs, Enron was able to avoid consolidating these entities even though it kept a 97 percent ownership in them. The FASB has since clarified the accounting rules for SPEs, which it calls Variable Interest Entities (VIEs).[6]

eBay's notes also provide detailed information about the company's acquisitions, including Bill Me Later, Inc., Stubhub, Inc., and Skype, in 2006, 2007, and 2008. Such disclosures help users assess the impact of the investments.

Ethics of Investing

When a company engages in investment transactions, there is always the possibility that its employees may use their knowledge about the transactions for personal gain. In the United States, **insider trading**, or making use of inside information for personal gain, is unethical and illegal. Before a publicly held company releases significant information about an investment to its stockholders and the general public, its officers and employees are not allowed to buy or sell stock in the company or in the firm whose shares the company is buying. Only after the information is released to the public can insiders engage in such trading. The Securities and Exchange Commission vigorously prosecutes any individual,

A bear and a bull guard the Frankfurt Stock Exchange in Germany. In 1995, Germany outlawed insider trading, eliminating what had been considered a management perk. It also required companies to warn investors of potential bad news. "In the U.S., the [SEC] has always been pretty ruthless with companies that didn't come clean, and it will be interesting to see what happens here," says Marco Becht, co-author of *The Control of Corporate Europe*.

Courtesy of Eberhard Streichan/ Corbis.

whether employed by the company in question or not, who buys or sells shares of a publicly held company based on information not yet available to the public.

Not all countries prohibit insider trading. Until recently, insider trading was legal in Germany, but with the goal of expanding its securities markets, that country reformed its securities laws. It established the Federal Authority for Securities Trading (FAST), in part to oversee insider trading. However, only seven FAST staff members handle investigations of insider trading, as compared with the more than fifty staff members who handle the SEC's investigations.[7] Other countries continue to permit insider trading.

STOP & APPLY >

Indicate whether each phrase listed below is most closely related to (a) trading securities, (b) available-for-sale securities, (c) held-to-maturity securities, (d) noninfluential and noncontrolling ownership, (e) influential but noncontrolling ownership, or (f) controlling ownership:

1. No significant influence over investee
2. Securities bought and sold for short-term profit
3. Ability to make decisions for investee
4. Significant influence over investee
5. Securities that may be sold at any time
6. Debt securities that will be held until they are repaid

SOLUTION

1. d; 2. a; 3. f; 4. e; 5. b; 6. c

Short-Term Investments in Equity Securities

LO2 Explain the financial reporting implications of short-term investments.

As we pointed out earlier, all trading securities are short-term investments, while available-for-sale securities may be either short-term or long-term.

Trading Securities

Trading securities are frequently bought and sold to generate profits on short-term changes in their prices. They are classified as current assets on the balance sheet and are valued at fair value, which is usually the same as market value. An increase or decrease in the fair value of a company's total trading portfolio (the group of securities it holds for trading purposes) is included in net income in the accounting period in which the increase or decrease occurs.

For example, suppose Norman Company buys 5,000 shares of **IBM** for $450,000 ($90 per share) and 5,000 shares of **Microsoft** for $150,000 ($30 per share) on October 25, 2010. The purchase is made for trading purposes—that is, Norman's management intends to realize a gain by holding the shares for only a short period. The entry in journal form to record the investment at cost is as follows:

Purchase

A	= L + SE
+600,000	
−600,000	

2010			
Oct. 25	Short-Term Investments	600,000	
	Cash		600,000
	Investment in stocks for trading ($450,000 + $150,000 = $600,000)		

Assume that at year end, IBM's stock price has decreased to $80 per share and Microsoft's has risen to $32 per share. The trading portfolio is now valued at $560,000:

Security	*Market Value*	*Cost*	*Gain (Loss)*
IBM (5,000 shares)	$400,000	$450,000	
Microsoft (5,000 shares)	160,000	150,000	
Totals	$560,000	$600,000	($40,000)

Because the current fair value of the portfolio is $40,000 less than the original cost of $600,000, the following adjusting entry is needed:

Year-End Adjustment

A	= L +	SE
−40,000		−40,000

2010			
Dec. 31	Unrealized Loss on Short-Term Investments	40,000	
	Allowance to Adjust Short-Term Investments to Market		40,000
	Recognition of unrealized loss on trading portfolio		

Study Note

The Allowance to Adjust Short-Term Investments to Market account is never changed when securities are sold. It changes only when an adjusting entry is made at year end.

The unrealized loss will appear on the income statement as a reduction in income. The loss is unrealized because the securities have not been sold; if unrealized gains occur, they are treated the same way. The Allowance to Adjust Short-Term Investments to Market account appears on the balance sheet as a contra-asset, as follows:

Short-term investments (at cost)	$600,000
Less allowance to adjust short-term investments to market	40,000
Short-term investments (at market)	$560,000

or, more simply,

Short-term investments (at market value, cost is $600,000)	$560,000

If Norman sells its 5,000 shares of Microsoft for $35 per share on March 2, 2011, a realized gain on trading securities is recorded as follows:

Sale

A	= L +	SE
+175,000		+25,000
−150,000		

2011			
Mar. 2	Cash	175,000	
	Short-Term Investments		150,000
	Gain on Sale of Investments		25,000
	Sale of 5,000 shares of Microsoft for $35 per share; cost was $30 per share		

The realized gain will appear on the income statement. Note that the realized gain is unaffected by the adjustment for the unrealized loss at the end of 2010. The two transactions are treated independently. If the stock had been sold for less than cost, a realized loss on investments would have been recorded. Realized losses also appear on the income statement.

Now let's assume that during 2011, Norman buys 1,000 shares of **Apple Computer** at $132 per share and has no transactions involving its shares of IBM.

FOCUS ON BUSINESS PRACTICE

How Can Even a Big Company Make an Accounting Mistake?

Like many companies, **General Electric**, one of America's largest corporations, protects itself against future increases in interest rates on debt by hedging its debt transactions with *derivatives*, which are agreements to buy or sell stocks, bonds, or other securities in the future. A derivative can be set up in such a way that it has no value and therefore entails no gain or loss. But when a derivative has value, it is considered a trading security and a money-making (or money-losing) tool rather than a true hedge; in this case, any gain or loss that results from valuing the derivative at fair value must be reported on the income statement. General Electric thought it had no gains or losses on its derivatives, but when it recalculated their value over a two-year period, it found that it had gains amounting to about $.02 per share in each year. When the company issued a press release reporting the error, its CFO stated that "there are no exceptions to hedge accounting.... At the end of the day, the standard is the standard."[8]

Also assume that by December 31, 2011, the price of IBM's stock has risen to $95 per share, or $5 per share more than the original cost, and that Apple's stock price has fallen to $122, or $10 less than the original cost. We can now analyze Norman's trading portfolio as follows:

Security	*Market Value*	*Cost*	*Gain (Loss)*
IBM (5,000 shares)	$475,000	$450,000	
Apple (1,000 shares)	122,000	132,000	
Totals	$597,000	$582,000	$15,000

The market value of Norman's trading portfolio now exceeds the cost by $15,000 ($597,000 − $582,000). This amount represents the targeted ending balance for the Allowance to Adjust Short-Term Investments to Market account. Recall that at the end of 2010, that account had a credit balance of $40,000, meaning that the market value of the trading portfolio was less than the cost. Because no entries are made to the account during 2011, it retains its balance until adjusting entries are made at the end of the year. The adjustment for 2011 must be $55,000—enough to result in a debit balance of $15,000 in the allowance account:

Year-End Adjustment

A	= L +	SE
+55,000		+55,000

2011			
Dec. 31	Allowance to Adjust Short-Term Investments to Market	55,000	
	Unrealized Gain on Short-Term Investments		55,000
	Recognition of unrealized gain on trading portfolio ($40,000 + $15,000 = $55,000)		

Study Note

The entry in the Allowance to Adjust Short-Term Investments to Market account is equal to the change in the market value. Compute the new allowance, and then compute the amount needed to change the account. The unrealized loss or gain is the other half of the entry.

The 2011 ending balance of Norman's allowance account can be determined as follows:

Allowance to Adjust Short-Term Investments to Market			
Dec. 31, 2011 Adj.	55,000	Dec. 31, 2010 Bal.	40,000
Dec. 31, 2011 Bal.	15,000		

The balance sheet presentation of short-term investments is as follows:

Short-term investments (at cost)	$582,000
Plus allowance to adjust short-term investments to market	15,000
Short-term investments (at market)	$597,000

or, more simply,

Short-term investments (at market value, cost is $582,000)	$597,000

If the company also has held-to-maturity securities that will mature within one year, they are included in short-term investments at cost adjusted for the effects of interest.

Available-for-Sale Securities

Short-term available-for-sale securities are accounted for in the same way as trading securities with two exceptions: (1) an unrealized gain or loss is reported as a special item in the stockholders' equity section of the balance sheet, not as a gain or loss on the income statement; (2) if a decline in the value of a security is considered permanent, it is charged as a loss on the income statement.

For example, **eBay**'s summary of significant accounting policies contains the following statement: "Unrealized gains and losses [on available-for-sale securities] are excluded from earnings and reported as a component of comprehensive income (loss)." The company's statement of comprehensive income shows unrealized gains on investments of $589.6 million in 2007 and unrealized losses on investments of $464.2 million in 2008. In addition, eBay's income statement shows impairment charges of $1.4 billion in 2007. The $1.4 billion represents the amount by which the carrying value of goodwill associated with its Skype Technologies (voice-over Internet) division exceeded its fair value. The company reported no impairment charges in 2008.[9]

STOP & APPLY >

Park Corporation began investing in trading securities in 2009. At the end of 2009, it had the following trading portfolio:

Security	*Cost*	*Market Value*
Apple (1,000 shares)	$100,000	$200,000
Delta Air Lines (20,000 shares)	240,000	160,000
Totals	$340,000	$360,000

Prepare the necessary year-end adjusting entry on December 31 and the entry for the sale of all the Delta shares on the following May 1 for $200,000.

SOLUTION

2009			
Dec. 31	Allowance to Adjust Short-Term Investments to Market	20,000	
	Unrealized Gain on Short-Term Investments		20,000
	Recognition of unrealized gain on trading securities		
2010			
May 1	Cash	200,000	
	Loss on Sale of Investments		40,000
	Short-Term Investments		240,000
	Sales of 200,000 shares of Delta Air Lines at less than cost		

Long-Term Investments in Equity Securities

LO3 Explain the financial reporting implications of long-term investments in stock and the cost-adjusted-to-market and equity methods used to account for them.

The accounting treatment of long-term investments in equity securities, such as common stock, depends on the extent to which the investing company can exercise control over the other company.

Noninfluential and Noncontrolling Investment

As noted earlier, available-for-sale securities are debt or equity securities that cannot be classified as trading or held-to-maturity securities. When long-term equity securities are involved, a further criterion for classifying them as available for sale is that they be noninfluential and noncontrolling investments of less than 20 percent of the voting stock. Accounting for long-term available-for-sale securities requires using the **cost-adjusted-to-market method**. With this method, the securities are initially recorded at cost and are thereafter adjusted periodically for changes in market value by using an allowance account.[10]

Available-for-sale securities are classified as long term if management intends to hold them for more than one year. When accounting for long-term available-for-sale securities, the unrealized gain or loss resulting from the adjustment is not reported on the income statement. Instead, the gain or loss is reported as a special item in the stockholders' equity section of the balance sheet and in the disclosure of comprehensive income.

At the end of each accounting period, the total cost and the total market value of these long-term stock investments must be determined. If the total market value is less than the total cost, the difference must be credited to a contra-asset account called Allowance to Adjust Long-Term Investments to Market. Because of the long-term nature of the investment, the debit part of the entry, which represents a decrease in value below cost, is treated as a temporary decrease and does not appear as a loss on the income statement. It is shown in a contra-stockholders' equity account called Unrealized Loss on Long-Term Investments.* Thus, both of these accounts are balance sheet accounts. If the market value exceeds the cost, the allowance account is added to Long-Term Investments, and the unrealized gain appears as an addition to stockholders' equity.

When a company sells its long-term investments in stock, the difference between the sale price and the cost of the stock is recorded as a realized gain or loss on the income statement. Dividend income from such investments is recorded by a debit to Cash and a credit to Dividend Income. For example, assume these facts about the long-term stock investments of Hoska Corporation:

June 1, 2010	Paid cash for the following long-term investments: 5,000 shares of Murcia Corporation common stock (representing 2 percent of outstanding stock) at $25 per share; 2,500 shares of Rava Corporation common stock (representing 3 percent of outstanding stock) at $15 per share.
Dec. 31, 2010	Quoted market prices at year end: Murcia common stock, $21; Rava common stock, $17.
Apr. 1, 2011	Change in policy required the sale of 1,000 shares of Murcia common stock at $23.
July 1, 2011	Received cash dividend from Rava equal to $0.20 per share.
Dec. 31, 2011	Quoted market prices at year end: Murcia common stock, $24; Rava common stock, $13.

Study Note

Hoska's sale of stock on April 1, 2011, was the result of a change in policy. This illustrates that intent is often the only difference between long-term investments and short-term investments.

*If the decrease in market value of a long-term investment is deemed permanent or if the investment is deemed impaired, the decline or impairment is recorded by debiting a loss account on the income statement instead of the Unrealized Loss account.

Entries in journal form to record these transactions are as follows:

Investment

A	= L +	SE
+162,500		
−162,500		

2010			
June 1	Long-Term Investments	162,500	
	Cash		162,500
	Investments in Murcia common stock (5,000 shares × $25 = $125,000) and Rava common stock (2,500 shares × $15 = $37,500)		

Year-End Adjustment

A	= L +	SE
−15,000		−15,000

2010			
Dec. 31	Unrealized Loss on Long-Term Investments	15,000	
	Allowance to Adjust Long-Term Investments to Market		15,000
	To record reduction of long-term investment to market		

This adjustment involves the following computations:

Company	*Shares*	*Market Price*	*Total Market*	*Total Cost*
Murcia	5,000	$21	$105,000	$125,000
Rava	2,500	17	42,500	37,500
			$147,500	$162,500

Total Cost − Total Market Value = $162,500 − $147,500 = $15,000

Other entries are as follows:

Sale

A	= L +	SE
+23,000		−2,000
−25,000		

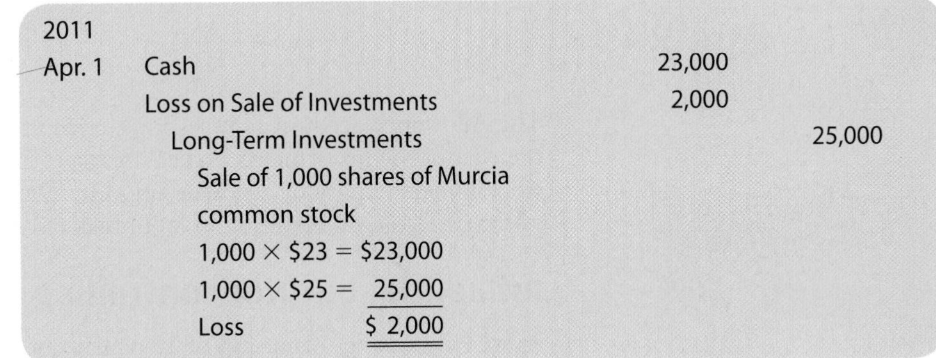

2011			
Apr. 1	Cash	23,000	
	Loss on Sale of Investments	2,000	
	Long-Term Investments		25,000
	Sale of 1,000 shares of Murcia common stock 1,000 × $23 = $23,000 1,000 × $25 = 25,000 Loss $ 2,000		

Dividend Received

A	= L +	SE
+500		+500

2011			
July 1	Cash	500	
	Dividend Income		500
	Receipt of cash dividend from Rava stock 2,500 × $0.20 = $500		

Year-End Adjustment

A	= L +	SE
+6,000		+6,000

2011			
Dec. 31	Allowance to Adjust Long-Term Investments to Market	6,000	
	Unrealized Loss on Long-Term Investments		6,000
	To record the adjustment in long-term investments so it is reported at market		

The adjustment equals the previous balance ($15,000 from the December 31, 2010, entry) minus the new balance ($9,000), or $6,000. The new balance of $9,000 is the difference at the present time between the total market value and the total cost of all investments. It is figured as follows:

Company	*Shares*	*Market Price*	*Total Market*	*Total Cost*
Murcia	4,000	$24	$ 96,000	$100,000
Rava	2,500	13	32,500	37,500
			$128,500	$137,500

Total Cost − Total Market Value = $137,500 − $128,500 = $9,000

The Allowance to Adjust Long-Term Investments to Market and the Unrealized Loss on Long-Term Investments are reciprocal contra accounts, each with the same dollar balance, as shown by the effects of these transactions on the T accounts:

CONTRA-ASSET ACCOUNT

ALLOWANCE TO ADJUST LONG-TERM INVESTMENTS TO MARKET

Dec. 31, 2011 Adj.	6,000	Dec. 31, 2010 Bal.	15,000
		Dec. 31, 2011 Bal.	9,000

CONTRA-STOCKHOLDERS' EQUITY ACCOUNT

UNREALIZED LOSS ON LONG-TERM INVESTMENTS

Dec. 31, 2010 Bal.	15,000	Dec. 31, 2011 Adj.	6,000
Dec. 31, 2011 Bal.	9,000		

The Allowance account reduces long-term investments by the amount by which the cost of the investments exceeds market; the Unrealized Loss account reduces stockholders' equity by a similar amount. The opposite effects will exist if market value exceeds cost, resulting in an unrealized gain.

Influential but Noncontrolling Investment

As we have noted, ownership of 20 percent or more of a company's voting stock is considered sufficient to influence the company's operations. When that is the case, the **equity method** should be used to account for the stock investment. The equity method presumes that an investment of 20 percent or more is not a passive investment and that the investor should therefore share proportionately in the success or failure of the company. The three main features of this method are as follows:

1. The investor records the original purchase of the stock at cost.
2. The investor records its share of the company's periodic net income as an increase in the Investment account, with a corresponding credit to an income

account. Similarly, it records its share of a periodic loss as a decrease in the Investment account, with a corresponding debit to a loss account.

3. When the investor receives a cash dividend, the asset account Cash is increased, and the Investment account is decreased.

eBay owns a minority interest of approximately 25 percent in **craigslist.inc.**, an online community featuring classified ad forums. Because the investment is more than 20 percent, eBay is presumed to have significant influence over craigslist's operations. Thus, eBay uses the equity method to account for the investment and classifies this investment and others that use the equity method as long-term investments.[11]

To illustrate the equity method, suppose that on January 1 of the current year, Shafer Corporation acquired 40 percent of Nica Corporation's voting common stock for $90,000. With this share of ownership, Shafer can exert significant influence over Nica's operations. During the year, Nica reported net income of $40,000 and paid cash dividends of $10,000. Shafer recorded these transactions as follows:

Investment

A	= L +	SE
+90000		
−90,000		

Investment in Nica Corporation	90,000	
Cash		90,000
Investment in Nica Corporation common stock		

Recognition of Income

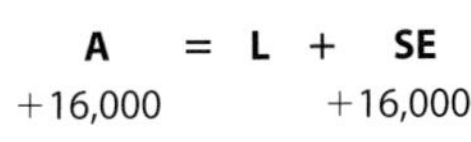

Investment in Nica Corporation	16,000	
Income, Nica Corporation Investment		16,000
Recognition of 40% of income reported by Nica Corporation		
40% × $40,000 = $16,000		

Receipt of Cash Dividend

A	= L +	SE
+4,000		
−4,000		

Cash	4,000	
Investment in Nica Corporation		4,000
Cash dividend from Nica Corporation		
40% × $10,000 = $4,000		

The balance of the investment in Nica Corporation account after these transactions is $102,000, as shown here:

Investment in Nica Corporation

Investment	90,000	Dividend Received	4,000
Share of Income	16,000		
Bal.	102,000		

Study Note

Under the equity method, dividends received represent a return on investment and decrease the Investment account with a credit entry.

The share of income is reported as a separate line item on the income statement as a part of income from operations. The dividends received affect cash flows from operating activities on the statement of cash flows. The reported income exceeds the cash received by $12,000 ($16,000 − $4,000).

FOCUS ON BUSINESS PRACTICE

Accounting for International Joint Ventures

When U.S. companies make investments abroad, they often find it wise or necessary to partner with a local company or with the government of the country. Some countries require that their citizens own a minimum percentage of each business. In other countries—among them, Brazil, China, India, and the former United Soviet Socialist Republics—the government has traditionally had a share of ownership. Such business arrangements are usually called *joint ventures*. Because the resulting enterprise is jointly owned, it is appropriate to treat the U.S. company's status as "influential but noncontrolling." Thus, the most appropriate accounting method for these arrangements is the equity method.

Controlling Investment Some investing firms that own less than 50 percent of a company's voting stock exercise such powerful influence that for all practical purposes, they control the policies of the other company. Nevertheless, ownership of more than 50 percent of the voting stock is required for accounting recognition of control. When a firm has a controlling interest in another company, a parent-subsidiary relationship is said to exist. The investing company is the **parent company**; the other company is a **subsidiary**.

Because a parent company and its subsidiaries are separate legal entities, each prepares separate financial statements. However, because of their special relationship, they are viewed for external financial reporting purposes as a single economic entity. For this reason, the FASB requires that they combine their financial statements into a single set of statements called **consolidated financial statements**.[12] For example, in its summary of significant accounting policies, **eBay** states that "the accompanying financial statements are consolidated and include the financial statements of eBay and our majority-owned subsidiaries. All significant intercompany balances and transactions have been eliminated in consolidation."[13]

Study Note

Parents and subsidiaries are separate legal entities even though they combine their financial reports at year end.

STOP & APPLY >

Maj Corporation has the following long-term investments:

1. 40 percent of the common stock of Fastrak Corporation
2. 16 percent of the common stock of Pepper, Inc.
3. 80 percent of the nonvoting preferred stock of Sanddex Corporation
4. 100 percent of the common stock of its financing subsidiary, LP, Inc.
5. 75 percent of the common stock of the Canadian company Canoil Company.
6. 40 percent of the common stock of the Mexican company Border Assembly Company

For each of these investments, tell which of the following methods should be used for external financial reporting:

a. Cost-adjusted-to-market method
b. Equity method
c. Consolidation of parent and subsidiary financial statements

SOLUTION

1. b; 2. a; 3. a; 4. c; 5. c; 6. b

Consolidated Financial Statements

LO4 Explain the financial reporting implications of consolidated financial statements.

Most major corporations find it convenient for economic, legal, tax, or other reasons to operate in parent-subsidiary relationships. When we speak of a large company, such as **PepsiCo** or **IBM**, we generally think of the parent company, not of its many subsidiaries. Potential investors, however, want a clear financial picture of the total economic entity. The main purpose of consolidated financial statements is to give such a view of the parent and subsidiary firms by treating them as if they were one company. On a consolidated balance sheet, the Inventory account includes the inventory held by the parent and all its subsidiaries. Similarly, on the consolidated income statement, the Sales account is the total revenue from sales by the parent and all its subsidiaries. This overview helps management, stockholders, and creditors of the parent company judge the company's progress in meeting its goals.

Consolidated Balance Sheet

The **acquisition method** of preparing consolidated financial statements combines similar accounts from the separate statements of the parent and the subsidiaries. Some accounts result from transactions between the parent and the subsidiary—for example, sales and purchases between the two entities, and debt owed by one of the entities to the other. It is not appropriate to include these accounts in the consolidated financial statements; the sales and purchases are only transfers between different parts of the business, and the payables and receivables do not represent amounts due to or receivable from outside parties. For this reason, it is important that certain **eliminations** be made. These eliminations avoid the duplication of accounts and reflect the financial position and operations from the standpoint of a single entity. Eliminations appear only on the work sheets used in preparing consolidated financial statements. They are never shown in the accounting records of either the parent or the subsidiary.

Study Note

As separate entities, the parent and subsidiary maintain individual accounting records. Work sheet eliminations remove only duplications that occur in consolidation and the effects of intercompany transactions.

Another good example of accounts that result from transactions between a parent and its subsidiary is the Investment in Subsidiary account on the parent's balance sheet and the stockholders' equity accounts of the subsidiary. When the balance sheets of the two companies are combined, these accounts must be eliminated to avoid duplicating them in the consolidated financial statements.

To illustrate the preparation of a consolidated balance sheet under the acquisition method, we use the following balance sheet data for Parent Company and Subsidiary Company:

Accounts	*Parent Company*	*Subsidiary Company*
Cash	$ 50,000	$12,500
Other assets	380,000	30,000
Total assets	$430,000	$42,500
Liabilities	$ 30,000	$ 5,000
Common stock	300,000	27,500
Retained earnings	100,000	10,000
Total liabilities and stockholders' equity	$430,000	$42,500

100 Percent Purchase at Book Value Suppose that Parent Company purchases 100 percent of the stock of Subsidiary Company for an amount exactly equal to Subsidiary's book value. The book value of Subsidiary Company is

$37,500 ($42,500 − $5,000). Parent Company would record the purchase as follows:

A	= L + SE
+37,500	
−37,500	

Investment in Subsidiary Company	37,500	
Cash		37,500
Purchase of 100 percent of Subsidiary Company at book value		

It is helpful to use a work sheet like the one shown in Exhibit 12-1 in preparing consolidated financial statements. Note that the balance of Parent Company's Cash account is now $12,500 and that Investment in Subsidiary Company is shown as an asset in Parent Company's balance sheet, reflecting the purchase of the subsidiary. To prepare a consolidated balance sheet, it is necessary to eliminate the investment in the subsidiary, as shown in elimination entry **1** in Exhibit 12-1. This entry accomplishes two things: It eliminates the double counting that would take place when the net assets of the two companies are combined, and it eliminates the stockholders' equity section of Subsidiary Company.

As we have pointed out, the theory underlying consolidated financial statements is that parent and subsidiary are a single entity. Thus, the stockholders' equity section of the consolidated balance sheet is the same for Parent Company and Subsidiary Company.

So, after eliminating the Investment in Subsidiary Company account and the stockholders' equity accounts of the subsidiary, we can take the information from the Consolidated Balance Sheet column in Exhibit 12-1 and present it in the following form:

Parent and Subsidiary Companies
Consolidated Balance Sheet
As of Acquisition Date

Cash	$ 25,000	Liabilities	$ 35,000
Other assets	410,000	Common stock	300,000
		Retained earnings	100,000
Total assets	$435,000	Total liabilities and stockholders' equity	$435,000

Less Than 100 Percent Purchase at Book Value When a parent company purchases less than 100 percent but more than 50 percent of a subsidiary's voting stock, it will have control over the subsidiary, and it must prepare consolidated financial statements. It must also account for the interests of the subsidiary's stockholders who own less than 50 percent of the voting stock. These are the minority stockholders, and their **minority interest** must appear on the consolidated balance sheet (as part of stockholders' equity) as an amount equal to their percentage of ownership times the subsidiary's net assets.[14]

Study Note

When the elimination entry is made, all of the subsidiary's stockholders' equity accounts are eliminated. The percentage not owned by the parent company is assigned to minority interest.

Suppose that Parent Company buys 90 percent of Subsidiary Company's voting stock for $33,750. In this case, the portion of the company purchased has a book value of $33,750 (90% × $37,500). The work sheet used to prepare the consolidated balance sheet appears in Exhibit 12-2. The elimination is made just as in Exhibit 12-1, except that the minority interest must be accounted for. All of the Investment in Subsidiary Company account ($33,750) is eliminated against all of Subsidiary Company's stockholders' equity accounts (totaling $37,500). The difference ($3,750, or 10% × $37,500) is set as minority interest.

There are two ways to classify minority interest on a consolidated balance sheet. One way is to place the entry between long-term liabilities and stockholders'

EXHIBIT 12-1 Work Sheet for Preparing a Consolidated Balance Sheet

Parent and Subsidiary Companies
Work Sheet for Consolidated Balance Sheet
As of Acquisition Date

Accounts	Balance Sheet, Parent Company	Balance Sheet, Subsidiary Company	Eliminations Debit	Eliminations Credit	Consolidated Balance Sheet
Cash	12,500	12,500			25,000
Investment in subsidiary company	37,500			(1) 37,500	—
Other assets	380,000	30,000			410,000
Total assets	430,000	42,500			435,000
Liabilities	30,000	5,000			35,000
Common stock	300,000	27,500	(1) 27,500		300,000
Retained earnings	100,000	10,000	(1) 10,000		100,000
Total liabilities and stockholders' equity	430,000	42,500	37,500	37,500	435,000

(1) Elimination of intercompany investment

EXHIBIT 12-2 Work Sheet Showing Elimination When Purchase Is for Less than 100 Percent Ownership

Parent and Subsidiary Companies
Work Sheet for Consolidated Balance Sheet
As of Acquisition Date

Accounts	Balance Sheet, Parent Company	Balance Sheet, Subsidiary Company	Eliminations Debit	Eliminations Credit	Consolidated Balance Sheet
Cash	16,250	12,500			28,750
Investment in subsidiary company	33,750			(1) 33,750	—
Other assets	380,000	30,000			410,000
Total assets	430,000	42,500			438,750
Liabilities	30,000	5,000			35,000
Common stock	300,000	27,500	(1) 27,500		300,000
Retained earnings	100,000	10,000	(1) 10,000		100,000
Minority interest	—	—		(1) 3,750	3,750
Total liabilities and stockholders' equity	430,000	42,500	37,500	37,500	438,750

(1) Elimination of intercompany investment. Minority interest equals 10 percent of subsidiary's total stockholders' equity.

equity. The other way is to consider the stockholders' equity section as consisting of minority interest and the parent company's stockholders' equity, as shown here:

Minority interest	$ 3,750
Common stock	300,000
Retained earnings	100,000
Total stockholders' equity	$403,750

Purchase at More or Less than Book Value The purchase price of a business depends on many factors, such as the current market price, the relative strength of the buyer's and seller's bargaining positions, and the prospects for future earnings. Thus, it is only by chance that the purchase price of a subsidiary equals the book value of its equity. Usually, it does not.

Study Note

Regardless of the circumstances, the Investment in Subsidiary Company account must be eliminated completely and should not appear on the consolidated balance sheet.

For example, a parent company may pay more than the subsidiary's book value for a controlling interest if the subsidiary's assets are understated. This happens when the historical cost less depreciation of the subsidiary's assets does not reflect current market values. The parent may also pay more than book value if the subsidiary has something the parent wants, such as an important technical process, a new and different product, or a new market. On the other hand, the parent may pay less than book value if the subsidiary's assets are not worth their depreciated cost. It may also pay less than book value if heavy losses suffered by the subsidiary have caused its stock price to drop.

The Accounting Principles Board has provided the following guidelines for consolidating a purchased subsidiary and its parent when the parent pays more than book value for its investment in the subsidiary:

> First, all identifiable assets acquired . . . and liabilities assumed in a business combination . . . should be assigned a portion of the cost of the acquired company, normally equal to their fair values at date of acquisition.
>
> Second, the excess of the cost of the acquired company over the sum of the amounts assigned to identifiable assets acquired less liabilities assumed should be recorded as goodwill.[15]

As explained in the chapter on long-term assets, goodwill is carried on the balance sheet at cost and is subject to an annual impairment test. **eBay** describes its treatment of goodwill as follows:

> Goodwill represents the excess of the purchase price over the fair value of the net tangible and identifiable intangible assets acquired. Intangible assets resulting from the acquisition of entities accounted for using the purchase method of accounting are estimated by management. . . . Goodwill is not subject to amortization, but is subject to at least an annual assessment for impairment, applying a fair-value based test.[16]

Study Note

Goodwill is recorded when the purchase price of a business exceeds the fair market value of the net assets purchased.

To illustrate the application of these principles, suppose that Parent Company purchases 100 percent of Subsidiary Company's voting stock for $46,250, or $8,750 more than book value. Parent Company considers $5,000 of the $8,750 to be due to the increased value of Subsidiary's other assets and $3,750 of the $8,750 to be due to the overall strength that Subsidiary Company would add to Parent Company's organization. The work sheet used to prepare the consolidated balance sheet appears in Exhibit 12-3. All of the Investment in Subsidiary Company ($46,250) has been eliminated against all of Subsidiary Company's stockholders' equity ($37,500). The excess of cost over book value ($8,750) has been debited in the amounts of $5,000 to Other Assets and $3,750 to a new account called **Goodwill**, or *Goodwill from Consolidation*.

EXHIBIT 12-3 Work Sheet Showing Elimination When Purchase Cost Is Greater than Book Value

Parent and Subsidiary Companies
Work Sheet for Consolidated Balance Sheet
As of Acquisition Date

Accounts	Balance Sheet, Parent Company	Balance Sheet, Subsidiary Company	Eliminations Debit	Eliminations Credit	Consolidated Balance Sheet
Cash	3,750	12,500			16,250
Investment in subsidiary company	46,250			(1) 46,250	—
Other assets	380,000	30,000	(1) 5,000		415,000
Goodwill	—	—	(1) 3,750		3,750
Total assets	430,000	42,500			435,000
Liabilities	30,000	5,000			35,000
Common stock	300,000	27,500	(1) 27,500		300,000
Retained earnings	100,000	10,000	(1) 10,000		100,000
Total liabilities and stockholders' equity	430,000	42,500	46,250	46,250	435,000

(1) Elimination of intercompany investment. Excess of cost over book value ($46,250 − $37,500 = $8,750) is allocated to Other Assets ($5,000) and Goodwill ($3,750).

The amount of goodwill is determined as follows:

Cost of investment in subsidiary	$46,250
Book value of subsidiary	37,500
Excess of cost over book value	$ 8,750
Portion of excess attributable to undervalued other assets of subsidiary	5,000
Portion of excess attributable to goodwill	$ 3,750

Study Note

In this example, neither company has goodwill on its balance sheet. Goodwill is "created" when consolidated statements are prepared.

On the consolidated balance sheet, goodwill appears as an asset representing the portion of the excess of the cost of the investment over book value that cannot be allocated to any specific asset. Other assets appears on the consolidated balance sheet at the combined total of $415,000 ($380,000 + $30,000 + $5,000).

When the parent company pays less than book value for its investment in the subsidiary, the excess of book value over cost of the investment be used to lower the carrying value of the subsidiary's long-term assets. The reasoning behind this is that market values of long-lived assets (other than marketable securities) are among the least reliable of estimates, since a ready market does not usually exist for such assets.

Intercompany Receivables and Payables If a subsidiary owes money to the parent company, there will be a receivable on the parent company's individual balance sheet and a payable on the subsidiary company's individual balance sheet. Conversely, if a parent owes money to a subsidiary, there will be a receivable on the subsidiary's balance sheet and a payable on the parent's balance sheet. When a consolidated balance sheet is prepared, both the receivable and the payable should be eliminated because from the viewpoint of the consolidated entity, neither the asset nor the liability exists. In other words, it does not make sense for a company to owe money to itself. The eliminating entry is made on the work sheet by debiting the payable and crediting the receivable for the amount of the intercompany loan.

Consolidated Income Statement

A consolidated income statement is prepared by combining the revenues and expenses of the parent and subsidiary companies. The procedure is the same as the one used to prepare a consolidated balance sheet—that is, intercompany transactions are eliminated to prevent double counting of revenues and expenses. The following intercompany transactions affect the consolidated income statement:

1. Sales and purchases of goods and services between parent and subsidiary
2. Income and expenses related to loans, receivables, or bond indebtedness between parent and subsidiary
3. Other income and expenses from intercompany transactions.

Study Note

Intercompany sales or purchases are not revenues or expenses to the consolidated entity. True revenues and expenses occur only when transactions are with parties outside the firm.

To illustrate the eliminating entries, suppose that Parent Company sold $60,000 of goods to Subsidiary Company, which in turn sold all the goods to others. Subsidiary Company paid Parent Company $1,000 interest on a loan.

The work sheet in Exhibit 12-4 shows how to prepare a consolidated income statement. Because the purpose of the eliminating entries is to treat the two companies as a single entity, it is important to include in Sales only sales made to outsiders and to include in Cost of Goods Sold only purchases made from outsiders. This goal is met with the first eliminating entry, which eliminates the $60,000 of intercompany sales and purchases by a debit of that amount to Sales

EXHIBIT 12-4 Work Sheet for Preparing a Consolidated Income Statement

Parent and Subsidiary Companies
Work Sheet for Consolidated Income Statement
For the Year Ended December 31, 2010

Accounts	Income Statement, Parent Company	Income Statement, Subsidiary Company	Eliminations Debit	Eliminations Credit	Consolidated Income Statement
Sales	215,000	100,000	(1) 60,000		255,000
Other revenues	30,000	5,000	(2) 1,000		34,000
Total revenues	245,000	105,000			289,000
Cost of goods sold	105,000	75,000		(1) 60,000	120,000
Other expenses	70,000	25,000		(2) 1,000	94,000
Total costs and expenses	175,000	100,000			214,000
Net income	70,000	5,000	61,000	61,000	75,000

(1) Elimination of intercompany sales and purchases
(2) Elimination of intercompany interest income and interest expense

and a credit of that amount to Cost of Goods Sold. As a result, only sales to outsiders ($255,000) and purchases from outsiders ($120,000) are included in the Consolidated Income Statement column. The intercompany interest income and expense are eliminated by a debit to Other Revenues and a credit to Other Expenses.

Public corporations also prepare consolidated statements of stockholders' equity and consolidated statements of cash flows. For examples of these statements, see the **CVS** annual report in the Supplement to Chapter 1.

Restatement of Foreign Subsidiary Financial Statements

Companies often expand by establishing or buying foreign subsidiaries. Such companies are called **multinational** or **transnational corporations**. If a company owns more than 50 percent of a foreign subsidiary and thus exercises control, the foreign subsidiary should be included in the consolidated financial statements. The consolidation procedure is the same as the one for domestic subsidiaries, except that the foreign subsidiary's statements must be restated in the reporting currency before consolidation takes place. The **reporting currency** is the currency in which the consolidated financial statements are presented, which for U.S. companies is usually the U.S. dollar. For example, **eBay** purchased a German firm and an Indian firm in 2004. Clearly, it makes no sense to combine the assets of German and Indian subsidiaries stated in euros and rupees with the assets of the U.S. parent company stated in dollars. Thus, **restatement** of the subsidiaries' statements into the currency of the parent company is necessary. After restatement, the parent's and subsidiaries' statements can be consolidated in the usual way.

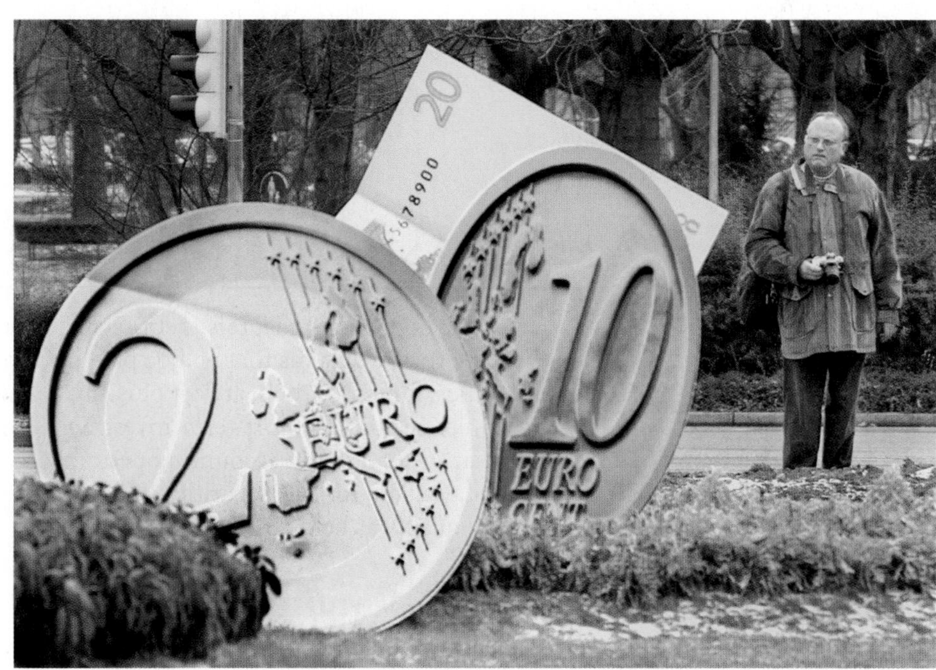

An art installation of euro currency in Ludwigsburg, Germany, preceded the adoption of the Euro on January 1, 2002, as the only form of legal tender in twelve European countries. When a U.S. company owns more than 50 percent of a foreign company, it must prepare consolidated financial statements. The statements of the foreign subsidiary must be restated in dollars—not euros or other foreign currencies—before consolidation can take place.

Courtesy of Roland Tarcillion/Getty Images.

STOP & APPLY >

S Company has total stockholders' equity of $50,000. Fill in the dollar amounts for each of the following investments by P Company in S's common stock:

	Goodwill	Minority Interest
1. P Company pays $50,000 for 100% of S Company's common stock, and S Company's net assets are fairly valued at $50,000.	______	______
2. P Company pays $60,000 for 100% of S Company's common stock, and S Company's net assets are fairly valued at $50,000.	______	______
3. P Company pays $60,000 for 100% of S Company's common stock, and S Company's net assets are fairly valued at $60,000.	______	______
4. P Company pays $40,000 for 80% of S Company's common stock, and S Company's net assets are fairly valued at $50,000.	______	______
5. P Company pays $50,000 for 80% of S Company's common stock, and S Company's net assets are fairly valued at $62,500.	______	______

SOLUTION

	Goodwill	Minority Interest
1.	0	0
2.	$10,000	0
3.	0	0
4.	0	$10,000
5.	0	$12,500

Investments in Debt Securities

LO5 Explain the financial reporting implications of debt investments.

As noted in previous chapters, debt securities are considered financial instruments because they are claims that will be paid in cash. When a company purchases debt securities, it records them at cost plus any commissions and fees. Like investments in equity securities, short-term investments in debt securities are valued at fair value at the end of the accounting period and are accounted for as trading securities or available-for-sale securities. However, the accounting treatment is different if they qualify as held-to-maturity securities.

Study Note

Any brokerage costs or other costs involved in acquiring securities are part of the cost of the securities.

Held-to-Maturity Securities

As we noted earlier, held-to-maturity securities are debt securities that management intends to hold to their maturity date. Such securities are recorded at cost and are valued on the balance sheet at cost adjusted for the effects of interest. For example, suppose that on December 1, 2010, Espinosa Company pays $48,500 for U.S. Treasury bills, which are short-term debt of the federal government.

The bills will mature in 120 days at $50,000. Espinosa would make the following entry in journal form:

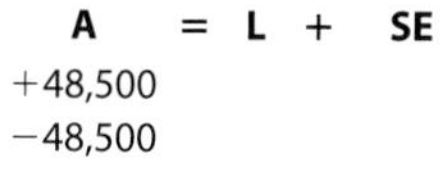

A	= L +	SE
+48,500		
−48,500		

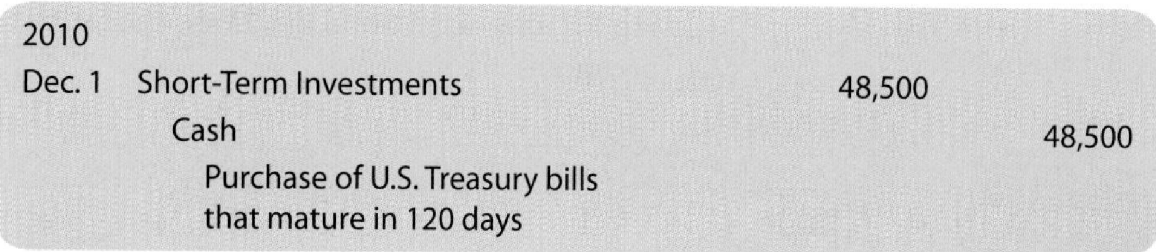

2010			
Dec. 1	Short-Term Investments	48,500	
	Cash		48,500
	Purchase of U.S. Treasury bills that mature in 120 days		

At Espinosa's year end on December 31, the entry in journal form to accrue the interest income earned to date would be as follows:

A	= L +	SE
+375		+375

2010			
Dec. 31	Short-Term Investments	375	
	Interest Income		375
	Accrual of interest on U.S. Treasury bills $1,500 × 30/120 = $375		

On December 31, the U.S. Treasury bills would be shown on the balance sheet as a short-term investment at their amortized cost of $48,875 ($48,500 + $375). When Espinosa receives the maturity value on March 31, 2011, the entry in journal form is as follows:

A	= L +	SE
+50,000		+1,125
−48,875		

2011			
Mar. 31	Cash	50,000	
	Short-Term Investments		48,875
	Interest Income		1,125
	Receipt of cash at maturity of U.S. Treasury bills and recognition of related income		

Long-Term Investments in Bonds

Like all investments, investments in bonds are recorded at cost, which, in this case, is the price of the bonds plus the broker's commission. When bonds are purchased between interest payment dates, the purchaser must also pay an amount equal to the interest that has accrued on the bonds since the last interest payment date. Then, on the next interest payment date, the purchaser receives an interest payment for the whole period. The payment for accrued interest should be recorded as a debit to Interest Income, which will be offset by a credit to Interest Income when the semiannual interest is received.

Subsequent accounting for a corporation's long-term bond investments depends on the classification of the bonds. If the company plans to hold the bonds until they are paid off on their maturity date, they are considered held-to-maturity securities. Except in industries like insurance and banking, it is unusual for companies to buy the bonds of other companies with the express purpose of holding them until they mature, which can be in 10 to 30 years. Thus, most long-term bond investments are classified as available-for-sale securities, meaning that the company plans to sell them at some point before their maturity date. Such bonds are accounted for at fair value, much as equity or stock investments

> **Study Note**
> The fair value of bonds is closely related to interest rates. An increase in interest rates lowers the fair value of bonds, and vice versa.

are; fair value is usually the market value. When bonds are intended to be held to maturity, they are accounted for not at fair value but at cost, adjusted for the amortization of their discount or premium. The procedure is similar to accounting for long-term bond liabilities, except that separate accounts for discounts and premiums are not used.

STOP & APPLY >

On Aug. 31, Jason Company invested $49,000 in U.S. Treasury bills. The bills mature in 120 days at $50,000. Prepare entries in journal form to record the purchase on Aug. 31; the adjustment to accrue interest on Sept. 30, which is the end of the fiscal year; and the receipt of cash at the maturity date of Dec. 28.

SOLUTION

Date	Account	Debit	Credit
Aug. 31	Short-Term Investments	49,000	
	Cash		49,000
	Investment in 120-day U.S. Treasury bills		
Sept. 30	Short-Term Investments	250	
	Interest Income		250
	Accrual of interest on U.S. Treasury bills		
	$1,000 × 30/120 = $250		
Dec. 28	Cash	50,000	
	Short-Term Investments		49,250
	Interest Income		750
	Receipt of cash at maturity of U.S. Treasury bills		
	and recognition of related interest income		

A LOOK BACK AT

▸ EBAY, INC.

As shown in the Financial Highlights at the beginning of the chapter, short- and long-term investments and goodwill from acquisitions constitute a large portion of the total assets on **eBay**'s balance sheet. The company's investments also have important effects on its income statement and statement of cash flows. To fully evaluate eBay's performance, users of its financial statements must address the following questions:

- What are the effects of eBay's investments on its financial performance?
- How does eBay's acquisition of other companies affect its financial performance?

As we pointed out in this chapter, eBay classifies both short- and long-term investments as available-for-sale securities and reports them at fair value on its balance sheet. It reports the difference between unrealized gains and losses in other comprehensive income (a component of stockholders' equity) and subjects its equity investments to an impairment test, which can be recorded as a loss on the income statement if a decline in an investment's value is deemed permanent.

In the case of eBay, the company had unrealized gains in 2008 of only $40,522 million and had no impairments. Because a majority of eBay's investments are debt securities, interest income is a significant component—almost 25 percent—of the company's income from operations. The investing section of its statement of cash flows reveals that in 2008, eBay spent about $108 million on investments.

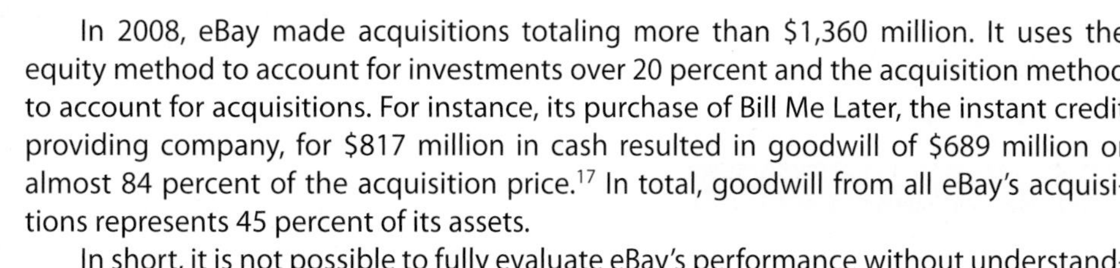

In 2008, eBay made acquisitions totaling more than $1,360 million. It uses the equity method to account for investments over 20 percent and the acquisition method to account for acquisitions. For instance, its purchase of Bill Me Later, the instant credit providing company, for $817 million in cash resulted in goodwill of $689 million or almost 84 percent of the acquisition price.[17] In total, goodwill from all eBay's acquisitions represents 45 percent of its assets.

In short, it is not possible to fully evaluate eBay's performance without understanding the effect that investments and acquisitions have on that performance.

Review Problem

Consolidated Balance Sheet: Less than 100 Percent Ownership

LO4

In a cash transaction on June 30, 2010, Lapa Company purchased 90 percent of the outstanding stock of Poklad Company for $381,600. Directly after the acquisition, the balance sheets of the two companies were as follows:

	A	B	C	D	E
1				Lapa	Poklad
2			Assets	Company	Company
3	Cash			$ 200,000	$ 24,000
4	Accounts receivable			325,000	120,000
5	Inventory			500,000	260,000
6	Investment in Poklad Company			381,600	—
7	Plant and equipment (net)			750,000	440,000
8	Other assets			25,000	80,000
9	Total assets			$2,181,600	$924,000
10					
11			Liabilities and Stockholders' Equity		
12	Accounts payable			$ 400,000	$200,000
13	Long-term debt			500,000	300,000
14	Common stock			1,000,000	400,000
15	Retained earnings			281,600	24,000
16	Total liabilities and stockholders' equity			$2,181,600	$924,000
17					

The following information is also available:

1. Poklad Company's other assets represent a long-term investment in Lapa Company's long-term debt. Poklad purchased the debt for an amount equal to Lapa's carrying value of the debt.
2. Lapa Company owes Poklad Company $50,000 for services rendered.

Required

Prepare a work sheet for a consolidated balance sheet as of the acquisition date.

Answers to Review Problem

Lapa and Poklad Companies
Work Sheet for Consolidated Balance Sheet
June 30, 2010

	Balance Sheet						Consolidated
	Lapa	Poklad	Eliminations				Balance
Accounts	**Company**	**Company**	**Debit**		**Credit**		**Sheet**
Cash	200,000	24,000					224,000
Accounts receivable	325,000	120,000			(3)	50,000	395,000
Inventory	500,000	260,000					760,000
Investment in Poklad Company	381,600	—			(1)	381,600	—
Plant and equipment (net)	750,000	440,000					1,190,000
Other assets	25,000	80,000			(2)	80,000	25,000
Total assets	2,181,600	924,000					2,594,000
Accounts payable	400,000	200,000	(3)	50,000			550,000
Long-term debt	500,000	300,000	(2)	80,000			720,000
Common stock	1,000,000	400,000	(1)	400,000			1,000,000
Retained earnings	281,600	24,000	(1)	24,000			281,600
Minority interest	—	—			(1)	42,400	42,400
Total liabilities and stockholders' equity	2,181,600	924,000		554,000		554,000	2,594,000

(1) Elimination of intercompany investment. Minority interest equals 10 percent of Poklad Company's stockholders' equity [10% × ($400,000 + $24,000) = $42,400]

(2) Elimination of intercompany long-term debt.

(3) Elimination of intercompany receivables and payables.

LO1 Identify and explain the management issues related to investments.

Investments are recorded on the date on which the transaction occurs, at which time there is either a transfer of funds or a definite obligation to pay. Investments are recorded at cost, or purchase price, including any commissions or fees. After the purchase, the balance sheet value of investments is adjusted to reflect subsequent conditions, including an option for fair value.

Investments are classified as short term or long term; as trading, available-for-sale, or held-to-maturity securities; and as noninfluential and noncontrolling, influential but noncontrolling, or controlling investments. These classifications play an important role in accounting for investments. Noninfluential and noncontrolling investments represent less than 20 percent ownership of a company; influential but noncontrolling investments represent 20 percent to 50 percent ownership; and controlling investments represent more than 50 percent ownership.

A company should disclose its accounting policies for investments and related details in the notes to its financial statements.

Managers and other employees must avoid using their knowledge of their company's planned investment transactions for personal gain.

LO2 Explain the financial reporting implications of short-term investments.

Short-term investments in stocks are classified as trading securities or available-for-sale securities. Trading securities are debt or equity securities that are bought and held principally for the purpose of being sold in the near term. They are classified as current assets on the balance sheet and are valued at fair value. Unrealized gains or losses on trading securities appear on the income statement.

Available-for-sale securities are debt or equity securities that do not meet the criteria for either trading or held-to-maturity securities. They are accounted for in the same way as trading securities with two exceptions: (1) an unrealized gain or loss is reported as a special item in the stockholders' equity section of the balance sheet; (2) if a decline in the value of a security is considered permanent, it is charged as a loss on the income statement.

LO3 Explain the financial reporting implications of long-term investments in stock and the cost-adjusted-to-market and equity methods used to account for them.

The cost-adjusted-to-market method is used to account for noninfluential and noncontrolling investments in stock. With this method, investments are initially recorded at cost and are then adjusted to market value by using an allowance account. The equity method is used to account for influential but noncontrolling investments. With this method, the investment is initially recorded at cost and is then adjusted for the investor's share of the company's net income or loss and subsequent dividends.

Consolidated financial statements are required when an investing company has legal and effective control over another company. Control exists when the parent company owns more than 50 percent of the voting stock of the subsidiary company.

LO4 Explain the financial reporting implications of consolidated financial statements.

Consolidated financial statements are useful to investors and others because they treat the parent company and its subsidiaries as an integrated economic unit. When a consolidated balance sheet is prepared at the date of acquisition, a work sheet entry is made to eliminate the investment from the parent company's financial statements and the stockholders' equity section of the subsidiary's financial statements. The assets and liabilities of the two companies are combined. If the parent owns less than 100 percent of the subsidiary, minority interest equal to the percentage of the subsidiary owned by minority stockholders multiplied by the subsidiary's net assets appears on the consolidated balance sheet. If the cost of the parent's investment in the subsidiary is greater than the subsidiary's book value, an amount equal to the excess of cost over book value is allocated to undervalued subsidiary assets and to goodwill. If the cost of the parent's investment in the subsidiary is less than book value, the excess of book value over cost should be used to reduce the book value of the subsidiary's long-term assets (other than long-term marketable securities).

When consolidated income statements are prepared, intercompany sales, purchases, interest income, interest expense, and other income and expenses from intercompany transactions must be eliminated to avoid double counting of these items.

The financial statements of foreign subsidiaries must be restated in terms of the parent company's reporting currency before consolidated financial statements can be prepared.

LO5 Explain the financial reporting implications of debt investments.

Held-to-maturity securities are debt securities that management intends to hold to their maturity date; they are valued on the balance sheet at cost adjusted for the effects of interest. Long-term investments in bonds fall into two categories: available-for-sale securities, which are recorded at cost and subsequently accounted for at fair value, and held-to-maturity securities.

REVIEW of Concepts and Terminology

The following concepts and terms were introduced in this chapter:

Acquisition method 593 (LO4)

Available-for-sale securities 581 (LO1)

Consolidated financial statements 592 (LO3)

Control 582 (LO1)

Cost-adjusted-to-market method 588 (LO3)

Eliminations 593 (LO4)

Equity method 590 (LO3)

Fair value 580 (LO1)

Goodwill 596 (LO4)

Held-to-maturity securities 581 (LO1)

Insider trading 583 (LO1)

Marketable securities 580 (LO1)

Minority interest 594 (LO4)

Multinational or transnational corporations 599 (LO4)

Parent company 592 (LO3)

Reporting currency 599 (LO4)

Restatement 599 (LO4)

Short-term investments 580 (LO1)

Significant influence 582 (LO1)

Subsidiary 592 (LO3)

Trading securities 581 (LO1)

CHAPTER ASSIGNMENTS

BUILDING Your Basic Knowledge and Skills

Short Exercises

LO2 Trading Securities

SE 1. Market Corporation began investing in trading securities in 2009. At the end of 2009, it had the following trading portfolio:

Security	Cost	Market Value
IBM (10,000 shares)	$440,000	$660,000
GAP (5,000 shares)	200,000	150,000
Totals	$640,000	$810,000

Prepare the necessary year-end adjusting entry on December 31 and the entry for the sale of all the GAP shares on the following March 23 for $190,000 in journal form.

LO3 Cost-Adjusted-to-Market Method

SE 2. On December 31, 2009, the market value of Logan Tech Company's portfolio of long-term available-for-sale securities was $320,000. The cost of these securities was $285,000. Prepare the entry in journal form to adjust the portfolio to market at year end, assuming that the company did not have any long-term investments prior to 2009.

LO3 Cost-Adjusted-to-Market Method

SE 3. Refer to your answer to **SE 2**. Assume that on December 31, 2010, the cost of Logan Tech Company's portfolio of long-term available-for-sale securities was $285,000 and that its market value was $245,000. Prepare the entry in journal form to record the 2010 year-end adjustment.

LO3 Equity Method

SE 4. Perk Company owns 30 percent of Storm Company. In 2009, Storm Company earned $120,000 and paid $80,000 in dividends. Prepare entries in journal form for Perk Company's records on December 31 to reflect this information. Assume that the dividends are received on December 31.

LO3 Methods of Accounting for Long-Term Investments

SE 5. For each of the investments listed below, tell which of the following methods should be used for external financial reporting: (a) cost-adjusted-to-market method, (b) equity method, (c) consolidation of parent and subsidiary financial statements.

1. 49 percent investment in Ramir Corporation
2. 51 percent investment in Fur Corporation
3. 5 percent investment in Baker Corporation

LO4 Purchase of 100 Percent at Book Value

SE 6. Omega Corporation buys 100 percent ownership of Family Season Corporation for $200,000. At the time of the purchase, Family Season's stockholders' equity consisted of $40,000 in common stock and $160,000 in retained earnings. Omega's stockholders' equity consisted of $400,000 in common stock and $800,000 in retained earnings. After the purchase, what would be the amount, if any, of the following accounts on the consolidated balance sheet: goodwill, minority interest, common stock, and retained earnings?

LO4 **Purchase of Less than 100 Percent at Book Value**

SE 7. Assume the same facts as in **SE 6** except that Omega purchased 80 percent of Family Season Corporation for $160,000. After the purchase, what would be the amount, if any, of the following accounts on the consolidated balance sheet: goodwill, minority interest, common stock, and retained earnings?

LO4 **Purchase of 100 Percent at More than Book Value**

SE 8. Assume the same facts as in **SE 6** except that the purchase of 100 percent of Family Season Corporation was for $240,000. After the purchase, what would be the amount, if any, of the following accounts on the consolidated balance sheet: goodwill, minority interest, common stock, and retained earnings? Assume that the fair value of Family Season's net assets equals their book value.

LO4 **Intercompany Transactions**

SE 9. X Company owns 100 percent of Y Company. The following are accounts from the balance sheets and income statements of both companies:

	X Company	Y Company
Accounts receivable	$ 230,000	$150,000
Accounts payable	180,000	90,000
Sales	1,200,000	890,000
Cost of goods sold	710,000	540,000

What would be the combined amount of each of the above accounts on the consolidated financial statements assuming the following additional information? (1) Y Company sold to X Company merchandise at cost in the amount of $270,000; (2) X Company sold all the merchandise it bought from Y Company to customers, but it still owes Y Company $60,000 for the merchandise.

LO5 **Held-to-Maturity Securities**

SE 10. On May 31, Fournier Company invested $98,000 in U.S. Treasury bills. The bills mature in 120 days at $100,000. Prepare entries in journal form to record the purchase on May 31; the adjustment to accrue interest on June 30, which is the end of the fiscal year; and the receipt of cash at the maturity date of September 28.

Exercises

LO1 LO2 LO3 **Discussion Questions**

E 1. Develop brief answers to each of the following questions:

1. Where in the financial statements are investment transactions reported?
2. What would cause an Allowance to Adjust Short-Term Investments to Market account that has a negative (credit) balance at the beginning of the year to have a positive (debit) balance at the end of the year?
3. When a company uses the equity method to record its proportionate share of the income and dividends of a company in which it has invested, what are the cash flow effects?

LO4 LO5 **Discussion Questions**

E 2. Develop brief answers to each of the following questions:

1. Under what conditions would a company have both minority interest and goodwill in a consolidation?

2. Why must the financial statements of foreign subsidiaries be restated?
3. What is the logic behind treating held-to-maturity securities different from any other investment?

LO2 Trading Securities

E 3. Owen Corporation, which has begun investing in trading securities, engaged in the following transactions:

Jan. 6 Purchased 7,000 shares of Google stock, $60 per share.
Feb. 15 Purchased 9,000 shares of Starbucks, $44 per share.

At year end on June 30, Google was trading at $80 per share, and Starbucks was trading at $36 per share.

Record the entries for the purchases. Then record the necessary year-end adjusting entry. (Include a schedule of the trading portfolio cost and market in the explanation.) Also record the entry in journal form for the sale of all the Starbucks shares on August 20 for $32 per share. Is the last entry affected by the June 30 adjustment?

LO3 Long-Term Investments

E 4. Canalle Corporation has the following portfolio of long-term available-for-sale securities at year end, December 31, 2010:

Company	Percentage of Voting Stock Held	Cost	Year-End Market Value
K Corporation	4	$160,000	$190,000
L Corporation	12	750,000	550,000
M Corporation	5	60,000	110,000
Total		$970,000	$850,000

Both the Unrealized Loss on Long-Term Investments account and the Allowance to Adjust Long-Term Investments to Market account currently have a balance of $80,000 from the last accounting period. Prepare T accounts with a beginning balance for each of these accounts. Record the effects of the above information on the accounts and determine the ending balances.

LO3 Long-Term Investments: Cost-Adjusted-to-Market and Equity Methods

E 5. On January 1, Caviar Corporation purchased, as long-term investments, 8 percent of the voting stock of Union Corporation for $500,000 and 45 percent of the voting stock of Boss Corporation for $4 million. During the year, Union Corporation had earnings of $200,000 and paid dividends of $80,000. Boss Corporation had earnings of $600,000 and paid dividends of $400,000. The market value did not change for either investment during the year. Which of these investments should be accounted for using the cost-adjusted-to-market method? Which should be accounted for using the equity method? At what amount should each investment be carried on the balance sheet at year end? Give a reason for each choice.

LO3 Long-Term Investments: Equity Method

E 6. On January 1, 2010, Huang Corporation acquired 40 percent of the voting stock of Lee Corporation, an amount sufficient to exercise significant influence over Lee Corporation's activities, for $2,400,000 in cash. On December 31, Huang determined that Lee paid dividends of $400,000 but incurred a net loss of $200,000 for 2010. Prepare entries in T account form to reflect this information.

LO3 **Methods of Accounting for Long-Term Investments**

E 7. Teague Corporation has the following long-term investments:

1. 60 percent of the common stock of Oho Corporation
2. 13 percent of the common stock of Salt, Inc.
3. 50 percent of the nonvoting preferred stock of Kluz Corporation
4. 100 percent of the common stock of its financing subsidiary, LP, Inc.
5. 35 percent of the common stock of the French company Merli
6. 70 percent of the common stock of the Canadian company Ontario Cannery

For each of these investments, tell which of the following methods should be used for external financial reporting, and why:

a. Cost-adjusted-to-market method
b. Equity method
c. Consolidation of parent and subsidiary financial statements

LO4 **Elimination Entry for a Purchase at Book Value**

E 8. R&M Manufacturing Company purchased 100 percent of the common stock of Bonn Manufacturing Company for $1,200,000. Bonn's stockholders' equity included common stock of $800,000 and retained earnings of $400,000. Prepare the eliminating entry in journal form that would appear on the work sheet for consolidating the balance sheets of these two entities as of the acquisition date.

LO4 **Elimination Entry and Minority Interest**

E 9. The stockholders' equity section of Veritas Corporation's balance sheet appeared as follows on December 31:

Common stock, $10 par value, 40,000 shares authorized and issued	$400,000
Retained earnings	48,000
Total stockholders' equity	$448,000

Midas Manufacturing Company owns 80 percent of Veritas's voting stock and paid $11.20 per share. In journal form, prepare the entry (including minority interest) to eliminate Midas' investment and Veritas's stockholders' equity that would appear on the work sheet used in preparing the consolidated balance sheet for the two firms.

LO4 **Consolidated Balance Sheet with Goodwill**

E 10. On September 1, 2010, A Company purchased 100 percent of the voting stock of B Company for $480,000 in cash. The separate condensed balance sheets immediately after the purchase were as follows:

	A Company	B Company
Other assets	$1,103,000	$544,500
Investment in B Company	480,000	—
Total assets	$1,583,000	$544,500
Liabilities	$ 435,500	$ 94,500
Common stock	500,000	150,000
Retained earnings	647,500	300,000
Total liabilities and stockholders' equity	$1,583,000	$544,500

Prepare a work sheet for preparing the consolidated balance sheet immediately after A Company acquired control of B Company. Assume that any excess cost of A Company's investment in the subsidiary over book value is attributable to goodwill from consolidation.

LO4 **Preparation of Consolidated Income Statement**

E 11. Lowell Company has owned 100 percent of Rich Company since 2009. The income statements of these two companies for the year ended December 31, 2010, follow.

	Lowell Company	Rich Company
Net sales	$3,000,000	$1,200,000
Cost of goods sold	1,500,000	800,000
Gross margin	$1,500,000	$ 400,000
Less: Selling expenses	$ 500,000	$ 100,000
General and administrative expenses	600,000	200,000
Total operating expenses	$1,100,000	$ 300,000
Income from operations	$ 400,000	$ 100,000
Other income	120,000	—
Net income	$ 520,000	$ 100,000

The following is additional information: (1) Rich Company purchased $560,000 of inventory from Lowell Company, which it had sold to Rich customers by the end of the year. (2) Rich Company leased its building from Lowell Company for $120,000 per year. Prepare a consolidated income statement work sheet for the two companies for the year ended December 31, 2010. Income taxes have been ignored.

LO5 **Held-to-Maturity Securities**

E 12. Jolanta Company experiences heavy sales in the summer and early fall, after which time it has excess cash to invest until the next spring. On November 1, 2009, the company invested $388,000 in U.S. Treasury bills. The bills mature in 180 days at $400,000. Prepare entries in journal form to record the purchase on November 1; the adjustment to accrue interest on December 31, which is the end of the fiscal year; and the receipt of cash at the maturity date of April 30.

Problems

LO1 LO2 **Accounting for Investments**

P 1. Karas Gas Corporation is a successful oil and gas exploration business in the southwestern United States. At the beginning of 2010, the company made investments in three companies that perform services in the oil and gas industry. The details of each of these investments follow.

Karas Gas purchased 200,000 shares of Shore Service Corporation at a cost of $16 per share. Shore has 3 million shares outstanding and during 2010 paid dividends of $0.80 per share on earnings of $1.60 per share. At the end of the year, Shore's shares were selling for $24 per share.

Karas Gas also purchased 4 million shares of Speed Drilling Company at $8 per share. Speed has 20 million shares outstanding. In 2010, Speed paid a dividend of $0.40 per share on earnings of $0.80 per share. During the year, the president of Karas Gas was appointed to Speed's board of directors. At the end of the year, Speed's stock was selling for $12 per share.

In another action, Karas Gas purchased 2 million shares of Tom Oil Field Supplies Company's 10 million outstanding shares at $12 per share. The president of Karas Gas sought membership on Tom's board of directors but was rebuffed when a majority of shareholders stated they did not want to be associated with Karas Gas. Tom paid a dividend of $0.80 per share and reported a net income of only $0.40 per share for the year. By the end of the year, its stock price had dropped to $4 per share.

Required

1. For each investment, make entries in journal form for (a) initial investment, (b) receipt of cash dividend, and (c) recognition of income (if appropriate).
2. What adjusting entry (if any) is required at the end of the year?
3. Assuming that Karas Gas sells its investment in Tom after the first of the year for $6 per share, what journal entry would be made?
4. Assuming no other transactions occur and that the market value of Karas Gas's investment in Shore exceeds cost by $4,800,000 at the end of the second year, what adjusting entry (if any) would be required?
5. User insight ▶ What principal factors were considered in determining how to account for Karas Gas's investments? Should they be shown on the balance sheet as short-term or long-term investments? What factors affect this decision?

LO3 Long-Term Investments: Equity Method

P 2. Basic Company owns 40 percent of the voting stock of Oslo Company. The investment account for this company on Basic's balance sheet had a balance of $600,000 on January 1, 2010. During 2010, the Oslo Company reported the following quarterly earnings and dividends paid:

Quarter	Earnings	Dividends Paid
1	$ 80,000	$ 40,000
2	60,000	40,000
3	160,000	40,000
4	(40,000)	40,000
	$260,000	$160,000

Basic Company exercises a significant influence over Oslo's operations and therefore uses the equity method to account for its investment.

Required

1. Prepare a T account for Basic's investment in Oslo. Enter the beginning balance, the relevant entries for the year in total, and the ending balance.
2. User insight ▶ What is the effect and placement of the entries in requirement 1 on Basic Company's earnings as reported on the income statement?
3. User insight ▶ What is the effect and placement of the entries in requirement 1 on the statement of cash flows?
4. User insight ▶ How would the effects on the statements differ if Basic's ownership represented only a 10 percent share of Oslo?

LO4 Consolidated Balance Sheet: Cost Exceeding Book Value

P 3. The balance sheets of Sail and Ivan Companies as of December 31, 2010, appear on the next page.

	Sail Company	Ivan Company
Assets		
Cash	$ 200,000	$ 60,000
Accounts receivable	275,000	600,000
Investment in Ivan Company	700,000	—
Property, plant, and equipment (net)	685,000	450,000
Total assets	$1,860,000	$1,110,000
Liabilities and Stockholders' Equity		
Accounts payable	$ 475,000	$ 535,000
Common stock, $20 par value	925,000	500,000
Retained earnings	460,000	75,000
Total liabilities and stockholders' equity	$1,860,000	$1,110,000

Assume that Sail Company purchased 100 percent of Ivan's common stock for $700,000 immediately prior to December 31, 2010. Also assume that $50,000 of the excess of cost over book value is attributable to the increased value of Ivan Company's property, plant, and equipment. Sail considers the rest of the excess to be goodwill.

Required

1. Prepare a work sheet for preparing a consolidated balance sheet as of the acquisition date.

User insight ▶ 2. If you were reading Sail's consolidated balance sheet, what account would indicate that Sail paid more than fair value for Ivan and where would you find it on the balance sheet? Also, would you expect the amount of this account to change from year-to-year? What would cause it to change?

LO4 Consolidated Balance Sheet: Less than 100 Percent Ownership

P 4. In a cash transaction, Gil Company purchased 70 percent of the outstanding stock of Cat Company for $296,800 cash on June 30, 2010. Immediately after the acquisition, the separate balance sheets of the companies appeared as shown at the top of the next page.

Additional information: (a) Cat Company's other assets represent a long-term investment in Gil Company's long-term debt. The debt was purchased for an amount equal to Gil's carrying value of the debt. (b) Gil Company owes Cat Company $40,000 for services rendered.

Required

1. Prepare a work sheet for preparing a consolidated balance sheet as of the acquisition date.

User insight ▶ 2. If you were reading Gil's consolidated balance sheet, what account would indicate that Gil owned less than 100 percent of Cat and where would you find it on the balance sheet?

	Gil Company	Cat Company
Assets		
Cash	$ 160,000	$ 24,000
Accounts receivable	260,000	120,000
Inventory	400,000	260,000
Investment in Cat Company	296,800	—
Property, plant, and equipment (net)	600,000	440,000
Other assets	20,000	80,000
Total assets	$1,736,800	$924,000
Liabilities and Stockholders' Equity		
Accounts payable	$ 320,000	$200,000
Long-term debt	400,000	300,000
Common stock, $10 par value	800,000	400,000
Retained earnings	216,800	24,000
Total liabilities and stockholders' equity	$1,736,800	$924,000

Alternate Problems

LO3 **Long-Term Investments: Equity Method**

P 5. Snow Corporation owns 35 percent of the voting stock of Nivella Corporation. The Investment account on Snow's books as of January 1, 2010, was $360,000. During 2010, Nivella reported the following quarterly earnings and dividends:

Quarter	Earnings	Dividends Paid
1	$ 80,000	$ 50,000
2	120,000	50,000
3	60,000	50,000
4	(40,000)	50,000
	$220,000	$200,000

Because of the percentage of voting shares Snow owns, it can exercise significant influence over the operations of Nivella Corporation. Therefore, Snow Corporation must account for the investment using the equity method.

Required

1. Prepare a T account for Snow Corporation's investment in Nivella, and enter the beginning balance, the relevant entries for the year in total, and the ending balance.
2. User insight ▶ What is the effect and placement of the entries in requirement **1** on Snow Corporation's earnings as reported on the income statement?
3. User insight ▶ What is the effect and placement of the entries in requirement 1 on the statement of cash flows?
4. User insight ▶ How would the effects on the statements differ if Snow's ownership represented only a 15 percent share of Nivella?

LO4 **Consolidated Balance Sheet: Cost Exceeding Book Value**

P 6. The balance sheets of Ola and Jake Companies as of December 31, 2010, appear below.

	Ola Company	Jake Company
Assets		
Cash	$ 60,000	$ 40,000
Accounts receivable	100,000	30,000
Investment in Jake Company	350,000	—
Property, plant, and equipment (net)	100,000	180,000
Total assets	$610,000	$250,000
Liabilities and Stockholders' Equity		
Accounts payable	$110,000	$ 30,000
Common stock, $20 par value	400,000	200,000
Retained earnings	100,000	20,000
Total liabilities and stockholders' equity	$610,000	$250,000

Assume that Ola Company purchased 100 percent of Jake's common stock for $350,000 immediately prior to December 31, 2010. Also assume that $80,000 of the excess of cost over book value is attributable to the increased value of Jake Company's property, plant, and equipment. The rest of the excess is considered by Ola Company to be goodwill.

Required

1. Prepare a work sheet for preparing a consolidated balance sheet as of the acquisition date.

User insight ▶

2. If you were reading Ola's consolidated balance sheet, what account would indicate that Ola paid more than fair value for Jake and where would you find it on the balance sheet? Also, would you expect the amount of this account to change from year-to-year? What would cause it to change?

LO3 **Long-Term Investment Transactions**

P 7. On January 2, 2009, the Healey Company made several long-term investments in the voting stock of various companies. It purchased 10,000 shares of Zima at $4.00 a share, 15,000 shares of Kane at $6.00 a share, and 6,000 shares of Rodriguez at $9.00 a share. Each investment represents less than 20 percent of the voting stock of the company. The remaining securities transactions of Healey during 2009 were as follows:

May 5	Purchased with cash 6,000 shares of Drennan stock for $6.00 per share. This investment represents less than 20 percent of the Drennan voting stock.
July 16	Sold the 10,000 shares of Zima stock for $3.60 per share.
Sept. 30	Purchased with cash 5,000 additional shares of Kane for $6.40 per share. This investment still represents less than 20 percent of the voting stock.
Dec. 31	The market values per share of the stock in the Long-Term Investments account were as follows: Kane, $6.50; Rodriguez, $8.00; and Drennan, $4.00.

Healey's transactions in securities during 2010 were as follows:

Feb. 1	Received a cash dividend from Kane of $.20 per share.
July 15	Sold the 6,000 Rodriguez shares for $8.00 per share.
Aug. 1	Received a cash dividend from Kane of $.20 per share.
Sept. 10	Purchased 3,000 shares of Parmet Company for $14.00 per share. This investment represents less than 20 percent of the voting stock of the company.
Dec. 31	The market values per share of the stock in the Long-Term Investments account were as follows: Kane, $6.50; Drennan, $5.00; and Parmet, $13.00.

Required

1. Prepare entries in journal form to record all of Healey Company's transactions in long-term investments during 2009 and 2010.

User insight ▶ 2. Assume that Healey increased its ownership in Kane to 25 percent and its ownership in Parmet to 60 percent in 2011. How would these actions affect the methods used to account for the investments?

LO2 LO5 **Held-to-Maturity and Trading Securities**

P 8. During certain periods, Yang Company invests its excess cash until it is needed. During 2010 and 2011, Yang engaged in these transactions:

2010

Jan. 16	Invested $146,000 in 120-day U.S. Treasury bills that had a maturity value of $150,000.
Apr. 15	Purchased 10,000 shares of King Tools common stock at $40 per share and 5,000 shares of Mellon Gas common stock at $30 per share as trading securities.
May 16	Received maturity value of U.S. Treasury bills in cash.
June 2	Received dividends of $2.00 per share from King Tools and $1.50 per share from Mellon Gas.
June 30	Made year-end adjusting entry for trading securities. Market price per share for King Tools is $32; for Mellon Gas, it is $35.
Nov. 14	Sold all the shares of King Tools for $42 per share.

2011

Feb. 15	Purchased 9,000 shares of MKD Communications for $50 per share.
Apr. 1	Invested $195,500 in 120-day U.S. Treasury bills that had a maturity value of $200,000.
June 1	Received dividends of $2.20 per share from Mellon Gas.
30	Made year-end adjusting entry for held-to-maturity securities.
30	Made year-end adjusting entry for trading securities. Market price of Mellon Gas shares is $33 per share and of MKD Communications shares is $60 per share.

Required

1. Prepare entries in journal form to record the preceding transactions, assuming that Yang Company's fiscal year ends on June 30.
2. Show the balance sheet presentation of short-term investments on June 30, 2011.

User insight ▶ 3. Explain the following statement: "Held-to-maturity and trading securities are opposites in terms of investment strategy and thus require opposite accounting treatments."

ENHANCING Your Knowledge, Skills, and Critical Thinking

LO2 LO3 **Understanding Investment Accounting**

C 1. Dell Computer Corporation has significant investment activities. The following items are from Dell's 2009 financial statements (in millions):[18]

Short-term investments	$ 740
Long-term investments	454
Investment income	134
Purchase of investments	1,584
Sales of investments	2,333
Change in unrealized gains (losses) on long-term investments, net	(29)

Dell states that all debt and equities securities are classified as available-for-sale and are subject to an annual impairment test.

1. Where would you find each of the above items in Dell Computer's financial statements?
2. What value (cost or fair value) would you expect the first two items on Dell's balance sheet to represent?
3. What are impairments, and how do they differ from unrealized losses on long-term investments?

LO4 **Goodwill and Minority Interest**

C 2. DreamWorks Animation makes well-known animated films like *Shrek 2*. Two items on the company's 2008 balance sheet are as follows:[19]

Goodwill	$34,216
Minority interest	2,941

1. What is the difference between goodwill and minority interest and where do these items appear on the balance sheet?
2. The amount of goodwill did not change from 2007 to 2008. Assuming no new acquisitions or sales, what would cause the amount of goodwill to change from year to year? Would it increase or decrease?

LO2 **Accounting for Short-Term Investments**

C 3. Malam Christmas Tree Company's business—the growing and selling of Christmas trees—is seasonal. By January 1, after its heavy selling season, the company has cash on hand that will not be needed for several months. It has minimal expenses from January to October and heavy expenses during the harvest and shipping months of November and December. The company's management follows the practice of investing the idle cash in marketable securities, which can be sold when funds are needed for operations. The company's fiscal year ends on June 30.

On January 10 of the current year, Malam has cash of $597,300 on hand. It keeps $20,000 on hand for operating expenses and invests the rest as follows:

$100,000 three-month Treasury bills	$ 97,800
5,000 shares of Ford Motor Co. ($10 per share)	50,000
5,000 shares of McDonald's ($25 per share)	125,000
4,350 shares of IBM ($70 per share)	304,500
Total short-term investments	$577,300

On February 10 and May 10, Malam receives quarterly cash dividends from each company in which it has invested: $0.10 per share from Ford Motor Co., $0.14 per share from McDonald's, and $0.20 per share from IBM. The Treasury bills are redeemed at face value on April 10. On June 1, management sells 1,000 shares of McDonald's at $28 per share.

On June 30, the market values of the investments are as follows:

Ford Motor Co.	$11 per share
McDonald's	$23 per share
IBM	$65 per share

Malam receives another quarterly dividend from each company on August 10. It sells all its remaining shares on November 1 at the following prices:

Ford Motor Co.	$ 9 per share
McDonald's	$22 per share
IBM	$80 per share

1. Record the investment transactions that occurred on January 10, February 10, April 10, May 10, and June 1. The Treasury bills are accounted for as held-to-maturity securities, and the stocks are trading securities. Prepare the required adjusting entry on June 30 and record the investment transactions on August 10 and November 1.
2. Explain how the short-term investments would be shown on the balance sheet on June 30.
3. After November 1, what is the balance of Allowance to Adjust Short-Term Investments to Market, and what will happen to this account next June?
4. What is your assessment of Malam Christmas Tree Company's strategy with regard to idle cash?

LO2 Investments in Derivatives

C 4. Refer to the annual report of **CVS** and the financial statements of **Southwest Airlines Co.** in the Supplement to Chapter 1. Refer to comprehensive income (loss) in each company's statement of shareholders' equity. Which item for each company refers to derivatives (a type of investment involving future contracts)? What causes either an unrealized gain or loss to occur? In the case of Southwest, find the accounting policy with regard to financial derivatives instruments in Note 1 to the financial statements. What problem does Southwest's management face in determining the fair market value of its derivatives? How does management solve the problem?

LO1 Insider Trading

C 5. Refer to the discussion about insider trading in this chapter to answer the following questions:

1. What does *insider trading* mean?
2. Why do you think insider trading is illegal in the United States and in Germany?
3. Why do you think insider trading is permissible in some other countries?
4. Can you think of any reasons why insider trading should be permitted in the United States?

LO3 LO4 **Comparison of Two Recent Acquisitions**

C 6. Mergers and acquisitions are in the news almost every day. Go to the website for **MSNBC** and scan recent headlines to locate two articles related to one company purchasing or making an offer to purchase another company. Read the articles and summarize the nature of the actual or proposed acquisition. What are the companies' names? What industry are they in? What is the dollar amount of the acquisition? How will the acquisition be paid for—in cash, stock, or a combination of cash and stock? In what ways are the acquisitions similar? How do they differ? Be prepared to present your findings in class.

LO1 LO2 LO3 **Identification of Investments and Resulting Gains and Losses**

C 7. Microsoft, one of the most successful businesses in the history of commerce, has accumulated a large investment portfolio, which in a recent year consisted of the following (in millions):[20]

Cash and cash equivalents	$ 6,076
Short-term investments-available-for-sale	25,371
Long-term investments—equity securities	4,933
Total investments	$36,380

In addition, during the 2009 fiscal year Microsoft had net realized losses on investments of $125 million, $862 million of impairments, unrealized losses of $285 million, and unrealized gains of $1,089 million.

Divide into at least seven groups to discuss each of the four types of investments and the three types of gains or losses. Each group should discuss the nature of each gain or loss and the nature of the investment that gave rise to it. Discuss where each investment and gain or loss would appear in the financial statements. Be prepared to present your group's findings in class.

LO1 **Presentation on Investment Classification and Valuation**

C 8. The classification and valuation of investments can be confusing for someone not familiar with classifying investments. Suppose you have been asked to make a short (five-minute) presentation that explains this classification scheme. Develop a one-page outline with talking points that explains the three types of short-term and long-term investments and how they are valued at year end. Then briefly cover how accounting for long-term investments depends on the level and percentage of ownership. Be prepared to give your presentation in class or to a small group.

CHAPTER

13

The Corporate Income Statement and the Statement of Stockholders' Equity

Focus on Financial Statements

INCOME STATEMENT

Revenues

− Expenses

= Net Income

STATEMENT OF RETAINED EARNINGS

Opening Balance

+ Net Income

− Dividends

= Retained Earnings

BALANCE SHEET

Assets	Liabilities
	Equity

A = L + E

STATEMENT OF CASH FLOWS

Operating activities
+ Investing activities
+ Financing activities
= Change in Cash
+ Starting Balance
= Ending Cash Balance

Net income from income statement is on statement of retained earnings; retained earnings is often component on statement of stockholders' equity.

As we pointed out in an earlier chapter, earnings management—the practice of manipulating revenues and expenses to achieve a specific outcome—is unethical when companies use it to create misleading financial statements. Users of financial statements consider the possibility of earnings management by assessing the quality, or sustainability, of a company's earnings. To do so, they evaluate how the components of the company's income statement affect earnings. In this chapter, we focus on those components. We also cover earnings per share, the statement of stockholders' equity, stock dividends and stock splits, and book value per share.

LEARNING OBJECTIVES

LO1 Define *quality of earnings*, and identify the components of a corporate income statement. (pp. 622–628)

LO2 Show the relationships among income taxes expense, deferred income taxes, and net of taxes. (pp. 629–632)

LO3 Compute earnings per share. (pp. 632–635)

LO4 Define *comprehensive income*, and describe the statement of stockholders' equity. (pp. 635–638)

LO5 Account for stock dividends and stock splits. (pp. 638–643)

LO6 Calculate book value per share. (pp. 643–644)

DECISION POINT ▸ A USER'S FOCUS MOTOROLA, INC.

Motorola, a well-known maker of cell phones and other telecommunications equipment, has had its ups and downs in recent years. As shown in its Financial Highlights, the company had good earnings in 2006 but a big decrease in revenue and an operating loss in 2007 and in 2008. These results reflect the initial success of the Razr phone, followed by the company's difficulty in extending the phone's popularity, and costs related to reorganization and separation of business.[1]

How does one use complex income statements like Motorola's to evaluate a company's performance? It is not enough to simply look at the "bottom line" (i.e., net earnings) or even at net sales and operating income. To gain a proper perspective on a company's performance, one must examine the components of its income statement.

MOTOROLA'S FINANCIAL HIGHLIGHTS (In millions)

	2008	2007	2006
Net sales	$30,146	$36,622	$42,847
Operating earnings (loss)	(2,391)	(553)	4,092
Net earnings (loss)	(4,244)	(49)	3,661
Basic earnings per share			
Continuing operations	(1.87)	(0.05)	1.33
Discontinued operations	—	0.03	0.17
	(1.87)	(0.02)	1.50
Cash flows from operating activities	242	785	3,499

- ▸ What items other than normal operating activities contributed to Motorola's performance?
- ▸ What does the company's income statement indicate about its quality of earnings?
- ▸ How does one put the various measures of performance (some of which are shown in Motorola's financial highlights) in perspective?

Performance Measurement: Quality of Earnings Issues

LO1 Define *quality of earnings*, and identify the components of a corporate income statement.

Net income (net earnings) is the measure most commonly used to evaluate a company's performance. In fact, a survey of 2,000 members of the Association for Investment Management and Research indicated that the two most important economic measures in evaluating common stocks were expected changes in earnings per share and expected return on equity.[2] Net income is a key component of both measures.

Because of the importance of net income, or the "bottom line," in measuring a company's prospects, there is significant interest in evaluating the quality of the net income figure, or the **quality of earnings**. The quality of a company's earnings refers to the substance of earnings and their sustainability into future accounting periods. For example, if earnings increase because of a gain on the sale of an asset, this portion of earnings will not be sustained in the future.

The accounting estimates and methods that a company uses affect the quality of its earnings, as do these components of the income statement:

- Gains and losses on transactions
- Write-downs and restructurings
- Nonoperating items

Because management has choices in the content and positioning of these income statement components, there is a potential for managing earnings to achieve specific income targets. It is therefore critical for users of income statements to understand these factors and take them into consideration when evaluating a company's performance.

Study Note

It is important to know which items included in earnings are recurring and which are one-time items. Income from continuing operations before nonoperating items gives a clear signal about future results. In assessing a company's future earnings potential, nonoperating items are excluded because they are not expected to continue.

Exhibit 13-1 shows the components of a typical corporate income statement. Net income or loss (the "bottom line" of the income statement) includes all revenues, expenses, gains, and losses over the accounting period. When a company has both continuing and discontinued operations, the operating income section is called **income from continuing operations**. Income from continuing operations before income taxes may include gains or losses on the sale of assets, write-downs, and restructurings. The income taxes expense section of the statement is subject to special accounting rules.

As you can see in Exhibit 13-1, the section of a corporate income statement that follows income taxes contains such nonoperating items as discontinued operations and extraordinary gains (or losses). Another item that may appear in this section is the write-off of goodwill when its value has been impaired. Earnings per share information appears at the bottom of the statement.

FOCUS ON BUSINESS PRACTICE

Why Do Investors Study Quality of Earnings?

Analysts for **Twentieth Century Mutual Funds**, a major investment company now merged with **American Century Investments Corporation**, make adjustments to a company's reported financial performance to create a more accurate picture of the company's ongoing operations. For example, suppose a paper manufacturer reports earnings of $1.30 per share. Further investigation, however, shows that the per share number includes a one-time gain on the sale of assets, which accounts for an increase of $0.25 per share. Twentieth Century would list the company as earning only $1.05 per share. "These kinds of adjustments help assure long-term decisions aren't based on one-time events."[3]

EXHIBIT 13-1 Corporate Income Statement

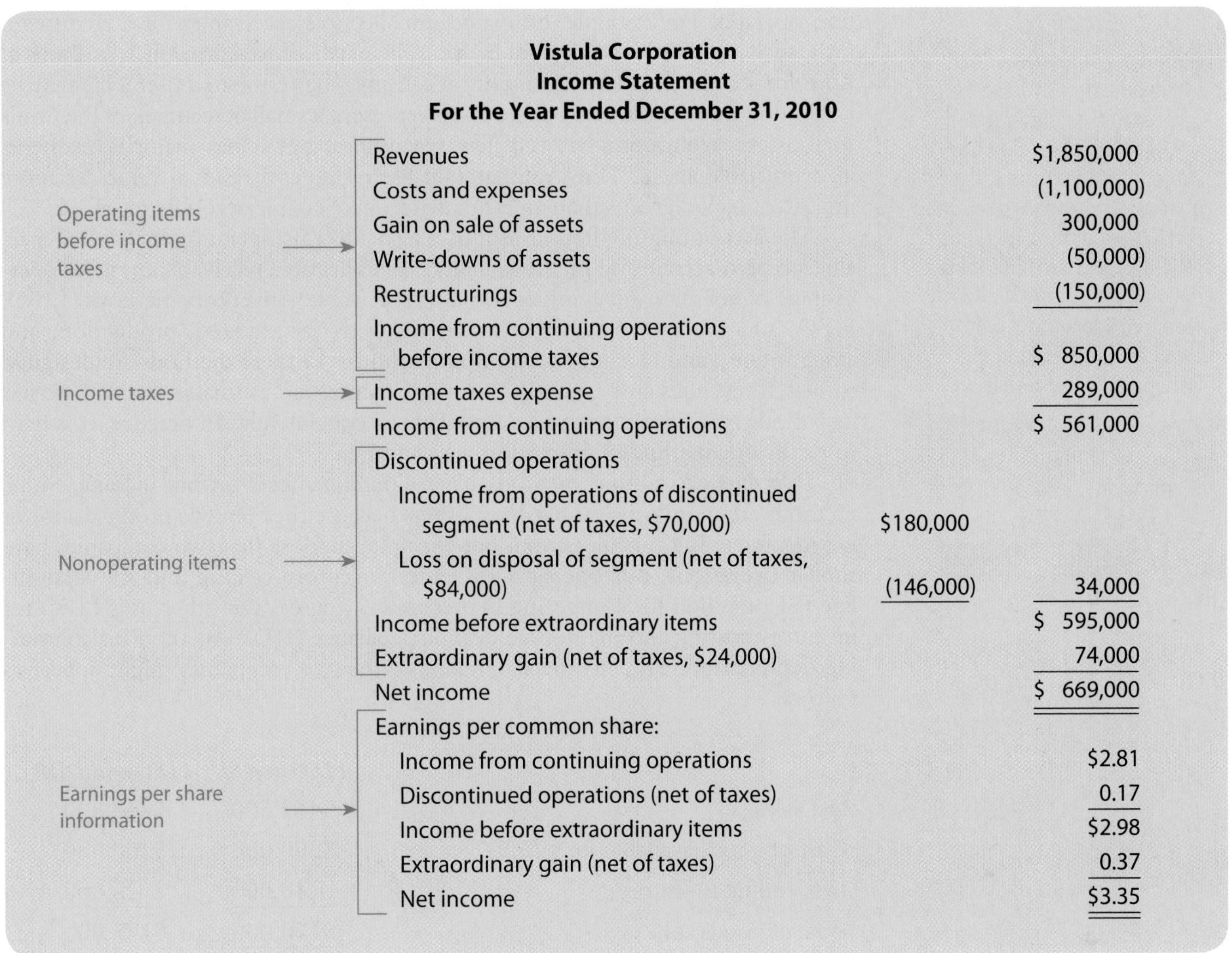

Vistula Corporation
Income Statement
For the Year Ended December 31, 2010

Operating items before income taxes	Revenues		$1,850,000
	Costs and expenses		(1,100,000)
	Gain on sale of assets		300,000
	Write-downs of assets		(50,000)
	Restructurings		(150,000)
	Income from continuing operations before income taxes		$ 850,000
Income taxes	Income taxes expense		289,000
	Income from continuing operations		$ 561,000
Nonoperating items	Discontinued operations		
	Income from operations of discontinued segment (net of taxes, $70,000)	$180,000	
	Loss on disposal of segment (net of taxes, $84,000)	(146,000)	34,000
	Income before extraordinary items		$ 595,000
	Extraordinary gain (net of taxes, $24,000)		74,000
	Net income		$ 669,000
Earnings per share information	Earnings per common share:		
	Income from continuing operations		$2.81
	Discontinued operations (net of taxes)		0.17
	Income before extraordinary items		$2.98
	Extraordinary gain (net of taxes)		0.37
	Net income		$3.35

The Effect of Accounting Estimates and Methods

Users of financial statements need to be aware of the impact that accounting estimates and methods have on the income that a firm reports. As you know, to comply with the matching rule, accountants must assign revenues and expenses to the periods in which they occur. If they cannot establish a direct relationship between revenues and expenses, they systematically allocate the expenses among the accounting periods that benefit from them, and in doing so, they must make estimates and exercise judgment. An accounting estimate should be based on realistic assumptions, but there is latitude in making the estimate, and the final judgment will affect the net income that appears on a company's income statement.

For example, when a company acquires an asset, the accountant must estimate the asset's useful life. Technological obsolescence could shorten the asset's expected useful life, and regular maintenance and repairs could lengthen it. Although the actual useful life cannot be known with certainty until some future date, the accountant's estimate of it affects both current and future operating income. Other areas that require accounting estimates include the residual value of assets, uncollectible accounts receivable, sales returns, total units of production, total recoverable units of natural resources, amortization periods, warranty claims, and environmental cleanup costs.

Study Note

Although companies in the same industry may have comparable earnings, their quality of earnings may not be comparable. To assess the quality of a company's reported earnings, you must know the estimates and methods it uses to compute income. Generally accepted accounting principles allow several methods, all yielding different results.

The importance of accounting estimates depends on the industry in which a firm operates. For example, estimated uncollectible receivables for a credit card firm, such as **American Express**, or for a financial services firm, such as **Bank of America**, can have a material impact on earnings, but estimated useful life may be less important because depreciable assets represent a small percentage of the firm's total assets. **Walgreens** has very few receivables, but it has major investments in depreciable assets. Thus, estimates of useful life and residual value are more important to Walgreens than an estimate of uncollectible accounts receivable.

The accounting methods a firm uses also affect its operating income. Generally accepted accounting methods include uncollectible receivable methods (percentage of net sales and aging of accounts receivable), inventory methods (LIFO, FIFO, and average-cost), depreciation methods (accelerated, production, and straight-line), and revenue recognition methods. All these methods are designed to match revenues and expenses, but the expenses are estimates, and the period or periods benefited cannot be demonstrated conclusively. In practice, it is hard to justify one method of estimation over another.

Different accounting methods have different effects on net income. Some methods are more conservative than others because they tend to produce a lower net income in the current period. For example, suppose that two companies have similar operations, but one uses FIFO for inventory costing and the straight-line (SL) method for computing depreciation, whereas the other uses LIFO for inventory costing and the double-declining-balance (DDB) method for computing depreciation. The income statements of the two companies might appear as follows:

	FIFO and SL	*LIFO and DDB*
Net sales	$462,500	$462,500
Cost of goods available for sale	$200,000	$200,000
Less ending inventory	30,000	25,000
Cost of goods sold	$170,000	$175,000
Gross margin	$292,500	$287,500
Less depreciation expense	$ 20,000	$ 40,000
Less other expenses	85,000	85,000
Total operating expenses	$105,000	$125,000
Income from continuing operations before income taxes	$187,500	$162,500

The income from continuing operations before income taxes for the firm that uses LIFO and DDB is lower because in periods of rising prices, the LIFO method produces a higher cost of goods sold, and in the early years of an asset's useful life, accelerated depreciation yields a higher depreciation expense. The result is lower operating income. However, future operating income should be higher.

Although the choice of accounting method does not affect cash flows except for possible differences in income taxes, the $25,000 difference in operating income stems solely from the choice of accounting methods. Estimates of the useful lives and residual values of plant assets could lead to an even greater difference. In practice, of course, differences in net income occur for many reasons, but the user of financial statements must be aware of the discrepancies that can occur as a result of the accounting methods used in preparing the statements. In

FOCUS ON BUSINESS PRACTICE

Beware of the "Bottom Line!"

In the second quarter of 2007, **McDonald's** posted its second-ever loss: $711.7 million. Is this cause for concern? In fact, it is misleading: the company is actually in a period of rapidly growing revenues and profits. The loss resulted from a one-time, noncash impairment of $1.6 billion, related to investments in Latin America. In another example, **Campbell Soup** showed unrealistically positive results in a recent year. Its income jumped by 31 percent, due to a tax settlement and an accounting restatement. Without these items, its revenue and income would have been up less than 1 percent, and soup sales—its main product—actually dropped by 6 percent. The lesson to be learned is to look beyond the "bottom line" to the components of the income statement when evaluating a company's performance.[4]

general, an accounting method or estimate that results in lower current earnings produces a better quality of operating income.

The latitude that companies have in their choice of accounting methods and estimates could cause problems in the interpretation of financial statements were it not for the conventions of full disclosure and consistency. As noted in an earlier chapter, full disclosure requires management to explain the significant accounting policies used in preparing the financial statements in a note to the statements. Consistency requires that the same accounting procedures be followed from year to year. If a change in procedure is made, the nature of the change and its monetary effect must be explained in a note. For instance, in a note to its financial statements, **Motorola** discloses that it uses the FIFO method for inventory accounting and a combination of straight-line and accelerated depreciation methods for various groups of long-term assets.

Gains and Losses

When a company sells or otherwise disposes of operating assets or marketable securities, a gain or loss generally results. Although these gains or losses appear in the operating section of the income statement, they usually represent one-time events. They are not sustainable, ongoing operations, and management often has some choice as to their timing. Thus, from an analyst's point of view, they should be ignored when considering operating income.

Write-downs and Restructurings

When management decides that an asset is no longer of value to the company, a write-down or restructuring occurs.

- A **write-down**, also called a *write-off*, is a reduction in the value of an asset below its carrying value on the balance sheet.
- A **restructuring** is the estimated cost of a change in a company's operations. It usually involves the closing of facilities and the laying off of personnel.

Both write-downs and restructurings reduce current operating income and boost future income by shifting future costs to the current accounting period. They are often an indication of poor management decisions in the past, such as paying too much for the assets of another company or making operational changes that do not work out. Companies sometimes take all possible losses in the current year so that future years will be "clean" of these costs. Such "big

FOCUS ON BUSINESS PRACTICE

Can You Believe "Pro Forma" Earnings?

Companies must report earnings in accordance with GAAP, but many also report "pro forma" earnings. Pro forma reporting of earnings, in the words of one analyst, means that they "have thrown out the bad stuff."[5] In other words, when companies report pro forma earnings, they are telling the investment community to ignore one-time losses and nonoperating items, which may reflect bad decisions in the past. In the late 1990s, technology firms with high growth rates and volatile or low earnings and firms that unexpectedly miss earnings targets widely relied on pro forma results. More recent research has shown that after the bubble burst in 2001–2002 and after the **Enron** collapse, the number of companies reporting pro forma earnings declined significantly.[6] The investment community learned that GAAP earnings are a better benchmark of a company's performance because they are based on recognized standards used by all companies, whereas there is no generally accepted way to report pro forma earnings. They are whatever the company wants you to see.

baths," as they are called, commonly occur when a company is having a bad year. They also often occur in years when there is a change in management. The new management takes a "big bath" in the current year so it can show improved results in future years.

In a recent year, 35 percent of 600 large companies had write-downs of tangible assets, and 42 percent had restructurings. Another 112 percent had write-downs or charges related to intangible assets, often involving goodwill.[7]

Nonoperating Items

The nonoperating items that appear on the income statement include discontinued operations and extraordinary gains and losses, both of which can significantly affect net income. In Exhibit 13-1, earnings per common share for income from continuing operations are $2.81, but when all the nonoperating items are taken into consideration, net income per share is $3.35. **Discontinued operations** are segments of a business, such as a separate major line of business, or serve a separate class of customer that is no longer part of a company's operations. To make it easier to evaluate a company's ongoing operations, generally accepted accounting principles require that gains and losses from discontinued operations be reported separately on the income statement.

In Exhibit 13-1, the disclosure of discontinued operations has two parts. One part shows that after the decision to discontinue, the income from operations of the disposed segment was $180,000 (net of $70,000 taxes). The other part shows that the loss from the disposal of the segment was $146,000 (net of $84,000 tax savings). (The computation of the gains or losses involved in discontinued operations is covered in more advanced accounting courses.)

Extraordinary items are "events or transactions that are distinguished by their unusual nature *and* by the infrequency of their occurrence."[8] Items usually treated as extraordinary include the following:

1. An uninsured loss from flood, earthquake, fire, or theft
2. A gain or loss resulting from the passage of a new law
3. The expropriation (taking) of property by a foreign government

In Exhibit 13-1, the extraordinary gain was $74,000 after taxes of $24,000.

Quality of Earnings and Cash Flows

The reason for considering quality of earnings issues is to assess how various components of the income statement affect cash flows and performance measures affected by earnings, such as profit margin, return on assets, and return on equity. Generally, except for their effect on income taxes, gains and losses, asset write-downs, restructurings, and nonoperating items have no effect on cash flows because the cash for these items has already been expended. Thus, the focus of analysis is on sustainable earnings, which generally have a relationship to future cash flows.

Because **Motorola** has a history of reporting nonrecurring special items, including restructuring expenses and investment and inventory write-offs, analysts have questioned the quality of its earnings.[9] Recently, the company had 7 straight years of such items. The nonrecurring special items in Motorola's income statement, shown in Exhibit 13-2, include other charges, gains on sales of investments and businesses, and earnings from discontinued operations. However, if you look back at Motorola's Financial Highlights at the start of this chapter, you will see that the company's cash flows from operating activities were positive even in 2007 when it suffered net losses but they were not greater than net earnings in 2008 and 2006 by a factor of more than 2 to 1. By this measure, Motorola's earnings are of relatively weaker quality.

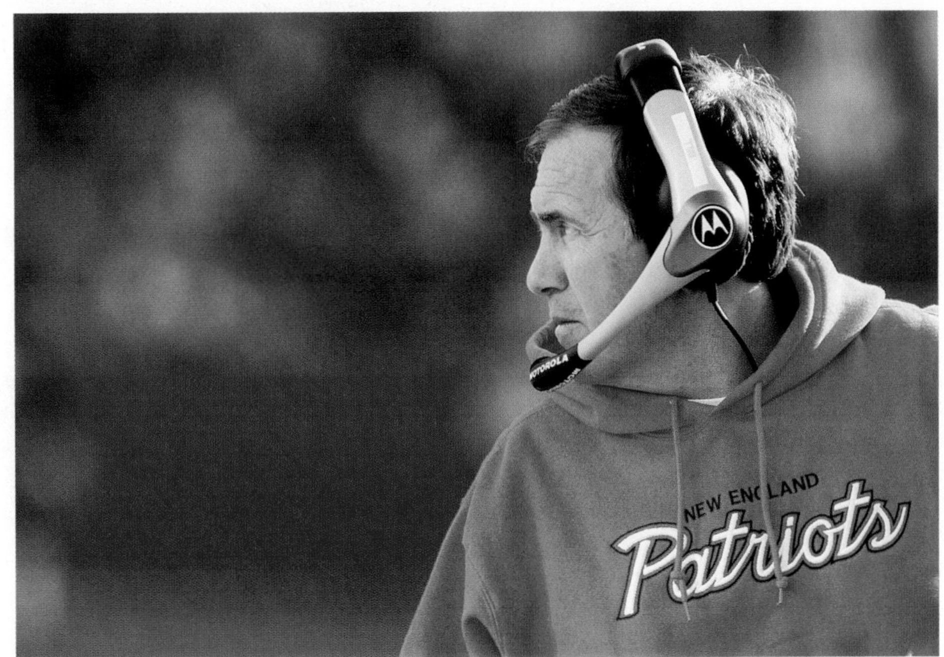

Motorola provides communications equipment to the National Football League. Shown here wearing a Motorola headset is Bill Belichick, head coach of the New England Patriots. Despite Motorola's sluggish results in recent years, its CEO pointed out in 2005 that the company's quality of earnings had improved from year to year. *Quality of earnings* refers to the substance and sustainability of earnings into future accounting periods.

Courtesy of Bernie Nunez/Getty Images.

EXHIBIT 13-2 Motorola's Income Statement

	Year Ended December 31		
(In millions)	**2008**	**2007**	**2006**
Net sales	**$30,146**	$36,622	$42,847
Cost of sales	**21,751**	26,670	30,120
Gross margin	**8,395**	$ 9,952	$12,727
Selling, general, and administrative costs	**$ 4,330**	$ 5,092	$ 4,504
Research and development expenditures	**4,109**	4,429	4,106
Other charges (income)	**2,347**	984	25
Operating earnings (loss)	**$ (2,391)**	$ (553)	$ 4,092
Other income (expense):			
Interest income, net	**$ 48**	$ 91	$ 326
Gains on sales of investments and businesses, net	**82**	50	41
Other	**(376)**	22	51
Total other income (expense)	**$ (246)**	$ 163	$ 518
Earnings (loss) from continuing operations before income taxes	**$ (2,637)**	$ (390)	$ 4,610
Income tax expense (benefit)	**1,607**	(285)	1,349
Earnings (loss) from continuing operations	**$ (4,244)**	$ (105)	$ 3,261
Earnings from discontinued operations, net of tax	**—**	56	400
Net earnings (loss)	**$ (4,244)**	$ (49)	$ 3,661

Note: Highlighted items are discussed in the text.
Source: Motorola, Inc., *Annual Report*, 2008.

& APPLY >

Assume the following data apply to Ace, Inc.: net sales, $180,000; cost of goods sold, $87,500; loss from discontinued operations (net of income tax benefit of $17,500), $50,000; loss on disposal of discontinued operations (net of income tax benefit of $4,000), $12,500; operating expenses, $32,500; income taxes expense on continuing operations, $25,000. From this information, prepare the company's income statement for the year ended December 31, 2011. (Ignore earnings per share information.)

SOLUTION

Ace, Inc.
Income Statement
For the Year Ended December 31, 2011

Net sales		$180,000
Cost of goods sold		87,500
Gross margin		$ 92,500
Operating expenses		32,500
Income from continuing operations before income taxes		$ 60,000
Income taxes expense		25,000
Income from continuing operations		$ 35,000
Discontinued operations		
Loss from discontinued operations (net of taxes, $17,500)	($50,000)	
Loss on disposal of discontinued operations (net of taxes, $4,000)	(12,500)	(62,500)
Net loss		($ 27,500)

Income Taxes

LO2 Show the relationships among income taxes expense, deferred income taxes, and net of taxes.

Corporations determine their taxable income (the amount on which they pay taxes) by deducting allowable expenses from taxable income. The federal tax laws determine which expenses corporations may deduct. (Rules for calculating and reporting taxable income in specialized industries, such as banking, insurance, mutual funds, and cooperatives, are highly technical and may vary significantly from the ones we discuss in this chapter.)

Table 13-1 shows the tax rates that apply to a corporation's taxable income. A corporation with taxable income of $70,000 would have a federal income tax liability of $12,500: $7,500 (the tax on the first $50,000 of taxable income) plus $5,000 (25 percent of the $20,000 earned in excess of $50,000).

Income taxes expense is recognized in the accounting records on an accrual basis. It may or may not equal the amount of taxes a corporation actually pays. The amount a corporation pays is determined by the rules of the income tax code. As we noted earlier in the text, small businesses often keep both their accounting records and tax records on a cash basis, so that the income taxes expense on their income statements equals their income taxes. This practice is acceptable as long as the difference between the income calculated on an accounting basis and the income calculated for tax purposes is not material. However, the purpose of accounting is not to determine taxable income and tax liability, but to determine net income in accordance with GAAP.

> **Study Note**
>
> Many people think is illegal to keep accounting records on a different basis from income tax records. However, the internal Revenue Code and GAAP often do not agree. To work with two conflicting sets of guidelines, the accountant must keep two sets of records.

Management has an incentive to use methods that minimize its firm's tax liability. But accountants, who are bound by accrual accounting and the materiality concept, cannot let tax procedures dictate their method of preparing financial statements if the result would be misleading. The difference between accounting income and taxable income, especially in large businesses, can be material. This discrepancy can result from differences in the timing of the recognition of revenues and expenses under accrual accounting and the tax method. The following are some possible variations:

	Accrual Accounting	*Tax Method*
Expense recognition	Accrual or deferral	At time of expenditure
Accounts receivable	Allowance	Direct charge-off
Inventories	Average-cost	FIFO
Depreciation	Straight-line	Accelerated cost recovery

TABLE 13-1
Tax Rate Schedule for Corporations, 2008

Taxable Income		**Tax Liability**	
Over	**But Not Over**		**Of the Amount Over**
	$ 50,000	0 + 15%	—
$ 50,000	75,000	$ 7,500 + 25%	$ 50,000
75,000	100,000	13,750 + 34%	75,000
100,000	335,000	22,250 + 39%	100,000
335,000	10,000,000	113,900 + 34%	335,000
10,000,000	15,000,000	3,400,000 + 35%	10,000,000
15,000,000	18,333,333	5,150,000 + 38%	15,000,000
18,333,333	—	6,416,667 + 35%	18,333,333

Note: Tax rates are subject to change by Congress.

Deferred Income Taxes

Study Note

The discrepancy between GAAP-based tax expense and Internal Revenue code-based tax liability creates the need for the Deferred Income Taxes account

Income tax allocation is the method used to accrue income taxes expense on the basis of accounting income when accounting income and taxable income differ. The account used to record the difference between income taxes expense and income taxes payable is called **Deferred Income Taxes**. For example, in the income statement in Exhibit 13-1, Vistula Corporation has income taxes expense on income from continuing operations of $289,000. Suppose, however, that Vistula's actual income taxes payable are $184,000. The following entry in journal form shows how income tax allocation would treat this situation:

A	=	L	+	SE
		+184,000		−289,000
		+105,000		

Dec. 31	Income Taxes Expense	289,000	
	Income Taxes Payable		184,000
	Deferred Income Taxes		105,000
	To record estimated current and deferred income taxes		

Study Note

Deferred Income Taxes is classified as a liability when it has a credit balance and as an asset when it has a debit balance. It is further classified as either current or long-term depending on when it is expected to reverse.

In other years, Vistula's Income Taxes Payable may exceed its Income Taxes Expense. In this case, the entry is the same except that Deferred Income Taxes is debited.

The Financial Accounting Standards Board has issued specific rules for recording, measuring, and classifying deferred income taxes.[10] Deferred income taxes are recognized for the estimated future tax effects resulting from temporary differences in the valuation of assets, liabilities, equity, revenues, expenses, gains, and losses for tax and financial reporting purposes. Temporary differences include revenues and expenses or gains and losses that are included in taxable income before or after they are included in financial income. In other words, the recognition point for revenues, expenses, gains, and losses is not the same for tax and financial reporting.

For example, advance payments for goods and services, such as magazine subscriptions, are not recognized as income until the products are shipped. However, for tax purposes, advance payments are usually recognized as revenue when cash is received. As a result, taxes paid exceed taxes expense, which creates a deferred income taxes asset (or prepaid taxes).

Classification of deferred income taxes as current or noncurrent depends on the classification of the asset or liability that created the temporary difference. For example, the deferred income taxes asset mentioned above would be classified as current if unearned subscription revenue were classified as a current liability. On the other hand, the temporary difference arising from depreciation is related to a long-term depreciable asset. Therefore, the resulting deferred income taxes would be classified as long-term. If a temporary difference is not related to an asset or liability, it is classified as current or noncurrent based on its expected date of reversal. (Temporary differences and the classification of deferred income taxes that results are covered in depth in more advanced courses.)

Each year, the balance of the Deferred Income Taxes account is evaluated to determine whether it still accurately represents the expected asset or liability in light of legislated changes in income tax laws and regulations.

In any given year, the amount a company pays in income taxes is determined by subtracting (or adding) the deferred income taxes for that year from (or to) income taxes expense. In subsequent years, the amount of deferred income taxes can vary based on changes in tax laws and rates.

A survey of the financial statements of 600 large companies indicates the importance of deferred income taxes to financial reporting. About 68 percent reported deferred income taxes with a credit balance in the long-term liability section of their balance sheets.[11]

Net of Taxes

The phrase **net of taxes** indicates that taxes (usually income taxes) have been taken into account in reporting an item in the financial statements. The phrase is used in a corporate income statement when a company has items that must be disclosed in a separate section. Each such item should be reported net of the applicable income taxes to avoid distorting the income taxes expense associated with ongoing operations and the resulting net operating income.

For example, assume that a corporation with operating income before income taxes of $240,000 has a total tax expense of $132,000 and that the total income includes a gain of $200,000 on which a tax of $60,000 is due. Also assume that the gain is not part of the corporation's normal operations and must be disclosed separately on the income statement as an extraordinary item. This is how the income taxes expense would be reported on the income statement:

Operating income before income taxes	$240,000
Income taxes expense	72,000
Income before extraordinary item	$168,000
Extraordinary gain (net of taxes, $60,000)	140,000
Net income	$308,000

If all the income taxes expense were deducted from operating income before income taxes, both the income before extraordinary item and the extraordinary gain would be distorted.

The procedure is the same in the case of an extraordinary loss. For example, given the same facts except that the income taxes expense is only $12,000 because of a $200,000 extraordinary loss, the result is a $60,000 tax savings:

Operating income before income taxes	$240,000
Income taxes expense	72,000
Income before extraordinary item	$168,000
Extraordinary loss (net of taxes, $60,000)	(140,000)
Net income	$ 28,000

In Exhibit 13-1, the total of the income tax items for Vistula Corporation is $299,000. That amount is allocated among five statement components, as follows:

Income taxes expense on income from continuing operations	$289,000
Income taxes on income from a discontinued segment	70,000
Income tax savings on the loss on the disposal of the segment	(84,000)
Income taxes on extraordinary gain	24,000
Total income taxes expense	$299,000

STOP & APPLY >

Jose Corporation reported the following accounting income before income taxes, income taxes expense, and net income for 2010 and 2011:

	2011	2010
Income before income taxes	$42,000	$42,000
Income taxes expense	13,245	13,245
Net income	$28,755	$28,755

On the balance sheet, deferred income taxes liability increased by $5,760 in 2010 and decreased by $2,820 in 2011.

1. How much was actually payable in income taxes for 2010 and 2011?
2. Prepare entries in journal form to record estimated current and deferred income taxes for 2010 and 2011.

SOLUTION

1. Income taxes calculated:

	2011	2010
Income taxes expense	$13,245	$13,245
Decrease (increase) in deferred income taxes	2,820	(5,760)
Income taxes payable	$16,065	$ 7,485

2. Entries prepared:

2010	Income Taxes Expense	13,245	
	Deferred Income Taxes		5,760
	Income Taxes Payable		7,485
	To record estimated current and deferred income taxes for 2010		
2011	Income Taxes Expense	13,245	
	Deferred Income Taxes	2,820	
	Income Taxes Payable		16,065
	To record estimated current and deferred income taxes for 2011		

Earnings per Share

LO3 Compute earnings per share.

Study Note

Earnings per share is a measure of a corporation's profitability. It is one of the most closely watched financial ratios in the business world. Its disclosure on the income statement is required.

Readers of financial statements use earnings per share to judge a company's performance and to compare it with the performance of other companies. Because this information is so important, the Accounting Principles Board concluded that earnings per share of common stock should be presented on the face of the income statement.[12] As shown in Exhibit 13-1, this information is usually disclosed just below net income.

A corporate income statement always shows earnings per share for income from continuing operations and other major components of net income. For example, if a company has a gain or loss on discontinued operations or on extraordinary items, its income statement may present earnings per share amounts for the gain or loss.

Exhibit 13-3 shows how **Motorola** presents earnings per share on its income statement. As you can see, the statement covers three years, and discontinued operations had a positive effect on earnings per share in two years. However,

EXHIBIT 13-3
Motorola's Earnings per Share Presentation

	Years Ended December 31		
	2008	**2007**	**2006**
Earnings (loss) per common share:			
Basic:			
Continuing operations	**($1.87)**	($0.05)	$1.33
Discontinued operations	—	0.03	0.17
	($1.87)	($0.02)	$1.50
Diluted:			
Continuing operations	**($1.87)**	($0.05)	$1.30
Discontinued operations	—	0.03	0.16
	($1.87)	($0.02)	$1.46
Weighted averages common shares outstanding:			
Basic	**2,265.4**	2,312.7	2,446.3
Diluted	**2,265.4**	2,312.7	2,504.2

Source: Motorola, Inc., *Annual Report,* 2008.

the earnings per share for continuing operations is a better indicator of the company's future performance. The company is discontinuing some operations by selling or otherwise disposing of noncore divisions. Note that earnings per share are reported as basic and diluted.

Basic Earnings per Share

Basic earnings per share is the net income applicable to common stock divided by the weighted-average number of common shares outstanding. To compute this figure, one must determine if the number of common shares outstanding changed during the year and if the company paid dividends on preferred stock.

When a company has only common stock and the number of shares outstanding is the same throughout the year, the earnings per share computation is simple. Exhibit 13-1 shows that Vistula Corporation had net income of $669,000. If Vistula had 200,000 shares of common stock outstanding during the entire year, the earnings per share of common stock would be computed as follows:

$$\text{Earnings per Share} = \frac{\$669{,}000}{200{,}000 \text{ Shares}} = \$3.35^{*} \text{ per Share}$$

If the number of shares outstanding changes during the year, it is necessary to figure the weighted-average number of shares outstanding for the year. Suppose that from January 1 to March 31, Vistula Corporation had 200,000 shares outstanding; from April 1 to September 30, it had 240,000 shares outstanding; and from October 31 to December 31, it had 260,000 shares outstanding. The

*This number is rounded, as are some other results of computations that follow.

weighted-average number of common shares outstanding and basic earnings per share would be determined this way:

200,000 shares × $^3/_{12}$ year	50,000
240,000 shares × $^6/_{12}$ year	120,000
260,000 shares × $^3/_{12}$ year	65,000
Weighted-average common shares outstanding	235,000

$$\text{Basic Earnings per Share} = \frac{\text{Net Income}}{\text{Weighted-Average Common Shares Outstanding}}$$

$$= \frac{\$669{,}000}{235{,}000 \text{ Shares}} = \$2.85 \text{ per Share}$$

If a company has nonconvertible preferred stock outstanding, the dividend for that stock must be subtracted from net income before earnings per share for common stock are computed. For example, suppose that Vistula Corporation has preferred stock on which it pays an annual dividend of $47,000. Earnings per share on common stock would be $2.65 [($669,000 − $47,000) ÷ 235,000 shares].

Diluted Earnings per Share

Companies can have a simple capital structure or a complex capital structure.

- A company has a **simple capital structure** if it has no preferred stocks, bonds, or stock options that can be converted to common stock. A company with a simple capital structure computes earnings per share as shown above.
- A company that has issued securities or stock options that can be converted to common stock has a **complex capital structure**. These securities and options have the potential of diluting the earnings per share of common stock.

Potential dilution means that the conversion of stocks or bonds or the exercise of stock options can increase the total number of shares of common stock that a company has outstanding and thereby reduce a current stockholder's proportionate share of ownership in the company. For example, suppose that a person owns 10,000 shares of a company's common stock, which equals 2 percent of the outstanding shares of 500,000. Now suppose that holders of convertible bonds convert the bonds into 100,000 shares of stock. The person's 10,000 shares would then equal only 1.67 percent (10,000 ÷ 600,000) of the outstanding shares. In addition, the added shares outstanding would lower earnings per share and would most likely lower market price per share.

When a company has a complex capital structure, it must report two earnings per share figures: basic earnings per share and diluted earnings per share.[13]

Diluted earnings per share are calculated by adding all potentially dilutive securities to the denominator of the basic earnings per share calculation. This figure shows stockholders the maximum potential effect of dilution on their ownership position. As you can see in Exhibit 13-3, the dilution effect for **Motorola** is not large, only 4 cents per share in 2006 ($1.50 − $1.46) and none in 2007 and 2008 the company's only dilutive securities are a relatively few stock options.

During 2011, Sasha Corporation reported a net income of $1,529,500. On January 1, 2011, Sasha had 350,000 shares of common stock outstanding, and it issued an additional 210,000 shares of common stock on October 1. The company has a simple capital structure.

1. Determine the weighted-average number of common shares outstanding.
2. Compute earnings per share.

SOLUTION

1. Weighted-average number of common shares outstanding:

350,000 shares × 9/12	262,500
560,000 shares × 3/12	140,000
Weighted-average number of common shares outstanding	402,500

2. Earnings per share:
   $1,529,500 ÷ 402,500 Shares = $3.80

Comprehensive Income and the Statement of Stockholders' Equity

LO4 Define *comprehensive income*, and describe the statement of stockholders' equity.

The concept of comprehensive income and the statement of stockholders' equity provide further explanation of the income statement and the balance sheet and serve as links between those two statements.

Comprehensive Income

Some items that are not stock transactions affect stockholders' equity. These items, which come from sources other than stockholders and that account for the change in a company's equity during an accounting period, are called **comprehensive income**. Comprehensive income includes net income, changes in unrealized investment gains and losses, and other items affecting equity, such as foreign currency translation adjustments. The FASB holds that these changes in stockholders' equity should be summarized as income for a period.[14] Companies may report comprehensive income and its components in a separate financial statement, as **eBay** does in Exhibit 13-4, or as a part of another financial statement.

EXHIBIT 13-4 eBay's Statement of Comprehensive Income

	Year Ended December 31		
(In thousands)	2008	2007	2006
Net income	$1,779,474	$1,082,043	$1,125,639
Other comprehensive income			
Foreign currency translation	(553,490)	(140,459)	588,150
Unrealized gains (losses) on investments, net	(464,171)	1,922	8,327
Unrealized gains (losses) on cash flow hedges	40,522	1,297	(194)
Estimated tax provision on above items	179,348	(1,272)	(3,216)
Net change in other comprehensive income	(797,791)	(138,512)	593,097
Comprehensive income	$ 981,683	$ 943,531	$1,718,706

Source: eBay Inc., *Annual Report*, 2008.

In a recent survey of 600 large companies, 579 reported comprehensive income. Of these, 83 percent reported comprehensive income in the statement of stockholders' equity (as in Exhibit 13-5), 13 percent reported it in a separate statement, and only 4 percent reported it in the income statement.[15]

The Statement of Stockholders' Equity

Study Note

The statement of stockholders' equity is a labeled calculation of the change in each stockholders' equity account over an accounting period.

The **statement of stockholders' equity**, also called the *statement of changes in stockholders' equity*, summarizes changes in the components of the stockholders' equity section of the balance sheet. Most companies use this statement in place of the statement of retained earnings because it reveals much more about the stockholders' equity transactions that took place during the accounting period.

For example, in Crisanti Corporation's statement of stockholders' equity in Exhibit 13-5, the first line shows the beginning balance of each account in the stockholders' equity section of the balance sheet. Each subsequent line discloses the effects of transactions on those accounts. Crisanti had a net income of \$540,000 and a foreign currency translation loss of \$20,000, which it reported as accumulated other comprehensive income. These two items together resulted in comprehensive income of \$520,000.

EXHIBIT 13-5 Statement of Stockholders' Equity

Crisanti Corporation
Statement of Stockholders' Equity
For the Year Ended December 31, 2010

	Preferred Stock \$100 Par Value 8% Convertible	Common Stock \$10 Par Value	Additional Paid-In Capital	Retained Earnings	Treasury Stock	Accumulated Other Comprehensive Income	Total
Balance, December 31, 2009	\$800,000	\$600,000	\$ 600,000	\$1,200,000			\$3,200,000
Net income				540,000			540,000
Foreign currency translation adjustment						(\$20,000)	(20,000)
Issuance of 10,000 shares of common stock		100,000	400,000				500,000
Conversion of 2,000 shares of preferred stock to 6,000 shares of common stock	(200,000)	60,000	140,000				—
10 percent stock dividend on common stock, 7,600 shares		76,000	304,000	(380,000)			—
Purchase of 1,000 shares of treasury stock					(\$48,000)		(48,000)
Cash dividends							
Preferred stock				(48,000)			(48,000)
Common stock				(95,200)			(95,200)
Balance, December 31, 2010	\$600,000	\$836,000	\$1,444,000	\$1,216,800	(\$48,000)	(\$20,000)	\$4,028,800

Study Note

The ending balances on the statement of stockholders' equity are transferred to the stockholders' equity section of the balance sheet.

Crisanti's statement of stockholders' equity also shows that during 2010, the firm issued 10,000 shares of common stock for $500,000, had a conversion of $200,000 of preferred stock to common stock, declared and issued a 10 percent stock dividend on common stock, purchased treasury stock for $48,000, and paid cash dividends on both preferred and common stock. The ending balances of the accounts appear at the bottom of the statement. Those accounts and balances make up the stockholders' equity section of Crisanti's balance sheet on December 31, 2010, as shown in Exhibit 13-6.

Retained Earnings

The Retained Earnings column in Exhibit 13-5 has the same components as the statement of retained earnings. As we explained earlier in the text, **retained earnings** represent the claims by stockholders to assets that arise from the earnings of the business. Retained earnings equal a company's profits since its inception, minus any losses, dividends to stockholders, or transfers to contributed capital.

It is important to remember that retained earnings are not the assets themselves. The existence of retained earnings means that assets generated by profitable operations have been kept in the company to help it grow or meet other business needs. A credit balance in Retained Earnings is *not* directly associated with a specific amount of cash or designated assets. Rather, it means that assets as a whole have increased.

Study Note

A *deficit* is a negative (debit) balance in Retained Earnings. It is not the same as a net loss, which reflects a firm's performance in just one accounting period.

Retained Earnings can have a debit balance. Generally, this happens when a company's dividends and subsequent losses are greater than its accumulated profits from operations. In this case, the company is said to have a **deficit** (debit balance) in Retained Earnings. A deficit is shown in the stockholders' equity section of the balance sheet as a deduction from contributed capital.

EXHIBIT 13-6
Stockholders' Equity Section of a Balance Sheet

Crisanti Corporation
Balance Sheet
December 31, 2010

Stockholders' Equity

Contributed capital		
Preferred stock, $100 par value, 8 percent convertible, 20,000 shares authorized, 6,000 shares issued and outstanding		$ 600,000
Common stock, $10 par value, 200,000 shares authorized, 83,600 shares issued, 82,600 shares outstanding	$ 836,000	
Additional paid-in capital	1,444,000	2,280,000
Total contributed capital		$2,880,000
Retained earnings		1,216,800
Total contributed capital and retained earnings		$4,096,800
Less: Treasury stock, common (1,000 shares, at cost)	$ 48,000	
Foreign currency translation adjustment	20,000	68,000
Total stockholders' equity		$4,028,800

Indicate which of the following items would appear on the statement of stockholders' equity:

a. Preferred stock cash dividends
b. Loss on disposal of segment
c. Issuance of common stock
d. Stock dividend
e. Income taxes expense
f. Purchase of treasury stock
g. Income from continuing operations
h. Net income
i. Accumulated other comprehensive income

SOLUTION

a, c, d, f, h, and i would appear on the statement of stockholders' equity.

Stock Dividends and Stock Splits

LO5 Account for stock dividends and stock splits.

Two transactions that commonly modify the content of stockholders' equity are stock dividends and stock splits. In the discussion that follows, we describe how to account for both kinds of transactions.

Stock Dividends

A **stock dividend** is a proportional distribution of shares among a corporation's stockholders. Unlike a cash dividend, a stock dividend involves no distribution of assets, and so it has no effect on a firm's assets or liabilities. A board of directors may declare a stock dividend for the following reasons:

1. To give stockholders some evidence of the company's success without affecting working capital, which would be the case if it paid a cash dividend.
2. To reduce the stock's market price by increasing the number of shares outstanding. (This goal is, however, more often met by a stock split.)
3. To make a nontaxable distribution to stockholders. Stock dividends that meet certain conditions are not considered income and are thus not taxed.
4. To increase the company's permanent capital by transferring an amount from retained earnings to contributed capital.

A stock dividend does not affect total stockholders' equity. Basically, it transfers a dollar amount from retained earnings to contributed capital. The amount transferred is the fair market value (usually, the market price) of the additional shares that the company issues. The laws of most states specify the minimum value of each share transferred, which is normally the minimum legal capital (par or stated value). When stock distributions are small—less than 20 to 25 percent of a company's outstanding common stock—generally accepted accounting principles hold that market value reflects their economic effect better than par or stated value. For this reason, market price should be used to account for small stock dividends.[16]

Study Note

The declaration of a stock dividend results in a reshuffling of stockholders' equity—that is, a portion of retained earnings is converted to contributed capital (by closing the Stock Dividends account). Total stockholders' equity is not affected.

To illustrate how to account for a stock dividend, suppose that stockholders' equity in Rivera Corporation is as follows:

Study Note

For a small stock dividend, the portion of retained earnings transferred is determined by multiplying the number of shares to be distributed by the stock's market price on the declaration date.

Contributed capital	
Common stock, $5 par value, 50,000 shares authorized, 15,000 shares issued and outstanding	$ 75,000
Additional paid-in capital	15,000
Total contributed capital	$ 90,000
Retained earnings	450,000
Total stockholders' equity	$540,000

Now suppose that on February 24, the market price of Rivera's stock is $20 per share, and on that date, its board of directors declares a 10 percent stock dividend to be distributed on March 31 to stockholders of record on March 15. No entry is needed for the date of record (March 15). The entries in journal form for the declaration and distribution of the stock dividend are as follows:

Declaration Date

A = L + SE
−30,000
+ 7,500
+22,500

Date	Account	Debit	Credit
Feb. 24	Stock Dividends	30,000	
	Common Stock Distributable		7,500
	Additional Paid-In Capital		22,500
	Declared a 10 percent stock dividend on common stock, distributable on March 31 to stockholders of record on March 15: 15,000 shares × 0.10 = 1,500 shares 1,500 shares × $20/share = $30,000 1,500 shares × $5/share = $7,500		

Date of Distribution

A = L + SE
−7,500
+7,500

Date	Account	Debit	Credit
Mar. 31	Common Stock Distributable	7,500	
	Common Stock		7,500
	Distributed a stock dividend of 1,500 shares		

This stock dividend permanently transfers the market value of the stock, $30,000, from retained earnings to contributed capital and increases the number of shares outstanding by 1,500.

The Stock Dividends account is used to record the total amount of the stock dividend. When the Stock Dividends account is closed to Retained Earnings at the end of the accounting period, Retained Earnings is reduced by the amount of the stock dividend. The Common Stock Distributable account is credited for the par value of the stock to be distributed (1,500 × $5 = $7,500).

In addition, when the market value is greater than the par value of the stock, the Additional Paid-In Capital account must be credited for the amount by which the market value exceeds the par value. In our example, the total market value of the stock dividend ($30,000) exceeds the total par value ($7,500) by $22,500. On the date of distribution, the Common Stock Distributable account is debited, and the Common Stock account is credited for the par value of the stock ($7,500).

Study Note

Common Stock Distributable is a contributed capital (stockholders' equity) account, not a liability account. When the shares are issued, Common Stock Distributable is converted to the Common Stock account.

Common Stock Distributable is not a liability account because there is no obligation to distribute cash or other assets. The obligation is to distribute additional shares of capital stock. If financial statements are prepared between the declaration date and the date of distribution, Common Stock Distributable should be reported as part of contributed capital:

Contributed capital	
Common stock, $5 par value, 50,000 shares authorized, 15,000 shares issued and outstanding	$ 75,000
Common stock distributable, 1,500 shares	7,500
Additional paid-in capital	37,500
Total contributed capital	$120,000
Retained earnings	420,000
Total stockholders' equity	$540,000

This example demonstrates the following points:

1. Total stockholders' equity is the same before and after the stock dividend.
2. The assets of the corporation are not reduced, as they would be by a cash dividend.
3. The proportionate ownership in the corporation of any individual stockholder is the same before and after the stock dividend.

To illustrate these points, suppose a stockholder owns 500 shares before the stock dividend. After the corporation distributes the 10 percent stock dividend, this stockholder would own 550 shares, as shown in the partial balance sheet that follows.

	Stockholders' Equity	
	Before Dividend	**After Dividend**
Common stock	$ 75,000	$ 82,500
Additional paid-in capital	15,000	37,500
Total contributed capital	$ 90,000	$120,000
Retained earnings	450,000	420,000
Total stockholders' equity	$ 540,000	$540,000
Shares outstanding	15,000	16,500
Stockholders' equity per share	$ 36.00	$ 32.73
	Stockholders' Investment	
Shares owned	500	550
Shares outstanding	15,000	16,500
Percentage of ownership	3⅓%	3⅓%
Proportionate investment ($540,000 × 3⅓%)	$18,000	$ 18,000

Study Note

When a stock dividend greater than 20 to 25 percent is declared, the transfer from retained earnings is based on the stock's par or stated value, not on its market value.

Both before and after the stock dividend, stockholders' equity totals $540,000, and the stockholder owns 3⅓ percent of the company. The proportionate investment (stockholders' equity times percentage of ownership) remains at $18,000.

All stock dividends have an effect on the market price of a company's stock. But some stock dividends are so large that they have a material effect. For example, a 50 percent stock dividend would cause the market price of the stock to drop about 33 percent because the increase is now one-third of shares outstanding. The AICPA has decided that large stock dividends—those greater than 20 to 25 percent—should be accounted for by transferring the par or stated value of the stock on the declaration date from retained earnings to contributed capital.[17]

Stock Splits

> **Study Note**
> Stock splits and stock dividends reduce earnings per share because they increase the number of shares issued and outstanding. Cash dividends have no effect on earnings per share.

A **stock split** occurs when a corporation increases the number of shares of stock issued and outstanding and reduces the par or stated value proportionally. A company may plan a stock split when it wants to lower its stock's market value per share and increase the demand for the stock at this lower price. It may do so if the market price has become so high that it hinders the trading of the stock or if it wants to signal to the market its success in achieving its operating goals.

Nike achieved these strategic objectives in 2009 fiscal year by increasing its cash dividend and declaring a 2-for-1 stock split in fiscal 2007 and increasing its cash dividend.[18] After the stock split, the number of the company's outstanding shares doubled, thereby cutting the share price from about $80 per share to $40 per share. The stock split left each stockholder's total wealth unchanged but increased the income stockholders received from dividends. The stock split was a sign that Nike has continued to do well.

To illustrate a stock split, suppose that Rivera Corporation has 15,000 shares of $5.00 par value stock outstanding and the market value is $70.00 per share. The corporation plans a 2-for-1 split. This split will lower the par value to $2.50 per share and increase the number of shares outstanding to 30,000. A stockholder who previously owned 200 shares of the $5.00 par value stock would own 400 shares of the $2.50 par value stock after the split. When a stock split occurs, the market value tends to fall in proportion to the increase in outstanding shares of stock. For example, Rivera's 2-for-1 stock split would cause the price of its stock to drop by approximately 50 percent, to about $35.00. It would also halve earnings per share and cash dividends per share (unless the board increased the dividend). The lower price and increase in shares tend to promote the buying and selling of shares.

A stock split does not increase the number of shares authorized, nor does it change the balances in the stockholders' equity section of the balance sheet. It simply changes the par value and number of shares issued, both shares outstanding and treasury stock. Thus, an entry is unnecessary. However, it is appropriate to document the change with a memorandum entry in the general journal. For example:

July 15	The 15,000 shares of $5 par value common stock issued and outstanding were split 2 for 1, resulting in 30,000 shares of $2.50 par value common stock issued and outstanding.

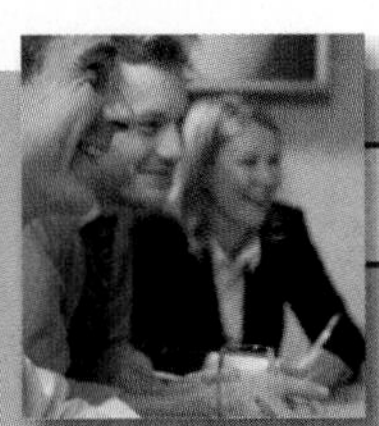

FOCUS ON BUSINESS PRACTICE

Do Stock Splits Help Increase a Company's Market Price?

Stock splits tend to follow the market. When the market went up dramatically in 1998, 1999, and 2000, there were record numbers of stock splits—more than 1,000 per year. At the height of the market in early 2000, stock splitters included such diverse companies as **Alcoa**, **Apple Computer**, **Chase Manhattan**, **Intel**, **NVIDIA**, **Juniper Networks**, and **Tiffany & Co.** Some analysts liken stock splits to the air a chef whips into a mousse: it doesn't make it any sweeter, just frothier. There is no fundamental reason a stock should go up because of a stock split. When **Rambus Inc.**, a developer of high-speed memory technology, announced a four-for-one split on March 10, 2000, its stock rose more than 50 percent, to $471 per share.[19] But when the market deflated in 2001, its stock dropped to less than $10 per share. Research shows that stock splits have no long-term effect on stock prices.

The change for Rivera Corporation is as follows:

Before Stock Split

Contributed capital	
Common stock, $5 par value, 50,000 shares authorized; 15,000 shares issued and outstanding	$ 75,000
Additional paid-in capital	15,000
Total contributed capital	$ 90,000
Retained earnings	450,000
Total stockholders' equity	$540,000

After Stock Split

Contributed capital	
Common stock, $2.50 par value, 50,000 shares authorized, 30,000 shares issued and outstanding	$ 75,000
Additional paid-in capital	15,000
Total contributed capital	$ 90,000
Retained earnings	450,000
Total stockholders' equity	$540,000

Study Note

A stock split affects only the calculation of common stock. In this case, there are twice as many shares after the split, but par value is half of what it was.

Although the per share amount of stockholders' equity is half as much after the split, each stockholder's proportionate interest in the company remains the same.

If the number of split shares will exceed the number of authorized shares, the corporation's board of directors must secure state and stockholders' approval before it can issue the additional shares.

How do stock splits affect stockholders? In a recent year, almost 10 percent of large companies declared stock splits. In most cases, stockholders received one additional share for each share owned (2 for 1). Since there are now twice as many shares, the market value of the stock will drop to about half, and each stockholder's interest in the company will be in the same proportion as before the split. Thus, a stockholder's wealth and ownership interest in the company are not materially affected by a stock split.

Courtesy of Corbis UK – Fancy/Alamy.

Abbie Corporation's board of directors declared a 2 percent stock dividend applicable to the outstanding shares of its $10 par value common stock, of which 1,000,000 shares are authorized, 300,000 are issued, and 100,000 are held in the treasury. It then declared a 2–for-1 stock split on issued shares. How many authorized, issued, and treasury shares existed after each of these transactions? What is the par value per share?

SOLUTION

Stock dividend applies to outstanding shares:
(300,000 shares − 100,000 shares) × 0.02 = 4,000 shares

Stock split applies to all issued shares:
304,000 shares × 2 = 608,000 shares

Authorized shares are unchanged (1,000,000, but par value is now $5 per share); issued shares are 608,000; and outstanding shares are 208,000 (200,000 + 8,000).

Book Value

LO6 Calculate book value per share.

The word *value* is associated with shares of stock in several ways. Par value or stated value is set when the stock is authorized, and it establishes a company's legal capital. Neither par value nor stated value has any relationship to a stock's book value or market value. The **book value** of stock represents a company's total assets less its liabilities. It is simply the stockholders' equity in a company or, to put it another way, it represents a company's net assets. The **book value per share** is therefore the equity of the owner of one share of stock in the net assets of a company. That value, of course, generally does not equal the amount a stockholder receives if the company is sold or liquidated because in most cases, assets are recorded at historical cost, not at their current market value.

If a company has only common stock outstanding, book value per share is calculated by dividing stockholders' equity by the number of common shares outstanding. Common stock distributable is included in the number of shares outstanding, but treasury stock is not. For example, if a firm has total stockholders' equity of $2,060,000 and 58,000 shares outstanding, the book value per share of its common stock would be $35.52 ($2,060,000 ÷ 58,000 shares).

If a company has both preferred and common stock, determining the book value per share is not so simple. Generally, the preferred stock's call value (or par value, if a call value is not specified) and any dividends in arrears are subtracted from stockholders' equity to determine the equity pertaining to common stock. As an illustration, refer to the stockholders' equity section of Crisanti Corporation's balance sheet in Exhibit 13-6. If Crisanti has no dividends in arrears and its preferred stock is callable at $105, the equity pertaining to its common stock would be calculated as follows:

Total stockholders' equity	$4,028,800
Less equity allocated to preferred stockholders (6,000 shares × $105)	630,000
Equity pertaining to common stockholders	$3,398,800

As indicated in Exhibit 13-6, Crisanti has 82,600 shares of common stock outstanding (83,600 shares issued less 1,000 shares of treasury stock). Its book values per share are computed as follows:

Preferred stock: $630,000 ÷ 6,000 Shares = $105 per Share
Common stock: $3,398,800 ÷ 82,600 Shares = $41.15 per Share

If we assume the same facts except that Crisanti's preferred stock is 8 percent cumulative and that one year of dividends is in arrears, the stockholders' equity would be allocated as follows:

Total stockholders' equity		$4,028,800
Less call value of outstanding preferred shares	$630,000	
Dividends in arrears ($600,000 × 0.08)	48,000	
Equity allocated to preferred stockholders		678,000
Equity pertaining to common stockholders		$3,350,800

The book values per share would then be as follows:

Preferred stock: $678,000 ÷ 6,000 Shares = $113 per Share
Common stock: $3,350,800 ÷ 82,600 Shares = $40.57 per Share

STOP & APPLY >

Using the data from the stockholders' equity section of Park Corporation's balance sheet shown below, compute the book value per share for both the preferred and common stock.

Contributed capital	
Preferred stock, $100 par value, 6 percent cumulative, 20,000 shares authorized, 2,000 shares issued and outstanding*	$ 200,000
Common stock, $5 par value, 200,000 shares authorized, 100,000 shares issued and outstanding	500,000
Additional paid-in capital	300,000
Total contributed capital	$1,000,000
Retained earnings	500,000
Total stockholders' equity	$1,500,000

* The preferred stock is callable at $104 per share, and one year's dividends are in arrears.

SOLUTION

Preferred stock book value per share:
$104 + $6 = $110

Common stock book value per share:
[$1,500,000 − (2,000 preferred shares × $110)] ÷ 100,000 common shares = $12.80

A LOOK BACK AT ▸ MOTOROLA, INC.

In this chapter's Decision Point, we observed that in evaluating a company's performance, it is important to look beyond "bottom line" earnings and other common indicators of performance. We pointed out that to gain a proper perspective on a company's performance, one must examine the components of its income statement. Users of **Motorola**'s income statement should ask questions like the following:

- What items other than normal operating activities contributed to Motorola's performance?
- What does the company's income statement indicate about its quality of earnings?
- How does one put the various measures of performance (some of which are shown in Motorola's financial highlights) in perspective?

The astute user of Motorola's income statement, shown in Exhibit 13-2, will take the following into account:

- *Other charges,* which appear in the operating section of Motorola's income statement, were present in all three years. These charges had a material effect on the company's performance in 2008 when they reduced operating income by over $2.3 billion, causing an operating loss. They were also significant in 2007, but less important in 2006.
- Gains on sales of investments and businesses occurred in all three years. Although such gains increase income, they lower the quality of earnings because they are one-time events, and the income they produce will not be sustained in the future. The analyst should therefore ignore them.
- Motorola had earnings from discontinued operations only in 2007 and 2006 fiscal years. Earnings from discontinued operations increase earnings, but these earnings are not likely to be repeated in future years. When a company eliminates unprofitable operations, it does so with the expectation of better results in the future.

To put Motorola's performance in perspective, the company's operating earnings performance has deteriorated significantly over the three-year period. All is not negative though. As may be seen in the Financial Highlights at the beginning of the chapter, Motorola's operations produced decreasing but positive cash flows.

Review Problem

Comprehensive Stockholders' Equity Transactions

LO4 LO5 LO6

The stockholders' equity of Kowalski Company on June 30, 2010, was as follows:

Contributed capital	
Common stock, no par value, $6 stated value, 500,000 shares authorized, 125,000 shares issued and outstanding	$ 750,000
Additional paid-in capital	410,000
Total contributed capital	$1,160,000
Retained earnings	485,000
Total stockholders' equity	$1,645,000

Stockholders' equity transactions in the next fiscal year were as follows:

a. The board of directors declared a 2-for-1 stock split.
b. The board of directors obtained authorization to issue 25,000 shares of $100 par value, 6 percent noncumulative preferred stock, callable at $104.
c. Issued 6,000 shares of common stock for a building appraised at $48,000.

d. Purchased 4,000 shares of the company's common stock for $32,000.
e. Issued 10,000 shares of preferred stock for $100 per share.
f. Sold 2,500 shares of treasury stock for $17,500.
g. Declared cash dividends of $6 per share on preferred stock and $0.20 per share on common stock.
h. Declared a 10 percent stock dividend on common stock to be distributed after the end of the fiscal year. The market value was $10 per share.
i. Closed net income for the year, $170,000.
j. Closed the Dividends and Stock Dividends accounts to Retained Earnings.

Required

1. Record the stockholders' equity components of the preceding transactions in T accounts. Indicate when there is no entry.
2. Prepare the stockholders' equity section of the company's balance sheet on June 30, 2011.
3. Compute the book values per share of common stock on June 30, 2010 and 2011, and of preferred stock on June 30, 2011, using the end-of-year shares outstanding.

Answers to Review Problem

1. Entries in T accounts:

a. No entry (memorandum in journal)
b. No entry (memorandum in journal)

	A	B	C	D	E	F	G	H	I
1		**Preferred Stock**					**Common Stock**		
2			e.	1,000,000				Beg. Bal.	750,000
3								c.	18,000
4								End. Bal.	768,000
5									
6		**Common Stock Distributable**					**Additional Paid-In Capital**		
7			h.	76,350				Beg. Bal.	410,000
8								c.	30,000
9								h.	178,150
10								End. Bal.	618,150
11									
12		**Retained Earnings**					**Treasury Stock**		
13	f.	2,500	Beg. Bal.	485,000		d.	32,000	f.	20,000
14	j.	365,400	i.	170,000		End. Bal.	12,000		
15			End. Bal.	287,100					
16									
17		**Dividends**					**Stock Dividends**		
18	g.	110,900*	j.	110,900		h.	254,500**	j.	254,500
19									
20	*10,000 × $6 =		$ 60,000			**254,500 shares × 0.10 × $10 = $254,500			
21	254,500 × $0.20 =		50,900						
22			$110,900						
23									

2. Stockholders' equity section of the balance sheet:

	A	B	C	D
1		**Kowalski Company**		
2		**Balance Sheet**		
3		**June 30, 2011**		
4				
5		**Stockholders' Equity**		
6	Contributed capital			
7		Preferred stock, $100 par value, 6 percent		
8		noncumulative, 25,000 shares authorized,		
9		10,000 shares issued and outstanding		$ 1,000,000
10		Common stock, no par value, $3 stated value,		
11		500,000 shares authorized, 256,000 shares		
12		issued, 254,500 shares outstanding	$768,000	
13		Common stock distributable, 25,450 shares	76,350	
14		Additional paid-in capital	618,150	1,462,500
15		Total contributed capital		$2,462,500
16	Retained earnings			287,100
17	Total contributed capital and retained earnings			$2,749,600
18	Less: Treasury stock (1,500 shares, at cost)			12,000
19	Total stockholders' equity			$2,737,600
20				

3. Book values:

June 30, 2010
Common Stock: $1,645,000 ÷ 125,000 shares = $13.16 per share
June 30, 2011
Preferred Stock: Call price of $104 per share equals book value per share
Common Stock:
($2,737,600 − $1,040,000) ÷ (254,500 shares + 25,450 shares)
$1,697,600 ÷ 279,950 shares = $6.06 per share (rounded)

LO1 Define *quality of earnings*, and identify the components of a corporate income statement.

The quality of earnings refers to the substance of earnings and their sustainability into future accounting periods. The quality of a company's earnings may be affected by the accounting methods and estimates it uses and by the gains and losses, write-downs and restructurings, and nonoperating items that it reports on its income statement.

When a company has both continuing and discontinued operations, the operating income section of its income statement is called income from continuing operations. Income from continuing operations before income taxes is affected by choices of accounting methods and estimates and may contain gains and losses on the sale of assets, write-downs, and restructurings. The income taxes expense section of the statement is subject to special accounting rules. The lower part of the statement may contain such nonoperating items as discontinued operations and extraordinary gains and losses. Earnings per share information appears at the bottom of the statement.

The reason for considering quality of earnings issues is to assess their effect on cash flows and performance measures. Except for possible income tax effects, gains and losses, asset write-downs, restructurings, and nonoperating items generally have no effect on cash flows. However, quality of earnings issues can affect key performance ratios like profit margin, return on assets, and return on equity because the cash for these items has already been expended.

LO2 Show the relationships among income taxes expense, deferred income taxes, and net of taxes.

Income taxes expense is the tax applicable to income from operations on an accrual basis. Income tax allocation is necessary when there is a material difference between accrual-based accounting income and taxable income—that is, between the income taxes expense reported on the income statement and actual income tax liability. The difference between income taxes expense and income taxes payable is debited or credited to an account called Deferred Income Taxes. The phrase *net of taxes* indicates that taxes have been taken into account in reporting an item in the financial statements.

LO3 Compute earnings per share.

Readers of financial statements use earnings per share to evaluate a company's performance and to compare it with the performance of other companies. Earnings per share of common stock are presented on the face of the income statement. The amounts are computed by dividing the income applicable to common stock by the number of common shares outstanding for the year. If the number of shares outstanding varied during the year, the weighted-average number of common shares outstanding is used in the computation. A company that has a complex capital structure must disclose both basic and diluted earnings per share on the face of its income statement.

LO4 Define *comprehensive income*, and describe the statement of stockholders' equity.

Comprehensive income includes all items from sources other than stockholders that account for changes in stockholders' equity during an accounting period. The statement of stockholders' equity summarizes changes over the period in each component of the stockholders' equity section of the balance sheet. This statement reveals much more than the statement of retained earnings does about the transactions that affect stockholders' equity.

LO5 Account for stock dividends and stock splits. A stock dividend is a proportional distribution of shares among a corporation's stockholders. The following is a summary of the key dates and accounting treatments of stock dividends:

Key Date	Stock Dividend
Declaration date	Debit Stock Dividends for the market value of the stock to be distributed (if the stock dividend is small), and credit Common Stock Distributable for the stock's par value and Additional Paid-In Capital for the excess of the market value over the stock's par value.
Record date	No entry is needed.
Date of distribution	Debit Common Stock Distributable and credit Common Stock for the par value of the stock.

A company usually declares a stock split to reduce the market value of its stock and thereby improve the demand for the stock. Because the par value of the stock normally decreases in proportion to the number of additional shares issued, a stock split has no effect on the dollar amount in stockholders' equity. A stock split does not require an entry in journal form, but a memorandum entry in the general journal is appropriate.

LO6 Calculate book value per share. Book value per share is stockholders' equity per share. It is calculated by dividing stockholders' equity by the number of common shares outstanding. When a company has both preferred and common stock, the call or par value of the preferred stock and any dividends in arrears are deducted from stockholders' equity before dividing by the common shares outstanding.

REVIEW of Concepts and Terminology

The following concepts and terms were introduced in this chapter:

Book value 643 (LO6)

Complex capital structure 634 (LO3)

Comprehensive income 635 (LO4)

Deferred Income Taxes 630 (LO2)

Deficit 637 (LO4)

Discontinued operations 626 (LO1)

Extraordinary items 626 (LO1)

Income from continuing operations 622 (LO1)

Income tax allocation 630 (LO2)

Net of taxes 631 (LO2)

Quality of earnings 622 (LO1)

Restructuring 625 (LO1)

Retained earnings 637 (LO4)

Simple capital structure 634 (LO3)

Statement of stockholders' equity 636 (LO4)

Stock dividend 638 (LO5)

Stock split 641 (LO5)

Write-down 625 (LO1)

Key Ratios

Basic earnings per share 633 (LO3)

Book value per share 643 (LO6)

Diluted earnings per share 634 (LO3)

CHAPTER ASSIGNMENTS

BUILDING Your Basic Knowledge and Skills

Short Exercises

LO1 **Quality of Earnings**

SE 1. Each of the items listed below is a quality of earnings issue. Indicate whether the item is (a) an accounting method, (b) an accounting estimate, or (c) a nonoperating item. For any item for which the answer is (a) or (b), indicate which alternative is usually the more conservative choice.

1. LIFO versus FIFO
2. Extraordinary loss
3. 10-year useful life versus 15-year useful life
4. Straight-line versus accelerated method
5. Discontinued operations
6. Immediate write-off versus amortization
7. Increase versus decrease in percentage of uncollectible accounts

LO1 **Corporate Income Statement**

SE 2. Assume that Jefferson Company's chief financial officer gave you the following information: net sales, $360,000; cost of goods sold, $175,000; loss from discontinued operations (net of income tax benefit of $35,000), $100,000; loss on disposal of discontinued operations (net of income tax benefit of $8,000), $25,000; operating expenses, $65,000; income taxes expense on continuing operations, $50,000. From this information, prepare the company's income statement for the year ended June 30, 2010. (Ignore earnings per share information.)

LO2 **Corporate Income Tax Rate Schedule**

SE 3. Using the corporate tax rate schedule in Table 13-1, compute the income tax liability for taxable income of (1) $800,000 and (2) $40,000,000.

LO3 **Earnings per Share**

SE 4. During 2010, Wells Corporation reported a net income of $1,338,400. On January 1, Wells had 720,000 shares of common stock outstanding. The company issued an additional 480,000 shares of common stock on August 1. In 2010, the company had a simple capital structure. During 2011, there were no transactions involving common stock, and the company reported net income of $1,740,000. Determine the weighted-average number of common shares outstanding for 2010 and 2011. Also compute earnings per share for 2010 and 2011.

LO4 **Statement of Stockholders' Equity**

SE 5. Refer to the statement of stockholders' equity for Crisanti Corporation in Exhibit 13-5 to answer the following questions: (1) At what price per share were the 5,000 shares of common stock sold? (2) What was the conversion price per share of the common stock? (3) At what price was the common stock selling on the date of the stock dividend? (4) At what price per share was the treasury stock purchased?

LO4 LO5 **Effects of Stockholders' Equity Actions**

SE 6. Tell whether the following actions will increase, decrease, or have no effect on total assets, total liabilities, and total stockholders' equity: (1) Declaration of a stock dividend; (2) Declaration of a cash dividend; (3) Stock split; (4) Purchase of treasury stock.

LO5 **Stock Dividends**

SE 7. On February 15, Asher Corporation's board of directors declared a 2 percent stock dividend applicable to the outstanding shares of its $10 par value common stock, of which 400,000 shares are authorized, 260,000 are issued, and 40,000 are held in the treasury. The stock dividend was distributed on March 15 to stockholders of record on March 1. On February 15, the market value of the common stock was $15 per share. On March 30, the board of directors declared a $.50 per share cash dividend. No other stock transactions have occurred. Record, as necessary, the transactions of February 15, March 1, March 15, and March 30.

LO5 **Stock Split**

SE 8. On August 10, 2010, the board of directors of Karton Inc. declared a 3-for-1 stock split of its $9 par value common stock, of which 200,000 shares were authorized and 62,500 were issued and outstanding. The market value on that date was $60 per share, the balance of additional paid-in capital was $1,500,000, and the balance of retained earnings was $1,625,000. Prepare the stockholders' equity section of the company's balance sheet after the stock split. What entry, if any, is needed to record the stock split?

LO6 **Book Value for Preferred and Common Stock**

SE 9. Using data from Soong Corporation's partial balance sheet below, compute the book value per share for both the preferred and the common stock.

Contributed capital	
Preferred stock, $100 par value, 8 percent cumulative, 20,000 shares authorized, 1,000 shares issued and outstanding*	$ 100,000
Common stock, $10 par value, 200,000 shares authorized, 80,000 shares issued and outstanding	800,000
Additional paid-in capital	1,032,000
Total contributed capital	$1,932,000
Retained earnings	550,000
Total stockholders' equity	$2,482,000

*The preferred stock is callable at $108 per share, and one year's dividends are in arrears.

Exercises

LO1 LO2 **Discussion Questions**

E 1. Develop brief answers to each of the following questions:

1. In what way is selling an investment for a gain potentially a negative in evaluating quality of earnings?
2. Is it unethical for new management to take an extra large write-off (a "big bath") in order to reduce future costs? Why or why not?
3. What is an argument against the recording of deferred income taxes?
4. Why is it useful to disclose discontinued operations separately on the income statement?

LO3 LO4 LO5 LO6 **Discussion Questions**

E 2. Develop brief answers to each of the following questions:

1. What is one way a company can improve its earnings per share without improving its earnings or net income?
2. Why is comprehensive income a part of stockholders' equity?

3. Upon receiving shares of stock from a stock dividend, why should the stockholder not consider the value of the stock as income?
4. What is the effect of a stock dividend or a stock split on book value per share?

LO1 **Effect of Alternative Accounting Methods**

E 3. At the end of its first year of operations, a company calculated its ending merchandise inventory according to three different accounting methods, as follows: FIFO, $95,000; average-cost, $90,000; LIFO, $86,000. If the company used the average-cost method, its net income for the year would be $34,000.

1. Determine net income if the company used the FIFO method.
2. Determine net income if the company used the LIFO method.
3. Which method is more conservative?
4. Will the consistency convention be violated if the company chooses to use the LIFO method? Why or why not?
5. Does the full-disclosure convention require disclosure of the inventory method used in the financial statements?

LO1 **Corporate Income Statement**

E 4. Assume that Cetnar Company's chief financial officer gave you the following information: net sales, $1,900,000; cost of goods sold, $1,050,000; extraordinary gain (net of income taxes of $3,500), $12,500; loss from discontinued operations (net of income tax benefit of $30,000), $50,000; loss on disposal of discontinued operations (net of income tax benefit of $13,000), $35,000; selling expenses, $50,000; administrative expenses, $40,000; income taxes expense on continuing operations, $300,000. From this information, prepare the company's income statement for the year ended June 30, 2010. (Ignore earnings per share information.)

LO1 **Corporate Income Statement**

E 5. The items below are components of Patel Company's income statement for the year ended December 31, 2010. Recast the income statement in proper multistep form, including allocating income taxes to appropriate items (assume a 30 percent income tax rate) and showing earnings per share figures (100,000 shares outstanding).

Sales	$555,000
Cost of goods sold	(275,000)
Operating expenses	(112,500)
Restructuring	(55,000)
Total income taxes expense for period	(89,550)
Income from discontinued operations	80,000
Gain on disposal of discontinued operations	70,000
Extraordinary gain	36,000
Net income	$208,950
Earnings per share	$ 2.09

LO2 **Corporate Income Tax Rate Schedule**

E 6. Using the corporate tax rate schedule in Table 13-1, compute the income tax liability for the following situations:

Situation	Taxable Income
A	$ 70,000
B	85,000
C	320,000

LO2 **Income Tax Allocation**

E 7. Fabio Corporation's income statement showed the following data for 2009 and 2010:

	2010	2009
Income before income taxes	$280,000	$280,000
Income taxes expense	88,300	88,300
Net income	$191,700	$191,700

On the balance sheet, deferred income taxes liability increased by $38,400 in 2009 and decreased by $18,800 in 2010.

1. How much did Fabio actually pay in income taxes for 2009 and 2010?
2. Prepare entries in journal form to record income taxes expense for 2009 and 2010.

LO3 **Earnings per Share**

E 8. During 2009, Arthur Corporation reported a net income of $3,059,000. On January 1, Arthur had 2,800,000 shares of common stock outstanding. The company issued an additional 1,680,000 shares of common stock on October 1. In 2009, the company had a simple capital structure. During 2010, there were no transactions involving common stock, and the company reported net income of $4,032,000.

1. Determine the weighted-average number of common shares outstanding each year.
2. Compute earnings per share for each year.

LO4 **Statement of Stockholders' Equity**

E 9. The stockholders' equity section of Erich Corporation's balance sheet on December 31, 2010, follows.

Contributed capital	
Common stock, $2 par value, 500,000 shares authorized, 400,000 shares issued and outstanding	$ 800,000
Additional paid-in capital	1,200,000
Total contributed capital	$2,000,000
Retained earnings	4,200,000
Total stockholders' equity	$6,200,000

Prepare a statement of stockholders' equity for the year ended December 31, 2011, assuming these transactions occurred in sequence in 2011:

a. Issued 10,000 shares of $100 par value, 9 percent cumulative preferred stock at par after obtaining authorization from the state.
b. Issued 40,000 shares of common stock in connection with the conversion of bonds having a carrying value of $600,000.
c. Declared and issued a 2 percent common stock dividend. The market value on the date of declaration was $14 per share.
d. Purchased 10,000 shares of common stock for the treasury at a cost of $16 per share.
e. Earned net income of $460,000.
f. Declared and paid the full year's dividend on preferred stock and a dividend of $0.40 per share on common stock outstanding at the end of the year.
g. Had foreign currency translation adjustment of minus $100,000.

LO5 **Entries: Stock Dividends**

E 10. Snols Company has 30,000 shares of its $1 par value common stock outstanding. Record in journal form the following transactions as they relate to the company's common stock:

July	17	Declared a 10 percent stock dividend on common stock to be distributed on August 10 to stockholders of record on July 31. Market value of the stock was $5 per share on this date.
	31	Date of record.
Aug.	10	Distributed the stock dividend declared on July 17.
Sept.	1	Declared a $0.50 per share cash dividend on common stock to be paid on September 16 to stockholders of record on September 10.

LO5 **Stock Split**

E 11. Fernandez Company currently has 500,000 shares of $1 par value common stock authorized with 200,000 shares outstanding. The board of directors declared a 2-for-1 split on May 15, 2010, when the market value of the common stock was $2.50 per share. The retained earnings balance on May 15 was $700,000. Additional paid-in capital on this date was $20,000. Prepare the stockholders' equity section of the company's balance sheet before and after the stock split. What entry, if any, would be necessary to record the stock split?

LO5 **Stock Split**

E 12. On January 15, 2010, the board of directors of Tower International declared a 3-for-1 stock split of its $12 par value common stock, of which 3,200,000 shares were authorized and 800,000 were issued and outstanding. The market value on that date was $45 per share. On the same date, the balance of additional paid-in capital was $16,000,000, and the balance of retained earnings was $32,000,000. Prepare the stockholders' equity section of the company's balance sheet before and after the stock split. What entry, if any, is needed to record the stock split?

LO6 **Book Value for Preferred and Common Stock**

E 13. Below is the stockholders' equity section of Hegel Corporation's balance sheet. Determine the book value per share for both the preferred and the common stock.

Contributed capital	
Preferred stock, $100 per share, 6 percent cumulative, 10,000 shares authorized, 200 shares issued and outstanding*	$ 20,000
Common stock, $5 par value, 100,000 shares authorized, 10,000 shares issued, 9,000 shares outstanding	50,000
Additional paid-in capital	28,000
Total contributed capital	$ 98,000
Retained earnings	95,000
Total contributed capital and retained earnings	$193,000
Less: Treasury stock, common (1,000 shares at cost)	15,000
Total stockholders' equity	$178,000

*The preferred stock is callable at $105 per share, and one year's dividends are in arrears.

Problems

LO1 **Effect of Alternative Accounting Methods**

P 1. Matka Company began operations in 2010. At the beginning of the year, the company purchased plant assets of $450,000, with an estimated useful life of ten years and no residual value. During the year, the company had net sales of $650,000, salaries expense of $100,000, and other expenses of $40,000, excluding depreciation. In addition, Matka Company purchased inventory as follows:

Jan. 15	200 units at $400	$ 80,000
Mar. 20	100 units at $408	40,800
June 15	400 units at $416	166,400
Sept. 18	300 units at $412	123,600
Dec. 9	150 units at $420	63,000
Total	1,150 units	$473,800

At the end of the year, a physical inventory disclosed 250 units still on hand. The managers of Matka Company know they have a choice of accounting methods, but they are unsure how those methods will affect net income. They have heard of the FIFO and LIFO inventory methods and the straight-line and double-declining-balance depreciation methods.

Required

1. Prepare two income statements for Matka Company, one using the FIFO and straight-line methods and the other using the LIFO and double-declining-balance methods. Ignore income taxes.
2. Prepare a schedule accounting for the difference in the two net income figures obtained in requirement **1**.

User insight ▶ 3. What effect does the choice of accounting method have on Matka's inventory turnover? What conclusions can you draw? Use the year-end balance to compute the ratio.

User insight ▶ 4. How does the choice of accounting methods affect Matka's return on assets? Assume the company's only assets are cash of $40,000, inventory, and plant assets. Use year-end balances to compute the ratios. Is your evaluation of Matka's profitability affected by the choice of accounting methods?

LO1 LO2 LO3 **Corporate Income Statement**

P 2. Information concerning operations of Camping Gear Corporation during 2010 is as follows:

a. Administrative expenses, $90,000
b. Cost of goods sold, $420,000
c. Extraordinary loss from an earthquake (net of taxes, $36,000), $60,000
d. Sales (net), $900,000
e. Selling expenses, $80,000
f. Income taxes expense applicable to continuing operations, $105,000

Required

1. Prepare the corporation's income statement for the year ended December 31, 2010, including earnings per share information. Assume a weighted average of 50,000 common shares outstanding during the year.

User insight ▶ 2. Which item in Camping Gear Corporation's income statement affects the company's quality of earnings? Why does it have an effect on quality of earnings?

LO1 LO2 LO3

Corporate Income Statement and Evaluation of Business Operations

P 3. During 2010, Vitos Corporation engaged in two complex transactions to improve the business—selling off a division and retiring bonds. The company has always issued a simple single-step income statement, and the accountant has accordingly prepared the December 31 year-end income statements for 2009 and 2010, as shown below.

Vitos Corporation
Income Statements
For the Years Ended December 31, 2010 and 2009

	2010	**2009**
Net sales	$ 2,000,000	$ 2,400,000
Cost of goods sold	(1,100,000)	(1,200,000)
Operating expenses	(450,000)	(300,000)
Income taxes expense	(358,200)	(270,000)
Income from operations of a discontinued segment	320,000	
Gain on disposal of discontinued segment	280,000	
Extraordinary gain on retirement of bonds	144,000	
Net income	$ 835,800	$ 630,000
Earnings per share	$ 2.09	$ 1.58

Joseph Vitos, the president of Vitos Corporation, is pleased to see that both net income and earnings per share increased by almost 33 percent from 2009 to 2010 and he intends to announce to the company's stockholders that the plan to improve the business has been successful.

Required

1. Recast the 2010 and 2009 income statements in proper multistep form, including allocating income taxes to appropriate items (assume a 30 percent income tax rate) and showing earnings per share figures (400,000 shares outstanding).

User insight ▶

2. What is your assessment of Vitos Corporation's plan and business operations in 2010?

LO4 LO5

Dividends, Stock Splits, and Stockholders' Equity

P 4. The stockholders' equity section of Lim Mills, Inc., as of December 31, 2009, was as follows:

Contributed capital	
Common stock, $3 par value, 1,000,000 shares authorized, 80,000 shares issued and outstanding	$240,000
Additional paid-in capital	75,000
Total contributed capital	$315,000
Retained earnings	240,000
Total stockholders' equity	$555,000

A review of the stockholders' equity records of Lim Mills, Inc., disclosed the following transactions during 2010:

Mar.	25	The board of directors declared a 5 percent stock dividend to stockholders of record on April 20 to be distributed on May 1. The market value of the common stock was $21 per share.
Apr.	20	Date of record for stock dividend.
May	1	Issued stock dividend.
Sept.	10	Declared a 3-for-1 stock split.
Dec.	15	Declared a 10 percent stock dividend to stockholders of record on January 15 to be distributed on February 15. The market price on this date is $9 per share.

Required

1. Record the stockholders' equity components of the transactions for Lim Mills, Inc., in T accounts.
2. Prepare the stockholders' equity section of the company's balance sheet as of December 31, 2010. Assume net income for 2010 is $494,000.

User insight ▶

3. If you owned 2,000 shares of Lim Mills stock on March 1, 2010, how many shares would you own on February 15, 2011? Would your proportionate share of the ownership of the company be different on the latter date than it was on the former date? Explain your answer.

LO4 LO5 LO6

Comprehensive Stockholders' Equity Transactions

KA K/R KLOOSTER & ALLEN

P 5. On December 31, 2010, the stockholders' equity section of Koval Company's balance sheet appeared as follows:

Contributed capital	
Common stock, $8 par value, 400,000 shares authorized, 120,000 shares issued and outstanding	$ 960,000
Additional paid-in capital	2,560,000
Total contributed capital	$3,520,000
Retained earnings	1,648,000
Total stockholders' equity	$5,168,000

The following are selected transactions involving stockholders' equity in 2011:

Jan.	4	The board of directors obtained authorization for 40,000 shares of $40 par value noncumulative preferred stock that carried an indicated dividend rate of $4 per share and was callable at $42 per share.
	14	The company sold 24,000 shares of the preferred stock at $40 per share and issued another 4,000 in exchange for a building valued at $160,000.
Mar.	8	The board of directors declared a 2-for-1 stock split on the common stock.
Apr.	20	After the stock split, the company purchased 6,000 shares of common stock for the treasury at an average price of $12 per share.
May	4	The company sold 2,000 of the shares purchased on April 20, at an average price of $16 per share.
July	15	The board of directors declared a cash dividend of $4 per share on the preferred stock and $0.40 per share on the common stock.

July 25	Date of record.
Aug. 15	Paid the cash dividend.
Nov. 28	The board of directors declared a 15 percent stock dividend when the common stock was selling for $20 per share to be distributed on January 5 to stockholders of record on December 15.
Dec. 15	Date of record for the stock dividend.

Required

1. Record the above transactions in journal form.
2. Prepare the stockholders' equity section of the company's balance sheet as of December 31, 2011. Net loss for 2011 was $436,000. (**Hint**: Use T accounts to keep track of transactions.)

User insight ▶ 3. Compute the book value per share for preferred and common stock (including common stock distributable) on December 31, 2010 and 2011, using end-of-year shares outstanding. What effect would you expect the change in book value to have on the market price per share of the company's stock?

Alternate Problems

LO4 LO5 Dividends and Stock Split Transactions and Stockholder's Equity

P 6. The stockholders' equity section of Acerin Moving and Storage Company's balance sheet as of December 31, 2010, appears below.

Contributed capital	
Common stock, $2 par value, 6,000,000 shares authorized, 1,000,000 shares issued and outstanding	$2,000,000
Additional paid-in capital	800,000
Total contributed capital	$2,800,000
Retained earnings	2,160,000
Total stockholders' equity	$4,960,000

The company engaged in the following stockholders' equity transactions during 2010:

Mar. 5	Declared a $0.40 per share cash dividend to be paid on April 6 to stockholders of record on March 20.
20	Date of record.
Apr. 6	Paid the cash dividend.
June 17	Declared a 10 percent stock dividend to be distributed August 17 to stockholders of record on August 5. The market value of the stock was $14 per share.
Aug. 5	Date of record for the stock dividend.
17	Distributed the stock dividend.
Oct. 2	Split its stock 2 for 1.
Dec. 27	Declared a cash dividend of $0.20 payable January 27, 2011, to stockholders of record on January 14, 2011.

Required

1. Record the 2010 transactions in journal form.
2. Prepare the stockholders' equity section of Acerin Moving and Storage Company's balance sheet as of December 31, 2010. Assume net income for the year is $800,000.

User insight ▶ 3. If you owned some shares of Acerin, would you expect the total value of your shares to go up or down as a result of the stock dividends and stock split? What intangibles might affect the stock value?

LO1 LO2 LO3

Corporate Income Statement

P 7. Income statement information for Nguyen Corporation in 2009 is as follows:

a. Administrative expenses, $110,000
b. Cost of goods sold, $440,000
c. Extraordinary loss from a storm (net of taxes, $10,000), $20,000
d. Income taxes expense, continuing operations, $42,000
e. Net sales, $890,000
f. Selling expenses, $190,000

Required

1. Prepare Nguyen Corporation's income statement for 2009, including earnings per share, assuming a weighted average of 100,000 shares of common stock outstanding for 2009.

User insight ▶ 2. Which item in Nguyen Corporation's income statement affects the company's quality of earnings? Why does it have this effect?

LO4 LO5 LO6

Comprehensive Stockholders' Equity Transactions

P 8. On December 31, 2010, the stockholders' equity section of Tsang Company's balance sheet appeared as follows:

Contributed capital	
Common stock, $8 par value, 200,000 shares authorized, 60,000 shares issued and outstanding	$ 480,000
Additional paid-in capital	1,280,000
Total contributed capital	$1,760,000
Retained earnings	824,000
Total stockholders' equity	$2,584,000

The following are selected transactions involving stockholders' equity in 2011: On January 4, the board of directors obtained authorization for 20,000 shares of $40 par value noncumulative preferred stock that carried an indicated dividend rate of $4 per share and was callable at $42 per share. On January 14, the company sold 12,000 shares of the preferred stock at $40 per share and issued another 2,000 in exchange for a building valued at $80,000. On March 8, the board of directors declared a 2-for-1 stock split on the common stock. On April 20, after the stock split, the company purchased 3,000 shares of common stock for the treasury at an average price of $12 per share; 1,000 of these shares subsequently were sold on May 4 at an average price of $16 per share. On July 15, the board of directors declared a cash dividend of $4 per share on the preferred stock and $.40 per share on the common stock. The date of record was July 25. The dividends were paid on August 15.

The board of directors declared a 15 percent stock dividend on November 28, when the common stock was selling for $20. The date of record for the stock dividend was December 15, and the dividend was to be distributed on January 5.

Required

1. Record the above transactions in journal form.
2. Prepare the stockholders' equity section of the company's balance sheet as of December 31, 2011. Net loss for 2011 was $218,000. (**Hint**: Use T accounts to keep track of transactions.)

User insight ▶

3. Compute the book value per share for preferred and common stock (including common stock distributable) on December 31, 2010 and 2011, using end-of-year shares outstanding. What effect would you expect the change in book value to have on the market price per share of the company's stock?

LO1 **Effect of Alternative Accounting Methods**

P 9. Zeigler Company began operations in 2010. At the beginning of the year, the company purchased plant assets of $900,000, with an estimated useful life of ten years and no residual value. During the year, the company had net sales of $1,300,000, salaries expense of $200,000, and other expenses of $80,000, excluding depreciation. In addition, Zeigler Company purchased inventory as follows:

Jan. 15	400 units at $400	$160,000
Mar. 20	200 units at $408	81,600
June 15	800 units at $416	332,800
Sept. 18	600 units at $412	247,200
Dec. 9	300 units at $420	126,000
Total	2,300 units	$947,600

At the end of the year, a physical inventory disclosed 500 units still on hand. The managers of Zeigler Company know they have a choice of accounting methods, but they are unsure how those methods will affect net income. They have heard of the FIFO and LIFO inventory methods and the straight-line and double-declining-balance depreciation methods.

Required

1. Prepare two income statements for Zeigler Company, one using the FIFO and straight-line methods and the other using the LIFO and double-declining-balance methods. Ignore income taxes.
2. Prepare a schedule accounting for the difference in the two net income figures obtained in requirement **1**.

User insight ▶

3. What effect does the choice of accounting method have on Zeigler's inventory turnover? What conclusions can you draw? Use the year-end balance to compute the ratio.

User insight ▶

4. How does the choice of accounting methods affect Zeigler's return on assets? Assume the company's only assets are cash of $80,000, inventory, and plant assets. Use year-end balances to compute the ratios. Is your evaluation of Zeigler's profitability affected by the choice of accounting methods?

ENHANCING Your Knowledge, Skills, and Critical Thinking

LO5 **Stock Split**

C 1. When **Croc's**, the shoe company, reported in early 2007 that its first quarter earnings had increased from the previous year, its stock price jumped to over $80 per share. At the same time, the company announced a 2-for-1 stock split.[20] What is a stock split and what effect does it have on the company's stockholders' equity? What effect will it likely have on the market value of the company's stock? In light of your answers, do you think the stock split is positive for the company and for its stockholders?

LO1 **Classic Quality of Earnings Case**

C 2. On Tuesday, January 19, 1988, **IBM** reported greatly increased earnings for the fourth quarter of 1987. Despite this reported gain in earnings, the price of IBM's stock on the New York Stock Exchange declined by $6 per share to $111.75. In sympathy with this move, most other technology stocks also declined.[21]

IBM's fourth-quarter net earnings rose from $1.39 billion, or $2.28 a share, to $2.08 billion, or $3.47 a share, an increase of 49.6 percent and 52.2 percent over the same period a year earlier. Management declared that these results demonstrated the effectiveness of IBM's efforts to become more competitive and that, despite the economic uncertainties of 1988, the company was planning for growth.

The apparent cause of the stock price decline was that the huge increase in income could be traced to nonrecurring gains. Investment analysts pointed out that IBM's high earnings stemmed primarily from such factors as a lower tax rate. Despite most analysts' expectations of a tax rate between 40 and 42 percent, IBM's was a low 36.4 percent, down from the previous year's 45.3 percent. Analysts were also disappointed in IBM's revenue growth. Revenues within the United States were down, and much of the company's growth in revenues came through favorable currency translations, increases that might not be repeated. In fact, some estimates of IBM's fourth-quarter earnings attributed $0.50 per share to currency translations and another $0.25 to tax-rate changes.

Other factors contributing to IBM's rise in earnings were one-time transactions, such as the sale of Intel Corporation stock and bond redemptions, along with a corporate stock buyback program that reduced the amount of stock outstanding in the fourth quarter by 7.4 million shares.

The analysts were concerned about the quality of IBM's earnings. Identify four quality of earnings issues reported in the case and the analysts' concern about each. In percentage terms, what is the impact of the currency changes on fourth-quarter earnings? Comment on management's assessment of IBM's performance. Do you agree with management? (Optional question: What has IBM's subsequent performance been?) Be prepared to discuss your answers in class.

LO1 LO4 **Interpretation of Statement of Stockholders' Equity**

C 3. The consolidated statement of stockholders' equity for Jackson Electronics, Inc., a manufacturer of a broad line of electrical components, is presented on the next page. It has nine summary transactions.

Jackson Electronics, Inc.
Consolidated Statement of Stockholders' Equity
For the Year Ended September 30, 2011
(In thousands)

	Preferred Stock	Common Stock	Additional Paid-In Capital	Retained Earnings	Treasury Stock, Common	Accumulated Other Comprehensive Income	Total
Balance at September 30, 2010	$2,756	$3,902	$14,149	$119,312	($ 942)		$139,177
(1) Net income				18,753			18,753
(2) Unrealized gain on available for sale securities						$12,000	12,000
(3) Redemption and retirement of preferred stock (27,560 shares)	(2,756)						(2,756)
(4) Stock options exercised (89,000 shares)		89	847				936
(5) Purchases of common stock for treasury (501,412 shares)					(12,552)		(12,552)
(6) Issuance of common stock (148,000 shares) in exchange for convertible subordinated debentures		148	3,635				3,783
(7) Issuance of common stock (715,000 shares) for cash		715	24,535				25,250
(8) Issuance of 500,000 shares of common stock in exchange for investment in Electrix Company shares		500	17,263				17,763
(9) Cash dividends—common stock ($0.80 per share)				(3,086)			(3,086)
Balance at September 30, 2011	$ —	$5,354	$60,429	$134,979	($13,494)	$12,000	$199,268

1. Show that you understand it by preparing an explanation for each transaction. In each case, if applicable, determine the average price per common share. At times, you will have to make assumptions about an offsetting part of the entry. For example, assume debentures (long-term bonds) are recorded at face value and that employees pay cash for stock purchased under company incentive plans.
2. Define comprehensive income and determine the amount for Jackson Electronics.

LO2 **Analysis of Income Taxes from Annual Report**

C 4. In its 2009 annual report, **Nike, Inc.**, the athletic sportswear company, provided the following data about its current and deferred income tax provisions (in millions):

	2009
Current income taxes due	$ 763.9
Deferred income taxes	(294.1)
Total provision for income taxes	$469.8

1. What were the 2009 income taxes on the income statement? Record in journal form the overall income tax liability for 2009, using income tax allocation procedures.
2. Nike's balance sheet contains both deferred income tax assets and deferred tax liabilities. How do such deferred income tax assets arise? How do such deferred income tax liabilities arise? Given the definition of assets and liabilities, do you see a potential problem with the company's classifying deferred income taxes as a liability? Why or why not?

LO4 LO5 LO6 **Analyzing Effects of Stockholders' Equity Transactions**

K/R

C 5. Kolmeyer Steel Corporation (KSC) is a small specialty steel manufacturer located in northern Alabama. The Kolmeyer family has owned the company for several generations. Robert Kolmeyer is a major shareholder in KSC by virtue of his having inherited 200,000 shares of common stock in the company. Kolmeyer has not shown much interest in the business because of his enthusiasm for archaeology. However, when he received the minutes of the last board of directors meeting, he questioned a number of transactions involving stockholders' equity. He asks you as a person with knowledge of accounting to help him interpret the effect of these transactions on his interest in KSC.

You begin by examining the stockholders' equity section of KSC's December 31, 2010, balance sheet, which appears at the top of the next page. Then you read these relevant parts of the minutes of the board of directors meeting on December 15, 2011:

Item A The president reported the following transactions involving the company's stock during the last quarter:

October 15. Sold 500,000 shares of authorized common stock through the investment banking firm of T.R. Kendall at a net price of $50 per share.

November 1. Purchased 100,000 shares for the corporate treasury from Lucy Kolmeyer at a price of $55 per share.

Item B The board declared a 2-for-1 stock split (accomplished by halving the par value and doubling each stockholder's shares), followed by a 10 percent stock dividend. The board then declared a cash dividend of $2 per share on the resulting shares. Cash dividends are declared on outstanding shares and shares distributable. All these transactions are applicable to stockholders of record on December 20 and are payable on January 10. The market value of KSC stock on the board meeting date after the stock split was estimated to be $30.

Item C The chief financial officer stated that he expected the company to report net income for the year of $4,000,000.

Kolmeyer Steel Corporation
Balance Sheet
December 31, 2010
Stockholders' Equity

Contributed capital	
Common stock, $10 par value, 5,000,000 shares authorized, 1,000,000 shares issued and outstanding	$10,000,000
Additional paid-in capital	25,000,000
Total contributed capital	$35,000,000
Retained earnings	20,000,000
Total stockholders' equity	$55,000,000

1. Prepare a stockholders' equity section of KSC's balance sheet as of December 31, 2011 that reflects the above transactions. (**Hint**: Use T accounts to analyze the transactions. Also use a T account to keep track of the shares of common stock outstanding.)
2. Write a memorandum to Robert Kolmeyer that shows the book value per share and Kolmeyer's percentage of ownership at the beginning and end of the year. Explain the difference and state whether Kolmeyer's position has improved during the year. Tell why or why not and state how Kolmeyer may be able to maintain his percentage of ownership.

LO1 LO4 **Corporate Income Statement and Statement of Stockholders' Equity**

C 6. Refer to the **CVS** annual report in the Supplement to Chapter 1 to answer the following questions:

1. Does CVS have discontinued operations or extraordinary items? Are there any items that would lead you to question the quality of CVS's earnings? Would you say the income statement for CVS is relatively simple or relatively complex? Why?
2. What transactions most often affect the stockholders' equity section of the CVS balance sheet? (**Hint:** Examine the corporation's statements of stockholders' equity.)

LO6 **Book Value and Market Value**

C 7. Refer to the **CVS** annual report and the financial statements for **Southwest Airlines Co.** in the Supplement to Chapter 1. Compute the 2008 and 2007 book value per share for both companies and compare the results to the average stock price of each in the fourth quarter of 2008 as shown in the notes to the financial statements. Southwest's average price per share was $11.01 in 2008 and $13.59 in 2007. How do you explain the differences in book value per share, and how do you interpret their relationship to market prices?

LO5 **Ethics and Stock Dividends**

C 8. For 20 years, Armand Service Corporation, a public corporation that has promoted itself to investors as a stable, reliable company, has paid a cash dividend every quarter. Recent competition from Asian companies has negatively affected the company's earnings and cash flows. As a result, Judy Armand, president of the company, is proposing that the board of directors declare a stock dividend of

5 percent this year instead of a cash dividend. She stated: "This will maintain our consecutive dividend record and will not require any cash outflow." What is the difference between a cash dividend and a stock dividend? Why does a corporation usually distribute either kind of dividend, and how does each affect the financial statements? Is the action that Judy Armand proposed ethical? Why or why not?

LO1 LO3 LO4

Comparison of Comprehensive Income Disclosures

C 9. When the FASB ruled that public companies should report comprehensive income, it did not issue specific guidelines for how this amount and its components should be disclosed. Choose two companies in the same industry. Go to the annual reports on the websites of the two companies you have selected. In the latest annual report, look at the financial statements. How have your two companies reported comprehensive income—as part of the income statement, as part of stockholders' equity, or as a separate statement? What items create a difference between net income and comprehensive income? Is comprehensive income greater or less than net income? Is comprehensive income more volatile than net income? Which measure of income is used to compute basic earnings per share?

CHAPTER

14 The Statement of Cash Flows

Focus on Financial Statements

INCOME STATEMENT

Revenues

– Expenses

= Net Income

STATEMENT OF RETAINED EARNINGS

Opening Balance

+ Net Income

– Dividends

= Retained Earnings

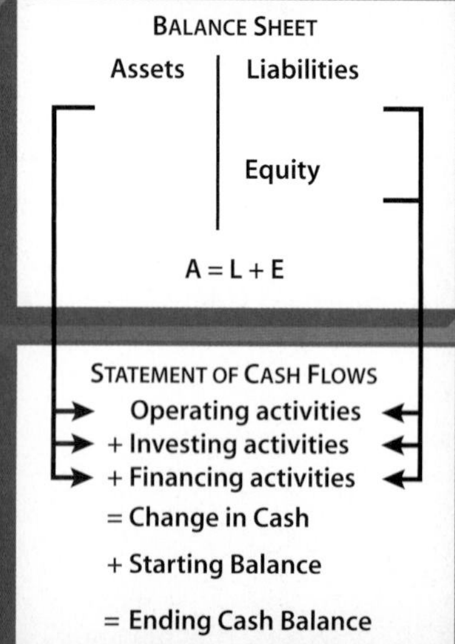

Changes in all noncash balance sheet accounts are used to explain changes in cash.

Cash flows are the lifeblood of a business. They enable a company to pay expenses, debts, employees' wages, and taxes, and to invest in the assets it needs for its operations. Without sufficient cash flows, a company cannot grow and prosper. Because of the importance of cash flows, one must be alert to the possibility that items may be incorrectly classified in a statement of cash flows and that the statement may not fully disclose all pertinent information. This chapter identifies the classifications used in a statement of cash flows and explains how to analyze the statement.

LEARNING OBJECTIVES

LO1 Describe the principal purposes and uses of the statement of cash flows, and identify its components. (pp. 668–673)

LO2 Analyze the statement of cash flows. (pp. 673–677)

LO3 Use the indirect method to determine cash flows from operating activities. (pp. 678–684)

LO4 Determine cash flows from investing activities. (pp. 684–687)

LO5 Determine cash flows from financing activities. (pp. 688–692)

DECISION POINT ► A USER'S FOCUS AMAZON.COM, INC.

- ► Are operations generating sufficient operating cash flows?
- ► Is the company growing by investing in long-term assets?
- ► Has the company had to borrow money or issue stock to finance its growth?

Founded in 1995, **Amazon.com, Inc.**, is now the largest on-line merchandising company in the world and one of the 500 largest companies in the United States. The company's financial focus is on "long-term sustainable growth" in cash flows.

Strong cash flows are critical to achieving and maintaining liquidity. If cash flows exceed the amount a company needs for operations and expansion, it will not have to borrow additional funds. It can use its excess cash to reduce debt, thereby lowering its debt to equity ratio and improving its financial position. That, in turn, can increase the market value of its stock, which will increase shareholders' value.

The Financial Highlights below summarize key components of Amazon.com's statement of cash flows.[1]

AMAZON.COM'S FINANCIAL HIGHLIGHTS:
Consolidated Statement of Cash Flows (In millions)

	2008	2007	2006
Net cash provided by operating activities	$ 1,697	$1,405	$ 702
Net cash provided by (used in) investing activities	(1,199)	42	(333)
Net cash provided by (used in) financing activities	(198)	50	(400)
Foreign currency effects	(70)	20	40
Increase (decrease) in cash and equivalents	$ 230	$1,517	$ 9

Overview of the Statement of Cash Flows

LO1 Describe the principal purposes and uses of the statement of cash flows, and identify its components.

> **Study Note**
> Money market accounts, commercial paper (short-term notes), and U.S. Treasury bills are considered cash equivalents because they are highly liquid, temporary (90 days or less) holding places for cash not currently needed to operate the business.

The **statement of cash flows** shows how a company's operating, investing, and financing activities have affected cash during an accounting period. It explains the net increase (or decrease) in cash during the period. For purposes of preparing this statement, **cash** is defined as including both cash and cash equivalents. **Cash equivalents** are investments that can be quickly converted to cash; they have a maturity of 90 days or less when they are purchased. They include money market accounts, commercial paper, and U.S. Treasury bills. A company invests in cash equivalents to earn interest on cash that would otherwise be temporarily idle.

Suppose, for example, that a company has $1,000,000 that it will not need for 30 days. To earn a return on this amount, the company could place the cash in an account that earns interest (such as a money market account), lend the cash to another corporation by purchasing that corporation's short-term notes (commercial paper), or purchase a short-term obligation of the U.S. government (a Treasury bill).

Because cash includes cash equivalents, transfers between the Cash account and cash equivalents are not treated as cash receipts or cash payments. On the statement of cash flows, cash equivalents are combined with the Cash account. Cash equivalents should not be confused with short-term investments, or marketable securities. These items are not combined with the Cash account on the statement of cash flows; rather, purchases of marketable securities are treated as cash outflows, and sales of marketable securities are treated as cash inflows.

Purposes of the Statement of Cash Flows

The primary purpose of the statement of cash flows is to provide information about a company's cash receipts and cash payments during an accounting period. A secondary purpose is to provide information about a company's operating, investing, and financing activities during the accounting period. Some information about those activities may be inferred from other financial statements, but the statement of cash flows summarizes *all* transactions that affect cash.

Uses of the Statement of Cash Flows

The statement of cash flows is useful to management, as well as to investors and creditors.

- Management uses the statement of cash flows to assess liquidity, to determine dividend policy, and to evaluate the effects of major policy decisions involving investments and financing. Examples include determining if short-term financing is needed to pay current liabilities, deciding whether to raise or lower dividends, and planning for investing and financing needs.
- Investors and creditors use the statement to assess a company's ability to manage cash flows, to generate positive future cash flows, to pay its liabilities, to pay dividends and interest, and to anticipate its need for additional financing.

Classification of Cash Flows

The statement of cash flows has three major classifications: operating, investing, and financing activities. The components of these activities are illustrated in Figure 14-1 and summarized below.

1. **Operating activities** involve the cash inflows and outflows from activities that enter into the determination of net income. Cash inflows in this category include cash receipts from the sale of goods and services and from the sale of

FIGURE 14-1 Classification of Cash Inflows and Cash Outflows

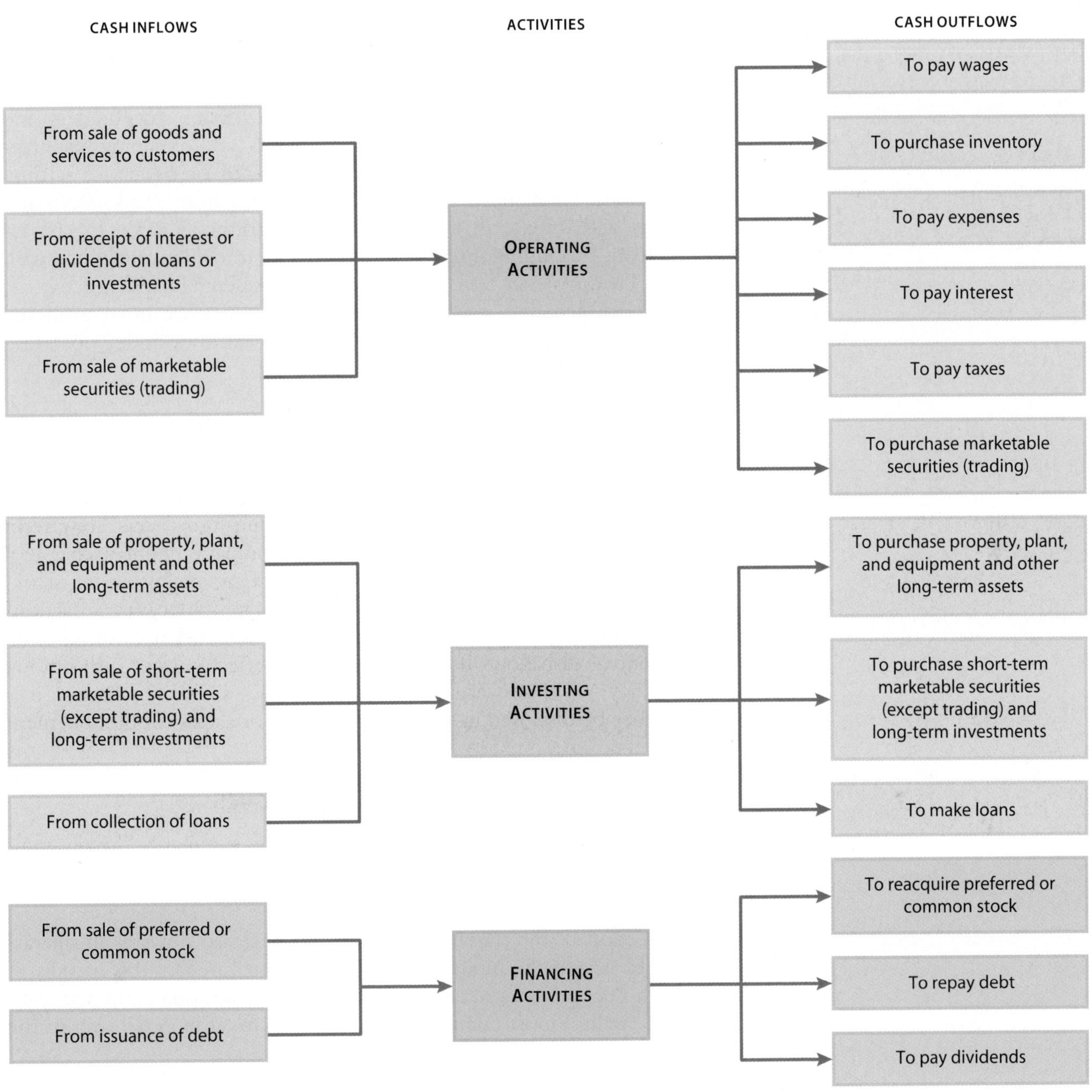

trading securities. Trading securities are a type of marketable security that a company buys and sells for the purpose of making a profit in the near term. Cash inflows also include interest and dividends received on loans and investments. Cash outflows include cash payments for wages, inventory, expenses, interest, taxes, and the purchase of trading securities. In effect, accrual-based income from the income statement is changed to reflect cash flows.

2. **Investing activities** involve the acquisition and sale of property, plant, and equipment and other long-term assets, including long-term investments. They also involve the acquisition and sale of short-term marketable securities, other than trading securities, and the making and collecting of loans.

Study Note

Operating activities involve the day-to-day sale of goods and services, investing activities involve long-term assets and investments, and financing activities deal with stockholders' equity accounts and debt (borrowing).

Cash inflows include the cash received from selling marketable securities and long-term assets and from collecting on loans. Cash outflows include the cash expended on purchasing these securities and assets and the cash lent to borrowers.

3. **Financing activities** involve obtaining resources from stockholders and providing them with a return on their investments, and obtaining resources from creditors and repaying the amounts borrowed or otherwise settling the obligations. Cash inflows include the proceeds from stock issues and from short- and long-term borrowing. Cash outflows include the repayments of loans (excluding interest) and payments to owners, including cash dividends. Treasury stock transactions are also considered financing activities. Repayments of accounts payable or accrued liabilities are not considered repayments of loans; they are classified as cash outflows under operating activities.

Required Disclosure of Noncash Investing and Financing Transactions

Companies occasionally engage in significant **noncash investing and financing transactions**. These transactions involve only long-term assets, long-term liabilities, or stockholders' equity. For instance, a company might exchange a long-term asset for a long-term liability, settle a debt by issuing capital stock, or take out a long-term mortgage to purchase real estate. Noncash transactions represent significant investing and financing activities, but they are not reflected on the statement of cash flows because they do not affect current cash inflows or outflows. They will, however, affect future cash flows. For this reason, it is required that they be disclosed in a separate schedule or as part of the statement of cash flows.

Format of the Statement of Cash Flows

The Financial Highlights at the beginning of the chapter summarize the key components of **Amazon.com**'s statement of cash flows. Exhibit 14-1 presents the full statement.

- The first section of the statement of cash flows is cash flows from operating activities. When the indirect method is used to prepare this section, it begins with net income and ends with cash flows from operating activities. This is the method most commonly used; we discuss it in detail later in the chapter.
- The second section, cash flows from investing activities, shows cash transactions involving capital expenditures (for property and equipment) and loans. Cash outflows for capital expenditures are usually shown separately from cash inflows from their disposal, as they are in Amazon.com's statement. However, when the inflows are not material, some companies combine these two lines to show the net amount of outflow.
- The third section, cash flows from financing activities, shows debt and common stock transactions, as well as payments for dividends and treasury stock.
- A reconciliation of the beginning and ending balances of cash appears at the bottom of the statement. These cash balances will tie into the cash balances of the balance sheets.

EXHIBIT 14-1 Consolidated Statements of Cash Flows

Amazon.com, Inc.
Consolidated Statements of Cash Flows

	For the Years Ended		
(In millions)	**2008**	**2007**	**2006**
Operating Activities			
Net income	$ 645	$ 476	$ 190
Adjustments to reconcile net income to net cash from operating activities:			
Depreciation and amortization	287	246	205
Stock-based compensation	275	185	101
Deferred income taxes	(5)	(99)	22
Excess tax benefits from stock-based compensation	(159)	(257)	(102)
Other	(60)	22	2
Cumulative effect of change in accounting principle	—	—	—
Changes in operating assets and liabilities:			
Inventories	(232)	(303)	(282)
Accounts receivable, net and other	(218)	(255)	(103)
Accounts payable	812	928	402
Accrued expenses and other	247	429	241
Additions to unearned revenue and other	105	33	26
Net cash provided by operating activities	$ 1,697	$ 1,405	$ 702
Investing Activities			
Purchases of fixed assets, including software and website development	$ (333)	$ (224)	$ (216)
Acquisitions, net of cash received and other	(494)	(75)	(32)
Sales and maturities of marketable securities and other investments	1,305	1,271	1,845
Purchases of marketable securities and other investments	(1,677)	(930)	(1,930)
Net cash provided by (used in) investing activities	$(1,199)	$ 42	$ (333)
Financing Activities			
Proceeds from exercises of stock options	$ 11	$ 91	$ 35
Excess tax benefits from exercises of stock options	159	257	102
Common stock repurchased (Treasury stock)	(100)	(248)	(252)
Proceeds from long-term debt and other	87	24	98
Repayments of long-term debt and capital lease obligations	(355)	(74)	(383)
Net cash provided by (used in) financing activities	$ (198)	$ 50	$ (400)
Foreign-currency effect on cash and cash equivalents	$ (70)	$ 20	$ 40
Net (Decrease) Increase in Cash and Cash Equivalents	$ 230	$ 1,517	$ 9
Cash and Cash Equivalents, beginning of year	2,539	1,022	1,013
Cash and Cash Equivalents, end of year	$ 2,769	$ 2,539	$ 1,022

Source: Amazon.com, Inc., *Annual Report*, 2008 (adapted).

FOCUS ON BUSINESS PRACTICE

IFRS

How Universal Is the Statement of Cash Flows?

Despite the importance of the statement of cash flows in assessing the liquidity of companies in the United States, there has been considerable variation in its use and format in other countries. For example, in many countries, the statement shows the change in working capital rather than the change in cash and cash equivalents. Although the European Union's principal directives for financial reporting do not address the statement of cash flows, international accounting standards require it, and international financial markets expect it to be presented. As a result, most multinational companies include the statement in their financial reports. Most European countries adopted the statement of cash flows when the European Union adopted international accounting standards.

Ethical Considerations and the Statement of Cash Flows

Although cash inflows and outflows are not as subject to manipulation as earnings are, managers are acutely aware of users' emphasis on cash flows from operations as an important measure of performance. Thus, an incentive exists to overstate these cash flows.

In earlier chapters, we cited an egregious example of earnings management. As you may recall, by treating operating expenses of about $10 billion over several years as purchases of equipment, **WorldCom** reduced reported expenses and improved reported earnings. In addition, by classifying payments of operating expenses as investments on the statement of cash flows, it was able to show an improvement in cash flows from operations. The inclusion of the expenditures in the investing activities section did not draw special attention because the company normally had large capital expenditures.

Another way a company can show an apparent improvement in its performance is through lack of transparency, or lack of full disclosure, in its financial statements. For instance, securitization—the sale of batches of accounts receivable—is clearly a means of financing, and the proceeds from it should be shown in the financing section of the statement of cash flows. However, because the accounting standards are somewhat vague about where these proceeds should go, some companies net the proceeds against the accounts receivable in the operating section of the statement and bury the explanation in the notes to the financial statements. By doing so, they make collections of receivables in the operating activities section look better than they actually were. It is not illegal to do this, but from an ethical standpoint, it obscures the company's true performance.

STOP & APPLY >

Filip Corporation engaged in the transactions listed below. Identify each transaction as (a) an operating activity, (b) an investing activity, (c) a financing activity, (d) a noncash transaction, or (e) not on the statement of cash flows. (Assume the indirect method is used.)

1. Purchased office equipment.
2. Decreased accounts receivable.
3. Sold land at cost.
4. Issued long-term bonds for plant assets.

(continued)

5. Increased inventory.
6. Issued common stock.
7. Repurchased common stock.
8. Issued notes payable.
9. Increased taxes payable.
10. Purchased a 60-day Treasury bill.
11. Purchased a long-term investment.
12. Declared and paid a cash dividend.

SOLUTION

1. b; 2. a; 3. b; 4. d; 5. a; 6. c; 7. c; 8. c; 9. a; 10. e (cash equivalent); 11. b; 12. c

Analyzing Cash Flows

LO2 Analyze the statement of cash flows.

Like the analysis of other financial statements, an analysis of the statement of cash flows can reveal significant relationships. Two areas on which analysts focus when examining a company's statement of cash flows are cash-generating efficiency and free cash flow.

Can a Company Have Too Much Cash?

Before the bull market ended in 2007, many companies had accumulated large amounts of cash. **ExxonMobil**, **Microsoft**, and **Cisco Systems**, for example, had amassed more than $100 billion in cash. At that time, the average large company in the United States had 7 percent of its assets in cash.

Increased cash can be a benefit or a potential risk. Many companies put their cash to good use. Of course they are wise to have cash on hand for emergencies. They may also invest in productive assets, conduct research and development, pay off debt, buy back stock, or pay dividends. Sometimes, however, shareholders suffer when executives are too conservative and keep the money in low-paying money market accounts or make unwise acquisitions. For the user of financial statements, the lesson is that it is important to look closely at the components of the statement of cash flows to see how management is spending its cash.[2]

Cash-Generating Efficiency

Managers accustomed to evaluating income statements usually focus on the bottom-line result. While the level of cash at the bottom of the statement of cash flows is certainly an important consideration, such information can be obtained from the balance sheet. The focal point of cash flow analysis is on cash inflows and outflows from operating activities. These cash flows are used in ratios that measure **cash-generating efficiency**, which is a company's ability to generate cash from its current or continuing operations. The ratios that analysts use to compute cash-generating efficiency are cash flow yield, cash flows to sales, and cash flows to assets.

In this section, we compute these ratios for **Amazon.com** in 2008 using data for net income and net cash flows from Exhibit 14-1 and the following information from Amazon.com's 2008 annual report. (All dollar amounts are in millions.)

	2008	2007	2006
Net sales	$19,166	$14,835	$10,711
Total assets	8,314	6,485	4,363

Cash flow yield is the ratio of net cash flows from operating activities to net income:

$$\text{Cash Flow Yield} = \frac{\text{Net Cash Flows from Operating Activities}}{\text{Net Income}}$$

$$= \frac{\$1{,}697}{\$645}$$

$$= 2.6 \text{ times*}$$

For most companies, the cash flow yield should exceed 1.0. In 2008, Amazon.com performed much better than this minimum. With a cash flow yield of 2.6 times, Amazon.com generated about $2.60 of cash for every dollar of net income.

The cash flow yield needs to be examined carefully. Keep in mind, for instance, that a firm with significant depreciable assets should have a cash flow yield greater than 1.0 because depreciation expense is added back to net income to arrive at cash flows from operating activities. If special items, such as discontinued operations, appear on the income statement and are material, income from continuing operations should be used as the denominator. Also, an artificially high cash flow yield may result because a firm has very low net income, which is the denominator in the ratio.

Cash flows to sales is the ratio of net cash flows from operating activities to sales:

$$\text{Cash Flows to Sales} = \frac{\text{Net Cash Flows from Operating Activities}}{\text{Sales}}$$

$$= \frac{\$1{,}697}{\$19{,}166}$$

$$= 8.9\%\text{*}$$

Thus, Amazon.com generated positive cash flows to sales of 8.9 percent. Another way to state this result is that every dollar of sales generates 8.9 cents in cash.

Cash flows to assets is the ratio of net cash flows from operating activities to average total assets:

$$\text{Cash Flows to Assets} = \frac{\text{Net Cash Flows from Operating Activities}}{\text{Average Total Assets}}$$

$$= \frac{\$1{,}697}{(\$8{,}314 + \$6{,}485) \div 2}$$

$$= 22.9\%\text{*}$$

At 22.9 percent, Amazon.com's cash flows to assets ratio indicates that for every dollar of assets, the company generates almost 23 cents. This excellent result is higher than its cash flows to sales ratio because of its good asset turnover ratio (sales ÷ average total assets) of 2.6 times (22.9% ÷ 8.9%). Cash flows to sales and cash flows to assets are closely related to the profitability measures of profit margin and return on assets. They exceed those measures by the amount of the cash flow yield ratio because cash flow yield is the ratio of net cash flows from operating activities to net income.

---

*Rounded.

Asking the Right Questions About the Statement of Cash Flows

Most readers of financial statements are accustomed to looking at the "bottom line" to get an overview of a company's financial status. They look at total assets on the balance sheet and net income on the income statement. However, the statement of cash flows requires a different approach because the bottom line of cash on hand does not tell the reader very much; changes in the components of the statement during the year are far more revealing.

In interpreting a statement of cash flows, it pays to know the right questions to ask. To illustrate, let's use **Amazon.com** as an example.

- In our discussion of cash flow yield, we saw that Amazon.com generated about $2.60 of cash from operating activities for every dollar of net income in 2008. What are the primary reasons that cash flows from operating activities differed from net income?

For Amazon.com, the largest positive items in 2008 were accounts payable and depreciation. They are added to net income for different reasons. Accounts payable represents an increase in the amount owed to creditors, whereas depreciation represents a noncash expense that is deducted in arriving at net income. Amazon.com's two largest negative items were increases in inventories and receivables. As a growing company, Amazon.com was managing its operating cycle by generating cash from creditors to pay for increases in inventories and receivables.

- Amazon.com had a large decrease in cash from investing activities in 2008. What were its most important investing activities other than capital expenditures?

The company was managing its investing activities by making active use of investments. Sales of marketable securities and other investments were not sufficient to offset the purchase of marketable securities and other investments and the purchase of various assets; therefore, the cash flow from investing activities was negative.

- Amazon.com's financing activities showed a small decrease in cash in 2008. How did the company manage its financing activities during that fiscal year?

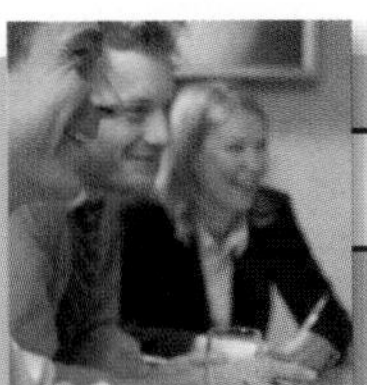

FOCUS ON BUSINESS PRACTICE

Cash Flows Tell All

In early 2001, the telecommunications industry began one of the biggest market crashes in history. Could it have been predicted? The capital expenditures that telecommunications firms must make for equipment, such as cable lines and computers, are sizable. When the capital expenditures (a negative component of free cash flow) of 41 telecommunications companies are compared with their cash flows from sales over the six years preceding the crash, an interesting pattern emerges. In the first three years, both capital expenditures and cash flows from sales were about 20 percent of sales. In other words, operations were generating enough cash flows to cover capital expenditures. Although cash flows from sales in the next three years stayed at about 20 percent of sales, free cash flows turned very negative, and almost half of capital expenditures had to be financed by debt instead of operations, making these companies more vulnerable to the downturn in the economy that occurred in 2001[3] and especially in 2008. The predictive reliability of free cash flow was confirmed in a later study that showed that of 100 different measures, stock price to free cash flow was the best predictor of future increases in stock price.[4]

Construction firms must make large capital expenditures for plant assets, such as the equipment shown here. These expenditures are a negative component of free cash flow, which is the amount of cash that remains after deducting the funds a company needs to operate at its planned level. In 2007, negative free cash flows forced a number of construction firms to rely heavily on debt to finance their capital expenditures, thus increasing their vulnerability to the economic downturn of 2008.

Courtesy R, 2009/Used under license from Shutterstock.com.

Exercise of stock options and the tax effects of stock-based compensation provided funds to buy back treasury stock and pay off some long-term debt, but the inflows were less than the outflows. Because of its good cash flow from operations, Amazon.com did not need long-term financing.

Free Cash Flow

As we noted in an earlier chapter, **free cash flow** is the amount of cash that remains after deducting the funds a company must commit to continue operating at its planned level. If free cash flow is positive, it means that the company has met all of its planned cash commitments and has cash available to reduce debt or to expand. A negative free cash flow means that the company will have to sell investments, borrow money, or issue stock in the short term to continue at its planned level; if a company's free cash flow remains negative for several years, it may not be able to raise cash by issuing stocks or bonds. On the statement of cash flows, cash commitments for current and continuing operations, interest, and income taxes are incorporated in cash flows from current operations.

Amazon.com has a stated primary financial objective of "long-term sustainable growth in free cash flow."[5] The company definitely achieved this objective in 2008. Its free cash flow for this year is computed as follows (in millions):

Study Note

The computation for free cash flow sometimes uses net capital expenditures in place of (Purchases of Plant Assets + Sales of Plant Assets).

Free Cash Flow = Net Cash Flows from Operating Activities − Dividends − Purchases of Plant Assets + Sales of Plant Assets

= \$1,697 − \$0 − \$333 + \$0

= \$1,364

Purchases of plant assets (capital expenditures) and sales (dispositions) of plant assets, if any, appear in the investing activities section of the statement of cash

FOCUS ON BUSINESS PRACTICE

What Do You Mean, "Free Cash Flow"?

Because the statement of cash flows has been around for less than 20 years, no generally accepted analyses have yet been developed. For example, the term *free cash flow* is commonly used in the business press, but there is no agreement on its definition. An article in *Forbes* defines *free cash flow* as "cash available after paying out capital expenditures and dividends, but *before taxes and interest*"[6] [emphasis added]. An article in *The Wall Street Journal* defines it as "operating income less maintenance-level capital expenditures."[7] The definition with which we are most in agreement is the one used in *BusinessWeek*: free cash flow is net cash flows from operating activities less net capital expenditures and dividends. This "measures truly discretionary funds—company money that an owner could pocket without harming the business."[8]

flows. Dividends, if any, appear in the financing activities section. Amazon.com is a growing company and does not have material sales of plant assets and does not pay dividends. The company's positive free cash flow of $1,364 million was due primarily to its strong operating cash flow of $1,697 million. Consequently, the company does not have to borrow money to expand.

Because cash flows can vary from year to year, analysts should look at trends in cash flow measures over several years. It is also important to consider the effect of seasonality on a company's sales. Because Amazon.com's sales peak toward the end of the year, the cash situation at that time may not be representative of the rest of the year. For example, Amazon.com's management states that

> Our cash, cash equivalents, and marketable securities balances typically reach their highest level [at the end of each year.] This operating cycle results in a corresponding increase in accounts payable at December 31. Our accounts payable balance generally declines during the first three months of the year, resulting in a corresponding decline in our cash . . ."[9]

& APPLY >

In 2011, Monfort Corporation had year-end assets of $2,400,000, sales of $2,000,000, net income of $400,000, net cash flows from operating activities of $360,000, dividends of $100,000, purchases of plant assets of $200,000, and sales of plant assets of $50,000. In 2010, year-end assets were $2,200,000. Calculate cash flow yield, cash flows to sales, cash flows to assets, and free cash flow.

SOLUTION

$$\text{Cash Flow Yield} = \frac{\$360{,}000}{\$400{,}000} = 0.9 \text{ times}$$

$$\text{Cash Flows to Sales} = \frac{\$360{,}000}{\$2{,}000{,}000} = 0.18, \text{ or } 18\%$$

$$\text{Cash Flows to Assets} = \frac{\$360{,}000}{(\$2{,}400{,}000 + \$2{,}200{,}000) \div 2} = 0.16, \text{ or } 16\% \text{ (rounded)}$$

$$\text{Free Cash Flow} = \$360{,}000 - \$100{,}000 - \$200{,}000 + \$50{,}000 = \$110{,}000$$

Operating Activities

LO3 Use the indirect method to determine cash flows from operating activities.

CASH FLOW

To demonstrate the preparation of the statement of cash flows, we will work through an example step by step. The data for this example are presented in Exhibit 14-2, which shows Laguna Corporation's income statement for 2010, and in Exhibit 14-3, which shows Laguna's balance sheets for December 31, 2010 and 2009. Exhibit 14-3 shows the balance sheet accounts that we use for analysis and whether the change in each account is an increase or a decrease.

The first step in preparing the statement of cash flows is to determine cash flows from operating activities. The income statement indicates how successful a company has been in earning an income from its operating activities, but because that statement is prepared on an accrual basis, it does not reflect the inflow and outflow of cash related to operating activities. Revenues are recorded even though the company may not yet have received the cash, and expenses are recorded even though the company may not yet have expended the cash. Thus, to ascertain cash flows from operations, the figures on the income statement must be converted from an accrual basis to a cash basis.

There are two methods of accomplishing this:

Study Note

The direct and indirect methods relate only to the operating activities section of the statement of cash flows. They are both acceptable for financial reporting purposes.

- The **direct method** adjusts each item on the income statement from the accrual basis to the cash basis. The result is a statement that begins with cash receipts from sales and interest and deducts cash payments for purchases, operating expenses, interest payments, and income taxes to arrive at net cash flows from operating activities.
- The **indirect method** does not require the adjustment of each item on the income statement. It lists only the adjustments necessary to convert net income to cash flows from operations.

The direct and indirect methods always produce the same net figure. The average person finds the direct method easier to understand because its presentation of operating cash flows is more straightforward than that of the indirect method. However, the indirect method is the overwhelming choice of most companies and accountants. A survey of large companies shows that 99 percent use this method.[10]

EXHIBIT 14-2
Income Statement

Laguna Corporation
Income Statement
For the Year Ended December 31, 2010

Sales		$698,000
Cost of goods sold		520,000
Gross margin		$178,000
Operating expenses (including depreciation expense of $37,000)		147,000
Operating income		$ 31,000
Other income (expenses)		
Interest expense	($23,000)	
Interest income	6,000	
Gain on sale of investments	12,000	
Loss on sale of plant assets	(3,000)	(8,000)
Income before income taxes		$ 23,000
Income taxes expense		7,000
Net income		$ 16,000

EXHIBIT 14-3 Comparative Balance Sheets Showing Changes in Accounts

Laguna Corporation
Comparative Balance Sheets
December 31, 2010 and 2009

	2010	2009	Change	Increase or Decrease
Assets				
Current assets				
Cash	$ 46,000	$ 15,000	$ 31,000	Increase
Accounts receivable (net)	47,000	55,000	(8,000)	Decrease
Inventory	144,000	110,000	34,000	Increase
Prepaid expenses	1,000	5,000	(4,000)	Decrease
Total current assets	$238,000	$185,000	$ 53,000	
Investments	$115,000	$127,000	($ 12,000)	Decrease
Plant assets	$715,000	$505,000	$210,000	Increase
Less accumulated depreciation	(103,000)	(68,000)	(35,000)	Increase
Total plant assets	$612,000	$437,000	$175,000	
Total assets	$965,000	$749,000	$216,000	
Liabilities				
Current liabilities				
Accounts payable	$ 50,000	$ 43,000	$ 7,000	Increase
Accrued liabilities	12,000	9,000	3,000	Increase
Income taxes payable	3,000	5,000	(2,000)	Decrease
Total current liabilities	$ 65,000	$ 57,000	$ 8,000	
Long-term liabilities				
Bonds payable	295,000	245,000	50,000	Increase
Total liabilities	$360,000	$302,000	$ 58,000	
Stockholders' Equity				
Common stock, $5 par value	$276,000	$200,000	$ 76,000	Increase
Additional paid-in capital	214,000	115,000	99,000	Increase
Retained earnings	140,000	132,000	8,000	Increase
Treasury stock	(25,000)	0	(25,000)	Increase
Total stockholders' equity	$605,000	$447,000	$158,000	
Total liabilities and stockholders' equity	$965,000	$749,000	$216,000	

From an analyst's perspective, the indirect method is superior to the direct method because it begins with net income and derives cash flows from operations; the analyst can readily identify the factors that cause cash flows from operations. From a company's standpoint, the indirect method is easier and less expensive to prepare. For these reasons, we use the indirect method in our example.

As Figure 14-2 shows, the indirect method focuses on adjusting items on the income statement to reconcile net income to net cash flows from operating

FIGURE 14-2 Indirect Method of Determining Net Cash Flows from Operating Activities

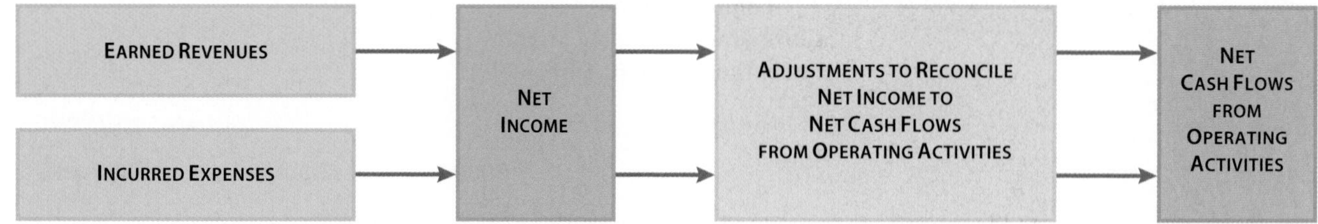

activities. These items include depreciation, amortization, and depletion; gains and losses; and changes in the balances of current asset and current liability accounts. The schedule in Exhibit 14-4 shows the reconciliation of Laguna Corporation's net income to net cash flows from operating activities. We discuss each adjustment in the sections that follow.

Depreciation

> **Study Note**
> Operating expenses on the income statement include depreciation expense, which does not require a cash outlay.

The investing activities section of the statement of cash flows shows the cash payments that the company made for plant assets, intangible assets, and natural resources during the accounting period. Depreciation expense, amortization expense, and depletion expense for these assets appear on the income statement as allocations of the costs of the original purchases to the current accounting period. The amount of these expenses can usually be found in the income statement or in a note to the financial statements. As you can see in Exhibit 14-2, Laguna Corporation's income statement discloses depreciation expense of $37,000, which would have been recorded as follows:

A	= L +	SE
−37,000		−37,000

Depreciation Expense	37,000	
Accumulated Depreciation		37,000
To record annual depreciation on plant assets		

Even though depreciation expense appears on the income statement, it involves no outlay of cash and so does not affect cash flows in the current period. Thus, to arrive at cash flows from operations on the statement of cash flows,

FOCUS ON BUSINESS PRACTICE IFRS

The Direct Method May Become More Important

At present, the direct method of preparing the operating section of the statement of cash flows is not important, but this may change if the International Accounting Standards Board (IASB) has its way. As mentioned earlier in the text, 99 percent of public companies in the United States presently use the indirect method to show the operating activities section of the statement of cash flows. However, in the interest of converging U.S. GAAP with international financial reporting standards (IFRS), the IASB is promoting the use of the direct method, even though it is more costly for companies to prepare. IFRS will continue to require a reconciliation of net income and net cash flows from operating activities similar to what is now done in the indirect method. **CVS**'s statement of cash flows, as shown in the Supplement to Chapter 1, is one of the few U.S. companies to use the direct method with a reconciliation. Thus, its approach is very similar to what all companies may do if IFRS are adopted in the United States.

EXHIBIT 14-4
Schedule of Cash Flows from Operating Activities: Indirect Method

Laguna Corporation
Schedule of Cash Flows from Operating Activities
For the Year Ended December 31, 2010

Cash flows from operating activities		
Net income		$16,000
Adjustments to reconcile net income to net cash flows from operating activities		
Depreciation	$37,000	
Gain on sale of investments	(12,000)	
Loss on sale of plant assets	3,000	
Changes in current assets and current liabilities		
Decrease in accounts receivable	8,000	
Increase in inventory	(34,000)	
Decrease in prepaid expenses	4,000	
Increase in accounts payable	7,000	
Increase in accrued liabilities	3,000	
Decrease in income taxes payable	(2,000)	14,000
Net cash flows from operating activities		$30,000

an adjustment is needed to increase net income by the amount of depreciation expense shown on the income statement.

Gains and Losses

> **Study Note**
> Gains and losses by themselves do not represent cash flows; they are merely bookkeeping adjustments. For example, when a long-term asset is sold, it is the proceeds (cash received), not the gain or loss, that constitute cash flow.

Like depreciation expense, gains and losses that appear on the income statement do not affect cash flows from operating activities and need to be removed from this section of the statement of cash flows. The cash receipts generated by the disposal of the assets that resulted in the gains or losses are included in the investing activities section of the statement of cash flows. Thus, to reconcile net income to cash flows from operating activities (and prevent double counting), gains and losses must be removed from net income.

For example, on its income statement, Laguna Corporation shows a $12,000 gain on the sale of investments. This amount is subtracted from net income to reconcile net income to net cash flows from operating activities. The reason for doing this is that the $12,000 is included in the investing activities section of the statement of cash flows as part of the cash from the sale of the investment. Because the gain has already been included in the calculation of net income, the $12,000 gain must be subtracted to prevent double counting.

Laguna's income statement also shows a $3,000 loss on the sale of plant assets. This loss is already reflected in the sale of plant assets in the investing activities section of the statement of cash flows. Thus, the $3,000 is added to net income to reconcile net income to net cash flows from operating activities.

Changes in Current Assets

Decreases in current assets other than cash have positive effects on cash flows, and increases in current assets have negative effects on cash flows. A decrease in a current asset frees up invested cash, thereby increasing cash flow. An increase in a current asset consumes cash, thereby decreasing cash flow. For example, look at Laguna Corporation's income statement and balance sheets in Exhibits 14-2 and 14-3. Note that net sales in 2010 were $698,000 and that Accounts Receivable decreased by $8,000. Thus, collections were $8,000 more than sales recorded for the year, and the total cash received from sales was $706,000 ($698,000 + $8,000 = $706,000). The effect on Accounts Receivable can be illustrated as follows:

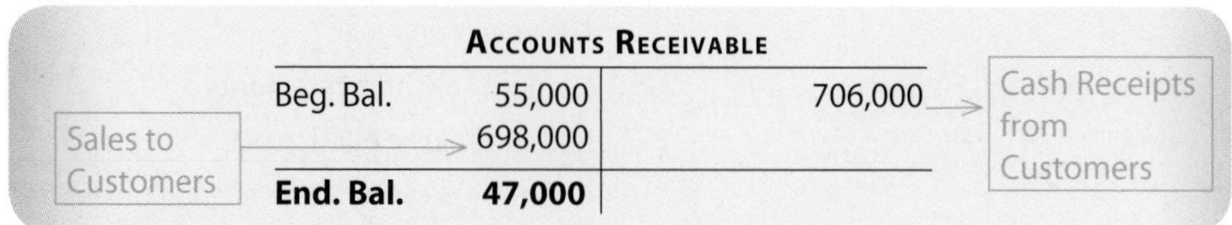

To reconcile net income to net cash flows from operating activities, the $8,000 decrease in Accounts Receivable is added to net income.

Inventory can be analyzed in the same way. For example, Exhibit 14-3 shows that Laguna's Inventory account increased by $34,000 between 2009 and 2010. This means that Laguna expended $34,000 more in cash for purchases than it included in cost of goods sold on its income statement. Because of this expenditure, net income is higher than net cash flows from operating activities, so $34,000 must be deducted from net income. By the same logic, the decrease of $4,000 in Prepaid Expenses shown on the balance sheets must be added to net income to reconcile net income to net cash flows from operations.

Changes in Current Liabilities

The effect that changes in current liabilities have on cash flows is the opposite of the effect of changes in current assets. An increase in a current liability represents a postponement of a cash payment, which frees up cash and increases cash flow in the current period. A decrease in a current liability consumes cash, which decreases cash flow. To reconcile net income to net cash flows from operating activities, increases in current liabilities are added to net income, and decreases are deducted. For example, Exhibit 14-3 shows that from 2009 to 2010, Laguna's accounts payable increased by $7,000. This means that Laguna paid $7,000 less to creditors than the amount indicated in the cost of goods sold on its income statement. The following T account illustrates this relationship:

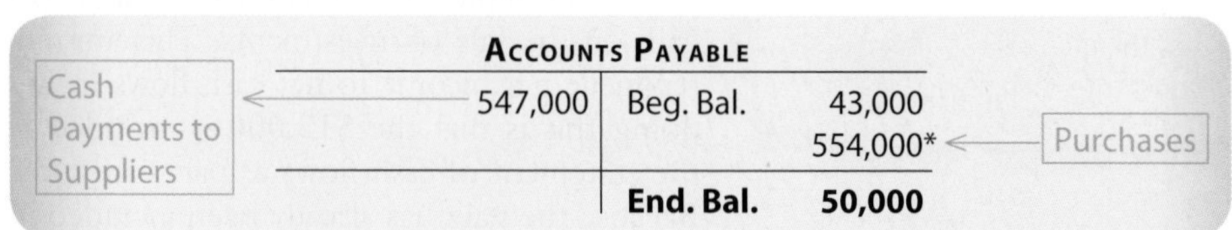

Thus, $7,000 must be added to net income to reconcile net income to net cash flows from operating activities. By the same logic, the increase of $3,000 in accrued liabilities shown on the balance sheets must be added to net income, and the decrease of $2,000 in income taxes payable must be deducted from net income.

---

*Purchases = Cost of Goods Sold ($520,000) + Increase in Inventory ($34,000)

Schedule of Cash Flows from Operating Activities

In summary, Exhibit 14-4 shows that by using the indirect method, net income of $16,000 has been adjusted by reconciling items totaling $14,000 to arrive at net cash flows from operating activities of $30,000. This means that although Laguna's net income was $16,000, the company actually had net cash flows of $30,000 available from operating activities to use for purchasing assets, reducing debts, and paying dividends. The treatment of income statement items that do not affect cash flows can be summarized as follows:

	Add to or Deduct from Net Income
Depreciation expense	Add
Amortization expense	Add
Depletion expense	Add
Losses	Add
Gains	Deduct

The following summarizes the adjustments for increases and decreases in current assets and current liabilities:

	Add to Net Income	*Deduct from Net Income*
Current assets		
Accounts receivable (net)	Decrease	Increase
Inventory	Decrease	Increase
Prepaid expenses	Decrease	Increase
Current liabilities		
Accounts payable	Increase	Decrease
Accrued liabilities	Increase	Decrease
Income taxes payable	Increase	Decrease

FOCUS ON BUSINESS PRACTICE

What Is EBITDA, and Is It Any Good?

Some companies and analysts like to use EBITDA (an acronym for Earnings Before Interest, Taxes, Depreciation, and Amortization) as a short-cut measure of cash flows from operations. But recent events have caused many analysts to reconsider this measure of performance. For instance, when **WorldCom** transferred $3.8 billion from expenses to capital expenditures in one year, it touted its EBITDA; at the time, the firm was, in fact, nearly bankrupt. The demise of **Vivendi**, the big French company that imploded when it did not have enough cash to pay its debts and that also touted its EBIDTA, is another reason that analysts have had second thoughts about relying on this measure of performance.

Some analysts are now saying that EBITDA is "to a great extent misleading" and that it "is a confusing metric.... Some take it for a proxy for profits and some take it for a proxy for cash flow, and it's neither."[11] Cash flows from operations and free cash flow, both of which take into account interest, taxes, and depreciation, are better and more comprehensive measures of a company's cash-generating efficiency.

For the year ended June 30, 2010, Hoffer Corporation's net income was $7,400. Its depreciation expense was $2,000. During the year, its Accounts Receivable increased by $4,400, Inventories increased by $7,000, Prepaid Rent decreased by $1,400, Accounts Payable increased by $14,000, Salaries Payable increased by $1,000, and Income Taxes Payable decreased by $600. The company also had a gain on the sale of investments of $1,800. Use the indirect method to prepare a schedule of cash flows from operating activities.

SOLUTION

Hoffer Corporation
Schedule of Cash Flows from Operating Activities
For the Year Ended June 30, 2010

Cash flows from operating activities		
Net income		$ 7,400
Adjustments to reconcile net income to net cash flows from operating activities		
Depreciation	$ 2,000	
Gain on sale of investments	(1,800)	
Changes in current assets and current liabilities		
Increase in accounts receivable	(4,400)	
Increase in inventories	(7,000)	
Decrease in prepaid rent	1,400	
Increase in accounts payable	14,000	
Increase in salaries payable	1,000	
Decrease in income taxes payable	(600)	4,600
Net cash flows from operating activities		$12,000

Investing Activities

LO4 Determine cash flows from investing activities.

To determine cash flows from investing activities, accounts involving cash receipts and cash payments from investing activities are examined individually. The objective is to explain the change in each account balance from one year to the next.

Although investing activities center on the long-term assets shown on the balance sheet, they also include any short-term investments shown under current assets on the balance sheet and any investment gains and losses on the income statement. The balance sheets in Exhibit 14-3 show that Laguna had no short-term investments and that its long-term assets consisted of investments and plant assets. The income statement in Exhibit 14-2 shows that Laguna had a gain on the sale of investments and a loss on the sale of plant assets.

The following transactions pertain to Laguna's investing activities in 2010:

1. Purchased investments in the amount of $78,000.
2. Sold for $102,000 investments that cost $90,000.
3. Purchased plant assets in the amount of $120,000.
4. Sold for $5,000 plant assets that cost $10,000 and that had accumulated depreciation of $2,000.
5. Issued $100,000 of bonds at face value in a noncash exchange for plant assets.

Study Note

Investing activities involve long-term assets and short- and long-term investments. Inflows and outflows of cash are shown in the investing activities section of the statement of cash flows.

In the following sections, we analyze the accounts related to investing activities to determine their effects on Laguna's cash flows.

Investments

Our objective in this section is to explain Laguna Corporation's $12,000 decrease in investments. We do this by analyzing the increases and decreases in Laguna's Investments account to determine their effects on the Cash account.

Item **1** in the list of Laguna's transactions states that its purchases of investments totaled $78,000 during 2010. This transaction, which caused a $78,000 decrease in cash flows, is recorded as follows:

A	= L +	SE
+78,000		
−78,000		

	Debit	Credit
Investments	78,000	
Cash		78,000
Purchase of investments		

Item **2** states that Laguna sold investments that cost $90,000 for $102,000. This transaction resulted in a gain of $12,000. It is recorded as follows:

A	= L +	SE
+102,000		+12,000
− 90,000		

	Debit	Credit
Cash	102,000	
Investments		90,000
Gain on Sale of Investments		12,000
Sale of investments for a gain		

Study Note

The $102,000 price obtained, not the $12,000 gained, constitutes the cash flow.

The effect of this transaction is a $102,000 increase in cash flows. Note that the gain on the sale is included in the $102,000. This is the reason we excluded it in computing cash flows from operations. If it had been included in that section, it would have been counted twice. We have now explained the $12,000 decrease in the Investments account during 2010, as illustrated in the following T account:

INVESTMENTS

Beg. Bal.	127,000	Sales	90,000
Purchases	78,000		
End. Bal.	**115,000**		

The cash flow effects of these transactions are shown in the investing activities section of the statement of cash flows as follows:

Purchase of investments	($ 78,000)
Sale of investments	102,000

Purchases and sales are listed separately as cash outflows and inflows to give analysts a complete view of investing activity. However, some companies prefer to list them as a single net amount. If Laguna Corporation had short-term investments or marketable securities, the analysis of cash flows would be the same.

Plant Assets

For plant assets, we have to explain changes in both the Plant Assets account and the related Accumulated Depreciation account. Exhibit 14-3 shows that from 2009 to 2010, Laguna Corporation's plant assets increased by $210,000 and that accumulated depreciation increased by $35,000.

Item **3** in the list of Laguna's transactions in 2010 states that the company purchased plant assets totaling $120,000. This entry records the cash outflow:

A	= L	+ SE
+120,000		
−120,000		

Plant Assets	120,000	
Cash		120,000
Purchase of plant assets		

Item **4** states that Laguna Corporation sold plant assets that cost $10,000 and that had accumulated depreciation of $2,000 for $5,000. Thus, this transaction resulted in a loss of $3,000. The entry to record it is as follows:

A	= L	+ SE
+ 5,000		−3,000
+ 2,000		
−10,000		

Cash	5,000	
Accumulated Depreciation	2,000	
Loss on Sale of Plant Assets	3,000	
Plant Assets		10,000
Sale of plant assets at a loss		

Study Note

Even though Laguna had a loss on the sale of plant assets, it realized a positive cash flow of $5,000, which will be reported in the investing activities section of its statement of cash flows. When the indirect method is used, the loss is eliminated with an "add-back" to net income.

Note that in this transaction, the positive cash flow is equal to the amount of cash received, $5,000. The loss on the sale of plant assets is included in the investing activities section of the statement of cash flows and excluded from the operating activities section by adjusting net income for the amount of the loss. The amount of a loss or gain on the sale of an asset is determined by the amount of cash received and does not represent a cash outflow or inflow.

The investing activities section of Laguna's statement of cash flows reports the firm's purchase and sale of plant assets as follows:

Purchase of plant assets	($120,000)
Sale of plant assets	5,000

Cash outflows and cash inflows are listed separately here, but companies sometimes combine them into a single net amount, as they do the purchase and sale of investments.

Item **5** in the list of Laguna's transactions is a noncash exchange that affects two long-term accounts, Plant Assets and Bonds Payable. It is recorded as follows:

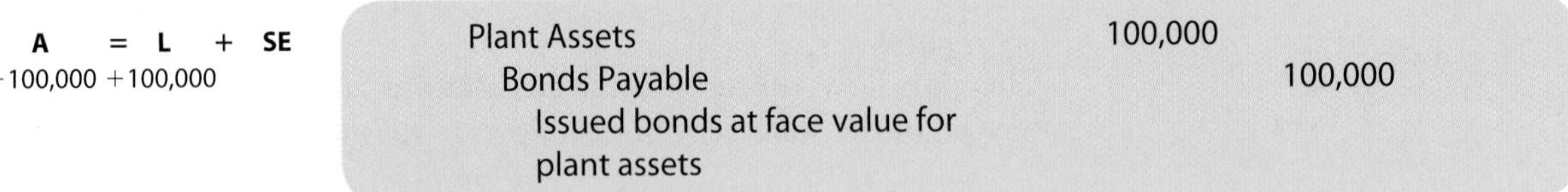

A	= L	+ SE
+100,000	+100,000	

Plant Assets	100,000	
Bonds Payable		100,000
Issued bonds at face value for plant assets		

Although this transaction does not involve an inflow or outflow of cash, it is a significant transaction involving both an investing activity (the purchase of plant assets) and a financing activity (the issue of bonds payable). Because one purpose of the statement of cash flows is to show important investing and financing activities, the transaction is listed at the bottom of the statement of cash flows or in a separate schedule, as follows:

Schedule of Noncash Investing and Financing Transactions

Issue of bonds payable for plant assets	$100,000

We have now accounted for all the changes related to Laguna's plant asset accounts. The following T accounts summarize these changes:

Plant Assets			
Beg. Bal.	505,000	Sales	10,000
Cash Purchase	120,000		
Noncash Purchase	100,000		
End. Bal.	**715,000**		

Accumulated Depreciation			
Sale	2,000	Beg. Bal.	68,000
		Dep. Exp.	37,000
		End. Bal.	**103,000**

Had the balance sheet included specific plant asset accounts (e.g., Equipment and the related accumulated depreciation account) or other long-term asset accounts (e.g., Intangibles), the analysis would have been the same.

STOP & APPLY >

The following T accounts show Matiz Company's plant assets and accumulated depreciation at the end of 2010:

Plant Assets			
Beg. Bal.	65,000	Disposals	23,000
Purchases	33,600		
End. Bal.	**75,600**		

Accumulated Depreciation			
Disposals	14,700	Beg. Bal.	34,500
		Depreciation	10,200
		End. Bal.	**30,000**

Matiz's income statement shows a gain on the sale of plant assets of $4,400. Compute the amounts that should be shown as cash flows from investing activities, and show how they should appear on Matiz's 2010 statement of cash flows.

SOLUTION

Cash flows from investing activities:

Purchase of plant assets	($33,600)
Sale of plant assets	12,700

The T accounts show total purchases of plant assets of $33,600, which is an outflow of cash, and disposal of plant assets that cost $23,000 and that had accumulated depreciation of $14,700. The income statement shows a $4,400 gain on the sale of the plant assets. The cash inflow from the disposal was as follows:

Plant assets	$23,000
Less accumulated depreciation	14,700
Book value	$ 8,300
Add gain on sale	4,400
Cash inflow from sale of plant assets	$12,700

Because the gain on the sale is included in the $12,700 in the investing activities section of the statement of cash flows, it should be deducted from net income in the operating activities section.

Financing Activities

LO5 Determine cash flows from financing activities.

Determining cash flows from financing activities is very similar to determining cash flows from investing activities, but the accounts analyzed relate to short-term borrowings, long-term liabilities, and stockholders' equity. Because Laguna Corporation does not have short-term borrowings, we deal only with long-term liabilities and stockholders' equity accounts.

The following transactions pertain to Laguna's financing activities in 2010:

1. Issued $100,000 of bonds at face value in a noncash exchange for plant assets.
2. Repaid $50,000 of bonds at face value at maturity.
3. Issued 15,200 shares of $5 par value common stock for $175,000.
4. Paid cash dividends in the amount of $8,000.
5. Purchased treasury stock for $25,000.

Bonds Payable

Exhibit 14-3 shows that Laguna's Bonds Payable account increased by $50,000 in 2010. Both items **1** and **2** in the list above affect this account. We analyzed item **1** in connection with plant assets, but it also pertains to the Bonds Payable account. As we noted, this transaction is reported on the schedule of noncash investing and financing transactions. Item **2** results in a cash outflow, which is recorded as follows:

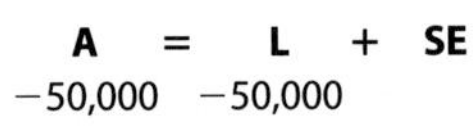

A	=	L	+	SE
−50,000		−50,000		

Bonds Payable	50,000	
Cash		50,000
Repayment of bonds at face value at maturity		

This appears in the financing activities section of the statement of cash flows as follows:

Repayment of bonds ($50,000)

The following T account explains the change in Bonds Payable:

Bonds Payable

Repayment	50,000	Beg. Bal.	245,000
		Noncash Issue	100,000
		End. Bal.	**295,000**

If Laguna Corporation had any notes payable, the analysis would be the same.

Common Stock

Like the Plant Asset account and its related accounts, accounts related to stockholders' equity should be analyzed together. For example, the Additional Paid-In Capital account should be examined along with the Common Stock account. In 2010, Laguna's Common Stock account increased by $76,000, and its Additional Paid-In Capital account increased by $99,000. Item **3** in the list of Laguna's transactions, which states that the company issued 15,200 shares of $5 par value common stock for $175,000, explains these increases. The entry in journal form to record the cash inflow is as follows:

FOCUS ON BUSINESS PRACTICE

How Much Cash Does a Company Need?

Some kinds of industries are more vulnerable to downturns in the economy than others. Historically, because of the amount of debt they carry and their large interest and loan payments, companies in the airline and automotive industries have been hard hit by economic downturns. But research has shown that high-tech companies with large amounts of intangible assets are also hard hit. Biotechnology, pharmaceutical, and computer hardware and software companies can lose up to 80 percent of their value in times of financial stress. In contrast, companies with large amounts of tangible assets, such as oil companies and railroads, can lose as little as 10 percent. To survive during economic downturns, it is very important for high-tech companies to use their cash-generating efficiency to build cash reserves. It makes sense for these companies to hoard cash and not pay dividends to the extent that companies in other industries do.[12]

A	= L +	SE
+175,000		+76,000
		+99,000

Cash	175,000	
Common Stock		76,000
Additional Paid-In Capital		99,000
Issued 15,200 shares of $5 par value common stock		

This appears in the financing activities section of the statement of cash flows as follows:

Issuance of common stock $175,000

The following analysis of this transaction is all that is needed to explain the changes in the two accounts during 2010:

Common Stock			Additional Paid-In Capital		
	Beg. Bal.	200,000		Beg. Bal.	115,000
	Issue	76,000		Issue	99,000
	End. Bal.	**276,000**		**End. Bal.**	**214,000**

Retained Earnings

At this point, we have dealt with several items that affect retained earnings. The only item affecting Laguna's retained earnings that we have not considered is the payment of $8,000 in cash dividends (item **4** in the list of Laguna's transactions). At the time it declared the dividend, Laguna would have debited its Dividends account. After paying the dividend, it would have closed the Dividends account to Retained Earnings and recorded the closing with the following entry:

A	= L +	SE
		−8,000
		+8,000

Retained Earnings	8,000	
Dividends		8,000
To close the Dividends account		

Cash dividends would be displayed in the financing activities section of Laguna's statement of cash flows as follows:

Payment of dividends ($8,000)

High-tech companies with large amounts of intangible assets can lose up to 80 percent of their value in times of financial stress. As a hedge against economic downturns, these companies need to build cash reserves, and they may therefore choose to hoard cash rather than pay dividends.

Courtesy of NICOLAS ASFOURI/AFP/Getty Images.

Study Note

It is dividends paid, not dividends declared, that appear on the statement of cash flows.

This T account shows the change in the Retained Earnings account:

Retained Earnings			
Dividends	8,000	Beg. Bal.	132,000
		Net Income	16,000
		End. Bal.	**140,000**

Treasury Stock

As we noted in the chapter on contributed capital, many companies buy back their own stock on the open market. These buybacks use cash, as this entry shows:

A	= L +	SE
−25,000		−25,000

	Dr.	Cr.
Treasury Stock	25,000	
Cash		25,000

Study Note

The purchase of treasury stock qualifies as a financing activity, but it is also a cash outflow.

This use of cash is classified in the statement of cash flows as a financing activity:

Purchase of treasury stock ($25,000)

The T account for this transaction is as follows:

Treasury Stock			
Purchase	25,000		

We have now analyzed all Laguna Corporation's income statement items, explained all balance sheet changes, and taken all additional information into account. Exhibit 14-5 shows how our data are assembled in Laguna's statement of cash flows.

EXHIBIT 14-5
Statement of Cash Flows: Indirect Method

Laguna Corporation
Statement of Cash Flows
For the Year Ended December 31, 2010

Cash flows from operating activities		
Net income		$ 16,000
Adjustments to reconcile net income to net cash flows from operating activities		
Depreciation	$ 37,000	
Gain on sale of investments	(12,000)	
Loss on sale of plant assets	3,000	
Changes in current assets and current liabilities		
Decrease in accounts receivable	8,000	
Increase in inventory	(34,000)	
Decrease in prepaid expenses	4,000	
Increase in accounts payable	7,000	
Increase in accrued liabilities	3,000	
Decrease in income taxes payable	(2,000)	14,000
Net cash flows from operating activities		$ 30,000
Cash flows from investing activities		
Purchase of investments	($ 78,000)	
Sale of investments	102,000	
Purchase of plant assets	(120,000)	
Sale of plant assets	5,000	
Net cash flows from investing activities		(91,000)
Cash flows from financing activities		
Repayment of bonds	($ 50,000)	
Issuance of common stock	175,000	
Payment of dividends	(8,000)	
Purchase of treasury stock	(25,000)	
Net cash flows from financing activities		92,000
Net increase in cash		$ 31,000
Cash at beginning of year		15,000
Cash at end of year		$ 46,000

Schedule of Noncash Investing and Financing Transactions

Issue of bonds payable for plant assets	$100,000

STOP & APPLY >

During 2011, F & K Company issued $1,000,000 in long-term bonds at par, repaid $200,000 of notes payable at face value, issued notes payable of $40,000 for equipment, paid interest of $40,000, paid dividends of $25,000, and repurchased common stock in the amount of $50,000. Prepare the cash flows from financing activities section of the statement of cash flows.

SOLUTION

Cash flows from financing activities	
Issuance of long-term bonds	$1,000,000
Repayment of notes payable	(200,000)
Payment of dividends	(25,000)
Purchase of treasury stock	(50,000)
Net cash flows from financing activities	$ 725,000

Note: Interest is an operating activity. The exchange of the notes payable for equipment is a noncash investing and financing transaction.

A LOOK BACK AT

▸ AMAZON.COM, INC.

As we pointed out in this chapter's Decision Point, strong cash flows are a basic ingredient in **Amazon.com**'s plans for the future. Strong cash flows enable a company to achieve and maintain liquidity, to expand, and to increase the value of its shareholders' investments. A company's statement of cash flows provides information essential to evaluating the strength of its cash flows and its liquidity.

A user of Amazon.com's statement of cash flows would want to ask the following questions:

- Are operations generating sufficient operating cash flows?
- Is the company growing by investing in long-term assets?
- Has the company had to borrow money or issue stock to finance its growth?

Using data from Exhibit 14-1, which presents Amazon.com's statements of cash flows, we can answer these questions. We can gauge Amazon.com's ability to generate cash flows from operations by calculating its cash flow yields in 2008 and 2007:

Cash Flow Yield		2008	2007

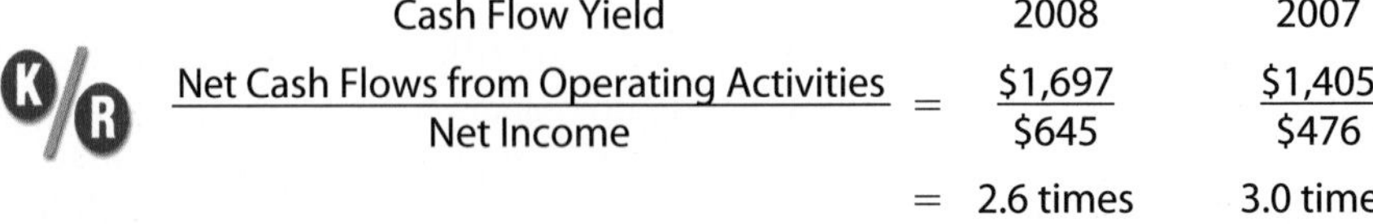

$$\frac{\text{Net Cash Flows from Operating Activities}}{\text{Net Income}} = \frac{\$1{,}697}{\$645} \qquad \frac{\$1{,}405}{\$476}$$

$$= 2.6 \text{ times} \qquad 3.0 \text{ times}$$

As you can see, Amazon.com's cash flow yield decreased somewhat over the two years, from 3.0 to 2.6 times, but both years easily exceeded the 1.0 level normally considered the minimum acceptable cash flow yield. Although both net cash flows from activities and net income increased significantly from 2007 to 2008, net income grew more rapidly.

Free cash flow measures the sufficiency of cash flows in a different way, and as mentioned earlier in the chapter, it is a key financial objective for Amazon.com's

management. The computations below show that the company is meeting its objectives. Its free cash flow grew by almost $700 million from 2007 to 2008:

Free Cash Flow		2008	2007
Net Cash Flows from Operating Activities − Dividends − Purchases of Plant Assets + Sales of Plant Assets	=	\$1,697 − \$0 − \$333 + \$0	\$1,405 − \$0 − \$224 + \$0
	=	\$1,364	\$1,181

An examination of Amazon.com' s statement of cash flows in Exhibit 14-1 shows how the company is investing its free cash flow. In addition to investing in long-term assets ($333 million in 2008 and $224 million in 2007), the company decreased its investment in marketable securities. Thus, the company did not have to rely on borrowing money (because repayments exceeded proceeds from debt) or issuing stock to finance its growth. In fact, although it did not pay a cash dividend, Amazon.com did repurchase common stock in the amount of $100 million in 2008. Finally, it increased its balance of cash and cash equivalents from $2,539 million in 2007 to $2,769 million in 2008. One must conclude that Amazon.com is a very successful and growing company. It will be interesting to see if it can keep up its success.

Review Problem

The Statement of Cash Flows

LO2 LO3 LO4 LO5

Lopata Corporation's income statement for 2011 and its comparative balance sheets for 2011 and 2010 are presented on the next page. The company's records for 2011 provide this additional information:

a. Sold long-term investments that cost $35,000 for a gain of $6,250; made other long-term investments in the amount of $10,000.
b. Purchased five acres of land to build a parking lot for $12,500.
c. Sold equipment that cost $18,750 and that had accumulated depreciation of $12,650 at a loss of $1,150; purchased new equipment for $15,000.
d. Repaid notes payable in the amount of $50,000; borrowed $15,000 by signing new notes payable.
e. Converted $50,000 of bonds payable into 3,000 shares of common stock.
f. Reduced the Mortgage Payable account by $10,000.
g. Declared and paid cash dividends of $25,000.
h. Purchased treasury stock for $5,000.

Required

1. Prepare a statement of cash flows using the indirect method.
2. Compute cash flow yield, cash flows to sales, cash flows to assets, and free cash flow for 2011.

Lopata Corporation Income Statement For the Year Ended December 31, 2011		
Net sales		$825,000
Cost of goods sold		460,000
Gross margin		$365,000
Operating expenses (including depreciation expense of $6,000 on buildings and $11,550 on equipment and amortization expense of $2,400)		235,000
Operating income		$130,000
Other income		
Interest expense	($27,500)	
Dividend income	1,700	
Gain on sale of investments	6,250	
Loss on disposal of equipment	(1,150)	(20,700)
Income before income taxes		$109,300
Income taxes expense		26,100
Net income		$ 83,200

Lopata Corporation Comparative Balance Sheets December 31, 2011 and 2010				
	2011	2010	Change	Increase or Decrease
Assets				
Cash	$ 52,925	$ 60,925	($ 8,000)	Decrease
Accounts receivable (net)	148,000	157,250	(9,250)	Decrease
Inventory	161,000	150,500	10,500	Increase
Prepaid expenses	3,900	2,900	1,000	Increase
Long-term investments	18,000	43,000	(25,000)	Decrease
Land	75,000	62,500	12,500	Increase
Buildings	231,000	231,000	—	—
Accumulated depreciation, buildings	(45,500)	(39,500)	(6,000)	Increase
Equipment	79,865	83,615	(3,750)	Decrease
Accumulated depreciation, equipment	(21,700)	(22,800)	1,100	Decrease
Intangible assets	9,600	12,000	(2,400)	Decrease
Total assets	$712,090	$741,390	($29,300)	
Liabilities and Stockholders' Equity				
Accounts payable	$ 66,875	$116,875	($50,000)	Decrease
Notes payable (current)	37,850	72,850	(35,000)	Decrease
Accrued liabilities	2,500	—	2,500	Increase
Income taxes payable	10,000	—	10,000	Increase
Bonds payable	105,000	155,000	(50,000)	Decrease
Mortgage payable	165,000	175,000	(10,000)	Decrease
Common stock, $10 par value	200,000	170,000	30,000	Increase
Additional paid-in capital	45,000	25,000	20,000	Increase
Retained earnings	104,865	46,665	58,200	Increase
Treasury stock	(25,000)	(20,000)	(5,000)	Increase
Total liabilities and stockholders' equity	$712,090	$741,390	($29,300)	

Answers to Review Problem

1. Statement of cash flows using the indirect method:

	A	B	C	D	E
1			**Lopata Corporation**		
2			**Statement of Cash Flows**		
3			**For the Year Ended December 31, 2011**		
4					
5	**Cash flows from operating activities**				
6	Net income				$83,200
7	Adjustments to reconcile net income to net cash flows				
8	from operating activities				
9		Depreciation expense, buildings		$ 6,000	
10		Depreciation expense, equipment		11,550	
11		Amortization expense, intangible assets		2,400	
12		Gain on sale of investments		(6,250)	
13		Loss on disposal of equipment		1,150	
14		Changes in current assets and current liabilities			
15			Decrease in accounts receivable	9,250	
16			Increase in inventory	(10,500)	
17			Increase in prepaid expenses	(1,000)	
18			Decrease in accounts payable	(50,000)	
19			Increase in accrued liabilities	2,500	
20			Increase in income taxes payable	10,000	(24,900)
21	Net cash flows from operating activities				$58,300
22	**Cash flows from investing activities**				
23	Sale of long-term investments			$41,250[a]	
24	Purchase of long-term investments			(10,000)	
25	Purchase of land			(12,500)	
26	Sale of equipment			4,950[b]	
27	Purchase of equipment			(15,000)	
28	Net cash flows from investing activities				8,700
29	**Cash flows from financing activities**				
30	Repayment of notes payable			($50,000)	
31	Issuance of notes payable			15,000	
32	Reduction in mortgage			(10,000)	
33	Dividends paid			(25,000)	
34	Purchase of treasury stock			(5,000)	
35	Net cash flows from financing activities				(75,000)
36	Net (decrease) in cash				($ 8,000)
37	Cash at beginning of year				60,925
38	Cash at end of year				$52,925
39					
40			**Schedule of Noncash Investing and Financing Transactions**		
41	Conversion of bonds payable into common stock				$50,000
42					
43	a	$35,000 + $6,250 (gain) = $41,250			
44	b	$18,750 − $12,650 = $6,100 (book value) − $1,150 (loss) = $4,950			

2. Cash flow yield, cash flows to sales, cash flows to assets, and free cash flow for 2011:

$$\text{Cash Flow Yield} = \frac{\$58{,}300}{\$83{,}200} = 0.7 \text{ times}$$

$$\text{Cash Flows to Sales} = \frac{\$58{,}300}{\$825{,}000} = 7.1\%$$

$$\text{Cash Flows to Assets} = \frac{\$58{,}300}{(\$712{,}090 + \$741{,}390) \div 2} = 8.0\%$$

$$\text{Free Cash Flow} = \$58{,}300 - \$25{,}000 - \$12{,}500 - \$15{,}000 + \$4{,}950 = \$10{,}750$$

LO1 Describe the principal purposes and uses of the statement of cash flows, and identify its components.

The statement of cash flows shows how a company's operating, investing, and financing activities have affected cash during an accounting period. For the statement of cash flows, *cash* is defined as including both cash and cash equivalents. The primary purpose of the statement is to provide information about a firm's cash receipts and cash payments during an accounting period. A secondary purpose is to provide information about a firm's operating, investing, and financing activities. Management uses the statement to assess liquidity, determine dividend policy, and plan investing and financing activities. Investors and creditors use it to assess the company's cash-generating ability.

The statement of cash flows has three major classifications: (1) operating activities, which involve the cash effects of transactions and other events that enter into the determination of net income; (2) investing activities, which involve the acquisition and sale of marketable securities and long-term assets and the making and collecting of loans; and (3) financing activities, which involve obtaining resources from stockholders and creditors and providing the former with a return on their investments and the latter with repayment. Noncash investing and financing transactions are also important because they affect future cash flows; these exchanges of long-term assets or liabilities are of interest to potential investors and creditors.

LO2 Analyze the statement of cash flows.

In examining a company's statement of cash flows, analysts tend to focus on cash-generating efficiency and free cash flow. Cash-generating efficiency is a firm's ability to generate cash from its current or continuing operations. The ratios used to measure cash-generating efficiency are cash flow yield, cash flows to sales, and cash flows to assets. Free cash flow is the cash that remains after deducting the funds a firm must commit to continue operating at its planned level. These commitments include current and continuing operations, interest, income taxes, dividends, and capital expenditures.

LO3 Use the indirect method to determine cash flows from operating activities.

The indirect method adjusts net income for all items in the income statement that do not have cash flow effects (such as depreciation, amortization, and gains and losses on sales of assets) and for changes in liabilities that affect operating cash flows. Generally, increases in current assets have a negative effect on cash flows, and decreases have a positive effect. Conversely, increases in current liabilities have a positive effect on cash flows, and decreases have a negative effect.

LO4 Determine cash flows from investing activities.

Investing activities involve the acquisition and sale of property, plant, and equipment and other long-term assets, including long-term investments. They also involve the acquisition and sale of short-term marketable securities, other than trading securities, and the making and collecting of loans. Cash flows from investing activities are determined by analyzing the cash flow effects of changes in each account related to investing activities. The effects of gains and losses reported on the income statement must also be considered.

LO5 Determine cash flows from financing activities.

Determining cash flows from financing activities is almost identical to determining cash flows from investing activities. The difference is that the accounts analyzed relate to short-term borrowings, long-term liabilities, and stockholders' equity. After the changes in the balance sheet accounts from one accounting period to the next have been explained, all the cash flow effects should have been identified.

REVIEW of Concepts and Terminology

The following concepts and terms were introduced in this chapter:

Cash 668 (LO1)

Cash equivalents 668 (LO1)

Cash-generating efficiency 673 (LO2)

Direct method 678 (LO3)

Financing activities 670 (LO1)

Free cash flow 676 (LO2)

Indirect method 678 (LO3)

Investing activities 669 (LO1)

Noncash investing and financing transactions 670 (LO1)

Operating activities 668 (LO1)

Statement of cash flows 668 (LO1)

Key Ratios

Cash flows to assets 674 (LO2)

Cash flows to sales 674 (LO2)

Cash flow yield 674 (LO2)

CHAPTER ASSIGNMENTS

BUILDING Your Basic Knowledge and Skills

Short Exercises

LO1 **Classification of Cash Flow Transactions**

SE 1. The list that follows itemizes Furlong Corporation's transactions. Identify each as (a) an operating activity, (b) an investing activity, (c) a financing activity, (d) a noncash transaction, or (e) none of the above.

1. Sold land.
2. Declared and paid a cash dividend.
3. Paid interest.
4. Issued common stock for plant assets.
5. Issued preferred stock.
6. Borrowed cash on a bank loan.

LO2 **Cash-Generating Efficiency Ratios and Free Cash Flow**

SE 2. In 2010, Ross Corporation had year-end assets of $550,000, sales of $790,000, net income of $90,000, net cash flows from operating activities of $180,000, purchases of plant assets of $120,000, and sales of plant assets of $20,000, and it paid dividends of $40,000. In 2009, year-end assets were $500,000. Calculate the cash-generating efficiency ratios of cash flow yield, cash flows to sales, and cash flows to assets. Also calculate free cash flow.

LO2 **Cash-Generating Efficiency Ratios and Free Cash Flow**

SE 3. Examine the cash flow measures in requirement **2** of the Review Problem in this chapter. Discuss the meaning of these ratios.

LO3 **Computing Cash Flows from Operating Activities: Indirect Method**

SE 4. Wachowski Corporation had a net income of $33,000 during 2010. During the year, the company had depreciation expense of $14,000. Accounts Receivable increased by $11,000, and Accounts Payable increased by $5,000. Those were the company's only current assets and current liabilities. Use the indirect method to determine net cash flows from operating activities.

LO3 **Computing Cash Flows from Operating Activities: Indirect Method**

SE 5. During 2010, Minh Corporation had a net income of $144,000. Included on its income statement were depreciation expense of $16,000 and amortization expense of $1,800. During the year, Accounts Receivable decreased by $8,200, Inventories increased by $5,400, Prepaid Expenses decreased by $1,000, Accounts Payable decreased by $14,000, and Accrued Liabilities decreased by $1,700. Use the indirect method to determine net cash flows from operating activities.

LO4 **Cash Flows from Investing Activities and Noncash Transactions**

SE 6. During 2010, Howard Company purchased land for $375,000. It paid $125,000 in cash and signed a $250,000 mortgage for the rest. The company also sold a building that originally cost $90,000, on which it had $70,000 of accumulated depreciation, for $95,000 cash, making a gain of $75,000. Prepare the cash flows from investing activities section and the schedule of noncash investing and financing transactions of the statement of cash flows.

LO5 **Cash Flows from Financing Activities**

SE 7. During 2010, Arizona Company issued $500,000 in long-term bonds at 96, repaid $75,000 of bonds at face value, paid interest of $40,000, and paid dividends of $25,000. Prepare the cash flows from the financing activities section of the statement of cash flows.

LO1 LO3 LO4 LO5 **Identifying Components of the Statement of Cash Flows**

SE 8. Assuming the indirect method is used to prepare the statement of cash flows, tell whether each of the following items would appear (a) in cash flows from operating activities, (b) in cash flows from investing activities, (c) in cash flows from financing activities, (d) in the schedule of noncash investing and financing transactions, or (e) not on the statement of cash flows at all:

1. Dividends paid
2. Cash receipts from customers
3. Decrease in accounts receivable
4. Sale of plant assets
5. Gain on sale of investments
6. Issue of stock for plant assets
7. Issue of common stock
8. Net income

Exercises

LO1 LO2 **Discussion Questions**

E 1. Develop brief answers to each of the following questions:

1. Which statement is more useful—the income statement or the statement of cash flows?
2. How would you respond to someone who says that the most important item on the statement of cash flows is the change in the cash balance for the year?
3. If a company's cash flow yield is less than 1.0, would its cash flows to sales and cash flows to assets be greater or less than profit margin and return on assets, respectively?

LO3 LO4 LO5 **Discussion Questions**

E 2. Develop brief answers to each of the following questions:

1. If a company has positive earnings, can cash flows from operating activities ever be negative?
2. Which adjustments to net income in the operating activities section of the statement of cash flows are directly related to cash flows in other sections?
3. In computing free cash flow, what is an argument for treating the purchases of treasury stock like dividend payments?

LO1 **Classification of Cash Flow Transactions**

E 3. Koral Corporation engaged in the transactions listed below. Identify each transaction as (a) an operating activity, (b) an investing activity, (c) a financing activity, (d) a noncash transaction, or (e) not on the statement of cash flows. (Assume the indirect method is used.)

1. Declared and paid a cash dividend.
2. Purchased a long-term investment.
3. Increased accounts receivable.
4. Paid interest.
5. Sold equipment at a loss.
6. Issued long-term bonds for plant assets.
7. Increased dividends receivable.
8. Issued common stock.
9. Declared and issued a stock dividend.
10. Repaid notes payable.
11. Decreased wages payable.
12. Purchased a 60-day Treasury bill.
13. Purchased land.

LO2 **Cash-Generating Efficiency Ratios and Free Cash Flow**

E 4. In 2011, Heart Corporation had year-end assets of $1,200,000, sales of $1,650,000, net income of $140,000, net cash flows from operating activities of $195,000, dividends of $60,000, purchases of plant assets of $250,000, and sales of plant assets of $45,000. In 2010, year-end assets were $1,050,000. Calculate free cash flow and the cash-generating efficiency ratios of cash flow yield, cash flows to sales, and cash flows to assets.

LO3 **Cash Flows from Operating Activities: Indirect Method**

E 5. The condensed single-step income statement for the year ended December 31, 2010, of Sunderland Chemical Company, a distributor of farm fertilizers and herbicides, appears as follows:

Sales		$13,000,000
Less: Cost of goods sold	$7,600,000	
Operating expenses (including depreciation of $820,000).	3,800,000	
Income taxes expense	400,000	11,800,000
Net income		$ 1,200,000

Selected accounts from Sunderland Chemical Company's balance sheets for 2010 and 2009 are as follows:

	2010	2009
Accounts receivable	$2,400,000	$1,700,000
Inventory	840,000	1,020,000
Prepaid expenses	260,000	180,000
Accounts payable	960,000	720,000
Accrued liabilities	60,000	100,000
Income taxes payable	140,000	120,000

Present in good form a schedule of cash flows from operating activities using the indirect method.

LO3 **Computing Cash Flows from Operating Activities: Indirect Method**

E 6. During 2010, Diaz Corporation had net income of $41,000. Included on its income statement were depreciation expense of $2,300 and amortization expense of $300. During the year, Accounts Receivable increased by $3,400, Inventories decreased by $1,900, Prepaid Expenses decreased by $200, Accounts Payable increased by $5,000, and Accrued Liabilities decreased by $450. Determine net cash flows from operating activities using the indirect method.

LO3 **Preparing a Schedule of Cash Flows from Operating Activities: Indirect Method**

E 7. For the year ended June 30, 2010, net income for Silk Corporation was $7,400. Depreciation expense was $2,000. During the year, Accounts Receivable increased by $4,400, Inventories increased by $7,000, Prepaid Rent decreased by $1,400, Accounts Payable increased by $14,000, Salaries Payable increased by $1,000, and Income Taxes Payable decreased by $600. Use the indirect method to prepare a schedule of cash flows from operating activities.

LO4 Computing Cash Flows from Investing Activities: Investments

E 8. CUD Company's T account for long-term available-for-sale investments at the end of 2010 is as follows:

INVESTMENTS			
Beg. Bal.	152,000	Sales	156,000
Purchases	232,000		
End. Bal.	**228,000**		

In addition, CUD Company's income statement shows a loss on the sale of investments of $26,000. Compute the amounts to be shown as cash flows from investing activities and show how they are to appear in the statement of cash flows.

LO4 Computing Cash Flows from Investing Activities: Plant Assets

E 9. The T accounts for plant assets and accumulated depreciation for CUD Company at the end of 2010 are as follows:

PLANT ASSETS			
Beg. Bal.	260,000	Disposals	92,000
Purchases	134,400		
End. Bal.	**302,400**		

ACCUMULATED DEPRECIATION			
Disposals	58,800	Beg. Bal.	138,000
		Depreciation	40,800
		End. Bal.	**120,000**

In addition, CUD Company's income statement shows a gain on sale of plant assets of $17,600. Compute the amounts to be shown as cash flows from investing activities and show how they are to appear on the statement of cash flows.

LO5 Determining Cash Flows from Financing Activities: Notes Payable

E 10. All transactions involving Notes Payable and related accounts of Pearl Company during 2010 are recorded as follows:

Cash	18,000	
Notes Payable		18,000
Bank loan		

Patent	30,000	
Notes Payable		30,000
Purchase of patent by issuing note payable		

Notes Payable	5,000	
Interest Expense	500	
Cash		5,500
Repayment of note payable at maturity		

Determine the amounts of the transactions affecting financing activities and show how they are to appear on the statement of cash flows for 2010.

LO3 LO4 LO5 **Preparing the Statement of Cash Flows: Indirect Method**

E 11. Olbrot Corporation's income statement for the year ended June 30, 2010 and its comparative balance sheets for June 30, 2010 and 2009 follow.

Olbrot Corporation
Income Statement
For the Year Ended June 30, 2010

Sales	$244,000
Cost of goods sold	148,100
Gross margin	$ 95,900
Operating expenses	45,000
Operating income	$ 50,900
Interest expense	2,800
Income before income taxes	$ 48,100
Income taxes expense	12,300
Net income	$ 35,800

Olbrot Corporation
Comparative Balance Sheets
June 30, 2010 and 2009

	2010	2009
Assets		
Cash	$139,800	$ 25,000
Accounts receivable (net)	42,000	52,000
Inventory	86,800	96,800
Prepaid expenses	6,400	5,200
Furniture	110,000	120,000
Accumulated depreciation, furniture	(18,000)	(10,000)
Total assets	$367,000	$289,000
Liabilities and Stockholders' Equity		
Accounts payable	$ 26,000	$ 28,000
Income taxes payable	2,400	3,600
Notes payable (long-term)	74,000	70,000
Common stock, $10 par value	230,000	180,000
Retained earnings	34,600	7,400
Total liabilities and stockholders' equity	$367,000	$289,000

Olbrot issued a $44,000 note payable for purchase of furniture; sold furniture that cost $54,000 with accumulated depreciation of $30,600 at carrying value; recorded depreciation on the furniture for the year, $38,600; repaid a note in the amount of $40,000; issued $50,000 of common stock at par value; and paid dividends of $8,600. Prepare Olbrot's statement of cash flows for the year 2010 using the indirect method.

Problems

LO1 Classification of Cash Flow Transactions

P 1. Analyze each transaction listed in the table that follows and place X's in the appropriate columns to indicate the transaction's classification and its effect on cash flows using the indirect method.

	Cash Flow Classification				Effect on Cash Flows		
Transaction	**Operating Activity**	**Investing Activity**	**Financing Activity**	**Noncash Transaction**	**Increase**	**Decrease**	**No Effect**
1. Paid a cash dividend.							
2. Decreased accounts receivable.							
3. Increased inventory.							
4. Incurred a net loss.							
5. Declared and issued a stock dividend.							
6. Retired long-term debt with cash.							
7. Sold available-for-sale securities at a loss.							
8. Issued stock for equipment.							
9. Decreased prepaid insurance.							
10. Purchased treasury stock with cash.							
11. Retired a fully depreciated truck (no gain or loss).							
12. Increased interest payable.							
13. Decreased dividends receivable on investment.							
14. Sold treasury stock.							
15. Increased income taxes payable.							
16. Transferred cash to money market account.							
17. Purchased land and building with a mortgage.							

LO1 Interpreting and Analyzing the Statement of Cash Flows

P 2. The comparative statements of cash flows for Executive Style Corporation, a manufacturer of high-quality suits for men, appear on the following page. To expand its markets and familiarity with its brand, the company attempted a new strategic diversification in 2010 by acquiring a chain of retail men's stores in outlet malls. Its plan was to expand in malls around the country, but department stores viewed the action as infringing on their territory.

Executive Style Corporation
Statement of Cash Flows
For the Years Ended December 31, 2010 and 2009
(In thousands)

	2010	2009
Cash flows from operating activities		
Net income (loss)	($ 21,545)	$ 38,015
Adjustments to reconcile net income to net cash flows from operating activities		
Depreciation	$ 35,219	$ 25,018
Loss on closure of retail outlets	35,000	—
Changes in current assets and current liabilities		
Decrease (increase) in accounts receivable	50,000	(44,803)
Decrease (increase) in inventory	60,407	(51,145)
Decrease (increase) in prepaid expenses	1,367	2,246
Increase (decrease) in accounts payable	30,579	1,266
Increase (decrease) in accrued liabilities	1,500	(2,788)
Increase (decrease) in income taxes payable	(8,300)	(6,281)
	$205,772	($ 76,487)
Net cash flows from operating activities	$184,227	($ 38,472)
Cash flows from investing activities		
Capital expenditures, net	($ 16,145)	($ 33,112)
Purchase of Retail Division, cash portion	—	(201,000)
Net cash flows from investing activities	($ 16,145)	($ 234,112)
Cash flows from financing activities		
Increase (decrease) in notes payable to banks	($123,500)	$ 228,400
Reduction in long-term debt	(9,238)	(10,811)
Payment of dividends	(22,924)	(19,973)
Purchase of treasury stock	—	(12,500)
Net cash flows from financing activities	($155,662)	$ 85,116
Net increase (decrease) in cash	$ 12,420	($ 87,468)
Cash at beginning of year	16,032	103,500
Cash at end of year	$ 28,452	$ 16,032

Schedule of Noncash Investing and Financing Transactions

Issue of bonds payable for retail acquisition		$ 50,000

Required

Evaluate the success of the company's strategy by answering the questions that follow.

1. What are the primary reasons cash flows from operating activities differ from net income? What is the effect on the acquisition in 2009? What conclusions can you draw from the changes in 2010?
2. Compute free cash flow for both years. What was the total cost of the acquisition? Is the company able to finance expansion in 2009 by generating internal cash flow? What was the situation in 2010?
3. User insight ▶ What are the most significant financing activities in 2009? How did the company finance the acquisition? Do you think this is a good strategy? What other issues might you question in financing activities?
4. User insight ▶ Based on results in 2010, what actions was the company forced to take and what is your overall assessment of the company's diversification strategy?

LO2 LO3 LO4 LO5

Statement of Cash Flows: Indirect Method

P 3. The comparative balance sheets for Arif Fabrics, Inc., for December 31, 2010 and 2009 appear below.

Arif Fabrics, Inc.
Comparative Balance Sheets
December 31, 2010 and 2009

	2010	2009
Assets		
Cash	$ 94,560	$ 27,360
Accounts receivable (net)	102,430	75,430
Inventory	112,890	137,890
Prepaid expenses	—	20,000
Land	25,000	—
Building	137,000	—
Accumulated depreciation–building	(15,000)	—
Equipment	33,000	34,000
Accumulated depreciation–equipment	(14,500)	(24,000)
Patents	4,000	6,000
Total assets	$479,380	$276,680
Liabilities and Stockholders' Equity		
Accounts payable	$ 10,750	$ 36,750
Notes payable (current)	10,000	—
Accrued liabilities	—	12,300
Mortgage payable	162,000	—
Common stock, $10 par value	180,000	150,000
Additional paid-in capital	57,200	37,200
Retained earnings	59,430	40,430
Total liabilities and stockholders' equity	$479,380	$276,680

Additional information about Arif Fabrics's operations during 2010 is as follows: (a) net income, $28,000; (b) building and equipment depreciation expense amounts, $15,000 and $3,000, respectively; (c) equipment that cost $13,500 with accumulated depreciation of $12,500 sold at a gain of $5,300; (d) equipment purchases, $12,500; (e) patent amortization, $3,000; purchase of patent, $1,000; (f) funds borrowed by issuing notes payable, $25,000; notes payable repaid, $15,000; (g) land and building purchased for $162,000 by signing a mortgage for the total cost; (h) 1,500 shares of $20 par value common stock issued for a total of $50,000; and (i) paid cash dividend, $9,000.

Required

1. Using the indirect method, prepare a statement of cash flows for Arif Fabrics.
2. User insight ▶ Why did Arif Fabrics have an increase in cash of $67,200 when it recorded net income of only $28,000? Discuss and interpret.
3. User insight ▶ Compute and assess cash flow yield and free cash flow for 2010. What is your assessment of Arif's cash-generating ability?

LO2 LO3 LO4 LO5

Statement of Cash Flows: Indirect Method

P 4. The comparative balance sheets for Lopez Ceramics, Inc., for December 31, 2010 and 2009 are presented on the next page. During 2010, the company had net income of $48,000 and building and equipment depreciation expenses

Lopez Ceramics, Inc.
Comparative Balance Sheets
December 31, 2010 and 2009

	2010	2009
Assets		
Cash	$ 128,800	$ 152,800
Accounts receivable (net)	369,400	379,400
Inventory	480,000	400,000
Prepaid expenses	7,400	13,400
Long-term investments	220,000	220,000
Land	180,600	160,600
Building	600,000	460,000
Accumulated depreciation, building	(120,000)	(80,000)
Equipment	240,000	240,000
Accumulated depreciation, equipment	(58,000)	(28,000)
Intangible assets	10,000	20,000
Total assets	$2,058,200	$1,938,200
Liabilities and Stockholders' Equity		
Accounts payable	$ 235,400	$ 330,400
Notes payable (current)	20,000	80,000
Accrued liabilities	5,400	10,400
Mortgage payable	540,000	400,000
Bonds payable	500,000	380,000
Common stock	650,000	650,000
Additional paid-in capital	40,000	40,000
Retained earnings	127,400	97,400
Treasury stock	(60,000)	(50,000)
Total liabilities and stockholders' equity	$2,058,200	$1,938,200

of $40,000 and $30,000, respectively. It amortized intangible assets in the amount of $10,000; purchased investments for $58,000; sold investments for $75,000, on which it recorded a gain of $17,000; issued $120,000 of long-term bonds at face value; purchased land and a warehouse through a $160,000 mortgage; paid $20,000 to reduce the mortgage; borrowed $30,000 by issuing notes payable; repaid notes payable in the amount of $90,000; declared and paid cash dividends in the amount of $18,000; and purchased treasury stock in the amount of $10,000.

Required

1. Using the indirect method, prepare a statement of cash flows for Lopez Ceramics, Inc.
2. User insight ▶ Why did Lopez Ceramics experience a decrease in cash in a year in which it had a net income of $48,000? Discuss and interpret.
3. User insight ▶ Compute and assess cash flow yield and free cash flow for 2010. Why is each of these measures important in assessing cash-generating ability?

LO2 LO3 LO4 LO5 **Statement of Cash Flows: Indirect Method**

P 5. Wu Corporation's comparative balance sheets as of December 31, 2011 and 2010 and its income statement for the year ended December 31, 2011 are presented on the next page.

Wu Company
Comparative Balance Sheets
December 31, 2011 and 2010

	2011	2010
Assets		
Cash	$164,800	$ 50,000
Accounts receivable (net)	165,200	200,000
Merchandise inventory	350,000	450,000
Prepaid rent	2,000	3,000
Furniture and fixtures	148,000	144,000
Accumulated depreciation, furniture and fixtures	(42,000)	(24,000)
Total assets	$788,000	$823,000
Liabilities and Stockholders' Equity		
Accounts payable	$143,400	$200,400
Income taxes payable	1,400	4,400
Notes payable (long-term)	40,000	20,000
Bonds payable	100,000	200,000
Common stock, $20 par value	240,000	200,000
Additional paid-in capital	181,440	121,440
Retained earnings	81,760	76,760
Total liabilities and stockholders' equity	$788,000	$823,000

Wu Company
Income Statement
For the Year Ended December 31, 2011

Sales		$1,609,000
Cost of goods sold		1,127,800
Gross margin		$ 481,200
Operating expenses (including depreciation expense of $46,800)		449,400
Income from operations		$ 31,800
Other income (expenses)		
Gain on sale of furniture and fixtures	$ 7,000	
Interest expense	(23,200)	(16,200)
Income before income taxes		$ 15,600
Income taxes expense		4,600
Net income		$ 11,000

During 2011, Wu Corporation engaged in these transactions:

a. Sold at a gain of $7,000 furniture and fixtures that cost $35,600, on which it had accumulated depreciation of $28,800.
b. Purchased furniture and fixtures in the amount of $39,600.
c. Paid a $20,000 note payable and borrowed $40,000 on a new note.
d. Converted bonds payable in the amount of $100,000 into 4,000 shares of common stock.
e. Declared and paid $6,000 in cash dividends.

Required

1. Using the indirect method, prepare a statement of cash flows for Wu Corporation. Include a supporting schedule of noncash investing transactions and financing transactions.

User insight ▶ 2. What are the primary reasons for Wu Corporation's large increase in cash from 2010 to 2011, despite its low net income?

User insight ▶ 3. Compute and assess cash flow yield and free cash flow for 2011. Compare and contrast what these two performance measures tell you about Wu's cash-generating ability.

Alternate Problems

LO1

Classification of Cash Flow Transactions

P 6. Analyze each transaction listed in the table that follows and place X's in the appropriate columns to indicate the transaction's classification and its effect on cash flows using the indirect method.

	Cash Flow Classification				Effect on Cash Flows		
Transaction	**Operating Activity**	**Investing Activity**	**Financing Activity**	**Noncash Transaction**	**Increase**	**Decrease**	**No Effect**
1. Increased accounts payable.							
2. Decreased inventory.							
3. Increased prepaid insurance.							
4. Earned a net income.							
5. Declared and paid a cash dividend.							
6. Issued stock for cash.							
7. Retired long-term debt by issuing stock.							
8. Purchased a long-term investment with cash.							
9. Sold trading securities at a gain.							
10. Sold a machine at a loss.							
11. Retired fully depreciated equipment.							
12. Decreased interest payable.							
13. Purchased available-for-sale securities (long-term).							
14. Decreased dividends receivable.							
15. Decreased accounts receivable.							
16. Converted bonds to common stock.							
17. Purchased 90-day Treasury bill.							

LO2 LO3 LO4 LO5

KA KLOOSTER & ALLEN

K/R

Statement of Cash Flows: Indirect Method

P 7. Ortega Corporation's income statement for the year ended June 30, 2010 and its comparative balance sheets as of June 30, 2010 and 2009 appear on the next page. During 2010, the corporation sold at a loss of $4,000 equipment that cost $24,000, on which it had accumulated depreciation of $17,000. It also

Ortega Corporation
Income Statement
For the Year Ended June 30, 2010

Sales		$4,040,900
Cost of goods sold		3,656,300
Gross margin		$ 384,600
Operating expenses (including depreciation expense of $60,000)		189,200
Income from operations		$ 195,400
Other income (expenses)		
Loss on sale of equipment	($ 4,000)	
Interest expense	(37,600)	(41,600)
Income before income taxes		$ 153,800
Income taxes expense		34,200
Net income		$ 119,600

Ortega Corporation
Comparative Balance Sheets
June 30, 2010 and 2009

	2010	2009
Assets		
Cash	$167,000	$ 20,000
Accounts receivable (net)	100,000	120,000
Inventory	180,000	220,000
Prepaid expenses	600	1,000
Property, plant, and equipment	628,000	552,000
Accumulated depreciation, property, plant, and equipment	(183,000)	(140,000)
Total assets	$892,600	$773,000
Liabilities and Stockholders' Equity		
Accounts payable	$ 64,000	$ 42,000
Notes payable (due in 90 days)	30,000	80,000
Income taxes payable	26,000	18,000
Mortgage payable	360,000	280,000
Common stock, $5 par value	200,000	200,000
Retained earnings	212,600	153,000
Total liabilities and stockholders' equity	$892,600	$773,000

purchased land and a building for $100,000 through an increase of $100,000 in Mortgage Payable; made a $20,000 payment on the mortgage; repaid notes but borrowed an additional $30,000 through the issuance of a new note payable of $80,000; and declared and paid a $60,000 cash dividend.

Required

1. Using the indirect method, prepare a statement of cash flows. Include a supporting schedule of noncash investing and financing transactions.

User insight ▶ 2. What are the primary reasons for Ortega Corporation's large increase in cash from 2009 to 2010?

User insight ▶ 3. Compute and assess cash flow yield and free cash flow for 2010. How would you assess the corporation's cash-generating ability?

LO2 LO3 **Statement of Cash Flows: Indirect Method**

LO4 LO5 **P 8.** The comparative balance sheets for Sharma Fabrics, Inc., for December 31, 2011 and 2010 appear below.

Sharma Fabrics, Inc.
Comparative Balance Sheets
December 31, 2011 and 2010

	2011	2010
Assets		
Cash	$189,120	$ 54,720
Accounts receivable (net)	204,860	150,860
Inventory	225,780	275,780
Prepaid expenses	—	40,000
Land	50,000	—
Building	274,000	—
Accumulated depreciation–building	(30,000)	—
Equipment	66,000	68,000
Accumulated depreciation–equipment	(29,000)	(48,000)
Patents	8,000	12,000
Total assets	$958,760	$553,360
Liabilities and Stockholders' Equity		
Accounts payable	$ 21,500	$ 73,500
Notes payable (current)	20,000	—
Accrued liabilities	—	24,600
Mortgage payable	324,000	—
Common stock, $10 par value	360,000	300,000
Additional paid-in capital	114,400	74,400
Retained earnings	118,860	80,860
Total liabilities and stockholders' equity	$958,760	$553,360

Additional information about Sharma Fabrics's operations during 2011 is as follows: (a) net income, $56,000; (b) building and equipment depreciation expense amounts, $30,000 and $6,000, respectively; (c) equipment that cost $27,000 with accumulated depreciation of $25,000 sold at a gain of $10,600; (d) equipment purchases, $25,000; (e) patent amortization, $6,000; purchase of patent, $2,000; (f) funds borrowed by issuing notes payable, $50,000; notes payable repaid, $30,000; (g) land and building purchased for $324,000 by signing a mortgage for the total cost; (h) 3,000 shares of $20 par value common stock issued for a total of $100,000; and (i) paid cash dividend, $18,000.

Required

1. Using the indirect method, prepare a statement of cash flows for Sharma Fabrics, Inc.

User insight ▶ 2. Why did Sharma Fabrics have an increase in cash of $134,400 when it recorded net income of only $56,000? Discuss and interpret.

User insight ▶ 3. Compute and assess cash flow yield and free cash flow for 2011. What is your assessment of Sharma's cash-generating ability?

LO2 LO3 LO4 LO5

Statement of Cash Flows: Indirect Method

P 9. The comparative balance sheets for Karidis Ceramics, Inc., for December 31, 2012 and 2011 are presented below.

Karidis Ceramics, Inc.
Comparative Balance Sheets
December 31, 2012 and 2011

	2012	2011
Assets		
Cash	$ 257,600	$ 305,600
Accounts receivable (net)	738,8 00	758,800
Inventory	960,000	800,000
Prepaid expenses	14,800	26,800
Long-term investments	440,000	440,000
Land	361,200	321,200
Building	1,200,000	920,000
Accumulated depreciation–building	(240,000)	(160,000)
Equipment	480,000	480,000
Accumulated depreciation–equipment	(116,000)	(56,000)
Intangible assets	20,000	40,000
Total assets	$4,116,400	$3,876,400
Liabilities and Stockholders' Equity		
Accounts payable	$ 470,800	$ 660,800
Notes payable (current)	40,000	160,000
Accrued liabilities	10,800	20,800
Mortgage payable	1,080,000	800,000
Bonds payable	1,000,000	760,000
Common stock	1,300,000	1,300,000
Additional paid-in capital	80,000	80,000
Retained earnings	254,800	194,800
Treasury stock	(120,000)	(100,000)
Total liabilities and stockholders' equity	$4,116,400	$3,876,400

During 2012, the company had net income of $96,000 and building and equipment depreciation expenses of $80,000 and $60,000, respectively. It amortized intangible assets in the amount of $20,000; purchased investments for $116,000; sold investments for $150,000, on which it recorded a gain of $34,000; issued $240,000 of long-term bonds at face value; purchased land and a warehouse through a $320,000 mortgage; paid $40,000 to reduce the mortgage; borrowed $60,000 by issuing notes payable; repaid notes payable in the amount of $180,000; declared and paid cash dividends in the amount of $36,000; and purchased treasury stock in the amount of $20,000.

Required

1. Using the indirect method, prepare a statement of cash flows for Karidis Ceramics, Inc.

User insight ▶ 2. Why did Karidis Ceramics experience a decrease in cash in a year in which it had a net income of $96,000? Discuss and interpret.

User insight ▶ 3. Compute and assess cash flow yield and free cash flow for 2012. Why is each of these measures important in assessing cash-generating ability?

ENHANCING Your Knowledge, Skills, and Critical Thinking

LO1 LO3 EBITDA and the Statement of Cash Flows

C 1. When **Fleetwood Enterprises, Inc.**, a large producer of recreational vehicles and manufactured housing, warned that it might not be able to generate enough cash to satisfy debt requirements and could be in default of a loan agreement, its cash flow, defined in the financial press as "EBITDA" (earnings before interest, taxes, depreciation, and amortization), was a negative $2.7 million. The company would have had to generate $17.7 million in the next accounting period to comply with the loan terms.[13] To what section of the statement of cash flows does EBITDA most closely relate? Is EBITDA a good approximation for this section of the statement of cash flows? Explain your answer, which should include an identification of the major differences between EBITDA and the section of the statement of cash flows you chose.

LO2 Anatomy of a Disaster

C 2. On October 16, 2001, Kenneth Lay, then chairman and CEO of **Enron Corporation**, announced the company's earnings for the first nine months of 2001 as follows:

> Our 26 percent increase in recurring earnings per diluted share shows the very strong results of our core wholesale and retail energy businesses and our natural gas pipelines. The continued excellent prospects in these businesses and Enron's leading market position make us very confident in our strong earnings outlook.[14]

Less than six months later, the company filed for the biggest bankruptcy in U.S. history. Its stock dropped to less than $1 per share, and a major financial scandal was underway.

Presented on the next page is Enron's statement of cash flows for the first nine months of 2001 and 2000 (restated to correct the previous accounting errors). Assume you report to an investment analyst who has asked you to analyze this statement for clues as to why the company went under.

1. For the two time periods shown, compute the cash-generating efficiency ratios of cash flow yield, cash flows to sales (Enron's revenues were $133,762 million in 2001 and $55,494 million in 2000), and cash flows to assets (use total assets of $61,783 million for 2001 and $64,926 million for 2000). Also compute free cash flows for the two years.
2. Prepare a memorandum to the investment analyst that assesses Enron's cash-generating efficiency in light of the chairman's remarks and that evaluates the company's available free cash flow, taking into account its financing activities. Identify significant changes in Enron's operating items and any special operating items that should be considered. Include your computations as an attachment.

Enron Corporation
Statement of Cash Flows
For the Nine Months Ended September 30, 2001 and 2000

(In millions)	**2001**	**2000**
Cash Flows from Operating Activities		
Reconciliation of net income to net cash provided by operating activities		
Net income	$ 225	$ 797
Cumulative effect of accounting changes, net of tax	(19)	0
Depreciation, depletion and amortization	746	617
Deferred income taxes	(134)	8
Gains on sales of non-trading assets	(49)	(135)
Investment losses	768	0
Changes in components of working capital		
Receivables	987	(3,363)
Inventories	1	339
Payables	(1,764)	2,899
Other	464	(455)
Trading investments		
Net margin deposit activity	(2,349)	541
Other trading activities	173	(555)
Other, net	198	(566)
Net Cash Provided by (Used in) Operating Activities	$ (753)	$ 127
Cash Flows from Investing Activities		
Capital expenditures	$(1,584)	$(1,539)
Equity investments	(1,172)	(858)
Proceeds from sales of non-trading investments	1,711	222
Acquisition of subsidiary stock	0	(485)
Business acquisitions, net of cash acquired	(82)	(773)
Other investing activities	(239)	(147)
Net Cash Used in Investing Activities	$(1,366)	$(3,580)
Cash Flows from Financing Activities		
Issuance of long-term debt	$ 4,060	$ 2,725
Repayment of long-term debt	(3,903)	(579)
Net increase in short-term borrowings	2,365	1,694
Issuance of common stock	199	182
Net redemption of company-obligated preferred securities of subsidiaries	0	(95)
Dividends paid	(394)	(396)
Net (acquisition) disposition of treasury stock	(398)	354
Other financing activities	(49)	(12)
Net Cash Provided by Financing Activities	$ 1,880	$ 3,873
Increase (Decrease) in Cash and Cash Equivalents	$ (239)	$ 420
Cash and Cash Equivalents, Beginning of Period	1,240	333
Cash and Cash Equivalents, End of Period	$ 1,001	$ 753

Source: Adapted from Enron Corporation, SEC filings, 2001.

LO2 **Cash-Generating Efficiency Ratios and Free Cash Flow**

C 3. The data that follow pertain to two of Japan's best-known and most successful companies, **Sony Corporation** and **Panasonic, Inc.**[15] (Numbers are in billions of yen.)

	Sony Corporation		Panasonic, Inc.	
	2009	2008	2009	2008
Sales	¥ 7,730	¥ 8,871	¥ 7,766	¥ 9,069
Net income	(99)	369	(379)	282
Average total assets	12,284	12,135	6,924	7,671
Net cash flows from operating activities	407	758	117	466
Dividends paid	43	25	83	69
Purchases of plant assets	496	475	522	419
Sales of plant assets	153	145	40	151

Calculate the ratios of cash flow yield, cash flows to sales, and cash flows to assets, as well as free cash flow, for the two years, for both Sony Corporation and Panasonic, Inc. Which company is most efficient in generating cash flow? Which company has the best year-to-year trend? Which company do you think will most probably need external financing?

LO2 LO3 LO4 LO5 **Analysis of Cash Flow Difficulty**

C 4. Sol Stein, certified public accountant, has just given his employer Sing Moy, the president of Moy Print Gallery, Inc., the income statement that appears below.

Moy Print Gallery, Inc.
Income Statement
For the Year Ended December 31, 2010

Sales	$ 884,000
Cost of goods sold	508,000
Gross margin	$ 376,000
Operating expenses (including depreciation expense of $20,000)	204,000
Operating income	$ 172,000
Interest expense	24,000
Income before income taxes	$ 148,000
Income taxes expense	28,000
Net income	$ 120,000

After examining the statement, Moy said to Stein, "Sol, the statement seems to be well done, but what I need to know is why I don't have enough cash to pay my bills this month. You show that I earned $120,000 in 2010, but I have only $24,000 in the bank. I know I bought a building on a mortgage and paid a cash dividend of $48,000, but what else is going on?"

Stein replied, "To answer your question, we have to look at comparative balance sheets and prepare another type of statement. Take a look at these balance sheets." The statement handed to Moy appears on the next page.

1. To what other statement is Stein referring? From the information given, prepare the additional statement using the indirect method.
2. Moy Print Gallery, Inc., has a cash problem despite profitable operations. Why is this the case?

Moy Print Gallery, Inc.
Comparative Balance Sheets
December 31, 2010 and 2009

	2010	2009
Assets		
Cash	$ 24,000	$ 40,000
Accounts receivable (net)	178,000	146,000
Inventory	240,000	180,000
Prepaid expenses	10,000	14,000
Building	400,000	—
Accumulated depreciation	(20,000)	—
Total assets	$832,000	$380,000
Liabilities and Stockholders' Equity		
Accounts payable	$ 74,000	$ 96,000
Income taxes payable	6,000	4,000
Mortgage payable	400,000	—
Common stock	200,000	200,000
Retained earnings	152,000	80,000
Total liabilities and stockholders' equity	$832,000	$380,000

Analysis of the Statement of Cash Flows

C 5. Refer to the statement of cash flows in the **CVS** annual report to answer the following questions:

1. Does CVS use the indirect method of reporting cash flows from operating activities? Other than net earnings, what are the most important factors affecting the company's cash flows from operating activities? Explain the trend of each of these factors.
2. Based on the cash flows from investing activities from 2006 to 2008, would you say that CVS is a contracting or an expanding company? Explain your answer.
3. Has CVS used external financing during 2006 to 2008? If so, where did it come from?

LO1 LO2 LO3 LO4 LO5

Cash Flows Analysis

C 6. Refer to the **CVS** annual report and the financial statements of **Southwest Airlines Co.** in the Supplement to Chapter 1. Calculate for two years each company's cash flow yield, cash flows to sales, cash flows to assets, and free cash flow. At the end of 2006, Southwest's total assets were $13,460 million and CVS's total assets were $20,574.1 million.

Discuss and compare the trends of the cash-generating ability of CVS and Southwest. Comment on each company's change in cash and cash equivalents over the two-year period.

LO2

Ethics and Cash Flow Classifications

C 7. Specialty Metals, Inc., a fast-growing company that makes metals for equipment manufacturers, has an $800,000 line of credit at its bank. One section in the credit agreement says that the ratio of cash flows from operations to interest expense must exceed 3.0. If this ratio falls below 3.0, the company must reduce the balance outstanding on its line of credit to one-half the total line if the funds borrowed against the line of credit exceed one-half of the total line.

After the end of the fiscal year, during a meeting with the president of the company, the controller made the following statement: "We will not meet the ratio requirements on our line of credit in 2010 because interest expense was $1.2 million and cash flows from operations were $3.2 million. Also, we have borrowed 100 percent of our line of credit. We do not have the cash to reduce the credit line by $400,000."

The president replied, "This is a serious situation. To pay our ongoing bills, we need our bank to increase our line of credit, not decrease it. What can we do about this?"

"Do you recall the $500,000 two-year note payable for equipment?" answered the controller. "It is now classified as 'Proceeds from Notes Payable' in cash flows provided from financing activities in the statement of cash flows. If we moved it to cash flows from operations and called it 'Increase in Payables,' it would increase cash flows from operations to $3.7 million and put us over the limit."

"Well, do it," ordered the president. "It surely doesn't make any difference where it appears on the statement. It is an increase in both places. It would be much worse for our company in the long term if we failed to meet this ratio requirement."

What is your opinion of the controller and president's reasoning? Is the president's order ethical? Who benefits and who is harmed if the controller follows the president's order? What alternatives are available to management? What would you do?

LO2 **Follow-up Analysis of Cash Flows**

C 8. Go to **CVS Caremark Corporation**'s website and find the statement of cash flows in its latest annual report. Compare it with the 2008 statement in the Supplement to Chapter 1 by doing the following:

1. Identify major changes in operating, investing, and financing activities.
2. Read management's financial review of cash flows.
3. Calculate the cash flow ratios (cash flow yield, cash flows to sales, cash flows to assets) and free cash flow for the most recent year.

How does CVS's cash flow performance differ between these two years? Be prepared to discuss your conclusions in class.

LO1 LO2 **Alternative Uses of Cash**

C 9. Perhaps because of hard times in their start-up years, companies in the high-tech sector of American industry seem more prone than those in other sectors to building up cash reserves. For example, companies like **Cisco Systems**, **Intel**, **Dell**, and **Oracle** have amassed large cash balances.[16]

Assume you work for a company in the high-tech industry that has built up a substantial amount of cash. The company is still growing through development of new products, has some debt, and has never paid a dividend or bought treasury stock. The price of the company's stock is lagging. Write a one-page memo to the CEO that outlines at least four strategies for using the company's cash to improve the company's financial outlook.

CHAPTER 15

The Changing Business Environment: A Manager's Perspective

The Management Process

PLAN

- ▷ **Formulate mission statement.**
- ▷ **Set strategic, tactical, and operating performance objectives and measures.**

PERFORM

- ▷ **Manage ethically.**
- ▷ **Measure value chain and supply chain performance.**

EVALUATE

- ▷ **Compare actual performance with performance levels established in planning stage.**
- ▷ **Use tools of continuous improvement.**

COMMUNICATE

- ▷ **Prepare business plan.**
- ▷ **Prepare accurate financial statements.**
- ▷ **Communicate information clearly and ethically.**

How managers plan, perform, evaluate, and report business can affect us all.

Management is expected to ensure that the organization uses its resources wisely, operates profitably, pays its debts, and abides by laws and regulations. To fulfill these expectations, managers establish the goals, objectives, and strategic plans that guide and control the organization's operating, investing, and financing activities. In this chapter, we describe the approaches that managers have developed to meet the challenges of today's changing business environment and the role that management accounting plays in meeting those challenges in an ethical manner.

LEARNING OBJECTIVES

LO1 Distinguish management accounting from financial accounting and explain how management accounting supports the management process. (pp. 720–727)

LO2 Describe the value chain and its usefulness in analyzing a business. (pp. 727–731)

LO3 Identify the management tools used for continuous improvement. (pp. 731–735)

LO4 Explain the balanced scorecard and its relationship to performance measures. (pp. 735–738)

LO5 Identify the standards of ethical conduct for management accountants. (pp. 738–740)

DECISION POINT ▸ A MANAGER'S FOCUS WAL-MART STORES, INC.

If organizations are to prosper, they must identify the factors that are critical to their success. Key success factors include:

- satisfying customer needs,
- developing efficient operating processes,
- fostering career paths for employees, and
- being an innovative leader in marketing products and services.

Wal-Mart's managers balance these factors when they plan, perform, evaluate, and report on their company's success. Wal-Mart's long-time leader, Lee Scott, summed up his company's strategy this way: "What we look at is, when you end the year, did you produce the record results you wanted and are you positioned to do that again next year?"[1]

- ▸ What is Wal-Mart's strategic plan?
- ▸ What management accounting tools does Wal-Mart use to stay ahead of its competitors?
- ▸ What role does management accounting play in Wal-Mart's endeavors?

The Role of Management Accounting

LO1 Distinguish management accounting from financial accounting and explain how management accounting supports the management process.

To plan and control an organization's operations, to measure its performance, and to make decisions about products or services and many other internal control and governance matters, managers need accurate and timely accounting information. The role of management accounting is to provide an information system that enables managers and persons throughout an organization:

- to make informed decisions,
- to be more effective at their jobs, and
- to improve the organization's performance.

In 2008, the Institute of Management Accountants (IMA) updated the definition of **management accounting** as follows:

> Management accounting is a profession that involves partnering in management decision making, devising planning and performance management systems, and providing expertise in financial reporting and control to assist management in the formulation and implementation of an organization's strategy.[2]

This definition recognizes that regulation, globalization, and technology changes have redefined the management accountant's role from a traditional compliance, number-focused one to that of a strategic business partner within an organization. Thus, the importance of nonfinancial information has increased significantly. Today, management accounting information includes nonfinancial data as well as financial data in performance management, planning and budgeting, corporate governance, risk management, and internal controls.

Management Accounting and Financial Accounting: A Comparison

Both management accounting and financial accounting assist decision makers by identifying, measuring, and processing relevant information and communicating this information through reports. Both provide managers with key measures of a company's performance and with cost information for valuing inventories on the balance sheet. Despite the overlap in their functions, management accounting and financial accounting differ in a number of ways. Table 15-1 summarizes these differences.

The primary users of management accounting information are people inside the organization, whereas financial accounting takes the actual results of management decisions about operating, investing, and financing activities and prepares financial statements for parties outside the organization—owners or stockholders, lenders, customers, and governmental agencies. Although these reports are prepared primarily for external use, managers also rely on them in evaluating an organization's performance.

Because management accounting reports are for internal use, their format can be flexible, driven by the user's needs. They may report either historical or future-oriented information without any formal guidelines or restrictions. In contrast, financial accounting reports, which focus on past performance, must follow generally accepted accounting principles as specified by the Securities and Exchange Commission (SEC).

The information in management accounting reports may be objective and verifiable, expressed in monetary terms or in physical measures of time or objects; the information may be based on estimates, and in such cases, it will be more subjective. In contrast, the statements that financial accounting provides must be based on objective and verifiable information, which is generally historical in nature and measured in monetary terms. Management accounting reports are

Study Note

Management accounting is *not* a subordinate activity to financial accounting. Rather, it is a process that includes financial accounting, tax accounting, information analysis, and other accounting activities.

Study Note

Financial accounting must adhere to the conventions of consistency and comparability to ensure the usefulness of information to parties outside the firm. Management accounting, on the other hand, can use innovative analyses and presentation techniques to enhance the usefulness of information to people within the firm.

TABLE 15-1 Comparison of Management Accounting and Financial Accounting

Areas of Comparison	Management Accounting	Financial Accounting
Primary users	Managers, employees, supply-chain partners	Owners or stockholders, lenders, customers, governmental agencies
Report format	Flexible, driven by user's needs	Based on generally accepted accounting principles
Purpose of reports	Provide information for planning, control, performance measurement, and decision making	Report on past performance
Nature of information	Objective and verifiable for decision making; more subjective for planning (relies on estimates); confidential and private	Objective and verifiable; publicly available
Units of measure	Monetary at historical or current market or projected values; physical measures of time or number of objects	Monetary at historical and current market values
Frequency of reports	Prepared as needed; may or may not be on a periodic basis	Prepared on a periodic basis

prepared as often as needed—annually, quarterly, monthly, or even daily. Financial statements, on the other hand, are prepared and distributed periodically, usually on a quarterly and annual basis.

Management Accounting and the Management Process

Although management actions differ from organization to organization, they generally follow a four-stage management process. As illustrated at the beginning of this chapter and in the chapters that follow, the four stages of this process are:

- planning,
- performing,
- evaluating, and
- communicating.

Management accounting is essential in each stage of the process as managers make business decisions.

Planning Figure 15-1 shows the overall framework in which planning takes place. The overriding goal of a business is to increase the value of the stakeholders' interest in the business. The goal specifies the business's end point, or ideal state. For example, **Wal-Mart**'s end point is "to become the worldwide leader in retailing."

A company's **mission statement** describes the fundamental way in which the company will achieve its goal of increasing stakeholders' value. It also expresses the company's identity and unique character. Wal-Mart's mission statement says that it wants "to give ordinary folk the chance to buy the same things as rich people."

The mission statement is essential to the planning process, which must consider how to add value through strategic objectives, tactical objectives, and operating objectives.

FIGURE 15-1
Overview of the Planning Framework

- **Strategic objectives** are broad, long-term goals that determine the fundamental nature and direction of a business and that serve as a guide for decision making. Strategic objectives involve such basic issues as what a company's main products or services will be, who its primary customers will be, and where it will operate. They stake out the strategic position that a company will occupy in the market—whether it will be a cost leader, quality leader, or niche satisfier. Wal-Mart's The Company of the Future: Fact Sheet[3] lays out three issues Wal-Mart will focus on in the future: health care, energy efficiency, and ethical sourcing. For healthcare, the stated strategic goal is that every American should have access to quality affordable health care. Notice how this goal stakes out Wal-Mart's position as the low cost leader in health care.
- **Tactical objectives** are mid-term goals that position an organization to achieve its long-term strategies. These objectives, which usually cover a three- to five-year period, lay the groundwork for attaining the company's strategic objectives. To implement its health care strategy, Wal-Mart is working with physicians and other providers to increase electronic prescriptions, is providing electronic health records to its employees and their families, and is contracting with other firms to manage their prescription benefit programs.
- **Operating objectives** are short-term goals that outline expectations for the performance of day-to-day operations. Operating objectives link to performance targets and specify how success will be measured. Wal-Mart's operating objectives for health care include: increasing the number of electronic prescriptions filled to 8 million by the end of 2008, providing private health records to all past and current employees and their families by 2010, and saving other companies more than $100 million in prescription benefit costs.

These health care objectives are in addition to Wal-Mart's central focus on increasing sales, earnings per share, and real profit dollars everyday—as evidenced by the daily posting of the company's stock price in every store.

To develop strategic, tactical, and operating objectives, managers must formulate a business plan. A **business plan** is a comprehensive statement of how a company will achieve its objectives. It is usually expressed in financial terms in the form of budgets, and it often includes performance goals for individuals, teams, products, or services.

EXAMPLE. Let's suppose that Vanna Lang is about to open a retail grocery store called Good Foods Store. Lang's goal is to obtain an income from the business and to increase the value of her investment in it. After reading about how traditional grocers are being squeezed out by low-cost competitors like **Wal-Mart** and quality-focused stores like **Whole Foods Market**, Lang has made the following decisions about Good Foods Store:

- Good Foods Store's mission is to attract upscale customers and retain them by selling high-quality foods and providing excellent service in a pleasant atmosphere.
- Lang's strategic objectives call for buying high-quality fresh foods from local growers and international distributors and reselling these items to consumers.
- Her tactical objectives include implementing a stable supply chain of high-quality suppliers and a database to track customers' preferences.
- Her operating objectives call for courteous and efficient customer service. To measure performance in this area, she decides to keep a record of the number and type of complaints about poor customer service.

Before Lang can open her store, she needs to apply to a local bank for a start-up loan. To do so, she must have a business plan that provides a full description of the business, including a complete operating budget for the first two years of operations. The budget must include a forecasted income statement, a forecasted statement of cash flows, and a forecasted balance sheet for both years.

Because Lang does not have a financial background, she consults a local accounting firm for help in developing her business plan. To provide relevant input for the plan, she has to determine the types of products she wants to sell; the volume of sales she anticipates; the selling price for each product; the monthly costs of leasing or purchasing facilities, employing personnel, and maintaining the facilities; and the number of display counters, storage units, and cash registers that she will need.

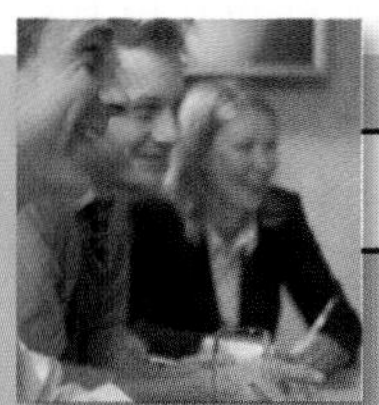

FOCUS ON BUSINESS PRACTICE

What's Going on in the Grocery Business?

Sales at large supermarket chains, such as **Kroger**, **Safeway**, and **Albertson's**, have been flat and profits weak because both ends of their customer market are being squeezed. Large-scale retailers like **Wal-Mart** and **Costco** are attracting cost-conscious grocery shoppers, and upscale grocery customers are being lured to specialty grocers like **Trader Joe's** and **Whole Foods Market**. Albertson's strategy to combat its flat sales and profits was to sell itself to other retailers, like **Supervalu** and **CVS**, to form larger businesses. Other grocery chains are reconsidering their company's mission and strategic options by adding new products and services, such as walk-in medical clinics, closing stores and downsizing, or entering new geographic markets.[4]

Performing Planning alone does not guarantee satisfactory operating results. Management must implement the business plan in ways that make optimal use of available resources in an ethical manner. Smooth operations require one or more of the following:

- Hiring and training personnel
- Matching human and technical resources to the work that must be done
- Purchasing or leasing facilities
- Maintaining an inventory of products for sale
- Identifying operating activities, or tasks, that minimize waste and improve the quality of products or services

Managers execute the business plan by overseeing the company's daily operations. In small companies like Vanna Lang's, managers generally have frequent direct contact with their employees. They supervise them and interact with them to help them learn a task or improve their performance. In larger, more complex organizations, there is usually less direct contact between managers and employees. Instead of directly observing employees, managers in large companies like **Wal-Mart** monitor their employees' performance by measuring the time taken to complete an activity (such as how long it takes to process customer sales) or the frequency of an activity (such as the number of customers served per hour).

Critical to managing any retail business is a thorough understanding of its supply chain. As Figure 15-2 shows, the **supply chain** (also called the *supply network*) is the path that leads from the suppliers of the materials from which a product is made to the final consumer. In the supply chain for grocery stores, food and other items flow from growers and suppliers to manufacturers or distributors to retailers to consumers. The supply chain expresses the links between businesses—growers to vendors to the business to their customers.

EXAMPLE. Let's assume that Good Foods Store is now open for business. The budget prepared for the store's first two years of operation expresses in monetary terms how the business plan should be executed. Items that relate to the business plan appear in the budget and become authorizations for expenditures. They include such matters as spending on store fixtures, hiring employees, developing advertising campaigns, and pricing items for special sales. Lang's knowledge of her supply chain allows her to coordinate deliveries from local growers and international distributors so that she meets the demands of her customers without having too much or too little inventory on hand.

Evaluating When managers evaluate operating results, they compare the organization's actual performance with the performance levels they established in the planning stage. They earmark any significant variations for further analysis so that they can correct the problems. If the problems are the result of a change in the organization's operating environment, the managers may revise the original

FIGURE 15-2 The Supply Chain

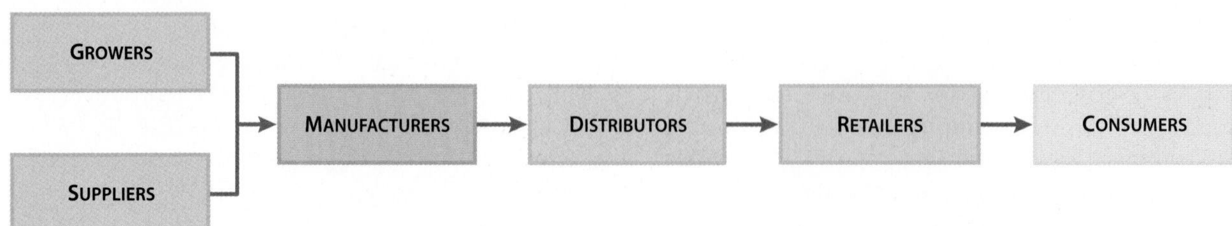

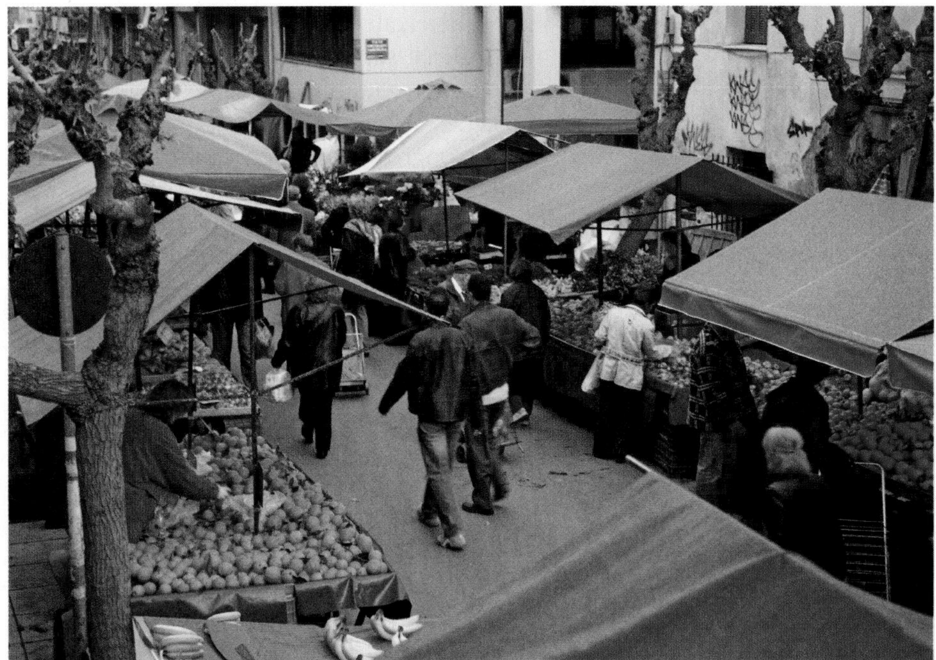

The supply chain is the path that links producers to stores to the final consumer. In the supply chain for grocery stores, fruits and vegetables flow from growers and suppliers to manufacturers or distributors to retailers to consumers. The supply chain for this farmer's market is much shorter: grower to consumer.

Courtesy of Vasiliki/iStockphoto.

objectives. Ideally, the adjustments made in the evaluation stage will improve the company's performance.

EXAMPLE. To evaluate how well Good Foods Store is doing, Vanna Lang will compare the amounts estimated in the budget with actual results. If any differences appear, she will analyze why they have occurred. The reasons for these differences may lead Lang to change parts of her original business plan. In addition to reviewing employees' performance with regard to financial goals, such as avoiding waste, Lang will want to review how well her employees served customers. As noted earlier, she decided to monitor service quality by keeping a record of the number and type of complaints about poor customer service. Her review of this record may help her develop new and better strategies.

Communicating Whether accounting reports are prepared for internal or external use, they must provide accurate information and clearly communicate this information to the reader. Inaccurate or confusing internal reports can have

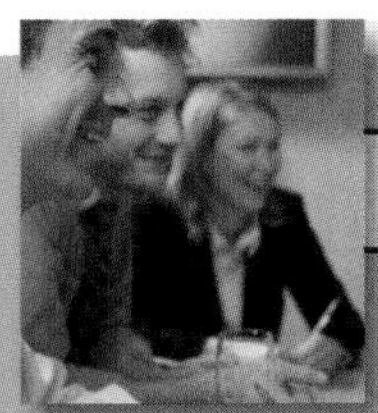

FOCUS ON BUSINESS PRACTICE

What Is Management's Responsibility for the Financial Statements?

Top-level managers have not only an ethical responsibility to ensure that the financial statements issued by their companies adhere to the principles of full disclosure and transparency; today, they have a legal responsibility as well. The Securities and Exchange Commission (SEC) requires the chief executive officers and chief financial officers of companies filing reports with the SEC to certify that those reports contain no untrue statements and include all facts needed to ensure that the reports are not misleading. In addition, the SEC requires managers to ensure that the information in reports filed with the SEC "is recorded, processed, summarized and reported on a timely basis."[5]

a negative effect on a company's operations. Full disclosure and transparency in financial statements issued to external parties is a basic concept of generally accepted accounting principles, and violation of this principle can result in stiff penalties. After the reporting violations by **Enron**, **WorldCom**, and other companies, Congress passed legislation that requires the top management of companies that file financial statements with the Securities and Exchange Commission to certify that these statements are accurate. The penalty for issuing false public reports can be loss of compensation, fines, and jail time.

The key to producing accurate and useful internal and external reports whose meaning is transparent to the reader is to apply the four *w's*: why, who, what, and when.

- **Why?** Know the purpose of the report. Focus on it as you write.
- **Who?** Identify the audience for your report. Communicate at a level that matches your readers' understanding of the issue and their familiarity with accounting information. A detailed, informal report may be appropriate for your manager, but a more concise summary may be necessary for other audiences, such as the president or board of directors of your organization.
- **What?** What information is needed, and what method of presentation is best? Select relevant information from reliable sources. You may draw information from pertinent documents or from interviews with knowledgeable managers and employees. The information should be not only relevant but also easy to read and understand. You may need to include visual aids, such as bar charts or graphs, to present the information clearly.
- **When?** Know the due date for the report. Strive to prepare an accurate report on a timely basis. If the report is urgently needed, you may have to sacrifice some accuracy in the interest of timeliness.

EXAMPLE. Assume that Vanna Lang has asked her company's accountant, Sal Chavez, to prepare financial statements and internal reports. In the financial statements that are prepared:

- The purpose—or *why*—is to report on the financial health of Good Foods Store.
- Lang, her bank and other creditors, and potential investors are the *who*.
- The *what* consists of disclosures about assets, liabilities, product costs, and sales.
- The required reporting deadline for the accounting period answers the question of *when*.

Lang will also want periodic internal reports on various aspects of her store's operations. For example, a monthly report may summarize the costs of ordering products from international distributors and the related shipping charges. If the costs in the monthly reports appear to be too high, she may ask for a special study. The results of such a study might result in a memorandum report like the one shown in Exhibit 15-1.

In summary, management accounting can provide a constant stream of relevant information. Compare Lang's activities and information needs with the plan, perform, evaluate, and communicate steps of the management process. She started with a business plan, implemented the plan, and evaluated the results. Accounting information helped her develop her business plan, communicate that plan to her bank and employees, evaluate the performance of her employees, and report the results of operations. As you can see, accounting plays a critical role in managing the operations of any organization.

EXHIBIT 15-1
A Management Accounting Report

Memorandum

When: Today's Date

Who: To: V. Lang, Good Foods Store
From: Sal Chavez, Accountant

Why: Re: International Distributors Ordering and Shipping Costs—Analysis and Recommendations

What: As you requested, I have analyzed the ordering and shipping costs incurred when buying from international distributors. I found that during the past year, these costs were 9 percent of sales, or $36,000.

On average, we are placing about two orders per week, or eight orders per month. Placing each order requires about two and one-half hours of an employee's time. Further, the international distributors charge a service fee for each order, and shippers charge high rates for orders as small as ours.

My recommendations are (1) to reduce orders to four per month (the products' freshness will not be affected if we order at least once a week) and (2) to begin placing orders through the international distributors' websites (our international distributors do not charge a service fee for online orders). If we follow these recommendations, I project that the costs of receiving products will be reduced to 4 percent of sales, or $16,000, annually—a savings of $20,000.

& APPLY >

Indicate whether each of the following characteristics relates to management accounting (MA) or financial accounting (FA):

1. Focuses on various segments of the business entity
2. Demands objectivity
3. Relies on the criterion of usefulness rather than formal guidelines in reporting information
4. Measures units in historical dollars
5. Reports information on a regular basis
6. Uses only monetary measures for reports
7. Adheres to generally accepted accounting principles
8. Prepares reports whenever needed

SOLUTION
1. MA; 2. FA; 3. MA; 4. FA; 5. FA; 6. FA; 7. FA; 8. MA

Value Chain Analysis

LO2 Describe the value chain and its usefulness in analyzing a business.

Each step in the making of a product or the delivery of a service can be thought of as a link in a chain that adds value to the product or service. This concept of how a business fulfills its mission and objectives is known as the **value chain**. As shown in Figure 15-3, the steps that add value to a product or service—which range from research and development to customer service—are known as **primary processes**. The value chain also includes **support services**, such as legal services and management accounting. These services facilitate the primary processes but do not add value to the final product or service. Their roles are critical, however, to making the primary processes as efficient and effective as possible.

FIGURE 15-3
The Value Chain

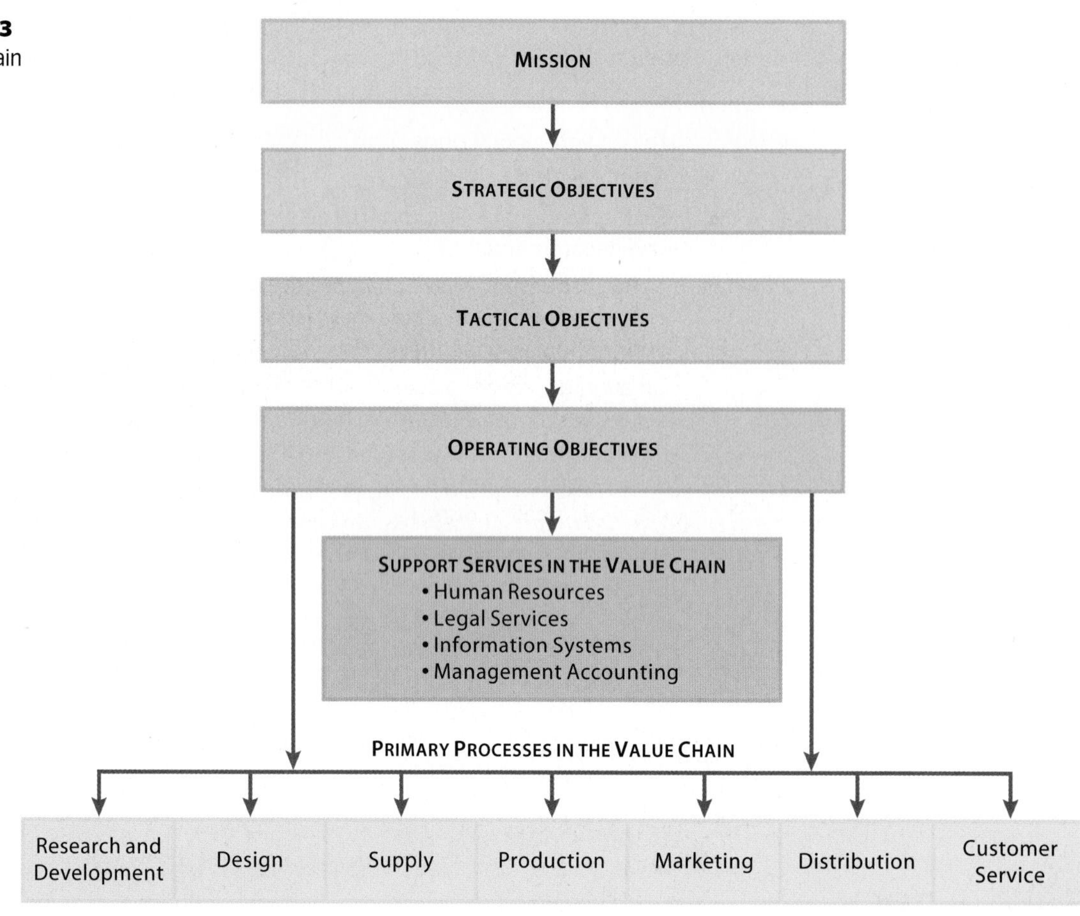

Primary Processes and Support Services

EXAMPLE. Let's assume that Good Foods Store has had some success, and Vanna Lang now wants to determine the feasibility of making and selling her own brand of candy. The primary processes that will add value to the new candy are as follows:

- ***Research and development:*** developing new and better products or services. Lang plans to add value by developing a candy that has less sugar content than similar confections.
- ***Design:*** creating improved and distinctive shapes, labels, or packages for products. For example, a package that is attractive and that describes the desirable features of Lang's new candy will add value to the product.
- ***Supply:*** purchasing materials for products or services. Lang will want to purchase high-quality sugar, chocolate, and other ingredients for the candy, as well as high-quality packaging.
- ***Production:*** manufacturing the product or service. To add value to the new candy, Lang will want to implement efficient manufacturing and packaging processes.
- ***Marketing:*** communicating information about the products or services and selling them. Attractive advertisements will facilitate sale of the new candy to customers.

- *Distribution:* delivering the product or service to the customer. Courteous and efficient service for in-store customers will add value to the product. Lang may also want to accommodate Internet customers by providing shipping.
- *Customer service:* following up with service after sales or providing warranty service. For example, Lang may offer free replacement of any candy that does not satisfy the customer. She could also use questionnaires to measure customer satisfaction.

The support services that provide the infrastructure for the primary processes are as follows:

- *Human resources:* hiring and training employees to carry out all the functions of the business. Lang will need to hire and train personnel to make the new candy.
- *Legal services:* maintaining and monitoring all contracts, agreements, obligations, and other relationships with outside parties. For example, Lang will want legal advice when applying for a trademark for the new candy's name and when signing contracts with suppliers.
- *Information systems:* establishing and maintaining technological means of controlling and communicating within the organization. Lang will want a computerized accounting system that keeps not only financial records but customer information as well.
- *Management accounting:* provides essential information in any business.

Advantages of Value Chain Analysis

An advantage of value chain analysis is that it allows a company to focus on its core competencies. A **core competency** is the thing that a company does best. It is what gives a company an advantage over its competitors. For example, **Wal-Mart** is known for having the lowest prices; that is its core competency.

> **Study Note**
> A company cannot succeed by trying to do everything at the highest level. It has to focus on its core competencies to give customers the best value.

A common result of value chain analysis is outsourcing, which can also be of benefit to a business. **Outsourcing** is the engagement of other companies to perform a process or service in the value chain that is not among an organization's core competencies. For instance, Wal-Mart outsources its inventory management to its vendors, who monitor and stock Wal-Mart's stores and warehouses.

Managers and Value Chain Analysis

In today's competitive global business environment, analysis of the value chain is critical to most companies' survival. Managers at Wal-Mart and other organizations must provide the highest value to customers at the lowest cost, and low cost often equates with the speed at which the primary processes of the value chain are executed. Time to market is very important.

Managers must also make the services that support the primary processes as efficient as possible. These services are essential and cannot be eliminated, but because they do not add value to the final product, they must be implemented as economically as possible. Businesses have been making progress in this area. For example, over the past ten years, the cost of the accounting function in many companies as a percentage of total revenue has declined from 6 percent to 2 percent. Technology has played a big role in making this economy possible.

EXAMPLE. To determine whether manufacturing and selling her own brand of candy will be profitable, Vanna Lang will need accurate information about the cost of the candy. She knows that if her candy is to be competitive, she cannot sell it for more than $10 per pound. Further, she has an idea of how much

EXHIBIT 15-2
Value Chain Analysis

Good Foods Store
Projected Costs of New Candy
June

Primary Process	Initial Costs per Pound	Revised Costs per Pound
Research and development	$0.25	$0.25
Design	0.10	0.10
Supply	1.10	0.60
Production	4.50	3.50
Marketing	0.50	0.50
Distribution	0.90	0.90
Customer service	0.65	0.65
Total cost	$8.00	$6.50

candy she can sell in the first year. Based on this information, her accountant, Sal Chavez, analyzes the value chain and projects the initial costs per pound shown in Exhibit 15-2. The total cost of $8 per pound worries Lang because with a selling price of $10, it leaves only $2, or 20 percent of revenue, to cover all the support services and provide a profit. Lang believes that if the enterprise is to be successful, this percentage, called the *margin*, must be at least 35 percent. Since the selling price is constrained by the competition, she must find a way to reduce costs.

- Option 1: Chavez tells her that the company could achieve a lower total cost per pound by selling a higher volume of candy, but that is not realistic for the new product. He also points out that the largest projected costs in the store's value chain are for supply and production. Because Lang plans to order ingredients from a number of suppliers, her orders would not be large enough to qualify for quantity discounts and savings on shipping. Using a single supplier could reduce the supply cost by $0.50 per unit.
- Option 2: Another way of reducing the cost of production would be to outsource this process to a candy manufacturer, whose high volume of products would allow it to produce the candy at a much lower cost than could be done at Good Foods Store. Outsourcing would reduce the production cost to $3.50 per unit. Thus, the total unit cost would be reduced to $6.50, as shown in Exhibit 15-2. This per unit cost would enable the company to sell the candy at a competitive $10 per pound and make the targeted margin of 35 percent ($3.50 ÷ $10.00).

This value chain analysis illustrates two important points. First, Good Food Store's mission is as a retailer. The company has no experience in making candy. Manufacturing candy would require a change in the company's mission and major changes in the way it does business.

Second, outsourcing portions of the value chain that are not part of a business's core competency is often the best business policy. Since Good Foods Store does not have a core competency in manufacturing candy, it would not be competitive in this field. Vanna Lang would be better off having an experienced candy manufacturer produce the candy according to her specifications and then selling the candy under her store's label. As Lang's business grows, increased volume may allow her to reconsider undertaking the manufacture of candy.

STOP & APPLY >

The following unit costs were determined by dividing the total costs of each component by the number of products produced. From these unit costs, determine the total cost per unit of primary processes and the total cost per unit of support services.

Research and development	$ 1.25
Human resources	1.35
Design	0.15
Supply	1.10
Legal services	0.40
Production	4.00
Marketing	0.80
Distribution	0.90
Customer service	0.65
Information systems	0.75
Management accounting	0.10
Total cost per unit	$11.45

SOLUTION

Primary Processes:

Research and development	$1.25
Design	0.15
Supply	1.10
Production	4.00
Marketing	0.80
Distribution	0.90
Customer service	0.65
Total cost per unit	$8.85

Support Services:

Human resources	$1.35
Legal services	0.40
Information systems	0.75
Management accounting	0.10
Total cost per unit	$2.60

Continuous Improvement

LO3 Identify the management tools used for continuous improvement.

Today, managers in all parts of the world have ready access to international markets and to current information for informed decision making. As a result, global competition has increased significantly. One of the most valuable lessons gained from this increase in competition is that management cannot afford to become complacent. The concept of **continuous improvement** evolved to avoid such complacency. Organizations that adhere to continuous improvement are never satisfied with what is; they constantly seek improved quality and lower cost through better methods, products, services, processes, or resources. In response to this concept, several important management tools have emerged. These tools help companies remain competitive by focusing on continuous improvement of business methods.

Management Tools for Continuous Improvement

Among the management tools that companies use are the just-in-time operating philosophy, total quality management, activity-based management, and the theory of constraints.

Just-in-Time Operating Philosophy The **just-in-time (JIT) operating philosophy** requires that all resources—materials, personnel, and facilities—be acquired and used only when they are needed. Its objectives are to improve productivity and eliminate waste.

In a JIT environment, production processes are consolidated and workers are trained to be multiskilled so that they can operate several different machines. Materials and supplies are delivered just at the time they are needed in the production process, which significantly reduces inventories of materials. Production is usually started only when an order is received, and the ordered goods are shipped when completed, which reduces the inventories of finished goods.

When manufacturing companies adopt the JIT operating philosophy, the management system is called **lean production** since it reduces production time and costs, investment in materials inventory, and materials waste, and it results in higher-quality goods. Funds that are no longer invested in inventory can be redirected according to the goals of the company's business plan. JIT methods help retailers like **Wal-Mart** and manufacturers like **Harley-Davidson** assign more accurate costs to their products and identify the costs of waste and inefficient operation. Wal-Mart for example, requires vendors to restock inventory often and pays them only when the goods sell. This minimizes the funds invested in inventory and allows the retailer to focus on offering high-demand merchandise at attractive prices.

Total Quality Management **Total quality management (TQM)** requires that all parts of a business focus on quality. TQM's goal is the improved quality of products or services and the work environment. Workers are empowered to make operating decisions that improve quality in both areas. All employees are tasked to spot possible causes of poor quality, use resources efficiently and effectively to improve quality, and reduce the time needed to complete a task or provide a service.

TQM, like the JIT operating philosophy, focuses on improving product or service quality by identifying and reducing or eliminating the causes of waste. Like JIT, TQM results in reduced waste of materials, higher-quality goods, and lower production costs in manufacturing environments.

To determine the impact of poor quality on profits, TQM managers use accounting information about the **costs of quality**. The costs of quality include both the costs of achieving quality (such as training costs and inspection costs) and the costs of poor quality (such as the costs of rework and of handling customer complaints). Managers use information about the costs of quality:

- to relate their organization's business plan to its daily operating activities,
- to stimulate improvement by sharing this information with all employees,
- to identify opportunities for reducing costs and customer dissatisfaction, and
- to determine the costs of quality relative to net income.

For retailers like Wal-Mart and Good Foods Store, TQM results in a quality customer experience before, during, and after the sale.

Activity-Based Management **Activity-based management (ABM)** is an approach to managing an organization that identifies all major activities or tasks involved in making a product or service, determines the resources consumed by each of those activities and why the resources are used, and categorizes the activities as either adding value to a product or service or not adding value.

Activities that add value to a product or service, as perceived by the customer, are known as **value-adding activities**. All other activities are called **nonvalue-adding activities**; they add cost to a product or service but do not increase its market value. ABM eliminates nonvalue-adding activities that do not support the organization; those that do support the organization are focal points for cost reduction. ABM results in reduced costs, reduced waste of resources, increased efficiency, and increased customer satisfaction.

ABM includes a management accounting practice called activity-based costing. **Activity-based costing (ABC)**:

- identifies all of an organization's major operating activities (both production and nonproduction),
- traces costs to those activities or cost pools, and
- assigns costs to the products or services that use the resources supplied by those activities.

The advantage to using ABC is that ABC produces more accurate costs than traditional cost allocation methods, which leads to improved decision making.

Theory of Constraints According to the **theory of constraints (TOC)**, limiting factors, or bottlenecks, occur during the production of any product or service, but once managers identify such a constraint, they can focus their attention and resources on it and achieve significant improvements. TOC thus helps managers set priorities for how they spend their time and resources. In identifying constraints, managers rely on the information that management accounting provides.

EXAMPLE. Suppose Vanna Lang wants to increase sales of store-roasted coffees. After reviewing management accounting reports, she concludes that the limited production capacity of her equipment—a roaster that can roast only 100 pounds of coffee beans per hour—limits the sales of the store's coffee. To overcome this constraint, she can rent or purchase a second roaster. The increase in production will enable her to increase coffee sales.

Achieving Continuous Improvement

JIT, TQM, ABM, and TOC all make a contribution to continuous improvement, as shown in Figure 15-4. In the just-in-time operating environment, management wages war on wasted time, wasted resources, and wasted space. All employees are encouraged to look for ways of improving processes and saving time. Total quality management focuses on improving the quality of the product or service and the work environment. It pursues continuous improvement by reducing the number of defective products and the time needed to complete a task or provide a service. Activity-based management seeks continuous improvement by emphasizing the ongoing reduction or elimination of nonvalue-adding activities. The theory of constraints helps managers focus resources on efforts that will produce the most effective improvements.

Each of these management tools can be used individually, or parts of them can be combined to create a new operating environment. They are applicable in service businesses, such as banking, as well as in manufacturing and retail businesses. By focusing attention on continuous improvement and fine-tuning of operations, they contribute to the same results in any organization:

- a reduction in product or service costs and delivery time,
- an improvement in the quality of the product or service, and
- an increase in customer satisfaction.

FIGURE 15-4 The Continuous Improvement Environment

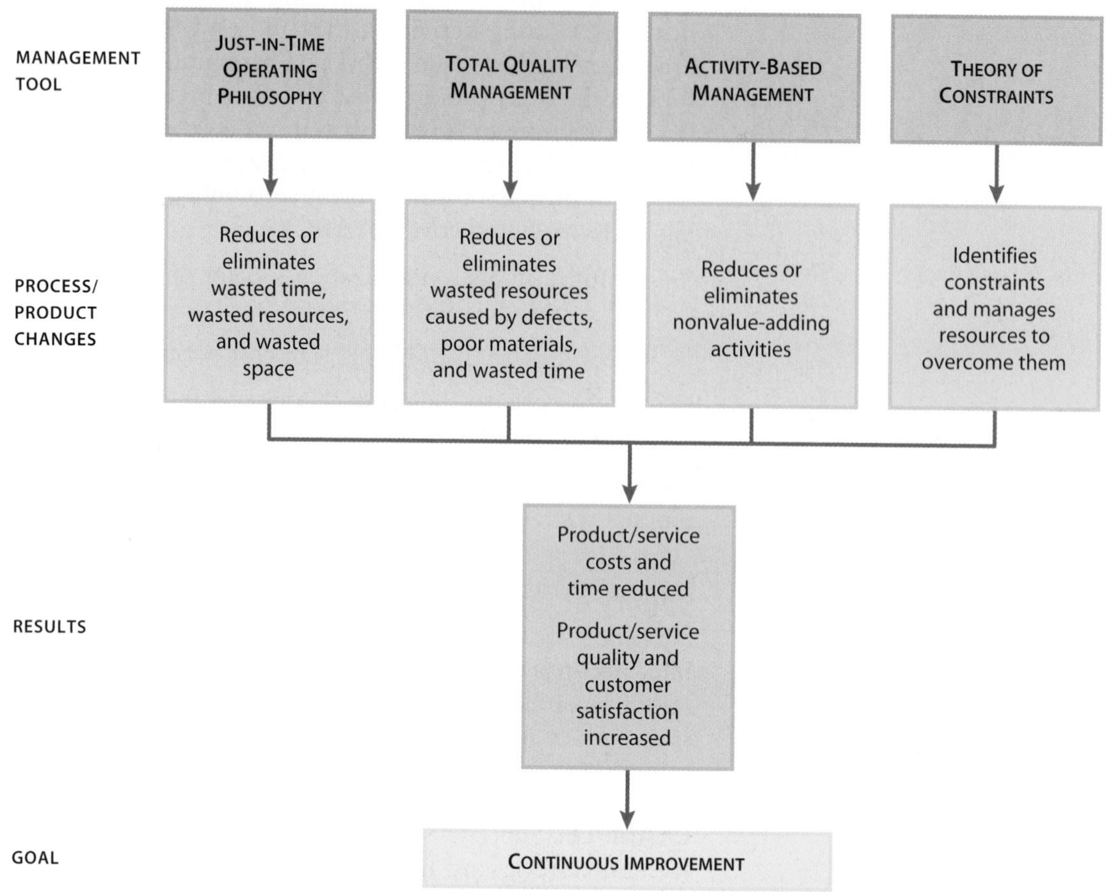

STOP & APPLY >

Recently, you dined with four chief financial officers (CFOs) who were attending a seminar on management tools and approaches to improving operations. During dinner, the CFOs shared information about their organizations' current operating environments. Excerpts from the dinner conversation appear below. Indicate whether each excerpt describes activity-based management (ABM), the just-in-time (JIT) operating philosophy, total quality management (TQM), or the theory of constraints (TOC).

CFO 1: We think quality can be achieved through carefully designed production processes. We focus on minimizing the time needed to move, store, queue, and inspect our materials and products. We've reduced inventories by purchasing and using materials only when they're needed.

CFO 2: Your approach is good. But we're more concerned with our total operating environment, so we have a strategy that asks all employees to contribute to the quality of both our products and our work environment. We focus on eliminating poor product quality by reducing waste and inefficiencies in our current operating methods.

(continued)

CFO 3: Our organization has adopted a strategy for producing high-quality products that incorporates many of your approaches. We also want to manage our resources effectively, and we do it by monitoring operating activities. We analyze all activities to eliminate or reduce the ones that don't add value to products.

CFO 4: All of your approaches are good, but how do you set priorities for your management efforts? We find that we achieve the greatest improvements by focusing our time and resources on the bottlenecks in our production processes.

SOLUTION

CFO 1: JIT; CFO 2: TQM; CFO 3: ABM; CFO 4: TOC

Performance Measures: A Key to Achieving Organizational Objectives

LO4 Explain the balanced scorecard and its relationship to performance measures.

Performance measures are quantitative tools that gauge an organization's performance in relation to a specific goal or an expected outcome. Performance measures may be financial or nonfinancial.

- Financial performance measures include return on investment, net income as a percentage of sales, and the costs of poor quality as a percentage of sales. Such measures use monetary information to gauge the performance of a profit-generating organization or its segments—its divisions, departments, product lines, sales territories, or operating activities.
- Nonfinancial performance measures include the number of times an activity occurs or the time taken to perform a task. Examples are number of customer complaints, number of orders shipped the same day, and the time taken to fill an order. Such performance measures are useful in reducing or eliminating waste and inefficiencies in operating activities.

Using Performance Measures in the Management Process

Managers use performance measures in all stages of the management process.

- In the planning stage, they establish performance measures that will support the organization's mission and the objectives of its business plan, such as reducing costs and increasing quality, efficiency, timeliness, and customer satisfaction. As you will recall from earlier in the chapter, Vanna Lang selected the number of customer complaints as a performance measure to monitor the quality of service at Good Foods Store.
- As managers perform their duties, they use the performance measures they established in the planning stage to guide and motivate employees and to assign costs to products, departments, and operating activities. Vanna Lang will record the number of customer complaints during the year. She can group the information by type of complaint or by the employee involved in the service.
- When evaluating performance, managers use the information that performance measures have provided to analyze significant differences between actual and planned performance and to identify ways of improving performance. By comparing the actual and planned number of customer complaints, Lang can identify problem areas and develop solutions.

- When communicating with stakeholders, managers use information derived from performance measurement to report results and develop new budgets. If Lang needed formal reports, she could prepare performance evaluations based on this information.

The Balanced Scorecard

Study Note

The balanced scorecard focuses all perspectives of a business on accomplishing the business's mission.

Study Note

The balanced scorecard provides a way of linking the lead performance indicators of employees, internal business processes, and customer needs to the lag performance indicator of external financial results. In other words, if managers can foster excellent performance for three of the stakeholder groups, good financial results will occur for the investor stakeholder group.

If an organization is to achieve its mission and objectives, it must identify the areas in which it needs to excel and establish measures of performance in these critical areas. As we have indicated, effective performance measurement requires an approach that uses both financial and nonfinancial measures that are tied to a company's mission and objectives. One such approach that has gained wide acceptance is the balanced scorecard.

The **balanced scorecard** is a framework that links the perspectives of an organization's four stakeholder groups to the organization's mission, objectives, resources, and performance measures. The four stakeholder groups are as follows:

- Stakeholders with a financial perspective (owners, investors, and creditors) value improvements in financial measures, such as net income and return on investment.
- Stakeholders with a learning and growth perspective (employees) value high wages, job satisfaction, and opportunities to fulfill their potential.
- Stakeholders who focus on the business's internal processes value the safe and cost-effective production of high-quality products.
- Stakeholders with a customer perspective value high-quality products that are low in cost.

Although their perspectives differ, these stakeholder groups may be interested in the same measurable performance goals. For example, holders of both the customer and internal business processes perspectives are interested in performance that results in high-quality products.

EXAMPLE. Figure 15-5 applies the balanced scorecard to Good Foods Store. The company's mission is to be the food store of choice in the community. This mission is at the center of the company's balanced scorecard. Surrounding it are the four interrelated perspectives.

- ***Learning and Growth:*** At the base of the scorecard is the learning and growth perspective. Here, part of the objective, or performance goal, is to provide courteous service. Because training employees in customer service should result in courteous service, performance related to this objective can be measured in terms of how many employees have received training. The number of customer complaints is another measure of courteous service.
- ***Internal Business Processes:*** From the perspective of internal business processes, the objective is to help achieve the company's mission by managing the supply chain efficiently, which should contribute to customer satisfaction. Efficiency in the ordering process can be measured by recording the number of orders placed with distributors each month and the number of times per month that customers ask for items that are not in stock.
- ***Customer:*** If the objectives of the learning and growth and internal business processes perspectives are met, this should result in attracting customers and

FIGURE 15-5 The Balanced Scorecard for Good Foods Store

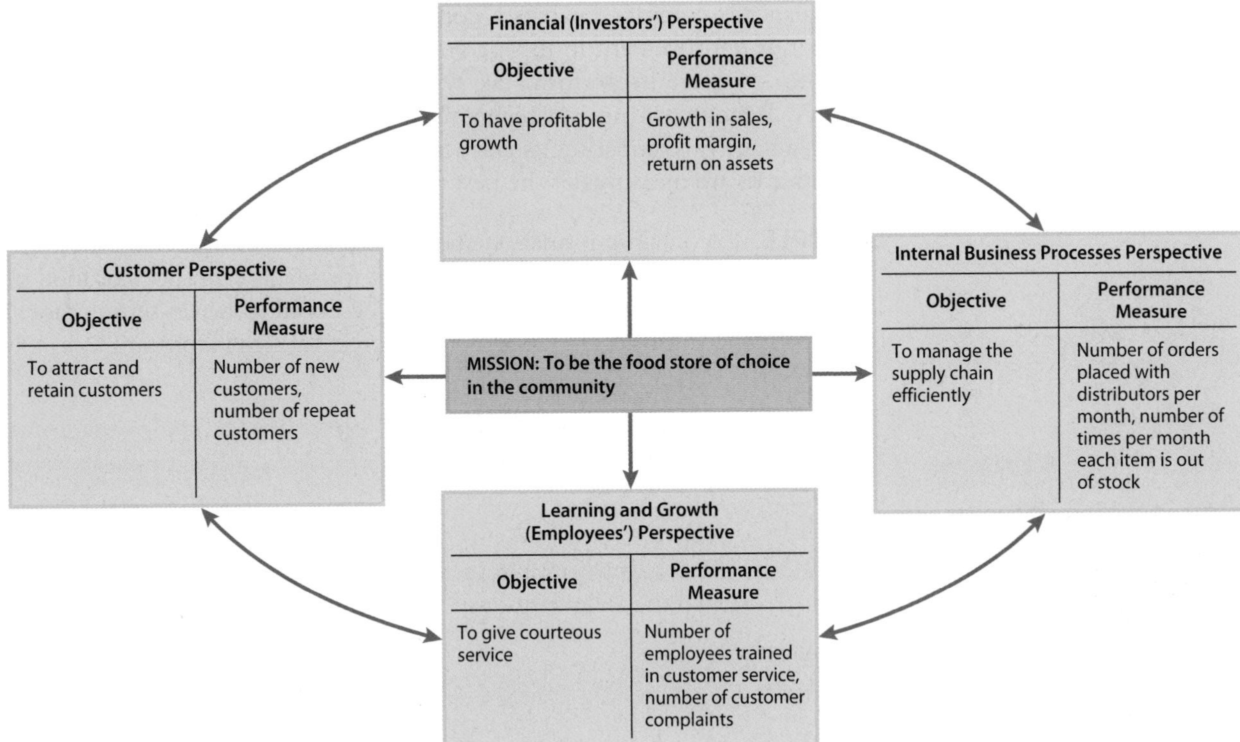

Source: Adapted from Robert S. Kaplan and David P. Norton, "The Balanced Scorecard: Measures That Drive Performance," *Harvard Business Review*, July–August 2005.

retaining them, which is the objective of the customer perspective. Performance related to this objective is measured by tracking the number of new customers and the number of repeat customers.

- ***Financial:*** Satisfied customers should help achieve the objective of the financial perspective, which is profitable growth. Profitable growth is measured by growth in sales, profit margin, and return on assets.

FOCUS ON BUSINESS PRACTICE

How Does the Balanced Scorecard Measure Success at Futura Industries?

Futura Industries is not a famous company, but it is one of the best. Based in Utah, it is rated as that state's top privately owned employer and serves a high-end niche in such diverse markets as floor coverings, electronics, transportation, and shower doors. In achieving its success, Futura uses the balanced scorecard. Futura has developed the following performance measures:

- Employee turnover is a measure of learning and growth.
- Percentage of sales from new products and total production cost per standard hour are measures of the company's internal processes.
- The number of customers' complaints and percentage of materials returned are the measures of customer satisfaction.
- Income and gross margin are among the measures of financial performance.[6]

Benchmarking

The balanced scorecard enables a company to determine whether it is making continuous improvement in its operations. But to ensure its success, a company must also compare its performance with that of similar companies in the same industry. **Benchmarking** is a technique for determining a company's competitive advantage by comparing its performance with that of its closest competitors. **Benchmarks** are measures of the best practices in an industry.

EXAMPLE. To obtain information about benchmarks in the retail grocery industry, Vanna Lang might join a trade association for small retail shops or food stores. Information about these benchmarks would be useful to her in setting targets for the performance measures in Good Foods Store's balanced scorecard.

STOP & APPLY >

Connie's Takeout caters to young professionals who want a good meal at home but do not have time to prepare it. Connie's has developed the following business objectives:

1. To provide fast, courteous service
2. To manage the inventory of food carefully
3. To have repeat customers
4. To be profitable and grow

Connie's has also developed the following performance measures:

5. Growth in revenues per quarter and net income
6. Average unsold food at the end of the business day as a percentage of the total food purchased that day
7. Average customer time at the counter before being waited on
8. Percentage of customers who have shopped in the store before

Match each of these objectives and performance measures with the four perspectives of the balanced scorecard: financial perspective, learning and growth perspective, internal business processes perspective, and customer perspective.

SOLUTION

Financial perspective: 4, 5; learning and growth perspective: 1, 7; internal business processes perspective: 2, 6; customer perspective: 3, 8

Standards of Ethical Conduct

LO5 Identify the standards of ethical conduct for management accountants.

Managers balance the interests of external parties (e.g., customers, owners, suppliers, governmental agencies, and the local community) when they make decisions about the proper use of organizational resources and the financial reporting of their actions. When ethical conflicts arise, management accountants have a responsibility to help managers balance those interests. For example, **Wal-Mart**'s goal is to provide customers with low-cost, durable, and safe products. It also seeks ethical and environmentally responsible global sourcing with its suppliers. But its suppliers may differ with Wal-Mart's management on these goals as they pursue maximum profits in countries where social and environmental standards are lax or nonexistent. These conflicting supplier/purchaser interests have prompted Wal-Mart to:

- Announce that it will only work with suppliers who maintain Wal-Mart standards throughout their relationship.

FOCUS ON BUSINESS PRACTICE

How to Blow the Whistle on Fraud

According to **PricewaterhouseCoopers**'s fourth biennial survey of more than 5,400 companies in 40 countries, eradicating fraud is extremely difficult. Despite increased attention to fraud detection systems and stronger internal controls, half of the companies interviewed had fallen victim to some type of fraud in the previous two years. The average cost of the fraud was about $3.2 million per company. Fraud appeared most likely to happen in Africa, North America, and Central-Eastern Europe.

The Sarbanes-Oxley Act of 2002 requires that all publicly traded companies have an anonymous incident reporting system. Such a system can help prevent fraud, as can hotlines that provide guidance on ethical dilemmas involved in reporting fraud. An example of such an ethics hotline is the one that the Institute of Management Accountants instituted in 2002. However, PricewaterhouseCoopers's study found that the best fraud deterrents were a company-wide risk management system with a continuous proactive fraud-monitoring component and a strong ethical culture to which all employees subscribe.[8]

- Start building a framework of social and environmental standards for all global retailers.
- Call for a single third party auditing system for everyone to assure compliance with these new standards.[7]

To be viewed credibly by the various parties who rely on the information they provide, management accountants must adhere to the highest standards of performance. To provide guidance, the Institute of Management Accountants has issued standards of ethical conduct for practitioners of management accounting and financial management. Those standards, presented in Exhibit 15-3, emphasize that management accountants have responsibilities in the areas of competence, confidentiality, integrity, and credibility.

EXHIBIT 15-3 Statement of Ethical Professional Practice

Members of IMA shall behave ethically. A commitment to ethical professional practice includes: overarching principles that express our values, and standards that guide our conduct.

PRINCIPLES

IMA's overarching ethical principles include: Honesty, Fairness, Objectivity, and Responsibility. Members shall act in accordance with these principles and shall encourage others within their organizations to adhere to them.

STANDARDS

A member's failure to comply with the following standards may result in disciplinary action.

I. COMPETENCE

Each member has a responsibility to:

1. Maintain an appropriate level of professional expertise by continually developing knowledge and skills.
2. Perform professional duties in accordance with relevant laws, regulations, and technical standards.
3. Provide decision support information and recommendations that are accurate, clear, concise, and timely.
4. Recognize and communicate professional limitations or other constraints that would preclude responsible judgment or successful performance of an activity.

(continued)

EXHIBIT 15-3 *(Continued)*

II. CONFIDENTIALITY

Each member has a responsibility to:

1. Keep information confidential except when disclosure is authorized or legally required.
2. Inform all relevant parties regarding appropriate use of confidential information. Monitor subordinates' activities to ensure compliance.
3. Refrain from using confidential information for unethical or illegal advantage.

III. INTEGRITY

Each member has a responsibility to:

1. Mitigate actual conflicts of interest. Regularly communicate with business associates to avoid apparent conflicts of interest. Advise all parties of any potential conflicts.
2. Refrain from engaging in any conduct that would prejudice carrying out duties ethically.
3. Abstain from engaging in or supporting any activity that might discredit the profession.

IV. CREDIBILITY

Each member has a responsibility to:

1. Communicate information fairly and objectively.
2. Disclose all relevant information that could reasonably be expected to influence an intended user's understanding of the reports, analyses, or recommendations.
3. Disclose delays or deficiencies in information, timeliness, processing, or internal controls in conformance with organization policy and/or applicable law.

RESOLUTION OF ETHICAL CONFLICT

In applying the Standards of Ethical Professional Practice, you may encounter problems identifying unethical behavior or resolving an ethical conflict. When faced with ethical issues, you should follow your organization's established policies on the resolution of such conflict. If these policies do not resolve the ethical conflict, you should consider the following courses of action:

Discuss the issue with your immediate supervisor except when it appears that the supervisor is involved. In that case, present the issue to the next level. If you cannot achieve a satisfactory resolution, submit the issue to the next management level. If your immediate superior is the chief executive officer or equivalent, the acceptable reviewing authority may be a group such as the audit committee, executive committee, board of directors, board of trustees, or owners. Contact with levels above the immediate superior should be initiated only with your superior's knowledge, assuming he or she is not involved. Communication of such problems to authorities or individuals not employed or engaged by the organization is not considered appropriate, unless you believe there is a clear violation of the law.

Clarify relevant ethical issues by initiating a confidential discussion with an IMA Ethics Counselor or other impartial advisor to obtain a better understanding of possible courses of action.

Consult your own attorney as to legal obligations and rights concerning the ethical conflict.

Source: IMA Statement of Ethical Professional Practice, Institute of Management Accountants, www.imanet.org. Reprinted by permission.

Rank in order of importance the management accountant's four areas of responsibility: competence, confidentiality, integrity, and credibility. Explain the reasons for your ranking.

SOLUTION

Rankings will vary depending on the reasoning used concerning the four areas of responsibility. Ranking differences between individuals also reinforces the fact that we approach ethical behavior in a variety of ways and why a code of ethics is necessary.

A LOOK BACK AT ▸ WAL-MART STORES, INC.

The Decision Point at the beginning of this chapter focused on **Wal-Mart**, a company whose mission is to give ordinary folk the chance to buy the same things as rich people around the world. It posed these questions:

- What is Wal-Mart's strategic plan?
- What management accounting tools does Wal-Mart use to stay ahead of its competitors?
- What role does management accounting play in Wal-Mart's endeavors?

Wal-Mart's strategic plan focuses on achieving the company's objective of being the low-cost leader in the markets that it enters. This strategy drives the way Wal-Mart's managers address stakeholder perspectives, as well as how they formulate tactical and operating plans. To stay agile, flexible, and ahead of its competitors, Wal-Mart uses management tools like supply and value chains to standardize requirements and procedures and keep the costs of doing business low. These cost containment measures demonstrate Wal-Mart's resolve to remain an industry leader. But what role does management accounting play in this endeavor?

Management accounting provides the information necessary for effective decision making. Wal-Mart's managers use management accounting information in making decisions about everything from entering new markets like health care, to selecting vendors and products, to developing and implementing new supply-chain processes, to pricing and marketing its goods.

Management accounting also provides Wal-Mart's managers with objective data that they can use to measure the company's performance in terms of its key success factor—cost. Among the management accounting tools used are budgets, which set daily operating goals and provide targets for evaluating a store's performance. As Wal-Mart strives to improve its sales, earnings per share, and profitability by maintaining its record of successes, it will continue to rely on the information that management accounting provides.

Review Problem

Supply Chain and Value Chain Analysis
LO2

Wal-mart sells hundreds of prescription drugs for $4.00 for a 30-day supply. Suppose Medicine for All manufactures generic prescription drugs and currently sells them for $3.00 for a 30-day supply. Wal-Mart will buy these drugs if Medicine for All lowers its price to $2.00. However, if Medicine for All lowers its price with the current cost structure, it will lose money. Medicine for Alls management applies value chain analysis to the company's operations in an effort to reduce costs and attract Wal-Mart's business. A study by the company's management accountant has determined the following per unit costs for primary processes:

Primary Process	Cost per Unit
Research and development	$0.50
Design	0.25
Supply	0.35
Production	0.50
Advertising and marketing	0.55
Distribution	0.20
Customer service	0.05
Total cost	$2.40

To generate a gross margin large enough for the company to cover its operating costs and earn a profit, Medicine for All must lower its total cost per 30-day supply for primary processes to less than $1.60. After analyzing operations, management believes the following cost reduction proposals for primary processes are possible:

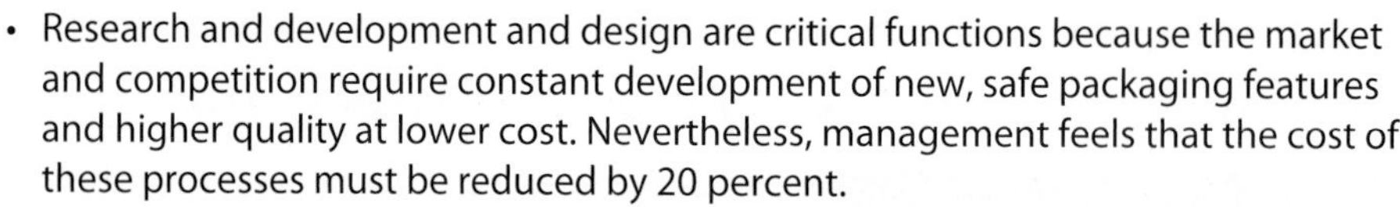

- Research and development and design are critical functions because the market and competition require constant development of new, safe packaging features and higher quality at lower cost. Nevertheless, management feels that the cost of these processes must be reduced by 20 percent.
- Five different suppliers currently provide the components for the generic medicines. Ordering these components from just two suppliers and negotiating lower prices could result in a savings of 30 percent.
- The generic drugs are currently manufactured in Mexico. By shifting production to China, the unit cost of production can be lowered by 40 percent.
- Management believes that by working with Wal-Mart they can cut their advertising and marketing budgets by 70 percent.
- Distribution costs are already very low, but management will set a target of reducing the cost by 10 percent.
- Customer support and service has been a weakness of the company and has resulted in lost sales. Management therefore proposes increasing the cost per unit of customer support to Wal-Mart by 50 percent.

Required

1. Prepare a table showing Medicine for All's current cost of primary processes and the projected cost per 30-day supply based on management's proposals for cost reduction.
2. Will management's proposals for cost reduction achieve the targeted total cost of less than $1.60 per 30-day supply?
3. Manager insight: What are the company's support services? What role should these services play in the value chain analysis?

Answers to Review Problem

1.

	Current Cost per 30-Day Supply	Percentage (Decrease) Increase	Projected Cost per 30-Day Supply*
Research and development	$0.50	(20%)	$0.400
Design	0.25	(20%)	0.200
Supply	0.35	(30%)	0.245
Production	0.50	(40%)	0.300
Advertising and marketing	0.55	(70%)	0.165
Distribution	0.20	(10%)	0.180
Customer service	0.05	50%	0.075
Total	$2.40		$1.565

*Computations: $0.50 × (100% − 20%) = $0.40; $0.25 × (100% − 20%) = $0.20; $0.35 × (100% − 30%) = $0.245; $0.50 × (100% − 40%) = $0.30; $0.55 × (100% − 70%) = $0.165; $0.20 × (100% − 10%) = $0.18; and $0.05 × (100% + 50%) = $0.075.

2. Yes, $1.565 is lower than $1.60. Accept Wal-Mart's offer.
3. The support services are human resources, legal services, information systems, and management accounting. The analysis has not mentioned these services, which are necessary but do not provide direct value to the final product. Management should analyze these functions carefully to see if they can be reduced.

LO1 Distinguish management accounting from financial accounting and explain how management accounting supports the management process.

Management accounting involves partnering with management in decision making, devising planning and performance management systems, and providing expertise in financial reporting and control to assist management in the formulation and implementation of an organization's strategy.

Management accounting reports provide information for planning, control, performance measurement, and decision making to managers and employees when they need such information. These reports have a flexible format; they can present either historical or future-oriented information expressed in dollar amounts or physical measures. In contrast, financial accounting reports provide information about an organization's past performance to owners, lenders, customers, and governmental agencies on a periodic basis. Financial accounting reports follow strict guidelines defined by generally accepted accounting principles.

Management accounting supports each stage of the management process. When managers plan, they work with management accounting to establish strategic, tactical, and operating objectives that reflect their company's mission and to formulate a comprehensive business plan for achieving those objectives. The plan is usually expressed in financial terms in the form of budgets. When managers implement the plan, they use the information provided in the budgets to manage the business in the context of its supply chain. In evaluating performance, managers compare actual performance with planned performance and take steps to correct any problems. Reports reflect the results of planning, executing, and evaluating operations and may be prepared for external or internal use.

LO2 Describe the value chain and its usefulness in analyzing a business.

The value chain conceives of each step in the production of a product or the delivery of a service as a link in a chain that adds value to the product or service. These value-adding steps—research and development, design, supply, production, marketing, distribution, and customer service—are known as primary processes. The value chain also includes support services—human resources, legal services, information services, and management accounting. Support services facilitate the primary processes but do not add value to the final product. Value chain analysis enables a company to focus on its core competencies. Parts of the value chain that are not core competencies are frequently outsourced.

LO3 Identify the management tools used for continuous improvement.

Management tools for continuous improvement include the just-in-time (JIT) operating philosophy, total quality management (TQM), activity-based management (ABM), and the theory of constraints (TOC). These tools are designed to help businesses meet the demands of global competition by reducing resource waste and costs and by improving product or service quality, thereby increasing customer satisfaction.

Management accounting responds to a just-in-time operating environment by providing an information system that is sensitive to changes in production processes. In a total quality management environment, management accounting provides information about the costs of quality. Activity-based management's assignment of overhead costs to products or services relies on the accounting practice known as activity-based costing (ABC). In businesses that use the theory of constraints, management accounting identifies process or product constraints.

LO4 Explain the balanced scorecard and its relationship to performance measures. The balanced scorecard links the perspectives of an organization's stakeholder groups—financial (investors and owners), learning and growth (employees), internal business processes, and customers—to the organization's mission, objectives, resources, and performance measures. Performance measures are used to assess whether the objectives of each of the four perspectives are being met. Benchmarking is a technique for determining a company's competitive advantage by comparing its performance with that of its industry peers.

LO5 Identify the standards of ethical conduct for management accountants. The Statement of Ethical Professional Practice emphasizes the Institute of Management Accounting members' responsibilities in the areas of competence, confidentiality, integrity, and credibility. These standards of conduct help management accountants recognize and avoid situations that could compromise their ability to supply management with accurate and relevant information.

REVIEW of Concepts and Terminology

The following concepts and terms were introduced in this chapter:

Activity-based costing (ABC) 733 (LO3)

Activity-based management (ABM) 732 (LO3)

Balanced scorecard 736 (LO4)

Benchmarking 738 (LO4)

Benchmarks 738 (LO4)

Business plan 723 (LO1)

Continuous improvement 731 (LO3)

Core competency 729 (LO2)

Costs of quality 732 (LO3)

Just-in-time (JIT) operating philosophy 732 (LO3)

Lean production 732 (LO3)

Management accounting 720 (LO1)

Mission statement 721 (LO1)

Nonvalue-adding activities 733 (LO3)

Operating objectives 722 (LO1)

Outsourcing 729 (LO2)

Performance measures 735 (LO4)

Primary processes 727 (LO2)

Strategic objectives 722 (LO1)

Supply chain 724 (LO1)

Support services 727 (LO2)

Tactical objectives 722 (LO1)

Theory of constraints (TOC) 733 (LO3)

Total quality management (TQM) 732 (LO3)

Value-adding activities 733 (LO3)

Value chain 727 (LO2)

CHAPTER ASSIGNMENTS

BUILDING Your Basic Knowledge and Skills

Short Exercises

LO1 **Management Accounting Versus Financial Accounting**

SE 1. Management accounting differs from financial accounting in a number of ways. Indicate whether each of the following characteristics relates to management accounting (MA) or financial accounting (FA):

1. Publically reported
2. Forward looking
3. Usually confidential
4. Complies with accounting standards
5. Reports past performance
6. Uses physical measures as well as monetary ones for reports
7. Focus on business decision making
8. Driven by user needs

LO1 **Strategic Positioning**

SE 2. Organizations stake out different strategic positions to add value and achieve success. Some strive to be low-cost leaders like **Wal-Mart**, while others become the high-end quality leaders like **Whole Foods Market**. Identify which of the following organizations are low-cost leaders (C) and which are quality leaders (Q):

1. **Tiffany & Co.**
2. **Yale University**
3. Local community college
4. **Lexus**
5. **Kia**
6. Rent-a-Wreck
7. **Hertz Rental Cars**
8. **Pepsi-Cola**
9. Store-brand soda

LO1 **The Management Process**

SE 3. Indicate whether each of the following management activities in a department store is part of planning (PL), performing (PE), evaluating (E), or communicating (C):

1. Completing a balance sheet and income statement at the end of the year
2. Training a clerk to complete a cash sale
3. Meeting with department managers to develop performance measures for sales personnel
4. Renting a local warehouse to store excess inventory of clothing
5. Evaluating the performance of the shoe department by examining the significant differences between its actual and planned expenses for the month
6. Preparing an annual budget of anticipated sales for each department and the entire store

LO1 **Report Preparation**

SE 4. Molly Metz, president of Metz Industries, asked controller Rick Caputo to prepare a report on the use of electricity by each of the organization's five divisions. Increases in electricity costs in the divisions ranged from 20 to 35 percent over the past year. What questions should Rick ask before he begins his analysis?

LO1 LO2 **The Supply Chain and the Value Chain**

SE 5. Indicate whether each of the following is part of the supply chain (SC), a primary process (PP) in the value chain, or a support service (SS) in the value chain:

1. Human resources
2. Research and development
3. Supplier
4. Management accounting
5. Customer service
6. Retailer

LO2 **The Value Chain**

SE 6. The following unit costs were determined by dividing the total costs of each component by the number of products produced. From these unit costs, determine the total cost per unit of primary processes and the total cost per unit of support services.

Research and development	$ 1.40
Human resources	1.45
Design	0.15
Supply	1.10
Legal services	0.50
Production	4.00
Marketing	0.80
Distribution	0.90
Customer service	0.65
Information systems	0.85
Management accounting	0.20
Total cost per unit	$12.00

LO3 **JIT and Continuous Improvement**

SE 7. The just-in-time operating environment focuses on reducing or eliminating the waste of resources. Resources include physical assets such as machinery and buildings, labor time, and materials and parts used in the production process. Choose one of those resources and describe how it could be wasted. How can an organization prevent the waste of that resource? How can the concept of continuous improvement be implemented to reduce the waste of that resource?

LO3 **TQM and Value**

SE 8. DUDs Dry Cleaners recently adopted total quality management. Dee Mathias, the owner, has hired you as a consultant. Classify each of the following activities as either value-adding (V) or nonvalue-adding (NV):

1. Providing same-day service
2. Closing the store on weekends
3. Providing free delivery service
4. Having a seamstress on site
5. Making customers pay for parking

LO4 **The Balanced Scorecard: Stakeholder Values**

SE 9. In the balanced scorecard approach, stakeholder groups with different perspectives value different performance goals. Sometimes, however, they may be interested in the same goal. Indicate which stakeholder groups—financial (F), learning and growth (L), internal business processes (P), and customers (C)—value the following performance goals:

1. High wages
2. Safe products

3. Low-priced products
4. Improved return on investment
5. Job security
6. Cost-effective production processes

LO5 **Ethical Conduct**

SE 10. Topher Sones, a management accountant for Beauty Cosmetics Company, has lunch every day with his friend Joel Saikle, who is a management accountant for Glowy Cosmetics, Inc., a competitor of Beauty Cosmetics. Last week, Topher couldn't decide how to treat some information in a report he was preparing, so he discussed it with Joel. Is Topher adhering to the ethical standards of management accountants? Defend your answer.

Exercises

LO1 **Management Accounting Versus Financial Accounting**

E 1. Explain this statement: "It is impossible to distinguish the point at which financial accounting ends and management accounting begins."

LO1 **Management Accounting**

E 2. In 1982, the IMA defined management accounting as follows:

> The process of identification, measurement, accumulation, analysis, preparation, interpretation, and communication of financial information used by management to plan, evaluate, and control within the organization and to assure appropriate use of and accountability for its resources.[9]

Compare this definition with the updated one that appears in LO 1. How has the emphasis changed?

LO1 **The Management Process**

E 3. Indicate whether each of the following management activities in a community hospital is part of planning (PL), performing (PE), evaluating (E), or communicating (C):

1. Leasing five ambulances for the current year
2. Comparing the actual number with the planned number of patient days in the hospital for the year
3. Developing a strategic plan for a new pediatric wing
4. Preparing a report showing the past performance of the emergency room
5. Developing standards, or expectations, for performance in the hospital admittance area for next year
6. Preparing the hospital's balance sheet and income statement and distributing them to the board of directors
7. Maintaining an inventory of bed linens and bath towels
8. Formulating a corporate policy for the treatment and final disposition of hazardous waste materials
9. Preparing a report on the types and amounts of hazardous waste materials removed from the hospital in the last three months
10. Recording the time taken to deliver food trays to patients

LO1 **Report Preparation**

E 4. John Jefferson is the sales manager for Sunny Greeting Cards, Inc. At the beginning of the year, the organization introduced a new line of humorous birthday cards to the U.S. market. Management held a strategic planning meeting on August 31 to discuss next year's operating activities. One item on the agenda was to review the success of the new line of cards and decide if there was a need to change the selling price or to stimulate sales volume in the five sales territories. Jefferson was asked to prepare a report addressing those issues and to present it at the meeting. His report was to include the profits generated in each sales territory by the new card line only.

On August 31, Jefferson arrived at the meeting late and immediately distributed his report to the strategic planning team. The report consisted of comments made by seven of Jefferson's leading sales representatives. The comments were broad in scope and touched only lightly on the success of the new card line. Jefferson was pleased that he had met the deadline for distributing the report, but the other team members were disappointed in the information he provided.

Using the four *w's* for report presentation, comment on Jefferson's effectiveness in preparing his report.

LO1 **The Supply Chain**

E 5. In recent years, **United Parcel Service (UPS)** (www.ups-scs.com/solutions/casestudies.html) has been positioning itself as a solver of supply-chain issues. Visit its website and read one of the case studies related to its supply-chain solutions. Explain how UPS helped improve the supply chain of the business featured in the case.

LO1 **The Planning Framework**

E 6. Edward Ortez has just opened a company that imports fine ceramic gifts from Mexico and sells them over the Internet. In planning his business, Ortez did the following:

1. Listed his expected expenses and revenues for the first six months of operations
2. Decided that he wanted the company to provide him with income for a good lifestyle and funds for retirement
3. Determined that he would keep his expenses low and generate enough revenues during the first two months of operations so that he would have a positive cash flow by the third month
4. Decided to focus his business on providing customers with the finest Mexican ceramics at a favorable price
5. Developed a complete list of goals, objectives, procedures, and policies relating to how he would find, buy, store, sell, and ship goods and collect payment
6. Decided not to have a retail operation but to rely solely on the Internet to market the products
7. Decided to expand his website to include ceramics from other Central American countries over the next five years

Match each of Ortez's actions to the components of the planning framework: goal, mission, strategic objectives, tactical objectives, operating objectives, business plan, and budget.

LO2 **The Value Chain**

E 7. As mentioned in **E 6**, Edward Ortez recently opened his own company. He has been thinking of ways to improve the business. Here is a list of the actions that he will be undertaking:

1. Engaging an accountant to help analyze progress in meeting the objectives of the company
2. Hiring a company to handle payroll records and employee benefits
3. Developing a logo for labeling and packaging the ceramics
4. Making gift packages by placing gourmet food products in ceramic pots and wrapping them in plastic
5. Engaging an attorney to write contracts
6. Traveling to Mexico himself to arrange for the purchase of products and their shipment back to the company

7. Arranging new ways of taking orders over the Internet and shipping the products
8. Keeping track of the characteristics of customers and the number and types of products they buy
9. Following up with customers to see if they received the products and if they are happy with them
10. Arranging for an outside firm to keep the accounting records
11. Distributing brochures that display the ceramics and refer to the website

Classify each of Ortez's actions as one of the value chain's primary processes—research and development, design, supply, production, marketing, distribution, or customer service—or as a support service—human resources, legal services, information systems, or management accounting. Of the 11 actions, which are the most likely candidates for outsourcing? Why?

LO1 LO2 The Supply Chain and Value Chain

E 8. The items in the following list are associated with a hotel. Indicate which are part of the supply chain (S) and which are part of the value chain (V).

1. Travel agency
2. Housekeeping supplies
3. Special events and promotions
4. Customer service
5. Travel bureau website
6. Tour agencies

LO1 LO3 Management Reports

E 9. The reports that follow are from a grocery store. Which report would be used for financial purposes, and which would be used for activity-based decision making? Why?

Salaries	$ 1,000	Scan grocery purchases	$ 3,000
Equipment	2,200	Stock fruit	1,000
Freight	5,000	Bake rye bread	500
Supplies	800	Operate salad bar	2,500
Use and occupancy	1,000	Stock can goods	2,000
		Collapse cardboard boxes	1,000
Total	$10,000	Total	$10,000

LO2 The Value Chain

E 10. As shown in the data that follow, a producer of ceiling fans has determined the unit cost of its most popular model. From these unit costs, determine the total cost per unit of primary processes and the total cost per unit of support services.

Research and development	$ 5.00
Human resources	4.50
Design	1.50
Supply	1.00
Legal services	0.50
Production	4.50
Marketing	2.00
Distribution	2.50
Customer service	6.50
Information systems	1.80
Management accounting	0.20
Total cost per unit	$30.00

LO3 Comparison of ABM and JIT

E 11. The following are excerpts from a conversation between two managers about their companies' management systems. Identify the manager who works for a company that emphasizes ABM and the one who works for a company that emphasizes a JIT system.

Manager 1: We try to manage our resources effectively by monitoring operating activities. We analyze all major operating activities, and we focus on reducing or eliminating the ones that don't add value to our products.

Manager 2: We're very concerned with eliminating waste. We've designed our operations to reduce the time it takes to move, store, queue, and inspect materials. We've also reduced our inventories by buying and using materials only when we need them.

LO4 The Balanced Scorecard

E 12. Tim's Bargain Basement sells used goods at very low prices. Tim has developed the following business objectives:

1. To buy only the inventory that sells
2. To have repeat customers
3. To be profitable and grow
4. To keep employee turnover low

Tim also developed the following performance measures:

5. Growth in revenues and net income per quarter
6. Average unsold goods at the end of the business day as a percentage of the total goods purchased that day
7. Number of unemployment claims
8. Percentage of customers who have shopped in the store before

Match each of these objectives and performance measures with the four perspectives of the balanced scorecard: financial perspective, learning and growth perspective, internal business processes perspective, and customer perspective.

LO4 The Balanced Scorecard

E 13. Your college's overall goal is to add value to the communities it serves. In light of that goal, match each of the following stakeholders' perspectives with the appropriate objective:

Perspective	Objective
1. Financial (investors)	a. Adding value means that the faculty engages in meaningful teaching and research.
2. Learning and growth (employees)	b. Adding value means that students receive their degrees in four years.
3. Internal business processes	c. Adding value means that the college has winning sports teams.
4. Customers	d. Adding value means that fund-raising campaigns are successful.

LO5 Ethical Conduct

E 14. Katrina Storm went to work for NOLA Industries five years ago. She was recently promoted to cost accounting manager and now has a new boss, Vickery

Howe, the corporate controller. Last week, Storm and Howe went to a two-day professional development program on international accounting standards changes. During the first hour of the first day's program, Howe disappeared and Storm didn't see her again until the cocktail hour. The same thing happened on the second day. During the trip home, Storm asked Howe if she had enjoyed the conference. She replied: "Katrina, the golf course was excellent. You play golf. Why don't you join me during the next conference? I haven't sat in on one of those sessions in ten years. This is my R&R time. Those sessions are for the new people. My experience is enough to keep me current. Plus, I have excellent people to help me as we adjust our accounting system to the international changes being implemented."

Does Katrina Storm have an ethical dilemma? If so, what is it? What are her options? How would you solve her problem? Be prepared to defend your answer.

LO5 Corporate Ethics

E 15. To answer the following questions, conduct a search of several companies' websites: (1) Does the company have an ethics statement? (2) Does it express a commitment to environmental or social issues? (3) In your opinion, is the company ethically responsible? Select one of the companies you researched and write a brief description of your findings.

Problems

LO1 Report Preparation

P 1. Clothing Industries, Inc. is deciding whether to expand its line of women's clothing called Sami Pants. Sales in units of this product were 22,500, 28,900, and 36,200 in 2010, 2011, and 2012, respectively. The product has been very profitable, averaging 35 percent profit (above cost) over the three-year period. The company has 10 sales representatives covering seven states in the North. Production capacity at present is about 40,000 pants per year. There is adequate plant space for additional equipment, and the labor needed can be easily hired and trained.

The organization's management is made up of four vice presidents: the vice president of marketing, the vice president of production, the vice president of finance, and the vice president of management information systems. Each vice president is directly responsible to the president, Jefferson Henry.

Required

1. What types of information will Henry need before he can decide whether to expand the Sami Pants line?
2. Assume that one report needed to support Henry's decision is an analysis of sales, broken down by sales representative, over the past three years. How would each of the four *w's* pertain to this report?
3. Design a format for the report described in requirement **2**.

LO2 The Value Chain

P 2. Reigle Electronics is a manufacturer of cell phones, a highly competitive business. Reigle's phones carry a price of $99, but competition forces the company to offer significant discounts and rebates. As a result, the average price of Reigle's cell phones has dropped to around $50, and the company is losing money. Management is applying value chain analysis to the company's operations in an effort to reduce costs and improve product quality. A study by the company's management accountant has determined the following per unit costs for primary processes:

Primary Process	Cost per Unit
Research and development	$ 2.50
Design	3.50
Supply	4.50
Production	6.70
Marketing	8.00
Distribution	1.90
Customer service	0.50
Total cost	$27.60

To generate a gross margin large enough for the company to cover its overhead costs and earn a profit, Reigle must lower its total cost per unit for primary processes to no more than $20. After analyzing operations, management reached the following conclusions about primary processes:

- Research and development and design are critical functions because the market and competition require constant development of new features with "cool" designs at lower cost. Nevertheless, management feels that the cost per unit of these processes must be reduced by 10 percent.
- Six different suppliers currently provide the components for the cell phones. Ordering these components from just two suppliers and negotiating lower prices could result in a savings of 15 percent.
- The cell phones are currently manufactured in Mexico. By shifting production to China, the unit cost of production can be lowered by 20 percent.
- Most cell phones are sold through wireless communication companies that are trying to attract new customers with low-priced cell phones. Management believes that these companies should bear more of the marketing costs and that it is feasible to renegotiate its marketing arrangements with them so that they will bear 35 percent of the current marketing costs.
- Distribution costs are already very low, but management will set a target of reducing the cost per unit by 10 percent.
- Customer service is a weakness of the company and has resulted in lost sales. Management therefore proposes increasing the cost per unit of customer service by 50 percent.

Required

1. Prepare a table showing the current cost per unit of primary processes and the projected cost per unit based on management's proposals for cost reduction.
2. Manager insight ▶ Will management's proposals for cost reduction achieve the targeted total cost per unit? What further steps should management take to reduce costs? Which steps that management is proposing do you believe will be the most difficult to accomplish?
3. Manager insight ▶ What are the company's support services? What role should these services play in the value chain analysis?

LO2 The Value Chain and Core Competency

P 3. Medic Products Company (MPC) is known for developing innovative and high-quality products for use in hospitals and medical and dental offices. Its latest product is a nonporous, tough, and very thin disposable glove that will not leak or split and molds tightly to the hand, making it ideal for use in medical and dental procedures. MPC buys the material it uses in making the gloves from another company, which manufactures it according to MPC's exact specifications and quality standards. MPC makes two models of the glove—one white and one transparent—in its own plant and sells them through independent agents who represent various manufacturers. When an agent informs MPC of a sale, MPC ships the order directly to the buyer. MPC advertises the gloves in professional journals and gives free samples to physicians and dentists. It provides a product warranty and periodically surveys users about the product's quality.

Required

1. Briefly explain how MPC accomplishes each of the primary processes in the value chain.
2. What is a core competency? Which one of the primary processes would you say is MPC's core competency? Explain your choice.

LO4 The Balanced Scorecard and Benchmarking

P 4. Howski Associates is an independent insurance agency that sells business, automobile, home, and life insurance. Maya Howski, senior partner of the agency, recently attended a workshop at the local university in which the balanced scorecard was presented as a way of focusing all of a company's functions on its mission. After the workshop, she met with her managers in a weekend brainstorming session. The group determined that Howski Associates' mission was to provide high-quality, innovative, risk-protection services to individuals and businesses. To ensure that the agency would fulfill this mission, the group established the following objectives:

- To provide a sufficient return on investment by increasing sales and maintaining the liquidity needed to support operations
- To add value to the agency's services by training employees to be knowledgeable and competent
- To retain customers and attract new customers
- To operate an efficient and cost-effective office support system for customer agents

To determine the agency's progress in meeting these objectives, the group established the following performance measures:

- Number of new ideas for customer insurance
- Percentage of customers who rate services as excellent
- Average time for processing insurance applications
- Number of dollars spent on training
- Growth in revenues for each type of insurance
- Average time for processing claims
- Percentage of employees who complete 40 hours of training during the year
- Percentage of new customer leads that result in sales
- Cash flow
- Number of customer complaints
- Return on assets
- Percentage of customers who renew policies
- Percentage of revenue devoted to office support system (information systems, accounting, orders, and claims processing)

Required

1. Prepare a balanced scorecard for Howski Associates by stating the agency's mission and matching its four objectives to the four stakeholder perspectives: the financial, learning and growth, internal business processes, and customer perspectives. Indicate which of the agency's performance measures would be appropriate for each objective.

Manager insight ▶ 2. Howski Associates is a member of an association of independent insurance agents that provides industry statistics about many aspects of operating an insurance agency. What is benchmarking, and in what ways would the industry statistics assist Howski Associates in further developing its balanced scorecard?

LO5 **Professional Ethics**

P 5. Taylor Zimmer is the controller for Value Corporation. He has been with the company for 17 years and is being considered for the job of chief financial officer. His boss, who is the current chief financial officer and former company controller, will be Value Corporation's new president. Zimmer has just discussed the year-end closing with his boss, who made the following statement during their conversation: "Taylor, why are you being so inflexible? I'm only asking you to postpone the $2,500,000 write-off of obsolete inventory for 10 days so that it won't appear on this year's financial statements. Ten days! Do it. Your promotion is coming up, you know. Make sure you keep all the possible outcomes in mind as you complete your year-end work. Oh, and keep this conversation confidential—just between you and me. Okay?"

Required

1. Identify the ethical issue or issues involved.
2. What do you believe is the appropriate solution to the problem? Be prepared to defend your answer.

Alternate Problems

LO1 **Report Preparation**

P 6. Daisy Flowers recently purchased Yardworks, Inc., a wholesale distributor of equipment and supplies for lawn and garden care. The organization, which is headquartered in Baltimore, has four distribution centers that service 14 eastern states. The centers are located in Boston, Massachusetts; Rye, New York; Reston, Virginia; and Lawrenceville, New Jersey. The company's profits for 2010, 2011, and 2012 were $225,400, $337,980, and $467,200, respectively.

Shortly after purchasing the organization, Flowers appointed people to the following positions: vice president, marketing; vice president, distribution; corporate controller; and vice president, research and development. Flowers called a meeting of this management group. She wants to create a deluxe retail lawn and garden center that would include a large, fully landscaped plant and tree nursery. The purposes of the retail center would be (1) to test equipment and supplies before selecting them for sales and distribution and (2) to showcase the effects of using the company's products. The retail center must also make a profit on sales.

Required

1. What types of information will Flowers need before deciding whether to create the retail lawn and garden center?
2. To support her decision, Flowers will need a report from the vice president of research and development analyzing all possible plants and trees that could be planted and their ability to grow in the places where the new retail center might be located. How would each of the four *w's* pertain to this report?
3. Design a format for the report in requirement **2**.

LO2 **The Value Chain**

P 7. Soft Spot is a manufacturer of futon mattresses. Soft Spot's mattresses are priced at $60, but competition forces the company to offer significant discounts and rebates. As a result, the average price of the futon mattress has dropped to around $50, and the company is losing money. Management is applying value chain analysis to the company's operations in an effort to reduce costs and improve product quality. A study by the company's management accountant has determined the following per unit costs for primary processes and support services:

Primary Process	Cost per Unit
Research and development	$ 5.00
Design	3.00
Supply	4.00
Production	16.00
Marketing	6.00
Distribution	7.00
Customer service	1.00
Total cost per unit	$42.00
Support Service	
Human resources	$ 2.00
Information services	5.00
Management accounting	1.00
Total cost per unit	$ 8.00

To generate a gross margin large enough for the company to cover its overhead costs and earn a profit, Soft Spot must lower its total cost per unit for primary processes to no more than $32.00 and its support services to no more than $5.00. After analyzing operations, management reached the following conclusions about primary processes and support services:

- Research and development and design are critical functions because the market and competition require constant development of new features with "cool" designs at lower cost. Nevertheless, management feels that the cost per unit of these processes must be reduced by 20 percent.
- Ten different suppliers currently provide the components for the futons. Ordering these components from just two suppliers and negotiating lower prices could result in a savings of 15 percent.
- The futons are currently manufactured in Mali. By shifting production to China, the unit cost of production can be lowered by 40 percent.
- Management believes that by selling to large retailers like **Wal-Mart** it is feasible to lower current marketing costs by 25 percent.
- Distribution costs are already very low, but management will set a target of reducing the cost per unit by 10 percent.
- Customer service and support to large customers are key to keeping their business. Management therefore proposes increasing the cost per unit of customer service by 20 percent.
- By outsourcing its support services, management projects a 20 percent drop in these costs.

Required

1. Prepare a table showing the current cost per unit of primary processes and support services and the projected cost per unit based on management's proposals.

Manager insight ▶ 2. Will management's proposals achieve the targeted total cost per unit? What further steps should management take to reduce costs?

Manager insight ▶ 3. What role should the company's support services play in the value chain analysis?

LO2 **The Value Chain and Core Competency**

P 8. Sports Products Company (SPC) is known for developing innovative high-quality shoes for lacrosse. Its latest patented product is a tough, all-weather, and very flexible shoe. SPC buys the material it uses in making the shoes from another company, which manufactures it according to SPC's exact specifications and quality standards. SPC makes two models of the shoe—one white and one black—in its own plant. SPC sells them through independent distributors who represent various manufacturers. When a distributor informs SPC of a sale, SPC ships the order directly to the buyer. SPC advertises the shoes in sports magazines and gives free samples to well-known lacrosse players who endorse its products. It provides a product warranty and periodically surveys users about the product's quality.

Required

1. Briefly explain how SPC accomplishes each of the primary processes in the value chain.
2. What is a core competency? Which one of the primary processes would you say is SPC's core competency? Explain your choice.

LO4 **The Balanced Scorecard and Benchmarking**

P 9. Resource College is a liberal arts school that provides local residents the opportunity to take college courses and earn bachelor's degrees. Yolanda Howard, the school's provost, recently attended a workshop in which the balanced scorecard was presented as a way of focusing all of an organization's functions on its mission. After the workshop, she met with her administrative staff and college deans in a weekend brainstorming session. The group determined that the college's mission was to provide high-quality courses and degrees to individuals to add value to their lives. To ensure that the college would fulfill this mission, the group established the following objectives:

- To provide a sufficient return on investment by increasing tuition revenues and maintaining the liquidity needed to support operations
- To add value to the college's courses by encouraging faculty to be lifelong learners
- To retain students and attract new students
- To operate efficient and cost-effective student support systems

To determine the college's progress in meeting these objectives, the group established the following performance measures:

- Number of faculty publications
- Percentage of students who rate college as excellent
- Average time for processing student applications
- Number of dollars spent on professional development
- Growth in revenues for each department
- Average time for processing transcript requests
- Percentage of faculty who annually do 40 hours of professional development
- Percentage of new student leads that result in enrollment
- Cash flow
- Number of student complaints
- Return on assets
- Percentage of returning students
- Percentage of revenue devoted to student services systems (registrar, computer services, financial aid, and student health)

Required

1. Prepare a balanced scorecard for Resource College by stating the college's mission and matching its four objectives to the four stakeholder perspectives: the financial, learning and growth, internal business processes, and customer perspectives.
2. Indicate which of the college's performance measures would be appropriate for each objective.

LO3 LO5 Ethics and JIT Implementation

P 10. For almost a year, WEST Company has been changing its manufacturing process from a traditional to a JIT approach. Management has asked for employees' assistance in the transition and has offered bonuses for suggestions that cut time from the production operation. Don Hanley and Jerome Obbo each identified a time-saving opportunity and turned in their suggestions to their manager, Sam Knightly.

Knightly sent the suggestions to the committee charged with reviewing employees' suggestions, which inadvertently identified them as being Knightly's own. The committee decided that the two suggestions were worthy of reward and voted a large bonus for Knightly. When notified of this, Knightly could not bring himself to identify the true authors of the suggestions.

When Hanley and Obbo heard about Knightly's bonus, they confronted him with his fraudulent act and expressed their grievances. He told them that he needed the recognition to be eligible for an upcoming promotion and promised that if they kept quiet about the matter, he would make sure that they both received significant raises.

Required

1. Should Hanley and Obbo keep quiet? What other options are open to them?
2. How should Knightly have dealt with Hanley's and Obbo's complaints?

ENHANCING Your Knowledge, Skills, and Critical Thinking

LO1 Management Information

C 1. Obtain a copy of a recent annual report of a publicly held organization in which you have a particular interest. (Copies of annual reports are available at your campus library, at a local public library, on the Internet, or by direct request to an organization.) Assume that you have just been appointed to a middle-management position in a division of the organization you have chosen. You are interested in obtaining information that will help you better manage the activities of your division, and you have decided to study the contents of the annual report in an attempt to learn as much as possible.

You particularly want to know about the following: (1) size of inventory maintained; (2) ability to earn income; (3) reliance on debt financing; (4) types, volume, and prices of products or services sold; (5) type of production process used; (6) management's long-range strategies; (7) success (profitability) of the division's various product lines; (8) efficiency of operations; and (9) operating details of your division.

1. Write a brief description of the organization and its products or services and activities.
2. Based on a review of the financial statements and the accompanying disclosure notes, prepare a written summary of information pertaining to items 1 through 9 above.

3. Can you find any of the information in which you are interested in other sections of the annual report? If so, which information, and in which sections of the report is it?
4. The annual report also includes other types of information that you may find helpful in your new position. In outline form, summarize this additional information.

LO1 **Management Information Needs**

C 2. In **C 1**, you examined your new employer's annual report and found some useful information. However, you are interested in knowing whether your division's products or services are competitive, and you were unable to find the necessary information in the annual report.

1. What kinds of information about your competition do you want to find?
2. Why is this information relevant? (Link your response to a particular decision about your organization's products or services. For example, you might seek information to help you determine a new selling price.)
3. From what sources could you obtain the information you need?
4. When would you want to obtain this information?
5. Create a report that will communicate your findings to your superior.

LO1 **Report Preparation**

C 3. The registrar's office of Mainland College is responsible for maintaining a record of each student's grades and credits for use by students, instructors, and administrators.

1. Assume that you are a manager in the registrar's office and that you recently joined a team of managers to review the grade-reporting process. Explain how you would prepare a report of grades for students' use and the same report for instructors' use by answering the following questions:
   a. Who will read the grade report?
   b. Why is the grade report necessary?
   c. What information should the grade report contain?
   d. When is the grade report due?
2. Why does the information in a grade report for students' use and in a grade report for instructors' use differ?
3. Visit the registrar's office of your school in person or through your school's website. Obtain a copy of your grade report and a copy of the form that the registrar's office uses to report grades to instructors. Compare the information that these reports supply with the information you listed in question **1**. Explain any differences.
4. What can the registrar's office do to make sure that its grade reports are effective in communicating all necessary information to readers?

LO4 **Management Information Needs**

C 4. McDonald's is a leading competitor in the fast-food restaurant business. One component of McDonald's marketing strategy is to increase sales by expanding its foreign markets. At present, McDonald's restaurants operate in over 100 countries. In making decisions about opening restaurants in foreign markets, the company uses quantitative and qualitative financial and nonfinancial information. The following types of information would be important to such a decision: the cost of a new building (quantitative financial information), the estimated number of hamburgers to be sold in the first year (quantitative nonfinancial information), and site desirability (qualitative information).

Suppose you are a member of McDonald's management team that must decide whether to open a new restaurant in England. Identify at least two examples each of the (a) quantitative financial, (b) quantitative nonfinancial, and (c) qualitative information that you will need before you can make a decision.

LO1 LO4 Performance Measures and the Balanced Scorecard

C 5. Working in a group of four to six students, select a local business. The group should become familiar with the background of the business by interviewing its manager or accountant. Each group member should identify several performance objectives for the business and link each objective with a specific stakeholder's perspective from the balanced scorecard. (Select at least one performance objective for each perspective.) For each objective, ask yourself, "If I were the manager of the business, how would I set performance measures for each objective?" Then prepare an email stating the business's name, location, and activities and your linked performance objective and perspectives. Also list possible measures for each performance objective.

In class, members of the group should compare their individual emails and compile them into a group report by having each group member assume a different stakeholder perspective (add government and community if you want more than four perspectives). Each group should be ready to present all perspectives and the group's report on performance objectives and measures in class.

LO1 LO3 Cookie Company (Continuing Case)

C 6. Each of the rest of the chapters in this text includes a "cookie company" case that shows how you could operate your own cookie business. In this chapter, you will express your company's mission statement; set strategic, tactical, and operating objectives; decide on a name for your business; and identify management tools you might consider using to run your business.

1. In researching how to start and run a cookie business, you found the following three examples of cookie company mission statements:
   - To provide cheap cookies that taste great and fast courteous service!
   - Our mission is to make the best chocolate chip cookies that you have ever tasted.
   - Handmaking the best in custom cookie creations.

   a. Consider which of the mission statements most closely expresses what you want your company's identity and unique character to be. Why?
   b. Will your business focus on cost, quality, or satisfying a specific need?
   c. Write your company's mission statement.
2. Based on your mission statement, describe your broad long-term strategic objectives:
   - What will be your main products?
   - Who will be your primary customers?
   - Where will you operate your business?
3. You made the following decisions about your business:
   - To list expected expenses and revenues for the first six months of operations
   - To keep expenses low and generate enough revenues during the first two months of operations to have a positive cash flow by the third month
   - To develop a complete list of goals, objectives, procedures, and policies relating to how to find, buy, store, sell, and ship goods and collect payment
   - To rely solely on the Internet to market products
   - To expand the ecommerce website to include 20 varieties of cookies over the next five years

   Match each of the above to the following components of the planning framework: strategic objectives, tactical objectives, operating objectives, business plan, and budget.
4. What will be the name of your cookie company?
5. Which of the management tools listed in the chapter might you consider using to operate your business? Why?

CHAPTER

16

Cost Concepts and Cost Allocation

The Management Process

PLAN

- ▷ **Classify costs.**
- ▷ **Compute predetermined overhead rates.**

PERFORM

- ▷ **Flow service and product-related costs through the inventory accounts.**
- ▷ **Allocate overhead using either the traditional or ABC approach.**
- ▷ **Compute the unit cost of a product or service.**

EVALUATE

- ▷ **Compare actual and allocated overhead amounts.**
- ▷ **Dispose of the under/over-applied overhead into Cost of Goods Sold account.**

COMMUNICATE

- ▷ **Prepare external reports (service, retail, and manufacturing income statements).**
- ▷ **Prepare internal management reports to monitor and manage costs.**

How managers use cost information to solve, "How much does it cost?" can result in differing answers.

In this chapter, we describe how managers use information about costs, classify costs, compile product unit costs, and allocate overhead costs using the traditional method.

LEARNING OBJECTIVES

LO1 **Explain how managers classify costs and how they use these cost classifications.** (pp. 762–765)

LO2 **Compare how service, retail, and manufacturing organizations report costs on their financial statements and how they account for inventories.** (pp. 766–769)

LO3 **Describe the flow of costs through a manufacturer's inventory accounts.** (pp. 770–774)

LO4 **Define *product unit cost,* and compute the unit cost of a product or service.** (pp. 774–778)

LO5 **Define *cost allocation,* and explain how the traditional method of allocating overhead costs figures into calculating product or service unit cost.** (pp. 779–784)

DECISION POINT ▸ A MANAGER'S FOCUS THE HERSHEY COMPANY

▸ How do managers at Hershey's determine the cost of a candy bar?

▸ How do managers use cost information?

With net sales of $4.9 billion, **The Hershey Company** does indeed fulfill its mission statement of "bringing sweet moments of Hershey happiness to the world everyday." To have achieved that and to continue doing it, Hershey's managers must know a lot about the costs of producing and selling its Reese's, KitKat, Twizzlers, Kisses, Jolly Rancher, Ice Breakers, and other products. Go to Hershey's website (www.Hersheys.com) to have a tour of the world's largest chocolate factory and to view how Reese's Peanut Butter Cups, Twizzler Twists, Mounds, Heath, or PayDay are made.

Cost Information

LO1 Explain how managers classify costs and how they use these cost classifications.

One of a company's primary goals is to be profitable. Because a company's owners expect to earn profits, managers have a responsibility to use the company's resources wisely and to generate revenues that will exceed the costs of the company's operating, investing, and financing activities. In this chapter, we focus on costs related to the operating activities of manufacturing, retail, and service organizations. We begin by looking at how managers in these different organizations use information about costs.

Managers' Use of Cost Information

Managers use information about operating costs to plan, perform, evaluate, and communicate the results of operating activities.

- Service organization managers find the estimated cost of services helpful in monitoring profitability and making decisions about such matters as bidding on future business, lowering or negotiating their fees, or dropping one of their services.
- In retail organizations, such as Good Foods Store, which we used as an example in the last chapter, managers work with the estimated cost of merchandise purchases to predict gross margin, operating income, and value of merchandise sold. They also use this information to make decisions about matters like reducing selling prices for clearance sales, lowering selling prices for bulk sales, or dropping a product line.
- Managers at manufacturing companies like **Hershey's** use estimated product costs to predict the gross margin and operating income on sales and to make decisions about such matters as dropping a product line, outsourcing the manufacture of a part to another company, bidding on a special order, or negotiating a selling price. In this chapter, we will use The Choice Candy Company, the hypothetical manufacturer of gourmet chocolate candy bars, to illustrate how managers of manufacturing companies use cost information.

Cost Information and Organizations

All organizations use cost information to determine profits and selling prices and to value inventories. Ultimately, a company is profitable only when its revenues from sales or services rendered exceed all its costs. But different types of organizations have different types of product or service costs.

- Service organizations like **Southwest Airlines** need information about the costs of providing services, which include the costs of labor and related overhead.
- Retail organizations like **Wal-Mart** and Good Foods Store need information about the costs of purchasing products for resale. These costs include adjustments for freight-in costs, purchase returns and allowances, and purchase discounts.
- Manufacturing organizations like **Hershey's** and The Choice Candy Company need information about the costs of manufacturing products. Product costs include the costs of direct materials, direct labor, and overhead.

Cost Classifications and Their Uses

A single cost can be classified and used in several ways, depending on the purpose of the analysis. Figure 16-1 provides an overview of commonly used cost classifications. These classifications enable managers to do the following:

1. Control costs by determining which are traceable to a particular cost object, such as a service or product.
2. Calculate the number of units that must be sold to achieve a certain level of profit (cost behavior).

FIGURE 16-1 Overview of Cost Classifications

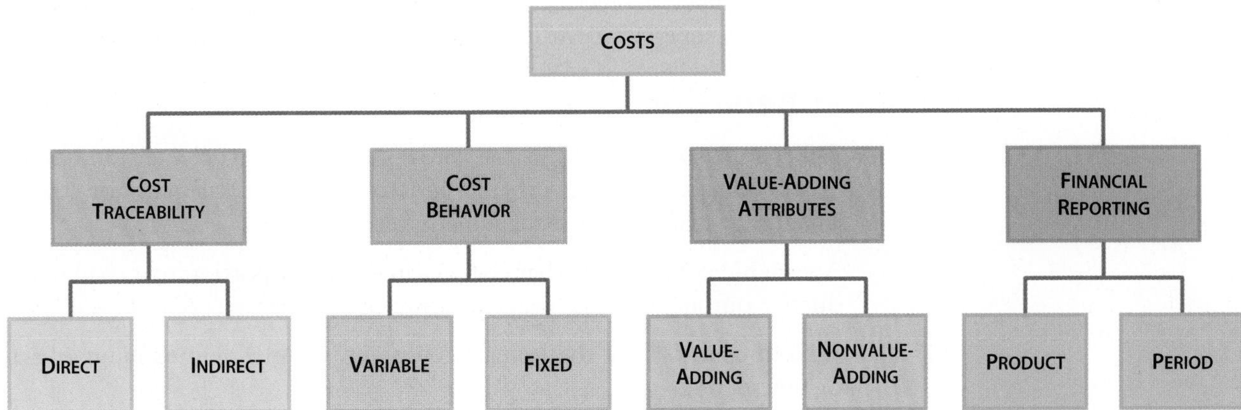

3. Identify the costs of activities that do and do not add value to a product or service.
4. Classify costs for the preparation of financial statements.

Cost Traceability

Managers trace costs to cost objects, such as products or services, sales territories, departments, or operating activities, to develop a fairly accurate measurement of costs.

- **Direct costs** are costs that can be conveniently and economically traced to a cost object. For example, the wages of workers who make candy bars can be conveniently traced to a particular batch because of time cards and payroll records. Similarly, the cost of chocolate's main ingredients—chocolate liquor, cocoa butter, sugar, and milk—can be easily traced.
- **Indirect costs** are costs that cannot be conveniently and economically traced to a cost object. Some examples include the nails used in furniture, the salt used in candy, and the rivets used in airplanes. For the sake of accuracy, however, these indirect costs must be included in the cost of a product or service. Because they are difficult to trace or an insignificant amount, management uses a formula to assign them to cost objects.

The following examples illustrate cost objects and their direct and indirect costs in service, retail, and manufacturing organizations:

- ***Service organization:*** In organizations such as an accounting firm, costs can be traced to a specific service, such as preparation of tax returns. Direct costs for such a service include the costs of government reporting forms, computer usage, and the accountant's labor. Indirect costs include the costs of supplies, office rental, utilities, secretarial labor, telephone usage, and depreciation of office furniture.
- ***Retail organization:*** Costs for organizations such as Good Foods Store can be traced to a department. For example, the direct costs of the produce department include the costs of fruits and vegetables and the wages of employees working in that department. Indirect costs include the costs of utilities to cool the produce displays and the storage and handling of the produce.
- ***Manufacturing organization:*** Costs for organizations such as The Choice Candy Company can be traced to the product. Direct costs include the costs

of the materials and labor needed to make the candy. Indirect costs include the costs of utilities, depreciation of plant and equipment, insurance, property taxes, inspection, supervision, maintenance of machinery, storage, and handling.

Cost Behavior

Managers are also interested in the way costs respond to changes in volume or activity. By analyzing those variable and fixed patterns of behavior, they gain information to make better management decisions.

- A **variable cost** is a cost that changes in direct proportion to a change in productive output (or some other measure of volume).
- A **fixed cost** is a cost that remains constant within a defined range of activity or time period.

All types of organizations have variable and fixed costs. Here are a few examples:

> **Study Note**
> Notice in each of these examples that as more products or services are produced and sold, the variable costs increase proportionately. Fixed costs, however, remain the same for a specified period.

- Because the number of passengers drives the consumption of food and beverages on a flight, the cost of peanuts and beverages is a variable cost for **Southwest Airlines**. Fixed costs include the depreciation on the plane and the salaries and benefits of the flight and ground crews.
- The variable costs of Good Foods Store include the cost of groceries sold and any sales commissions. Fixed costs include the costs of building and lot rental, depreciation on store equipment, and the manager's salary.
- The variable costs of The Choice Candy Company include the costs of direct materials (e.g., sugar, cocoa), direct labor wages, indirect materials (e.g., salt), and indirect labor (e.g., inspection and maintenance labor). Fixed costs include the costs of supervisors' salaries and depreciation on buildings.

Value-Adding Versus Nonvalue-Adding Costs

Costs incurred to improve the quality of a product are value-adding costs if the customer is willing to pay more for the higher-quality product or service; otherwise, they are nonvalue-adding costs because they do not increase its market value.

- A **value-adding cost** is the cost of an activity that increases the market value of a product or service.
- A **nonvalue-adding cost** is the cost of an activity that adds cost to a product or service but does not increase its market value.

Managers examine the value-adding attributes of their company's operating activities and, wherever possible, reduce or eliminate activities that do not directly add value to the company's products or services. For example, the costs of administrative activities, such as accounting and human resource management, are nonvalue-adding costs. Because they are necessary for the operation of the business, they are monitored closely but cannot be eliminated.

> **Study Note**
> Product costs and period costs can be explained by using the matching rule. Product costs must be charged to the period in which the product generates revenue, and period costs are charged against the revenue of the current period.

Cost Classifications for Financial Reporting

For purposes of preparing financial statements, managers classify costs as product costs or period costs.

- **Product costs**, or *inventoriable* costs, are costs assigned to inventory; they include direct materials, direct labor, and overhead. Product costs appear on the income statement as cost of goods sold and on the balance sheet as inventory.

TABLE 16-1 Examples of Cost Classifications for a Candy Manufacturer

Cost Examples	Traceability to Product	Cost Behavior	Value Attribute	Financial Reporting
Sugar for candy	Direct	Variable	Value-adding	Product (direct materials)
Labor for mixing	Direct	Variable	Value-adding	Product (direct labor)
Labor for supervision	Indirect	Fixed	Nonvalue-adding	Product (overhead)
Depreciation on mixing machine	Indirect	Fixed	Value-adding	Product (overhead)
Sales commission	—*	Variable	Value-adding†	Period
Accountant's salary	—*	Fixed	Nonvalue-adding	Period

*Sales commissions and accountants' salaries cannot be directly or indirectly traced to a cost object; they are not product costs.

†Sales commissions can be value-adding because customers' perceptions of the salesperson and the selling experience can strongly affect their perceptions of the product's market value.

- **Period costs**, or *noninventoriable* costs, are costs of resources used during the accounting period that are not assigned to products. They appear as operating expenses on the income statement. For example, among the period costs listed on the income statement are selling, administrative, and general expenses.

Table 16-1 shows how some costs of a candy manufacturer can be classified in terms of traceability, behavior, value attribute, and financial reporting.

STOP & APPLY >

Indicate whether each of the following costs for a gourmet chocolate candy maker is a product or a period cost, a variable or a fixed cost, a value-adding or a nonvalue-adding cost, and, if it is a product cost, a direct or an indirect cost of the candy:

Cost Classification			
Product or Period	**Variable or Fixed**	**Value-Adding or Nonvalue-Adding**	**Direct or Indirect**
Product	Variable	Value-adding	Direct

1. Chocolate
2. Office rent
3. Candy chef wages
4. Dishwasher wages
5. Pinch of salt
6. Utilities to run mixer

SOLUTION

	Cost Classification			
	Product or Period	**Variable or Fixed**	**Value-Adding or Nonvalue-Adding**	**Direct or Indirect**
Chocolate	Product	Variable	Value-adding	Direct
Office rent	Period	Fixed	Nonvalue-adding	—
Candy chef wages	Product	Variable	Value-adding	Direct
Dishwasher wages	Product	Variable	Value-adding	Indirect
Pinch of salt	Product	Variable	Value-adding	Indirect
Utilities to run mixer	Product	Variable	Value-adding	Indirect

Financial Statements and the Reporting of Costs

LO2 Compare how service, retail, and manufacturing organizations report costs on their financial statements and how they account for inventories.

Managers prepare financial statements at least once a year to communicate the results of their management activities for the period. The key to preparing an income statement or a balance sheet in any kind of organization is determining its cost of goods or services sold and the value of its inventories, if any.

Income Statement and Accounting for Inventories

Remember that all organizations—service, retail, and manufacturing—use the following income statement format:

$$\text{Sales} - \begin{matrix}\text{Cost of Sales}\\ \text{or}\\ \text{Cost of Goods Sold}\end{matrix} = \begin{matrix}\text{Gross}\\ \text{Margin}\end{matrix} - \begin{matrix}\text{Operating}\\ \text{Expenses}\end{matrix} = \text{Operating Income}$$

Figure 16-2 compares the financial statements of service, retail, and manufacturing organizations. Note in particular the differences in inventory accounts and cost of goods sold. As pointed out earlier, product costs, or inventoriable costs, appear as inventory on the balance sheet and as cost of goods sold on the income statement. Period costs, also called *noninventoriable costs* or *selling, administrative, and general expenses,* are reflected in the operating expenses on the income statement.

Because the operations of service and retail organizations differ from those of manufacturers, the accounts presented in their financial statements differ as well.

- Service organizations like **Southwest Airlines** and **United Parcel Service (UPS)** sell services and not products; they maintain no inventories for sale or resale. As a result, unlike manufacturing and retail organizations, they have no inventory accounts on their balance sheets.

Suppose that Good Foods Store, the retail shop that we used as an example in the last chapter, employs UPS to deliver its products. The cost of sales for UPS would include the wages and salaries of personnel plus the expense of the trucks, planes, supplies, and anything else that UPS uses to deliver packages for Good Foods Store.

- Retail organizations, such as **Wal-Mart** and Good Foods Store, which purchase products ready for resale, maintain just one inventory account on the balance sheet. Called the Merchandise Inventory account, it reflects the costs of goods held for resale.

Suppose that Good Foods Store had a balance of $3,000 in its Merchandise Inventory account at the beginning of the year. During the year, its purchases of food products totaled $23,000 (adjusted for purchase discounts, returns and allowances, and freight-in). At year-end, its Merchandise Inventory balance was $4,500. The cost of goods sold was thus $21,500.

- Manufacturing organizations like The Choice Candy Company, which make products for sale, maintain three inventory accounts on the balance sheet: the Materials Inventory, Work in Process Inventory, and Finished Goods Inventory accounts. The Materials Inventory account shows the cost of materials that have been purchased but not used in the production process. During the production process, the costs of manufacturing the product are accumulated in the Work in Process Inventory account; the balance of this account represents the costs of the unfinished product. Once the product is complete and ready for sale, its cost is transferred to the Finished Goods Inventory account; the balance in this account is the cost of the unsold completed product.

FIGURE 16-2 Financial Statements of Service, Retail, and Manufacturing Organizations

	Service Company	Retail Company		Manufacturing Company	
Income Statement	Sales – Cost of sales = Gross margin – Operating expenses = Operating income	Sales – Cost of goods sold* = Gross margin – Operating expenses = Operating income		Sales – Cost of goods sold† = Gross margin – Operating expenses = Operating income	
		*Cost of goods sold: Beginning merchandise inventory + Net cost of purchases = Cost of goods available for sale – Ending merchandise inventory = Cost of goods sold		†Cost of goods sold: Beginning finished goods inventory + Cost of goods manufactured = Cost of goods available for sale – Ending finished goods inventory = Cost of goods sold	
Balance Sheet (current assets section)	No inventory accounts	One inventory account: Merchandise Inventory (finished product ready for sale)		Three inventory accounts: Materials Inventory (unused materials) Work in Process Inventory (unfinished product) Finished Goods Inventory (finished product ready for sale)	
Example with numbers		Income Statement:		Income Statement:	
		Beg. merchandise inventory	$ 3,000	Beg. finished goods inventory	$ 52,000
		+ Net cost of purchases	23,000	+ Cost of goods manufactured	144,000
		= Cost of goods available for sale	$26,000	= Cost of goods available for sale	$196,000
		– End. merchandise inventory	4,500	– End. finished goods inventory	78,000
		= Cost of goods sold	$21,500	= Cost of goods sold	$118,000
		Balance Sheet:		Balance Sheet:	
		Merchandise inventory, ending	$ 4,500	Finished goods inventory, ending	$ 78,000

Suppose that The Choice Candy Company had a balance of $52,000 in its Finished Goods Inventory account at the beginning of the year. During the year, the cost of the products that the company manufactured totaled $144,000. At year end, its Finished Goods Inventory balance was $78,000. The cost of goods sold was thus $118,000.

Statement of Cost of Goods Manufactured

The key to preparing an income statement for a manufacturing organization is computing its cost of goods sold, which means that you must first determine the cost of goods manufactured. This dollar amount is calculated on the **statement of cost of goods manufactured**, a special report based on an analysis of the Work in Process Inventory account. At the end of an accounting period, the flow of all manufacturing costs incurred during the period is summarized in this statement. Exhibit 16-1 shows The Choice Candy Company's statement of cost of goods manufactured for the year.

It is helpful to think of the statement of cost of goods manufactured as being developed in three steps:

Step 1. ***Compute the cost of direct materials used during the accounting period.*** As shown in Exhibit 16-1, add the beginning balance in the Materials Inventory account to the direct materials purchased. The subtotal

($300,000) represents the cost of direct materials available for use during the accounting period. Next, subtract the ending balance of the Materials Inventory account from the cost of direct materials available for use. The difference is the cost of direct materials used during the period.

Step 2. ***Calculate total manufacturing costs for the period.*** As shown in Exhibit 16-1, the costs of direct materials used and direct labor are added to total overhead costs incurred during the period to arrive at total manufacturing costs.

Study Note

An alternative to the cost of goods manufactured calculation uses the cost flow concept that is discussed in LO3.

Step 3. ***Determine total cost of goods manufactured for the period.*** As shown in Exhibit 16-1, add the beginning balance in the Work in Process Inventory account to total manufacturing costs to arrive at the total cost of work in process during the period. From this amount, subtract the ending balance in the Work in Process Inventory account to arrive at the cost of goods manufactured.

EXHIBIT 16-1
Statement of Cost of Goods Manufactured and Partial Income Statement for a Manufacturing Organization

The Choice Candy Company
Statement of Cost of Goods Manufactured
For the Year 2011

Direct materials used		
Beginning materials inventory	$100,000	
Direct materials purchased	200,000	
Cost of direct materials available for use	$300,000	
Less ending materials inventory	50,000	
Step 1: Cost of direct materials used		$250,000
Direct labor		120,000
Overhead		60,000
Step 2: Total manufacturing costs		$430,000
Add beginning work in process inventory		20,000
Total cost of work in process during the year		$450,000
Less ending work in process Inventory		150,000
Step 3: Cost of goods manufactured		$300,000

The Choice Candy Company
Income Statement
For the Year 2011

Sales		$500,000
Cost of goods sold		
Beginning finished goods inventory	$ 78,000	
Cost of goods manufactured	300,000	
Cost of goods available for sale	$378,000	
Less ending finished goods inventory	138,000	
Cost of goods sold		240,000
Gross margin		$260,000
Selling and administrative expenses		160,000
Operating income		$100,000

Cost of Goods Sold and a Manufacturer's Income Statement

Study Note

It is important not to confuse the cost of goods manufactured with the cost of goods sold.

Exhibit 16-1 shows the relationship between The Choice Candy Company's income statement and its statement of cost of goods manufactured. The total amount of the cost of goods manufactured during the period is carried over to the income statement, where it is used to compute the cost of goods sold. The beginning balance of the Finished Goods Inventory account is added to the cost of goods manufactured to arrive at the total cost of goods available for sale during the period. The cost of goods sold is then computed by subtracting the ending balance in Finished Goods Inventory (what was not sold) from the total cost of goods available for sale (what was available for sale). The cost of goods sold is considered an expense in the period in which the goods are sold.

STOP & APPLY >

Given the following information, compute the ending balances of the Materials Inventory, Work in Process Inventory, and Finished Goods Inventory accounts:

Materials inventory, beginning balance	$ 230
Work in process inventory, beginning balance	250
Finished goods inventory, beginning balance	380
Direct materials purchased	850
Direct materials placed into production	740
Direct labor costs	970
Overhead costs	350
Cost of goods completed	1,230
Cost of goods sold	935

SOLUTION

Materials Inventory, ending balance:	
Materials Inventory, beginning balance	$ 230
Direct materials purchased	850
Direct materials placed into production	(740)
Materials Inventory, ending balance	$ 340
Work in Process Inventory, ending balance:	
Work in Process Inventory, beginning balance	$ 250
Direct materials placed into production	740
Direct labor costs	970
Overhead costs	350
Cost of goods completed	(1,230)
Work in Process Inventory, ending balance	$1,080
Finished Goods Inventory, ending balance:	
Finished Goods Inventory, beginning balance	$ 380
Cost of goods completed	1,230
Cost of goods sold	(935)
Finished Goods Inventory, ending balance	$ 675

Inventory Accounts in Manufacturing Organizations

LO3 Describe the flow of costs through a manufacturer's inventory accounts.

Transforming materials into finished products ready for sale requires a number of production and production-related activities. A manufacturing organization's accounting system tracks these activities as product costs flowing through the Materials Inventory, Work in Process Inventory, and Finished Goods Inventory accounts.

- The **Materials Inventory account** shows the balance of the cost of unused materials.
- The **Work in Process Inventory account** shows the manufacturing costs that have been incurred and assigned to partially completed units of product.
- The **Finished Goods Inventory account** shows the costs assigned to all completed products that have not been sold.

Document Flows and Cost Flows Through the Inventory Accounts

Managers accumulate and report manufacturing costs based on documents pertaining to production and production-related activities. Figure 16-3 summarizes the typical relationships among the production activities, the documents for each of the three cost elements, and the inventory accounts affected by the activities. Looking at the relationship between activities and documents provides insight into how costs flow through the three inventory accounts and when an activity must be recorded in the accounting records.

To illustrate document flow and changes in inventory balances for production activities in Figure 16-3, we continue with our example of The Choice Candy Company, a typical manufacturing business.

Purchase of Materials

- The purchasing process starts with a *purchase request* prepared on a computer form which is submitted electronically for specific quantities of materials needed in the manufacturing process but not currently available in the materials storeroom. A qualified manager approves the request online. Based on the information in the purchase request, the Purchasing Department prepares a computer-generated *purchase order* and sends it to a supplier.
- When the materials arrive, an employee on the receiving dock examines the materials and enters the information into the company database as a *receiving report.* The system matches the information on the receiving report with the descriptions and quantities listed on the purchase order. A materials handler moves the newly arrived materials from the receiving area to the materials storeroom.
- The Choice Candy Company's accounting department receives a *vendor's invoice* from the supplier requesting payment for the purchased materials. The cost of those materials increases the balance of the Materials Inventory account and an account payable is recognized. If all documents match, payment is authorized to be made.

Production of Goods

- When candy bars are scheduled for production, the storeroom clerk receives a *materials request form.* In addition to showing authorization, it describes the types and quantities of materials that the storeroom clerk is to send to the production area, and it authorizes the release of those materials from the materials inventory into production.

FIGURE 16-3 Activities, Documents, and Cost Flows Through the Inventory Accounts of a Manufacturing Organization

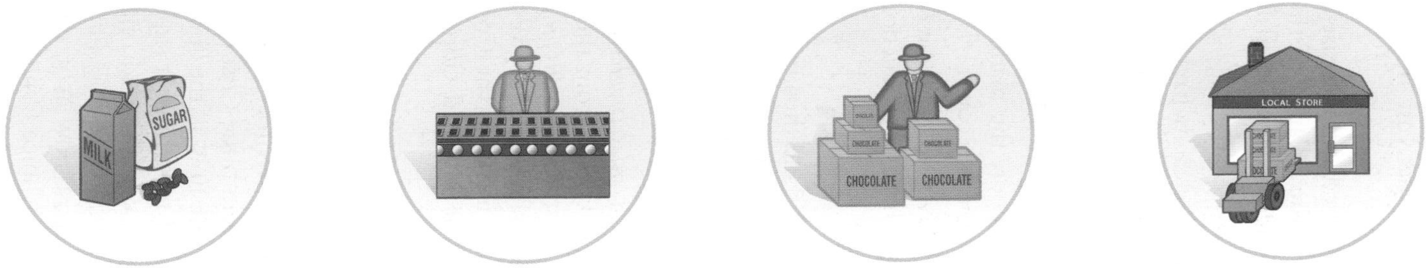

	PURCHASE OF MATERIALS	PRODUCTION OF GOODS	PRODUCT COMPLETION	PRODUCT SALE
ACTIVITIES	• Purchase, receive, inspect, and store materials. • Confirm receipt of materials. • Match documents.	• Move materials to production area. • Convert materials into finished product using direct labor and overhead.	• Move completed products to finished goods storage area and store until sold. • Move sold units to shipping.	• Ship products sold to customer.
DOCUMENTS	• Purchase request • Purchase order • Receiving report • Vendor's invoice	• Materials request form • Time card • Job order cost card	• Job order cost card	• Sales invoice • Shipping document • Job order cost card
INVENTORY ACCOUNTS (RELATED DOCUMENTS)	MATERIALS INVENTORY Debit: Cost of materials purchased (vendor's invoice) Credit: Cost of materials used in production (materials request form)	WORK IN PROCESS INVENTORY Debit: Cost of materials used in production (materials request form); Cost of direct labor (time card); Cost of overhead Credit: Cost of completed products (job order cost card)	FINISHED GOODS INVENTORY Debit: Cost of completed products (job order cost card) Credit: Cost of sold units (job order cost card)	COST OF GOODS SOLD Debit: Cost of sold units (job order cost card)

- If all is in order, the storeroom clerk has the materials handler move the materials to the production floor.
  - The cost of the direct materials transferred will increase the balance of the Work in Process Inventory account and decrease the balance of the Materials Inventory account.
  - The cost of the indirect materials transferred will increase the balance of the Overhead account and decrease the balance of the Materials Inventory account. (We discuss overhead in more detail later in this chapter.)
- Each of the production employees who make the candy bars prepares a *time card* to record the number of hours he or she has worked on this and other orders each day.
  - The costs of the direct labor used to manufacture the candy bars increase the balance of the Work in Process Inventory account.
  - The costs of the indirect labor used to support the manufacture of the candy bars increase the balance of the Overhead account.
- A *job order cost card* can be used to record all direct material, direct labor, and overhead costs incurred as the products move through production.

Product Completion and Sale

- Employees place completed candy bars in cartons and then move the cartons to the finished goods storeroom, where they are kept until they are shipped to customers. The cost of the completed candy bars increases the balance of the Finished Goods Inventory account and decreases the balance of the Work in Process Inventory account.
- When candy bars are sold, a clerk prepares a *sales invoice,* and another employee fills the order by removing the candy bars from the storeroom, packaging them, and shipping them to the customer. A *shipping document* shows the quantity of the products that are shipped and gives a description of them. The cost of the candy bars sold increases the Cost of Goods Sold account and decreases the balance of the Finished Goods Inventory account.

The Manufacturing Cost Flow

Manufacturing cost flow is the flow of manufacturing costs (direct materials, direct labor, and overhead) through the Materials Inventory, Work in Process Inventory, and Finished Goods Inventory accounts into the Cost of Goods Sold account. A defined, structured manufacturing cost flow is the foundation for product costing, inventory valuation, and financial reporting. It supplies all the information necessary to prepare the statement of cost of goods manufactured and compute the cost of goods sold, as shown in Exhibit 16-1.

Figure 16-4 summarizes the manufacturing cost flow as it relates to the inventory accounts and production activity of The Choice Candy Company for the year ended December 31. To show the basic flows in this example, we assume that all materials can be traced directly to the candy bars. This means that there are no indirect materials in the Materials Inventory account. We also work with the actual amount of overhead, rather than an estimated amount.

Materials Inventory Because there are no indirect materials in this case, the Materials Inventory account shows the balance of unused direct materials. The cost of direct materials purchased increases the balance of the Materials Inventory account, and the cost of direct materials used by the Production Department decreases it.

Figure 16-4 shows the flows of material purchased and used through the Materials Inventory T account.

Work in Process Inventory The Work in Process Inventory account records the balance of partially completed units of the product.

- As direct materials and direct labor enter the production process, their costs are added to the Work in Process Inventory account. The cost of overhead for the current period is also added.
- The total costs of direct materials, direct labor, and overhead incurred and transferred to work in process inventory during an accounting period are called **total manufacturing costs** (also called *current manufacturing costs*). These costs increase the balance of the Work in Process Inventory account.
- The cost of all units completed and moved to finished goods inventory during an accounting period is the **cost of goods manufactured**. The cost of goods manufactured for the period decreases the balance of the Work in Process Inventory account.

Figure 16-4 recaps the inflows of direct materials, direct labor, and overhead into the Work in Process Inventory T account and the resulting outflow of completed product costs.

Finished Goods Inventory The Finished Goods Inventory account holds the balance of costs assigned to all completed products that a manufacturing company has not yet sold. The cost of goods manufactured increases the balance, and the cost of goods sold decreases the balance.

Figure 16-4 shows the inflow of cost of goods manufactured and the outflow of cost of goods sold to the Finished Goods Inventory T account.

Study Note

When costs are transferred from one inventory account to another in a manufacturing company, they remain assets. They are on the balance sheet and are not expensed on the income statement until the finished goods are sold.

Study Note

Materials Inventory and Work in Process Inventory support the production process, while Finished Goods Inventory supports the sales and distribution functions.

FIGURE 16-4 Manufacturing Cost Flow: An Example Using Actual Costing for The Choice Candy Company

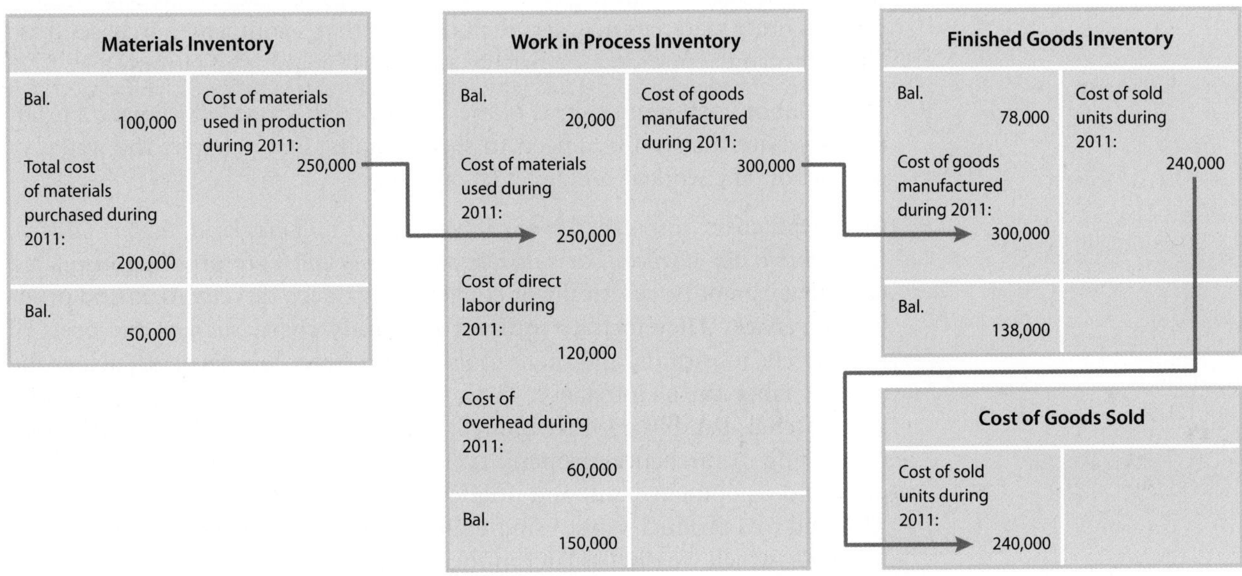

STOP & APPLY >

Given the following information, use T accounts to compute the ending balances of the Materials Inventory, Work in Process Inventory, and Finished Goods Inventory accounts:

Materials Inventory, beginning balance	$ 230
Work in Process Inventory, beginning balance	250
Finished Goods Inventory, beginning balance	380
Direct materials purchased	850
Direct materials (DM) placed into production (used)	740
Direct labor (DL) costs	970
Overhead (OH) costs	350
Cost of goods completed (COGM)	1,230
Cost of goods sold (COGS)	935

SOLUTION

Material Inventory

Beg.	230	Used	740
Purchased	850		
End.	**340**		

Work in Process Inventory

Beg.	250	COGM	1,230
DM	740		
DL	970		
OH	350		
End.	**1,080**		

Finished Goods Inventory

Beg.	380	COGS	935
COGM	1,230		
End.	**675**		

Elements of Product Costs

LO4 Define *product unit cost,* and compute the unit cost of a product or service.

As noted above, product costs include all costs related to the manufacturing process. The three elements of product cost are direct materials costs, direct labor costs, and overhead costs.

- **Direct materials costs** are the costs of materials used in making a product that can be conveniently and economically traced to specific units of the product. Some examples of direct materials are the meat and bun in hamburgers, the oil and additives in a gallon of gasoline, and the sugar used in making candy. Direct materials may also include parts that a company purchases from another manufacturer, e.g., a battery and windshield for an automobile.
- **Direct labor costs** are the costs of the hands-on labor needed to make a product or service that can be traced to specific units. For example, the wages of production-line workers are direct labor costs.
- **Overhead costs** (also called *service overhead, factory overhead, factory burden, manufacturing overhead,* or *indirect production costs*) are production-related costs that cannot be practically or conveniently traced directly to an end product or service. They include **indirect materials costs**, such as the costs of nails, rivets, lubricants, and small tools, and **indirect labor costs**, such as the costs of labor for maintenance, inspection, engineering design, supervision, and materials handling. Other indirect manufacturing costs include the costs of building maintenance, property taxes, property insurance, depreciation on plant and equipment, rent, and utilities. As indirect costs, overhead costs are allocated to a product's cost using either traditional or activity-based costing methods, which we discuss later in the chapter.

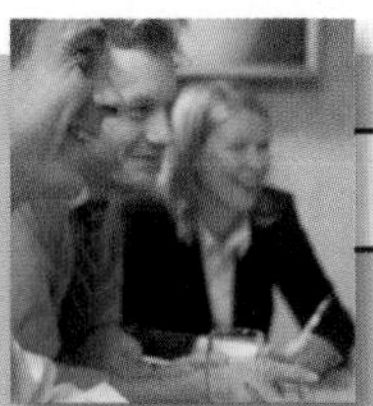

FOCUS ON BUSINESS PRACTICE

Has Technology Shifted the Elements of Product Costs?

New technology and manufacturing processes have created new patterns of product costs. The three elements of product costs are still direct materials, direct labor, and overhead, but the percentage that each contributes to the total cost of a product has changed. From the 1950s through the 1970s, direct labor was the dominant element, making up over 40 percent of total product cost, while direct materials contributed 35 percent and overhead, around 25 percent. Thus, direct costs, traceable to the product, accounted for 75 percent of total product cost. Improved production technology caused a dramatic shift in the three product cost elements. Machines replaced people, significantly reducing direct labor costs. Today, only 50 percent of the cost of a product is directly traceable to the product; the other 50 percent is overhead, an indirect cost.

To illustrate product costs and the manufacturing process, we'll refer again to The Choice Candy Company. Maggie Evans, the company's founder and president, has identified the following elements of the product cost of one candy bar:

- *Direct materials costs:* costs of sugar, chocolate, and wrapper
- *Direct labor costs:* costs of labor used in making the candy bar
- *Overhead costs:* indirect materials costs, including the costs of salt and flavorings; indirect labor costs, including the costs of labor to move materials to the production area and to inspect the candy bars during production; other indirect overhead costs, including depreciation on the building and equipment, utilities, property taxes, and insurance

Prime Costs and Conversion Costs

The three elements of manufacturing costs can be grouped into prime costs and conversion costs.

- **Prime costs** are the primary costs of production; they are the sum of the direct materials costs and direct labor costs.
- **Conversion costs** are the costs of converting direct materials into a finished product; they are the sum of direct labor costs and overhead costs.

These classifications are important for understanding the costing methods discussed in later chapters. Figure 16-5 summarizes the relationships among the product cost classifications presented so far.

Computing Product Unit Cost

Product unit cost is the cost of manufacturing a single unit of a product. It is made up of the costs of direct materials, direct labor, and overhead. These three cost elements are accumulated as a batch or production run of products is being produced. When the batch or run has been completed, the product unit cost is computed by dividing the total cost of direct materials, direct labor, and overhead

FIGURE 16-5
Relationships Among Product Cost Classifications

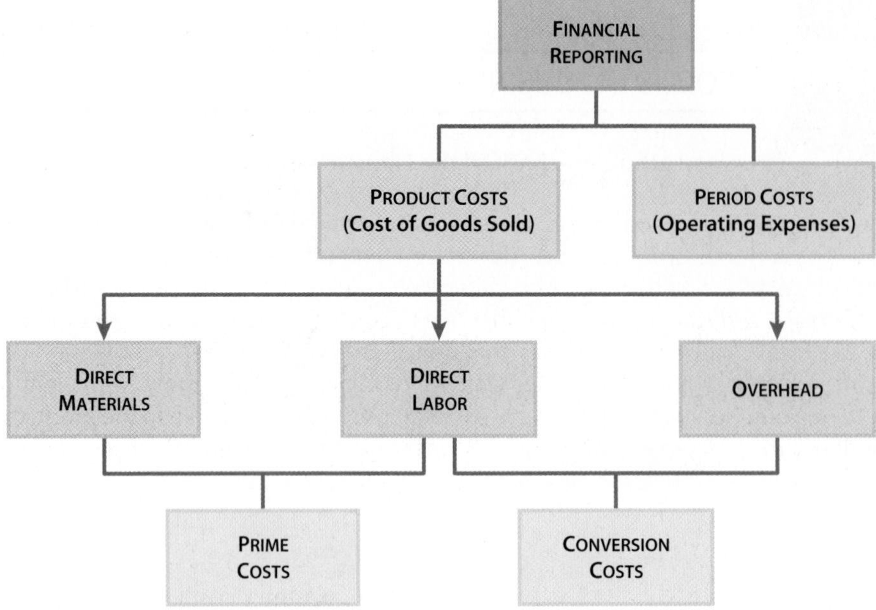

by the total number of units produced, or by determining the cost per unit for each element of the product cost and summing those per unit costs.

$$\text{Product Unit Cost} = \frac{\text{Direct Materials Cost} + \text{Direct Labor Cost} + \text{Overhead Cost}}{\text{Number of Units Produced}}$$

or

$$\text{Product Unit Cost} = \text{Direct Materials Cost per Unit} + \text{Direct Labor Cost per Unit} + \text{Overhead Cost per Unit}$$

Product Cost Measurement Methods

How products flow physically and how costs are incurred do not always match. For example, The Choice Candy Company physically produces candy bars 24 hours a day, 7 days a week, but the accounting department only does accounting 8 hours a day, 5 days a week. Because product cost data must be available 24/7, managers may use estimates or predetermined standards to compute product costs during the period. At the end of the period, these estimates are reconciled with the actual product costs so actual product costs appear in the financial statements. Here are the three methods managers and accountants can use to calculate product unit cost:

- Actual costing method,
- Normal costing method, or
- Standard costing method.

Table 16-2 summarizes how these three product cost-measurement methods use actual and estimated costs.

Actual Costing Method The **actual costing** method uses the actual costs of direct materials, direct labor, and overhead when they become known to calculate the product unit cost. This means, many times, waiting until the end of the

TABLE 16-2
Use of Actual and Estimated Costs in Three Cost-Measurement Methods

Product Cost Elements	Actual Costing	Normal Costing	Standard Costing
Direct materials	Actual costs	Actual costs	Estimated costs
Direct labor	Actual costs	Actual costs	Estimated costs
Overhead	Actual costs	Estimated costs	Estimated costs

Study Note
Many management decisions require estimates of future costs. Managers often use actual cost as a basis for estimating future cost.

period when all the cost data are available. For most companies, this is not practical. Notice in the following example that product unit cost is computed after the job was completed and all cost information was known.

The Choice Candy Company produced 3,000 candy bars on December 28 for Good Foods Store. Sara Kearney, the company's accountant, calculated that the actual costs for the order were direct materials, $540; direct labor, $420; and overhead, $210. The actual product unit cost for the order was $0.39, calculated as follows:

Actual direct materials ($540 ÷ 3,000 candy bars)	$0.18
Actual direct labor ($420 ÷ 3,000 candy bars)	0.14
Actual overhead ($210 ÷ 3,000 candy bars)	0.07
Actual product cost per candy bar ($1,170 ÷ 3,000 candy bars)	$0.39

Study Note
The use of normal costing is widespread, since many overhead bills, such as utility bills, are not received until after products or services are produced and sold.

Normal Costing Method The **normal costing** method combines the easy-to-track actual direct costs of materials and labor with estimated overhead costs to determine a product unit cost.

- The normal costing method is simple and allows a smoother, more even assignment of overhead costs to production during an accounting period than is possible with the actual costing method.
- However, at the end of the accounting period, any difference between the estimated and actual costs must be identified and removed so that the financial statements show only the actual product costs.

Assume that Sara Kearney used normal costing to price the Good Foods Store order for 3,000 candy bars and that overhead was applied to the product's cost using an estimated rate of 60 percent of direct labor costs. In this case, the costs for the order would include the actual direct materials cost of $540, the actual direct labor cost of $420, and an estimated overhead cost of $252 ($420 × 60%). The product unit cost would be $0.40:

Actual direct materials ($540 ÷ 3,000 candy bars)	$0.18
Actual direct labor ($420 ÷ 3,000 candy bars)	0.14
Estimated overhead ($252 ÷ 3,000 candy bars)	0.08
Normal product cost per candy bar ($1,212 ÷ 3,000 candy bars)	$0.40

Standard Costing Method The **standard costing** method uses estimated or standard costs of direct materials, direct labor, and overhead to calculate the product unit cost.

- Managers sometimes need product cost information before the accounting period begins so that they can control the cost of operating activities or price a proposed product for a customer. In such situations, product unit costs must be estimated, and the standard costing method can be helpful.

- Standard costing is very useful in performance management and evaluation because a manager can compare actual and standard costs to compute the variances. We cover standard costing in more detail in another chapter.

Assume that The Choice Candy Company is placing a bid to manufacture 2,000 candy bars for a new customer. From standard cost information developed at the beginning of the period, Kearney estimates the following costs: $0.20 per unit for direct materials, $0.15 per unit for direct labor, and $0.09 per unit for overhead (assuming a standard overhead rate of 60 percent of direct labor cost). The standard cost per unit would be $0.44:

Standard direct materials	$0.20
Standard direct labor	0.15
Standard overhead ($0.15 × 60%)	0.09
Standard product cost per candy bar	$0.44

Computing Service Unit Cost

Study Note

Any material costs in a service organization would be for supplies used in providing services. Because these are indirect materials costs, they are included in overhead.

Delivering products, representing people in courts of law, selling insurance policies, and computing people's income taxes are typical of the services performed in many service organizations. Like other services, these are labor-intensive processes supported by indirect materials or supplies, indirect labor, and other overhead costs.

- The most important cost in a service organization is the direct cost of labor that can be traceable to the service rendered.
- The indirect costs incurred in performing a service are similar to those incurred in manufacturing a product. They are classified as overhead.
- These service costs appear on service organizations' income statements as cost of sales.

STOP & APPLY >

Fickle Picking Services provides inexpensive, high-quality labor for farmers growing vegetable and fruit crops. In September, Fickle Picking Services paid laborers $4,000 to harvest 500 acres of apples. The company incurred overhead costs of $2,400 for apple-picking services in September. This amount included the costs of transporting the laborers to the orchards; of providing facilities, food, and beverages for the laborers; and of scheduling, billing, and collecting from the farmers. Of this amount, 50 percent was related to picking apples. Compute the cost per acre to pick apples.

SOLUTION

Total cost to pick apples:	$4,000 + (0.50 × $2,400) = $5,200
Cost per acre to pick apples:	$5,200 ÷ 500 acres = $10.40 per acre

Cost Allocation

LO5 Define *cost allocation,* and explain how the traditional method of allocating overhead costs figures into calculating product or service unit cost.

As noted earlier, the costs of direct materials and direct labor can be easily traced to a product or service, but overhead costs are indirect costs that must be collected and allocated in some manner.

- **Cost allocation** is the process of assigning a collection of indirect costs, such as overhead, to a specific **cost object**, such as a product or service, a department, or an operating activity, using an allocation base known as a cost driver.
- A **cost driver** might be direct labor hours, direct labor costs, units produced, or another activity base that has a cause-and-effect relationship with the cost.
- As the cost driver increases in volume, it causes the **cost pool**—the collection of indirect costs assigned to a cost object—to increase in amount.

Suppose The Choice Candy Company has a machine maintenance cost pool. The cost pool consists of overhead costs needed to maintain the machines, the cost object is the candy product, and the cost driver is machine hours. As more machine hours are used to maintain the machines, the amount of the cost pool increases, thus increasing the costs assigned to the candy product.

Allocating the Costs of Overhead

Allocating overhead costs to products or services is a four-step process that corresponds to the four stages of the management process:

1. *Planning.* In the first step, managers estimate overhead costs and calculate a rate at which they will assign those costs to products or services.
2. *Performing.* In the second step, this rate is applied to products or services as overhead costs are incurred and recorded during production.
3. *Evaluating.* In the third step, actual overhead costs are recorded as they are incurred, and managers calculate the difference between the estimated (or applied) and actual costs.
4. *Communicating.* In the fourth step, managers report on this difference.

Figure 16-6 summarizes these four steps in terms of their timing, the procedures involved, and the entries they require. It also shows how the cost flows in the various steps affect the accounting records.

Step 1. ***Planning the overhead rate.*** Before a period begins, managers determine cost pools and cost drivers and calculate a **predetermined overhead rate** by dividing the cost pool of total estimated overhead costs by the total estimated cost driver level.

- Grouping all estimated overhead costs into one cost pool and using direct labor hours or machine hours as the cost driver results in a single, plantwide overhead rate.
- This step requires no entry because no business activity has occurred.

Step 2. ***Applying the overhead rate.*** As units of the product or service are produced during the period, the estimated overhead costs are assigned to the product or service using the predetermined overhead rate.

- The predetermined overhead rate is multiplied by the actual cost driver level (e.g., the actual number of direct labor hours used to complete the product). The purpose of this calculation is to assign a consistent overhead cost to each unit produced during the period.
- An entry records the allocation of overhead. The entry to apply overhead to a product is recorded as a debit or increase to the Work in Process Inventory account and a credit or decrease to the Overhead account.

FIGURE 16-6
Allocating Overhead Costs: A Four-Step Process

Year 2010 — January 1 — Year 2011 — December 31

	Step 1: Planning the Overhead Rate	Step 2: Applying the Overhead Rate	Step 3: Recording Actual Overhead Costs	Step 4: Reconciling Applied and Actual Overhead Costs
Timing and Procedure	Before the accounting period begins, determine cost pools and cost drivers. Calculate the overhead rate by dividing the cost pool of total estimated overhead costs by the total estimated cost driver level.	During the accounting period, as units are produced, apply overhead costs to products by multiplying the predetermined overhead rate for each cost pool by the actual cost driver level for that pool. Record costs.	Record actual overhead costs as they are incurred during the accounting period.	At the end of the accounting period, calculate and reconcile the difference between applied and actual overhead costs.
Entry	None	Increase Work in Process Inventory account and decrease Overhead account: Dr. Work in Process Inventory XX Cr. Overhead XX	Increase Overhead account and decrease asset accounts or increase contra-asset or liability accounts: Dr. Overhead XX Cr. Various Accounts XX	Entry will vary depending on how costs have been applied. If overapplied, increase Overhead and decrease Cost of Goods Sold. If underapplied, increase Cost of Goods Sold and decrease Overhead.

Cost Flow Through the Accounts

Step 2:

Overhead

Debit	Credit
	Overhead applied using predetermined rate

Work in Process Inventory

Debit	Credit
Overhead applied using predetermined rate	

Step 3:

Overhead

Debit	Credit
Actual overhead costs recorded	

Various Asset and Liability Accounts

Debit	Credit
	Actual overhead costs recorded

Step 4:

Overapplied:
Overhead

Debit	Credit
Actual overhead costs recorded	Overhead applied using predetermined rate
Overapplied	
Bal. $0	

Cost of Goods Sold

Debit	Credit
Bal.	**Overapplied**
Actual Bal.	

Underapplied:
Overhead

Debit	Credit
Actual overhead costs recorded	Overhead applied using predetermined rate
	Underapplied
Bal. $0	

Cost of Goods Sold

Debit	Credit
Bal.	
Underapplied	
Actual Bal.	

Step 3. ***Recording actual overhead costs.*** The actual overhead costs are recorded as they are incurred during the period.

- These costs include the actual costs of indirect materials, indirect labor, depreciation, property taxes, and other production costs.
- The entry made for the actual overhead costs records a debit in the Overhead account and a credit in the asset, contra-asset, or liability accounts affected.

Step 4. ***Reconciling the applied and actual overhead amounts.*** At the end of the period, the difference between the applied and actual overhead costs is calculated and reconciled.

Overapplied Overhead If the overhead costs applied to production during the period are greater than the actual overhead costs, the difference in the amounts represents **overapplied overhead costs**.

- If this difference is immaterial, the Overhead account is debited or increased and the Cost of Goods Sold or Cost of Sales account is credited or decreased by the difference.
- If the difference is material for the products produced, adjustments are made to the accounts affected—that is, the Work in Process Inventory, Finished Goods Inventory, and Cost of Goods Sold accounts.

Underapplied Overhead If the overhead costs applied to production during the period are less than the actual overhead costs, the difference represents **underapplied overhead costs**.

- If the difference is immaterial, the Cost of Goods Sold or Cost of Sales account is debited or increased and the Overhead account is credited or decreased by this difference.
- If the difference is material for the products produced, adjustments are made to the accounts affected—that is, the Work in Process Inventory, Finished Goods Inventory, and Cost of Goods Sold accounts.

Actual Cost of Goods Sold or Cost of Sales The adjustment for overapplied or underapplied overhead costs is necessary to reflect the actual overhead costs on the income statement.

Allocating Overhead: The Traditional Approach

The traditional approach to applying overhead costs to a product or service is to use a single plantwide overhead rate.

- This approach is especially useful when companies manufacture only one product or a few very similar products that require the same production processes and production-related activities, such as setup, inspection, and materials handling.
- The total overhead costs constitute one cost pool, and a traditional activity base—such as direct labor hours, direct labor costs, machine hours, or units of production—is the cost driver.

As we continue with our example of The Choice Candy Company, let's assume that the company will be selling two product lines in the coming year—plain candy bars and candy bars with nuts—and that Sara Kearney chooses direct labor hours as the cost driver. Kearney estimates that total overhead costs for the next year will be $20,000 and that total direct labor hours (DLH) worked will be 400,000 hours.

Table 16-3 summarizes the first two steps in the traditional approach to allocating overhead costs.

Step 1. ***Planning the overhead rate.*** Kearney uses the following formula to compute the rate at which overhead costs will be applied:

$$\text{Predetermined Overhead Rate} = \frac{\$20{,}000}{400{,}000 \text{ DLH}} = \$0.05 \text{ per DLH}$$

Step 2. ***Applying the overhead rate.*** Kearney applies the predetermined overhead rate to the products. During the year, The Choice Candy Company actually uses 250,000 direct labor hours to produce 100,000 plain candy bars and 150,000 direct labor hours to produce 50,000 candy bars with nuts.

- The portion of the overhead cost applied to the plain candy bars totals \$12,500 (\$0.05 × 250,000 DLH), or \$0.13 per unit (\$12,500 ÷ 100,000 units).
- The portion of overhead applied to the candy bars with nuts totals \$7,500 (\$0.05 × 150,000 DLH), or \$0.15 per unit (\$7,500 ÷ 50,000 units).

Product Unit Cost Using the Normal Costing Approach Kearney also wants to calculate the product unit cost for the accounting period using normal costing. She gathers the following data for the two product lines:

TABLE 16-3 Allocating Overhead Costs and Calculating Product Unit Cost: Traditional Approach

Step 1. Calculate overhead rate for cost pool:

$$\frac{\text{Estimated Total Overhead Costs}}{\text{Estimated Total Cost Driver Level}} = \frac{\$20{,}000}{400{,}000 \text{ (DLH)}} = \$0.05 \text{ per DLH}$$

Step 2. Apply predetermined overhead rate to products:

	Plain Candy Bars	Candy Bars with Nuts
	Predetermined Overhead Rate × Actual Cost Driver Level = Cost Applied to Production	Predetermined Overhead Rate × Actual Cost Driver Level = Cost Applied to Production
Overhead applied: \$0.05 per DLH	\$0.05 × 250,000 DLH = \$12,500	\$0.05 × 150,000 DLH = \$7,500
Overhead cost per unit: Cost Applied ÷ Number of Units	\$12,500 ÷ 100,000 = \$0.13*	\$7,500 ÷ 50,000 = \$0.15

Product unit cost using normal costing:

	Plain Candy Bars	Candy Bars with Nuts
Product costs per unit:		
Direct materials	\$0.18	\$0.21
Direct labor	0.14	0.16
Applied overhead	0.13	0.15
Total product unit cost	\$0.45	\$0.52

*Rounded.

	Plain Candy Bars	*Candy Bars with Nuts*
Actual direct materials cost per unit	$0.18	$0.21
Actual direct labor cost per unit	0.14	0.16
Prime cost per unit	$0.32	$0.37

At the bottom of Table 16-3 is Kearney's calculation of the normal product unit cost for each product line consisting of its prime costs plus applied overhead. The product unit cost of the candy bar with nuts ($0.52) is higher than the plain candy bar's cost ($0.45) because producing the candy bar with nuts required more expensive materials and more labor time.

Step 3. ***Recording actual overhead costs.*** Kearney records the actual overhead costs as they were incurred during the year. The actual overhead costs totaled $19,800. The entry she made records a debit in the Overhead account and a credit in the asset, contra-asset, or liability accounts affected.

Step 4. ***Reconciling the applied and actual overhead amounts.*** Kearney compares the actual and applied overhead costs to compute the amount of underapplied or overapplied overhead:

	Actual	*Applied*	*Overapplied*
Overhead Costs	$19,800	$20,000	$200

Study Note

Don't make the mistake of thinking that because a cost is not traced directly to a product, it is not a product cost. All manufacturing costs, both direct and indirect, are product costs.

Actual Cost of Goods Sold Cost of Goods Sold will be reduced by the $200 of overapplied overhead costs. The adjustment is necessary to reflect the actual overhead costs on the income statement.

Allocating Overhead: The ABC Approach

Activity-based costing (ABC) is a more accurate method of assigning overhead costs to products or services than the traditional approach. It categorizes all indirect costs by activity, traces the indirect costs to those activities, and assigns activity costs to products or services using a cost driver related to the cause of the cost.

- A company that uses ABC identifies production-related activities or tasks and the events and circumstances that cause, or drive, those activities, such as number of inspections or maintenance hours. As a result, many smaller activity pools are created from the single overhead cost pool used in the traditional method.
- This means that managers will calculate many rates. There will be an overhead rate, or activity cost rate, for each activity pool, which must be applied to products or services produced.
- Managers must select an appropriate number of activity pools instead of the traditional plantwide rate for overhead.

ABC will improve the accuracy of product or service cost estimates for organizations. More careful cost allocation means that managers will have better information for decision making.

STOP & APPLY >

1. Compute the predetermined overhead rate for the Sample Service Company if its estimated overhead costs for the coming year will be $15,000 and 5,000 direct labor hours will be worked.
2. Calculate the amount of overhead costs applied by the Sample Service Company to one of its jobs if the job required 10 direct labor hours to complete.
3. Compute the total cost of the job if prime (direct material and direct labor) costs incurred by Sample Service Company to complete it were $60. If the job contained 5 units of service, what is the unit cost?
4. Using the traditional overhead rate computed in Step 1, determine the total amount of overhead applied to operations during the year if Sample Service Company compiles a total of 4,900 labor hours worked.
5. If Sample Company's actual overhead costs for the year are $14,800, compute the amount of under- or overapplied overhead for the year. Will the Cost of Goods Sold account be increased or decreased to correct the under- or overapplication of overhead?

SOLUTION

1. $$\text{Predetermined Overhead Rate} = \frac{\text{Estimated Overhead Costs}}{\text{Estimated Direct Labor Hours}} = \frac{\$15{,}000}{5{,}000\ \text{DLH}} = \$3.00 \text{ per DLH}$$

2. Overhead Costs Applied = Predetermined Overhead Rate × Actual Hours Worked

   $3 per DLH × 10 Actual Direct Labor Hours Worked = $30

3. Total Cost = Actual Direct Materials Cost + Actual Direct Labor Cost + Applied Overhead Cost

   = $60 + $30 = $90

   $$\text{Unit Cost} = \frac{\text{Total Cost of Job}}{\text{Units Produced}} = \frac{\$90}{5\ \text{units}} = \$18 \text{ per unit}$$

4. Overhead Costs Applied = Predetermined Overhead Rate × Actual Hours Worked During Year

   = $3 per DLH × 4,900 Actual Direct Labor Hours Worked

   = $14,700

5. Overhead Costs Applied = $14,700

   Actual Overhead Costs = 14,800

   Underapplied Overhead = $ 100, which will increase the Cost of Goods Sold account

A LOOK BACK AT ▸ THE HERSHEY COMPANY

In this chapter's Decision Point, we posed these questions:

- How do managers at Hershey's determine the cost of a candy bar?
- How do managers use cost information?

To determine the cost of a candy bar, managers at **The Hershey Company** must conduct complex analyses of many product costs, as well as costs that are unrelated to products. They analyze both the traceable costs of direct labor and materials and the indirect costs needed to support candy production. They also consider any other relevant selling, administrative, or general operating costs that relate to the candy bars.

Classifying and analyzing costs helps managers make decisions that will sustain Hershey's profitability. All costs must be analyzed in terms of their traceability and behavior and in terms of whether they add value and how they affect the financial statements. Because many costs cannot be directly traced to specific candy products, managers must use a method of allocation to assign them. Possibilities include the traditional allocation method and the activity-based costing method discussed in this chapter.

Review Problem

Calculating Cost of Goods Manufactured: Three Fundamental Steps

LO2 LO4

Assume that one of The Hershey Company's factories produces 50-pound blocks of dark chocolate and that it needs to prepare a year-end balance sheet and income statement, as well as a statement of cost of goods manufactured. During the year, the factory purchased $361,920 of direct materials. The factory's direct labor costs for the year were $99,085 (10,430 hours at $9.50 per hour); its indirect labor costs totaled $126,750 (20,280 hours at $6.25 per hour). Account balances for the year were as follows:

Account	Balance
Plant Supervision	$ 42,500
Factory Insurance	8,100
Utilities, Factory	29,220
Depreciation–Factory Building	46,200
Depreciation–Factory Equipment	62,800
Factory Security	9,460
Factory Repair and Maintenance	14,980
Selling and Administrative Expenses	76,480
Materials Inventory, beginning	26,490
Work in Process Inventory, beginning	101,640
Finished Goods Inventory, beginning	148,290
Materials Inventory, ending	24,910
Work in Process Inventory, ending	100,400
Finished Goods Inventory, ending	141,100

Required

1. Compute the cost of materials used during the year.
2. Given the cost of materials used, compute the total manufacturing costs for the year.

3. Given the total manufacturing costs for the year, compute the cost of goods manufactured during the year.
4. If 13,397 units (1 unit = 50-pound block of dark chocolate) were manufactured during the year, what was the actual product unit cost? (Round your answer to two decimal places.)

Answers to Review Problem

1. Cost of materials used:

Materials inventory, beginning	$ 26,490
Direct materials purchased	361,920
Cost of materials available for use	$388,410
Less materials inventory, ending	24,910
Cost of materials used	$363,500

2. Total manufacturing costs:

Cost of materials used		$363,500
Direct labor costs		99,085
Overhead costs		
Indirect labor	$126,750	
Plant supervision	42,500	
Factory insurance	8,100	
Utilities, factory	29,220	
Depreciation–factory building	46,200	
Depreciation–factory equipment	62,800	
Factory security	9,460	
Factory repair and maintenance	14,980	
Total overhead costs		340,010
Total manufacturing costs		$802,595

3. Cost of goods manufactured:

Total manufacturing costs	$802,595
Add work in process inventory, beginning	101,640
Total cost of work in process during the year	$904,235
Less work in process inventory, ending	100,400
Cost of goods manufactured	$803,835

4. Actual product unit cost:

$$\frac{\text{Cost of Goods Manufactured}}{\text{Number of Units Manufactured}} = \frac{\$803{,}835}{13{,}397 \text{ units}} = \$60.00^*$$

*Rounded.

LO1 Explain how managers classify costs and how they use these cost classifications.

Managers in manufacturing, retail, and service organizations use information about operating costs and product or service costs to prepare budgets, make pricing and other decisions, calculate variances between estimated and actual costs, and communicate results.

A single cost can be classified as a direct or an indirect cost, a variable or a fixed cost, a value-adding or a nonvalue-adding cost, and a product or a period cost. These cost classifications enable managers to control costs by tracing them to cost objects, to calculate the number of units that must be sold to obtain a certain level of profit, to identify the costs of activities that do and do not add value to a product or service, and to prepare financial statements for parties outside the organization.

LO2 Compare how service, retail, and manufacturing organizations report costs on their financial statements and how they account for inventories.

Because the operations of service, retail, and manufacturing organizations differ, their financial statements differ as well. A service organization maintains no inventory accounts on its balance sheet. The cost of sales on its income statement reflects the net cost of the services sold. A retail organization, which purchases products ready for resale, maintains only a Merchandise Inventory account, which is used to record and account for items in inventory. The cost of goods sold is simply the difference between the cost of goods available for sale and the ending merchandise inventory. A manufacturing organization, because it creates a product, maintains three inventory accounts: Materials Inventory, Work in Process Inventory, and Finished Goods Inventory. Manufacturing costs flow through all three inventory accounts. During the accounting period, the cost of completed products is transferred to the Finished Goods Inventory account, and the cost of units that have been manufactured and sold is transferred to the Cost of Goods Sold account.

LO3 Describe the flow of costs through a manufacturer's inventory accounts.

The flow of costs through the inventory accounts begins when costs for direct materials, direct labor, and overhead are incurred. Materials costs flow first into the Materials Inventory account, which is used to record the costs of materials when they are received and again when they are issued for use in a production process. All manufacturing-related costs—direct materials, direct labor, and overhead—are recorded in the Work in Process Inventory account as the production process begins. When products are completed, their costs are transferred from the Work in Process Inventory account to the Finished Goods Inventory account. Costs remain in the Finished Goods Inventory account until the products are sold, at which time they are transferred to the Cost of Goods Sold account.

LO4 Define *product unit cost,* and compute the unit cost of a product or service.

Direct materials costs are the costs of materials used in making a product that can be conveniently and economically traced to specific product units. Direct labor costs include all labor costs needed to make a product or service that can be traced to specific product units. All other production-related costs are classified and accounted for as overhead costs. Such costs cannot be easily traced to end products or services, so a cost allocation method is used to assign them to products or services.

When a batch of products has been completed, the product unit cost is computed by dividing the total cost of direct materials, direct labor, and overhead by the total number of units produced. The product unit cost can be calculated using the actual, normal, or standard costing method. Under actual costing, the actual costs of direct materials, direct labor, and overhead are used to compare the product unit cost. Under normal costing, the actual costs of direct materials and direct labor are combined with the estimated cost of overhead to determine the product unit cost. Under standard costing, the estimated costs of direct materials, direct labor, and overhead are used to calculate the product unit cost. The components of product cost may be classified as prime costs or conversion costs. Prime costs are the primary costs of production; they are the sum of direct materials costs and direct labor costs. Conversion costs are the costs of converting direct materials into finished products; they are the sum of direct labor costs and overhead costs.

Because no products are manufactured in the course of providing services, service organizations have no materials costs. They do, however, have both direct labor costs and overhead costs, which are similar to those in manufacturing organizations. To determine the cost of performing a service, professional labor and service-related overhead costs are included in the analysis.

LO5 Define *cost allocation,* and explain how the traditional method of allocating overhead costs figures into calculating product or service unit cost.

Cost allocation is the process of assigning collected indirect costs to a specific cost object using an allocation base known as a cost driver. The allocation of overhead costs requires the pooling of overhead costs that are affected by a common activity and the selection of a cost driver whose activity level causes a change in the cost pool. A cost pool is the collection of overhead costs assigned to a cost object. A cost driver is an activity base that causes the cost pool to increase in amount as the cost driver increases.

Allocating overhead is a four-step process that involves planning a rate at which overhead costs will be assigned to products or services, assigning overhead costs at this predetermined rate to products or services during production, recording actual overhead costs as they are incurred, and reconciling the difference between the actual and applied overhead costs. The Cost of Goods Sold or Cost of Sales account is corrected for an amount of over- or underapplied overhead costs assigned to the products or services. In manufacturing companies, if the difference is material, adjustments are made to the Work in Process Inventory, Finished Goods Inventory, and Cost of Goods Sold accounts.

The traditional method applies overhead costs to a product or service by estimating one predetermined overhead rate and multiplying that rate by the actual cost driver level. The product or service unit cost is computed either by dividing the total product or service cost (the sum of the total applied overhead cost and the actual costs of direct materials and direct labor) by the total number of units produced or by determining the cost per unit for each element of the product's or service's cost and summing those per unit costs.

When ABC is used, overhead costs are grouped into a number of cost pools related to specific activities. For each activity pool, cost drivers are identified, and cost driver levels are estimated. Each activity cost rate is calculated by dividing the estimated activity pool amount by the estimated cost driver level. Overhead, which is divided into the activity pools, is applied to the product or service by multiplying the various activity cost rates by their actual cost driver levels. The product or service unit cost is computed by dividing the total product or service cost (the sum of the total applied cost pools and the actual costs of direct materials and direct labor) by the total number of units produced.

REVIEW of Concepts and Terminology

The following concepts and terms were introduced in this chapter:

Activity-based costing (ABC) 783 (LO5)

Actual costing 776 (LO4)

Conversion costs 775 (LO4)

Cost allocation 779 (LO5)

Cost driver 779 (LO5)

Cost object 779 (LO5)

Cost of goods manufactured 773 (LO3)

Cost pool 779 (LO5)

Direct costs 763 (LO1)

Direct labor costs 774 (LO4)

Direct materials costs 774 (LO4)

Finished Goods Inventory account 770 (LO3)

Fixed cost 764 (LO1)

Indirect costs 763 (LO1)

Indirect labor costs 774 (LO4)

Indirect materials costs 774 (LO4)

Manufacturing cost flow 772 (LO3)

Materials Inventory account 770 (LO3)

Nonvalue-adding cost 764 (LO1)

Normal costing 777 (LO4)

Overapplied overhead costs 781 (LO5)

Overhead costs 774 (LO4)

Period costs 765 (LO1)

Predetermined overhead rate 779 (LO5)

Prime costs 775 (LO4)

Product costs 764 (LO1)

Product unit cost 775 (LO4)

Standard costing 777 (LO4)

Statement of cost of goods manufactured 767 (LO2)

Total manufacturing costs 773 (LO3)

Underapplied overhead costs 781 (LO5)

Value-adding cost 764 (LO1)

Variable cost 764 (LO1)

Work in Process Inventory account 770 (LO3)

CHAPTER ASSIGNMENTS

BUILDING Your Basic Knowledge And Skills

Short Exercises

LO1 Cost Classifications

SE 1. Indicate whether each of the following is a direct cost (D), an indirect cost (ID), or neither (N) and a variable (V) or a fixed (F) cost. Also indicate whether each adds value (VA) or does not add value (NVA) to the product and whether each is a product cost (PD) or a period cost (PER).

1. Production supervisor's salary
2. Sales commission
3. Wages of a production-line worker

LO2 Income Statement for a Manufacturing Organization

SE 2. Using the following information from Char Company, prepare an income statement through operating income for the year:

Sales	$900,000
Finished goods inventory, beginning	45,000
Cost of goods manufactured	585,000
Finished goods inventory, ending	60,000
Operating expenses	275,000

LO3 Cost Flow in a Manufacturing Organization

SE 3. Given the following information, compute the ending balances of the Materials Inventory, Work in Process Inventory, and Finished Goods Inventory accounts:

Materials Inventory, beginning balance	$ 23,000
Work in Process Inventory, beginning balance	25,750
Finished Goods Inventory, beginning balance	38,000
Direct materials purchased	85,000
Direct materials placed into production	74,000
Direct labor costs	97,000
Overhead costs	35,000
Cost of goods manufactured	123,000
Cost of goods sold	93,375

LO3 Document Flows in a Manufacturing Organization

SE 4. Identify the document needed to support each of the following activities in a manufacturing organization:

1. Placing an order for direct materials with a supplier
2. Recording direct labor time at the beginning and end of each work shift
3. Receiving direct materials at the shipping dock
4. Recording the costs of a specific job requiring direct materials, direct labor, and overhead
5. Issuing direct materials into production
6. Billing the customer for a completed order
7. Fulfilling a request from the Production Scheduling Department for the purchase of direct materials

LO4 Elements of Manufacturing Costs

E 5. Dalston Lui, the accountant at Brightlight, Inc., must group the costs of manufacturing candles. Indicate whether each of the following items should be classified as direct materials (DM), direct labor (DL), overhead (O), or none of these (N). Also indicate whether each is a prime cost (PC), a conversion cost (CC), or neither (N).

1. Depreciation of the cost of vats to hold melted wax
2. Cost of wax
3. Rent on the factory where candles are made
4. Cost of George's time to dip the wicks into the wax
5. Cost of coloring for candles
6. Cost of Ray's time to design candles for Halloween
7. Sam's commission to sell candles to Candles Plus

LO4 Computation of Product Unit Cost

E 6. What is the product unit cost for Job 14, which consists of 300 units and has total manufacturing costs of direct materials, $4,500; direct labor, $7,500; and overhead, $3,600? What are the prime costs and conversion costs per unit?

LO5 Calculation of Underapplied or Overapplied Overhead

SE 7. At year end, records show that actual overhead costs incurred were $25,870 and the amount of overhead costs applied to production was $27,000. Identify the amount of under- or overapplied overhead, and indicate whether the Cost of Goods Sold account should be increased or decreased to reflect actual overhead costs.

LO5 Computation of Overhead Rate

SE 8. Compute the overhead rate per service request for the Maintenance Department if estimated overhead costs are $18,290 and the number of estimated service requests is 3,100.

LO5 Allocation of Overhead to Production

SE 9. Calculate the amount of overhead costs applied to production if the predetermined overhead rate is $4 per direct labor hour and 1,200 direct labor hours were worked.

Exercises

LO1 The Management Process and Operating Costs

E 1. Indicate whether each of the following activities takes place during the planning (PL), performing (PE), evaluating (E), or communicating (C) stage of the management process:

1. Changing regular price to clearance price
2. Reporting results to appropriate personnel
3. Preparing budgets of operating costs
4. Comparing estimated and actual costs to determine variances

LO1 Cost Classifications

E 2. Indicate whether each of the following costs for a bicycle manufacturer is a product or a period cost, a variable or a fixed cost, a value-adding or a nonvalue-adding cost, and, if it is a product cost, a direct or an indirect cost of the bicycle:

	Cost Classification			
Example	**Product or Period**	**Variable or Fixed**	**Value-Adding or Nonvalue-Adding**	**Direct or Indirect**
Bicycle tire	Product	Variable	Value-adding	Direct

1. Depreciation on office computer
2. Labor to assemble bicycle
3. Labor to inspect bicycle
4. Internal auditor's salary
5. Lubricant for wheels

LO2 **Comparison of Income Statement Formats**

E 3. Indicate whether each of these equations applies to a service organization (SER), a retail organization (RET), or a manufacturing organization (MANF):

1. Cost of Goods Sold = Beginning Merchandise Inventory + Net Cost of Purchases − Ending Merchandise Inventory
2. Cost of Sales = Net Cost of Services Sold
3. Cost of Goods Sold = Beginning Finished Goods Inventory + Cost of Goods Manufactured − Ending Finished Goods Inventory

LO2 **Statement of Cost of Goods Manufactured**

E 4. During August, Radio Company's purchases of direct materials totaled $139,000; direct labor for the month was 3,400 hours at $8.75 per hour. Radio also incurred the following overhead costs: utilities, $5,870; supervision, $16,600; indirect materials, $6,750; depreciation, $6,200; insurance, $1,830; and miscellaneous, $1,100.

Beginning inventory accounts were as follows: Materials Inventory, $48,600; Work in Process Inventory, $54,250; and Finished Goods Inventory, $38,500. Ending inventory accounts were as follows: Materials Inventory, $50,100; Work in Process Inventory, $48,400; and Finished Goods Inventory, $37,450.

From the information given, prepare a statement of cost of goods manufactured.

LO2 **Statement of Cost of Goods Manufactured and Cost of Goods Sold**

E 5. Treetop Corp. makes irrigation sprinkler systems for tree nurseries. Ramsey Roe, Treetop's new controller, can find only the following partial information for the past year:

	Oak Division	Loblolly Division	Maple Division	Spruce Division
Direct materials used	$3	$ 7	$ g	$ 8
Total manufacturing costs	6	d	h	14
Overhead	1	3	2	j
Direct labor	a	6	4	4
Ending work in process inventory	b	3	2	5
Cost of goods manufactured	7	20	12	1
Beginning work in process inventory	2	e	3	k
Ending finished goods inventory	2	6	i	9
Beginning finished goods inventory	3	f	5	7
Cost of goods sold	c	18	13	9

Using the information given, compute the unknown values. List the accounts in the proper order, and show subtotals and totals as appropriate.

LO2 Characteristics of Organizations

E 6. Indicate whether each of the following is typical of a service organization (SER), a retail organization (RET), or a manufacturing organization (MANF):

1. Maintains only one balance sheet inventory account
2. Maintains no balance sheet inventory accounts
3. Maintains three balance sheet inventory accounts
4. Purchases products ready for resale
5. Designs and makes products for sale
6. Sells services
7. Determines the net cost of services sold
8. Includes the cost of goods manufactured in calculating cost of goods sold
9. Includes the net cost of purchases in calculating cost of goods sold

LO2 Missing Amounts—Manufacturing

E 7. Presented below are incomplete inventory and income statement data for Toliver Corporation. Determine the missing amounts.

	Cost of Goods Sold	Cost of Goods Manufactured	Beginning Finished Goods Inventory	Ending Finished Goods Inventory
1.	$ 10,000	$12,000	$ 1,000	?
2.	$140,000	?	$45,000	$60,000
3.	?	$89,000	$23,000	$20,000

LO2 Inventories, Cost of Goods Sold, and Net Income

E 8. The data presented below are for a retail organization and a manufacturing organization.

1. Fill in the missing data for the retail organization:

	First Quarter	Second Quarter	Third Quarter	Fourth Quarter
Sales	$9	$ e	$15	$ k
Gross margin	a	4	5	1
Ending merchandise inventory	5	f	5	m
Beginning merchandise inventory	4	g	h	5
Net cost of purchases	b	7	9	n
Operating income	3	2	i	2
Operating expenses	c	2	2	4
Cost of goods sold	5	6	j	11
Cost of goods available for sale	d	12	15	15

2. Fill in the missing data for the manufacturing organization:

	First Quarter	Second Quarter	Third Quarter	Fourth Quarter
Ending finished goods inventory	$a	$ 3	$ h	$ 6
Cost of goods sold	6	3	5	1
Operating income	1	3	1	m
Cost of goods available for sale	8	d	10	13
Cost of goods manufactured	5	e	i	8
Gross margin	4	f	j	7
Operating expenses	3	g	5	6
Beginning finished goods inventory	b	2	3	n
Sales	c	10	k	14

LO3 Documentation

E 9. Waltz Company manufactures music boxes. Seventy percent of its products are standard items produced in long production runs. The other 30 percent are special orders with specific requests for tunes. The latter cost from three to six times as much as the standard product because they require additional materials and labor.

Reza Seca, the controller, recently received a complaint memorandum from Iggy Paulo, the production supervisor, about the new network of source documents that has been added to the existing cost accounting system. The new documents include a purchase request, a purchase order, a receiving report, and a materials request. Paulo claims that the forms create extra work and interrupt the normal flow of production.

Prepare a written memorandum from Reza Seca to Iggy Paulo that fully explains the purpose of each type of document.

LO3 Cost Flows and Inventory Accounts

E 10. For each of the following activities, identify the inventory account (Materials Inventory, Work in Process Inventory, or Finished Goods Inventory), if any, that is affected. If an inventory account is affected, indicate whether the account balance will increase or decrease. (*Example:* Moved completed units to finished goods inventory. *Answer:* Increase Finished Goods Inventory; decrease Work in Process Inventory.) If no inventory account is affected, use "None of these" as your answer.

1. Moved materials requested by production
2. Sold units of product
3. Purchased and received direct materials for production
4. Used direct labor and overhead in the production process
5. Received payment from customer
6. Purchased office supplies and paid cash
7. Paid monthly office rent

LO4 Unit Cost Determination

E 11. The Pattia Winery is one of the finest wineries in the country. One of its famous products is a red wine called Old Vines. Recently, management has become concerned about the increasing cost of making Old Vines and needs to determine if the current selling price of $10 per bottle is adequate. The winery wants to achieve a 25 percent gross profit on the sale of each bottle. The information on the next page is given to you for analysis.

1. Compute the unit cost per bottle for materials, labor, and overhead.
2. How would you advise management regarding the price per bottle of wine?
3. Compute the prime costs per unit and the conversion costs per unit.

Batch size	10,550 bottles
Costs	
Direct materials	
Olen Millot grapes	$22,155
Chancellor grapes	9,495
Bottles	5,275
Total direct materials costs	$36,925
Direct labor	
Pickers/loaders	$ 2,110
Crusher	422
Processors	8,440
Bottler	13,293
Total direct labor costs	$24,265
Overhead	
Depreciation–equipment	$ 2,743
Depreciation–building	5,275
Utilities	1,055
Indirect labor	6,330
Supervision	7,385
Supplies	9,917
Repairs	1,477
Miscellaneous	633
Total overhead costs	$34,815
Total production costs	$96,005

LO4 Unit Costs in a Service Business

E 12. Walden Green provides custom farming services to owners of 5-acre wheat fields. In July, he earned $2,400 by cutting, turning, and baling 3,000 bales. In the same month, he incurred the following costs: gas, $150; tractor maintenance, $115; and labor, $600. His annual tractor depreciation is $1,500. What was Green's cost per bale? What was his revenue per bale? Should he increase the amount he charges for his services?

LO5 Computation of Overhead Rate

E 13. The overhead costs that Lucca Industries, Inc., used to compute its overhead rate for the past year are as follows:

Indirect materials and supplies	$ 79,200
Repairs and maintenance	14,900
Outside service contracts	17,300
Indirect labor	79,100
Factory supervision	42,900
Depreciation–machinery	85,000
Factory insurance	8,200
Property taxes	6,500
Heat, light, and power	7,700
Miscellaneous overhead	5,760
Total overhead costs	$346,560

The allocation base for the past year was 45,600 total machine hours. For the next year, all overhead costs except depreciation, property taxes, and miscellaneous overhead are expected to increase by 10 percent. Depreciation should increase by 12 percent, and property taxes and miscellaneous overhead are expected to increase by 20 percent. Plant capacity in terms of machine hours used will increase by 4,400 hours.

1. Compute the past year's overhead rate. (Carry your answer to three decimal places.)
2. Compute the overhead rate for next year. (Carry your answer to three decimal places.)

LO5 Computation and Application of Overhead Rate

E 14. Compumatics specializes in the analysis and reporting of complex inventory costing projects. Materials costs are minimal, consisting entirely of operating supplies (DVDs, inventory sheets, and other recording tools). Labor is the highest single expense, totaling $693,000 for 75,000 hours of work last year. Overhead costs for last year were $916,000 and were applied to specific jobs on the basis of labor hours worked. This year the company anticipates a 25 percent increase in overhead costs. Labor costs will increase by $130,000, and the number of hours worked is expected to increase by 20 percent.

1. Determine the total amount of overhead anticipated this year.
2. Compute the overhead rate for this year. (Round your answer to the nearest cent.)
3. During April of this year, 11,980 labor hours were worked. Calculate the overhead amount assigned to April production.

LO5 Disposition of Overapplied Overhead

E 15. At the end of this year, Compumatics had compiled a total of 89,920 labor hours worked. The actual overhead incurred was $1,143,400.

1. Using the overhead rate computed in **E 14**, determine the total amount of overhead applied to operations during the year.
2. Compute the amount of overapplied overhead for the year.
3. Will the Cost of Goods Sold account be increased or decreased to correct the overapplication of overhead?

LO2 Problems

A Manufacturing Organization's Balance Sheet

P 1. The following information is from the trial balance of Mills Manufacturing Company:

	Debit	Credit
Cash	$ 34,000	
Accounts Receivable	27,000	
Materials Inventory, ending	31,000	
Work in Process Inventory, ending	47,900	
Finished Goods Inventory, ending	54,800	
Production Supplies	5,700	
Small Tools	9,330	
Land	160,000	
Factory Building	575,000	
Accumulated Depreciation–Factory Building		$ 199,000
Factory Equipment	310,000	
Accumulated Depreciation–Factory Equipment		137,000
Patents	33,500	
Accounts Payable		26,900
Insurance Premiums Payable		6,700
Income Taxes Payable		41,500
Mortgage Payable		343,000
Common Stock		200,000
Retained Earnings		334,130
	$1,288,230	$1,288,230

Required

1. Manufacturing organizations use asset accounts that are not needed by retail organizations.
   a. List the titles of the asset accounts that are specifically related to manufacturing organizations.
   b. List the titles of the asset, liability, and equity accounts that you would see on the balance sheets of both manufacturing and retail organizations.
2. Assuming that the following information reflects the results of operations for the year, calculate the (a) gross margin, (b) cost of goods sold, (c) cost of goods available for sale, and (d) cost of goods manufactured:

Operating income	$138,130
Operating expenses	53,670
Sales	500,000
Finished goods inventory, beginning	50,900

Manager insight ▶ 3. Does Mills Manufacturing use the periodic or perpetual inventory system?

LO4 Computation of Unit Cost

P 2. Carola Industries, Inc., manufactures discs for several of the leading recording studios in the United States and Europe. Department 60 is responsible for the electronic circuitry within each disc. Department 61 applies the plastic-like surface to the discs and packages them for shipment. Carola recently produced 4,000 discs for the Milo Company. In fulfilling this order, the departments incurred the following costs:

	Department	
	60	61
Direct materials used	$29,440	$3,920
Direct labor	6,800	2,560
Overhead	7,360	4,800

1. Compute the unit cost for each department.
2. Compute the total unit cost for the Milo Company order.

Manager insight ▶

3. The selling price for this order was $14 per unit. Was the selling price adequate? List the assumptions and/or computations upon which you based your answer. What suggestions would you make to Carola Industries' management about the pricing of future orders?
4. Compute the prime costs and conversion costs per unit for each department.

LO5 Allocation of Overhead

P 3. Natural Cosmetics Company applies overhead costs on the basis of machine hours. The overhead rate is computed by analyzing data from the previous year to determine the percentage change in costs. Thus, this year's overhead rate will be based on the percentage change multiplied by last year's costs.

	Last Year
Machine hours	57,360
Overhead costs	
Indirect labor	$ 23,530
Employee benefits	28,600
Manufacturing supervision	18,480
Utilities	14,490
Factory insurance	7,800
Janitorial services	12,100
Depreciation–factory and machinery	21,300
Miscellaneous overhead	7,475
Total overhead	$133,775

This year the cost of utilities is expected to increase by 40 percent over the previous year; the cost of indirect labor, employee benefits, and miscellaneous overhead is expected to increase by 30 percent over the previous year; the cost of insurance and depreciation is expected to increase by 20 percent over the previous year; and the cost of supervision and janitorial services is expected to increase by 10 percent over the previous year. Machine hours are expected to total 68,832.

Required

1. Compute the projected costs and the overhead rate for this year, using the information about expected cost increases. (Carry your answer to three decimal places.)
2. Jobs completed during this year and the machine hours used were as follows:

Job No.	Machine Hours
2214	12,300
2215	14,200
2216	9,800
2217	13,600
2218	11,300
2219	8,100

Determine the amount of overhead to be applied to each job and to total production during this year. (Round answers to whole dollars.)

3. Actual overhead costs for this year were $165,845. Was overhead underapplied or overapplied? By how much? Should the Cost of Goods Sold account be increased or decreased to reflect actual overhead costs?

LO5 Allocation of Overhead

P 4. Byte Computer Company, a manufacturing organization, has just completed an order that Grater, Ltd., placed for 80 computers. Direct materials, purchased parts, and direct labor costs for the Grater order are as follows:

Cost of direct materials	$36,750.00	Direct labor hours	220
Cost of purchased parts	$21,300.00	Average direct labor pay rate	$15.25

Overhead costs were applied at a single, plantwide overhead rate of 270 percent of direct labor dollars.

Required

Using the traditional costing method, compute the total cost of the Grater order.

Alternate Problems

LO2 Statement of Cost of Goods Manufactured

P 5. Dillo Vineyards, a large winery in Texas, produces a full line of varietal wines. The company, whose fiscal year begins on November 1, has just completed a record-breaking year. Its inventory account balances on October 31 of this year were Materials Inventory, $1,803,800; Work in Process Inventory, $2,764,500; and Finished Goods Inventory, $1,883,200. At the beginning of the year, the inventory account balances were Materials Inventory, $2,156,200; Work in Process Inventory, $3,371,000; and Finished Goods Inventory, $1,596,400.

During the fiscal year, the company's purchases of direct materials totaled $6,750,000. Direct labor hours totaled 142,500, and the average labor rate was $8.20 per hour. The following overhead costs were incurred during the year: depreciation–plant and equipment, $685,600; indirect labor, $207,300; property tax, plant and equipment, $94,200; plant maintenance, $83,700; small tools, $42,400; utilities, $96,500; and employee benefits, $76,100.

Required

Prepare a statement of cost of goods manufactured for the fiscal year ended October 31.

LO4 Unit Costs in a Service Business

P 6. Municipal Hospital relies heavily on cost data to keep its pricing structures in line with those of its competitors. The hospital provides a wide range of services, including intensive care, intermediate care, and a neonatal nursery. Joo Young, the hospital's controller, is concerned about the profits generated by the 30-bed intensive care unit (ICU), so she is reviewing current billing procedures for that unit. The focus of her analysis is the hospital's billing per ICU patient day. This billing equals the per diem cost of intensive care plus a 40 percent markup to cover other operating costs and generate a profit. ICU patient costs include the following:

Doctors' care	2 hours per day @ $360 per hour (actual)
Special nursing care	4 hours per day @ $85 per hour (actual)
Regular nursing care	24 hours per day @ $28 per hour (average)
Medications	$237 per day (average)
Medical supplies	$134 per day (average)
Room rental	$350 per day (average)
Food and services	$140 per day (average)

One other significant ICU cost is equipment, which is about $185,000 per room. Young has determined that the cost per patient day for the equipment is $179.

Wiley Dix, the hospital director, has asked Young to compare the current billing procedure with another that uses industry averages to determine the billing per patient day.

Required

1. Compute the cost per patient per day.
2. Compute the billing per patient day using the hospital's existing markup rate. (Round answers to whole dollars.)
3. Industry averages for markup rates are as follows:

Equipment	30%	Medications	50%
Doctors' care	50	Medical supplies	50
Special nursing care	40	Room rental	30
Regular nursing care	50	Food and services	25

Using these rates, compute the billing per patient day. (Round answers to the nearest whole dollars.)

4. Based on your findings in requirements **2** and **3**, which billing procedure would you recommend? Why?

LO5 Allocation of Overhead

P 7. Lund Products, Inc., uses a predetermined overhead rate in its production, assembly, and testing departments. One rate is used for the entire company; it is based on machine hours. The rate is determined by analyzing data from the previous year to determine the percentage change in costs. Thus this year's overhead rate will be based on the percentage change multiplied by last year's costs. Lise Jensen is about to compute the rate for this year using the following data:

	Last Year's Costs
Machine hours	41,800
Overhead costs	
Indirect materials	$ 57,850
Indirect labor	25,440
Supervision	41,580
Utilities	11,280
Labor-related costs	9,020
Depreciation, factory	10,780
Depreciation, machinery	27,240
Property taxes	2,880
Insurance	1,920
Miscellaneous overhead	4,840
Total overhead	$192,830

This year the cost of indirect materials is expected to increase by 30 percent over the previous year. The cost of indirect labor, utilities, machinery depreciation, property taxes, and insurance is expected to increase by 20 percent over the previous year. All other expenses are expected to increase by 10 percent over the previous year. Machine hours for this year are estimated at 45,980.

Required

1. Compute the projected costs and the overhead rate for this year using the information about expected cost increases. (Round your answer to three decimal places.)
2. During this year, Lund Products completed the following jobs using the machine hours shown:

Job No.	Machine Hours	Job No.	Machine Hours
H–142	7,840	H–201	10,680
H–164	5,260	H–218	12,310
H–175	8,100	H–304	2,460

   Determine the amount of overhead applied to each job. What was the total overhead applied during this year? (Round answers to the nearest dollar.)
3. Actual overhead costs for this year were $234,485. Was overhead underapplied or overapplied this year? By how much? Should the Cost of Goods Sold account be increased or decreased to reflect actual overhead costs?
4. At what point during this year was the overhead rate computed? When was it applied? Finally, when was underapplied or overapplied overhead determined and the Cost of Goods Sold account adjusted to reflect actual costs?

LO5 Allocation of Overhead

P 8. Fraser Products, Inc., which produces copy machines for wholesale distributors in the Pacific Northwest, has just completed packaging an order from Kent Company for 150 Model 14 machines. Direct materials, purchased parts, and direct labor costs for the Kent order are as follows:

Cost of direct materials	$17,450.00
Cost of purchased parts	$14,800.00
Direct labor hours	140
Average direct labor pay rate	$16.50

Overhead costs were applied at a single, plantwide overhead rate of 240 percent of direct labor dollars.

Required

Using the traditional costing approach, compute the total cost of the Kent order.

ENHANCING Your Knowledge, Skills, and Critical Thinking

LO1 Cost Classifications

C 1. Visit a local fast-food restaurant. Observe all aspects of the operation and take notes on the entire process. Describe the procedures used to take, process, and fill an order and deliver the food to the customer. Based on your observations, make a list of the costs incurred by the restaurant. Then create a table similar to Table 16-1, in which you classify the costs you have identified by their traceability (direct or indirect), cost behavior (variable or fixed), value attribute (value-adding or nonvalue-adding), and implications for financial reporting (product or period costs). Be prepared to discuss your findings in class.

LO2 Financial Performance Measures

C 2. Tarbox Manufacturing Company makes sheet metal products for heating and air conditioning installations. Its statements of cost of goods manufactured and income statements for the last two years are presented below and on the next page.

Tarbox Manufacturing Company
Statements of Cost of Goods Manufactured
For the Years Ended December 31

	This Year		Last Year	
Direct materials used				
Materials inventory, beginning	$ 91,240		$ 93,560	
Direct materials purchased (net)	987,640		959,940	
Cost of direct materials available for use	$1,078,880		$1,053,500	
Less materials inventory, ending	95,020		91,240	
Cost of direct materials used		$ 983,860		$ 962,260
Direct labor		571,410		579,720
Overhead				
Indirect labor	$ 182,660		$ 171,980	
Power	34,990		32,550	
Insurance	22,430		18,530	
Supervision	125,330		120,050	
Depreciation	75,730		72,720	
Other overhead costs	41,740		36,280	
Total overhead		482,880		452,110
Total manufacturing costs		$2,038,150		$1,994,090
Add work in process inventory, beginning		148,875		152,275
Total cost of work in process during the period		$2,187,025		$2,146,365
Less work in process inventory, ending		146,750		148,875
Cost of goods manufactured		$2,040,275		$1,997,490

Tarbox Manufacturing Company
Income Statements
For the Years Ended December 31

		This Year		Last Year
Sales		$2,942,960		$3,096,220
Cost of goods sold				
Finished goods inventory, beginning	$ 142,640		$ 184,820	
Cost of goods manufactured	2,040,275		1,997,490	
Cost of goods available for sale	$2,182,915		$ 2,182,310	
Less finished goods inventory, ending	186,630		142,640	
Total cost of goods sold		1,996,285		2,039,670
Gross margin		$ 946,675		$1,056,550
Selling and administrative expenses				
Sales salaries and commission expense	$ 394,840		$ 329,480	
Advertising expense	116,110		194,290	
Other selling expenses	82,680		72,930	
Administrative expenses	242,600		195,530	
Total selling and administrative expenses		836,230		792,230
Income from operations		$ 110,445		$ 264,320
Other revenues and expenses				
Interest expense		54,160		56,815
Income before income taxes		$ 56,285		$ 207,505
Income taxes expense		19,137		87,586
Net income		$ 37,148		$ 119,919

For the past several years, the company's income has been declining. You have been asked to comment on why the ratios for Tarbox's profitability have deteriorated.

1. In preparing your comments, compute the following ratios for each year:
   a. Ratios of cost of direct materials used to total manufacturing costs, direct labor to total manufacturing costs, and total overhead to total manufacturing costs. (Round to one decimal place.)
   b. Ratios of sales salaries and commission expense, advertising expense, other selling expenses, administrative expenses, and total selling and administrative expenses to sales. (Round to one decimal place.)
   c. Ratios of gross margin to sales and net income to sales. (Round to one decimal place.)
2. From your evaluation of the ratios computed in 1, state the probable causes of the decline in net income.
3. What other factors or ratios do you believe should be considered in determining the cause of the company's decreased income?

LO1 **Management Decision about a Supporting Service Function**

C 3. As the manager of grounds maintenance for Latchey, a large insurance company in Missouri, you are responsible for maintaining the grounds surrounding the company's three buildings, the six entrances to the property, and the recreational facilities, which include a golf course, a soccer field, jogging and bike paths, and tennis, basketball, and volleyball courts. Maintenance includes gardening (watering, planting, mowing, trimming, removing debris, and so on) and land improvements (e.g., repairing or replacing damaged or worn concrete and gravel areas).

Early in January, you receive a memo from the president of Latchey requesting information about the cost of operating your department for the last 12 months. She has received a bid from Xeriscape Landscapes, Inc., to perform the gardening activities you now perform. You are to prepare a cost report that will help her decide whether to keep gardening activities within the company or to outsource the work.

1. Before preparing your report, answer the following questions:
   a. What kinds of information do you need about your department?
   b. Why is this information relevant?
   c. Where would you go to obtain this information (sources)?
   d. When would you want to obtain this information?
2. Draft a report showing only headings and line items that best communicate the costs of your department. How would you change your report if the president asked you to reduce the costs of operating your department?
3. One of your department's cost accounts is the Maintenance Expense–Garden Equipment account.
   a. Is this a direct or an indirect cost?
   b. Is it a product or a period cost?
   c. Is it a variable or a fixed cost?
   d. Does the activity add value to Latchey's provision of insurance services?
   e. Is it a budgeted or an actual cost in your report?

LO2 **Management Information Needs**

C 4. The H&W Pharmaceuticals Corporation manufactures most of its three pharmaceutical products in Indonesia. Inventory balances for March and April are as follows:

	March 31	April 30
Materials Inventory	$258,400	$228,100
Work in Process Inventory	138,800	127,200
Finished Goods Inventory	111,700	114,100

During April, purchases of direct materials, which include natural materials, basic organic compounds, catalysts, and suspension agents, totaled $612,600. Direct labor costs were $160,000, and actual overhead costs were $303,500. Sales of the company's three products for April totaled $2,188,400. General and administrative expenses were $362,000.

1. Prepare a statement of cost of goods manufactured and an income statement through operating income for the month ended April 30.
2. Why is it that the total manufacturing costs do not equal the cost of goods manufactured?
3. What additional information would you need to determine the profitability of each of the three product lines?
4. Indicate whether each of the following is a product cost or a period cost:
   a. Import duties for suspension agent materials
   b. Shipping expenses to deliver manufactured products to the United States

c. Rent for manufacturing facilities in Jakarta
d. Salary of the American production-line manager working at the Indonesian manufacturing facilities
e. Training costs for an Indonesian accountant

LO4 **Preventing Pollution and the Costs of Waste Disposal**

C 5. Lake Weir Power Plant provides power to a metropolitan area of 4 million people. Sundeep Guliani, the plant's controller, has just returned from a conference on the Environmental Protection Agency's regulations concerning pollution prevention. She is meeting with Alton Guy, the president of the company, to discuss the impact of the EPA's regulations on the plant.

"Alton, I'm really concerned. We haven't been monitoring the disposal of the radioactive material we send to the Willis Disposal Plant. If Willis is disposing of our waste material improperly, we could be sued," said Guliani. "We also haven't been recording the costs of the waste as part of our product cost. Ignoring those costs will have a negative impact on our decision about the next rate hike."

"Sundeep, don't worry. I don't think we need to concern ourselves with the waste we send to Willis. We pay the company to dispose of it. The company takes it off our hands, and it's their responsibility to manage its disposal. As for the cost of waste disposal, I think we would have a hard time justifying a rate increase based on a requirement to record the full cost of waste as a cost of producing power. Let's just forget about waste and its disposal as a component of our power cost. We can get our rate increase without mentioning waste disposal," replied Guy.

What responsibility for monitoring the waste disposal practices at the Willis Disposal Plant does Lake Weir Power Plant have? Should Guliani take Guy's advice to ignore waste disposal costs in calculating the cost of power? Be prepared to discuss your response.

LO4 LO5 **Cookie Company (Continuing Case)**

C 6. In the "Cookie Company" case in the last chapter, you prepared a mission statement for your company. You also set its strategic, tactical, and operating objectives; decided on its name; and identified the tools you might use to run it. Here, you will form a company team and assign roles to team members, set cookie specifications, decide on a cookie recipe, and answer some questions about product costs.

1. Join with 4 or 5 other students in the class to form a company team. (Your instructor may assign groups or allow students to organize their own teams.)
   - Determine team members' tasks, and make team assignments (e.g., mixer, baker, quality controller, materials purchaser, accountant, marketing manager).
   - Assign each task an hourly pay rate or monthly salary based on your team's perception of the job market for the task involved.
   - Give the plan compiled thus far to your instructor and all team members in writing.
2. As a team, determine cookie specifications: quality, size, appearance, and special features (such as types of chips or nuts), as well as quantity and packaging.
3. As a team, select a cookie recipe that best fits the company's mission.
4. As a team, answer the following questions and submit the answers to your instructor:
   - Will your company use actual or normal costing when computing the cost per cookie? Explain your answer.
   - List the types of costs that your company will classify as overhead.

CHAPTER

17 Costing Systems: Job Order Costing

The Management Process

PLAN

- ▷ **Select the costing system that is best for the business's products or services.**
- ▷ **Estimate a job's costs, price, and profit.**
- ▷ **Select the period's predetermined overhead rate(s).**

PERFORM

- ▷ **Track product cost flows using job order cost cards and inventory accounts.**
- ▷ **Compute a job's actual revenue, costs, and profit.**
- ▷ **Compute a job's cost per unit.**

EVALUATE

- ▷ **Analyze performance by comparing job estimates with actual job costs.**

COMMUNICATE

- ▷ **Prepare job estimates for potential customers.**
- ▷ **Prepare internal management reports to manage and monitor jobs.**

Companies that produce made-to-order products or services use a job order costing system to account for costs and determine unit cost.

A product costing system is expected to provide unit cost information, to supply cost data for management decisions, and to furnish ending values for the Materials, Work in Process, and Finished Goods Inventory accounts. Managers will select a job order costing system, a process costing system, or a hybrid of the two systems. In this chapter, we describe job order costing, including how to prepare job order cost cards and how to compute product unit cost. We also describe how job order costing differs from process costing. Process costing will be covered in the next chapter.

LEARNING OBJECTIVES

LO1 Explain why unit cost is important in the management process. (pp. 808–809)

LO2 Distinguish between the two basic types of product costing systems, and identify the information that each provides. (pp. 809–811)

LO3 Explain the cost flow in a manufacturer's job order costing system. (pp. 811–817)

LO4 Prepare a job order cost card, and compute a job order's product or service unit cost. (pp. 817–820)

DECISION POINT ▸ A MANAGER'S FOCUS COLD STONE CREAMERY, INC.

- ▸ Is the product costing system that is used for custom-made items appropriate for mass-produced items?
- ▸ What performance measures would be most useful in evaluating the results of each type of product?

However you like your ice cream, **Cold Stone Creamery** can create it for you. The personalized process begins on a frozen granite countertop with high-quality ice cream, which is freshly made every day, and your choice of mix-ins—chocolate, candy, nuts, fruit, and even homemade cake batter. Once the customer selects the mix-in, the server "spades" the ingredients together into a unique creation in one of three sizes—Like It, Love It, or Gotta Have It. To view many examples of this personalized process from around the world, search YouTube. Cold Stone has no immediate plans to create a mass-produced product for sale in grocery stores or other retail establishments. But, as you will see in this chapter, if it did create such a product, Cold Stone would need to adjust its product costing system, as well as performance measures.

Product Unit Cost Information and the Management Process

LO1 Explain why unit cost is important in the management process.

Managers depend on relevant and reliable information about costs to manage their organizations. Although they vary in their approaches, managers share the same basic concerns as they move through the management process.

Planning

During the planning process, having knowledge of unit costs helps managers of both manufacturing and service companies set reasonable selling prices and estimate the cost of their products or services.

- Products: In manufacturing companies, such as **Cold Stone Creamery**, **Toyota**, and **Levi Strauss & Co.**, managers use unit cost information to develop budgets, establish product prices, and plan production volumes.
- Services: In service organizations, such as **Century 21**, **H&R Block**, and **UPS**, managers use cost information to develop budgets, establish prices, set sales goals, and determine human resource needs.

Performing

Managers make decisions every day about controlling costs, managing the company's activity volume, ensuring quality, and negotiating prices. They use timely cost and volume information and actual unit costs to support their decisions.

- In manufacturing companies, managers use information about costs to decide whether to drop a product line, add a production shift, outsource the manufacture of a subassembly to another company, bid on a special order, or negotiate a selling price.
- In service organizations, managers use cost information to make decisions about bidding on jobs, dropping a current service, outsourcing a task to an independent contractor, adding staff, or negotiating a price.

Evaluating

When managers evaluate results, they watch for changes in cost and quality. They compare actual and targeted total and unit costs, assess relevant price and volume information, and then adjust their planning and decision-making strategies.

- For example, if a service business's unit cost has risen, managers may break the unit cost down into its many components to analyze where costs can be cut or how the service can be performed more efficiently.

Communicating

Internal and external users analyze the data in the performance evaluation reports prepared by managers to determine whether the business is achieving cost goals for their organization's products or services.

- When managers report to stakeholders, they prepare financial statements.
- In manufacturing companies, managers use product unit costs to determine inventory balances for the organization's balance sheet and the cost of goods sold for its income statement.
- In service organizations, managers use unit costs of services to determine cost of sales for the income statement.
- When managers prepare internal performance evaluation reports, they compare actual unit costs with targeted costs, as well as actual and targeted nonfinancial measures of performance.

STOP & APPLY >

Shelley's Kennel provides pet boarding. Shelley, the owner of the kennel, must make several business decisions soon. Write *yes* or *no* to indicate whether knowing the cost to board one animal for one day (i.e., the product unit cost) can help Shelley answer these questions:

1. Is the daily boarding fee high enough to cover the kennel's costs?
2. How much profit will the kennel make if it boards an average of 10 dogs per day for 50 weeks?
3. What costs can be reduced to make the kennel's boarding fee competitive with that of its competitor?

SOLUTION

1. Yes; 2. Yes; 3. Yes

Product Costing Systems

LO2 Distinguish between the two basic types of product costing systems, and identify the information that each provides.

To meet managers' needs for cost information, it is necessary to have a highly reliable product costing system specifically designed to record and report the organization's operations.

A **product costing system** is a set of procedures used to account for an organization's product costs and to provide timely and accurate unit cost information for pricing, cost planning and control, inventory valuation, and financial statement preparation.

- The product costing system enables managers to track costs throughout the management process.
- It provides a structure for recording the revenue earned from sales and the costs incurred for direct materials, direct labor, and overhead.

Two basic types of product costing systems have been developed: job order costing systems and process costing systems. Table 17-1 summarizes the characteristics of both costing systems.

TABLE 17-1
Characteristics of Job Order Costing and Process Costing Systems

Job Order Costing System	Process Costing System
Traces manufacturing costs to a specific job order	Traces manufacturing costs to processes, departments, or work cells and then assigns the costs to products manufactured
Measures the cost of each completed unit	Measures costs in terms of units completed during a specific period
Uses a single Work in Process Inventory account to summarize the cost of all job orders	Uses several Work in Process Inventory accounts, one for each process, department, or work cell
Typically used by companies that make unique or special-order products, such as customized publications, built-in cabinets, or made-to-order draperies	Typically used by companies that make large amounts of similar products or liquid products or that have long, continuous production runs of identical products, such as makers of paint, soft drinks, candy, bricks, and paper

Businesses that make special-order items, such as the kitchen cabinets shown here, use a job order costing system. With such a system, the costs of direct materials (e.g., the wood used in framing the cabinets), direct labor, and overhead (e.g., insurance and depreciation on tools and vehicles) are traced to a specific batch of products or job order. All costs are recorded on a job order cost card.

Courtesy of George Peters/ istockphoto.com.

A **job order costing system** is used by companies that make unique or special-order products, such as personalized ice cream creations, specially built cabinets, made-to-order draperies, or custom-tailored suits.

- It uses a single Work in Process Inventory account to record the costs of all job orders.
- It traces the costs of direct materials, direct labor, and overhead to a specific batch of products or a specific **job order** (i.e., a customer order for a specific number of specially designed, made-to-order products) by using job order cost cards.
- A **job order cost card** is usually an electronic or paper document on which all costs incurred in the production of a particular job order are recorded. The costs that a job order costing system gathers are used to measure the cost of each completed unit.

Study Note

In job order costing, costs are traced to jobs; in process costing, costs are traced to production processes.

A **process costing system** is used by companies that produce large amounts of similar products or liquid products or that have long, continuous production runs of identical products. Makers of paint, soft drinks, candy, bricks, paper, and gallon containers of ice cream would use such a system.

- It first traces the costs of direct materials, direct labor, and overhead to processes, departments or work cells and then assigns the costs to the products manufactured by those processes, departments, or work cells during a specific period.
- It uses several Work in Process Inventory accounts, one for each process, department, or work cell.

In reality, few production processes are a perfect match for either a job order costing system or a process costing system. The typical product costing system therefore combines parts of job order costing and process costing to create a hybrid system known as an **operations costing system** designed specifically for an organization's production process.

- For example, an automobile maker like **Toyota** may use process costing to track the costs of manufacturing a standard car and job order costing to track the costs of customized features, such as a convertible top or a stick shift.

FOCUS ON BUSINESS PRACTICE

Why Does Toyota Use a Hybrid Product Costing System?

Thanks to its virtual production line, **Toyota** can now manufacture custom vehicles in five days. Computer software allows Toyota to calculate the exact number of parts needed at each precise point on its production line for a certain mix of cars. The mix can be modified up to five days in advance of actual production, allowing Toyota to modify a production run to include custom orders. With its virtual production line and a hybrid product costing system, Toyota has an advantage over its competitors.

STOP & APPLY >

State whether a job order costing system or a process costing system would typically be used to account for the costs of the following:

1. Manufacturing golf tees
2. Manufacturing custom-designed fencing for a specific golf course
3. Providing pet grooming
4. Manufacturing golf balls
5. Manufacturing dog food
6. Providing private golf lessons

SOLUTION

1. Process; 2. Job; 3. Job; 4. Process; 5. Process; 6. Job

Job Order Costing in a Manufacturing Company

LO3 Explain the cost flow in a manufacturer's job order costing system.

> **Study Note**
>
> In a job order costing system, the specific job or batch of product, *not* a department or work cell, is the focus of cost accumulation.

A job order costing system is a system that traces the costs of a specific order or batch of products to provide timely, accurate cost information and to facilitate the smooth and continuous flow of that information. A basic part of a job order costing system is the set of procedures, electronic documents, and accounts that a company uses when it incurs costs for direct materials, direct labor, and overhead. Job order cost cards and cost flows through the inventory accounts form the core of a job order costing system.

To study the cost flows in a job order costing system, let's look at how Jonas Lytton, the owner of Augusta Custom Golf Carts, Inc., operates his business. Augusta builds both customized and general-purpose golf carts.

- The direct materials costs for a golf cart include the costs of a cart frame, wheels, upholstered seats, a windshield, a motor, and a rechargeable battery.
- Direct labor costs include the wages of the two production workers who assemble the golf carts.
- Overhead includes indirect materials costs for upholstery zippers, cloth straps to hold equipment in place, wheel lubricants, screws and fasteners, and silicon to attach the windshield. It also includes indirect labor costs for moving materials to the production area and inspecting a golf cart during its

construction; depreciation on the manufacturing plant and equipment used to make the golf carts; and utilities, insurance, and property taxes related to the manufacturing plant.

Exhibit 17-1 shows the flow of each of these costs. Notice that the beginning balance in the Materials Inventory account means that there are already direct and indirect materials in the materials storeroom. The beginning balance in Work in Process Inventory means that Job CC is in production (with specifics given in the job order cost card). The zero beginning balance in Finished Goods Inventory means that all previously completed golf carts have been shipped.

Materials

When Augusta receives or expects to receive a sales order, the purchasing process begins with a request for specific quantities of direct and indirect materials that are needed for the order but are not currently available in the materials storeroom. When the new materials arrive at Augusta, the Accounting Department records the materials purchased by making an entry in journal form that debits or increases the balance of the Materials Inventory account and credits either the Cash or Accounts Payable account (depending on whether the purchase was for cash or credit):

	Dr.	Cr.
Materials Inventory	XX	
Cash or Accounts Payable		XX

Study Note

It is often helpful to understand the process of tracking production costs as they flow through the three inventory accounts and the entries that are triggered by the organization's source documents. The entries that track product cost flows are provided as background.

During the month, Augusta made two purchases on credit. As shown in Exhibit 17-1, these purchases increase the debit balances in the Materials Inventory account and increase the credit balances in the Accounts Payable account.

- In transaction **1**, the company purchased cart frames costing $572 and wheels costing $340 for a total of $912 from one of its vendors.
- In transaction **2**, the company purchased indirect materials costing $82 from another vendor.

When golf carts are scheduled for production, requested materials are sent to the production area. To record the flow of direct materials requested from the Materials Inventory account into the Work in Process Inventory account, the entry in journal form is:

	Dr.	Cr.
Work in Process Inventory	XX	
Materials Inventory		XX

To record the flow of indirect materials requested from the Materials Inventory account into the Overhead account, the entry in journal form is:

	Dr.	Cr.
Overhead	XX	
Materials Inventory		XX

During the month, Augusta processes requests for direct and indirect materials. Notice that the direct materials requested appear as a debit in the Work in Process Inventory account, and as a credit in the Materials Inventory account.

EXHIBIT 17-1 The Job Order Costing System—Augusta Custom Golf Carts, Inc.

Materials Inventory

Beg. Bal.	1,230	(3)	1,880
(1)	912	(3)	96
(2)	82		
End. Bal.	**248**		

Payroll Payable

		(4)	1,640
		(5)	760
		End. Bal.	**2,400**

Overhead

(3)	96	(8)	1,394
(5)	760		
(6)	295		
(7)	240		
	1,391		1,394
(11)	3		
End. Bal.	—		

Cash

		(6)	295
		End. Bal.	**295**

Accounts Receivable

(10)	3,000		
End. Bal.	**3,000**		

Accumulated Depreciation

		(7)	240
		End. Bal.	**240**

Work in Process Inventory

Beg. Bal.	400	(9)	3,880
(3)	1,880		
(4)	1,640		
(8)	1,394		
End. Bal.	**1,434**		

Finished Goods Inventory

Beg. Bal.	—	(10)	1,940
(9)	3,880		
End. Bal.	**1,940**		

Cost of Goods Sold

(10)	1,940	(11)	3
End. Bal.	**1,937**		

Accounts Payable

		(1)	912
		(2)	82
		End. Bal.	**994**

Sales

		(10)	3,000
		End. Bal.	**3,000**

Notice that the indirect materials requested appear as a debit to the Overhead account instead of to a Work in Process Inventory account.

Transaction **3** shows the request for $1,880 of direct materials for the production of two jobs. These costs are also recorded on the corresponding job order cost cards.

- Job CC, a batch run of two general-purpose golf carts already in production, required $1,038 of the additional direct materials.
- Job JB, a customized golf cart made to the specifications of an individual customer, Alex Special, required $842 of the direct materials.

In addition, transaction **3** accounts for the $96 of indirect materials requested for production as a $96 debit to Overhead and a $96 credit to Materials Inventory.

Labor

Every pay period, the payroll costs are recorded. In general, the payroll costs include salaries and wages for direct and indirect labor as well as for nonproduction-related employees. As noted earlier, Augusta's two production employees assemble the golf carts. Several other employees support production by moving materials and inspecting the products. The following entry in journal form records the payroll:

	Dr.	Cr.
Work in Process Inventory (direct labor costs)	XX	
Overhead (indirect labor costs)	XX	
Selling and Administrative Expenses (nonproduction-related salary and wage costs)	XX	
Payroll Payable		XX

Transactions **4** and **5** show the total production-related wages earned by employees during the period.

- Transaction **4** shows the total direct labor cost of $1,640 ($1,320 for Job CC and $320 for Job JB) as a debit to the Work in Process Inventory account and a credit to Augusta's Payroll Payable account.
- Transaction **5** shows that the indirect labor cost of $760 flows to the Overhead account instead of to a particular job. The corresponding credit is to Augusta's Payroll Payable account.

Overhead

Thus far, indirect materials and indirect labor have been the only costs debited to the Overhead account. Other actual indirect production costs, such as utilities, property taxes, insurance, and depreciation, are also charged to the Overhead account as they are incurred during the period. In general, the entry in journal form to incur actual overhead costs appears as:

	Dr.	Cr.
Overhead	XX	
Cash or Accounts Payable		XX
Accumulated Depreciation		XX

- Transaction **6** shows that other indirect costs amounting to $295 were paid.
- Transaction **7** records the $240 of production-related depreciation. The corresponding credit is to Augusta's Accumulated Depreciation account for $240.

During the period, to recognize all product-related costs for a job, an overhead cost estimate is applied to a job using a predetermined rate. The entry in journal form to apply overhead using a predetermined rate is:

	Dr.	Cr.
Work in Process Inventory	XX	
Overhead		XX

Based on its budget and past experience, Augusta currently uses a predetermined overhead rate of 85 percent of direct labor costs.

In transaction **8**, total overhead of $1,394 is applied, with $1,122 going to Job CC (85 percent of $1,320) and $272 going to Job JB (85 percent of $320).

- The Work in Process Inventory account is debited for $1,394 (85 percent of $1,640; see transaction **4**), and the Overhead account is credited for the applied overhead of $1,394.

Completed Units

When a custom job or a batch of general-purpose golf carts is completed and ready for sale, the products are moved from the manufacturing area to the finished goods. To record the cost flow of completed products from the Work in Process Inventory account into the Finished Goods Inventory account, the entry in journal form is:

	Dr.	Cr.
Finished Goods Inventory	XX	
Work in Process Inventory		XX

As shown in transaction **9**, when Job CC is completed, its cost of $3,880 is transferred from the Work in Process Inventory account to the Finished Goods Inventory account by debiting Finished Goods Inventory for $3,880 and crediting Work in Process Inventory for $3,880. Its job order cost card is also completed and transferred to the finished goods file.

Sold Units

Study Note

In this example, the company uses a perpetual inventory system. In a periodic inventory system, the cost of goods sold is calculated at the end of the period.

When a company uses a perpetual inventory system, as Augusta does, two accounting entries are made when products are sold. One is prompted by the sales invoice and records the quantity and selling price of the products sold. The other entry, prompted by the delivery of products to a customer, records the quantity and cost of the products shipped. These two entries follow.

	Dr.	Cr.
Cash or Accounts Receivable (sales price × units sold)	XX	
Sales (sales price × units sold)		XX

	Dr.	Cr.
Cost of Goods Sold (unit cost × units sold)	XX	
Finished Goods Inventory (unit cost × units sold)		XX

In transaction **10**, the $1,940 cost of the one general-purpose golf cart that was sold during the period is transferred from the Finished Goods Inventory account to the Cost of Goods Sold account.

- The Finished Goods Inventory account has an ending balance of $1,940 for the one remaining unsold cart.
- The $3,000 sales price of the golf cart sold on account is also recorded in Accounts Receivable.

Reconciliation of Overhead Costs

Study Note

Why do financial statements require the reconciliation of overhead costs? Financial statements report actual cost information; therefore, estimated overhead costs applied during the accounting period must be adjusted to reflect actual overhead costs.

To prepare financial statements at the end of the accounting period, the Cost of Goods Sold account must reflect actual product costs, including actual overhead. Thus, the Overhead account must be reconciled every period.

- ***Underapplied overhead:*** As you learned in a previous chapter, if at the end of the accounting period the actual overhead debit balance exceeds the applied overhead credit balance, then the Overhead account is said to be underapplied and the debit balance must be closed to the Cost of Goods Sold account. Here is the entry in journal form:

	Dr.	Cr.
Cost of Goods Sold	XX	
Overhead		XX

- ***Overapplied overhead:*** If the actual overhead cost for the period is less than the estimated overhead that was applied during the period, then the Overhead account is overapplied and the credit balance must be closed to the Cost of Goods Sold account. Here is the entry in journal form:

	Dr.	Cr.
Overhead	XX	
Cost of Goods Sold		XX

- In transaction **11**, since the actual overhead cost for the period ($1,391) is less than the overhead that was applied during the period ($1,394), the $3 credit balance must be closed to the Cost of Goods Sold account. The overapplied amount will reduce Cost of Goods Sold and it will then reflect the actual overhead costs incurred. Thus, $3 is deducted from the Cost of Goods Sold account, making the ending balance of that account $1,937.

STOP & APPLY >

Partial operating data for Sample Company are presented below. Sample Company's management has set the predetermined overhead rate for the current year at 60 percent of direct labor costs.

Account/Transaction	October
Beginning Materials Inventory	$ 4,000
Beginning Work in Process Inventory	6,000
Beginning Finished Goods Inventory	2,000
Direct materials used	16,000
Direct materials purchased	a
Direct labor costs	24,000
Overhead applied	b
Cost of units completed	c
Cost of Goods Sold	50,000
Ending Materials Inventory	3,000
Ending Work in Process Inventory	10,000
Ending Finished Goods Inventory	d

Using T accounts and the data provided, compute the unknown values. Show all your computations.

(continued)

SOLUTION

MATERIALS INVENTORY

Beg. Bal.	4,000	Used	16,000
(a) Purchased	15,000		
End. Bal.	**3,000**		

WORK IN PROCESS INVENTORY

Beg. Bal.	6,000	(c) Cost of units completed	50,400
Direct materials used	16,000		
Direct labor	24,000		
(b) Overhead applied	14,400*		
End. Bal.	**10,000**		

FINISHED GOODS INVENTORY

Beg. Bal.	2,000	Cost of goods sold	50,000
(c) Cost of units completed	50,400		
(d) **End. Bal.**	**2,400**		

*$24,000 × 60% = $14,400

A Job Order Cost Card and the Computation of Unit Cost

LO4 Prepare a job order cost card, and compute a job order's product or service unit cost.

As is evident from the preceding discussion, job order cost cards play a key role in a job order costing system. Each job being worked on has a job order cost card. As costs are incurred, they are classified by job and recorded on the appropriate card.

A Manufacturer's Job Order Cost Card and the Computation of Unit Cost

As you can see in Figure 17-1, a manufacturer's job order cost card has space for direct materials, direct labor, and overhead costs. It also includes the job order number, product specifications, the name of the customer, the date of the order, the projected completion date, and a cost summary. As a job incurs direct materials and direct labor costs, its job order cost card is updated. Overhead is also posted to the job order cost card at the predetermined rate.

- Job order cost cards for incomplete jobs make up the Work in Process Inventory account. To ensure correctness, the ending balance in the Work in Process Inventory account is compared with the total of the costs shown on the job order cost cards.

A job order costing system simplifies the calculation of product unit costs. When a job is finished, the costs of direct materials, direct labor, and overhead that have been recorded on its job order cost card are totaled.

- The product unit cost is computed by dividing the total costs for the job by the number of good (i.e., salable) units produced. The product unit cost is entered on the job order cost card and will be used to value items in inventory. The job order cost card in Figure 17-1 shows the costs for completed Job CC. Two golf carts were produced at a total cost of $3,880, so the product unit cost was $1,940.

FIGURE 17-1
Job Order Cost Card for a Manufacturing Company

Job Order: CC

JOB ORDER COST CARD
Augusta Custom Golf Carts, Inc.
Spring Hill, Florida

Customer: Stock **Batch:** X **Custom:**
Specifications: Two general-purpose golf carts
Date of Order: 2/26/11
Date of Completion: 3/6/11

Costs Charged to Job	Previous Months	Current Month	Cost Summary
Direct materials	$165	$1,038	$1,203
Direct labor	127	1,320	1,447
Overhead (85% of direct labor cost)	108	1,122	1,230
Totals	$400	$3,480	$3,880
Units completed			÷ 2
Product unit cost			$1,940

Job Order Costing in a Service Organization

Many service organizations use a job order costing system to compute the cost of rendering services. The most important cost for a service organization is labor, which is carefully accounted for through the use of time cards. The cost flow of services is similar to the cost flow of manufactured products. Job order cost cards are used to keep track of the costs incurred for each job. Job costs include labor, materials and supplies, and service overhead.

To cover these costs and earn a profit, many service organizations base jobs on **cost-plus contracts**. Such contracts require the customer to pay all costs incurred in performing the job plus a predetermined amount of profit, which is based on the amount of costs incurred. When the job is complete, the costs on the completed job order cost card become the cost of services. The cost of services is adjusted at the end of the accounting period for the difference between the applied service overhead costs and the actual service overhead costs.

To illustrate how a service organization uses a job order costing system, let's assume that a company called Dream Golf Retreats earns its revenue by designing and selling golf retreat packages to corporate clients. Figure 17-2 shows Dream Golf Retreats' job order cost card for the Work Corporation. Costs have been categorized into three separate activities: planning, golf activities, and non-golf activities.

- The service overhead cost for planning is 40 percent of planning labor costs, and the service overhead cost for golf activities is 50 percent of on-site labor costs.
- Total costs incurred for this job were $5,400.

FIGURE 17-2 Job Order Cost Card for a Service Organization

Job Order: 2011-A7

JOB ORDER COST CARD
Dream Golf Retreats

Customer: Work Corporation **Batch:** **Customer:** X
Specifications: Golf retreat for 45 executives
Date of Order: 3/24/11 **Date of Completion:** 4/8/11

Costs Charged to Job		**Previous Months**	**Current Month**	**Total Cost**
Planning				
Supplies		$ 100	$ —	$ 100
Labor		850		850
Overhead	(40% of planning labor costs)	340	—	340
Totals		$1,290		$1,290
Golf Activities				
Supplies		$ 970	$1,200	$2,170
Labor		400	620	1,020
Overhead	(50% of on-site labor costs)	200	310	510
Totals		$1,570	$2,130	$3,700
Non-Golf Activities				
Cost of outsourcing		$ 90	$ 320	$ 410
Totals		$ 90	$ 320	$ 410

Cost Summary to Date		**Total Cost**
Planning		$1,290
Golf Activities		3,700
Non-Golf Activities		410
Total		$5,400
Profit Margin	(15% of total cost)	810
Job Revenue		$6,210

Study Note

Job order cost cards for service businesses record costs by activities done for the job. The activity costs may include supplies, labor, and overhead.

Dream Golf Retreats' cost-plus contract with Work Corporation has a 15 percent profit guarantee. Therefore, $810 of profit margin is added to the total cost to arrive at the total contract revenue of $6,210, which is the amount billed to the Work Corporation.

Complete the following job order cost card for five custom-built cabinets:

Job Order 16

Job Order Cost Card
Unique Cupboards, LLP
Sample City, Oregon

Customer:	Brian Tofer	Batch: ___	Custom: X
Specifications:	5 custom cabinets		
Date of Order:	5/4/2011	Date of Completion:	6/8/2011

Costs Charged to Job	**Previous Months**	**Current Month**	**Cost Summary**
Direct materials	$3,500	$2,800	$?
Direct labor	2,300	1,600	?
Overhead applied	1,150	800	?
Totals	$?	$?	$?
Units completed			÷ ?
Product unit cost			$?

SOLUTION

Job Order 16

Job Order Cost Card
Unique Cupboards, LLP
Sample City, Oregon

Customer:	Brian Tofer	Batch: ___	Custom: X
Specifications:	5 custom cabinets		
Date of Order:	5/4/2011	Date of Completion:	6/8/2011

Costs Charged to Job	**Previous Months**	**Current Month**	**Cost Summary**
Direct materials	$3,500	$2,800	$ 6,300
Direct labor	2,300	1,600	3,900
Overhead applied	1,150	800	1,950
Totals	$6,950	$5,200	$12,150
Units completed			÷ 5
Product unit cost			$ 2,430

A LOOK BACK AT

▸ COLD STONE CREAMERY, INC.

The Decision Point at the beginning of this chapter focused on **Cold Stone Creamery**, a company known for its custom ice cream and cake creations. It posed these questions:

- Is the product costing system that is used for custom-made items appropriate for mass-produced items?
- What performance measures would be most useful in evaluating the results of each type of product?

Whether a product costing system is appropriate depends on the nature of the production process. Because the production of custom-made items and the production of mass-produced items involve different processes, they generally require different costing systems.

- When a product is custom-made, it is possible to use a job order costing system, which collects the costs of each order.
- When a product is mass-produced, the costs of a specific unit cannot be collected because there is a continuous flow of similar products. In this case a process costing system is used, and costs are collected by process, department, or work cell.

Thus, if Cold Stone Creamery were to introduce mass-produced cakes or quarts of ice cream for sale in grocery stores or other retail establishments, it would have to adjust its costing system to determine the product cost of a unit. It would also have to use different performance measures. Its management can now measure the profitability of each personalized order by comparing the order's cost and price. But if a mass-produced product were introduced, management would measure performance by comparing the budgeted and actual costs for a process, department, or work cell.

Review Problem

Job Order Costing
LO4

Suppose one of **Cold Stone Creamery**'s stores has begun hosting parties at its location. It uses job order cost cards to keep track of the costs of each party. Job costs (direct materials and supplies, direct labor, and service overhead) are categorized under three activities: planning and design, party, and cleanup. The service overhead charge for planning and design is 30 percent of the party planner's labor costs, and the service overhead charge for the party is 50 percent of the cost of the cake created for the party.

The manager has tracked all costs of the Happy Birthday Billy job, and now that the work is finished, it is time to complete the job order cost card. It is a cost-plus contract with a 25 percent profit guarantee. The costs for the job are as follows:

Costs During June	
Planning and design	
Supplies	$12.00
Party planner labor	25.00
Party	
Cake creation	21.50
Direct labor	16.00
Cleanup	
Janitorial service cost	35.25

Required

1. Create the job order cost card for the Happy Birthday Billy job.

2. What amount will the manager bill for the job?
3. Using the format of the Work in Process Inventory account in Exhibit 17-1, reconstruct the beginning balance and costs for the current month.

Answers to Review Problem

1. Job order cost card for the Happy Birthday Billy job:

Job Order Cost Card
Cold Stone Creamery, Inc.

Customer:	Happy Birthday Billy	Batch: ____	Custom: X
Specifications:	Birthday party		
Date of Order:	5/28/2011	Date of Completion:	6/5/2011

Costs Charged to Job	**Current Month**	**Total Cost**
Planning and design		
Supplies	$ 12.00	$12.00
Party planner labor	25.00	25.00
Overhead (30% of planning labor costs)	7.50	7.50
Totals	$ 44.50	$44.50
Party		
Cake creation	$ 21.50	$21.50
Direct labor	16.00	16.00
Overhead (50% of cake creation cost)	10.75	10.75
Totals	$ 48.25	$48.25
Cleanup		
Janitorial service costs	$ 35.25	$35.25
Totals	$ 35.25	$35.25
Cost Summary to Date		
Planning and design	$ 44.50	
Party	48.25	
Cleanup	35.25	
Total	$128.00	
Profit margin (25% of total cost)	32.00	
Job revenue	$160.00	

2. The manager will bill $160.00 for this job.
3. Beginning balance and costs for the current month:

Work in Process Inventory

Beg. Bal.	—	Completed	128.00
Planning and design			
Supplies	12.00		
Party planner labor	25.00		
Overhead	7.50		
Party			
Cake creation	21.50		
Direct labor	16.00		
Overhead	10.75		
Cleanup			
Janitorial service costs	35.25		
End. Bal.	—		

STOP & REVIEW >

LO1 Explain why unit cost is important in the management process.

When managers plan, information about costs helps them develop budgets, establish prices, set sales goals, plan production volumes, estimate product or service unit costs, and determine human resource needs. Daily, managers use cost information to make decisions about controlling costs, managing the company's volume of activity, ensuring quality, and negotiating prices. When managers evaluate results, they analyze actual and targeted information to evaluate performance and make any necessary adjustments to their planning and decision-making strategies. When managers communicate with stakeholders, they use unit costs to determine inventory balances and the cost of goods or services sold for the financial statements. They also analyze internal reports that compare the organization's measures of actual and targeted performance to determine whether cost goals for products or services are being achieved.

LO2 Distinguish between the two basic types of product costing systems, and identify the information that each provides.

A job order costing system is a product costing system used by companies that make unique, custom, or special-order products. Such a system traces the costs of direct materials, direct labor, and overhead to a specific batch of products or to a specific job order. A job order costing system measures the cost of each complete unit and summarizes the cost of all jobs in a single Work in Process Inventory account that is supported by job order cost cards.

A process costing system is a product costing system used by companies that produce large amounts of similar products or liquid products or that have long, continuous production runs of identical products. Such a system first traces the costs of direct materials, direct labor, and overhead to processes, departments, or work cells and then assigns the costs to the products manufactured by those processes, departments, or work cells. A process costing system uses several Work in Process Inventory accounts, one for each department, process, or work cell.

LO3 Explain the cost flow in a manufacturer's job order costing system.

In a manufacturer's job order costing system, the costs of materials are first charged to the Materials Inventory account. The various actual overhead costs are debited to the Overhead account. As products are manufactured, the costs of direct materials and direct labor are debited to the Work in Process Inventory account and are recorded on each job's job order cost card. Overhead costs are applied and debited to the Work in Process Inventory account and credited to the Overhead account using a predetermined overhead rate. They, too, are recorded on the job order cost card. When products and jobs are completed, the costs assigned to them are transferred to the Finished Goods Inventory account. Then, when the products are sold and shipped, their costs are transferred to the Cost of Goods Sold account.

LO4 Prepare a job order cost card, and compute a job order's product or service unit cost.

All costs of direct materials, direct labor, and overhead for a particular job are accumulated on a job order cost card. When the job has been completed, those costs are totaled. The total is then divided by the number of good units produced to find the product unit cost for that order. The product unit cost is entered on the job order cost card and will be used to value items in inventory.

Many service organizations use a job order costing system to track the costs of labor, materials and supplies, and service overhead to specific customer jobs. Labor is an important cost for service organizations, but their materials costs are usually negligible. To cover their costs and earn a profit, service organizations often base jobs on cost-plus contracts, which require the customer to pay all costs incurred plus a predetermined amount of profit.

REVIEW of Concepts and Terminology

The following concepts and terms were introduced in this chapter:

Cost-plus contracts 818 (LO4)

Job order 810 (LO2)

Job order cost card 810 (LO2)

Job order costing system 810 (LO2)

Operations costing system 810 (LO2)

Process costing system 810 (LO2)

Product costing system 809 (LO2)

CHAPTER ASSIGNMENTS

BUILDING Your Basic Knowledge and Skills

Short Exercises

LO1 **Uses of Product Costing Information**

SE 1. Silly Putter Miniature Golf provides 36 holes of miniature golf. Dan, the owner of the golf course, must make several business decisions soon. Write *yes* or *no* to indicate whether knowing the cost to play one golf game (i.e., the product unit cost) can help Dan answer these questions:

1. Is the fee for playing a golf game high enough to cover the related cost?
2. How much profit will Silly Putter make if it sells an average of 100 games per day for 50 weeks?
3. What costs can be reduced to make the fee competitive with that of its competitor?

LO2 **Companies That Use Job Order Costing**

SE 2. Write *yes* or *no* to indicate whether each of the following companies would typically use a job order costing system:

1. Soft-drink producer
2. Jeans manufacturer
3. Submarine contractor
4. Office building contractor
5. Stuffed-toy maker

LO2 **Job Order Versus Process Costing Systems**

SE 3. State whether a job order costing system or a process costing system would typically be used to account for the costs of the following:

1. Manufacturing bottles of water
2. Manufacturing custom-designed swimming pools
3. Providing babysitting
4. Manufacturing one-size-fits-all flip-flop shoes
5. Manufacturing canned food
6. Providing accounting services

LO3 **Transactions in a Manufacturer's Job Order Costing System**

SE 4. For each of the following transactions, state which account(s) would be debited and credited in a job order costing system:

1. Purchased materials on account, $12,890
2. Charged direct labor to production, $3,790
3. Requested direct materials for production, $6,800
4. Applied overhead to jobs in process, $3,570

LO3 **Transactions in a Manufacturer's Job Order Costing System**

SE 5. Enter the following transactions into T accounts:

1. Incurred $34,000 of direct labor and $18,000 of indirect labor
2. Applied overhead based on 12,680 labor hours @ $6.50 per labor hour

LO3 **Accounts for Job Order Costing**

SE 6. Identify the accounts in which each of the following transactions for Acorn Furniture, a custom manufacturer of oak tables and chairs, would be debited and credited:

1. Issued oak materials into production for Job ABC
2. Recorded direct labor time for the first week in February for Job ABC
3. Purchased indirect materials from a vendor on account
4. Received a production-related electricity bill
5. Applied overhead to Job ABC
6. Completed but did not yet sell Job ABC

LO4 **Product Unit Cost**

SE 7. Write *yes* or *no* to indicate whether each of the following costs is included in a product unit cost. Then explain your answers.

1. Direct materials costs
2. Fixed overhead costs
3. Variable selling costs
4. Fixed administrative costs
5. Direct labor costs
6. Variable overhead costs

LO4 **Computation of Product Unit Cost**

SE 8. Complete the following job order cost card for six custom-built computer systems:

Job Order 168

Job Order Cost Card
Keeper 3000
Apache City, North Dakota

Customer: Brian Patcher Batch: ____ Custom: X
Specifications: 6 Custom-Built Computer Systems
Date of Order: 4/4/2011 Date of Completion: 6/8/2011

Costs Charged to Job	Previous Months	Current Month	Cost Summary
Direct materials	$3,540	$2,820	$?
Direct labor	2,340	1,620	?
Overhead applied	2,880	2,550	?
Totals	$?	$?	$?
Units completed			÷ ?
Product unit cost			$?

LO4 **Job Order Costing in a Service Organization**

SE 9. For each of the following transactions, state which account(s) would be debited and credited in a job order costing system for a desert landscaping business:

1. Charged customer for landscape design
2. Purchased cactus plants and gravel on credit for one job
3. Paid three employees to prepare soil for gravel
4. Paid for rental equipment to move gravel to job site

LO4 **Job Order Costing with Cost-Plus Contracts**

SE 10. Complete the following job order cost card for an individual tax return:

Job Order 2011-A7

Job Order Cost Card
Doremus Tax Service
Puyallup, Washington

Customer: Arthur Farnsworth Batch: ____ Custom: X
Specifications: Annual Individual Tax Return
Date of Order: 3/24/2011 Date of Completion: 4/8/2011

Costs Charged to Job	Previous Months	Current Month	Total Cost
Client interview			
Supplies	$10	$ —	$?
Labor	50	60	?
Overhead (40% of interview labor costs)	20	24	?
Totals	$?	$?	$?
Preparation of return			
Supplies	$—	$ 16	$?
Computer time	—	12	?
Labor	—	240	?
Overhead (50% of preparation labor costs)	—	120	?
Totals	$—	$?	$?
Delivery			
Postage	$—	$ 12	$?
Totals	$—	$?	$?

Cost Summary to Date	Total Cost
Client interview	$?
Preparation of return	?
Delivery	?
Total	$?
Profit margin (25% of total cost)	?
Job revenue	$?

Exercises

LO2 **Product Costing**

E 1. Bell Printing Company specializes in wedding invitations. Bell needs information to budget next year's activities. Write *yes* or *no* to indicate whether each of the following costs is likely to be available in the company's product costing system:

1. Cost of paper and envelopes
2. Printing machine setup costs
3. Depreciation of printing machinery
4. Advertising costs
5. Repair costs for printing machinery
6. Costs to deliver stationery to customers
7. Office supplies costs
8. Costs to design a wedding invitation
9. Cost of ink
10. Sales commissions

LO2 **Costing Systems: Industry Linkage**

E 2. Which of the following products would typically be accounted for using a job order costing system? Which would typically be accounted for using a process costing system? (a) Paint, (b) jelly beans, (c) jet aircraft, (d) bricks, (e) tailor-made suit, (f) liquid detergent, (g) helium gas canisters used to inflate balloons, and (h) aluminum compressed-gas cylinders with a special fiberglass wrap for a Mount Everest expedition.

LO2 **Costing Systems: Industry Linkage**

E 3. Which of the following products would typically be accounted for using a job order costing system? Which would typically be accounted for using a process costing system? (a) Standard nails, (b) television sets, (c) printed wedding invitations, (d) a limited edition of lithographs, (e) flea collars for pets, (f) personal marathon training program, (g) breakfast cereal, and (h) an original evening gown.

LO3 **Job Order Cost Flow**

E 4. The three product cost elements—direct materials, direct labor, and overhead—flow through a job order costing system in a structured, orderly fashion. Specific accounts are used to verify and record cost information. Write a paragraph describing the cost flow in a job order costing system.

LO3 **Work in Process Inventory: T Account Analysis**

E 5. On June 30, New Haven Company's Work in Process Inventory account showed a beginning balance of $29,400. The Materials Inventory account showed a beginning balance of $240,000. Production activity for July was as follows: Direct materials costing $238,820 were requested for production; total manufacturing payroll was $140,690, of which $52,490 was used to pay for indirect labor; indirect materials costing $28,400 were purchased and used; and overhead was applied at a rate of 150 percent of direct labor costs.

1. Record New Haven's materials, labor, and overhead costs for July in T accounts.
2. Compute the ending balance in the Work in Process Inventory account. Assume a transfer of $461,400 to the Finished Goods Inventory account during the period.

LO3 **T Account Analysis with Unknowns**

E 6. Partial operating data for Merton Company are presented below. Management has set the predetermined overhead rate for the current year at 120 percent of direct labor costs.

Account/Transaction	June	July
Beginning Materials Inventory	a	e
Beginning Work in Process Inventory	$ 89,605	f
Beginning Finished Goods Inventory	79,764	$ 67,660
Direct materials requested	59,025	g
Materials purchased	57,100	60,216
Direct labor costs	48,760	54,540
Overhead applied	b	h
Cost of units completed	c	231,861
Cost of Goods Sold	166,805	i
Ending Materials Inventory	32,014	27,628
Ending Work in Process Inventory	d	j
Ending Finished Goods Inventory	67,660	30,515

Using T accounts and the data provided, compute the unknown values. Show all your computations.

LO3 **T Account Analysis with Unknowns**

E 7. Partial operating data for Charing Cross Company are presented below. Charing Cross Company's management has set the predetermined overhead rate for the current year at 80 percent of direct labor costs.

Account/Transaction	December
Beginning Materials Inventory	$ 42,000
Beginning Work in Process Inventory	66,000
Beginning Finished Goods Inventory	29,000
Direct materials used	168,000
Direct materials purchased	a
Direct labor costs	382,000
Overhead applied	b
Cost of units completed	c
Cost of Goods Sold	808,000
Ending Materials Inventory	38,000
Ending Work in Process Inventory	138,600
Ending Finished Goods Inventory	d

Using T accounts and the data provided, compute the unknown values. Show all your computations.

LO4 **Job Order Cost Card and Computation of Product Unit Cost**

E 8. In January, the Cabinet Company worked on six job orders for specialty kitchen cabinets. It began Job A-62 for Zeke Cabinets, Inc., on January 10, 2011 and completed it on January 24, 2011. Partial data for Job A-62 are as follows:

	Costs	Machine Hours Used
Direct materials		
Cedar	$7,900	
Pine	6,320	
Hardware	2,930	
Assembly supplies	988	
Direct labor		
Sawing	2,840	120
Shaping	2,200	220
Finishing	2,250	180
Assembly	2,890	50

The Cabinet Company produced a total of 34 cabinets for Job A-62. Its current predetermined overhead rate is $21.60 per machine hour. From the information given, prepare a job order cost card and compute the job order's product unit cost. (Round to whole dollars.)

LO4 **Computation of Product Unit Cost**

E 9. Using job order costing, determine the product unit cost based on the following costs incurred during March: liability insurance, manufacturing, $2,500; rent, sales office, $2,900; depreciation, manufacturing equipment, $6,100; direct materials, $32,650; indirect labor, manufacturing, $3,480;

indirect materials, $1,080; heat, light, and power, manufacturing, $1,910; fire insurance, manufacturing, $2,600; depreciation, sales equipment, $4,250; rent, manufacturing, $3,850; direct labor, $18,420; manager's salary, manufacturing, $3,100; president's salary, $5,800; sales commissions, $8,250; and advertising expenses, $2,975. The Inspection Department reported that 48,800 good units were produced during March. Carry your answer to two decimal places.

LO4 **Computation of Product Unit Cost**

E 10. Wild Things, Inc., manufactures custom-made stuffed animals. Last month the company produced 4,540 stuffed bears with stethoscopes for the local children's hospital to sell at a fund-raising event. Using job order costing, determine the product unit cost of a stuffed bear based on the following costs incurred during the month: manufacturing utilities, $500; depreciation on manufacturing equipment, $450; indirect materials, $300; direct materials, $1,300; indirect labor, $800; direct labor, $2,400; sales commissions, $3,000; president's salary, $4,000; insurance on manufacturing plant, $600; advertising expense, $500; rent on manufacturing plant, $5,000; rent on sales office, $4,000; and legal expense, $250. Carry your answer to two decimal places.

LO4 **Computation of Product Unit Cost**

E 11. Arch Corporation manufactures specialty lines of women's apparel. During February, the company worked on three special orders: A-25, A-27, and B-14. Cost and production data for each order are as follows:

	Job A-25	Job A-27	Job B-14
Direct materials			
Fabric Q	$10,840	$12,980	$17,660
Fabric Z	11,400	12,200	13,440
Fabric YB	5,260	6,920	10,900
Direct labor			
Garment maker	8,900	10,400	16,200
Layout	6,450	7,425	9,210
Packaging	3,950	4,875	6,090
Overhead			
(120% of direct labor costs)	?	?	?
Number of units produced	700	775	1,482

1. Compute the total cost associated with each job. Show the subtotals for each cost category.
2. Compute the product unit cost for each job. (Round your computations to the nearest cent.)

LO4 **Job Order Costing in a Service Organization**

E 12. A job order cost card for Hal's Computer Services appears at the top of the next page. Complete the missing information. The profit factor in the organization's cost-plus contract is 30 percent of total cost.

Job Order Cost Card
Hal's Computer Services

Customer:	James Lowe
Job Order No.:	8-324
Contract Type:	Cost-Plus
Type of Service:	Software Installation and Internet Interfacing
Date of Completion:	October 6, 2011

Costs Charged to Job	**Total Cost**
Software installation services	
Installation labor	$300
Service overhead (? % of installation labor costs)	?
Total	$450
Internet services	
Internet labor	$200
Service overhead (20% of Internet labor costs)	40
Total	$?

Cost Summary to Date	**Total Cost**
Software installation services	$?
Internet services	?
Total	$?
Profit margin (30% of total cost)	?
Contract revenue	$?

LO4 **Job Order Costing in a Service Organization**

E 13. A job order cost card for Miniblinds by Jenny appears below. Complete the missing information. The profit factor in the company's cost-plus contract is 50 percent of total cost.

Job Order Cost Card
Miniblinds by Jenny

Customer:	Carmen Sawyer
Job Order No.:	8-482
Contract Type:	Cost-Plus
Type of Service:	Miniblind Installation and Design
Date of Completion:	June 12, 2011

Costs Charged to Job	**Total Cost**
Installation services	
Installation labor	$445
Service overhead (80% of installation labor costs)	?
Total	$?
Designer services	
Designer labor	$200
Service overhead (? % of designer labor costs)	?
Total	$400

Cost Summary to Date	**Total Cost**
Installation services	$?
Designer services	?
Total	$?
Profit margin (50% of total cost)	?
Contract revenue	$?

LO4 Job Order Costing in a Service Organization

E 14. Personal Shoppers, Inc., relieves busy women executives of the stress of shopping for clothes by taking an inventory of a client's current wardrobe and shopping for her needs for the next season or a special event. The company charges clients $30 per hour for the service plus the cost of the clothes purchased. It pays its employees various hourly wage rates.

During September, Personal Shoppers worked with three clients. It began Job 9-3, for Lucinda Mapley, on September 3, 2011 and completed the job on September 30, 2011. Using the partial data that follow, prepare the job order cost card. What amount of profit will Personal Shoppers make on this job?

Costs Charged to Job	Costs	Hours	Other
In-person consultation			
Supplies	$ 30		
Labor ($10 per hour)		4	
Overhead (10% of in-person labor costs)			
Shopping			
Purchases	$560		
Labor ($15 per hour)		8	
Overhead (25% of shopping labor costs)			
Telephone consultations			
Cell phone calls ($1 per call)			6 calls
Labor ($6 per hour)		2	
Overhead (50% of telephone labor costs)			

Problems

LO3 T Account Analysis with Unknowns

P 1. Flagstaff Enterprises makes flagpoles. Dan Dalripple, the company's new controller, can find only the following partial information for the past two months:

Account/Transaction	May	June
Beginning Materials Inventory	$ 36,240	$ e
Beginning Work in Process Inventory	56,480	f
Beginning Finished Goods Inventory	44,260	g
Materials purchased	a	96,120
Direct materials requested	82,320	h
Direct labor costs	b	72,250
Overhead applied	53,200	i
Cost of units completed	c	221,400
Cost of Goods Sold	209,050	j
Ending Materials Inventory	38,910	41,950
Ending Work in Process Inventory	d	k
Ending Finished Goods Inventory	47,940	51,180

The current year's predetermined overhead rate is 80 percent of direct labor cost.

Required

Using the data provided and T accounts, compute the unknown values.

LO3 Job Order Costing: T Account Analysis

P 2. Par Carts, Inc., produces special-order golf carts, so Par Carts uses a job order costing system. Overhead is applied at the rate of 90 percent of direct labor cost. The following is a list of transactions for January, 2011:

Jan. 1 Purchased direct materials on account, $215,400.
2 Purchased indirect materials on account, $49,500.
4 Requested direct materials costing $193,200 (all used on Job X) and indirect materials costing $38,100 for production.
10 Paid the following overhead costs: utilities, $4,400; manufacturing rent, $3,800; and maintenance charges, $3,900.
15 Recorded the following gross wages and salaries for employees: direct labor, $120,000 (all for Job X); indirect labor, $60,620.
15 Applied overhead to production.
19 Purchased indirect materials costing $27,550 and direct materials costing $190,450 on account.
21 Requested direct materials costing $214,750 (Job X, $178,170; Job Y, $18,170; and Job Z, $18,410) and indirect materials costing $31,400 for production.
31 Recorded the following gross wages and salaries for employees: direct labor, $132,000 (Job X, $118,500; Job Y, $7,000; Job Z, $6,500); indirect labor, $62,240.
31 Applied overhead to production.
31 Completed and transferred Job X (375 carts) and Job Y (10 carts) to finished goods inventory; total cost was $855,990.
31 Shipped Job X to the customer; total production cost was $824,520 and sales price was $996,800.
31 Recorded these overhead costs (adjusting entries): prepaid insurance expired, $3,700; property taxes (payable at year end), $3,400; and depreciation–machinery, $15,500.

Required

1. Record the entries for all transactions in January using T accounts for the following: Materials Inventory, Work in Process Inventory, Finished Goods Inventory, Overhead, Cash, Accounts Receivable, Prepaid Insurance, Accumulated Depreciation–Machinery, Accounts Payable, Payroll Payable, Property Taxes Payable, Sales, and Cost of Goods Sold. Use job order cost cards for Job X, Job Y, and Job Z. Determine the partial account balances. Assume no beginning inventory balances. Also assume that when the payroll was recorded, entries were made to the Payroll Payable account.
2. Compute the amount of underapplied or overapplied overhead as of January 31, 2011 and transfer it to the Cost of Goods Sold account.
3. Why should the Overhead account's underapplied or overapplied overhead be transferred to the Cost of Goods Sold account?

LO3 LO4 Job Order Cost Flow

P 3. On May 31, the inventory balances of Princess Designs, a manufacturer of high-quality children's clothing, were as follows: Materials Inventory, $21,360; Work in Process Inventory, $15,112; and Finished Goods Inventory, $17,120. Job order cost cards for jobs in process as of June 30 had these totals:

Job No.	Direct Materials	Direct Labor	Overhead
24-A	$1,596	$1,290	$1,677
24-B	1,492	1,380	1,794
24-C	1,984	1,760	2,288
24-D	1,608	1,540	2,002

The predetermined overhead rate is 130 percent of direct labor costs. Materials purchased and received in June were as follows:

June 4	$33,120
June 16	28,600
June 22	31,920

Direct labor costs for June were as follows:

June 15 payroll	$23,680
June 29 payroll	25,960

Direct materials requested by production during June were as follows:

June 6	$37,240
June 23	38,960

On June 30, Princess Designs sold on account finished goods with a 75 percent markup over cost for $320,000.

Required

1. Using T accounts for Materials Inventory, Work in Process Inventory, Finished Goods Inventory, Overhead, Accounts Receivable, Payroll Payable, Sales, and Cost of Goods Sold, reconstruct the transactions in June.
2. Compute the cost of units completed during the month.
3. What was the total cost of goods sold during June?
4. Determine the ending inventory balances.
5. Jobs 24-A and 24-C were completed during the first week of July. No additional materials costs were incurred, but Job 24-A required $960 more of direct labor, and Job 24-C needed an additional $1,610 of direct labor. Job 24-A was composed of 1,200 pairs of trousers; Job 24-C, of 950 shirts. Compute the product unit cost for each job. (Round your answers to two decimal places.)

LO4 **Job Order Costing in a Service Organization**

P 4. Riley & Associates is a CPA firm located in Clinton, Kansas. The firm deals primarily in tax and audit work. For billing of major audit engagements, it uses cost-plus contracts, and its profit factor is 25 percent of total job cost. Costs are accumulated for three primary activities: preliminary analysis, fieldwork, and report development. Current service overhead rates based on billable hours are preliminary analysis, $12 per hour; fieldwork, $20 per hour; and report development, $16 per hour. Supplies are treated as direct materials and are traceable to each engagement. Audits for three clients—Fulcrum, Inc., Rainy Day Bakeries, and Our Place Restaurants—are currently in process. During March, 2011 costs related to these projects were as follows:

	Fulcrum, Inc.	Rainy Day Bakeries	Our Place Restaurants
Beginning Balances			
Preliminary analysis	$1,160	$2,670	$2,150
Fieldwork	710	1,980	3,460
Report development	—	1,020	420
Costs During March			
Preliminary analysis			
Supplies	$ 710	$ 430	$ 200
Labor: hours	60	10	12
dollars	$1,200	$ 200	$ 240

Fieldwork			
Supplies	$ 450	$1,120	$ 890
Labor: hours	120	240	230
dollars	$4,800	$9,600	$9,200
Report development			
Supplies	$ 150	$ 430	$ 390
Labor: hours	30	160	140
dollars	$ 900	$4,800	$4,200

Required

1. Using the format shown in this chapter's Review Problem, create the job order cost card for each of the three audit engagements.
2. Riley & Associates will complete the audits of Rainy Day Bakeries and Our Place Restaurants by the end of March. What will the billing amount for each of those audit engagements be?
3. What is the March ending balance of Riley & Associates' Audit in Process account?

LO4 **Job Order Costing in a Service Organization**

P 5. Peruga Engineering Company specializes in designing automated characters and displays for theme parks. It uses cost-plus profit contracts, and its profit factor is 30 percent of total cost.

Peruga uses a job order costing system to track the costs of developing each job. Costs are accumulated for three primary activities: bid and proposal, design, and prototype development. Current service overhead rates based on engineering hours are as follows: bid and proposal, $18 per hour; design, $22 per hour; and prototype development, $20 per hour. Supplies are treated as direct materials, traceable to each job. Peruga worked on three jobs, P-12, P-15, and P-19, during January, 2011. The following table shows the costs for those jobs:

	P-12	P-15	P-19
Beginning Balances			
Bid and proposal	$2,460	$2,290	$ 940
Design	1,910	460	—
Prototype development	2,410	1,680	—
Costs During January			
Bid and proposal			
Supplies	$ —	$ 280	$2,300
Labor: hours	12	20	68
dollars	$ 192	$ 320	$1,088
Design			
Supplies	$ 400	$ 460	$ 290
Labor: hours	64	42	26
dollars	$1,280	$ 840	$ 520
Prototype development			
Supplies	$6,744	$7,216	$2,400
Labor: hours	120	130	25
dollars	$2,880	$3,120	$ 600

Required

1. Using the format in the answer to requirement **1** of this chapter's Review Problem, create the job order cost card for each of the three jobs.
2. Peruga completed Jobs P-12 and P-15, and the customers approved the prototype products. Customer A plans to produce 12 special characters using the design and specifications created by Job P-12. Customer B plans to make 18 displays from the design developed by Job P-15. What dollar amount will each customer use as the cost of design for each of those products (i.e., what is the product unit cost for Jobs P-12 and P-15)? (Round to the nearest dollar.)
3. What is the January ending balance of Peruga's Contract in Process account for the three jobs?

Manager insight ▶ 4. Rank the jobs in order from most costly to least costly based on each job's total cost. From the rankings of cost, what observations can you make?

Manager insight ▶ 5. Speculate on the price that Peruga should charge for such jobs.

Alternate Problems

LO3 T Account Analysis with Unknowns

P 6. Hard Core Enterprises makes peripheral equipment for computers. Emily Vit, the company's new controller, can find only the following partial information for the past two months:

Account/Transaction	July	August
Beginning Materials Inventory	$ 52,000	$ e
Beginning Work in Process Inventory	24,000	f
Beginning Finished Goods Inventory	36,000	g
Materials purchased	a	31,000
Direct materials requested	77,000	h
Direct labor costs	b	44,000
Overhead applied	53,200	i
Cost of units completed	c	167,000
Cost of Goods Sold	188,000	j
Ending Materials Inventory	27,000	8,000
Ending Work in Process Inventory	d	k
Ending Finished Goods Inventory	12,000	19,000

The current year's predetermined overhead rate is 110 percent of direct labor cost.

Required

Using the data provided and T accounts, compute the unknown values.

LO3 Job Order Costing: T Account Analysis

P 7. Rhile Industries, Inc., produces colorful and stylish nursing uniforms. During September, 2011 Rhile Industries completed the following transactions:

Sept. 1 Purchased direct materials on account, $59,400.
3 Requested direct materials costing $26,850 for production (all for Job A).
4 Purchased indirect materials for cash, $22,830.
8 Issued checks for the following overhead costs: utilities, $4,310; manufacturing insurance, $1,925; and repairs, $4,640.

Sept. 10 Requested direct materials costing $29,510 (all used on Job A) and indirect materials costing $6,480 for production.

15 Recorded the following gross wages and salaries for employees: direct labor, $62,900 (all for Job A); indirect labor, $31,610; manufacturing supervision, $26,900; and sales commissions, $32,980.

15 Applied overhead to production at a rate of 120 percent of direct labor cost.

22 Paid the following overhead costs: utilities, $4,270; maintenance, $3,380; and rent, $3,250.

23 Recorded the purchase on account and receipt of $31,940 of direct materials and $9,260 of indirect materials.

27 Requested $28,870 of direct materials (Job A, $2,660; Job B, $8,400; Job C, $17,810) and $7,640 of indirect materials for production.

30 Recorded the following gross wages and salaries for employees: direct labor, $64,220 (Job A, $44,000; Job B, $9,000; Job C, $11,220); indirect labor, $30,290; manufacturing supervision, $28,520; and sales commissions, $36,200.

30 Applied overhead to production at a rate of 120 percent of direct labor cost.

30 Completed and transferred Job A (58,840 units) and Job B (3,525 units) to finished goods inventory; total cost was $322,400.

30 Shipped Job A to the customer; total production cost was $294,200, and sales price was $418,240.

30 Recorded the following adjusting entries: $2,680 for depreciation–manufacturing equipment; and $1,230 for property taxes, manufacturing, payable at month end.

Required

1. Record the entries for all Rhile's transactions in September using T accounts for the following: Materials Inventory, Work in Process Inventory, Finished Goods Inventory, Overhead, Cash, Accounts Receivable, Accumulated Depreciation–Manufacturing Equipment, Accounts Payable, Payroll Payable, Property Taxes Payable, Sales, Cost of Goods Sold, and Selling and Administrative Expenses. Use job order cost cards for Job A, Job B, and Job C. Determine the partial account balances. Assume no beginning inventory balances. Assume also that when payroll was recorded, entries were made to the Payroll Payable account. (Round your answers to the nearest whole dollar.)
2. Compute the amount of underapplied or overapplied overhead for September and transfer it to the Cost of Goods Sold account.
3. Why should the Overhead account's underapplied or overapplied overhead be transferred to the Cost of Goods Sold account?

LO3 LO4 Job Order Cost Flow

P 8. Laurence Norton is the chief financial officer of Rotham Industries, a company that makes special-order sound systems for home theaters. His records for February revealed the following information:

Beginning inventory balances	
Materials Inventory	$27,450
Work in Process Inventory	22,900
Finished Goods Inventory	19,200
Direct materials purchased and received	
February 6	$ 7,200
February 12	8,110
February 24	5,890
Direct labor costs	
February 14	$13,750
February 28	13,230
Direct materials requested for production	
February 4	$ 9,080
February 13	5,940
February 25	7,600

Job order cost cards for jobs in process on February 28 had the following totals:

Job No.	Direct Materials	Direct Labor	Overhead
AJ-10	$3,220	$1,810	$2,534
AJ-14	3,880	2,110	2,954
AJ-15	2,980	1,640	2,296
AJ-16	4,690	2,370	3,318

The predetermined overhead rate for the month was 140 percent of direct labor costs. Sales for February totaled $152,400, which represented a 70 percent markup over the cost of production.

Required

1. Using T accounts for Materials Inventory, Work in Process Inventory, Finished Goods Inventory, Overhead, Accounts Receivable, Payroll Payable, Sales, and Cost of Goods Sold, reconstruct the transactions in February.
2. Compute the cost of units completed during the month.
3. What was the total cost of goods sold during February?
4. Determine the ending balances in the inventory accounts.
5. During the first week of March, Jobs AJ-10 and AJ-14 were completed. No additional direct materials costs were incurred, but Job AJ-10 needed $720 more of direct labor, and Job AJ-14 needed an additional $1,140 of direct labor. Job AJ-10 was 40 units; Job AJ-14, 55 units. Compute the product unit cost for each completed job (round to two decimal places).

LO4 Job Order Costing in a Service Organization

P 9. Locust Lodge, a restored 1920s lodge located in Alabama, caters and serves special events for businesses and social occasions. The company earns 60 percent of its revenue from weekly luncheon meetings of local clubs like Rotary. The remainder of its business comes from bookings for weddings and receptions.

Locust Lodge uses job order cost cards to keep track of the costs incurred. Job costs are separated into three categories: food and beverage, labor, and facility overhead. The facility overhead cost for weekly events is 10 percent of food and beverage costs, the facility overhead cost for sit-down receptions is 40 percent of food and beverage costs, and the facility overhead cost for stand-up receptions is 20 percent of food and beverage costs. Accumulated costs for three Locust Lodge clients in the current quarter are as follows:

	Food and Beverage	Labor	Facility Overhead
Tuesday Club meetings	Last month: $2,000 This month: $2,500	Last month: $200 This month: $250	Last month: ? This month: ?
Doar-Turner engagement and wedding parties	Last month: $3,000 This month: $8,000 Both sit-down affairs	Last month: $1,000 This month: $2,000	Last month: ? This month: ?
Reception for the new president	This month: $5,000 A stand-up affair	This month: $1,000	This month: ?

The number of attendees served at Tuesday Club meetings is usually 200 per month. The Doar-Turner parties paid for 500 guests. The organizers of the reception for the new president paid for 1,000 invitees.

Required

1. Using the format shown in this chapter's Review Problem, create a job order cost card for each of the three clients.
2. Calculate the total cost of each of the three jobs on its job order cost card.
3. Calculate the cost per attendee for each job.

Manager insight ▶ 4. Rank the jobs in order from most costly to least costly based on each job's total cost and on the cost per attendee. From the rankings of cost, what observations are you able to make?

Manager insight ▶ 5. Speculate on the price that Locust Lodge should charge for such jobs.

LO4 Job Order Costing in a Service Organization

P 10. Refer to assignment **P 5** in this chapter. Peruga Engineering Company needs to analyze its jobs in process during the month of January.

Required

1. Using Excel's Chart Wizard and the job order cost cards that you created for Jobs P-12, P-15, and P-19, prepare a bar chart that compares the bid and proposal costs, design costs, and prototype development costs of the jobs. The suggested format to use for the information table necessary to complete the bar chart is as follows:

	A	B	C	D	E
1	1		P-12	P-15	P-19
2	2	Bid and proposal			
3	3	Design			
4	4	Prototype development			
5	5	Total job cost			
6					

2. Examine the chart you prepared in requirement **1**. List some reasons for the differences between the costs of the various jobs.

ENHANCING Your Knowledge, Skills, and Critical Thinking

LO1 Interpreting Nonfinancial Data

C 1. Eagle Manufacturing supplies engine parts to Cherokee Cycle Company, a major U.S. manufacturer of motorcycles. Like all of Cherokee's suppliers, Eagle has always added a healthy profit margin to its cost when quoting selling prices to Cherokee. Recently, however, several companies have offered to supply engine parts to Cherokee for lower prices than Eagle has been charging.

Because Eagle Manufacturing wants to keep Cherokee Cycle Company's business, a team of Eagle's managers analyzed their company's product costs and decided to make minor changes in the company's manufacturing process. No new equipment was purchased, and no additional labor was required. Instead, the machines were rearranged, and some of the work was reassigned.

To monitor the effectiveness of the changes, Eagle introduced three new performance measures to its information system: inventory levels, lead time (total time required for a part to move through the production process), and productivity (number of parts manufactured per person per day). Eagle's goal was to reduce the quantities of the first two performance measures and to increase the quantity of the third.

A section of a recent management report, shown below, summarizes the quantities for each performance measure before and after the changes in the manufacturing process were made.

Measure	Before	After	Improvement
Inventory in dollars	$21,444	$10,772	50%
Lead time in minutes	17	11	35%
Productivity (parts per person per day)	515	1,152	124%

1. Do you believe that Eagle improved the quality of its manufacturing process and the quality of its engine parts? Explain your answer.
2. Can Eagle lower its selling price to Cherokee? Explain your answer.
3. Did the introduction of the new measures affect the design of the product costing system? Explain your answer.
4. Do you believe that the new measures caused a change in Eagle's cost per engine part? If so, how did they cause the change?

LO1 LO2 Product Costing Systems and Nonfinancial Data

C 2. Refer to the information in **C1**. Jordan Smith, the president of Eagle Manufacturing, wants to improve the quality of the company's operations and products. She believes waste exists in the design and manufacture of standard engine parts. To begin the improvement process, she has asked you to (1) identify the sources of such waste, (2) develop performance measures to account for the waste, and (3) estimate the current costs associated with the waste. She has asked you to submit a memo of your findings within two weeks so that she can begin strategic planning to revise the price at which Eagle sells engine parts to Cherokee.

You have identified two sources of costly waste. The Production Department is redoing work that was not done correctly the first time, and the Engineering Design Department is redesigning products that were not initially designed to customer specifications. Having improper designs has caused the company to buy parts that are not used in production. You have also obtained the following information from the product costing system:

Direct labor costs	$673,402
Engineering design costs	124,709
Indirect labor costs	67,200
Depreciation on production equipment	84,300
Supervisors' salaries	98,340
Direct materials costs	432,223
Indirect materials costs	44,332

1. In preparation for writing your memo, answer the following questions:
   a. For whom are you preparing the memo? What is the appropriate length of the memo?
   b. Why are you preparing the memo?
   c. What information is needed for the memo? Where can you get this information? What performance measure would you suggest for each activity? Is the accounting information sufficient for your memo?
   d. When is the memo due? What can be done to provide accurate and timely information?
2. Prepare an outline of the sections you would want to include in your memo.

LO3 Job Order Costing

C 3. Many businesses accumulate costs for each job performed. Examples of businesses that use a job order costing system include print shops, car repair shops, health clinics, and kennels.

Visit a local business that uses job order costing, and interview the owner, manager, or accountant about the job order process and the documents the business uses to accumulate product costs. Write a paper that summarizes the information you obtained. Include the following in your summary:

1. The name of the business and the type of operations performed
2. The name and position of the individual you interviewed
3. A description of the process of starting and completing a job
4. A description of the accounting process and the documents used to track a job
5. Your responses to these questions:
   a. Did the person you interviewed know the actual amount of direct materials, direct labor, and overhead charged to a particular job? If the job includes some estimated costs, how are the estimates calculated? Do the costs affect the determination of the selling price of the product or service?
   b. Compare the documents discussed in this chapter with the documents used by the company you visited. How are they similar, and how are they different?
   c. In your opinion, does the business record and accumulate its product costs effectively? Explain.

LO4 **Costing Procedures and Ethics**

C 4. Kevin Rogers, the production manager of Stitts Metal Products Company, entered the office of controller Ed Harris and asked, "Ed, what gives here? I was charged for 330 direct labor hours on Job AD22, and my records show that we spent only 290 hours on that job. That 40-hour difference caused the total cost of direct labor and overhead for the job to increase by over $5,500. Are my records wrong, or was there an error in the direct labor assigned to the job?"

Harris replied, "Don't worry about it, Kevin. This job won't be used in your quarterly performance evaluation. Job AD22 was a federal government job, a cost-plus contract, so the more costs we assign to it, the more profit we make. We decided to add a few hours to the job in case there is some follow-up work to do. You know how fussy the feds are." What should Kevin Rogers do? Discuss Ed Harris's costing procedure.

LO1 LO4 **Role of Cost Information in Software Development**

C 5. Software development companies frequently have a problem: When is "good enough" good enough? How many hours should be devoted to developing a new product? The industry's rule of thumb is that developing and shipping new software takes six to nine months. To be the first to market, a company must develop and ship products much more quickly than the industry norm. One performance measure that is used to answer the "good enough" question is a calculation based on the economic value (not cost) of what a company's developers create. The computation takes the estimated current market valuation of a firm and divides it by the number of product developers in the firm, to arrive at the market value created per developer. Some companies refine this calculation further to determine the value that each developer creates per workday. One company has estimated this value to be $10,000. Thus, for one software development company, "good enough" focuses on whether a new product's potential justifies an investment of time by someone who is worth $10,000 per day.

The salary cost of the company's developers is not used in the "good enough" calculation. Why is that cost not relevant?

LO4 **Cookie Company (Continuing Case)**

C 6. In the "Cookie Company" case in the last chapter, your team selected a cookie recipe for your company. In this chapter, your team will use that recipe to bake a batch of cookies, collect cost and time performance data related to the baking, create a marketing display for your company, and vote for the class's favorite cookie during an in-class cookie taste test. The goal of the taste test is to have your team's product voted the "best in class." One rule of the contest is that you may not vote for your own team's product.

1. Design a job measurement document that includes at least the following measures: cost per cookie; number of cookies produced (= number meeting specs + number rejected + number sampled for quality control + unexplained differences); size of cookies before baking; size of cookies after baking; and total throughput time (= mix time + [bake time for one cookie sheet × number of cookie sheets processed] + packaging time + downtime + cleanup time).
2. Design a job order cost card for your company that resembles one of those displayed in this chapter.
3. Using the recipe your team selected and assigning duties as described in the last chapter, bake a batch of cookies, and complete the job measurement document and job order cost card.
   - Assume an overhead rate of $2 for every $1 of direct material cost.
   - Assign direct labor cost for each production task based on the hourly rate or a monthly salary previously determined by your team.

4. Create a marketing display for your cookie product, and bring it to class on the day of the taste test. The marketing display should include 20 cookies on a plate or napkin and a poster that displays your company's name and mission statement, cookie recipe, job measurement document, and job order cost card.
5. During class, each student should look at all the marketing displays, taste 2 or 3 cookies and, on a ballot provided by your instructor, rank taste test results by giving 1 to the best cookie tasted, 2 to the next best, and so on. Students must sign their ballots before they turn them in to the instructor. (Remember, you cannot cast a vote for your own team's entry.) Your instructor will tabulate the ballots and announce the winning team.
6. Finally, write a review of your team members' efforts, and give it to your instructor.

CHAPTER

18 Costing Systems: Process Costing

The Management Process

PLAN

- ▷ **Select the costing system that is best for the business's products.**
- ▷ **Prepare budgets for production departments where process costs will be tracked.**

PERFORM

- ▷ **Track product cost flows through departments or processes.**
- ▷ **Prepare process cost reports every period for each production department or process using either FIFO or the average costing approach.**
- ▷ **Record the entries to transfer costs on to the next department or to finished goods inventory.**

EVALUATE

- ▷ **Analyze performance by comparing budget and actual department costs.**

COMMUNICATE

- ▷ **Prepare financial statements using the cost information provided by process costing.**
- ▷ **Prepare internal management reports to manage and monitor processes and departments.**

Companies that produce identical products use a process costing system to account for costs and determine unit cost.

As we noted in the previous chapter, a product costing system is expected to provide unit cost information, to supply cost data for management decisions, and to furnish ending values for the Materials Inventory, Work in Process Inventory, and Finished Goods Inventory accounts. In this chapter, we focus on the process costing system, which is used by companies that make large amounts of similar products or liquid products. We also describe product flow patterns, equivalent production, and the preparation of process cost reports.

LEARNING OBJECTIVES

LO1 **Describe the process costing system, and identify the reasons for its use.** (pp. 846–847)

LO2 **Relate the patterns of product flows to the cost flow methods in a process costing environment, and explain the role of the Work in Process Inventory accounts.** (pp. 847–849)

LO3 **Define *equivalent production,* and compute equivalent units.** (pp. 849–852)

LO4 **Prepare a process cost report using the FIFO costing method.** (pp. 852–859)

LO5 **Prepare a process cost report using the average costing method.** (pp. 859–863)

DECISION POINT ▸ A MANAGER'S FOCUS DEAN FOODS

Dean Foods is the largest milk processor and distributor of milk and other dairy products in the United States. Its products are made in over 100 plants under such popular brands as Meadow Gold, Land of Lakes, Pet, Garelick Farms, Silk, and Horizon Organic. In this chapter we explain why a company like Dean Foods should use a process costing system to provide managers with relevant information. To learn more about Dean Foods go to http://www.deanfoods.com

- ▸ Why is a process costing system appropriate for Dean Foods?
- ▸ How does a process costing system facilitate management decisions?

The Process Costing System

LO1 Describe the process costing system, and identify the reasons for its use.

Study Note

In process costing, costs are traced to production processes, whereas in job order costing, costs are traced to jobs.

As we noted earlier, a **process costing system** is a product costing system used by companies that make large amounts of similar products or liquid products or that have long, continuous production runs of identical products. Companies that produce paint, beverages, chocolate syrup, computer chips, milk, paper, and gallon containers of ice cream are typical users of a process costing system.

Since one gallon of chocolate ice cream is identical to the next gallon, they should cost the same amount to produce. A process costing system first accumulates the costs of direct materials, direct labor, and overhead for each process, department, or work cell and then assigns those costs to the products produced during a particular period.

Managers use process costing in every stage of the management process:

- When managers plan, they use information about past and projected product costing and customer preferences to decide what a product should cost. After they have determined a target number of units to be sold, all product-related costs for that targeted number of units can be computed and used in the budget.
- During the period, managers track product and cost flows through their departments or processes and prepare process cost reports to assign production costs to the products manufactured.
- When managers evaluate performance, they compare targeted costs with actual costs. If costs have exceeded expectations, managers analyze why this has occurred and adjust their planning and decision-making strategies.
- When managers communicate with external stakeholders, they use actual units produced and costs incurred to value inventory on the balance sheet and cost of goods sold on the income statement. Managers are also interested in internal reports on whether goals for product costs are being achieved.

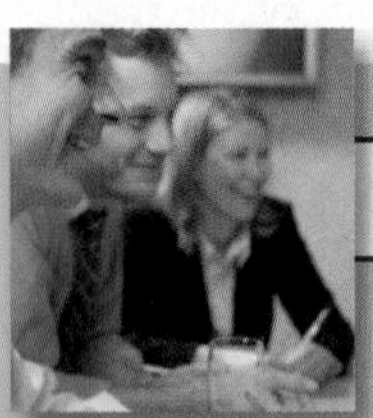

FOCUS ON BUSINESS PRACTICE

What Kinds of Companies Use Process Costing?

Process costing is appropriate for companies in many types of industries. The following list provides some examples:

Industry	*Company*	*Industry*	*Company*
Aluminum	**Alcoa, Inc.**	Foods	**Kellogg Company**
Beverages	**Coors**	Machinery	**Caterpillar Inc.**
Building materials	**Owens Corning**	Oil and gas	**ExxonMobil**
Chemicals	**Dow Chemicals**	Plastic products	**Tupperware**
Computers	**Apple Computer**	Soft drinks	**Coca-Cola**

STOP & APPLY >

Indicate whether the manufacturer of each of the following products should use a job order costing system or a process costing system to accumulate product costs:

a. Milk bottles
b. Chocolate milk
c. Nuclear submarines
d. Generic drugs

SOLUTION

a. Process; b. Process; c. Job order; d. Process

Patterns of Product Flows and Cost Flow Methods

LO2 Relate the patterns of product flows to the cost flow methods in a process costing environment, and explain the role of the Work in Process Inventory accounts.

During production in a process costing environment, products flow in a first-in, first-out (FIFO) fashion through several processes, departments, or work cells, and they may undergo many different combinations of operations. Figure 18-1 illustrates a simple linear production flow; it shows how milk is produced in a series of three processing steps, or departments. Each department has its own Work in Process Inventory account to accumulate the direct material, direct labor, and overhead costs associated with it.

- Homogenization department: Raw milk from the cow must be mixed to evenly distribute the butterfat. The homogenized milk and its associated cost then become the direct materials for the next department.
- Pasteurization department: The homogenized milk is heated to 145 degrees to kill the bacteria found in raw milk. The homogenized, pasteurized milk and all associated costs are then transferred to the packaging department.

FIGURE 18-1 Product Flows in a Process Costing Environment

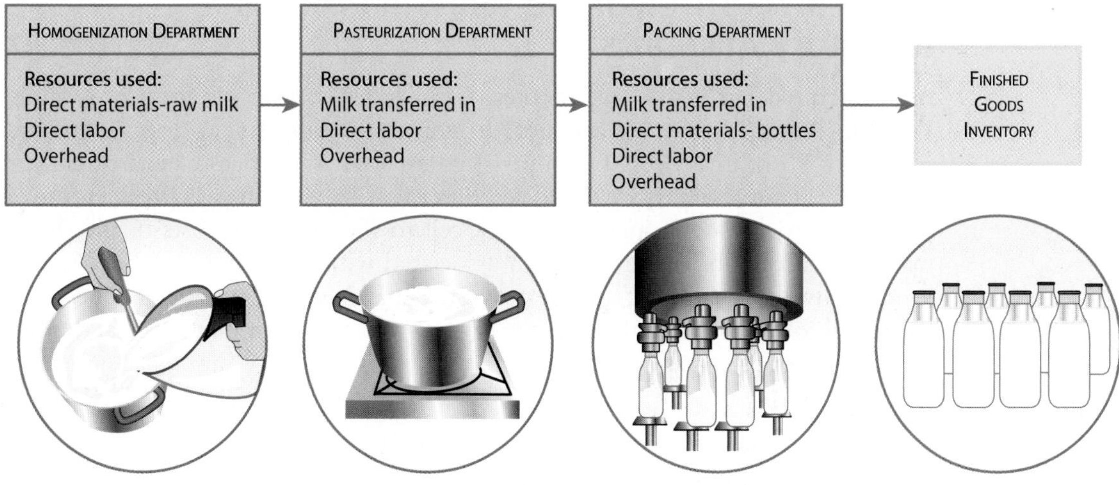

- Packaging department: The milk is put into bottles and transferred to Finished Goods Inventory since it is now ready for sale.

The product unit cost of a bottle of milk is the sum of the cost elements in all three departments.

Process costing environments can be more or less complex than the one we have just described, but even in simple process costing environments, production generally involves a number of separate manufacturing processes, departments, or work cells. For example, the separate processes involved in manufacturing cookies include the mixing department, the baking department, and the packaging department.

As products pass through each manufacturing process, department, or work cell, the process costing system accumulates their costs and passes them on to the next process, department, or work cell. At the end of every accounting period, each manufacturing process, department, or work cell generates a report that assigns the costs that have accumulated during the period to the units that have transferred out of it and to the units that are still a part of its work in process. Managers use this report, called a **process cost report**, to assign costs by using a cost allocation method, such as the FIFO (first-in, first-out) costing method or the average costing method.

- In the **FIFO costing method**, the cost flow follows the logical physical flow of production—that is, the costs assigned to the first materials processed are the first costs transferred out when those materials flow to the next process, department, or work cell. Thus, in Figure 18-1, the costs assigned to the homogenized milk would be the first costs transferred to the pasteurization department.
- In contrast, the **average costing method** assigns an average cost to all products made during an accounting period; this method thus uses total cost averages and does not try to match cost flow with the physical flow of production.

We discuss process cost reports that use the FIFO and average costing methods later in this chapter.

Cost Flows Through the Work in Process Inventory Accounts

As we pointed out in the last chapter, a job order costing system uses a single Work in Process Inventory account. In contrast, a process costing system has a separate Work in Process Inventory account for each process, department, or work cell. These accounts are the focal point of process costing. As products move from one process, department, or work cell to the next, the costs of the direct materials, direct labor, and overhead associated with them flow to the Work in Process Inventory account of that process, department, or work cell. The entry in journal form to record the transfer of product costs from one process, department, or work cell to another is:

	Dr.	Cr.
Work in Process Inventory (next department)	XX	
Work in Process Inventory (this department)		XX

Once the products are completed, packaged, and ready for sale, their costs are transferred to the Finished Goods Inventory account. The entry in journal form to record the transfer of the completed product costs out of Work in Process Inventory into Finished Goods Inventory is:

	Dr.	Cr.
Finished Goods Inventory	XX	
Work in Process Inventory (last department)		XX

As you will learn later in this chapter, the costs associated with these entries are calculated in a process cost report for the process, department, or work cell.

STOP & APPLY >

Milk Smoothies, Inc., uses an automated mixing machine in its Mixing Department to combine three raw materials into a product called Strawberry Smoothie Mix. Total costs charged to the Mixing Department's Work in Process Inventory account during the month were $210,000. There were no units in beginning or ending work in process inventory. What is the entry in journal form to transfer the units completed to Finished Goods Inventory?

SOLUTION

Finished Goods Inventory	210,000	
Work in Process Inventory (Mixing Department)		210,000

Computing Equivalent Production

LO3 Define *equivalent production,* and compute equivalent units.

A process costing system makes no attempt to associate costs with particular job orders. Instead, it assigns the costs incurred in a process, department, or work cell to the units worked on during an accounting period by computing an average cost per unit of effort. To compute the unit cost, the total cost of direct materials, direct labor, and overhead is divided by the total number of units worked on during the period. Thus, exactly how many units were worked on during the period is a critical question. Do we count only units started and completed during the period? Or should we include partially completed units in the beginning work in process inventory? And what about incomplete products in the ending work in process inventory?

These questions relate to the concept of equivalent production. **Equivalent production** (also called *equivalent units*) is a measure that applies a percentage-of-completion factor to partially completed units to calculate the equivalent number of whole units produced during a period for each type of input (i.e., direct materials, direct labor, and overhead).

- The number of equivalent units produced is the sum of (1) total units started and completed during the period and (2) an amount representing the work done on partially completed products in both the beginning and the ending work in process inventories.

FIGURE 18-2 Computation of Equivalent Production

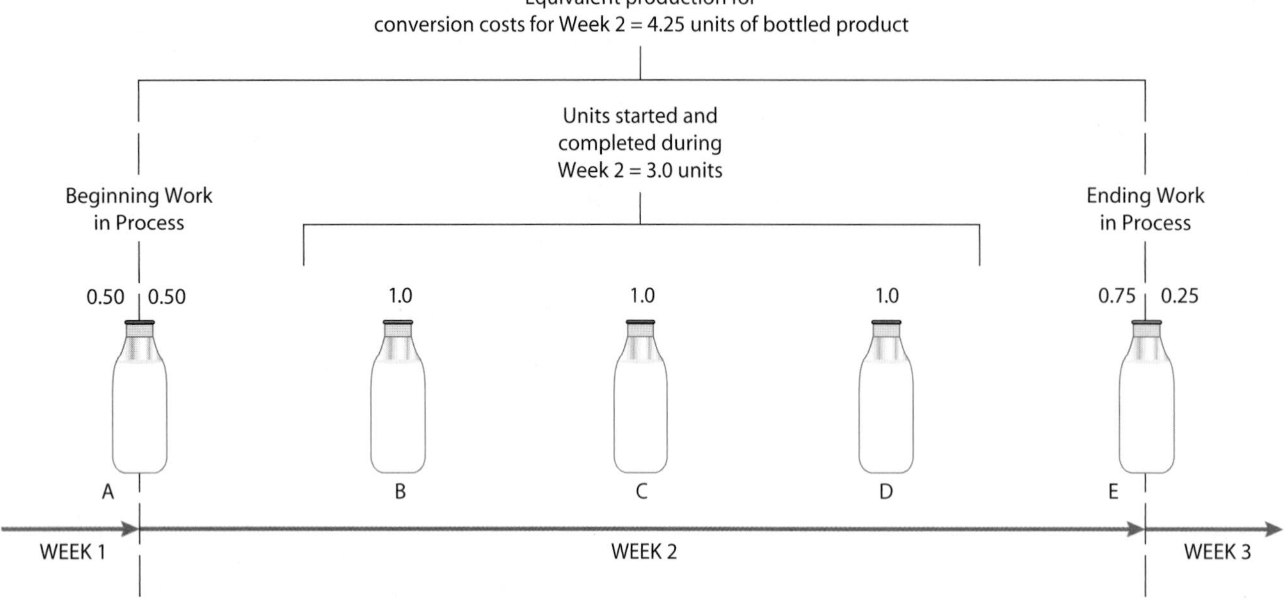

Note: Conversion costs (the cost of direct labor and overhead) are incurred uniformly as each physical unit of drink moves through production. Equivalent production for Week 2 is 4.25 units for conversion costs. But direct materials costs are all added to production at the beginning of the process. Because four physical units of drinks entered production in Week 2, equivalent production for the week is 4.0 units of effort for direct materials costs.

> **Study Note**
> Direct materials are sometimes added at stages of production other than the beginning (e.g., chocolate chips are added to batter at the end of the mixing process).

Equivalent production must be computed separately for each type of input because of differences in the ways in which costs are incurred.

- Direct materials are usually added to production at the beginning of the process.
- The costs of direct labor and overhead are often incurred uniformly throughout the production process. Thus, it is convenient to combine direct labor and overhead when calculating equivalent units. These combined costs are called **conversion costs** (also called *processing costs*).

We will explain the computation of equivalent production by using a simplified example. One of the products Milk Products Company makes is a pint-sized, bottled milk drink. As illustrated in Figure 18-2, the company started Week 2 with one half-completed drink in process. During Week 2, it started and completed three drinks, and at the end of Week 2, it had one drink that was three-quarters completed.

Equivalent Production for Direct Materials

At Milk Products, all direct materials, including liquids and bottles, are added at the beginning of production. Thus, the drink that was half-completed at the beginning of Week 2 had had all its direct materials added during the previous week.

- No direct materials costs for this drink are included in the computation of Week 2's equivalent units for the beginning inventory units.

> **Study Note**
> The number of units started and completed is not the same as the total number of units completed during the period. Total units completed include both units in beginning work in process inventory that were completed and units started and completed.

During Week 2, work began on four new drinks—the three drinks that were completed and the drink that was three-quarters completed at week's end. Because all direct materials are added at the beginning of the production process, all four drinks were 100 percent complete with regard to direct materials at the end of Week 2.

- Thus, for Week 2, the equivalent production for direct materials was 4.0 units. This figure includes direct materials for both the 3.0 units that were started and completed and the 1.0 unit that was three-quarters completed.

Equivalent Production for Conversion Costs

> **Study Note**
> Work in the current period is applied to three distinct product groups: units in beginning work in process inventory, which must be completed; goods started and completed during the period; and goods started but not completed by the end of the accounting period.

Because conversion costs at Milk Products are incurred uniformly throughout the production process, the equivalent production for conversion costs during Week 2 consists of three components: the cost to finish the half-completed unit in beginning work in process inventory (0.50), the cost to begin and finish three completed units (3.0), and the cost to begin work on the three-quarters-completed unit in ending work in process inventory (0.75).

▶ For Week 2, the total equivalent production for conversion costs was 4.25 units (0.50 of beginning inventory + 3.0 of units started and completed + 0.75 of ending inventory).

In reality, Milk Products would make many more drinks during an accounting period and would have many more partially completed drinks in its beginning and ending work in process inventories. The number of partially completed drinks would be so great that it would be impractical to take a physical count of them. So, instead of taking a physical count, Milk Products would estimate an average percentage of completion for all drinks in process.

Summary of Equivalent Production

The following is a recap of the current equivalent production for direct materials and conversion costs for the period for Milk Products:

	Physical Units	Equivalent Units of Effort: Direct Materials		Equivalent Units of Effort: Conversion Costs	
Beginning inventory	1.00				
Units started this period	4.00				
Units to be accounted for	5.00				
Beginning inventory	1.00	—	0%	0.50	50%
Units started and completed	3.00	3.00	100%	3.00	100%
Ending inventory	1.00	1.00	100%	0.75	75%
Units accounted for	5.00	4.00		4.25	

STOP & APPLY >

Milk Smoothies, Inc., adds direct materials at the start of the production process and adds conversion costs uniformly throughout this process. Given the following information from Milk Smoothie's records for July, compute the current period's equivalent units of production:

Units in beginning inventory: 2,000
Units started during the period: 13,000
Units partially completed: 500
Percentage of completion of beginning inventory: 100% for direct materials; 40% for conversion costs
Percentage of completion of ending work in process inventory: 100% for direct materials; 70% for conversion costs.

(continued)

SOLUTION

Milk Smoothies, Inc.
For the Month Ended July 31

	Physical Units	Equivalent Units of Effort			
		Direct Materials		Conversion Costs	
Beginning inventory	2,000				
Units started this period	13,000				
Units to be accounted for	15,000				
Beginning inventory	2,000	—	0%	1,200	60%
Units started and completed	12,500	12,500	100%	12,500	100%
Ending inventory	500	500	100%	350	70%
Units accounted for	15,000	13,000		14,050	

Preparing a Process Cost Report Using the FIFO Costing Method

LO4 Prepare a process cost report using the FIFO costing method.

Study Note

The FIFO method focuses on the work done in the current period only.

As we mentioned earlier, a process cost report, such as the one shown in Exhibit 18-1, is a report that managers use to track and analyze costs for a process, department, or work cell in a process costing system. In a process cost report that uses the FIFO costing method, the cost flow follows the logical physical flow of production—that is, the costs assigned to the first products processed are the first costs transferred out when those products flow to the next process, department, or work cell.

As illustrated in Exhibit 18-1, the preparation of a process cost report involves five steps. The first two steps account for the units of product being processed:

Step 1. ***Account for physical units.***

Step 2. ***Account for equivalent units of effort.***

The next two steps account for the costs of the direct materials, direct labor, and overhead being incurred:

Step 3. ***Account for the costs incurred.***

Step 4. ***Compute the cost per equivalent unit.***

The final step assigns costs to products being transferred out of the area and to those remaining behind in ending work in process inventory:

Step 5. ***Assign costs to cost of goods manufactured and ending inventory.***

Accounting for Units

Managers must account for the physical flow of products through their areas (Step 1) before they can compute equivalent production for the accounting period (Step 2). To continue with the Milk Products example, assume the following facts for the accounting period of February:

- The beginning work in process inventory consists of 6,200 partially completed units (60 percent processed in the previous period).
- During the period, the 6,200 units in beginning inventory were completed, and 57,500 units were started into production.

EXHIBIT 18-1 Process Cost Report: FIFO Costing Method

Step 1: *Account for physical units.*

Beginning inventory (units started last period)	6,200
Units started this period	57,500
Units to be accounted for	63,700

Step 2: *Account for equivalent units.*

	Physical Units	Direct Materials	% Incurred During Period	Conversion Costs	% Incurred During Period
		Current Equivalent Units of Effort			
Beginning inventory (units completed this period)	6,200	—	0%	2,480	40%
Units started and completed this period	52,500	52,500	100%	52,500	100%
Ending inventory (units started but not completed this period)	5,000	5,000	100%	2,250	45%
Units accounted for	63,700	57,500		57,230	

Step 3: *Account for costs.*

	Total Costs		Direct Materials		Conversion Costs
Beginning inventory	$ 41,540	=	$ 20,150	+	$ 21,390
Current costs	510,238	=	189,750	+	320,488
Total costs	$551,778				

Step 4: *Compute cost per equivalent unit.*

			Direct Materials		Conversion Costs
Current Costs / Equivalent Units			$189,750 / 57,500		$320,488 / 57,230
Cost per equivalent unit	$8.90	=	$3.30	+	$5.60

Step 5: *Assign costs to cost of goods manufactured and ending inventory.*

Cost of goods manufactured and transferred out:					
From beginning inventory	$ 41,540				
Current costs to complete	13,888	=	$0	+	(2,480 × $5.60)
Units started and completed this period	467,250	=	(52,500 × $3.30)	+	(52,500 × $5.60)
Cost of goods manufactured	$522,678		*(No rounding necessary)*		
Ending inventory	29,100	=	(5,000 × $3.30)	+	(2,250 × $5.60)
Total costs	$551,778				

WORK IN PROCESS INVENTORY ACCOUNT: COST RECAP

Beg. Bal.	41,540	522,678 (Cost of goods manufactured and transferred out)
Direct materials	189,750	
Conversion costs	320,488	
End. Bal.	**29,100**	

WORK IN PROCESS INVENTORY ACCOUNT: UNIT RECAP

Beg. Bal.	6,200	58,700 (FIFO units transferred out from the 6,200 in beginning inventory plus the 52,500 started and completed)
Units started	57,500	
End. Bal.	**5,000**	

- Of the 57,500 units started during the period, 52,500 units were completed. The other 5,000 units remain in ending work in process inventory and are 45 percent complete.

Step 1. In Step 1 of Exhibit 18-1, Milk Products' department manager computes the total units to be accounted for by adding the 6,200 units in beginning inventory to the 57,500 units started into production during this period. These 63,700 units are the actual physical units that the manager is responsible for during the period.

Step 1 continues accounting for physical units. As shown in Exhibit 18-1, the 6,200 units in beginning inventory that were completed during the period, the 52,500 units that were started and finished in the period, and the 5,000 units remaining in the department at the end of the period are summed, and the total is listed as "units accounted for." (Note that the "units accounted for" must equal the "units to be accounted for" in Step 1.)

Study Note

The percentage of completion for beginning work in process inventory is the amount of work completed during the previous period. Under FIFO, the amount of effort required to complete beginning work in process inventory is the relevant percentage.

Step 2. The units accounted for in Step 1 are used to compute equivalent production for the department's direct materials and conversion costs for the month, as described below.

- ***Beginning Inventory*** Because all direct materials are added at the beginning of the production process, the 6,200 partially completed units that began February as work in process were already 100 percent complete in regard to direct materials. They were 60 percent complete in regard to conversion costs on February 1. The remaining 40 percent of their conversion costs were incurred as they were completed during the month. Thus, as shown in the "Conversion Costs" column of Exhibit 18-1, the equivalent production for their conversion costs is 2,480 units (6,200 × 40%).

Study Note

Units in beginning work in process inventory represent work accomplished in the previous accounting period that has already been assigned a certain portion of its total cost. Those units must be completed in the current period, incurring additional costs.

- ***Units Started and Completed During the Period*** All the costs of the 52,500 units started and completed during February were incurred during this accounting period. Thus, the full amount of 52,500 is entered as the equivalent units for both direct materials costs and conversion costs.

- ***Ending Inventory*** Because the materials for the 5,000 drinks still in process at the end of February were added when the drinks went into production during the month, the full amount of 5,000 is entered as the equivalent units for direct materials costs. However, these drinks are only 45 percent complete in terms of conversion costs. Thus, as shown in the "Conversion Costs" column of Exhibit 18-1, the equivalent production for their conversion costs is 2,250 units (5,000 × 45%).

- ***Totals*** Step 2 is completed by summing all the physical units to be accounted for, all equivalent units for direct materials costs, and all equivalent units for conversion costs. Exhibit 18-1 shows that for February, Milk Products accounted for 63,700 units. Equivalent units for direct materials costs totaled 57,500, and equivalent units for conversion costs totaled 57,230. Once Milk Products knows February's equivalent unit amounts, it can complete the remaining three steps in the preparation of a process cost report.

Accounting for Costs

Thus far, we have focused on accounting for units of productive output—in our example, bottled milk drinks. We now turn our focus to cost information.

- Step 3 in preparing a process cost report involves accumulating and analyzing all costs charged to the Work in Process Inventory account of each production process, department, or work cell.
- In Step 4, the cost per equivalent unit for direct materials costs and conversion costs is computed.

The following information about Milk Products' manufacture of drinks during February enables us to complete Steps 3 and 4:

Work in Process Inventory		
Costs from beginning inventory:		
Direct materials costs	20,150	
Conversion costs	21,390	
Current period costs:		
Direct materials costs	189,750	
Conversion costs	320,488	

Step 3. As shown in Exhibit 18-1, all costs for the period are accumulated in the Total Costs column. Beginning inventory's direct materials costs of \$20,150 are added to its conversion costs of \$21,390 to determine the total cost of beginning inventory (\$41,540). Current period costs for direct materials (\$189,750) are added to conversion costs (\$320,488) to determine the total current manufacturing costs (\$510,238). The grand total of \$551,778 is the sum of beginning inventory costs (\$41,540) and current period costs (\$510,238). Notice that only the Total Costs column is totaled. Because only the current period costs for direct materials and conversion are used in Step 4, there is no need to find the total costs of the direct materials and conversion costs columns in Step 3.

Step 4. The direct materials costs and conversion costs for the current period are divided by their respective units of equivalent production to arrive at the cost per equivalent unit. Prior period costs attached to units in beginning inventory are not included in these computations because the FIFO costing method uses a separate costing analysis for each accounting period. (The FIFO method treats the costs of beginning inventory separately, in Step 5.) Exhibit 18-1 shows that the total current cost of \$8.90 per equivalent unit consists of \$3.30 per equivalent unit for direct materials costs (\$189,750 ÷ 57,500 equivalent units) plus \$5.60 per equivalent unit for conversion costs (\$320,488 ÷ 57,230 equivalent units). (Note that the equivalent units are taken from Step 2 of Exhibit 18-1.)

Study Note

The cost per equivalent unit using the FIFO method measures the current cost divided by current effort. Notice in Exhibit 18-1 that the cost of beginning work in process inventory is omitted.

Assigning Costs

Step 5. Step 5 in the preparation of a process costing report uses information from Steps 2 and 4 to assign costs, as shown in Exhibit 18-1. This final step determines the costs that are transferred out either to the next production process, department, or work cell or to the Finished Goods Inventory account (i.e., the cost of goods manufactured), as well as the costs that remain in the ending balance in the Work in Process Inventory account. The total costs assigned to units completed and transferred out and to ending inventory must equal the total costs in Step 3.

> **Study Note**
> The process cost report is developed for the purpose of assigning a value to one transaction: the transfer of goods from one department to another or to finished goods inventory. The ending balance in the Work in Process Inventory account represents the costs that remain after this transfer.

- ***Cost of Goods Manufactured and Transferred Out*** Step 5 in Exhibit 18-1 shows that the costs transferred to the Finished Goods Inventory account include the $41,540 in direct materials and conversion costs for completing the 6,200 units in beginning inventory. Step 2 in the exhibit shows that 2,480 equivalent units of conversion costs were required to complete these 6,200 units. Because the equivalent unit conversion cost for February is $5.60, the cost to complete the units carried over from January is $13,888 (2,480 units × $5.60).

Each of the 52,500 units started and completed in February cost $8.90 to produce. Their combined cost of $467,250 is added to the $41,540 and $13,888 of costs required to produce the 6,200 units from beginning inventory to arrive at the total of $522,678 that is transferred to the Finished Goods Inventory account. The entry resulting from doing the process cost report for February is:

	Dr.	Cr.
Finished Goods Inventory	522,678	
Work in Process Inventory		522,678

> **Study Note**
> All costs must be accounted for, including both costs from beginning inventory and costs incurred during the current period. All costs must be assigned to either ending inventory or the goods transferred out.

- ***Ending Inventory*** All costs remaining in Milk Products Company's Work in Process Inventory account after the cost of goods manufactured has been transferred out represent the costs of the drinks still in production at the end of February. As shown in Step 5 of Exhibit 18-1, the balance of $29,100 in the ending Work in Process Inventory is made up of $16,500 of direct materials costs (5,000 units × $3.30 per unit) and $12,600 of conversion costs (2,250 × $5.60 per unit).

> **Study Note**
> Rounding product unit costs to even dollars may lead to a significant difference in total costs, giving the impression that costs have been miscalculated. Carry product unit costs to two decimal places where appropriate.

Rounding Differences As you perform Step 5 in any process cost report, remember that the total costs in Steps 3 and 5 must always be the same number. In Exhibit 18-1, for example, they are both $551,778.

- If the total costs in Steps 3 and 5 are not the same, first check for omission of any costs and for calculation errors.
- If that does not solve the problem, check whether any rounding was necessary in computing the costs per equivalent unit in Step 4. If rounding was done in Step 4, rounding differences will occur when assigning costs in Step 5. In that case, adjust the total costs transferred out for any rounding difference so that the total costs in Step 5 equal the total costs in Step 3.

Recap of Work in Process Inventory Account When the process cost report is complete, an account recap may be prepared to show the effects of the report on the Work in Process Inventory account for the period. Two recaps of Milk Products' Work in Process Inventory account for February—one for costs and one for units—appear at the bottom of Exhibit 18-1.

Process Costing for Two or More Production Departments

In our example, Milk Products Company has only one production department for making milk drinks, so it needs only one Work in Process Inventory account. However, a company that has more than one production process or department to make various products must have a Work in Process Inventory account for each process or department.

For instance, when processing raw milk, a milk producer like **Dean Foods**, has a production department for homogenization, another for pasteurization, and another for packaging needs, which requires three Work in Process Inventory accounts.

- When products flow from the Homogenization Department to the Pasteurization Department, their costs flow from the Homogenization Department's Work in Process Inventory account to the Pasteurization Department's Work in Process Inventory account.
- The costs transferred into the Pasteurization Department's Work in Process Inventory account are treated in the same way as the cost of direct materials added at the beginning of the production process.
- When production flows to the Packaging Department, the accumulated costs (incurred in the two previous departments) are transferred to that department's Work in Process Inventory account.
- At the end of the accounting period, a separate process cost report is prepared for each department.

Pop Chewing Gum Company produces bubble gum. Direct materials are blended at the beginning of the manufacturing process. No materials are lost in the process, so one kilogram of materials input produces one kilogram of bubble gum. Direct labor and overhead costs are incurred uniformly throughout the blending process.

- On June 30, 16,000 units were in process. All direct materials had been added, but the units were only 70 percent complete in regard to conversion costs. Direct materials costs of $8,100 and conversion costs of $11,800 were attached to the beginning inventory.
- During July, 405,000 kilograms of materials were used at a cost of $202,500. Direct labor charges were $299,200, and overhead costs applied during July were $284,000.
- The ending work in process inventory was 21,600 kilograms. All direct materials have been added to those units, and 25 percent of the conversion costs have been assigned. Output from the Blending Department is transferred to the Packaging Department.

Required

1. Prepare a process cost report using the FIFO costing method for the Blending Department for July.
2. Identify the amount that should be transferred out of the Work in Process Inventory account, and state where those dollars should be transferred. What is the entry in journal form?

(continued)

SOLUTION

1. FIFO Process Cost Report for the Blending Department for July:

Pop Chewing Gum Company
Blending Department
Process Cost Report: FIFO Method
For the Month Ended July 31

Step 1: *Account for physical units.*

Beginning inventory (units started last period)	16,000
Units started this period	405,000
Units to be accounted for	421,000

Step 2: *Account for equivalent units.*

		Current Equivalent Units of Effort			
	Physical Units	**Direct Materials**	**% Incurred During Period**	**Conversion Costs**	**% Incurred During Period**
Beginning inventory (units completed this period)	16,000	—	0%	4,800	30%
Units started and completed this period	383,400	383,400	100%	383,400	100%
Ending inventory (units started but not completed this period)	21,600	21,600	100%	5,400	25%
Units accounted for	421,000	405,000		393,600	

Step 3: *Account for costs.*

	Total Costs				
Beginning inventory	$ 19,900	=	$ 8,100	+	$ 11,800
Current costs	785,700	=	202,500	+	583,200
Total costs	$805,600				

Step 4: *Compute cost per equivalent unit.*

Current Costs / Equivalent Units			$202,500 / 405,000		$583,200 / 393,600
Cost per equivalent unit	$1.98	=	$0.50	+	$1.48*

**Rounded to nearest cent.*

Step 5: *Assign costs to cost of goods manufactured and ending inventory.*

Cost of goods manufactured and transferred out:			
From beginning inventory	$ 19,900		
Current costs to complete	7,104	=	$0 + (4,800 × $1.48)
Units started and completed this period	759,132	=	(383,400 × $0.50) + (383,400 × $1.48)
Cost of goods manufactured	$786,808		*[Cost of goods manufactured must be $786,808 (add rounding of $672) since Total costs = Ending inventory + Cost of goods manufactured]*
Ending inventory	18,792	=	(21,600 × $0.50) + (5,400 × $1.48)
Total costs	$805,600		

WORK IN PROCESS INVENTORY ACCOUNT: COST RECAP

Beg. Bal.	19,900	786,808 (Cost of goods manufactured and transferred out)
Direct materials	202,500	
Conversion costs	583,200	
End. Bal.	**18,792**	

WORK IN PROCESS INVENTORY ACCOUNT: UNIT RECAP

Beg. Bal.	16,000	399,400 (FIFO units transferred out from the 16,000 in beginning inventory plus the 383,400 started and completed)
Units started	405,000	
End. Bal.	**21,600**	

(continued)

2. The amount of $786,808 should be transferred to the Work in Process Inventory account of the Packaging Department. The entry in journal form is:

Work in Process Inventory (Packaging Department)	786,808	
Work in Process Inventory (Blending Department)		786,808

Preparing a Process Cost Report Using the Average Costing Method

LO5 Prepare a process cost report using the average costing method.

When a process cost report uses the average costing method, cost flows do not follow the logical physical flow of production as they do when the FIFO method is used. Instead, the costs in beginning inventory are combined with current period costs to compute an average product unit cost. Preparing a process cost report using the average costing method involves the same five steps as preparing one using the FIFO method, but the procedures for completing the steps differ.

We now return to the example of Milk Products Company making milk drinks, but this time we assume that Milk Products uses the average costing method of process costing.

Accounting for Units

Step 1. Step 1 of a process cost report, which accounts for the physical units in a production process, department, or work cell during an accounting period, is identical for the average costing and FIFO costing methods. The physical units in beginning inventory are added to the physical units started during the period to arrive at "units to be accounted for." In Step 1 of Exhibit 18-2, Milk Products' department manager computes the 63,700 total units to be accounted for by adding the 6,200 units in beginning inventory to the 57,500 units started into production in this period.

Step 2. Step 2 also accounts for production during the period in terms of units. After the number of units completed and transferred to finished goods inventory and the number of units in ending inventory have been added to arrive at "units accounted for," the equivalent units in terms of direct materials costs and conversion costs are computed, as described below.

- ***Units Completed and Transferred Out*** As you can see in Exhibit 18-2, the average costing method treats both the direct materials costs and the conversion costs of the 58,700 units completed in February (6,200 units from beginning inventory + 52,500 started this period) as if they were incurred in the current period. Thus, the full amount of 58,700 is entered as the equivalent units for these costs. In contrast, as shown in Exhibit 18-1, the FIFO costing method disregards the previous period costs of units started in the last period and calculates only the equivalent units required in the current period to complete the units in beginning inventory.
- ***Ending Inventory*** The average costing method treats ending inventory in exactly the same way as the FIFO costing method. Because all direct materials are added at the beginning of the production process, the full amount of 5,000 is entered as the equivalent units for direct materials cost. Because the 5,000 units in ending inventory are only 45 percent complete in terms of conversion costs, the amount of equivalent units is 2,250 (5,000 × 45%).

EXHIBIT 18-2 Process Cost Report: Average Costing Method

Step 1: *Account for physical units.*

	Physical Units
Beginning inventory (units started last period)	6,200
Units started this period	57,500
Units to be accounted for	63,700

Step 2: *Account for equivalent units.*

	Physical Units	Total Equivalent Units of Effort: Direct Materials	% Incurred During Period	Conversion Costs	% Incurred During Period
Units completed and transferred out	58,700	58,700	100%	58,700	100%
Ending inventory (units started but not completed this period)	5,000	5,000	100%	2,250	45%
Units accounted for	63,700	63,700		60,950	

Step 3: *Account for costs.*

	Total Costs		Direct Materials		Conversion Costs
Beginning inventory	$ 41,540	=	$ 20,150	+	$ 21,390
Current costs	510,238	=	189,750	+	320,488
Total costs	$551,778		$209,900		$341,878

Step 4: *Compute cost per equivalent unit.*

	Total Costs		Direct Materials		Conversion Costs
Total Costs / Equivalent Units			$209,900 / 63,700		$341,878 / 60,950
Cost per equivalent unit	$8.91	=	$3.30*	+	$5.61*
			Rounded to nearest cent.		*Rounded to nearest cent.*

Step 5: *Assign costs to cost of goods manufactured and ending*

Cost of goods manufactured and transferred out: $522,655 = (58,700 × $3.30) + (58,700 × $5.61)

[Cost of goods manufactured must be $522,655 (less rounding of $362)] since Total costs = Ending inventory + Cost of Goods Manufactured)

Ending inventory: 29,123* = (5,000 × $3.30) + (2,250 × $5.61)

Rounded.

Total costs: $551,778

Work in Process Inventory Account: Cost Recap

Beg. Bal.	41,540	522,655 (Cost of goods manufactured and transferred out)
Direct materials	189,750	
Conversion costs	320,488	
End. Bal.	**29,123**	

Work in Process Inventory Account: Unit Recap

Beg. Bal.	6,200	58,700 (Units transferred out)
Units started	57,500	
End. Bal.	**5,000**	

- ***Totals*** Whether the FIFO costing method or the average costing method is used, Step 2 in a process cost report is completed by summing all the physical units to be accounted for, all equivalent units for direct materials costs, and all equivalent units for conversion costs. Exhibit 18-2 shows that for the month of February, Milk Products accounted for 63,700 physical units. Equivalent units for direct materials costs totaled 63,700, and equivalent units for conversion costs totaled 60,950.

Accounting for Costs

As we noted in our discussion of process cost reports that use the FIFO method, Step 3 of the report accumulates and analyzes all costs in the Work in Process Inventory account, and Step 4 computes the cost per equivalent unit for direct materials costs and conversion costs. You may recall from the discussion that the costs of Milk Products' beginning inventory were $20,150 for direct materials and $21,390 for conversion. Current period costs were $189,750 for direct materials and $320,488 for conversion.

Step 3. If you compare Exhibit 18-2 with Exhibit 18-1, you will see that the average costing and FIFO costing methods deal with Step 3 in the same manner. All direct materials costs and conversion costs for beginning inventory and the current period are accumulated in the Total Costs column. The total of $551,778 consists of $209,900 in direct materials costs and $341,878 in conversion costs.

Step 4. Step 4 computes the cost per equivalent unit for direct materials costs and conversion costs by dividing the total of these costs by their respective equivalent units. The $8.91 total cost per equivalent unit consists of $3.30 per equivalent unit for direct materials ($209,900 ÷ 63,700 equivalent units) plus $5.61 per equivalent unit for conversion ($341,878 ÷ 60,950 equivalent units).

- Notice that the cost per equivalent unit for both direct materials and conversion costs has been rounded to the nearest cent. In this text, any rounding differences are assigned to the units transferred out in Step 5.

- Notice also that the average costing and FIFO costing methods use different numerators and denominators in Step 4. Average costing divides *total* cost by *total* equivalent units, whereas FIFO divides *current* costs by *current* equivalent units.

Assigning Costs

Step 5. Using information from Steps 2 and 4, Step 5 of a process cost report assigns direct materials and conversion costs to the units transferred out and to the units still in process at the end of the period. As noted above, any rounding issues that arise in completing Step 5 are included in units completed and transferred out. Milk Products completes Step 5 as described next.

- ***Cost of Goods Manufactured and Transferred Out*** As shown in Exhibit 18-2, the costs of the units completed and transferred out are assigned by multiplying the equivalent units for direct materials and conversion costs (accounted for in Step 2) by their respective cost per equivalent unit (computed in Step 4) and then totaling these assigned values. Thus, the $522,655 assigned to cost of goods manufactured and transferred out includes $193,710 of direct materials costs (58,700 equivalent units × $3.30 cost per equivalent unit) plus $329,307 of conversion costs (58,700 equivalent units × $5.61 cost per equivalent unit). In this case, because the costs per equivalent unit were rounded in Step 4, a rounding difference of $362 has been deducted from the total cost. The $522,655 of transferred costs will go to the Finished Goods Inventory account, since the goods are ready for sale. The entry in journal form resulting from doing the process cost report for February is:

	Dr.	Cr.
Finished Goods Inventory	522,655	
Work in Process Inventory		522,655

- ***Ending Inventory*** The costs of the units in ending work in process inventory are assigned in the same way as the costs of cost of goods manufactured and transferred out. As you can see in Exhibit 18-2, the total of $29,123 assigned to ending inventory includes $16,500 of direct materials costs (5,000 equivalent units × $3.30 cost per equivalent unit) plus $12,623 (rounded) of conversion costs (2,250 equivalent units × $5.61 cost per equivalent unit). The $29,123 will appear as the ending balance in this department's Work in Process Inventory account.

Recap of Work in Process Inventory Account As we noted earlier, when a process cost report is complete, an account recap may be prepared to show the effects of the report on the Work in Process Inventory account for the period. Exhibit 18-2 includes a cost recap and a unit recap of Milk Products' Work in rocess Inventory account for February.

& APPLY >

Pop Chewing Gum Company produces bubble gum. Direct materials are blended at the beginning of the manufacturing process. No materials are lost in the process, so one kilogram of materials input produces one kilogram of bubble gum. Direct labor and overhead costs are incurred uniformly throughout the blending process.

- On June 30, 16,000 units were in process. All direct materials had been added, but the units were only 70 percent complete in regard to conversion costs. Direct materials costs of $8,100 and conversion costs of $11,800 were attached to the beginning inventory.
- During July, 405,000 kilograms of materials were used at a cost of $202,500. Direct labor charges were $299,200, and overhead costs applied during July were $284,000.
- The ending work in process inventory was 21,600 kilograms. All direct materials have been added to those units, and 25 percent of the conversion costs have been assigned. Output from the Blending Department is transferred to the Packaging Department.

Required

1. Prepare a process cost report using the average costing method for the Blending Department for July.
2. Identify the amount that should be transferred out of the Work in Process Inventory account, and state where those dollars should be transferred. What is the entry in journal form?

(continued)

SOLUTION

1. Average Costing Process Cost Report–Blending Department for July:

Pop Chewing Gum Company
Blending Department
Process Cost Report: Average Costing Method
For the Month Ended July 31

				Total Equivalent Units of Effort			
		Physical Units		**Direct Materials Costs**	**% Incurred During Period**	**Conversion Costs**	**% Incurred During Period**
Step 1: *Account for physical units.*	Beginning inventory (units started last period)	16,000					
	Units started this period	405,000					
	Units to be accounted for	421,000					
Step 2: *Account for equivalent units.*	Units completed and transferred out	399,400		399,400	100%	399,400	100%
	Ending inventory (units started but not completed this period)	21,600		21,600	100%	5,400	25%
	Units accounted for	421,000		421,000		404,800	
Step 3: *Account for costs.*		**Total Costs**					
	Beginning inventory	$ 19,900	=	$ 8,100	+	$ 11,800	
	Current costs	785,700	=	202,500	+	583,200	
	Total costs	$805,600		$210,600		$595,000	
Step 4: *Compute cost per equivalent unit.*	Total Costs / Equivalent Units			$210,600 / 421,000		$595,000 / 404,800	
	Cost per equivalent unit	$1.97	=	$0.50*	+	$1.47*	
				**Rounded to nearest cent*		**Rounded to nearest cent*	
Step 5: *Assign costs to cost of goods manufactured and ending inventory.*	Cost of goods manufactured and transferred out	$786,862 *(Add rounding $44)*	=	(399,400 × $0.50)	+	(399,400 × $1.47)	
	Ending inventory	18,738	=	(21,600 × $0.50)	+	(5,400 × $1.47)	
	Total costs	$805,600					

Work in Process Inventory Account: Cost Recap

Beg. Bal.	19,900	786,862 (Cost of goods manufactured and transferred out)
Direct materials	202,500	
Conversion costs	583,200	
End. Bal.	**18,738**	

Work in Process Inventory Account: Unit Recap

Beg. Bal.	16,000	399,400 (Units transferred out)
Units started	405,000	
End. Bal.	**21,600**	

2. The amount of $786,862 should be transferred to the Work in Process Inventory account of the Packaging Department. The entry in journal form is:

Work in Process Inventory (Packaging Department)	786,862	
Work in Process Inventory (Blending Department)		786,862

A LOOK BACK AT  DEAN FOODS

The Decision Point at the beginning of this chapter focused on **Dean Foods**, a company known as a leader in the field of milk products. It posed these questions:

- Why is a process costing system appropriate for Dean Foods?
- How does a process costing system facilitate management decisions?

Because there is a continuous flow of similar products during the process of producing milk and milk products, the most appropriate costing system for Dean Foods is a process costing system. Such a system accumulates costs by process, department, or work cell and assigns them to the products as they pass through the production system. A process costing system provides the information that Dean Foods' management needs to make sound product decisions.

Review Problem

Process Costing Using the FIFO Costing and Average Costing Methods

LO4 LO5

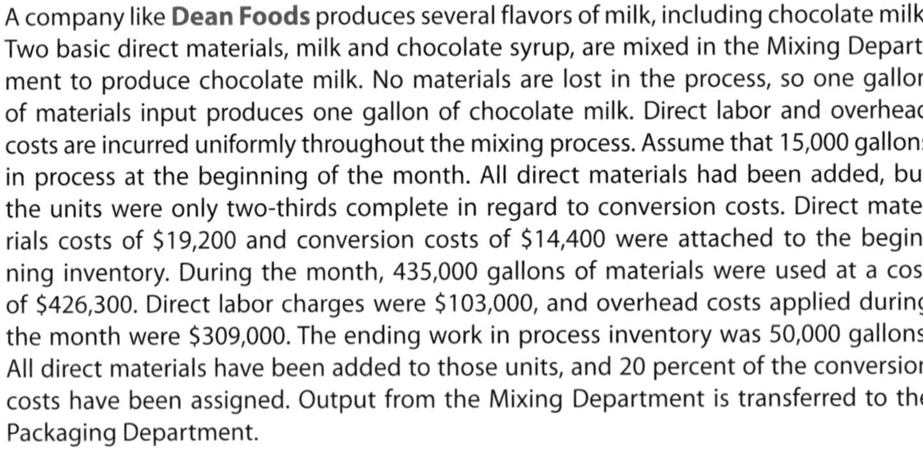

A company like **Dean Foods** produces several flavors of milk, including chocolate milk. Two basic direct materials, milk and chocolate syrup, are mixed in the Mixing Department to produce chocolate milk. No materials are lost in the process, so one gallon of materials input produces one gallon of chocolate milk. Direct labor and overhead costs are incurred uniformly throughout the mixing process. Assume that 15,000 gallons in process at the beginning of the month. All direct materials had been added, but the units were only two-thirds complete in regard to conversion costs. Direct materials costs of \$19,200 and conversion costs of \$14,400 were attached to the beginning inventory. During the month, 435,000 gallons of materials were used at a cost of \$426,300. Direct labor charges were \$103,000, and overhead costs applied during the month were \$309,000. The ending work in process inventory was 50,000 gallons. All direct materials have been added to those units, and 20 percent of the conversion costs have been assigned. Output from the Mixing Department is transferred to the Packaging Department.

Required

1. Using the FIFO costing method, prepare a process cost report for the Mixing Department for the month.
2. What amount should be transferred out of the Work in Process Inventory account, and where should those dollars be transferred? What is the entry in journal form?
3. Using the average costing method, repeat requirement **1**.
4. Answer the questions in requirement **2** as they apply to the process cost report that you prepared in requirement **3**.

Answers to Review Problem

1. Process cost report prepared using the FIFO costing method:

Mixing Department
Process Cost Report—FIFO Costing Method
For the Month

Beginning inventory	15,000
Units started this period	435,000
Units to be accounted for	450,000

		Current Equivalent Units of Effort			
	Physical Units	**Direct Materials Costs**	**% Incurred During Period**	**Conversion Costs**	**% Incurred During Period**
Beginning inventory	15,000	—	0%	5,000	33%
Units started and completed	385,000	385,000	100%	385,000	100%
Ending inventory	50,000	50,000	100%	10,000	20%
Units accounted for	450,000	435,000		400,000	

	Total Costs				
Beginning inventory	$ 33,600	=	$ 19,200	+	$ 14,400
Current costs	838,300	=	426,300	+	412,000
Total costs	$871,900				
Current Costs / Equivalent Units			$426,300 / 435,000		$412,000 / 400,000
Cost per equivalent unit	$2.01	=	$0.98	+	$1.03

Cost of goods manufactured and transferred out:			
From beginning inventory	$ 33,600		
Current costs to complete	5,150	=	$0 (5,000 × $1.03)
Units started and completed	773,850	=	(385,000 × $0.98) + (385,000 × $1.03)
Cost of goods manufactured	$812,600		
Ending inventory	59,300	=	(50,000 × $0.98) + (10,000 × $1.03)
Total costs	$871,900		

2. The amount of $812,600 should be transferred to the Work in Process Inventory account of the Packaging Department. The entry in journal form is:

Work in Process (Packaging Inventory Department)	812,600	
Work in Process (Mixing Inventory Department)		812,600

3. Process cost report using the average costing method:

Mixing Department
Process Cost Report—Average Costing Method
For the Month

Beginning inventory	15,000				
Units started this period	435,000				
Units to be accounted for	450,000				

		Total Equivalent Units of Effort			
	Physical Units	**Direct Materials Costs**	**% Incurred During Period**	**Conversion Costs**	**% Incurred During Period**
Units completed and transferred out	400,000	400,000	100%	400,000	100%
Ending inventory	50,000	50,000	100%	10,000	20%
Units accounted for	450,000	450,000		410,000	

	Total Costs				
Beginning inventory	$ 33,600	=	$ 19,200	+	$ 14,400
Current costs	838,300	=	426,300	+	412,000
Total costs	$871,900		$445,500		$426,400
Total Costs / Equivalent Units			$445,500 / 450,000		$426,400 / 410,000
Cost per equivalent unit	$2.03	=	$0.99	+	$1.04
Cost of goods manufactured and transferred out	$812,000	=	(400,000 × $0.99)	+	(400,000 × $1.04)
Ending inventory	59,900	=	(50,000 × $0.99)	+	(10,000 × $1.04)
Total costs	$871,900				

4. The amount of $812,000 should be transferred to the Work in Process Inventory account of the Packaging Department. The entry in journal form is:

Work in Process (Packaging Inventory Department)	812,000	
Work in Process (Mixing Inventory Department)		812,000

LO1 Describe the process costing system, and identify the reasons for its use.

A process costing system is a product costing system used by companies that produce large amounts of similar products or liquid products or that have long, continuous production runs of identical products. Because these companies have a continuous production flow, it would be impractical for them to use a job order costing system, which tracks costs to a specific batch of products or a specific job order. In contrast to a job order costing system, a process costing system accumulates the costs of direct materials, direct labor, and overhead for each process, department, or work cell and assigns those costs to the products as they are produced during a particular period.

The product costs provided by a process costing system play a key role in the management process. When managers plan, they use past and projected information about product costs to set selling prices and prepare budgets. Each day, managers use cost information to make decisions about controlling costs, managing the company's volume of activity, ensuring quality, and negotiating prices. Actual costs are incurred as units are produced, so actual unit costs can be computed. When managers evaluate performance results, they compare targeted costs with actual costs. When managers communicate with external stakeholders, they use actual units produced and costs incurred to value inventory on the balance sheet and cost of goods sold on the income statement. They also analyze internal reports that compare the organization's measures of actual and targeted performance to determine whether cost goals for products or services are being achieved.

LO2 Relate the patterns of product flows to the cost flow methods in a process costing environment, and explain the role of the Work in Process Inventory accounts.

During production in a process costing environment, products flow in a first-in, first-out (FIFO) fashion through several processes, departments, or work cells. As they do, the process costing system accumulates their costs and passes them on to the next process, department, or work cell. At the end of every accounting period, the system generates a report that assigns the costs that have accumulated during the period to the units that have transferred out of the process, department, or work cell and to the units that are still work in process. The process cost report may assign costs by using the FIFO costing method, in which the costs assigned to the first products processed are the first costs transferred out when those products flow to the next process, department, or work cell, or the average costing method, which assigns an average cost to all products made during an accounting period.

The Work in Process Inventory accounts are the focal point of a process costing system. Each production process, department, or work cell has its own Work in Process Inventory account. All costs charged to that process, department, or work cell flow into its Work in Process Inventory account. A process cost report prepared at the end of every accounting period assigns the costs that have accumulated during the period to the units that have flowed out of the process, department, or work cell (the cost of goods transferred out) and to the units that are still in process (the cost of ending inventory).

LO3 Define *equivalent production,* and compute equivalent units.

Equivalent production is a measure that applies a percentage-of-completion factor to partially completed units to compute the equivalent number of whole units produced in an accounting period for each type of input. Equivalent units are computed from (1) units in the beginning work in process inventory and their percentage of completion, (2) units started and completed during the period, and (3) units in the ending work in process inventory and their percentage of completion. The computation of equivalent units differs depending on whether the FIFO method or the average costing method is used.

LO4 Prepare a process cost report using the FIFO costing method.

In a process cost report that uses the FIFO costing method, the cost flow follows the logical physical flow of production—that is, the costs assigned to the first products processed are the first costs transferred when those products flow to the next process, department, or work cell. Preparation of a process cost report involves five steps. Steps 1 and 2 account for the physical flow of products and compute the equivalent units of production. Once equivalent production has been determined, the focus of the report shifts to accounting for costs. In Step 3, all direct materials costs and conversion costs for the current period are added to arrive at total costs. In Step 4, the cost per equivalent unit for both direct materials costs and conversion costs is found by dividing those costs by their respective equivalent units. In Step 5, costs are assigned to the units completed and transferred out during the period, as well as to the ending work in process inventory. The costs assigned to units completed and transferred out include the costs incurred in the preceding period and the conversion costs that were needed to complete those units during the current period. That amount is added to the total cost of producing all units started and completed during the period. The result is the total cost transferred out for the units completed during the period. Step 5 also assigns costs to units still in process at the end of the period by multiplying their direct materials costs and conversion costs by their respective equivalent units. The total equals the balance in the Work in Process Inventory account at the end of the period.

LO5 Prepare a process cost report using the average costing method.

The average costing method is an alternative method of accounting for production costs in a manufacturing environment characterized by a continuous production flow. The difference between a process costing report that uses the FIFO method and one that uses the average costing method is that the latter does not differentiate when work was done on inventory. When the average costing method is used, the costs in beginning inventory are averaged with the current period costs to compute the product unit costs. These costs are used to value the ending balance in Work in Process Inventory and the goods completed and transferred out of the process, department, or work cell.

REVIEW of Concepts and Terminology

The following concepts and terms were introduced in this chapter:

Average costing method 848 (LO2)

Conversion costs 850 (LO3)

Equivalent production 849 (LO3)

FIFO costing method 848 (LO2)

Process cost report 848 (LO2)

Process costing system 846 (LO1)

CHAPTER ASSIGNMENTS

BUILDING Your Basic Knowledge and Skills

Short Exercises

LO1 **Process Costing Versus Job Order Costing**

SE 1. Indicate whether the manufacturer of each of the following products should use a job order costing system or a process costing system to accumulate product costs:

1. Plastics
2. Ocean cruise ships
3. Cereal
4. Medical drugs for veterinary practices

LO1 **Process Costing Versus Job Order Costing**

SE 2. Indicate whether each of the following is a characteristic of job order costing or of process costing:

1. Several Work in Process Inventory accounts are used, one for each department or work cell in the process.
2. Costs are grouped by process, department, or work cell.
3. Costs are measured for each completed job.
4. Only one Work in Process Inventory account is used.
5. Costs are measured in terms of units completed in specific time periods.
6. Costs are assigned to specific jobs or batches of product.

LO2 **Process Costing and a Work in Process Inventory Account**

SE 3. Chemical Pro uses an automated mixing machine in its Mixing Department to combine three raw materials into a product called Triogo. On average, each unit of Triogo contains $3 of Material X, $6 of Material Y, $9 of Material Z, $2 of direct labor, and $12 of overhead. Total costs charged to the Mixing Department's Work in Process Inventory account during the month were $208,000. There were no units in beginning or ending work in process inventory. How many units were completed and transferred to Finished Goods Inventory during the month?

LO3 **Equivalent Production: FIFO Costing Method**

SE 4. Blue Blaze adds direct materials at the beginning of its production process and adds conversion costs uniformly throughout the process. Given the following information from Blue Blaze's records for July and using Steps 1 and 2 of the FIFO costing method, compute the equivalent units of production:

Units in beginning inventory	3,000
Units started during the period	17,000
Units partially completed	2,500
Percentage of completion of ending work in process inventory	100% for direct materials; 70% for conversion costs
Percentage of completion of beginning inventory	100% for direct materials; 40% for conversion costs

LO4 **Determining Unit Cost: FIFO Costing Method**

SE 5. Using the information from **SE 4** and the following data, compute the total cost per equivalent unit:

	Beginning Work in Process	Costs for the Period
Direct materials	$20,400	$7,600
Conversion costs	32,490	2,545

LO4 **Assigning Costs: FIFO Costing Method**

SE 6. Using the data in **SE 4** and **SE 5**, assign costs to the units transferred out and to the units in ending inventory for July.

LO5 **Equivalent Production: Average Costing Method**

SE 7. Using the same data as in **SE 4** but Steps 1 and 2 of the average costing method, compute the equivalent units of production for the month.

LO5 **Determining Unit Cost: Average Costing Method**

SE 8. Using the average costing method and the information from **SE 4**, **SE 5**, and **SE 7**, compute the total cost per equivalent unit.

LO5 **Assigning Costs: Average Costing Method**

SE 9. Using the data in **SE 4**, **SE 5**, **SE 7**, and **SE 8** and assuming that Blue Blaze uses the average costing method, assign costs to the units completed and transferred out and to the units in ending inventory for July.

LO5 **Equivalent Production: Average Costing Method**

SE 10. Red Company adds direct materials at the beginning of its production process and adds conversion costs uniformly throughout the process. Given the following information from Red Company's records for July, compute the current period's equivalent units of production for direct materials and conversion costs:

Units in beginning inventory: 2,000

Units started during the period: 13,000

Units partially completed: 500

Percentage of completion of beginning inventory: 100% for direct materials; 40% for conversion costs

Percentage of completion of ending work in process inventory: 100% for direct materials; 70% for conversion costs

Exercises

LO1 **Process Costing Versus Job Order Costing**

E 1. Indicate whether the manufacturer of each of the following products should use a job order costing system or a process costing system to accumulate product costs:

1. Paint
2. Fruit juices
3. Tailor-made suits
4. Milk
5. Coffee cups printed with your school insignia
6. Paper
7. Roller coaster for a theme park
8. Posters for a fund-raising event

LO2 **Use of Process Costing Information**

E 2. Tom's Bakery makes a variety of cakes, cookies, and pies for distribution to five major chains of grocery stores in the area. The company uses a standard manufacturing process for all items except special-order cakes. It currently uses a process costing system. Tom, the owner of the company, has some urgent questions, which are listed at the top of the next page. Which of these questions can be answered using information from a process costing system? Which can be best answered using information from a job order costing system? Explain your answers.

1. How much does it cost to make one chocolate cheesecake?
2. Did the cost of making special-order cakes exceed the cost budgeted for this month?
3. What is the value of the pie inventory at the end of June?
4. What were the costs of the cookies sold during June?
5. At what price should Tom's Bakery sell its famous brownies to the grocery store chains?
6. Were the planned production costs of $3,000 for making pies in June exceeded?

LO2 **Work in Process Inventory Accounts in Process Costing Systems**

E 3. Gilbert, Inc., which uses a process costing system, makes a chemical used as a food preservative. The manufacturing process involves Departments A and B. The company had the following total costs and unit costs for completed production last month, when it manufactured 10,000 pounds of the chemical. Neither Department A nor Department B had any beginning or ending work in process inventories.

	Total Cost	Unit Cost
Department A		
Direct materials	$10,000	$1.00
Direct labor	2,600	0.26
Overhead	1,300	0.13
Total costs	$13,900	$1.39
Department B		
Direct materials	$ 3,000	$0.30
Direct labor	700	0.07
Overhead	1,000	0.10
Total costs	$ 4,700	$0.47
Totals	$18,600	$1.86

1. How many Work in Process Inventory accounts would Gilbert use?
2. What dollar amount of the chemical's production cost was transferred from Department A to Department B last month?
3. What dollar amount was transferred from Department B to the Finished Goods Inventory account?
4. What dollar amount is useful in determining a selling price for 1 pound of the chemical?

LO3 **Equivalent Production: FIFO Costing Method**

E 4. McQuary Stone Company produces bricks. Although the company has been in operation for only 12 months, it already enjoys a good reputation. During its first 12 months, it put 600,000 bricks into production and completed and transferred 586,000 bricks to finished goods inventory. The remaining bricks were still in process at the end of the year and were 60 percent complete.

The company's process costing system adds all direct materials costs at the beginning of the production process; conversion costs are incurred uniformly throughout the process. From this information, compute the equivalent units of production for direct materials and conversion costs for the company's first year, which ended December 31. Use the FIFO costing method.

LO3 **Equivalent Production: FIFO Costing Method**

E 5. O'Leon Enterprises makes Perfect Shampoo for professional hair stylists. On July 31, it had 5,200 liters of shampoo in process that were 80 percent complete in regard to conversion costs and 100 percent complete in regard to direct materials costs. During August, it put 212,500 liters of direct materials into production. Data for Work in Process Inventory on August 31 were as follows: shampoo, 4,500 liters; stage of completion, 60 percent for conversion costs and 100 percent for direct materials. From this information, compute the equivalent units of production for direct materials and conversion costs for the month. Use the FIFO costing method.

LO3 **Equivalent Production: FIFO Costing Method**

E 6. Paper Savers Corporation produces wood pulp that is used in making paper. The following data pertain to the company's production of pulp during September:

		Percentage Complete	
	Tons	Direct Materials	Conversion Costs
Work in process, Aug. 31	40,000	100%	60%
Placed into production	250,000	—	—
Work in process, Sept. 30	80,000	100%	40%

Compute the equivalent units of production for direct materials and conversion costs for September using the FIFO costing method.

LO4 **Work in Process Inventory Accounts: Total Unit Cost**

E 7. Scientists at Anschultz Laboratories, Inc., have just perfected Dentalite, a liquid substance that dissolves tooth decay. The substance, which is generated by a complex process involving five departments, is very expensive. Cost and equivalent unit data for the latest week are as follows (units are in ounces):

	Direct Materials		Conversion Costs	
Dept.	Dollars	Equivalent Units	Dollars	Equivalent Units
A	$12,000	1,000	$33,825	2,050
B	21,835	1,985	13,065	1,005
C	23,896	1,030	20,972	2,140
D	—	—	22,086	2,045
E	—	—	15,171	1,945

From these data, compute the unit cost for each department and the total unit cost of producing 1 ounce of Dentalite.

LO4 **Determining Unit Cost: FIFO Costing Method**

E 8. Reuse Cookware, Inc., manufactures sets of heavy-duty pots. It has just completed production for August. At the beginning of August, its Work in Process Inventory account showed direct materials costs of $31,700 and conversion costs of $29,400. The cost of direct materials used in August was $275,373; conversion costs were $175,068. During the month, the company started and completed 15,190 sets. For August, a total of 16,450 equivalent sets for direct materials and 16,210 equivalent sets for conversion costs have been computed.

From this information, determine the cost per equivalent set for August. Use the FIFO costing method.

LO4 Assigning Costs: FIFO Costing Method

E 9. The Bakery produces tea cakes. It uses a process costing system. In March, its beginning inventory was 450 units, which were 100 percent complete for direct materials costs and 10 percent complete for conversion costs. The cost of beginning inventory was $655. Units started and completed during the month totaled 14,200. Ending inventory was 410 units, which were 100 percent complete for direct materials costs and 70 percent complete for conversion costs. Costs per equivalent unit for March were $1.40 for direct materials costs and $0.80 for conversion costs.

From this information, compute the cost of goods transferred to the Finished Goods Inventory account, the cost remaining in the Work in Process Inventory account, and the total costs to be accounted for. Use the FIFO costing method.

LO4 Process Cost Report: FIFO Costing Method

E 10. Toy Country Corporation produces children's toys using a liquid plastic formula and a continuous production process. In the company's toy truck work cell, the plastic is heated and fed into a molding machine. The molded toys are then cooled and trimmed and sent to the packaging work cell. All direct materials are added at the beginning of the process. In November, the beginning work in process inventory was 420 units, which were 40 percent complete; the ending balance was 400 units, which were 70 percent complete.

During November, 15,000 units were started into production. The Work in Process Inventory account had a beginning balance of $937 for direct materials costs and $370 for conversion costs. In the course of the month, $35,300 of direct materials were added to the process, and $31,760 of conversion costs were assigned to the work cell. Using the FIFO costing method, prepare a process cost report that computes the equivalent units for November, the product unit cost for the toys, and the ending balance in the Work in Process Inventory account.

LO5 Equivalent Production: Average Costing Method

E 11. Using the data in **E 4** and assuming that the company uses the average costing method, compute the equivalent units of production for direct materials and conversion costs for the year ended December 31.

LO5 Equivalent Production: Average Costing Method

E 12. Using the data in **E 5** and assuming that the company uses the average costing method, compute the equivalent units of production for direct materials and conversion for August.

LO5 Equivalent Production: Average Costing Method

E 13. Using the data in **E 6** and assuming that the company uses the average costing method, compute the equivalent units of production for direct materials and conversion for September.

LO5 Determining Unit Cost: Average Costing Method

E 14. Using the data in **E 8** and the average costing method, determine the cost per equivalent set for August. Assume equivalent sets are 16,900 for direct materials costs and 17,039 for conversion costs.

LO5 Process Cost Report: Average Costing Method

E 15. Using the data in **E 10** and the average costing method, prepare a process cost report that computes the equivalent units for November, the product unit cost for the toys, and the ending balance in the Work in Process Inventory account.

Problems

LO4 LO5 Process Costing: FIFO Costing and Average Costing Methods

P 1. Lightning Industries specializes in making Flash, a high-moisture, low-alkaline wax used to protect and preserve skis. The company began producing a new, improved brand of Flash on January 1. Materials are introduced at the beginning of the production process. During January, 15,300 pounds were used at a cost of $46,665. Direct labor of $17,136 and overhead costs of $25,704 were incurred uniformly throughout the month. By January 31, 13,600 pounds of Flash had been completed and transferred to the finished goods inventory (1 pound of input equals 1 pound of output). Since no spoilage occurred, the leftover materials remained in production and were 40 percent complete on average.

Required

1. Using the FIFO costing method, prepare a process cost report for January.
2. From the information in the process cost report, identify the amount that should be transferred out of the Work in Process Inventory account, and state where those dollars should be transferred.
3. Repeat requirements **1** and **2** using the average costing method.

LO4 Process Costing: FIFO Costing Method

P 2. Liquid Extracts Company produces a line of fruit extracts for home use in making wine, jams and jellies, pies, and meat sauces. Fruits enter the production process in pounds; the product emerges in quarts (1 pound of input equals 1 quart of output). On May 31, 4,250 units were in process. All direct materials had been added, and the units were 70 percent complete for conversion costs. Direct materials costs of $4,607 and conversion costs of $3,535 were attached to the units in beginning work in process inventory. During June, 61,300 pounds of fruit were added at a cost of $71,108. Direct labor for the month totaled $19,760, and overhead costs applied were $31,375. On June 30, 3,400 units remained in process. All direct materials for these units had been added, and 50 percent of conversion costs had been incurred.

Required

1. Using the FIFO costing method, prepare a process cost report for June.
2. From the information in the process cost report, identify the amount that should be transferred out of the Work in Process Inventory account, and state where those dollars should be transferred.

LO4 Process Costing: One Process and Two Time Periods—FIFO Costing Method

P 3. Wash Clean Laboratories produces biodegradable liquid detergents that leave no soap film. The production process has been automated, so the product can now be produced in one operation instead of in a series of heating, mixing, and cooling operations. All direct materials are added at the beginning of the process, and conversion costs are incurred uniformly throughout the process. Operating data for July and August are as follows:

	July	August
Beginning work in process inventory		
Units (pounds)	2,300	3,050
Direct materials	$ 4,699	?*
Conversion costs	$ 1,219	?*
Production during the period		
Units started (pounds)	31,500	32,800
Direct materials	$65,520	$66,912
Conversion costs	$54,213	$54,774
Ending work in process inventory		
Units (pounds)	3,050	3,600

*From calculations at end of July.

The beginning work in process inventory was 30 percent complete for conversion costs. The ending work in process inventory for July was 60 percent complete; for August, it was 50 percent complete. Assume that the loss from spoilage and evaporation was negligible.

Required

1. Using the FIFO costing method, prepare a process cost report for July.
2. From the information in the process cost report, identify the amount that should be transferred out of the Work in Process Inventory account, and state where those dollars should be transferred.
3. Repeat requirements **1** and **2** for August.

LO5 **Process Costing: Average Costing Method and Two Time Periods**

P 4. Lid Corporation produces a line of beverage lids. The production process has been automated, so the product can now be produced in one operation rather than in the three operations that were needed before the company purchased the automated machinery. All direct materials are added at the beginning of the process, and conversion costs are incurred uniformly throughout the process. Operating data for May and June are as follows:

	May	June
Beginning work in process inventory		
Units (May: 40% complete)	220,000	?
Direct materials	$ 3,440	$ 400
Conversion costs	$ 6,480	$ 420
Production during the month		
Units started	24,000,000	31,000,000
Direct materials	$45,000	$93,200
Conversion costs	$66,000	$92,796
Ending work in process inventory		
Units (May: 70% complete; June: 60% complete)	200,000	320,000

1. Using the average costing method, prepare process cost reports for May and June. (Round unit costs to three decimal places; round all other costs to the nearest dollar.)
2. From the information in the process cost report for May, identify the amount that should be transferred out of the Work in Process Inventory account, and state where those dollars should be transferred.
3. Compare the product costing results for June with the results for May. What is the most significant change? What are some of the possible causes of this change?

LO5 **Process Costing: Average Costing Method**

P 5. Hurricane Products, Inc., makes high-vitamin, calorie-packed wafers that are popular among professional athletes because they supply quick energy. The company produces the wafers in a continuous flow, and it uses a process costing system based on the average costing method. It recently purchased several automated machines so that the wafers can be produced in a single department. All direct materials are added at the beginning of the process. The costs for the machine operators' labor and production-related overhead are incurred uniformly throughout the process.

In February, the company put a total of 231,200 liters of direct materials into production at a cost of $294,780. Two liters of direct materials were used to produce one unit of output (one unit = 144 wafers). Direct labor costs for February were $60,530, and overhead was $181,590. The beginning work in process inventory for February was 14,000 units, which were 100 percent complete for direct materials and 20 percent complete for conversion costs. The total cost of those units was $55,000, $48,660 of which was assigned to the cost of direct materials. The ending work in process inventory of 12,000 units was fully complete for direct materials but only 30 percent complete for conversion costs.

Required

1. Using the average costing method and assuming no loss due to spoilage, prepare a process cost report for February.
2. From the information in the process cost report, identify the amount that should be transferred out of the Work in Process Inventory account, and state where those dollars should be transferred.

Alternate Problems

LO4 LO5 Process Costing: FIFO Costing and Average Costing Methods

P 6. Sunshine Soda Company manufactures and sells several different kinds of soft drinks. Direct materials (sugar syrup and artificial flavor) are added at the beginning of production in the Mixing Department. Direct labor and overhead costs are applied to products throughout the process. For August, beginning inventory for the citrus flavor was 2,400 gallons, 80 percent complete. Ending inventory was 3,600 gallons, 50 percent complete. Production data show 240,000 gallons started during August. A total of 238,800 gallons was completed and transferred to the Bottling Department. Beginning inventory costs were $600 for direct materials and $676 for conversion costs. Current period costs were $57,600 for direct materials and $83,538 for conversion costs.

Required

1. Using the FIFO costing method, prepare a process cost report for the Mixing Department for August.
2. From the information in the process cost report, identify the amount that should be transferred out of the Work in Process Inventory account, and state where those dollars should be transferred.
3. Repeat requirements **1** and **2** using the average costing method.

LO4 Process Costing: FIFO Costing Method

P 7. Canned fruits and vegetables are the main products made by Good Foods, Inc. All direct materials are added at the beginning of the Mixing Department's process. When the ingredients have been mixed, they go to the Cooking Department. There the mixture is heated to 100° Celsius and simmered for 20 minutes. When cooled, the mixture goes to the Canning Department for final processing. Throughout the operations, direct labor and overhead costs are incurred uniformly. No direct materials are added in the Cooking Department. Cost data and other information for the Mixing Department for January are as follows:

Production Cost Data	Direct Materials	Conversion Costs
Mixing Department		
Beginning inventory	$ 28,560	$ 5,230
Current period costs	450,000	181,200
Work in process inventory		
Beginning inventory		
Mixing Department (40% complete)	5,000 liters	
Ending inventory		
Mixing Department (60% complete)	6,000 liters	
Unit production data		
Units started during January	90,000 liters	
Units transferred out during January	89,000 liters	

Assume that no spoilage or evaporation loss took place during January.

Required

1. Using the FIFO costing method, prepare a process cost report for the Mixing Department for January.

Manager insight ▶ 2. Explain how the analysis for the Cooking Department will differ from the analysis for the Mixing Department.

LO4 Process Costing: One Process and Two Time Periods—FIFO Costing Method

P 8. Honey Dews Company produces organic honey, which it sells to health food stores and restaurants. The company owns thousands of beehives. No direct materials other than honey are used. The production operation is a simple one. Impure honey is added at the beginning of the process and flows through a series of filterings, leading to a pure finished product. Costs of labor and overhead are incurred uniformly throughout the filtering process. Production data for April and May are as follows:

	April	May
Beginning work in process inventory		
Units (liters)	7,100	12,400
Direct materials	$ 2,480	?*
Conversion costs	$ 5,110	?*
Production during the period		
Units started (liters)	288,000	310,000
Direct materials	$100,800	$117,800
Conversion costs	$251,550	$277,281
Ending work in process inventory		
Units (liters)	12,400	16,900

*From calculations at end of April.

The beginning work in process inventory for April was 80 percent complete for conversion costs, and ending work in process inventory was 20 percent complete. The ending work in process inventory for May was 30 percent complete for conversion costs. Assume that there was no loss from spoilage or evaporation.

Required

1. Using the FIFO method, prepare a process cost report for April.
2. From the information in the process cost report, identify the amount that should be transferred out of the Work in Process Inventory account, and state where those dollars should be transferred.
3. Repeat requirements **1** and **2** for May.

LO5 Process Costing: Average Costing Method and Two Time Periods

P 9. Carton Corporation produces a line of beverage cartons. The production process has been automated, so the product can now be produced in one operation rather than in the three operations that were needed before the company purchased the automated machinery. All direct materials are added at the beginning of the process, and conversion costs are incurred uniformly throughout the process. Operating data for July and August are as follows:

	July	August
Beginning work in process inventory		
Units (July: 20% complete)	20,000	?
Direct materials	$20,000	$6,000
Conversion costs	$30,000	$6,000
Production during the month		
Units started	70,000	90,000
Direct materials	$34,000	$59,000
Conversion costs	$96,000	$130,800
Ending work in process inventory		
Units (July: 40% complete; August: 60% complete)	10,000	25,000

1. Using the average costing method, prepare process cost reports for July and August. (Round unit costs to two decimal places; round all other costs to the nearest dollar.)
2. From the information in the process cost report for July, identify the amount that should be transferred out of the Work in Process Inventory account, and state where those dollars should be transferred.
3. Compare the product costing results for August with the results for July. What is the most significant change? What are some of the possible causes of this change?

LO5 Process Costing: Average Costing Method

P 10. Many of the products made by Wireless Plastics Company are standard telephone replacement parts that require long production runs and are produced continuously. A unit for Wireless Plastics is a box of parts. During April, direct materials for 25,250 units were put into production. Total cost of direct materials used during April was $2,273,000. Direct labor costs totaled $1,135,000, and overhead was $2,043,000. The beginning work in process inventory contained 1,600 units, which were 100 percent complete for direct materials costs and 60 percent complete for conversion costs. Costs attached to the units in beginning inventory totaled $232,515, which included $143,500 of direct materials costs. At the end of the month, 1,250 units were in ending inventory; all direct materials had been added, and the units were 70 percent complete for conversion costs.

Required

1. Using the average costing method and assuming no loss due to spoilage, prepare a process cost report for April.
2. From the information in the process cost report, identify the amount that should be transferred out of the Work in Process Inventory account, and state where those dollars should be transferred.

ENHANCING Your Knowledge, Skills, and Critical Thinking

LO1 Concept of Process Costing Systems

C 1. For more than 60 years, **Dow Chemical Company** has made and sold a tasteless, odorless, and calorie-free substance called Methocel. When heated, this liquid plastic (methyl cellulose) has the unusual characteristic (for plastics) of becoming a gel that resembles cooked egg whites. It is used in over 400 food products, including gravies, soups, and puddings. It was also used as wampa drool in *The Empire Strikes Back* and dinosaur sneeze in *Jurassic Park*. What kind of costing system is most appropriate for the manufacture of Methocel? Why is that system most appropriate? Describe the system, and include in the description a general explanation of how costs are determined.

LO1 LO2 Continuing Professional Education

C 2. Paula Woodward is the head of the Information Systems Department at Moreno Manufacturing Company. Roland Randolph, the company's controller, is meeting with her to discuss changes in data gathering that relate to the company's new flexible manufacturing system. Woodward opens the conversation by saying, "Roland, the old job order costing methods just will not work with the new flexible manufacturing system. The new system is based on continuous product flow, not batch processing. We need to change to a process costing system for both data gathering and product costing. Otherwise, our product costs will be way off, and it will affect our pricing decisions. I found out about the need for this change at a professional seminar I attended last month. You should have been there with me."

Randolph responds, "Paula, who is the accounting expert here? I know what product costing approach is best for this situation. Job order costing has provided accurate information for this product line for more than 15 years. Why should we change just because we've purchased a new machine? We've purchased several machines for this line over the years. And as for your seminar, I don't need to learn about costing methods. I was exposed to them all when I studied management accounting back in the late 1970s."

Is Randolph's behavior ethical? If not, what has he done wrong? What can Woodward do if Randolph continues to refuse to update the product costing system?

LO3 LO4 Analysis of Product Cost

C 3. Ready Tire Corporation makes several lines of automobile and truck tires. The company operates in a competitive marketplace, so it relies heavily on cost data from its FIFO-based process costing system. It uses that information to set prices for its most competitive tires. The company's radial line has lost some of its market share during each of the past four years. Management believes that price breaks allowed by the company's three biggest competitors are the main reason for the decline in sales.

The company controller, Sara Birdsong, has been asked to review the product costing information that supports pricing decisions on the radial line. In preparing her report, she collected the following data for last year, the most recent full year of operations:

		Units	Dollars
Equivalent units	Direct materials	84,200	
	Conversion costs	82,800	
Manufacturing costs:	Direct materials		$1,978,700
	Direct labor		800,400
	Overhead		1,600,800
Unit cost data:	Direct materials		23.50
	Conversion costs		29.00
Work in process inventory:			
Beginning (70% complete)		4,200	
Ending (30% complete)		3,800	

Units started and completed last year totaled 80,400. Attached to the beginning Work in Process Inventory account were direct materials costs of $123,660 and conversion costs of $57,010. Birdsong found that little spoilage had occurred. The proper cost allowance for spoilage was included in the predetermined overhead rate of $2 per direct labor dollar. The review of direct labor cost revealed, however, that $90,500 had been charged twice to the production account, the second time in error. This resulted in overly high overhead costs being charged to the production account.

The radial has been selling for $92 per tire. This price was based on last year's unit data plus a 75 percent markup to cover operating costs and profit. The company's three main competitors have been charging about $87 for a tire of comparable quality. The company's process costing system adds all direct materials at the beginning of the process, and conversion costs are incurred uniformly throughout the process.

1. Identify what inaccuracies in costs, inventories, and selling prices result from the company's cost-charging error.

2. Prepare a revised process cost report for last year. Round unit costs to two decimal places. Round total costs to whole dollars.
3. What should have been the minimum selling price per tire this year?
4. Suggest ways of preventing such errors in the future.

LO4 Setting a Selling Price

C 4. For the past four years, three companies have dominated the soft drink industry, holding a combined 85 percent of market share. Wonder Cola, Inc., ranks second nationally in soft drink sales. Its management is thinking about introducing a new low-calorie drink called Null Cola.

Wonder soft drinks are processed in a single department. All ingredients are added at the beginning of the process. At the end of the process, the beverage is poured into bottles that cost $0.24 per case produced. Direct labor and overhead costs are applied uniformly throughout the process.

Corporate controller Adam Daneen believes that costs for the new cola will be very much like those for the company's Cola Plus drink. Last year, he collected the following data about Cola Plus:

	Units*	Costs
Work in process inventory		
January 1†	2,200	
Direct materials costs		$ 2,080
Conversion costs		620
December 31‡	2,000	
Direct materials costs		1,880
Conversion costs		600
Units started during year	458,500	
Costs for year		
Liquid materials added		430,990
Direct labor and overhead		229,400
Bottles		110,068

*Each unit is a 24-bottle case.
†50% complete.
‡60% complete.

The company's variable general administrative and selling costs are $1.10 per unit. Fixed administrative and selling costs are assigned to products at the rate of $0.50 per unit. Each of Wonder Cola's two main competitors is already marketing a diet cola. Company A's product sells for $4.10 per unit; Company B's, for $4.05. All costs are expected to increase by 10 percent in the next three years. Wonder Cola tries to earn a profit of at least 15 percent on the total unit cost.

1. What factors should Wonder Cola, Inc., consider in setting a unit selling price for a case of Null Cola?
2. Using the FIFO costing method, compute (a) equivalent units for direct materials, cases of bottles, and conversion costs; (b) the total production cost per unit; and (c) the total cost per unit of Cola Plus for the year.
3. What is the expected unit cost of Null Cola for the year?
4. Recommend a unit selling price range for Null Cola, and give the reason(s) for your choice.

LO2 LO3 LO4 Using the Process Costing System

C 5. You are the production manager for Great Grain Corporation, a manufacturer of four cereal products. The company's best-selling product is Smackaroos, a sugar-coated puffed rice cereal. Yesterday, Clark Winslow, the controller, reported that the production cost for each box of Smackaroos has increased approximately 22 percent in the last four months. Because the company is unable to increase the selling price for a box of Smackaroos, the increased production costs will reduce profits significantly.

Today, you received a memo from Gilbert Rom, the company president, asking you to review your production process to identify inefficiencies or waste that can be eliminated. Once you have completed your analysis, you are to write a memo presenting your findings and suggesting ways to reduce or eliminate the problems. The president will use your information during a meeting with the top management team in ten days.

You are aware of previous problems in the Baking Department and the Packaging Department. Winslow has provided you with process cost reports for the two departments. He has also given you the following detailed summary of the cost per equivalent unit for a box of Smackaroos cereal:

	April	May	June	July
Baking Department				
Direct materials	$1.25	$1.26	$1.24	$1.25
Direct labor	0.50	0.61	0.85	0.90
Overhead	0.25	0.31	0.34	0.40
Department totals	$2.00	$2.18	$2.43	$2.55
Packaging Department				
Direct materials	$0.35	$0.34	$0.33	$0.33
Direct labor	0.05	0.05	0.04	0.06
Overhead	0.10	0.16	0.15	0.12
Department totals	$0.50	$0.55	$0.52	$0.51
Total cost per equivalent unit	$2.50	$2.73	$2.95	$3.06

1. In preparation for writing your memo, answer the following questions:
   a. For whom are you preparing the memo? Does this affect the length of the memo? Explain.
   b. Why are you preparing the memo?
   c. What actions should you take to gather information for the memo? What information is needed? Is the information that Winslow provided sufficient for analysis and reporting?
   d. When is the memo due? What can be done to provide accurate, reliable, and timely information?
2. Based on your analysis of the information that Winslow provided, where is the main problem in the production process?
3. Prepare an outline of the sections you would want in your memo.

LO1 Cookie Company (Continuing Case)

C 6. In this segment of our continuing case, you are considering whether process costing is more appropriate for your cookie company than job order costing. List reasons why your company may choose to use process costing instead of job order costing.

CHAPTER

19

Value-Based Systems: ABM and Lean

The Management Process

PLAN

- ▷ Identify activities that add value to products and services.
- ▷ Identify the resources necessary to perform value-adding activities.
- ▷ Conduct process value analysis of current business to identify improvement opportunities.
- ▷ Develop a business plan focused on value-enhanced products and services where waste is eliminated.
- ▷ Set value and waste goals and select key performance indicators of success.

PERFORM

- ▷ Implement plan to achieve goals.
- ▷ Measure value chain and supply-chain performance.
- ▷ Eliminate waste in products and business processes.

EVALUATE

- ▷ Assess if value enhancement and waste elimination goals are being met.
- ▷ Revise business plan as a result of management analysis.

COMMUNICATE

- ▷ Prepare external reports that summarize performance.
- ▷ Prepare internal planning, performance, and analysis reports.

Managers can use ABM and/or a lean approach to add value for their customers.

To remain competitive in today's challenging business environment, companies have had to rethink their organizational processes and basic operating methods. Managers focus on creating value for their customers. They design their internal value chain and external supply chain to provide customer-related, activity-based information; to track costs; and to eliminate waste and inefficiencies. In this chapter, we describe two systems that help managers improve operating processes and make better decisions: activity-based management and the lean operating philosophy.

LEARNING OBJECTIVES

LO1 **Explain why managers use value-based systems, and discuss the relationship of these systems to the supply chain and value chain.** (pp. 884–888)

LO2 **Define *activity-based costing,* and explain how a cost hierarchy and a bill of activities are used.** (pp. 888–891)

LO3 **Define the elements of a lean operation, and identify the changes in inventory management that result when a firm adopts its just-in-time operating philosophy.** (pp. 892–896)

LO4 **Define and apply *backflush costing,* and compare the cost flows in traditional and backflush costing.** (pp. 896–899)

LO5 **Compare ABM and lean operations as value-based systems.** (p. 900)

DECISION POINT ▶ A MANAGER'S FOCUS LA-Z-BOY, INC.

La-Z-Boy, Inc., makes thousands of built-to-order sofas and chairs each week in its U.S. plants, and it generally delivers them less than three weeks after customers have placed their orders with a retailer. This gives La-Z-Boy a significant advantage over its competitors. Critical factors in the company's success are the speed of its supply chain and its use of value-based systems.

- ▶ How have value-based systems helped La-Z-Boy, Inc., improve its production processes and reduce delivery time?
- ▶ How do La-Z-Boy's managers plan to maintain the company's status as the leading manufacturer of upholstered products?

Value-Based Systems and Management

LO1 Explain why managers use value-based systems, and discuss the relationship of these systems to the supply chain and value chain.

Many companies, including **La-Z-Boy, Inc.**, are rethinking how to operate in volatile business environments that are strongly influenced by customer demands. Managers realize that value-based systems, rather than traditional cost-based systems, provide the information they need. **Value-based systems** are information systems that provide customer-related, activity-based information. Value-based systems focus on eliminating waste as companies produce and deliver quality products and services demanded by customers. Managers can use value-based information to compare the value created by products or services with the **full product cost**, which includes not only the costs of direct materials and direct labor, but also the costs of all production and nonproduction activities required to satisfy the customer. For example, the full product cost of a La-Z-Boy recliner or sofa includes the cost of the frame and upholstery, as well as the costs of taking the sales order, processing the order, packaging and shipping the furniture, and providing subsequent customer service for warranty work.

Creating value by satisfying customers' needs for quality, reasonable price, and timely delivery requires that managers do the following:

- Work with suppliers and customers.
- View the organization as a collection of value-adding activities.
- Use resources for value-adding activities.
- Reduce or eliminate non-value-adding activities.
- Know the total cost of creating value for a customer.

Each company in a supply chain is a customer of an earlier supplier. The furniture maker shown here would be a customer of a supplier of high-quality wood and perhaps of a metal manufacturer, caning supplier, and leather manufacturer. His customer might be a furniture wholesaler or retail store. The retail store, which sells the furniture to customers, is the final link in the supply chain.

Courtesy of PhotostoGO.com.

If an organization's business plan focuses on providing products or services that customers esteem, then managers will work both externally and internally to manage their supply chain and value chains, respectively.

- Externally, with suppliers and customers, managers will find ways of improving quality, reducing costs, and shortening delivery time.
- Internally, managers will find the best ways of using resources to create and maintain the value of their products or services. This requires matching resources to the operating activities that add value to a product or service. Managers will examine all business activities involved in value creation for waste, including research and development, design, supply, production, storage, sales and marketing, distribution, and customer service.

Value Chains and Supply Chains

As we noted earlier in the text, a **value chain** is a sequence of activities inside the organization, also known as *primary processes,* that add value to a company's product or service; the value chain also includes support services, such as management accounting, that facilitate the primary processes. Managers see their organization's internal value chain as part of a larger system that includes the value chains of suppliers and customers. This larger system is the **supply chain**—the path that leads from the suppliers of the materials from which a product is made to the final customer. The supply chain (also called the *supply network*) includes both suppliers and suppliers' suppliers, and customers and customers' customers. It links businesses together in a relationship chain of business to business to business.

As Figure 19-1 shows, in the supply chain for a furniture company like La-Z-Boy, a cotton farmer supplies cotton to the upholstery manufacturer, which supplies upholstery to the furniture manufacturer. The furniture manufacturer supplies furniture to furniture stores, which in turn supply furniture to the final

FIGURE 19-1 The Supply Chain and Value Chain in a Furniture Company

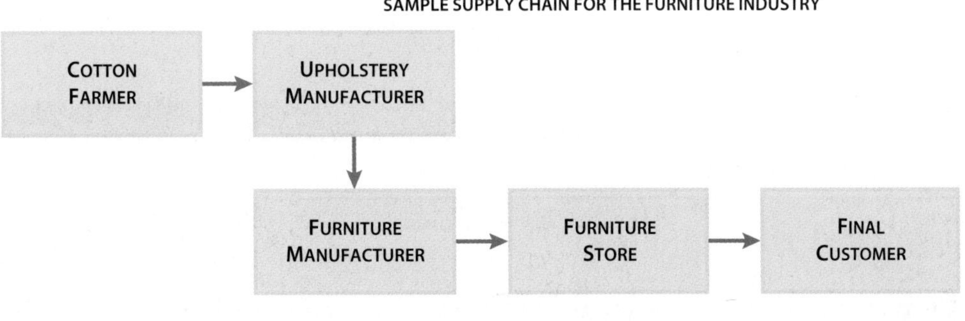

SAMPLE VALUE CHAIN FOR THE FURNITURE MANUFACTURER

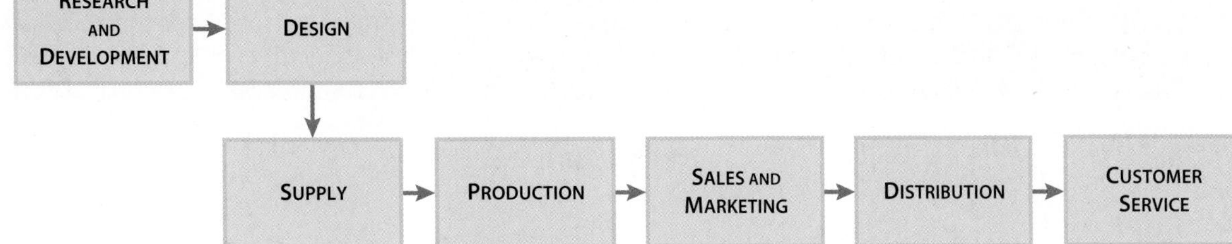

customers. Each organization in this supply chain is a customer of an earlier supplier, and each has its own value chain.

The sequence of primary processes in the value chain varies from company to company depending on a number of factors, including the size of the company and the types of products or services that it sells. Figure 19-1 also shows the primary processes that add value for a furniture manufacturer—research and development, design, supply, production, sales and marketing, distribution, and customer service.

Understanding value chains and supply chains gives managers a better grasp of their company's internal and external operations. Managers who understand the supply chain and how their company's value-adding activities fit into their suppliers' and customers' value chains can see their company's role in the overall process of creating and delivering products or services. When organizations work cooperatively with others in their supply chain, they can develop new processes that reduce the total costs of their products or services.

For example, La-Z-Boy, places computers for online order entry in its sofa kiosks located in indoor shopping malls. The computers streamline the processing of orders and make the orders more accurate. In this case, even though La-Z-Boy incurs the cost of the computers, the total cost of making and delivering furniture decreases because the cost of order processing decreases.

Process Value Analysis

Process value analysis (PVA) is a technique that managers use to identify and link all the activities involved in the value chain. It analyzes business processes by relating activities to the events that prompt those activities and to the resources that the activities consume. PVA forces managers to look critically at all phases of their operations. PVA improves cost traceability and results in significantly more accurate product costs, which in turn improves management decisions and increases profitability. By using PVA to identify non-value-adding activities, companies can reduce their costs and redirect their resources to value-adding activities.

FOCUS ON BUSINESS PRACTICE

What Is VBM?

Value-based management (VBM) is a long-term strategy that many businesses use to reward managers who create and sustain shareholder wealth and value. In other words, VBM encourages managers to think like business owners. Three elements are essential for a successful VBM program. First, VBM must have the full support of top management. Second, performance and compensation must be linked, because "what gets measured and rewarded gets done." Finally, everyone involved must understand the what, why, and how of the program. Since a variety of VBM approaches exist, each company can tailor its VBM performance metrics and implementation strategy to meet its particular needs.[1]

Value-Adding and Non-Value-Adding Activities

Study Note

The customer's perspective governs whether an activity adds value to a product or service. To minimize costs, managers continuously seek to improve processes and activities. To manage the cost of an activity, they can reduce the activity's frequency or eliminate it entirely.

A **value-adding activity** is one that adds value to a product or service as perceived by the customer. In other words, if customers are willing to pay for the activity, it adds value to the product or service. Examples include designing the components of a new recliner, assembling the recliner, and upholstering it.

A **non-value-adding activity** is one that adds cost to a product or service but does not increase its market value. Managers eliminate non-value-adding activities that are not essential to an organization and reduce the costs of those that are essential, such as legal services, management accounting, machine repair, materials handling, and building maintenance. For example, inspection costs can be reduced if an inspector samples one of every three reclining mechanisms received from a supplier rather than inspecting every mechanism. If the supplier is a reliable source of high-quality mechanisms, such a reduction in inspection activity is appropriate.

Another way managers can reduce costs is to outsource an activity—that is, to have it done by another company that is more competent at the work and can perform it at a lower cost. For example, many companies outsource purchasing, accounting, and the maintenance of their information systems. Some activities can be eliminated completely if business processes are changed.

Value-Based Systems

In this chapter, we explore two types of value-based systems—activity-based management (ABM) and lean operations. Both can be used together or separately to eliminate waste and manage activities.

Study Note

ABM and lean operations focus on value-adding activities—not costs—to increase income.

- They create opportunities to improve the nonfinancial performance measures as well as cost information supplied to managers.
- They help managers view their organization as a collection of activities. Value-based cost information helps managers improve operating processes and make better pricing decisions.

Activity-Based Management

As you may recall from an earlier chapter, **activity-based management (ABM)** is an approach to managing an organization that identifies all major operating activities, determines the resources consumed by each activity and the cause of the resource usage, and categorizes the activities as either adding value to a product or service or not adding value. ABM focuses on reducing or eliminating non-value-adding activities.

- Because it provides financial and performance information at the activity level, ABM is useful both for strategic planning and for making tactical and operational decisions about business segments, such as product lines, market segments, and customers.
- It also helps managers eliminate waste and inefficiencies and redirect resources to activities that add value to the product or service.

Activity-based costing (ABC) is the tool used in an ABM environment to assign activity costs to cost objects. ABC helps managers make better pricing decisions, inventory valuations, and profitability decisions.

Managing Lean Operations

A **lean operation** focuses on eliminating waste in an organization. In other words, business processes should focus on what a customer is willing to pay for. Lean operations emphasize the elimination of three kinds of waste:

- Waste that can be eliminated proactively through good planning and design of the product or service and the production processes for making it.
- Waste that can be eliminated during production by smart production scheduling and consistently following standardized product and processing plans to ensure quality.
- Waste that can be eliminated by management analysis of the actions of workers and machines in the process of making products and services.

Just-in-time (JIT) is one of the key strategies of a lean operation to reorganize production activities and manage inventory. JIT will be discussed later in the chapter.

STOP & APPLY >

The reports that follow are from a furniture store. Which report would be used for financial purposes, and which would be used for activity-based decision making? Why?

Salaries/Commissions	$1,400	Enter sales orders	$1,000
Equipment	1,200	Attend sales training	1,000
Office Supplies	300	Create ad campaign	1,500
Rent	1,000	Maintain website	500
Insurance	1,000	Resolve problems	900
Total	$4,900	Total	$4,900

SOLUTION

The report on the left is the financial report because it is organized by costs. The report on the right is the ABM report because it is organized by activities or tasks. Thus, the ABM report enables managers to focus on reducing non-value-adding activities.

Activity-Based Costing

LO2 Define *activity-based costing*, and explain how a cost hierarchy and a bill of activities are used.

As access to value chain data has improved, managers have refined the issue of how to assign costs fairly to products or services to determine unit costs. You may recall from an earlier chapter that traditional methods of allocating overhead costs to products use such cost drivers as direct labor hours, direct labor costs, or machine hours and one overhead rate. More than 20 years ago, organizations began realizing that these methods did not assign overhead costs to their product lines accurately and that the resulting inaccuracy in product unit costs was causing poor pricing decisions and poor control of overhead costs. In their search for more accurate product costing, many organizations embraced activity-based costing.

> **Study Note**
> ABC can be used to allocate all the various costs that make up overhead and nonmanufacturing activity costs as well.

> **Study Note**
> ABC reflects the cause-and-effect relationships between costs and individual processes, products, services, or customers.

As we noted earlier, activity-based costing (ABC) is a tool of ABM. It is a method of assigning costs that calculates a more accurate product cost than traditional methods. It does so by categorizing all indirect costs by activity, tracing the indirect costs to those activities, and assigning those costs to products or services using a cost driver related to the cause of the cost.

Activity-based costing is an important tool of activity-based management because it improves the accuracy in allocating activity-driven costs to cost objects (i.e., products or services). To implement activity-based costing, managers:

1. Identify and classify each activity.
2. Estimate the cost of resources for each activity.
3. Identify a cost driver for each activity and estimate the quantity of each cost driver.
4. Calculate an activity cost rate for each activity.
5. Assign costs to cost objects based on the level of activity required to make the product or provide the service.

While ABC does increase the accuracy of cost information and gives managers greater control over the costs they manage, it does have its limitations, including the following:

- High measurement costs necessary to collect accurate data from many activities instead of just one overhead account may make ABC too costly.
- Some costs are difficult to assign to a specific activity or cost object since they benefit the business in general (e.g., the president's salary) and should not be arbitrarily allocated.
- ABC allocations may add undue complexity and complications to controlling costs.

The Cost Hierarchy and the Bill of Activities

Two tools used in implementing ABC are a cost hierarchy and a bill of activities.

Cost Hierarchy A **cost hierarchy** is a framework for classifying activities according to the level at which their costs are incurred. Many companies use this framework to allocate activity-based costs to products or services. In a manufacturing company, the cost hierarchy typically has four levels: the unit level, the batch level, the product level, and the facility level.

- **Unit-level activities** are performed each time a unit is produced and are generally considered variable costs. For example, when a furniture manufacturer like **La-Z-Boy** installs a recliner mechanism in a chair, unit-level activities include the direct material cost of the recliner mechanism and direct labor connecting the mechanism to the chair frame. Because each chair contains only one mechanism, these activities have a direct correlation to the number of chairs produced.
- **Batch-level activities** are performed each time a batch or production run of goods is produced. Examples of batch-level activities include setup and materials handling for the production run of a certain style of recliner. These activities vary with the number of batches prepared or production runs completed.

TABLE 19-1
Sample Activities in Cost Hierarchies

Activity Level	Furniture Manufacturer: Recliner Mechanism Installation
Unit level	Install mechanism
	Test mechanism
Batch level	Set up installation process
	Move mechanisms
	Inspect mechanisms
Product level	Redesign installation process
Facility level	Provide facility maintenance, lighting, and security

- **Product-level activities** are performed to support a particular product line. Examples of product-level activities include implementing design, engineering, or marketing changes for a particular brand of product. These activities vary with the number of brands or product designs a company has.
- **Facility-level activities** are performed to support a facility's general manufacturing process and are generally fixed costs. Examples for a furniture manufacturer include maintaining, lighting, securing, and insuring the factory. These activities are generally a fixed amount for a certain time period.

Note that the frequency of activities varies across levels and that the cost hierarchy includes both value-adding and non-value-adding activities. Service organizations can also use a cost hierarchy to group their activities; the four levels typically are the unit level, the batch level, the service level, and the operations level. Table 19-1 lists examples of activities in the cost hierarchies of a manufacturing company like La-Z-Boy.

Study Note
A bill of activities summarizes costs relating to a product or service and supports the calculation of the product or service unit cost.

Bill of Activities Once managers have created the cost hierarchy, they group the activities into the specified levels and prepare a summary of the activity costs assigned to the selected cost objects. A **bill of activities** is a list of activities and related costs that is used to compute the costs assigned to activities and the product unit cost. More complex bills of activities group activities into activity pools and include activity cost rates and the cost driver levels used to assign costs to cost objects. A bill of activities may be used as the primary document or as a supporting schedule to calculate the product unit cost in both job order and process costing systems and in both manufacturing and service businesses.

Furniture Corporation has received an order for 10 recliner chairs from FurnitureTown, LLC. A partially complete bill of activities for that order appears on the next page. Fill in the missing data.

(continued)

Bill of Activities for FurnitureTown, LLC, Order

Activity	Activity Cost Rate	Cost Driver Level	Activity Cost
Unit level			
Parts production	$50 per machine hour	5 machine hours	$?
Assembly	$30 per direct labor hour	10 direct labor hours	?
Packing	$35 per unit	10 units	?
Batch level			
Work setup	$25 per setup	4 setups	?
Product level			
Product design	$160 per design hour	20 design hours	?
Facility level			
Building occupancy	200% of assembly labor cost	?	?
Total activity costs assigned to job			$?
Total job units			÷ 0
Activity costs per unit (total activity costs ÷ total units)			$?
Job cost summary:			
Direct materials			$1,000
Purchased parts			500
Activity costs			?
Total cost of order			$?
Product unit cost (total cost ÷ 10 units)			**$?**

SOLUTION

Bill of Activities for FurnitureTown, LLC Order

Activity	Activity Cost Rate	Cost Driver Level	Activity Cost
Unit level			
Parts production	$50 per machine hour	5 machine hours	$ 250
Assembly	$30 per direct labor hour	10 direct labor hours	300
Packing	$35 per unit	10 units	350
Batch level			
Work setup	$25 per setup	4 setups	100
Product level			
Product design	$160 per design hour	2 design hours	320
Facility level			
Building occupancy	200% of assembly labor cost	$300	600
Total activity costs assigned to job			$1,920
Total job units			÷ 10
Activity costs per unit (total activity costs ÷ total units)			$ 192
Job cost summary:			
Direct materials			$1,000
Purchased parts			500
Activity costs			1,920
Total cost of order			$3,420
Product unit cost (total cost ÷ 10 units)			**$ 342**

The New Operating Environment and Lean Operations

LO3 Define the elements of a lean operation, and identify the changes in inventory management that result when a firm adopts its just-in-time operating philosophy.

To achieve lean operations, managers focus on the elimination of waste. They must redesign their company's operating systems, plant layout, and basic management methods to conform to several basic concepts:

- Simple is better.
- The quality of the product or service is critical to customer satisfaction.
- The work environment must emphasize continuous improvement.
- Maintaining large inventories wastes resources and may hide poor work.
- Activities or functions that do not add value to a product or service should be eliminated or reduced.
- Goods should be produced only when needed.
- Workers must be multiskilled and must participate in eliminating waste.
- Building and maintaining long-term relationships with suppliers is important.

Application of these elements creates a lean operation throughout the company's value chain and guides all employees' work. Piecemeal attempts at lean operations have proved disastrous when the implementation focused on a few lean tools and methodologies instead of emphasizing how to think lean throughout the organization.

Just-in-Time (JIT)

Study Note

Traditional environments emphasize *functional* departments that tend to group similar activities together (e.g., repairs and maintenance).

Traditionally, companies operated with large amounts of inventory. They stored finished goods in anticipation of customers' orders; purchased materials infrequently but in large amounts; had long production runs with infrequent setups; manufactured large batches of products; and trained each member of their work forces to perform a limited number of tasks. Managers determined that changes in how inventory was processed were necessary because

- Large amounts of an organization's space and money were tied up in inventory.
- The source of poor-quality materials, products, or services was hard to pinpoint.

FOCUS ON BUSINESS PRACTICE

The Evolution to Lean Operations

- Eli Whitney perfected the concept of interchangeable parts in 1799, when he produced 10,000 muskets for the U.S. Army for the low price of $13.40 per musket.
- In the late 1890s, Frederick W. Taylor used his ideas of scientific management to standardize work through time studies.
- In the early twentieth century, Frank and Lillian Galbraith (parents of the authors of *Cheaper by the Dozen*) focused on eliminating waste by studying worker motivation and using motion studies and process charting.
- Starting in 1910, Henry Ford and Charles E. Sorensen arranged all the elements of manufacturing into a continuous system called the *production line*.
- After World War II, Taichii Ohno and Shigeo Shingo recognized the importance of inventory management, and they perfected the Toyota production system, from which lean production developed.[2]

- The number of non-value-adding activities was growing.
- Accounting for the manufacturing process was becoming ever more complex.

A lean operation embraces the **just-in-time (JIT) operating philosophy**, which requires that all resources—materials, personnel, and facilities—be acquired and used only as needed to create value for customers. A JIT environment reveals waste and eliminates it by adhering to the principles described below.

Minimum Inventory Levels In the traditional manufacturing environment, parts, materials, and supplies are purchased far in advance and stored until the production department needs them. In contrast, in a JIT environment, materials and parts are purchased and received only when they are needed. The JIT approach lowers costs by reducing the space needed for inventory storage, the amount of materials handling, and the amount of inventory obsolescence. It also reduces the need for inventory control facilities, personnel, and recordkeeping. In addition, it significantly decreases the amount of work in process inventory and the amount of working capital tied up in all inventories.

Study Note

Pull-through production represents a change in concept. Instead of producing goods in anticipation of customers' needs, customers' orders trigger the production process.

Pull-Through Production The JIT operating philosophy requires **pull-through production**, a system in which a customer's order triggers the purchase of materials and the scheduling of production for the products that have been ordered. In contrast, with the **push-through method** used in traditional manufacturing operations, products are manufactured in long production runs and stored in anticipation of customers' orders. With pull-through production, the size of a customer's order determines the size of a production run, and the company purchases materials and parts as needed. Inventory levels are kept low, but machines must be set up more frequently as different job are worked on.

Study Note

In the JIT environment, normal operating activities—setup, production, and maintenance—still take place. But the timing of those activities is altered to promote smoother operations and to minimize downtime.

Quick Setup and Flexible Work Cells In the past, managers felt that it was more cost-effective to produce large batches of goods because producing small batches increases the number of machine setups. The success of JIT disproved this. By placing machines in more efficient locations and standardizing setups, setup time can be minimized.

In a traditional factory layout, similar machines are grouped together, forming functional departments. Products are routed through these departments in sequence, so that all necessary operations are completed in order. This process can take several days or weeks, depending on the size and complexity of the job. By changing the factory layout so that all the machines needed for sequential processing are placed together, the JIT operating philosophy may cut the manufacturing time of a product from days to hours, or from weeks to days. The new cluster of machinery forms a flexible **work cell**, an autonomous production line that can perform all required operations efficiently and continuously. The flexible work cell handles a "family of products"—that is, products of similar shape or size. Product families require minimal setup changes as workers move from one job to the next. The more flexible the work cell is, the greater its potential to minimize total production time.

A Multiskilled Work Force In the flexible work cells of a JIT environment, one worker may be required to operate several types of machines simultaneously. The worker may have to set up and retool the machines and even perform routine maintenance on them. A JIT operating philosophy thus requires a multiskilled work force, and multiskilled workers have been very effective in contributing to high levels of productivity.

Study Note
That inspections are necessary is an admission that problems with quality do occur. Continuous inspection throughout production as opposed to inspection only at the end creates awareness of a problem at the point where it occurs.

High Levels of Product Quality A JIT environment results in high-quality products because high-quality direct materials are used and inspections are made throughout the production process. In a JIT environment, inspection as a separate step does not add value to a product, so inspection is incorporated into ongoing operations. A JIT machine operator inspects the products as they pass through the manufacturing process. If the operator detects a flaw, he or she shuts down the work cell to prevent the production of similarly flawed products while the cause of the problem is being determined. The operator either fixes the problem or helps others find a way to correct it. This integrated inspection procedure, combined with high-quality materials, produces high-quality finished goods.

Study Note
Although separate inspection costs are reduced in a JIT operating environment, some additional time is added to production because the machine operator is now performing the inspection function. The objectives are to reduce *total* costs and to increase quality.

Effective Preventive Maintenance When a company rearranges its machinery into flexible work cells, each machine becomes an integral part of its cell. If one machine breaks down, the entire work cell stops functioning, and the product cannot easily be routed to another machine while the malfunctioning machine is being repaired. Continuous JIT operations therefore require an effective system of preventive maintenance. Preventing machine breakdowns is considered more important and more cost-effective than keeping machines running continuously. Machine operators are trained to perform minor repairs when they detect problems. Machines are serviced regularly—much as an automobile is—to help guarantee continued operation. The machine operator conducts routine maintenance during periods of downtime between orders. (Remember that in a JIT setting, the work cell does not operate unless there is a customer order for the product. Machine operators take advantage of such downtime to perform routine maintenance.)

Continuous Improvement of the Work Environment

Study Note
The JIT operating philosophy must be adopted by everyone in a company before its total benefits can be realized.

A JIT operating philosophy fosters loyalty among workers, who are likely to see themselves as part of a team because they are so deeply involved in the production process. Machine operators must have the skills to run several types of machines, detect defective products, suggest measures to correct problems, and maintain the machinery within their work cells. In addition, each worker is encouraged to suggest improvements to the production process. In Japanese, this is called *kaizen,* meaning "good change." Companies with a JIT operating philosophy receive thousands of employee suggestions and implement a high percentage of them, and they reward workers for suggestions that improve the process. Such an environment fosters workers' initiative and benefits the company.

Accounting for Product Costs in a JIT Operating Environment

When a firm shifts to lean operations and adopts a JIT operating philosophy, managers must take a new approach to evaluating costs and controlling operations. The changes in the operations will affect how costs are determined and what measures are used to monitor performance.

When a company adopts a JIT operating philosophy, the work cells and the goal of reducing or eliminating non-value-adding activities change the way costs are classified and assigned.

Classifying Costs The traditional production process can be divided into five time frames:

Processing time	The actual amount of time spent working on a product
Inspection time	The time spent looking for product flaws or reworking defective units

Moving time	The time spent moving a product from one operation or department to another
Queue time	The time a product spends waiting to be worked on once it arrives at the next operation or department
Storage time	The time a product spends in materials inventory, work in process inventory, or finished goods inventory

In product costing under JIT, costs associated with processing time are classified as either direct materials costs or conversion costs. **Conversion costs** are the sum of the direct labor costs and overhead costs incurred by a production department, work cell, or other work center. According to JIT, costs associated with inspection, moving, queue, and storage time should be reduced or eliminated because they do not add value to the product.

Assigning Costs In a JIT operating environment, managers focus on **throughput time**, the time it takes to move a product through the entire production process. Measures of product movement, such as machine time, are used to apply conversion costs to products.

Sophisticated computer monitoring of the work cells allows many costs to be traced directly to the cells in which products are manufactured. As Table 19-2 shows, several costs that in a traditional environment are treated as indirect costs and applied to products using an overhead rate are treated as the direct costs of a JIT work cell. Because the products that a work cell manufactures are similar in nature, direct materials and conversion costs should be nearly uniform for each product in a cell.

- The costs of repairs and maintenance, materials handling, operating supplies, utilities, and supervision can be traced directly to work cells as they are incurred.
- Depreciation charges are based on units of output, not on time, so depreciation can be charged directly to work cells based on the number of units produced.
- Building occupancy costs, insurance premiums, and property taxes remain indirect costs and must be assigned to the work cells for inclusion in the conversion cost.

TABLE 19-2
Direct and Indirect Costs in Traditional and JIT Environments

	Costs in a Traditional Environment	Costs in a JIT Environment
Direct materials	Direct	Direct
Direct labor	Direct	Direct
Repairs and maintenance	Indirect	Direct to work cell
Materials handling	Indirect	Direct to work cell
Operating supplies	Indirect	Direct to work cell
Utilities costs	Indirect	Direct to work cell
Supervision	Indirect	Direct to work cell
Depreciation	Indirect	Direct to work cell
Supporting service functions	Indirect	Mostly direct to work cell
Building occupancy	Indirect	Indirect
Insurance and taxes	Indirect	Indirect

The cost categories in the following list are typical of a furniture manufacturer. Identify each cost as direct or indirect, assuming that it was incurred in (1) a traditional manufacturing setting and (2) a JIT environment. State the reasons for changes in classification.

	Traditional Setting	JIT Setting	Reason for Change
Direct materials			
Direct labor			
Supervisory salaries			
Electrical power			
Operating supplies			
Purchased parts			
Employee benefits			
Indirect labor			
Insurance and taxes, plant			

SOLUTION

	Traditional Setting	JIT Setting	Reason for Change
Direct materials	Direct	Direct	
Direct labor	Direct	Direct	
Supervisory salaries	Indirect	Direct	Traceable to work cell
Electrical power	Indirect	Direct	Traceable to work cell
Operating supplies	Indirect	Direct	Traceable to work cell
Purchased parts	Direct	Direct	
Employee benefits	Indirect	Direct	Traceable to work cell
Indirect labor	Indirect	Direct	Traceable to work cell
Insurance and taxes, plant	Indirect	Indirect	

Backflush Costing

LO4 Define and apply *backflush costing,* and compare the cost flows in traditional and backflush costing.

Managers in a lean operating environment are continuously seeking ways of reducing wasted resources and wasted time. So far, we have focused on how they can trim waste from operations, but they can reduce waste in other areas as well, including the accounting process. Because a lean operation reduces labor costs, the accounting system can combine the costs of direct labor and overhead into the single category of conversion costs, and because in JIT, materials arrive just in time to be used in the production process, there is little reason to maintain a separate Materials Inventory account. Thus, by simplifying cost flows through the accounting records, it is possible to reduce the time it takes to record and account for the costs of the manufacturing process.

A lean organization can also streamline its accounting process by using backflush costing. In **backflush costing,** all product costs are first accumulated in the Cost of Goods Sold account; at the end of the accounting period, they are "flushed back," or worked backward, into the appropriate inventory accounts. By having all product costs flow straight to a final destination and working back to determine the proper balances for the inventory accounts at the end of the period, this method saves recording time. As illustrated in Figure 19-2, it eliminates the need to record several transactions that must be recorded in traditional operating environments.

> **Study Note**
> Backflush costing eliminates the need to make journal entries during the period to track cost flows through the production process as the product is made.

FIGURE 19-2 Comparison of Cost Flows in Traditional and Backflush Costing

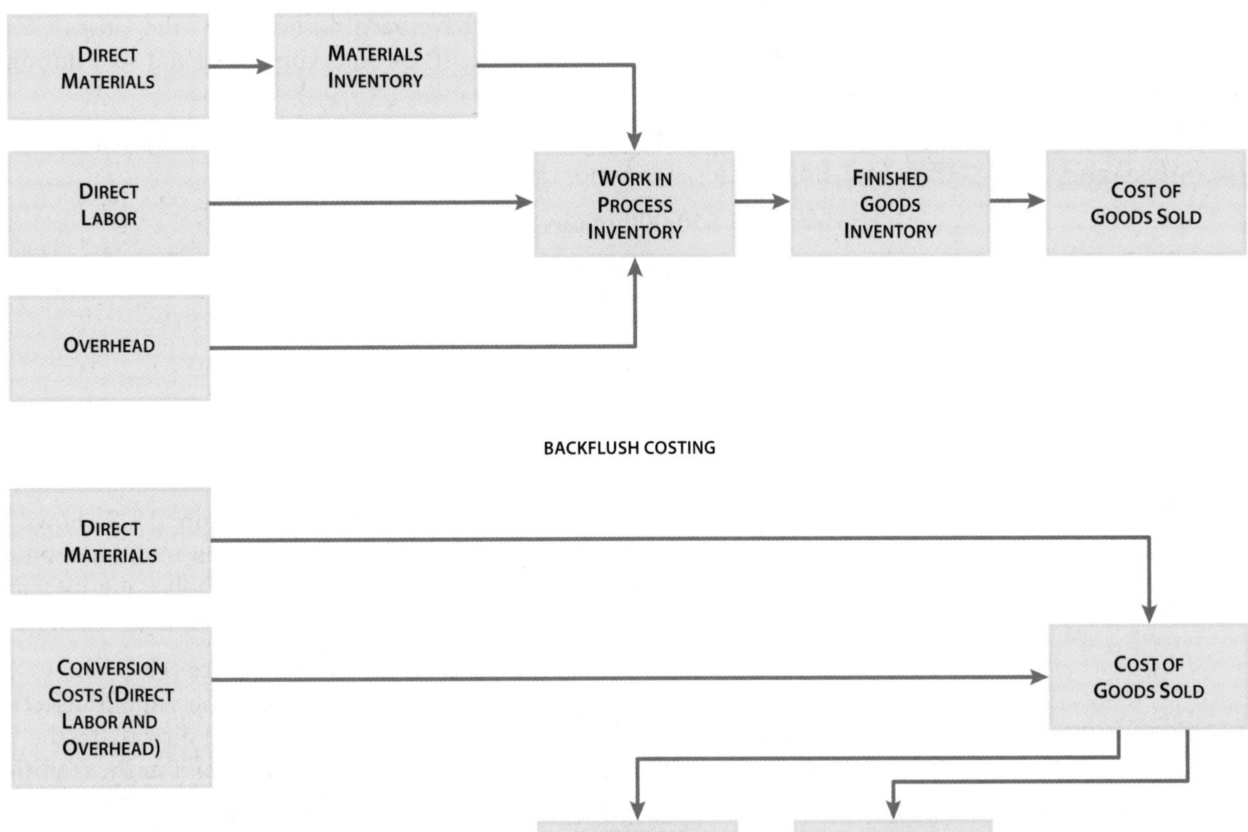

In a traditional environment, costs are tracked through the various production departments as products or services move through the production process.

Traditional costing methods:

- When direct materials arrive at a factory, their costs flow into the Materials Inventory account.
- When the direct materials are requisitioned into production, their costs flow into the Work in Process Inventory account. When direct labor is used, its costs are added to the Work in Process Inventory account. Overhead is applied to production using a base like direct labor hours, machine hours, or number of units produced and is added to the other costs in the Work in Process Inventory account.
- At the end of the manufacturing process, the costs of the finished units are transferred to the Finished Goods Inventory account, and when the units are sold, their costs are transferred to the Cost of Goods Sold account.

JIT costing method:

- In a JIT setting, direct materials arrive just in time to be placed into production. As you can see in Figure 19-2, when backflush costing is used, the direct materials costs and the conversion costs (direct labor and overhead) are immediately charged to the Cost of Goods Sold account.

Study Note

In backflush costing, entries to the Work in Process Inventory and Finished Goods Inventory accounts are made at the end of the period.

- At the end of the period, the costs of goods in work in process inventory and in finished goods inventory are determined, and those costs are flushed back to the Work in Process Inventory account and the Finished Goods Inventory account. Once those costs have been flushed back, the Cost of Goods Sold account contains only the costs of units completed and sold during the period.

To illustrate, assume that the following transactions occurred at one of **La-Z-Boy**'s factories last month:

1. Purchased $20,000 of direct materials on account.
2. Used all of the direct materials in production during the month.
3. Incurred direct labor costs of $8,000.
4. Applied $24,000 of overhead to production.
5. Completed units costing $51,600 during the month.
6. Sold units costing $51,500 during the month.

- ***Traditional costing methods:*** The top diagram in Figure 19-3 shows how these transactions would be entered in T accounts when traditional product costing is used. You can trace the flow of each cost by following its transaction number.
- ***JIT costing method:*** The bottom diagram in Figure 19-3 shows how backflush costing in a JIT environment would treat the same transactions. The cost of direct materials (Transaction 1) is charged directly to the Cost of Goods Sold account. Transaction 2, which is included in the traditional method, is not included when backflush costing is used because there is no Materials Inventory account. The costs of direct labor (Transaction 3) and overhead (Transaction 4) are combined and transferred to the Cost of Goods Sold account. The total in the Cost of Goods Sold account is then $52,000 ($20,000 for direct materials and $32,000 for conversion costs).

Once all product costs for the period have been entered in the Cost of Goods Sold account, the amounts to be transferred back to the inventory accounts are calculated.

- The amount transferred to the Finished Goods Inventory account is the difference between the cost of units sold (Transaction 6) and the cost of completed units (Transaction 5) ($51,600 − $51,500 = $100).
- The remaining difference in the Cost of Goods Sold account represents the cost of the work that is still in production at the end of the period. It is the amount charged to the Cost of Goods Sold account during the period less the actual cost of goods finished during the period (Transaction 5) [($20,000 + $8,000 + $24,000) − $51,600 = $400]; this amount is transferred to the Work in Process Inventory account.

Notice that the ending balance in the Cost of Goods Sold account, $51,500, is the same as the ending balance when traditional costing is used. The difference is that backflush costing enabled us to use fewer accounts and to avoid recording several transactions.

FIGURE 19-3 Cost Flows Through T Accounts in Traditional and Backflush Costing

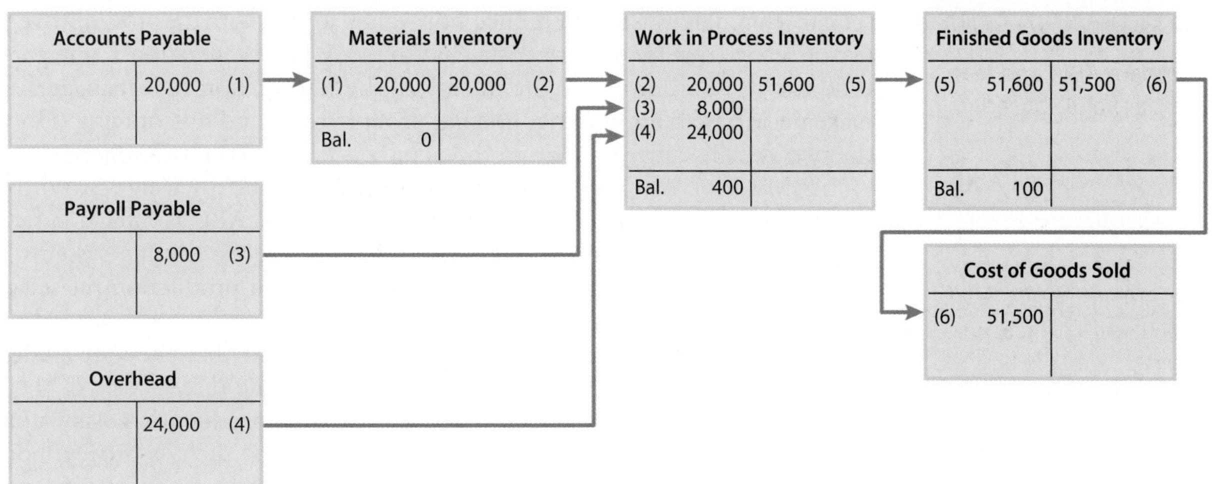

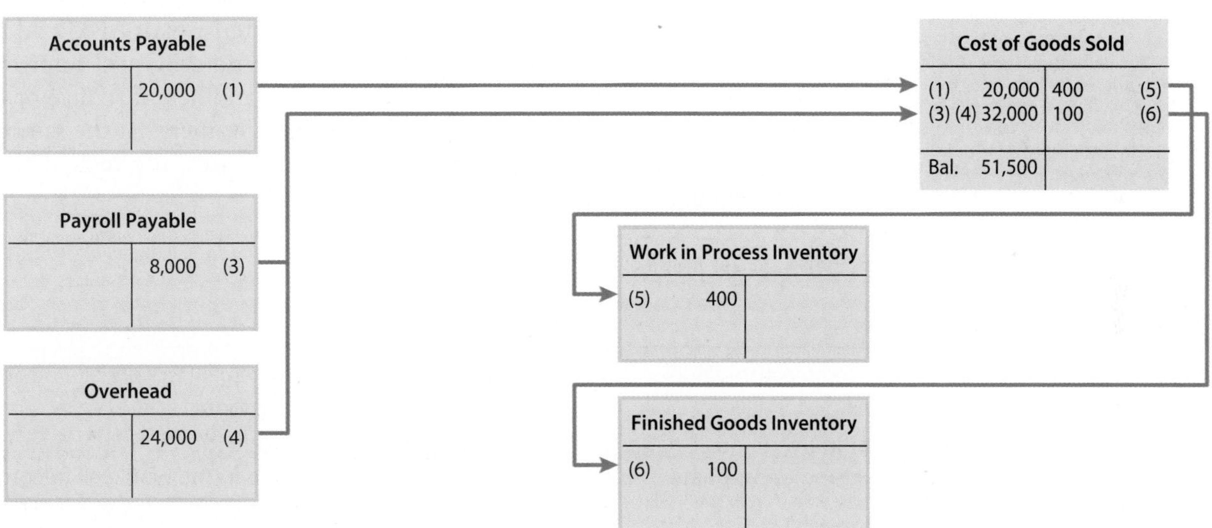

STOP & APPLY >

For work done during August, Plush Furniture Company, incurred direct materials costs of $123,450 and conversion costs of $265,200. The company employs a just-in-time operating environment and backflush costing.

At the end of August, it was determined that the Work in Process Inventory account had been assigned $980 of costs, and the ending balance of the Finished Goods Inventory account was $1,290. There were no beginning inventory balances. How much was charged to the Cost of Goods Sold account during August? What was the ending balance of the Cost of Goods Sold account?

SOLUTION

A total of $388,650 ($123,450 + $265,200) was charged to the Cost of Goods Sold account during August. The ending balance of Cost of Goods Sold was $386,380 ($388,650 − $980 − $1,290).

Comparison of ABM and Lean

LO5 Compare ABM and lean operations as value-based systems.

ABM and lean have several things in common. As value-based systems, both analyze processes and identify value-adding and non-value-adding activities. Both seek to eliminate waste and reduce non-value-adding activities to improve product or service quality, reduce costs, and improve an organization's efficiency and productivity. Both improve the quality of the information that managers use to make decisions about bidding, pricing, product lines, and outsourcing. However, the two systems differ in their methods of costing and cost assignment.

ABM's tool, ABC, calculates product or service cost by using cost drivers to assign the indirect costs of production to cost objects. ABC is often a fairly complex accounting method used with job order and process costing systems. Note that the ABC method can also be used to examine non-production-related activities, such as marketing and shipping.

> **Study Note**
> ABM's primary goal is to calculate product or service cost accurately. Lean's primary goal is to eliminate waste in business processes.

Lean uses JIT and reorganizes many activities so that they are performed within work cells. The costs of those activities become direct costs of the work cell and of the products made in that cell. The total production costs within the cell can then be assigned by using simple cost drivers, such as process hours or direct materials cost. Companies that have implemented lean operations may use backflush costing rather than job order costing or process costing. This approach focuses on the output at the end of the production process and simplifies the accounting system. Table 19-3 summarizes the characteristics of ABM and lean.

A company can use both ABM and lean. ABM and ABC will improve the accuracy of the company's product or service costing and help it reduce or eliminate business activities that do not add value for its customers. At the same time, the company can apply lean thinking to simplify processes, use resources effectively, and eliminate waste.

TABLE 19-3 Comparison of ABM and Lean Activity-Based Systems

	ABM	Lean
Primary purpose	To eliminate or reduce non-value-adding activities	To eliminate or reduce waste in all aspects of a business, including its processes and products or services
Cost assignment	Uses ABC to assign overhead costs to the product by using appropriate cost drivers	Uses JIT and reorganizes production activities into work cells; overhead costs incurred in the work cell become direct costs of the cell's products
Costing method	Integrates ABC with job order or process costing to calculate product costs	May use backflush costing to calculate product costs
Limitation	ABC can involve costly data collection and complex allocations	Requires management to think differently and use different performance measures

& APPLY >

Couch Potato, Inc., produces futon mattresses. The company recently changed from a traditional production environment to just-in-time work cells. Would you recommend the use of ABM/ABC or backflush costing for tracking product costs? Explain your choice.

SOLUTION

Because the company produces similar products, it lends itself well to backflush costing for the calculation of product costs. A company that makes a variety of products with differing activity choices in a job order setting is better served by the more accurate and more complex procedures of ABM/ABC product costing.

A LOOK BACK AT ▶ LA-Z-BOY

In this chapter's Decision Point, we asked the following questions:

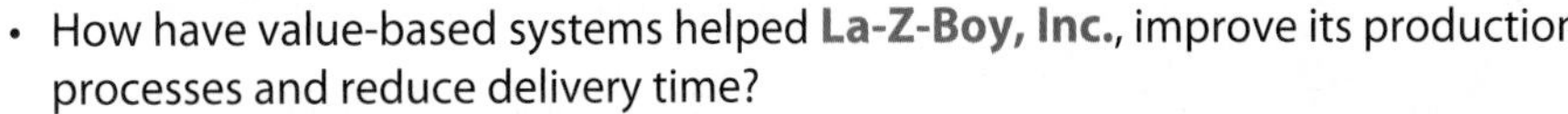

- How have value-based systems helped **La-Z-Boy, Inc.**, improve its production processes and reduce delivery time?

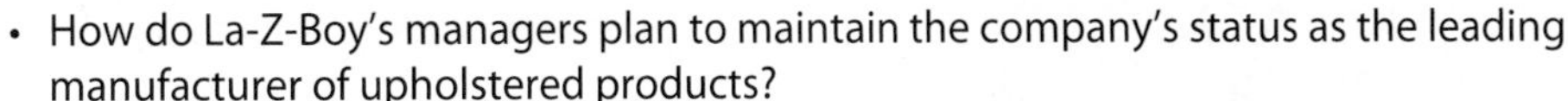

- How do La-Z-Boy's managers plan to maintain the company's status as the leading manufacturer of upholstered products?

La-Z-Boy's managers use activity-based management (ABM) and a lean operating environment to identify and reduce or eliminate activities that do not add value to the company's products. These systems focus on minimizing waste, reducing costs, and improving profitability. The continuous flow of information that ABM and JIT provide has enabled La-Z-Boy's managers to improve the company's production processes. They are able to adjust their labor needs each week to meet order requirements; to schedule timely deliveries from suppliers, thus maintaining appropriate inventory levels; and to keep track of the company's fleet of delivery trucks.

La-Z-Boy's disciplined monitoring of order, production, and delivery activities gives the company its competitive edge today and in the future. By using ABM and lean thinking, La-Z-Boy has achieved higher productivity than other furniture manufacturers and is able to offer more than 40,000 product variations.[3]

Review Problem

Activity-Based Costing LO2

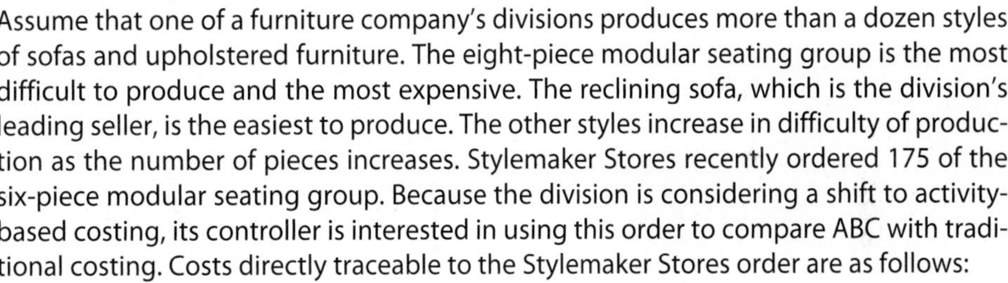

Assume that one of a furniture company's divisions produces more than a dozen styles of sofas and upholstered furniture. The eight-piece modular seating group is the most difficult to produce and the most expensive. The reclining sofa, which is the division's leading seller, is the easiest to produce. The other styles increase in difficulty of production as the number of pieces increases. Stylemaker Stores recently ordered 175 of the six-piece modular seating group. Because the division is considering a shift to activity-based costing, its controller is interested in using this order to compare ABC with traditional costing. Costs directly traceable to the Stylemaker Stores order are as follows:

Direct materials	$57,290
Purchased parts	$76,410
Direct labor hours	1,320
Average direct labor pay rate per hour	$14.00

With the traditional costing approach, the controller applies overhead costs at a rate of 320 percent of direct labor costs.

For activity-based costing of the Stylemaker Stores order, the controller uses the following data:

Activity	Cost Driver	Activity Cost Rate	Activity Usage
Product design	Engineering hours	$62 per engineering hour	76 engineering hours
Work cell setup	Number of setups	$90 per setup	16 setups
Parts production	Machine hours	$38 per machine hour	380 machine hours
Assembly	Assembly labor hours	$40 per assembly labor hour	500 assembly labor hours
Product simulation	Testing hours	$90 per testing hour	28 testing hours
Packaging and shipping	Product units	$26 per unit	175 units
Building occupancy	Direct labor cost	125% of direct labor cost	$18,480 direct labor cost

Required

1. Use the traditional costing approach to compute the total cost and product unit cost of the Stylemaker Stores order.
2. Using the cost hierarchy for manufacturing companies, classify each activity of the Stylemaker Stores order according to the level at which it occurs.
3. Prepare a bill of activities for the operating costs, and use ABC to compute the total cost and product unit cost.
4. What is the difference between the product unit cost you computed using the traditional approach and the one you computed using ABC? Does the use of ABC guarantee cost reduction for every order?

Answers to Review Problem

1. Traditional costing approach:

Direct materials	$ 57,290
Purchased parts	76,410
Direct labor	18,480
Overhead (320% of direct labor cost)	59,136
Total cost of order	$ 211,316
Product unit cost (total costs ÷ 175 units)	$1,207.52

2. Activities classified by level of the manufacturing cost hierarchy:

Unit level:	Parts production
	Assembly
	Packaging and shipping
Batch level:	Work cell setup
Product level:	Product design
	Product simulation
Facility level:	Building occupancy

3. Bill of activities and total cost and product unit cost computed with ABC:

Bill of Activities
Stylemaker Stores Order

Activity	Activity Cost Rate	Cost Driver Level	Activity Cost
Unit level			
Parts production	$38 per machine hour	380 machine hours	$ 14,440
Assembly	$40 per assembly labor hour	500 assembly labor hours	20,000
Packaging and shipping	$26 per unit	175 units	4,550
Batch level			
Work cell setup	$90 per setup	16 setups	1,440
Product level			
Product design	$62 per engineering hour	76 engineering hours	4,712
Product simulation	$90 per testing hour	28 testing hours	2,520
Facility level			
Building occupancy	125% of direct labor cost	$18,480 direct labor cost	23,100
Total activity costs assigned to job			$ 70,762
Total job units			÷ 175
Activity costs per unit (total activity costs ÷ total units)			$ 404.35*
Cost summary			
Direct materials			$ 57,290
Purchased parts			76,410
Activity costs (includes labor and overhead)			70,762
Total cost of order			$ 204,462
Product unit cost (total cost of order ÷ 175 units)			$1,168.35*

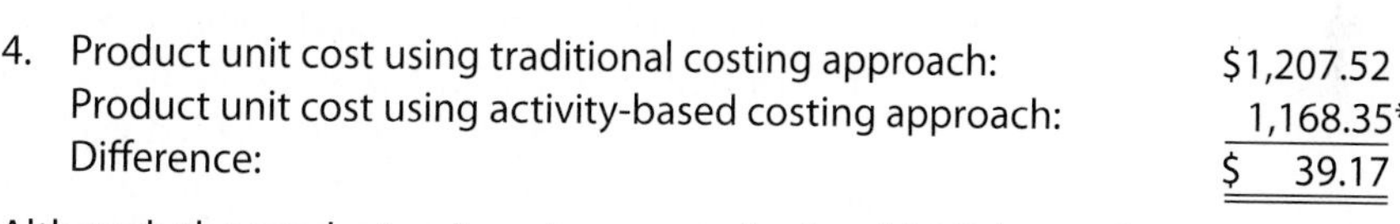

4. Product unit cost using traditional costing approach: $1,207.52
   Product unit cost using activity-based costing approach: 1,168.35*
   Difference: $ 39.17

Although the product unit cost computed using ABC is lower than the one computed using the traditional costing approach, ABC does not guarantee cost reduction for every product. It does improve cost traceability, which often identifies products that are "undercosted" or "overcosted" by a traditional product costing system.

*Rounded.

& REVIEW >

LO1 Explain why managers use value-based systems, and discuss the relationship of these systems to the supply chain and value chain.

A value-based system categorizes activities as either adding value to a product or service or not adding value. It enables managers to see their organization as a collection of value-creating activities (a value chain) that operates as part of a larger system that includes suppliers' and customers' value chains (a supply chain). This perspective helps managers work cooperatively both inside and outside their organizations to reduce costs by eliminating waste and inefficiencies and by redirecting resources toward value-adding activities. PVA is a technique that managers use to identify and link all the activities involved in the value chain. It analyzes business processes by relating activities to the events that prompt the activities and to the resources that the activities consume. A value-adding activity adds value to a product or service as perceived by the customer. A non-value-adding activity adds cost to a product or service but does not increase its market value.

LO2 Define *activity-based costing,* and explain how a cost hierarchy and a bill of activities are used.

Activity-based costing (ABC) is a method of assigning costs that calculates a more accurate product cost than traditional methods do. It does so by categorizing all indirect costs by activity, tracing the indirect costs to those activities, and assigning those costs to products using a cost driver related to the cause of the cost. To implement ABC, managers (1) identify and classify each activity, (2) estimate the cost of resources for each activity, (3) identify a cost driver for each activity and estimate the quantity of each cost driver, (4) calculate an activity cost rate for each activity, and (5) assign costs to cost objects based on the level of activity required to make the product or provide the service. ABC's primary disadvantage is that it is costly to implement.

Two tools—a cost hierarchy and a bill of activities—help in the implementation of ABC. To create a cost hierarchy, managers classify activities into four levels. Unit-level activities are performed each time a unit is produced. Batch-level activities are performed each time a batch of goods is produced. Product-level activities are performed to support a particular product line or brand. Facility-level activities are performed to support a facility's general manufacturing process. A bill of activities is then used to compute the costs assigned to activities and the product or service unit cost.

LO3 Define the elements of a lean operation, and identify the changes in inventory management that result when a firm adopts its just-in-time operating philosophy.

Lean operation's objective is to eliminate waste. One of its basic principles is to operate production on a just-in-time (JIT) basis. The elements of a JIT environment are minimum inventory levels, pull-through production, quick setup and flexible work cells, a multiskilled work force, high levels of product quality, effective preventive maintenance, and continuous improvement of the work environment.

In product costing under JIT, processing costs are classified as either direct materials costs or conversion costs. The costs associated with inspection time, moving time, queue time, and storage time are reduced or eliminated. With computerized monitoring of the work cells, many costs that are treated as indirect or overhead costs in traditional manufacturing settings become direct costs because they can be traced directly to work cells. The only costs that remain indirect costs and must be assigned to the work cells are those that cannot be linked to a specific work cell—in other words, those associated with building occupancy, insurance, and property taxes.

LO4 Define and apply *backflush costing*, and compare the cost flows in traditional and backflush costing.

In backflush costing, all product costs are first accumulated in the Cost of Goods Sold account; at the end of the accounting period, they are "flushed back," or worked backward, into the appropriate inventory accounts. Backflush costing is commonly used to account for product costs in a JIT operating environment. It differs from the traditional costing approach, which records the costs of materials purchased in the Materials Inventory account and uses the Work in Process Inventory account to record the costs of direct materials, direct labor, and overhead during the production process. The objective of backflush costing is to save recording time, which cuts costs.

LO5 Compare ABM and lean operations as value-based systems.

As value-based systems, both ABM and lean seek to eliminate waste and reduce non-value-adding activities. However, they differ in their approaches to cost assignment and calculation of product cost. ABM uses ABC to assign indirect costs to products using cost drivers; lean uses JIT to reorganize activities so that they are performed within work cells, and the overhead costs incurred in a work cell become direct costs of the products made in that cell. ABM uses job order or process costing to calculate product costs, whereas lean may use backflush costing.

REVIEW of Concepts and Terminology

The following concepts and terms were introduced in this chapter:

Activity-based costing (ABC) 887 (LO1)

Activity-based management (ABM) 887 (LO1)

Backflush costing 896 (LO4)

Batch-level activities 889 (LO2)

Bill of activities 890 (LO2)

Conversion costs 895 (LO3)

Cost hierarchy 889 (LO2)

Facility-level activities 890 (LO2)

Full product cost 884 (LO1)

Inspection time 894 (LO3)

Just-in-time (JIT) operating philosophy 893 (LO3)

Lean operation 888 (LO1)

Moving time 895 (LO3)

Non-value-adding activity 887 (LO1)

Processing time 894 (LO3)

Process value analysis (PVA) 886 (LO1)

Product-level activities 890 (LO2)

Pull-through production 893 (LO3)

Push-through method 893 (LO3)

Queue time 895 (LO3)

Storage time 895) (LO3)

Supply chain 885 (LO1)

Throughput time 895 (LO3)

Unit-level activities 889 (LO2)

Value-adding activity 887 (LO1)

Value-based systems 884 (LO1)

Value chain 885 (LO1)

Work cell 893 (LO3)

CHAPTER ASSIGNMENTS

BUILDING Your Basic Knowledge and Skills

Short Exercises

LO1 **Activity-Based Systems**

SE 1. Thom Lutz started a retail clothing business two years ago. Lutz's first year was very successful, but sales dropped 50 percent in the second year. A friend who is a business consultant analyzed Lutz's business and came up with two basic reasons for the decline in sales: (1) Lutz has been placing orders late in each season, and (2) shipments of clothing have been arriving late and in poor condition. What measures can Lutz take to improve his business and persuade customers to return?

LO1 **The Value Chain**

SE 2. Which of the following activities would be part of the value chain of a manufacturing company? Which activities do not add value?

1. Product marketing
2. Machine drilling
3. Materials storage
4. Product design
5. Product packing
6. Cost accounting
7. Moving work in process
8. Inventory control

LO1 **The Supply Chain**

SE 3. Jack DuBois is developing plans to open a restaurant called Ribs 'n Slaw. He has located a building and will lease all the furniture and equipment he needs for the restaurant. Food Servers, Inc. will supply all the restaurant's personnel. Identify the components of Ribs 'n Slaw's supply chain.

LO1 **Value-Adding and Non-Value-Adding Activities**

SE 4. Indicate whether the following activities of a submarine sandwich shop are value-adding (V) or non-value-adding (NV):

1. Purchasing sandwich ingredients
2. Storing condiments
3. Making sandwiches
4. Cleaning up the shop
5. Making home deliveries
6. Accounting for sales and costs

LO2 **The Cost Hierarchy**

SE 5. Engineering design is an activity that is vital to the success of any motor vehicle manufacturer. Identify the level at which engineering design would be classified in the cost hierarchy used with ABC for each of the following:

1. A maker of unique editions of luxury automobiles
2. A maker of built-to-order city and county emergency vehicles (orders are usually placed for 10 to 12 identical vehicles)
3. A maker of a line of automobiles sold throughout the world

LO2 **The Cost Hierarchy**

SE 6. Match the four levels of the cost hierarchy to the following activities of a blue jeans manufacturer that uses activity-based management:

1. Routine maintenance of sewing machines
2. Designing a pattern for a new style
3. Sewing seams on a garment
4. Producing 100 jeans of a certain style in a certain size

LO3 **Elements of a JIT Operating Environment**

SE 7. Maintaining minimum inventory levels and using pull-through production are important elements of a just-in-time operating environment. How does pull-through production help minimize inventories?

LO3 **Product Costing Changes in a JIT Environment**

SE 8. Aromatherapy Products Company is in the process of adopting the just-in-time operating environment for its lotion-making operations. Indicate which of the following overhead costs are non-value-adding costs (NVA) and which can be traced directly to the new lotion-making work cell (D):

1. Storage containers for work in process inventory
2. Insurance on the storage warehouse
3. Machine electricity
4. Machine repairs
5. Depreciation of the storage container moving equipment
6. Machine setup labor

LO4 **Backflush Costing**

SE 9. For work done during August, Pansey Company incurred direct materials costs of $120,000 and conversion costs of $260,000. The company employs a just-in-time operating philosophy and backflush costing. At the end of August, it was determined that the Work in Process Inventory account had been assigned $900 of costs, and the ending balance of the Finished Goods Inventory account was $1,300. There were no beginning inventory balances. How much was charged to the Cost of Goods Sold account during August? What was the ending balance of that account?

LO5 **Comparison of ABM and Lean**

SE 10. Hwang Corp. recently installed three just-in-time work cells in its screen-making division. The work cells will make large quantities of similar products for major window and door manufacturers. Should Hwang use lean with JIT and backflush costing or ABM and ABC to account for product costs? Defend your choice of system.

Exercises

LO1 **Management Reports**

E 1. The reports that follow are from a department in an insurance company. Which report would be used for financial purposes, and which would be used for activity-based decision making? Why?

Salaries	$ 1,400	Enter claims into system	$ 2,000
Equipment	1,200	Analyze claims	1,000
Travel expenses	8,000	Suspend claims	1,500
Supplies	300	Receive inquiries	1,500
Use and occupancy	3,000	Resolve problems	400
		Process batches	3,000
		Determine eligibility	4,000
		Make copies	200
		Write correspondence	100
		Attend training	200
Total	$13,900	Total	$13,900

LO1 **The Supply Chain and Value Chain**

E 2. Indicate which of the following persons and activities associated with a lawn and garden nursery are part of the supply chain (S) and which are part of the value chain (V):

1. Plant and tree vendor
2. Purchasing potted trees
3. Computer and software company
4. Creating marketing plans
5. Advertising company
6. Scheduling delivery trucks
7. Customer service

LO1 **The Supply Chain and Value Chain**

E 3. The items in the following list are associated with a bank. Indicate which are part of the supply chain (S) and which are part of the value chain (V).

1. Federal Reserve Bank
2. Student loan processing
3. Investment services
4. ATM
5. Customer

LO1 **Value Analysis**

E 4. Libbel Enterprises has been in business for 30 years. Last year, the company purchased Chemcraft Laboratory and entered the chemical processing business. Libbel's controller prepared a process value analysis of the new operation and identified the following activities:

New product research	Product sales	Product bottling process
Design testing	Packaging process	Product warranty work
Materials storage	Materials inspection	Product engineering
Product curing process	New product marketing	Purchasing of direct materials
Product scheduling	Product inspection	Finished goods storage
Product spoilage	Product delivery	Cleanup of processing areas
Customer follow-up	Materials delivery	Product mixing process

Identify the value-adding activities in this list, and classify them into the activity areas of the value chain illustrated in Figure 19-1. Prepare a separate list of the non-value-adding activities.

LO1 **Value-Adding Activities**

E 5. When Courtney Tybee prepared a process value analysis for her company, she identified the following primary activities. Identify the value-adding activities (VA) and the non-value-adding activities (NVA).

1. Production scheduling
2. Customer follow-up
3. Materials moving
4. Product inspection
5. Engineering design
6. Product marketing
7. Product sales
8. Materials storage

LO2 **The Cost Hierarchy**

E 6. Copia Electronics makes speaker systems. Its customers range from new hotels and restaurants that need specifically designed sound systems to nationwide retail outlets that order large quantities of similar products. The following activities are part of the company's operating process:

New retail product design	Purchasing of materials	Assembly labor
Retail product marketing	Building repair	Assembly line setup
Unique system design	Retail sales commissions	Building security
Unique system packaging	Bulk packing of orders	Facility supervision

Classify each activity as unit level (UL), batch level (BL), product level (PL), or facility level (FL).

LO2 **Bill of Activities**

E 7. Lake Corporation has received an order for handheld computers from Union, LLC. A partially complete bill of activities for that order appears below. Fill in the missing data.

Lake Corporation
Bill of Activities for Union, LLC
Order Form

Activity	Activity Cost Rate	Cost Driver Level	Activity Cost
Unit level			
Parts production	$50 per machine hour	200 machine hours	$?
Assembly	$20 per direct labor hour	100 direct labor hours	?
Packaging and shipping	$12.50 per unit	400 units	?
Batch level			
Work cell setup	$100 per setup	16 setups	?
Product level			
Product design	$60 per engineering hour	80 engineering hours	?
Product simulation	$80 per testing hour	30 testing hours	?
Facility level			
Building occupancy	200% of assembly labor cost	?	?
Total activity costs assigned to job			$?
Total job units			÷ 400
Activity costs per unit (total activity costs ÷ total units)			$?
Cost summary			
Direct materials			$60,000
Purchased parts			80,000
Activity costs			?
Total cost of order			$?
Product unit cost (total cost ÷ 400 units)			$?

LO2 **Activity Cost Rates**

E 8. Compute the activity cost rates for materials handling, assembly, and design based on these data:

Materials	
Cloth	$26,000
Fasteners	4,000
Purchased parts	40,000
Materials handling	
Labor	8,000
Equipment depreciation	5,000
Electrical power	2,000
Maintenance	6,000
Assembly	
Machine operators	5,000

Design	
Labor	$ 5,000
Electrical power	1,000
Overhead	8,000

Output totaled 40,000 units. Each unit requires three machine hours of effort. Materials handling costs are allocated to the products based on direct materials cost. Design costs are allocated based on units produced. Assembly costs are allocated based on 500 machine operator hours. [**Hint**: Activity cost rate = (Total activity costs ÷ Total allocation base). Examples of an allocation base include total dollars of materials, total machine operator hours, or total units of output.]

LO3 Elements of a Lean Operating Environment

E 9. The following numbered items are concepts that underlie value-based systems, such as ABM and lean. Match each concept to the related lettered element(s) of a lean operating environment.

1. Business processes are simplified.
2. The quality of the product or service is critical.
3. Employees are cross-trained.
4. Large inventories waste resources and may hide bad work.
5. Goods should be produced only when needed.
6. Equipment downtime is minimized.

a. Minimum inventory levels
b. Pull-through production
c. Quick machine setups and flexible work cells
d. A multiskilled work force
e. High levels of product quality
f. Effective preventive maintenance

LO3 Comparison of Traditional Manufacturing Environments and JIT

E 10. Identify which of the following exist in a traditional manufacturing environment and which exist in a JIT environment:

1. Large amounts of inventory
2. Complex manufacturing processes
3. A multiskilled labor force
4. Flexible work cells
5. Push-through production methods
6. Materials purchased infrequently but in large lot sizes
7. Infrequent setups

LO3 Direct and Indirect Costs in JIT and Traditional Manufacturing Environments

E 11. The cost categories in this list are typical of many manufacturing operations:

Direct materials:	Direct labor	Depreciation–machinery
Sheet steel	Engineering labor	Supervisory salaries
Iron castings	Indirect labor	Electrical power
Assembly parts:	Operating supplies	Insurance and taxes–plant
Part 24RE6	Small tools	President's salary
Part 15RF8	Depreciation–plant	Employee benefits

Identify each cost as direct or indirect, assuming that it was incurred in (1) a traditional manufacturing setting and (2) a JIT environment. State the reasons for changes in classification.

LO4 **Backflush Costing**

E 12. Conda Products Company implemented a JIT work environment in its trowel division eight months ago, and the division has been operating at near capacity since then. At the beginning of May, Work in Process Inventory and Finished Goods Inventory had zero balances. The following transactions took place last week:

May 28	Ordered, received, and used handles and sheet metal costing $11,340.
29	Direct labor costs incurred, $5,400.
29	Overhead costs incurred, $8,100.
30	Completed trowels costing $24,800.
31	Sold trowels costing $24,000.

Using backflush costing, calculate the ending balance in the Work in Process Inventory and Finished Goods Inventory accounts.

LO4 **Backflush Costing**

E 13. Good Morning Enterprises produces digital alarm clocks. It has a just-in-time assembly process and uses backflush costing to record production costs. Overhead is assigned at a rate of $17 per assembly labor hour. There were no beginning inventories in March. During March, the following operating data were generated:

Cost of direct materials purchased and used	$53,200
Direct labor costs incurred	$27,300
Overhead costs assigned	?
Assembly hours worked	3,840 hours
Ending work in process inventory	$1,050
Ending finished goods inventory	$960

Using T accounts, show the flow of costs through the backflush costing system. What is the total cost of goods sold in March?

LO5 **Comparison of ABM and Lean**

E 14. Identify each of the following as a characteristic of ABM or lean:

1. Backflush costing
2. ABC used to assign overhead costs to the product cost
3. ABC integrated with job order or process costing systems
4. Complexity reduced by using work cells, minimizing inventories, and reducing or eliminating non-value-adding activities
5. Activities reorganized so that they are performed within work cells

LO5 **Comparison of ABM and Lean**

E 15. The following are excerpts from a conversation between two managers about their companies' activity-based systems. Identify the manager who works for a company that emphasizes ABM and the one who works for a company that emphasizes a lean system.

Manager 1: We try to manage our resources effectively by monitoring operating activities. We analyze all major operating activities, and we focus on reducing or eliminating the ones that don't add value to our products. Our product costs are more accurate since we allocate activity costs to products and services.

Manager 2: We're very concerned with eliminating waste to reduce costs. We've designed our operations in flexible work cells to reduce the time it takes to move, store, queue, and inspect materials. We've also reduced our inventories by buying and using materials only when we need them.

Problems

LO1 The Value Chain and Process Value Analysis

P 1. Lindstrom Industries, Inc. produces chain saws, weed whackers, and lawn mowers for major retail chains. Lindstrom makes these products to order in large quantities for each customer. It has adopted activity-based management, and its controller is in the process of developing an ABC system. The controller has identified the following primary activities of the company:

Product delivery	Production–assembly
Customer follow-up	Engineering design
Materials and parts purchasing	Product inspection
Materials storage	Processing areas cleanup
Materials inspection	Product marketing
Production–drilling	Building maintenance
Product packaging	Product sales
Product research	Product rework
Finished goods storage	Production–grinding
Production–machine setup	Personnel services
Materials moving	Production scheduling

Required

1. Identify the activities that do not add value to Lindstrom's products.
2. Assist the controller's analysis by grouping the value-adding activities into the activity areas of the value chain shown in Figure 19-1.

Manager insight ▶

3. State whether each non-value-adding activity is necessary or unnecessary. Suggest how each unnecessary activity could be reduced or eliminated.

LO2 Activity-Based Costing

P 2. Boulware Products, Inc. produces printers for wholesale distributors. It has just completed packaging an order from Shawl Company for 450 printers. Before the order is shipped, the controller wants to compare the unit costs computed under the company's new activity-based costing system with the unit costs computed under its traditional costing system. Boulware's traditional costing system assigned overhead costs at a rate of 240 percent of direct labor cost.

Data for the Shawl order are as follows: direct materials, $17,552; purchased parts, $14,856; direct labor hours, 140; and average direct labor pay rate per hour, $17.

Data for activity-based costing related to processing direct materials and purchased parts for the Shawl order are as follows:

Activity	Cost Driver	Activity Cost Rate	Activity Usage
Engineering systems design	Engineering hours	$28 per engineering hour	18 engineering hours
Setup	Number of setups	$36 per setup	12 setups
Parts production	Machine hours	$37 per machine hour	82 machine hours
Product assembly	Assembly hours	$42 per assembly hour	96 assembly hours
Packaging	Number of packages	$5.60 per package	150 packages
Building occupancy	Machine hours	$10 per machine hour	82 machine hours

Required

1. Use the traditional costing approach to compute the total cost and the product unit cost of the Shawl order.
2. Using the cost hierarchy, identify each activity as unit level, batch level, product level, or facility level.
3. Prepare a bill of activities for the activity costs.
4. Use ABC to compute the total cost and product unit cost of the Shawl order.

Manager insight ▶ 5. What is the difference between the product unit cost you computed using the traditional approach and the one you computed using ABC? Does the use of ABC guarantee cost reduction for every order?

LO2 Activity Cost Rates

P 3. Noir Company produces four versions of its model J17-21 bicycle seat. The four versions have different shapes, but their processing operations and production costs are identical. During July, these costs were incurred:

Direct materials	
Leather	$25,430
Metal frame	39,180
Bolts	3,010
Materials handling	
Labor	8,232
Equipment depreciation	4,410
Electrical power	2,460
Maintenance	5,184
Assembly	
Direct labor	13,230
Engineering design	
Labor	4,116
Electrical power	1,176
Engineering overhead	7,644
Overhead	
Equipment depreciation	7,056
Indirect labor	30,870
Supervision	17,640
Operating supplies	4,410
Electrical power	10,584
Repairs and maintenance	21,168
Building occupancy overhead	52,920

July's output totaled 29,400 units. Each unit requires three machine hours of effort. Materials handling costs are allocated to the products based on direct materials cost, engineering design costs are allocated based on units produced, and overhead is allocated based on machine hours. Assembly costs are allocated based on direct labor hours, which are estimated at 882 for July.

During July, Noir Company completed 520 bicycle seats for Job 142. The activity usage for Job 142 was as follows: direct materials, $1,150; direct labor hours, 15.

Required

1. Compute the following activity cost rates: (a) materials handling cost rate; (b) assembly cost rate, (c) engineering design cost rate, and (d) overhead rate.

2. Prepare a bill of activities for Job 142.
3. Use activity-based costing to compute the job's total cost and product unit cost.

LO3 Direct and Indirect Costs in Lean and Traditional Manufacturing Environments

P 4. Funz Company, which produces wooden toys, is about to adopt a lean operating environment. In anticipation of the change, Letty Hernandez, Funz's controller, prepared the following list of costs for December:

Wood	$1,200	Insurance–plant	$ 324
Bolts	32	President's salary	4,000
Small tools	54	Engineering labor	2,700
Depreciation–plant	450	Utilities	1,250
Depreciation–machinery	275	Building occupancy	1,740
Direct labor	2,675	Supervision	2,686
Indirect labor	890	Operating supplies	254
Purchased parts	58	Repairs and maintenance	198
Materials handling	74	Employee benefits	2,654

Required

1. Identify each cost as direct or indirect, assuming that it was incurred in a traditional manufacturing setting.
2. Identify each cost as direct or indirect, assuming that it was incurred in a lean environment.
3. Assume that the costs incurred in the lean environment are for a work cell that completed 1,250 toy cars in December. Compute the total direct cost and the direct cost per unit for the cars produced.

LO4 Backflush Costing

P 5. Automotive Parts Company produces 12 parts for car bodies and sells them to three automobile assembly companies in the United States. The company implemented lean operating and costing procedures three years ago. Overhead is applied at a rate of $26 per work cell hour used. All direct materials and purchased parts are used as they are received.

One of the company's work cells produces automobile fenders that are completely detailed and ready to install when received by the customer. The cell is operated by four employees and involves a flexible manufacturing system with 14 workstations. Operating details for February for this cell are as follows:

Beginning work in process inventory	—
Beginning finished goods inventory	$420
Cost of direct materials purchased on account and used	$213,400
Cost of parts purchased on account and used	$111,250
Direct labor costs incurred	$26,450
Overhead costs assigned	?
Work cell hours used	8,260
Costs of goods completed during February	$564,650
Ending work in process inventory	$1,210
Ending finished goods inventory	$670

Required

1. Using T accounts, show the cost flows through a backflush costing system.
2. Using T accounts, show the cost flows through a traditional costing system.
3. What is the total cost of goods sold for the month?

Alternate Problems

LO1 LO2 The Value Chain and Process Value Analysis

P 6. Direct Marketing Inc. (DMI) offers database marketing strategies to help companies increase their sales. DMI's basic package of services includes the design of a mailing piece (either a Direct Mailer or a Store Mailer), creation and maintenance of marketing databases containing information about the client's target group, and a production process that prints a promotional piece and prepares it for mailing. In its marketing strategies, DMI targets working women ages 25 to 54 who are married with children and who have an annual household income in excess of $50,000. DMI has adopted activity-based management, and its controller is in the process of developing an ABC system. The controller has identified the following primary activities of the company:

Use database of customers	Accounting
Service sales	Mailer assembly
Deliver mailers to post office	Process orders
Supplies storage	Purchase supplies
Client follow-up	Design mailer
Database research trends	Building maintenance
Schedule order processing	Processing cleanup
Personnel	Mailer rework

Required

1. Identify the activities that do not add value to DMI's services.
2. Assist the controller's analysis by grouping the value-adding activities into the activity areas of the value chain shown in Figure 19-1.
3. Manager insight ▶ State whether each non-value-adding activity is necessary or unnecessary. Suggest how each unnecessary activity could be reduced or eliminated.

LO2 Activity-Based Costing

P 7. Kauli Company produces cellular phones. It has just completed an order for 10,000 phones placed by Stay Connect, Ltd. Kauli recently shifted to an activity-based costing system, and its controller is interested in the impact that the ABC system had on the Stay Connect order. Data for that order are as follows: direct materials, $36,950; purchased parts, $21,100; direct labor hours, 220; average direct labor pay rate per hour, $15.

Under Kauli's traditional costing system, overhead costs were assigned at a rate of 270 percent of direct labor cost.

Data for activity-based costing for the Stay Connect order are as follows:

Activity	Cost Driver	Activity Cost Rate	Activity Usage
Electrical engineering design	Engineering hours	$19 per engineering hour	32 engineering hours
Setup	Number of setups	$29 per setup	11 setups
Parts production	Machine hours	$26 per machine hour	134 machine hours
Product testing	Number of tests	$32 per test	52 tests
Packaging	Number of packages	$0.0374 per package	10,000 packages
Building occupancy	Machine hours	$9.80 per machine hour	134 machine hours
Assembly	Direct labor hours	$15 per direct labor hour	220 direct labor hours

Required

1. Use the traditional costing approach to compute the total cost and the product unit cost of the Stay Connect order.
2. Using the cost hierarchy, identify each activity as unit level, batch level, product level, or facility level.
3. Prepare a bill of activities for the activity costs.
4. Use ABC to compute the total cost and product unit cost of the Stay Connect order.

Manager insight ▶

5. What is the difference between the product unit cost you computed using the traditional approach and the one you computed using ABC? Does the use of ABC guarantee cost reduction for every order?

LO2 **Activity Cost Rates**

P 8. Meanwhile Company produces three models of aluminum skateboards. The models have minor differences, but their processing operations and production costs are identical. During June, these costs were incurred:

Direct materials	
Aluminum frame	$162,524
Bolts	3,876
Purchased parts	
Wheels	74,934
Decals	5,066
Materials handling *(assigned based on direct materials cost)*	
Labor	17,068
Utilities	4,438
Maintenance	914
Depreciation	876
Assembly line *(assigned based on labor hours)*	
Labor	46,080
Setup *(assigned based on number of setups)*	
Labor	6,385
Supplies	762
Overhead	3,953
Product testing *(assigned based on number of tests)*	
Labor	2,765
Supplies	435
Building occupancy *(assigned based on machine hours)*	
Insurance	5,767
Depreciation	2,452
Repairs and maintenance	3,781

For June, output totaled 32,000 skateboards. Each board required 1.5 machine hours of effort. During June, Meanwhile's assembly line worked 2,304 hours, performed 370 setups and 64,000 product tests, and completed an order for 1,000 skateboards placed by Whatever Toys Company. The job incurred costs of $5,200 for direct materials and $2,500 for purchased parts. It required 3 setups, 2,000 tests, and 72 assembly line hours.

Required

1. Compute the following activity cost rates:
   a. Materials handling cost rate
   b. Assembly line cost rate

c. Setup cost rate
d. Product testing cost rate
e. Building occupancy cost rate
2. Prepare a bill of activities for the Whatever Toys job.
3. Use activity-based costing to compute the job's total cost and product unit cost. (Round your answer to two decimal places.)

LO3 **Direct and Indirect Costs in Lean and Traditional Manufacturing Environments**

P 9. Caffene Company, which processes coffee beans into ground coffee, is about to adopt a lean operating environment. In anticipation of the change, Hattie Peralto, Caffene's controller, prepared the following list of costs for the month:

Coffee beans	$5,000	Insurance–plant	$ 300
Bags	100	President's salary	4,000
Small tools	80	Engineering labor	1,700
Depreciation–plant	400	Utilities	1,250
Depreciation–grinder	200	Building occupancy	1,940
Direct labor	1,000	Supervision	400
Indirect labor	300	Operating supplies	205
Labels	20	Repairs and maintenance	120
Materials handling	75	Employee benefits	500

Required

1. Identify each cost as direct or indirect, assuming that it was incurred in a traditional manufacturing setting.
2. Identify each cost as direct or indirect, assuming that it was incurred in a just-in-time (JIT) environment.
3. Assume that the costs incurred in the JIT environment are for a work cell that completed 5,000 1-pound bags of coffee during the month. Compute the total direct cost and the direct cost per unit for the bags produced.

LO4 **Backflush Costing**

P10. Reilly Corporation produces metal fasteners using six work cells, one for each of its product lines. It implemented just-in-time operations and costing methods two years ago. Overhead is assigned using a rate of $14 per machine hour for the Machine Snap Work Cell. There were no beginning inventories on April 1. All direct materials and purchased parts are used as they are received. Operating details for April for the Machine Snap Work Cell are as follows:

Cost of direct materials purchased on account and used	$104,500
Cost of parts purchased on account and used	$78,900
Direct labor costs incurred	$39,000
Overhead costs assigned	?
Machine hours used	12,220
Costs of goods completed during April	$392,540
Ending work in process inventory	$940
Ending finished goods inventory	$1,020

Required

1. Using T accounts, show the flow of costs through a backflush costing system.
2. Using T accounts, show the flow of costs through a traditional costing system.
3. What is the total cost of goods sold for April using a traditional costing system?

ENHANCING Your Knowledge, Skills, and Critical Thinking

LO1 LO2

ABM and ABC in a Service Business

C 1. MUF, a CPA firm, has provided audit and tax services to businesses in the London area for over 50 years. Recently, the firm decided to use ABM and activity-based costing to assign its overhead costs to those service functions. Gemma Fior, the company's controller, is interested in seeing how the change from the traditional to the activity-based costing approach affects the average cost per audit job. The following information has been provided to assist in the comparison:

Total direct labor costs	£400,000
Other direct costs	120,000
Total direct costs	£520,000

The traditional costing approach assigned overhead costs at a rate of 120 percent of direct labor costs.

Data for activity-based costing of the audit function are as follows:

Activity	Cost Driver	Activity Cost Rate	Activity Usage
Professional development	Number of employees	£2,000 per employee	50 employees
Administration	Number of jobs	£1,000 per job	50 jobs
Client development	Number of new clients	£5,000 per new client	29 new clients

1. Using direct labor cost as the cost driver, calculate the total costs for the audit function. What is the average cost per job?
2. Using activity-based costing to assign overhead, calculate the total costs for the audit function. What is the average cost per job?
3. Calculate the difference in total costs between the two approaches. Why would activity-based costing be the better approach for assigning overhead to the audit function?
4. Your instructor will divide the class into groups to work through the case. One student from each group should present the group's findings to the class.

LO2

ABC and Selling and Administrative Expenses

C 2. Sandee Star, the owner of Star Bakery, wants to know the profitability of each of her bakery's customer groups. She is especially interested in the State Institutions customer group, which is one of the company's largest. Currently, the bakery is selling doughnuts and snack foods to ten state institutions in three states. The controller has prepared the following income statement for the State Institutions customer group:

Star Bakery
Income Statement for State Institutions Customer Group
For the Year Ended December 31

Sales ($5 per case × 50,000 cases)	$250,000
Cost of goods sold ($3.50 per case × 50,000 cases)	175,000
Gross margin	$ 75,000
Less: Selling and administrative activity costs	94,750
Operating income (loss) contributed by State Institutions customer group	($ 19,750)

Activity	Activity Cost Rate	Actual Cost Driver Level	Activity Cost
Make sales calls	$60 per sales call	60 sales calls	$ 3,600
Prepare sales orders	10 per sales order	900 sales orders	9,000
Handle inquiries	5 per minute	1,000 minutes	5,000
Ship products	1 per case sold	50,000 cases	50,000
Process invoices	20 per invoice	950 invoices	19,000
Process credits	20 per notice	40 notices	800
Process billings and collections	7 per billing	1,050 billings	7,350
Total selling and administrative activity costs			$ 94,750

The controller has also provided budgeted information about selling and administrative activities for the State Institutions customer group. For this year, the planned activity cost rates and the annual cost driver levels for each selling and administrative activity are as follows:

Activity	Planned Activity Cost Rate	Planned Annual Cost Driver Level
Make sales calls	$60 per sales call	59 sales calls
Prepare sales orders	10 per sales order	850 sales orders
Handle inquiries	5.10 per minute	1,000 minutes
Ship products	0.60 per case sold	50,000 cases
Process invoices	1 per invoice	500 invoices
Process credits	10 per notice	5 notices
Process billings and collections	4 per billing	600 billings

You have been called in as a consultant on the State Institutions customer group.

1. Calculate the planned activity cost for each activity.
2. Calculate the differences between the planned activity cost and the State Institutions customer group's activity costs for this year.
3. From your evaluation of the differences calculated in **2** and your review of the income statement, identify the non-value-adding activities and state which selling and administrative activities should be examined.
4. What actions might the company take to reduce the costs of non-value-adding selling and administrative activities?

LO2 ABC in Planning and Control

C 3. Refer to the income statement in **C 2** for the State Institutions customer group for the year ended December 31. Sandee Star, the owner of Star Bakery, is in the process of budgeting income for next year. She has asked the controller to prepare a budgeted income statement for the State Institutions customer group. She estimates that the selling price per case, the number of cases sold, the cost of goods sold per case, and the activity costs for making sales calls, preparing sales orders, and handling inquiries will remain the same next year. She has contracted with a new freight company to ship the 50,000 cases at $0.60 per case sold. She has also analyzed the procedures for invoicing, processing credits, billing, and collecting and has decided that it would be less expensive for a customer service agency to do the work. The agency will charge the bakery 1.5 percent of the total sales revenue.

1. Prepare a budgeted income statement for the State Institutions customer group for next year; the year ends December 31.
2. Refer to the information in **C 2.** Assuming that the planned activity cost rate and planned annual cost driver level for each selling and administrative activity remain the same next year, calculate the planned activity cost for each activity.
3. Calculate the differences between the planned activity costs (determined in **2**) and the State Institutions customer group's budgeted activity costs for next year (determined in **1**).
4. Evaluate the results of changing freight companies and outsourcing the customer service activities.

LO3 Lean in a Service Business

C 4. The initiation banquet for new members of your business club is being held at an excellent restaurant. You are sitting next to two college students who are majoring in marketing. In discussing the accounting course they are taking, they mention that they are having difficulty understanding the lean philosophy. They have read that the elements of a company's operating system support the concepts of simplicity, continuous improvement, waste reduction, timeliness, and efficiency. They realize that to understand lean thinking in a complex manufacturing environment, they must first understand lean in a simpler context. They ask you to explain the philosophy and provide an example.

Briefly explain the lean philosophy. Apply the elements of a JIT operating system to the restaurant where the banquet is being held. Do you believe the lean philosophy applies in all restaurant operations? Explain your answer.

LO3 Activities, Cost Drivers, and JIT

C 5. Fifteen years ago, Bruce Sable, together with 10 financial supporters, founded Sable Corporation. Located in Atlanta, the company originally manufactured roller skates, but 12 years ago, on the advice of its marketing department, it switched to making skateboards. More than 4 million skateboards later, Sable Corporation finds itself an industry leader in both volume and quality. To retain market share, it has decided to automate its manufacturing process. It has ordered flexible manufacturing systems for wheel assembly and board shaping. Manual operations will be retained for board decorating because some hand painting is involved. All operations will be converted to a just-in-time environment.

Bruce Sable wants to know how the JIT approach will affect the company's product costing practices and has called you in as a consultant.

1. Summarize the elements of a JIT environment.
2. How will the automated systems change product costing?
3. What are some cost drivers that the company should employ? In what situations should it employ them?

LO1 LO2 LO3 LO5

Cookie Company (Continuing Case)

C 6. As we continue with this case, assume that your company has been using a continuous manufacturing process to make chocolate chip cookies. Demand has been so great that the company has built a special plant that makes only custom-ordered cookies. The cookies are shaped by machines but vary according to the customer's specific instructions. Ten basic sizes of cookies are produced and then customized. Slight variations in machine setup produce the different sizes.

In the past six months, several problems have developed. Even though a computer-controlled machine is used in the manufacturing process, the company's backlog is growing rapidly, and customers are complaining that delivery is too slow. Quality is declining because cookies are being pushed through production without proper inspection. Working capital is tied up in excessive amounts of inventory and storage space. Workers are complaining about the pressure to produce the backlogged orders. Machine breakdowns are increasing. Production control reports are not useful because they are not timely and contain irrelevant information. The company's profitability and cash flow are suffering.

Assume that you have been appointed CEO and that the company has asked you to analyze its problems. The board of directors asks that you complete your preliminary analysis quickly so that you can present it to the board at its midyear meeting.

1. In memo form, prepare a preliminary report recommending specific changes in the manufacturing processes.
2. In preparing the report, answer the following questions:
   a. Why are you preparing the report? What is its purpose?
   b. Who is the audience for this report?
   c. What kinds of information do you need to prepare the report, and where will you find it (i.e., what sources will you use)?
   d. When do you need to obtain the information?

CHAPTER

20 Cost Behavior Analysis

The Management Process

PLAN

- ▷ **Identify costs as variable, fixed, or mixed.**
- ▷ **Use cost formulas to develop business plans and budgets.**

PERFORM

- ▷ **Record actual cost and sales data.**
- ▷ **Prepare scattergraphs to verify cost behavior classifications.**
- ▷ **Develop cost formulas based on actual cost data using one or more methods.**
- ▷ **Determine the relevant range of the cost formula.**
- ▷ **Compute breakeven for single products or a mix of products.**

EVALUATE

- ▷ **Assess what-ifs and profit projections using C-V-P analysis.**
- ▷ **Determine if C-V-P assumptions are true.**

COMMUNICATE

- ▷ **Prepare external reports that summarize performance.**
- ▷ **Prepare contribution margin income statements for internal use.**

Analysis of cost behavior is important not only in achieving profitability but also in using resources wisely.

Knowing how costs will behave is essential for managers as they chart their organization's course. Managers commonly analyze alternative courses of action using cost behavior information so they can select the course that will best generate income for an organization's owners, maintain liquidity for its creditors, and use the organization's resources responsibly.

LEARNING OBJECTIVES

LO1 Define *cost behavior*, and identify variable, fixed, and mixed costs. (pp. 924–929)

LO2 Separate mixed costs into their variable and fixed components, and prepare a contribution margin income statement. (pp. 924–929)

LO3 Define *cost-volume-profit (C-V-P) analysis*, and discuss how managers use it as a tool for planning and control. (pp. 934–936)

LO4 Define *breakeven point*, and use contribution margin to determine a company's breakeven point for multiple products. (pp. 936–940)

LO5 Use C-V-P analysis to project the profitability of products and services. (pp. 941–944)

DECISION POINT ▸ A MANAGER'S FOCUS FLICKR

- How does Flickr decide which services to offer?
- Why do Flickr's managers analyze cost behavior?

The types of products and services that a company offers often vary from year to year depending on customers' preferences. For example, **Flickr**, which is today a very popular website for sharing personal photographs, evolved from an online game for multiple players called *Game Neverending* that was launched in 2002. The game was shelved in 2004, and the tools used in developing it were then used to develop a multiuser chat room with photo exchange capabilities. The chat room was eventually dropped as Flikr began focusing more on photo exchange. The site currently claims to host more than 4 billion images, and it offers two types of accounts: Free and Pro. It provides not only public and private photo and video storage but also a web services suite and an online community platform. The on-going challenge for Flickr's management is to offer a mix of services that appeals to customers and that allows the company to optimize its resources and profits.

Cost Behavior and Management

LO1 Define *cost behavior,* and identify variable, fixed, and mixed costs.

Cost behavior—the way costs respond to changes in volume or activity—is a factor in almost every decision managers make. Managers commonly use it to analyze alternative courses of action so they can select the course that will best generate income for an organization's owners, use resources wisely, and maintain liquidity for its creditors. The management process described on the first page of this chapter explains how managers use cost behavior when they plan, perform, evaluate, and communicate.

Service businesses like **Flickr**, **Facebook**, and **Google** find cost behavior analyses useful when planning the optimal mix of services to offer. For example, before officially adding a new feature, Google's managers analyze its cost behavior in their online Google Labs to gather user data and feedback.

During the year, managers collect cost behavior data and use it in decision making. Managers must understand and anticipate cost behavior to determine the impact of their actions on operating income and resource optimization. For example, Google's managers must understand the changes in income that can result from buying new, more productive servers or launching an online advertising product like AdWords or AdSense.

When evaluating operations and preparing reports for various product or service lines or geographic regions, managers in all types of organizations analyze how changes in cost and sales affect the profitability of product lines, sales territories, customers, departments, and other segments.

Although our focus in this chapter is on cost behavior as it relates to products and services, cost behavior can also be observed in selling, administrative, and general activities. For example, increases in the number of shipments affect shipping costs; the number of units sold or total sales revenue affects the cost of sales commissions; and the number of customers billed affects total billing costs. If managers can predict how costs behave, whether they are product- or service-related or are for selling, administrative, or general activities, then costs become manageable.

The Behavior of Costs

Some costs vary with volume or operating activity (variable costs). Others remain fixed as volume changes (fixed costs). Between those two extremes are costs that exhibit characteristics of each type (mixed costs).

FOCUS ON BUSINESS PRACTICE

A Different Kind of Company

Google's informal motto is simple: "Don't be evil." In the preface to its Code of Conduct, Google states that "being a different kind of company" depends on employees' applying the company's core values "in all aspects of [their] lives as Google employees."[1]

The company's Code of Conduct provides ethical guidelines in the following areas:

- Serving users
- Respecting each other
- Avoiding conflicts of interest
- Preserving confidentiality
- Maintaining books and records
- Protecting Google's assets
- Obeying the law

> **Study Note**
>
> Variable costs change in *direct proportion* to changes in activity; that is, they increase *in total* with an increase in volume and decrease *in total* with a decrease in volume, but they remain the same on a *per unit* basis.

Variable Costs Total costs that change in direct proportion to changes in productive output (or any other measure of volume) are called **variable costs**. In a previous chapter we referred to them as unit-level activities since the cost is incurred each time a unit is produced or a service is delivered. For example, direct materials, direct labor, operating supplies, and gasoline are variable costs.

Total variable cost costs go up or down as volume increases or decreases, but the cost per unit remains unchanged, as demonstrated in Figure 20-1 by the linear relationship between direct labor and units produced. Notice the relationship graphs as a straight line. In the figure, each unit of output requires \$2.50 of labor cost. Total labor costs grow in direct proportion to the increase in units of output. For two units, total labor costs are \$5.00; for six units, the organization incurs \$15.00 in labor costs.

The **variable cost formula** for variable cost behavior is that of a straight line: $Y = a(X)$, where Y is total variable cost, a is the variable rate per unit, and X is the units produced. The cost formula for direct labor in Figure 20-1 is:

$$\text{Total Direct Labor Costs} = \$2.50 \times \text{Units Produced}$$

Figure 20-2 illustrates other examples of variable costs. All those costs—whether incurred by a manufacturer like **La-Z-Boy** or **Intel**; a service business like **Flickr**, **Facebook**, or **Google**; or a merchandiser like **Wal-Mart**—are variable based on either productive output or total sales.

Because variable costs increase or decrease in direct proportion to volume or output, it is important to know an organization's operating capacity. **Operating capacity** is the upper limit of an organization's productive output capability, given its existing resources. It describes just what an organization can accomplish in a given period. In our discussions, we assume that operating capacity is constant and that all activity occurs within the limits of current operating capacity.

There are three common measures, or types, of operating capacity: theoretical, or ideal, capacity; practical capacity; and normal capacity.

FIGURE 20-1
A Common Variable Cost Behavior Pattern: A Linear Relationship

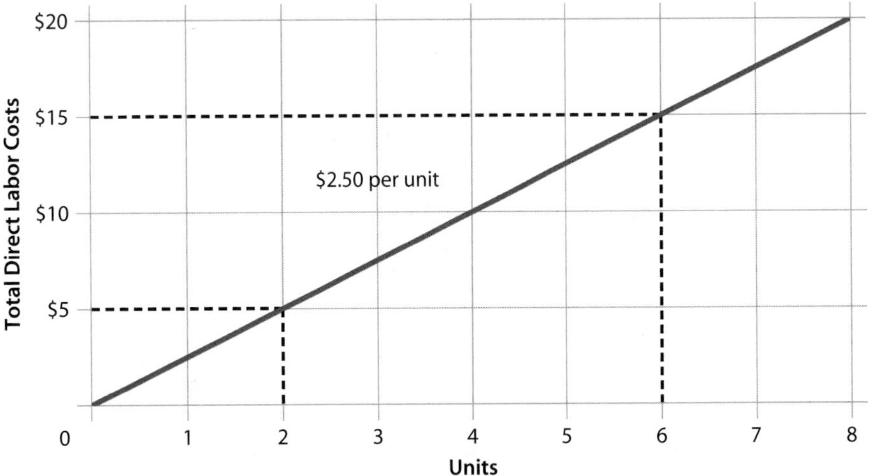

FIGURE 20-2 Examples of Variable, Fixed, and Mixed Costs

Costs	Manufacturing Company—Tire Manufacturer	Merchandising Company—Department Store	Service Company—Bank
VARIABLE	Direct materials Direct labor (hourly) Indirect labor (hourly) Operating supplies Small tools	Merchandise to sell Sales commissions Shelf stockers (hourly)	Computer equipment leasing (based on usage) Computer operators (hourly) Operating supplies Data storage disks
FIXED	Depreciation–machinery and building Insurance premiums Labor (salaried) Supervisory salaries Property taxes (on machinery and building)	Depreciation–equipment and building Insurance premiums Buyers (salaried) Supervisory salaries Property taxes (on equipment and building)	Depreciation–furniture and fixtures Insurance premiums Salaries: Programmers Systems designers Bank administrators Rent–buildings
MIXED	Electrical power Telephone Heat	Electrical power Telephone Heat	Electrical power Telephone Heat

- **Theoretical (ideal) capacity** is the maximum productive output for a given period in which all machinery and equipment are operating at optimum speed, without interruption. No company ever actually operates at such an ideal level.
- **Practical capacity** is theoretical capacity reduced by normal and expected work stoppages, such as machine breakdowns; downtime for retooling, repairs, and maintenance; and employees' breaks. Practical capacity is sometimes called *engineering capacity* and is used primarily as a planning goal of what could be produced if all went well, but no company ever actually operates at such a level.
- **Normal capacity** is the average annual level of operating capacity needed to meet expected sales demand. Normal capacity is the realistic measure of what an organization is *likely* to produce, not what it *can* produce. Thus, each variable cost should be related to an appropriate measure of normal capacity. For example, operating costs can be related to machine hours used or total units produced, and sales commissions usually vary in direct proportion to total sales dollars.

Study Note

An activity base is often called *denominator activity or cost driver*; it is the activity for which relationships are established. The basic relationships should not change greatly if activity fluctuates around the level of denominator activity.

The basis for measuring the activity of variable costs should be carefully selected for two reasons:

- First, an appropriate activity base simplifies cost planning and control.
- Second, managers must combine (aggregate) many variable costs with the same activity base so that the costs can be analyzed in a reasonable way. Such aggregation also provides information that allows management to predict future costs.

The general guide for selecting an activity base is to relate costs to their most logical or causal factor. For example, direct material and direct labor costs should be considered variable in relation to the number of units produced.

Study Note

Because fixed costs are expected to hold relatively constant over the entire relevant range of activity, they can be described as the costs of providing capacity.

Fixed Costs **Fixed costs** behave very differently from variable costs. Fixed costs are total costs that remain constant within a relevant range of volume or activity. **Relevant range** is the span of activity in which a company expects to operate. Within the relevant range, it is assumed that both total fixed costs and per unit variable costs are constant. In a previous chapter we referred to fixed costs as facility-level activities. Look back at Figure 20-2 for examples of fixed costs. The manufacturer, the department store, and the bank all incur depreciation costs and fixed annual insurance premiums. In addition, all salaried personnel have fixed earnings for a particular period. The manufacturer and the department store own their buildings and pay annual property taxes, and the bank pays an annual fixed rental charge for the use of its building.

Study Note

Cost behavior is closely linked to the concept of cost control. In the short run, it is generally easier to control variable costs than fixed costs.

According to economic theory, all costs tend to be variable in the long run; thus, as the examples in Figure 20-2 suggest, a cost is fixed only within a limited period. A change in plant capacity, labor needs, or other production factors causes fixed costs to increase or decrease. Management usually considers a one-year period when planning and controlling costs; thus fixed costs are expected to be constant within that period.

Of course, fixed costs change when activity exceeds the relevant range. These costs are called *step costs* or *step-variable*, *step-fixed*, or *semifixed costs*. A **step cost** remains constant in a relevant range of activity and increases or decreases in a step-like manner when activity is outside the relevant range.

For example, assume that one customer support team at My Media Place, a company like **Flickr**, has the capacity to handle up to 500,000 customer incidents per 8-hour shift. The relevant range, then, is from 0 to 500,000 units. Unfortunately, volume has increased to more than 500,000 incidents per 8-hour shift, taxing current equipment capacity and the quality of customer care. My Media Place must add another customer support team to handle the additional volume. Figure 20-3 shows this behavior pattern. The fixed costs for the first 500,000 units of production are $4,000. Those costs hold steady at $4,000 for any level of output within the relevant range. But if output goes above 500,000 units, another team must be added, pushing fixed costs to $8,000.

Fixed cost behavior expressed mathematically in the **fixed cost formula** is a horizontal line in the relevant range: $Y = b$, where Y is total fixed cost and b is the fixed cost in the relevant range. The fixed cost formula for up to 500,000 units in Figure 20-3 is:

$$\text{Total Fixed Costs} = \$4{,}000$$

On a per unit basis, fixed costs go down as volume goes up, as long as a firm is operating within the relevant range of activity. Look at how the customer

FIGURE 20-3
A Common Step-Like Fixed Cost Behavior Pattern

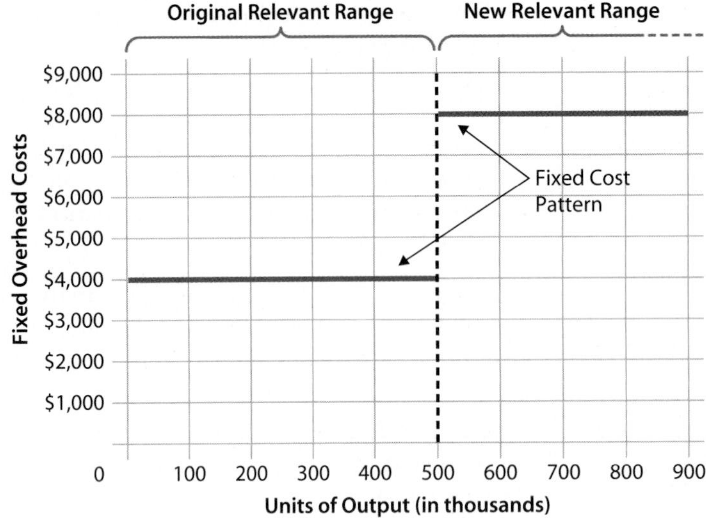

support team's costs per unit fall as the volume of activity increases within the relevant range:

Volume of Activity	*Support Team Cost per Unit*
100,000 units	\$4,000 ÷ 100,000 = \$0.0400
300,000 units	\$4,000 ÷ 300,000 = \$0.0133*
500,000 units	\$4,000 ÷ 500,000 = \$0.0080
600,000 units	\$8,000 ÷ 600,000 = \$0.0133*

*Rounded.

At 600,000 units, the activity level is above the relevant range, which means another team must be added; thus, the per unit cost changes to \$0.0133.

Study Note
Mixed costs are common in businesses.

Mixed Costs **Mixed costs** have both variable and fixed cost components. Part of a mixed cost changes with volume or usage, and part is fixed over a particular period. Look back at Figure 20-2 for examples of mixed costs. The manufacturer, the department store, and the bank all incur electric, telephone, and heat costs that have both variable and fixed cost components. For example, electric costs include charges per kilowatt-hour used plus a basic monthly service charge. The kilowatt-hour charges are variable because they depend on the amount of use; the monthly service charge is a fixed cost.

Figure 20-4 depicts an organization's total electricity costs. The monthly bill begins with a fixed service charge and increases as kilowatt-hours are consumed.

FIGURE 20-4
Behavior Patterns of Mixed Costs

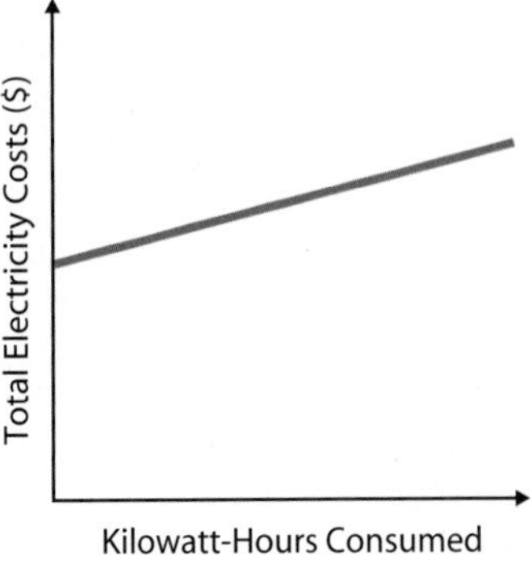

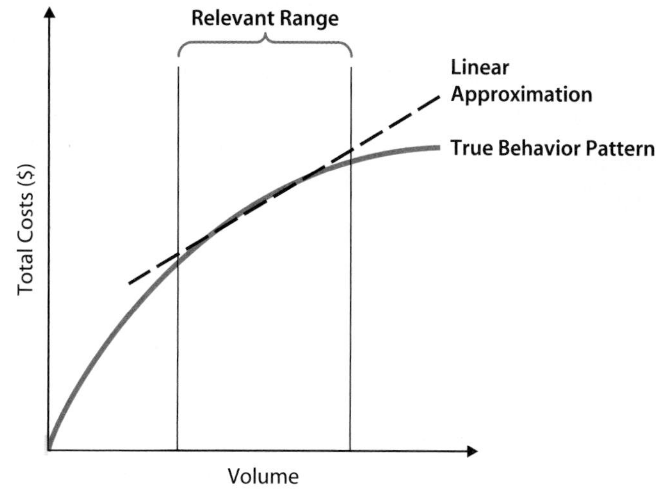

FIGURE 20-5
The Relevant Range and Linear Approximation

Mixed cost behavior is expressed mathematically in the **mixed cost formula**, which is the linear equation $Y = a(X) + b$, where Y is total mixed cost, a the variable rate per unit, X the units produced, and b the fixed cost for the period.

Many mixed costs vary with operating activity in a nonlinear fashion. To simplify cost analysis procedures and make mixed costs easier to use, accountants have developed a method of converting nonlinear costs into linear ones. Called *linear approximation*, this method relies on the concept of relevant range. Under that concept, many nonlinear costs can be estimated using the linear approximation approach illustrated in Figure 20-5. Those estimated costs can then be treated as part of the other variable and fixed costs.

Study Note

Nonlinear costs can be roughly estimated by treating them as if they were linear (variable) costs within set limits of volume.

A linear approximation of a nonlinear cost is not a precise measure, but it allows the inclusion of nonlinear costs in cost behavior analysis, and the loss of accuracy is usually not significant. The goal is to help management estimate costs and prepare budgets, and linear approximation helps accomplish that goal.

STOP & APPLY >

Indicate whether each of the following costs is usually variable (V) or fixed (F):

1. Operating supplies
2. Real estate taxes
3. Gasoline for a delivery truck
4. Property insurance
5. Depreciation expense of computers (calculated with the straight-line method)
6. Depreciation expense of machinery (calculated with the units-of-production method)

SOLUTION

1. V; 2. F; 3. V; 4. F; 5. F; 6. V

Mixed Costs and the Contribution Margin Income Statement

LO2 Separate mixed costs into their variable and fixed components, and prepare a contribution margin income statement.

For cost planning and control purposes, mixed costs must be divided into their variable and fixed components. The separate components can then be grouped with other variable and fixed costs for analysis. Four methods are commonly used to separate mixed cost components: the engineering, scatter diagram, high-low, and statistical methods.

- Because the results yielded by each of these four methods are likely to differ, managers often use multiple approaches to find the best possible estimate for a mixed cost.

The Engineering Method

The **engineering method** is used to separate costs into their fixed and variable components by performing a step-by-step analysis of the tasks, costs, and processes involved. This type of analysis is sometimes called a *time and motion study*. The engineering method is expensive because it is so detailed, and it is generally used to estimate the cost of activities or new products. For example, the U.S. Postal Service conducts periodic audits of how many letters a postal worker should be able to deliver on a particular mail route within a certain period.

The Scatter Diagram Method

When there is doubt about the behavior pattern of a particular cost, especially a mixed cost, it helps to plot past costs and related measures of volume in a scatter diagram. A **scatter diagram** is a chart of plotted points that helps determine whether a linear relationship exists between a cost item and its related activity measure. It is a form of linear approximation. If the diagram suggests a linear relationship, a cost line can be imposed on the data by either visual means or statistical analysis. For example, suppose that My Media Place incurred the following machine hours and electricity costs last year:

Like most businesses, the U.S. Postal Service is concerned about delivery time. To determine how many deliveries a postal worker should be able to make within a certain period, it conducts periodic audits using the engineering method (a type of analysis that is also known as a time and motion study).

Courtesy of Michelle Malven/ istockphoto.com.

Month	*Machine Hours*	*Electricity Costs*
January	6,250	$ 24,000
February	6,300	24,200
March	6,350	24,350
April	6,400	24,600
May	6,300	24,400
June	6,200	24,300
July	6,100	23,900
August	6,050	23,600
September	6,150	23,950
October	6,250	24,100
November	6,350	24,400
December	6,450	24,700
Totals	75,150	$290,500

Figure 20-6 shows a scatter diagram of these data. The diagram suggests a linear relationship between machine hours and the cost of electricity. If we were to add a line to the diagram to represent the linear relationship, the estimated fixed electricity cost would occur at the point at which the line intersects the vertical axis, or $23,200 of fixed monthly electric costs. The variable cost per machine hour can be estimated by determining the slope of the line, much as is done in Step 1 of the high-low method.

The High-Low Method

The **high-low method** is a common, three-step approach to determining the variable and fixed components of a mixed cost. It is based on the premise that only two data points are necessary to define a linear cost-volume relationship, $Y = a(X) + b$, where Y is total mixed cost, a is the variable rate per unit, X is the volume level, and b is the total fixed cost for the period. It is a relatively crude method since it uses only the high and low data observations to predict cost behavior.

- The disadvantage of this method is that if one or both data points are not representative of the remaining data set, the estimate of variable and fixed costs may not be accurate.
- Its advantage is that it can be used when only limited data are available.

FIGURE 20-6
Scatter Diagram of Machine Hours and Electricity Costs

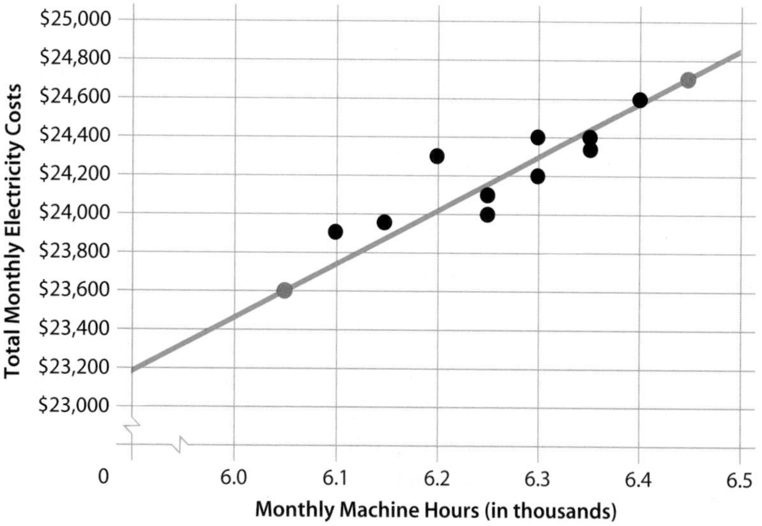

Study Note

A scatter diagram shows how closely volume and costs are correlated. A tight, closely associated group of data is better suited to linear approximation than a random or circular pattern of data points.

The method involves three steps:

1. Find the variable rate—that is, the a in $Y = a(X) + b$.
2. Find the total fixed costs—that is, the b in $Y = a(X) + b$.
3. Express the cost formula to estimate total costs within the relevant range:

$Y = a(X) + b$, or Total Cost = Variable Rate(Volume Level) + Fixed Costs

Using My Media Place's last 12 months of machine usage and electric cost data, here is a step-by-step example of how to use the high-low method:

Step 1. *Find the variable rate.*

> **Study Note**
>
> Step 1 is also how you compute the slope of a line, that is, Change in $Y \div$ Change in X.

- Select the periods of highest and lowest activity within the accounting period. In our example, the highest-volume machine-hour month was in December and the lowest was in August.
- Find the difference between the highest and lowest amounts for both the machine hours and their related electricity costs.
- Compute the variable rate, that is, the variable cost per machine hour, by dividing the difference in cost by the difference in machine hours.

Volume	*Month*	*Activity Level (X)*	*Cost (Y)*
High	December	6,450 hours	$24,700
Low	August	6,050 hours	23,600
Difference		400 hours	$ 1,100

Variable Cost per Machine Hour = $1,100 ÷ 400 Machine Hours
= $2.75 per Machine Hour

Step 2. *Find the total fixed costs.* Compute total fixed costs for a month by putting the known variable rate and the information from the month with the highest volume into the cost formula and solve for the total fixed costs:

Total Fixed Costs = Total Costs − Total Variable Costs
Total Fixed Costs for December = $24,700.00 − (6,450 Hours × $2.75)
= $6,962.50

You can check your answer by recalculating total fixed costs using the month with the lowest activity. Total fixed costs will be the same:

Total Fixed Costs for August = $23,600.00 − (6,050 Hours × $2.75)
= $6,962.50

Step 3. *Express the cost formula to estimate the total costs within the relevant range.*

Total Electricity Costs per Month = $2.75 per Machine Hour + $6,962.50

Remember that the cost formula will work only within the relevant range. In this example, the formula would work for amounts between 6,050 machine hours and 6,450 machine hours. To estimate the electricity costs for machine hours outside the relevant range (in this case, below 6,050 machine hours or above 6,450 machine hours), a new cost formula must be calculated.

Statistical Methods

Statistical methods, such as **regression analysis**, mathematically describe the relationship between costs and activities and are used to separate mixed costs into variable and fixed components. Because all data observations are used, the resulting linear equation is more representative of cost behavior than either the high-low or scatter diagram methods. Regression analysis can be performed using one or more activities to predict costs. For example, overhead costs can be predicted using only machine hours (a simple regression analysis), or they can be predicted using both machine hours and labor hours (a multiple regression analysis) because both activities affect overhead.

We leave further description of regression analysis to statistics courses, which provide detailed coverage of this method.

Contribution Margin Income Statements

Once an organization's costs are classified as being either variable or fixed, the traditional income statement can be reorganized into a more useful format for internal operations and decision making. Table 20-1 compares the structure of a traditional and a contribution margin income statement (sometimes referred to as a *variable costing income statement*). A **contribution margin income statement** is formatted to emphasize cost behavior rather than organizational functions. All variable costs related to production, selling, and administration are subtracted from sales to determine the total **contribution margin (CM)** (i.e., the amount that remains after all variable costs are subtracted from sales). All fixed costs related to production, selling, and administration are subtracted from the total contribution margin to determine operating income.

Although a traditional income statement and a contribution margin income statement arrive at the same operating income, the traditional approach divides costs into product and period costs, whereas the contribution margin approach divides costs into variable and fixed costs.

The contribution margin income statement enables managers to view revenue and cost relationships on a per unit basis or as a percentage of sales. If managers understand these relationships as expressed by the contribution margin income statement, then they can determine how many units they must sell to avoid losing money, or what the sales price per unit must be to cover costs, or what their profits will be for a certain dollar amount of sales revenue. In the next section, you will learn about cost-volume-profit analysis as a tool for planning and control. Table 20-2 shows the two ways a contribution margin income statement can be presented.

TABLE 20-1
Comparison of Income Statements

Traditional Income Statement	Contribution Margin Income Statement
Sales revenue	Sales revenue
– Cost of goods sold, variable	– Cost of goods sold, variable
– Cost of goods sold, fixed	– Operating expenses, variable
= Gross margin	= Contribution margin
– Operating expenses, variable	– Cost of goods sold, fixed
– Operating expenses, fixed	– Operating expenses, fixed
= Operating income	= Operating income

TABLE 20-2 Contribution Margin Income Statement

	Per unit Relationships	As a Percentage of Sales
Sales revenue	Sales price per unit × Units sold	Sales revenue ÷ Sales revenue
Less variable costs	– Variable rate per unit × Units sold	– Variable costs ÷ Sales revenue
Contribution margin	= Contribution margin per unit × Units sold	= Contribution margin ÷ Sales revenue
Less fixed costs	– Total fixed costs	– Fixed costs
Operating income	= $XXXXX	= Operating income

STOP & APPLY >

Using the high-low method and the following information, compute the monthly variable cost per kilowatt-hour and the monthly fixed electricity cost for a local business. Finally, express the monthly electricity cost formula and its relevant range.

Month	Kilowatt-Hours Used	Electricity Costs
April	90	$450
May	80	430
June	70	420

SOLUTION

Volume	Month	Activity Level	Cost
High	April	90 hours	$450
Low	June	70 hours	420
Difference		20 hours	$ 30

Variable cost per kilowatt-hour = $30 ÷ 20 hours
= $1.50 per hour

Fixed costs for April: $450 − (90 × $1.50) = $315
Fixed costs for June: $420 − (70 × $1.50) = $315

Monthly electricity costs = ($1.50 × Hours) + $315. The cost formula can be used for hourly activity between 70 and 90 hours per month.

Cost-Volume-Profit Analysis

LO3 Define *cost-volume-profit (C-V-P) analysis*, and discuss how managers use it as a tool for planning and control.

Cost-volume-profit (C-V-P) analysis is an examination of the cost behavior patterns that underlie the relationships among cost, volume of output, and profit. C-V-P analysis usually applies to a single product, product line, or division of a company. For that reason, *profit*, which is only part of an entire company's operating income, is the term used in the C-V-P equation. The equation is expressed as

$$\text{Sales Revenue} - \text{Variable Costs} - \text{Fixed Costs} = \text{Profit}$$
$$S - VC - FC = P$$

Study Note

One of the important benefits of C-V-P analysis is that it allows managers to adjust different variables and to evaluate how these changes affect profit.

or as

$$\text{Sales Price(Units Sold)} - \text{Variable Rate(Units Sold)} - \text{Fixed Costs} = \text{Profit}$$
$$SP(X) - VR(X) - FC = P$$

For example, suppose My Media Place wants to make a profit of $50,000 on one of its services. The service sells for $95.50 per unit and has variable costs of $80 per unit. If 4,000 units are sold during the period, what were the fixed costs? Use the equation $SP(X) - VR(X) - FC = P$ to solve for the unknown fixed costs.

$$\$95.50(4{,}000) - \$80(4{,}000) - FC = \$50{,}000$$
$$\$382{,}000 - \$320{,}000 - FC = \$50{,}000$$
$$FC = \$12{,}000$$

In cases involving the income statement of an entire company, the term *operating income* is more appropriate than *profit.* In the context of C-V-P analysis, however, *profit* and *operating income* mean the same thing.

C-V-P analysis is a tool for both planning and control. The techniques and the problem-solving procedures involved in the process express relationships among revenue, sales mix, cost, volume, and profit. Those relationships provide a general model of financial activity that managers can use for short-range planning and for evaluating performance and analyzing alternative courses of action.

For planning, managers can use C-V-P analysis to calculate operating income when sales volume is known, or they can determine the level of sales needed to reach a targeted amount of operating income. C-V-P analysis is used extensively in budgeting as well, and is also a way of measuring how well an organization's departments are performing. At the end of a period, sales volume and related actual costs are analyzed to find actual operating income. A department's performance is measured by comparing actual costs with expected costs—costs that have been computed by applying C-V-P analysis to actual sales volume. The result is a performance report on which managers can base the control of operations.

In addition, managers use C-V-P analysis to measure the effects of alternative courses of action, such as changing variable or fixed costs, expanding or contracting sales volume, and increasing or decreasing selling prices. C-V-P analysis is useful in making decisions about product pricing, product mix (when an organization makes more than one product or offers more than one service), adding or dropping a product line, and accepting special orders.

C-V-P analysis has many applications, all of which managers use to plan and control operations effectively. However, it is useful only under certain conditions and only when certain assumptions hold true. Those conditions and assumptions are as follows:

1. The behavior of variable and fixed costs can be measured accurately.
2. Costs and revenues have a close linear approximation throughout the relevant range. For example, if costs rise, revenues rise proportionately.
3. Efficiency and productivity hold steady within the relevant range of activity.
4. Cost and price variables also hold steady during the period being planned.
5. The sales mix does not change during the period being planned.
6. Production and sales volume are roughly equal.

If one or more of these conditions and assumptions are absent, the C-V-P analysis may be misleading.

STOP & APPLY >

A local business wants to make a profit of $10,000 each month. It has variable costs of $5 per unit and fixed costs of $20,000 per month. How much must it charge per unit if 6,000 units are sold?

SOLUTION

Using the equation SP(X) − VR(X) − FC = P to set up and solve for the unknown sales price:

$$\text{SP}(6{,}000) - \$5(6{,}000) - \$20{,}000 = \$10{,}000$$

$$\text{SP} = \frac{\$5(6{,}000) + \$20{,}000 + \$10{,}000}{6{,}000 \text{ Units}} = \frac{\$60{,}000}{6{,}000} = \$10 \text{ per Unit}$$

Breakeven Analysis

LO4 Define *breakeven point*, and use contribution margin to determine a company's breakeven point for multiple products.

Breakeven analysis uses the basic elements of cost-volume-profit relationships. The **breakeven point** is the point at which total revenues equal total costs. It is thus the point at which an organization can begin to earn a profit. When a new venture or product line is being planned, the likelihood of the project's success can be quickly measured by finding its breakeven point. If, for instance, the breakeven point is 24,000 units and the total market is only 25,000 units, the margin of safety would be very low, and the idea should be considered carefully. The **margin of safety** is the number of sales units or amount of sales dollars by which actual sales can fall below planned sales without resulting in a loss—in this example, 1,000 units.

Sales (S), variable costs (VC), and fixed costs (FC) are used to compute the breakeven point, which can be stated in terms of sales units or sales dollars. The general equation for finding the breakeven point is as follows:

$$\text{S} - \text{VC} - \text{FC} = \$0$$

or as

$$\text{SP}(X) - \text{VR}(X) - \text{FC} = \$0$$

Suppose, for example, that one of the services My Media Place sells is website setups. Variable costs are $50 per unit, and fixed costs average $20,000 per year. A unit is a basic website setup which sells for $90.

- ***Breakeven in sales units:*** Given this information, we can compute the breakeven point for website setup services in sales units (X equals sales units):

$$\begin{aligned} \text{S} - \text{VC} - \text{FC} &= \$0 \\ \$90X - \$50X - \$20{,}000 &= \$0 \\ \$40X &= \$20{,}000 \\ X &= 500 \text{ Units} \end{aligned}$$

- ***Breakeven in sales dollars:*** We can also compute breakeven in sales dollars since sales price multiplied by breakeven in sales units equals breakeven in sales dollars:

$$\$90 \times 500 \text{ Units} = \$45{,}000$$

FIGURE 20-7
Graphic Breakeven Analysis for My Media Place

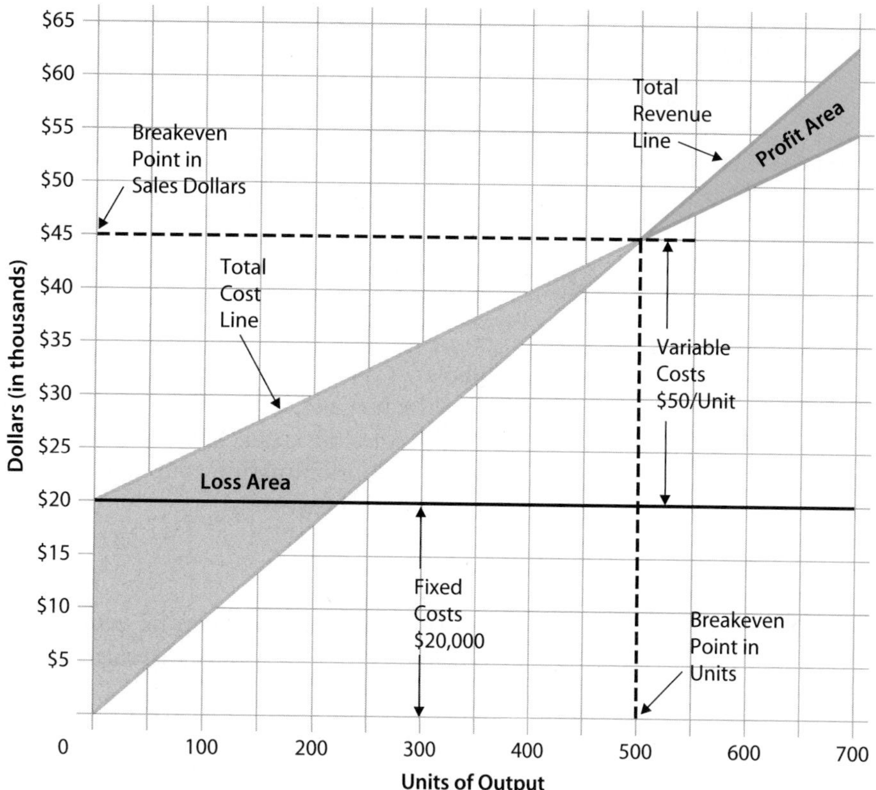

- ***Breakeven by scatter diagram:*** In addition, we can make a rough estimate of the breakeven point using a scatter diagram. This method is less exact, but it does yield meaningful data. Figure 20-7 shows a breakeven graph for My Media Place. As you can see there, the graph has five parts:

  1. A horizontal axis for units of output
  2. A vertical axis for dollars
  3. A line running horizontally from the vertical axis at the level of fixed costs
  4. A total cost line that begins at the point where the fixed cost line crosses the vertical axis and slopes upward to the right (The slope of the line depends on the variable cost per unit.)
  5. A total revenue line that begins at the origin of the vertical and horizontal axes and slopes upward to the right (The slope depends on the selling price per unit.)

At the point at which the total revenue line crosses the total cost line, revenues equal total costs. The breakeven point, stated in either sales units or dollars of sales, is found by extending broken lines from this point to the axes. As Figure 20-7 shows, My Media Place will break even when it has sold 500 website setups for $45,000.

Study Note

Contribution margin equals sales minus variable costs, whereas gross margin equals sales minus the cost of goods sold.

Using an Equation to Determine the Breakeven Point

A simpler method of determining the breakeven point uses contribution margin in an equation. You will recall from our discussion of the contribution margin income statement that the contribution margin (CM) is the amount that remains after all variable costs are subtracted from sales:

$$S - VC = CM$$

Study Note

The maximum contribution a unit of product or service can make is its selling price. After paying for itself (variable costs), a product or service provides a contribution margin to help pay total fixed costs and then earn a profit.

A product line's contribution margin represents its net contribution to paying off fixed costs and earning a profit. Profit (P) is what remains after fixed costs are paid and subtracted from the contribution margin:

$$\text{CM} - \text{FC} = \text{P}$$

The example that follows uses the contribution margin income statement approach to organize the facts and to determine the profitability of one of My Media Place's products.

Symbols		Units Produced and Sold		
		250	**500**	**750**
S	Sales revenue ($90 per unit)	$22,500	$45,000	$67,500
VC	Less variable costs ($50 per unit)	12,500	25,000	37,500
CM	Contribution margin ($40 per unit)	$10,000	$20,000	$30,000
FC	Less fixed costs	20,000	20,000	20,000
P	Profit (loss)	($10,000)	$ 0	$10,000

The breakeven point (BE) can be expressed as the point at which contribution margin minus total fixed costs equals zero (or the point at which contribution margin equals total fixed costs).

- ***Breakeven in sales units:*** In terms of units of product, the equation for the breakeven point looks like this:

$$(\text{CM per Unit} \times \text{BE Units}) - \text{FC} = \$0$$

It can also be expressed like this:

$$\text{BE Units} = \frac{\text{FC}}{\text{CM per unit}}$$

To show how the formula works, we use the data for My Media Place:

$$\text{BE Units} = \frac{\text{FC}}{\text{CM per unit}} = \frac{\$20{,}000}{\$90 - \$50} = \frac{\$20{,}000}{\$40} = 500 \text{ Units}$$

- ***Breakeven in sales dollars:*** The breakeven point in total sales dollars may be determined by multiplying the breakeven point in units by the selling price (SP) per unit:

$$\text{BE Dollars} = \text{SP} \times \text{BE Units} = \$90 \times 500 \text{ Units} = \$45{,}000$$

  - An alternative way of determining the breakeven point in total sales dollars is to divide the fixed costs by the contribution margin ratio. The contribution margin ratio is the contribution margin divided by the selling price:

$$\text{CM Ratio} = \frac{\text{CM}}{\text{SP}} = \frac{\$40}{\$90} = 0.444^*, \text{ or } 4/9$$

$$\text{BE Dollars} = \frac{\text{FC}}{\text{CM Ratio}} = \frac{\$20{,}000}{0.444} = \$45{,}045^*$$

The Breakeven Point for Multiple Products

To satisfy the needs of different customers, most companies sell a variety of products or services that often have different variable and fixed costs and different

*Rounded.

FIGURE 20-8
Sales Mix for My Media Place

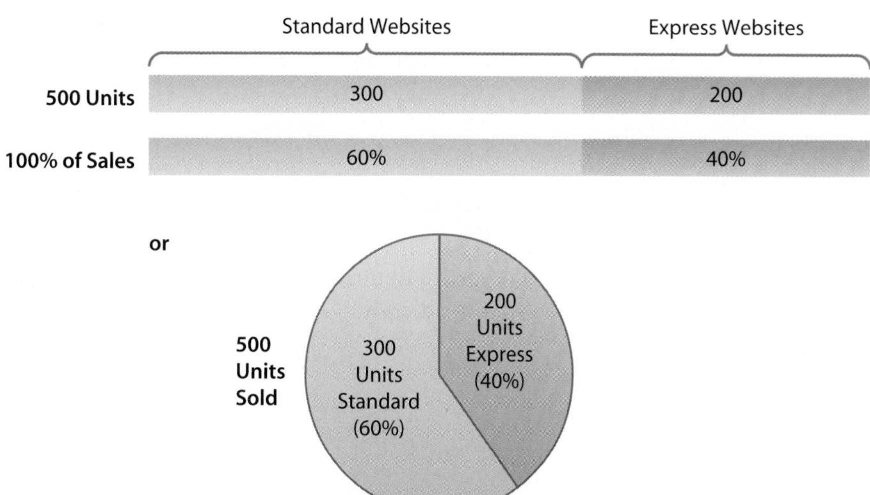

> **Study Note**
> A company's sales mix can be very dynamic. If the mix is constantly changing, an assumption of stability may undermine the C-V-P analysis.

selling prices. To calculate the breakeven point for each product, its unit contribution margin must be weighted by the sales mix. The **sales mix** is the proportion of each product's unit sales relative to the company's total unit sales.

Let's assume that My Media Place sells two types of websites: standard and express. If the company sells 500 units, of which 300 units are standard and 200 are express, the sales mix would be 3:2. For every three standard websites sold, two express websites are sold. The sales mix can also be stated in percentages. Of the 500 units sold, 60 percent (300 ÷ 500) are standard sales, and 40 percent (200 ÷ 500) are express sales (see Figure 20-8).

The breakeven point for multiple products can be computed in three steps:

1. Compute the weighted-average contribution margin.
2. Calculate the weighted-average breakeven point.
3. Calculate the breakeven point for each product.

To illustrate, we will use My Media Place's sales mix of 60 percent standard websites to 40 percent express websites and total fixed costs of $32,000; the selling price, variable cost, and contribution margin per unit for each product line are shown in Step 1 below.

Step 1. *Compute the weighted-average contribution margin.* To do so, multiply the contribution margin for each product by its percentage of the sales mix, as follows:

	Selling Price		*Variable Costs*		*Contribution Margin (CM)*		*Percentage of Sales Mix*		*Weighted-Average CM*
Standard	$90	−	$50	=	$40	×	60%	=	$24
Express	$40	−	$20	=	$20	×	40%	=	8
Weighted-average contribution margin									$32

Step 2. *Calculate the weighted-average breakeven point.* Divide total fixed costs by the weighted-average contribution margin:

Weighted-Average Breakeven Point = Total Fixed Costs ÷ Weighted-Average Contribution Margin
= $32,000 ÷ $32
= 1,000 Units

Step 3. *Calculate the breakeven point for each product.* Multiply the weighted-average breakeven point by each product's percentage of the sales mix:

	Weighted-Average Breakeven Point		*Sales Mix*		*Breakeven Point*
Standard	1,000 units	×	60%	=	600 units
Express	1,000 units	×	40%	=	400 units

To verify, determine the contribution margin of each product and subtract the total fixed costs:

Contribution Margin		
Standard	600 × $40 =	$24,000
Express	400 × $20 =	8,000
Total contribution margin		$32,000
Less fixed costs		32,000
Profit		$ 0

& APPLY >

Using the contribution margin approach, find the breakeven point in units for a local business's two products. Product M's selling price per unit is $20, and its variable cost per unit is $11. Product N's selling price per unit is $12, and its variable cost per unit is $6. Fixed costs are $24,000, and the sales mix of Product M to Product N is 2:1.

SOLUTION

Step 1.

	Selling Price		Variable Costs		Contribution Margin (CM)		Percentage of Sales Mix		Weighted-Average CM
M	$20	–	$11	=	$9	×	66.7%	=	$6
N	$12	–	$ 6	=	$6	×	33.3%	=	2
Weighted-average contribution margin									$8

Step 2.

Weighted-Average Breakeven Point = $24,000 ÷ $8.00 = 3,000 Units

Step 3. Breakeven point for each product line:

		Weighted-Average Breakeven Point	×	Sales Mix	=	Breakeven Point
M	=	3,000 Units	×	0.667	=	2,000 Units
N	=	3,000 Units	×	0.333	=	1,000 Units

Check: Contribution Margin

Product M	=	2,000	×	$9	=	$18,000
Product N	=	1,000	×	$6	=	6,000
Total contribution margin						$24,000
Less fixed costs						24,000
Profit						$ 0

Using C-V-P Analysis to Plan Future Sales, Costs, and Profits

LO5 Use C-V-P analysis to project the profitability of products and services.

The primary goal of a business venture is not to break even; it is to generate profits. C-V-P analysis adjusted for targeted profit can be used to estimate the profitability of a venture. This approach is excellent for "what-if" analysis, in which managers select several scenarios and compute the profit that may be anticipated from each. Each scenario generates a different amount of profit or loss.

For instance, what if sales increase by 17,000 units? What effect will the increase have on profit? What if sales increase by only 6,000 units? What if fixed costs are reduced by $14,500? What if the variable unit cost increases by $1.40?

Applying C-V-P to Target Profits

To illustrate two ways a business can apply C-V-P analysis to target profits, assume that My Media Place has set $4,000 in profit as this year's goal. If all the data in our earlier example remain the same, how many websites must My Media Place sell to reach the targeted profit?

- ***Contribution margin approach:***

$$\begin{aligned} S &= VC + FC + P \\ \$90X &= \$50X + \$20{,}000 + \$4{,}000 \\ \$40X &= \$24{,}000 \\ X &= 600 \text{ Units} \end{aligned}$$

- ***Equation approach:*** Add the targeted profit to the numerator of the contribution margin breakeven equation and solve for targeted sales in units:

$$\text{Targeted Sales Units} = \frac{FC + P}{\text{CM per Unit}}$$

The number of sales units My Media Place needs to generate $4,000 in profit is computed this way:

$$\text{Targeted Sales Units} = \frac{FC + P}{\text{CM per Unit}} = \frac{\$20{,}000 + \$4{,}000}{\$40} = \frac{\$24{,}000}{\$40}$$

$$= 600 \text{ Units}$$

To summarize My Media Place's plans for the coming year, a contribution margin income statement can be used. As you can see in the contribution margin income statement for My Media Place shown below, the focus of such a statement is on cost behavior, *not* cost function. (As we noted earlier, in income statements, the term *operating income* is more appropriate than *profit.*)

My Media Place's planning team wants to consider three alternatives to the original plan shown in the statement. In the following sections, we examine each

Contribution Margin Income Statement
For the Year Ended December 31

	Per Unit	Total for 600 Units
Sales revenue	$90	$54,000
Less variable costs	50	30,000
Contribution margin	$40	$24,000
Less fixed costs		20,000
Operating income		$ 4,000

of these alternatives and its impact on projected operating income. In the summary, we review our work from a strategic management perspective and analyze the different breakeven points of the three alternatives.

What-If Alternative 1: Decrease Variable Costs, Increase Sales Volume What if website design labor were outsourced? Based on the planning team's research, the direct labor cost of a website would decrease by $3 to $47 and sales volume would increase by 10 percent to 660 units. How does this alternative affect operating income?

	Per Unit	*Total for 660 Units*
Sales revenue	$90	$59,400
Less variable costs	47	31,020
Contribution margin	$43	$28,380
Less fixed costs		20,000
Operating income		$ 8,380
Alternative 1:		
Increase in operating income ($8,380 – $4,000)		$ 4,380

What-If Alternative 2: Increase Fixed Costs, Increase Sales Volume What if the Marketing Department suggests that a $500 increase in advertising costs would increase sales volume by 5 percent to 630 units? How does this alternative affect operating income?

	Per Unit	*Total for 630 Units*
Sales revenue	$90	$56,700
Less variable costs	50	31,500
Contribution margin	$40	$25,200
Less fixed costs		20,500
Operating income		$ 4,700
Alternative 2:		
Increase in operating income ($4,700 – $4,000)		$ 700

What-If Alternative 3: Increase Selling Price, Decrease Sales Volume What is the impact of a $10 increase in selling price on the company's operating income? If the selling price is increased, the planning team estimates that the sales volume will decrease by 15 percent to 510 units. How does this alternative affect operating income?

	Per Unit	*Total for 510 Units*
Sales revenue	$100	$51,000
Less variable costs	50	25,500
Contribution margin	$ 50	$25,500
Less fixed costs		20,000
Operating income		$ 5,500
Alternative 3:		
Increase in operating income ($5,500 – $4,000)		$ 1,500

Study Note

Remember that the breakeven point provides a rough estimate of the number of units that must be sold to cover the total costs.

Comparative Summary In preparation for a meeting, the planning team at My Media Place compiled the summary presented in Exhibit 20-1. It compares the three alternatives with the original plan and shows how changes in variable and fixed costs, selling price, and sales volume affect the breakeven point.

- Note that the decrease in variable costs (direct materials) proposed in Alternative 1 increases the contribution margin per unit (from $40 to $43), which reduces the breakeven point. Because fewer sales dollars are required to cover variable costs, the breakeven point is reached sooner than in the original plan—at a sales volume of 466 units rather than at 500 units.
- In Alternative 2, the increase in fixed costs has no effect on the contribution margin per unit, but it does require the total contribution margin to cover more fixed costs before reaching the breakeven point. Thus, the breakeven point is higher than in the original plan—513 units as opposed to 500.
- The increase in selling price in Alternative 3 increases the contribution margin per unit, which reduces the breakeven point. Because more sales dollars are available to cover fixed costs, the breakeven point of 400 units is lower than the breakeven point in the original plan.

From a strategic standpoint, which plan should the planning team choose? If they want the highest operating income, they will choose Alternative 1. If, however, they want the company to begin generating operating income more quickly, they will choose the plan with the lowest breakeven point, Alternative 3.

Additional qualitative information may help the planning team make a better decision. Will customers perceive that the quality of the website is lower if the company outsources the web work, as proposed in Alternative 1? Will increased expenditures on advertising yield a 5 percent increase in sales volume, as Alternative 2 suggests? Will the increase in selling price suggested in Alternative 3 create more than a 15 percent decline in unit sales?

Quantitative information is essential for planning, but managers must also be sensitive to qualitative factors, such as product quality, reliability and quality of suppliers, and availability of human and technical resources.

EXHIBIT 20-1
Comparative Summary of Alternatives at My Media Place

	Original Plan	Alternative 1	Alternative 2	Alternative 3
	Totals for 600 Units	Decrease Direct Materials Costs for 660 Units	Increase Advertising Costs for 630 Units	Increase Selling Price for 510 Units
Sales revenue	$54,000	$59,400	$56,700	$51,000
Less variable costs	30,000	31,020	31,500	25,500
Contribution margin	$24,000	$28,380	$25,200	$25,500
Less fixed costs	20,000	20,000	20,500	20,000
Operating income	$ 4,000	$ 8,380	$ 4,700	$ 5,500
Breakeven point in whole units (FC ÷ CM)				
$20,000 ÷ $40 =	500			
$20,000 ÷ $43 =		466*		
$20,500 ÷ $40 =			513*	
$20,000 ÷ $50 =				400

*Rounded up to next whole unit.

STOP & APPLY >

Assume a local real estate appraisal business is planning its home appraisal activities for the coming year. The manager estimates that her variable costs per appraisal will be $220, monthly fixed costs are $16,200, and service fee revenue will be $400 per appraisal. How many appraisals will the business have to perform each month to achieve a targeted profit of $18,000 per month?

SOLUTION

$$
\begin{aligned}
\text{Let } X &= \text{Targeted Sales in Units} \\
\text{S} - \text{VC} - \text{FC} &= \text{P} \\
\$400X - \$220X - \$16{,}200 &= \$18{,}000 \\
\$180X &= \$34{,}200 \\
X &= 190 \text{ Appraisals per Month}
\end{aligned}
$$

A LOOK BACK AT ▸ FLICKR

The Decision Point at the beginning of this chapter focused on **Flickr**, a company whose business is continually evolving to meet customers' preferences. It posed these questions:

- How does Flickr decide which services to offer?
- Why do Flickr's managers analyze cost behavior?

In Flickr's quest to add services its subscribers want, its managers must consider the variable and fixed costs of producing those services and the effect that they would have on resource usage and profitability. To ensure that their decisions about adding services will profit the company and make the best use of its resources, the managers must analyze cost behavior. They may use a variety of methods and formulas to separate mixed costs into their variable and fixed components. With an understanding of cost behavior patterns, they can use cost-volume-profit analysis to evaluate "what-if" scenarios and to determine selling prices that cover both fixed and variable costs and take into account the variability of demand for their company's services.

Review Problem

Breakeven Analysis and Profitability Planning
LO4 LO5

Suppose a company like Flickr is considering entering the online digital lockbox business by renting server space to customers to store any type of computer file. The company's managers believe this business has a large potential market as more individuals and small businesses are moving their file backups to secure online servers that can be accessed around the clock. Here is a summary of data projections for this business:

Selling price per year per customer account:	$95
Direct supplies	$23
Direct labor	8
Overhead	6
Selling expense	5
Variable costs per unit	$42
Overhead	$195,000
Advertising	55,000
Administrative expense	68,000
Total annual fixed costs	$318,000

Required

1. Compute the annual breakeven point in customer accounts.
2. Suppose managers projects sales to 6,500 customer accounts next year. If that projection is accurate, how much profit will the company realize?
3. To improve profitability, management is considering the following four alternative courses of action. (In performing the required steps, use the figures from items **1** and **2**, and treat each alternative independently.)
   a. Calculate the number of digital lockbox accounts that must be sold to generate a targeted profit of $95,400. Assume that costs and selling price remain constant.
   b. Calculate the operating income if the company increases the number of accounts sold by 20 percent and cuts the selling price by $5 per account.
   c. Determine the number of accounts that must be sold to break even if advertising costs (fixed costs) increase by $47,700.
   d. Find the number of accounts that must be sold to generate a targeted profit of $120,000 if variable costs decrease by 10 percent.

Answers to Review Problem

1. Annual breakeven point in customer accounts:

$$\text{Breakeven Units} = \frac{\text{FC}}{\text{CM per Unit}} = \frac{\$318{,}000}{\$95 - \$42} = \frac{\$318{,}000}{\$53} = 6{,}000 \text{ Units}$$

2. Profit from sale of 6,500 accounts:

Units sold	6,500
Units required to break even	6,000
Units over breakeven	500

$$\text{Profit} = \$53 \text{ per unit} \times 500 = \$26{,}500$$

Contribution margin equals sales minus all variable costs. Contribution margin per account equals the amount left to cover fixed costs and earn a profit after variable costs have been subtracted from sales dollars. If all fixed costs have been absorbed by the time breakeven is reached, the entire contribution margin of each unit sold in excess of breakeven represents profit.

3. a. Number of accounts that must be sold to generate a targeted profit of $95,400:

$$\text{Targeted Sales Units} = \frac{\text{FC} + \text{P}}{\text{CM per Unit}}$$

$$\frac{\$318{,}000 + \$95{,}400}{\$53} = \frac{\$413{,}400}{\$53} = 7{,}800 \text{ Units}$$

   b. Operating income if account sales increase 20 percent and selling price per account decreases by $5:

Sales revenue [7,800 (6,500 × 1.20) accounts at $90 per account]	$702,000
Less variable costs (7,800 units × $42)	327,600
Contribution margin	$374,400
Less fixed costs	318,000
Operating income	$ 56,400

c. Number of accounts needed to break even if advertising costs (fixed costs) increase by $47,700:

$$\text{BE Units} = \frac{\text{FC}}{\text{CM per Unit}}$$

$$\frac{\$318{,}000 + \$47{,}700}{\$53} = \frac{\$365{,}700}{\$53} = 6{,}900 \text{ Units}$$

d. Number of accounts that must be sold to generate a targeted profit of $120,000 if variable costs decrease by 10 percent:

$$\text{CM per Account} = \$95.00 - (\$42.00 \times 0.90) = \$95.00 - \$37.80 = \$57.20$$

$$\text{Targeted Sales Units} = \frac{\text{FC} + \text{P}}{\text{CM per Unit}}$$

$$\frac{\$318{,}000 + \$120{,}000}{\$57.20} = \frac{\$438{,}000}{\$57.20} = 7{,}658 \text{ Units*}$$

*Note that the answer is rounded up to the next whole unit.

STOP & REVIEW >

LO1 Define *cost behavior*, and identify variable, fixed, and mixed costs.

Cost behavior is the way costs respond to changes in volume or activity. Some costs vary in relation to volume or operating activity; other costs remain fixed as volume changes. Cost behavior depends on whether the focus is total costs or cost per unit. Total costs that change in direct proportion to changes in productive output (or any other volume measure) are called *variable costs.* They include hourly wages, the cost of operating supplies, direct materials costs, and the cost of merchandise. Total *fixed costs* remain constant within a relevant range of volume or activity. They change only when volume or activity exceeds the relevant range—for example, when new equipment or new buildings must be purchased, higher insurance premiums and property taxes must be paid, or additional supervisory personnel must be hired to accommodate increased activity. A *mixed cost*, such as the cost of electricity, has both variable and fixed cost components.

LO2 Separate mixed costs into their variable and fixed components, and prepare a contribution margin income statement.

For cost planning and control, mixed costs must be separated into their variable and fixed components. To separate them, managers use a variety of methods, including the engineering, scatter diagram, high-low, and statistical methods. When preparing a contribution margin income statement, all variable costs related to production, selling, and administration are subtracted from sales to determine the total contribution margin; then, all fixed costs are subtracted from the total contribution margin to determine operating income.

LO3 Define *cost-volume-profit (C-V-P) analysis*, and discuss how managers use it as a tool for planning and control.

Cost-volume-profit analysis is an examination of the cost behavior patterns that underlie the relationships among cost, volume of output, and profit. It is a tool for both planning and control. The techniques and problem-solving procedures involved in C-V-P analysis express relationships among revenue, sales mix, cost, volume, and profit. Those relationships provide a general model of financial activity that management can use for short-range planning and for evaluating performance and analyzing alternatives.

LO4 Define *breakeven point*, and use contribution margin to determine a company's breakeven point for multiple products.

The *breakeven point* is the point at which total revenues equal total costs—in other words, the point at which net sales equal variable costs plus fixed costs. Once the number of units needed to break even is known, the number can be multiplied by the product's selling price to determine the breakeven point in sales dollars. *Contribution margin* is the amount that remains after all variable costs have been subtracted from sales. A product's contribution margin represents its net contribution to paying off fixed costs and earning a profit. The breakeven point in units can be computed by using the following formula:

$$\text{BE Units} = \frac{\text{FC}}{\text{CM per Unit}}$$

Sales mix is used to calculate the breakeven point for each product when a company sells more than one product.

LO5 Use C-V-P analysis to project the profitability of products and services.

The addition of targeted profit to the breakeven equation makes it possible to plan levels of operation that yield the targeted profit. The formula in terms of contribution margin is

$$\text{Targeted Sales Units} = \frac{\text{FC} + \text{P}}{\text{CM per Unit}}$$

C-V-P analysis, whether used by a manufacturing company or a service organization, enables managers to select several "what-if" scenarios and evaluate the outcome of each to determine which will generate the desired amount of profit.

REVIEW of Concepts and Terminology

The following concepts and terms were introduced in this chapter:

Breakeven point 936 (LO4)

Contribution margin (CM) 933 (LO2)

Contribution margin income statement 933 (LO2)

Cost behavior 924 (LO1)

Cost-volume-profit (C-V-P) analysis 934 (LO3)

Engineering method 930 (LO2)

Fixed cost formula 927 (LO1)

Fixed costs 927 (LO1)

High-low method 931 (LO2)

Margin of safety 936 (LO4)

Mixed cost formula 929 (LO1)

Mixed costs 928 (LO1)

Normal capacity 926 (LO1)

Operating capacity 925 (LO1)

Practical capacity 926 (LO1)

Regression analysis 933 (LO2)

Relevant range 927 (LO1)

Sales mix 939 (LO4)

Scatter diagram 930 (LO2)

Step cost 927 (LO1)

Theoretical (ideal) capacity 926 (LO1)

Variable cost formula 925 (LO1)

Variable costs 925 (LO1)

CHAPTER ASSIGNMENTS

BUILDING Your Basic Knowledge and Skills

Short Exercises

LO1 **Concept of Cost Behavior**

SE 1. Dapper Hat Makers is in the business of designing and producing specialty hats. The material used for derbies costs $4.50 per unit, and Dapper pays each of its two full-time employees $360 per week. If Employee A makes 15 derbies in one week, what is the variable cost per derby, and what is this worker's fixed cost per derby? If Employee B makes only 12 derbies in one week, what are this worker's variable and fixed costs per derby?

LO1 **Identification of Variable, Fixed, and Mixed Costs**

SE 2. Identify the following as (a) fixed costs, (b) variable costs, or (c) mixed costs:

1. Direct materials
2. Electricity
3. Operating supplies
4. Personnel manager's salary
5. Factory building rent

LO2 **Mixed Costs: High-Low Method**

SE 3. Using the high-low method and the following information, compute the monthly variable cost per telephone hour and total fixed costs for Sadiko Corporation.

Month	Telephone Hours Used	Telephone Costs
April	96	$4,350
May	93	4,230
June	105	4,710

LO2 **Contribution Margin Income Statement**

SE 4. Prepare a contribution margin income statement if DeLuca, Inc., wants to make a profit of $20,000. It has variable costs of $8 per unit and fixed costs of $12,000. How much must it charge per unit if 4,000 units are sold?

LO4 **Breakeven Analysis in Units and Dollars**

SE 5. How many units must Braxton Company sell to break even if the selling price per unit is $8.50, variable costs are $4.30 per unit, and fixed costs are $3,780? What is the breakeven point in total dollars of sales?

LO4 **Contribution Margin in Units**

SE 6. Using the contribution margin approach, find the breakeven point in units for Norcia Consumer Products if the selling price per unit is $11, the variable cost per unit is $6, and the fixed costs are $5,500.

LO4 **Contribution Margin Ratio**

SE 7. Compute the contribution margin ratio and the breakeven point in total sales dollars for Wailley Products if the selling price per unit is $16, the variable cost per unit is $6, and the fixed costs are $6,250.

LO4 **Breakeven Analysis for Multiple Products**

SE 8. Using the contribution margin approach, find the breakeven point in units for Sardinia Company's two products. Product A's selling price per unit is $10, and its variable cost per unit is $4. Product B's selling price per unit is $8, and its variable cost per unit is $5. Fixed costs are $15,000, and the sales mix of Product A to Product B is 2:1.

LO4 LO5 **Contribution Margin and Projected Profit**

SE 9. If Oui Watches sells 300 watches at $48 per watch and has variable costs of $18 per watch and fixed costs of $4,000, what is the projected profit?

LO2 **Monthly Costs and the High-Low Method**

SE 10. Guy Spy, a private investigation firm, investigated 91 cases in December and had the following costs: direct labor, $190 per case; and service overhead of $20,840. Service overhead for October was $21,150; for November, it was $21,350. The number of cases investigated during October and November was 93 and 97, respectively. Compute the variable and fixed cost components of service overhead using the high-low method. Then determine the variable and fixed costs per case for December. (Round to nearest dollar where necessary.)

Exercises

LO1 **Identification of Variable and Fixed Costs**

E 1. Indicate whether each of the following costs of productive output is usually (a) variable or (b) fixed:

1. Packing materials for stereo components
2. Real estate taxes
3. Gasoline for a delivery truck
4. Property insurance
5. Depreciation expense of buildings (calculated with the straight-line method)
6. Supplies
7. Indirect materials
8. Bottles used to package liquids
9. License fees for company cars
10. Wiring used in radios
11. Machine helper's wages
12. Wood used in bookcases
13. City operating license
14. Machine depreciation based on machine hours used
15. Machine operator's hourly wages
16. Cost of required outside inspection of each unit produced

LO1 **Variable Cost Analysis**

E 2. Zero Time Oil Change has been in business for six months. The company pays $0.50 per quart for the oil it uses in servicing cars. Each job requires an average of 4 quarts of oil. The company estimates that in the next three months, it will service 240, 288, and 360 cars.

1. Compute the cost of oil for each of the three months and the total cost for all three months.

Month	Cars to Be Serviced	Required Quarts/Car	Cost/Quart	Total Cost/Month
1	240	4	$0.50	_____
2	288	4	0.50	_____
3	360	4	0.50	_____
Three-month total	888			_____

2. Complete the following sentences by choosing the words that best describe the cost behavior at Zero Time Oil Change:
   a. Cost per unit (increased, decreased, remained constant).
   b. Total variable cost per month (increased, decreased) as the quantity of oil used (increased, decreased).

LO2 Mixed Costs: High-Low Method

E 3. Whitehouse Company manufactures major appliances. Because of growing interest in its products, it has just had its most successful year. In preparing the budget for next year, its controller compiled these data:

Month	Volume in Machine Hours	Electricity Cost
July	6,000	$ 60,000
August	5,000	53,000
September	4,500	49,500
October	4,000	46,000
November	3,500	42,500
December	3,000	39,000
Six-month total	26,000	$290,000

Using the high-low method, determine the variable electricity cost per machine hour and the monthly fixed electricity cost. Estimate the total variable electricity costs and fixed electricity costs if 4,800 machine hours are projected to be used next month.

LO2 Mixed Costs: High-Low Method

E 4. When Jerome Company's monthly costs were $75,000, sales were $80,000; when its monthly costs were $60,000, sales were $50,000. Use the high-low method to develop a monthly cost formula for Jerome's coming year.

LO2 LO4 Contribution Margin Income Statement and Ratio

E 5. Senora Company manufactures a single product that sells for $110 per unit. The company projects sales of 500 units per month. Projected costs are as follows:

Type of Cost	Manufacturing	Nonmanufacturing
Variable	$10,000	$5,000
Nonvariable	$12,500	$7,500

1. Prepare a contribution margin income statement for the month.
2. What is the contribution margin ratio?
3. What volume, in terms of units, must the company sell to break even?

LO4 LO5 Contribution Margin Income Statement and C-V-P Analysis

E 6. Using the data in the contribution margin income statement for Sedona, Inc., that appears at the top of the next page, calculate (1) selling price per unit, (2) variable costs per unit, and (3) breakeven point in units and in sales dollars.

Sedona, Inc. Contribution Margin Income Statement For the Year Ended December 31		
Sales (10,000 units)		$16,000,000
Less variable costs		
Cost of goods sold	$8,000,000	
Selling, administrative, and general	4,000,000	
Total variable costs		12,000,000
Contribution margin		$ 4,000,000
Less fixed costs		
Overhead	$1,200,000	
Selling, administrative, and general	800,000	
Total fixed costs		2,000,000
Operating income		$ 2,000,000

LO4 **Graphic Breakeven Analysis**

E 7. Identify the letter of the point, line segment, or area of the breakeven graph shown below that correctly completes each of the following statements:

1. The maximum possible operating loss is
   a. A c. B
   b. D d. F
2. The breakeven point in sales dollars is
   a. C c. A
   b. D d. G
3. At volume F, total contribution margin is
   a. C c. E
   b. D d. G
4. Operating income is represented by area
   a. KDL c. BDC
   b. KCJ d. GCJ
5. At volume J, total fixed costs are represented by
   a. H c. I
   b. G d. J
6. If volume increases from F to J, the change in total costs is
   a. HI minus DE c. BC minus DF
   b. DF minus HJ d. AB minus DE

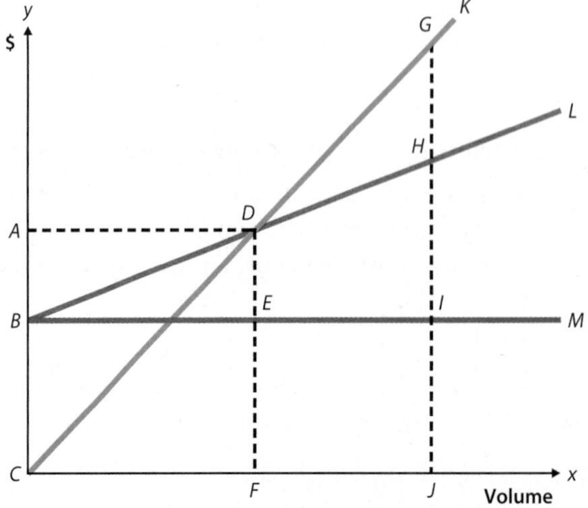

LO4 **Breakeven Analysis**

E 8. Techno Designs produces head covers for golf clubs. The company expects to generate a profit next year. It anticipates fixed manufacturing costs of $126,500 and fixed general and administrative expenses of $82,030 for the year. Variable manufacturing and selling costs per set of head covers will be $4.65 and $2.75, respectively. Each set will sell for $13.40.

1. Compute the breakeven point in sales units.
2. Compute the breakeven point in sales dollars.
3. If the selling price is increased to $14 per unit and fixed general and administrative expenses are cut by $33,465, what will the new breakeven point be in units?
4. Prepare a graph to illustrate the breakeven point computed in **2**.

LO4 LO5 **Breakeven Analysis and Pricing**

E 9. McLennon Company has a plant capacity of 100,000 units per year, but its budget for this year indicates that only 60,000 units will be produced and sold. The entire budget for this year is as follows:

Sales (60,000 units at $4)		$240,000
Less cost of goods produced (based on production of 60,000 units)		
Direct materials (variable)	$60,000	
Direct labor (variable)	30,000	
Variable ovesrhead costs	45,000	
Fixed overhead costs	75,000	
Total cost of goods produced		210,000
Gross margin		$ 30,000
Less selling and administrative expenses		
Selling (fixed)	$24,000	
Administrative (fixed)	36,000	
Total selling and administrative expenses		60,000
Operating income (loss)		($ 30,000)

1. Given the budgeted selling price and cost data, how many units would McLennon have to sell to break even? (**Hint:** Be sure to consider selling and administrative expenses.)
2. Market research indicates that if McLennon were to drop its selling price to $3.80 per unit, it could sell 100,000 units. Would you recommend the drop in price? What would the new operating income or loss be?

LO4 **Breakeven Point for Multiple Products**

E 10. Saline Aquarium, Inc., manufactures and sells aquariums, water pumps, and air filters. The sales mix is 1:2:2 (i.e., for every one aquarium sold, two water pumps and two air filters are sold). Using the contribution margin approach, find the breakeven point in units for each product. The company's fixed costs are $26,000. Other information is as follows:

	Selling Price per Unit	Variable Costs per Unit
Aquariums	$60	$25
Water pumps	20	12
Air filters	10	3

LO4 Breakeven Point for Multiple Products

E 11. Hamburgers and More, Inc., sells hamburgers, drinks, and fries. The sales mix is 1:3:2 (i.e., for every one hamburger sold, three drinks and two fries are sold). Using the contribution margin approach, find the breakeven point in units for each product. The company's fixed costs are $2,040. Other information is as follows:

	Selling Price per Unit	Variable Costs per Unit
Hamburgers	$0.99	$0.27
Drinks	0.99	0.09
Fries	0.99	0.15

LO4 Sales Mix Analysis

E 12. Ella Mae Simpson is the owner of a hairdressing salon in Palm Coast, Florida. Her salon provides three basic services: shampoo and set, permanents, and cut and blow dry. The following are its operating results from the past quarter:

Type of Service	Number of Customers	Total Sales	Contribution Margin in Dollars
Shampoo and set	1,200	$24,000	$14,700
Permanents	420	21,000	15,120
Cut and blow dry	1,000	15,000	10,000
	2,620	$60,000	$39,820
Total fixed costs			30,000
Profit			$ 9,820

Compute the breakeven point in units based on the weighted-average contribution margin for the sales mix.

LO4 LO5 Contribution Margin and Profit Planning

E 13. Target Systems, Inc., makes heat-seeking missiles. It has recently been offered a government contract from which it may realize a profit. The contract purchase price is $130,000 per missile, but the number of units to be purchased has not yet been decided. The company's fixed costs are budgeted at $3,973,500, and variable costs are $68,500 per unit.

1. Compute the number of units the company should agree to make at the stated contract price to earn a profit of $1,500,000.
2. Using a lighter material, the variable unit cost can be reduced by $1,730, but total fixed overhead will increase by $27,500. How many units must be produced to make $1,500,000 in profit?
3. Given the figures in **2**, how many additional units must be produced to increase profit by $1,264,600?

LO5 Planning Future Sales

E 14. Short-term automobile rentals are the specialty of ASAP Auto Rentals, Inc. Average variable operating costs have been $12.50 per day per automobile. The company owns 60 automobiles. Fixed operating costs for the next year are expected to be $145,500. Average daily rental revenue per automobile is expected to be $34.50. Management would like to earn a profit of $47,000 during the year.

1. Calculate the total number of daily rentals the company must have during the year to earn the targeted profit.
2. On the basis of your answer to **1**, determine the average number of days each automobile must be rented.

3. Determine the total revenue needed to achieve the targeted profit of $47,000.
4. What would the total rental revenue be if fixed operating costs could be lowered by $5,180 and the targeted profit increased to $70,000?

LO2 LO5 **Cost Behavior in a Service Business**

E 15. Luke Ricci, CPA, is the owner of a firm that provides tax services. The firm charges $50 per return for the direct professional labor involved in preparing standard short-form tax returns. In January, the firm prepared 850 such returns; in February, 1,000; and in March, 700. Service overhead (telephone and utilities, depreciation on equipment and building, tax forms, office supplies, and wages of clerical personnel) for January was $18,500; for February, $20,000; and for March, $17,000.

1. Determine the variable and fixed cost components of the firm's Service Overhead account.
2. What would the estimated total cost per tax return be if the firm prepares 825 standard short-form tax returns in April?

LO5 **C-V-P Analysis in a Service Business**

E 16. Flossmoor Inspection Service specializes in inspecting cars that have been returned to automobile leasing companies at the end of their leases. Flossmoor's charge for each inspection is $50; its average cost per inspection is $15. Tony Lomangeno, Flossmoor's owner, wants to expand his business by hiring another employee and purchasing an automobile. The fixed costs of the new employee and automobile would be $3,000 per month. How many inspections per month would the new employee have to perform to earn Lomangeno a profit of $1,200?

Problems

LO1 LO2 LO5 **Cost Behavior and Projection for a Service Business**

P 1. Power Brite Painting Company specializes in refurbishing exterior painted surfaces that have been hard hit by humidity and insect debris. It uses a special technique, called pressure cleaning, before priming and painting the surface. The refurbishing process involves the following steps:

1. Unskilled laborers trim all trees and bushes within two feet of the structure.
2. Skilled laborers clean the building with a high-pressure cleaning machine, using about 6 gallons of chlorine per job.
3. Unskilled laborers apply a coat of primer.
4. Skilled laborers apply oil-based exterior paint to the entire surface.

On average, skilled laborers work 12 hours per job, and unskilled laborers work 8 hours. The refurbishing process generated the following operating results during the year on 628 jobs:

Skilled labor	$20 per hour
Unskilled labor	$8 per hour
Gallons of chlorine used	3,768 gallons at $5.50 per gallon
Paint primer	7,536 gallons at $15.50 per gallon
Paint	6,280 gallons at $16 per gallon
Depreciation of paint-spraying equipment	$600 per month depreciation
Lease of two vans	$800 per month total
Rent on storage building	$450 per month

Data on utilities for the year are as follows:

Month	Number of Jobs	Cost	Hours Worked
January	42	$ 3,950	840
February	37	3,550	740
March	44	4,090	880
April	49	4,410	980
May	54	4,720	1,080
June	62	5,240	1,240
July	71	5,820	1,420
August	73	5,890	1,460
September	63	5,370	1,260
October	48	4,340	960
November	45	4,210	900
December	40	3,830	800
Totals	628	$55,420	12,560

Required

1. Classify the costs as variable, fixed, or mixed.
2. Using the high-low method, separate mixed costs into their variable and fixed components. Use total hours worked as the basis.
3. Compute the average cost per job for the year. (**Hint:** Divide the total of all costs for the year by the number of jobs completed.)
4. Project the average cost per job for next year if variable costs per job increase 20 percent.

Manager insight ▶ 5. Why can actual utility costs vary from the amount computed using the utilities cost formula (requirement **2**)?

LO4 LO5 **Breakeven Analysis**

P 2. Luce & Morgan, a law firm in downtown Jefferson City, is considering opening a legal clinic for middle- and low-income clients. The clinic would bill at a rate of $18 per hour. It would employ law students as paraprofessional help and pay them $9 per hour. Other variable costs are anticipated to be $5.40 per hour, and annual fixed costs are expected to total $27,000.

Required

1. Compute the breakeven point in billable hours.
2. Compute the breakeven point in total billings.
3. Find the new breakeven point in total billings if fixed costs should go up by $2,340.
4. Using the original figures, compute the breakeven point in total billings if the billing rate decreases by $1 per hour, variable costs decrease by $0.40 per hour, and fixed costs go down by $3,600.

LO4 LO5 **Planning Future Sales: Contribution Margin Approach**

P 3. Icon Industries is considering a new product for its Trophy Division. The product, which would feature an alligator, is expected to have global market appeal and to become the mascot for many high school and university athletic teams. Expected variable unit costs are as follows: direct materials, $18.50; direct labor, $4.25; production supplies, $1.10; selling costs, $2.80; and other, $1.95. Annual fixed costs are depreciation, building, and equipment, $36,000; advertising, $45,000; and other, $11,400. Icon Industries plans to sell the product for $55.00.

Required

1. Using the contribution margin approach, compute the number of units the company must sell to (a) break even and (b) earn a profit of $70,224.

2. Using the same data, compute the number of units that must be sold to earn a profit of $139,520 if advertising costs rise by $40,000.
3. Using the original information and sales of 10,000 units, compute the selling price the company must use to make a profit of $131,600. (**Hint:** Calculate contribution margin per unit first.)

Manager insight ▶

4. According to the vice president of marketing, Albert Flora, the most optimistic annual sales estimate for the product would be 15,000 units, and the highest competitive selling price the company can charge is $52 per unit. How much more can be spent on fixed advertising costs if the selling price is $52, if the variable costs cannot be reduced, and if the targeted profit for 15,000 unit sales is $251,000?

LO4 LO5 **Breakeven Analysis and Planning Future Sales**

P 4. Write Company has a maximum capacity of 200,000 units per year. Variable manufacturing costs are $12 per unit. Fixed overhead is $600,000 per year. Variable selling and administrative costs are $5 per unit, and fixed selling and administrative costs are $300,000 per year. The current sales price is $23 per unit.

Required

1. What is the breakeven point in (a) sales units and (b) sales dollars?
2. How many units must Write Company sell to earn a profit of $240,000 per year?
3. A strike at one of the company's major suppliers has caused a shortage of materials, so the current year's production and sales are limited to 160,000 units. To partially offset the effect of the reduced sales on profit, management is planning to reduce fixed costs to $841,000. Variable cost per unit is the same as last year. The company has already sold 30,000 units at the regular selling price of $23 per unit.
   a. What amount of fixed costs was covered by the total contribution margin of the first 30,000 units sold?
   b. What contribution margin per unit will be needed on the remaining 130,000 units to cover the remaining fixed costs and to earn a profit of $210,000 this year?

LO4 LO5 **Planning Future Sales for a Service Business**

P 5. Lending Hand Financial Corporation is a subsidiary of Gracey Enterprises. Its main business is processing loan applications. Last year, Bettina Brent, the manager of the corporation's loan department, established a policy of charging a $250 fee for every loan application processed. Next year's variable costs have been projected as follows: loan consultant's wages, $15.50 per hour (a loan application takes 5 hours to process); supplies, $2.40 per application; and other variable costs, $5.60 per application. Annual fixed costs include depreciation of equipment, $8,500; building rental, $14,000; promotional costs, $12,500; and other fixed costs, $8,099.

Required

1. Using the contribution margin approach, compute the number of loan applications the company must process to (a) break even and (b) earn a profit of $14,476.
2. Using the same approach and assuming promotional costs increase by $5,662, compute the number of applications the company must process to earn a profit of $20,000.
3. Assuming the original information and the processing of 500 applications, compute the loan application fee the company must charge if the targeted profit is $41,651.

Manager insight ▶ 4. Brent's staff can handle a maximum of 750 loan applications. How much more can be spent on promotional costs if the highest fee tolerable to the customer is \$280, if variable costs cannot be reduced, and if the targeted profit for the loan applications is \$50,000?

Alternate Problems

LO1 LO2 LO5

Mixed Costs

P 6. Officials of the Hidden Hills Golf and Tennis Club are in the process of preparing a budget for the year ending December 31. Because Ramon Saud, the club treasurer, has had difficulty with two expense items, the process has been delayed by more than four weeks. The two items are mixed costs—expenses for electricity and for repairs and maintenance—and Saud has been having trouble breaking them down into their variable and fixed components.

An accountant friend has suggested that he use the high-low method to divide the costs into their variable and fixed parts. The spending patterns and activity measures related to each cost during the past year are as follows:

	Electricity Expense		Repairs and Maintenance	
Month	Amount	Kilowatt-Hours	Amount	Labor Hours
January	\$ 7,500	210,000	\$ 7,578	220
February	8,255	240,200	7,852	230
March	8,165	236,600	7,304	210
April	8,960	268,400	7,030	200
May	7,520	210,800	7,852	230
June	7,025	191,000	8,126	240
July	6,970	188,800	8,400	250
August	6,990	189,600	8,674	260
September	7,055	192,200	8,948	270
October	7,135	195,400	8,674	260
November	8,560	252,400	8,126	240
December	8,415	246,600	7,852	230
Totals	\$92,550	2,622,000	\$96,416	2,840

Required

1. Using the high-low method, compute the variable cost rates used last year for each expense. What was the monthly fixed cost for electricity and for repairs and maintenance?
2. Compute the total variable cost and total fixed cost for each expense category for last year.
3. Saud believes that in the coming year, the electricity rate will increase by \$0.005 and the repairs rate, by \$1.20. Usage of all items and their fixed cost amounts will remain constant. Compute the projected total cost for each category. How will the cost increases affect the club's profits and cash flow?

LO4 LO5

Breakeven Analysis

P 7. At the beginning of each year, the Accounting Department at Moon Glow Lighting, Ltd., must find the point at which projected sales revenue will equal total budgeted variable and fixed costs. The company produces custom-made, low-voltage outdoor lighting systems. Each system sells for an average of \$435. Variable costs per unit are \$210. Total fixed costs for the year are estimated to be \$166,500.

Required

1. Compute the breakeven point in sales units.
2. Compute the breakeven point in sales dollars.
3. Find the new breakeven point in sales units if the fixed costs go up by $10,125.
4. Using the original figures, compute the breakeven point in sales units if the selling price decreases to $425 per unit, fixed costs go up by $15,200, and variable costs decrease by $15 per unit.

LO4 LO5 Planning Future Sales: Contribution Margin Approach

P 8. Garden Marbles manufactures birdbaths, statues, and other decorative items, which it sells to florists and retail home and garden centers. Its design department has proposed a new product, a statue of a frog, that it believes will be popular with home gardeners. Expected variable unit costs are direct materials, $9.25; direct labor, $4.00; production supplies, $0.55; selling costs, $2.40; and other, $3.05. The following are fixed costs: depreciation, building, and equipment, $33,000; advertising, $40,000; and other, $6,000. Management plans to sell the product for $29.25.

Required

1. Using the contribution margin approach, compute the number of statues the company must sell to (a) break even and (b) earn a profit of $50,000.
2. Using the same data, compute the number of statues that must be sold to earn a profit of $70,000 if advertising costs rise by $20,000.
3. Using the original data and sales of 15,000 units, compute the selling price the company must charge to make a profit of $100,000.
4. (Manager insight ▶) According to the vice president of marketing, Yvonne Palmer, if the price of the statues is reduced and advertising is increased, the most optimistic annual sales estimate is 25,000 units. How much more can be spent on fixed advertising costs if the selling price is reduced to $28.00 per statue, if the variable costs cannot be reduced, and if the targeted profit for sales of 25,000 statues is $120,000?

LO4 LO5 Breakeven Analysis and Planning Future Sales

P 9. Peerless Company has a maximum capacity of 500,000 units per year. Variable manufacturing costs are $25 per unit. Fixed overhead is $900,000 per year. Variable selling and administrative costs are $5 per unit, and fixed selling and administrative costs are $300,000 per year. The current sales price is $36 per unit.

Required

1. What is the breakeven point in (a) sales units and (b) sales dollars?
2. How many units must Peerless Company sell to earn a profit of $600,000 per year?
3. A strike at one of the company's major suppliers has caused a shortage of materials, so the current year's production and sales are limited to 400,000 units. To partially offset the effect of the reduced sales on profit, management is planning to reduce fixed costs to $1,000,000. Variable cost per unit is the same as last year. The company has already sold 30,000 units at the regular selling price of $36 per unit.
   a. What amount of fixed costs was covered by the total contribution margin of the first 30,000 units sold?
   b. What contribution margin per unit will be needed on the remaining 370,000 units to cover the remaining fixed costs and to earn a profit of $300,000 this year?

LO5 Planning Future Sales for a Service Business

P 10. Home Mortgage Inc.'s primary business is processing mortgage loan applications. Last year, Jenna Jason, the manager of the mortgage application department, established a policy of charging a $500 fee for every loan application processed. Next year's variable costs have been projected as follows: mortgage processor wages, $30 per hour (a mortgage application takes 3 hours to process); supplies, $10 per application; and other variable costs, $15 per application. Annual fixed costs include depreciation of equipment, $5,000; building rental, $34,000; promotional costs, $45,000; and other fixed costs, $20,000.

Required

1. Using the contribution margin approach, compute the number of loan applications the company must process to (a) break even and (b) earn a profit of $50,000.
2. Using the same approach and assuming promotional costs increase by $5,400, compute the number of applications the company must process to earn a profit of $60,000.
3. Assuming the original information and the processing of 500 applications, compute the loan application fee the company must charge if the targeted profit is $40,000.
4. Manager insight ▶ Jason's staff can handle a maximum of 750 loan applications. How much more can be spent on promotional costs if the highest fee tolerable to the customer is $400, if variable costs cannot be reduced, and if the targeted profit for the loan applications is $50,000?

ENHANCING Your Knowledge, Skills, and Critical Thinking

LO4 Breaking Even and Ethics

C 1. Lesley Chomski is the supervisor of the New Product Division of MCO Corporation. Her annual bonus is based on the success of new products and is computed on the number of sales that exceed each new product's projected breakeven point. In reviewing the computations supporting her most recent bonus, Chomski found that although an order for 7,500 units of a new product called R56 had been refused by a customer and returned to the company, the order had been included in the bonus calculations. She later discovered that the company's accountant had labeled the return an overhead expense and had charged the entire cost of the returned order to the plantwide Overhead account. The result was that product R56 appeared to exceed breakeven by more than 5,000 units and Chomski's bonus from this product amounted to over $1,000. What actions should Chomski take? Be prepared to discuss your response in class.

LO1 LO4 Cost Behavior and Contribution Margin

C 2. Visit a local fast-food restaurant. Observe all aspects of the operation and take notes on the entire process. Describe the procedures used to take, process, and fill an order and deliver the order to the customer. Based on your observations, make a list of the costs incurred by the operation. Identify at least three variable costs and three fixed costs. Can you identify any potential mixed costs? Why is the restaurant willing to sell a large drink for only a few cents more than a medium drink? How is the restaurant able to offer a "value meal" (e.g., sandwich, drink, and fries) for considerably less than those items would cost if they were bought separately? Bring your notes to class and be prepared to discuss your findings.

Your instructor will divide the class into groups to discuss the case. Summarize your group's discussion, and ask one member of the group to present the summary to the rest of the class.

LO3 LO4 **C-V-P Analysis**

C 3. Based in Italy, Datura, Ltd., is an international importer-exporter of pottery with distribution centers in the United States, Europe, and Australia. The company was very successful in its early years, but its profitability has since declined. As a member of a management team selected to gather information for Datura's next strategic planning meeting, you have been asked to review its most recent contribution margin income statement for the year ended December 31, 2010, which appears below.

Datura, Ltd.
Contribution Margin Income Statement
For the Year Ended December 31, 2010

Sales revenue		€13,500,000
Less variable costs		
Purchases	€6,000,000	
Distribution	2,115,000	
Sales commissions	1,410,000	
Total variable costs		9,525,000
Contribution margin		€ 3,975,000
Less fixed costs		
Distribution	€ 985,000	
Selling	1,184,000	
General and administrative	871,875	
Total fixed costs		3,040,875
Operating income		€ 934,125

In 2010, Datura sold 15,000 sets of pottery.

1. For each set of pottery sold in 2010, calculate the (a) selling price, (b) variable purchases cost, (c) variable distribution cost, (d) variable sales commission, and (e) contribution margin.
2. Calculate the breakeven point in units and in sales euros.
3. Historically, Datura's variable costs have been about 60 percent of sales. What was the ratio of variable costs to sales in 2010? List three actions Datura could take to correct the difference.
4. How would fixed costs have been affected if Datura had sold only 14,000 sets of pottery in 2010?

LO5 **C-V-P Analysis Applied**

C 4. Refer to the information in **C 3**. In January 2011, Sophia Callas, the president of Datura, Ltd., conducted a strategic planning meeting. During the meeting, Phillipe Mazzeo, vice president of distribution, noted that because of a new contract with an international shipping line, the company's fixed distribution costs for 2011 would be reduced by 10 percent and its variable distribution costs by 4 percent. Gino Roma, vice president of sales, offered the following information:

> We plan to sell 15,000 sets of pottery again in 2011, but based on review of the competition, we are going to lower the selling price to €890 per set. To encourage increased sales, we will raise sales commissions to 12 percent of the selling price.

Sophia Callas is concerned that the changes described by Roma and Mazzeo may not improve operating income sufficiently in 2011. If operating income does not increase by at least 10 percent, she will want to find other ways to reduce the company's costs. She asks you to evaluate the situation in a written report. Because it is already January of 2011 and changes need to be made quickly, she requests your report within five days.

1. Prepare a budgeted contribution margin income statement for 2011. Your report should show the budgeted (estimated) operating income based on the information provided above and in **C 3**. Will the changes improve operating income sufficiently? Explain.
2. In preparation for writing your report, answer the following questions:
   a. Why are you preparing the report?
   b. Who needs the report?
   c. What sources of information will you use?
   d. When is the report due?

LO5 Planning Future Sales

C 5. As noted in **C 3,** Datura, Ltd., sold 15,000 sets of pottery in 2010. As noted in **C 4**, in 2011, Datura's strategic planning team targeted sales of 15,000 sets of pottery, reduced the selling price to €890 per set, increased sales commissions to 12 percent of the selling price, and decreased fixed distribution costs by 10 percent and variable distribution costs by 4 percent. It was assumed that all other costs would stay the same.

Based on an analysis of these changes, Sophia Callas, Datura's president, is concerned that the proposed strategic plan will not meet her goal of increasing Datura's operating income by 10 percent over last year's income and that the operating income will be less than last year's income. She has come to you for spreadsheet analysis of the proposed strategic plan and for analysis of a special order she just received from an Australian distributor for 4,500 sets of pottery. The order's selling price, variable purchases cost per unit, sales commission, and total fixed costs will be the same as for the rest of the business, but the variable distribution costs will be €160 per unit.

Using an Excel spreadsheet, complete the following tasks:

1. Calculate the targeted operating income for 2011 using just the proposed strategic plan.
2. Prepare a budgeted contribution margin income statement for 2011 based on just the strategic plan. Do you agree with Datura's president that the company's projected operating income for 2011 will be less than the operating income for 2010? Explain your answer.
3. Calculate the total contribution margin from the Australian sales.
4. Prepare a revised budgeted contribution margin income statement for 2011 that includes the Australian order. (**Hint:** Combine the information from **2** and **3** above.)
5. Does Datura need the Australian sales to achieve its targeted operating income for 2011?

LO1 LO2 Cookie Company (Continuing Case)

C 6. In this segment of our continuing "cookie company" case, you will classify the costs of the business as variable, fixed, or mixed; use the high-low method to evaluate utility costs; and prepare a contribution margin income statement.

1. Review your cookie recipe and the overhead costs you identified in Chapter 16, and classify the costs as variable, fixed, or mixed costs.

2. Obtain your electric bills for three months, and use the high-low method's cost formula to determine the monthly cost of electricity—that is, monthly electric cost = variable rate per kilowatt-hour + monthly fixed cost. If you do not receive an electric bill, use the following information:

Month	Kilowatt-Hours Used	Electric Costs
August	1,439	$202
September	1,866	230
October	1,146	158

3. Prepare a daily contribution margin income statement based on the following assumptions:

   Cookie Company makes only one kind of cookie and sells it for $1.00 per unit. The company projects sales of 500 units per day. Projected daily costs are as follows:

Type of Cost	Manufacturing	Nonmanufacturing
Variable	$100	$50
Nonvariable	120	60

   a. What is the contribution margin ratio?
   b. What volume, in terms of units, must the company sell to break even each day?

CHAPTER

21 The Budgeting Process

The Management Process

PLAN

- **Review strategic, tactical, and operating objectives.**
- **Analyze and forecast sales.**
- **Analyze costs and determine cost formulas.**
- **Prepare operating budgets.**
- **Prepare financial budgets.**

PERFORM

- **Implement budgets to grant authority and responsibility for operating objectives.**

EVALUATE

- **Compare actual results with budgets; revise budgets if needed.**

COMMUNICATE

- **Prepare internal budget reports that summarize and analyze performance.**
- **Prepare pro forma financial statements for external use.**

Budgeting is not only an essential part of planning; it also helps managers control, evaluate, and report on operations.

When managers develop budgets, they match their organizational goals with the resources necessary to accomplish those goals. During the budgeting process, they evaluate operational, tactical, value chain, and capacity issues; assess how resources can be used efficiently; and develop contingency budgets as business conditions change. In this chapter, we describe the budgeting process, identify the elements of a master budget, and demonstrate how managers prepare operating budgets and financial budgets.

LEARNING OBJECTIVES

LO1 Define *budgeting,* and explain budget basics. (pp. 966–969)

LO2 Identify the elements of a master budget in different types of organizations and the guidelines for preparing budgets. (pp. 969–973)

LO3 Prepare the operating budgets that support the financial budgets. (pp. 973–980)

LO4 Prepare a budgeted income statement, a cash budget, and a budgeted balance sheet. (pp. 981–987)

DECISION POINT ▶ A MANAGER'S FOCUS FRAMERICA CORPORATION

- ▶ How does Framerica Corporation translate long-term goals into operating objectives?
- ▶ What is the effect of Framerica's budgeting process?

Framerica Corporation is one of the leading manufacturers of picture frames in North America. Its innovations, which include profile-wrapping capabilities and finishes, have revolutionized the methods used in producing picture frames. Because Framerica believes its work force is its most valuable asset, one of its priorities is to help employees attain their personal goals.

One highly effective way of achieving congruence between a company's goals and objectives and employees' personal aspirations is a participative budgeting process—an ongoing dialogue that involves personnel at all levels of a company in making budgeting decisions. This dialogue provides both managers and lower-level employees with insight into the company's current activities and future direction and motivates them to improve their own performance, which, in turn, improves the company's performance.

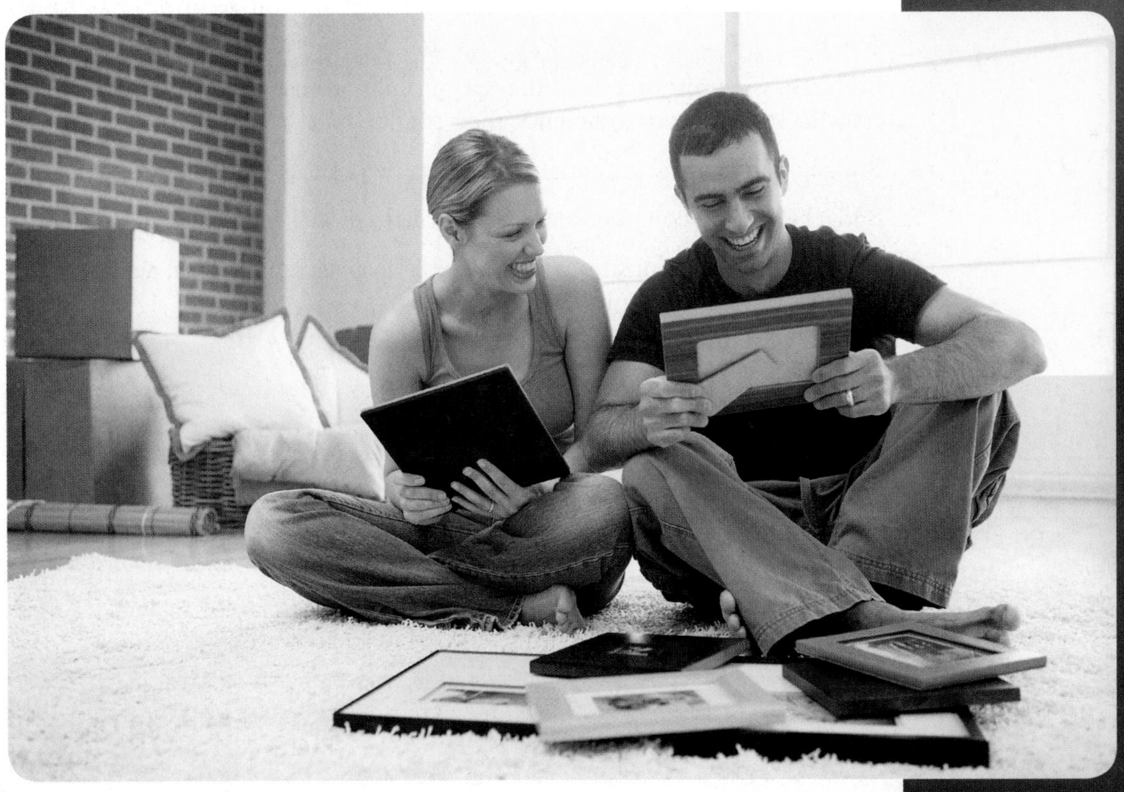

The Budgeting Process

LO1 Define *budgeting,* and explain budget basics.

Study Note

For-profit organizations often use the term *profit planning* rather than *budgeting.*

Budgeting is the process of identifying, gathering, summarizing, and communicating financial and nonfinancial information about an organization's future activities. It is an essential part of the continuous planning that an organization must do to accomplish its long-term goals. The budgeting process provides managers of all types of organizations—including for-profit organizations and not-for-profit organizations—the opportunity to match their organizational goals with the resources necessary to accomplish those goals.

Budgets—plans of action based on forecasted transactions, activities, and events—are synonymous with managing an organization. They are essential to accomplishing the goals articulated in an organization's strategic plan. They are used to communicate information, coordinate activities and resource usage, motivate employees, and evaluate performance. For example, a board of directors may use budgets to determine managers' areas of responsibility and to measure managers' performance in those areas.

Budgets are, of course, also used to manage and account for cash. Such budgets establish targeted levels of cash receipts and limits on the spending of cash for particular purposes.

Advantages of Budgeting

Budgeting is advantageous for organizations, because:

1. Budgets foster organizational communication.
2. Budgets ensure a focus both on future events and on resolving day-to-day issues.
3. Budgets assign resources and the responsibility to use them wisely to managers who are held accountable for their results.
4. Budgets can identify potential constraints before they become problems.
5. Budgets facilitate congruence between organizational and personal goals.
6. Budgets define organizational goals and objectives numerically, against which actual performance results can be evaluated.

FOCUS ON BUSINESS PRACTICE

What Can Cause the Planning Process to Fail?

When chief financial officers were asked what caused their planning process to fail, these were the six factors they most commonly cited:[1]

- An inadequately defined strategy
- No clear link between strategy and the operational budget
- Lack of individual accountability for results
- Lack of meaningful performance measures
- Inadequate pay for performance
- Lack of appropriate data

Budgeting and Goals

Long-Term Goals **Strategic planning** is the process by which management establishes an organization's long-term goals. These goals define the strategic direction that an organization will take over a ten-year period and are the basis for making annual operating plans and preparing budgets. Long-term goals cannot be vague; they must set specific tactical targets and timetables and assign operating responsibility for achieving the goals to specific personnel. For example, a long-term goal for a company that currently holds only 4 percent of its product's market share might specify that the vice president of marketing is to develop strategies to ensure that the company controls 10 percent of the market in five years and 15 percent by the end of ten years.

Study Note

As plans are formulated for time periods closer to the current date, they become more specific and quantified. The annual budget is a very specific plan of action.

Short-Term Goals Annual operating plans involve every part of an enterprise and are much more detailed than long-term strategic plans. To formulate an annual operating plan, an organization must restate its long-term goals in terms of what it needs to accomplish during the next year. The process entails making decisions about sales and profit targets, human resource needs, and the introduction of new products or services. The short-term goals identified in an annual operating plan are the basis of an organization's operating budgets for the year.

Budgeting Basics

Once long- and short-term goals have been decided, the organization's controller and **budget committee**, which includes many top managers, play a central role in coordinating the budgeting process. Together, they set the basics of the budgeting process, including assigning budget authority, inviting employee participation, selecting the budget period, and implementing the budget.

Budget Authority Every budget and budget line item is associated with a specific role or job in an organization. For example, a department manager is responsible for the department's budget, and the marketing vice president is responsible for what is spent on advertising.

Since managers responsibilities and budget authority are linked, managers must explain or take corrective action for any deviations between their budgets and actual results. Responsibility accounting, which will be discussed in greater detail in the next chapter, authorizes managers to take control of and be held accountable for the revenues and expenses in their budgets. It assigns resources and the responsibility to use them wisely to managers. If managers do not have budget authority, they lack the control necessary to accomplish their duties and cannot be held accountable for results. The concept of responsibility accounting holds managers accountable for only those budget items that they actually control.

Participation Because an organization's main activities—such as production, sales, and employee training—take place at its lower levels, the information necessary for establishing a budget flows from the employees and supervisors of those activities through middle managers to senior executives. Each person in this chain of communication thus plays a role in developing a budget, as well as in implementing it. If these individuals feel that they have a voice in setting the budget targets, they will be motivated to ensure that their departments attain those targets and stay within the budget. If they do not feel that they have a role in the budgeting process, motivation will suffer. The key to a successful budget is therefore **participative budgeting**, a process in which personnel at all levels of an organization actively engage in making decisions about the budget. Participative budgeting depends on joint decision making; without it the budgeting process will be authoritative rather than participative. Without input from personnel at all operational levels, the budget targets may be unrealistic and impossible to attain.

Budget Period Budgets, like the company's fiscal period, generally cover a one-year period of time. An annual operating budget may be divided further by an organization into monthly or quarterly periods depending on how detailed the information needs are. In this chapter, you will be working with both monthly and quarterly budgets.

The organization's controller and budget committee decide whether they will use a static or continuous budgeting process. **Static budgets** are prepared once a year and do not change during the annual budget period. To ensure that its managers have continuously updated operating data against which to measure performance, an organization may select an ongoing budgeting process, called a continuous budget. A **continuous budget** is a forward-rolling budget that summarizes budgets for the next 12 months. Each month, managers prepare a budget for the same month next year. Thus, the budget is continuously reviewed and revised during the year.

Budget Approach Traditional budgeting approaches require managers to justify only budget changes over the past year. An alternative to traditional budgeting is zero-based budgeting. **Zero-based budgeting** requires that every budget item be justified annually, not just the changes. So each year the budget is built from scratch.

Budget Implementation The budget committee and the controller have overall responsibility for budget implementation. The budget committee oversees each stage in the preparation of the organization's overall budget, mediates any departmental disputes that may arise in the process, and gives final approval to the budget. The makeup of the committee ensures that the budgeting process has a companywide perspective.

A budget may have to go through many revisions before it includes all planning decisions and has the approval of the budget committee. Once the committee approves the budget, periodic reports from department managers allow the committee to monitor the company's progress in attaining budget targets.

Successful budget implementation depends on two factors—clear communication and the support of top management. To ensure their cooperation in implementing the budget, all key persons involved must know what roles they are expected to play and must have specific directions on how to achieve their performance goals. Thus, the controller and other members of the budget committee must be very clear in communicating performance expectations and budget targets. Equally important, top management must show support for the budget and encourage its implementation. The process will succeed only if middle- and lower-level managers are confident that top management is truly interested in the outcome and is willing to reward personnel for meeting the budget targets. Today, many organizations have employee incentive plans that tie the achievement of budget targets to bonuses or other types of compensation.

Study Note

Because good communication can eliminate many of the problems that typically arise in the budgeting process, company-wide dialogue is extremely important.

Randi Quelle is the manager of the electronics department in a large discount store. During a recent meeting, Quelle and her supervisor agreed that Quelle's goal for the next year would be to increase by 20 percent the number of flat-screen televisions sold. The department sold 500 TV sets last year. Two sales persons currently work for Quelle. What types of budgets should Quelle use to help her achieve her sales goal? What kinds of information should those budgets provide?

SOLUTION

Budgets and information that might be useful include:

1. Breakdown by month of last year's sales to use as a guide to build this year's monthly targets. This would include seasonal sales information.
2. Budgets by sales person, which may indicate a need for a third sales person.
3. Inventory and purchasing information.
4. Budgets of sales promotion and advertising.
5. Information on customer flow and the best times to sell.

The Master Budget

LO2 Identify the elements of a master budget in different types of organizations and the guidelines for preparing budgets.

A **master budget** consists of a set of operating budgets and a set of financial budgets that detail an organization's financial plans for a specific accounting period, generally a year. When a master budget covers an entire year, some of the operating and financial budgets may show planned results by month or by quarter.

- As the term implies, **operating budgets** are plans used in daily operations. They are also the basis for preparing the **financial budgets**, which are projections of financial results for the accounting period.
- Financial budgets include a budgeted income statement, a capital expenditures budget, a cash budget, and a budgeted balance sheet.

Study Note

Budgeted financial statements are often referred to as *forecasted financial statements, pro forma financial statements,* or *forward-looking financial statements.*

The budgeted financial statements—that is, the budgeted income statement and budgeted balance sheet—are also called **pro forma financial statements**, meaning that they show projections rather than actual results. Pro forma financial statements are often used to communicate business plans to external parties.

If, for example, you wanted to obtain a bank loan so that you could start a new business, you would have to present the bank with a pro forma, or budgeted, income statement and balance sheet showing that you could repay the loan with cash generated by profitable operations.

Preparation of a Master Budget

Suppose you have started your own business. Whether it is a manufacturing, retail, or service organization, to manage it effectively, you would prepare a master budget each period. A master budget provides the information needed to match long-term goals to short-term activities and to plan the resources needed to ensure an organization's profitability and liquidity.

Figures 21-1, 21-2, and 21-3 display the elements of a master budget for a manufacturing organization, a retail organization, and a service organization, respectively. As these illustrations indicate, the process of preparing a master budget is similar in all three types of organizations in that each prepares a set of

FIGURE 21-1 Preparation of a Master Budget for a Manufacturing Organization

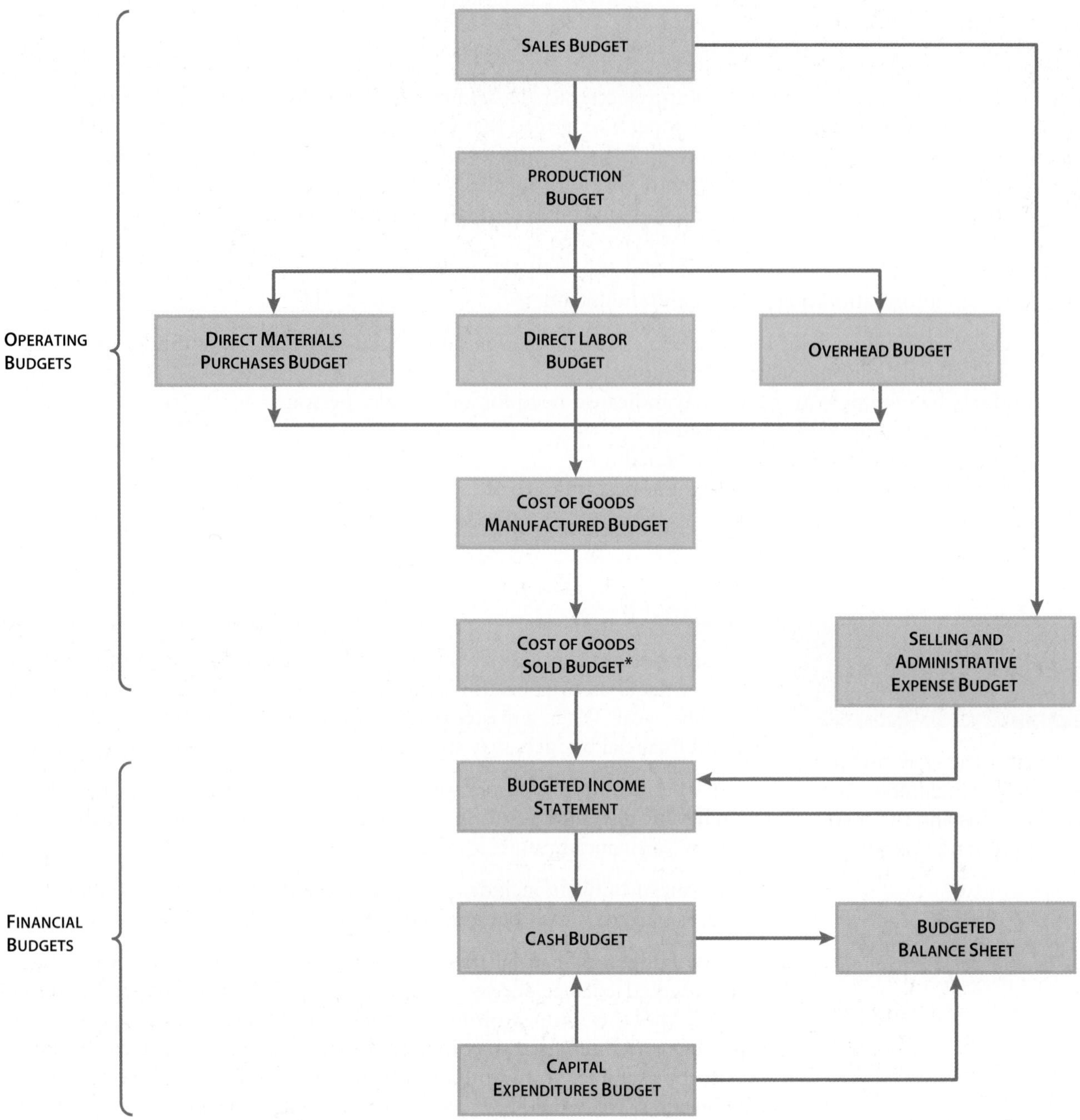

*Some organizations choose to include the cost of goods sold budget in the budgeted income statement.

operating budgets that serve as the basis for preparing the financial budgets. The process differs mainly in the kinds of operating budgets that each type of organization prepares.

- The operating budgets of manufacturing organizations, such as **Framerica**, include budgets for sales, production, direct materials, direct labor, overhead, selling and administrative expenses, and cost of goods manufactured.
- Retail organizations, such as **Michaels**, **Talbots**, and **Lowe's**, prepare a sales budget, a purchases budget, a selling and administrative expense budget, and a cost of goods sold budget.

FIGURE 21-2
Preparation of a Master Budget for a Retail Organization

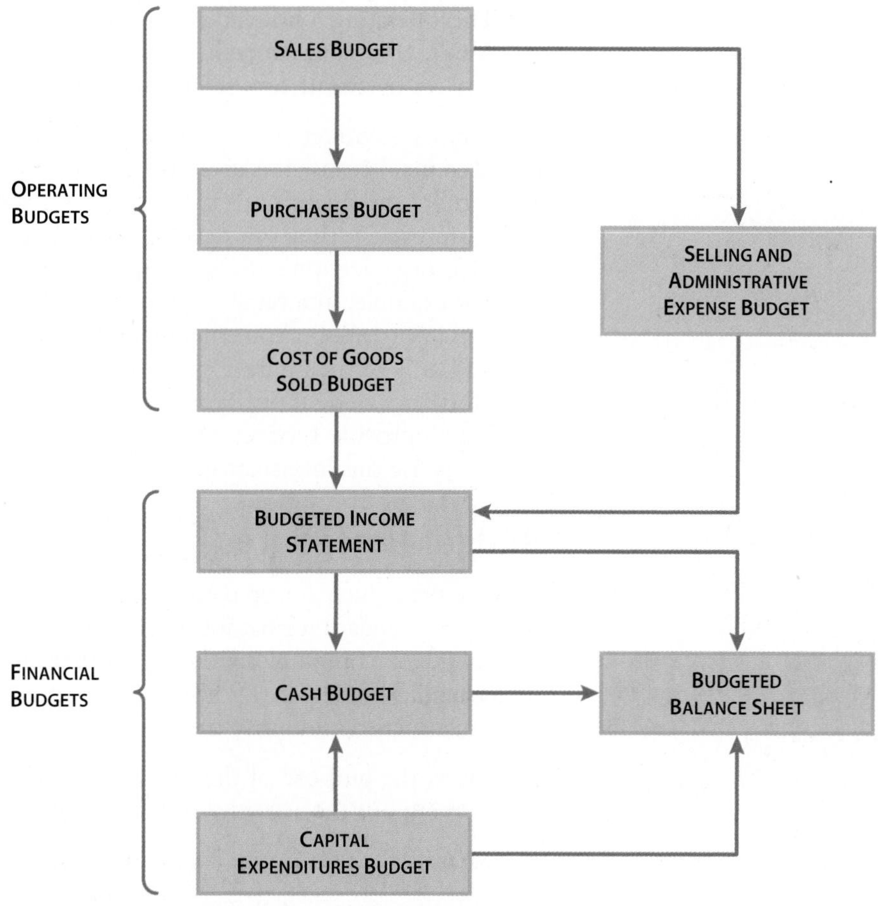

FIGURE 21-3 Preparation of a Master Budget for a Service Organization

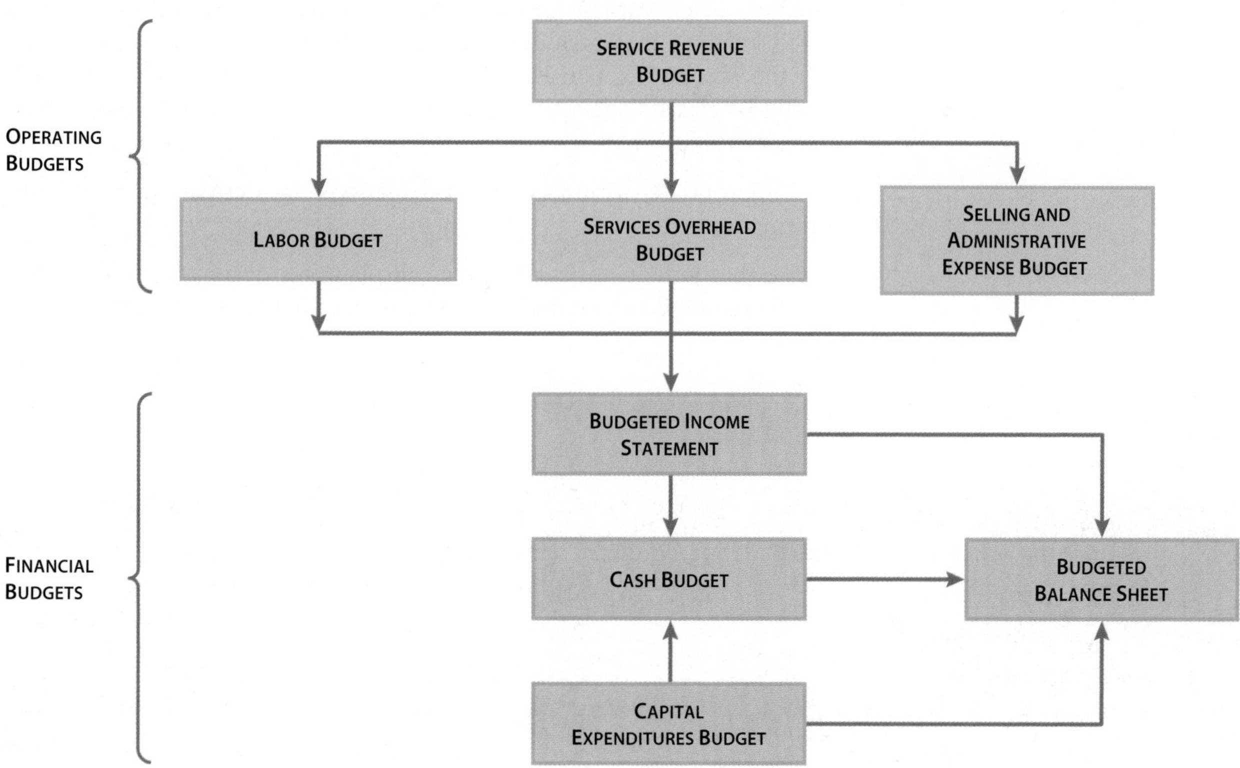

- The operating budgets of service organizations, such as **Enterprise Rent-A-Car**, **UPS**, and **Amtrak**, include budgets for service revenue (sales), labor, services overhead, and selling and administrative expenses.

The sales budget (or in service organizations, the service revenue budget) is prepared first because it is used to estimate sales volume and revenues. Once managers know the quantity of products or services to be sold and how many sales dollars to expect, they can develop other budgets that will enable them to manage their organization's resources so that they generate profits on those sales.

For example, in a retail organization, the purchases budget provides managers with information about the quantity of merchandise needed to meet the sales demand and yet maintain a minimum level of inventory. In a service organization, the labor budget provides information about the labor hours and labor rates needed to provide services and generate the revenues planned for each period; managers use this information in scheduling services and setting prices.

Budget Procedures

Because procedures for preparing budgets vary from organization to organization, there is no standard format for budget preparation. The only universal requirement is that budgets communicate the appropriate information to the reader in a clear and understandable manner. By keeping that in mind and using the following guidelines, managers can improve the quality of budgets in any type of organization:

1. Know the purpose of the budget, and clearly identify who is responsible for carrying out the activities in the budget.
2. Identify the user group and its information needs.
3. Identify sources of accurate, meaningful budget information. Such information may be gathered from documents or from interviews with employees, suppliers, or managers who work in the related areas.
4. Establish a clear format for the budget. A budget should begin with a clearly stated heading that includes the organization's name, the type of budget, and the accounting period under consideration. The budget's components should be clearly labeled, and the unit and financial data should be listed in an orderly manner.
5. Use appropriate formulas and calculations in deriving the quantitative information.
6. Revise the budget until it includes all planning decisions. Several revisions may be required before the final version is ready for distribution.

STOP & APPLY >

Identify the order in which the following budgets are prepared:

1. Overhead budget
2. Production budget
3. Direct labor budget
4. Direct materials purchases budget
5. Sales budget
6. Budgeted balance sheet
7. Cash budget
8. Budgeted income statement

(continued)

SOLUTION

1. Sales budget
2. Production budget
3. Direct materials purchases budget, direct labor budget, and overhead budget
4. Budgeted income statement
5. Cash budget
6. Budgeted balance sheet

Operating Budgets

LO3 Prepare the operating budgets that support the financial budgets.

Although procedures for preparing operating budgets vary, the tools used in the process do not. In this section, we use a frame-making company, called Framecraft Company, to illustrate how a manufacturing organization prepares its operating budgets. Because Framecraft Company makes only one product—a plastic picture frame—it prepares only one of each type of operating budget. Organizations that manufacture a variety of products or provide many types of services may prepare either separate operating budgets or one comprehensive budget for each product or service.

The Sales Budget

Study Note

The sales budget is the only budget based on an estimate of customer demand. Other budgets for the period are prepared from it and are based on the numbers it provides.

As we indicated earlier, the first step in preparing a master budget is to prepare a sales budget. A **sales budget** is a detailed plan, expressed in both units and dollars, that identifies the sales expected during an accounting period. Sales managers use this information to plan sales- and marketing-related activities and to determine their human, physical, and technical resource needs. Accountants use the information to determine estimated cash receipts for the cash budget.

The following equation is used to determine the total budgeted sales:

$$\text{Total Budgeted Sales} = \text{Estimated Selling Price per Unit} \times \text{Estimated Sales in Units}$$

Although the calculation is easy, selecting the best estimates for the selling price per unit and the sales demand in units can be difficult.

- An estimated selling price below the current selling price may be needed if competitors are currently selling the same product or service at lower prices or if the organization wants to increase its share of the market.
- On the other hand, if the organization has improved the quality of its product or service by using more expensive materials or processes, the estimated selling price may have to be higher than the current price.

The estimated sales volume is very important because it will affect the level of operating activities and the amount of resources needed for operations. To help estimate sales volume, managers often use a **sales forecast**, which is a projection of sales demand (the estimated sales in units) based on an analysis of external and internal factors. The external factors include:

1. The state of the local and national economies
2. The state of the industry's economy
3. The nature of the competition and its sales volume and selling price

EXHIBIT 21-1
Sales Budget

Framecraft Company
Sales Budget
For the Year Ended December 31

	Quarter				
	1	**2**	**3**	**4**	**Year**
Sales in units	10,000	30,000	10,000	40,000	90,000
× Selling price per unit	× $5	× $5	× $5	× $5	× $5
Total sales	$50,000	$150,000	$50,000	$200,000	$450,000

Internal factors taken into consideration in a sales forecast include:

1. The number of units sold in prior periods
2. The organization's credit policies
3. The organization's collection policies
4. The organization's pricing policies
5. Any new products that the organization plans to introduce to the market
6. The capacity of the organization's manufacturing facilities

Exhibit 21-1 illustrates Framecraft Company's sales budget for the year. The budget shows the estimated number of unit sales and dollar revenue amounts for each quarter and for the entire year. Because a sales forecast indicated a highly competitive marketplace, Framecraft's managers have estimated a selling price of $5 per unit. The sales forecast also indicated highly seasonal sales activity; the estimated sales volume therefore varies from 10,000 to 40,000 per quarter.

The Production Budget

A **production budget** is a detailed plan showing the number of units that a company must produce to meet budgeted sales and inventory needs. Production managers use this information to plan for the materials and human resources that production-related activities will require. To prepare a production budget, managers must know the budgeted number of unit sales (which is specified in the sales budget) and the desired level of ending finished goods inventory for each period in the budget year. That level is often stated as a percentage of the next period's budgeted unit sales.

For example, Framecraft Company's desired level of ending finished goods inventory is 10 percent of the next quarter's budgeted unit sales. (Its desired level of beginning finished goods inventory is 10 percent of the current quarter's budgeted unit sales.)

The following formula identifies the production needs for each accounting period:

$$\text{Total Production Units} = \text{Budgeted Sales in Units} + \text{Desired Units of Ending Finished Goods Inventory} - \text{Desired Units of Beginning Finished Goods Inventory}$$

Exhibit 21-2 shows Framecraft Company's production budget for the year. Notice that each quarter's desired total units of ending finished goods inventory become the next quarter's desired total units of beginning finished goods inventory.

EXHIBIT 21-2
Production Budget

Framecraft Company
Production Budget
For the Year Ended December 31

	Quarter				
	1	**2**	**3**	**4**	**Year**
Sales in units	10,000	30,000	10,000	40,000	90,000
Plus desired units of ending finished goods inventory	3,000	1,000	4,000	1,500	1,500
Desired total units	13,000	31,000	14,000	41,500	91,500
Less desired units of beginning finished goods inventory	1,000	3,000	1,000	4,000	1,000
Total production units	12,000	28,000	13,000	37,500	90,500

- Because unit sales of 15,000 are budgeted for the first quarter of next year, the ending finished goods inventory for the fourth quarter of the year is 1,500 units (0.10 × 15,000 units), which is the same as the desired number of units of ending finished goods inventory for the entire year.
- Similarly, the number of desired units for the first quarter's beginning finished goods inventory—1,000—is the same as the desired number of units of beginning finished goods inventory for the entire year.

The Direct Materials Purchases Budget

A **direct materials purchases budget** is a detailed plan that identifies the quantity of purchases required to meet budgeted production and inventory needs and the costs associated with those purchases. A purchasing department uses this information to plan purchases of direct materials. Accountants use the same information to estimate cash payments to suppliers.

To prepare a direct materials purchases budget, managers must know what production needs will be in each accounting period in the budget; this information is provided by the production budget. They must also know the desired level of the direct materials inventory for each period and the per unit cost of direct materials. The desired level of ending direct materials inventory is usually stated as a percentage of the next period's production needs.

For example, Framecraft's desired level of ending direct materials inventory is 20 percent of the next quarter's budgeted production needs. (Its desired level of beginning direct materials inventory is 20 percent of the current quarter's budgeted production needs.)

The following three steps are involved in preparing a direct materials purchases budget:

Step 1. Calculate each period's total production needs in units of direct materials. Plastic is the only direct material used in Framecraft Company's picture frames; each frame requires 10 ounces. Framecraft's managers therefore calculate units of production needs in ounces; they multiply the number of frames budgeted for production in a quarter by the 10 ounces of plastic that each frame requires.

Step 2. Determine the quantity of direct materials to be purchased during each accounting period in the budget using the following formula:

Total Units of Direct Materials to Be Purchased	=	Total Production Needs in Units of Direct Materials	+	Desired Units of Ending Direct Materials Inventory	−	Desired Units of Beginning Direct Materials Inventory

Step 3. Calculate the cost of the direct materials purchases by multiplying the total number of unit purchases by the direct materials cost. Framecraft's Purchasing Department has estimated the cost of the plastic used in the picture frames at $0.05 per ounce.

Exhibit 21-3 shows Framecraft's direct materials purchases budget for the year. Notice that each quarter's desired units of ending direct materials inventory become the next quarter's desired units of beginning direct materials inventory.

- The company's budgeted number of units for the first quarter of the following year is 150,000 ounces; its ending direct materials inventory for the fourth quarter of this year is therefore 30,000 ounces (0.20 × 150,000 ounces), which is the same as the number of desired units of ending direct materials inventory for the entire year.
- Similarly, the number of desired units for the first quarter's beginning direct materials inventory—24,000 ounces—is the same as the beginning amount for the entire year.

EXHIBIT 21-3
Direct Materials Purchases Budget

Framecraft Company
Direct Materials Purchases Budget
For the Year Ended December 31

	Quarter				
	1	**2**	**3**	**4**	**Year**
Total production units	12,000	28,000	13,000	37,500	90,500
× 10 ounces per unit	× 10	× 10	× 10	× 10	× 10
Total production needs in ounces	120,000	280,000	130,000	375,000	905,000
Plus desired ounces of ending direct materials inventory	56,000	26,000	75,000	30,000	30,000
	176,000	306,000	205,000	405,000	935,000
Less desired ounces of beginning direct materials inventory	24,000	56,000	26,000	75,000	24,000
Total ounces of direct materials to be purchased	152,000	250,000	179,000	330,000	911,000
× Cost per ounce	× $0.05	× $0.05	× $0.05	× $0.05	× $0.05
Total cost of direct materials purchases	$ 7,600	$ 12,500	$ 8,950	$ 16,500	$ 45,550

EXHIBIT 21-4
Direct Labor Budget

Framecraft Company
Direct Labor Budget
For the Year Ended December 31

	Quarter 1	Quarter 2	Quarter 3	Quarter 4	Year
Total production units	12,000	28,000	13,000	37,500	90,500
× Direct labor hours per unit	× 0.10	× 0.10	× 0.10	× 0.10	× 0.10
Total direct labor hours	1,200	2,800	1,300	3,750	9,050
× Direct labor cost per hour	× $6	× $6	× $6	× $6	× $6
Total direct labor cost	$ 7,200	$16,800	$ 7,800	$22,500	$54,300

The Direct Labor Budget

A **direct labor budget** is a detailed plan that estimates the direct labor hours needed during an accounting period and the associated costs. Production managers use estimated direct labor hours to plan how many employees will be required during the period and the hours that each will work, and accountants use estimated direct labor costs to plan for cash payments to the workers. Managers of human resources use the information in a direct labor budget in deciding whether to hire new employees or reduce the existing work force and also as a guide in training employees and preparing schedules of employee fringe benefits.

The following two steps are used to prepare a direct labor budget:

Step 1. Estimate the total direct labor hours by multiplying the estimated direct labor hours per unit by the anticipated units of production (see Exhibit 21-2).

Step 2. Calculate the total budgeted direct labor cost by multiplying the estimated total direct labor hours by the estimated direct labor cost per hour. A company's human resources department provides an estimate of the hourly labor wage.

$$\text{Total Budgeted Direct Labor Costs} = \text{Estimated Total Direct Labor Hours} \times \text{Estimated Direct Labor Cost per Hour}$$

Exhibit 21-4 shows how Framecraft Company uses these formulas to estimate the total direct labor cost. Framecraft's Production Department needs an estimated one-tenth (0.10) of a direct labor hour to complete one unit. Its Human Resources Department estimates a direct labor cost of $6 per hour.

The Overhead Budget

An **overhead budget** is a detailed plan of anticipated manufacturing costs, other than direct materials and direct labor costs, that must be incurred to meet budgeted production needs. It has two purposes: to integrate the overhead cost budgets developed by the managers of production and production-related departments and to group information for the calculation of overhead rates for the next accounting period. The format for presenting information in an overhead budget is flexible. Grouping information by activities is useful for organizations that use activity-based costing. This approach makes it easier for accountants to determine the application rates for each cost pool.

EXHIBIT 21-5
Overhead Budget

Framecraft Company Overhead Budget For the Year Ended December 31	Quarter				
	1	2	3	4	Year
Variable overhead costs					
Factory supplies	$ 2,160	$ 5,040	$ 2,340	$ 6,750	$ 16,290
Employee benefits	2,880	6,720	3,120	9,000	21,720
Inspection	1,080	2,520	1,170	3,375	8,145
Maintenance and repairs	1,920	4,480	2,080	6,000	14,480
Utilities	3,600	8,400	3,900	11,250	27,150
Total variable overhead costs	$11,640	$27,160	$12,610	$36,375	$ 87,785
Fixed overhead costs					
Depreciation–machinery	$ 2,810	$ 2,810	$ 2,810	$ 2,810	$ 11,240
Depreciation–building	3,225	3,225	3,225	3,225	12,900
Supervision	9,000	9,000	9,000	9,000	36,000
Maintenance and repairs	2,150	2,150	2,150	2,150	8,600
Other overhead expenses	3,175	3,175	3,175	3,175	12,700
Total fixed overhead costs	$20,360	$20,360	$20,360	$20,360	$ 81,440
Total overhead costs	$32,000	$47,520	$32,970	$56,735	$169,225

As Exhibit 21-5 shows, Framecraft Company prefers to group overhead information into variable and fixed costs to facilitate C-V-P analysis. The single overhead rate is the estimated total overhead costs divided by the estimated total direct labor hours.

For example, Framecraft's predetermined overhead rate is $18.70* per direct labor hour ($169,225 ÷ 9,050 direct labor hours), or $1.87 per unit produced ($18.70 per direct labor hour × 0.10 direct labor hour per unit). The variable portion of the overhead rate is $9.70 per direct labor hour ($87,785 ÷ 9,050 direct labor hours), which includes factory supplies, $1.80; employee benefits, $2.40; inspection, $0.90; maintenance and repairs, $1.60; and utilities, $3.00.

The Selling and Administrative Expense Budget

> **Study Note**
> Remember that selling and administrative expenses are period costs, not product costs.

A **selling and administrative expense budget** is a detailed plan of operating expenses, other than those related to production, that are needed to support sales and overall operations during an accounting period. Accountants use this budget to estimate cash payments for products or services not used in production-related activities.

Framecraft Company's selling and administrative expense budget appears in Exhibit 21-6. The company groups its selling and administrative expenses into variable and fixed components for purposes of cost behavior analysis, C-V-P analysis, and profit planning.

*Rounded.

EXHIBIT 21-6
Selling and Administrative Expense Budget

Framecraft Company
Selling and Administrative Expense Budget
For the Year Ended December 31

	Quarter 1	Quarter 2	Quarter 3	Quarter 4	Year
Variable selling and administrative expenses					
Delivery expenses	$ 800	$ 2,400	$ 800	$ 3,200	$ 7,200
Sales commissions	1,000	3,000	1,000	4,000	9,000
Accounting	700	2,100	700	2,800	6,300
Other administrative expenses	400	1,200	400	1,600	3,600
Total variable selling and administrative expenses	$ 2,900	$ 8,700	$ 2,900	$11,600	$ 26,100
Fixed selling and administrative expenses					
Sales salaries	$ 4,500	$ 4,500	$ 4,500	$ 4,500	$ 18,000
Executive salaries	12,750	12,750	12,750	12,750	51,000
Depreciation–office equipment	925	925	925	925	3,700
Taxes and insurance	1,700	1,700	1,700	1,700	6,800
Total fixed selling and administrative expenses	$19,875	$19,875	$19,875	$19,875	$ 79,500
Total selling and administrative expenses	$22,775	$28,575	$22,775	$31,475	$105,600

For example, Framecraft Company's estimated variable selling and administrative expense rate is $0.29 per unit sold, which includes delivery expenses, $0.08; sales commissions, $0.10; accounting, $0.07; and other administrative expenses, $0.04.

The Cost of Goods Manufactured Budget

A **cost of goods manufactured budget** is a detailed plan that summarizes the estimated costs of production during an accounting period. The sources of information for total manufacturing costs are the direct materials, direct labor, and overhead budgets. Most manufacturing organizations anticipate some work in process at the beginning or end of the period covered by a budget. However, Framecraft Company has a policy of no work in process on December 31 of any year. Exhibit 21-7 summarizes the company's estimated costs of production for the year. (The right-hand column of the exhibit shows the sources of key data.)

The budgeted, or standard, product unit cost for one picture frame is rounded to $2.97 ($268,775 ÷ 90,500 units).

EXHIBIT 21-7
Cost of Goods Manufactured Budget

Framecraft Company
Cost of Goods Manufactured Budget
For the Year Ended December 31

			Source of Data
Direct materials used			
Direct materials inventory, beginning	$ 1,200*		**Exhibit 21-3**
Purchases	45,550		**Exhibit 21-3**
Cost of direct materials available for use	$46,750		
Less direct materials inventory, ending	1,500*		**Exhibit 21-3**
Cost of direct materials used		$ 45,250	
Direct labor costs		54,300	**Exhibit 21-4**
Overhead costs		169,225	**Exhibit 21-5**
Total manufacturing costs		$268,775	
Work in process inventory, beginning		—†	
Less work in process inventory, ending		—†	
Cost of goods manufactured		$268,775	

*The desired direct materials inventory balance at the beginning of the year is $1,200 (24,000 ounces × $0.05 per ounce); at year end, it is $1,500 (30,000 ounces × $0.05 per ounce).
†It is the company's policy to have no units in process at the beginning or end of the year.

STOP & APPLY >

Sample Company is preparing a production budget for the year. The company's policy is to maintain a finished goods inventory equal to one-half of the next month's sales. Sales of 4,000 units are budgeted for April. Use the following monthly production budget for the first quarter to determine how many units should be produced in January, February, and March:

	January	February	March
Sales in units	3,000	2,400	6,000
Add desired units of ending finished goods inventory	?	?	?
Desired total units			
Less desired units of beginning finished goods inventory	?	?	?
Total production units	?	?	?

SOLUTION

	January	February	March
Sales in units	3,000	2,400	6,000
Add desired units of ending finished goods inventory	1,200	3,000	2,000
Desired total units	4,200	5,400	8,000
Less desired units of beginning finished goods inventory	1,500	1,200	3,000
Total production units	2,700	4,200	5,000

Financial Budgets

LO4 Prepare a budgeted income statement, a cash budget, and a budgeted balance sheet.

With revenues and expenses itemized in the operating budgets, an organization's controller is able to prepare the financial budgets, which, as we noted earlier, are projections of financial results for the accounting period. Financial budgets include a budgeted income statement, a capital expenditures budget, a cash budget, and a budgeted balance sheet.

The Budgeted Income Statement

A **budgeted income statement** projects an organization's net income for an accounting period based on the revenues and expenses estimated for that period. Exhibit 21-8 shows Framecraft Company's budgeted income statement for the year. The company's expenses include 8 percent interest paid on a $70,000 note payable and income taxes paid at a rate of 30 percent.

Information about projected sales and costs comes from several operating budgets, as indicated by the right-hand column of Exhibit 21-8, which identifies the sources of key data and makes it possible to trace how Framecraft Company's budgeted income statement was developed.

At this point, you can review the overall preparation of the operating budgets and the budgeted income statement by comparing the preparation flow in Figure 21-2 with the budgets in Exhibits 21-1 through 21-8. You will notice that Framecraft Company has no budget for cost of goods sold; that information is included in its budgeted income statement.

EXHIBIT 21-8
Budgeted Income Statement

Framecraft Company
Budgeted Income Statement
For the Year Ended December 31

			Source of Data
Sales		$450,000	**Exhibit 21-1**
Cost of goods sold			
Finished goods inventory, beginning	$ 2,970		**Exhibit 21-2**
Cost of goods manufactured	268,775		**Exhibit 21-7**
Cost of goods available for sale	$271,745		
Less finished goods inventory, ending	4,455		**Exhibit 21-2**
Cost of goods sold		267,290	
Gross margin		$182,710	
Selling and administrative expenses		105,600	**Exhibit 21-6**
Income from operations		$ 77,110	
Interest expense (8% × $70,000)		5,600	
Income before income taxes		$ 71,510	
Income taxes expense (30%)		21,453	
Net income		$ 50,057	

Note: Finished goods inventory balances assume that product unit costs were the same in both years:

Beginning	Ending
1,000 units (Exhibit 21-2)	1,500 units (Exhibit 21-2)
× $2.97*	× $2.97*
$2,970	$4,455

*$268,775 ÷ 90,500 units (Exhibits 21-7 and 21-2) = $2.97 (Rounded)

The Capital Expenditures Budget

A **capital expenditures budget** is a detailed plan outlining the anticipated amount and timing of capital outlays for long-term assets during an accounting period. Managers rely on the information in a capital expenditures budget when making decisions about such matters as buying equipment, building a new plant, purchasing and installing a materials handling system, or acquiring another business. Framecraft Company's capital expenditures budget for the year includes $30,000 for the purchase of a new frame-making machine. The company plans to pay $15,000 in the first quarter of the year, when the order is placed, and $15,000 in the second quarter of the year, when it receives the machine. This information is necessary for preparing the company's cash budget. We discuss capital expenditures in more detail in a later chapter.

The Cash Budget

A **cash budget** is a projection of the cash that an organization will receive and the cash that it will pay out during an accounting period. It summarizes the cash flow prospects of all transactions considered in the master budget. The information that the cash budget provides enables managers to plan for short-term loans when the cash balance is low and for short-term investments when the cash balance is high. Table 21-1 shows how the elements of a cash budget relate to operating, investing, and financing activities.

A cash budget excludes planned noncash transactions, such as depreciation expense, amortization expense, issuance and receipt of stock dividends, uncollectible accounts expense, and gains and losses on sales of assets. Some organizations also exclude deferred taxes and accrued interest from the cash budget.

The following formula is useful in preparing a cash budget:

$$\begin{matrix}\text{Estimated} \\ \text{Ending Cash} \\ \text{Balance}\end{matrix} = \begin{matrix}\text{Total} \\ \text{Estimated} \\ \text{Cash Receipts}\end{matrix} - \begin{matrix}\text{Total} \\ \text{Estimated} \\ \text{Cash Payments}\end{matrix} + \begin{matrix}\text{Estimated} \\ \text{Beginning Cash} \\ \text{Balance}\end{matrix}$$

Estimates of cash receipts are based on information from several sources. Among these sources are the sales budget, the budgeted income statement, cash budgets from previous periods, cash collection records and analyses of collection trends, and records

TABLE 21-1
Elements of a Cash Budget

Activities	Cash Receipts from	Cash Payments for
Operating	Cash sales	Purchases of materials
	Cash collections on credit sales	Direct labor
	Interest income from investments	Overhead expenses
	Cash dividends from investments	Selling and administrative expenses
		Interest expense
		Income taxes
Investing	Sale of investments	Purchases of investments
	Sale of long-term assets	Purchases of long-term assets
Financing	Proceeds from loans	Loan repayments
	Proceeds from issue of stock	Cash dividends to stockholders
	Proceeds from issue of bonds	Retirement of bonds
		Purchases of treasury stock

Note: Classifications of cash receipts and cash payments correspond to those in a statement of cash flows.

pertaining to notes, stocks, and bonds. Information used in estimating cash payments comes from the operating budgets, the budgeted income statement, the capital expenditures budget, the previous year's financial statements, and loan records.

In estimating cash receipts and cash payments for the cash budget, many organizations prepare supporting schedules. For example, Framecraft Company's controller converts credit sales to cash inflows and purchases made on credit to cash outflows and then discloses those conversions on schedules that support the cash budget. The schedule in Exhibit 21-9 shows the cash that Framecraft Company expects to collect from customers during the year.

- Cash sales represent 20 percent of the company's expected sales; the other 80 percent are credit sales.
- Experience has shown that Framecraft collects payments for 60 percent of all credit sales in the quarter of sale, 30 percent in the quarter following sale, and 10 percent in the second quarter following sale.

As you can see in Exhibit 21-9, Framecraft's balance of accounts receivable was $48,000 at the beginning of the budget year. The company expects to collect $38,000 of that amount in the first quarter and the remaining $10,000 in the second quarter. At the end of the budget year, the estimated ending balance of accounts receivable is $68,000—that is, $4,000 from the third quarter's credit sales [($50,000 × 0.80) × 0.10] plus $64,000 from the fourth quarter's sales [($200,000 × 0.80) × 0.40]. The expected cash collections for each quarter and for the year appear in the total cash receipts section of the cash budget.

Exhibit 21-10 shows Framecraft's schedule of expected cash payments for direct materials during the year. This information is summarized in the first line of the cash payments section of the company's cash budget. Framecraft pays 50 percent of the invoices it receives in the quarter of purchase and the other 50 percent in the following quarter.

The beginning balance of accounts payable for the first quarter is given at $4,200. At the end of the budget year, the estimated ending balance of accounts payable is $8,250 (50 percent of the $16,500 of direct materials purchases in the fourth quarter).

EXHIBIT 21-9
Schedule of Expected Cash Collections from Customers

Framecraft Company
Schedule of Expected Cash Collections from Customers
For the Year Ended December 31

	Quarter				
	1	**2**	**3**	**4**	**Year**
Accounts receivable, beginning	$38,000	$ 10,000	$ —	$ —	$ 48,000
Cash sales	10,000	30,000	10,000	40,000	90,000
Collections of credit sales					
First quarter ($40,000)	24,000	12,000	4,000		40,000
Second quarter ($120,000)		72,000	36,000	12,000	120,000
Third quarter ($40,000)			24,000	12,000	36,000
Fourth quarter ($160,000)				96,000	96,000
Total cash to be collected from customers	$72,000	$124,000	$74,000	$160,000	$430,000

EXHIBIT 21-10
Schedule of Expected Cash Payments for Direct Materials

Framecraft Company
Schedule of Expected Cash Payments for Direct Materials
For the Year Ended December 31

	Quarter				
	1	2	3	4	Year
Accounts payable, beginning	$4,200	$ —	$ —	$ —	$ 4,200
First quarter ($7,600)	3,800	3,800			7,600
Second quarter ($12,500)		6,250	6,250		12,500
Third quarter ($8,950)			4,475	4,475	8,950
Fourth quarter ($16,500)				8,250	8,250
Total cash payments for direct materials	$8,000	$10,050	$10,725	$12,725	$41,500

Framecraft's cash budget for the year appears in Exhibit 21-11. It shows the estimated cash receipts and cash payments for the period, as well as the cash increase or decrease. The cash increase or decrease plus the period's beginning cash balance equals the ending cash balance anticipated for the period. As you can see in Exhibit 21-11, the beginning cash balance for the first quarter is $20,000. This amount is also the beginning cash balance for the year.

Note that each quarter's budgeted ending cash balance becomes the next quarter's beginning cash balance. Also note that equal income tax payments are made quarterly. You can trace the development of this budget by referring to the data sources listed in the exhibit.

Many organizations maintain a minimum cash balance to provide a margin of safety against uncertainty. If the ending cash balance on the cash budget falls below the minimum level required, short-term borrowing may be necessary to cover planned cash payments during the year. If the ending cash balance is significantly larger than the organization needs, it may invest the excess cash in short-term securities to generate additional income.

For example, if Framecraft Company wants a minimum of $10,000 cash available at the end of each quarter, its balance of $7,222 at the end of the first quarter indicates that there is a problem. Framecraft's management has several options for handling this problem. It can borrow cash to cover the first quarter's cash needs, delay purchasing the new extrusion machine until the second quarter, or reduce some of the operating expenses. On the other hand, the balance at the end of the fourth quarter may be higher than the company wants, in which case management might invest a portion of the idle cash in short-term securities.

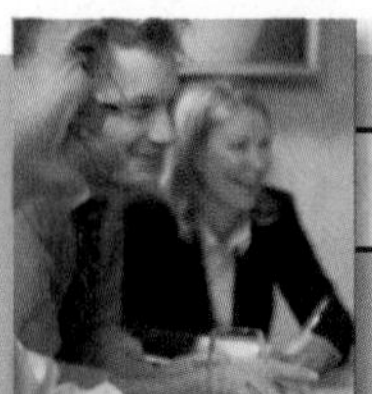

FOCUS ON BUSINESS PRACTICE

Can Budgeting Lead to a Breakdown in Corporate Ethics?

When budgets are used to force performance results, as they were at **WorldCom**, breaches in corporate ethics can occur. One former WorldCom employee described the situation at that company as follows: "You would have a budget, and he [WorldCom CEO Bernard Ebbers] would mandate that you had to be 2% under budget. Nothing else was acceptable."[2] This type of restrictive budget policy appears to have been a factor in many of the corporate scandals that occurred in the last decade.

EXHIBIT 21-11 Cash Budget

Framecraft Company **Cash Budget** **For the Year Ended December 31**						**Source of Data**
	Quarter					
	1	**2**	**3**	**4**	**Year**	
Cash receipts						
Cash collections from customers	$ 72,000	$124,000	$74,000	$160,000	$430,000	**Exhibit 21-9**
Total cash receipts	$ 72,000	$124,000	$74,000	$160,000	$430,000	
Cash payments						
Direct materials	$ 8,000	$ 10,050	$10,725	$ 12,725	$ 41,500	**Exhibit 21-10**
Direct labor	7,200	16,800	7,800	22,500	54,300	**Exhibit 21-4**
Factory supplies	2,160	5,040	2,340	6,750	16,290	**Exhibit 21-5**
Employee benefits	2,880	6,720	3,120	9,000	21,720	
Inspection	1,080	2,520	1,170	3,375	8,145	
Variable maintenance and repairs	1,920	4,480	2,080	6,000	14,480	
Utilities	3,600	8,400	3,900	11,250	27,150	
Supervision	9,000	9,000	9,000	9,000	36,000	
Fixed maintenance and repairs	2,150	2,150	2,150	2,150	8,600	
Other overhead expenses	3,175	3,175	3,175	3,175	12,700	
Delivery expenses	800	2,400	800	3,200	7,200	**Exhibit 21-6**
Sales commissions	1,000	3,000	1,000	4,000	9,000	
Accounting	700	2,100	700	2,800	6,300	
Other administrative expenses	400	1,200	400	1,600	3,600	
Sales salaries	4,500	4,500	4,500	4,500	18,000	
Executive salaries	12,750	12,750	12,750	12,750	51,000	
Taxes and insurance	1,700	1,700	1,700	1,700	6,800	
Capital expenditures*	15,000	15,000			30,000	
Interest expense	1,400	1,400	1,400	1,400	5,600	**Exhibit 21-8**
Income taxes	5,363	5,363	5,363	5,364	21,453	
Total cash payments	$ 84,778	$117,748	$74,073	$123,239	$399,838	
Cash increase (decrease)	$(12,778)	$ 6,252	$ (73)	$ 36,761	$ 30,162	
Beginning cash balance	20,000	7,222	13,474	13,401	20,000	
Ending cash balance	$ 7,222	$ 13,474	$13,401	$ 50,162	$ 50,162	

*The company plans to purchase an extrusion machine costing $30,000 and to pay for it in two installments of $15,000 each in the first and second quarters of the year.

The Budgeted Balance Sheet

A **budgeted balance sheet** projects an organization's financial position at the end of an accounting period. It uses all estimated data compiled in the course of preparing a master budget and is the final step in that process. Exhibit 21-12 presents Framecraft Company's budgeted balance sheet at the end of the budget year. Again, the data sources are listed in the exhibit. The beginning balances for Land, Notes Payable, Common Stock, and Retained Earnings were $50,000, $70,000, $150,000, and $50,810, respectively.

EXHIBIT 21-12
Budgeted Balance Sheet

Framecraft Company
Budgeted Balance Sheet
December 31

				Source of Data
Assets				
Current assets				
Cash		$ 50,162		**Exhibit 21-11**
Accounts receivable		68,000[a]		**Exhibit 21-9**
Direct materials inventory		1,500		**Exhibit 21-7**
Work in process inventory		—		**Exhibit 21-7, Note**
Finished goods inventory		4,455		**Exhibit 21-8, Note**
Total current assets			$124,117	
Property, plant, and equipment				
Land		$ 50,000		
Plant and equipment[b]	$200,000			
Less accumulated depreciation[c]	45,000	155,000		
Total property, plant, and equipment			205,000	
Total assets			$329,117	
Liabilities				
Current liabilities				
Accounts payable			$ 8,250[d]	**Exhibit 21-10, Note**
Total current liabilities			$ 8,250	
Long-term liabilities				
Notes payable			70,000	
Total liabilities			$ 78,250	
Stockholders' Equity				
Common stock		$150,000		
Retained earnings[e]		100,867		
Total stockholders' equity			250,867	
Total liabilities and stockholders' equity			$329,117	

[a]The accounts receivable balance at year end is $68,000: $4,000 from the third quarter's sales [($50,000 × 0.80) × 0.10] plus $64,000 from the fourth quarter's sales [($200,000 × 0.80) × 0.40].

[b]The plant and equipment balance includes the $30,000 purchase of an extrusion machine.

[c]The accumulated depreciation balance includes depreciation expense of $27,840 for machinery, building, and office equipment ($11,240, $12,900, and $3,700, respectively).

[d]At year end, the estimated ending balance of accounts payable is $8,250 (50 percent of the $16,500 of direct materials purchases in the fourth quarter).

[e]The retained earnings balance at December 31 equals the beginning retained earnings balance plus the net income projected for the year ($50,810 and $50,057, respectively).

Sample Corporation's budgeted balance sheet for the beginning of the coming year shows total assets of $5,000,000 and total liabilities of $2,000,000. Common stock and retained earnings make up the entire stockholders' equity section of the balance sheet. Common stock remains at its beginning balance of $1,500,000. The projected net income for the year is $350,000. The company plans to pay no cash dividends. What is the balance of retained earnings at the beginning and end of the year?

SOLUTION

Using the accounting equation A = L + SE (knowing that common stock + retained earnings makes up the entire SE) and the information given:

Beginning retained earnings:

$5,000,000 = $2,000,000 + $1,500,000 + Beginning Retained Earnings

Thus, the beginning balance of retained earnings is $1,500,000.

Ending retained earnings:

Beginning retained earnings	$1,500,000
+ Net income	350,000
− Dividends	0
Ending retained earnings	$1,850,000

A LOOK BACK AT ▸ FRAMERICA CORPORATION

In this chapter's Decision Point, we noted that one of **Framerica Corporation**'s priorities is to help employees attain their personal goals. We also noted that a participatory budgeting process is a highly effective way of achieving congruence between a company's goals and objectives and employees' personal aspirations. We asked these questions:

- How does Framerica Corporation translate long-term goals into operating objectives?
- What is the effect of Framerica's budgeting process?

As you know after reading this chapter, budgets translate a company's long-term goals into annual operating objectives. Because the budgets express these goals and objectives in concrete terms, managers and employees are able to act in ways that will achieve them. Budgets also give managers and employees a means of monitoring the results of their actions. At companies like Framerica, the ongoing dialogue about strategy that is part of the participative budgeting process fosters rapid improvements in productivity and customer service, as well as innovation in product and market development.

Review Problem

Preparing a Cash Budget

LO4

Suppose a company like **Framerica Corporation** has an Info Processing Division that provides database management services for the professional photographers who buy its frames. The division uses state-of-the-art equipment and employs five information specialists. Each specialist works an average of 160 hours a month. The division's controller has compiled the following information:

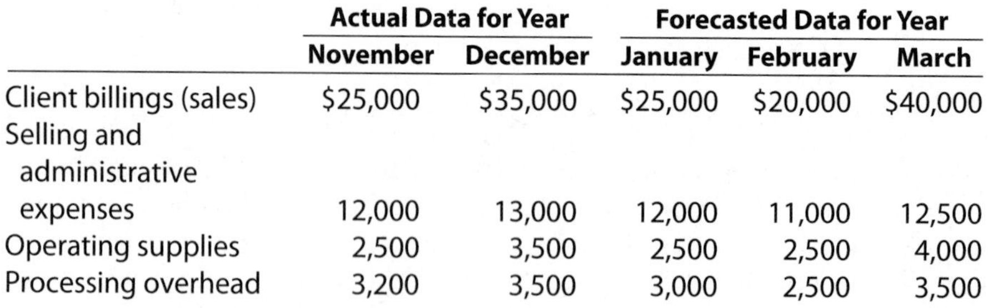

	Actual Data for Year		Forecasted Data for Year		
	November	December	January	February	March
Client billings (sales)	$25,000	$35,000	$25,000	$20,000	$40,000
Selling and administrative expenses	12,000	13,000	12,000	11,000	12,500
Operating supplies	2,500	3,500	2,500	2,500	4,000
Processing overhead	3,200	3,500	3,000	2,500	3,500

Of the client billings, 60 percent are collected during the month of sale, 30 percent are collected in the first month following the sale, and 10 percent are collected in the second month following the sale. Operating supplies are paid for in the month of purchase. Selling and administrative expenses and processing overhead are paid in the month following the cost's incurrence.

The division has a bank loan of $12,000 at a 12 percent annual interest rate. Interest is paid monthly, and $2,000 of the loan principal is due on February 28 of next year. Income taxes of $4,550 for this calendar year are due and payable on March 15 of next year. The information specialists earn $8.50 an hour, and all payroll-related employee benefit costs are included in processing overhead. The division anticipates no capital expenditures for the first quarter of the coming year. It expects its cash balance on December 31 of this year to be $13,840.

Required

Prepare a monthly cash budget for the Info Processing Division for the three-month period ending March 31 of next year. Comment on whether the ending cash balances are adequate for the division's cash needs.

Answers to Review Problem

Info Processing Division
Monthly Cash Budgets
For the Quarter Ended March 31

	January	February	March	Quarter
Total cash receipts	$28,000	$23,000	$32,500	$83,500
Cash payments				
Operating supplies	$ 2,500	$ 2,500	$ 4,000	$ 9,000
Direct labor	6,800	6,800	6,800	20,400
Selling & admin. expenses	13,000	12,000	11,000	36,000
Processing overhead	3,500	3,000	2,500	9,000
Interest expense	120	120	100	340
Loan payment	—	2,000	—	2,000
Income tax payment	—	—	4,550	4,550
Total cash payments	$25,920	$26,420	$28,950	$81,290
Cash increase (decrease)	$ 2,080	($ 3,420)	$ 3,550	$ 2,210
Beginning cash balance	13,840	15,920	12,500	13,840
Ending cash balance	$15,920	$12,500	$16,050	$16,050

The details supporting the individual computations in this cash budget are as follows:

	January	February	March
Client billings			
November	$ 2,500	—	—
December	10,500	$ 3,500	—
January	15,000	7,500	$ 2,500
February	—	12,000	6,000
March	—	—	24,000
	$28,000	$23,000	$32,500
Operating supplies			
Paid for in the month purchased	$ 2,500	$ 2,500	$ 4,000
Direct labor			
5 employees × 160 hours a month × $8.50 an hour	6,800	6,800	6,800
Selling and administrative expenses			
Paid in the month following incurrence	13,000	12,000	11,000
Processing overhead			
Paid in the month following incurrence	3,500	3,000	2,500
Interest expense			
January and February = 1% of $12,000	120	120	—
March = 1% of $10,000	—	—	100
Loan payment	—	2,000	—
Income tax payment	—	—	4,550

The ending cash balances of $15,920, $12,500, and $16,050 for January, February, and March, respectively, appear to be comfortable but not too large for the Info Processing Division.

LO1 Define *budgeting*, and explain budget basics.

Budgeting is the process of identifying, gathering, summarizing, and communicating financial and nonfinancial information about an organization's future activities. Budgeting is not only an essential part of planning; it also helps managers control, evaluate, and report on operations. When managers develop budgets, they match their organizational goals with the resources necessary to accomplish those goals. During the budgeting process, they evaluate operational, tactical, value chain, and capacity issues; assess how resources can be efficiently used; and develop contingency budgets as business conditions change. During the budget period, budgets authorize managers to use resources and provide guidelines to control costs. When managers assess performance, they can compare actual operating results to budget plans and evaluate the variances. Participative budgeting, a process in which personnel at all levels actively engage in making decisions about the budget, is key to a successful budget.

Budgets can be static, meaning they do not change during the annual budget period, or continuous, meaning they are a forward-moving budget for the next 12 months. Traditional budgeting approaches require managers to justify only budget changes over the past year. An alternative to traditional budgeting is a zero-based budgeting approach, which requires every budget item to be justified, not just the changes.

A budget committee made up of top management has overall responsibility for budget implementation. The company's controller and the budget committee oversee each stage in the preparation of the master budget, mediate any departmental disputes that may arise during the process, and give final approval to the budget. After the master budget is approved, periodic reports from department managers enable the committee to monitor the progress the company is making in attaining budget targets.

LO2 Identify the elements of a master budget in different types of organizations and the guidelines for preparing budgets.

A master budget consists of a set of operating budgets and a set of financial budgets that detail an organization's financial plans for a specific accounting period. The operating budgets serve as the basis for preparing the financial budgets, which include a budgeted income statement, a capital expenditures budget, a cash budget, and a budgeted balance sheet.

The operating budgets of a manufacturing organization include budgets for sales, production, direct materials purchases, direct labor, overhead, selling and administrative expenses, and cost of goods manufactured. The operating budgets of a retail organization include budgets for sales, purchases, selling and administrative expenses, and cost of goods sold. The operating budgets of a service organization include budgets for service revenue, labor, services overhead, and selling and administrative expenses.

The guidelines for preparing budgets include identifying the purpose of the budget, the user group and its information needs, and the sources of budget information; establishing a clear format for the budget; and using appropriate formulas and calculations to derive the quantitative information.

LO3 Prepare the operating budgets that support the financial budgets.

The initial step in preparing a master budget in any type of organization is to prepare a sales budget. Once sales have been estimated, the manager of a manufacturing organization's production department is able to prepare a budget that shows how many units of products must be manufactured to meet the projected sales volume. With that information in hand, other managers are able to prepare budgets for direct materials purchases, direct labor, overhead, selling and administrative expenses, and cost of goods manufactured. A cost of goods sold budget may be prepared separately, or it may be included in the cost of goods manufactured budget for a manufacturing organization. The operating budgets supply the information needed to prepare the financial budgets.

LO4 Prepare a budgeted income statement, a cash budget, and a budgeted balance sheet.

With estimated revenues and expenses itemized in the operating budgets, a controller is able to prepare the financial budgets. A budgeted income statement projects an organization's net income for a specific accounting period. A capital expenditures budget estimates the amount and timing of the organization's capital outlays during the period. A cash budget projects its cash receipts and cash payments for the period. Estimates of cash receipts and payments are needed to prepare a cash budget. Information about cash receipts comes from several sources, including the sales budget, the budgeted income statement, and various financial records. Sources of information about cash payments include the operating budgets, the budgeted income statement, and the capital expenditures budget. The difference between the total estimated cash receipts and total estimated cash payments is the cash increase or decrease anticipated for the period. That total plus the period's beginning cash balance equals the ending cash balance. The final step in developing a master budget is to prepare a budgeted balance sheet, which projects the organization's financial position at the end of the accounting period. All budgeted data are used in preparing this statement.

REVIEW of Concepts and Terminology

The following concepts and terms were introduced in this chapter:

Budget committee 967 (LO1)

Budgeted balance sheet 985 (LO4)

Budgeted income statement 981 (LO4)

Budgeting 966 (LO1)

Budgets 966 (LO1)

Capital expenditures budget 982 (LO4)

Cash budget 982 (LO4)

Continuous budget 968 (LO1)

Cost of goods manufactured budget 979 (LO3)

Direct labor budget 977 (LO3)

Direct materials purchases budget 975 (LO3)

Financial budgets 969 (LO2)

Master budget 969 (LO2)

Operating budgets 969 (LO2)

Overhead budget 977 (LO3)

Participative budgeting 968 (LO1)

Production budget 974 (LO3)

Pro forma financial statements 969 (LO2)

Sales budget 973 (LO3)

Sales forecast 973 (LO3)

Selling and administrative expense budget 978 (LO3)

Static budgets 968 (LO1)

Strategic planning 967 (LO1)

Zero-based budgeting 968 (LO1)

CHAPTER ASSIGNMENTS

BUILDING Your Basic Knowledge and Skills

Short Exercises

LO1 **Budgeting in a Retail Organization**

SE 1. Sam Zubac is the manager of the shoe department in a discount department store. During a recent meeting, Zubac and his supervisor agreed that Zubac's goal for the next year would be to increase the number of pairs of shoes sold by 20 percent. The department sold 8,000 pairs of shoes last year. Two sales people currently work for Zubac. What types of budgets should Zubac use to help him achieve his sales goal? What kinds of information should those budgets provide?

LO1 **Budgetary Control**

SE 2. Andi Kures owns a tree nursery. She analyzes her business's results by comparing actual operating results with figures budgeted at the beginning of the year. When the business generates large profits, she often overlooks the differences between actual and budgeted data. But when profits are low, she spends many hours analyzing the differences. If you owned Kures's business, would you use her approach to budgetary control? If not, what changes would you make?

LO2 LO3 **Components of a Master Budget**

SE 3. A master budget is a compilation of forecasts for the coming year or operating cycle made by various departments or functions within an organization. What is the most important forecast made in a master budget? List the reasons for your answer. Which budgets must managers prepare before they can prepare a direct materials purchases budget?

LO3 **Production Budget**

SE 4. Isobel Law, the controller for Aberdeen Lock Company, is preparing a production budget for the year. The company's policy is to maintain a finished goods inventory equal to one-half of the following month's sales. Sales of 7,000 locks are budgeted for April. Complete the monthly production budget for the first quarter:

	January	February	March
Sales in units	5,000	4,000	6,000
Add desired units of ending finished goods inventory	2,000	?	?
Desired total units	7,000		
Less desired units of beginning finished goods inventory	?	?	?
Total production units	4,500	?	?

LO3 **Preparing an Operating Budget**

SE 5. Ulster Company expects to sell 50,000 units of its product in the coming year. Each unit sells for $45. Sales brochures and supplies for the year are expected to cost $9,000. Two sales representatives cover the southeast region. Each representative's base salary is $20,000, and each earns a sales commission of 5 percent of the selling price of the units he or she sells. The sales representatives supply their own transportation; they are reimbursed for travel at a rate of

$0.60 per mile. The company estimates that the sales representatives will drive a total of 75,000 miles next year. From the information provided, calculate Ulster Company's budgeted selling expenses for the coming year.

LO3 LO4 **Budgeted Gross Margin**

SE 6. Operating budgets for the Paolo Company reveal the following information: net sales, $450,000; beginning materials inventory, $23,000; materials purchased, $185,000; beginning work in process inventory, $64,700; beginning finished goods inventory, $21,600; direct labor costs, $34,000; overhead applied, $67,000; ending work in process inventory, $61,200; ending materials inventory, $18,700; and ending finished goods inventory, $16,300. Compute Paolo Company's budgeted gross margin.

LO4 **Estimating Cash Collections**

SE 7. KDP Insurance Company specializes in term life insurance contracts. Cash collection experience shows that 30 percent of billed premiums are collected in the month before they are due, 60 percent are paid in the month in which they are due, and 6 percent are paid in the month following their due date. Four percent of the billed premiums are paid late (in the second month following their due date) and include a 10 percent penalty payment. Total billing notices in January were $58,000; in February, $62,000; in March, $66,000; in April, $65,000; in May, $60,000; and in June, $62,000. How much cash does the company expect to collect in May?

LO4 **Cash Budget**

SE 8. The projections of direct materials purchases that follow are for the Stromboli Corporation.

	Purchases on Account	Cash Purchases
December, 2010	$40,000	$20,000
January, 2011	60,000	30,000
February, 2011	50,000	25,000
March, 2011	70,000	35,000

The company pays for 60 percent of purchases on account in the month of purchase and 40 percent in the month following the purchase. Prepare a monthly schedule of expected cash payments for direct materials for the first quarter of 2011.

LO4 **Cash Budget**

SE 9. Alberta Limited needs a cash budget for the month of November. The following information is available:

a. The cash balance on November 1 is $6,000.
b. Sales for October and November are $80,000 and $60,000, respectively. Cash collections on sales are 30 percent in the month of sale and 65 percent in the month after the sale; 5 percent of sales are uncollectible.
c. General expenses budgeted for November are $25,000 (depreciation represents $2,000 of this amount).
d. Inventory purchases will total $30,000 in October and $40,000 in November. The company pays for half of its inventory purchases in the month of purchase and for the other half the month after purchase.
e. The company will pay $4,000 in cash for office furniture in November. Sales commissions for November are budgeted at $12,000.
f. The company maintains a minimum ending cash balance of $4,000 and can borrow from the bank in multiples of $100. All loans are repaid after 60 days.

Prepare a cash budget for Alberta Limited for the month of November.

LO4 **Budgeted Balance Sheet**

SE 10. Wellman Corporation's budgeted balance sheet for the coming year shows total assets of $4,650,000 and total liabilities of $1,900,000. Common stock and retained earnings make up the entire stockholders' equity section of the balance sheet. Common stock remains at its beginning balance of $1,500,000. The projected net income for the year is $349,600. The company pays no cash dividends. What is the balance of retained earnings at the beginning of the budget period?

Exercises

LO1 **Characteristics of Budgets**

E 1. You recently attended a workshop on budgeting and overheard the following comments as you walked to the refreshment table:

1. "Budgets are the same regardless of the size of an organization or management's role in the budgeting process."
2. "Budgets can include financial or nonfinancial data. In our organization, we plan the number of hours to be worked and the number of customer contacts we want our sales people to make."
3. "All budgets are complicated. You have to be an expert to prepare one."
4. "Budgets don't need to be highly accurate. No one in our company stays within a budget anyway."

Do you agree or disagree with each comment? Explain your answers.

LO1 **Budgeting and Goals**

E 2. Effective planning of long- and short-term goals has contributed to the success of Multitasker Calendars, Inc. Described below are the actions that the company's management team took during a recent planning meeting. Indicate whether the goals related to those actions are short-term or long-term.

1. In forecasting the next 10-year period, the management team considered economic and industry forecasts, employee–management relationships, and the structure and role of management.
2. Based on the 10-year forecast, the team made decisions about next year's sales and profit targets.

LO1 **Budgeting and Goals**

E 3. Assume that you work in the accounting department of a small wholesale warehousing company. Inspired by a recent seminar on budgeting, the company's president wants to develop a budgeting system and has asked you to direct it. Identify the points concerning the initial steps in the budgeting process that you should communicate to the president. Concentrate on principles related to long-term goals and short-term goals.

LO2 LO3 LO4 **Components of a Master Budget**

E 4. Identify the order in which the following budgets are prepared. Use the letter *a* to indicate the first budget to be prepared, *b* for the second, and so on.

1. Production budget
2. Direct labor budget
3. Direct materials purchases budget
4. Sales budget
5. Budgeted balance sheet
6. Cash budget
7. Budgeted income statement

LO3 **Sales Budget**

E 5. Quarterly and annual sales for this year for Steen Manufacturing Company follow. Prepare a sales budget for next year for the company based on the estimated percentage increases shown by product class. Show both quarterly and annual totals for each product class.

Steen Manufacturing Company
Actual Sales Revenue
For the Year Ended December 31

Product Class	January–March	April–June	July–September	October–December	Annual Totals	Estimated Percent Increases by Product Class
Marine products	$ 44,500	$ 45,500	$ 48,200	$ 47,900	$ 186,100	10%
Mountain products	36,900	32,600	34,100	37,200	140,800	5%
River products	29,800	29,700	29,100	27,500	116,100	30%
Hiking products	38,800	37,600	36,900	39,700	153,000	15%
Running products	47,700	48,200	49,400	49,900	195,200	25%
Biking products	65,400	65,900	66,600	67,300	265,200	20%
Totals	$263,100	$259,500	$264,300	$269,500	$1,056,400	

LO3 **Production Budget**

E 6. Santa Fe Corporation produces and sells a single product. Expected sales for September are 12,000 units; for October, 15,000 units; for November, 9,000 units; for December, 10,000 units; and for January, 14,000 units. The company's desired level of ending finished goods inventory at the end of a month is 10 percent of the following month's sales in units. At the end of August, 1,200 units were on hand. How many units need to be produced in the fourth quarter?

LO3 **Direct Materials Purchases Budget**

E 7. The U-Z Door Company manufactures garage door units. The units include hinges, door panels, and other hardware. Prepare a direct materials purchases budget for the first quarter of the year based on budgeted production of 16,000 garage door units. Sandee Morton, the controller, has provided the information that follows.

Hinges	4 sets per door	$11.00 per set
Door panels	4 panels per door	$27.00 per panel
Other hardware	1 lock per door	$31.00 per lock
	1 handle per door	$22.50 per handle
	2 roller tracks per door	$16.00 per set of 2 roller tracks
	8 rollers per door	$ 4.00 per roller

Assume no beginning or ending quantities of direct materials inventory.

LO3 Direct Materials Purchases Budget

E 8. Hard Corporation projects sales of $230,000 in May, $250,000 in June, $260,000 in July, and $240,000 in August. Since the dollar value of the company's cost of goods sold is generally 65 percent of total sales, cost of goods sold is $149,500 in May, $162,500 in June, $169,000 in July, and $156,000 in August. The dollar value of its desired ending inventory is 25 percent of the following month's cost of goods sold.

Compute the total purchases in dollars budgeted for June and the total purchases in dollars budgeted for July.

LO3 Direct Labor Budget

E 9. Paige Metals Company has two departments—Cutting and Grinding—and manufactures three products. Budgeted unit production for the coming year is 21,000 of Product T, 36,000 of Product M, and 30,000 of Product B. The company is currently analyzing direct labor hour requirements for the coming year. Data for each department are as follows:

	Cutting	Grinding
Estimated hours per unit		
Product T	1.1	0.5
Product M	0.6	2.9
Product B	3.2	1.0
Hourly labor rate	$9	$7

Prepare a direct labor budget for the coming year that shows the budgeted direct labor costs for each department and for the company as a whole.

LO3 Overhead Budget

E 10. Carole Dahl is chief financial officer of the Phoenix Division of Dahl Corporation, a multinational company with three operating divisions. As part of the budgeting process, Dahl's staff is developing the overhead budget for next year. The division estimates that it will manufacture 50,000 units during the year. The budgeted cost information is as follows:

	Variable Rate per Unit	Total Fixed Costs
Indirect materials	$1.00	
Indirect labor	4.00	
Supplies	0.40	
Repairs and maintenance	3.00	$ 40,000
Electricity	0.10	20,000
Factory supervision		180,000
Insurance		25,000
Property taxes		35,000
Depreciation–machinery		82,000
Depreciation–building		72,000

Using these data, prepare the division's overhead budget for next year.

LO4 Cash Collections

E 11. Dacahr Bros., Inc., is an automobile maintenance and repair company with outlets throughout the western United States. Henley Turlington, the company controller, is starting to assemble the cash budget for the fourth quarter. Projected sales for the quarter are as follows:

	On Account	Cash
October	$452,000	$196,800
November	590,000	214,000
December	720,500	218,400

Cash collection records pertaining to sales on account indicate the following collection pattern:

Month of sale	40%
First month following sale	30
Second month following sale	28
Uncollectible	2

Sales on account during August were $346,000. During September, sales on account were $395,000.

Compute the amount of cash to be collected from customers during each month of the fourth quarter.

LO4 Cash Collections

E 12. XYZ Company collects payment on 50 percent of credit sales in the month of sale, 40 percent in the month following sale, and 5 percent in the second month following the sale. Its sales budget is as follows:

Month	Cash Sales	Credit Sales
May	$20,000	$ 40,000
June	40,000	60,000
July	60,000	80,000
August	80,000	100,000

Compute XYZ Company's total cash collections in July and its total cash collections in August.

LO4 Cash Budget

E 13. SABA Enterprises needs a cash budget for the month of June. The following information is available:

a. The cash balance on June 1 is $4,000.
b. Sales for May and June are $50,000 and $40,000, respectively. Cash collections on sales are 40 percent in the month of sale and 50 percent in the month after the sale; 10 percent of sales are uncollectible.
c. General expenses budgeted for June are $20,000 (depreciation represents $1,000 of this amount).
d. Inventory purchases will total $40,000 in May and $30,000 in June. The company pays for half of its inventory purchases in the month of purchase and for the other half the month after purchase.
e. The company will pay $5,000 in cash for office furniture in June. Sales commissions for June are budgeted at $6,000.
f. The company maintains a minimum ending cash balance of $4,000 and can borrow from the bank in multiples of $100. All loans are repaid after 60 days.

Prepare a cash budget for SABA Enterprises for the month of June.

LO4 Cash Budget

E 14. Tex Kinkaid's dream was to develop the biggest produce operation with the widest selection of fresh fruits and vegetables in northern Texas. Within three years of opening Minigarden Produce, Inc., Kincaid accomplished his objective. Kinkaid has asked you to prepare monthly cash budgets for Minigarden Produce for the quarter ended September 30.

Credit sales to retailers in the area constitute 80 percent of Minigarden Produce's business; cash sales to customers at the company's retail outlet make up the other 20 percent. Collection records indicate that Minigarden Produce collects payment on 50 percent of all credit sales during the month of sale, 30 percent in the month after the sale, and 20 percent in the second month after the sale.

The company's total sales in May were $66,000; in June, they were $67,500. Anticipated sales in July are $69,500; in August, $76,250; and in September, $84,250. The company's purchases are expected to total $43,700 in July, $48,925 in August, and $55,725 in September. The company pays for all purchases in cash.

Projected monthly costs for the quarter include $1,040 for heat, light, and power; $375 for bank fees; $1,925 for rent; $1,120 for supplies; $1,705 for depreciation of equipment; $1,285 for equipment repairs; and $475 for miscellaneous expenses. Other projected costs for the quarter are salaries and wages of $18,370 in July, $19,200 in August, and $20,300 in September.

The company's cash balance at June 30 was $2,745. It has a policy of maintaining a minimum monthly cash balance of $1,500.

1. Prepare a monthly cash budget for Minigarden Produce, Inc., for the quarter ended September 30.
2. Should Minigarden Produce anticipate taking out a loan during the quarter? If so, how much should it borrow, and when?

LO4 **Budgeted Income Statement**

E 15. Delft House, Inc., a multinational company based in Amsterdam, organizes and coordinates art shows and auctions throughout the world. Its budgeted and actual costs for last year are as follows:

	Budgeted Cost	Actual Cost
Salaries expense, staging	€ 480,000	€ 512,800
Salaries expense, executive	380,000	447,200
Travel costs	640,000	652,020
Auctioneer services	540,000	449,820
Space rental costs	251,000	246,580
Printing costs	192,000	182,500
Advertising expense	169,000	183,280
Insurance, merchandise	84,800	77,300
Insurance, liability	64,000	67,100
Home office costs	209,200	219,880
Shipping costs	105,000	112,560
Miscellaneous	25,000	25,828
Total operating expenses	€3,140,000	€3,176,868
Net receipts	€6,200,000	€6,369,200

Delft House, Inc., has budgeted the following fixed costs for the coming year: executive salaries, €440,000; advertising expense, €190,000; merchandise insurance, €80,000; and liability insurance, €68,000. Additional information pertaining to the operations of Delft House, Inc., in the coming years is as follows:

a. Net receipts are estimated at €6,400,000.
b. Salaries expense for staging will increase 20 percent over the actual figures for the last year.

c. Travel costs are expected to be 11 percent of net receipts.
d. Auctioneer services will be billed at 9.5 percent of net receipts.
e. Space rental costs will be 20 percent higher than the amount budgeted in the last year.
f. Printing costs are expected to be €190,000.
g. Home office costs are budgeted for €230,000.
h. Shipping costs are expected to be 20 percent higher than the amount budgeted in the last year.
i. Miscellaneous expenses for the coming year will be budgeted at €28,000.

Because the company sells only services, it has expenses only and no cost of sales. (Net receipts equal gross margin.)

1. Using a 40 percent income tax rate, prepare the company's budgeted income statement for the coming year.
2. Should the budget committee be worried about the trend in the company's operations? Explain your answer.

Problems

LO3 Preparing Operating Budgets

P 1. The principal product of Yangsoo Enterprises, Inc., is a multipurpose hammer that carries a lifetime guarantee. Listed next are cost and production data for the Yangsoo hammer.

Direct materials
Anodized steel: 2 kilograms per hammer at $1.60 per kilogram
Leather strapping for the handle: 0.5 square meter per hammer at $4.40 per square meter

Direct labor
Forging operation: $12.50 per labor hour; 6 minutes per hammer
Leather-wrapping operation: $12.00 per direct labor hour; 12 minutes per hammer

Overhead
Forging operation: rate equals 70 percent of department's direct labor dollars
Leather-wrapping operation: rate equals 50 percent of department's direct labor dollars

In October, November, and December, Yangsoo Enterprises expects to produce 108,000, 104,000, and 100,000 hammers, respectively. The company has no beginning or ending balances of direct materials inventory or work in process inventory for the year.

Required

1. For the three-month period ending December 31, prepare monthly production cost information for the Yangsoo hammer. Classify the costs as direct materials, direct labor, or overhead, and show your computations.
2. Prepare a cost of goods manufactured budget for the hammer. Show monthly cost data and combined totals for the quarter for each cost category.

LO3 LO4 Preparing a Comprehensive Budget

P 2. Bertha's Bathworks produces hair and bath products. Its biggest customer is a national retail chain that specializes in such products. Bertha Jackson, the owner of Bertha's Bathworks, would like to have an estimate of the company's net income in the coming year.

Required

Project Bertha's Bathworks' net income next year by completing the operating budgets and budgeted income statement that follow.

1. Sales Budget:

Bertha's Bathworks
Sales Budget
For the Year Ended December 31

	Quarter				
	1	**2**	**3**	**4**	**Year**
Sales in units	4,000	3,000	5,000	5,000	17,000
× Selling price per unit	× $5	× ?	× ?	× ?	× ?
Total sales	$20,000	?	?	?	?

2. Production Budget:

Bertha's Bathworks
Production Budget
For the Year Ended December 31

	Quarter				
	1	**2**	**3**	**4**	**Year**
Sales in units	4,000	?	?	?	?
Plus desired units of ending finished goods inventory*	**300**	?	?	**600**	**600**
Desired total units	4,300				
Less desired units of beginning finished goods inventory†	**400**	?	?	?	**400**
Total production units	3,900	?	?	?	?

*Desired units of ending finished goods inventory = 10% of next quarter's budgeted sales.

†Desired units of beginning finished goods inventory = 10% of current quarter's budgeted sales.

3. Direct Materials Purchases Budget:

Bertha's Bathworks
Direct Materials Purchases Budget
For the Year Ended December 31

	Quarter 1	Quarter 2	Quarter 3	Quarter 4	Year
Total production units	3,900	3,200	5,000	5,100	17,200
× 3 ounces per unit	× 3	× ?	× ?	× ?	× ?
Total production needs in ounces	11,700	?	?	?	?
Plus desired ounces of ending direct materials inventory*	**1,920**	?	?	**3,600**	**3,600**
	13,620	?	?	?	?
Less desired ounces of beginning direct materials inventory†	**2,340**	?	?	?	**2,340**
Total ounces of direct materials to be purchased	11,280	?	?	?	?
× Cost per ounce	×$0.10	× ?	× ?	× ?	× ?
Total cost of direct materials purchases	$ 1,128	?	?	?	?

*Desired ounces of ending direct materials inventory = 20% of next quarter's budgeted production needs in ounces.

†Desired ounces of beginning direct materials inventory = 20% of current quarter's budgeted production needs in ounces.

4. Direct Labor Budget:

Bertha's Bathworks
Direct Labor Budget
For the Year Ended December 31

	Quarter 1	Quarter 2	Quarter 3	Quarter 4	Year
Total production units	3,900	?	?	?	?
× Direct labor hours per unit	×0.10	× ?	× ?	× ?	× ?
Total direct labor hours	390	?	?	?	?
× Direct labor cost per hour	× $7	× ?	× ?	× ?	× ?
Total direct labor cost	$2,730	?	?	?	?

5. Overhead Budget:

Bertha's Bathworks
Overhead Budget
For the Year Ended December 31

	Quarter				
	1	**2**	**3**	**4**	**Year**
Variable overhead costs					
Factory supplies ($0.05)	$ 195	?	?	?	?
Employee benefits ($0.25)	975	?	?	?	?
Inspection ($0.10)	390	?	?	?	?
Maintenance and repairs ($0.15)	585	?	?	?	?
Utilities ($0.05)	195	?	?	?	?
Total variable overhead costs	$2,340	?	?	?	?
Fixed overhead costs					
Depreciation–machinery	$ 500	?	?	?	?
Depreciation–building	700	?	?	?	?
Supervision	1,800	?	?	?	?
Maintenance and repairs	400	?	?	?	?
Other overhead expenses	600	?	?	?	?
Total fixed overhead costs	$4,000	?	?	?	?
Total overhead costs	$6,340	?	?	?	?

Note: The figures in parentheses are variable costs per unit.

6. Selling and Administrative Expense Budget:

Bertha's Bathworks
Selling and Administrative Expense Budget
For the Year Ended December 31

	Quarter				
	1	**2**	**3**	**4**	**Year**
Variable selling and administrative expenses					
Delivery expenses ($0.10)	$ 400	?	?	?	?
Sales commissions ($0.15)	600	?	?	?	?
Accounting ($0.05)	200	?	?	?	?
Other administrative expenses ($0.20)	800	?	?	?	?
Total variable selling and administrative expenses	$2,000	?	?	?	?
Fixed selling and administrative expenses					
Sales salaries	$5,000	?	?	?	?
Depreciation, office equipment	900	?	?	?	?
Taxes and insurance	1,700	?	?	?	?
Total fixed selling and administrative expenses	$7,600	?	?	?	?
Total selling and administrative expenses	$9,600	?	?	?	?

Note: The figures in parentheses are variable costs per unit.

7. Cost of Goods Manufactured Budget:

Bertha's Bathworks
Cost of Goods Manufactured Budget
For the Year Ended December 31

Direct materials used		
Direct materials inventory, beginning	?	
Purchases during the year	?	
Cost of direct materials available for use	?	
Less direct materials inventory, ending	?	
Cost of direct materials used		?
Direct labor costs		?
Overhead costs		?
Total manufacturing costs		?
Work in process inventory, beginning		?
Less work in process inventory, ending*		?
Cost of goods manufactured		?
Manufactured Cost per Unit = Cost of Goods Manufactured ÷ Units Produced		?

*It is the company's policy to have no units in process at the end of the year.

8. Budgeted Income Statement:

Bertha's Bathworks
Budgeted Income Statement
For the Year Ended December 31

Sales		?
Cost of goods sold		
Finished goods inventory, beginning	?	
Cost of goods manufactured	?	
Cost of goods available for sale	?	
Less finished goods inventory, ending	?	
Cost of goods sold		?
Gross margin		?
Selling and administrative expenses		?
Income from operations		?
Income taxes expense (30%)*		?
Net income		?

*The figure in parentheses is the company's income tax rate.

LO4 Basic Cash Budget

P 3. Felasco Nurseries, Inc., has been in business for six years and has four divisions. Ethan Poulis, the corporation's controller, has been asked to prepare a cash budget for the Southern Division for the first quarter. Projected data supporting this budget follow.

Sales (60% on credit)		Purchases	
November	$160,000	December	$ 86,800
December	200,000	January	124,700
January	120,000	February	99,440
February	160,000	March	104,800
March	140,000		

Collection records of accounts receivable have shown that 30 percent of all credit sales are collected in the month of sale, 60 percent in the month following the sale, and 8 percent in the second month following the sale; 2 percent of the sales are uncollectible. All purchases are paid for in the month after the purchase. Salaries and wages are projected to be $25,200 in January, $33,200 in February, and $21,200 in March. Estimated monthly costs are utilities, $4,220; collection fees, $1,700; rent, $5,300; equipment depreciation, $5,440; supplies, $2,480; small tools, $3,140; and miscellaneous, $1,900.

Each of the corporation's divisions maintains a $6,000 minimum cash balance. As of December 31, the Southern Division had a cash balance of $9,600.

Required

1. Prepare a monthly cash budget for Felasco Nurseries' Southern Division for the first quarter.

Manager insight ▶ 2. Should Felasco Nurseries anticipate taking out a loan for the Southern Division during the quarter? If so, how much should it borrow, and when?

LO4 **Cash Budget**

P 4. Security Services Company provides security monitoring services. It employs five security specialists. Each specialist works an average of 160 hours a month. The company's controller has compiled the following information:

	Actual Data for Last Year		Forecasted Data for Next Year		
	November	December	January	February	March
Security billings (sales)	$30,000	$35,000	$25,000	$20,000	$30,000
Selling and administrative expenses	10,000	11,000	9,000	8,000	10,500
Operating supplies	2,500	3,500	2,500	2,000	3,000
Service overhead	3,000	3,500	3,000	2,500	3,000

Sixty percent of the client billings are cash sales collected during the month of sale; 30 percent are collected in the first month following the sale; and 10 percent are collected in the second month following the sale. Operating supplies are paid for in the month of purchase. Selling and administrative expenses and service overhead are paid in the month following the cost's incurrence.

The company has a bank loan of $12,000 at a 12 percent annual interest rate. Interest is paid monthly, and $2,000 of the loan principal is due on February 28. Income taxes of $4,500 for the last calendar year are due and payable on March 15. The five security specialists each earn $8.50 an hour, and all payroll-related employee benefit costs are included in service overhead. The company anticipates no capital expenditures for the first quarter of the coming year. It expects its cash balance on December 31 to be $13,000.

Required

Prepare a monthly cash budget for Security Services Company for the three-month period ended March 31.

LO4 **Budgeted Income Statement and Budgeted Balance Sheet**

P 5. Moontrust Bank has asked the president of Wishware Products, Inc., for a budgeted income statement and budgeted balance sheet for the quarter ended June 30. These pro forma financial statements are needed to support Wishware Products' request for a loan.

Wishware Products routinely prepares a quarterly master budget. The operating budgets prepared for the quarter ending June 30 have provided the following information: Projected sales for April are $220,400; for May, $164,220; and for June, $165,980. Direct materials purchases for the period are estimated at $96,840; direct materials usage, at $102,710; direct labor expenses, at $71,460; overhead, at $79,940; selling and administrative expenses, at $143,740; capital expenditures, at $125,000 (to be spent on June 29); cost of goods manufactured, at $252,880; and cost of goods sold, at $251,700.

Balance sheet account balances at March 31 were as follows: Accounts Receivable, $26,500; Materials Inventory, $23,910; Work in Process Inventory, $31,620; Finished Goods Inventory, $36,220; Prepaid Expenses, $7,200; Plant, Furniture, and Fixtures, $498,600; Accumulated Depreciation–Plant, Furniture, and Fixtures, $141,162; Patents, $90,600; Accounts Payable, $39,600; Notes Payable, $105,500; Common Stock, $250,000; and Retained Earnings, $207,158.

Projected monthly cash balances for the second quarter are as follows: April 30, $20,490; May 31, $35,610; and June 30, $45,400. During the quarter, accounts receivable are expected to increase by 30 percent, patents to go up by $6,500, prepaid expenses to remain constant, and accounts payable to go down by 10 percent (Wishware Products will make a $5,000 payment on a note payable, $4,100 of which is principal reduction). The federal income tax rate is 34 percent, and the second quarter's tax is paid in July. Depreciation for the quarter will be $6,420, which is included in the overhead budget. The company will pay no dividends.

Required

1. Prepare a budgeted income statement for the quarter ended June 30. Round answers to the nearest dollar.
2. Prepare a budgeted balance sheet as of June 30.

Alternate Problems

LO3 **Preparing Operating Budgets**

P 6. The principal product of Waterworks, Inc., is a metal water bottle that carries a lifetime guarantee. Listed here are cost and production data for the water bottle.

Direct materials
- Stainless steel: 0.25 kilogram per bottle at $8.00 per kilogram
- Clip for the handle: 1 per bottle at $0.10 each

Direct labor
- Stamping operation: $30 per labor hour; 2 minutes per bottle

Overhead
- Stamping operation: rate equals 70 percent of department's direct labor dollars

In January, February, and March, Waterworks expects to produce 200,000, 225,000, and 150,000 bottles, respectively. The company has no beginning or ending balances of direct materials inventory or work in process inventory for the year.

Required

1. For the three-month period ending March 31, prepare monthly production cost information for the metal water bottle. Classify the costs as direct materials, direct labor, or overhead, and show your computations.
2. Prepare a cost of goods manufactured budget for the water bottle. Show monthly cost data and combined totals for the quarter for each cost category.

LO3 LO4 **Preparing a Comprehensive Budget**

P 7. The Bottled Water Company has been bottling and selling water since 1940. Ginnie Adams, the current owner of The Bottled Water Company, would like to know how a new product would affect the company's net income in the coming year.

Required

Calculate The Bottled Water Company's net income for the new product in the coming year by completing the operating budgets and budgeted income statement that follow.

1. Sales Budget:

The Bottled Water Company
Sales Budget
For the Year Ended December 31

	Quarter				
	1	**2**	**3**	**4**	**Year**
Sales in units	40,000	30,000	50,000	55,000	175,000
× Selling price per unit	× $1	× ?	× ?	× ?	× ?
Total sales	$40,000	?	?	?	?

2. Production Budget:

The Bottled Water Company
Production Budget
For the Year Ended December 31

	Quarter				
	1	**2**	**3**	**4**	**Year**
Sales in units	40,000	?	?	?	?
Plus desired units of ending finished goods inventory*	3,000	?	?	6,000	6,000
Desired total units	43,000				
Less desired units of beginning finished goods inventory†	4,000	?	?	?	4,000
Total production units	39,000	?	?	?	?

*Desired units of ending finished goods inventory = 10% of next quarter's budgeted sales.

†Desired units of beginning finished goods inventory = 10% of current quarter's budgeted sales.

3. Direct Materials Purchases Budget:

The Bottled Water Company
Direct Materials Purchases Budget
For the Year Ended December 31

	Quarter				
	1	**2**	**3**	**4**	**Year**
Total production units	39,000	32,000	50,500	55,500	?
× 20 ounces per unit	× 20	× ?	× ?	× ?	× ?
Total production needs in ounces	780,000	?	?	?	?
Plus desired ounces of ending direct materials inventory*	128,000	?	?	240,000	240,000
	908,000	?	?	?	?
Less desired ounces of beginning direct materials inventory†	156,000	?	?	?	156,000
Total ounces of direct materials to be purchased	752,000	?	?	?	?
× Cost per ounce	× $0.01	× ?	× ?	× ?	× ?
Total cost of direct materials purchases	$ 7,520	?	?	?	?

*Desired ounces of ending direct materials inventory = 20% of next quarter's budgeted production needs in ounces.

†Desired ounces of beginning direct materials inventory = 20% of current quarter's budgeted production needs in ounces.

4. Direct Labor Budget:

The Bottled Water Company
Direct Labor Budget
For the Year Ended December 31

	Quarter				
	1	**2**	**3**	**4**	**Year**
Total production units	39,000	?	?	?	?
× Direct labor hours per unit	× 0.001	× ?	× ?	× ?	× ?
Total direct labor hours	39.0	?	?	?	?
× Direct labor cost per hour	× $8	× ?	× ?	× ?	× ?
Total direct labor cost	$ 312	?	?	?	?

5. Overhead Budget:

The Bottled Water Company
Overhead Budget
For the Year Ended December 31

	Quarter				
	1	2	3	4	Year
Variable overhead costs					
Factory supplies ($0.01)	$ 390	?	?	?	?
Employee benefits ($0.05)	1,950	?	?	?	?
Inspection ($0.01)	390	?	?	?	?
Maintenance and repairs ($0.02)	780	?	?	?	?
Utilities ($0.01)	390	?	?	?	?
Total variable overhead costs	$3,900	?	?	?	?
Total fixed overhead costs	1,500	?	?	?	?
Total overhead costs	$5,400	?	?	?	?

Note: The figures in parentheses are variable costs per unit.

6. Selling and Administrative Expense Budget:

The Bottled Water Company
Selling and Administrative Expense Budget
For the Year Ended December 31

	Quarter				
	1	2	3	4	Year
Variable selling and administrative expenses					
Delivery expenses ($0.01)	$ 400	?	?	?	?
Sales commissions ($0.02)	800	?	?	?	?
Accounting ($0.01)	400	?	?	?	?
Other administrative expenses ($0.01)	400	?	?	?	?
Total variable selling and administrative expenses	$2,000	?	?	?	?
Total fixed selling and administrative expenses	5,000	?	?	?	?
Total selling and administrative expenses	$7,000	?	?	?	?

Note: The figures in parentheses are variable costs per unit.

7. Cost of Goods Manufactured Budget:

The Bottled Water Company
Cost of Goods Manufactured Budget
For the Year Ended December 31

Direct materials used		
Direct materials inventory, beginning	?	
Purchases during the year	?	
Cost of direct materials available for use	?	
Less direct materials inventory, ending		?
Cost of direct materials used		?
Direct labor costs		?
Overhead costs		?
Total manufacturing costs		?
Work in process inventory, beginning*		0
Less work in process inventory, ending*		0
Cost of goods manufactured		?
Manufactured Cost per Unit = Cost of Goods Manufactured ÷ Units Produced		?

*It is the company's policy to have no units in process at the end of the year.

8. Budgeted Income Statement:

The Bottled Water Company
Budgeted Income Statement
For the Year Ended December 31

Sales		?
Cost of goods sold		
Finished goods inventory, beginning	?	
Cost of goods manufactured	?	
Cost of goods available for sale	?	
Less finished goods inventory, ending	?	
Cost of goods sold		?
Gross margin		?
Selling and administrative expenses		?
Income from operations		?
Income taxes expense (30%)*		?
Net income		?

*The figure in parentheses is the company's income tax rate.

LO4 Comprehensive Cash Budget

P 8. Located in Telluride, Colorado, Wellness Centers, Inc., emphasizes the benefits of regular workouts and the importance of physical examinations. The corporation operates three fully equipped fitness centers, as well as a medical center that specializes in preventive medicine. The data that follow pertain to the corporation's first quarter.

Cash Receipts

Memberships: December, 870; January, 880; February, 910; March, 1,030
Membership dues: $90 per month, payable on the 10th of the month
(80 percent collected on time; 20 percent collected one month late)
Medical examinations: January, $35,610; February, $41,840; March, $45,610
Special aerobics classes: January, $4,020; February, $5,130; March, $7,130
High-protein food sales: January, $4,890; February, $5,130; March, $6,280

Cash Payments

Salaries and wages:
Corporate officers: 2 at $12,000 per month
Physicians: 2 at $7,000 per month
Nurses: 3 at $2,900 per month
Clerical staff: 2 at $1,500 per month
Aerobics instructors: 3 at $1,100 per month
Clinic staff: 6 at $1,700 per month
Maintenance staff: 3 at $900 per month
Health-food servers: 3 at $750 per month

Purchases:
Muscle-toning machines: January, $14,400; February, $13,800
(no purchases in March)
Pool supplies: $520 per month
Health food: January, $3,290; February, $3,460; March, $3,720
Medical supplies: January, $10,400; February, $11,250; March, $12,640
Medical uniforms and disposable garments: January, $7,410; February, $3,900; March, $3,450
Medical equipment: January, $11,200; February, $3,400; March $5,900
Advertising: January, $2,250; February, $1,190; March, $2,450
Utilities expense: January, $5,450; February, $5,890; March, $6,090

Insurance:
Fire: January, $3,470
Liability: March, $3,980

Property taxes: $3,760 due in January
Federal income taxes: Last year's taxes of $21,000 due in March
Miscellaneous: January, $2,625; February, $2,800; March, $1,150

Wellness Centers' controller anticipates that the beginning cash balance on January 1 will be $9,840.

Required

Prepare a cash budget for Wellness Centers, Inc., for the first quarter of the year. Use *January, February, March,* and *Quarter* as the column headings.

LO4 Cash Budget

P 9. FM Company provides fraud monitoring services. It employs four fraud specialists. Each specialist works an average of 200 hours a month. The company's controller has compiled the following information:

	Actual Data for Last Year		Forecasted Data for Next Year		
	November	December	January	February	March
Billings (sales)	$100,000	$80,000	$60,000	$50,000	$70,000
Selling and administrative expenses	15,000	12,000	8,000	7,000	10,000
Operating supplies	2,500	3,500	2,500	2,000	3,000
Service overhead	14,000	13,500	13,000	12,500	13,000

Seventy percent of the client billings are cash sales collected during the month of sale; 20 percent are collected in the first month following the sale; and 10 percent are collected in the second month following the sale. Operating supplies are paid in the month of purchase. Selling and administrative expenses and service overhead are paid in the month the cost is incurred.

The company has a bank loan of $12,000 at a 6 percent annual interest rate. Interest is paid monthly, and $2,000 of the loan principal is due on February 28. Income taxes of $6,500 for last calendar year are due and payable on March 15. The four security specialists each earn $48.00 an hour, and all payroll-related employee benefit costs are included in service overhead. The company anticipates no capital expenditures for the first quarter of the coming year. It expects its cash balance on December 31 to be $10,000.

Required

Prepare a monthly cash budget for FM Company for the three-month period ended March 31.

LO4 Budgeted Income Statement and Budgeted Balance Sheet

P 10. Stillwater Video Company, Inc., produces and markets two popular video games, *High Range* and *Star Boundary.* The closing account balances on the company's balance sheet for last year are as follows: Cash, $18,735; Accounts Receivable, $19,900; Materials Inventory, $18,510; Work in Process Inventory, $24,680; Finished Goods Inventory, $21,940; Prepaid Expenses, $3,420; Plant and Equipment, $262,800; Accumulated Depreciation–Plant and Equipment, $55,845; Other Assets, $9,480; Accounts Payable, $52,640; Mortgage Payable, $70,000; Common Stock, $90,000; and Retained Earnings, $110,980.

Operating budgets for the first quarter of the coming year show the following estimated costs: direct materials purchases, $58,100; direct materials usage, $62,400; direct labor expense, $42,880; overhead, $51,910; selling expenses, $35,820; general and administrative expenses, $60,240; cost of goods manufactured, $163,990; and cost of goods sold, $165,440. Estimated ending cash balances are as follows: January, $34,610; February, $60,190; and March, $54,802. The company will have no capital expenditures during the quarter.

Sales are projected to be $125,200 in January, $105,100 in February, and $112,600 in March. Accounts receivable are expected to double during the quarter, and accounts payable are expected to decrease by 20 percent. Mortgage payments for the quarter will total $6,000, of which $2,000 will be interest expense. Prepaid expenses are expected to go up by $20,000, and other assets are projected to increase by 50 percent over the budget period. Depreciation for plant and equipment (already included in the overhead budget) averages 5 percent of total plant and equipment per year. Federal income taxes (34 percent of profits) are payable in April. The company pays no dividends.

Required

1. Prepare a budgeted income statement for the quarter ended March 31.
2. Prepare a budgeted balance sheet as of March 31.

ENHANCING Your Knowledge, Skills, and Critical Thinking

LO1 LO2 Policies for Budget Development

C 1. Hector Corporation is a manufacturing company with annual sales of $25 million. Its budget committee has created the following policy that the company uses each year in developing its master budget for the following calendar year:

May	The company's controller and other members of the budget committee meet to discuss plans and objectives for next year. The controller conveys all relevant information from this meeting to division managers and department heads.
June	Division managers, department heads, and the controller meet to discuss the corporate plans and objectives for next year. They develop a timetable for developing next year's budget data.
July	Division managers and department heads develop budget data. The vice president of sales provides them with final sales estimates, and they complete monthly sales estimates for each product line.
August	Estimates of next year's monthly production activity and inventory levels are completed. Division managers and department heads communicate these estimates to the controller, who distributes them to other operating areas.
September	All operating areas submit their revised budget data. The controller integrates their labor requirements, direct materials requirements, unit cost estimates, cash requirements, and profit estimates into a preliminary master budget.
October	The budget committee meets to discuss the preliminary master budget and to make any necessary corrections, additions, or deletions. The controller incorporates all authorized changes into a final draft of the master budget.
November	The controller submits the final draft to the budget committee for approval. If the committee approves it, it is distributed to all corporate officers, division managers, and department heads.

1. Comment on this policy.
2. What changes would you recommend?

LO1 LO3 Ethical Considerations in Budgeting

C 2. Javier Gonzales is the manager of the Repairs and Maintenance Department of JG Industries. He is responsible for preparing his department's annual budget. Most managers in the company inflate their budget numbers by at least 10 percent because their bonuses depend upon how much below budget their departments operate. Gonzales turned in the following information for his department's budget for next year to the company's budget committee:

	Budget This Year	Actual This Year	Budget Next Year
Supplies	$ 20,000	$ 16,000	$ 24,000
Labor	80,000	82,000	96,000
Utilities	8,500	8,000	10,200
Tools	12,500	9,000	15,000
Hand-carried equipment	25,000	16,400	30,000
Cleaning materials	4,600	4,200	5,520
Miscellaneous	2,000	2,100	2,400
Totals	$152,600	$137,700	$183,120

Because the figures for next year are 20 percent above those in this year's budget, the budget committee questioned them. Gonzales defended them by saying that he expects a significant increase in activity in his department next year.

What do you think are the real reasons for the increase in the budgeted amounts? What ethical considerations enter into this situation?

LO4 **Budgeting for Cash Flows**

C 3. The nature of a company's business affects its need to budget for cash flows. **H&R Block** is a service company whose main business is preparing tax returns. Most tax returns are prepared after January 31 and before April 15. For a fee and interest, the company will advance cash to clients who are due refunds. The clients are expected to repay the cash advances when they receive their refunds. Although H&R Block has some revenues throughout the year, it devotes most of the nontax season to training potential employees in tax preparation procedures and to laying the groundwork for the next tax season.

Toys "R" Us is a toy retailer whose sales are concentrated in October, November, and December of one year and January of the next year. Sales continue at a steady but low level during the rest of the year. The company purchases most of its inventory between July and September.

Johnson & Johnson sells the many health care products that it manufactures to retailers, and the retailers sell them to the final customer. Johnson & Johnson offers retailers credit terms.

Discuss the nature of cash receipts and cash disbursements over a calendar year in the three companies we have just described. What are some key estimates that the management of these companies must make when preparing a cash budget?

LO1 LO4 **Budgeting Procedures**

C 4. Since Rood Enterprises inaugurated participative budgeting 10 years ago, everyone in the organization—from maintenance personnel to the president's staff—has had a voice in the budgeting process. Until recently, participative budgeting has worked in the best interests of the company as a whole. Now, however, it is becoming evident that some managers are using the practice solely to benefit their own divisions. The budget committee has therefore asked you, the company's controller, to analyze this year's divisional budgets carefully before incorporating them into the company's master budget.

The Motor Division was the first of the company's six divisions to submit its budget request for next year. The division's budgeted income statement appears at the top of the next page.

Rood Enterprises
Motor Division
Budgeted Income Statement
For the Years Ended December 31

	Budget for This Year	Budget for Next Year	Increase (Decrease)
Net sales			
Radios	$ 850,000	$ 910,000	$ 60,000
Appliances	680,000	740,000	60,000
Telephones	270,000	305,000	35,000
Miscellaneous	84,400	90,000	5,600
Net sales	$1,884,400	$2,045,000	$160,600
Less cost of goods sold	750,960	717,500*	(33,460)
Gross margin	$1,133,440	$1,327,500	$194,060
Operating expenses			
Wages			
Warehouse	$ 94,500	$ 102,250	$ 7,750
Purchasing	77,800	84,000	6,200
Delivery/shipping	69,400	74,780	5,380
Maintenance	42,650	45,670	3,020
Salaries			
Supervisory	60,000	92,250	32,250
Executive	130,000	164,000	34,000
Purchases, supplies	17,400	20,500	3,100
Maintenance	72,400	82,000	9,600
Depreciation	62,000	74,750†	12,750
Building rent	96,000	102,500	6,500
Sales commissions	188,440	204,500	16,060
Insurance			
Fire	12,670	20,500	7,830
Liability	18,200	20,500	2,300
Utilities	14,100	15,375	1,275
Taxes			
Property	16,600	18,450	1,850
Payroll	26,520	41,000	14,480
Miscellaneous	4,610	10,250	5,640
Total operating expenses	$1,003,290	$1,173,275	$169,985
Income from operations	$ 130,150	$ 154,225	$ 24,075

*Less expensive merchandise will be purchased in the next year to boost profits.

†Depreciation is increased because additional equipment must be bought to handle increased sales.

1. Recast the Motor Division's budgeted income statement in the following format (round percentages to two places):

	Budget for This Year		Budget for Next Year	
Account	**Amount**	**Percentage of Net Sales**	**Amount**	**Percentage of Net Sales**

2. Actual results for this year revealed the following information about revenues and cost of goods sold:

	Amount	Percentage of Net Sales
Net sales		
Radios	$ 780,000	43.94
Appliances	640,000	36.06
Telephones	280,000	15.77
Miscellaneous	75,000	4.23
Net sales	$1,775,000	100.00
Less cost of goods sold	763,425	43.01
Gross margin	$1,011,575	56.99

On the basis of this information and your analysis in **1**, what do you think the budget committee should say to the managers of the Motor Division? Identify any specific areas of the budget that may need to be revised, and explain why the revision is needed.

LO3 LO4 **The Budgeting Process**

C 5. Refer to our development of Framecraft Company's master budget in this chapter. Suppose that because of a new customer in Canada, the company's management has decided to increase budgeted sales in the first quarter by 5,000 units. The expenses for this sale will include direct materials, direct labor, variable overhead, and variable selling and administrative expenses. The delivery expense for the Canadian customer will be $0.18 per unit rather than the regular $0.08 per unit. The desired units of beginning finished goods inventory will remain at 1,000 units.

1. Using an Excel spreadsheet, revise Framecraft Company's budgeted income statement and the operating budgets that support it to reflect the changes described above. (Round manufactured cost per unit to three decimals.)
2. What was the change in income from operations? Would you recommend accepting the order from the Canadian customer? If so, why?

LO1 LO2 **Cookie Company (Continuing Case)**

LO4 **C 6.** In this segment of our continuing case, you have decided to open a store where you will sell your company's cookies, as well as coffee, tea, and other beverages. You believe that the store will be able to provide excellent service and undersell the local competition. To fund operations, you are applying for a loan from the Small Business Administration. The loan application requires you to submit two financial budgets—a pro forma income statement and a pro forma balance sheet—within six weeks.

How do the four *w*'s of preparing an accounting report apply in this situation—that is, *why* are you preparing these financial budgets, *who* needs them, *what* information do you need to prepare them, and *when* are they due?

CHAPTER 22

Performance Management and Evaluation

The Management Process

PLAN

- ▷ **Translate the organization's mission and vision into operational objectives from multiple stakeholders' perspectives.**
- ▷ **Select performance measures for objectives.**
- ▷ **Establish targets for each performance objective.**

PERFORM

- ▷ **Balance the needs of all stakeholders when making decisions.**
- ▷ **Improve performance by tracking causal relationships among objectives, measures, and targets.**

EVALUATE

- ▷ **Compare financial and nonfinancial results with performance targets.**
- ▷ **Analyze results and take corrective actions.**

COMMUNICATE

- ▷ **Prepare reports of interest to stakeholder groups.**

Managers use multiple evaluation metrics to analyze and manage performance.

If managers want satisfactory results, they must understand the cause-and-effect relationships between their actions and their organization's overall performance. By measuring and tracking the relationships that they are responsible for, managers can improve performance and thereby add value for all of their organization's stakeholders. In this chapter, we describe the role of the balanced scorecard, responsibility accounting, and economic value added as they relate to performance management and evaluation. We also point out how managers can use a wide range of financial and nonfinancial data to manage and evaluate performance more effectively.

LEARNING OBJECTIVES

LO1 **Define a *performance management and evaluation system*, and describe how the balanced scorecard aligns performance with organizational goals.** (pp. 1018–1021)

LO2 **Define *responsibility accounting*, and describe the role that responsibility centers play in performance management and evaluation.** (pp. 1021–1025)

LO3 **Prepare performance reports for cost centers using flexible budgets and for profit centers using variable costing.** (pp. 1026–1029)

LO4 **Prepare performance reports for investment centers using the traditional measures of return on investment and residual income and the newer measure of economic value added.** (pp. 1029–1035)

LO5 **Explain how properly linked performance incentives and measures add value for all stakeholders in performance management and evaluation.** (pp. 1035–1038)

DECISION POINT ▸ A MANAGER'S FOCUS VAIL RESORTS

- ▸ How do managers at Vail Resorts link performance measures and set performance targets to achieve performance objectives?
- ▸ How do they use the PEAKS system and its integrated database to improve performance management and evaluation?

Vail Resorts includes five vacation spots: Vail, Breckenridge, Keystone, Heavenly, and Beaver Creek. To help guests enjoy all the activities that these places offer, Vail Resorts instituted its PEAKS system. PEAKS is an all-in-one card that guests at the five resort areas can use to pay for lift tickets, skiing and snowboarding lessons, equipment rentals, dining, and more.

Guests like the PEAKS system's convenience and its program for earning points toward free or reduced-rate lift tickets, dining, and lodging. After enrolling, members receive a picture identification card with radio frequency technology that is scanned each time they ride the ski lifts, attend ski school, or charge purchases, meals, or lodging.[1]

Managers at Vail Resorts like the PEAKS system because it enables them to collect huge amounts of information—both financial and nonfinancial—in a simple way and because the data have so many uses. New data are entered in the system each time a guest's card is scanned. Those data then become part of an integrated management information system that managers use to measure and evaluate the performance of their resorts in many ways.

Performance Measurement

LO1 Define a *performance management and evaluation system*, and describe how the balanced scorecard aligns performance with organizational goals.

A **performance management and evaluation system** is a set of procedures that account for and report on both financial and nonfinancial performance so that a company can identify how well it is doing, where it is going, and what improvements will make it more profitable.

What to Measure, How to Measure

Performance measurement is the use of quantitative tools to gauge an organization's performance in relation to a specific goal or an expected outcome. For performance measurement to succeed, managers must be able to distinguish between what is being measured and the actual measures used to monitor performance. For instance, product or service quality is not a performance measure. It is part of a management strategy: Management wants to produce the highest-quality product or service possible, given the resources available. Product or service quality thus is what management wants to measure.

> **Study Note**
>
> What a manager measures for example, quality—is not the same as the actual measures used to monitor performance—for example, the number of defective units per hour.

To measure product or service quality, managers must collaborate with other managers to develop a group of measures, such as the balanced scorecard, that will identify changes in product or service quality and help employees determine what needs to be done to improve quality.

Other Measurement Issues

Each organization must develop a set of performance measures that is appropriate to its situation. In addition to answering the basic questions of what to measure and how to measure, management must consider a variety of other issues, including the following:

- What performance measures can be used?
- How can managers monitor the level of product or service quality?
- How can managers monitor production and other business processes to identify areas that need improvement?
- How can managers measure customer satisfaction?
- How can managers monitor financial performance?
- Are there other stakeholders to whom a manager is accountable?
- What performance measures do government entities impose on the company?
- How can a manager measure the company's effect on the environment?

FOCUS ON BUSINESS PRACTICE

"Old" Doesn't Mean "Out of Date"

The *tableau de bord*, or "dashboard," was developed by French engineers around 1900 as a concise performance measurement system that helped managers understand the cause-and-effect relationships between their decisions and the resulting performance. The indicators, both financial and nonfinancial, allowed managers at all levels to monitor their progress in terms of the mission and objectives of their unit and of their company overall. Like a set of nested Russian dolls, each unit's key success factors and key performance indicators were integrated with those of other units. The dashboard continues to encourage a performance measurement system that focuses on and supports an organization's strategic plan.[2]

Organizational Goals and the Balanced Scorecard

The **balanced scorecard**, developed by Robert S. Kaplan and David R Norton, is a framework that links the perspectives of an organization's four basic stakeholder groups—financial (investors), learning and growth (employees), internal business processes, and customers—with the organization's mission and vision, performance measures, strategic and tactical plans, and resources. To succeed, an organization must add value for all groups in both the short and the long term. Thus, an organization will determine each group's objectives and translate them into performance measures that have specific, quantifiable performance targets. Ideally, managers should be able to see how their actions contribute to the achievement of organizational goals and understand how their compensation is related to their actions. The balanced scorecard assumes that an organization will get only what it measures.

The Balanced Scorecard and Management

To illustrate how managers use the balanced scorecard, we will refer to **Vail Resorts**' PEAKS system, which we described in the Decision Point.

Planning During the planning stage, the balanced scorecard provides a framework that enables managers to translate their organization's vision and strategy into operational terms. Managers evaluate the company's vision from the perspective of each stakeholder group and seek to answer one key question for each group:

- ***Financial (investors):*** To achieve our organization's vision, how should we appear to our shareholders?
- ***Learning and growth (employees):*** To achieve our organization's vision, how should we sustain our ability to improve and change?
- ***Internal business processes:*** To succeed, in which business processes must our organization excel?
- ***Customers:*** To achieve our organization's vision, how should we appeal to our customers?

Study Note

The alignment of an organization's strategy with all the perspectives of the balanced scorecard results in performance objectives that benefit all stakeholders.

These key questions align the organization's strategy from all perspectives. The answers to the questions result in performance objectives that are mutually beneficial to all stakeholders. Once the organization's objectives are set, managers can select performance measures and set performance targets to translate the objectives into an action plan. For example, if Vail Resorts' collective vision and strategy is to please guests, its managers might establish the following overall objectives:

Perspective	*Objective*
Financial (investors)	Increase guests' spending at the resort.
Learning and growth (employees)	Continually cross-train employees in each other's duties to sustain premium-quality service for guests.
Internal business processes	Leverage market position by introducing and improving innovative marketing and technology-driven advances that clearly benefit guests.
Customers	Create new premium-price experiences and facilities for vacations in all seasons.

These overall objectives are then translated into specific performance objectives and measures for specific managers. Figure 22-1 summarizes how Vail

FIGURE 22-1 Sample Balanced Scorecard of Linked Objectives, Performance Measures, and Targets

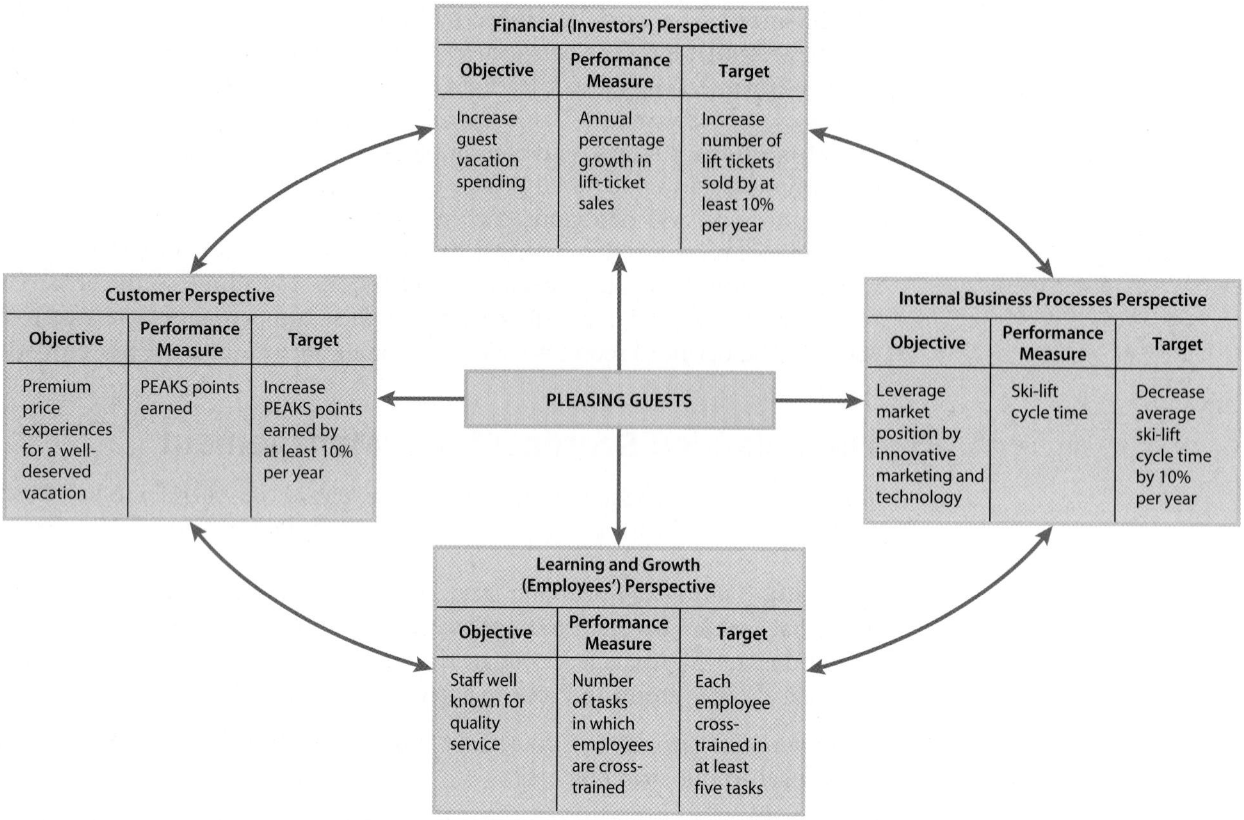

Financial (Investors') Perspective

Objective	Performance Measure	Target
Increase guest vacation spending	Annual percentage growth in lift-ticket sales	Increase number of lift tickets sold by at least 10% per year

Customer Perspective

Objective	Performance Measure	Target
Premium price experiences for a well-deserved vacation	PEAKS points earned	Increase PEAKS points earned by at least 10% per year

PLEASING GUESTS

Internal Business Processes Perspective

Objective	Performance Measure	Target
Leverage market position by innovative marketing and technology	Ski-lift cycle time	Decrease average ski-lift cycle time by 10% per year

Learning and Growth (Employees') Perspective

Objective	Performance Measure	Target
Staff well known for quality service	Number of tasks in which employees are cross-trained	Each employee cross-trained in at least five tasks

Source: Adapted from Robert S. Kaplan and David P. Norton, "Using the Balanced Scorecard as a Strategic Management System," *Harvard Business Review*, January–February 1996.

Resort's managers might link their organization's vision and strategy to objectives, then link the objectives to logical performance measures, and, finally, set performance targets for a ski lift manager. As a result, a ski lift manager will have a variety of performance measures that balance the perspectives and needs of all stakeholders.

Performing Managers use the mutually agreed-upon strategic and tactical objectives for the entire organization as the basis for decision making within their individual areas of responsibility. This practice ensures that they consider the needs of all stakeholder groups and shows how measuring and managing performance for some stakeholder groups can lead to improved performance for another stakeholder group. Specifically, improving the performance of indicators like internal business processes and learning and growth will create improvements for customers, which in turn will result in improved financial performance. For example, when making decisions about available ski lift capacity, the ski lift manager at Vail Resorts will balance such factors as lift ticket sales, snow conditions, equipment reliability, trained staff availability, and length of wait for ski lifts.

When managers understand the causal and linked relationship between their actions and their company's overall performance, they can see new ways to be more effective. For example, a ski lift manager may hypothesize that shorter waiting lines for the ski lifts would improve customer satisfaction and lead to more visits to the ski lift. The manager could test this possible cause-and-effect relationship by measuring and tracking the length of ski lift waiting lines and the number of visits to the ski lift. If a causal relationship exists, the manager can improve the performance of the ski lift operation by doing everything possible to ensure that waiting lines are short because a quicker ride to the top will result in improved results for the operation and for other perspectives as well.

Evaluating Managers compare performance objectives and targets with actual results to determine if the targets were met, what measures need to be changed, and what strategies or objectives need revision. For example, the ski lift manager at Vail Resorts would analyze the reasons for performance gaps and make recommendations to improve the performance of the ski lift area.

Communicating A variety of reports enable managers to monitor and evaluate performance measures that add value for stakeholder groups. For example, the database makes it possible to prepare financial performance reports, customer PEAKS statements, internal business process reports for targeted performance measures and results, and performance appraisals of individual employees.

The balanced scorecard adds dimension to the management process. Managers plan, perform, evaluate, and communicate the organization's performance from multiple perspectives. By balancing the needs of all stakeholders, managers are more likely to achieve their objectives in both the short and the long term.

STOP & APPLY >

Molly Sams wants to measure customer satisfaction within her sales region. Link an appropriate performance measure with each balanced scorecard perspective.

Customer Satisfaction	Possible Performance Measures
1. Financial (investors)	a. Number of cross-trained staff
2. Learning and growth (employees)	b. Customer satisfaction rating
3. Internal business processes	c. Time lapse from order to delivery
4. Customers	d. Dollar sales to repeat customers

SOLUTION

1. d; 2. a; 3. c; 4. b

Responsibility Accounting

LO2 Define *responsibility accounting*, and describe the role that responsibility centers play in performance management and evaluation.

As part of their performance management systems, many organizations assign resources to specific areas of responsibility and track how the managers of those areas use those resources. For example, **Vail Resorts** assigns resources to its Lodging, Dining, Retail and Rental, Ski School, and Real Estate divisions and holds the managers of those divisions responsible for generating revenue and managing costs. Within each division, other managers are assigned responsibility for such areas as Children and Adult Ski School, Snowboard School, or Private Lessons. All managers at all levels are then evaluated in terms of their ability to manage their areas of responsibility in keeping with the organization's goals.

To assist in performance management and evaluation, many organizations use responsibility accounting. **Responsibility accounting** is an information system that classifies data according to areas of responsibility and reports each area's activities by including only the revenue, cost, and resource categories that the assigned manager can control. A **responsibility center** is an organizational unit whose manager has been assigned the responsibility of managing a portion of the organization's resources. The activities of a responsibility center dictate the extent of a manager's responsibility.

A report for a responsibility center should contain only the costs, revenues, and resources that the manager of that center can control. Such costs and revenues are called **controllable costs and revenues** because they are the result of a manager's actions, influence, or decisions. A responsibility accounting system ensures that managers will not be held responsible for items that they cannot change.

Types of Responsibility Centers

There are five types of responsibility centers: (1) cost centers, (2) discretionary cost centers, (3) revenue centers, (4) profit centers, and (5) investment centers. The key characteristics of the five types of responsibility centers are summarized in Table 22-1.

Cost Centers A responsibility center whose manager is accountable only for controllable costs that have well-defined relationships between the center's resources and certain products or services is called a **cost center**.

Manufacturing companies like **Apple Computer** use cost centers to manage assembly plants, where the relationship between the costs of resources (direct material, direct labor) and the resulting products is well defined. Service organizations use cost centers to manage activities in which resources are clearly linked with a service that is provided at no additional charge. For example, in nursing

Research and development units, such as the one shown here, are a type of discretionary cost center in which a manager is accountable for costs only and the relationship between resources and products or services produced is not well defined. A common performance measure used to evaluate research and development activities is the number of patents obtained.

Courtesy of Image Source/Getty Images.

TABLE 22-1
Types of Responsibility Centers

Responsibility Center	Manager Accountable For	How Performance Is Measured	Examples
Cost center	Only controllable costs, where there are well-defined links between the costs of resources and the resulting products or services	Compare actual costs with flexible and master budget costs Analyze resulting variances	Product: Manufacturing assembly plants Service: Food service for hospital patients
Discretionary cost center	Only controllable costs; the links between the costs of resources and the resulting products or services are *not* well defined	Compare actual noncost-based measures with targets Determine compliance with preapproved budgeted spending limits	Product or service: Administrative activities such as accounting, human resources, and research and development
Revenue center	Revenue generation	Compare actual revenue with budgeted revenue Analyze resulting variances	Product: Phone or e-commerce sales for pizza delivery Service: Reservation center on Internet
Profit center	Operating income resulting from controllable revenues and costs	Compare actual variable costing income statement with the budgeted income statement	Product or service: Local store of a national chain
Investment center	Controllable revenues, costs, and the investment of resources to achieve organizational goals	Return on investment Residual income Economic value added	Product: A division of a multinational corporation Service: A national office of a multinational consulting firm

homes and hospitals, there is a clear relationship between the costs of food and direct labor and the number of inpatient meals served.

The performance of a cost center is usually evaluated by comparing an activity's actual cost with its budgeted cost and analyzing the resulting variances. You will learn more about this performance evaluation process in the chapter on standard costing.

Discretionary Cost Centers A responsibility center whose manager is accountable for costs only and in which the relationship between resources and the products or services produced is not well defined is called a **discretionary cost center**. Departments that perform administrative activities, such as accounting, human resources, and legal services, are typical examples of discretionary cost centers. These centers, like cost centers, have approved budgets that set spending limits.

Because the spending and use of resources in discretionary cost centers are not clearly linked to the production of a product or service, cost-based measures usually cannot be used to evaluate performance (although such centers are penalized if they exceed their approved budgets). For example, among the performance measures used to evaluate the research and development activities are the number of patents obtained and the number of cost-saving innovations that are developed.

At service organizations, such as the **United Way**, a common measure of administrative activities is how low their costs are as a percentage of total contributions.

Revenue Centers A responsibility center whose manager is accountable primarily for revenue and whose success is based on its ability to generate revenue is called a **revenue center**. Examples of revenue centers are **Hertz**'s national car reservation center and the clothing retailer **Nordstrom**'s ecommerce order department.

A revenue center's performance is usually evaluated by comparing its actual revenue with its budgeted revenue and analyzing the resulting variances. Performance measures at both manufacturing and service organizations may include sales dollars, number of customer sales, or sales revenue per minute.

Profit Centers A responsibility center whose manager is accountable for both revenue and costs and for the resulting operating income is called a **profit center**. A good example is a local store of a national chain, such as **Wal-Mart** or **Jiffy Lube**.

The performance of a profit center is usually evaluated by comparing the figures on its actual income statement with the figures on its master or flexible budget income statement.

Investment Centers A responsibility center whose manager is accountable for profit generation and can also make significant decisions about the resources that the center uses is called an **investment center**. For example, the president of **Harley-Davidson**'s Buell subsidiary and the president of **Brinker International**'s Chili's Grill and Bar can control revenues, costs, and the investment of assets to achieve organizational goals.

The performance of these centers is evaluated using such measures as return on investment, residual income, and economic value added. These measures are used in all types of organizations, both manufacturing and nonmanufacturing, and are discussed later in this chapter.

Organizational Structure and Performance Management

Much can be learned about an organization by examining how its managers organize activities and resources. A company's organizational structure formalizes its lines of managerial authority and control. An **organization chart** is a visual representation of an organization's hierarchy of responsibility for the purposes of management control. Within an organization chart, the five types of responsibility centers are arranged by level of management authority and control.

By examining a typical corporate organization chart, you can see how a responsibility accounting system works. Figure 22-2 shows part of the management structure for the Restaurant Division of a major hospitality corporation. Notice that the figure shows examples of all five types of responsibility centers.

FIGURE 22-2 Partial Organization Chart of a Restaurant Division

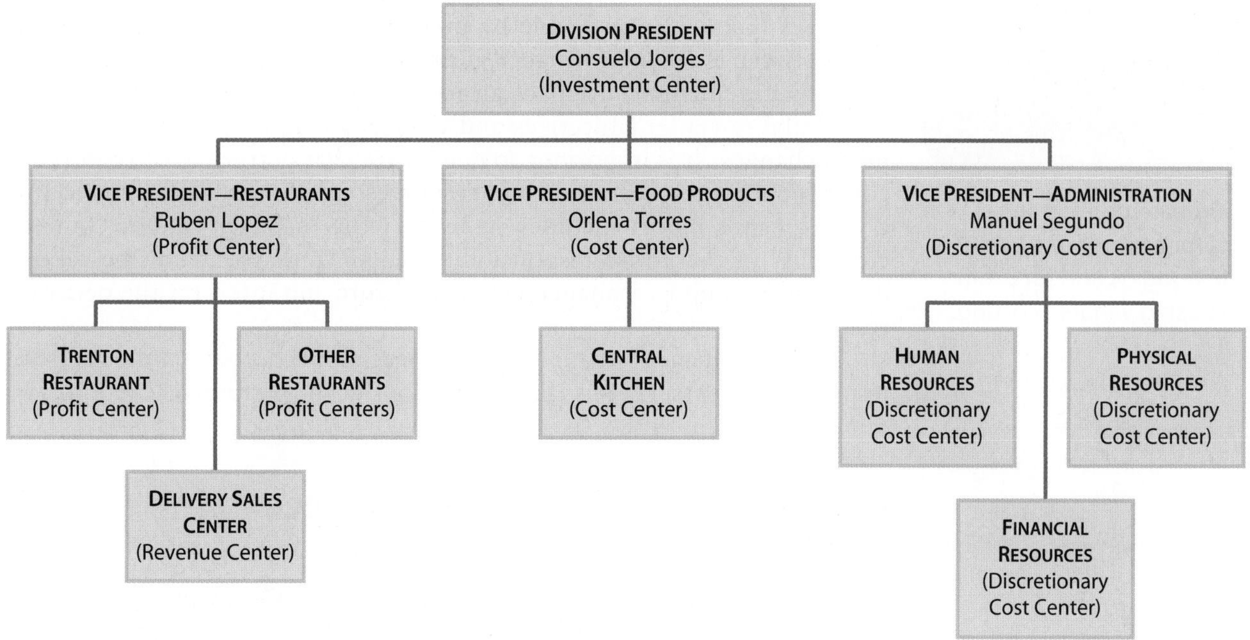

In a responsibility accounting system, the performance reports for each level of management are tailored to each manager's individual needs for information. As information moves up the organizational chart, it is usually condensed. Performance reporting by responsibility level enables an organization to trace the source of a cost, revenue, or resource to the manager who controls it and to evaluate that manager's performance accordingly.

& APPLY >

Identify the most appropriate type of responsibility center for each of the following organizational units:

1. A pizza store in a pizza chain
2. The ticket sales center of a major airline
3. The food service function at a nursing home
4. A subsidiary of a business conglomerate
5. The information technology area of a company

SOLUTION

1. Profit center
2. Revenue center
3. Cost center
4. Investment center
5. Discretionary cost center

Performance Evaluation of Cost Centers and Profit Centers

LO3 Prepare performance reports for cost centers using flexible budgets and for profit centers using variable costing.

Study Note

Only controllable items should be included on a manager's performance report.

Because performance reports contain information about costs, revenues, and resources that are controllable by individual managers, they allow comparisons between actual performance and budget expectations. Such comparisons allow management to evaluate an individual's performance with respect to responsibility center objectives and companywide objectives and to recommend changes. It is important to emphasize that performance reports should contain only costs, revenues, and resources that the manager can control. If a performance report includes items that the manager cannot control, the credibility of the entire responsibility accounting system can be called into question. It is up to management to structure and interpret the performance results fairly.

The content and format of a performance report depend on the nature of the responsibility center. Let us take a closer look at the performance reports for cost centers and profit centers.

Evaluating Cost Center Performance Using Flexible Budgeting

In the Restaurant Division whose organization is shown in Figure 22-2, the Central Kitchen is where the food products that the restaurants sell are prepared. It is a cost center because its costs have well-defined relationships with the resulting products, which are then transferred to the restaurants for further processing and sale. To ensure that the central kitchen is meeting its performance goals, the manager will evaluate the performance of each food item produced. A separate report on each product will compare its actual costs with the corresponding amounts from the budget.

The Central Kitchen's performance report on House Dressing is presented in Exhibit 22-1. It compares data from the master budget (prepared at the beginning of the period) with the actual results for the period. As you can see, actual costs exceeded budgeted costs. Most managers would consider such a cost overrun significant. But was there really a cost overrun? The amounts budgeted in the master budget are based on an output of 1,000 units of dressing; however, the actual output was 1,200 units of dressing.

To judge the central kitchen's performance accurately, the company's managers must change the budgeted data in the master budget to reflect an output of 1,200 units. They can do this by using a flexible budget.

A **flexible budget** (also called a *variable budget*) is a summary of expected costs for a range of activity levels. Unlike a static budget, a flexible budget provides forecasted data that can be adjusted for changes in the level of output.

- A flexible budget is derived by multiplying actual unit output by predetermined unit costs for each cost item in the report.
- The flexible budget is used primarily as a cost control tool in evaluating performance at the end of a period, as in Exhibit 22-1.

In the next chapter, you will learn that favorable (positive, or F) and unfavorable (negative, or U) variances between actual costs and the flexible budget can be further examined by using standard costing to compute specific variances for direct materials, direct labor, and variable and fixed overhead. Also, you will use the flexible budget as a cost control tool to evaluate performance.

EXHIBIT 22-1
Central Kitchen's Performance Report on House Dressing

	Actual Results	Variance	Flexible Budget	Variance	Master Budget
Gallons produced	**1,200**	**0**	**1,200**	200 **(F)**	**1,000**
Center costs					
Direct materials ($0.25 per gallon)	$312	$12 (U)	$300	$50 (U)	$250
Direct labor ($0.05 per gallon)	72	12 (U)	60	10 (U)	50
Variable overhead ($0.03 per gallon)	33	3 (F)	36	6 (U)	30
Fixed overhead	2	3 (F)	5	0	5
Total cost	$419	$18 (U)	$401	$66 (U)	$335
Performance measures					
Defect-free gallons to total produced	0.98	0.01 (U)	N/A	N/A	0.99
Average throughput time per gallon	11 minutes	1 minute (F)	N/A	N/A	12 minutes

Note: In this exhibit and others that appear later in this chapter, (F) indicates a favorable variance, and (U) indicates an unfavorable variance.

Evaluating Profit Center Performance Using Variable Costing

Restaurants are profit centers since each is accountable for its own revenues and costs and for the resulting operating income. A profit center's performance is usually evaluated by comparing its actual income statement results to its budgeted income statement.

Variable costing is a method of preparing profit center performance reports that classifies a manager's controllable costs as either variable or fixed. Variable costing produces a variable costing income statement instead of a traditional income statement (also called a *full costing* or *absorption costing* or *traditional income statement*), which is used for external reporting purposes.

A variable costing income statement is the same as a contribution margin income statement, whose format you may recall from its use in cost-volume-profit analysis. Such an income statement is useful in performance management and evaluation because it focuses on cost variability and the profit center's contribution to operating income.

A variable costing income statement differs from the traditional income statement prepared for financial reporting, as shown by the two income statements in Exhibit 22-2 for Trenton Restaurant, which is part of the Restaurant Divison. In the traditional income statement, all manufacturing costs are assigned to cost of goods sold; in the variable costing income statement, only the variable manufacturing costs are included.

- Under variable costing, direct materials costs, direct labor costs, and variable overhead costs are the only cost elements used to compute variable cost of goods sold.

EXHIBIT 22-2
Variable Costing Income Statement Versus Traditional Income Statement for Trenton Restaurant

Variable Costing Income Statement		**Traditional Income Statement**	
Sales	$2,500	Sales	$2,500
Variable cost of goods sold	1,575	Cost of goods sold	1,745
Variable selling expenses	325	($1,575 + $170 = $1,745)	
Contribution margin	$ 600	Gross margin	$ 755
Fixed manufacturing costs	170	Variable selling expenses	325
Fixed selling expenses	230	Fixed selling expenses	230
Profit center operating income	$ 200	Profit center operating income	$ 200

- Fixed manufacturing costs are considered costs of the current accounting period. Notice that fixed manufacturing costs are listed with fixed selling expenses after the contribution margin has been computed.

In addition to tracking financial performance measures, a manager of a profit center may want to measure and evaluate nonfinancial information—for example, the number of food orders processed and the average amount of a sales order at the Trenton Restaurant. The resulting report, based on variable costing and flexible budgeting, is shown in Exhibit 22-3.

Although performance reports vary in format depending on the type of responsibility center, they have some common themes:

- All responsibility center reports compare actual results to budgeted figures and focus on the differences.
- Often, comparisons are made to a flexible budget as well as to the master budget.
- Only the items that the manager can control are included in the performance report.
- Nonfinancial measures are also examined to achieve a more balanced view of the manager's responsibilities.

EXHIBIT 22-3 Performance Report Based on Variable Costing and Flexible Budgeting for the Trenton Restaurant

	Actual Results	**Variance**	**Flexible Budget**	**Variance**	**Master Budget**
Meals served	**750**	**0**	**750**	**250 (U)**	**1,000**
Sales (average meal $2.85)	$2,500.00	$362.50 (F)	$2,137.50	$712.50 (U)	$2,850.00
Controllable variable costs					
Variable cost of goods sold ($1.50)	1,575.00	450.00 (U)	1,125.00	375.00 (F)	1,500.00
Variable selling expenses ($0.40)	325.00	25.00 (U)	300.00	100.00 (F)	400.00
Contribution margin	$ 600.00	$112.50 (U)	$ 712.50	$237.50 (U)	$ 950.00
Controllable fixed costs					
Fixed manufacturing expenses	170.00	30.00 (F)	200.00	0.00	200.00
Fixed selling expenses	230.00	20.00 (F)	250.00	0.00	250.00
Profit center operating income	$ 200.00	$ 62.50 (U)	$ 262.50	$237.50 (U)	$ 500.00
Other nonfinancial performance measures					
Number of orders processed	300	50 (F)	N/A	N/A	250
Average sales order	$8.34	$3.06 (U)	N/A	N/A	$11.40

STOP & APPLY >

Complete the following performance report for a profit center for the month ended December 31:

	Actual Results	Variance	Master Budget
Sales	$?	$ 20 (F)	$ 120
Controllable variable costs			
Variable cost of goods sold	25	10 (U)	?
Variable selling and administrative expenses	15	?	5
Contribution margin	$100	$?	$ 100
Controllable fixed costs	?	10 (F)	60
Profit center income	$ 50	$ 10 (F)	$?
Performance measures			
Number of orders processed	50	20 (F)	?
Average daily sales	$?	$0.66 (F)	$4.00
Number of units sold	100	40 (F)	?

SOLUTION

Profit Center
For the Month Ended December 31

	Actual Results	Variance	Master Budget
Sales	$ 140	$ 20 (F)	$ 120
Controllable variable costs			
Variable cost of goods sold	25	10 (U)	15
Variable selling and administrative expenses	15	10 (U)	5
Contribution margin	$ 100	$ 0	$ 100
Controllable fixed costs	50	10 (F)	60
Profit center operating income	$ 50	$ 10 (F)	$ 40
Performance measures			
Number of orders processed	50	20 (F)	30
Average daily sales	$4.66	$0.66 (F)	$4.00
Number of units sold	100	40 (F)	60

Performance Evaluation of Investment Centers

LO4 Prepare performance reports for investment centers using the traditional measures of return on investment and residual income and the newer measure of economic value added.

The evaluation of an investment center's performance requires more than a comparison of controllable revenues and costs with budgeted amounts. Because the managers of investment centers also control resources and invest in assets, other performance measures must be used to hold them accountable for revenues, costs, and the capital investments that they control. In this section, we focus on the traditional performance evaluation measures of return on investment and residual income and the relatively new performance measure of economic value added.

Return on Investment

Traditionally, the most common performance measure that takes into account both operating income and the assets invested to earn that income is **return on investment (ROI)**. Return on investment is computed as follows:

EXHIBIT 22-4
Performance Report Based on Return on Investment for the Restaurant Division

	Actual Results	Variance	Master Budget
Operating income	$610	$280 (U)	$ 890
Assets invested	$800	$200 (F)	$1,000
Performance measure			
ROI	76%	13% (U)	89%

ROI = Operating Income ÷ Assets Invested

$890 ÷ $1,000 = 0.89, or 89%

$610 ÷ $800 = 0.76, or 76%*

*Rounded.

$$\text{Return on Investment (ROI)} = \frac{\text{Operating Income}}{\text{Assets Invested}}$$

In this formula, *assets invested* is the average of the beginning and ending asset balances for the period.

Properly measuring the income and the assets specifically controlled by a manager is critical to the quality of this performance measure. Using ROI, it is possible to evaluate the manager of any investment center, whether it is an entire company or a unit within a company such as a subsidiary, division, or other business segment.

For example, assume that the Restaurant Division had actual operating income of $610 and that the average assets invested were $800. The master budget called for $890 in operating income and $1,000 in invested assets. As shown in Exhibit 22-4, the budgeted ROI for the division would be 89 percent, and the actual ROI would be 76 percent. The actual ROI was lower than the budgeted ROI because the division's actual operating income was lower than expected relative to the actual assets invested.

For investment centers, the ROI computation is really the aggregate measure of many interrelationships. The basic ROI equation, Operating Income ÷ Assets Invested, can be rewritten to show the many elements within the aggregate ROI number that a manager can influence. Two important indicators of performance are profit margin and asset turnover. **Profit margin** is the ratio of operating income to sales; it represents the percentage of each sales dollar that results in profit. **Asset turnover** is the ratio of sales to average assets invested; it indicates the productivity of assets, or the number of sales dollars generated by each dollar invested in assets.

Study Note

Profit margin focuses on the income statement, and asset turnover focuses on the balance sheet aspects of ROI.

Return on investment is equal to profit margin multiplied by asset turnover:

$$\text{ROI} = \text{Profit Margin} \times \text{Asset Turnover}$$

$$\text{ROI} = \frac{\text{Operating Income}}{\text{Sales}} \times \frac{\text{Sales}}{\text{Assets Invested}} = \frac{\text{Operating Income}}{\text{Assets Invested}}$$

Profit margin and asset turnover help explain changes in return on investment for a single investment center or differences in return or investment among investment centers. Therefore, the formula ROI = Profit Margin × Asset Turnover is useful for analyzing and interpreting the elements that make up a business's overall return on investment.

Du Pont, one of the first organizations to recognize the many interrelationships that affect ROI, designed a formula similar to the one diagrammed in Figure 22-3. You can see that ROI is affected by a manager's decisions about pricing, product

FIGURE 22-3 Factors Affecting the Computation of Return on Investment

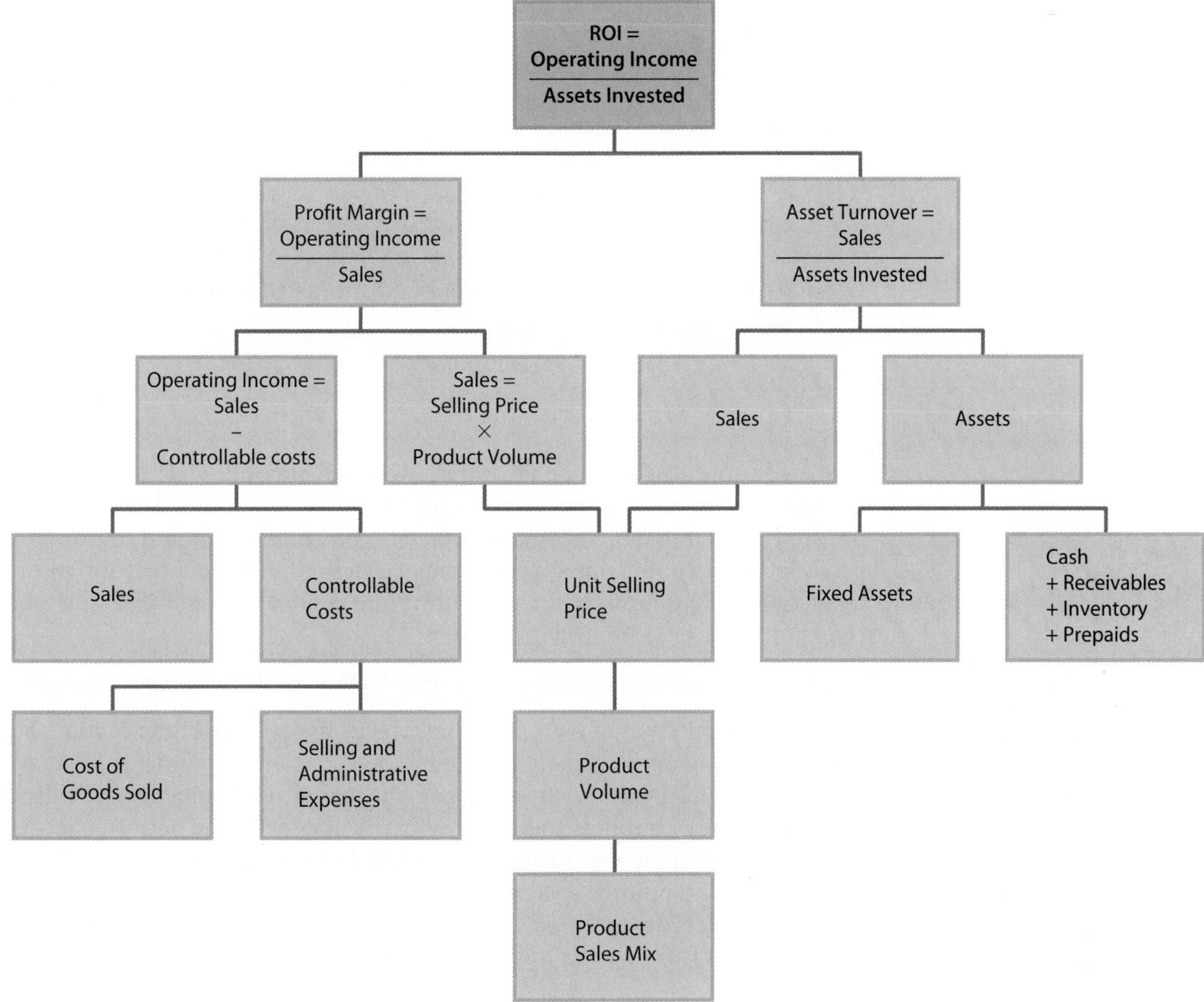

sales mix, capital budgeting for new facilities, product sales volume, and other financial matters. In essence, a single ROI number is a composite index of many cause-and-effect relationships and interdependent financial elements. A manager can improve ROI by increasing sales, decreasing costs, or decreasing assets.

Drawbacks Because of the many factors that affect ROI, management should use this measure cautiously in evaluating performance. If ROI is overemphasized, investment center managers may react by making business decisions that favor their personal ROI performance at the expense of companywide profits or the long-term success of other investment centers. To avoid such problems, other performance measures should always be used in conjunction with ROI—for example, comparisons of revenues, costs, and operating income with budget amounts or past trends; sales growth percentages; market share percentages; or other key variables in the organization's activity. ROI should also be compared with budgeted goals and with past ROI trends because changes in this ratio over time can be more revealing than any single number.

Residual Income

Because of the pitfalls of using return on investment as a performance measure, other approaches to evaluating investment centers have evolved. Residual income

EXHIBIT 22-5
Performance Report Based on Residual Income for the Restaurant Division

	Actual Results	Variance	Master Budget
Operating income	$610	$280 (U)	$ 890
Assets invested	$800	$200 (F)	$1,000
Desired ROI			20%
Performance measures			
ROI	76%	13% (U)	89%
Residual income	$450	$240 (U)	$ 690

Residual Income = Operating Income − (Desired ROI × Assets Invested)

$890 − 20%($1,000) = $690

$610 − 20%($800) = $450

Study Note

ROI is expressed as a percentage, and RI is expressed in dollars.

is one of those performance measures. **Residual income (RI)** is the operating income that an investment center earns above a minimum desired return on invested assets. Residual income is not a ratio but a dollar amount: the amount of profit left after subtracting a predetermined desired income target for an investment center. The formula for computing the residual income of an investment center is

Residual Income = Operating Income − (Desired ROI × Assets Invested)

As in the computation of ROI, assets invested is the average of the center's beginning and ending asset balances for the period.

The desired RI will vary from investment center to investment center depending on the type of business and the level of risk assumed. The performance report based on residual income for the Restaurant Division is shown in Exhibit 22-5. Assume that the residual income performance target is to exceed a 20 percent return on assets invested in the division. Note that the division's residual income is $450, which was lower than the $690 that was projected in the master budget.

Comparisons with other residual income figures will strengthen the analysis. To add context to the analysis of the division and its manager, questions such as the following need to be answered: How did the division's residual income this year compare with its residual income in previous years? Did the actual residual income exceed the budgeted residual income? How did this division's residual income compare with the amounts generated by other investment centers of the company?

Drawbacks Caution is called for when using residual income to compare investment centers within a company. For their residual income figures to be comparable, all investment centers must have equal access to resources and similar asset investment bases. Some managers may be able to produce larger residual incomes simply because their investment centers are larger rather than because their performance is better. Like ROI, RI has some flaws.

Economic Value Added

More and more businesses are using the shareholder wealth created by an investment center, or the **economic value added (EVA)**, as an indicator of performance. The calculation of EVA, a registered trademark of the consulting

EXHIBIT 22-6
Performance Report Based on Economic Value Added for the Restaurant Division

	Actual Results	Variance	Master Budget
Performance measures			
ROI	76%	13% (U)	89%
Residual income	$450	$240 (U)	$690
Economic value added	$334		

Economic Value Added = After-Tax Operating Income − [Cost of Capital × (Total Assets − Current Liabilities)]
$400 − 12%($800 − $250) = $334

firm **Stern Stewart & Company**, can be quite complex because it makes various cost of capital and accounting principles adjustments. You will learn more about the cost of capital in the chapter that discusses capital investment decisions. However, for the purposes of computing EVA, the **cost of capital** is the minimum desired rate of return on an investment, such as the assets invested in an investment center.

Basically, the computation of EVA is similar to the computation of residual income, except that after-tax operating income is used instead of pretax operating income, and a cost of capital percentage is multiplied by the center's invested assets less current liabilities instead of a desired ROI percentage being multiplied by invested assets. Also, like residual income, the economic value added is expressed in dollars. The formula is

EVA = After-Tax Operating Income − [Cost of Capital × (Total Assets − Current Liabilities)]

A very basic computation of economic value added for the Restaurant Division is shown in Exhibit 22-6. The report assumes that the division's after-tax operating income is $400, its cost of capital is 12 percent, its total assets are $800, and its current liabilities are $250.

- The report shows that the division has added $334 to its economic value after taxes and cost of capital. In other words, the division produced after-tax profits of $334 in excess of the cost of capital required to generate those profits.

The factors that affect the computation of economic value added are illustrated in Figure 22-4. An investment center's economic value is affected by managers' decisions on pricing, product sales volume, taxes, cost of capital, capital investments, and other financial matters.

- In essence, the EVA number is a composite index drawn from many cause-and-effect relationships and interdependent financial elements.
- A manager can improve the economic value of an investment center by increasing sales, decreasing costs, decreasing assets, or lowering the cost of capital.

Drawbacks Because many factors affect the economic value of an investment center and its cost of capital, management should be cautious when drawing conclusions about performance. The evaluation will be more meaningful if the current economic value added is compared to EVAs from previous periods, target EVAs, and EVAs from other investment centers.

FIGURE 22-4 Factors Affecting the Computation of Economic Value Added

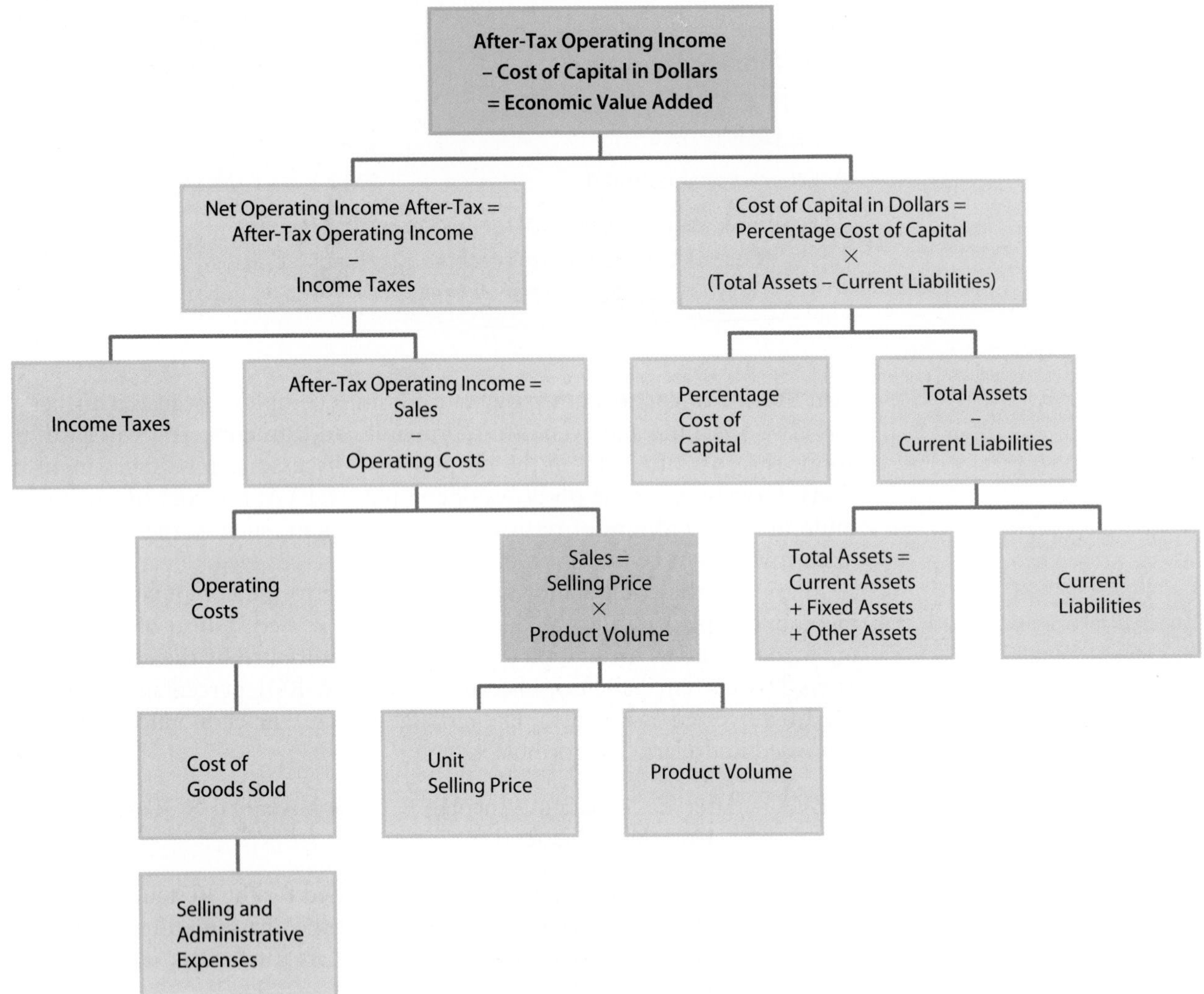

The Importance of Multiple Performance Measures

In summary, to be effective, a performance management system must consider both operating results and multiple performance measures, such as return on investment, residual income, and economic value added. Comparing actual results to budgeted figures adds meaning to the evaluation. Performance measures such as ROI, RI, and EVA indicate whether an investment center is effective in coordinating its own goals with companywide goals because these measures take into account both operating income and the assets used to produce that income. However, all three measures are limited by their focus on short-term financial performance.

- To obtain a fuller picture, management needs to break these three measures down into their components, analyze such information as responsibility center income over time, and compare current results to the targeted amounts in the flexible or master budget.
- In addition, the analysis of such nonfinancial performance indicators as average throughput time, employee turnover, and number of orders processed will ensure a more balanced view of a business's well-being and how to improve it.

Brew Mountain Company sells coffee and hot beverages. Its Coffee Cart Division sells to skiers as they come off the mountain. The balance sheet for the Coffee Cart Division showed that the company had invested assets of $30,000 at the beginning of the year and $50,000 at the end of the year. During the year, the division's operating income was $80,000 on sales of $120,000.

a. Compute the division's residual income if the desired ROI is 20 percent.

b. Compute the return on investment for the division.

c. Compute the economic value added for Brew Mountain Company if total corporate assets are $600,000, current liabilities are $80,000, after-tax operating income is $70,000, and the cost of capital is 12 percent.

SOLUTION

a. $80,000 − {20% × [($30,000 + $50,000) ÷ 2]} = $72,000

b. $80,000 ÷ [($30,000 + $50,000) ÷ 2] = 200%

c. $70,000 − [12% × ($600,000 − $80,000)] = $7,600

Performance Incentives and Goals

LO5 Explain how properly linked performance incentives and measures add value for all stakeholders in performance management and evaluation.

The effectiveness of a performance management and evaluation system depends on how well it coordinates the goals of responsibility centers, managers, and the entire company. Two factors are key to the successful coordination of goals:

- The logical linking of goals to measurable objectives and targets
- The tying of appropriate compensation incentives to the achievement of the targets—that is, performance-based pay

Linking Goals, Performance Objectives, Measures, and Performance Targets

The causal links among an organization's goals, performance objectives, measures, and targets must be apparent. For example, if a company seeks to be an environmental steward, as **Vail Resorts** does, it may choose the following linked goal, objective, measure, and performance target:

Goal	*Objective*	*Measure*	*Performance Target*
To be an environmental steward	To reduce, reuse, and recycle	Number of tons recycled per year	To recycle at least one pound per guest

You may recall that the balanced scorecard also links objectives, measures, and targets, as shown earlier in Figure 22-1.

FOCUS ON BUSINESS PRACTICE

Pay-for-Performance Reality Check

Many service businesses, such as the CPA firm **Meyners + Company**, assume that aligning staff performance and compensation with the business's core values and competencies is a simple matter. But for Meyners, it turned out that administering a pay-for-performance program was time-consuming and data-intensive. Based on a survey of the entire firm four years after the program was inaugurated, the pay-for-performance structure was simplified, and employees were offered other types of incentives.[3]

Performance-Based Pay

The tying of appropriate compensation incentives to performance targets increases the likelihood that the goals of responsibility centers, managers, and the entire organization will be well coordinated. Unfortunately, this linkage does not always happen. Responsibility center managers are more likely to achieve their performance targets if their compensation depends on it. **Performance-based pay** is the linking of employee compensation to the achievement of measurable business targets.

Cash bonuses, awards, profit-sharing plans, and stock options are common types of incentive compensation.

- Cash bonuses are usually given to reward an individual's short-term performance. A bonus may be stated as a fixed dollar amount or as a percentage of a target figure, such as 5 percent of operating income or 10 percent of the dollar increase in operating income.
- An award may be a trip or some other form of recognition for desirable individual or group performance. For example, many companies sponsor a trip for all managers who have met their performance targets during a specified period. Other companies award incentive points that employees may redeem for goods or services. (Notice that awards can be used to encourage both short-term and long-term performance.)
- Profit-sharing plans reward employees with a share of the company's profits.
- Employees often receive company stock as recognition of their contribution to a profitable period. Using stock as a reward encourages employees to think and act as both investors and employees and encourages a stable work force. In terms of the balanced scorecard, employees assume two stakeholder perspectives and take both a short- and a long-term viewpoint. Companies use stock to motivate employees to achieve financial targets that increase the company's stock price.

The Coordination of Goals

What performance incentives and measures should a company use to manage and evaluate performance? What actions and behaviors should an organization reward? Which incentive compensation plans work best? The answers to such questions depend on the facts and circumstances of each organization. To determine

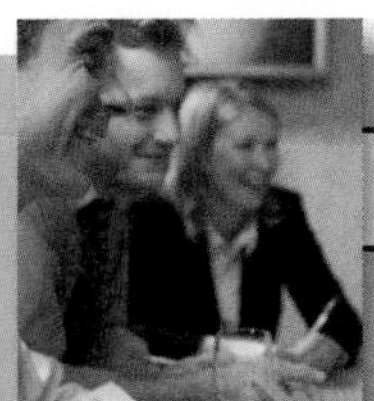

FOCUS ON BUSINESS PRACTICE

Aligning Incentives Among Supply-Chain Partners

A study of more than 50 supply networks found that misaligned performance incentives are often the cause of inventory buildups or shortages, misguided sales efforts, and poor customer relations. A supply chain works only if the partners work together effectively by adopting revenue-sharing contracts, using technology to track shared information, and/or working with intermediaries to build trust. Such incentives among supply-chain partners must be reassessed periodically as business conditions change.[4]

the right performance incentives for their organization, employees and managers must answer several questions:

- When should the reward be given—now or sometime in the future?
- Whose performance should be rewarded—that of responsibility centers, individual managers, or the entire company?
- How should the reward be computed?
- On what should the reward be based?
- What performance criteria should be used?
- Does our performance incentive plan address the interests of all stakeholders?

The effectiveness of a performance management and evaluation system relies on the coordination of responsibility center, managerial, and company goals. Performance can be optimized by linking goals to measurable objectives and targets and by tying appropriate compensation incentives to the achievement of the targets. Each organization's unique circumstances will determine the correct mix of measures and compensation incentives for that organization. If management values the perspectives of all of its stakeholder groups, its performance management and evaluation system will balance and benefit all interests.

STOP & APPLY >

Necessary Toys, Inc., has adopted the balanced scorecard to motivate its managers to work toward the companywide goal of leading its industry in innovation. Identify the four stakeholder perspectives that would link to the following objectives, measures, and targets:

Perspective	Objective	Measure	Target
	Profitable new products	New-product ROI	New-product ROI of at least 75 percent
	Work force with cutting-edge skills	Percentage of employees cross-trained on work-group tasks	100 percent of work group cross-trained on new tasks within 30 days
	Agile product design and production processes	Time to market (the time between a product idea and its first sales)	Time to market less than one year for 80 percent of product introductions
	Successful product introductions	New-product market share	Capture 80 percent of new-product market within one year

SOLUTION

Goal: Company leads its industry in innovation

Perspective	Objective	Measure	Target
Financial (investors)	Profitable new products	New-product ROI	New-product ROI of at least 75 percent
Learning and growth (employees)	Work force with cutting-edge skills	Percentage of employees cross-trained on work-group tasks	100 percent of work group cross-trained on new tasks within 30 days
Internal business processes	Agile product design and production processes	Time to market (the time between a product idea and its first sales)	Time to market less than one year for 80 percent of product introductions
Customers	Successful product introductions	New-product market share	Capture 80 percent of new-product market within one year

A LOOK BACK AT ▸ **VAIL RESORTS**

In this chapter's Decision Point, we asked these questions:

- How do managers at **Vail Resorts** link performance measures and set performance targets to achieve performance objectives?
- How do they use the PEAKS system and its integrated database to improve performance management and evaluation?

Managers at Vail Resorts link their organization's vision and strategy to their performance objectives; they then link the objectives to logical performance measures; and, finally, they set performance targets. A balanced scorecard approach enables them to consider the perspectives of all the organization's stakeholders: financial (investors), learning and growth (employees), internal business processes, and customers.

As we indicated in the Decision Point, Vail Resorts' managers like the PEAKS all-in-one-card system because it is a quick and easy way of collecting huge amounts of valuable and versatile information. Whenever a guest's card is scanned, new data enter the system and become part of an integrated management information system that allows managers to measure and control costs, quality, and performance in all of the resort's areas. The system's ability to store both financial and nonfinancial data about all aspects of the resort enables managers to learn about and balance the interests of all the organization's stakeholders. The managers can then use the information to answer traditional financial questions about such matters as the cost of sales and the value of inventory (e.g., food ingredients in the resort's restaurants and the merchandise in its shops) and to obtain performance data about the resort's activities, products, services, and customers. In addition, the system provides managers with timely feedback about their performance, which encourages continuous improvement.

Review Problem

Evaluating Profit Center and Investment Center Performance

LO3 LO4 LO5

Assume that a company like **Vail Resorts** has just acquired Winter Wonderland, a full-service resort and spa. When Vail investigated Winter Wonderland, it learned the following: Mary Fortenberry, the resort's general manager, is responsible for guest activities, administration, and food and lodging. In addition, she is solely responsible for the resort's capital investments. The organization chart below shows the resort's various activities and the levels of authority that Fortenberry has established:

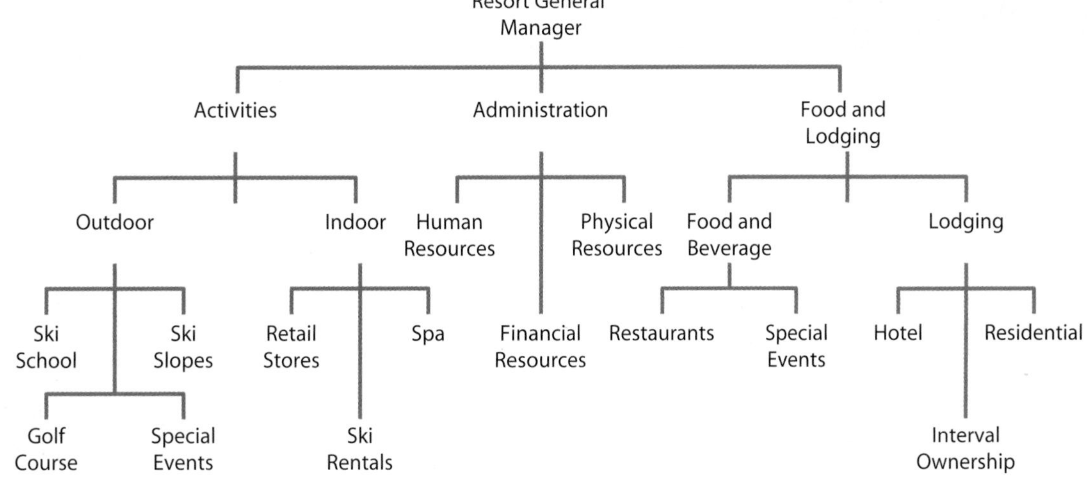

Three divisional managers receive compensation based on their division's performance and have the authority to make employee compensation decisions for their division. Alexandra Patel manages the Food and Lodging Division. The Food and Lodging Division's master budget and actual results for the year ended June 30 follow.

	Master Budget	Actual Results
Winter Wonderland Resort		
Food and Lodging Division		
For the Year Ended June 30		
(Dollar amounts in thousands)		
Guest days	4,000	4,100
Sales	$38,000	$40,000
Variable cost of sales	24,000	25,000
Variable selling and administrative expenses	4,000	4,250
Fixed cost of sales	2,000	1,800
Fixed selling and administrative expenses	2,500	2,500

Required

1. What types of responsibility centers are Administration, Food and Lodging, and Resort General Manager?
2. Assume that Food and Lodging is a profit center. Prepare a performance report using variable costing and flexible budgeting. Determine the variances between actual results and the corresponding figures in the flexible budget and the master budget.
3. Assume that the divisional managers have been assigned responsibility for capital expenditures and that their divisions are thus investment centers. Food and Lodging is expected to generate a desired ROI of at least 30 percent on average assets invested of $10,000,000.
   a. Compute the division's return on investment and residual income using the average assets invested in both the actual and budget calculations.
   b. Using the ROI and residual income, evaluate Alexandra Patel's performance as divisional manager.
4. Compute the division's actual economic value added if the division's assets are $12,000,000, current liabilities are $3,000,000, after-tax operating income is $4,500,000, and the cost of capital is 20 percent.

Answers to Review Problem

1. Administration: discretionary cost center; Food and Lodging: profit center; Resort General Manager: investment center

2. Performance report:

Winter Wonderland Resort Food and Lodging Division For the Year Ended June 30 (Dollar amounts in thousands)							
	Actual Results	**Variance**		**Flexible Budget**	**Variance**		**Master Budget**
Guest days	4,100	—		4,100	100	(F)	4,000
Sales	$40,000	$1,050	(F)	$38,950	$950	(F)	$38,000
Controllable variable costs							
Variable cost of sales	25,000	400	(U)	24,600	600	(U)	24,000
Variable selling and administrative expenses	4,250	150	(U)	4,100	100	(U)	4,000
Contribution margin	$10,750	$ 500	(F)	$10,250	$250	(F)	$10,000
Controllable fixed costs							
Fixed cost of sales	1,800	200	(F)	2,000	—		2,000
Fixed selling and administrative expenses	2,500	—		2,500	—		2,500
Division operating income	$ 6,450	$ 700	(F)	$ 5,750	$250	(F)	$ 5,500

3. a. *Return on investment*

   Actual results: $6,450,000 ÷ $10,000,000 = 64.50%

   Flexible budget: $5,750,000 ÷ $10,000,000 = 57.50%

   Master budget: $5,500,000 ÷ $10,000,000 = 55.00%

   Residual income

   Actual results: $6,450,000 − 30%($10,000,000) = $3,450,000

   Flexible budget: $5,750,000 − 30%($10,000,000) = $2,750,000

   Master budget: $5,500,000 − 30%($10,000,000) = $2,500,000

   b. Alexandra Patel's performance as the divisional manager of Food and Lodging exceeds company performance expectations. Actual ROI was 64.5 percent, whereas the company expected an ROI of 30 percent and the flexible budget and the master budget showed projections of 57.5 percent and 55.0 percent, respectively. Residual income also exceeded expectations. The Food and Lodging Division generated $3,450,000 in residual income when the flexible budget and master budget had projected RIs of $2,750,000 and $2,500,000, respectively. The performance report for the division shows 100 more guest days than had been anticipated and a favorable controllable fixed cost variance. As a manager, Patel will investigate the unfavorable variances associated with her controllable variable costs.

4. Economic value added:

   $4,500,000 − 20%($12,000,000 − $3,000,000) = $2,700,000

LO1 Define a *performance management and evaluation system,* and describe how the balanced scorecard aligns performance with organizational goals.

An effective performance management and evaluation system accounts for and reports on both financial and nonfinancial performance so that a company can ascertain how well it is doing, where it is going, and what improvements will make it more profitable. Each company must develop a set of performance measures appropriate to its specific needs. Besides answering basic questions about what to measure and how to measure, managers must consider a variety of other issues. They must collaborate to develop a group of measures, such as the balanced scorecard, that will help them determine how to improve performance.

The balanced scorecard is a framework that links the perspectives of an organization's four basic stakeholder groups—financial, learning and growth, internal business processes, and customers—with its mission and vision, performance measures, strategic and tactical plans, and resources. Ideally, managers should see how their actions help to achieve organizational goals and understand how their compensation is linked to their actions. The balanced scorecard assumes that an organization will get what it measures.

LO2 Define *responsibility accounting,* and describe the role that responsibility centers play in performance management and evaluation.

Responsibility accounting classifies data according to areas of responsibility and reports each area's activities by including only the revenue, cost, and resource categories that the assigned manager can control. There are five types of responsibility centers: cost, discretionary cost, revenue, profit, and investment. Performance reporting by responsibility center allows the source of a cost, revenue, or resource to be traced to the manager who controls it and thus makes it easier to evaluate a manager's performance.

LO3 Prepare performance reports for cost centers using flexible budgets and for profit centers using variable costing.

Performance reports contain information about the costs, revenues, and resources that individual managers can control. The content and format of a performance report depend on the nature of the responsibility center.

The performance of a cost center can be evaluated by comparing its actual costs with the corresponding amounts in the flexible and master budgets. A flexible budget is a summary of anticipated costs for a range of activity levels. It provides forecasted cost data that can be adjusted for changes in the level of output. A flexible budget is derived by multiplying actual unit output by predetermined standard unit costs for each cost item in the report.

The performance of a profit center is usually evaluated by comparing the profit center's actual income statement results with its budgeted income statement. When variable costing is used, the controllable costs of the profit center's manager are classified as variable or fixed. The resulting performance report takes the form of a contribution margin income statement. The variable costing income statement is useful because it focuses on cost variability and the profit center's contribution to operating income.

LO4 Prepare performance reports for investment centers using the traditional measures of return on investment and residual income and the newer measure of economic value added.

Traditionally, the most common performance measure has been return on investment (ROI). The basic formula is ROI = Operating Income ÷ Assets Invested. Return on investment can also be examined in terms of profit margin and asset turnover. In this case, ROI = Profit Margin × Asset Turnover, where Profit Margin = Operating Income ÷ Sales, and Asset Turnover = Sales ÷ Assets Invested. Residual income (RI) is the operating income that an investment center earns above a minimum desired return on invested assets. It is expressed as a dollar amount: Residual Income = Operating Income − (Desired ROI × Assets

Invested). It is the amount of profit left after subtracting a predetermined desired income target for an investment. Today, businesses are increasingly using the shareholder wealth created by an investment center, or economic value added (EVA), as a performance measure. The calculation of economic value added can be quite complex because of the various adjustments it involves. Basically, it is similar to the calculation of residual income: EVA = After-Tax Operating Income − Cost of Capital in Dollars. A manager can improve the economic value of an investment center by increasing sales, decreasing costs, decreasing assets, or lowering the cost of capital.

LO5 Explain how properly linked performance incentives and measures add value for all stakeholders in performance management and evaluation.

The effectiveness of a performance management and evaluation system depends on how well it coordinates the goals of responsibility centers, managers, and the entire company. Performance can be optimized by linking goals to measurable objectives and targets and tying appropriate compensation incentives to the achievement of those targets. Common types of incentive compensation are cash bonuses, awards, profit-sharing plans, and stock options. If management values the perspectives of all of its stakeholder groups, its performance management and evaluation system will balance and benefit all interests.

REVIEW of Concepts and Terminology

The following concepts and terms were introduced in this chapter:

Balanced scorecard 1019 (LO1)

Controllable costs and revenues 1022 (LO2)

Cost center 1022 (LO2)

Cost of capital 1033 (LO4)

Discretionary cost center 1023 (LO2)

Flexible budget 1026 (LO3)

Investment center 1024 (LO2)

Organization chart 1024 (LO2)

Performance-based pay 1036 (LO5)

Performance management and evaluation system 1018 (LO1)

Performance measurement 1018 (LO1)

Profit center 1024 (LO2)

Responsibility accounting 1021 (LO2)

Responsibility center 1022 (LO2)

Revenue center 1024 (LO2)

Variable costing 1027 (LO3)

Key Ratios

Asset turnover 1030 (LO4)

Economic value added (EVA) 1032 (LO4)

Profit margin 1030 (LO4)

Residual income (RI) 1032 (LO4)

Return on investment (ROI) 1029 (LO4)

CHAPTER ASSIGNMENTS

BUILDING Your Basic Knowledge and Skills

Short Exercises

LO1 Balanced Scorecard

SE 1. One of your college's overall goals is customer satisfaction. In light of that goal, match each of the following stakeholders' perspectives with the appropriate objective:

Perspective	Objective
1. Financial (investors)	a. Customer satisfaction means that the faculty (employees) engages in cutting-edge research.
2. Learning and growth	b. Customer satisfaction means that students receive their degrees in four years.
3. Internal business processes	c. Customer satisfaction means that the college has a winning athletics program.
4. Customers	d. Customer satisfaction means that fund-raising campaigns are successful.

LO2 Responsibility Centers

SE 2. Identify each of the following as a cost center, a discretionary cost center, a revenue center, a profit center, or an investment center:

1. The manager of center A is responsible for generating cash inflows and incurring costs with the goal of making money for the company. The manager has no responsibility for assets.
2. Center B produces a product that is not sold to an external party but transferred to another center for further processing.
3. The manager of center C is responsible for the telephone order operations of a large retailer.
4. Center D designs, produces, and sells products to external parties. The manager makes both long-term and short-term decisions.
5. Center E provides human resource support for the other centers in the company.

LO2 Controllable Costs

SE 3. Ha Kim is the manager of the Paper Cutting Department in the Northwest Division of Striking Paper Products. Identify each of the following costs as either controllable or not controllable by Kim:

1. Lumber Department hauling costs
2. Salaries of cutting machine workers
3. Cost of cutting machine parts
4. Cost of electricity for the Northwest Division
5. Vice president's salary

LO3 Cost Center Performance Report

SE 4. Complete the following performance report for cost center C for the month ended December 31:

	Actual Results	Variance	Flexible Budget	Variance	Master Budget
Units produced	80	0	?	(20) U	100
Center costs					
Direct materials	$ 84	$?	$ 80	$?	$100
Direct labor	150	?	?	40 (F)	200
Variable overhead	?	20 (U)	240	?	300
Fixed overhead	270	?	250	?	250
Total cost	$?	$34 (U)	$?	$120 (F)	$850
Performance measures					
Defect-free units to total produced	80%	?	N/A	N/A	90%
Average throughput time per unit	11 minutes	?	N/A	N/A	10 minutes

LO3 **Profit Center Performance Report**

SE 5. Complete this performance report for profit center P for the month ended December 31:

	Actual Results	Variance	Master Budget
Sales	$?	$ 20 (F)	$ 120
Controllable variable costs			
Variable cost of goods sold	25	10 (U)	?
Variable selling and administrative expenses	15	?	5
Contribution margin	$100	$?	$ 100
Controllable fixed costs	?	20 (F)	60
Profit center operating income	$ 60	$ 20 (F)	$?
Performance measures			
Number of orders processed	50	20 (F)	?
Average daily sales	$?	$0.68 (F)	$4.00
Number of units sold	100	40 (F)	?

LO4 **Return on Investment**

SE 6. Complete the profit margin, asset turnover, and return on investment calculations for investment centers D and V

	Subsidiary D	Subsidiary V
Sales	$1,650	$2,840
Operating income	$180	$210
Average assets invested	$940	$1,250
Profit margin	?	7.39%
Asset turnover	1.76 times	?
ROI	?	?

LO4 **Return on Investment**

SE 7. Complete the average assets invested, profit margin, asset turnover, and return on investment calculations for investment centers J and K on the next page.

	Subsidiary J	Subsidiary K
Sales	$2,000	$2,000
Operating income	$500	$800
Beginning assets invested	$4,000	$500
Ending assets invested	$6,000	$1,500
Average assets invested	$?	$?
Profit margin	25%	?
Asset turnover	?	2 times
ROI	?	?

LO4 **Residual Income**

SE 8. Complete the operating income, ending assets invested, average assets invested, and residual income calculations for investment centers H and F:

	Subsidiary H	Subsidiary F
Sales	$20,000	$25,000
Operating income	$1,500	$?
Beginning assets invested	$4,000	$500
Ending assets invested	$6,000	$?
Average assets invested	$?	$1,000
Desired ROI	20%	20%
Residual income	$?	$600

LO4 **Economic Value Added**

SE 9. Complete the current liabilities, total assets−current liabilities, and economic value added calculations for investment centers M and N:

	Subsidiary M	Subsidiary N
Sales	$15,000	$18,000
After-tax operating income	$1,000	$1,100
Total assets	$4,000	$5,000
Current liabilities	$1,000	$?
Total assets − current liabilities	$?	$3,500
Cost of capital	15%	15%
Economic value added	$?	$?

LO5 **Coordination of Goals**

SE 10. One of your college's goals is customer satisfaction. In view of that goal, identify each of the following as a linked objective, a measure, or a performance target:

1. To have successful fund-raising campaigns
2. Number of publications per year per tenure-track faculty
3. To increase the average donation by 10 percent
4. Average number of dollars raised per donor
5. To have faculty engage in cutting-edge research
6. To increase the number of publications per faculty member by at least one per year

Exercises

LO1 **Balanced Scorecard**

E 1. Biggs Industries is considering adopting the balanced scorecard and has compiled the following list of possible performance measures. Select the balanced scorecard perspective that best matches each performance measure.

Performance Measure	Balanced Scorecard Perspective
1. Residual income	a. Financial (investors)
2. Customer satisfaction rating	b. Learning and growth (employees)
3. Employee absentee rate	c. Internal business processes
4. Growth in profits	d. Customers
5. On-time deliveries	
6. Manufacturing processing time	

LO1 Balanced Scorecard

E 2. Valient Online Products is considering adopting the balanced scorecard and has compiled the following list of possible performance measures. Select the balanced scorecard perspective that best matches each performance measure.

Performance Measure	Balanced Scorecard Perspective
1. Economic value added	a. Financial (investors)
2. Employee turnover	b. Learning and growth (employees)
3. Average daily sales	c. Internal business processes
4. Defect-free units	d. Customers
5. Number of repeat customer visits	
6. Employee training hours	

LO1 Performance Measures

E 3. Beva Washington wants to measure her division's product quality. Link an appropriate performance measure with each balanced scorecard perspective.

Product Quality	Possible Performance Measures
1. Financial (investors)	a. Number of defective products returned
2. Learning and growth (employees)	b. Number of products failing inspection
3. Internal business processes	c. Increased market share
4. Customers	d. Savings from employee suggestions

LO1 Performance Measures

E 4. Sam Yu wants to measure customer satisfaction within his region. Link an appropriate performance measure with each balanced scorecard perspective.

Customer Satisfaction	Possible Performance Measures
1. Financial (investors)	a. Number of staff promotions
2. Learning and growth (employees)	b. Number of repeat customers
3. Internal business processes	c. Number of process improvements
4. Customers	d. Percentage sales increase over last period

LO2 Responsibility Centers

E 5. Identify the most appropriate type of responsibility center for each of the following organizational units:

1. A manufacturing department of a large corporation
2. An eye clinic in a community hospital
3. The South American division of a multinational company
4. The food preparation plant of a large restaurant chain
5. The catalog order department of a retailer

LO2 **Controllable Costs**

E 6. Angel Sweets produces pies. The company has the following three-tiered manufacturing structure:

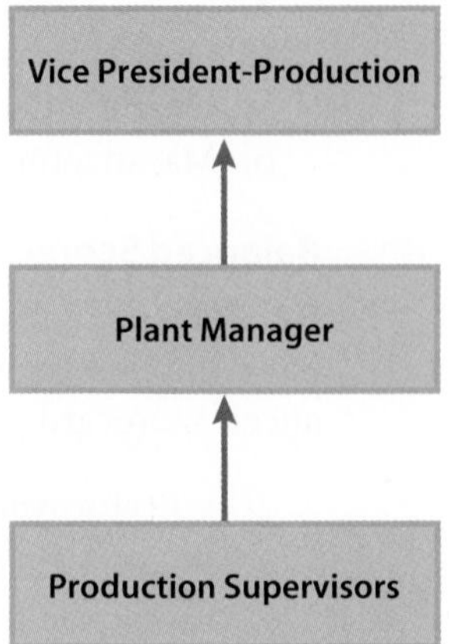

Identify the manager responsible for each of the following costs:

1. Repair and maintenance costs
2. Materials handling costs
3. Direct labor
4. Supervisors' salaries
5. Maintenance of plant grounds
6. Depreciation–equipment
7. Plant manager's salary
8. Cost of materials used
9. Storage of finished goods
10. Property taxes–plant
11. Depreciation–plant

LO2 **Organization Chart**

E 7. Happy Industries wants to formalize its management structure by designing an organization chart. The company has a president, a board of directors, and two vice presidents. Four discretionary cost centers—Financial Resources, Human Resources, Information Resources, and Physical Resources—report to one of the vice presidents. The other vice president has one manufacturing plant with three subassembly areas reporting to her. Draw the company's organization chart.

LO3 **Performance Reports**

E 8. Jackie Jefferson, a new employee at Handown, Inc., is learning about the various types of performance reports. Describe the typical contents of a performance report for each type of responsibility center.

LO3 **Variable Costing Income Statement**

E 9. Vegan, LLC, owns a chain of gourmet vegetarian take-out markets. Last month, Store Q generated the following information: sales, $890,000; direct materials, $220,000; direct labor, $97,000; variable overhead, $150,000; fixed overhead, $130,000; variable selling and administrative expenses, $44,500; and fixed selling expenses, $82,300. There were no beginning or ending inventories. Average daily sales (25 business days) were $35,600. Customer orders processed totaled 15,000.

Vegan had budgeted monthly sales of $900,000; direct materials, $210,000; direct labor, $100,000; variable overhead, $140,000; fixed overhead, $140,000; variable selling and administrative expenses, $45,000; and fixed selling expenses, $60,000. Store Q had been projected to do $36,000 in daily sales and process 16,000 customer orders. Using this information, prepare a performance report for Store Q.

LO3 **Variable Costing Income Statement**

E 10. The income statement in the traditional reporting format for Green Products, Inc., for the year ended December 31, is as follows:

Green Products, Inc. Income Statement For the Year Ended December 31	
Sales	$296,400
Cost of goods sold	112,750
Gross margin	$183,650
Selling expenses	
Variable	69,820
Fixed	36,980
Administrative expenses	27,410
Operating income	$ 49,440

Total fixed manufacturing costs for the year were $16,750. All administrative expenses are considered to be fixed.

Using this information, prepare an income statement for Green Products, Inc., for the year ended December 31, using the variable costing format.

LO3 Performance Report for a Cost Center

E 11. Archer, LLC, owns a blueberry processing plant. Last month, the plant generated the following information: blueberries processed, 50,000 pounds; direct materials, $50,000; direct labor, $10,000; variable overhead, $12,000; and fixed overhead, $13,000. There were no beginning or ending inventories. Average daily pounds processed (25 business days) were 2,000. Average rate of processing was 250 pounds per hour.

At the beginning of the month, Archer had budgeted costs of blueberries, $45,000; direct labor, $10,000; variable overhead, $14,000; and fixed overhead, $14,000. The monthly master budget was based on producing 50,000 pounds of blueberries each month. This means that the plant had been projected to process 2,000 pounds daily at the rate of 240 pounds per hour.

Using this information, prepare a performance report for the month for the blueberry processing plant. Include a flexible budget and a computation of variances in your report. Indicate whether the variances are favorable (F) or unfavorable (U) to the performance of the plant.

LO4 Investment Center Performance

E 12. Momence Associates is evaluating the performance of three divisions: Maple, Oaks, and Juniper. Using the following data, compute the return on investment and residual income for each division, compare the divisions' performance, and comment on the factors that influenced performance:

	Maple	Oaks	Juniper
Sales	$100,000	$100,000	$100,000
Operating income	$10,000	$10,000	$20,000
Assets invested	$25,000	$12,500	$25,000
Desired ROI	40%	40%	40%

LO4 Economic Value Added

E 13. Leesburg, LLP, is evaluating the performance of three divisions: Lake, Sumter, and Poe. Using the data that appear on the next page, compute the economic value added by each division, and comment on each division's performance.

	Lake	Sumter	Poe
Sales	$100,000	$100,000	$100,000
After-tax operating income	$10,000	$10,000	$20,000
Total assets	$25,000	$12,500	$25,000
Current liabilities	$5,000	$5,000	$5,000
Cost of capital	15%	15%	15%

LO5 Performance Incentives

E 14. Dynamic Consulting is advising Solid Industries on the short-term and long-term effectiveness of cash bonuses, awards, profit sharing, and stock as performance incentives. Prepare a chart identifying the effectiveness of each incentive as either long-term or short-term or both.

LO5 Goal Congruence

E 15. Serious Toys, Inc., has adopted the balanced scorecard to motivate its managers to work toward the companywide goal of leading its industry in innovation. Identify the four stakeholder perspectives that would link to the following objectives, measures, and targets:

Perspective	Objective	Measure	Target
	Profitable new products	New product RI	New-product RI of at least $100,000
	Work force with cutting-edge skills	Percentage of employees cross-trained on work-group tasks	90 percent of work-group cross-trained on new tasks within 10 days
	Agile production processes	Time to market (the time between a product idea and its first sales)	Time to market less than 6 months for 80% of product introductions
	Successful product introductions	New-product market share	Capture 75% of new product market within 6 months

Problems

LO2 LO3 Evaluating Cost Center Performance

P 1. Beverage Products, LLC, manufactures metal beverage containers. The division that manufactures soft-drink beverage cans for the North American market has two plants that operate 24 hours a day, 365 days a year. The plants are evaluated as cost centers. Small tools and supplies are considered variable overhead. Depreciation and rent are considered fixed overhead. The master budget for a plant and the operating results of the two North American plants, East Coast and West Coast, are as follows:

	Master Budget	East Coast	West Coast
Center costs			
Rolled aluminum ($0.01)	$4,000,000	$3,492,000	$5,040,000
Lids ($0.005)	2,000,000	1,980,000	2,016,000
Direct labor ($0.0025)	1,000,000	864,000	1,260,000
Small tools and supplies ($0.0013)	520,000	432,000	588,000
Depreciation and rent	480,000	480,000	480,000
Total cost	$8,000,000	$7,248,000	$9,384,000

Performance measures			
Cans processed per hour	45,662	41,096	47,945
Average daily pounds of scrap metal	5	6	7
Cans processed (in millions)	400	360	420

Required

1. Prepare a performance report for the East Coast plant. Include a flexible budget and variance analysis.
2. Prepare a performance report for the West Coast plant. Include a flexible budget and variance analysis.
3. Compare the two plants, and comment on their performance.

Manager insight ▶ 4. Explain why a flexible budget should be prepared.

LO3 **Traditional and Variable Costing Income Statements**

P 2. Roofing tile is the major product of the Tops Corporation. The company had a particularly good year, as shown by its operating data. It sold 88,400 cases of tile. Variable cost of goods sold was $848,640; variable selling expenses were $132,600; fixed overhead was $166,680; fixed selling expenses were $152,048; and fixed administrative expenses were $96,450. Selling price was $18 per case. There were no partially completed jobs in process at the beginning or the end of the year. Finished goods inventory had been used up at the end of the previous year.

Required

1. Prepare the calendar year-end income statement for the Tops Corporation using the traditional reporting format.
2. Prepare the calendar year-end income statement for the Tops Corporation using the variable costing format.

LO2 LO3 LO4 **Evaluating Profit Center and Investment Center Performance**

P 3. Bobbie Howell, the managing partner of the law firm Howell, Bagan, and Clark, LLP, makes asset acquisition and disposal decisions for the firm. As managing partner, she supervises the partners in charge of the firm's three branch offices. Those partners have the authority to make employee compensation decisions. The partners' compensation depends on the profitability of their branch office. Victoria Smith manages the City Branch, which has the following master budget and actual results for the year:

	Master Budget	Actual Results
Billed hours	5,000	4,900
Revenue	$250,000	$254,800
Controllable variable costs		
Direct labor	120,000	137,200
Variable overhead	40,000	34,300
Contribution margin	$ 90,000	$ 83,300
Controllable fixed costs		
Rent	30,000	30,000
Other administrative expenses	45,000	42,000
Branch operating income	$ 15,000	$ 11,300

Required

1. Assume that the City Branch is a profit center. Prepare a performance report that includes a flexible budget. Determine the variances between actual results, the flexible budget, and the master budget.

2. Evaluate Victoria Smith's performance as manager of the City Branch.
3. Assume that the branch managers are assigned responsibility for capital expenditures and that the branches are thus investment centers. City Branch is expected to generate a desired ROI of at least 30 percent on average invested assets of $40,000.
   a. Compute the branch's return on investment and residual income.
   b. Using the ROI and residual income, evaluate Victoria Smith's performance as branch manager. (Manager insight ▶)

LO4 **Return on Investment and Residual Income**

P 4. Ornamental Iron is a division of Iron Foundry Company. Its balance sheets and income statements for the past two years appear below.

Iron Foundry Company
Ornamental Iron Division
Balance Sheet
December 31

	This Year	Last Year
Assets		
Cash	$ 5,000	$ 3,000
Accounts receivable	10,000	8,000
Inventory	30,000	32,000
Other current assets	600	600
Plant assets	128,300	120,300
Total assets	$173,900	$163,900
Liabilities and Stockholders' Equity		
Current liabilities	$ 13,900	$ 10,000
Long-term liabilities	90,000	93,900
Stockholders' equity	70,000	60,000
Total liabilities and stockholders' equity	$173,900	$163,900

Iron Foundry Company
Ornamental Iron Division
Income Statement
For the Years Ended December 31

	This Year	Last Year
Sales	$180,000	$160,000
Cost of goods sold	100,000	90,000
Selling and administrative expenses	27,500	26,500
Operating income	$ 52,500	$ 43,500
Income taxes expense	17,850	14,790
Net income	$ 34,650	$ 28,710

Required

1. Compute the division's profit margin, asset turnover, and return on investment for this year and last year. Beginning total assets for last year were $157,900. Round to two decimal places.
2. The desired return on investment for the division has been set at 12 percent. Compute Ornamental Iron's residual income for this year and last year.
3. The cost of capital for the division is 8 percent. Compute the division's economic value added for this year and last year.

Manager insight ▶ 4. Before drawing conclusions about this division's performance, what additional information would you want?

LO4 **Return on Investment and Economic Value Added**

P 5. The balance sheet for the New Products Division of NuBone Corporation showed invested assets of $200,000 at the beginning of the year and $300,000 at the end of the year. During the year, the division's operating income was $12,500 on sales of $500,000.

Required

1. Compute the division's residual income if the desired ROI is 6 percent.
2. Compute the following performance measures for the division: (a) profit margin, (b) asset turnover, and (c) return on investment
3. Recompute the division's ROI under each of the following independent assumptions:
   a. Sales increase from $500,000 to $600,000, causing operating income to rise from $12,500 to $30,000.
   b. Invested assets at the beginning of the year are reduced from $200,000 to $100,000.
   c. Operating expenses are reduced, causing operating income to rise from $12,500 to $20,000.
4. Compute NuBone's EVA if total corporate assets are $500,000, current liabilities are $80,000, after-tax operating income is $50,000, and the cost of capital is 8 percent.

Alternate Problems

LO2 LO3 **Evaluating Cost Center Performance**

P 6. Plastic Products, LLC, manufactures plastic beverage bottles. The division that manufactures water bottles for the North American market has two plants that operate 24 hours a day, 365 days a year. The plants are evaluated as cost centers. Small tools and supplies are considered variable overhead. Depreciation and rent are considered fixed overhead. The master budget for a plant and the operating results of the two North American plants, North and South, are as follows:

	Master Budget	North Actual	South Actual
Center costs			
Plastic pellets ($0.009)	$4,500,000	$3,880,000	$5,500,000
Caps ($0.004)	2,000,000	1,990,000	2,000,000
Direct labor ($0.002)	1,000,000	865,000	1,240,000
Small tools and supplies ($0.0005)	250,000	198,000	280,000
Depreciation and rent	450,000	440,000	480,000
Total cost	$8,200,000	$7,373,000	$9,500,000

Performance measures			
Bottles processed per hour	69,450	62,000	70,250
Average daily pounds of scrap	5	6	7
Bottles processed (in millions)	500	450	520

Required

1. Prepare a performance report for the North plant. Include a flexible budget and variance analysis.
2. Prepare a performance report for the South plant. Include a flexible budget and variance analysis.
3. Compare the two plants, and comment on their performance.

Manager insight ▶ 4. Explain why a flexible budget should be prepared.

LO3 **Traditional and Variable Costing Income Statements**

P 7. Interior designers often use the deluxe carpet products of Lux Mills, Inc. The Maricopa blend is the company's top product line. In March, Lux produced and sold 174,900 square yards of Maricopa blend. Factory operating data for the month included variable cost of goods sold of $2,623,500 and fixed overhead of $346,875. Other expenses were variable selling expenses, $166,155; fixed selling expenses, $148,665; and fixed general and administrative expenses, $231,500. Total sales revenue equaled $3,935,250. All production took place in March, and there was no work in process at month end. Goods are usually shipped when completed.

Required

1. Prepare the March income statement for Lux Mills, Inc., using the traditional reporting format.
2. Prepare the March income statement for Lux Mills, Inc., using the variable costing format.

LO2 LO3 LO4 **Return on Investment and Residual Income**

P 8. Portia Carter is the president of a company that owns six multiplex movie theaters. Carter has delegated decision-making authority to the theater managers for all decisions except those relating to capital expenditures and film selection. The theater managers' compensation depends on the profitability of their theaters. Max Burgman, the manager of the Park Theater, had the following master budget and actual results for the month:

	Master Budget	Actual Results
Tickets sold	120,000	110,000
Revenue–tickets	$ 840,000	$ 880,000
Revenue–concessions	480,000	330,000
Total revenue	$1,320,000	$1,210,000
Controllable variable costs		
Concessions	120,000	99,000
Direct labor	420,000	330,000
Variable overhead	540,000	550,000
Contribution margin	$ 240,000	$ 231,000
Controllable fixed costs		
Rent	55,000	55,000
Other administrative expenses	45,000	50,000
Theater operating income	$ 140,000	$ 126,000

Required

1. Assuming that the theaters are profit centers, prepare a performance report for the Park Theater. Include a flexible budget. Determine the variances between actual results, the flexible budget, and the master budget.
2. Evaluate Burgman's performance as manager of the Park Theater.
3. Assume that the managers are assigned responsibility for capital expenditures and that the theaters are thus investment centers. Park Theater is expected to generate a desired ROI of at least 6 percent on average invested assets of $2,000,000.
   a. Compute the theater's return on investment and residual income.
   b. Using the ROI and residual income, evaluate Burgman's performance as manager. (Manager insight ▶)

LO4 Return on Investment and Residual Income

P 9. The financial results for the past two years for ABB Company, follow.

ABB Company
Balance Sheet
December 31

	This Year	Last Year
Assets		
Cash	$ 9,000	$ 4,000
Accounts receivable	40,000	50,000
Inventory	30,000	25,000
Other current assets	1,000	1,000
Plant assets	120,000	100,000
Total assets	$200,000	$180,000
Liabilities and Stockholders' Equity		
Current liabilities	$ 10,000	$ 10,000
Long-term Liabilities	20,000	10,000
Stockholders' equity	170,000	160,000
Total liabilities and stockholders' equity	$200,000	$180,000

ABB Company
Income Statement
For the Years Ended
December 31

	This Year	Last Year
Sales	$250,000	$200,000
Cost of goods sold	150,000	115,000
Selling and administrative expenses	30,000	25,000
Operating income	$ 70,000	$ 60,000
Income taxes expense	21,000	18,000
Net income	$ 49,000	$ 42,000

Required

1. Compute the company's profit margin, asset turnover, and return on investment for this year and last year. Beginning total assets for last year were $160,000. Round to two decimal places.

2. The desired return on investment for the company has been set at 10 percent. Compute ABB's residual income for this year and last year.
3. The cost of capital for the company is 5 percent. Compute the company's economic value added for this year and last year.

Manager insight ▶ 4. Before drawing conclusions about this company's performance, what additional information would you want?

LO4 **Return on Investment and Economic Value Added**

P 10. Micanopy Company makes replicas of Indian artifacts. The balance sheet for the Arrowhead Division showed that the company had invested assets of $300,000 at the beginning of the year and $500,000 at the end of the year. During the year, Arrowhead Division's operating income was $80,000 on sales of $1,200,000.

Required

1. Compute Arrowhead Division's residual income if the desired ROI is 20 percent.
2. Compute the following performance measures for the division: (a) profit margin, (b) asset turnover, and (c) return on investment.
3. Compute Micanopy Company's economic value added if total corporate assets are $6,000,000, current liabilities are $800,000, after-tax operating income is $750,000, and the cost of capital is 12 percent.

ENHANCING Your Knowledge, Skills, and Critical Thinking

LO1 **Balanced Scorecard Results**

C 1. IT, Inc., has adopted the balanced scorecard approach to motivate the managers of its product divisions to work toward the companywide goal of leading its industry in innovation. The corporation's selected performance measures and scorecard results are as follows:

Measure	Division A	Division B	Division C	Performance Target
New product ROI	80%	75%	70%	75%
Employees cross-trained in new tasks within 30 days	95	96	94	100
New product's time to market less than one year	85	90	86	80
New product's market share one year after introduction	50	100	80	80

Can you effectively compare the performance of the three divisions against the targets? What other measures mentioned in this chapter are needed to evaluate performance effectively?

LO1 LO2 **Responsibility Centers**

C 2. Wood4Fun makes wooden playground equipment for the institutional and consumer markets. The company strives for low-cost, high-quality production because it operates in a highly competitive market in which product price is set by the marketplace and is not based on production costs. The company is organized into responsibility centers. The vice president of manufacturing is responsible for three manufacturing plants. The vice president of sales is responsible for four sales regions. Recently, these two vice presidents began to disagree about whether the manufacturing plants are cost centers or profit centers. The vice president of manufacturing views the plants as cost centers because the managers of the plants control only product-related costs. The vice president of sales believes the plants are profit centers because product quality and product cost strongly affect company profits.

1. Identify the controllable performance that Wood4Fun values and wants to measure. Give at least three examples of performance measures that Wood4-Fun could use to monitor such performance.
2. For the manufacturing plants, what type of responsibility center is most consistent with the controllable performance Wood4Fun wants to measure?
3. For the sales regions, what type of responsibility center is most appropriate?

LO1 LO2 LO3 LO5

Types of Responsibility Centers

C 3. Yuma Foods acquired Aldo's Tortillas several years ago. Aldo's has continued to operate as an independent company, except that Yuma Foods has exclusive authority over capital investments, production quantity, and pricing decisions because Yuma has been Aldo's only customer since the acquisition. Yuma uses return on investment to evaluate the performance of Aldo's manager. The most recent performance report is as follows:

Yuma Foods
Performance Report for Aldo's Tortillas
For the Year Ended June 30

Sales	$6,000
Variable cost of goods sold	3,000
Variable administrative expenses	1,000
Variable corporate expenses (% of sales)	600
Contribution margin	$1,400
Fixed overhead (includes depreciation of $100)	400
Fixed administrative expenses	500
Operating income	$ 500
Average assets invested	$5,500
Return on investment	9.09%*

*Rounded.

1. Analyze the items listed in the performance report, and identify the items that Aldo controls and those that Yuma controls. In your opinion, what type of responsibility center is Aldo's Tortillas? Explain your response.
2. Prepare a revised performance report for Aldo's Tortillas and an accompanying memo to the president of Yuma Foods that explains why it is important to change the content of the report. Cite some basic principles of responsibility accounting to support your recommendation.

LO1 LO4 LO5

Economic Value Added and Performance

C 4. Sevilla Consulting offers environmental consulting services worldwide. The managers of branch offices are rewarded for superior performance with bonuses based on the economic value that the office adds to the company. Last year's operating results for the entire company and for its three offices, expressed in millions of U.S. dollars, are as follows:

	Worldwide	Europe	Americas	Asia
Cost of capital	9%	10%	8%	12%
Total assets	$210	$70	$70	$70
Current liabilities	$80	$10	$40	$30
After-tax operating income	$15	$5	$5	$5

1. Compute the economic value added for each office worldwide. What factors affect each office's economic value added? How can an office improve its economic value added?
2. If managers' bonuses are based on economic value added to office performance, what specific actions will managers be motivated to take?
3. Is economic value added the only performance measure needed to evaluate investment centers adequately? Explain your response.

LO4 Return on Investment and Residual Income

C 5. Suppose Alexandra Patel, the manager of the Food and Lodging Division at Winter Wonderland Resort, has hired you as a consultant to help her examine her division's performance under several different circumstances.

1. Type the data that follow into an Excel spreadsheet to compute the division's actual return on investment and residual income. (Data are from parts **3** and **4** of this chapter's Review Problem.) Match your data entries to the rows and columns shown below. (**Hint:** Remember to format each cell for the type of numbers it holds, such as percentage, currency, or general.)

	A	B	C	D
1				**Investment Center**
2				**Food and Lodging Division**
3				**Actual Results**
4	Sales			$40,000,000
5	Operating income			$ 6,450,000
6	Average assets invested			$10,000,000
7	Desired ROI			30%
8	Return on Investment			=(D5/D6)
9	Profit Margin			=(D5/D4)
10	Asset Turnover			=(D4/D6)
11	Residual Income			=[D5-(D7*D6)]
12				

2. Patel would like to know how the figures would change if Food and Lodging had a desired ROI of 40 percent and average assets invested of $10,000,000. Revise your spreadsheet from **1** to compute the division's return on investment and residual income under those conditions.
3. Patel also wants to know how the figures would change if Food and Lodging had a desired ROI of 30 percent and average assets invested of $12,000,000. Revise your spreadsheet from **1** to compute the division's return on investment and residual income under those conditions.
4. Does the use of formatted spreadsheets simplify the computation of ROI and residual income? Do such spreadsheets make it easier to perform "what-if" analyses?

LO4 Cookie Company (Continuing Case)

C 6. As we continue with this case, assume that your cookie store is now part of a national chain. The store has been consistently profitable, and sales remain satisfactory despite a temporary economic downturn in your area.

At the first of the year, corporate headquarters set a targeted return on investment of 20 percent for your store. The store currently averages $140,000 in invested assets (beginning invested assets, $130,000; ending invested assets, $150,000) and is projected to have an operating income of $30,800. You are considering whether to take one or both of the following actions before the end of the year:

- Hold off recording and paying $5,000 in bills owed until the start of the next fiscal year.
- Write down to zero value $3,000 in store inventory (nonperishable containers) that you have been unable to sell.

Currently, your bonus is based on store profits. Next year, corporate headquarters is changing its performance incentive program so that bonuses will be based on a store's actual return on investment.

1. What effect would each of the actions that you are considering have on the store's operating income this year? (**Hint:** Use Figure 22-3 to trace the effects.) In your opinion, is either action unethical?
2. Independent of question 1, how would the inventory write-down affect next year's income and return on investment if the inventory is sold for $4,000 next year, when corporate headquarters changes its performance incentive plan for store managers? In your opinion, do you have an ethical dilemma?

CHAPTER

23

Standard Costing and Variance Analysis

The Management Process

PLAN

- ▷ **Prepare the operating budgets, and determine standard costs.**
- ▷ **Establish cost-based goals for products and services.**

PERFORM

- ▷ **Apply cost standards as work is performed in cost centers.**
- ▷ **Collect actual cost data.**

EVALUATE

- ▷ **Use flexible budgets to evaluate manager's performance.**
- ▷ **Calculate variances between standard and actual costs for direct materials, direct labor, variable overhead, and fixed overhead.**
- ▷ **Determine their causes and take corrective action.**

COMMUNICATE

- ▷ **Prepare cost center performance reports using standard costing.**
- ▷ **Prepare comparative analyses of flexible budgets to actual results for materials, labor, and overhead.**

Use standard costing and flexible budgets to evaluate the performance cost centers.

Standard costs are useful tools for management because they are based on realistic estimates of operating costs. Managers use them to develop budgets, to control costs, and to prepare reports. Because of their usefulness in comparing planned and actual costs, standard costs have usually been most closely associated with the performance evaluation of cost centers. In this chapter, we describe how standard costs are computed and how managers use the variances between standard and actual costs to evaluate performance and control costs.

LEARNING OBJECTIVES

LO1 **Define *standard costs*, explain how standard costs are developed, and compute a standard unit cost.** (pp. 1062–1066)

LO2 **Prepare a flexible budget, and describe how managers use variance analysis to control costs.** (pp. 1066–1070)

LO3 **Compute and analyze direct materials variances.** (pp. 1071–1073)

LO4 **Compute and analyze direct labor variances.** (pp. 1074–1077)

LO5 **Compute and analyze overhead variances.** (pp. 1077–1084)

LO6 **Explain how variances are used to evaluate managers' performance.** (pp. 1085–1087)

DECISION POINT ▸ A MANAGER'S FOCUS iROBOT CORPORATION

▸ How does setting performance standards help managers control costs?

▸ How do managers use standard costs to evaluate the performance of cost centers?

Known for its floor-cleaning home robots, Roomba and Scooba, **iRobot Corporation** is a leader in the emerging robotics industry. Its PackBot, a combat-proven mobile robot, has saved many lives by performing hazardous reconnaissance, search, and bomb disposal duties in battle zones worldwide. As iRobot develops the next generation of robots for military, industrial, and home use, its managers will continue to keep the business highly profitable by using design specifications to set standard costs for the company's product lines. Managers in all types of companies use these figures as performance targets and as benchmarks against which to measure actual spending trends and monitor changes in business conditions.

Standard Costing

LO1 Define *standard costs,* explain how standard costs are developed, and compute a standard unit cost.

Standard costs are realistic estimates of costs based on analyses of both past and projected operating costs and conditions. They are usually stated in terms of cost per unit. They provide a standard, or predetermined, performance level for use in **standard costing,** a method of cost control that also includes a measure of actual performance and a measure of the difference, or **variance,** between standard and actual performance. This method of measuring and controlling costs differs from the actual and normal costing methods in that it uses estimated costs exclusively to compute all three elements of product cost—direct materials, direct labor, and overhead.

Standard costing is especially effective for managing cost centers. You may recall that a cost center is a responsibility center in which there are well-defined links between the cost of the resources (direct materials, direct labor, and overhead) and the resulting products or services.

A disadvantage to using standard costing is that it can be expensive because the estimated costs are based not just on past costs, but also on engineering estimates, forecasted demand, worker input, time and motion studies, and type and quality of direct materials. However, this method can be used in any type of business. Both manufacturers and service businesses can use standard costing in conjunction with a job order costing, process costing, or activity-based costing system.

Standard Costs and Managers

Study Note

Standard costs are necessary for planning and control. Budgets are developed from standard costs, and performance is measured against them.

As we noted in the introduction to this chapter, standard costs are useful tools for management. Managers use them to develop budgets, to control costs, and to prepare reports. Because of their usefulness in comparing planned and actual costs, standard costs have usually been most closely associated with the performance evaluation of cost centers.

In recent years, the increasing automation of manufacturing processes has caused a significant decrease in direct labor costs and a corresponding decline in the importance of labor-related standard costs and variances. As a result, managers at manufacturing companies, which once used standard costing for all three elements of product cost, may now apply this method only to direct materials and overhead.

Today, many service organizations' managers also use standard costing. Although a service organization has no direct materials costs, labor and overhead costs are very much a part of providing services, and standard costing is an effective way of planning and controlling them.

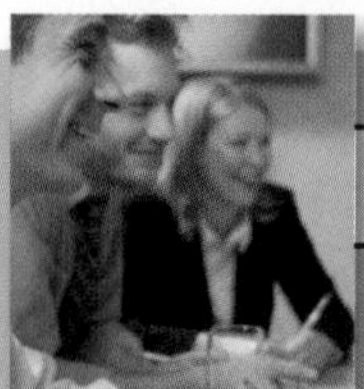

FOCUS ON BUSINESS PRACTICE

Why Go on a Factory Tour?

If you've had some manufacturing experience, you probably understand the importance of standard costing and variance analysis. If you haven't had any manufacturing experience, you can gain insight into the importance of cost planning and control by visiting a factory. Consult your local chamber of commerce for factory tours near you. You can also tour factories online. Check out the virtual production tour of jelly beans at www.jellybelly.com or see how chocolate is made at www.hersheys.com.

Computing Standard Costs

A fully integrated standard costing system uses standard costs for all the elements of product cost: direct materials, direct labor, and overhead. Inventory accounts for materials, work in process, and finished goods, as well as the Cost of Goods Sold account, are maintained and reported in terms of standard costs, and standard unit costs are used to compute account balances. Actual costs are recorded separately so that managers can compare what should have been spent (the standard costs) with the actual costs incurred in the cost center.

A standard unit cost for a manufactured product has the following six elements:

- Price standard for direct materials
- Quantity standard for direct materials
- Standard for direct labor rate
- Standard for direct labor time
- Standard for variable overhead rate
- Standard for fixed overhead rate

To compute a standard unit cost, it is necessary to identify and analyze each of these elements. (A standard unit cost for a service includes only the elements that relate to direct labor and overhead.)

Standard Direct Materials Cost

The **standard direct materials cost** is found by multiplying the price standard for direct materials by the quantity standard for direct materials. For example, if the price standard for a certain item is $2.75 and a specific job calls for a quantity standard of 8 of the items, the standard direct materials cost for that job is computed as follows:

Standard Direct Materials Cost	=	Direct Materials Price Standard	×	Direct Materials Quantity Standard
$22.00	=	$2.75	×	8

The **direct materials price standard** is a careful estimate of the cost of a specific direct material in the next accounting period. An organization's purchasing agent or its purchasing department is responsible for developing price standards for all direct materials and for making the actual purchases. When estimating a direct materials price standard, the purchasing agent or department must take into account all possible price increases, changes in available quantities, and new sources of supply.

The **direct materials quantity standard** is an estimate of the amount of direct materials, including scrap and waste, that will be used in an accounting period. It is influenced by product engineering specifications, the quality of direct materials, the age and productivity of machinery, and the quality and experience of the work force. Production managers or management accountants usually establish and monitor standards for direct materials quantity, but engineers, purchasing agents, and machine operators may also contribute to the development of these standards.

Standard Direct Labor Cost

The **standard direct labor cost** for a product, task, or job order is calculated by multiplying the standard wage for direct labor by the standard hours of direct labor. For example, if the standard direct labor rate is $8.40 per hour and a product takes 1.5 standard direct labor hours to produce, the product's standard direct labor cost is computed as follows:

$$\begin{array}{ccccc} \text{Standard Direct} & = & \text{Direct Labor} & \times & \text{Direct Labor} \\ \text{Labor Cost} & & \text{Rate Standard} & & \text{Time Standard} \\ \$12.60 & = & \$8.40 & \times & 1.5 \text{ hours} \end{array}$$

Study Note

Both the direct labor rate standard and the direct labor time standard are based on an average of the different levels of skilled workers, and both are related to the production of one unit or batch.

The **direct labor rate standard** is the hourly direct labor rate that is expected to prevail during the next accounting period for each function or job classification. Although rate ranges are established for each type of worker and rates vary within those ranges according to each worker's experience and length of service, an average standard rate is developed for each task. Even if the person making the product is paid more or less than the standard rate, the standard rate is used to calculate the standard direct labor cost. Standard labor rates are fairly easy to develop because labor rates are either set by a labor union contract or defined by the company.

The **direct labor time standard** is the expected labor time required for each department, machine, or process to complete the production of one unit or one batch of output. In many cases, standard time per unit is a small fraction of an hour. Current time and motion studies of workers and machines, as well as records of their past performance, provide the data for developing this standard. The direct labor time standard should be revised whenever a machine is replaced or the quality of the labor force changes.

Standard Overhead Cost

The **standard overhead cost** is the sum of the estimates of variable and fixed overhead costs in the next accounting period. It is based on standard overhead rates that are computed in much the same way as the predetermined overhead rate that we discussed in an earlier chapter. Unlike that rate, however, the standard overhead rate has two parts, one for variable costs and one for fixed costs. The reason for computing the standard variable and fixed overhead rates separately is that their cost behavior differs.

The **standard variable overhead rate** is computed by dividing the total budgeted variable overhead costs by an expression of capacity, such as the number of standard machine hours or standard direct labor hours. (Other bases may be used if machine hours or direct labor hours are not good predictors, or drivers, of variable overhead costs.) For example, using standard machine hours as the base, the formula is as follows:

$$\frac{\text{Standard Variable}}{\text{Overhead Rate}} = \frac{\text{Total Budgeted Variable Overhead Costs}}{\text{Expected Number of Standard Machine Hours}}$$

The **standard fixed overhead rate** is computed by dividing the total budgeted fixed overhead costs by an expression of capacity, usually normal capacity in terms of standard hours or units. The denominator is expressed in the same terms as the variable overhead rate. For example, using normal capacity in terms of standard machine hours as the denominator, the formula is as follows:

$$\text{Standard Fixed Overhead Rate} = \frac{\text{Total Budgeted Fixed Overhead Costs}}{\text{Normal Capacity in Terms of Standard Machine Hours}}$$

Recall that normal capacity is the level of operating capacity needed to meet expected sales demand. Using it as the application base ensures that all fixed overhead costs have been applied to units produced by the time normal capacity is reached.

Total Standard Unit Cost

Using standard costs eliminates the need to calculate unit costs from actual cost data every week or month or for each batch of goods produced. Once standard costs for direct materials, direct labor, and variable and fixed overhead have been developed, a total standard unit cost can be computed at any time.

To illustrate how standard costs are used to compute total unit cost, let's suppose that a company called ICU, Inc., has adapted **iRobot Corporation**'s technology to create Watch Dog, a robot used for home surveillance. ICU, Inc., has recently updated the standards for this line of robots. Direct materials price standards are now $9.20 per square foot for casing materials and $20.17 for each mechanism. Direct materials quantity standards are 0.025 square foot of casing materials per robot and one mechanism per robot. Direct labor time standards are 0.01 hour per robot for the Case Stamping Department and 0.05 hour per robot for the Assembly Department. Direct labor rate standards are $8.00 per hour for the Case Stamping Department and $10.20 per hour for the Assembly Department. Standard manufacturing overhead rates are $12.00 per direct labor hour for the standard variable overhead rate and $9.00 per direct labor hour for the standard fixed overhead rate. The standard cost of making one robot would be computed in the following manner:

Direct materials costs:	
Casing ($9.20 per sq. ft. × 0.025 sq. ft.)	$ 0.23
One mechanism	20.17
Direct labor costs:	
Case Stamping Department ($8.00 per hour × 0.01 hour per robot)	0.08
Assembly Department ($10.20 per hour × 0.05 hour per robot)	0.51
Variable overhead ($12.00 per hour × 0.06 hour per robot)	0.72
Total standard variable cost of one robot	$21.71
Fixed overhead ($9.00 per hour × 0.06 hour per robot)	0.54
Total standard cost of one robot	$22.25

Study Note

The total standard cost of $22.25 represents the *desired* cost of producing one robot.

The total standard cost of producing a watch like this or a robot like the Watch Dog represents the desired production cost. It is based on the standards established for direct materials costs, direct labor costs, and variable and fixed overhead.

Courtesy of Timothy Goodwin/ istockphoto.com.

STOP & APPLY >

Using the following information, compute the standard unit cost of a 5-pound bag of sugar:

Direct materials quantity standard	5 pounds per unit
Direct materials price standard	$0.05 per pound
Direct labor time standard	0.01 hour per unit
Direct labor rate standard	$10.00 per hour
Variable overhead rate standard	$0.15 per machine hour
Fixed overhead rate standard	$0.10 per machine hour
Machine hour standard	0.5 hour per unit

SOLUTION

Direct materials cost ($0.05 × 5 pounds)	$0.25
Direct labor cost ($10.00 × 0.01 hour)	0.10
Variable overhead ($0.15 × 0.5 machine hour)	0.08
Fixed overhead ($0.10 × 0.5 machine hour)	0.05
Total standard unit cost	$0.48

Variance Analysis

LO2 Prepare a flexible budget, and describe how managers use variance analysis to control costs.

Managers in all types of organizations constantly compare the costs of what was expected to happen with the costs of what actually did happen. By examining the differences, or variances, between standard and actual costs, they can gather much valuable information. **Variance analysis** is the process of computing the differences between standard costs and actual costs and identifying the causes of those differences. In this section, we look at how managers use flexible budgets to improve the accuracy of variance analysis and how they use variance analysis to control costs.

The Role of Flexible Budgets in Variance Analysis

The accuracy of variance analysis depends to a large extent on the type of budget that managers use when comparing variances. Static, or fixed, budgets forecast revenues and expenses for just one level of sales and just one level of output. The budgets that make up a master budget are usually based on a single level of output, but many things can happen over an accounting period that will cause actual output to differ from the estimated output. If a company produces more products than predicted, total production costs will almost always be greater than predicted. When that is the case, a comparison of actual production costs with fixed budgeted costs will inevitably show variances.

The performance report in Exhibit 23-1 compares data from the static master budget of ICU, Inc., with the actual costs of the company's Watch Division, the division responsible for manufacturing the surveillance robots, for the year ended December 31. As you can see, actual costs exceeded budgeted costs by $5,539. On the face of it, most managers would consider such a cost overrun significant. But was there really a cost overrun? The budgeted amounts are based on an output of 17,500 units; however, the actual output was 19,100 units.

To judge the division's performance accurately, the company's managers must change the budgeted data to reflect an output of 19,100 units. They can do this by using a flexible budget. A **flexible budget** (also called a *variable budget*) is a summary of expected costs for a range of activity levels. Unlike a static budget, a flexible budget provides forecasted data that can be adjusted for changes in

EXHIBIT 23-1
Performance Report Using Data from a Static Budget

ICU, Inc.
Performance Report—Watch Division
For the Year Ended December 31

Cost Category	Budgeted Costs*	Actual Costs†	Difference Under (Over) Budget
Direct materials	$357,000	$361,000	($4,000)
Direct labor	10,325	11,779	(1,454)
Variable overhead			
Indirect materials	3,500	3,600	(100)
Indirect labor	5,250	5,375	(125)
Utilities	1,750	1,810	(60)
Other	2,100	2,200	(100)
Fixed overhead			
Supervisory salaries	4,000	3,500	500
Depreciation	2,000	2,000	—
Utilities	450	450	—
Other	3,000	3,200	(200)
Totals	$389,375	$394,914	($5,539)

*Budgeted costs are based on an output of 17,500 units.
†Actual output was 19,100 units.

the level of output. The flexible budget is used primarily as a cost control tool in evaluating performance at the end of a period.

A flexible budget for ICU's Watch Division appears in Exhibit 23-2. It shows the estimated costs for 15,000, 17,500, and 20,000 units of output. The total cost of a variable cost item is found by multiplying the number of units produced by the item's per unit cost. For example, if the Watch Division produces 15,000 units, direct materials will cost $306,000 (15,000 units × $20.40).

An important element in this exhibit is the **flexible budget formula**, an equation that determines the expected, or budgeted, cost for any level of output. Its components include a per unit amount for variable costs and a total amount for fixed costs. (In Exhibit 23-2, the $21.71 variable cost per unit is computed in the far right column, and the $9,450 is found in the section on fixed overhead costs.) Using the flexible budget formula, you can create a budget for the Watch Division for any level of output in the range of levels given.

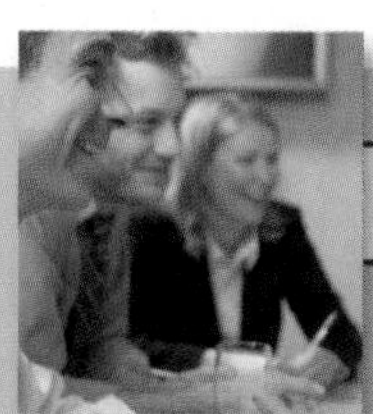

FOCUS ON BUSINESS PRACTICE

Why Complicate the Flexible Budget?

Because of the database capabilities of enterprise resource management (ERM) systems and the principles of resource consumption accounting (RCA), the flexible budget has become more complicated. This new and more complex version of a flexible budget is called *authorized reporting*. Authorized reporting is like a flexible budget in that it restates an accounting period's costs in terms of different levels of output, but it enhances cost restatement by taking into account all the factors that can influence a cost's behavior. With its sophisticated cost analyses, authorized reporting is a more relevant yardstick for cost comparison and control than the traditional flexible budget.[1]

EXHIBIT 23-2
Flexible Budget for Evaluation of Overall Performance

ICU, Inc.
Flexible Budget—Watch Division
For the Year Ended December 31

	Units Produced*			Variable Cost per Unit†
Cost Category	**15,000**	**17,500**	**20,000**	
Direct materials	$306,000	$357,000	$408,000	$20.40
Direct labor	8,850	10,325	11,800	0.59
Variable overhead				
Indirect materials	3,000	3,500	4,000	0.20
Indirect labor	4,500	5,250	6,000	0.30
Utilities	1,500	1,750	2,000	0.10
Other	1,800	2,100	2,400	0.12
Total variable costs	$325,650	$379,925	$434,200	$21.71
Fixed overhead				
Supervisory salaries	$ 4,000	$ 4,000	$ 4,000	
Depreciation	2,000	2,000	2,000	
Utilities	450	450	450	
Other	3,000	3,000	3,000	
Total fixed overhead costs	$ 9,450	$ 9,450	$ 9,450	
Total costs	$335,100	$389,375	$443,650	

Flexible budget formula:

Total Budgeted Costs = (Variable Cost per Unit × Number of Units Produced) + Budgeted Fixed Costs
= ($21.71 × Units Produced) + $9,450

*Flexible budgets are commonly used only for overhead costs; when they are, machine hours or direct labor hours are used in place of units produced.

†Computed by dividing the dollar amount in any column by the respective level of output.

Study Note

Flexible budgets allow managers to compare budgeted and actual costs at the same level of output.

The performance report in Exhibit 23-3 is based on data from the flexible budget shown in Exhibit 23-2. Variable unit costs have been multiplied by the 19,100 units actually produced to arrive at the total flexible budgeted costs, and fixed overhead information has been carried over from Exhibit 23-2. In this report, actual costs are $29,197 less than the amount budgeted. In other words, when we use a flexible budget at the end of the period, we find that the performance of the Watch Division in this period actually exceeded budget targets by $29,197.

Using Variance Analysis to Control Costs

As Figure 23-1 shows, using variance analysis to control costs is a four-step process. First, managers compute the amount of the variance. If the amount is insignificant—meaning that actual operating results are close to those anticipated—no corrective action is needed. If the amount is significant, then managers analyze the variance to identify its cause. In identifying the cause, they are usually able to pinpoint the activities that need to be monitored. They then select performance measures that will enable them to track those activities, analyze the results, and determine the action needed to correct the problem. Their final step is to take the appropriate corrective action.

EXHIBIT 23-3
Performance Report Using Data from a Flexible Budget

ICU, Inc.
Performance Report—Watch Division
For the Year Ended December 31

Cost Category (Variable Unit Cost)	Budgeted Costs*	Actual Costs	Difference Under (Over) Budget
Direct materials ($20.40)	$389,640	$361,000	$28,640
Direct labor ($0.59)	11,269	11,779	(510)
Variable overhead			
Indirect materials ($0.20)	3,820	3,600	220
Indirect labor ($0.30)	5,730	5,375	355
Utilities ($0.10)	1,910	1,810	100
Other ($0.12)	2,292	2,200	92
Fixed overhead			
Supervisory salaries	4,000	3,500	500
Depreciation	2,000	2,000	—
Utilities	450	450	—
Other	3,000	3,200	(200)
Totals	$424,111	$394,914	$29,197

*Budgeted costs are based on an output of 19,100 units.

Although computing the amount of a variance is important, it is also important to remember that this computation does nothing to prevent the variance from recurring. To control costs, managers must determine the cause of the variance and select performance measures that will help them track the problem and find the best solution for it.

FIGURE 23-1
Variance Analysis: A Four-Step Approach to Controlling Costs

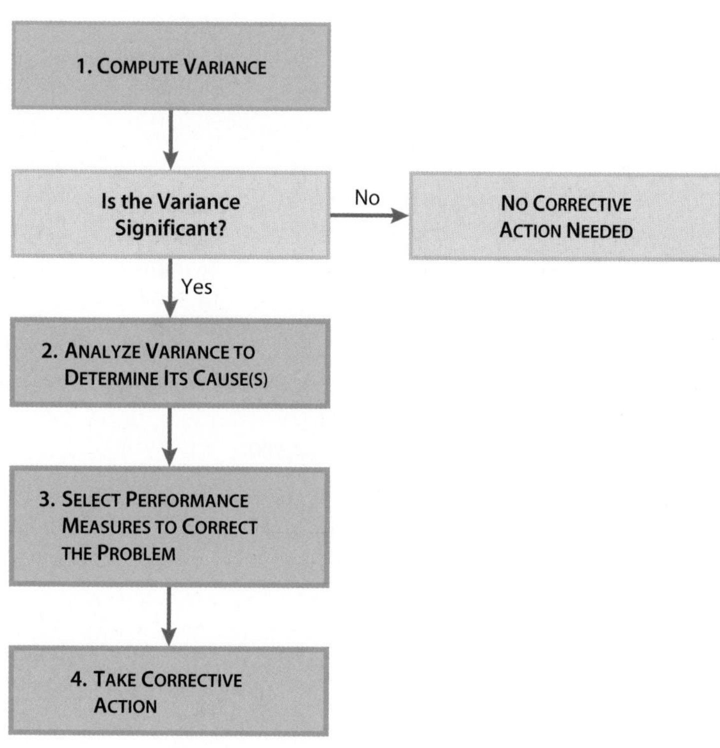

As we focus on the computation and analysis of cost center variances in the next sections, we follow the steps outlined in Figure 23-1. We limit our analysis to eight variances, two for each of the cost categories of direct materials, direct labor, variable overhead, and fixed overhead. We give examples of operating problems that might cause each of these variances to occur. We also identify some financial and nonfinancial performance measures that can be used to track the cause of a variance and that can be helpful in correcting it.

STOP & APPLY >

Keel Company's fixed overhead costs for the year are expected to be as follows: depreciation, $72,000; supervisory salaries, $92,000; property taxes and insurance, $26,000; and other fixed overhead, $14,500. Total fixed overhead is thus expected to be $204,500. Variable costs per unit are expected to be as follows: direct materials, $16.50; direct labor, $8.50; operating supplies, $2.60; indirect labor, $4.10; and other variable overhead costs, $3.20.

Prepare a flexible budget for the following levels of production: 18,000 units, 20,000 units, and 22,000 units. What is the flexible budget formula for the year ended December 31?

SOLUTION

Keel Company
Flexible Budget
For the Year Ended December 31

	Units Produced			
Cost Category	**18,000**	**20,000**	**22,000**	**Variable Cost per Unit**
Direct materials	$297,000	$330,000	$363,000	$16.50
Direct labor	153,000	170,000	187,000	8.50
Variable overhead				
Operating supplies	46,800	52,000	57,200	2.60
Indirect labor	73,800	82,000	90,200	4.10
Other	57,600	64,000	70,400	3.20
Total variable costs	$628,200	$698,000	$767,800	$34.90
Fixed overhead				
Depreciation	$ 72,000	$ 72,000	$ 72,000	
Supervisory salaries	92,000	92,000	92,000	
Property taxes and insurance	26,000	26,000	26,000	
Other	14,500	14,500	14,500	
Total fixed overhead	$204,500	$204,500	$204,500	
Total costs	$832,700	$902,500	$972,300	

Flexible budget formula for the year ended December 31:
Total Budgeted Costs = ($34.90 × Units Produced) + $204,500

Computing and Analyzing Direct Materials Variances

LO3 Compute and analyze direct materials variances.

To control cost center operations, managers compute and analyze variances for whole cost categories, such as total direct materials costs, as well as variances for elements of those categories, such as the price and quantity of each direct material. The more detailed their analysis of direct materials variances is, the more effective they will be in controlling costs.

Computing Direct Materials Variances

The **total direct materials cost variance** is the difference between the standard cost and actual cost of direct materials used to produce the salable units; it is also referred to as the *good units produced*. To illustrate how this variance is computed, let us assume that a manufacturer called Cambria Company makes leather bags to carry the Watch Dog robots. Each bag should use 4 feet of leather (standard quantity), and the standard price of leather is $6.00 per foot. During August, Cambria Company purchased 760 feet of leather costing $5.90 per foot and used the leather to produce 180 bags.

Given these facts, the total direct materials cost variance for Cambria is calculated as follows:

Standard cost

Standard Price × Standard Quantity =	
$6.00 per foot × (180 bags × 4 feet per bag) =	
$6.00 per foot × 720 feet =	$4,320

Less actual cost

Actual Price × Actual Quantity =	
$5.90 per foot × 760 feet =	4,484
Total direct materials cost variance =	$ 164 (U)

Study Note

It is just as important to identify whether a variance is favorable or unfavorable as it is to compute the variance. This information is necessary for analyzing the variance and taking corrective action.

Here, actual cost exceeds standard cost. The situation is unfavorable, as indicated by the U in parentheses after the dollar amount. An F means a favorable situation.

To find the area or people responsible for the variance, the total direct materials cost variance must be broken down into two parts: the direct materials price variance and the direct materials quantity variance. The **direct materials price variance** (also called the *direct material spending* or *rate variance*) is the difference between the standard price and the actual price per unit multiplied by the actual quantity purchased.

Study Note

The direct materials price variance measures the difference between the standard cost and the actual cost of purchased materials. It is not concerned with the quantity of materials used in the production process.

For Cambria Company, the direct materials price variance is computed as follows:

Standard price	$6.00
Less actual price	5.90
Difference per foot	$0.10 (F)

Direct Materials Price Variance = (Standard Price − Actual Price) × Actual Quantity
= $0.10 × 760 feet
= $76 (F)

Because the price that the company paid for the direct materials was less than the standard price it expected to pay, the variance is favorable.

The **direct materials quantity variance** (also called the *direct material efficiency* or *usage variance*) is the difference between the standard quantity allowed and the actual quantity used multiplied by the standard price. For Cambria, it is computed as follows:

Standard quantity allowed (180 bags × 4 feet per bag)	720 feet
Less actual quantity	760 feet
Difference	40 feet (U)

Direct Materials Quantity Variance = Standard Price × (Standard Quantity Allowed − Actual Quantity)
= \$6 × 40 feet
= \$240 (U)

Because more leather than the standard quantity was used in the production process, the direct materials quantity variance is unfavorable.

Summary of Direct Material Variances If the calculations are correct, the net of the direct materials price variance and the direct materials quantity variance should equal the total direct materials cost variance. The following check shows that the variances were computed correctly:

Direct materials price variance	\$ 76 (F)
Direct materials quantity variance	240 (U)
Total direct materials cost variance	\$164 (U)

Variance analyses are sometimes easier to interpret in diagram form. Figure 23-2 illustrates our analysis of Cambria Company's direct materials variances. Notice that although direct materials are purchased at actual cost, they are entered in the Materials Inventory account at standard price; thus, the direct materials price variance of

FIGURE 23-2
Diagram of Direct Materials Variance Analysis

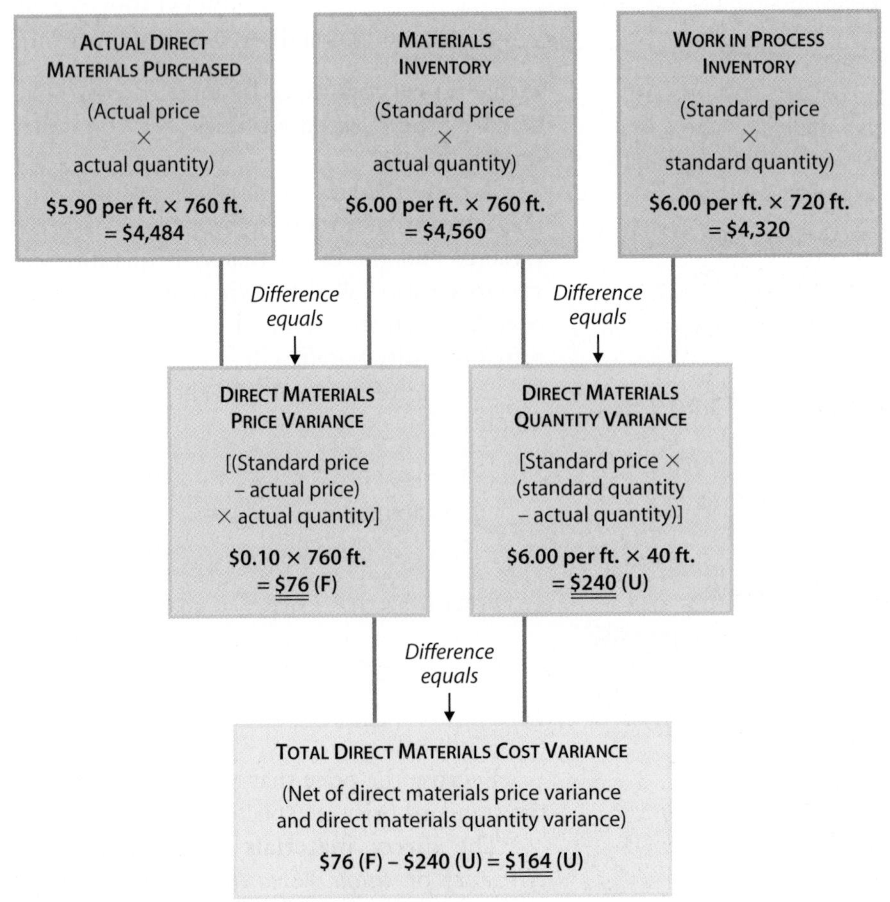

$76 (F) is obvious when the costs are recorded. As Figure 23-2 shows, the standard price multiplied by the standard quantity is the amount entered in the Work in Process Inventory account.

Analyzing and Correcting Direct Materials Variances

Cambria Company's managers were concerned because the company had been experiencing direct materials price variances and quantity variances for some time; moreover, as our analysis shows, the price variances were always favorable and the quantity variances were always unfavorable. By tracking the purchasing activity for three months, the managers discovered that the company's purchasing agent, without any authorization, had been purchasing a lower grade of leather at a reduced price. After careful analysis, the engineering manager determined that the substitute leather was not appropriate and that the company should resume purchasing the grade of leather originally specified. In addition, an analysis of scrap and rework revealed that the inferior quality of the substitute leather was causing the unfavorable quantity variance. By tracking the purchasing activity, Cambria's managers were able to solve the problems the company had been having with direct materials variances.

& APPLY >

Using the following information, compare the actual and standard cost and usage data for the production of 5-pound bags of sugar, and compute the direct materials price and direct materials quantity variances using formulas or diagram form:

Direct materials quantity standard	5 pounds per unit
Direct materials price standard	$0.05 per pound
Direct materials purchased and used	55,100 pounds
Price paid for direct materials	$0.04 per pound
Number of good units produced	11,000 units

SOLUTION

Direct Materials Price Variance = (Standard Price − Actual Price) × Actual Quantity
= ($0.05 − $0.04) × 55,100 pounds
= $0.01 × 55,100 pounds = $551 (F)

Direct Materials Quantity Variance = Standard Price × (Standard Quantity − Actual Quantity)
= $0.05 × [(11,000 × 5 pounds) − 55,100 pounds]
= $0.05 × (55,000 pounds − 55,100 pounds) = $5 (U)

Diagram Form:

	Actual Price × Actual Quantity		Standard Price × Actual Quantity		Standard Price × Standard Quantity
Direct Materials	$2,204[a]	Price Variance	$2,755[b]	Quantity Variance	$2.750[c]
		$551 (F)		$5 (U)	

[a] $0.04 × 55,100 = $2,204
[b] $0.05 × 55,100 = $2,755
[c] $0.05 × (11,000 × 5) = $2,750

Computing and Analyzing Direct Labor Variances

LO4 Compute and analyze direct labor variances.

The procedure for computing and analyzing direct labor cost variances parallels the procedure for finding direct materials variances. Again, the more detailed the analysis is, the more effective managers will be in controlling costs.

Computing Direct Labor Variances

The **total direct labor cost variance** is the difference between the standard direct labor cost for good units produced and actual direct labor costs. (*Good units* are the total units produced less units that are scrapped or need to be reworked—in other words, the salable units.) At Cambria Company, each leather bag requires 2.4 standard direct labor hours, and the standard direct labor rate is \$8.50 per hour. During August, 450 direct labor hours were used to make 180 bags at an average pay rate of \$9.20 per hour.

Based on these facts, the total direct labor cost variance is computed as follows:

Standard cost

Standard Rate × Standard Hours Allowed =

\$8.50 × (180 bags × 2.4 hours per bag) =

\$8.50 × 432 hours = \$3,672

Less actual cost

Actual Rate × Actual Hours =

\$9.20 × 450 hours = 4,140

Total direct labor cost variance = \$ 468 (U)

Both the actual direct labor hours per bag and the actual direct labor rate varied from the standard. For effective performance evaluation, management must know how much of the total cost arose from different direct labor rates and how much from different numbers of direct labor hours. This information is found by computing the direct labor rate variance and the direct labor efficiency variance.

The **direct labor rate variance** (also called the *direct labor spending variance*) is the difference between the standard direct labor rate and the actual direct labor rate multiplied by the actual direct labor hours worked. For Cambria, it is computed as follows:

Standard rate	\$8.50
Less actual rate	9.20
Difference per hour	\$0.70 (U)

Direct Labor Rate Variance = (Standard Rate − Actual Rate) × Actual Hours

= \$0.70 × 450 hours

= \$315 (U)

Study Note

The computation of the direct labor rate variance is very similar to the computation of the direct materials price variance. Computations of the direct labor efficiency variance and the direct materials quantity variance are also similar.

The **direct labor efficiency variance** (also called the *direct labor quantity* or *usage variance*) is the difference between the standard direct labor hours allowed for good units produced and the actual direct labor hours worked multiplied by the standard direct labor rate. For Cambria, it is computed this way:

Standard hours allowed (180 bags × 2.4 hours per bag)	432 hours
Less actual hours	450 hours
Difference	18 hours (U)

Direct Labor Efficiency Variance = Standard Rate × (Standard Hours Allowed − Actual Hours)
= $8.50 × 18 hours
= $153 (U)

Summary of Direct Labor Variances If the calculations are correct, the net of the direct labor rate variance and the direct labor efficiency variance should equal the total direct labor cost variance. The following check shows that the variances were computed correctly:

Direct labor rate variance	$315 (U)
Direct labor efficiency variance	153 (U)
Total direct labor cost variance	$468 (U)

Figure 23-3 summarizes our analysis of Cambria Company's direct labor variances. Unlike direct materials variances, the direct labor rate and efficiency variances are usually computed and recorded at the same time.

FIGURE 23-3
Diagram of Direct Labor Variance Analysis

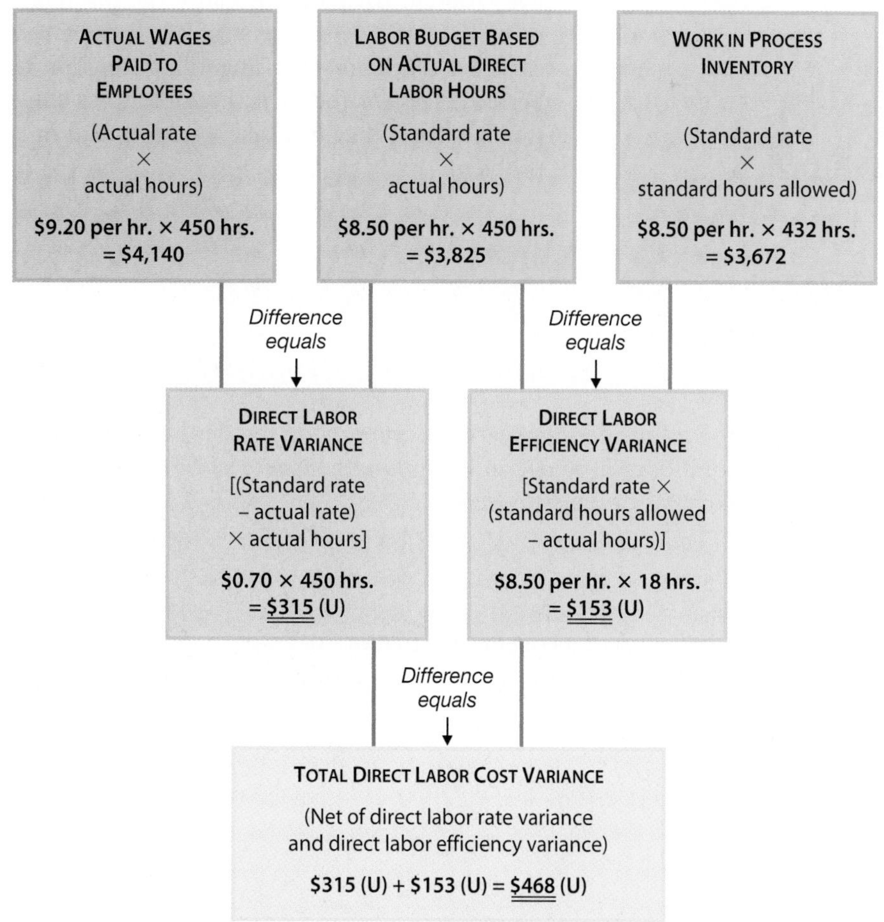

FOCUS ON BUSINESS PRACTICE

What Do You Get When You Cross a Vacuum Cleaner with a Gaming Console?

The transfer of technology ideas used for government purposes to home use is common—for example, the Internet and computers. But, what about transferring technology from home use to the battlefield? **iRobot Corporation** applied the technology it uses in its Roomba vacuum cleaner to create small unmanned ground vehicles. These robots, such as the PackBot, have cameras that see both during the day and at night, flexible treads that allow them to climb stairs, and radio links that connect them to an operator at a gaming-like console and to the military command center.[2]

Analyzing and Correcting Direct Labor Variances

Because Cambria Company's direct labor rate variance and direct labor efficiency variance were unfavorable, its managers investigated the causes of these variances. An analysis of employee time cards revealed that the Bag Assembly Department had replaced an assembly worker who was ill with a machine operator from another department. The machine operator made $9.20 per hour, whereas the assembly worker earned the standard $8.50 per hour rate. When questioned about the unfavorable efficiency variance, the assembly supervisor identified two causes. First, the machine operator had to learn assembly skills on the job, so his assembly time was longer than the standard time per bag. Second, the materials handling people were partially responsible because they delivered parts late on five different occasions. Because the machine operator was a temporary replacement, Cambria's managers took no corrective action, but they decided to keep a close eye on the materials handling function by tracking delivery times and number of delays for the next three months. Once they have collected and analyzed the new data, they will take whatever action is needed to correct the scheduling problem.

STOP & APPLY >

Using the following information, compare the standard cost and usage data for the production of 5-pound bags of sugar, and compute the direct labor rate and direct labor efficiency variances using formulas or diagram form:

Direct labor time standard	0.01 hour per unit
Direct labor rate standard	$10.00 per hour
Direct labor hours used	100 hours
Total cost of direct labor	$1,010
Number of good units produced	11,000 units

(continued)

SOLUTION

Direct Labor Rate Variance

$$= (\text{Standard Rate} - \text{Actual Rate}) \times \text{Actual Hours}$$
$$= [\$10.00 \div (\$1{,}010 \div 100 \text{ hours})] \times 100 \text{ hours}$$
$$= (\$10.00 - \$10.10) \times 100 \text{ hours}$$
$$= \$0.10 \times 100 \text{ hours} = \underline{\underline{\$10.00}} \text{ (U)}$$

Direct Labor Efficiency Variance

$$= \text{Standard Rate} \times (\text{Standard Hours Allowed} - \text{Actual Hours})$$
$$= \$10.00 \times [(11{,}000 \times 0.01 \text{ hour}) - 100 \text{ hours}]$$
$$= \$10.00 \times (110 \text{ hours} - 100 \text{ hours})$$
$$= \$10.00 \times 10 \text{ hours} = \underline{\underline{\$100.00}} \text{ (F)}$$

Diagram Form:

	Actual Rate × Actual Hours		Standard Rate × Actual Hours		Standard Rate × Standard Hours
Direct Labor	$1,010[a]	Rate Variance	$1,000[b]	Efficiency Variance	$1,100[c]
		$10.00 (U)		$100.00 (F)	

[a] $10.10 × 100 = $1,010
[b] $10.00 × 100 = $1,000
[c] $10.00 × (11,000 × 0.01 hour) = $1,100

Computing and Analyzing Overhead Variances

LO5 Compute and analyze overhead variances.

Many types of variable and fixed overhead costs may contribute to variances from standard costs. Controlling these costs is more difficult than controlling direct materials and direct labor costs because the responsibility for overhead costs is hard to assign. Fixed overhead costs may be unavoidable past costs, such as depreciation and lease expenses; they are therefore not under the control of any department manager. If variable overhead costs can be related to departments or activities, however, some control is possible.

Using a Flexible Budget to Analyze Overhead Variances

Earlier in the chapter, we described the flexible budget that the managers of ICU, Inc., use to evaluate overall performance. That budget, shown in Exhibit 23-2, is based on units of output. Cambria Company's managers also use a flexible budget, but to analyze overhead costs only. As you can see in Exhibit 23-4, Cambria's flexible budget uses direct labor hours as the expression of activity. Thus, variable costs vary with the number of direct labor hours worked. Total fixed overhead costs remain constant. The flexible budget formula in such cases is as follows:

$$\text{Total Budgeted Overhead Costs} = (\text{Variable Costs per Direct Labor Hour} \times \text{Number of Direct Labor Hours}) + \text{Budgeted Fixed Overhead Costs}$$

EXHIBIT 23-4
Flexible Budget for Evaluation of Overhead Costs

Cambria Company
Flexible Budget—Overhead
Bag Assembly Department
For an Average One-Month Period

	Direct Labor Hours (DLH)			
Cost Category	**400**	**432**	**500**	**Variable Cost per DLH**
Budgeted variable overhead				
Indirect materials	$ 600	$ 648	$ 750	$1.50
Indirect Labor	800	864	1,000	2.00
Supplies	300	324	375	0.75
Utilities	400	432	500	1.00
Other	200	216	250	0.50
Total budgeted variable overhead costs	$2,300	$2,484	$2,875	$5.75
Budgeted fixed overhead				
Supervisory salaries	$ 600	$ 600	$ 600	
Depreciation	400	400	400	
Other	300	300	300	
Total budgeted fixed overhead costs	$1,300	$1,300	$1,300	
Total budgeted overhead costs	$3,600	$3,784	$4,175	

Flexible budget formula (based on a normal capacity of 400 direct labor hours):

Total Budgeted Overhead Costs = (Variable Costs per Direct Labor Hour × Number of DLH) + Budgeted Fixed Overhead Costs
= ($5.75 × Number of DLH) + $1,300

When applied to Cambria Company's data, the flexible budget formula is as follows:

Total Budgeted Overhead Costs = ($5.75 × Number of Direct Labor Hours) + $1,300

Cambria's flexible budget shows monthly overhead costs for 400, 432, and 500 direct labor hours.

To find the total monthly flexible budgeted overhead costs for the 180 bags produced, you simply insert the direct labor hours allowed in the flexible budget formula—for example ($5.75 × 432 direct labor hours) + $1,300 = $3,784.

Computing Overhead Variances

Analyses of overhead variances differ in degree of detail. The basic approach is to compute the **total overhead cost variance,** which is the difference between actual overhead costs and standard overhead costs applied. You may recall from a previous chapter how overhead was applied to production by using a standard overhead rate.

A standard overhead rate has two parts: a variable rate and a fixed rate. For Cambria Company, the standard variable rate is $5.75 per direct labor hour (from the flexible budget). The standard fixed overhead rate is found by dividing total budgeted fixed overhead ($1,300) by normal capacity set by the master budget at the beginning of the period. (Cambria's normal capacity is 400 direct labor hours.) The result is a fixed overhead rate of $3.25 per direct labor hour ($1,300 ÷ 400 hours). So, Cambria's total standard overhead rate is $9.00 per direct labor hour ($5.75 + $3.25).

Cambria Company's total overhead cost variance would be computed as follows:

Standard overhead costs applied to good units produced	
$9.00 per direct labor hour × (180 bags × 2.4 hr. per bag)	$3,888
Less actual overhead costs	4,100
Total overhead cost variance	$ 212 (U)

This amount can be divided into variable overhead variances and fixed overhead variances.

Variable Overhead Variances The **total variable overhead cost variance** is the difference between actual variable overhead costs and the standard variable overhead costs that are applied to good units produced using the standard variable rate. The procedure for finding this variance is similar to the procedure for finding direct materials and labor variances.

Figure 23-4 shows an analysis of Cambria Company's variable overhead variances. At Cambria, each leather bag requires 2.4 standard direct labor hours, and the standard variable overhead rate is $5.75 per direct labor hour. For example, during August, the company incurred $2,500 of variable overhead costs. The total variable overhead cost variance is computed as follows:

Overhead applied to good units produced	
Standard Variable Rate × Standard Labor Hours Allowed	=
$5.75 per hour × (180 bags × 2.4 hours per bag)	=
$5.75 × 432 hours	= $2,484
Less actual cost	2,500
Total variable overhead cost variance	= $ 16 (U)

Both the actual variable overhead and the direct labor hours per bag may vary from the standard. For effective performance evaluation, managers must know how much of the total cost arose from variable overhead spending deviations and how much from variable overhead application deviations (i.e., applied and actual direct labor hours). This information is found by computing the variable overhead spending variance and the variable overhead efficiency variance.

The **variable overhead spending variance** (also called the *variable overhead rate variance*) is computed by multiplying the actual hours worked by the difference between actual variable overhead costs and the standard variable overhead rate. For Cambria, it is computed as follows:

Variable Overhead Spending Variance = (Standard Variable Rate × Actual Hours Worked) − Actual Variable Overhead Cost
= ($5.75 × 450 hours) − $2,500.00
= $2,587.50 − $2,500.00
= $87.50 (F)

FIGURE 23-4
Diagram of Variable Overhead Variance Analysis

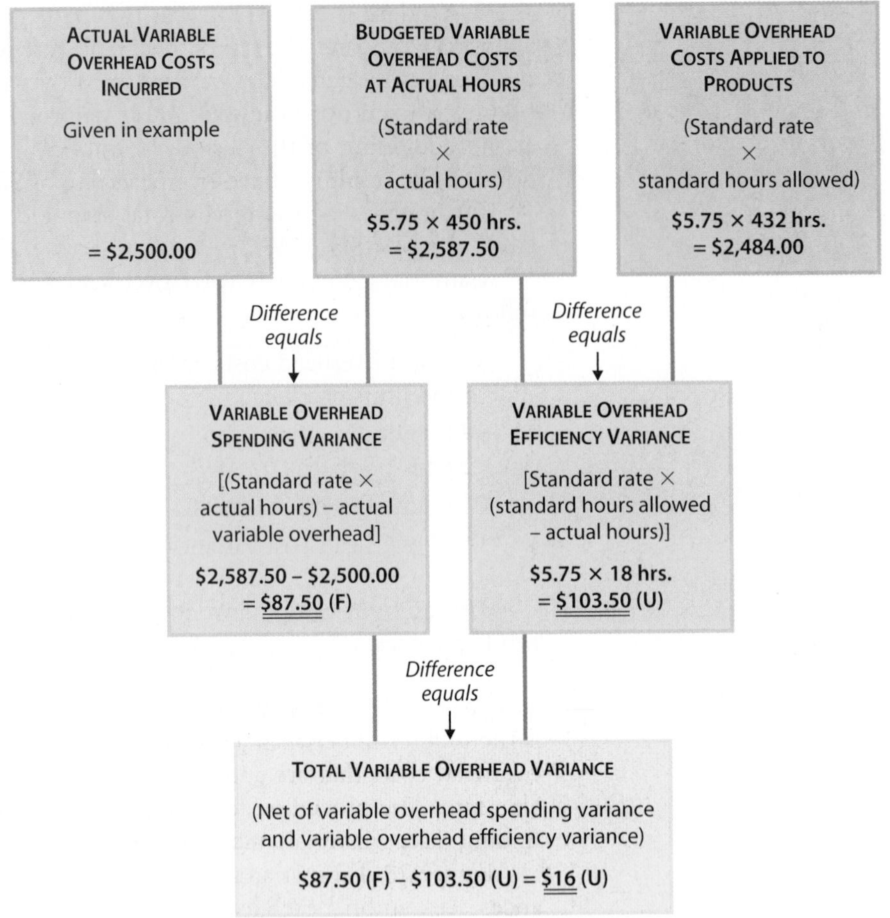

The **variable overhead efficiency variance** is the difference between the standard direct labor hours allowed for good units produced and the actual hours worked multiplied by the standard variable overhead rate per hour. For Cambria, it is computed as follows:

Standard direct labor hours allowed (180 bags × 2.4 hours per bag)	432 hours
Less actual hours	450 hours
Difference	18 hours (U)

Variable Overhead Efficiency Variance = Standard Variable Rate × (Standard Hours Allowed − Actual Hours)
= $5.75 × 18 hours
= $103.50 (U)

Summary of Variable Overhead Variances If the calculations are correct, the net of the variable overhead spending variance and the variable overhead efficiency variance should equal the total variable overhead variance. The following check shows that these variances have been computed correctly:

Variable overhead spending variance	$ 87.50 (F)
Variable overhead efficiency variance	103.50 (U)
Total variable overhead cost variance	$ 16.00 (U)

Fixed Overhead Variances The **total fixed overhead cost variance** is the difference between actual fixed overhead costs and the standard fixed overhead costs that are applied to good units produced using the standard fixed overhead rate. The procedure for finding this variance differs from the procedure used for finding direct materials, direct labor, and variable overhead variances.

Figure 23-5 shows an analysis of fixed overhead variances for Cambria Company. At Cambria, each bag requires 2.4 standard direct labor hours, and the standard fixed overhead rate is $3.25 per direct labor hour. As we noted earlier, the standard fixed overhead rate is found by dividing budgeted fixed overhead ($1,300) by normal capacity, which was set by the master budget at the beginning of the period. In this case, because normal capacity is 400 direct labor hours, the fixed overhead rate is $3.25 per direct labor hour ($1,300 ÷ 400 hours). For example, during August, Cambria incurred $1,600 of actual fixed overhead costs. The total fixed overhead variance is computed as follows:

Overhead applied to the good units produced	
Standard fixed rate × Standard direct labor hours allowed=	
$3.25 × (180 bags × 2.4 hours per bag) =	
$3.25 × 432 hours =	$1,404
Less actual cost	1,600
Total fixed overhead cost variance	= $ 196 (U)

FIGURE 23-5
Diagram of Fixed Overhead Variance Analysis

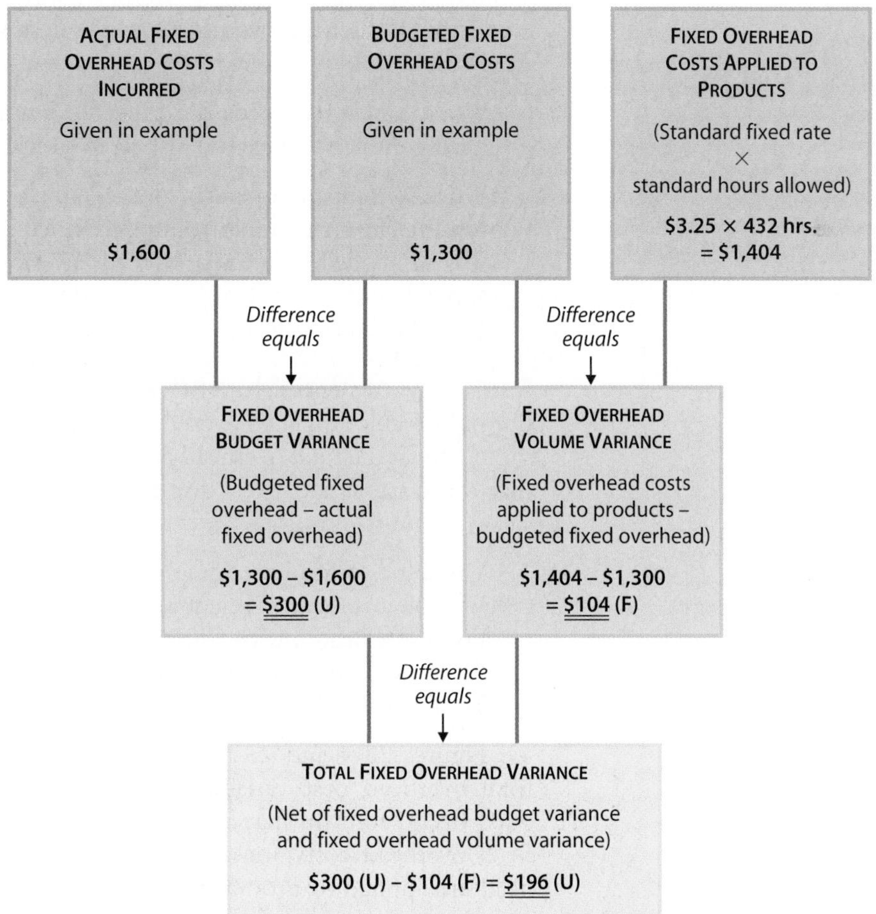

For effective performance evaluation, managers break down the total fixed overhead cost variance into two additional variances: the fixed overhead budget variance and the fixed overhead volume variance.

The **fixed overhead budget variance** (also called the *budgeted fixed overhead variance*) is the difference between budgeted and actual fixed overhead costs. For Cambria, it is computed as follows:

Fixed Overhead Budget Variance = Budgeted Fixed Overhead − Actual Fixed Overhead
= \$1,300 − \$1,600
= \$300 (U)

The **fixed overhead volume variance** is the difference between budgeted fixed overhead costs and the overhead costs that are applied to production using the standard fixed overhead rate. For Cambria, the fixed overhead volume variance is computed as follows:

Standard fixed overhead applied to good units produced		
\$3.25 per direct labor hour × (180 bags × 2.4 hours per bag)	\$1,404	
Less total budgeted fixed overhead	1,300	
Fixed overhead volume variance	\$ 104	(F)

Because the fixed overhead volume variance measures the use of existing facilities and capacity, a volume variance will occur if more or less than normal capacity is used. At Cambria Company, 400 direct labor hours are considered normal use of facilities. Because fixed overhead costs are applied on the basis of standard hours allowed, Cambria Company's overhead was applied on the basis of 432 hours, even though the fixed overhead rate was computed using 400 hours. Thus, more fixed costs would be applied to products than were budgeted.

- When capacity exceeds the expected amount, the result is a favorable overhead volume variance because fixed overhead was overapplied.
- When a company operates at a level below the normal capacity in units, the result is an unfavorable volume variance. Not all of the fixed overhead costs will be applied to units produced. In other words, fixed overhead is underapplied, and the cost of goods produced does not include the full budgeted cost of fixed overhead.

Summary of Variable and Fixed Overhead Variances If our calculations of variable and fixed overhead variances are correct, the net of these variances should equal the total overhead cost variance. Checking the computations, we find that the variable and fixed overhead variances do equal the total overhead cost variance:

Variable overhead spending variance	\$ 87.50	(F)
Variable overhead efficiency variance	103.50	(U)
Fixed overhead budget variance	300.00	(U)
Fixed overhead volume variance	104.00	(F)
Total overhead cost variance	\$212.00	(U)

Figures 23-4 and 23-5 summarize our analysis of overhead variances. The total overhead cost variance is also the amount of overapplied or underapplied overhead. You may recall from an earlier chapter that actual variable and fixed overhead costs are recorded as they occur, that variable and fixed overhead are applied to products as they are produced, and that the overapplied or underapplied overhead is computed and reconciled at the end of each accounting period. By breaking down the total overhead cost variance into variable and fixed variances, managers can more accurately control costs and reconcile their causes. An analysis of these two overhead variances will help explain why the amount of overhead applied to units produced is different from the actual overhead costs incurred.

Analyzing and Correcting Overhead Variances

In analyzing the unfavorable total overhead cost variance of $212, the manager of Cambria Company's Bag Assembly Department found causes for the variances that contributed to it:

- Although the variable overhead spending variance was favorable ($87.50 less than expected because of savings on purchases), the inefficiency of the machine operator who substituted for an assembly worker created unfavorable variances for both direct labor efficiency and variable overhead efficiency. As a result, the manager is going to consider the feasibility of implementing a program for cross-training employees.
- After reviewing the fixed overhead costs, the manager of the Bag Assembly Department concluded that higher-than-anticipated factory insurance premiums were the reason for the unfavorable fixed overhead budget variance and were the result of an increase in the number of insurance claims filed by employees. To obtain more specific information, the manager will study the insurance claims filed over a three-month period.
- Finally, since the 432 standard hours were well above the normal capacity of 400 direct labor hours, fixed overhead was overapplied, and it resulted in a $104(F) volume variance. The overutilization of capacity was traced to high demand that pressed the company to use almost all its capacity. Management decided not to do anything about the fixed overhead volume variance because it fell within an anticipated seasonal range.

& APPLY >

Sutherland Products uses standard costing. The following information about overhead was generated during August:

Standard variable overhead rate	$2 per machine hour
Standard fixed overhead rate	$3 per machine hour
Actual variable overhead costs	$443,200
Actual fixed overhead costs	$698,800
Budgeted fixed overhead costs	$700,000
Standard machine hours per unit produced	12
Good units produced	18,940
Actual machine hours	228,400

Compute the variable overhead spending and efficiency variances and the fixed overhead budget and volume variances using formulas or diagram form.

(continued)

SOLUTION

Variable overhead spending variance:

Budgeted variable overhead for actual hours	
Standard rate × actual hours worked ($2 × 228,400)	$456,800
Less actual variable overhead costs incurred	443,200
Variable overhead spending variance	$ 13,600 (F)

Variable overhead efficiency variance:

Variable overhead applied to good units produced	
Standard rate × standard hours allowed [$2 × (18,940 × 12)]	$454,560
Less budgeted variable overhead costs for actual hours	
Standard rate × actual hours worked ($2 × 228,400)	456,800
Variable overhead efficiency variance	$ 2,240 (U)

Diagram Form:

	Actual Variable Overhead Costs		Standard Rate × Actual Hours		Standard Rate × Standard Hours
Variable Overhead	$443,200	Spending Variance	$456,800[a]	Efficiency Variance	$454,560[b]
		$13,600 (F)		$2,240 (U)	

[a] $2 × 228,400 = $456,800
[b] $2 × (18,940 × 12) = $454,560

Fixed overhead budget variance:

Budgeted fixed overhead	$700,000
Less actual fixed overhead costs incurred	698,800
Fixed overhead budget variance	$ 1,200 (F)

Fixed overhead volume variance:

Fixed overhead applied to good units produced	
Standard rate × standard hours allowed [$3 × (18,940 × 12)]	$681,840
Less budgeted fixed overhead	700,000
Fixed overhead volume variance	$ 18,160 (U)

Diagram Form:

	Actual Fixed Overhead Costs		Budgeted Fixed Overhead Costs		Standard Rate × Standard Hours
Fixed Overhead	$698,800	Budget Variance	$700,000	Volume Variance	$681,840[a]
		$1,200 (F)		$18,160 (U)	

[a] $3 × (18,940 × 12) = $681,840

Using Cost Variances to Evaluate Managers' Performance

LO6 Explain how variances are used to evaluate managers' performance.

How effectively and fairly a manager's performance is evaluated depends on human factors—the people doing the evaluating—as well as on company policies. The evaluation process becomes more accurate when managerial performance reports include variances from standard costs.

To ensure that the evaluation of a manager's performance is effective and fair, a company's policies should be based on input from managers and employees and should specify the procedures that managers are to use when doing the following:

- Preparing operational plans
- Assigning responsibility for carrying out the operational plans
- Communicating the operational plans to key personnel
- Evaluating performance in each area of responsibility
- Identifying the causes of significant variances from the operational plan
- Taking corrective action to eliminate problems

Because variance analysis provides detailed data about differences between standard and actual costs and thus helps identify the causes of those differences, it is usually more effective at pinpointing efficient and inefficient operating areas than are basic comparisons of budgeted and actual data. A managerial performance report based on standard costs and related variances should identify the causes of each significant variance, the personnel involved, and the corrective actions taken. It should be tailored to the cost center manager's specific areas of responsibility and explain clearly how the manager's department met or did not meet operating expectations. Managers should be held accountable only for the cost areas under their control.

Exhibit 23-5 shows a performance report for the manager of Cambria Company's Bag Assembly Department. The report summarizes all cost data and variances for direct materials, direct labor, and overhead. In addition, it identifies the causes of the variances and the corrective actions taken. Such a report would enable a supervisor to review a cost center manager's actions and evaluate his or her performance.

A point to remember is that the mere occurrence of a variance does not indicate that a manager of a cost center has performed poorly. However, if a variance occurs consistently, and no cause is identified and no corrective action is taken, it may well indicate poor managerial performance.

Exhibit 23-5 shows that the causes of the variances have been identified and corrective actions have been taken, indicating that the manager of the Cambria Company's Bag Assembly Department has the operation under control.

EXHIBIT 23-5 Managerial Performance Report Using Variance Analysis

Cambria Company
Managerial Performance Report
Bag Assembly Department
For the Month Ended August 31

Productivity Summary:

Normal capacity in units	167 bags
Normal capacity in direct labor hours (DLH)	400 DLH*
Good units produced	180 bags
Performance level (standard hours allowed for good units produced)	432 DLH

*Rounded.

Cost and Variance Analysis:

	Standard Costs	Actual Costs	Total Variance	Variance Breakdown Amount	Variance Breakdown Type
Direct materials	$ 4,320	$ 4,484	$164 (U)	$ 76.00 (F)	Direct materials price variance
				240.00 (U)	Direct materials quantity variance
Direct labor	3,672	4,140	468 (U)	315.00 (U)	Direct labor rate variance
				153.00 (U)	Direct labor efficiency variance
Variable overhead	2,484	2,500	16 (U)	87.50 (F)	Variable overhead spending variance
				103.50 (U)	Variable overhead efficiency variance
Fixed overhead	1,404	1,600	196 (U)	300.00 (U)	Fixed overhead budget variance
				104.00 (F)	Fixed overhead volume variance
Totals	$11,880	$12,724	$844 (U)	$844.00 (U)	

Causes of Variances	Actions Taken
Direct materials price variance: New direct materials purchased at reduced price	New direct materials deemed inappropriate; resumed purchasing materials originally specified
Direct materials quantity variance: Poor quality of new direct materials	New direct materials deemed inappropriate; resumed using direct materials originally specified
Direct labor rate variance: Machine operator who had to learn assembly skills	Temporary replacement; no action taken on the job
Direct labor efficiency variance: Machine operator who had to learn assembly skills	Temporary replacement; no action taken on the job
Late delivery of parts to assembly floor	Material delivery times and number of delays being tracked
Variable overhead spending variance: Cost savings on purchases	No action necessary
Variable overhead efficiency variance: Machine operator who had to learn assembly skills on the job	A cross-training program for employees now under consideration
Fixed overhead budget variance: Large number of factory insurance claims	Study of insurance claims being conducted
Fixed overhead volume variance: High number of orders caused by demand	No action necessary

STOP & APPLY >

Jason Ponds, the production manager at WAWA Industries, recently received his performance report from Gina Rolando, the company's controller. The report contained the following information:

	Actual Cost	Standard Cost	Variance
Direct materials	$38,200	$36,600	$1,600 (U)
Direct labor	19,450	19,000	450 (U)
Variable overhead	62,890	60,000	2,890 (U)

Rolando asked Ponds to respond to his performance report. If you were Ponds, how would you respond? What additional information might you need to prepare your response?

SOLUTION

Ponds is responsible only for the direct materials quantity variance, the direct labor efficiency variance, and the variable overhead efficiency variance. Before he answers the controller's query, he needs to break down the total variances given to him into their individual variance amounts. Then, and only then, will he know how well or poorly he performed.

A LOOK BACK AT ► iROBOT CORPORATION

The Decision Point at the beginning of this chapter focused on **iRobot Corporation**, a manufacturer of robots for military, industrial, and home use. It asked these questions:

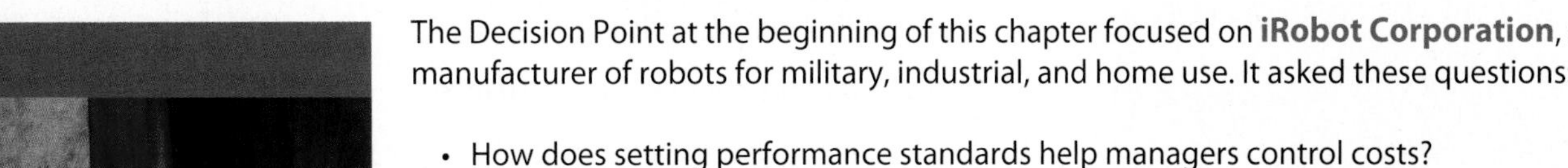

- How does setting performance standards help managers control costs?
- How do managers use standard costs to evaluate the performance of cost centers?

Managers base standard costs on realistic estimates of operating costs. They use these figures as performance targets and as benchmarks against which they measure actual spending trends. By analyzing variances between standard and actual costs, they gain insight into the causes of those differences. Once they have identified an operating problem that is causing a cost variance, they can devise a solution that results in better control of costs.

When evaluating the performance of cost centers, managers use standard costs to prepare a flexible budget, which will improve the accuracy of their variance analysis. This comparison of actual costs and a budget based on the same amount of output can provide managers with objective data that they can use to assess the center's performance in terms of its key success factor—cost.

Review Problem

Variance Analysis

LO1 LO3 LO4 LO5

Suppose a company makes a heavy-duty plastic bag for a 30-pound aerial robot. The bag is made in a single cost center using a standard costing system. The standard variable costs for one bag (a unit) are as follows:

Direct materials (3 sq. meters @ $12.50 per sq. meter)	$37.50
Direct labor (1.2 hours @ $9.00 per hour)	10.80
Variable overhead (1.2 hours @ $5.00 per direct labor hour)	6.00
Standard variable cost per unit	$54.30

The company's master budget was based on its normal capacity of 15,000 direct labor hours. Its budgeted fixed overhead costs for the year were $54,000. During the year, the company produced and sold 12,200 bags, and it purchased and used 37,500 square meters of direct materials; the purchase cost was $12.40 per square meter. The average labor rate was $9.20 per hour, and 15,250 direct labor hours were worked. The company actual variable overhead costs for the year were $73,200, and its fixed overhead costs were $55,000.

Required

Using the data given, compute the following using formulas or diagram form:

1. Standard hours allowed for good output
2. Standard fixed overhead rate
3. Direct materials cost variances:
   a. Direct materials price variance
   b. Direct materials quantity variance
   c. Total direct materials cost variance
4. Direct labor cost variances:
   a. Direct labor rate variance
   b. Direct labor efficiency variance
   c. Total direct labor cost variance
5. Variable overhead cost variances:
   a. Variable overhead spending variance
   b. Variable overhead efficiency variance
   c. Total variable overhead cost variance
6. Fixed overhead cost variances:
   a. Fixed overhead budget variance
   b. Fixed overhead volume variance
   c. Total fixed overhead cost variance

Answers to Review Problem

1. Standard Hours Allowed = Good Units Produced × Standard Direct Labor Hours per Unit
   = 12,200 Units × 1.2 Direct Labor Hours per Unit
   = 14,640 Hours

2. $$\text{Standard Fixed Overhead Rate} = \frac{\text{Budgeted Fixed Overhead Cost}}{\text{Normal Capacity}} = \frac{\$54{,}000}{15{,}000 \text{ Direct Labor Hours}}$$
   = $3.60 per Direct Labor Hour

3. Direct Materials Cost Variances:
   a. Direct Materials Price Variance:

Price difference:	Standard price	$12.50
	Less actual price	12.40
	Difference	$ 0.10 (F)

Direct Materials Price Variance = (Standard Price − Actual Price) × Actual Quantity
= $0.10 × 37,500 Sq. Meters
= $3,750 (F)

b. Direct Materials Quantity Variance:

Quantity difference: Standard quantity

(12,200 units × 3 sq. meters)	36,600 Sq. Meters
Less actual quantity	37,500 Sq. Meters
Difference	900 Sq. Meters (U)

Direct Materials Quantity Variance = Standard Price × (Standard Quantity − Actual Quantity)
= $12.50 per Sq. Meter × 900 Sq. Meters
= $11,250 (U)

c. Total Direct Materials Cost Variance:

Total Direct Materials Cost Variance = Net of Direct Materials Price Variance and Direct Materials Quantity Variance
= $3,750 (F) − $11,250 (U)
= $7,500 (U)

Diagram Form:

	Actual Price × Actual Quantity		Standard Price × Actual Quantity		Standard Price × Standard Quantity
Direct Materials	$12.40 × 37,500 = $465,000	**Price Variance**	$12.50 × 37,500 = $468,750	**Quantity Variance**	$12.50 × (12,200 × 3) = $457,500
		$3,750 (F)	**Total Direct Materials Cost Variance**	$11,250 (U)	
			$7,500 (U)		

4. Direct Labor Cost Variances:

a. Direct Labor Rate Variance:

Rate difference:	Standard labor rate	$9.00
	Less actual labor rate	9.20
	Difference	$0.20 (U)

Direct Labor Rate Variance = (Standard Rate − Actual Rate) × Actual Hours
= $0.20 × 15,250 hours
= $3,050 (U)

b. Direct Labor Efficiency Variance:

Difference in hours:	Standard hours allowed	14,640 hours*
	Less actual hours	15,250 hours
	Difference	610 hours (U)

Direct Labor Efficiency Variance = Standard Rate × (Standard Hours Allowed − Actual Hours)
= $9.00 per hour × 610 hours (U)
= $5,490 (U)

*12,200 units produced × 1.2 hours per unit = 14,640 hours.

c. Total Direct Labor Cost Variance:
Total Direct Labor Cost Variance = Net of Direct Labor Rate Variance and Direct Labor Efficiency Variance
= $3,050 (U) + $5,490 (U)
= $8,540 (U)

Diagram Form:

	Actual Rate × Actual Hours		Standard Rate × Actual Hours		Standard Rate × Standard Hours
Direct Labor	$9.20 × 15,250 = $140,300	**Rate Variance**	$9.00 × 15,250 = $137,250	**Efficiency Variance**	$9.00 × (12,200 × 1.2) = $131,760
		$3,050 (U)	**Total Direct Labor Cost Variance**	$5,490 (U)	
			$8,540 (U)		

5. Variable Overhead Cost Variances:
   a. Variable Overhead Spending Variance:

Standard variable rate × actual hours worked ($5.00 per hour × 15,250 labor hours)	$76,250
Less actual variable overhead costs incurred	73,200
Variable Overhead Spending Variance	$ 3,050 (F)

   b. Variable Overhead Efficiency Variance:

Variable overhead applied to good units produced (14,640 hours* × $5.00 per hour)	$73,200
Less budgeted variable overhead for actual hours (15,250 hours × $5.00 per hour)	76,250
Variable Overhead Efficiency Variance	$ 3,050 (U)

*12,200 units produced × 1.2 hours per unit = 14,640 hours.

   c. Total Variable Overhead Cost Variance:
   Total Variable Overhead Cost Variance = Net of Variable Overhead Spending Variance and Variable Overhead Efficiency Variance
   = $3,050 (F) − $3,050 (U)
   = $0

Diagram Form:

	Actual Variable Overhead Costs		Standard Rate × Actual Hours		Standard Rate × Standard Hours
Variable Overhead	$73,200	**Spending Variance**	$5.00 × 15,250 = $76,250	**Efficiency Variance**	$5.00 × (12,200 × 1.2) = $73,200
		$3,050 (F)	**Total Variable Overhead Cost Variance**	$3,050 (U)	
			$0		

6. Fixed Overhead Cost Variances:
   a. Fixed Overhead Budget Variance:

Budgeted fixed overhead	$54,000
Less actual fixed overhead	55,000
Fixed Overhead Budget Variance	$ 1,000 (U)

   b. Fixed Overhead Volume Variance:

Standard fixed overhead applied (14,640 labor hours × $3.60* per hour)	$52,704
Less total budgeted fixed overhead	54,000
Fixed Overhead Volume Variance	$ 1,296 (U)

   c. Total Fixed Overhead Cost Variance:

   Total Fixed Overhead Cost Variance = Net of Fixed Overhead Budget Variance and Fixed Overhead Volume Variance
   = $1,000 (U) + $1,296 (U)
   = $2,296 (U)

*From answer to requirement **2.**

Diagram Form:

	Actual Fixed Overhead Costs		**Budgeted Fixed Overhead Costs**		**Standard Rate × Standard Hours**
Fixed Overhead	$55,000	**Budget Variance**	$54,000	**Volume Variance**	$3.60 × (12,200 × 1.2) = $52,704
		$1,000 (U)	**Total Fixed Overhead Cost Variance**	$1,296 (U)	
			$2,296 (U)		

LO1 Define *standard costs,* explain how standard costs are developed, and compute a standard unit cost.

Standard costs are realistic estimates of costs based on analyses of both past and projected operating costs and conditions. They provide a standard, or predetermined, performance level for use in standard costing, a method of cost control that also includes a measure of actual performance and a measure of the variance between standard and actual performance.

A standard unit cost has six elements. A total standard unit cost is computed by adding the following costs: direct materials costs (direct materials price standard times direct materials quantity standard), direct labor costs (direct labor rate standard times direct labor time standard), and overhead costs (standard variable and standard fixed overhead rate times standard direct labor hours allowed per unit).

LO2 Prepare a flexible budget, and describe how managers use variance analysis to control costs.

A flexible budget is a summary of anticipated costs for a range of activity levels. It provides forecasted cost data that can be adjusted for changes in level of output. The variable cost per unit and total fixed costs presented in a flexible budget are components of the flexible budget formula, an equation that determines the budgeted cost for any level of output. A flexible budget improves the accuracy of variance analysis, which is a four-step approach to controlling costs. First, managers compute the amount of the variance. If the amount is significant, managers then analyze the variance to identify its cause. They then select performance measures that will enable them to track those activities, analyze the results, and determine the action needed to correct the problem. Their final step is to take the appropriate corrective action.

LO3 Compute and analyze direct materials variances.

The direct materials price variance is computed by finding the difference between the standard price and the actual price per unit and multiplying it by the actual quantity purchased. The direct materials quantity variance is the difference between the standard quantity that should have been used and the actual quantity used, multiplied by the standard price. An analysis of these variances enables managers to identify what is causing them and to formulate plans for correcting related operating problems.

LO4 Compute and analyze direct labor variances.

The direct labor rate variance is computed by determining the difference between the standard direct labor rate and the actual rate and multiplying it by the actual direct labor hours worked. The direct labor efficiency variance is the difference between the standard hours allowed for the number of good units produced and the actual hours worked multiplied by the standard direct labor rate. Managers analyze these variances to find the causes of differences between standard direct labor costs and actual direct labor costs.

LO5 Compute and analyze overhead variances.

The total overhead variance is equal to the amount of under- or overapplied overhead costs for an accounting period. An analysis of the variable and fixed overhead variances will help explain why the amount of overhead applied to units produced differs from the actual overhead costs incurred. The total overhead cost variance can be broken down into a variable overhead spending variance, a variable overhead efficiency variance, a fixed overhead budget variance, and a fixed overhead volume variance.

LO6 Explain how variances are used to evaluate managers' performance.

How effectively and fairly a manager's performance is evaluated depends on human factors—the people doing the evaluating—as well as on company policies. To ensure that performance evaluation is effective and fair, a company's evaluation policies should be based on input from managers and employees and should be specific about the procedures that managers are to follow. The evaluation process becomes more accurate when managerial performance reports for cost centers include variances from standard costs. A managerial performance report based on standard costs and related variances should identify the causes of each significant variance, along with the personnel involved and the corrective actions taken. It should be tailored to the cost center manager's specific areas of responsibility.

REVIEW of Concepts and Terminology

The following concepts and terms were introduced in this chapter:

CHAPTER ASSIGNMENTS

BUILDING Your Basic Knowledge and Skills

Short Exercises

LO1 **Uses of Standard Costs**

SE 1. Lago Corporation is considering adopting the standard costing method. Dan Sarkis, the manager of the Ohio Division, attended a corporate meeting at which Leah Rohr, the controller, discussed the proposal. Sarkis asked, "Leah, how will this new method benefit me? How will I use it?" Prepare Rohr's response to Sarkis.

LO1 **Purposes of Standard Costs**

SE 2. Suppose you are a management consultant and a client asks you why companies include standard costs in their cost accounting systems. Prepare your response, listing several purposes for using standard costs.

LO1 **Computing a Standard Unit Cost**

SE 3. Using the information that follows, compute the standard unit cost of Product MZW:

Direct materials quantity standard	5 pounds per unit
Direct materials price standard	$10.20 per pound
Direct labor time standard	0.2 hour per unit
Direct labor rate standard	$10.75 per hour
Variable overhead rate standard	$7.00 per machine hour
Fixed overhead rate standard	$11.00 per machine hour
Machine hour standard	3 hours per unit

LO2 **Analyzing Cost Variances**

SE 4. Garden Metal Works produces lawn sculptures. The company analyzes only variances that differ by more than 5 percent from the standard cost. The controller computed the following direct labor efficiency variances for March:

	Direct Labor Efficiency Variance	Standard Direct Labor Cost
Product 4	$1,240 (U)	$26,200
Product 6	3,290 (F)	41,700
Product 7	2,030 (U)	34,300
Product 9	1,620 (F)	32,560
Product 12	2,810 (U)	59,740

For each product, determine the variance as a percentage of the standard cost (round to one decimal place). Then identify the products whose variances should be analyzed and suggest possible causes for the variances.

LO2 **Preparing a Flexible Budget**

SE 5. Prepare a flexible budget for 10,000, 12,000, and 14,000 units of output, using the following information:

Variable costs	
Direct materials	$10.00 per unit
Direct labor	$3.00 per unit
Variable overhead	$5.00 per unit
Total budgeted fixed overhead	$80,800

LO3 **Direct Materials Variances**

SE 6. Using the standard unit costs that you computed in **SE 3** and the following actual cost and usage data, compute the direct materials price and direct materials quantity variances:

Direct materials purchased and used (pounds)	55,000
Price paid for direct materials	$10.00 per pound
Number of good units produced	11,000 units

LO4 **Direct Labor Variances**

SE 7. Using the standard unit costs that you computed in **SE 3** and the following actual cost and usage data, compute the direct labor rate and direct labor efficiency variances:

Direct labor hours used	2,250 hours
Total cost of direct labor	$24,750
Number of good units produced	11,000 units

LO5 **Overhead Variances**

SE 8. Weatherall Products uses standard costing. The following information about overhead was generated during August:

Standard variable overhead rate	$3.00 per machine hour
Standard fixed overhead rate	$3.10 per machine hour
Actual variable overhead costs	$680,100
Actual fixed overhead costs	$698,800
Budgeted fixed overhead costs	$700,000
Standard machine hours per unit produced	12
Good units produced	18,940
Actual machine hours	228,400

Compute the variable overhead spending and efficiency variances and the fixed overhead budget and volume variances.

LO5 **Fixed Overhead Rate and Variances**

SE 9. To the Point Manufacturing Company uses the standard costing method. The company's main product is a fine-quality fountain pen that normally takes 2.5 hours to produce. Normal annual capacity is 30,000 direct labor hours, and budgeted fixed overhead costs for the year were $15,000. During the year, the company produced and sold 14,000 units. Actual fixed overhead costs were $19,000. Compute the fixed overhead rate per direct labor hour, and determine the fixed overhead budget and volume variances.

LO6 **Evaluating Managerial Performance**

SE 10. Raul Tempest, the controller at GoTo Products, gave Jim Dodds, the production manager, a report containing the following information:

	Actual Cost	Standard Cost	Variance
Direct materials	$40,200	$38,200	$2,000 (U)
Direct labor	17,550	17,000	550 (U)
Variable overhead	52,860	50,000	2,860 (U)

Tempest asked for a response. If you were Dodds, how would you respond? What additional information might you need to prepare your response?

Exercises

LO1 **Uses of Standard Costs**

E 1. Summer Diaz has just assumed the duties of controller for Market Research Company. She is concerned that the company's methods of cost planning and control do not accurately track the operations of the business. She plans to suggest to the company's president, Sydney Tyson, that the company start using standard costing for budgeting and cost control. The new method could be incorporated into the existing accounting system. The anticipated cost of adopting it and training managers is around $7,500. Prepare a memo from Summer Diaz to Sydney Tyson that defines standard costing and outlines its uses and benefits.

LO1 **Computing Standard Costs**

E 2. Normal Corporation uses standard costing and is in the process of updating its direct materials and direct labor standards for Product 20B. The following data have been accumulated:

Direct materials In the previous period, 20,500 units were produced, and 32,800 square yards of direct materials at a cost of $122,344 were used to produce them.

Direct labor During the previous period, 57,400 direct labor hours were worked—34,850 hours on machine H and 22,550 hours on machine K. Machine H operators earned $9.40 per hour, and machine K operators earned $9.20 per hour last period. A new labor union contract calls for a 10 percent increase in labor rates for the coming period.

Using this information as the basis for the new standards, compute the direct materials quantity and price standards and the direct labor time and rate standards for each machine for the coming accounting period.

LO1 **Computing a Standard Unit Cost**

E 3. Weather Aerodynamics, Inc., makes electronically equipped weather-detecting balloons for university meteorology departments. Because of recent nationwide inflation, the company's management has ordered that standard costs be recomputed. New direct materials price standards are $700 per set for electronic components and $14.00 per square meter for heavy-duty canvas. Direct materials quantity standards include one set of electronic components and 100 square meters of heavy-duty canvas per balloon. Direct labor time standards are 26 hours per balloon for the Electronics Department and 21 hours per balloon for the Assembly Department. Direct labor rate standards are $21 per hour for the Electronics Department and $18 per hour for the Assembly Department. Standard overhead rates are $16 per direct labor hour for the standard variable overhead rate and $12 per direct labor hour for the standard fixed overhead rate. Using these production standards, compute the standard unit cost of one weather balloon.

LO2 **Preparing a Flexible Budget**

E 4. Keel Company's fixed overhead costs for the year are expected to be as follows: depreciation, $80,000; supervisory salaries, $92,000; property taxes and insurance, $26,000; and other fixed overhead, $14,500. Total fixed overhead is thus expected to be $212,500. Variable costs per unit are expected to be as follows: direct materials, $17.00; direct labor, $9.00; operating supplies, $3.00; indirect labor, $4.00; and other variable overhead costs, $2.50. Prepare a flexible budget for the following levels of production: 15,000 units, 20,000 units, and 25,000 units. What is the flexible budget formula for the year ended December 31?

LO3 Direct Materials Price and Quantity Variances

E 5. SITO Elevator Company manufactures small hydroelectric elevators with a maximum capacity of ten passengers. One of the direct materials used is heavy-duty carpeting for the floor of the elevator. The direct materials quantity standard for April was 8 square yards per elevator. During April, the purchasing agent purchased this carpeting at $11 per square yard; the standard price for the period was $12. Ninety elevators were completed and sold during the month; the Production Department used an average of 8.5 square yards of carpet per elevator. Calculate the company's direct materials price and quantity variances for carpeting for April.

LO3 Direct Materials Variances

E 6. Diekow Productions manufactured and sold 1,000 products at $11,000 each during the past year. At the beginning of the year, production had been set at 1,200 products; direct materials standards had been set at 100 pounds of direct materials at $2 per pound for each product produced. During the year, the company purchased and used 98,000 pounds of direct materials; the cost was $2.04 per pound. Calculate Diekow Production's direct materials price and quantity variances for the year.

LO4 Direct Labor Variances

E 7. At the beginning of last year, Diekow Productions set direct labor standards of 20 hours at $15 per hour for each product produced. During the year, 20,500 direct labor hours were actually worked at an average cost of $16 per hour. Using this information and the applicable information in **E 6**, calculate Diekow Production's direct labor rate and efficiency variances for the year.

LO4 Direct Labor Rate and Efficiency Variances

E 8. NEO Foundry, Inc., manufactures castings that other companies use in the production of machinery. For the past two years, NEO's best-selling product has been a casting for an eight-cylinder engine block. Standard direct labor hours per engine block are 1.8 hours. A labor union contract requires that the company pay all direct labor employees $14 per hour. During June, NEO produced 16,500 engine blocks. Actual direct labor hours and costs for the month were 29,900 hours and $433,550, respectively.

1. Compute the direct labor rate variance for eight-cylinder engine blocks during June.
2. Using the same data, compute the direct labor efficiency variance for eight-cylinder engine blocks during June. Check your answer, assuming that the total direct labor cost variance is $17,750 (U).

LO5 Variable Overhead Variances

E 9. At the beginning of last year, Diekow Productions set variable overhead standards of 10 machine hours at a rate of $10 per hour for each product produced. During the year, 10,800 machine hours were used at a cost of $10.20 per hour. Using this information and the applicable information in **E 6**, calculate Diekow Production's variable overhead spending and efficiency variances for the year.

LO5 Fixed Overhead Variances

E 10. At the beginning of last year, Diekow Productions set budgeted fixed overhead costs at $456,000. During the year, actual fixed overhead costs were $500,000. Using this information and the applicable information in **E 6**, calculate Diekow Production's fixed overhead budget and volume variances for the year. Assume that fixed overhead is applied based on units of product.

LO5 Variable Overhead Variances for a Service Business

E 11. Design Architects, LLP, billed clients for 6,000 hours of design work for the month. Actual variable overhead costs for the month were $315,000, and 6,250 hours were worked. At the beginning of the year, a variable overhead standard of $50 per design hour had been developed based on a budget of 5,000 design hours each month. Calculate Design Architects' variable overhead spending and efficiency variances for the month.

LO5 Fixed Overhead Variances for a Service Business

E 12. Engineering Associates billed clients for 11,000 hours of engineering work for the month. Actual fixed overhead costs for the month were $435,000, and 11,850 hours were worked. At the beginning of the year, a fixed overhead standard of $40 per engineering hour had been developed based on a budget of 10,000 engineering hours each month. Calculate Engineering Associates' fixed overhead budget and volume variances for the month.

LO5 Overhead Variances

E 13. Cedar Key Company produces handmade clamming buckets and sells them to distributors along the Gulf Coast of Florida. The company incurred $9,400 of actual overhead costs ($8,000 variable; $1,400 fixed) in May. Budgeted standard overhead costs for May were $4 of variable overhead costs per direct labor hour and $1,500 of fixed overhead costs. Normal capacity was set at 2,000 direct labor hours per month. In May, the company produced 10,100 clamming buckets by working 1,900 direct labor hours. The time standard is 0.2 direct labor hour per clamming bucket. Compute (1) the variable overhead spending and efficiency variances and (2) the fixed overhead budget and volume variances for May.

LO5 Overhead Variances

E 14. Suncoast Industries uses standard costing and a flexible budget for cost planning and control. Its monthly budget for overhead costs is $200,000 of fixed costs plus $5.20 per machine hour. Monthly normal capacity of 100,000 machine hours is used to compute the standard fixed overhead rate. During December, employees worked 105,000 machine hours. Only 98,500 standard machine hours were allowed for good units produced during the month. Actual overhead costs incurred during December totaled $441,000 of variable costs and $204,500 of fixed costs. Compute (1) the under- or overapplied overhead during December and (2) the variable overhead spending and efficiency variances and the fixed overhead budget and volume variances.

LO6 Evaluating Managerial Performance

E 15. Ron LaTulip oversees projects for ACE Construction Company. Recently, the company's controller sent him a performance report regarding the construction of the Campus Highlands Apartment Complex, a project that LaTulip supervised. Included in the report was an unfavorable direct labor efficiency variance of $1,900 for roof structures. What types of information does LaTulip need to analyze before he can respond to this report?

Problems

LO1 Computing and Using Standard Costs

P 1. Prefabricated houses are the specialty of Affordable Homes, Inc., of Corsicana, Texas. Although Affordable Homes produces many models, the company's best-selling model is the Welcome Home, a three-bedroom, 1,400-square-foot house with an impressive front entrance. Last year, the standard costs for the six basic direct materials used in manufacturing the entrance were as follows: wood framing materials, $2,140; deluxe front door, $480; door hardware, $260; exterior siding, $710; electrical materials, $580; and interior finishing materials, $1,520. Three types of direct labor are used to build the entrance: carpenter, 30 hours at $12 per hour; door specialist, 4 hours at $14 per hour; and electrician, 8 hours at $16 per hour. Last year, the company used an overhead rate of 40 percent of total direct materials cost.

This year, the cost of wood framing materials is expected to increase by 20 percent, and a deluxe front door will cost $496. The cost of the door hardware will increase by 10 percent, and the cost of electrical materials will increase by 20 percent. Exterior siding cost should decrease by $16 per unit. The cost of interior finishing materials is expected to remain the same. The carpenter's wages will increase by $1 per hour, and the door specialist's wages should remain the same. The electrician's wages will increase by $0.50 per hour. Finally, the overhead rate will decrease to 25 percent of total direct materials cost.

Required

1. Compute the total standard cost of direct materials per entrance for last year.
2. Using your answer to requirement **1**, compute the total standard unit cost per entrance for last year.
3. Compute the total standard unit cost per entrance for this year.

LO2 Preparing a Flexible Budget and Evaluating Performance

P 2. Home Products Company manufactures a complete line of kitchen glassware. The Beverage Division specializes in 12-ounce drinking glasses. Erin Fisher, the superintendent of the Beverage Division, asked the controller to prepare a report of her division's performance in April. The following report was handed to her a few days later:

Cost Category (Variable Unit Cost)	Budgeted Costs*	Actual Costs	Difference Under (Over) Budget
Direct materials ($0.10)	$ 5,000	$ 4,975	$ 25
Direct labor ($0.12)	6,000	5,850	150
Variable overhead			
Indirect labor ($0.03)	1,500	1,290	210
Supplies ($0.02)	1,000	960	40
Heat and power ($0.03)	1,500	1,325	175
Other ($0.05)	2,500	2,340	160
Fixed overhead			
Heat and power	3,500	3,500	—
Depreciation	4,200	4,200	—
Insurance and taxes	1,200	1,200	—
Other	1,600	1,600	—
Totals	$28,000	$27,240	$760

*Based on normal capacity of 50,000 units.

In discussing the report with the controller, Fisher stated, "Profits have been decreasing in recent months, but this report indicates that our production process is operating efficiently."

Required

1. Prepare a flexible budget for the Beverage Division using production levels of 45,000 units, 50,000 units, and 55,000 units.
2. What is the flexible budget formula?
3. Assume that the Beverage Division produced 46,560 units in April and that all fixed costs remained constant. Prepare a revised performance report similar to the one above, using actual production in units as a basis for the budget column.

Manager insight ▶ 4. Which report is more meaningful for performance evaluation, the original one above or the revised one? Why?

LO3 LO4 **Direct Materials and Direct Labor Variances**

P 3. Winners Trophy Company produces a variety of athletic awards, most of them in the form of trophies. Its deluxe trophy stands 3 feet tall above the base. The company's direct materials standards for the deluxe trophy include 1 pound of metal and 8 ounces of wood for the base. Standard prices for the year were $3.30 per pound of metal and $0.45 per ounce of wood. Direct labor standards for the deluxe trophy specify 0.2 hour of direct labor in the Molding Department and 0.4 hour in the Trimming/Finishing Department. Standard direct labor rates are $10.75 per hour in the Molding Department and $12.00 per hour in the Trimming/Finishing Department.

During January, the company made 16,400 deluxe trophies. Actual production data are as follows:

Direct materials	
Metal	16,640 pounds @ $3.25 per pound
Wood	131,400 ounces @ $0.48 per ounce
Direct labor	
Molding	3,400 hours @ $10.60 per hour
Trimming Finishing	6,540 hours @ $12.10 per hour

Required

1. Compute the direct materials price and quantity variances for metal and wood.
2. Compute the direct labor rate and efficiency variances for the Molding and the Trimming/Finishing Departments.

LO3 LO4 LO5 **Direct Materials, Direct Labor, and Overhead Variances**

P 4. The Doormat Division of Clean Sweep Company produces all-vinyl mats. Each doormat calls for 0.4 meter of vinyl material; the material should cost $3.10 per meter. Standard direct labor hours and labor cost per doormat are 0.2 hour and $1.84 (0.2 hour × $9.20 per hour), respectively. Currently, the division's standard variable overhead rate is $1.50 per direct labor hour, and its standard fixed overhead rate is $0.80 per direct labor hour.

In August, the division manufactured and sold 60,000 doormats. During the month, it used 25,200 meters of vinyl material; the total cost of the material was $73,080. The total actual overhead costs for August were $28,200, of which $18,200 was variable. The total number of direct labor hours worked was 10,800, and the factory payroll for direct labor for the month was $95,040. Budgeted fixed overhead for August was $9,280. Normal monthly capacity for the year was set at 58,000 doormats.

Required

1. Compute for August the (a) direct materials price variance, (b) direct materials quantity variance, (c) direct labor rate variance, (d) direct labor efficiency

variance, (e) variable overhead spending variance, (f) variable overhead efficiency variance, (g) fixed overhead budget variance, and (h) fixed overhead volume variance.

Manager insight ▶ 2. Prepare a performance report based on your variance analysis, and suggest possible causes for each variance.

LO5 **Overhead Variances**

P 5. Celine Corporation's accountant left for vacation before completing the monthly cost variance report. George Celine, the corporation's president, has asked you to complete the report. The following data are available to you (capacities are expressed in machine hours):

Actual machine hours	17,100
Standard machine hours allowed	17,500
Actual variable overhead	a
Standard variable overhead rate	$2.50
Variable overhead spending variance	$250 (F)
Variable overhead efficiency variance	b
Actual fixed overhead	c
Budgeted fixed overhead	$153,000
Fixed overhead budget variance	$1,300 (U)
Fixed overhead volume variance	$4,500 (F)
Normal capacity in machine hours	d
Standard fixed overhead rate	e
Fixed overhead applied	f

Required

Analyze the data and fill in the missing amounts. (**Hint:** Use the structure of Figures 23-4 and 23-5 to guide your analysis.)

Alternate Problems

LO1 **Computing Standard Costs for Direct Materials**

P 6. TickTock, Ltd., assembles clock movements for grandfather clocks. Each movement has four components: the clock facing, the clock hands, the time movement, and the spring assembly. For the current year, the company used the following standard costs: clock facing, $15.90; clock hands, $12.70; time movement, $66.10; and spring assembly, $52.50.

Prices of materials are expected to change next year. TickTock will purchase 60 percent of the facings from Company A at $18.50 each and the other 40 percent from Company B at $18.80 each. The clock hands, which are produced for TickTock by Hardware, Inc., will cost $15.50 per set next year. TickTock will purchase 30 percent of the time movements from Company Q at $68.50 each, 20 percent from Company R at $69.50 each, and 50 percent from Company S at $71.90 each. The manufacturer that supplies TickTock with spring assemblies has announced that it will increase its prices by 20 percent.

Required

1. Determine the total standard direct materials cost per unit for next year.
2. Suppose that because TickTock has guaranteed Hardware, Inc., that it will purchase 2,500 sets of clock hands next year, the cost of a set of clock hands has been reduced by 20 percent. Find the standard direct materials cost per clock.

Manager insight ▶ 3. Suppose that to avoid the increase in the cost of spring assemblies, TickTock purchased substandard ones from a different manufacturer at $50 each; 20 percent of them turned out to be unusable and could not be returned. Assuming that all other data remain the same, compute the standard direct materials unit cost. Spread the cost of the defective materials over the good units produced.

LO2 **Flexible Budgets and Performance Evaluation**

P 7. Cassen Realtors, Inc., specializes in the sale of residential properties. It earns its revenue by charging a percentage of the sales price. Commissions for sales persons, listing agents, and listing companies are its main costs. Business has improved steadily over the last 10 years. Bonnie Cassen, the managing partner of Cassen Realtors, receives a report summarizing the company's performance each year. The report for the most recent year appears below.

Cassen Realtors, Inc.
Performance Report
For the Year Ended December 31

	Budgeted*	Actual†	Difference Under (Over) Budget
Total selling fees	$2,052,000	$2,242,200	($190,200)
Variable costs			
Sales commissions	$1,102,950	$1,205,183	($102,233)
Automobile	36,000	39,560	(3,560)
Advertising	93,600	103,450	(9,850)
Home repairs	77,400	89,240	(11,840)
General overhead	656,100	716,970	(60,870)
	$1,966,050	$2,154,403	($188,353)
Fixed costs			
General overhead	60,000	62,300	(2,300)
Total costs	$2,026,050	$2,216,703	($190,653)
Operating income	$ 25,950	$ 25,497	$ 453

*Budgeted data are based on 180 units sold.
†Actual data for 200 units sold.

Required

1. Analyze the performance report. What does it say about the company's performance? Is the performance report reliable? Explain your answer.
2. Calculate the budgeted selling fee and budgeted variable costs per home sale.
3. Prepare a performance report using a flexible budget based on the actual number of home sales.

Manager insight ▶ 4. Analyze the report you prepared in requirement 3. What does it say about the company's performance? Is the report reliable? Explain your answer.

Manager insight ▶ 5. What recommendations would you make to improve the company's performance next year?

LO3 LO4 **Direct Materials and Direct Labor Variances**

P 8. Fruit Packaging Company makes plastic baskets for food wholesalers. Each basket requires 0.8 gram of liquid plastic and 0.6 gram of an additive that includes color and hardening agents. The standard prices are $0.15 per gram of liquid plastic and $0.09 per gram of additive. Two kinds of direct labor—molding and trimming/packing—are required to make the baskets. The direct labor time and rate standards for a batch of 100 baskets are as follows: molding, 1.0 hour per batch at an hourly rate of $12; and trimming/packing, 1.2 hours per batch at $10 per hour.

During the year, the company produced 48,000 baskets. It used 38,600 grams of liquid plastic at a total cost of $5,404 and 28,950 grams of additive at $2,895. Actual direct labor included 480 hours for molding at a total cost of $5,664 and 560 hours for trimming/packing at $5,656.

Required

1. Compute the direct materials price and quantity variances for both the liquid plastic and the additive.
2. Compute the direct labor rate and efficiency variances for the molding and trimming/packing processes.

LO3 LO4 LO5 LO6

Computing Variances and Evaluating Performance

P 9. Last year, Biomed Laboratories, Inc., researched and perfected a cure for the common cold. Called Cold-Gone, the product sells for $28.00 per package, each of which contains five tablets. Standard unit costs for this product were developed late last year for use this year. Per package, the standard unit costs were as follows: chemical ingredients, 6 ounces at $1.00 per ounce; packaging, $1.20; direct labor, 0.8 hour at $14.00 per hour; standard variable overhead, $4.00 per direct labor hour; and standard fixed overhead, $6.40 per direct labor hour. Normal capacity is 46,875 units per week.

In the first quarter of this year, demand for the new product rose well beyond the expectations of management. During those three months, the peak season for colds, the company produced and sold over 500,000 packages of Cold-Gone. During the first week in April, it produced 50,000 packages but used materials for 50,200 packages costing $60,240. It also used 305,000 ounces of chemical ingredients costing $292,800. The total cost of direct labor for the week was $579,600; direct labor hours totaled 40,250. Total variable overhead was $161,100, and total fixed overhead was $242,000. Budgeted fixed overhead for the week was $240,000.

Required

1. Compute for the first week of April (a) all direct materials price variances, (b) all direct materials quantity variances, (c) the direct labor rate variance, (d) the direct labor efficiency variance, (e) the variable overhead spending variance, (f) the variable overhead efficiency variance, (g) the fixed overhead budget variance, and (h) the fixed overhead volume variance.

Manager insight ▶

2. Prepare a performance report based on your variance analysis, and suggest possible causes for each significant variance.

LO5

Overhead Variances

P 10. Meantime Corporation's accountant left for vacation before completing the monthly cost variance report. Gillian Thornton, the corporation's president, has asked you to complete the report. The following data are available to you:

Actual machine hours	20,100
Standard machine hours allowed	20,500
Actual variable overhead	a
Standard variable overhead rate	$2.00
Variable overhead spending variance	$200 (F)
Variable overhead efficiency variance	b
Actual fixed overhead	c

Budgeted fixed overhead	$153,000
Fixed overhead budget variance	$500 (U)
Fixed overhead volume variance	$750 (F)
Normal capacity in machine hours	**d**
Standard fixed overhead rate	**e**
Fixed overhead applied	**f**

Required

Analyze the data and fill in the missing amounts. (**Hint:** Use the structure of Figures 23-4 and 23-5 to guide your analysis.)

ENHANCING Your Knowledge, Skills, and Critical Thinking

LO1 An Ethical Question Involving Standard Costs

C 1. Taylor Industries, Inc., develops standard costs for all its direct materials, direct labor, and overhead costs. It uses these costs to price products, cost inventories, and evaluate the performance of purchasing and production managers. It updates the standard costs whenever costs, prices, or rates change by 3 percent or more. It also reviews and updates all standard costs each December; this practice provides current standards that are appropriate for use in valuing year-end inventories on the company's financial statements.

Jody Elgar is in charge of standard costing at Taylor Industries. On November 30, she received a memo from the chief financial officer informing her that Taylor Industries was considering purchasing another company and that she and her staff were to postpone adjusting standard costs until late February; they were instead to concentrate on analyzing the proposed purchase.

In the third week of November, prices on more than 20 of Taylor Industries' direct materials had been reduced by 10 percent or more, and a new labor union contract had reduced several categories of labor rates. A revision of standard costs in December would have resulted in lower valuations of inventories, higher cost of goods sold because of inventory write-downs, and lower net income for the year. Elgar believed that the company was facing an operating loss and that the assignment to evaluate the proposed purchase was designed primarily to keep her staff from revising and lowering standard costs. She questioned the chief financial officer about the assignment and reiterated the need for updating the standard costs, but she was again told to ignore the update and concentrate on the proposed purchase. Elgar and her staff were relieved of the evaluation assignment in early February. The purchase never materialized.

Assess Jody Elgar's actions in this situation. Did she follow all ethical paths to solving the problem? What are the consequences of failing to adjust the standard costs?

LO1 LO2 Standard Costs and Variance Analysis

C 2. Domino's Pizza is a major purveyor of home-delivered pizzas. Although customers can pick up their orders at the shops where Domino's makes its pizzas, employees deliver most orders to customers' homes, and they use their own cars to do it.

Specify what standard costing for a Domino's pizza shop would entail. Where would you obtain the information for determining the cost standards? In what ways would the standards help in managing a pizza shop? If necessary to gain a better understanding of the operation, visit a pizzeria. (It does not have to be a Domino's.)

Your instructor will divide the class into groups to discuss the case. Summarize your group's discussion, and select one person from your group to report the group's findings to the class.

LO2 LO4 LO5 LO6

Preparing Performance Reports

C 3. Troy Corrente, the president of Forest Valley Spa, is concerned about the spa's operating performance during March. He budgeted his costs carefully so that he could reduce the annual membership fees. He now needs to evaluate those costs to make sure that the spa's profits are at the level he expected.

He has asked you, the spa's controller, to prepare a performance report on labor and overhead costs for March. He also wants you to analyze the report and suggest possible causes for any problems that you find. He wants to attend to any problems quickly, so he has asked you to submit your report as soon as possible. The following information for the month is available to you:

	Budgeted Costs	Actual Costs
Variable costs		
Operating labor	$10,880	$12,150
Utilities	2,880	3,360
Repairs and maintenance	5,760	7,140
Fixed overhead costs		
Depreciation, equipment	2,600	2,680
Rent	3,280	3,280
Other	1,704	1,860
Totals	$27,104	$30,470

Corrente's budget allows for eight employees to work 160 hours each per month. During March, nine employees worked an average of 150 hours each.

1. Answer the following questions:
   a. Why are you preparing this performance report?
   b. Who will use the report?
   c. What information do you need to develop the report? How will you obtain that information?
   d. When are the performance report and the analysis needed?
2. With the limited information available to you, compute the labor rate variance, the labor efficiency variance, and the variable and fixed overhead variances.
3. Prepare a performance report for the spa for March. Analyze the report, and suggest causes for any problems that you find.

LO2 LO5

Developing a Flexible Budget and Analyzing Overhead Variances

C 4. Ezelda Marva is the controller at FH Industries. She has asked you, her new assistant, to analyze the following data related to projected and actual overhead costs for October:

	Standard Variable Costs per Machine Hour (MH)	Actual Variable Costs in October
Indirect materials and supplies	$1.10	$ 2,380
Indirect machine setup labor	2.50	5,090
Materials handling	1.40	3,950
Maintenance and repairs	1.50	2,980
Utilities	0.80	1,490
Miscellaneous	0.10	200
Totals	$7.40	$16,090

(continued)

	Budgeted Fixed Overhead	Actual Fixed Overhead in October
Supervisory salaries	$ 3,630	$ 3,630
Machine depreciation	8,360	8,580
Other	1,210	1,220
Totals	$13,200	$13,430

For October, the number of good units produced was used to compute the 2,100 standard machine hours allowed.

1. Prepare a monthly flexible budget for operating activity at 2,000 machine hours, 2,200 machine hours, and 2,500 machine hours.
2. Develop a flexible budget formula.
3. The company's normal operating capacity is 2,200 machine hours per month. Compute the fixed overhead rate at this level of activity. Then break the rate down into rates for each element of fixed overhead.
4. Prepare a detailed comparative cost analysis for October. Include all variable and fixed overhead costs. Format your analysis by using columns for the following five elements: cost category, cost per machine hour, costs applied, actual costs incurred, and variance.
5. Develop an overhead variance analysis for October that identifies the variable overhead spending and efficiency variances and the fixed overhead budget and volume variances.
6. Prepare an analysis of the variances. Could a manager control some of the fixed costs? Defend your answer.

LO4 LO5 Standard Costing in a Service Company

C 5. Annuity Life Insurance Company (ALIC) markets several types of life insurance policies, but P20A—a permanent, 20-year life annuity policy—is its most popular. This policy sells in $10,000 increments and features variable percentages of whole life insurance and single-payment annuities, depending on the policyholder's needs and age. ALIC devotes an entire department to supporting and marketing the P20A policy. Because both the support staff and the sales persons contribute to each P20A policy, ALIC categorizes them as direct labor for purposes of variance analysis, cost control, and performance evaluation. For unit costing, each $10,000 increment is considered one unit; thus, a $90,000 policy is counted as nine units. Standard unit cost information for January is as follows:

Direct labor	
Policy support staff	
3 hours at $12.00 per hour	$ 36.00
Policy sales person	
8.5 hours at $14.20 per hour	120.70
Operating overhead	
Variable operating overhead	
11.5 hours at $26.00 per hour	299.00
Fixed operating overhead	
11.5 hours at $18.00 per hour	207.00
Standard unit cost	$662.70

Actual costs incurred for the 265 units sold during January were as follows:

Direct labor	
Policy support staff	
848 hours at $12.50 per hour	$10,600
Policy sales persons	
2,252.5 hours at $14.00 per hour	31,535
Operating overhead	
Variable operating overhead	78,440
Fixed operating overhead	53,400

Normal monthly capacity is 260 units, and the budgeted fixed operating overhead for January was $53,820.

1. Compute the standard hours allowed in January for policy support staff and policy sales persons.
2. What should the total standard costs for January have been? What were the total actual costs that the company incurred in January? Compute the total cost variance for the month.
3. Compute the direct labor rate and efficiency variances for policy support staff and policy sales persons.
4. Compute the variable and fixed operating overhead variances for January.
5. Identify possible causes for each variance and suggest possible solutions.

LO3 LO4 LO6

Cookie Company (Continuing Case)

C 6. In this segment of our continuing case, assume that you have been using standard costing to plan and control costs at your cookie store. In a meeting with your budget team, which includes managers and employees from the Purchasing, Product Design, and Production departments, you ask all team members to describe any operating problems they encountered in the last quarter. You explain that you will use this information to analyze the causes of significant cost variances that occurred during the quarter.

For each of the following situations, identify the direct materials and/or direct labor variance(s) that could be affected, and indicate whether the variances are favorable or unfavorable:

1. The production department uses highly skilled, highly paid workers.
2. Machines were improperly adjusted.
3. Direct labor personnel worked more carefully than they had in the past to manufacture the product.
4. The Product Design Department replaced a direct material with one that was less expensive and of lower quality.
5. The Purchasing Department bought higher-quality materials at a higher price.
6. A major supplier used a less-expensive mode of transportation to deliver the raw materials.
7. Work was halted for 2 hours because of a power failure.

CHAPTER 24

Short-Run Decision Analysis

The Management Process

PLAN

- ▷ **Discover a problem or a need.**
- ▷ **Identify all reasonable courses of action that can solve the problem or meet the need.**
- ▷ **Prepare a thorough analysis of each possible solution, identifying its total costs, savings, and other financial effects, as well as any qualitative effects.**
- ▷ **Select the best course of action.**

PERFORM

- ▷ **Make decisions that affect operations in the current period, including outsourcing, special order, segment profitability, sales mix, and sell or process-further decisions.**

EVALUATE

- ▷ **Examine each short-run decision and how it affected the organization.**
- ▷ **Identify and prescribe corrective action.**

COMMUNICATE

- ▷ **Prepare reports related to short-run decisions throughout the year.**

Managers use incremental analysis to make a variety of operating decisions throughout the year.

Managers use both financial and nonfinancial quantitative information to analyze the effects of past and potential business actions on their organization's resources and profits. Although many short-term business problems are unique and cannot be solved by following strict rules, managers often take predictable actions when making decisions that will affect their organizations in the short run. In this chapter, we describe those actions. We also explain how managers use incremental analysis in making various types of short-term decisions.

LEARNING OBJECTIVES

LO1 Describe how managers make short-run decisions using incremental analysis. (pp. 1110–1113)

LO2 Perform incremental analysis for outsourcing decisions. (pp. 1113–1115)

LO3 Perform incremental analysis for special order decisions. (pp. 1115–1117)

LO4 Perform incremental analysis for segment profitability decisions. (pp. 1118–1120)

LO5 Perform incremental analysis for sales mix decisions involving constrained resources. (pp. 1120–1123)

LO6 Perform incremental analysis for sell or process-further decisions. (pp. 1123–1125)

DECISION POINT ▸ A MANAGER'S FOCUS BANK OF AMERICA

- How do managers at Bank of America decide on new ways to increase business and protect customers' interests?
- How can incremental analysis help managers at Bank of America take advantage of the business opportunities that online banking offers?

Bank of America is one of the world's largest financial institutions. It serves large corporations, small and mid-sized businesses, governments, institutions, and individuals in over 150 countries. In the United States alone, it serves approximately 53 million individuals and small businesses. The bank has received numerous awards for online customer satisfaction and for its initiatives in preventing online fraud and identity theft. In 2009, more than 29 million of its customers did their banking online.

Managers at Bank of America believe the trend to online commerce is good for business. As customers gain confidence in dealing with their finances over the Internet, the bank's managers plan to offer more online products and services. In their quest to find safe and innovative ways to meet the needs of customers, managers at Bank of America make short-run decisions that affect the bank's profits, resources, and opportunities to increase online banking.

Short-Run Decision Analysis and the Management Process

LO1 Describe how managers make short-run decisions using incremental analysis.

Many of the decisions that managers make affect their organization's activities in the short run. Those decisions are the focus of this chapter. In making short-run decisions, managers need historical and estimated quantitative information that is both financial and nonfinancial in nature. Such information should be relevant, timely, and presented in a format that is easy to use in decision making.

Short-run decision analysis is the systematic examination of any decision whose effects will be felt over the course of the next year. The decision analysis must take into account the organization's strategic plan and tactical objectives, the related costs and revenues, as well as any relevant qualitative factors.

Although many business problems are unique and cannot be solved by following strict rules, managers frequently take four predictable actions when making short-run decisions:

1. Discover a problem or need.
2. Identify all reasonable courses of action that can solve the problem or meet the need.
3. Prepare a thorough analysis of each possible solution, identifying its total costs, savings, and other financial effects, as well as any qualitative factors.
4. Select the best course of action.

Later, managers review each decision to determine whether it produced the forecasted results by examining how it was carried out and how it affected the organization. If results fell short, they identify and prescribe corrective action. This postdecision audit supplies feedback about the results of the short-run decision. If the solution is not completely satisfactory or if the problem remains, the management process begins again.

In the course of a year, managers may make many short-run decisions, such as whether to make a product or service or buy it from an outside supplier, whether to accept a special order, whether to keep or drop an unprofitable segment, and whether to sell a product as is or process it further. If resources are limited, they may also have to decide on the most appropriate product mix. In making such decisions, managers analyze not only quantitative factors relating to profitability and liquidity; they also analyze qualitative factors. For example, the qualitative factors a bank might consider when deciding whether to keep or eliminate a branch location include the following:

- Competition (Do our competitors have a branch office located here?)
- Economic conditions (Is the community growing?)
- Social issues (Will keeping this branch benefit the community we serve?)
- Product or service quality (Can we attract more business because of the quality of service at this branch?)
- Timeliness (Does the branch promote customer service?)

Managers must identify and assess the importance of all such qualitative factors, as well as quantitative factors, when they make short-run decisions.

Incremental Analysis for Short-Run Decisions

Once managers have determined that a problem or need is worthy of consideration and have identified alternative courses of action, they must evaluate the effect that each alternative will have on their organization. The method of

FOCUS ON BUSINESS PRACTICE

How Much Does It Cost to Process a Check?

Banks today have several options for processing checks. They can outsource the processing of paper checks, use the quasi-paperless system of ATMs, or process transactions over the Internet. Bank managers have found that online banking substantially reduces transaction processing costs. According to a study by an international consulting firm, the cost of processing a transaction is 1 cent if the transaction is completed over the Internet, 27 cents if an ATM is used, and $1.07 if processed by a teller.[1]

Study Note

Incremental analysis is a technique used not only by businesses but also by individuals to solve daily problems.

comparing alternatives by focusing on the differences in their projected revenues and costs is called **incremental analysis**. If incremental analysis excludes revenues or costs that stay the same or that do not change between the alternatives, it is called *differential analysis.*

Irrelevant Costs and Revenues A cost that changes between alternatives is known as a **differential cost** (also called an *incremental cost*). For example, suppose that managers at Home State Bank, a local institution, are deciding which of two ATM machines—C or W—to buy. The ATMs have the same purchase price but different revenue and cost characteristics. The company currently owns ATM B, which it bought three years ago for $15,000 and which has accumulated depreciation of $9,000 and a book value of $6,000. ATM B is now obsolete as a result of advances in technology and cannot be sold or traded in.

A manager has prepared the following comparison of the annual revenue and operating cost estimates for the two new machines:

	ATM C	*ATM W*
Increase in revenue	$16,200	$19,800
Increase in annual operating costs		
Direct materials	4,800	4,800
Direct labor	2,200	4,100
Variable overhead	2,100	3,050
Fixed overhead (depreciation included)	5,000	5,000

Study Note

Sunk costs cannot be recovered and are irrelevant in short-run decision making.

The first step in the incremental analysis is to eliminate any irrelevant revenues and costs. *Irrelevant revenues* are those that will not differ between the alternatives. *Irrelevant costs* include sunk costs and costs that will not differ between the alternatives. A **sunk cost** is a cost that was incurred because of a previous decision and cannot be recovered through the current decision. An example of a sunk cost is the book value of ATM B. A manager might be tempted to say that the ATM should not be junked because the company still has $6,000 invested in it. However, the manager would be incorrect because the book value of the old ATM represents money that was spent in the past and so does not affect the decision about whether to replace the old ATM with a new one.

The old ATM would be of interest only if it could be sold or traded in, and if the amount received for it would be different, depending on which new ATM

EXHIBIT 24-1
Incremental Analysis

Home State Bank
Incremental Analysis

	ATM C	ATM W	Difference in Favor of ATM W
Increase in revenue	$16,200	$19,800	$3,600
Increase in annual operating costs that differ between alternatives			
Direct labor	$ 2,200	$ 4,100	($1,900)
Variable overhead	2,100	3,050	(950)
Total increase in operating costs	$ 4,300	$ 7,150	($2,850)
Resulting change in operating income	$11,900	$12,650	$ 750

was chosen. In that case, the amount of the sale or trade-in value would be relevant to the decision because it would affect the future cash flows of the alternatives. Two examples of an irrelevant cost in the financial data for ATMs C and W are the costs of direct materials and fixed overhead (depreciation included). These costs can also be eliminated from the analysis because they are the same under both alternatives.

Once the irrelevant revenues and costs have been identified, the incremental analysis can be prepared using only the differential revenues and costs that will change between the alternative ATMs, as shown in Exhibit 24-1. The analysis shows that ATM W would produce $750 more in operating income than ATM C. Because the costs of buying the two ATMs are the same, this report would favor the purchase of ATM W.

Opportunity Costs Because incremental analysis focuses on only the quantitative differences among the alternatives, it simplifies management's evaluation of a decision and reduces the time needed to choose the best course of action. However, incremental analysis is only one input to the final decision. Management needs to consider other issues. For instance, the manufacturer of ATM C might have a reputation for better quality or service than the manufacturer of ATM W. **Opportunity costs** are the benefits that are forfeited or lost when one alternative is chosen over another. For example, suppose Home State Bank offers a local plant nursery a high price for the land on which the nursery is located. The interest that could be earned from investing the cash proceeds of the land sale is an opportunity cost for the nursery owner. It is revenue that the nursery owner has chosen to forgo to continue operating the nursery in that location.

Study Note

Opportunity costs arise when the choice of one course of action eliminates the possibility of another course of action.

Opportunity costs often come into play when a company is operating at or near capacity and must choose which products or services to offer. For example, suppose that Home State Bank, which currently services 20,000 debit cards, has the option of offering 15,000 premium debit cards, which is a higher-priced product, but it cannot do both. The amount of income from the 20,000 debit cards is an opportunity cost of the premium debit cards.

Credit Banc has assembled the following monthly information related to the purchase of a new automated teller machine:

	Machine A	Machine B
Increase in revenue	$4,200	$5,100
Increase in annual operating costs		
Direct materials	1,200	1,200
Direct labor	1,200	1,600
Variable overhead	2,500	2,900
Fixed overhead (including depreciation)	1,400	1,400

Using incremental analysis and only relevant information, compute the difference in favor of the Machine B.

SOLUTION

Credit Banc
Incremental Analysis

	Machine A	Machine B	Difference in Favor of Machine B
Increase in revenue	$4,200	$5,100	$ 900
Increase in operating costs that differ between alternatives			
Direct labor	$1,200	$1,600	($ 400)
Variable overhead	2,500	2,900	(400)
Total increase in operating costs	$3,700	$4,500	($ 800)
Resulting change in operating income	$ 500	$ 600	$ 100

Incremental Analysis for Outsourcing Decisions

LO2 Perform incremental analysis for outsourcing decisions.

Outsourcing is the use of suppliers outside the organization to perform services or produce goods that could be performed or produced internally. **Make-or-buy decisions**, which are decisions about whether to make a part internally or buy it from an external supplier, may lead to outsourcing. However, a company may decide to outsource entire operating activities, such as warehousing or human resources, that have traditionally been performed in-house.

To improve operating income and compete effectively in global markets, many companies are focusing their resources on their core competencies—that is, the activities that they perform best. One way to obtain the financial, physical, human, and technological resources needed to emphasize those competencies is to outsource expensive nonvalue-adding activities. Strong candidates for outsourcing include payroll processing, training, managing fleets of vehicles, sales and marketing, custodial services, and information management. Many such areas involve either relatively low skill levels (such as payroll processing or custodial services) or highly specialized knowledge (such as information management) that could be better acquired from experts outside the company.

Outsourcing production or operating activities can reduce a company's investment in physical assets and human resources, which can improve cash flow. It can also help a company reduce its operating costs and improve operating income. For example, because **Amazon.com** outsources the distribution of most of its products, it has been able to reduce its storage and distribution costs enough to offer product discounts of up to 40 percent off the list price. It is also able to provide additional value-adding services, such as online reviews by customers, personalized recommendations, and discussions and interviews on current products.

Outsourcing Analysis In manufacturing companies, a common decision facing managers is whether to make or to buy some or all of the parts used in product assembly. The goal is to select the more profitable choice by identifying the costs of each alternative and their effects on revenues and existing costs. Managers need the following information for this analysis:

Information About Making	*Information About Buying*
Variable costs of making the item	Purchase price of item
Need for additional machinery	Rent or net cash flow to be generated from vacated space in the factory
Incremental fixed costs	Salvage value of unused machinery

To illustrate a manufacturer's outsourcing decision, let's suppose that for the past five years, Box Company has purchased packing cartons from an outside supplier at a cost of $1.25 per carton.

- The supplier has just informed Box Company that it is raising the price 20 percent, to $1.50 per carton, effective immediately.
- Box Company has idle machinery that could be adjusted to produce the cartons. Annual production and usage would be 20,000 cartons. The company estimates the cost of direct materials at $0.84 per carton. Workers, who will be paid $8.00 per hour, can process 20 cartons per hour ($0.40 per carton). The cost of variable overhead will be $4 per direct labor hour, and 1,000 direct labor hours will be required.
- Fixed overhead includes $4,000 of depreciation per year and $6,000 of other fixed costs.
- The company has space and machinery to produce the cartons; the machines are currently idle and will continue to be idle if the cartons are purchased.

Study Note

When performing an incremental analysis for an outsourcing decision, do not incorporate irrelevant information, such as depreciation and other fixed costs. Include only costs that change between the alternatives.

Should Box Company continue to outsource the cartons?

Exhibit 24-2 presents an incremental analysis of the two alternatives. All relevant costs are listed. Because the machinery has already been purchased and

EXHIBIT 24-2
Incremental Analysis: Outsourcing Decision

Box Company
Outsourcing Decision
Incremental Analysis

	Make	**Outsource**	**Difference in Favor of Make**
Direct materials (20,000 × $0.84)	$16,800	—	($16,800)
Direct labor (20,000 × $0.40)	8,000	—	(8,000)
Variable overhead (1,000 hours × $4)	4,000	—	(4,000)
Purchase price (20,000 × $1.50)	—	$30,000	30,000
Totals	$28,800	$30,000	$ 1,200

neither the machinery nor the required factory space has any other use, the depreciation costs and other fixed overhead costs are the same for both alternatives; therefore, they are not relevant to the decision. The cost of making the needed cartons is $28,800. The cost of buying 20,000 cartons at the increased purchase price will be $30,000. Since the company would save $1,200 by making the cartons, management will decide to make the cartons.

STOP & APPLY >

Office Associates, Inc., is currently operating at less than capacity. The company thinks it could cut costs by outsourcing office cleaning to an independent cleaning service for $75 a week. Currently, a general office worker is employed for $10 an hour to do light cleaning and other general office duties. Cleaning the office usually takes one hour a day to perform and consumes $10 of supplies, $2 of variable overhead, and $18 of fixed overhead each week. Should Office Associates, Inc., continue to perform office cleanings, or should it begin to outsource them?

SOLUTION

Costs per Cleaning	Continue to Perform Cleanings	Outsource Cleanings	Difference in Favor of Continuing to Perform Cleanings
Employee labor	$50	—	($50)
Supplies	10	—	(10)
Variable overhead	2	—	(2)
Outside cleaning service	—	$75	75
Totals	$62	$75	$13

Office Associates should continue to perform office cleanings itself.

Incremental Analysis for Special Order Decisions

LO3 Perform incremental analysis for special order decisions.

Study Note

A decision to accept a special order assumes that excess capacity exists to fulfill the order and that the order will not have an impact on regular sales orders.

Managers are often faced with **special order decisions**, which are decisions about whether to accept or reject special orders at prices below the normal market prices. Special orders usually involve large numbers of similar products that are sold in bulk. Before a firm accepts a special product order, it must be sure that excess capacity exists to complete the order and that the order will not reduce unit sales from its full-priced regular product line.

The objective of a special order decision is to determine whether a special order should be accepted. A special order should be accepted only if it maximizes operating income. In many situations, sales commission expenses are excluded from a special order decision analysis because the customer approached the company directly. In addition, the fixed costs of existing facilities usually do not change if a company accepts a special order, and therefore these costs are usually irrelevant to the decision. If additional fixed costs must be incurred to fill the special order, they would be relevant to the decision. Examples of relevant fixed costs are the purchase of additional machinery, an increase in supervisory help, and an increase in insurance premiums required by a specific order.

Special Order Analyses One approach to a special order decision is to compare the price of the special order with the relevant costs of producing, packaging, and shipping the order. The relevant costs include the variable costs, variable selling costs (if any), and other costs directly associated with the special order (e.g., freight, insurance, and packaging and labeling the product). Another approach to this kind of decision is to prepare a special order bid price by calculating a minimum selling price for the special order. The bid price must cover the relevant costs and an estimated profit.

For example, suppose Home State Bank has been approved to provide and service four ATMs at a special event. The event sponsors want the fee reduced to $0.50 per ATM transaction. At past special events, ATM use has averaged 2,000 transactions per machine. Home State Bank has located four idle ATMs and determined the following additional information:

ATM Cost Data for Annual Use of One Machine (400,000 Transactions)	
Direct materials	$0.10
Direct labor	0.05
Variable overhead	0.20
Fixed overhead ($100,000 ÷ 400,000)	0.25
Advertising ($60,000 ÷ 400,000)	0.15
Other fixed selling and administrative expenses ($120,000 ÷ 400,000)	0.30
Cost per transaction	$1.05
Regular fee per transaction	$1.50

Should Home State Bank accept the special event offer?

An incremental analysis of the decision in the contribution margin reporting format appears in Exhibit 24-3. The report shows the contribution margin for Home State Bank's operations both with and without the special order. Fixed costs are not included because the only costs affected by the order are direct materials, direct labor, and variable overhead.

- ***Price and relevant cost comparison:*** The net result of accepting the special order is a $1,200 increase in contribution margin (and, correspondingly, in

EXHIBIT 24-3
Incremental Analysis: Special Order Decision

Home State Bank
Special Order Decision
Incremental Analysis

	Without Order	With Order	Difference in Favor of Accepting Order
Sales	$2,400,000	$2,404,000	$ 4,000
Less variable costs			
Direct materials	$ 160,000	$ 160,800	($ 800)
Direct labor	80,000	80,400	(400)
Variable overhead	320,000	321,600	(1,600)
Total variable costs	$ 560,000	$ 562,800	($ 2,800)
Contribution margin	$1,840,000	$1,841,200	$ 1,200

operating income). The analysis reveals that Home State Bank should accept the special order. The $1,200 increase is verified by the following incremental analysis:

Special order sales [(2,000 transactions × 4) × $0.50]		$4,000
Less variable costs		
Direct materials (8,000 transactions × $0.10)	$ 800	
Direct labor (8,000 transactions × $0.05)	400	
Variable overhead (8,000 transactions × $0.20)	1,600	
Total variable costs		2,800
Special order contribution margin		$1,200

- ***Minimum bid price for special order:*** Now let us assume that the event sponsor asks Home State Bank what its minimum special order price is. If the incremental costs for the special order are $2,800, the relevant cost per transaction is $0.35 ($2,800 ÷ 8,000). The special order price should cover this cost and generate a profit. If Home State Bank would like to earn $800 from the special order, the special order price should be $0.45 [$0.35 cost per transaction plus $0.10 profit per transaction ($800 ÷ 8,000 transactions)].

Of course, the Home State Bank management's decisions must be consistent with the bank's strategic plan and tactical objectives, and it must take into account not only costs and revenues but also relevant qualitative factors. Qualitative factors that might influence the decision are (1) the impact of the special order on regular customers, (2) the potential of the special order to lead into new sales areas, and (3) the customer's ability to maintain an ongoing relationship that includes good ordering and paying practices.

STOP & APPLY >

Sample Company has received an order for Product EZ at a special selling price of $26 per unit (suggested retail price is $30). This order is over and above normal production, and budgeted production and sales targets for the year have already been exceeded. Capacity exists to satisfy the special order. No selling costs will be incurred in connection with this order. Unit costs to manufacture and sell Product EZ are as follows: direct materials, $7.00; direct labor, $10.00; variable overhead, $8.00; fixed manufacturing costs, $5.00; variable selling costs, $3.00; and fixed general and administrative costs, $9.00. Should Sample Company accept the order?

SOLUTION

Variable Costs to Produce Product EZ

Direct materials	$ 7.00
Direct labor	10.00
Variable overhead	8.00
Total variable costs to produce	$25.00

Sample Company should accept the special order because the offered price exceeds the variable manufacturing costs.

Incremental Analysis for Segment Profitability Decisions

LO4 Perform incremental analysis for segment profitability decisions.

Another type of operating decision that management must make is whether to keep or drop unprofitable segments, such as product lines, services, sales territories, divisions, departments, stores, or outlets. Management must select the alternative that maximizes operating income. The objective of the decision analysis is to identify the segments that have a negative segment margin so that managers can drop them or take corrective action.

A **segment margin** is a segment's sales revenue minus its direct costs (direct variable costs and direct fixed costs traceable to the segment). Such costs are assumed to be **avoidable costs**. An avoidable cost could be eliminated if management were to drop the segment.

- If a segment has a positive segment margin—that is, the segment's revenue is greater than its direct costs—it is able to cover its own direct costs and contribute a portion of its revenue to cover common costs and add to operating income. In that case, management should keep the segment.
- If a segment has a negative segment margin—that is, the segment's revenue is less than its direct costs—management should eliminate the segment.

However, certain common costs will be incurred regardless of the decision. Those are unavoidable costs, and the remaining segments must have sufficient contribution margin to cover their own direct costs and the common costs.

Segment Profitability Analysis An analysis of segment profitability includes the preparation of a segmented income statement using variable costing to identify variable and fixed costs. The fixed costs that are traceable to the segments are called *direct fixed costs.* The remaining fixed costs are *common costs* and are not assigned to segments.

Suppose Home State Bank wants to determine if it should eliminate its Safe Deposit Division. Managers prepare a segmented income statement, separating variable and fixed costs to calculate the contribution margin. They separate the total fixed costs of $84,000 further by directly tracing $55,500 to Bank Operations and $16,500 to the Safe Deposit Division; the remaining $12,000 are common fixed costs. The following segmented income statement shows the segment margins for Bank Operations and the Safe Deposit Division and the operating income for the total company:

Home State Bank
Segmented Income Statement
For the Year Ended December 31, 2011

	Bank Operations	Safe Deposit Division	Total Company
Sales	$135,000	$15,000	$150,000
Less variable costs	52,500	7,500	60,000
Contribution margin	$ 82,500	$ 7,500	$ 90,000
Less direct fixed costs	55,500	16,500	72,000
Segment margin	$ 27,000	($ 9,000)	$ 18,000
Less common fixed costs			12,000
Operating income			$ 6,000

EXHIBIT 24-4
Incremental Analysis:
Segment Profitability Decision

Home State Bank
Segment Profitability Decision
Incremental Analysis—Situation 1

	Keep Safe Deposit Division	Drop Safe Deposit Division	Difference in Favor of Dropping Safe Deposit Division
Sales	$150,000	$135,000	($15,000)
Less variable costs	60,000	52,500	7,500
Contribution margin	$ 90,000	$ 82,500	($ 7,500)
Less direct fixed costs	72,000	55,500	16,500
Segment margin	$ 18,000	$ 27,000	$ 9,000
Less common fixed costs	12,000	12,000	0
Operating income	$ 6,000	$ 15,000	$ 9,000

Home State Bank
Segment Profitability Decision
Incremental Analysis—Situation 2

	Keep Safe Deposit Division	Drop Safe Deposit Division	Difference in Opposition to Dropping Safe Deposit Division
Sales	$150,000	$108,000	($42,000)
Less variable costs	60,000	42,000	18,000
Contribution margin	$ 90,000	$ 66,000	($24,000)
Less direct fixed costs	72,000	55,500	16,500
Segment margin	$ 18,000	$ 10,500	($ 7,500)
Less common fixed costs	12,000	12,000	0
Operating income	$ 6,000	($ 1,500)	($ 7,500)

Exhibit 24-4 presents two situations. Situation 1 demonstrates that dropping the Safe Deposit Division will increase operating income by $9,000. Unless the bank can increase the division's segment margin by increasing sales revenue or by reducing direct costs, management should drop the segment. The incremental approach to analyzing this decision isolates the segment and focuses on its segment margin, as shown in the last column of the exhibit. The decision to drop a segment also requires a careful review of the other segments to see whether they will be affected.

Situation 2 in Exhibit 24-4 assumes that Bank Operation's sales volume and variable costs will decrease by 20 percent if management eliminates the Safe Deposit Division. The reduction in sales volume stems from the loss of customers who purchase products from both divisions. The analysis shows that dropping the division would reduce both the segment margin and the bank's operating income by $7,500. In this situation, Home State Bank would want to keep the Safe Deposit Division.

FOCUS ON BUSINESS PRACTICE

Why Banks Prefer Ebanking

After performing segment analysis of online banking and face-to-face banking, bank managers worldwide are encouraging customers to do their banking over the Internet. Banks have found that linking global Internet access with customer relationship management (CRM), customer-friendly financial software, and online bill payment in a secure banking environment can reduce costs, increase service and product availability, and boost earnings.[2]

STOP & APPLY >

Sample Company is evaluating its two divisions, East Division and West Division. Data for East Division include sales of \$500,000, variable costs of \$250,000, and fixed costs of \$400,000, 50 percent of which are traceable to the division. West Division's data for the same period include sales of \$600,000, variable costs of \$350,000, and fixed costs of \$450,000, 60 percent of which are traceable to the division.

Should either division be considered for elimination?

SOLUTION

	East Division	**West Division**	**Total Company**
Sales	\$500,000	\$600,000	\$1,100,000
Less variable costs	250,000	350,000	600,000
Contribution margin	\$250,000	\$250,000	\$ 500,000
Less direct fixed costs	200,000	270,000	470,000
Divisional income	\$ 50,000	(\$ 20,000)	\$ 30,000
Less common fixed costs			380,000
Operating income (loss)			(\$ 350,000)

The company should keep East Division because it is profitable. West Division does not seem to be profitable and should be considered for elimination. The home office and its very heavy overhead costs are causing the company's loss.

Incremental Analysis for Sales Mix Decisions

LO5 Perform incremental analysis for sales mix decisions involving constrained resources.

A company may not be able to provide the full variety of products or services that customers demand within a given time. Limits on resources like machine time or available labor may restrict the types or quantities of products or services that are available. Resource constraints can also be associated with other activities, such as inspection and equipment setup. The question is, Which products or services contribute the most to profitability in relation to the amount of capital assets or other constrained resources needed to offer those items? To satisfy customers' demands and maximize operating income, management will choose to offer the most profitable product or service first. To identify such products or services, managers calculate the contribution margin per constrained resource (such as labor hours or machine hours) for each product or service.

Study Note

When resources like direct materials, direct labor, or machine time are scarce, the goal is to maximize the contribution margin per unit of scarce resource.

Sales Mix Analysis The objective of a **sales mix decision** is to select the alternative that maximizes the contribution margin per constrained resource. The decision analysis, which uses incremental analysis to identify the relevant costs and revenues, consists of two steps:

Step 1. Calculate the contribution margin per unit for each product or service affected by the constrained resource. The contribution margin per unit equals the selling price per unit less the variable costs per unit.

Step 2. Calculate the contribution margin per unit of the constrained resource. The contribution margin per unit of the constrained resource equals the contribution margin per unit divided by the quantity of the constrained resource required per unit.

Suppose Home State Bank offers three types of loans: commercial loans, auto loans, and home loans. The product line data are as follows:

	Commercial Loans	*Auto Loans*	*Home Loans*
Current loan application demand	20,000	30,000	18,000
Processing hours per loan application	2.0	1.0	2.5
Loan origination fee	\$24.00	\$18.00	\$32.00
Variable processing costs	\$12.50	\$10.00	\$18.75
Variable selling costs	\$6.50	\$5.00	\$6.25

The current loan application capacity is 100,000 processing hours.

Question 1. Which loan type should be advertised and promoted first because it is the most profitable for the bank? Which should be second? Which last?

Exhibit 24-5 shows the sales mix analysis. It indicates that the auto loans should be promoted first because they provide the highest contribution margin per processing hour. Home loans should be second, and commercial loans should be last.

Question 2. How many of each type of loan should the bank sell to maximize its contribution margin based on the current loan application capacity of 100,000 processing hours? What is the total contribution margin for that combination?

To begin the analysis, compare the current loan application capacity with the total capacity required to meet the current loan demand. The company needs 115,000 processing hours to meet the current loan demand: 40,000 processing hours for commercial loans (20,000 loans × 2 processing hours per loan), 30,000 processing hours for auto loans (30,000 loans × 1 processing hour per loan), and 45,000 processing hours for home loans (18,000 loans × 2.5 processing hours per loan). Because that amount exceeds the current capacity of 100,000 processing hours, management must determine the sales mix that maximizes the company's contribution margin, which will also maximize its operating income.

EXHIBIT 24-5
Incremental Analysis: Sales Mix Decision Involving Constrained Resources

Home State Bank
Sales Mix Decision: Ranking the Order of Loans
Incremental Analysis

	Commercial Loans	Auto Loans	Home Loans
Loan origination fee per loan	$24.00	$18.00	$32.00
Less variable costs			
Processing	$12.50	$10.00	$18.75
Selling	6.50	5.00	6.25
Total variable costs	$19.00	$15.00	$25.00
Contribution margin per loan (A)	$ 5.00	$ 3.00	$ 7.00
Processing hours per loan (B)	÷ 2.0	÷ 1.0	÷ 2.5
Contribution margin per processing hour (A ÷ B)	$ 2.50	$ 3.00	$ 2.80

Home State Bank
Sales Mix Decision: Number of Units to Make
Incremental Analysis

	Processing Hours
Total processing hours available	100,000
Less processing hours to produce auto loans (30,000 loans × 1 processing hour per loan)	30,000
Balance of processing hours available	70,000
Less processing hours to produce home loans (18,000 loans × 2.5 processing hours per loan)	45,000
Balance of processing hours available	25,000
Less processing hours to produce commercial loans (12,500 loans × 2 processing hours per loan)	25,000
Balance of processing hours available	0

The calculations in the second part of Exhibit 24-5 show that Home State Bank should sell 30,000 auto loans, 18,000 home loans, and 12,500 commercial loans. The total contribution margin is as follows:

Auto loans (30,000 loans × $3.00 per loan)	$ 90,000
Home loans (18,000 loans × $7.00 per loan)	126,000
Commercial loans (12,500 loans × $5.00 per loan)	62,500
Total contribution margin	$278,500

STOP & APPLY >

Surf, Inc., makes three kinds of surfboards, but it has a limited number of machine hours available to make them. Product line data are as follows:

	Fiberglass	Plastic	Graphite
Machine hours per unit	4	1	2
Selling price per unit	$1,500	$800	$1,300
Variable manufacturing cost per unit	500	200	800
Variable selling costs per unit	200	350	200

In what order should the surfboard product lines be produced?

SOLUTION

	Fiberglass	Plastic	Graphite
Selling price per unit	$1,500	$800	$1,300
Less variable costs			
Manufacturing	$ 500	$200	$ 800
Selling	200	350	200
Total unit variable costs	$ 700	$550	$1,000
Contribution margin per unit (A)	$ 800	$250	$ 300
Machine hours per unit (B)	÷ 4	÷ 1	÷ 2
Contribution margin per machine hour (A ÷ B)	$ 200	$250	$ 150

Surf, Inc., should produce plastic surfboards first, then fiberglass surfboards, and finally graphite surfboards.

Incremental Analysis for Sell or Process-Further Decisions

LO6 Perform incremental analysis for sell or process-further decisions.

Study Note

Products are made by combining materials or by dividing materials, as in oil refining or ore extraction.

Some companies offer products or services that can either be sold in a basic form or be processed further and sold as a more refined product or service to a different market. For example, a meatpacking company processes cattle into meat and meat-related products, such as bones and hides. The company may choose to sell sides of beef and pounds of bones and hides to other companies for further processing. Alternatively, it could choose to cut and package the meat for immediate sale in grocery stores, process bone into fertilizer for gardeners, or tan hides into refined leather for purses.

A **sell or process-further decision** is a decision about whether to sell a joint product at the split-off point or sell it after further processing. **Joint products** are two or more products made from a common material or process that cannot be identified as separate products or services during some or all of the processing. Only at a specific point, called the **split-off point**, do joint products or services become separate and identifiable. At that point, a company may choose to sell the product or service as is or to process it into another form for sale to a different market.

Sell or Process-Further Analysis The objective of a sell or process-further decision is to select the alternative that maximizes operating income. The decision analysis entails calculating the incremental revenue, which is the difference between the total revenue if the product or service is sold at the split-off point and the total revenue if the product or service is sold after further processing. You then compare the incremental revenue with the incremental costs of processing further.

- If the incremental revenue is greater than the incremental costs of processing further, a decision to process the product or service further would be justified.
- If the incremental costs are greater than the incremental revenue, you would probably choose to sell the product or service at the split-off point.

Study Note

The common costs shared by two or more products before they are split off are called *joint costs.* Joint costs are irrelevant in a sell or process-further decision.

Be sure to ignore *joint costs* (or common costs) in your analysis, because they are incurred *before* the split-off point and do not change if further processing occurs. Although accountants assign joint costs to products or services when valuing inventories and calculating cost of goods sold, joint costs are not relevant to a sell or process-further decision and are omitted from the decision analysis.

For example, as part of the company's strategic plan, Home State Bank's management is looking for new markets for banking services, and management is considering whether it would be profitable to bundle banking services. Home State Bank is considering adding two levels of service, Premier Checking and Personal Banker, beyond its current Basic Checking account services. The three levels have the following bundled features:

- Basic Checking: Online checking account, debit card, and online bill payment with a required minimum average balance of $500
- Premier Checking: Paper and online checking, a debit card, a credit card, and a small life insurance policy equal to the maximum credit limit on the credit card for customers who maintain a minimum average balance of $1,000
- Personal Banker: All of the features of Premier Checking plus a safe deposit box, a $5,000 personal line of credit at the prime interest rate, financial investment advice, and a toaster upon opening the account for customers who maintain a minimum average balance of $5,000

Assume that the bank can earn sales revenue of 5 percent on its checking account balances and that the total cost of offering basic checking services is currently $50,000. The bank's accountant provided these data for each level of service:

Product	*Sales Revenue*	*Additional Costs*
Basic Checking	$ 25	$ 0
Premier Checking	50	30
Personal Banker	250	200

The decision analysis in Exhibit 24-6 indicates that the bank should offer Personal Banking services in addition to Basic Checking accounts. Notice that the $50,000 joint costs of Basic Checking were ignored because they are sunk costs that will not influence the decision.

As we noted earlier, the decision analysis must take into account the organization's strategic plan and tactical objectives. In this example, the decision to process services further supports the bank's strategic plan to expand into new markets. In making the final decision, management must also consider other factors, such as the bank's ability to obtain favorable returns on its bank deposit investments.

EXHIBIT 24-6
Incremental Analysis:
Sell or Process-Further Decision

Home State Bank
Sell or Process-Further Decision
Incremental Analysis

	Premier Checking	Personal Banker
Incremental revenue per account if processed further:		
Process further	$50	$250
Split-off—Basic Checking	25	25
Incremental revenue	$25	$225
Less incremental costs	30	200
Operating income (loss) from processing further	($ 5)	$ 25

STOP & APPLY >

In an attempt to provide superb customer service, Home Movie Rentals is considering expanding its product offerings from single movie or game rentals to complete movie or game evenings. Each evening would include a movie or game, candy, popcorn, and drinks. The accountant for Home Movie Rentals has compiled the following relevant information:

Product	Sales Revenue if No Additional Service	Sales Revenue if Processed Further	Additional Processing Costs
Movie	$2	$10	$5
Game	1	6	5

Determine which products Home Movie Rentals should offer.

SOLUTION

Incremental Revenue if Processed Further	Movie Evening	Game Evening
Process further	$10	$6
Split-off	2	1
Incremental revenue	$ 8	$5
Less incremental costs	5	5
Operating income from further processing	$ 3	$0

Home Movie Rentals should promote movie evenings first, then movies, and finally games or game evenings. There is no difference in profitability between the sale of games and the sale of game evenings.

A LOOK BACK AT ▶ BANK OF AMERICA

In this chapter's Decision Point, we commented on **Bank of America**'s online banking strategies. We asked the following questions:

- How do managers at Bank of America decide on new ways to increase business and protect customers' interests?
- How can incremental analysis help managers at Bank of America take advantage of the business opportunities that online banking offers?

As managers at Bank of America make short-term decisions about which alternatives to pursue that will increase business and give customers additional protection against fraud and identity theft, they will ask a number of questions—for example: When should bank products and services be outsourced? When should a special order for service be accepted? When is a bank segment profitable? When resource constraints exist, what is the best sales mix? When should bank products be sold as is or processed further into different products?

To answer such questions and determine what could happen under alternative courses of action, the bank's managers need pertinent information that they can use in incremental analysis. On that basis, they can make sound, ethical decisions that will protect the bank's customers and increase both its traditional and online business.

Review Problem

Segment Profitability

LO4

Suppose a loan officer at **Bank of America** has been analyzing Home Services, Inc., to determine whether the bank should grant it a loan. Home Services has been in business for ten years, and its services now include tree trimming and auto, boat, and tile floor repair. The following data pertaining to those services were available for analysis:

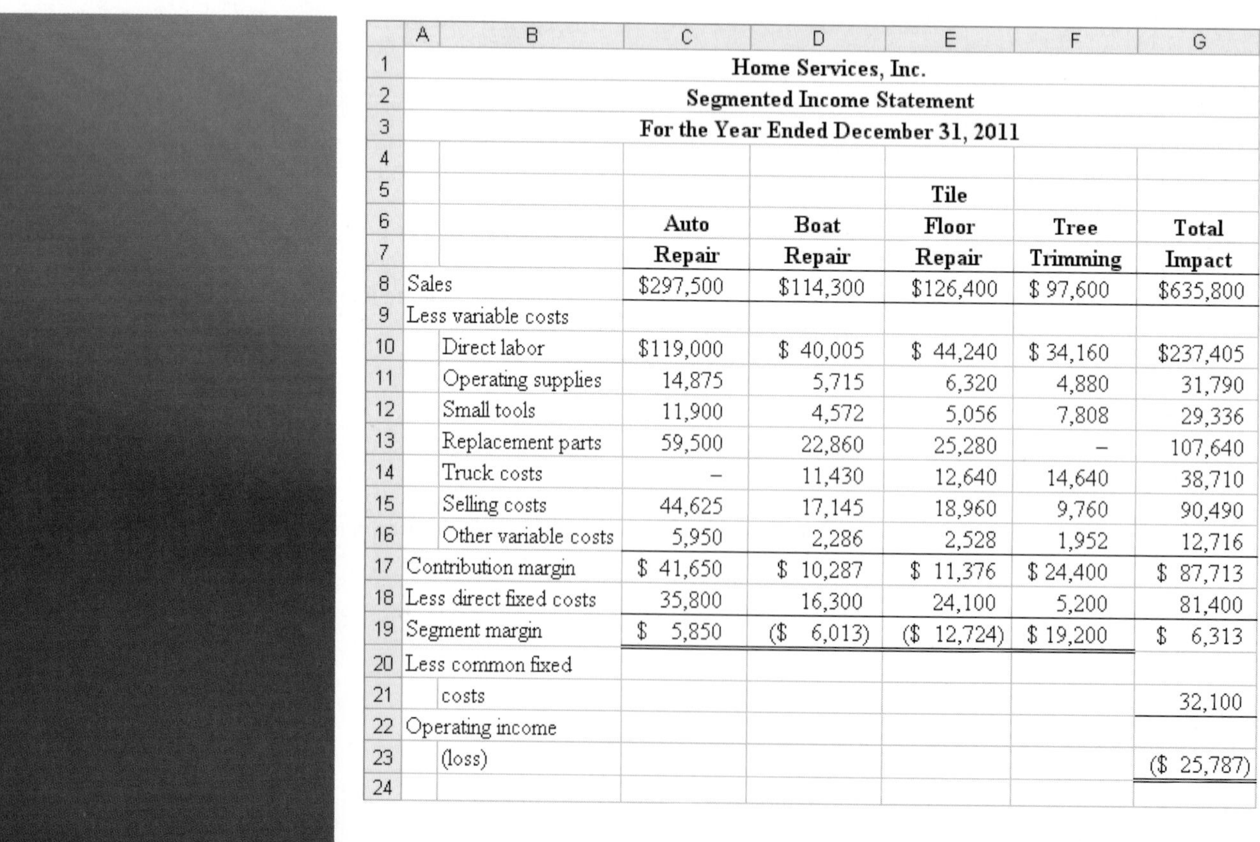

Home Services, Inc.
Segmented Income Statement
For the Year Ended December 31, 2011

	Auto Repair	Boat Repair	Tile Floor Repair	Tree Trimming	Total Impact
Sales	$297,500	$114,300	$126,400	$ 97,600	$635,800
Less variable costs					
Direct labor	$119,000	$ 40,005	$ 44,240	$ 34,160	$237,405
Operating supplies	14,875	5,715	6,320	4,880	31,790
Small tools	11,900	4,572	5,056	7,808	29,336
Replacement parts	59,500	22,860	25,280	–	107,640
Truck costs	–	11,430	12,640	14,640	38,710
Selling costs	44,625	17,145	18,960	9,760	90,490
Other variable costs	5,950	2,286	2,528	1,952	12,716
Contribution margin	$ 41,650	$ 10,287	$ 11,376	$ 24,400	$ 87,713
Less direct fixed costs	35,800	16,300	24,100	5,200	81,400
Segment margin	$ 5,850	($ 6,013)	($ 12,724)	$ 19,200	$ 6,313
Less common fixed costs					32,100
Operating income (loss)					($ 25,787)

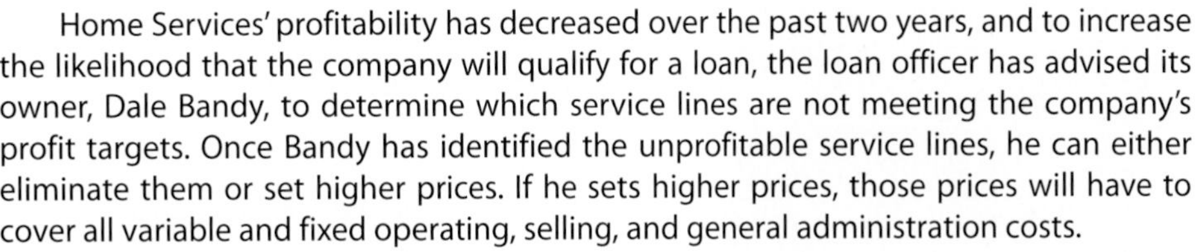

Home Services' profitability has decreased over the past two years, and to increase the likelihood that the company will qualify for a loan, the loan officer has advised its owner, Dale Bandy, to determine which service lines are not meeting the company's profit targets. Once Bandy has identified the unprofitable service lines, he can either eliminate them or set higher prices. If he sets higher prices, those prices will have to cover all variable and fixed operating, selling, and general administration costs.

Required

1. Analyze the performance of the four service lines. Should Dale Bandy eliminate any of them? Explain your answer.
2. Why might Bandy want to continue providing unprofitable service lines?
3. Identify possible causes of a service's poor performance. What actions do you think Bandy should take to make his company a better loan candidate?

Answers to Review Problem

1. In deciding whether to eliminate any of the four service lines, Dale Bandy should concentrate on those that have a negative segment margin. If the revenues from a service line are less than the sum of its variable and direct fixed costs, then other service lines must cover some of the losing line's costs and carry the burden of the common fixed costs.

   The segmented income statement on the opposite page indicates that Bandy will increase the company's operating income by $18,737 ($6,013 + $12,724) if he eliminates the boat and tile floor repair services, both of which have a negative segment margin. A decision to eliminate these services can also be supported by the following analysis:

	A	B	C	D	E
1			**Home Services, Inc.**		
2			**Segment Profitability Decision**		
3					
4					**Difference in**
5					**Favor of**
6			**Keep**	**Drop**	**Dropping**
7			**Boat Repair**	**Boat Repair**	**Boat Repair**
8			**and**	**and**	**and**
9			**Tile Floor Repair**	**Tile Floor Repair**	**Tile Floor Repair**
10	Sales		$635,800	$395,100	($240,700)
11	Less variable costs		548,087	329,050	219,037
12	Contribution margin		$ 87,713	$ 66,050	($ 21,663)
13	Less direct fixed costs		81,400	41,000	40,400
14	Segment margin		$ 6,313	$ 25,050	$ 18,737
15	Less common fixed costs		32,100	32,100	–
16	Operating income (loss)		($ 25,787)	($ 7,050)	$ 18,737

2. Bandy may want to continue offering the unprofitable service lines if their elimination would have a negative effect on the sale of the auto repair or tree trimming services.

3. The following are among the possible causes of a service's poor performance:
   a. Service fees set too low
   b. Inadequate advertising
   c. Excessively high direct labor costs
   d. Other variable costs excessively high
   e. Poor management of fixed costs
   f. Excessive supervision costs

   To improve profitability and make the company a better candidate for a bank loan, Bandy should eliminate nonvalue-adding costs, increase service fees, or increase the volume of services provided to customers.

LO1 Describe how managers make short-run decisions using incremental analysis.

Both quantitative information and qualitative information are important in short-run decision analysis. Such information should be relevant, timely, and presented in a format that is easy to use in decision making.

Incremental analysis helps managers compare alternative courses of action by focusing on the differences in projected revenues and costs. Any data that relate to future costs, revenues, or uses of resources and that will differ among alternative courses of action are considered relevant decision information. Examples of relevant information are projected sales or estimated costs, such as the costs of direct materials or direct labor, that differ for each alternative. The manager analyzes relevant information to determine which alternative contributes the most to profits or incurs the lowest costs. Only data that differ for each alternative are considered. Differential or incremental costs are costs that vary among alternatives and thus are relevant to the decision. Sunk costs are past costs that cannot be recovered; they are irrelevant to the decision process. Opportunity costs are revenue or income forgone as a result of choosing an alternative.

LO2 Perform incremental analysis for outsourcing decisions.

Outsourcing (including make-or-buy) decision analysis helps managers decide whether to use suppliers from outside the organization to perform services or provide goods that could be performed or produced internally. An incremental analysis of the expected costs and revenues for each alternative is used to identify the best alternative.

LO3 Perform incremental analysis for special order decisions.

A special order decision is a decision about whether to accept or reject a special order at a price below the normal market price. One approach is to compare the special order price with the relevant costs to see if a profit can be generated. Another approach is to prepare a special order bid price by calculating a minimum selling price for the special order. Generally, fixed costs are irrelevant to a special order decision because such costs are covered by regular sales activity and do not differ among alternatives.

LO4 Perform incremental analysis for segment profitability decisions.

Segment profitability decisions involve the review of segments of an organization, such as product lines, services, sales territories, divisions, or departments. Managers often must decide whether to add or drop a segment. A segment with a negative segment margin may be dropped. A segment margin is a segment's sales revenue minus its direct costs, which include variable costs and avoidable fixed costs. Avoidable costs are traceable to a specific segment. If the segment is eliminated, the avoidable costs will also be eliminated.

LO5 Perform incremental analysis for sales mix decisions involving constrained resources.

Sales mix decisions require the selection of the most profitable combination of sales items when a company makes more than one product or service using a common constrained resource. The product or service generating the highest contribution margin per constrained resource is offered and sold first.

LO6 Perform incremental analysis for sell or process-further decisions.

Sell or process-further decisions require managers to choose between selling a joint product at its split-off point or processing it into a more refined product. Managers compare the incremental revenues and costs of the two alternatives. Joint processing costs are irrelevant to the decision because they are identical for both alternatives. A product should be processed further only if the incremental revenues generated exceed the incremental costs incurred.

REVIEW of Concepts and Terminology

The following concepts and terms were introduced in this chapter:

Avoidable costs 1118 (LO4)

Differential cost 1111 (LO1)

Incremental analysis 1111 (LO1)

Joint products 1123 (LO6)

Make-or-buy decisions 1113 (LO2)

Opportunity costs 1112 (LO1)

Outsourcing 1113 (LO2)

Sales mix decision 1121 (LO5)

Segment margin 1118 (LO4)

Sell or process-further decision 1123 (LO6)

Short-run decision analysis 1110 (LO1)

Special order decisions 1115 (LO3)

Split-off point 1123 (LO6)

Sunk cost 1111 (LO1)

CHAPTER ASSIGNMENTS

BUILDING Your Knowledge Foundation

Short Exercises

LO1 **Qualitative and Quantitative Information in Short-Run Decision Analysis**

SE 1. The owner of Milo's, a Mexican restaurant, is deciding whether to take fish tacos off the menu. State whether each item of decision information that follows is qualitative or quantitative. If the information is quantitative, specify whether it is financial or nonfinancial.

1. The time needed to prepare the fish
2. The daily number of customers who order the tacos
3. Whether competing Mexican restaurants have this entrée on the menu
4. The labor cost of the chef who prepares the fish tacos
5. The fact that the president of a nearby company who brings ten guests with him each week always orders fish tacos

LO1 **Using Incremental Analysis**

SE 2. Pices Corporation has assembled the following information related to the purchase of a new automated postage machine:

	Posen Machine	Value Machine
Increase in revenue	$44,200	$49,300
Increase in annual operating costs		
Direct materials	12,200	12,200
Direct labor	10,200	10,600
Variable overhead	24,500	26,900
Fixed overhead (including depreciation)	12,400	12,400

Using incremental analysis and only relevant information, compute the difference in favor of the Value machine.

LO2 **Outsourcing Decision**

SE 3. Marc Company assembles products from a group of interconnecting parts. The company produces some of the parts and buys some from outside vendors. The vendor for Part X has just increased its price by 35 percent, to $10 per unit for the first 5,000 units and $9 per additional unit ordered each year. The company uses 7,500 units of Part X each year. Unit costs if the company makes the part are as follows:

Direct materials	$3.50
Direct labor	2.00
Variable overhead	4.00
Variable selling costs for the assembled product	3.75

Should Marc continue to purchase Part X or begin making it?

LO2 **Outsourcing Decision**

SE 4. Dental Associates, Inc., is currently operating at less than capacity. The company thinks it could cut costs by outsourcing dental cleaning to an independent dental hygienist for $50 per cleaning. Currently, a dental hygienist is employed for $30 an hour. A dental cleaning usually takes one hour to perform and consumes $10 of dental supplies, $8 of variable overhead, and $16 of fixed overhead. Should Dental Associates, Inc., continue to perform dental cleanings, or should it begin to outsource them?

LO3 **Special Order Decision**

SE 5. Hadley Company has received a special order for Product R3P at a selling price of $20 per unit. This order is over and above normal production, and budgeted production and sales targets for the year have already been exceeded. Capacity exists to satisfy the special order. No selling costs will be incurred in connection with this order. Unit costs to manufacture and sell Product R3P are as follows: direct materials, $7.60; direct labor, $3.75; variable overhead, $9.25; fixed overhead, $4.85; variable selling costs, $2.75; and fixed general and administrative costs, $6.75. Should Hadley Company accept the order?

LO3 **Special Order Decision**

SE 6. Smith Accounting Services is considering a special order that it received from one of its corporate clients. The special order calls for Smith to prepare the individual tax returns of the corporation's four-largest shareholders. The company has idle capacity that could be used to complete the special order. The following data have been gathered about the preparation of individual tax returns:

Materials cost per page	$1
Average hourly labor rate	$60
Standard hours per return	4
Standard pages per return	10
Variable overhead cost per page	$0.50
Fixed overhead cost per page	$0.50

Smith Accounting Services would be satisfied with a $40 gross profit per return. Compute the minimum bid price for the entire order.

LO4 **Segment Profitability Decision**

SE 7. Peruna Company is evaluating its two divisions, North Division and South Division. Data for North Division include sales of $530,000, variable costs of $290,000, and fixed costs of $260,000, 50 percent of which are traceable to the division. South Division's efforts for the same period include sales of $610,000, variable costs of $340,000, and fixed costs of $290,000, 60 percent of which are traceable to the division. Should Peruna Company consider eliminating either division? Is there any other problem that needs attention?

LO5 **Sales Mix Decision**

SE 8. Snow, Inc., makes three kinds of snowboards, but it has a limited number of machine hours available to make them. Product line data are as follows:

	Wood	Plastic	Graphite
Machine hours per unit	1.25	1.0	1.5
Selling price per unit	$100	$120	$200
Variable manufacturing cost per unit	$45	$50	$100
Variable selling costs per unit	$15	$26	$36

In what order should the snowboard product lines be produced?

LO6 **Sell or Process-Further Decision**

SE 9. Gomez Industries produces three products from a single operation. Product A sells for $4 per unit, Product B for $6 per unit, and Product C for $10 per unit. When B is processed further, there are additional unit costs of $3, and its new selling price is $10 per unit. Each product is allocated $2 of joint costs from the initial production operation. Should Product B be processed further, or should it be sold at the end of the initial operation?

LO6 Sell or Process-Further Decision

SE 10. In an attempt to provide superb customer service, Richard V. Meats is considering the expansion of its product offerings from whole hams and turkeys to complete ham and turkey dinners. Each dinner would include a carved ham or turkey, two side dishes, and six rolls or cornbread. The accountant for Richard V. Meats has compiled the following relevant information:

Product	Sales Revenue if No Additional Service	Sales Revenue if Processed Further	Additional Processing Costs
Ham	$30	$50	$15
Turkey	20	35	15

A cooked, uncarved ham costs Richard V. Meats $20 to produce, and a cooked, uncarved turkey costs $15 to prepare. Use incremental analysis to determine which products Richard V. Meats should offer.

Exercises

LO1 Incremental Analysis

E 1. Max Wayco, the business manager for Essey Industries, must select a new computer system for his assistant. Rental of Model A, which is similar to the model now being used, is $2,200 per year. Model B is a deluxe system that rents for $2,900 per year and will require a new desk for the assistant. The annual desk rental charge is $750. The assistant's salary of $1,200 per month will not change. If Model B is rented, $280 in annual software training costs will be incurred. Model B has greater capacity and is expected to save $1,550 per year in part-time wages. Upkeep and operating costs will not differ between the two models.

1. Identify the relevant data in this problem.
2. Prepare an incremental analysis to aid the business manager in his decision.

LO1 Incremental Analysis

E 2. The managers of Lennox Company must decide which of two mill blade grinders—Y or Z—to buy. The grinders have the same purchase price but different revenue and cost characteristics. The company currently owns Grinder X, which it bought three years ago for $15,000 and which has accumulated depreciation of $9,000 and a book value of $6,000. Grinder X is now obsolete as a result of advances in technology and cannot be sold or traded in.

The accountant has collected the following annual revenue and operating cost estimates for the two new machines:

	Grinder Y	Grinder Z
Increase in revenue	$16,000	$20,000
Increase in annual operating costs		
Direct materials	4,800	4,800
Direct labor	3,000	4,100
Variable overhead	2,100	3,000
Fixed overhead (depreciation included)	5,000	5,000

1. Identify the relevant data in this problem.
2. Prepare an incremental analysis to aid the managers in their decision.
3. Should the company purchase Grinder Y or Grinder Z?

LO2 Outsourcing Decision

E 3. One component of a radio produced by Audio Systems, Inc., is currently being purchased for $225 per 100 parts. Management is studying the possibility of manufacturing that component. Annual production at Audio is 70,000 units; fixed costs (all of which remain unchanged whether the part is made or purchased) are $38,500; and variable costs are $0.95 per unit for direct materials, $0.55 per unit for direct labor, and $0.60 per unit for variable overhead.

Using incremental analysis, decide whether Audio Systems, Inc., should manufacture the part or continue to purchase it from an outside vendor.

LO2 **Outsourcing Decision**

E 4. Sunny Hazel, the manager of Cyber Web Services, must decide whether to hire a new employee or to outsource some of the web design work to Ky To, a freelance graphic designer. If she hires a new employee, she will pay $32 per design hour for the employee to work 600 hours and incur service overhead costs of $2 per design hour. If she outsources the work to Ky To, she will pay $36 per design hour for 600 hours of work. She can also redirect the use of a computer and server to generate $4,000 in additional revenue from web page maintenance work.

Should Cyber Web Services hire a new designer or outsource the work to Ky To?

LO3 **Special Order Decision**

E 5. Antiquities, Ltd., produces antique-looking books. Management has just received a request for a special order for 2,000 books and must decide whether to accept it. Venus Company, the purchaser, is offering to pay $25.00 per book, which includes $3.00 per book for shipping costs.

The variable production costs per book include $9.20 for direct materials, $4.00 for direct labor, and $3.80 for variable overhead. The current year's production is 22,000 books, and maximum capacity is 25,000 books. Fixed costs, including overhead, advertising, and selling and administrative costs, total $80,000. The usual selling price is $25.00 per book. Shipping costs, which are additional, average $3.00 per book.

Determine whether Antiquities should accept the special order.

LO3 **Special Order Decision**

E 6. Jens Sporting Goods, Inc., manufactures a complete line of sporting equipment. Leiden Enterprises operates a large chain of discount stores. Leiden has approached Jens with a special order for 30,000 deluxe baseballs. Instead of being packaged separately, the balls are to be packed in boxes containing 500 baseballs each. Leiden is willing to pay $2.45 per baseball. Jens knows that annual expected production is 400,000 baseballs. It also knows that the current year's production is 410,000 baseballs and that the maximum production capacity is 450,000 baseballs. The following additional information is available:

Standard unit cost data for 400,000 baseballs	
Direct materials	$ 0.90
Direct labor	0.60
Overhead:	
Variable	0.50
Fixed ($100,000 ÷ 400,000)	0.25
Packaging per unit	0.30
Advertising ($60,000 ÷ 400,000)	0.15
Other fixed selling and administrative expenses ($120,000 ÷ 400,000)	0.30
Product unit cost	$ 3.00
Unit selling price	$ 4.00
Total estimated bulk packaging costs for special order (30,000 baseballs: 500 per box)	$2,500

1. Should Jens Sporting Goods, Inc., accept Leiden's offer?
2. What would be the minimum order price per baseball if Jens would like to earn a profit of $3,000 from the special order?

LO3 Special Order Decision

E 7. In September, a nonprofit organization, Toys for Homeless Children (THC), offers Virtually LLC $400 to prepare a custom web page to help the organization attract toy donations. The home page for the THC website will include special animated graphics of toys and stuffed animals. Virtually LLC estimates that it will take 12 design labor hours at $32 per design hour and 2 installation labor hours at $10 per installation hour to complete the job. Fixed costs are already covered by regular business. Should Virtually LLC accept THC's offer?

LO4 Elimination of Unprofitable Segment Decision

E 8. Guld's Glass, Inc., has three divisions: Commercial, Nonprofit, and Residential. The segmented income statement for last year revealed the following:

Guld's Glass, Inc.
Divisional Profit Summary and Decision Analysis

	Commercial Division	Nonprofit Division	Residential Division	Total Company
Sales	$290,000	$533,000	$837,000	$1,660,000
Less variable costs	147,000	435,000	472,000	1,054,000
Contribution margin	$143,000	$ 98,000	$365,000	$ 606,000
Less direct fixed costs	124,000	106,000	139,000	369,000
Segment margin	$ 19,000	($ 8,000)	$226,000	$ 237,000
Less common fixed costs				168,000
Operating income				$ 69,000

1. How will Guld's Glass be affected if the Nonprofit Division is dropped?
2. Assume the elimination of the Nonprofit Division causes the sales of the Residential Division to decrease by 10 percent. How will Guld's Glass be affected if the Nonprofit Division is dropped?

LO4 Elimination of Unprofitable Segment Decision

E 9. URL Services has two divisions: Basic Web Pages and Custom Web Pages. Ricky Vega, manager of Custom Web Pages, wants to find out why Custom Web Pages is not profitable. He has prepared the reports that appear on the next page.

1. How will URL Services be affected if the Custom Web Pages Division is eliminated?
2. How will URL Services be affected if the Design segment of Custom Web Pages is eliminated?
3. What should Ricky Vega do? What additional information would be helpful to him in making the decision?

URL Services
Segmented Income Statement
For the Year Ended December 31

	Basic Web Pages (1,000 units)	Custom Web Pages (200 units)	Total Company
Service revenue	$200,000	$150,000	$350,000
Less variable costs			
Direct professional labor: design	$ 32,000	$ 80,000	$112,000
Direct professional labor: install	30,000	4,000	34,000
Direct professional labor: maintain	15,000	36,000	51,000
Total variable costs	$ 77,000	$120,000	$197,000
Contribution margin	$123,000	$ 30,000	$153,000
Less direct fixed costs			
Depreciation on computer equipment	$ 6,000	$ 12,000	$ 18,000
Depreciation on servers	10,000	20,000	30,000
Total direct fixed costs	$ 16,000	$ 32,000	$ 48,000
Segment margin	$107,000	($ 2,000)	$105,000
Less common fixed costs			
Building rent			$ 24,000
Supplies			1,000
Insurance			3,000
Telephone			1,500
Website rental			500
Total common fixed costs			$ 30,000
Operating income			$ 75,000

Custom Web Pages Division
URL Services
Segment Profitability Decision
Incremental Analysis

	Design	Install	Maintain	Total
Service revenue	$60,000	$25,000	$65,000	$150,000
Less variable costs	80,000	4,000	36,000	120,000
Contribution margin	($20,000)	$21,000	$29,000	$ 30,000
Less direct fixed costs	6,000	13,000	13,000	32,000
Segment margin	($26,000)	$ 8,000	$16,000	($ 2,000)

LO5 **Scarce Resource Usage**

E 10. EZ, Inc., manufactures two products that require both machine processing and labor operations. Although there is unlimited demand for both products, EZ could devote all its capacities to a single product. Unit prices, cost data, and processing requirements follow.

	Product E	Product Z
Unit selling price	$70	$230
Unit variable costs	$30	$90
Machine hours per unit	0.4	1.4
Labor hours per unit	2.0	6.0

Next year, the company will be limited to 160,000 machine hours and 120,000 labor hours. Fixed costs for the year are $1,500,000.

1. Compute the most profitable combination of products to be produced next year.
2. Prepare an income statement using the contribution margin format for the product volume computed in **1**.

LO5 Sales Mix Decision

E 11. Grady Enterprises manufactures three computer games. They are called Rising Star, Ghost Master, and Road Warrior. The product line data are as follows:

	Rising Star	Ghost Master	Road Warrior
Current unit sales demand	20,000	30,000	18,000
Machine hours per unit	2.0	1.0	2.5
Selling price per unit	$24.00	$18.00	$32.00
Unit variable manufacturing costs	$12.50	$10.00	$18.75
Unit variable selling costs	$6.50	$5.00	$6.25

The current production capacity is 110,000 machine hours.

1. Which computer game should be manufactured first? Which should be manufactured second? Which last?
2. How many of each type of computer game should be manufactured and sold to maximize the company's contribution margin based on the current production activity of 110,000 machine hours? What is the total contribution margin for that combination?

LO5 Sales Mix Decision

E 12. Web Services, a small company owned by Simon Orozco, provides web page services to small businesses. His services include the preparation of basic pages and custom pages.

The following summary of information will be used to make several short-run decisions for Web Services:

	Basic Pages	Custom Pages
Service revenue per page	$200	$750
Variable costs per page	77	600
Contribution margin per page	$123	$150

Total annual fixed costs are $78,000.

One of Web Services' two graphic designers, Taylor Campbell, is planning to take maternity leave in July and August. As a result, there will be only one designer available to perform the work, and design labor hours will be a resource constraint. Orozco plans to help the other designer complete the projected 160 orders for basic pages and 30 orders for custom pages for those two months. However, he wants to know which type of page Web Services should advertise and market. Although custom pages have a higher contribution margin per service, each custom page requires 12.5 design hours, whereas basic pages require only 1 design hour per page. On which page type should his company focus? Explain your answer.

LO6 **Sell or Process-Further Decision**

E 13. H & L Beef Products, Inc., processes cattle. It can sell the meat as sides of beef or process it further into final cuts (steaks, roasts, and hamburger). As part of the company's strategic plan, management is looking for new markets for meat or meat by-products. The production process currently separates hides and bones for sale to other manufacturers. However, management is considering whether it would be profitable to process the hides into leather and the bones into fertilizer. The costs of the cattle and of transporting, hanging, storing, and cutting sides of beef are $125,000. The company's accountant provided these data:

Product	Sales Revenue if Sold at Split-Off	Sales Revenue if Sold After Further Processing	Additional Processing Costs
Meat	$100,000	$200,000	$80,000
Bones	20,000	40,000	15,000
Hides	50,000	55,000	10,000

Should the products be processed further? Explain your answer.

LO6 **Sell or Process-Further Decision**

E 14. Six Star Pizza manufactures frozen pizzas and calzones and sells them for $4 each. It is currently considering a proposal to manufacture and sell fully prepared products. The following relevant information has been gathered by management:

Product	Sales Revenue if No Additional Processing	Sales Revenue if Processed Further	Additional Processing Costs
Pizza	$4	$ 8	$5
Calzone	4	10	5

Use incremental analysis to determine which products Six Star should offer.

Problems

LO2 **Outsourcing Decision**

P 1. Stainless Refrigerator Company purchases ice makers and installs them in its products. The ice makers cost $138 per case, and each case contains 12 ice makers. The supplier recently gave advance notice that the price will rise by 50 percent immediately. Stainless Refrigerator Company has idle equipment that with only a few minor changes could be used to produce similar ice makers.

Cost estimates have been prepared under the assumption that the company could make the product itself. Direct materials would cost $100.80 per 12 ice makers. Direct labor required would be 10 minutes per ice maker at a labor rate of $18.00 per hour. Variable overhead would be $4.60 per ice maker. Fixed overhead, which would be incurred under either decision alternative, would be $32,420 a year for depreciation and $234,000 a year for other costs. Production and usage are estimated at 75,000 ice makers a year. (Assume that any idle equipment cannot be used for any other purpose.)

Required

1. Prepare an incremental analysis to determine whether the ice makers should be made within the company or purchased from the outside supplier at the higher price.
2. Compute the variable unit cost to (a) make one ice maker and (b) buy one ice maker.

LO3 **Special Order Decision**

P 2. On March 26, Sinker Industries received a special order request for 120 ten-foot aluminum fishing boats. Operating on a fiscal year ending May 31, the company already has orders that will allow it to produce at budget levels for the period. However, extra capacity exists to produce the 120 additional boats.

The terms of the special order call for a selling price of $675 per boat, and the customer will pay all shipping costs. No sales personnel were involved in soliciting the order.

The ten-foot fishing boat has the following cost estimates: direct materials, aluminum, two 4′ × 8′ sheets at $155 per sheet; direct labor, 14 hours at $15.00 per hour; variable overhead, $7.25 per direct labor hour; fixed overhead, $4.50 per direct labor hour; variable selling expenses, $46.50 per boat; and variable shipping expenses, $57.50 per boat.

Required

1. Prepare an analysis for the management of Sinker Industries to use in deciding whether to accept or reject the special order. What decision should be made?
2. To make an $8,000 profit on this order, what would be the lowest possible price that Sinker Industries could charge per boat?

LO4 **Segment Profitability Decision**

P 3. Sports, Inc., is a nationwide distributor of sporting equipment. The corporate president, Wesley Coldwell, is dissatisfied with corporate operating results, particularly those of the Spring Branch, and has asked the controller for more information. The controller prepared the following segmented income statement (in thousands of dollars) for the Spring Branch:

Sports, Inc., Spring Branch
Segmented Income Statement
For the Year Ended December 31
(Amounts in Thousands)

	Football Line	Baseball Line	Basketball Line	Spring Branch
Sales	$3,500	$2,500	$2,059	$8,059
Less variable costs	2,900	2,395	1,800	7,095
Contribution margin	$ 600	$ 105	$ 259	$ 964
Less direct fixed costs	300	150	159	609
Segment margin	$ 300	($ 45)	$ 100	$ 355
Less common fixed costs				450
Operating income (loss)				($ 95)

Coldwell is considering adding a new product line, Kite Surfing. The controller estimates that adding this line to the Spring Branch will increase sales by $300,000, variable costs by $150,000, and direct fixed costs by $20,000. The new product line will have no effect on common fixed costs.

Required

1. How will operating income be affected if the Baseball line is dropped?
2. How will operating income be affected if the Baseball line is kept and a Kite Surfing line is added?

3. If the Baseball line is dropped and the Kite Surfing line is added, sales of the Football line will decrease by 10 percent and sales of the Basketball line will decrease by 5 percent. How will those changes affect operating income?

Manager insight ▶ 4. What decision do you recommend? Explain.

LO5 Sales Mix Decision

P 4. Management at Generic Chemical Company is evaluating its product mix in an attempt to maximize profits. For the past two years, Generic has produced four products, and all have large markets in which to expand market share. Heinz Bexer, Generic's controller, has gathered data from current operations and wants you to analyze them for him. Sales and operating data are as follows:

	Product AZ1	Product BY7	Product CX5	Product DW9
Variable production costs	$71,000	$91,000	$91,920	$97,440
Variable selling costs	$10,200	$5,400	$12,480	$30,160
Fixed production costs	$20,400	$21,600	$29,120	$18,480
Fixed administrative costs	$3,400	$5,400	$6,240	$10,080
Total sales	$122,000	$136,000	$156,400	$161,200
Units produced and sold	85,000	45,000	26,000	14,000
Machine hours used*	17,000	18,000	20,800	16,800

*Generic's scarce resource, machine hours, is being used to full capacity.

Required

1. Compute the machine hours needed to produce one unit of each product.
2. Determine the contribution margin per machine hour for each product.
3. Which product line(s) should be targeted for market share expansion?

LO6 Sell or Process-Further Decision

P 5. Bagels, Inc., produces and sells 20 types of bagels by the dozen. Bagels are priced at $6.00 per dozen (or $0.50 each) and cost $0.20 per unit to produce. The company is considering processing the bagels further into two products: bagels with cream cheese and bagel sandwiches. It would cost an additional $0.50 per unit to produce bagels with cream cheese, and the new selling price would be $2.50 each. It would cost an additional $1.00 per sandwich to produce bagel sandwiches, and the new selling price would be $3.50 each.

Required

1. Identify the relevant per unit costs and revenues for the alternatives. Are there any sunk costs?
2. Based on the information in requirement **1**, should Bagels, Inc., expand its product offerings?
3. Suppose that Bagels, Inc., did expand its product line to include bagels with cream cheese and bagel sandwiches. Based on customer feedback, the company determined that it could further process those two products into bagels with cream cheese and fruit and bagel sandwiches with cheese. The company's accountant compiled the following information:

Product (per unit)	Sales Revenue if Sold with No Further Processing	Sales Revenue if Processed Further	Additional Processing Costs
Bagels with cream cheese	$2.50	$3.50	Fruit: $1.00
Bagel sandwiches	$3.50	$4.50	Cheese: $0.50

Perform an incremental analysis to determine if Bagels, Inc., should process its products further. Explain your findings.

Alternate Problems

LO2 Outsourcing Decision

P 6. Three Brothers Restaurant purchases cheesecakes and offers them as dessert items on its menu. The cheesecakes cost $24 each, and a cake contains 8 pieces. The supplier recently gave advance notice that the price will rise by 20 percent immediately. Three Brothers Restaurant has idle equipment that with only a few minor changes could be used to produce similar cheesecakes.

Cost estimates have been prepared under the assumption that the company could make the product itself. Direct materials would cost $7.00 per cheesecake. Direct labor required would be 0.5 hour per cheesecake at a labor rate of $24.00 per hour. Variable overhead would be $9.00 per cheesecake. Fixed overhead, which would be incurred under either decision alternative, would be $35,200 a year for depreciation and $230,000 a year for other costs. Production and usage are estimated at 3,600 cheesecakes a year. (Assume that any idle equipment cannot be used for any other purpose.)

Required

1. Prepare an incremental analysis to determine whether the cheesecakes should be made within the company or purchased from the outside supplier at the higher price.
2. Compute the variable unit cost to (a) make one cheesecake and (b) buy one cheesecake.

LO3 Special Order Decision

P 7. Keystone Resorts, Ltd., has approached Crystal Printers, Inc., with a special order to produce 300,000 two-page brochures. Most of Crystal's work consists of recurring short-run orders. Keystone Resorts is offering a one-time order, and Crystal has the capacity to handle the order over a two-month period.

The management of Keystone Resorts has stated that the company would be unwilling to pay more than $48 per 1,000 brochures. Crystal Printers' controller assembled the following cost data for this decision analysis: Direct materials (paper) would be $26.80 per 1,000 brochures; direct labor costs would be $6.80 per 1,000 brochures; direct materials (ink) would be $4.40 per 1,000 brochures; variable production overhead would be $6.20 per 1,000 brochures; machine maintenance (fixed cost) is $1.00 per direct labor dollar. Other fixed production overhead amounts to $2.40 per direct labor dollar. Variable packing costs would be $4.30 per 1,000 brochures. Also, the share of general and administrative expenses (fixed costs) to be allocated would be $5.25 per direct labor dollar.

Required

1. Prepare an analysis for Crystal Printers' management to use in deciding whether to accept or reject Keystone Resorts' offer. What decision should be made?
2. What is the lowest possible price Crystal Printers can charge per thousand and still make a $6,000 profit on the order?

LO4 Decision to Eliminate an Unprofitable Product

P 8. Seven months ago, Naib Publishing Company published its first book (Book N). Since then, Naib has added four more books to its product list (Books S, Q, X, and H). Management is considering proposals for three more new books, but editorial capacity limits the company to producing only seven books annually. Before deciding which of the proposed books to publish, management wants you to evaluate the performance of its existing book list. Recent revenue and cost data are as follows:

Naib Publishing Company
Product Profit and Loss Summary
For the Year Ended December 31

	Book N	Book S	Book Q	Book X	Book H	Company Totals
Sales	$813,800	$782,000	$634,200	$944,100	$707,000	$3,881,100
Less variable costs						
Materials and binding	$325,520	$312,800	$190,260	$283,230	$212,100	$1,323,910
Editorial services	71,380	88,200	73,420	57,205	80,700	370,905
Author royalties	130,208	125,120	101,472	151,056	113,120	620,976
Sales commissions	162,760	156,400	95,130	141,615	141,400	697,305
Other selling costs	50,682	44,740	21,708	18,334	60,700	196,164
Total variable costs	$740,550	$727,260	$481,990	$651,440	$608,020	$3,209,260
Contribution margin	$ 73,250	$ 54,740	$152,210	$292,660	$ 98,980	$ 671,840
Less total fixed costs	97,250	81,240	89,610	100,460	82,680	451,240
Operating income loss	($ 24,000)	($ 26,500)	$ 62,600	$192,200	$ 16,300	$ 220,600
Direct fixed costs included in total fixed costs above	$ 51,200	$ 65,100	$ 49,400	$ 69,100	$ 58,800	$ 293,600

Projected data for the three proposed new books are as follows: Book P, sales, $450,000, and contribution margin, $45,000; Book T, sales, $725,000, and contribution margin, ($25,200); Book R, sales, $913,200, and contribution margin, $115,500. Projected direct fixed costs are Book P, $5,000; Book T, $6,000; Book R, $40,000.

Required

1. Analyze the performance of the five books that the company is currently publishing.
2. Should Naib Publishing Company eliminate any of its present products? If so, which one(s)?
3. Identify the new books you would use to replace those eliminated. Justify your answer.

LO5 **Sales Mix Decision**

P 9. Dr. Massy, who specializes in internal medicine, wants to analyze his sales mix to find out how the time of his physician assistant, Consuela Ortiz, can be used to generate the highest operating income.

Ortiz sees patients in Dr. Massy's office, consults with patients over the telephone, and conducts a daily weight-loss support group attended by up to 50 patients. Statistics for the three services are as follows:

	Office Visits	Phone Calls	Weight-Loss Support Group
Maximum number of patient billings per day	20	40	50
Hours per billing	0.25	0.10	1.0
Billing rate	$50	$25	$10
Variable costs	$25	$12	$5

Ortiz works seven hours a day.

Required

1. Determine the best sales mix. Rank the services offered in order of their profitability.
2. Based on the ranking in requirement **1,** how much time should Ortiz spend on each service in a day? (**Hint:** Remember to consider the maximum number of patient billings per day.) What would be the daily total contribution margin generated by Ortiz?
3. Dr. Massy knows that the daily 60-minute meeting of the weight-loss support group has 50 patients and should continue to be offered. If the new ranking for the services is (1) weight-loss support group, (2) phone calls, and (3) office visits, how much time should Ortiz spend on each service in a day? What would be the total contribution margin generated by Ortiz, assuming the weight-loss support group has the maximum number of patient billings?

Manager insight ▶ 4. Which ranking would you recommend? What additional amount of total contribution margin would be generated if your recommendation were to be accepted?

LO6 **Sell or Process-Further Decision**

P 10. Marketeers, Inc., developed a promotional program for a large shopping center in Sunset Living, Arizona, a few years ago. Having invested $360,000 in developing the original promotion campaign, the firm is ready to present its client with an add-on contract offer that includes the original promotion areas of (1) a TV advertising campaign, (2) a series of brochures for mass mailing, and (3) a special rotating BIG SALE schedule for 10 of the 28 tenants in the shopping center. Presented below are the revenue terms from the original contract with the shopping center and the offer for the add-on contract, which extends the original contract terms.

	Original Contract Terms	Extended Contract Including Add-On Terms
TV advertising campaign	$520,000	$ 580,000
Brochure series	210,000	230,000
Rotating BIG SALE schedule	170,000	190,000
Totals	$900,000	$1,000,000

Marketeers, Inc., estimates that the following additional costs will be incurred by extending the contract:

	TV Campaign	Brochures	BIG SALE Schedule
Direct labor	$30,000	$ 9,000	$7,000
Variable overhead costs	22,000	14,000	6,000
Fixed overhead costs*	12,000	4,000	2,000

*80 percent are direct fixed costs applied to this contract.

Required

1. Compute the costs that will be incurred for each part of the add-on portion of the contract.

Manager insight ▶ 2. Should Marketeers, Inc., offer the add-on contract, or should it ask for a final settlement check based on the original contract only? Defend your answer.

Manager insight ▶ 3. If management of the shopping center indicates that the terms of the add-on contract are negotiable, how should Marketeers, Inc., respond?

ENHANCING Your Knowledge, Skills, and Critical Thinking

LO1 Defining and Identifying Relevant Information

C 1. Bob's Burgers is in the fast-food restaurant business. One component of its marketing strategy is to increase sales by expanding in foreign markets. It uses both financial and nonfinancial quantitative and qualitative information when deciding whether to open restaurants abroad. Bob's decided to open a restaurant in Prague (Czech Republic) five years ago. The following information helped the managers in making that decision:

Financial Quantitative Information
Operating information
  Estimated food, labor, and other operating costs (e.g., taxes, insurance, utilities, and supplies)
  Estimated selling price for each food item
Capital investment information
  Cost of land, building, equipment, and furniture
  Financing options and amounts

Nonfinancial Quantitative Information
Estimated daily number of customers, hamburgers to be sold, and number of employees
High-traffic time periods
Income of people living in the area
Ratio of population to number of restaurants in the market area
Traffic counts in front of similar restaurants in the area

Qualitative Information
Government regulations, taxes, duties, tariffs, political involvement in business operations
Property ownership restrictions
Site visibility
Accessibility of store location
Training process for local managers
Hiring process for employees
Local customs and practices

Bob's Burgers has hired you as a consultant and given you an income statement comparing the operating incomes of its five restaurants in Eastern Europe. You have noticed that the Prague location is operating at a loss (including unallocated fixed costs) and must decide whether to recommend closing that restaurant.

Review the information used in making the decision to open the restaurant. Identify the types of information that would also be relevant in deciding whether to close the restaurant. What period or periods of time should be reviewed in making your decision? What additional information would be relevant in making your decision?

LO1 Identifying Relevant Decision Information

C 2. Select two destinations for a one-week vacation, and gather information about them from brochures, magazines, travel agents, the Internet, and friends. Then list the relevant quantitative and qualitative information in order of its importance to your decision. Analyze the information, and select a destination.

Which factors were most important to your decision? Why? Which were least important? Why? How would the process of identifying relevant information differ if the president of your company asked you to prepare a budget for the next training meeting, to be held at a location of your choice?

Your instructor will divide the class into groups and ask each group to discuss this case. One student from each group will summarize his or her group's findings and debrief the entire class.

LO2 Ethics of a Make-or-Buy Decision

C 3. Tilly Issac is the assistant controller for Tagwell Corporation, a leading producer of home appliances. Her friend Zack Marsh is the supervisor of the firm's Cookware Department. Marsh has the authority to decide whether parts are purchased from outside vendors or manufactured in his department. Issac recently conducted an internal audit of the parts being manufactured in the Cookware Department, including a comparison of the prices currently charged by vendors for similar parts. She found more than a dozen parts that could be purchased for less than they cost the company to produce. When she approached Marsh about the situation, he replied that if those parts were purchased from outside vendors, two automated machines would be idle for several hours a week. Increased machine idle time would have a negative effect on his performance evaluation and could reduce his yearly bonus. He reminded Issac that he was in charge of the decision to make or purchase those parts and asked her not to pursue the matter any further.

What should Issac do in this situation? Discuss her options.

LO3 Special Order Decision

C 4. Metallica Can Opener Company is a subsidiary of Maltz Appliances, Inc. The can opener that Metallica produces is in strong demand. Sales this year are expected to be 1,000,000 units. Full plant capacity is 1,150,000 units, but 1,000,000 units are considered normal capacity for the current year. The following unit price and cost breakdown is applicable:

	Per Unit
Sales price	$22.50
Less manufacturing costs	
Direct materials	$ 6.00
Direct labor	2.50
Overhead, variable	3.50
Overhead, fixed	1.50
Total manufacturing costs	$13.50
Gross margin	$ 9.00
Less selling and administrative expenses	
Selling, variable	$ 1.50
Selling, fixed	1.00
Administrative, fixed	1.25
Packaging, variable*	0.75
Total selling and administrative expenses	$ 4.50
Operating income	$ 4.50

*Three types of packaging are available: deluxe, $0.75 per unit; plain, $0.50 per unit; and bulk pack, $0.25 per unit.

During November, the company received three requests for special orders from large chain-store companies. Those orders are not part of the budgeted 1,000,000 units for this year, but company officials think that sufficient capacity exists for one order to be accepted. Orders received and their terms are as follows: Order 1, 75,000 can openers @ $20.00 per unit, deluxe packaging; Order 2, 90,000 can openers @ $18.00 per unit, plain packaging; Order 3, 125,000 can openers @ $15.75 per unit, bulk packaging.

Because the orders were placed directly with company officials, no variable selling costs will be incurred.

1. Analyze the profitability of each of the three special orders.
2. Which special order should be accepted?

LO4 Decision to Add a New Department

C 5. The management at Transco Company is considering a proposal to install a third production department in its factory building. With the company's existing production setup, direct materials are processed through the Mixing Department to produce Materials A and B in equal proportions. The Shaping Department then processes Material A to yield Product C. Material B is sold as is at $20.25 per pound. Product C has a selling price of $100.00 per pound. There is a proposal to add a Baking Department to process Material B into Product D. It is expected that any quantity of Product D can be sold for $30.00 per pound.

Costs per pound under this proposal appear at the top of the next page.

	Mixing Department (Materials A and B)	Shaping Department (Product C)	Baking Department (Product D)
Costs from Mixing Department	—	$52.80	$13.20
Direct materials	$20.00	—	—
Direct labor	6.00	9.00	3.50
Variable overhead	4.00	8.00	4.00
Fixed overhead			
Traceable (direct, avoidable)	2.25	2.25	1.80
Allocated (common, unavoidable)	0.75	0.75	0.75
	$33.00	$72.80	$23.25

1. If (a) sales and production levels are expected to remain constant in the foreseeable future and (b) there are no foreseeable alternative uses for the factory space, should Transco Company add a Baking Department and produce Product D, if 100,000 pounds of D can be sold? Show calculations of incremental revenues and costs to support your answer.
2. List at least two qualitative reasons why Transco Company may not want to install a Baking Department and produce Product D, even if this decision appears profitable.
3. List at least two qualitative reasons why Transco Company may want to install a Baking Department and produce Product D, even if it appears that this decision is unprofitable. (CMA adapted)

LO3 LO4 LO6 **Cookie Company (Continuing Case)**

C 6. As the president of your cookie company, you are interested in how public companies with a segment that includes cookies report their operating results. Because public companies are required to report on their segments, it is possible to evaluate the performance of comparable segments of different companies.

Access the website of **Kraft Foods, Inc.**, which markets Nabisco cookies (www.kraftfoodscompany.com/About), and the website of **Kellogg Company**, which markets Keebler cookies (www2.kelloggs.com). Find information about these companies' major segments. Which segments are comparable, and which are not comparable? Which segments of these companies do you think include their brand of cookies?

CHAPTER

25

Capital Investment Analysis

The Management Process

PLAN

- **Carry out capital investment process:**
  1. **Identify capital investment needs.**
  2. **Prepare formal requests for capital investments.**
  3. **Perform preliminary screening of proposals.**
  4. **Establish the acceptance-rejection standard based on cost of capital.**
  5. **Evaluate proposals.**
  6. **Make decisions based on dollars available for capital investments.**

PERFORM

- **Implement capital investment decisions with proper controls.**

EVALUATE

- **Compare actual results with budget projections.**
- **Conduct postcompletion audit to determine if outcomes were achieved.**

COMMUNICATE

- **Prepare reports related to capital investment process.**

Managers use capital investment analysis to make long-term decisions that impact the business.

When deciding when and how much to spend on expensive, long-term projects, such as the construction of a new building or the installation of a new production system, managers apply capital investment analysis to ensure that they use resources wisely and that their choices make the maximum contribution to future profits. This chapter explains the net present value method and other methods of capital investment analysis that managers use when making decisions about long-term capital investments.

LEARNING OBJECTIVES

LO1 **Define *capital investment analysis*, state the purpose of the minimum rate of return, and identify the methods used to arrive at that rate.** (pp. 1150–1155)

LO2 **Identify the types of projected costs and revenues used to evaluate alternatives for capital investment.** (pp. 1155–1158)

LO3 **Apply the concept of the time value of money.** (pp. 1158–1162)

LO4 **Analyze capital investment proposals using the net present value method.** (pp. 1162–1164)

LO5 **Analyze capital investment proposals using the payback period method and the accounting rate-of-return method.** (pp. 1165–1168)

DECISION POINT ▶ A MANAGER'S FOCUS AIR PRODUCTS AND CHEMICALS INC.

- ▶ Why are capital investment decisions critical for a company like Air Products and Chemicals Inc.?
- ▶ In evaluating capital investment alternatives, how can managers at Air Products and Chemicals Inc. ensure a wise allocation of resources and minimize the risks involved in capital investments?

Air Products and Chemicals Inc. is an industrial producer of gases that are piped directly into steel mills and other factories; it has many small gas plants located near its customers. What makes Air Products and Chemicals competitive is its use of "lights-out" systems, which are unattended operations with remote operator access. These systems minimize on-site labor by having regional operators remotely monitor several gas plants from a computer at their homes. If a problem occurs with a machine, an operator can repair it remotely or visit the plant.

Air Products and Chemicals is not alone in turning on-site labor's lights off. Using systems that link machines to the Internet so that managers can monitor operations at any time and from anywhere is common not only in industries that produce identical products in high volume, but also when monitoring cellphone tower operations or vending machines. Automated systems of this kind are expensive, and managers must carefully weigh the risks involved in investing in them.

The Capital Investment Process

LO1 Define *capital investment analysis*, state the purpose of the minimum rate of return, and identify the methods used to arrive at that rate.

Among the most significant decisions that management must make are **capital investment decisions**, which are decisions about when and how much to spend on capital facilities and other long-term projects. Capital facilities and projects may include machinery, systems, or processes; new buildings or additions or renovations to existing buildings; entire new divisions or product lines; and distribution and software systems. For example, **Air Products and Chemicals Inc.** will make decisions about installing new equipment, replacing old equipment, expanding service by renovating or adding to existing equipment, buying a building, or acquiring another company.

Capital facilities and projects are expensive. A new factory or production system may cost millions of dollars and require several years to complete. Managers must make capital investment decisions carefully so that they select the alternatives that will contribute the most to future profits.

Capital Investment Analysis

Capital investment analysis, or *capital budgeting*, is the process of making decisions about capital investments. It consists of identifying the need for a capital investment, analyzing courses of action to meet that need, preparing reports for managers, choosing the best alternative, and allocating funds among competing needs. Every part of the organization participates in this process.

Study Note

Capital investment analysis is a decision process for the purchase of capital facilities, such as buildings and equipment.

- Financial analysts supply a target cost of capital or desired rate of return and an estimate of how much money can be spent annually on capital facilities.
- Marketing specialists predict sales trends and new product demands, which help in determining which operations need expansion or new equipment.
- Managers at all levels help identify facility needs and often prepare preliminary cost estimates for the desired capital investment.
- All then work together to implement the project selected and to keep the results within revenue and cost estimates.

The capital investment process involves the evaluation of alternative proposals for large capital investments, including considerations for financing the projects. Capital investment analyses affect both short-term and long-term planning. Figure 25-1 illustrates the time span of the capital expenditure planning process. Most companies have a long-term plan—that is, a projection of operations for the next five or ten years. Large capital investments should be an integral part of that plan. Anticipated additions or changes to product lines, replacements of equipment, and acquisitions of other companies are examples of items to be included in long-term capital investment plans.

Capital Budgets and Master Budgets One element of budgeting is a capital investment budget. The capital investment budget fits into both the long-term planning process and the capital investment process. Long-term plans are not very specific; they are expressed in broad, goal-oriented terms. Each annual budget must help accomplish the organization's long-term goals. Look again at Figure 25-1. Suppose that in 2015 Neighborhood Communications, a lights-out user like **Air Products and Chemicals**, plans to build a special-purpose cell phone tower.

- When the ten-year capital budget plan was developed, it included only a broad statement about a plan to purchase the machine. Nothing was specified about the cost of the machine or the anticipated operating details and costs.

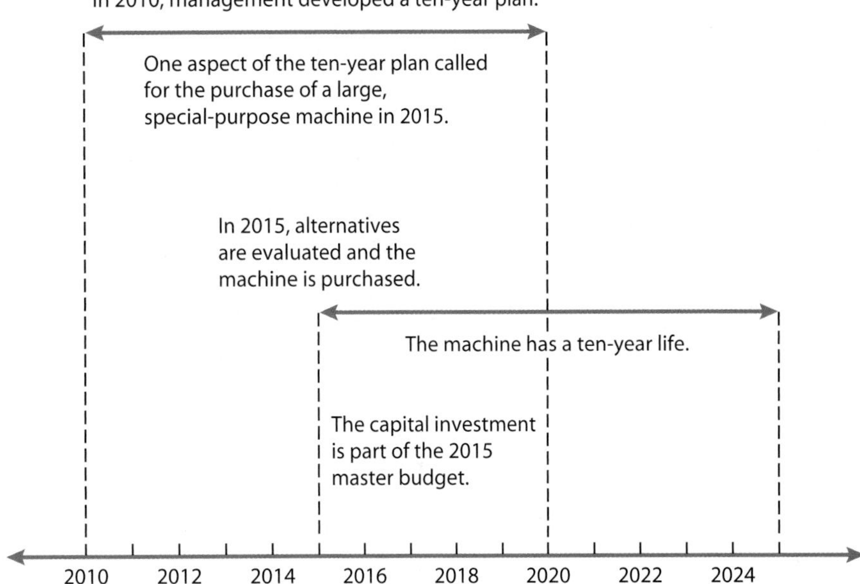

FIGURE 25-1
Time Span of the Capital Investment Planning Process

- Those details are contained in the annual master budget for 2015, and it is in 2015 that the capital investment analysis will occur.

So, although capital investment decisions that will affect the company for many years are discussed and estimates of future revenues and expenditures are made when the long-term plan is first developed, the capital investment analysis is performed in the period in which the expenditure will be made. This point is important to the understanding of capital investment analysis.

Capital Investment Analysis in the Management Process

Managers pay close attention to capital investments throughout the management process, as illustrated in the sidebar on the first page of this chapter. However, the greatest portion of capital investment analysis takes place when they plan. Each decision made about a capital investment is vitally important because it involves a large amount of money and commits a company to a course of action for years to come. For example, **Air Products and Chemicals** and Neighborhood Communications must make capital investment decisions that fit into their strategic plans. A series of poor decisions about capital investments can cause a company to fail.

To ensure high-quality capital investment decisions, managers follow six key steps when they plan.

> **Study Note**
> The six steps of capital investment analysis are performed for both long-term and short-term planning purposes.

Step 1. ***Identification of Capital Investment Needs*** Identifying the need for a new capital investment is the starting point of capital investment analysis. Managers identify capital investment opportunities from past sales experience, changes in sources and quality of materials, employees' suggestions, production bottlenecks caused by obsolete equipment, new production or distribution methods, or customer complaints. In addition, capital investment needs are identified through proposals to:

- Add new products to the product line.
- Expand capacity in existing product lines.

- Reduce production costs of existing products without altering operating levels.
- Automate existing production processes.

Step 2. ***Formal Requests for Capital Investments*** To enhance control over capital investments, managers prepare formal requests for new capital investments. Each request includes a complete description of the investment under review; the reasons a new investment is needed; the alternative means of satisfying the need; the timing, estimated costs, and related cost savings of each alternative; and the investment's engineering specifications, if necessary.

Step 3. ***Preliminary Screening*** Organizations that have several branches and a highly developed system for capital investment analysis require that all proposals go through preliminary screening. The purpose of preliminary screening is to ensure that the only proposals to receive serious review are those that both meet company strategic goals and produce the minimum rate of return set by management.

Step 4. ***Establishment of the Acceptance-Rejection Standard*** To attract and maintain funding for capital investments, an organization establishes an acceptance-rejection standard. Such a standard may be expressed as a minimum rate of return or a minimum cash flow payback period. If the number of acceptable requests for capital investments exceeds the funds available for such investments, the proposals must be ranked according to their rates of return. Acceptance-rejection standards are used to identify projects that are expected to yield inadequate or marginal returns. They also identify proposed projects for which high product demand and high financial returns are expected. Cost of capital information is often used to establish minimum rates of return on investments. The development of such rates is discussed later in this chapter.

Step 5. ***Evaluation of Proposals*** Proposals are evaluated by verifying decision variables and applying established proposal evaluation methods. The key decision variables are (1) expected life, (2) estimated cash flow, and (3) investment cost. Each variable in a proposal should be checked for accuracy. Three commonly used methods of evaluating proposed capital investments are:

- Net present value method
- Payback period method
- Accounting rate-of-return method

Using one or more evaluation methods and the minimum acceptance-rejection standard, management evaluates all proposals. In addition to this quantitative analysis, management will also consider qualitative factors, such as availability and training of employees, competition, anticipated future technological improvements, and the proposal's impact on other company operations.

Step 6. ***Capital Investment Decisions*** The proposals that meet the standards of the evaluation process are given to the appropriate manager for final review. When deciding which requests to implement, the manager must consider the funds available for capital investments. The acceptable proposals are ranked in order of net present value, payback period, or rate of return, and the highest-ranking proposals are funded first. Often there will not be enough money to fund all proposals. The final capital investment budget is then prepared by allocating funds to the selected proposals.

The Minimum Rate of Return on Investment

Most companies set a minimum rate of return, and any capital expenditure proposal that fails to produce that rate of return is automatically refused. The minimum rate of return is often referred to as a *hurdle rate* because it is the rate that must be exceeded, or hurdled. If none of the capital investment requests is expected to meet or exceed the minimum rate of return, or hurdle rate, all requests will be turned down.

Organizations set a minimum rate of return to guard their profitability. If the return from a capital investment falls below the minimum rate of return, the funds can be used more profitably in another part of the organization. Projects that produce poor returns will ultimately have a negative effect on an organization's profitability.

Cost of Capital

Study Note

Depending on the mixture of sources of capital, a company's cost of capital will vary.

Determining a minimum rate of return is not a simple task. The most widely used measure is the cost of capital. The **cost of capital** is the weighted-average rate of return that a company must pay to its long-term creditors and shareholders for the use of their funds. The components of cost of capital are the cost of debt, the cost of preferred stock, the cost of common stock, and the cost of retained earnings. Sophisticated methods may be used to determine these costs. However, in this discussion, we use a simplified definition of each cost:

- The cost of debt is the after-tax interest on the debt (interest times 1 minus the tax rate). The after-tax amount is used because the interest is tax-deductible.
- The cost of preferred stock is the full dividend rate because dividends are not tax-deductible.
- The cost of equity capital (common stock and retained earnings) is the return required by investors in the company.

Cost of Capital Calculation The cost of capital is computed in four steps:

1. Identify the cost of each source of capital.
2. Compute the proportion (percentage) of the organization's total amount of debt and equity that each source of capital represents.

FOCUS ON BUSINESS PRACTICE

Why Look Beyond the Cost of a Capital Investment?

Cost should not be the only factor when making a capital investment decision. International trade and logistics can also be very important, as **Koss Corporation**, a maker of high-fidelity headphones located in Milwaukee, Wisconsin, learned after moving much of its production to China, where costs were low. The move, however, caused a problem with making timely deliveries to customers, and the just-in-time inventory philosophy was abandoned to avoid customer backorders and dissatisfaction. Now, finished products are stacked in the Milwaukee factory to ensure against dockworker strikes and missed deliveries. Looking beyond the numbers is thus an important consideration in capital investment decisions.[1]

3. Multiply each source's cost by its proportion of the capital.
4. Total the weighted costs computed in Step **3**.

For example, suppose Neighborhood Communications' financing structure is as follows:

Cost of Capital	*Source of Capital*	*Amount*	*Proportion of Capital*
6%	Debt financing	$150,000	30%
8	Preferred stock	50,000	10
12	Common stock	200,000	40
12	Retained earnings	100,000	20
	Totals	$500,000	100%

The cost of capital of 9.8 percent would be computed as follows:

Source of Capital	*Cost of Capital*	×	*Proportion of Capital*	=	*Weighted Cost*
Debt financing	6%		30%		0.018
Preferred stock	8		10		0.008
Common stock	12		40		0.048
Retained earnings	12		20		0.024
Cost of capital					0.098

Other Measures for Determining Minimum Rate of Return

If cost of capital information is unavailable, management can use one of three less accurate but still useful amounts as the minimum rate of return.

- The first is the average total corporate return on investment. This measure is based on the notion that any capital investment that produces a lower return than the rate that the company has earned historically will negatively affect investors' perception of the firm's future market value.
- A second method is to use the industry's average cost of capital. Most sizable industry associations supply such information.
- As a last resort, a company might use the current bank lending rate. But because most companies are financed by both debt and equity, the bank lending rate seldom reflects an accurate rate of return.

Ranking Capital Investment Proposals

The requests for capital investments that a company receives usually exceed the funds available for capital investments. Even after management evaluates and selects proposals under the minimum acceptance-rejection standard, there are often too many proposals to fund adequately. At that point, managers must rank the proposals according to their rates of return, or profitability, and begin a second selection process.

Suppose that Neighborhood Communications has $4,500,000 to spend this year for capital improvements and that five acceptable proposals are competing for those funds. The company's current minimum rate of return is 18 percent, and it is considering the following proposals:

Project	*Rate of Return*	*Capital Investment*	*Cumulative Investment*
A	32%	$1,460,000	$1,460,000
B	30	1,890,000	3,350,000
C	28	460,000	3,810,000
D	24	840,000	4,650,000
E	22	580,000	5,230,000
Total		$5,230,000	

The proposals are listed in the order of their rates of return. As you can see, Projects A, B, and C have the highest rates of return and together will cost a total of $3,810,000. That leaves $690,000 in capital funds for other projects. Project D should be examined first to see if it could be implemented for $150,000 less. If not, then Project E should be selected. The selection of Projects A, B, C, and E means that $110,000 in capital funds will be uncommitted for the year.

STOP & APPLY >

Sample Industries is considering investing $20 million in a plant expansion. Management needs to know the average cost of capital to use in evaluating this capital investment decision. The company's capital structure consists of $2,000,000 of debt at 6 percent interest and $3,000,000 of stockholders' equity at 2 percent. What is Sample Industries' average cost of capital?

SOLUTION

The company's average cost of capital is 3.6 percent, which is computed as follows:

Source of Capital	Amount	Proportion of Capital		Cost of Capital		Weighted Cost
Debt	$20,000,000	40%	×	6%	=	0.024
Equity	30,000,000	60	×	2	=	0.012
Total	$50,000,000	100%				0.036

Measures Used in Capital Investment Analysis

LO2 Identify the types of projected costs and revenues used to evaluate alternatives for capital investment.

When evaluating a proposed capital investment, managers must predict how the new asset will perform and how it will benefit the company. Various measures are used to estimate the benefits to be derived from a capital investment.

Expected Benefits from a Capital Investment

Each capital investment analysis must include a measure of the expected benefit from the investment project. The measure of expected benefit depends on the method of analyzing capital investment alternatives.

Net Income One possible measure is net income, calculated in the usual way. Managers determine increases in net income resulting from the capital investment for each alternative.

Net Cash Flows and Cost Savings A more widely used measure of expected benefit is projected cash flows. **Net cash inflows** are the balance of increases in projected cash receipts over increases in projected cash payments resulting from a capital investment. In some cases, equipment replacement decisions involve situations in which revenues are the same among alternatives. In such cases, **cost savings** measure the benefits, such as reduced costs, from proposed capital investments.

Either net cash inflows or cost savings can be used as the basis for an evaluation, but the two measures should not be confused.

- If the analysis involves cash receipts, net cash inflows are used.
- If the analysis involves only cash outlays, cost savings are used.

Managers must measure and evaluate all the investment alternatives consistently.

Equal Versus Unequal Cash Flows

Projected cash flows may be the same for each year of an asset's life, or they may vary from year to year. Unequal annual cash flows are common and must be analyzed for each year of an asset's life. Proposed projects with equal annual cash flows require less detailed analysis. Both a project with equal cash flows and one with unequal cash flows are illustrated and explained later in this chapter.

Carrying Value of Assets

Carrying value is the undepreciated portion of the original cost of a fixed asset—that is, the asset's cost less its accumulated depreciation. Carrying value is also referred to as *book value*. When a decision to replace an asset is being evaluated, the carrying value of the old asset is irrelevant because it is a past, or historical, cost and will not be altered by the decision. Net proceeds from the asset's sale or disposal are relevant, however, because the proceeds affect cash flows and may differ for each alternative.

Depreciation Expense and Income Taxes

The techniques of capital investment analysis discussed in this chapter compare the relative benefits of proposed capital investments by measuring the cash receipts and payments for a facility or project. Income taxes alter the amount and timing of cash flows of projects under consideration by for-profit companies because corporate income tax rates vary and can change yearly. To assess the benefits of a capital project, a company must include the effects of taxes in its capital investment analyses. Depreciation expense is deductible when determining income taxes. (You may recall that the annual depreciation expense computation using the straight-line method is the asset's cost less its residual value, divided by the asset's useful life.) Thus, depreciation expense strongly influences the amount of income taxes that a company pays and can lead to significant tax savings.

To examine how taxes affect capital investment analysis, assume that Neighborhood Communications has a tax rate of 30 percent on taxable income. It is considering a capital project that will make the following annual contribution to operating income:

Cash revenues	$400,000
Cash expenses	(200,000)
Depreciation	(100,000)
Operating income before income taxes	$100,000
Income taxes at 30%	(30,000)
Operating income	$ 70,000

The net cash inflows for this project can be determined in either of two ways:

1. Net cash inflows—receipts and disbursements

Revenues (cash inflows)	$400,000
Cash expenses (outflows)	(200,000)
Income taxes (outflows)	(30,000)
Net cash inflows	$170,000

2. Net cash inflows—income adjustment procedure

Income after income taxes	$ 70,000
Add back noncash expenses (depreciation)	100,000
Less noncash revenues	—
Net cash inflows	$170,000

In both computations, the net cash inflows are $170,000, and the total effect of income taxes is to lower the net cash inflows by $30,000.

Disposal or Residual Values

Proceeds from the sale of an old asset are current cash inflows and are relevant to evaluating a proposed capital investment. Projected disposal or residual values of replacement equipment are also relevant because they represent future cash inflows and usually differ among alternatives. Remember that the residual value, sometimes called the *disposal* or *salvage value*, of an asset will be received at the end of the asset's estimated life.

STOP & APPLY >

Sample Company has a tax rate of 25 percent on taxable income. It is considering a capital project that will make the following annual contribution to operating income:

Cash revenues	$500,000
Cash expenses	(300,000)
Depreciation	(150,000)
Operating income before income taxes	$ 50,000
Income taxes at 25%	(12,500)
Operating income	$ 37,500

1. Determine the net cash inflows for this project in two different ways. Are net cash flows the same under either approach?
2. What is the impact of income taxes on net cash flows?

(continued)

SOLUTION

1. The net cash inflows for this project can be determined in two ways:

    a. Net cash inflows—receipts and disbursements

Revenues (cash inflows)	$500,000
Cash expenses (outflows)	(300,000)
Income taxes (outflows)	(12,500)
Net cash inflows	$187,500

    b. Net cash inflows—income adjustment procedure

Income after income taxes	$ 37,500
Add back noncash expenses (depreciation)	150,000
Less noncash revenues	—
Net cash inflows	$187,500

    In both computations, the net cash inflows are $187,500.

2. The total effect of income taxes is to lower the net cash inflows by $12,500.

The Time Value of Money

LO3 Apply the concept of the time value of money.

An organization has many options for investing capital besides buying plant assets. Consequently, management expects a plant asset to yield a reasonable return during its useful life. A key question in capital investment analysis is how to measure the return on a plant asset. One way is to look at the cash flows that the asset will generate during its useful life. When an asset has a long useful life, management will usually analyze those cash flows in terms of the time value of money. The **time value of money** is the concept that cash flows of equal dollar amounts separated by an interval of time have different present values because of the effect of compound interest. The notions of interest, present value, future value, and present value of an ordinary annuity are all related to the time value of money.

Interest

Study Note

Interest is a cost associated with the passage of time, whether or not there is a stated interest rate.

Interest is the cost associated with the use of money for a specific period of time. Because interest is a cost associated with time and "time is money," interest is an important consideration in any business decision.

- **Simple interest** is the interest cost for one or more periods when the amount on which the interest is computed stays the same from period to period.
- **Compound interest** is the interest cost for two or more periods when the amount on which interest is computed changes in each period to include all interest paid in previous periods. In other words, compound interest is interest earned on a principal sum that is increased at the end of each period by the interest for that period.

Example: Simple Interest You accept an 8 percent, $30,000 note due in 90 days. How much will you receive in total when the note comes due? The formula for calculating simple interest is as follows:

$$\begin{aligned}\text{Interest Expense} &= \text{Principal} \times \text{Rate} \times \text{Time}\\ &= \$30{,}000 \times 8/100 \times 90/360\\ &= \$600\end{aligned}$$

The total that you will receive is computed as follows:

$$\begin{aligned}\text{Total} &= \text{Principal} + \text{Interest}\\ &= \$30{,}000 + \$600\\ &= \$30{,}600\end{aligned}$$

If the interest is paid and the note is renewed for an additional 90 days, the interest calculation will remain the same.

Example: Compound Interest You make a deposit of $5,000 in a savings account that pays 6 percent interest. You expect to leave the principal and accumulated interest in the account for three years. What will be your account total at the end of three years? Assume that the interest is paid at the end of the year, that the interest is added to the principal at that time, and that this total in turn earns interest.

The amount at the end of three years is computed as follows:

(1)	*(2)*	*(3)*	*(4)*
Year	*Principal Amount at Beginning of Year*	*Annual Amount of Interest (col. 2 × 0.06)*	*Accumulated Amount at End of Year (col. 2 + col. 3)*
1	$5,000.00	$300.00	$5,300.00
2	5,300.00	318.00	5,618.00
3	5,618.00	337.08	5,955.08

At the end of three years, you will have $5,955.08 in your savings account. Note that the annual amount of interest increases each year by the interest rate times the interest of the previous year. For example, between year 1 and year 2, the interest increased by $18 ($318 − $300), which exactly equals 6 percent times $300.

Present Value

Suppose that you had the choice of receiving $100 today or one year from today. Intuitively, you would choose to receive the $100 today. Why? You know that if you have the $100 today, you can put it in a savings account to earn interest, so that you will have more than $100 a year from today.

▶ Therefore, we can say that an amount to be received in the future (future value) is not worth as much today as the same amount to be received today (present value) because of the cost associated with the passage of time.

Future value and present value are closely related. **Future value** is the amount that an investment will be worth at a future date if it is invested today at compound interest. **Present value** is the amount that must be invested today at a given rate of compound interest to produce a given future value.

Assume Neighborhood Communications needs $1,000 one year from now. How much should it invest today to achieve that goal if the interest rate is 5 percent? The following equation can be used to answer that question:

$$\begin{aligned}\text{Present Value} \times (1.0 + \text{Interest Rate}) &= \text{Future Value}\\ \text{Present Value} \times 1.05 &= \$1{,}000.00\\ \text{Present Value} &= \$1{,}000.00 \div 1.05\\ \text{Present Value} &= \$952.38^{*}\end{aligned}$$

*Rounded.

Thus, to achieve a future value of $1,000.00, a present value of $952.38 must be invested. Interest of 5 percent on $952.38 for one year equals $47.62, and the two amounts added together equal $1,000.00.

Present Value of a Single Sum Due in the Future

When more than one time period is involved, the calculation of present value is more complicated.

Assume Neighborhood Communications wants to be sure of having $4,000 at the end of three years. How much must the company invest today in a 5 percent savings account to achieve that goal? By adapting the preceding equation, the present value of $4,000 at compound interest of 5 percent for three years in the future may be computed as follows:

Year	*Amount at End of Year*		*Divide by*		*Present Value at Beginning of Year*
3	$4,000.00	÷	1.05	=	$3,809.52
2	3,809.52	÷	1.05	=	3,628.11
1	3,628.11	÷	1.05	=	3,455.34

Neighborhood Communications must invest a present value of $3,455.34 to achieve a future value of $4,000 in three years.

This calculation is made easier by using the appropriate table from the appendix on present value tables. In Table 1, we look down the 5 percent column until we reach period 3. There we find the factor 0.864. Multiplied by $1, this factor gives the present value of $1 to be received three years from now at 5 percent interest. Thus, we solve the previous problem as follows:

$$\text{Future Value} \times \text{Present Value Factor} = \text{Present Value}$$

$$\$4{,}000 \times 0.864 = \$3{,}456$$

Except for a rounding difference of $0.66, this gives the same result as the previous calculation.

Present Value of an Ordinary Annuity

It is often necessary to compute the present value of a series of receipts or payments. When we calculate the present value of equal amounts equally spaced over a period of time, we are computing the present value of an ordinary annuity. An

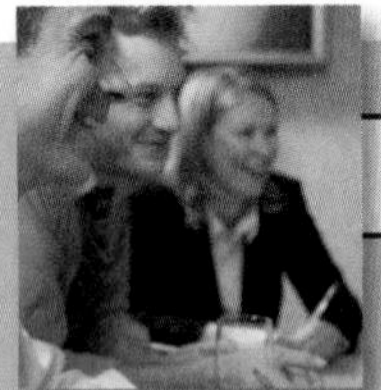

FOCUS ON BUSINESS PRACTICE

How Would You Decide Whether to Buy Rare Dinosaur Bones?

Not-for-profit organizations can use the techniques of capital investment analysis just as for-profit ones do. For example, the officers of the Field Museum in Chicago applied these techniques when they decided to bid at auction several years ago on the most complete skeleton of a *Tyrannosaurus rex* ever found. The museum bought the bones for $8.2 million and spent another $9 million to restore and install the dinosaur, named Sue. The museum projected that Sue would attract 1 million new visitors, who would produce $5 million in admissions and spend several more million dollars on food, gifts, and the like. After deducting operating costs, museum officials used discounted present values to calculate a return on investment of 10.5 percent. Given that the museum's cost of capital was 8.5 percent, Sue's purchase was considered a financial success. Sue has been extremely popular with the public and more than met the museum's attendance goals in the first year after installation.[2]

Study Note

The first payment of an ordinary annuity is always made at the end of the first year.

ordinary annuity is a series of equal payments or receipts that will begin one time period from the current date.

Suppose that Neighborhood Communications has sold a piece of property and is to receive $15,000 in three equal annual cash payments of $5,000, beginning one year from today. What is the present value of this sale, assuming a current interest rate of 5 percent?

This present value can be determined by calculating a separate present value for each of the three payments (using Table 1 in the appendix on present value tables) and summing the results, as follows:

Future Cash Receipts (Annuity)				*Present Value Factor at 5 Percent*		*Present*
Year 1	*Year 2*	*Year 3*		*(from Table 1)*		*Value*
$5,000			×	0.952	=	$ 4,760
	$5,000		×	0.907	=	4,535
		$5,000	×	0.864	=	4,320
Total Present Value						$13,615

The present value of this sale is $13,615. Thus, there is an implied interest cost (given the 5 percent rate) of $1,385 associated with the payment plan that allows the purchaser to pay in three installments. We can calculate this present value more easily by using Table 2 in the appendix on present value tables. We look down the 5 percent column until we reach period 3. There we find the factor 2.723. That factor, when multiplied by $1, gives the present value of a series of three $1 payments, spaced one year apart, at compound interest of 5 percent. Thus, we solve the problem as follows:

Periodic Payment	×	Present Value Factor	=	Present Value
$5,000	×	2.723	=	$13,615

This result is the same as the one computed earlier.

To summarize the example, if Neighborhood Communications is willing to accept a 5 percent rate of return, management will be equally satisfied to receive a single cash payment of $13,615 today or three equal annual cash payments of $5,000 spread over the next three years.

& APPLY >

For each of the following situations, identify the correct factor to use from Tables 1 or 2 in the appendix on present value tables. Also, compute the appropriate present value.

1. Annual net cash inflows of $35,000 for five years, discounted at 16 percent
2. An amount of $25,000 to be received at the end of ten years, discounted at 12 percent
3. The amount of $28,000 to be received at the end of two years, and $15,000 to be received at the end of years 4, 5, and 6, discounted at 10 percent

(continued)

SOLUTION

1. From Table 2 in the appendix on present value tables:

$35,000	×	3.274	=	$114,590

2. From Table 1 in the appendix on present value tables:

$25,000	×	0.322	=	$ 8,050

3. From Table 1 in the appendix on present value tables:

$28,000	×	0.826	=	$ 23,128
$15,000	×	0.683	=	10,245
$15,000	×	0.621	=	9,315
$15,000	×	0.564	=	8,460
Total				$ 51,148

The Net Present Value Method

LO4 Analyze capital investment proposals using the net present value method.

The **net present value method** evaluates a capital investment by discounting its future cash flows to their present values and subtracting the amount of the initial investment from their sum. All proposed capital investments are evaluated in the same way, and the projects with the highest net present value—the amount that exceeds the initial investment—are selected for implementation.

Advantages of the Net Present Value Method

Study Note

Because it is based on cash flow, the net present value method is widely used not only in business but also by individuals.

A significant advantage of the net present value method is that it incorporates the time value of money into the analysis of proposed capital investments. Future cash inflows and outflows are discounted by the company's minimum rate of return to determine their present values. The minimum rate of return should at least equal the company's average cost of capital.

When dealing with the time value of money, use discounting to find the present value of an amount to be received in the future. To determine the present values of future amounts of money, use Tables 1 and 2 in the appendix on present value tables. Remember:

- Table 1 deals with a single payment or amount.
- Table 2 is used for a series of equal periodic amounts.

Study Note

If the net present value is zero, the investment will earn the minimum rate of return.

Tables 1 and 2 are used to discount each future cash inflow and cash outflow over the life of the asset to the present. If the net present value is positive (the total of the discounted net cash inflows exceeds the cash investment at the beginning), the rate of return on the investment will exceed the company's minimum rate of return, or hurdle rate, and the project can be accepted. Conversely, if the net present value is negative (the cash investment at the beginning exceeds the discounted net cash inflows), the return on the investment is less than the minimum rate of return and the project should be rejected. If the net present value is zero (if discounted cash inflows equal discounted cash outflows), the project meets the minimum rate of return and can be accepted.

The Net Present Value Method Illustrated

Suppose that Neighborhood Communications is considering the purchase of a new cell phone antenna that will boost the power of cell phone signals in the area.

Study Note

When using the net present value method, remember to consider the present value of the residual or disposal value.

The company's minimum rate of return is 16 percent. Management must decide between two models.

- Model M costs $17,500 and will have an estimated residual value of $2,000 after five years. It is projected to produce cash inflows of $6,000, $5,500, $5,000, $4,500, and $4,000 during its five-year life.
- Model N costs $21,000 and will have an estimated residual value of $2,000. It is projected to produce cash inflows of $6,000 per year for five years.

Because Model M is expected to produce unequal cash inflows, Table 1 in the appendix on present value tables is used to determine the present value of each cash inflow from each year of the machine's life. The net present value of Model M is determined as follows:

Model M

Year	*Net Cash Inflows*	*16% Factor*	*Present Value*
1	$6,000	0.862	$ 5,172.00
2	5,500	0.743	4,086.50
3	5,000	0.641	3,205.00
4	4,500	0.552	2,484.00
5	4,000	0.476	1,904.00
Residual value	2,000	0.476	952.00
Total present value of cash inflows			$17,803.50
Less purchase price of Model M			17,500.00
Net present value			$ 303.50

All the factors for this analysis can be found in the column for 16 percent in Table 1. The factors are used to discount the individual cash flows, including the expected residual value, to the present. The amount of the investment in Model M is deducted from the total present value of the cash inflows to arrive at the net present value of $303.50. Since the entire investment of $17,500 in Model M is a cash outflow at the beginning—that is, at time zero—no discounting of the $17,500 purchase price is necessary.

- Because the net present value is positive, the proposed investment in Model M will achieve at least the minimum rate of return.

Because Model N is expected to produce equal cash receipts in each year of its useful life, Table 2 in the appendix on present value tables is used to determine the combined present value of those future cash inflows. However, Table 1 is used to determine the present value of the machine's residual value because it represents a single payment, not an annuity. The net present value of Model N is calculated as follows:

Model N

Year	*Net Cash Inflows*	*16% Factor*	*Present Value*
1–5	$6,000	3.274	$19,644.00
Residual value	2,000	0.476	952.00
Total present value of cash inflows			$20,596.00
Less purchase price of Model N			21,000.00
Net present value			($ 404.00)

FOCUS ON BUSINESS PRACTICE

What Is Total Cost of Ownership, and Why Is It Important?

The concept of total cost of ownership (TCO) was developed to determine the total lifetime costs of owning an information technology (IT) asset, such as a computer system. TCO includes both the direct and indirect costs associated with the acquisition, deployment, operation, support, and retirement of the asset. Today, TCO is the industry standard for evaluating and comparing the costs associated with long-lived asset acquisitions. For example, if you buy a printer, TCO includes the direct costs of buying the printer, the annual supplies costs of ink and paper, and the indirect costs of maintaining it. Thus, the decision about which printer to buy is not based solely on the cost of the printer, but on all costs related to it over its useful lifetime.

Table 2 is used to determine the factor of 3.274 (found in the column for 16 percent and the row for five periods). Because the residual value is a single inflow in the fifth year, the factor of 0.476 must be taken from Table 1 (the column for 16 percent and the row for five periods). The result is a net present value of ($404).

▶ Because the net present value is negative, the proposed investment in Model N will not achieve the minimum rate of return and should be rejected.

The two analyses show that Model M should be chosen because it has a positive net present value and would exceed the company's minimum rate of return. Model N should be rejected because it does not achieve the minimum rate of return. Model M is the better choice because it is expected to produce cash inflows sooner and will thus produce a proportionately greater present value.

STOP & APPLY >

Sample Communications, Inc., is considering the purchase of a new piece of data transmission equipment. Estimated annual net cash inflows for the new equipment are $575,000. The equipment costs $2 million, has a five-year life, and will have no residual value at the end of the five years. The company's minimum rate of return is 12 percent. Compute the net present value of the equipment. Should the company purchase it?

SOLUTION

Net Present Value = Present Value of Future Net Cash Inflows − Cost of Equipment
= ($575,000 × 3.605*) − $2,000,000
= $2,072,875 − $2,000,000
= $72,875

The solution is positive, so the company should purchase the equipment. A positive answer means that the investment will yield more than the minimum 12 percent return required by the company.

*From Table 2 in the appendix on present value tables.

Other Methods of Capital Investment Analysis

LO5 Analyze capital investment proposals using the payback period method and the accounting rate-of-return method.

The net present value method is the best method for capital investment analysis. However, two other commonly used methods provide rough guides to evaluating capital investment proposals. These methods are the payback period method and the accounting rate-of-return method.

The Payback Period Method

Because cash is an essential measure of a business's health, many managers estimate the cash flow that an investment will generate. Their goal is to determine the minimum time it will take to recover the initial investment. If two investment alternatives are being studied, management should choose the investment that pays back its initial cost in the shorter time. That period of time is known as the payback period, and the method of evaluation is called the **payback period method**. Although the payback period method is simple to use, its use has declined because it does not consider the time value of money.

Study Note

The payback period method measures the estimated length of time necessary to recover in cash the cost of an investment.

Payback Calculation The payback period is computed as follows:

$$\text{Payback Period} = \frac{\text{Cost of Investment}}{\text{Annual Net Cash Inflows}}$$

To apply the payback period method, suppose that Neighborhood Communications is interested in purchasing a new server that costs $51,000 and has a residual value of $3,000. Assume that estimates for the proposal include revenue increases of $17,900 a year and operating cost increases of $11,696 a year (including depreciation and taxes). To evaluate this proposed capital investment, use the following steps:

Step 1. Determine the cost of the investment. In the example, it is $51,000.

Step 2. Determine the annual net cash inflows, which are the annual cash revenues minus the cash expenses.

- Eliminate the effects of all noncash revenue and expense items included in the analysis of net income to determine cash revenues and cash expenses.
- In this case, the only noncash expense or revenue is machine depreciation. To eliminate it from operating expenses, you must first calculate depreciation expense. To calculate this amount, you must know the asset's life and the depreciation method. Suppose that Neighborhood Communications uses the straight-line method of depreciation, and the new server will have a ten-year service life. The annual depreciation is computed using this information and the facts given earlier, as follows:

$$\begin{aligned}\text{Annual Depreciation} &= \frac{\text{Cost} - \text{Residual Value}}{\text{Years}}\\ &= \frac{\$51{,}000 - \$3{,}000}{10 \text{ Years}}\\ &= \$4{,}800 \text{ per Year}\end{aligned}$$

- Thus, cash expenses are equal to the operating cost of $11,696 reduced by the depreciation expense of $4,800, or $6,896.
- The annual net cash inflows are $11,004, or cash revenue increases of $17,900 less cash expenses of $6,896.

Study Note

In computing the payback period, depreciation is omitted because it is a noncash expense.

Step 3. Compute the payback period.

$$\text{Payback Period} = \frac{\text{Cost of Machine}}{\text{Cash Revenue} - \text{Cash Expenses}}$$

$$= \frac{\$51{,}000}{\$17{,}900 - (\$11{,}696 - \$4{,}800)}$$

$$= \frac{\$51{,}000}{\$11{,}004}$$

$$= 4.6 \text{ Years*}$$

*Rounded.

If the company's desired payback period is five years or less, this proposal would be approved.

Unequal Annual Net Cash Inflows If a proposed capital investment has unequal annual net cash inflows, the payback period is determined by subtracting each annual amount (in chronological order) from the cost of the capital facility. When a zero balance is reached, the payback period has been determined. This will often occur in the middle of a year. The portion of the final year is computed by dividing the amount needed to reach zero (the unrecovered portion of the investment) by the entire year's estimated cash inflow. The Review Problem in this chapter illustrates that process.

Advantages and Disadvantages The payback period method is widely used because it is easy to compute and understand. It is especially useful in areas in which technology changes rapidly, such as in Internet companies, and when risk is high, such as when investing in emerging countries. However, the disadvantages of this approach far outweigh its advantages. First, the payback period method does not measure profitability. Second, it ignores differences in the present values of cash flows from different periods; thus, it does not adjust cash flows for the time value of money. Finally, the payback period method emphasizes the time it takes to recover the investment rather than the long-term return on the investment. It ignores all future cash flows after the payback period is reached.

The Accounting Rate-of-Return Method

The **accounting rate-of-return method** is an imprecise but easy way to measure the estimated performance of a capital investment, since it uses financial statement information. This method does not use an investment's cash flows but considers the financial reporting effects of the investment instead. The accounting rate-of-return method measures expected performance using two variables: (1) estimated annual net income from the project and (2) average investment cost.

Accounting Rate-of-Return Calculation The basic equation is as follows:

$$\text{Accounting Rate of Return} = \frac{\text{Average Annual Net Income}}{\text{Average Investment Cost}}$$

Step 1. Compute the average annual net income. Use the cost and revenue data prepared for evaluating the project—that is, revenues minus operating expenses (including depreciation and taxes).

Step 2. Compute the average investment cost in a proposed capital facility as follows:

$$\text{Average Investment Cost} = \left(\frac{\text{Total Investment} - \text{Residual Value}}{2}\right) + \text{Residual Value}$$

Study Note

Payback period is expressed in time, net present value is expressed in money, and accounting rate of return is expressed as a percentage.

Step 3. Compute the accounting rate of return.

To see how the accounting rate-of-return is used in evaluating a proposed capital investment, assume the same facts as before for Neighborhood Communications' interest in purchasing a server. Also assume that the company's management will consider only projects that promise to yield more than a 16 percent return. To determine if the company should invest in the machine, compute the accounting rate of return as follows:

$$\text{Accounting Rate of Return} = \frac{\$17{,}900 - \$11{,}696}{\left(\frac{\$51{,}000 - \$3{,}000}{2}\right) + \$3{,}000}$$

$$= \frac{\$6{,}204}{\$27{,}000}$$

$$= 23\%^*$$

*Rounded.

The projected rate of return is higher than the 16 percent minimum, so management should think seriously about making the investment.

Advantages and Disadvantages The accounting rate-of-return method has been widely used because it is easy to understand and apply, but it does have several disadvantages. First, because net income is averaged over the life of the investment, it is not a reliable figure; actual net income may vary considerably from the estimates. Second, the method is unreliable if estimated annual net incomes differ from year to year. Third, it ignores cash flows. Fourth, it does not consider the time value of money; thus, future and present dollars are treated as equal.

& APPLY >

Sample Communications, Inc., is considering the purchase of new data transmission equipment. Estimated annual net cash inflows from the new equipment are $575,000. The equipment costs $2 million and will have no residual value at the end of its five-year life. Compute the payback period for the equipment. Does this method yield a positive or negative response to the proposal to buy the equipment, assuming that the company has set a maximum payback period of four years?

SOLUTION

Payback Period = Cost of Investment ÷ Annual Net Cash Inflows
= $2,000,000 ÷ $575,000
= 3.5 Years*

*Rounded.

The piece of equipment should be purchased because its payback period is less than the company's maximum payback period of 4 years.

Sample Trucking is considering whether to purchase a delivery truck that will cost $26,000, last six years, and have an estimated residual value of $6,000. Average annual net income from the delivery truck is estimated at $4,000. Sample Trucking's owners want to earn an accounting rate of return of 20 percent. Compute the average investment cost and the accounting rate of return. Should the company make the investment?

(continued)

SOLUTION

$$\text{Average Investment Cost} = \left(\frac{\text{Total Investment} - \text{Residual Value}}{2}\right) + \text{Residual Value}$$

$$= \left(\frac{\$26{,}000 - \$6{,}000}{2}\right) + \$6{,}000 = \$16{,}000$$

$$\text{Accounting Rate-of-Return} = \frac{\text{Average Annual Net Income}}{\text{Average Investment Cost}}$$

$$= \frac{\$4{,}000}{\$16{,}000}$$

$$= 25\%$$

The project will exceed the desired return of 20% and should be undertaken.

A LOOK BACK AT ▸ AIR PRODUCTS AND CHEMICALS INC.

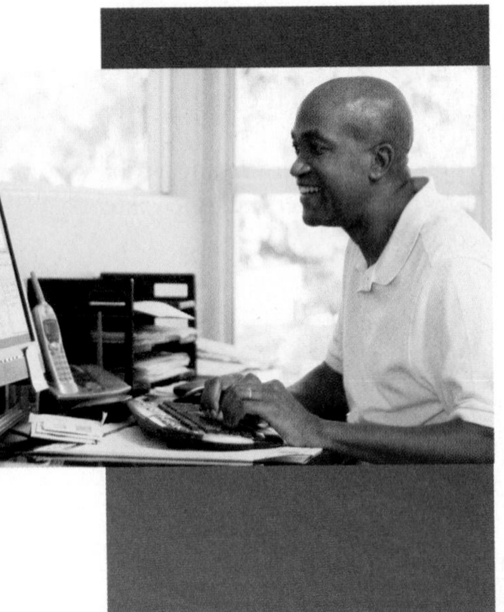

In this chapter's Decision Point, we asked the following questions:

- Why are capital investment decisions critical for a company like **Air Products and Chemicals Inc.**?
- In evaluating capital investment alternatives, how can managers at Air Products and Chemicals Inc. ensure a wise allocation of resources and minimize the risks involved in capital investments?

Capital investments require making decisions about long-term projects that may have positive or negative consequences for a company for many years. It is therefore essential to take a systematic approach to evaluating such projects. Companies like Air Products and Chemicals have many equipment and factory needs, and installing completely automated systems is costly. Thus, when deciding whether to invest their company's capital in an expensive project like an automated plant, managers must focus on making the best decisions possible by using methods of capital investment analysis, such as the net present value method, the payback period method, or the accounting rate-of-return method. With these methods, they can make wise resource choices and minimize the risks involved in the decision. Air Products and Chemicals' management typically evaluates each proposed investment alternative to determine if it will generate an adequate return for the company before making far-reaching capital investment decisions.

Review Problem

Capital Investment Analysis
LO2 LO3
LO4 LO5

Suppose that a company like **Air Products and Chemicals** is considering building a new lights-out facility and has gathered the following information:

Purchase price	$600,000
Residual value	$100,000
Desired payback period	3 years
Minimum rate of return	15%

The cash flow estimates are as follows:

Year	Cash Inflows	Cash Outflows	Net Cash Inflows	Projected Net Income
1	$ 500,000	$260,000	$240,000	$115,000
2	450,000	240,000	210,000	85,000
3	400,000	220,000	180,000	55,000
4	350,000	200,000	150,000	25,000
Totals	$1,700,000	$920,000	$780,000	$280,000

Required

1. Analyze the company's investment in the new facility using (a) the net present value method, (b) the payback period method, and (c) the accounting rate-of-return method.
2. Summarize your findings from requirement **1**, and recommend a course of action.

Answers to Review Problem

1. a. Net present value method (factors are from Table 1 in the appendix on present value tables):

Year	Net Cash Inflows	Present Value Factor	Present Value
1	$240,000	0.870	$208,800
2	210,000	0.756	158,760
3	180,000	0.658	118,440
4	150,000	0.572	85,800
4	100,000 (residual value)	0.572	57,200
Total present value			$629,000
Less cost of original investment			600,000
Net present value			$ 29,000

b. Payback period method:

Total cash investment		$ 600,000
Less cash flow recovery		
Year 1	$240,000	
Year 2	210,000	
Year 3 (5/6 of $180,000)	150,000	(600,000)
Unrecovered investment		$ 0

Payback period: 2.833 (2⅚) Years, or 2 Years, 10 Months.

c. Accounting rate-of-return method:

$$\text{Accounting Rate of Return} = \frac{\text{Average Annual Net Income}}{\text{Average Investment Cost}}$$

$$= \frac{\$280{,}000 \div 4}{\left(\frac{\$600{,}000 - \$100{,}000}{2}\right) + \$100{,}000}$$

$$= \frac{\$70{,}000}{\$350{,}000}$$

$$= 20\%$$

2. Summary of decision analysis:

	Decision Measures	
	Desired	**Calculated**
Net present value	—	$29,000
Accounting rate of return	15%	20%
Payback period	3 Years	2.833 Years

Based on the calculations in requirement **1,** the company should invest in the facility.

LO1 Define *capital investment analysis*, state the purpose of the minimum rate of return, and identify the methods used to arrive at that rate.

Capital investment decisions focus on when and how much to spend on capital facilities and other long-term projects. Capital investment analysis, often referred to as *capital budgeting*, consists of identifying the need for a capital investment, analyzing courses of action to meet that need, preparing reports for management, choosing the best alternative, and dividing funds among competing resource needs.

The minimum rate of return, or hurdle rate, is used as a screening mechanism to eliminate from further consideration capital investment requests with anticipated inadequate returns. Managers save time by quickly identifying substandard requests. The most commonly used measure for determining minimum rates of return is cost of capital. Other measures that are used less often are corporate return on investment, industry average return on investment, and bank lending rates.

LO2 Identify the types of projected costs and revenues used to evaluate alternatives for capital investment.

The accounting rate-of-return method requires measures of net income. Other methods of evaluating capital investments evaluate net cash inflows or cost savings. The analysis process must take into consideration whether each period's cash flows will be equal or unequal. Unless the after-income-tax effects on cash flows are being considered, carrying values and depreciation expense of assets awaiting replacement are irrelevant. Net proceeds from the sale of an old asset and estimated residual value of a new facility represent future cash flows and must be part of the estimated benefit of a project. Depreciation expense on replacement equipment is relevant to evaluations based on after-tax cash flows.

LO3 Apply the concept of the time value of money.

Cash flows of equal dollar amounts at different times have different values because of the effect of compound interest. This phenomenon is known as the time value of money. Of the evaluation methods discussed in this chapter, only the net present value method takes into account the time value of money.

LO4 Analyze capital investment proposals using the net present value method.

The net present value method incorporates the time value of money into the analysis of a proposed capital investment. A minimum required rate of return, usually the average cost of capital, is used to discount an investment's expected future cash flows to their present values. The present values are added together, and the amount of the initial investment is subtracted from their total. If the resulting amount, called the net present value, is positive, the rate of return on the investment will exceed the required rate of return, and the investment should be accepted. If the net present value is negative, the return on the investment will be less than the minimum rate of return, and the investment should be rejected.

LO5 Analyze capital investment proposals using the payback period method and the accounting rate-of-return method.

The payback period method of evaluating a capital investment focuses on the minimum length of time needed to get the amount of the initial investment back in cash. With the accounting rate-of-return method, managers evaluate two or more capital investment proposals and then select the alternative that yields the highest ratio of average annual net income to average cost of investment. Both methods are easy to use, but they are very rough measures that do not consider the time value of money. As a result, the net present value method is preferred.

REVIEW of Concepts and Terminology

The following concepts and terms were introduced in this chapter:

CHAPTER ASSIGNMENTS

BUILDING Your Basic Knowledge and Skills

Short Exercises

LO1 **Manager's Role in Capital Investment Decisions**

SE 1. The supervisor of the Logistics Department has suggested to the plant manager that a new machine costing $285,000 be purchased to improve material handling operations for the plant's newest product line. How should the plant manager proceed with this request?

LO1 **Average Cost of Capital**

SE 2. Gatwick Industries is considering a $1 million plant expansion. Management needs to know the average cost of capital to use in evaluating this capital investment decision. The company's capital structure consists of $3,000,000 of debt at 4 percent interest and $2,000,000 of stockholders' equity at 6 percent. What is Gatwick Industries' average cost of capital?

LO1 **Ranking Capital Investment Proposals**

SE 3. Zelolo Corp. has the following capital investment requests pending from its three divisions: Request 1, $60,000, 11 percent projected return; Request 2, $110,000, 14 percent projected return; Request 3, $130,000, 16 percent projected return; Request 4, $160,000, 13 percent projected return; Request 5, $175,000, 12 percent projected return; and Request 6, $230,000, 15 percent projected return. Zelolo's minimum rate of return is 13 percent, and $500,000 is available for capital investment this year. Which requests will be honored, and in what order?

LO2 **Capital Investment Analysis and Revenue Measures**

SE 4. Daize Corp. is analyzing a proposal to switch its factory over to a lights-out operation similar to the one discussed in this chapter's Decision Point. To do so, it must acquire a fully automated machine that will be able to produce an entire product line in a single operation. Projected annual net cash inflows from the machine are $180,000, and projected net income is $120,000. Why is the projected net income lower than the projected net cash inflows? Identify possible causes for the $60,000 difference.

LO3 **Time Value of Money**

SE 5. Heidi Layne recently inherited a trust fund from a distant relative. On January 2, the bank managing the trust fund notified Layne that she has the option of receiving a lump-sum check for $200,000 or leaving the money in the trust fund and receiving an annual year-end check for $20,000 for each of the next 20 years. Layne likes to earn at least a 5 percent return on her investments. What should she do?

LO4 **Residual Value and Present Value**

SE 6. Annelle Coiner is developing a capital investment analysis for her supervisor. The proposed capital investment has an estimated residual value of $5,500 at the end of its five-year life. The company uses an 8 percent minimum rate of return. What is the present value of the residual value? Use Table 1 in the appendix on present value tables.

LO4 **Capital Investment Decision: Net Present Value Method**

SE 7. Noway Jose Communications, Inc., is considering the purchase of a new piece of computerized data transmission equipment. Estimated annual net cash inflows for the new equipment are $590,000. The equipment costs $2 million, it has a five-year life, and it will have no residual value at the end of the five years. The company has a minimum rate of return of 12 percent. Compute the net present value of the piece of equipment. Should the company purchase it? Use Table 2 in the appendix on present value tables.

LO5 **Capital Investment Decision: Payback Period Method**

SE 8. Using the information about Noway Jose Communications, Inc., in **SE** 7, compute the payback period for the piece of equipment. Does this method yield a positive or a negative response to the proposal to buy the equipment, assuming that the company sets a maximum payback period of four years?

LO5 **Capital Investment Decision: Payback Period Method**

SE 9. East-West Cable, Inc., is considering the purchase of new data transmission equipment. Estimated annual cash revenues for the new equipment are $1 million, and operating costs (including depreciation of $400,000) are $825,000. The equipment costs $2 million, it has a five-year life, and it will have no residual value at the end of the five years. Compute the payback period for the piece of equipment. Does this method yield a positive or a negative response to the proposal to buy the equipment if the company has set a maximum payback period of four years?

LO5 **Capital Investment Decision: Accounting Rate-of-Return Method**

SE 10. Best Cleaners is considering whether to purchase a delivery truck that will cost $50,000, last six years, and have an estimated residual value of $5,000. Average annual net income from the delivery service is estimated to be $4,000. Best Cleaners' owners seek to earn an accounting rate of return of 10 percent. Compute the average investment cost and the accounting rate of return. Should the investment be made?

Exercises

LO1 **Capital Investment Analysis**

E 1. Genette Henderson was just promoted to supervisor of building maintenance for the Ford Valley Theater complex. Allpoints Entertainment, Inc., Henderson's employer, uses a company-wide system for evaluating capital investment requests from its 22 supervisors. Henderson has approached you, the corporate controller, for advice on preparing her first proposal. She would also like to become familiar with the entire decision-making process.

1. What advice would you give Henderson before she prepares her first capital investment proposal?
2. Explain the role of capital investment analysis in the management process, including the six key steps taken during planning.

LO1 **Minimum Rate of Return**

E 2. The controller of Olaf Corporation wants to establish a minimum rate of return and would like to use a weighted-average cost of capital. Current data about the corporation's financing structure are as follows: debt financing, 40 percent; preferred stock, 30 percent; common stock, 20 percent; and retained earnings, 10 percent. The cost of debt is 4 percent. The dividend rate on the preferred stock issue is 3 percent. The cost of common stock is 2 percent and the cost of retained earnings is 5 percent.

Compute the weighted-average cost of capital.

LO1 **Ranking Capital Investment Proposals**

E 3. Managers of the Emerald Bay Furniture Company have gathered all of the capital investment proposals for the year, and they are ready to make their final selections. The following proposals and related rate-of-return amounts were received during the period:

Project	Amount of Investment	Rate of Return (Percentage)
AB	$ 450,000	19
CD	500,000	28
EF	654,000	12
GH	800,000	32
IJ	320,000	23
KL	240,000	18
MN	180,000	16
OP	400,000	26
QR	560,000	14
ST	1,200,000	22
UV	1,600,000	20

Assume that the company's minimum rate of return is 15 percent and that $5,000,000 is available for capital investments during the year.

1. List the acceptable capital investment proposals in order of profitability.
2. Which proposals should be selected for this year?

LO2 **Income Taxes and Net Cash Flow**

E 4. Santa Cruz Company has a tax rate of 20 percent on taxable income. It is considering a capital project that will make the following annual contribution to operating income:

Cash revenues	$400,000
Cash expenses	(200,000)
Depreciation	(140,000)
Operating income before income taxes	$ 60,000
Income taxes at 20%	(12,000)
Operating income	$ 48,000

1. Determine the net cash inflows for this project in two different ways. Are net cash flows the same under either approach?
2. What is the impact of income taxes on net cash flows?

LO3 **Using the Present Values Tables**

E 5. For each of the following situations, identify the correct factor to use from Tables 1 or 2 in the appendix on present value tables. Also, compute the appropriate present value.

1. Annual net cash inflows of $5,000 for five years, discounted at 6 percent
2. An amount of $25,000 to be received at the end of ten years, discounted at 4 percent
3. The amount of $14,000 to be received at the end of two years, and $8,000 to be received at the end of years 4, 5, and 6, discounted at 10 percent

LO3 Using the Present Values Tables

E 6. For each of the following situations, identify the correct factor to use from Tables 1 or 2 in the appendix on present value tables. Also, compute the appropriate present value.

1. Annual net cash inflows of $22,500 for a period of twelve years, discounted at 14 percent
2. The following five years of cash inflows, discounted at 10 percent:

Year 1	$35,000	Year 4	$40,000
Year 2	20,000	Year 5	50,000
Year 3	30,000		

3. The amount of $70,000 to be received at the beginning of year 7, discounted at 14 percent

LO3 Present Value Computations

E 7. Two machines—Machine M and Machine P—are being considered in a replacement decision. Both machines have about the same purchase price and an estimated ten-year life. The company uses a 12 percent minimum rate of return as its acceptance-rejection standard. Following are the estimated net cash inflows for each machine.

Year	Machine M	Machine P
1	$12,000	$17,500
2	12,000	17,500
3	14,000	17,500
4	19,000	17,500
5	20,000	17,500
6	22,000	17,500
7	23,000	17,500
8	24,000	17,500
9	25,000	17,500
10	20,000	17,500
Residual value	14,000	12,000

1. Compute the present value of future cash flows for each machine, using Tables 1 and 2 in the appendix on present value tables.
2. Which machine should the company purchase, assuming that both involve the same capital investment?

LO4 Capital Investment Decision: Net Present Value Method

E 8. Qen and Associates wants to buy an automated coffee roaster/grinder/brewer. This piece of equipment would have a useful life of six years, would cost $218,500, and would increase annual net cash inflows by $57,000. Assume that there is no residual value at the end of six years. The company's minimum rate of return is 14 percent.

Using the net present value method, prepare an analysis to determine whether the company should purchase the machine. Use Tables 1 and 2 in the appendix on present value tables.

LO4 Capital Investment Decision: Net Present Value Method

E 9. H and Y Service Station is planning to invest in automatic car wash equipment valued at $240,000. The owner estimates that the equipment will increase annual net cash inflows by $46,000. The equipment is expected to have a ten-year useful life with an estimated residual value of $50,000. The company requires a 14 percent minimum rate of return.

Using the net present value method, prepare an analysis to determine whether the company should purchase the equipment. How important is the estimate of residual value to this decision? Use Tables 1 and 2 in the appendix on present value tables.

LO4 **Capital Investment Decision: Net Present Value Method**

E 10. Assume the same facts for H and Y Service Station as in **E 9**, except assume that the company requires a 20 percent minimum rate of return.

Using the net present value method, prepare an analysis to determine whether the company should purchase the equipment. Use Tables 1 and 2 in the appendix on present value tables.

LO5 **Capital Investment Decision: Payback Period Method**

E 11. Perfection Sound, Inc., a manufacturer of stereo speakers, is thinking about adding a new plastic-injection molding machine. This machine can produce speaker parts that the company now buys from outsiders. The machine has an estimated useful life of 14 years and will cost $425,000. The residual value of the new machine is $42,500. Gross cash revenue from the machine will be about $400,000 per year, and related cash expenses should total $310,050. Depreciation is estimated to be $30,350 annually. The payback period should be five years or less.

Use the payback period method to determine whether the company should invest in the new machine. Show your computations to support your answer.

LO5 **Capital Investment Decision: Payback Period Method**

E 12. Soaking Wet, Inc., a manufacturer of gears for lawn sprinklers, is thinking about adding a new fully automated machine. This machine can produce gears that the company now produces on its third shift. The machine has an estimated useful life of ten years and will cost $800,000. The residual value of the new machine is $80,000. Gross cash revenue from the machine will be about $520,000 per year, and related operating expenses, including depreciation, should total $500,000. Depreciation is estimated to be $80,000 annually. The payback period should be five years or less.

Use the payback period method to determine whether the company should invest in the new machine. Show your computations to support your answer.

LO5 **Capital Investment Decision: Accounting Rate-of-Return Method**

E 13. Assume the same facts as in **E 11** for Perfection Sound, Inc. Management has decided that only capital investments that yield at least a 20 percent return will be accepted.

Using the accounting rate-of-return method, decide whether the company should invest in the machine. Show all computations to support your decision.

LO5 **Capital Investment Decision: Accounting Rate-of-Return Method**

E 14. Assume the same facts as in **E 12** for Soaking Wet, Inc. Management has decided that only capital investments that yield at least a 5 percent return will be accepted.

Using the accounting rate-of-return method, decide whether the company should invest in the machine. Show all computations to support your decision.

LO5 Capital Investment Decision: Accounting Rate-of-Return Method

E 15. Boink Corporation manufactures metal hard hats for on-site construction workers. Recently, management has tried to raise productivity to meet the growing demand from the real estate industry. The company is now thinking about buying a new stamping machine. Management has decided that only capital investments that yield at least a 14 percent return will be accepted. The new machine would cost $325,000; revenue would increase by $98,400 per year; the residual value of the new machine would be $32,500; and operating cost increases (including depreciation) would be $75,000.

Using the accounting rate-of-return method, decide whether the company should invest in the machine. Show all computations to support your decision.

Problems

LO1 LO2 Minimum Rate of Return

P 1. Capital investment analysis is the main responsibility of Ginny Weiss, the special assistant to the controller of Nazzaro Manufacturing Company. During the previous 12-month period, the company's capital mix and the respective costs were as follows:

	Percentage of Total Financing	Cost of Capital
Debt financing	25%	7%
Preferred stock	15	9
Common stock	50	12
Retained earnings	10	12

Plans for the current year call for a 10 percent shift in total financing from common stock financing to debt financing. Also, the cost of debt financing is expected to increase to 8 percent, although the cost of the other types of financing will remain the same.

Weiss has already analyzed several proposed capital investments. Those projects and their projected rates of return are as follows: Project M, 9.5 percent; Equipment Item N, 8.5 percent; Product Line O, 15.0 percent; Project P, 6.9 percent; Product Line Q, 10.5 percent; Equipment Item R, 11.9 percent; and Project S, 11.0 percent.

Required

1. Using the expected adjustments to cost and capital mix, compute the weighted-average cost of capital for the current year.
2. Identify the proposed capital investments that should be implemented based on the cost of capital calculated in requirement **1.**

LO3 LO4 Net Present Value Method

P 2. Sonja and Sons, Inc., owns and operates a group of apartment buildings. Management wants to sell one of its older four-family buildings and buy a new building. The old building, which was purchased 25 years ago for $100,000, has a 40-year estimated life. The current market value is $80,000, and if it is sold, the cash inflow will be $67,675. Annual net cash inflows from the old building are expected to average $16,000 for the remainder of its estimated useful life.

The new building will cost $300,000. It has an estimated useful life of 25 years. Net cash inflows are expected to be $50,000 annually.

Assume that (1) all cash flows occur at year end, (2) the company uses straight-line depreciation, (3) the buildings will have a residual value equal to 10 percent of their purchase price, and (4) the minimum rate of return is 14 percent. Use Tables 1 and 2 in the appendix on present value tables.

Required

1. Compute the present value of future cash flows from the old building.
2. What will the net present value of cash flows be if the company purchases the new building?
3. Should the company keep the old building or purchase the new one?

Manager insight ▶ (3)

LO3 LO4

Net Present Value Method

P 3. The management of Better Plastics has recently been looking at a proposal to purchase a new plastic-injection-style molding machine. With the new machine, the company would not have to buy small plastic parts to use in production. The estimated useful life of the machine is 15 years, and the purchase price, including all setup charges, is $400,000. The residual value is estimated to be $40,000. The net addition to the company's cash inflow as a result of the savings from making the parts is estimated to be $70,000 a year. Better Plastics' management has decided on a minimum rate of return of 14 percent. Use Tables 1 and 2 in the appendix on present value tables.

Required

1. Using the net present value method to evaluate this capital investment, determine whether the company should purchase the machine. Support your answer.
2. If the management of Better Plastics had decided on a minimum rate of return of 16 percent, should the machine be purchased? Show all computations to support your answer.

Manager insight ▶ (2)

LO5

Accounting Rate-of-Return and Payback Period Methods

P 4. The Raab Company is expanding its production facilities to include a new product line, a sporty automotive tire rim. Tire rims can now be produced with little labor cost using new computerized machinery. The controller has advised management about two such machines. The details about each machine are as follows:

	XJS Machine	HZT Machine
Cost of machine	$500,000	$550,000
Residual value	50,000	55,000
Net income	34,965	40,670
Annual net cash inflows	91,215	90,170

The company's minimum rate of return is 12 percent. The maximum payback period is six years. (Where necessary, round calculations.)

Required

1. For each machine, compute the projected accounting rate of return.
2. Compute the payback period for each machine.
3. Based on the information from requirements **1** and **2**, which machine should be purchased? Why?

Manager insight ▶ (3)

LO3 LO4 LO5

Capital Investment Decision: Comprehensive

P 5. The Arcadia Manufacturing Company, based in Arcadia, Florida, is one of the fastest-growing companies in its industry. According to Ms. Prinze, the company's production vice president, keeping up-to-date with technological changes is what makes the company successful.

Prinze believes a new machine will fill an important need. The machine has an estimated useful life of four years, a purchase price of $250,000, and a residual value of $25,000. The company controller has estimated average annual net income of $11,250 and the following cash flows for the new machine:

	Cash Flow Estimates		
Year	Cash Inflows	Cash Outflows	Net Cash Inflows
1	$325,000	$250,000	$75,000
2	320,000	250,000	70,000
3	315,000	250,000	65,000
4	310,000	250,000	60,000

Prinze uses a 12 percent minimum rate of return and a three-year payback period for capital investment evaluation purposes.

Required

1. Analyze the data about the machine, and decide if the company should purchase it. Use the following evaluation approaches in your analysis: (a) the net present value method, (b) the accounting rate-of-return method, and (c) the payback period method. Use Tables 1 and 2 in the appendix on present value tables.
2. Summarize the information generated in requirement **1**, and make a recommendation to Prinze.

Alternate Problems

LO1 LO2 Minimum Rate of Return

P 6. Capital investment analysis is the main responsibility of the controller of Glory Company. During the previous 12-month period, the company's capital mix and the respective costs were as follows:

	Percentage of Total Financing	Cost of Capital
Debt financing	40%	2%
Preferred stock	10	3
Common stock	30	8
Retained earnings	20	6

Plans for the current year call for a 10 percent shift in total financing from debt financing to common stock financing. Also, the cost of debt financing is expected to increase to 4 percent, although the cost of the other types of financing will remain the same.

The controller has already analyzed several proposed capital investments. Those projects and their projected rates of return are as follows: Project M, 7.5 percent; Equipment Item N, 6.2 percent; Product Line O, 5.0 percent; Product Line P, 6.9 percent; Product Line Q, 1.5 percent; Equipment Item R, 3.9 percent; and Project S, 6.0 percent.

Required

1. Using the expected adjustments to cost and capital mix, compute the weighted-average cost of capital for the current year.
2. Identify the proposed capital investments that should be implemented based on the cost of capital calculated in requirement **1.**

LO3 LO4 **Comparison of Alternatives: Net Present Value Method**

P 7. City Sights, Ltd., operates a tour and sightseeing business. Its trademark is the use of trolley buses. Each vehicle has its own identity and is specially made for the company. Gridlock, the oldest bus, was purchased 15 years ago and has 5 years of its estimated useful life remaining. The company paid $25,000 for Gridlock, and the bus could be sold today for $20,000. Gridlock is expected to generate average annual net cash inflows of $24,000 for the remainder of its estimated useful life.

Management wants to replace Gridlock with a modern-looking vehicle called Phantom. Phantom has a purchase price of $140,000 and an estimated useful life of 20 years. Net cash inflows for Phantom are projected to be $40,000 per year.

Assume that (1) all cash flows occur at year end, (2) each vehicle's residual value equals 10 percent of its purchase price, and (3) the minimum rate of return is 10 percent. Use Tables 1 and 2 in the appendix on present value tables.

Required

1. Compute the present value of the future cash flows from Gridlock.
2. Compute the net present value of cash flows if Phantom were purchased.
3. Manager insight ▶ Should City Sights keep Gridlock or purchase Phantom?

LO3 LO4 **Net Present Value Method**

P 8. Mansion is a famous restaurant in the French Quarter of New Orleans. Bouillabaisse Sophie is Mansion's house specialty. Management is considering the purchase of a machine that would prepare all the ingredients, mix them automatically, and cook the dish to the restaurant's specifications. The machine will function for an estimated 12 years, and the purchase price, including installation, is $250,000. Estimated residual value is $25,000. This labor-saving device is expected to increase cash flows by an average of $42,000 per year during its estimated useful life. For capital investment decisions, the restaurant uses a 12 percent minimum rate of return. Use Tables 1 and 2 in the appendix on present value tables.

Required

1. Using the net present value method, determine if the company should purchase the machine. Support your answer.
2. Manager insight ▶ If management had decided on a minimum rate of return of 14 percent, should the machine be purchased? Show all computations to support your answer.

LO5 **Accounting Rate-of-Return and Payback Period Methods**

P 9. The Cute Car Company is expanding its production facilities to include a new product line, an energy-efficient sporty convertible. The car can be produced with little labor cost using computerized machinery. There are two such machines to choose from. The details about each machine are as follows:

	GoGo Machine	Autom Machine
Cost of machine	$300,000	$325,000
Residual value	30,000	32,500
Net income	25,000	30,000
Annual net cash inflows	60,000	50,000

The company's minimum rate of return is 15 percent. The maximum payback period is six years. (Where necessary, round calculations.)

Required

1. For each machine, compute the projected accounting rate of return.
2. Compute the payback period for each machine.

Manager insight ▶ 3. Based on the information from requirements **1** and **2**, which machine should be purchased? Why?

LO3 LO4 LO5 **Capital Investment Decision: Comprehensive**

P 10. Pressed Corporation wants to buy a new stamping machine. The machine will provide the company with a new product line: pressed rubber food trays for kitchens. Two machines are being considered; the data for each machine are as follows:

	ETZ Machine	LKR Machine
Cost of machine	$350,000	$370,000
Net income	$39,204	$48,642
Annual net cash inflows	$64,404	$75,642
Residual value	$28,000	$40,000
Estimated useful life in years	10	10

The company's minimum rate of return is 16 percent, and the maximum allowable payback period is 5.0 years.

Required

1. Compute the net present value for each machine.
2. Compute the accounting rate of return for each machine.
3. Compute the payback period for each machine.

Manager insight ▶ 4. From the information generated in requirements **1**, **2**, and **3**, decide which machine should be purchased. Why?

ENHANCING Your Knowledge, Skills, and Critical Thinking

LO1 **Evaluation of Proposed Capital Investments**

C 1. The board of directors of the Tanashi Corporation met to review a number of proposed capital investments that would improve the quality of company products. One production-line manager requested the purchase of new computer-integrated machines to replace the older machines in one of the ten production departments at the Tokyo plant. Although the manager had presented quantitative information to support the purchase of the new machines, the board members asked the following important questions:

1. Why do we want to replace the old machines? Have they deteriorated? Are they obsolete?
2. Will the new machines require less cycle time?
3. Can we reduce inventory levels or save floor space by replacing the old machines?
4. How expensive is the software used with the new machines?

5. Will we be able to find highly skilled employees to maintain the new machines? Or can we find workers who are trainable? What would it cost to train workers? Would the training disrupt the staff by causing relocations?
6. Would the implementation of the machines be delayed because of the time required to recruit and train new workers?
7. How would the new machines affect the other parts of the manufacturing systems? Would the company lose some of the flexibility in its manufacturing systems if it introduced the new machines?

The board members believe that the qualitative information needed to answer their questions could lead to the rejection of the project, even though it would have been accepted based on the quantitative information.

1. Identify the questions that can be answered with quantitative information. Give an example of the quantitative information that could be used.
2. Identify the questions that can be answered with qualitative information. Explain why this information could negatively influence the capital investment decision even though the quantitative information suggests a positive outcome.

LO3 LO4 Using Net Present Value

C 2. The McCall Syndicate owns four resort hotels in Europe. Because the Paris operation (Hotel 1) has been booming over the past five years, management has decided to build an addition to the hotel. This addition will increase the hotel's capacity by 20 percent. A construction company has bid to build the addition at a cost of $30,000,000. The building will have an increased residual value of $3,000,000.

Daj Van Dyke, the controller, has started an analysis of the net present value for the project. She has calculated the annual net cash inflows by subtracting the increase in cash operating expenses from the increase in cash inflows from room rentals. Her partially completed schedule follows:

Year	Net Cash Inflows
1–20 (each year)	$3,900,000

Capital investment projects must generate a 12 percent minimum rate of return to qualify for consideration.

Using net present value analysis, evaluate the proposal and make a recommendation to management. Explain how your recommendation would change if management were willing to accept a 10 percent minimum rate of return. Use Tables 1 and 2 in the appendix on present value tables.

LO4 Capital Investment Analysis

C 3. Automated teller machines (ATMs) have become common in the banking industry. San Angelo Federal Bank is planning to replace some old teller machines and has decided to use the York Machine. Nola Chavez, the controller, has prepared the analysis shown at the top of the next page. She has recommended the purchase of the machine based on the positive net present value shown in the analysis.

The York Machine has an estimated useful life of five years and an expected residual value of $35,000. Its purchase price is $385,000. Two existing ATMs, each having a carrying value of $25,000, can be sold to a neighboring bank for a total of $50,000. Annual operating cash inflows are expected to increase in the following manner:

Year 1	$79,900
Year 2	76,600
Year 3	79,900
Year 4	83,200
Year 5	86,500

San Angelo Federal Bank
Capital Investment Analysis
Net Present Value Method

Year	Net Cash Inflows	Present Value Factor	Present Value
1	$ 85,000	0.909	$ 77,265
2	80,000	0.826	66,080
3	85,000	0.751	63,835
4	90,000	0.683	61,470
5	95,000	0.621	58,995
5 (residual value)	35,000	0.621	21,735
Total present value			$349,380
Initial investment		$385,000	
Less proceeds from the sale of existing teller machines		50,000	
Net capital investment			(335,000)
Net present value			$ 14,380

The San Angelo Federal Bank uses straight-line depreciation. The minimum rate of return is 12 percent.

1. Analyze Chavez's work. What changes need to be made in her capital investment analysis?
2. What would be your recommendation to bank management about the purchase of the York Machine?

LO4 **Net Present Value of Cash Flows**

C 4. CPC Corporation is an international plumbing equipment and supply company located in southern California. The manager of the Pipe Division is considering the purchase of a computerized copper pipe machine that costs $120,000.

The machine has a six-year life, and its expected residual value after six years of use will be 10 percent of its original cost. Cash revenue generated by the new machine is projected to be $50,000 in year 1 and will increase by $10,000 each year for the next five years. Variable cash operating costs will be materials and parts, 25 percent of revenue; machine labor, 5 percent of revenue; and overhead, 15 percent of revenue. First-year sales and marketing cash outflows are expected to be $10,500 and will decrease by 10 percent each year over the life of the new machine. Anticipated cash administrative expenses will be $2,500 per year. The company uses a 15 percent minimum rate of return for all capital investment analyses.

1. Prepare an Excel spreadsheet to compute the net present value of the anticipated cash flows for the life of the proposed new machine. Use the following format:

		Projected Cash Outflows							
Future Time Period	Projected Cash Revenue	Materials and Parts	Machine Labor	Overhead	Sales and Marketing	Administrative Expenses	Projected Net Cash Inflows	15% Factor	Present Value

Should the company invest in the new machine?

2. After careful analysis, the controller has determined that the variable rate for materials and parts can be reduced to 22 percent of revenue. Will this reduction in cash outflow change the decision about investing in the new machine? Explain your answer.
3. The marketing manager has determined that the initial estimate of sales and marketing cash expenses was too high and has reduced that estimate by $1,000. The 10 percent annual reductions are still expected to occur. Together with the change in **2**, will this reduction affect the initial investment decision? Explain your answer.

LO4

Ethics, Capital Investment Decisions, and the New Globally Competitive Business Environment

C 5. Marika Jonssen is the controller of Bramer Corporation, a globally competitive producer of standard and custom-designed window units for the housing industry. As part of the corporation's move to become automated, Jonssen was asked to prepare a capital investment analysis for a robot-guided aluminum extruding and stamping machine. This machine would automate the entire window-casing manufacturing line. She has just returned from an international seminar on the subject of qualitative inputs into the capital investment decision process and is eager to incorporate those new ideas into the analysis. In addition to the normal net present value analysis (which produced a significant negative result), Jonssen factored in figures for customer satisfaction, scrap reduction, reduced inventory needs, and reputation for quality. With the additional information included, the analysis produced a positive response to the decision question.

When the chief financial officer finished reviewing Jonssen's work, he threw the papers on the floor and said, "What kind of garbage is this! You know it's impossible to quantify such things as customer satisfaction and reputation for quality. How do you expect me to go to the board of directors and explain your work? I want you to redo the entire analysis and follow only the traditional approach to net present value. Get it back to me in two hours!"

What is Jonssen's dilemma? What ethical courses of action are available to her?

LO2 LO3 LO4 LO5

Cookie Company (Continuing Case)

C 6. Suppose your cookie company is now a corporation that has granted franchises to more than 50 stores. Currently, only 10 of the 50 stores have computerized machines for mixing cookie dough. Because of a tremendous increase in demand for cookie dough, you, as the corporation's president, are considering purchasing 10 more computerized mixing machines by the end of this month. You are writing a memo evaluating this purchase that you will present at the board of directors' meeting next week.

According to your research, the 10 new machines will cost $320,000. They will function for an estimated five years and should have a $32,000 residual value. All of your corporation's capital investments are expected to produce a 20 percent minimum rate of return, and they should be recovered in three years or less. All fixed assets are depreciated using the straight-line method. The forecasted increase in operating results for the aggregate of the 10 new machines is as follows:

	Cash Flow Estimates	
Year	Cash Inflows	Cash Outflows
1	$310,000	$210,000
2	325,000	220,000
3	340,000	230,000
4	300,000	210,000
5	260,000	180,000

1. In preparation for writing your memo, answer the following questions:
   a. What kinds of information do you need to prepare this memo?
   b. Why is the information relevant?
   c. Where would you find the information?
   d. When would you want to obtain the information?
2. Analyze the purchase of the machines, and decide if your corporation should purchase them. Use (a) the net present value method, (b) the accounting rate-of-return method, and (c) the payback period method.

CHAPTER

26

Pricing Decisions, Including Target Costing and Transfer Pricing

The Management Process

PLAN

- **Identify the maximum price the market will accept and the minimum price the company can sustain.**
- **Set the external price for each product or service using either cost-based or market-based methods.**
- **Set internal transfer prices for products and services.**

PERFORM

- **Sell products or services at the set prices or on the auction market.**

EVALUATE

- **Analyze actual prices and profits versus targeted ones.**
- **Determine which pricing strategies were successful and which failed.**
- **Identify reasons for success or failure.**
- **Take necessary corrective actions.**

REPORT

- **Prepare reports to assess past pricing strategies and plan future strategies.**

The price managers set for products and services impacts business operations both internally and externally.

In this chapter, we examine the various approaches that managers use to establish the prices of goods and services. There are many such approaches; however, each approach may very well produce a different price for the same product or service. The process of establishing a correct price is, in fact, more of an art than a science. It depends on a manager's ability to analyze the marketplace and anticipate customers' reactions to a product or service and its price.

LEARNING OBJECTIVES

LO1 Identify the objectives and rules used to establish prices of goods and services, and relate pricing issues to the management process. (pp. 1188–1191)

LO2 Describe economic pricing concepts, including the auction-based pricing method used on the Internet. (pp. 1191–1194)

LO3 Use cost-based pricing methods to develop prices. (pp. 1194–1200)

LO4 Describe target costing, and use that concept to analyze pricing decisions and evaluate a new product opportunity. (pp. 1201–1204)

LO5 Describe how transfer pricing is used for transferring goods and services and evaluating performance within a division or segment. (pp. 1205–1209)

DECISION POINT ▸ A MANAGER'S FOCUS LAB 126

Lab 126, a subsidiary of **Amazon.com**, dominates the e-book market. Its latest product is the Kindle DX, a larger version of the original Kindle. These portable readers allow users to wirelessly download e-books and other digital media to a high-resolution electronic display; no computer is required. Kindle users can buy e-books online from Amazon.com for a small fee. Another of Lab 126's products, the Kindle for iPhone application, provides an easy-to-use interface that enables users of **Apple**'s iPhones and iPods to read Kindle books. Competition among Lab 126's products, the Sony Reader, and other e-book readers is very keen, and there is constant pressure to offer more technology-rich features to outdo competitors.

- ▸ Why do managers generally use several pricing approaches?
- ▸ Why might Lab 126's managers use target costing to establish a price for the Kindle?

The Pricing Decision and the Manager

LO1 Identify the objectives and rules used to establish prices of goods and services, and relate pricing issues to the management process.

As we have noted, establishing a correct price depends on a manager's ability to analyze the marketplace and anticipate customers' reactions to a product or service and its price.

Pricing Policies

Setting appropriate prices is one of the most difficult decisions that managers must make on a day-to-day basis. Because such decisions affect the long-term survival of any profit-oriented enterprise, a company's long-term objectives should include a pricing policy. A pricing policy is one way in which companies differentiate themselves from their competitors. Compare, for example, the pricing policies of luxury brands like **Lexus** and **Nordstrom** with those of cost-driven companies like **Toyota** or **Wal-Mart**. Consider also how prices are set on **eBay** and **Priceline.com.** Although all these companies are successful, their pricing policies differ significantly because each company has different pricing objectives.

In addition, companies may use pricing policies to differentiate among their own brands. For example, **Gap, Inc.**, uses price to differentiate the Gap brand from the brand of its subsidiary, **Old Navy**, and **Mercedes Benz** uses price to differentiate the Smart Car from the Mercedes. Thus, for each product brand, the company has identified the market segment that it intends to serve and has developed pricing objectives to meet the needs of that market.

Pricing Policy Objectives

Possible objectives of a pricing policy include the following:

1. ***Identifying and adhering to both short-run and long-run pricing strategies.*** Pricing strategies depend on many factors and conditions. The pricing strategies of companies that produce standard items or commodities for a competitive marketplace will differ from the pricing strategies of companies that make custom-designed items. In a competitive market, companies can reduce prices to draw sales away from competing companies. They can also continuously add value-enhancing features and upgrades to their products and services to create the impression that customers are receiving more for their money. In contrast, a company that makes custom-designed items can be more conservative in its pricing strategy.

2. ***Maximizing profits.*** Maximizing profits has traditionally been the underlying objective of any pricing policy.

3. ***Maintaining or gaining market share.*** One key indicator of profit potential is an increasing share of the market. Maintaining or gaining market share is closely related to pricing strategies. However, market share is important only if sales are profitable. To increase market share by reducing prices below cost can be economically disastrous unless such a move is accompanied by strategies that compensate for the lost revenues.

4. ***Setting socially responsible prices.*** Maximizing profits remains a dominant factor in price setting. However, to enhance their standing with the public and thus ensure their long-term survival, companies today also consider whether their prices are socially responsible. The pricing policies of many companies now take into consideration a variety of social concerns, including environmental factors, the influence of an aging population, legal constraints, and ethical issues.

5. ***Maintaining a minimum rate of return on investment.*** Organizations view each product or service as an investment. They will not invest in making a product or providing a service unless it will provide a minimum return. To maintain a minimum return on investment, an organization, when setting prices, adds a markup percentage to each product's costs of production. This markup percentage is closely related to the objective of profit maximization.

6. ***Being customer focused.*** Taking customers' needs into consideration when setting prices or increasing a product's value to customers is important for at least three reasons. These reasons are as follows:

   - Sensitivity to customers is necessary to sustain sales growth.
   - Customers' acceptance is crucial to success in a competitive market.
   - Prices should reflect the enhanced value that the company adds to the product or service, which is another way of saying that prices are customer-driven.

Pricing and the Management Process

For an organization to stay in business, its selling price must (1) be competitive with the competition's price, (2) be acceptable to customers, (3) recover all costs incurred in bringing the product or service to market, and (4) return a profit. If a manager deviates from any of these four pricing rules, there must be a specific short-run objective that accounts for the change. Breaking those pricing rules for a long period will force a company into bankruptcy. The sidebar on the first page of this chapter illustrates the elements of pricing that managers need to consider at each step in the management process.

External and Internal Pricing Factors

When making and evaluating pricing decisions, managers must consider many factors. As shown in Figure 26-1, some of those factors relate to the external market, and others relate to internal constraints.

- The external factors include demand for the product, customer needs, competition, and quantity and quality of competing products or services.
- The internal factors include constraints caused by costs, desired return on investment, quality and quantity of materials and labor, and allocation of scarce resources.

FIGURE 26-1
External and Internal Factors Affecting Pricing Decisions

WHEN MAKING AND EVALUATING PRICING DECISIONS

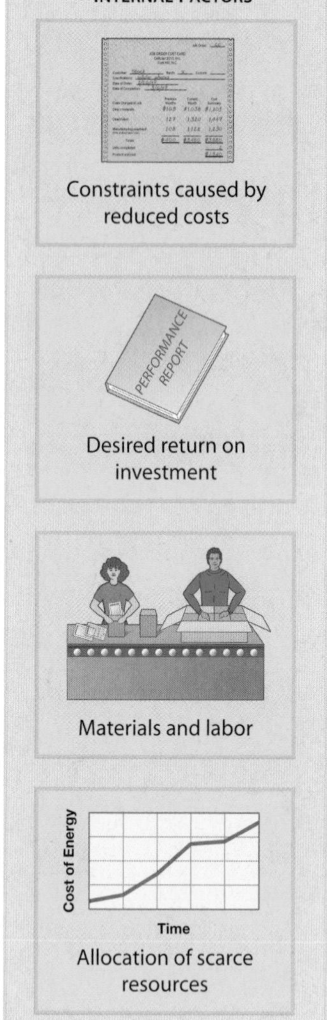

STOP & APPLY >

Towne's Tire Outlet features more than a dozen brands of tires. Two of the brands are Gripper and Roadster. Information about the two brands is as follows:

	Gripper	Roadster
Selling price:		
Single tire, installed	$125	$110
Set of four tires, installed	460	400
Cost per tire	90	60

As shown, selling prices include installation costs, which are $20 per tire.

1. Compute each brand's net unit selling price after installation for both a single tire and a set of four.
2. Was cost the main consideration in setting those prices?
3. What other factors could have influenced those prices?

(continued)

SOLUTION

1.

	Gripper		Roadster	
	One Tire	**Four Tires**	**One Tire**	**Four Tires**
Selling price	$125	$460	$110	$400
Less installation cost	20	80	20	80
Net selling price	$105	$380	$ 90	$320
Unit selling price	$105	$ 95	$ 90	$ 80

2. The Gripper tire costs the company $30 more than the Roadster tire, but there is only a $15 difference between the two selling prices. The low cost of the Roadster allows the company to sell it at a significantly lower price than the higher-cost Gripper. Therefore, customers perceive the Roadster to be a better purchase value than the Gripper. The company is not using cost as a major consideration in its pricing decisions.
3. Other pricing considerations include local competition, quality versus price, and demand for the tires.

Economic Pricing Concepts

LO2 Describe economic pricing concepts, including the auction-based pricing method used on the Internet.

The economic approach to pricing is based on microeconomic theory. Pricing plays a strong role in the concepts underlying microeconomic theory as it is practiced at individual firms. Every firm is in business to maximize profits. Although each product has its own set of revenues and costs, microeconomic theory states that profit will be greatest when the difference between total revenue and total cost is greatest.

Total Revenue and Total Cost Curves

It may seem that if a company could produce an infinite number of products, it would realize the maximum profit. But this is not the case, and microeconomic theory explains why. Figure 26-2A shows the economist's view of a breakeven chart. It contains two breakeven points, between which is a large space labeled "profit area."

Total Revenues Notice that the total revenue line is curved rather than straight. The theory behind this is that as a product is marketed, because of competition and other factors, price reductions will be necessary if the firm is to sell additional units. Total revenue will continue to increase, but the rate of increase will diminish as more units are sold. Therefore, the slope of the total revenue line declines, and the line curves toward the right.

Total Costs Costs react in an opposite way. Over the assumed relevant range, variable and fixed costs are fairly predictable, with fixed costs remaining constant and variable costs being the same per unit. The result is a straight line for total costs. However, following microeconomic theory, costs per unit will increase as more units are sold because fixed costs will change. As costs move into different relevant ranges, such fixed costs as supervision and depreciation increase, and competition causes marketing costs to rise. As the company pushes for more and more products from limited facilities, repair and maintenance costs also increase. And as the push from management increases, total costs per unit rise at an accelerating rate. The result is that the slope of the total cost line in Figure 26-2A increases, and the line begins curving upward. The total revenue line and the total cost line then cross again; beyond that point, the company suffers a loss on additional sales.

FIGURE 26-2
Microeconomic Pricing Theory

A. TOTAL REVENUE AND TOTAL COST CURVES

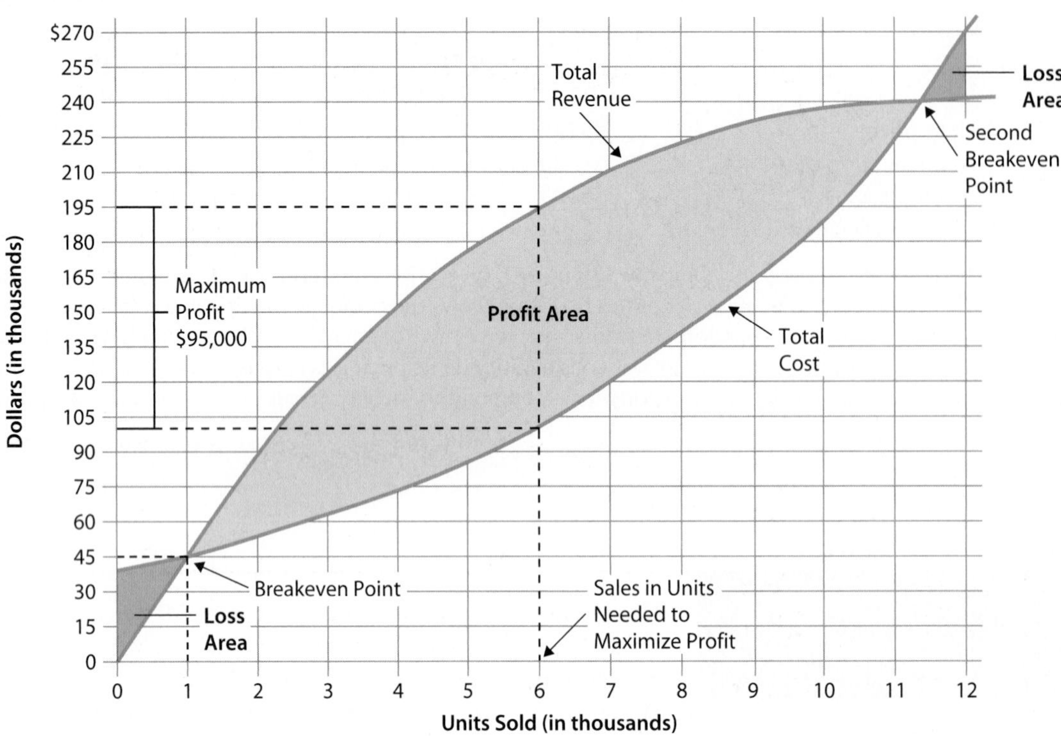

B. MARGINAL REVENUE AND MARGINAL COST CURVES

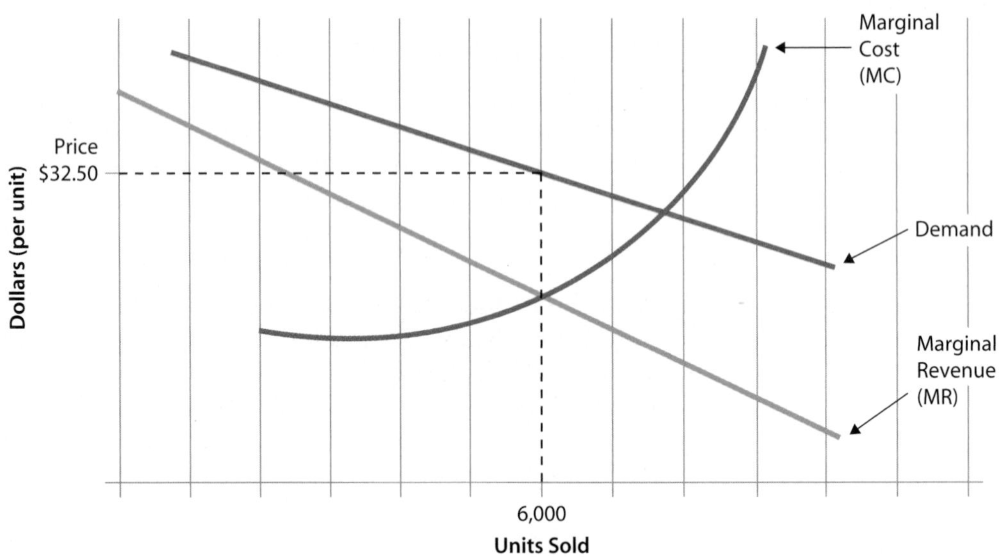

Profit Maximization Profits are maximized at the point where the difference between total revenue and total cost is the greatest. In Figure 26-2A, this point is 6,000 units of sales. At that sales level, total revenue will be $195,000; total cost, $100,000; and profit, $95,000. In theory, if one additional unit is sold, profit per unit will drop because total cost is rising at a faster rate than total revenues. As you can see, if the company sells 11,000 units, total profits will be almost entirely depleted by the rising costs. Therefore, 6,000 sales units is the optimal operating level, and the price charged at that level is the optimal price.

Marginal Revenue and Marginal Cost Curves

Economists use marginal revenue and marginal cost to help determine the optimal price for a product or service. **Marginal revenue** is the change in total revenue caused by a one-unit change in output. **Marginal cost** is the change in total cost caused by a one-unit change in output. Graphic curves for marginal revenue and marginal cost are created by measuring and plotting the rate of change in total revenue and total cost at various activity levels.

If you computed marginal revenue and marginal cost for each unit sold in our example and plotted them on a graph, the lines would resemble those in Figure 26-2B. Notice that the marginal cost line crosses the marginal revenue line at 6,000 units. After that point, profit per unit will decrease as additional units are sold. Marginal cost will exceed marginal revenue for each unit sold over 6,000. Profit will be maximized when the marginal revenue and marginal cost lines intersect. By projecting this point onto the product's demand curve, you can locate the optimal price, which is $32.50 per unit.

If all the information used in microeconomic theory were certain, picking the optimal price would be fairly easy. But most information used in such an analysis relies on projected amounts for unit sales, product costs, and revenues. Nevertheless, developing such an analysis usually highlights cost patterns and the unanticipated influences of demand. For this reason, it is important that managers consider the microeconomic approach to pricing when setting product prices. However, the results of this type of analysis should not be the only data relied on.

Auction-Based Pricing

In recent years, as a result of auctions hosted by Internet companies like **eBay**, **Yahoo**, and **Price-line.com**, auction-based pricing has skyrocketed in popularity. **Auction-based pricing** occurs in two ways: Either sellers post what they have to sell, ask for price bids, and accept a buyer's offer to purchase at a certain price, or buyers interested in buying something post what they want, ask for prices, and accept a seller's offer to sell at a certain price.

To illustrate the seller's auction-based price, suppose a corporation like **Intel** has an excess of silicon chips after a production run. The company posts a message on the Internet asking for the quantity of silicon chips that prospective buyers are willing to buy and the price that they are willing to pay. After the offers are received, the company prepares a demand curve of all offers and selects the one that best fits the quantity of silicon chips it has available for sale.

To illustrate the buyer's auction-based price, consider an individual who wants to fly round-trip to Europe on certain dates and posts his or her needs on one of the Internet's auction markets. After receiving the offers to sell round-trip tickets to Europe, the individual will accept the offer that best suits his or her needs.

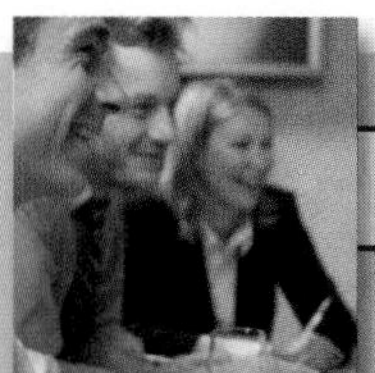

FOCUS ON BUSINESS PRACTICE

What's It Worth to Shop Online?

The Internet makes it possible to price efficiently at the level of marginal costs. For instance, at websites like **Priceline.com**, travelers pick a destination and a price they are willing to pay for air or hotel reservations.The price must be guaranteed by credit card. An airline or hotel has a limited amount of time to accept or reject the bid. If the bid is accepted, the buyer is obligated to pay for the air or hotel reservation. The hotels and airlines are often willing to accept the low bid prices because the marginal cost of filling an additional seat on an airplane or an extra room in a hotel is very low.

FOCUS ON BUSINESS PRACTICE

How Big a Problem Is Fraud on the Internet?

The Internet Fraud Complaint Center, which is co-sponsored by the Federal Bureau of Investigation, recently reported that 44.9 percent of the complaints it received were about Internet auction fraud, 19.0 percent were about nondelivery of merchandise/payment, and 4.9 percent were about check fraud. Other categories of complaints included credit/debit card fraud, confidence schemes, and financial institution fraud.

Auction-based pricing will continue to grow in importance as a result of the escalating amount of business that is being conducted over the Internet by both organizations and individuals. Just about anything can be bought or sold via the Internet.

STOP & APPLY >

Assume that a product has the total cost and total revenue curves pictured in Figure 26-2A. Also assume that the difference between total revenue and total cost is the same at the 4,000- and 9,000-unit levels. If you had to choose between those two levels of activity as goals for total sales over the life of the product, which would you prefer? Why?

SOLUTION

The 4,000-unit level is preferable. Given the same total profit will be made at both the 4,000- and the 9,000-unit levels, it does not make economic sense to produce the additional 5,000 units.

Cost-Based Pricing Methods

LO3 Use cost-based pricing methods to develop prices.

Managers may use a variety of pricing methods. A good starting point for developing a price is to base it on the cost of producing a good or service. Two pricing methods based on cost are gross margin pricing and return on assets pricing. Remember that in a competitive environment, market prices and conditions also influence price; however, if prices do not cover a company's costs, the company will eventually fail.

To illustrate the two methods of cost-based pricing, we will use Bookit Company as an example. Bookit buys parts from outside vendors and assembles them into very basic e-book readers. In the previous accounting period, the company produced 14,750 readers. The total costs and unit costs incurred follow.

	Total Costs	Unit Costs
Variable production costs		
Direct materials and parts	$ 88,500	$ 6.00
Direct labor	66,375	4.50
Variable overhead	44,250	3.00
Total variable production costs	$199,125	$13.50
Fixed overhead	154,875	10.50
Total production costs	$354,000	$24.00
Selling, general, and administrative expenses		
Selling expenses	$ 73,750	$ 5.00
General expenses	36,875	2.50
Administrative expenses	22,125	1.50
Total selling, general, and administrative expenses	$132,750	$ 9.00
Total costs and expenses	$486,750	$33.00

No changes in unit costs are expected this period. The desired profit for the period is $110,625. The company uses assets totaling $921,875 in producing the e-book readers and expects a 14 percent return on those assets.

Gross Margin Pricing

Study Note

The gross margin pricing method is also called the *income statement method.*

Gross margin pricing emphasizes the use of income statement information to determine a selling price. (Gross margin is the difference between sales and the total production costs of those sales.) In gross margin pricing, the price is computed using a markup percentage based on a product's total production costs. The markup percentage is designed to include all costs other than those used in the computation of gross margin. Therefore, the gross margin markup percentage covers selling, general, and administrative expenses and the desired profit. Because an accounting system often provides management with unit production cost data, both variable and fixed, this method of determining selling price can be easily applied.

Gross Margin Calculations With gross margin pricing, there are three ways of determining a price.

1. The first approach uses the two following formulas:

$$\text{Markup Percentage} = \frac{\text{Desired Profit} + \text{Total Selling, General, and Administrative Expenses}}{\text{Total Production Costs}}$$

$$\text{Gross Margin-Based Price} = \text{Total Production Costs per Unit} + (\text{Markup Percentage} \times \text{Total Production Costs per Unit})$$

For Bookit Company, the markup percentage and selling price are computed as follows:

$$\text{Markup Percentage} = \frac{\$110{,}625 + \$132{,}750}{\$354{,}000}$$

$$= 68.75\%$$

$$\text{Gross Margin-Based Price} = \$24.00 + (68.75\% \times \$24.00)$$

$$= \underline{\underline{\$40.50}}$$

The numerator in the markup percentage formula is the sum of the desired profit ($110,625) and the total selling, general, and administrative expenses ($132,750). The denominator contains all production costs: variable costs of $199,125 and fixed production costs of $154,875. The gross margin markup is 68.75 percent of total production costs, or $16.50. Adding $16.50 to the total production costs per unit yields a selling price of $40.50.

2. The second way to express the gross margin-based price is to state the formula in terms of a company's desire to recover all of its costs and make a profit. This approach ignores the computation of the markup percentage, achieves the same gross margin-based price, and is stated as follows:

$$\text{Gross Margin-Based Price} = \frac{\text{Total Production Costs} + \text{Total Selling, General, and Administrative Expenses} + \text{Desired Profit}}{\text{Total Units Produced}}$$

Using this formula, the gross margin-based price for Bookit Company is computed as follows:

$$\begin{aligned}\text{Gross Margin-Based Price} &= \frac{\$354{,}000 + \$132{,}750 + \$110{,}625}{14{,}750\ \text{Units}} \\ &= \$597{,}375 \div 14{,}750 \\ &= \underline{\underline{\$40.50}}\end{aligned}$$

Study Note

Gross margin-based price per unit equals total production, selling, general, and administrative costs per unit plus a desired profit per unit.

3. The third way the gross margin-based price can be determined is on a per unit basis:

$$\begin{aligned}\text{Gross Margin-Based Price} = {} & \text{Direct Materials} + \text{Direct Labor} \\ & + \text{Variable Overhead} + \text{Fixed Overhead} \\ & + \text{Selling, General, and Administrative Expenses} \\ & + \text{Desired Profit per Unit}\end{aligned}$$

Applying this formula to Bookit Company's data, the computations are as follows:

$$\begin{aligned}\text{Gross Margin-Based Price} &= \$6.00 + \$4.50 + \$3.00 + \$10.50 + \$5.00 \\ &\quad + \$2.50 + \$1.50 + (\$110{,}625 - 14{,}750) \\ &= \underline{\underline{\$40.50}}\end{aligned}$$

Return on Assets Pricing

Study Note

The return on assets pricing method is also known as the *balance sheet method.*

Return on assets pricing focuses on earning a specified rate of return on the assets employed in the operation. This changes the objective of the price determination process from earning a return on the income statement to earning a return on the business's resources on the balance sheet. Because this approach focuses on a desired minimum rate of return on assets, it is also known as the *balance sheet approach to pricing.*

Return on Assets Calculations There are two formulas to finding the return on assets price:

1. $$\begin{aligned}\text{Return on Assets-Based Price} = {} & \text{Total Costs and Expenses per Unit} \\ & + (\text{Desired Rate of Return} \\ & \times \text{Cost of Assets Employed per Unit})\end{aligned}$$

2. Return on Assets-Based Price = [(Total Production Costs + Total Selling, General, and Administrative Expenses) ÷ Units to Be Produced] + [Desired Rate of Return × (Total Cost of Assets Employed ÷ Units to Be Produced)]

Recall that Bookit Company has an asset base of $921,875. It plans to produce 14,750 units and would like to earn a 14 percent return on assets. If the company uses return on assets pricing, the selling price per unit would be calculated as follows:

Return on Assets-Based Price = $24.00 + $9.00
+ [14% × ($921,875 ÷ 14,750)]
= $41.75

or as

Return on Assets-Based Price = [($354,000 + $132,750) ÷ 14,750]
+ [14% × ($921,875 ÷ 14,750)]
= $33.00 + $8.75
= $41.75

Summary of Cost-Based Pricing Methods

Figure 26-3 summarizes the two cost-based pricing methods. If Bookit Company uses return on assets pricing and has a desired rate of return of 14 percent, it will need to set a higher selling price ($41.75) than it would under the gross margin method ($40.50).

Companies select their pricing methods based on their degree of trust in a cost base. The cost bases from which they can choose are (1) total product costs per unit and (2) total costs and expenses per unit.

- Often, total product costs per unit are readily available, which makes gross margin pricing a good way to compute selling prices. However, gross margin pricing depends on an accurate forecast of units because the fixed cost per unit portion of total production costs will vary if the actual number of units produced differs from the estimated number of units.
- Return on assets pricing is also a good pricing method if the assets used to manufacture a product can be identified and their cost determined. If this is not the case, the method yields inaccurate results.

FOCUS ON BUSINESS PRACTICE

Pricing a Six-Pack

The average cost of a six-pack of beer continues to rise. That's because **Anheuser-Busch**, maker of Bud Light and Budweiser—the world's largest-selling brands of beer—generally raises prices to keep pace with the consumer price index, and competitors have historically followed the company's price lead.[1]

FIGURE 26-3
Cost-Based Pricing Methods: Bookit Company

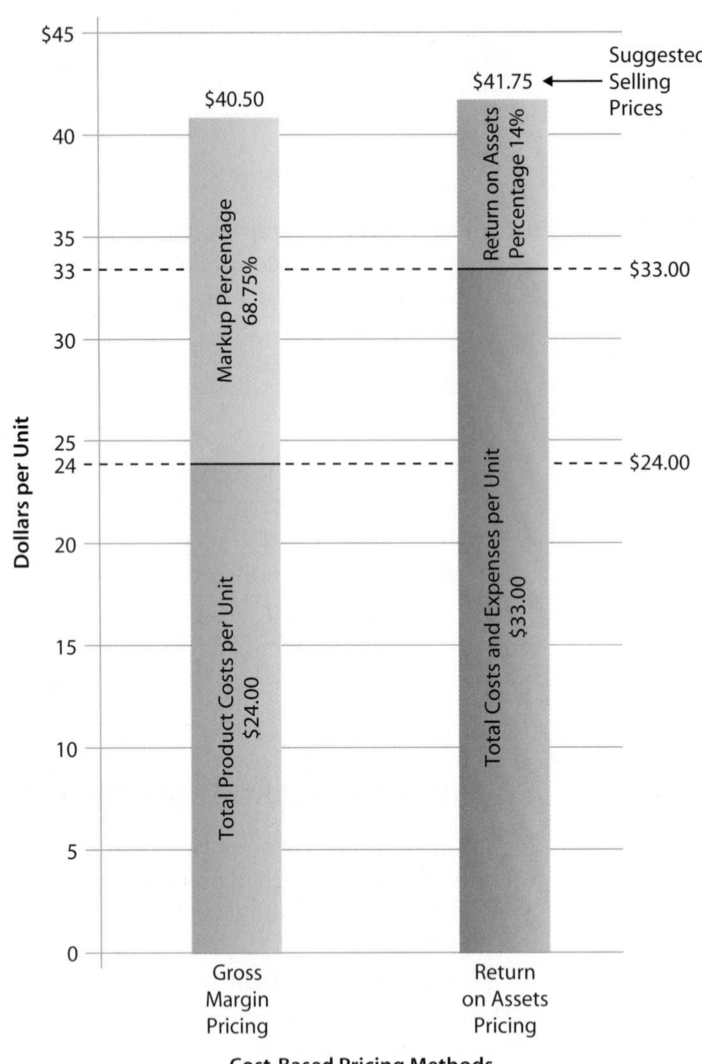

Pricing Services

A service business's approach to pricing differs from that of a manufacturer. Although a service has no physical substance, it must still be priced and billed to the customer. Most service organizations use a form of **time and materials pricing** (also known as *parts and labor pricing*) to arrive at the price of a service. With this method, service companies, such as appliance repair shops, home-remodeling specialists, and automobile repair shops, arrive at prices by using two computations: one for direct labor and one for materials and parts. Markup percentages are added to the costs of materials and labor to cover the cost of overhead and provide a profit factor. If the service does not require materials and parts, then only direct labor costs are used in developing the price. Professionals, such as attorneys, accountants, and consultants, apply a factor representing all overhead costs to the base labor costs to establish a price for their services.

> **Study Note**
> Time and materials pricing is also known as *parts and labor pricing.*

Time and Materials Price Calculation The formula used in time and materials pricing is as follows:

$$\text{Time and Materials Price} = \text{Material Cost per Unit} + \text{Markup \%} \times \text{Material Cost per Unit} + \text{Labor Cost per Unit} + \text{Markup\%} \times \text{Labor Cost per Unit}$$

To illustrate, suppose that the owner of an auto repair shop has just completed work on a customer's car. The parts used to repair the vehicle cost $840. The company's 40 percent markup rate on parts covers parts-related overhead costs and profit. The repairs required 4 hours of labor by a certified repair specialist, whose wages are $35 per hour. The company's overhead markup rate on labor is 80 percent. The repair shop will compute the bill as follows:

Repair parts used	$840	
Overhead charges: $840 × 40%	336	
Total parts charges		$1,176
Labor charges		
4 hours @ $35 per hour	$140	
Overhead charges: $140 × 80%	112	
Total labor charges		252
Total billing		$1,428

Factors Affecting Cost-Based Pricing Methods

In some areas of the economy, such as government contracts, cost-based pricing is widely used. Although a variety of cost-based methods may be used to mechanically compute a price, many factors external to the product or service still require a manager's attention. Once a cost-based price has been determined, the decision maker must consider such factors as competitors' prices, customers' expectations, and the cost of substitute products and services. Pricing is a risky part of operating a business, and care must be taken when establishing that all-important selling price.

Auto repair shops commonly use time and materials pricing (also called parts and labor pricing). This method involves computing the costs of direct labor and materials and adding percentage markups to those costs to cover overhead and provide a profit factor.

Courtesy of Kathy Wynn/Dreamstime.

STOP & APPLY >

Gillson Industries has just patented a new product called Gleam, an automobile wax for lasting protection against the elements. The company's controller has developed the following annual information for use in price determination meetings:

Variable production costs	$1,110,000
Fixed overhead	540,000
Selling expenses	225,000
General and administrative expenses	350,000
Desired profit	250,000
Cost of assets employed	1,000,000

Annual demand for the product is expected to be 250,000 cans. On average, the company now earns a 10 percent return on assets.

1. Compute the projected unit cost for one can of Gleam.
2. Using gross margin pricing, compute the markup percentage and selling price for one can.
3. Using return on assets pricing, compute the unit price for one can.

SOLUTION

1. Unit cost computed:

Costs Categories		**Total Projected Cost**
Variable production costs		$1,110,000
Fixed overhead		540,000
Total production costs		$1,650,000
Selling expenses		$ 225,000
General and administrative expenses		350,000
Total selling, general, and administrative expenses		$ 575,000
Total costs and expenses		$2,225,000
Units produced		250,000
Total cost per unit	($2,225,000 ÷ 250,000 units)	$ 8.90

2. Markup percentage and unit selling price computed, using gross margin pricing:

$$\text{Markup Percentage} = \frac{\text{Desired Profit + Total Selling, General, and Administrative Expenses}}{\text{Total Production Costs}}$$

$$= \frac{\$250{,}000 + \$575{,}000}{\$1{,}650{,}000} = 50.0\%$$

Gross Margin-Based Price = Total Production Costs per Unit + (Markup Percentage × Total Production Costs per Unit)
= ($1,650,000 ÷ 250,000) + [50.0% × ($1,650,000 ÷ 250,000)]
= $9.90

3. Unit selling price computed using return on assets pricing:

Return on Assets-Based Price = Total Costs and Expenses per Unit + (Desired Rate of Return × Cost of Assets Employed per Unit)

Return on Assets-Based Price = $8.90 + [10% × ($1,000,000 ÷ 250,000)]
= $8.90 + $0.40
= $9.30

Pricing Based on Target Costing

LO4 Describe target costing, and use that concept to analyze pricing decisions and evaluate a new product opportunity.

Target costing is a pricing method designed to enhance a company's ability to compete, especially in markets for new or emerging products, such as the e-book readers described in this chapter's Decision Point. This approach to pricing differs significantly from the cost-based methods that we discussed in the last section.

Instead of first determining the cost of a product or service and then adding a profit factor to arrive at a price, target costing reverses the procedure. Target costing (1) identifies the price at which a product will be competitive in the marketplace, (2) defines the desired profit to be made on the product, and (3) computes the target cost for the product by subtracting the desired profit from the competitive market price.

Study Note

Target costing is sometimes referred to as *target pricing*.

Target Costing Calculation The formula used in target costing is as follows:

$$\text{Target Price} - \text{Desired Profit} = \text{Target Cost}$$

Once the target cost has been established, the company's engineers and product designers use it as the maximum cost to be incurred for the materials and other resources needed to design and manufacture the product. It is their responsibility to create the product at or below its target cost.

Pricing based on target costing may not seem revolutionary, but a detailed look at its underlying principles reveals its strategic superiority:

- Target costing gives managers the ability to control or dictate the costs of a new product at the planning stage of the product's life cycle.
- In a competitive environment, the use of target costing enables managers to analyze a product's potential before they commit resources to its production.

Figure 26-4 compares the timing of a pricing decision that uses a traditional approach with one that uses target costing. The stages of the product life cycle, from the generation of the product idea to the final disposition of the product, are identified at the base of the figure.

Study Note

Remember that when desired profit is defined as a percentage of target cost, target price is equal to 100 percent of target cost *plus* the percentage of target cost desired as profit.

- When traditional cost-based pricing practices are used, prices cannot be set until production has taken place and costs have been incurred and analyzed. At that point, a profit factor is added to the product's cost, and the product is ready to be offered to customers.
- In contrast, under target costing, the pricing decision takes place immediately after the market research for a new product. The market research not only reveals the potential demand for the product but also identifies the maximum price that a customer would be willing to pay for it. Once the price is determined, target costing enables the company's engineers to design the product with a fixed maximum target cost on which to base the product's features.

Differences Between Cost-Based Pricing and Target Costing

One of the primary benefits of using target costing is the ability to design and build a product to a specific cost goal. The increased emphasis on product design allows a company to engineer the target cost into the product before manufacturing begins. A new product is designed only if its projected costs are equal to or lower than its

FIGURE 26-4
Comparison of Price Decision Timing

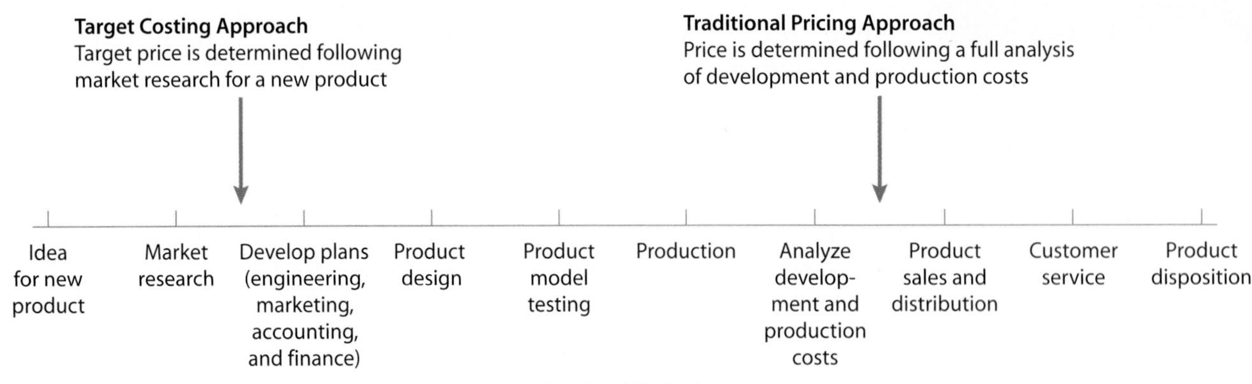

target cost. The company can thus focus on holding costs down while it plans and designs the product, before the costs are actually committed and incurred.

- **Committed costs** are the costs of design, development, engineering, testing, and production that are engineered into a product or service at the design stage of development.
- **Incurred costs** are the actual costs incurred in making the product.

When cost-based pricing is used, it is very difficult to control costs from the planning phase through the production phase. Under that approach, concern about reducing costs begins only after the product has been produced. This often leads to random efforts to cut costs, which can reduce product quality and further erode the customer base. Under target costing, the product is expected to produce a profit as soon as it is marketed. Cost-cutting improvements in a product's design and production methods can still be made, but profitability is built into the selling price from the beginning.

These shoppers at an **Ikea** store have a large selection of high-quality products to choose from. Target costing enables Ikea to offer its products at competitive prices and ensures that a product will earn a profit as soon as it is introduced. This method identifies the price at which a product will be competitive in the marketplace, defines the desired profit to be made on the product, and computes the target cost by subtracting the desired profit from the competitive market price.

Courtesy of AP Photo/Carlos Osorio

Companies like **Sony** and **Ikea** have used target costing successfully for years and have benefited from increased sales volume each time they have cut prices because of production improvements. These companies never sacrifice product quality.

Target Costing Analysis in an Activity-Based Management Environment

Study Note

Activity-based management (ABM) can be used successfully with target costing.

To see how a company that uses activity-based management implements target costing, consider Elsinore Company's approach to new product decisions. A customer is seeking price quotations for a special-purpose router and a wireless palm-sized tablet computer. The current market-price ranges for the two products are as follows: router, \$320–\$380 per unit; and tablet computer, \$750–\$850 per unit.

One of Elsinore's sales persons thinks that if the company could quote prices of \$300 for the router and \$725 for the tablet computer, it would get the order and gain a significant share of the market for those products. Elsinore's usual profit markup is 25 percent of total unit cost.

The company's design engineers and accountants put together these specifications and costs for the new products:

Activity-based cost rates	
Materials handling	\$ 1.30 per dollar of direct materials and purchased parts cost
Production	\$ 3.50 per machine hour
Product delivery	\$24.00 per router
	\$30.00 per computer

	Router	*Computer*
Projected unit demand	26,000	18,000
Per-unit data		
Direct materials cost	\$25.00	\$65.00
Purchased parts cost	\$15.00	\$45.00
Manufacturing labor		
Hours	2.6	4.8
Hourly labor rate	\$12.00	\$15.00
Assembly labor		
Hours	3.4	8.2
Hourly labor rate	\$14.00	\$16.00
Machine hours	12.8	28.4

The three steps used in arriving at the target cost are as follows:

1. ***Find the target cost per unit.*** The target cost for each product is computed as follows:

$$\text{Router} = \$300.00 \div 1.25 = \$240.00^{*}$$

$$\text{Computer} = \$725.00 \div 1.25 = \$580.00$$

$$^{*}\text{Target Price} - \text{Desired Profit} = \text{Target Cost}$$

$$\$300.00 - 0.25X = X$$

$$\$300.00 = 1.25X$$

$$X = \frac{\$300.00}{1.25} = \underline{\underline{\$240.00}}$$

2. ***Find the projected unit cost.*** The projected total unit cost of production and delivery is computed in the following way:

	Router	*Computer*
Direct materials cost	$ 25.00	$ 65.00
Purchased parts cost	15.00	45.00
Total cost of direct materials and parts	$ 40.00	$110.00
Manufacturing labor		
Router (2.6 hours × $12.00)	31.20	
Computer (4.8 hours × $15.00)		72.00
Assembly labor		
Router (3.4 hours × $14.00)	47.60	
Computer (8.2 hours × $16.00)		131.20
Activity-based costs		
Materials handling		
Router ($40.00 × $1.30)	52.00	
Computer ($110.00 × $1.30)		143.00
Production		
Router (12.8 machine hours × $3.50)	44.80	
Computer (28.4 machine hours × $3.50)		99.40
Product delivery		
Router	24.00	
Computer		30.00
Projected total unit cost	$239.60	$585.60

3. ***Make a decision.*** Using the target costing approach and the following data, we can determine whether Elsinore Company should produce the new products:

	Router	*Computer*
Target unit cost	$240.00	$580.00
Less projected unit cost	239.60	585.60
Difference	$ 0.40	($ 5.60)

The router can be produced below its target cost, so it should be produced. As currently designed, the tablet computer cannot be produced at or below its target cost, so Elsinore should either redesign it or drop plans to produce it.

STOP & APPLY >

Success Ltd. is considering a new product and must make a go or no-go decision when its planning team meets tomorrow. Market research shows that the unit selling price that would be agreeable to potential customers is $1,000, and the company's desired profit is 25 percent of target cost. The design engineer's preliminary estimate of the product's design, production, and distribution costs is $775 per unit. Using target costing, determine whether the company should market the new product.

SOLUTION

The company should market the new product. The target cost for the product is $800 ($1,000 ÷ 1.25). The engineer's projected cost is $775, or $25 below the amount needed to earn the desired profit.

Pricing for Internal Providers of Goods and Services

LO5 Describe how transfer pricing is used for transferring goods and services and evaluating performance within a division or segment.

So far in this chapter, we have focused on how a company sets prices for consumers outside the organization. We now turn our focus to the inside of an organization and look at how it prices its products and services for internal transfers between divisions or segments.

As a business grows, its day-to-day operations often become too complex to be managed by a single person. To make operations more manageable, the business is usually organized into divisions or operating segments, and a separate manager is assigned to control the operations of each segment. Such a business is called a **decentralized organization**. Each division or segment often sells its goods and services both inside and outside the organization.

For example, the beverage division of **Pepsico** sells its Pepsi drink products to internal customers like KFC and Taco Bell restaurants. It also sells to external customers like **Safeway** and **Wal-Mart**. And **Anheuser-Busch**'s beer segment produces and sells its products internally to Sea World amusement parks, as well as externally to unrelated entities like airlines and grocery stores.

Transfer Pricing

Study Note
Transfer pricing is not used for external pricing; it is used to set prices for transfers among a company's departments, divisions, or segments.

When divisions or segments within a company exchange goods or services and assume the role of customer or supplier for each other, they use transfer prices. A **transfer price** is the price at which goods and services are charged and exchanged between a company's divisions or segments. Transfer prices are an internal pricing mechanism that allows transactions between divisions or segments of a business to be measured and accounted for.

- Transfer prices affect the revenues and costs of the divisions involved.
- They do not affect the revenues and costs of the company as a whole.

The transfer price just shifts part of the profits from the divisions or centers that externally charge for their goods or services to the divisions or centers that do not externally bill for their services and products. Transfer pricing enables a business to assess both the internal and the external profitability of its products or services. The three basic kinds of transfer prices are cost-plus transfer prices, market transfer prices, and negotiated transfer prices.

Study Note
Cost-plus transfer pricing is similar to the gross margin pricing method.

Cost-Plus Transfer Price A **cost-plus transfer price** is based on either the full cost or the variable costs incurred by the producing division plus an agreed-on profit percentage. The weakness of the cost-plus pricing method is that cost recovery is guaranteed to the selling division. Guaranteed cost recovery prevents the company from detecting inefficient operating conditions and the incurrence of excessive costs, and it may even inappropriately reward inefficient divisions that incur excessive costs. This reduces overall company profitability and shareholder value.

Study Note
The market transfer price is also called the *external market price*.

Market Transfer Price A **market transfer price** is based on the price that could be charged if a segment could buy from or sell to an external party. Some experts believe that the use of a market transfer price is preferable to the other methods. It forces the division that is "selling," or transferring, the product or service to another division to be competitive with market conditions, and it does not penalize the "buying," or receiving, division by charging it a higher price than it would have to pay if it bought from outside the firm.

However, using market prices may lead the selling division to ignore negotiation attempts from the buying division manager and to sell directly to outside customers. If this causes an internal shortage of materials and forces the buying division to purchase materials from the outside, overall company profits may decline even if the selling division makes a profit. Such use of market prices works against a company's overall operating objectives. Therefore, when market prices are used to develop transfer prices, they are usually used only as a basis for negotiation.

Study Note

A negotiated transfer price is often used for internal pricing.

Negotiated Transfer Price A **negotiated transfer price** is arrived at through bargaining between the managers of the buying and selling divisions or segments. Such a transfer price may be based on an agreement to use a cost plus a profit percentage. The negotiated price will be between the negotiation floor (the selling division's variable cost) and the negotiation ceiling (the market price). This approach allows for cost recovery while still allowing the selling division to return a profit.

Developing a Transfer Price

To illustrate the development of the three kinds of transfer prices, let's consider the Simple Box Company, a firm that makes cardboard boxes. As shown in Figure 26-5, this company has two divisions: the Pulp Division and the Cardboard Division. The Pulp Division produces pulp for the Cardboard Division. The Cardboard Division may also purchase pulp from outside suppliers. Exhibit 26-1 shows the development of a cost-plus transfer price for the Pulp Division. The Pulp Division's manager has created a one-year budget based on the expectation that the Cardboard Division will require 480,000 pounds of pulp. Unit costs appear in the last column of Exhibit 26-1.

Cost-Plus Transfer Price Notice that allocated corporate overhead is not included in the computation of the transfer price. Only the variable costs of $11.85 ($3.30 + $0.70 + $1.60 + $2.40 + $1.90 + $1.95) and the fixed cost of $1.05 related to the Pulp Division are included. The profit markup of 10 percent adds $1.29, producing the final cost-plus transfer price of $14.19.

Market Value Price Management could now dictate that the $14.19 price be used. However, the Cardboard Division's manager could point out that it is possible to purchase pulp from an outside supplier for $13.00 per pound. Use of the $13.00 price would represent a market value approach.

FIGURE 26-5
Transfer Price Alternatives at Simple Box Company

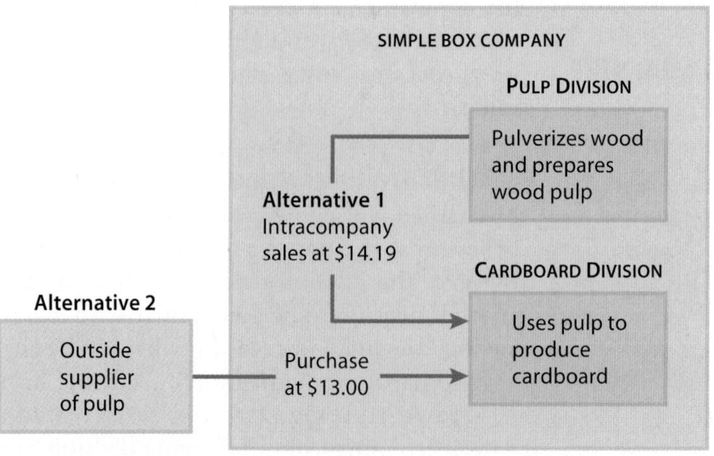

EXHIBIT 26-1
Transfer Price Computation

Simple Box Company
Pulp Division—Transfer Price Computation

Cost Categories	Budgeted Costs	Cost per Unit
Direct materials		
Wood	$1,584,000	$ 3.30
Scrap wood	336,000	0.70
Direct labor		
Shaving/cleaning	768,000	1.60
Pulverizing	1,152,000	2.40
Blending	912,000	1.90
Overhead		
Variable	936,000	1.95
Fixed	504,000	1.05
Subtotals	$6,192,000	$12.90
Costs allocated from corporate office	144,000	
Target profit, 10% of division's costs	619,200	1.29
Total costs and profit	$6,955,200	
Cost-plus transfer price		$14.19

Negotiated Transfer Price The best solution might be to agree on a negotiated transfer price between the variable costs of $11.85, the floor, and the outside market price of $13.00, the ceiling. The negotiation process will facilitate each manager's role in maximizing companywide profits and controlling his or her division's costs. Many times, the managers will split the difference and negotiate a price of $12.43* [($11.85 + $13.00)/2].

*Rounded.

Other Transfer Price Issues

In this example, both managers brought their concerns to the attention of top management, and a settlement was reached. The negotiated transfer price allows for the sharing of the final product's companywide profits between the divisions when the boxes are sold on the outside market. Such an approach is often used to maintain harmony within an organization.

Study Note
The use of transfer pricing encourages accountability for seller-customer relationships.

Additional issues may arise if the Cardboard Division chooses to purchase from outside suppliers. Because the Pulp Division has adequate capacity to fulfill the Cardboard Division's demands, it should sell to that division at any price that recovers its incremental costs. The incremental costs of intracompany sales include all variable costs of production and distribution plus any avoidable fixed costs that are directly traceable to intracompany sales. If the Cardboard Division can acquire products from outside suppliers at an annual cost that is less than the Pulp Division's incremental costs, then purchases should be made from the outside supplier because it will enhance the company's overall profits. Before making such a decision, a thorough analysis of the Pulp Division's operations should be conducted.

Using Transfer Prices to Measure Performance

Because a transfer price contains an estimated amount of profit, a manager's ability to meet a targeted profit can be measured. Although transfer prices are often

EXHIBIT 26-2
Performance Report Using Transfer Prices

Simple Box Company
Pulp Division—Performance Report
For March

	Budget	Actual	Difference Under/(Over) Budget
Sales to Carboard Division (42,000 lbs.)	$546,000	$546,000	$ 0
Costs Controllable by Manager			
Cost of goods sold			
Direct materials			
Wood	$138,600	$140,250	($1,650)
Scrap wood	29,400	29,750	(350)
Direct labor			
Shaving/cleaning	67,200	68,000	(800)
Pulverizing	100,800	102,000	(1,200)
Blending	79,800	80,750	(950)
Overhead			
Variable	81,900	82,875	(975)
Fixed	44,100	44,100	—
Total cost of goods sold	$541,800	$547,725	($5,925)
Gross margin from sales	$ 4,200	($ 1,725)	$5,925
Costs Uncontrollable by Manager			
Cost allocated from corporate office	12,600	12,600	—
Operating (loss)	($ 8,400)	($ 14,325)	$5,925

called *artificial* or *created* prices, they and their related policies are closely connected with performance evaluation.

When transfer prices are used, a division can be evaluated as a profit center, even if it does not sell to outsiders, because using transfer prices to value the division's output creates simulated revenues for the division. The operating income calculated in this way is not based on real sales to outsiders and is thus artificial. However, it is a valuable performance measure if the transfer prices are realistic and are determined using the methods described in this chapter.

Exhibit 26-2 shows a performance report for the Pulp Division of the Simple Box Company. The Pulp Division produced and transferred 42,000 pounds as budgeted at a negotiated transfer price of $13.00 per pound. The budgeted costs are based on the costs per unit in Exhibit 26-1. The performance report in Exhibit 26-2 shows that the Pulp Division's actual gross margin was ($1,725), whereas the budgeted gross margin was $4,200. The difference of $5,925 stems from cost overages in various materials, labor, and variable overhead accounts. Those differences will need to be investigated, as they would be for any division.

The use of transfer prices to simulate revenues, however, allows further evaluation. For instance, the measures of operating income (loss) can be compared with the amount of capital the company has invested in the Pulp Division to determine whether the division is making an adequate return on the company's investment, and the impact on the division of uncontrollable costs from the corporate office can be assessed.

& APPLY >

The Molding Process Division at Trophy Products has been treated as a cost center since the company was founded in 1968. Recently, management decided to change the performance evaluation approach and treat the company's processing divisions as profit centers. Each division is expected to earn a 20 percent profit on its total production costs. One of Trophy's products is a plastic base for a display chest. The Molding Process Division supplies this base to the Cabinet Process Division, and it also sells the base to another company. Molding's total production cost for the base is $27.40. It sells the base to the other company for $38.00. What should the transfer price for the plastic base be?

SOLUTION

In addition to the traditional approaches of transferring the product from one process to the next at variable or full cost, management should consider the following three options when setting the transfer price for the plastic base:

Cost plus profit:	$27.40 + ($27.40 × 20%) = $32.88
Market price:	$38.00
Negotiated price:	Any price between $32.88 and $38.00

Managers of the Molding Process Division have the option of selling the division's output to the outside company and earning more than the 20 percent minimum return. They should also be able to earn more than 20 percent internally. A price at the midpoint of the negotiated price range seems to be fair, $35.44.

A LOOK BACK AT ▸ LAB 126

In this chapter's Decision Point, we asked the following questions:

- Why do managers generally use several pricing approaches?
- Why might **Lab 126**'s managers use target costing to establish a price for the Kindle?

As you learned in this chapter, no one pricing method is superior, because each business and market segment differs. Successful managers, like those at Lab 126, therefore generally use several pricing approaches.

Early in the e-book reader market, there was little competition, and new models may have been priced to recover the product's cost and earn a certain amount of profit. Now that new products with desirable features, such as text-to-speech, are being introduced and the market has become very competitive, Lab 126's managers might use target costing to set a price for a new reader. To do so, they would subtract their desired profit from the proposed market price to arrive at the maximum target cost. A team of engineering, accounting, and sales managers would then analyze each proposed product feature to verify that the product could be designed and manufactured at or below the target cost.

Review Problem

Gross Margin Pricing

LO3

Suppose that The Undercovers Company makes a complete line of covers for e-book readers like the Kindle, including a plain cover, a deluxe cover, and a trendy cover. The covers are produced on an assembly line, beginning with the Stamping Department and continuing through the Sewing, Detailing, and Packaging departments. The projected costs of each cover and the percentages for assigning unavoidable fixed and common costs are as follows:

Cost Categories	Total Projected Costs	Plain Cover	Deluxe Cover	Trendy Cover
Direct materials				
Leather	$137,000	$62,500	$29,000	$45,500
Magnet	5,250	2,500	1,000	1,750
Clip	9,250	3,750	2,000	3,500
Package	70,500	30,000	16,000	24,500
Direct labor				
Stamping	53,750	22,500	12,000	19,250
Sewing	94,000	42,500	20,000	31,500
Detailing	107,500	45,000	24,000	38,500
Packaging	44,250	17,500	11,000	15,750
Indirect labor	173,000	77,500	36,000	59,500
Operating supplies	30,000	12,500	7,000	10,500
Variable overhead	90,500	40,000	19,000	31,500
Fixed overhead	120,000	45%	25%	30%
Distribution expenses	105,000	40%	20%	40%
Variable marketing expenses	123,000	$55,000	$26,000	$42,000
Fixed marketing expenses	85,400	40%	25%	35%
General and administrative expenses	47,600	40%	25%	35%

The Undercovers Company's policy is to earn a minimum of 30 percent over total cost on each type of cover produced. Expected sales for the year are: plain, 50,000 units; deluxe, 20,000 units; and trendy, 35,000 units. Assume no change in inventory levels, and round all answers to two decimal places.

Required

1. Using the gross margin pricing method, compute the selling price for each kind of cover.
2. The competition is selling a similar plain cover for around $14. Should this influence Undercover's pricing decision? Give reasons for your answer.

Answers to Review Problem

Before the selling prices are computed, the cost analysis must be completed and restructured to supply the information that is required for the pricing computations.

Cost Categories	Total Projected Costs	Plain Cover	Deluxe Cover	Trendy Cover
Total direct materials	$ 222,000	$ 98,750	$ 48,000	$ 75,250
Total direct labor	299,500	127,500	67,000	105,000
Indirect labor	173,000	77,500	36,000	59,500
Operating supplies	30,000	12,500	7,000	10,500
Variable overhead	90,500	40,000	19,000	31,500
Fixed overhead	120,000	54,000	30,000	36,000
Total production costs	$ 935,000	$410,250	$207,000	$317,750
Distribution expenses	$ 105,000	$ 42,000	$ 21,000	$ 42,000
Variable marketing expenses	123,000	55,000	26,000	42,000
Fixed marketing expenses	85,400	34,160	21,350	29,890
General and administrative expenses	47,600	19,040	11,900	16,660
Total selling, general, and administrative expenses	$ 361,000	$150,200	$ 80,250	$130,550
Total costs	$1,296,000	$560,450	$287,250	$448,300
Desired profit (30%)	$ 388,800	$168,135	$ 86,175	$134,490

1. Pricing using the gross margin approach:

Markup percentage formula:

$$\text{Markup Percentage} = \frac{\text{Desired Profit} + \text{Total Selling, General, and Administrative Expenses}}{\text{Total Production Costs}}$$

Gross margin pricing formula:

$$\text{Gross Margin-Based Price} = \text{Total Production Costs per Unit} + (\text{Markup Percentage} \times \text{Total Production Costs per Unit})$$

Plain: $$\text{Markup Percentage} = \frac{\$168{,}135 + \$150{,}200}{\$410{,}250} = 77.60\%^{*}$$

$$\text{Gross Margin-Based Price} = (\$410{,}250 \div 50{,}000) + [77.60\% \times (\$410{,}250 \div 50{,}000)] = \underline{\underline{\$14.57}}^{*}$$

Deluxe: $$\text{Markup Percentage} = \frac{\$86{,}175 + \$80{,}250}{\$207{,}000} = 80.40\%^{*}$$

$$\text{Gross Margin-Based Price} = (\$207{,}000 \div 20{,}000) + [80.40\% \times (\$207{,}000 \div 20{,}000)] = \underline{\underline{\$18.67}}^{*}$$

Trendy: $$\text{Markup Percentage} = \frac{\$134{,}490 + \$130{,}550}{\$317{,}750} = 83.41\%^{*}$$

$$\text{Gross Margin-Based Price} = (\$317{,}750 \div 35{,}000) + [83.41\% \times (\$317{,}750 \div 35{,}000)] = \underline{\underline{\$16.65}}^{*}$$

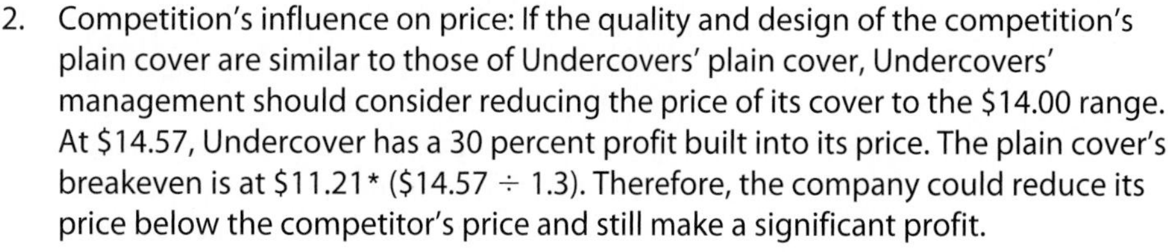

2. Competition's influence on price: If the quality and design of the competition's plain cover are similar to those of Undercovers' plain cover, Undercovers' management should consider reducing the price of its cover to the $14.00 range. At $14.57, Undercover has a 30 percent profit built into its price. The plain cover's breakeven is at $11.21* ($14.57 ÷ 1.3). Therefore, the company could reduce its price below the competitor's price and still make a significant profit.

---

*Rounded.

LO1 Identify the objectives and rules used to establish prices of goods and services, and relate pricing issues to the management process.

A company's long-run objectives should include statements on pricing policy. Possible pricing policy objectives include (1) identifying and adhering to both short-run and long-run pricing strategies, (2) maximizing profits, (3) maintaining or gaining market share, (4) setting socially responsible prices, (5) maintaining a minimum rate of return on investment, and (6) being customer focused.

During the management process, managers keep the following points in mind: a product's or service's selling price must (1) be competitive with the competition's price, (2) be acceptable to the customer, (3) recover all costs incurred in bringing the product or service to market, and (4) return a profit. If a manager deviates from any of these four pricing rules, there must be a specific short-run objective that accounts for the change. Breaking those pricing rules for a long period of time will force a company into bankruptcy.

LO2 Describe economic pricing concepts, including the auction-based pricing method used on the Internet.

The economic approach to pricing is based on microeconomic theory. Microeconomic theory states that profits will be maximized when the difference between total revenue and total cost is greatest. Total revenue then increases more slowly, because as a product is marketed, price reductions are necessary to sell more units. Total cost increases when larger quantities are produced because fixed costs change. To locate the point of maximum profit, marginal revenue and marginal cost must be computed and plotted. Profit is maximized at the point where the marginal revenue and marginal cost curves intersect. Auction-based pricing is growing in importance as a pricing mechanism as more companies and individuals are conducting business over the Internet. Basically, the Internet allows sellers and buyers to solicit bids and transact exchanges in an open market environment. An auction-based price is set by a willing buyer and seller in a sales transaction.

LO3 Use cost-based pricing methods to develop prices.

Cost-based pricing methods include gross margin pricing and return on assets pricing. Under these two methods, a markup representing a percentage of production costs or a desired rate of return is added to the total costs. A pricing method often used by service businesses is time and materials pricing. Although managers may depend on one or two traditional approaches to pricing, they often also factor in their own experience.

LO4 Describe target costing, and use that concept to analyze pricing decisions and evaluate a new product opportunity.

Target costing enhances a company's ability to compete in the global marketplace. Instead of first determining the cost of a product and then adding a profit factor to arrive at its price, target costing reverses the procedure. Target costing (1) identifies the price at which a product will be competitive in the marketplace, (2) defines the desired profit to be made on the product, and (3) computes the target cost for the product by subtracting the desired profit from the competitive market price. Target costing gives managers the ability to control or dictate the costs of a new product at the planning stage; under a traditional pricing system, managers cannot control costs until after the product has been manufactured. To identify a new product's target cost, the following formula is applied:

$$\text{Target Price} - \text{Desired Profit} = \text{Target Cost}$$

The target cost is then given to the engineers and product designers, who use it as a maximum cost to be incurred for materials and other resources needed to design and manufacture the product. It is their responsibility to create the product at or below its target cost. Sometimes, the cost requirements cannot be met. In such a case, the organization should try to adjust the product's design and the approach to production. If those attempts fail, the organization should either invest in new equipment and procedures or abandon its plans to market the product.

LO5 Describe how transfer pricing is used for transferring goods and services and evaluating performance within a division or segment.

A transfer price is the price at which goods and services are charged and exchanged between a company's divisions or segments. There are three primary approaches to developing transfer prices: (1) the price may be based on the cost of the item up to the point at which it is transferred to the next department or process; (2) the price may be based on market value if the item has an existing external market; or (3) the price may be negotiated by the managers of the buying and selling divisions. A cost-plus transfer price is the sum of costs incurred by the producing division plus an agreed-on profit percentage. A market-based transfer price is based on external market prices. In most cases, a negotiated transfer price is used, that is, a price is reached through bargaining between the managers of the selling and buying divisions. A division's performance may be evaluated by using transfer prices as the basis for determining revenues.

REVIEW of Concepts and Terminology

The following concepts and terms were introduced in this chapter:

Auction-based pricing 1193 (LO2)

Committed costs 1202 (LO4)

Cost-plus transfer price 1205 (LO5)

Decentralized organization 1205 (LO5)

Gross margin pricing 1195 (LO3)

Incurred costs 1202 (LO4)

Marginal cost 1193 (LO2)

Marginal revenue 1193 (LO2)

Market transfer price 1205 (LO5)

Negotiated transfer price 1206 (LO5)

Return on assets pricing 1196 (LO3)

Target costing 1201 (LO4)

Time and materials pricing 1198 (LO3)

Transfer price 1205 (LO5)

CHAPTER ASSIGNMENTS

BUILDING Your Basic Knowledge And Skills

Short Exercises

LO1 Rules for Establishing Prices

SE 1. Jason Kellam is planning to open a pizza restaurant next month in Flora, Alabama. He plans to sell his large pizzas for a base price of $18 plus $2 for each topping selected. When asked how he arrived at the base price, he said that his cousin developed that price for his pizza restaurant in New York City. What pricing rules has Jason Kellam not followed?

LO1 External Factors That Influence Prices

SE 2. Your client is about to introduce a very high-quality product that will remove an invasive form of pepper bush in the southern United States. The Marketing Department has established a price of $37 per gallon, and the company controller has projected total production, selling, and distribution costs of $26 per gallon. What other factors should your client consider before introducing the product into the marketplace?

LO2 Traditional Economic Pricing Concept

SE 3. You are to decide the total demand for a particular product. Assume that the product you are evaluating has the total cost and total revenue curves pictured in Figure 26-2A. Also assume that the difference between total revenue and total cost is the same at the 5,000- and 8,000-unit levels. If you had to choose between those two levels of activity as goals for total sales over the life of the product, which would you prefer? Why?

LO3 Cost-Based Price Setting

SE 4. The Windwalker Company has collected the following data for one of its product lines: total production costs, $300,000; total selling, general, and administrative expenses, $112,600; desired profit, $67,400; and production costs per unit, $40. Using the gross margin pricing method, compute a suggested selling price for this product that would yield the desired profit.

LO3 Pricing a Service

SE 5. Evan Nathan runs a home repair business. Recently he gathered the following cost information about the repair of a client's pool deck: replacement wood, $650; deck screws and supplies, $112; and labor, 12 hours at $14 per hour. Nathan applies a 40 percent overhead rate to all direct costs of a job. Compute the total billing price for the repair of the pool deck.

LO4 Committed Costs and Target Costing

SE 6. Nanci Osborne is a design engineer for Dash Enterprises. In a discussion about a proposed new product, Osborne stated that the product's projected target cost was $6.50 below the committed costs identified by design estimates. Given this information, should the company proceed with the new product? Explain your answer, and include a definition of committed cost in your analysis.

LO4 Pricing Using Target Costing

SE 7. JTZ Furniture is considering a new product and must make a go or no-go decision before tomorrow's planning team meeting. Market research shows that the unit selling price agreeable to potential customers is $1,600, and the company's desired profit is 22 percent of target cost. The design engineer's preliminary estimate of the product's design, production, and distribution costs is $1,380 per unit. Using target costing, determine whether the company should market the new product.

LO5 **Decision to Use Transfer Prices**

SE 8. The production process at Premier Castings includes eight processes, each of which is currently treated as a cost center with a specific set of operations to perform on each casting produced. Following the fourth process's operations, the rough castings have an external market. The fourth process must also supply the fifth process with its direct materials. The management of Premier Castings wants to develop a new approach to measuring process performance. Is Premier a candidate for using transfer prices? Explain your answer.

LO5 **Cost-Based Versus Market-Based Transfer Prices**

SE 9. Refer to the information in **SE 8**. Should Premier Castings use economic-based, cost-based, market-based, or negotiated transfer prices?

LO5 **Developing a Negotiated Transfer Price**

SE 10. The Cookie Dough Division at Sweet Products has been treated as a cost center since the company was founded. Recently, management decided to change the performance evaluation approach and treat its processing divisions as profit centers. Each division is expected to earn a 20 percent profit on its total production costs. One of Sweet's products is chocolate chip cookie dough. The Cookie Dough Division supplies this dough to the Packaged Cookies Divison, and it also sells it to another company. Cookie Dough's total production cost for the dough is $2.40 per pound. It sells the dough to the other company for $5.00 a pound. What should the transfer price for a pound of cookie dough be?

Exercises

LO1 **Pricing Policy Objectives**

E 1. Old Denim, Ltd., is an international clothing company that retails medium-priced goods. Its retail outlets are located throughout the United States, France, Germany, and Great Britain. Management wants to maintain the company's image of providing the highest possible quality at the lowest possible prices. Selling prices are developed to draw customers away from competitors' stores. First-of-the-month sales are regularly held at all stores, and customers are accustomed to this practice. Company buyers are carefully trained to seek out quality goods at inexpensive prices. Sales are targeted to increase a minimum of 5 percent per year. All sales should yield a 15 percent return on assets. Sales personnel are expected to wear Old Denim clothing while working, and all personnel can purchase clothing at 10 percent above cost. All stores are required to be clean and well organized. Competitors' prices are checked daily. Identify the pricing policy objectives of Old Denim, Ltd.

LO1 **External and Internal Pricing Factors**

E 2. Mobile Battery features more than a dozen brands of batteries in many sizes. Two of the brands are PowerPlus and SuperPower. The following information about the two brands was obtained:

	PowerPlus	SuperPower
Selling price:		
Battery, installed	$120	$110
Cost per battery	100	70

As shown, selling prices include installation costs. Each battery costs $10 to install.

1. Compute each brand's net unit selling price after installation.
2. Was cost the main consideration in setting those prices?
3. What other factors could have influenced those prices?

LO2 Traditional Economic Pricing Theory

E 3. Texaza, a product design firm, has just completed a contract to develop a wireless phone keychain. The phone keychain needs to be recharged only once a week and can be used worldwide. Initial fixed costs for this product are $4,000. The designers estimate that the product will break even at the $5,000/100-unit mark. Total revenues will again equal total costs at the $25,000/900-unit point. Marginal cost is expected to equal marginal revenue when 550 units are sold.

1. Sketch total revenue and total cost curves for this product. Mark the vertical axis at each $5,000 increment and the horizontal axis at each 100-unit increment.
2. Based on your total revenue and total cost curves in **1**, at what unit selling price will profits be maximized?

LO2 ebusiness

E 4. Visit the websites of **Priceline.com** and **eBay.com.** Write a brief comparison of each site's features. Which site do you prefer, and why?

LO3 Price Determination

E 5. Turley Industries has just patented a new toothpaste called Sparkle for lasting protection against tooth decay. The company's controller has developed the following annual information for use in price determination meetings:

Variable production costs	$ 900,000
Fixed overhead	500,000
Selling expenses	200,000
General and administrative expenses	125,000
Desired profit	375,000
Cost of assets employed	1,000,000

Annual demand for the product is expected to be 500,000 tubes. On average, the company now earns an 8 percent return on assets.

1. Compute the projected unit cost for one tube of Sparkle.
2. Using gross margin pricing, compute the markup percentage and selling price for one tube.
3. Using return on assets pricing, compute the unit price for one tube.

LO3 Pricing a Service

E 6. Texas has just passed a law making it mandatory to have every head of cattle inspected at least once a year for a variety of communicable diseases. Big Springs Enterprises is considering entering this inspection business. After extensive studies, Tex Autry, the owner of Big Springs Enterprises, has developed the following annual projections:

Direct service labor	$525,000
Variable service overhead costs	250,000
Fixed service overhead costs	225,000
Selling expenses	142,500
General and administrative expenses	157,500
Minimum desired profit	120,000
Cost of assets employed	750,000

Autry believes his company could inspect 250,000 head of cattle per year. On average, the company now earns a 16 percent return on assets.

1. Compute the projected cost of inspecting each head of cattle.
2. Determine the price to charge for inspecting each head of cattle. Use gross margin pricing.
3. Using return on assets pricing, compute the unit price to charge for this inspection service.

LO3 Cost-based Pricing

E 7. Hometown Bank is determining the price for its newest mini debit card. The card can be used at any retail outlet with a swipe reader and is small enough to attach to a key chain—no PIN number or signature is required. Sigrid Olmo has developed the following annual information for use in upcoming price determination meetings:

Variable processing costs	$50 million
Fixed processing costs	36 million
Selling expenses (fixed)	10 million
General and administrative expenses (fixed)	4 million
Desired profit	3 billion
Cost of assets employed	10 billion

Annual usage is expected to be 10 billion transactions. On average, the company now earns a 6 percent return on assets.

1. Compute the projected cost of one transaction.
2. Using gross margin pricing, compute the price to charge per transaction.
3. Using return on assets pricing, compute the price to charge per transaction.

LO3 Pricing Services

E 8. Gator Car Repair specializes in repairing hybrid cars. The company uses a 70 percent markup rate on parts to cover parts-related overhead costs and profit margin. It uses a 100 percent markup rate on labor to cover labor-related overhead costs and profit margin. Compute the bill for a recent job that used the following parts and labor:

Material and repair parts used	$550
Labor used	4 hours at $40 per hour

LO3 Time and Materials Pricing

E 9. Cruz's Home Remodeling Service specializes in refurbishing older homes. Last week Cruz was asked to bid on a remodeling job for the town's mayor. His list of materials and labor needed to complete the job is as follows:

Materials		Labor	
Lumber	$ 6,500	Carpenter	$2,000
Nails/bolts	160	Floor specialist	1,300
Paint	1,420	Painter	1,500
Glass	2,890	Supervisor	1,420
Doors	730	Helpers	1,680
Hardware	600	Total	$7,900
Supplies	400		
Total	$12,700		

The company uses an overhead markup percentage for materials (60 percent) and for labor (40 percent). Those markups cover all operating costs. In addition, Cruz expects to make at least a 25 percent profit on all jobs. Compute the price that Cruz should quote for the mayor's job.

LO4 **Target Costing and Pricing**

E 10. Environ Company has determined that its new fireplace screen would gain widespread customer acceptance if the company could price it at or under $90. Anticipated labor hours and costs for each unit of the new product are as follows:

Direct materials cost	$15
Direct labor cost	
Manufacturing labor	
Hours	1.2
Hourly labor rate	$12
Assembly labor	
Hours	1.5
Hourly labor rate	$10
Machine hours	2

The company currently uses the following three activity-based cost rates:

Materials handling	$1.30 per dollar of direct materials
Production	$3.00 per machine hour
Product delivery	$5.50 per unit

The company's minimum desired profit is 25 percent over total production and delivery cost. Compute the target cost for the new fireplace screen, and determine if the company should market it.

LO4 **Target Costing**

E 11. Assume the same facts as in **E 10** except that the company's minimum desired profit has been revised to 10 percent over production and delivery costs as a result of a recent economic downturn. Compute the revised target cost for the new fireplace screen, and determine if the company should market it.

LO4 **Target Costing**

E 12. Suppose that **Ikea**, the Swedish retailer, is developing a new chair targeted to sell for less than $100 and that it is considering the two production alternatives that follow. Rank the alternatives, assuming that the company's minimum desired profit is 30 percent over total production costs.

	Alternative A	Alternative B
Direct material costs	$35	$20
Direct labor cost	1 hour at $12 per hour	2 hours at $8 per hour
Overhead costs	200 percent of direct labor costs	$2 per dollar of direct materials

LO4 **Target Costing**

E 13. Management at Fox Valley Machine Tool Co. is considering the development of a new automated drill press called the AutoDrill. After conferring with the design engineers, the controller's staff assembled the following data about this product:

Target selling price	$6,000 per unit
Desired profit percentage	20% of total unit cost
Projected unit demand	4,500 units
Activity-based cost rates	
Materials handling	5% of direct materials and purchased parts cost
Engineering	$300 per unit for AutoDrill
Production and assembly	$50 per machine hour
Delivery	$570 per unit for AutoDrill
Marketing	$400 per unit for AutoDrill
Per-unit data	
Direct materials cost	$1,620
Purchased parts cost	$200
Manufacturing labor	
Hours	6
Hourly labor rate	$14
Assembly labor	
Hours	10
Hourly labor rate	$15
Machine hours	30

1. Compute the product's target cost.
2. Compute the product's projected unit cost based on the design engineers' estimates.
3. Should management produce and market the AutoDrill? Defend your answer.

LO5 **Transfer Price Comparison**

E 14. Mary Janus is developing a transfer price for the housing section of an automatic pool-cleaning device. The housing for the device is made in Department A. It is then passed on to Department D, where final assembly occurs. Unit costs for the housing are as follows:

Cost Categories	Unit Costs
Direct materials	$5.20
Direct labor	2.30
Variable overhead	1.30
Fixed overhead	2.60
Profit markup, 20% of cost	?

An outside vendor can supply the housing for $13.00 per unit.

1. Develop a cost-plus transfer price for the housing.
2. What should the transfer price be? Support your answer.

LO5 **Transfer Pricing**

E 15. Patch Watch Company's Seconds Store offers refurbished or factory seconds time-keeping products to the public at substantially reduced prices. The factory controller is developing transfer price alternatives to present to management to determine the best price to use when transferring products from the factory to the store, using the following data:

Unit price if sold to outside retailers	$25
Variable product cost per unit	10
Fixed product cost per unit	5
Seconds store profit markup	40%

1. What is the market-based transfer price alternative?
2. What is the minimum transfer price alternative?
3. Compute the cost-plus transfer price alternative assuming cost includes variable costs only.

Problems

LO3 **Pricing Decision**

P 1. Ed Vetz & Company specializes in the assembly of home appliances. One division focuses most of its efforts on assembling a standard toaster oven. Projected costs of this product are as follows:

Cost Description	Budgeted Costs
Toaster casings	$ 960,000
Electrical components	2,244,000
Direct labor	3,648,000
Variable indirect assembly costs	780,000
Fixed indirect assembly costs	1,740,000
Selling expenses	1,536,000
General operating expenses	840,000
Administrative expenses	816,000

The projected costs are based on an estimated demand of 600,000 toaster ovens peryear. The company wants to make a $1,260,000 profit.

Competitors have just published their wholesale prices for the coming year. They range from $21.60 to $22.64 per oven. The Vetz toaster oven is known for its high quality and modern look. It competes with products at the top end of the price range. Even with its reputation, however, every $.20 increase above the top competitor's price causes a drop in demand of 60,000 units below the original estimate. Assume that all price changes are in $.20 increments.

Required

1. Prepare a schedule of total projected costs and unit costs.
2. Use gross margin pricing to compute the anticipated selling price.
3. Based on competitors' prices, what should the Vetz toaster sell for (assume a constant unit cost)? Defend your answer. (**Hint**: Determine the total profit at various sales levels.)

Manager insight ▶ 4. Would your pricing structure in requirement **3** change if the company had only limited competition at its quality level? If so, in what direction? Explain why.

LO3 **Cost-Based Pricing**

P 2. Centered Publishing Company specializes in health awareness books. Because the field of health awareness is very competitive, Jay Rosenbek, the company's president, maintains a strict policy about selecting manuscripts to publish. Rosenbek wants to publish only books whose projected earnings are 20 percent above total projected costs. Three titles were accepted for publication during the year. The authors of those books are Tone, Tyme, and Klay. Projected costs for each book and allocation percentages for common costs are shown here.

Cost Categories	Tone Book	Tyme Book	Klay Book	Projected Costs
Direct labor	$146,250	$243,750	$97,500	$487,500
Royalty costs	$36,000	$60,000	$24,000	120,000
Printing costs	$74,580	$124,300	$49,720	248,600
Supplies	$10,260	$17,100	$6,840	34,200
Variable production costs	$42,600	$71,000	$28,400	142,000
Fixed production costs	35%	40%	25%	168,000
Distribution costs	30%	50%	20%	194,000
Marketing costs	$61,670	$90,060	$42,270	194,000
General and administrative costs	35%	40%	25%	52,400

Expected sales for the year are as follows: Tone, 26,000 copies; Tyme, 32,000 copies; and Klay, 20,000 copies.

Required

1. Prepare a cost analysis that computes the desired profit for each of the three books and in total.
2. Use gross margin pricing to compute the selling price for each book. (**Hint**: Treat royalty costs as production costs.)

Manager insight ▶ 3. If the competition's average selling price for a book similar to Klay's is $22, should this influence the pricing decision? Explain.

LO3 **Time and Materials Pricing in a Service Business**

P 3. Ace Maintenance, Inc., repairs heavy construction equipment and vehicles. Recently, the Shanti Construction Company had one of its giant earthmovers overhauled and its tires replaced. Repair work for a vehicle of that size usually takes from one week to ten days. The vehicle must be lifted up so that maintenance workers can gain access to the engine. Parts are normally so large that a crane must be used to put them into place.

The company uses the time and materials pricing system and data from the previous year to compute markup percentages for overhead related to parts and materials and overhead related to direct labor. It adds markups of 130 percent to the cost of materials and parts and 140 percent to the cost of direct labor to cover overhead and profit. The following materials, parts, and direct labor are needed to repair the giant earthmover:

Quantity	Unit Price	Hours	Hourly Rate
Materials and parts		Direct labor	
24 Spark plugs	$ 3.40	42 Mechanic hours	$18.20
20 Oil, quarts	2.90	54 Assistant mechanic hours	12.00
12 Hoses	11.60		
1 Water pump	764.00		
30 Coolant, quarts	6.50		
18 Clamps	5.90		
1 Distributor cap	128.40		
1 Carburetor	214.10		
4 Tires	820.00		

Required

Prepare a complete billing for this job. Include itemized amounts for each type of materials, parts, and direct labor. Follow the time and materials pricing approach, and show the total price for the job.

LO4 **Pricing Using Target Costing**

P 4. Young Joon Corp. is considering marketing two new graphing calculators, named Speed-Calc 4 and Speed-Calc 5. According to recent market research, the two products will surpass the current competition in both speed and quality and would be welcomed in the market. Customers would be willing to pay $98 for Speed-Calc 4 and $110 for Speed-Calc 5, based on their projected design capabilities. Both products have many uses, but the primary market interest comes from college students. Current production capacity exists for the manufacture and assembly of the two products. The company has a minimum desired profit of 25 percent above all costs for all of its products. Current activity-based cost rates are as follows:

Materials/parts handling	$1.20 per dollar of direct materials and purchased parts cost
Production	$8.00 per machine hour
Marketing/delivery	$4.40 per unit of Speed-Calc 4
	$6.20 per unit of Speed-Calc 5

Design engineering and accounting estimates to produce the two new products are as follows:

	Speed-Calc 4	Speed-Calc 5
Projected unit demand	100,000	80,000
Per-unit data		
Direct materials cost	$5.50	$7.50
Computer chip cost	$10.60	$11.70
Production labor		
Hours	1.2	1.3
Hourly labor rate	$16.00	$16.00
Assembly labor		
Hours	0.6	0.5
Hourly labor rate	$12.00	$12.00
Machine hours	1	1.2

Required

1. Compute the target costs for each product.
2. Compute the projected total unit cost of production and delivery.
3. Using the target costing approach, decide whether the products should be produced.

LO5 Developing Transfer Prices

P 5. Cylinder Company has two divisions, Glass Division and Instrument Division. For several years, Glass Division has manufactured a special glass container, which it sells to Instrument Division at the prevailing market price of $20. Glass Division produces the glass containers only for Instrument Division and does not sell the product to outside customers. Annual production and sales volume is 20,000 containers. A unit cost analysis for Glass Division showed the following:

Cost Categories	Costs per Container
Direct materials	$ 3.50
Direct labor, 1¼ hours	2.30
Variable overhead	7.50
Avoidable fixed costs: $30,000 ÷ 20,000	1.50
Corporate overhead: $18 per direct labor hour	4.50
Variable shipping costs	1.20
Unit cost	$20.50

Corporate overhead represents the allocated joint fixed costs of production—building depreciation, property taxes, insurance, and executives' salaries. A profit markup of 20 percent is used to determine transfer prices.

Required

1. What would be the appropriate transfer price for Glass Division to use in billing its transactions with Instrument Division?
2. If Glass Division decided to sell some containers to outside customers, would your answer to requirement **1** change? Defend your response.

Manager insight ▶

3. What factors concerning transfer price should management consider when transferring products between divisions?

Alternate Problems

LO3 Pricing Decision

P 6. Sumac & Oak's, Ltd., designs and assembles low-priced portable Internet devices. It estimates that there will be 235,000 requests for its most popular model. Budgeted costs for this product for the year are as follows:

Description	Budgeted Costs
Casing	$ 432,400
Battery chamber	545,200
Electronics	1,151,500
Direct labor	1,598,000
Variable indirect assembly costs	789,600
Fixed indirect assembly costs	338,400
Selling expenses	493,500
General operating expenses	183,300
Administrative expenses	126,900

The budget is based on the demand previously stated. The company wants to earn an annual operating income of $846,000.

Last week, four competitors released their wholesale prices for the year. Their prices are as follows: Competitor A, $25.68; Competitor B, $24.58; Competitor C, $23.96; Competitor D, $25.30

Sumac & Oak's portable devices are known for their high quality. However, every $1 price increase above the top competitor's price causes a 55,000-unit drop in demand from the original estimate. (Assume all price changes occur in $1 increments.)

Required

1. Prepare a schedule of total projected costs and unit costs.
2. Use gross margin pricing to compute the anticipated selling price.
3. Based on competitors' prices, what should Sumac & Oak's portable device sell for (assume a constant unit cost)? Defend your answer. (**Hint**: Determine the total operating income at various sales levels.)
4. Would your pricing structure in requirement **3** change if the company had only limited competition at this quality level? If so, in what direction? Explain why.

Manager insight ▶

LO3 **Pricing Decisions**

P 7. The Fastener Company manufactures office equipment for retail stores. Carol Watson, the vice president of marketing, has proposed that Fastener introduce two new products: an electric stapler and an electric pencil sharpener. Watson has requested that the Profit Planning Department develop preliminary selling prices for the two new products for her review.

Profit Planning has followed the company's standard policy for developing potential selling prices. It has used all data available for each product. The data accumulated by Profit Planning are as follows:

	Electric Stapler	Electric Pencil Sharpener
Estimated annual demand in units	16,000	12,000
Estimated unit manufacturing costs	$14.00	$15.00
Estimated unit selling and administrative expenses	$3.00	Not available
Assets employed in manufacturing	$160,000	Not available

Fastener plans to use an average of $1,200,000 in assets to support operations in the current year. The condensed budgeted income statement that follows reflects the planned return on assets of 20 percent ($240,000 ÷ $1,200,000) for the entire company for all products.

Fastener Company
Budgeted Income Statement
For the Year Ended May 31
(in thousands)

Revenue	$2,400
Cost of goods sold	1,440
Gross profit	$ 960
Selling and administrative expenses	720
Operating income	$ 240

Required

1. Calculate a potential selling price for (a) the stapler, using return on assets pricing, and (b) the pencil sharpener, using gross margin pricing.
2. Could a selling price for the electric pencil sharpener be calculated using return on assets pricing? Explain your answer.
3. Which of the two pricing methods—return on assets pricing or gross margin pricing—is more appropriate for decision analysis? Explain your answer.
4. (Manager insight ▶) Discuss the additional steps Carol Watson is likely to take in setting an actual selling price for each of the two products after she receives their potential selling prices (as calculated in requirement **1**.) (CMA adapted)

LO3 Time and Materials Pricing in a Service Business

P 8. Friendly Car Repair performs routine maintenance on rental vehicles. Recently, the local auto rental business had its fleet serviced. Friendly uses the time and materials pricing system and data from the previous year to compute markup percentages for overhead related to parts and materials and overhead related to direct labor. It adds markups of 100 percent to the cost of materials and parts and 120 percent to the cost of direct labor to cover overhead and profit. The following materials, parts, and direct labor are needed to repair the rental fleet:

Quantity	Unit Price	Hours	Hourly Rate
Materials and parts		Direct labor	
24 Spark plugs	$ 0.50	38 Mechanic hours	$28.20
50 Oil, quarts	2.50	61 Assistant mechanic hours	14.00
12 Hoses	11.20		
1 Sun visor	13.50		
36 Coolant, quarts	6.50		
4 Clamps	5.50		
5 Emergency kits	12.40		
40 Washer fluid	1.25		
4 Tires	300.00		

Required

Prepare a complete billing for this job. Include itemized amounts for each type of materials, parts, and direct labor. Follow the time and materials pricing approach, and show the total price for the job.

LO4 Pricing Using Target Costing

P 9. Clevenger Machine Tool Company designs and produces a line of high-quality machine tools and markets them throughout the world. Its main competition comes from French, British, and Korean companies. Five competitors have recently introduced two highly specialized machine tools, Y14 and Z33. The prices charged for Y14 range from $625 to $675 per tool, and the price range for Z33 is from $800 to $840 per tool. Clevenger is contemplating entering the market for these two products. Market research has indicated that if Clevenger can sell Y14 for $650 per tool and Z33 for $750 per tool, it will be successful in marketing the products worldwide. The company's profit markup is 25 percent over all costs to produce and deliver a product. Current activity-based cost rates are as follows:

Materials handling	\$ 1.30 per dollar of direct materials and purchased parts cost
Production	\$ 4.40 per machine hour
Product delivery	\$34.00 per unit of Yl4
	\$40.00 per unit of Z33

Design engineering and accounting estimates for the production of the two new products are as follows:

	Product Yl 4	Product Z33
Projected unit demand	75,000	95,000
Per-unit data		
Direct materials cost	\$50.00	\$60.00
Purchased parts cost	\$65.00	\$70.00
Manufacturing labor		
Hours	6.2	7.4
Hourly labor rate	\$14.00	\$14.00
Assembly labor		
Hours	4.6	9.2
Hourly labor rate	\$12.00	\$12.00
Machine hours	14	16

Required

1. Compute the target cost for each product.
2. Compute the total projected unit cost of producing and delivering each product.
3. Using target costing, decide whether the products should be produced.

LO5 Developing Transfer Prices

P 10. Sims Corporation produces sound equipment for home use. Its Research and Development (R&D) Division is responsible for continually evaluating and updating critical electronic parts used in the corporation's products. Two years ago, R&D took on the added responsibility of producing all microchip circuit boards for the company's sound equipment. One of Sims's specialties is a sound dissemination board (SDB) that greatly enhances the quality of Sims's speakers.

Demand for the SDB has increased significantly in the past year. As a result, R&D has increased its production and assembly labor force. Three outside customers now want to purchase the SDB. To date, R&D has been producing SDBs for internal use only.

The R&D controller wants to create a transfer price for the SDBs that will apply to all intracompany transfers. Estimated demand over the next six months is 235,000 SDBs for internal use and 165,000 SDBs for external customers, for a total of 400,000 units. The following data show cost projections for the next six months:

Materials and parts	\$2,600,000
Direct labor	1,920,000
Supplies	100,000
Indirect labor	580,000
Other variable overhead costs	200,000
Fixed overhead, SDBs	1,840,000
Other fixed overhead, corporate	560,000
Variable selling expenses, SDBs	1,480,000
Fixed selling expenses, corporate	520,000
General corporate operating expenses	880,000
Corporate administrative expenses	680,000

A profit markup of at least 20 percent must be added to total unit cost for internal transfer purposes. Outside customers are willing to pay $35 for each SDB. All categories of fixed costs are assumed to be unavoidable.

Required

1. Prepare a table that shows the total budgeted costs and the cost per unit for each component of the budget. Also show the profit markup and the cost-plus transfer price.

Manager insight ▶

2. Should R&D use the computed transfer price? Explain the factors that influenced your decision.

ENHANCING Your Knowledge, Skills, and Critical Thinking

LO1 LO2

Ethics in Pricing

C 1. Barnes Company has been doing business in Hong Kong for the past three years. The company produces leather handbags that are in great demand there. When Barnes's sales person Harriet Mackay was recently in Hong Kong, Kwan Cho, the purchasing agent for Shen Enterprises, approached her to arrange for a purchase of 2,500 handbags. Barnes's usual price is $75 per bag. Kwan Cho wanted to purchase the handbags at $65 per bag. After an hour of haggling, they agreed to a final price of $68 per item. When Makay returned to her hotel room after dinner, she found an envelope containing five new $100 bills and a note that said, "Thank you for agreeing to our order of 2,500 handbags at $68 per bag. My company's president wants you to have the enclosed gift for your fine service." Makay later learned that Kwan Cho was following her company's normal business practice. What should Harriet Makay do? Is the gift hers to keep? Be prepared to justify your opinion.

LO3 LO4

Product Pricing in a Foreign Market

C 2. Borner, Inc., is an international corporation that manufactures and sells home care products. Today a meeting is being held at corporate headquarters in New York City. The purpose of the meeting is to discuss changing the price of the laundry detergent the company manufactures and sells in Brazil. During the meeting, a conflict develops between Carl Dickson, the corporate sales manager, and José Cabral, the Brazilian Division's sales manager.

Dickson insists that the selling price of the laundry detergent should be increased to the equivalent of U.S. $3. This increase is necessary because the Brazilian Division's costs are higher than those of other international divisions. The Brazilian Division is paying high interest rates on notes payable for the acquisition of a new manufacturing plant. In addition, a stronger, more expensive ingredient has been introduced into the laundry detergent, which has caused the product cost to increase by $0.20.

Cabral believes that the laundry detergent's selling price should remain at $2.50 for several reasons. He argues that the market for laundry detergent in Brazil is highly competitive. Labor costs are low, and the costs of distribution are small because the target market is limited to the Rio de Janeiro metropolitan area. Inflation is extremely high in Brazil, and the Brazilian government continues to impose policies to control inflation. Because of these controls, Cabral insists, buyers will resist any price hikes.

1. What selling price do you believe Borner, Inc., should set for the laundry detergent? Explain your answer. Do you believe Borner should let the Brazilian Division set the selling price for laundry detergent in the future? When should corporate headquarters set prices?
2. Based on the information given above, should cost-based pricing or target costing be used to set the selling price for laundry detergent in Brazil? Explain your answer.

LO4 **Target Costing and the Internet**

C 3. Assume that you work for a company that wants to develop a product to compete with the Kindle. You have been assigned the task of using target costing to help in its development. Do a search for Kindle product reviews and product specifications and get price quotes. Why would your company's management want to use target costing to help in its development of a competitive e-book reader? What retail price would you suggest be used as a basis for target costing? Assuming a desired profit of 25 percent of selling price, what is the resulting target cost? What actions should the company take now?

LO4 **Target Costing**

C 4. Every Electronics, Inc., produces circuit boards for electronic devices that are made by more than a dozen customers. Competition among the producers of circuit boards is keen, with over 30 companies bidding on every job request from those customers. The circuit boards can vary widely in their complexity, and their unit prices can range from $250 to more than $500.

Every's controller is concerned that the cost planning projection for a new complex circuit board, the CX35, is almost 6 percent above its target cost. The controller has asked the Engineering Design Department to review its design and projections and come up with alternatives that will reduce the proposed product's costs to equal to or below the target cost. The following information was used to develop the initial cost projections:

Target selling price	$590.00	per unit
Desired profit percentage	25%	of total unit cost
Projected unit demand	13,600	units
Per-unit data		
Direct materials cost	$56.00	
Purchased parts cost	$37.00	
Manufacturing labor		
Hours	4.5	
Hourly labor rate	$14.00	
Assembly labor		
Hours	5.2	
Hourly labor rate	$15.00	
Machine hours	26	
Activity-based cost rates		
Materials handling	10%	of direct materials and purchased parts cost
Engineering	$13.50	per unit for CX35
Production	$8.20	per machine hour
Product delivery	$24.00	per unit for CX35
Marketing	$6.00	per unit for CX35

1. Compute the product's target cost.
2. Compute the product cost of the original estimate to verify that the controller's calculations were correct.
3. Rework the product cost calculations for each of the following alternatives recommended by the design engineers:
   a. Cut product quality, which will reduce direct materials cost by 20 percent and purchased parts cost by 15 percent.
   b. Increase the quality of direct materials, which will increase direct materials cost by 20 percent but will reduce machine hours by 10 percent, manufacturing labor hours by 16 percent, and assembly labor hours by 20 percent.
4. What decision should the management of Every Electronics, Inc., make about the new product? Defend your answer.

LO5 Transfer Pricing

C 5. Cirrus Industries, Inc., has two major operating divisions, the Cabinet Division and the Electronics Division. The company's main product is a deluxe console television set. The TV cabinets are manufactured by the Cabinet Division, and the Electronics Division produces all electronic components and assembles the sets. The company has a decentralized organizational structure.

The Cabinet Division not only supplies cabinets to the Electronics Division but also sells cabinets to other TV manufacturers. The following unit cost breakdown for a deluxe television cabinet was developed based on a typical sales order of 40 cabinets:

Direct materials	$ 32.00
Direct labor	15.00
Variable overhead	12.00
Fixed overhead	18.00
Variable selling expenses	9.00
Fixed selling expenses	6.00
Fixed general and administrative expenses	8.00
Total unit cost	$100.00

The Cabinet Division's usual profit margin is 20 percent, and the regular selling price of a deluxe cabinet is $120. The division's managers recently decided that $120 will also be the transfer price for all intracompany transactions.

Managers at the Electronics Division are unhappy with that decision. They claim that the Cabinet Division will show superior performance at the expense of the Electronics Division. Competition recently forced the company to lower its prices. Because of the newly established transfer price for the cabinet, the Electronics Division's portion of the profit margin on deluxe television sets was lowered to 18 percent. To counteract the new intracompany transfer price, the managers of the Electronics Division announced that effective immediately, all cabinets will be purchased from an outside supplier, in lots of 200 cabinets at a unit price of $110 per cabinet. The company president, Joe Springer, has called a meeting of both divisions to negotiate a fair intracompany transfer price. The following prices were listed as possible alternatives:

Current market price	$120 per cabinet
Current outside purchase price (This price is based on a large-quantity purchase discount. It will cause increased storage costs for the Electronics Division.)	$110 per cabinet
Total unit manufacturing costs plus a 20 percent profit margin: $77.00 + $15.40	$92.40 per cabinet
Total unit costs excluding variable selling expenses plus a 20 percent profit margin: $91.00 + $18.20	$109.20 per cabinet

1. What price should be established for intracompany transactions? Defend your answer by showing the shortcomings of each alternative.
2. If there were an outside market for all units produced by the Cabinet Division at the $120 price, would you change your answer to 1? Why?

LO5 Cookie Company (Continuing Case)

C 6. Your company produces cookies in a two-step process. The Mixing Division prepares the cookie dough and transfers it to the Baking Division, which bakes the cookies and packs all finished cookies for shipment.

At a recent meeting of your company's board of directors, the manager of the Baking Division made this statement: "That Mixing Division is robbing us blind!" Because of the board's concern about this statement, the company controller gathered the following data for the past year:

	Mixing Division	Baking Division
Sales		
Regular	$700,000	$1,720,000
Deluxe	900,000	3,300,000
Direct materials		
Cookie dough (from Mixing Division)	—	1,600,000
Cookie ingredients	360,000	—
Box inserts	—	660,000
Boxes	—	1,560,000
Direct labor	480,000	540,000
Variable overhead	90,000	240,000
Fixed divisional overhead—avoidable	150,000	210,000
Selling and general operating expenses	132,000	372,000
Company administrative expenses	84,000	108,000

During the year, the two divisions completed and transferred or shipped 200,000 regular cookie boxes and 150,000 deluxe cookie boxes. Transfer prices used by the Mixing Division were as follows:

Regular	$3.50
Deluxe	6.00

The regular box wholesales for $8.60 and the deluxe box for $22.00. The company uses a predetermined formula to allocate administrative costs to the divisions. Management has indicated that the transfer price should include a 20 percent profit factor on total division costs.

1. Prepare a performance report on the Mixing Division.
2. Prepare a performance report on the Baking Division.
3. Compute each division's rate of return on controllable costs and on total division costs.
4. Do you agree with the statement made by the manager of the Baking Division? Explain your response.
5. What procedures would you recommend to the board of directors?

CHAPTER

27 Quality Management and Measurement

The Management Process

PLAN

- ▷ **Formulate strategic and tactical plans that manage quality.**
- ▷ **Prepare operating forecasts.**
- ▷ **Prepare budgets.**

PERFORM

- ▷ **Implement personnel, resource, and activity decisions.**
- ▷ **Measure relevant and reliable data on quality.**
- ▷ **Minimize waste.**
- ▷ **Improve quality through quality control and quality assurance.**

EVALUATE

- ▷ **Assess performance measures of all business functions.**
- ▷ **Reward performance promptly.**
- ▷ **Take corrective actions.**
- ▷ **Analyze and revise performance measurement plans.**

REPORT

- ▷ **Customize reports for performance analysis and decision making.**

Managers focus on quality to compete successfully in today's marketplace.

Quality has many dimensions. Not only must a product or service be defect-free and dependable; it must also embody such intangibles as prestige and good taste. Managers must meet or exceed a variety of expectations about customer service and create innovative new products and services that anticipate the opportunities offered by an ever-changing marketplace. To compete successfully, managers need information that enables them to determine accurate product, service, and customer costs; to improve processes; and to provide timely feedback about their organization to all stakeholders. Such information can be produced only by an information system that captures both financial and nonfinancial information. In this chapter, we describe financial and nonfinancial measures of quality and how managers use these measures to evaluate operating performance.

LEARNING OBJECTIVES

LO1 **Describe a management information system, and explain how it enhances management decision making.** (pp. 1234–1236)

LO2 **Define *total quality management* (*TQM*), and identify financial and nonfinancial measures of quality.** (pp. 1236–1242)

LO3 **Use measures of quality to evaluate operating performance.** (pp. 1242–1246)

LO4 **Discuss the evolving concept of quality.** (pp. 1246–1248)

LO5 **Recognize the awards and organizations that promote quality.** (pp. 1248–1249)

DECISION POINT ► A MANAGER'S FOCUS AMAZON.COM

- ► How do Amazon.com's managers maintain the company's competitive edge?
- ► What measures of quality can Amazon.com use to evaluate operating performance?

Through its innovative approach to selling books and other merchandise online, **Amazon.com** has changed the rules of successful electronic retailing. To maintain a competitive advantage, the company's managers must have an information system that produces more than just financial data. They need an extensive information infrastructure that can capture all kinds of information in huge, secure databases. Amazon.com's databases contain trillions of bytes of information that the company can privately mine and use in multiple applications.

Customers of online retailing firms have come to expect not only innovative features but also a high standard of product reliability and service. Amazon.com can continue to challenge and experiment with the ever-evolving ecommerce business model only if its management information system remains on the cutting edge of database technology and produces pertinent information of the highest quality for its managers.

The Role of Management Information Systems in Quality Management

LO1 Describe a management information system, and explain how it enhances management decision making.

Many traditional management information systems contain only financial data and do not produce the sort of information that is necessary in today's competitive business environment. To compete successfully, managers need information that enables them to determine accurate product, service, and customer costs; improve processes; and provide timely feedback to all stakeholders about their organization. Such information can be produced only by an information system that captures both financial and nonfinancial information.

This kind of **management information system (MIS)** is a reporting system that identifies, monitors, and maintains continuous, detailed analyses of a company's activities and provides managers with timely measures of operating results. It is designed to support such management philosophies as lean operations, activity-based management (ABM), and total quality management (TQM).

The primary focus of an MIS is on the management of activities, not on costs. By focusing on activities, an MIS provides managers with improved knowledge of the processes for which they are responsible. Activity-related information that is needed to increase responsiveness to customers and reduce processing time is readily available. More accurate product and service costs lead to improved pricing decisions. Nonvalue-adding activities are highlighted, and managers can work to reduce or eliminate them. In addition to providing information about product profitability, an MIS can analyze the profitability of individual customers and look at all aspects of serving customers. Overall, the MIS identifies resource usage and cost for each activity and fosters managerial decisions that lead to continuous improvement throughout the organization.

Enterprise Resource Planning Systems

An MIS can be designed as a customized, informally linked series of systems for specific purposes, such as financial reporting, product costing, and business process measurement, or as a fully integrated database system known as an **enterprise resource planning (ERP) system**. An ERP system combines the management of all major business activities (e.g., purchasing, manufacturing, marketing, sales, logistics, and order fulfillment) with support activities (e.g., accounting and human resources) to form one easy-to-access, centralized data warehouse. An ERP system not only fosters communication within an organization; it can also communicate with other businesses' databases.

Study Note

The term *enterprise resource management* (ERM) can be used in place of *ERP*.

This chapter's Decision Point presents an example of an ERP system that has merged **Amazon.com**'s operating, financial, and management systems into one extensive information infrastructure. Because of its ability to access a variety of data types from multiple sources, both inside and outside the company, Amazon.com has developed a competitive advantage in achieving financial targets and quality results. Using improved knowledge of the activities and processes for which they are responsible, Amazon.com's managers have pinpointed resource usage and fostered managerial decisions that have led to continuous improvement throughout the organization.

Managers' Use of MIS

Like the managers at Amazon.com, business managers today use their management information systems' detailed, real-time financial and nonfinancial information about customers, inventory, resources, and the supply chain to manage quality. Without the flexibility and power of database management information systems like ERP, managers would be at a disadvantage in today's rapidly changing and highly competitive business environment.

FOCUS ON BUSINESS PRACTICE

How Do Health Care Professionals Measure Success?

The National Quality Measures Clearinghouse is a repository of evidence-based measures sponsored by the Agency for Healthcare Research and Quality and the U.S. Department of Health and Human Services. This database can be used to assess treatment quality and to view the recovery odds for various medical conditions. It lists by disease, medical condition, or treatment the quality measures that health care professionals use to evaluate medical success. For example, the bacterial pneumonia link discusses measures like hospital admission rates and response rates to various antibiotic regimens or vaccines. Visit the website at www.qualitymeasures.ahrq.gov.

Planning Managers use the MIS database to obtain relevant and reliable information for formulating strategic plans, making forecasts, and preparing budgets.

For example, managers at Amazon.com use their MIS to develop forecasts and budgets for existing operations and to create plans for new value-adding products and services.

Performing Managers use the financial and nonfinancial information in the MIS database to implement decisions about personnel, resources, and activities that will minimize waste and improve the quality of their organization's products or services.

At Amazon.com, managers use their supply-chain and value-chain software to manage operations in ways that ensure accurate order fulfillment and timely delivery.

Evaluating Managers identify and track financial and nonfinancial performance measures to evaluate all major business functions.

By enabling the timely comparison of actual performance with expected performance, Amazon.com's MIS allows managers to reward good performance promptly, take speedy corrective actions, and analyze and revise performance measurement plans.

Communicating Managers can use an MIS to generate customized reports that evaluate performance and provide useful information for decision making.

For example, managers at Amazon.com can consolidate customer profiles from their company's sophisticated database into a real-time report available on their desktops to continuously monitor the changing buying habits of their customers.

STOP & APPLY >

Lamar Remy has been asked to develop a plan for installing a management information system in his company. The president has already approved the concept and has given Remy the go-ahead. What kind of information will Remy need to give managers to help them with their decision making?

(continued)

SOLUTION

To help managers plan, Remy will need to make sure that the company's MIS database provides relevant and reliable information that managers can use to formulate strategic plans, make forecasts, and prepare budgets. To help managers perform, Remy will need to focus on expanding the collection of financial and nonfinancial data to improve personnel, resource, and activity decision making; minimize waste; and improve the quality of the company's products and services. To help managers evaluate, Remy will need to improve the identification and tracking of the performance measures the company uses to evaluate all business functions. To help managers communicate, Remy will need to improve the system's ability to generate customized reports that evaluate performance and provide useful information for decision making.

Financial and Nonfinancial Measures of Quality

LO2 Define *total quality management* (*TQM*), and identify financial and nonfinancial measures of quality.

Over the past two decades, organizations have defined quality in terms of what their customers value. Organizations believe that customers want the highest-quality goods and services and that customers' willingness to pay for high quality will result in improved organizational profits. As a result, organizations strive to exceed customers' expectations and improve the quality of their products or services. Quality is not something that a company can simply add at some point in the production process or assume will happen automatically. Inspections can detect bad products, but they do not ensure quality. Managers need reliable measures of quality to help them meet the goal of producing high-quality, reasonably priced products or services. They need to create a total quality management environment.

- **Total quality management (TQM)** is an organizational environment in which all business functions work together to build quality into the firm's products or services.

The first step toward creating a TQM environment is to identify and manage the financial measures of quality, or the costs of quality. The second step is to analyze operating performance using nonfinancial measures and to require that all business processes and products or services be improved continuously.

Financial Measures of Quality

To the average person, *quality* means that one product or service is better than another—perhaps because of its design, its durability, or some other attribute. In a business setting, however, **quality** is the result of an operating environment in which a product or service meets or conforms to a customer's specifications the first time it is produced or delivered.

The **costs of quality** are the costs that are specifically associated with the achievement or nonachievement of product or service quality. Total costs of quality include (1) the costs of good quality, incurred to ensure the successful development of a product or service, and (2) the costs of poor quality, incurred to transform a faulty product or service into one that is acceptable to the customer.

The costs of quality can make up a significant portion of a product's or service's total cost. Therefore, controlling the costs of quality strongly affects profitability. Today's managers should be able to identify the activities associated with improving quality and should be aware of the cost of resources used to achieve high quality.

Study Note

Costs of conformance include the costs of building quality into products and services by doing it right the first time.

The costs of quality have two components: the **costs of conformance**, which are the costs incurred to produce a quality product or service, and the **costs of nonconformance**, which are the costs incurred to correct defects in a product or service. Costs of conformance are made up of prevention costs and appraisal costs.

- **Prevention costs** are the costs associated with the prevention of defects and failures in products and services.
- **Appraisal costs** are the costs of activities that measure, evaluate, or audit products, processes, or services to ensure their conformance to quality standards and performance requirements.

The costs of nonconformance include internal failure costs and external failure costs.

- **Internal failure costs** are the costs incurred when defects are discovered before a product or service is delivered to a customer.
- **External failure costs** are costs incurred after the delivery of a defective product or service.

> **Study Note**
> Internal failure costs are costs incurred to correct mistakes found by the company. External failure costs are costs incurred to correct mistakes discovered by customers.

Table 27-1 gives examples of each cost category. Note that there is an inverse relationship between the costs of conformance and the costs of nonconformance. For example, if a company spends money on the costs of conformance, the costs of nonconformance should be reduced. However, if little attention is paid to the costs of conformance, the costs of nonconformance may escalate.

An organization's overall goal is to avoid costs of nonconformance because both internal and external failures affect customers' satisfaction and the organization's profitability. High initial costs of conformance are justified when they minimize the total costs of quality over the life of a product or service. Common quality ratios include: total cost of quality as a percentage of sales, the ratio of costs of conformance to total costs of quality, the ratio of costs of nonconformance to total costs of quality, and the costs of nonconformance as a percentage of sales.

Nonfinancial Measures of Quality

By measuring the costs of quality, a company learns how much it has spent in its efforts to improve product or service quality. But critics say that tracking historical data to monitor quality performance does little to enhance quality. What managers need is a measurement and evaluation system that signals poor quality early enough to allow problems to be corrected before a defective product or service reaches the customer. Implementing a policy of continuous improvement satisfies this need for early detection of poor quality and is the second stage of total quality management.

> **Study Note**
> Nonfinancial measures gauge quality and the value created throughout the supply and value chains.

Nonfinancial measures of performance, identified and reported to managers in a timely manner, are used to supplement cost-based measures. Although cost control is still an important consideration, a commitment to ongoing improvement encourages activities that enhance quality at every stage, from design to delivery. As explained earlier, those activities, or cost drivers, cause costs. By controlling the leading nonfinancial performance measures of activities, managers can ultimately maximize the resulting financial return from operations. Five categories of nonfinancial measures of quality are discussed in the following sections:

- Product design
- Vendor performance
- Production performance
- Delivery cycle time
- Customer satisfaction

TABLE 27-1
Financial Measures of Quality

Costs of Conformance to Customer Standards	
Prevention Costs	
Technical support for vendors	Quality-certified suppliers
Integrated system development	Quality circles
Quality improvement projects	Preventive maintenance
Quality training of employees	Statistical process control
Design review of products and processes	Process engineering
Appraisal Costs	
Inspection of materials, processes, and machines	Maintenance of test equipment
End-of-process sampling and testing	Quality audits of products and processes
Vendor audits and sample testing	Field testing
Costs of Nonconformance to Customer Standards	
Internal Failure Costs	
Scrap and rework	Failure analysis
Reinspection and retesting of rework	Inventory control and scheduling
Quality-related downtime	Downgrading because of defects
Scrap disposal losses	
External Failure Costs	
Lost sales	Returned goods and replacements
Restoration of reputation	Investigation of defects
Warranty claims and adjustments	Product recalls
Customer complaint processing	Product-liability settlements
Measures of Quality	
Total costs of quality as a percentage of net sales	
Ratio of costs of conformance to total costs of quality	
Ratio of costs of nonconformance to total costs of quality	
Costs of nonconformance as a percentage of net sales	

Product Design Problems with quality often are the result of poor design. Most automated production operations use **computer-aided design (CAD)**, a computer-based engineering system with a built-in program to detect product design flaws. Such computer programs automatically identify poorly designed parts or manufacturing processes, which means that engineers can correct these problems before production begins. Managers monitor the CAD reports on design flaws to ensure that products are properly designed and free of defects. Among the measures that they consider are the number and types of design defects detected, the average time between defect detection and correction, and the number of unresolved design defects at the time of product introduction.

Vendor Performance Companies have changed the way they do business with suppliers of materials. Instead of dealing with dozens of suppliers in a quest for the lowest cost, companies now analyze their vendors to determine which ones are most reliable, furnish high-quality goods, have a record of timely deliveries, and charge competitive prices. Once a company has identified such vendors, they become an integral part of the production team's effort to ensure a continuing supply of high-quality materials. Vendors may even contribute to product design to ensure that the correct materials are being used.

Managers use measures of quality (such as defect-free materials as a percentage of total materials received) and measures of delivery (such as timely deliveries as a percentage of total deliveries) to identify reliable vendors and monitor their performance.

Production Performance Management must always be concerned about the wasted time and money that can be traced to defective products, scrapped parts, machine maintenance, and downtime. To minimize such concerns, more and more companies have adopted **computer-integrated manufacturing (CIM) systems**, in which production and its support operations are coordinated by computers. Within a CIM system, computer-aided manufacturing (CAM) may be used to coordinate and control production activities, or a flexible manufacturing system (FMS) may be used to link together automated equipment into a computerized flexible production network.

In CIM systems, most direct labor hours are replaced by machine hours, and very little direct labor cost is incurred. In addition, a significant part of variable product cost is replaced by the cost of expensive machinery, a fixed cost. Today, the largest item on a company's balance sheet is often automated machinery and equipment. Each piece of equipment has a specific capacity, above which continuous operation is threatened. When managers evaluate such machines, their measures have two objectives:

1. To evaluate the performance of each piece of equipment in relation to its capacity
2. To evaluate the performance of maintenance personnel in following a prescribed maintenance program

Measures of production quality, parts scrapped, equipment utilization, machine downtime, and machine maintenance time help managers monitor production performance.

Delivery Cycle Time Companies today are extremely interested in the amount of time they take to respond to customers. To evaluate their responsiveness to customers, companies examine their **delivery cycle time**, which is the time between the acceptance of an order and the final delivery of the product or service. When a customer places an order, it is important for a sales person to be able to promise an accurate delivery date. Companies pay careful attention to delivery cycle time not only because on-time delivery is important to customers but also because a decrease in delivery cycle time can lead to a significant increase in income from operations.

The formula to compute delivery cycle time is:

$$\text{Delivery Cycle Time} = \text{Purchase-Order Lead Time} + \text{Production Cycle Time} + \text{Delivery Time}$$

Delivery cycle time consists of

- **Purchase-order lead time** (the time it takes a company to take and process an order and organize so that production can begin),
- **Production cycle time** (the time it takes to make a product), and
- **Delivery time** (the time between the completion of a product and its receipt by the customer).

Managers should establish measures that emphasize the importance of minimizing the purchase-order lead time, production cycle time, and delivery time for each order. They should also track the average purchase-order lead time, production cycle time, and delivery time for all orders. Trends should be highlighted, and reports should be readily available. Other measures designed to monitor delivery

TABLE 27-2
Nonfinancial Measures of Quality

Measures of Product Design Quality	
Product design flaws	Number and types of design defects detected
	Average time between defect detection and correction
	Number of unresolved design defects at time of product introduction
Measures of Vendor Performance	
Vendor quality	Defect-free materials as a percentage of total materials received; prepared for each vendor
Vendor delivery	Timely deliveries of materials as a percentage of total deliveries; prepared for each vendor
Measures of Production Performance	
Production quality	Number of defective products per thousand produced
Parts scrapped	Number and type of materials spoiled during production
Equipment utilization rate	Productive machine time as a percentage of total time available for production
Machine downtime	Amount of time each machine is idle
Machine maintenance time	Amount of time each machine is idle for maintenance and upgrades
Measures of Delivery Cycle Time	
On-time deliveries	Shipments received by promised date as a percentage of total shipments
Orders filled	Orders filled as a percentage of total orders received
Average process time	Average time required to make a product available for shipment
Average setup time	Average amount of time elapsed between the acceptance of an order and the beginning of production
Purchase-order lead time	Time it takes a company to process an order and organize so that production can begin
Production cycle time	Time it takes to make a product
Delivery time	Time between a product's completion and its receipt by customer
Delivery cycle time	Time between the acceptance of an order and the final delivery of the product or service (purchase-order lead time + production cycle time + delivery time)
Waste time	Production cycle time − (average process time + average setup time)
Production backlog	Number and type of units waiting to begin processing
Measures of Customer Satisfaction	
Customer complaints	Number and types of customer complaints
Warranty claims	Number and causes of claims
Returned orders	Shipments returned as a percentage of total shipments

cycle time include order backlogs, on-time delivery performance, percentage of orders filled, and waste time. The formula to compute waste time is:

$$\text{Waste Time} = \text{Production Cycle Time} - (\text{Average Process Time} + \text{Average Setup Time})$$

Customer Satisfaction The sale and shipment of a product does not mark the end of performance measurement. Customer follow-up helps in evaluating total customer satisfaction. Measures used to determine the degree of customer satisfaction include (1) the number and types of customer complaints, (2) the number and causes of warranty claims, and (3) the percentage of shipments returned by customers (or the percentage of shipments accepted by customers). Several companies have developed their own customer satisfaction indexes from these measures so that they can compare different product lines over different time periods.

Recap Table 27-2 lists specific examples of the many nonfinancial measures used to monitor quality. These measures help a company continuously produce higher-quality products, improve production processes, and reduce throughput time and costs.

Measuring Service Quality

The quality of services rendered can be measured and analyzed. Many of the costs of conformance and nonconformance for a product apply to the development and delivery of a service. Flaws in service design lead to poor-quality services. Timely service delivery is as important as timely product shipments. Customer satisfaction in a service business can be measured by services accepted or rejected, the number of complaints, and the number of returning customers. Poor service development leads to internal and external failure costs.

Many of the costs-of-quality categories and several of the nonfinancial measures of quality can be applied directly to services and can be adopted by any type of service company.

& APPLY >

Internal reports on quality at the EMCAP Publishing Company generated the following information for the Trade Division for the first three months of the year:

Total sales	$60,000,000
Costs of quality:	
Prevention	$ 523,000
Appraisal	477,000
Internal failure	1,360,000
External failure	640,000

Compute the following:

a. Total costs of quality as a percentage of sales

b. Ratio of costs of conformance to total costs of quality

c. Ratio of costs of nonconformance to total costs of quality

d. Costs of nonconformance as a percentage of total sales

(continued)

SOLUTION

Costs of Conformance = Prevention Costs + Appraisal Costs
= $523,000 + $477,000 = $1,000,000

Costs of Nonconformance = Internal Failure Costs + External Failure Costs
= $1,360,000 + $640,000 = $2,000,000

a. Total Costs of Quality as a Percentage of Sales = $3,000,000 ÷ $60,000,000 = 5%

b. Ratio of Costs of Conformance to Total Costs of Quality = Costs of Conformance ÷ (Costs of Conformance + Costs of Nonconformance)
= $1,000,000 ÷ ($1,000,000 + $2,000,000)
= 0.33 to 1

c. Ratio of Costs of Nonconformance to Total Costs of Quality = Costs of Nonconformance ÷ (Costs of Conformance + Costs of Nonconformance)
= $2,000,000 ÷ ($1,000,000 +$2,000,000)
= 0.67 to 1

d. Costs of Nonconformance as a Percentage of Total Sales = $2,000,000 ÷ $60,000,000 = 3.33%

Measuring Quality: An Illustration

LO3 Use measures of quality to evaluate operating performance.

Using many of the examples of the costs of quality identified in Table 27-1 and the nonfinancial measures of quality listed in Table 27-2, the following sections demonstrate how a company measures and evaluates its progress toward the goal of achieving total quality management.

Evaluating the Costs of Quality

As demonstrated in Exhibit 27-1, three companies—Able, Baker, and Cane—have taken different approaches to achieving product quality. All three companies are the same size, each having generated $15 million in sales last year.

Key Quality Performance Questions We can evaluate each company's approach to quality enhancement by analyzing the costs of quality and by answering the following questions:

- Which company is most likely to succeed in the competitive marketplace?
- Which company has serious problems with its products' quality?
- What do you think will happen to the total costs of quality for each company over the next five years? Why?

Exhibit 27-2 shows that each company spent between 10.22 and 10.48 percent of its sales dollars on these costs. The following discussion is based on that analysis:

- ***Which company is most likely to succeed in the competitive marketplace?*** Able Co. spent the most money on costs of quality. What is more important, however, is that the company spent 80 percent of that money on costs of conformance, which will reap benefits in years to come. The company's focus on the costs of conformance means that only a small amount had to be spent on internal and external failure costs. The resulting high-quality products will lead to high customer satisfaction.

EXHIBIT 27-1
Analysis of the Costs of Quality

	Able Co.	Baker Co.	Cane Co.
Annual Sales	$15,000,000	$15,000,000	$15,000,000
Costs of conformance to customer standards			
Prevention Costs			
Quality training of employees	$ 210,000	$ 73,500	$ 136,500
Process engineering	262,500	115,500	189,000
Design review of products	105,000	42,000	84,000
Preventive maintenance	157,500	84,000	115,500
Subtotal	$ 735,000	$ 315,000	$ 525,000
Appraisal Costs			
End-of-process sampling and testing	$ 126,000	$ 63,000	$ 73,500
Inspection of materials	199,500	31,500	115,500
Quality audits of products	84,000	21,000	42,000
Vendor audits and sample testing	112,500	52,500	63,000
Subtotal	$ 522,000	$ 168,000	$ 294,000
Total costs of conformance	$ 1,257,000	$ 483,000	$ 819,000
Costs of nonconformance to customer standards			
Internal Failure Costs			
Scrap and rework	$ 21,000	$ 189,000	$ 126,000
Reinspection of rework	15,750	126,000	73,500
Quality-related downtime	42,000	231,000	178,500
Scrap disposal losses	26,250	84,000	52,500
Subtotal	$ 105,000	$ 630,000	$ 430,500
External Failure Costs			
Warranty claims	$ 47,250	$ 94,500	$ 84,000
Returned goods and replacements	15,750	68,250	36,750
Investigation of defects	26,250	78,750	57,750
Customer complaint processing	120,750	178,500	126,000
Subtotal	$ 210,000	$ 420,000	$ 304,500
Total costs of nonconformance	$ 315,000	$ 1,050,000	$ 735,000
Total costs of quality	$ 1,572,000	$ 1,533,000	$ 1,554,000
Total costs of quality as a percentage of sales	10.48%	10.22%	10.36%
Ratio of costs of conformance to total costs of quality	0.80 to 1	0.32 to 1	0.53 to 1
Ratio of costs of nonconformance to total costs of quality	0.20 to 1	0.68 to 1	0.47 to 1
Costs of nonconformance as a percentage of sales	2.10%	7.00%	4.90%

Which company has serious problems with its products' quality? Baker Co. spent the least on costs of quality but that's not the reason it is in serious trouble. Over 68 percent of its costs of quality ($1,050,000 of a total of $1,533,000) was spent on internal and external failure costs. Scrap costs, reinspection costs, the cost of downtime, warranty costs, and customer complaint costs were all high. Baker's products are very low in quality, which will lead to hard times in the future.

EXHIBIT 27-2
Analysis of Nonfinancial Measures of Quality

	Able Co.	Baker Co.	Cane Co.
Vendor Performance			
Percentage of defect-free materials			
2011	98.20%	94.40%	95.20%
2012	98.40%	93.20%	95.30%
2013	98.60%	93.10%	95.20%
Production Performance			
Production quality level (product defects per million)			
2011	1,400	4,120	2,710
2012	1,340	4,236	2,720
2013	1,210	4,340	2,680
Delivery Cycle Time			
Percentage of on-time deliveries			
2011	94.20%	76.20%	84.10%
2012	94.60%	75.40%	84.00%
2013	95.40%	73.10%	83.90%
Customer Satisfaction			
Percentage of returned orders			
2011	1.30%	6.90%	4.20%
2012	1.10%	7.20%	4.10%
2013	0.80%	7.60%	4.00%
Number of customer complaints			
2011	22	189	52
2012	18	194	50
2013	12	206	46

▶ ***What do you think will happen to the total costs of quality for each company over the next five years? Why?***

Able Co. When money is spent on costs of conformance early in a product's life cycle, quality is integrated into the development and production processes. Once a high level of quality has been established, total costs of quality should be lower in future years. Able Co. seems to be in that position today.

Baker Co. Baker's costs of conformance will have to increase significantly if the company expects to stay in business. It is spending 7 percent of its sales revenue on internal and external failure costs. Because the marketplace is not accepting its products, its competitors have the upper hand and the company is in a weak position.

Cane Co. Cane Co. is taking a middle road. This company is spending a little more than half (53 percent) of its cost-of-quality dollars on conformance, so product quality should be increasing. However, the company is still incurring high internal and external failure costs. Cane's managers must learn to prevent such costs if they expect the company to remain competitive.

Evaluating Nonfinancial Measures of Quality

From the information presented in Exhibit 27-2, we can evaluate each company's experience in its pursuit of total quality management. That part of the exhibit presents nonfinancial measures for each company for three years—2011, 2012, and 2013. The trends shown there tend to support the findings in the analysis of the costs of quality in Exhibit 27-1.

Able Co. For Able Co., 98.2 percent of the materials received from suppliers in 2011 were of high quality, and the quality has been increasing over the three years. The product defect rate, measured in number of defects per million, has been decreasing rapidly, proof that the costs of conformance are having a positive effect. The percentage of on-time deliveries has been increasing, and both the percentage of returned orders and the number of customer complaints have been decreasing, which means that customer acceptance and satisfaction have been increasing.

Baker Co. Baker Co.'s experience is not encouraging. The number of high-quality shipments of materials from vendors has been decreasing, the product defect rate has been increasing (it seems to be out of control), on-time deliveries were bad to begin with and have been getting worse, more goods have been returned each year, and customer complaints have been on the rise. All those signs reflect the company's high costs of nonconformance.

Cane Co. Cane Co. is making progress toward higher quality, but its progress is very slow. Most of the nonfinancial measures show a very slight positive trend. More money needs to be spent on the costs of conformance.

A graphic analysis can be very useful when a manager is comparing the performance of several operating units. Mere columns of numbers do not always adequately depict differences in operating performance and may be difficult to interpret. In such cases, a chart or graph can help managers see what the data are saying. For example, the bar graph in Figure 27-1 illustrates the amounts that Able, Baker, and Cane are spending on costs of quality. It clearly shows that

- Able Co. is focusing on costs of conformance and has low costs of nonconformance.
- Baker Co., in contrast, is paying over $1,000,000 in costs of non-conformance because it has not tried to increase spending on prevention and appraisal.
- Cane Co. spends slightly more on costs of conformance than on costs of non-conformance, but, like Baker Co., it is spending too much on failure costs.

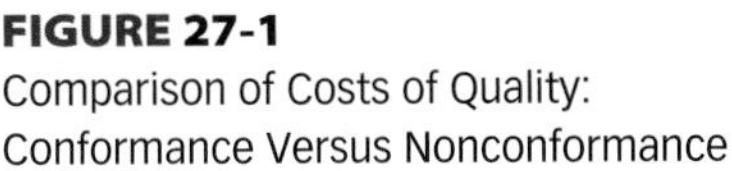

FIGURE 27-1
Comparison of Costs of Quality: Conformance Versus Nonconformance

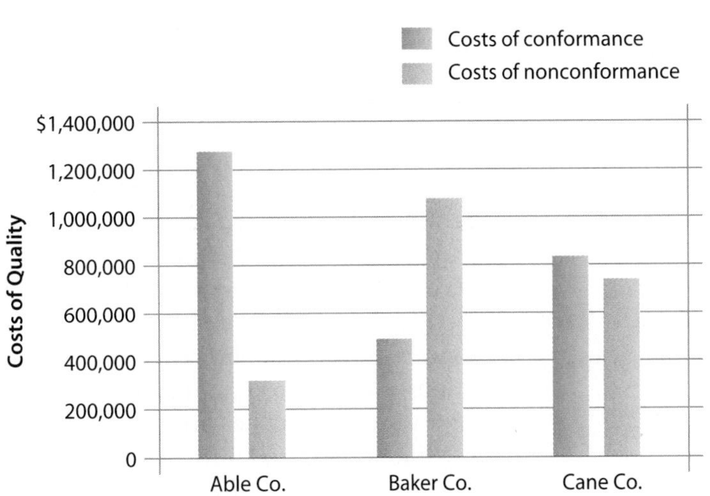

A corporation has two departments, Department C and Department D, that produce two separate product lines. The company has been implementing total quality management over the past year. Conformance and nonconformance cost ratios of quality for the year for each department are presented below. Which department is committed to TQM?

	Dept. C	Dept. D	Totals
Total costs of quality as a percentage of sales	5.00%	5.00%	5.00%
Ratio of costs of conformance to total costs of quality	0.70 to 1	0.35 to 1	0.51 to 1
Ratio of costs of nonconformance to total costs of quality	0.30 to 1	0.65 to 1	0.49 to 1
Costs of nonconformance as a percentage of sales	1.50%	3.25%	2.45%

SOLUTION

Department C is taking a more serious approach to implementing TQM. It is spending more than twice as much on costs of conformance as on costs of nonconformance. Department D is doing almost the opposite.

The Evolving Concept of Quality

LO4 Discuss the evolving concept of quality.

Much of what organizations now know about quality can be traced to past manufacturing initiatives. Before the advent of TQM over 20 years ago, managers assumed that there was a trade-off between the costs and the benefits of improving quality. In economic terms, a **return on quality (ROQ)** results when the marginal revenues possible from a higher-quality good or service exceed the marginal costs of providing that higher quality. In other words, managers must weigh the high costs of consistent quality against the resulting higher revenues, and they must base the quality standards for a good or service on the expected return on quality.

In the 1980s, quality gave organizations a competitive edge in the global marketplace. W. Edwards Deming and other advocates of TQM stressed improved quality as a means of enhancing an organization's efficiency and profits. As a result, managers focused on increasing customer satisfaction and product or service quality, and organizations recognized the value of producing highly reliable products. Companies emphasized **kaizen**, or the gradual and ongoing improvement of products and processes while reducing costs. Quality control methods such as statistical analysis, computer-aided design, and Six Sigma eliminated defects in the design and manufacture of products. Today more than 90 percent of the *Fortune* 500 companies use a combination of those methods.

The story of **Motorola** and its Six Sigma quality standard illustrates how product quality quickly improved. In 1978, Motorola was losing market share as a result of aggressive competition from high-quality Japanese goods. In response, Motorola set the goal of Six Sigma quality, which meant that Motorola's customers would perceive the company's products and services as perfect. It used the DMAIC (define, measure, analyze, improve, control) and DMADV (define, measure, analyze, design, verify) methods to improve both existing processes and new ones. Motorola applied the Six Sigma quality standard to all aspects of its operations—not just to production. Even Motorola's Corporate Finance Department measures defects per unit, tracking its number of errors per monthly close and the time it takes to close the books each month.

Thousands of companies, including **Amazon.com,** have embraced the data-driven approach of Six Sigma to reduce errors. But Six Sigma has its drawbacks,

The Walt Disney character Minnie Mouse interacts with customers waiting in line at Disney's Magic Kingdom in Orlando, Florida. Disney theme parks use characters to keep waiting customers amused, thereby maximizing customers' satisfaction with the theme park experience.

Courtesy of Joe Raedle/Getty Images.

including diminishing worker morale and invention, and many companies are rethinking Six Sigma as a business cure-all.

Two respected techniques made popular by Six Sigma, benchmarking and process mapping, are still widely used and allow managers to understand and measure quality improvements.

- **Benchmarking** is the measurement of the gap between the quality of a company's process and the quality of a parallel process at the best-in-class company. For example, Motorola improved its order-processing system by studying order processing at **Lands' End**.
- **Process mapping** is a method of using a flow diagram to indicate process inputs, outputs, constraints, and flows to help managers identify unnecessary efforts and inefficiencies in a business process. Quality problems and their causes are visually tracked using control charts, histograms, cause-and-effect diagrams, and Pareto diagrams. As a result, customer satisfaction with a product or service and with the buying experience both before and after the sale is enhanced.

Service businesses also recognize the importance of quality and seek to maximize customers' satisfaction with their services. For example, **Disney** theme parks minimize customers' impatience as they wait in long lines by having Disney characters interact and play with the crowd. A potential customer problem becomes another opportunity to deliver Disney magic.

In summary, a manager's concept of quality must continuously evolve to fulfill customers' needs and expectations and to meet the demands of the changing business environment. Quality has many dimensions. Not only must a product or service be defect-free and dependable; it must also embody such intangibles as prestige and good taste. Managers must meet or exceed a variety of expectations about customer service and create innovative new products and services that anticipate the opportunities offered by an ever-changing marketplace. The concept of quality means more than having zero defects in a product or service; it means doing everything possible to have zero defections of customers.

Ecommerce has changed the way goods and services are obtained. How do companies like **Amazon .com** continue to anticipate customer needs? To answer this question, visit Amazon.com's website.

SOLUTION

Ecommerce companies use their huge databases to spot customer trends and maintain their competitive advantage. Such innovations as customer-specific web pages, prepublication book sales, and rapid delivery have benefits for both the company and its customers.

Recognition of Quality

LO5 Recognize the awards and organizations that promote quality.

Many awards and organizations have been established to recognize and promote the importance of quality. Three of the most prestigious awards are the Deming prizes, the EFQM Excellence Award, and the Malcolm Baldrige Quality Award. In addition, the International Organization for Standardization works to promote quality standards worldwide.

Deming Prizes In 1951, the Japanese Union of Scientists and Engineers established the Deming Application Prize to honor individuals or groups who have contributed to the development and dissemination of total quality control. Consideration for the prize was originally limited to Japanese companies, but interest in it was so great that the rules were revised to allow the participation of companies outside Japan. Today, the organization awards several **Deming prizes** to companies and individuals who achieve distinctive results by carrying out total quality control.

EFQM Excellence Award Since the 1990s the nonprofit European Foundation for Quality Management has presented the **EFQM Excellence Award** annually to businesses and organizations operating in Europe that excel in quality management. The EFQM has also developed a quality framework called the EFQM Excellence Model to help businesses

- Define their vision and measurable goals.
- Understand business systems and their causal relationships and links.
- Identify and promote successful internal and external customer experiences.
- Self-assess their current organizational health.

Malcolm Baldrige National Quality Award In 1987, the U.S. Congress created the **Malcolm Baldrige National Quality Award** to recognize U.S. organizations for their achievements in quality and business performance and to raise awareness of the importance of quality and performance excellence. Organizations are evaluated on the basis of the Baldrige performance excellence criteria, standards that are divided into seven categories:

- Leadership
- Strategic planning
- Customer and market focus
- Measurement, analysis, and knowledge management
- Work force focus

- Process management
- Results

Thousands of organizations throughout the world accept the Baldrige criteria as the standards for performance excellence and use them for training and self-assessment, whether they plan to compete for the award or not. Award winners are showcased annually on the Internet (www.quality.nist.gov) and are encouraged to share their best practices with others.

ISO Standards The International Organization for Standardization (ISO) is a worldwide federation of national standards bodies (http://www.iso.org). It promotes standardization with a view to facilitating the international exchange of goods and services. For example, by developing a standard format for credit cards, standard film speed codes, and standard graphical symbols for use on equipment and diagrams, the ISO has saved time and money for both individuals and businesses worldwide.

Study Note

Some ISO standards vary between countries. For example, the standard size of computer paper in the United States is different from the standard size in European countries.

To standardize quality management and quality assurance, the ISO has developed families of standards that have been implemented by more than a million organizations in 175 countries. The two most popular standards families are ISO 9000 and ISO 14000. The **ISO 14000** series provides an environmental management framework to minimize the harmful environmental effects of business activities and continually improve environmental performance.

ISO 9000 is a set of guidelines for businesses that covers the design, development, production, final inspection and testing, installation, and servicing of products, processes, and services. Because many organizations do business only with ISO-certified companies, these guidelines have been adopted worldwide. To become ISO certified, an organization must pass a rigorous third-party audit of its manufacturing and service processes. As a result, certified companies have detailed documentation of their operations. There are eight quality management principles of ISO 9000:

- Customer focus
- Leadership
- Involvement of people
- Process approach
- System approach to management
- Continual involvement
- Factual approach to decision making
- Mutually beneficial supplier relationships

Some quality standards or principles appear to be comparable among the organizations that promote quality. List some of the shared principles.

SOLUTION

Quality principles shared by the Baldrige award and ISO include customer focus or customer and market focus; leadership; involvement of people or work force focus; process approach or process management; and factual approach to decision making or measurement, analysis, and knowledge management. There is some overlap in the other areas as well.

A LOOK BACK AT ▸ AMAZON.COM

This chapter's Decision Point posed the following questions:

- How do Amazon.com's managers maintain the company's competitive edge?
- What measures of quality can Amazon.com use to evaluate operating performance?

Doing business over the Internet has added a rich dimension to quality. At **Amazon .com**, the quality of a customer's experience is enhanced by the company's management information system. By maintaining customer profiles based on previous visits and purchases, Amazon.com can greet customers as they return to the site with a web page customized to their preferences. And by integrating its supply-chain software with its warehousing and data-mining applications, Amazon.com can ensure timely and efficient deliveries to its warehouses and its customers.

Amazon.com's managers also use their information system's highly developed infrastructure to meet the changing expectations of their diverse customer base. In assessing customer satisfaction and the responsiveness of the company's supply chain and value chain, these managers use both nonfinancial and financial measures. To maintain a competitive edge, they will continue to need detailed, real-time information, both financial and nonfinancial, about every aspect of the company's operations and the highly competitive environment of ecommerce.

Review Problem

Analysis of Nonfinancial Data LO2 LO3

Suppose that three months ago one of Amazon's subsidiaries installed a new manufacturing system in its New Products Division. A lean approach is now followed for everything from ordering materials and parts to product shipment and delivery. The division's superintendent is very interested in the initial results of the venture. The following data have been collected for your analysis:

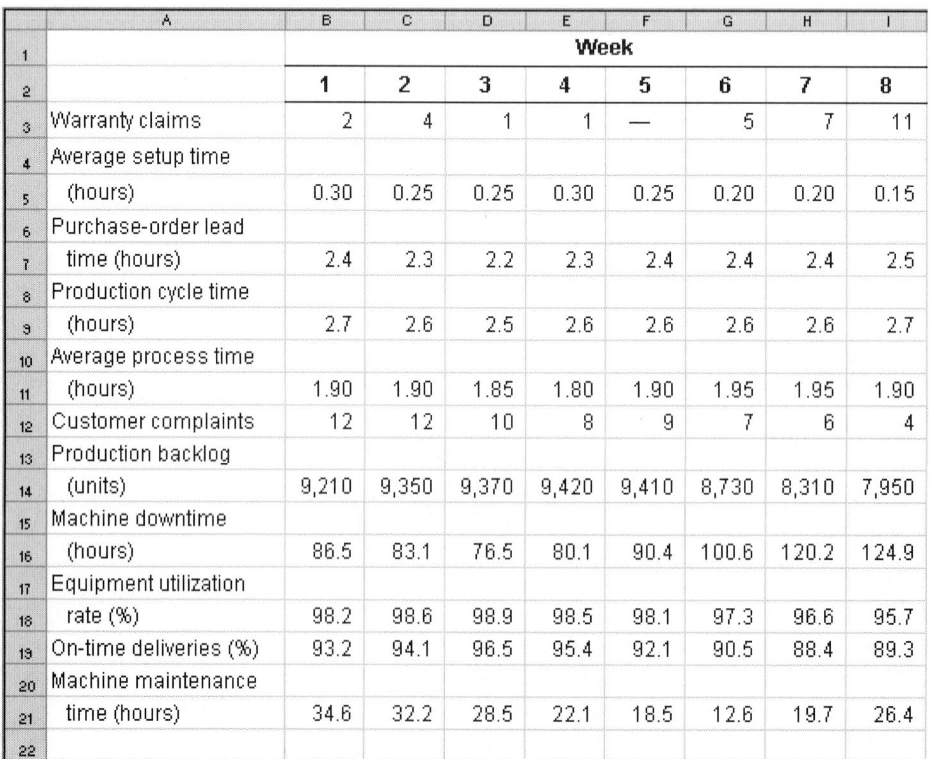

	A	B	C	D	E	F	G	H	I
1		Week							
2		1	2	3	4	5	6	7	8
3	Warranty claims	2	4	1	1	—	5	7	11
4	Average setup time								
5	(hours)	0.30	0.25	0.25	0.30	0.25	0.20	0.20	0.15
6	Purchase-order lead								
7	time (hours)	2.4	2.3	2.2	2.3	2.4	2.4	2.4	2.5
8	Production cycle time								
9	(hours)	2.7	2.6	2.5	2.6	2.6	2.6	2.6	2.7
10	Average process time								
11	(hours)	1.90	1.90	1.85	1.80	1.90	1.95	1.95	1.90
12	Customer complaints	12	12	10	8	9	7	6	4
13	Production backlog								
14	(units)	9,210	9,350	9,370	9,420	9,410	8,730	8,310	7,950
15	Machine downtime								
16	(hours)	86.5	83.1	76.5	80.1	90.4	100.6	120.2	124.9
17	Equipment utilization								
18	rate (%)	98.2	98.6	98.9	98.5	98.1	97.3	96.6	95.7
19	On-time deliveries (%)	93.2	94.1	96.5	95.4	92.1	90.5	88.4	89.3
20	Machine maintenance								
21	time (hours)	34.6	32.2	28.5	22.1	18.5	12.6	19.7	26.4
22									

Required

1. Analyze the nonfinancial measures of quality of the division for the eight-week period. Focus on the following areas of performance:
   a. Production performance
   b. Delivery cycle time
   c. Customer satisfaction
2. Summarize your findings in a report to the division's superintendent.

Answers to Review Problem

1. Analysis of nonfinancial measures of performance. The data given were reorganized as shown below, and one additional piece of information, average waste time, was calculated from the data.

			Week								Weekly
1											
2			1	2	3	4	5	6	7	8	Average
3	a.	**Production Performance**									
4		Machine downtime (hours)	86.5	83.1	76.5	80.1	90.4	100.6	120.2	124.9	95.3
5		Equipment utilization rate (%)	98.2	98.6	98.9	98.5	98.1	97.3	96.6	95.7	97.7
6		Machine maintenance time (hours)	34.6	32.2	28.5	22.1	18.5	12.6	19.7	26.4	24.3
7	b.	**Delivery Cycle Time**									
8		On-time deliveries (%)	93.2	94.1	96.5	95.4	92.1	90.5	88.4	89.3	92.4
9		Average setup time (hours)	0.30	0.25	0.25	0.30	0.25	0.20	0.20	0.15	0.24
10		Purchase-order lead time (hours)	2.4	2.3	2.2	2.3	2.4	2.4	2.4	2.5	2.4
11		Production cycle time (hours)	2.7	2.6	2.5	2.6	2.6	2.6	2.6	2.7	2.6
12		Average process time (hours)	1.90	1.90	1.85	1.80	1.90	1.95	1.95	1.90	1.89
13		Production backlog (units)	9,210	9,350	9,370	9,420	9,410	8,730	8,310	7,950	8,969
14		Average waste time (hours)	0.50	0.45	0.40	0.50	0.45	0.45	0.45	0.65	0.48
15	c.	**Customer Satisfaction**									
16		Customer complaints	12	12	10	8	9	7	6	4	8.5
17		Warranty claims	2	4	1	1	—	5	7	11	3.9
18											

2. Memorandum to the division superintendent:

   My analysis of the operating data for the division for the last eight weeks revealed the following:

   - ***Production Performance:*** Machine downtime is increasing. Also, the equipment utilization rate is down. Machine maintenance time originally decreased, but it has increased in the past two weeks. Department managers should be aware of these potential problem areas.
   - ***Delivery Cycle Time:*** We are having trouble maintaining the averages for delivery cycle time established eight weeks ago. On-time delivery percentages are slipping. Waste time is increasing, which is contrary to our goals. Backlogged orders are decreasing, which is a good sign from a lean viewpoint but could spell problems in the future. On the positive side, setup time seems to be under control. Emphasis needs to be placed on reducing lead time, cycle time, and process time.
   - ***Customer Satisfaction:*** Customer satisfaction seems to be improving, as the number of complaints is decreasing rapidly. However, warranty claims have risen significantly in the past three weeks, which may be a signal of quality problems.

   Overall, we can see good signs from the new equipment, but we need to pay special attention to all potential problem areas.

& REVIEW >

LO1 Describe a management information system, and explain how it enhances management decision making.

In a management information system (MIS), the primary focus is on the management of activities, not on costs. By focusing on activities, an MIS provides managers with improved knowledge of the processes for which they are responsible. The MIS pinpoints resource usage for each activity and fosters managerial decisions that lead to continuous improvement throughout the organization.

As managers plan, they use the MIS database to obtain relevant and reliable information for formulating strategic plans, making forecasts, and preparing budgets. When managers perform their duties, they use the financial and nonfinancial information in the MIS database to implement decisions about personnel, resources, and activities that will minimize waste and improve the quality of their organization's products or services. When they evaluate performance, managers identify and track financial and nonfinancial performance measures to evaluate all major business functions. By enabling the timely comparison of actual to expected performance, the MIS allows managers to reward performance promptly, take speedy corrective actions, and analyze and revise performance measurement plans. And when they communicate, managers are able to generate customized reports that evaluate performance and provide useful real-time information for decision making.

LO2 Define *total quality management* (*TQM*), and identify financial and nonfinancial measures of quality.

Total quality management is an organizational environment in which all business functions work together to build quality into a firm's products or services. The costs of quality are measures of the costs that are specifically related to the achievement or nonachievement of product or service quality. The costs of quality have two components. One is the cost of conforming to a customer's product or service standards by preventing defects and failures and by appraising quality and performance. The other is the cost of nonconformance—the costs incurred when defects are discovered before a product is shipped and the costs incurred after a defective product or faulty service is delivered to the customer.

The objective of TQM is to reduce or eliminate the costs of nonconformance, the internal and external failure costs that are associated with customer dissatisfaction. To this end, managers can justify high initial costs of conformance if they minimize the total costs of quality over the product's or service's life cycle.

LO3 Use measures of quality to evaluate operating performance.

Nonfinancial measures of quality are related to product design, vendor performance, production performance, delivery cycle time, and customer satisfaction. Those measures, together with the costs of quality, help a firm meet its goal of continuously improving product or service quality and the production process.

LO4 Discuss the evolving concept of quality.

A manager's concept of quality must continuously evolve to fulfill customers' needs and expectations and to meet the demands of the changing business environment. Quality has many dimensions that extend beyond the mere creation and delivery of a product or service. Managers must satisfy customers today and create innovative products and services for tomorrow. The evolving concept of quality means more than having zero defects in a product or service; it means doing everything possible to have zero defections of customers.

LO5 Recognize the awards and organizations that promote quality. The importance of quality has been acknowledged worldwide through the granting of numerous awards, certificates, and prizes for quality. Three of the most prestigious awards are the Deming prizes, the EFQM Excellence Award, and the Malcolm Baldrige Quality Award. In addition, the International Organization for Standardization promotes quality management through the ISO 9000 and 14000 families of standards.

REVIEW of Concepts and Terminology

The following concepts and terms were introduced in this chapter:

Appraisal costs 1237 (LO2)

Benchmarking 1247 (LO4)

Computer-aided design (CAD) 1238 (LO2)

Computer-integrated manufacturing (CIM) systems 1239 (LO2)

Costs of conformance 1236 (LO2)

Costs of nonconformance 1236 (LO2)

Costs of quality 1236 (LO2)

Delivery cycle time 1239 (LO2)

Delivery time 1239 (LO2)

Deming prizes 1248 (LO5)

EFQM Excellence Award 1248 (LO5)

Enterprise resource planning (ERP) system 1234 (LO1)

External failure costs 1237 (LO2)

Internal failure costs 1237 (LO2)

ISO 9000 1249 (LO5)

ISO 14000 1249 (LO5)

Kaizen 1246 (LO4)

Malcolm Baldrige National Quality Award 1248 (LO5)

Management information system (MIS) 1234 (LO1)

Prevention costs 1237 (LO2)

Process mapping 1247 (LO4)

Production cycle time 1239 (LO2)

Purchase-order lead time 1239 (LO2)

Quality 1236 (LO2)

Return on quality (ROQ) 1246 (LO4)

Total quality management (TQM) 1236 (LO2)

CHAPTER ASSIGNMENTS

BUILDING Your Basic Knowledge and Skills

Short Exercises

LO1 **Traits of a Management Information System**

SE 1. What kinds of information does a management information system capture? How do managers use such information?

LO1 **Continuous Improvement**

SE 2. Maxy Politt is the controller for Pratt Industries. She has been asked to develop a plan for installing a management information system in her company. The president has already approved the concept and has given Politt the go-ahead. What kind of information will Politt need to give managers to help them with their decision making?

LO2 **Costs of Quality in a Service Business**

SE 3. Elam Insurance Agency incurred the following activity costs related to service quality. Identify those that are costs of conformance (CC) and those that are costs of nonconformance (CN).

Policy processing improvements	$76,400
Customer complaints response	34,100
Policy writer training	12,300
Policy error losses	82,700
Policy proofing	39,500

LO2 **Measures of Quality**

SE 4. Internal reports on quality at the Lakeside Publishing Company generated the following information for the School Division for the first three months of the year:

Total sales	$50,000,000
Costs of quality:	
Prevention	$ 523,000
Appraisal	77,000
Internal failure	860,000
External failure	640,000

Compute the following:

a. Total costs of quality as a percentage of sales
b. Ratio of costs of conformance to total costs of quality
c. Ratio of costs of nonconformance to total costs of quality
d. Costs of nonconformance as a percentage of total sales

LO2 **Nonfinancial Measures of Quality**

SE 5. For a fast-food restaurant that specializes in deluxe cheeseburgers, identify two nonfinancial measures of good product quality and two nonfinancial measures of poor product quality.

LO2 **Vendor Quality**

SE 6. Cite some specific measures of vendor quality that Nick Michael could use when he installs a quality-certification program for the vendors that supply his company, Stamp It, Inc., with direct materials.

LO2 LO3 Measures of Delivery Cycle Time

SE 7. Quality Cosmetics, Inc., has developed a set of nonfinancial measures to evaluate on-time product delivery for one of its best-selling cosmetics. The following data have been generated for the past four weeks:

Week	Purchase-Order Lead Time	Production Cycle Time	Delivery Time
1	3.0 days	3.5 days	4.0 days
2	2.3 days	3.5 days	3.5 days
3	2.4 days	3.3 days	3.4 days
4	2.5 days	3.2 days	3.3 days

Compute total delivery cycle time for each week. Evaluate the delivery performance. Is there an area that needs management's attention?

LO4 Return on Quality

SE 8. For many years, June Pirolo has used return on quality (ROQ) to evaluate quality. What assumptions about quality did she make?

LO4 Quality and Cycle Time

SE 9. Motorola's Finance Department has adapted the concept of delivery cycle time to include the measurement of cycle times for processing customer credit memos, invoices, and orders. Why would such performance measures contribute to Motorola's quest for Six Sigma quality?

LO5 Quality Award Recipients

SE 10. What types of organizations are represented by recent recipients of the Malcolm Baldrige Award? Consult the website at http://www.quality.nist.gov.

Exercises

LO1 Adapting to Changing Information Needs

E 1. "What's all the fuss about managers' needing to focus on activities instead of costs?" demanded Sam Wards, the controller of Tyme Flies. "The bottom line is all that matters, and our company's current management information system is just fine for figuring that out. I know that our system is ten years old, but if it isn't broken, why should we fix it?" How would you respond to Sam Wards?

LO2 Costs of Conformance in a Service Business

E 2. Home Health Care, LLP, incurred the following service-related activity costs for the month. Prepare an analysis of the costs of conformance by identifying the prevention costs and appraisal costs, and compute the percentage of sales represented by prevention costs, appraisal costs, and total costs of conformance.

Total sales	$25,000
Quality training of employees	500
Vendor audits	400
Quality-certified vendors	100
Preventive maintenance	300
Quality sampling of services	200
Field testing of new services	250
Quality circles	50
Quality improvement projects	150
Technical service support	75
Inspection of services rendered	175

LO2 **Costs of Nonconformance in a Service Business**

E 3. Home Health Care, LLP, incurred the following service-related activity costs for the month. Prepare an analysis of the costs of nonconformance by identifying the internal failure costs and external failure costs, and compute the percentage of sales represented by internal failure costs, external failure costs, and total costs of nonconformance.

Total sales	$25,000
Reinspection of rework	50
Investigation of service defects	300
Lawsuits	0
Quality-related downtime	75
Failure analysis	50
Customer complaint processing	500
Retesting of service scheduling	25
Restoration of reputation	0
Lost sales	100
Replacement services	1,000

LO2 **Measures of Quality in a Service Business**

E 4. Rehab Health Care, LLC, incurred the following service-related activity costs for the month:

Total sales	$42,000
Customer complaint processing	1,200
Employee training	400
Reinspection and retesting	500
Design review of service procedures	300
Technical support	200
Investigation of service defects	800
Sample testing of vendors	100
Inspection of supplies	150
Quality audits	250
Quality-related downtime	300

Prepare an analysis of the costs of quality for Rehab Health Care, LLC. Categorize the costs as (a) costs of conformance, with subsets of prevention costs and appraisal costs, or (b) costs of nonconformance, with subsets of internal failure costs and external failure costs. Compute the percentage of sales represented by prevention costs, appraisal costs, total costs of conformance, internal failure costs, external failure costs, total costs of nonconformance, and total costs of quality. Also compute the ratio of costs of conformance to total costs of quality and the ratio of costs of nonconformance to total costs of quality.

LO2 LO3 **Costs of Quality**

E 5. Lager Corp. produces and supplies automotive manufacturers with the mechanisms used to adjust the positions of front seating units. Several competitors have recently entered the market, and management is concerned that the quality of the company's current products may be surpassed by the quality of the new competitors' products. The controller was asked to conduct an analysis of the efforts in January to improve product quality. His analysis generated the following costs of quality:

Training of employees	$22,400
Customer service	13,600
Reinspection of rework	28,000

Quality audits	$31,300
Design review	27,500
Warranty claims	67,100
Sample testing of materials	27,400
Returned goods	98,700
Preventive maintenance	26,500
Quality engineering	18,700
Setup for testing new products	42,100
Scrap and rework	76,500
Losses caused by vendor scrap	65,800
Product simulation	28,400

1. Prepare a detailed analysis of the costs of quality.
2. Comment on the company's current efforts to improve product quality.

LO2 LO3 Measuring Costs of Quality

E 6. A corporation has two departments that produce two separate product lines. The company has been implementing total quality management over the past year. Revenue and costs of quality for that year are presented below.

	Dept. G	Dept. H	Totals
Annual sales	$9,200,000	$11,000,000	$20,200,000
Costs of quality			
Prevention costs	$ 186,000	$ 124,500	$ 310,500
Appraisal costs	136,000	68,000	204,000
Internal failure costs	94,000	197,500	291,500
External failure costs	44,000	160,000	204,000
Totals	$ 460,000	$ 550,000	$ 1,010,000

Which department is taking a more serious approach to implementing TQM? Base your answer on the following computations:

a. Total costs of quality as a percentage of sales
b. Ratio of costs of conformance to total costs of quality
c. Ratio of costs of nonconformance to total costs of quality
d. Costs of nonconformance as a percentage of sales

LO2 Measures of Product Design Quality

E 7. Being first to market with its newest product, the pocket e-book, was the goal of management at Read It, Inc. Comment on how the company's measures of product design quality, which follow, compare with the industry benchmarks.

Measures of Product Design Quality	Read It, Inc.	Industry Benchmark
Number of design defects detected	50	50
Unresolved design defects at time of product introduction	10	5
Average time between defect detection and correction (hours)	4	8
Time to market (time from design idea to market) (days)	60	100

LO2 Measures of Vendor Performance

E 8. Hal Justin, the manager of a hotel that caters to traveling businesspeople, is reviewing the nonfinancial measures of quality for the hotel's dry-cleaning service. Six months ago, he contracted with a local dry-cleaning company to provide the service to hotel guests. The cleaner promised a four-hour turnaround on all dry-cleaning orders. Comment on the following measures for the last six months.

	January	February	March	April	May	June
Percentage of complaints	1%	2%	1%	2%	2%	1%
Percentage of on-time deliveries	100%	75%	100%	80%	85%	100%
Number of orders	300	400	400	500	600	600

LO2 Measures of Production Performance

E 9. Analyze the following nonfinancial measures of quality for Holiday Express, Inc., a supplier of mistletoe, for a recent four-week period. Focus specifically on measures of production performance.

Measures of Quality	Week 1	Week 2	Week 3	Week 4
Percentage of defective products per million produced	1.0%	0.8%	0.6%	0.5%
Equipment utilization rate	90%	91%	89%	90%
Machine downtime (hours)	12	10	13	12
Machine maintenance time (hours)	8	8	8	8
Machine setup time (hours)	4	2	5	4

LO2 Measures of Delivery Cycle Time

E 10. Compute the missing numbers for **a**, **b**, **c**, and **d** for the delivery cycle time for Companies M, N, Q, and P.

Company	Purchase-Order Lead Time	Production Cycle Time	Delivery Time	Total Delivery Cycle Time
M	a	2	1	4
N	2	4	b	9
Q	10	c	15	30
P	2	7	1	d

LO2 Analysis of Waste Time

E 11. Calculate the missing numbers for **a**, **b**, **c**, and **d** to analyze the waste time for the following orders. Comment on your findings.

Name of Order	Production Cycle Time	Average Process Time	Average Setup Time	Waste Time
Nguyen	6	a	1	1
Smith	b	9	4	2
Gomez	9	5	c	3
Patel	8	3	1	d

LO2 LO3 Nonfinancial Measures of Quality and TQM

E 12. "A satisfied customer is the most important goal of this company!" was the opening remark of the corporate president, Alice Nunes, at the monthly executive committee meeting of Santiago Company. The company manufactures tube products for customers in 16 western states. It has four divisions, each producing a different type of tubing material. Nunes, a proponent of total quality management, was reacting to the latest measures of quality from the four divisions. The data for the four divisions follow.

	Brass Division	Plastics Division	Aluminum Division	Copper Division	Company Averages
Vendor on-time delivery	97.20%	91.40%	98.10%	88.20%	93.73%*
Production quality rates (defective parts per million)	1,440	2,720	1,370	4,470	2,500
On-time shipments	89.20%	78.40%	91.80%	75.60%	83.75%
Returned orders	1.10%	4.60%	0.80%	6.90%	3.35%
Number of customer complaints	24	56	10	62	38
Number of warranty claims	7	12	4	14	9.3*

*Rounded.

Why was Nunes upset? Which division or divisions do not appear to have satisfied customers? What criteria did you use to make your decision?

LO4 Nonfinancial Data Analysis

E 13. Takada Company makes racing bicycles. Its Lightning model is considered the top of the line in the industry. Three months ago, to improve quality and reduce production time, Takada Company purchased and installed a computer-integrated manufacturing system for the Lightning model. Management is interested in cutting time in all phases of the delivery cycle. The controller's office gathered these data for the past four-week period:

	Week			
	1	2	3	4
Average process time (hours)	24.6	24.4	23.8	23.2
Average setup time (hours)	1.4	1.3	1.2	1.1
Customer complaints	7	6	8	9
Delivery time (hours)	34.8	35.2	36.4	38.2
On-time deliveries (%)	98.1	97.7	97.2	96.3
Production backlog (units)	8,230	8,340	8,320	8,430
Production cycle time (hours)	28.5	27.9	27.2	26.4
Purchase-order lead time (hours)	38.5	36.2	35.5	34.1
Warranty claims	2	3	3	2

Analyze the performance of the Lightning model for the four-week period, focusing specifically on product delivery cycle time and on customer satisfaction.

LO4 **Innovation and Quality**

E 14. Ecommerce has changed the way goods and services are obtained. How do companies like **Barnes and Noble** or **Borders** or **Books-A-Million** continue to anticipate customer needs? To answer this question, visit their websites.

LO5 **Quality Awards**

E 15. How do the Malcolm Baldrige Quality Award and the ISO 9000 standards differ? Consult their websites at www.quality.nist.gov and www.iso.org.

Problems

LO2 **Costs and Nonfinancial Measures of Quality**

P 1. Minturn Enterprises, Inc., operates as three autonomous companies, each with a chief executive officer who oversees its operations. At a recent corporate meeting, the company CEOs agreed to adopt total quality management and to track, record, and analyze their costs and nonfinancial measures of quality. All three companies are operating in highly competitive markets. Sales and quality-related data for September follow.

	Carbondale Company	Wolcott Company	Silverthorne Company
Annual sales	$11,600,000	$13,300,000	$10,800,000
Costs of quality			
Vendor audits	$ 69,000	$ 184,800	$ 130,800
Quality audits	58,900	115,550	141,700
Failure analysis	188,500	92,400	16,350
Design review of products	80,500	176,700	218,000
Scrap and rework	207,000	160,800	21,200
Quality-certified suppliers	49,200	105,600	231,600
Preventive maintenance	92,000	158,400	163,500
Warranty adjustments	149,550	105,600	49,050
Product recalls	201,250	198,000	80,050
Quality training of employees	149,500	237,600	272,500
End-of-process sampling and testing	34,500	145,200	202,700
Reinspection of rework	126,500	66,000	27,250
Returned goods	212,750	72,600	16,350
Customer complaint processing	109,250	162,450	38,150
Total costs of quality	$ 1,728,400	$ 1,981,700	$ 1,609,200
Nonfinancial measures of quality			
Number of warranty claims	61	36	12
Customer complaints	107	52	18
Defective parts per million	4,610	2,190	1,012
Returned orders	9.20%	4.10%	0.90%

Required

1. Prepare an analysis of the costs of quality for the three divisions. Categorize the costs as (a) costs of conformance, with subsets of prevention costs and appraisal costs, or (b) costs of nonconformance, with subsets of internal failure costs and external failure costs. Compute the total costs in each category for each company.

2. For each company compute the percentage of sales represented by prevention costs, appraisal costs, total costs of conformance, internal failure costs, external failure costs, total costs of nonconformance, and total costs of quality.
3. Interpret the cost-of-quality data for each company. Is its product of high or low quality? Why? Is each company headed in the right direction to be competitive?

Manager insight ▶
4. Evaluate the nonfinancial measures of quality in terms of customer satisfaction. Are the results consistent with your analysis in requirement 3? Explain your answer.

LO2 LO3 **Analysis of Nonfinancial Data**

P 2. Enterprises, Inc., manufactures several lines of small machinery. Before the company installed automated equipment, the total delivery cycle time for its Coin machine models averaged about three weeks. Last year, management decided to purchase a new computer-integrated manufacturing system for the Coin line. The following is a summary of operating data for the past eight weeks for the Coin line:

	Week							
	1	2	3	4	5	6	7	8
Average process time (hours)	7.20	7.20	7.10	7.40	7.60	7.20	6.80	6.60
Average setup time (hours)	2.20	2.20	2.10	1.90	1.90	1.80	2.00	1.90
Customer complaints	5	6	4	7	6	8	9	9
Delivery time (hours)	36.20	37.40	37.20	36.40	35.90	35.80	34.80	34.20
Equipment utilization rate (%)	98.10	98.20	98.40	98.10	97.80	97.60	97.80	97.80
Machine downtime (hours)	82.30	84.20	85.90	84.30	83.40	82.20	82.80	80.40
Machine maintenance time (hours)	50.40	52.80	49.50	46.40	47.20	45.80	44.80	42.90
On-time deliveries (%)	92.40	92.50	93.20	94.20	94.40	94.10	95.80	94.60
Production backlog (units)	15,230	15,440	15,200	16,100	14,890	13,560	13,980	13,440
Production cycle time (hours)	12.20	12.60	11.90	11.80	12.20	11.60	11.20	10.60
Purchase-order lead time (hours)	26.20	26.80	26.50	25.90	25.70	25.30	24.80	24.20
Warranty claims	2	2	3	2	3	4	3	3

Required

1. Analyze the performance of the Coin machine line for the eight-week period. Focus on performance in the following areas. Carry your answers to two decimal places.
   a. Production performance
   b. Delivery cycle time, including computations of delivery cycle time and waste time
   c. Customer satisfaction
2. Summarize your findings in a report to the company's president, Wilhem Devore.

LO2 **Costs of Quality**

P 3. Karen Setten, regional manager of Heavenly Pies, is evaluating the performance of four pie kitchens in her region. In accordance with the company's costs-of-quality standards of performance, the four locations provided these data for the past six months:

	Aspen	Basalt	Frisco	Dillon
Sales	$1,800,000	$1,500,000	$1,400,000	$1,200,000
Prevention costs	$ 32,000	$ 48,000	$ 16,000	$ 20,000
Appraisal costs	42,000	32,000	18,000	25,000
Internal failure costs	24,000	21,000	42,000	30,000
External failure costs	3,000	16,000	45,000	5,000
Total costs of quality	$ 131,000	$ 117,000	$ 121,000	$ 100,000

Required

1. For each location, compute the percentages of sales represented by prevention costs, appraisal costs, total costs of conformance, internal failure costs, external failure costs, total costs of nonconformance, and total costs of quality. Carry your answers to two decimal places.
2. For each location, calculate the ratio of costs of conformance to costs of quality and the ratio of costs of nonconformance to costs of quality.

Manager insight ▶ 3. Interpret the cost-of-quality data for each location. Rank the locations in terms of quality.

LO2 LO3 **Interpreting Measures of Quality**

P 4. Watts Corporation supplies electronic circuitry to major appliance manufacturers in all parts of the world. Producing a high-quality product in each of the company's four divisions is the mission of management. Each division is required to record and report its efforts to achieve quality in all of its primary product lines. The following information for the most recent three-month period was submitted to the chief financial officer:

	Glenwood Division		Lakes Division		Springs Division		Gilman Division	
	Amount	% of Revenue	Amount	% of Revenue	Amount	% of Revenue	Amount	% of Revenue
Costs of Quality								
Costs of Conformance								
Prevention costs:								
Quality training of employees	$ 4,400		$ 15,600		$ 23,600		$ 8,900	
Process engineering	3,100		19,700		45,900		9,400	
Preventive maintenance	5,800		14,400		13,800		11,100	
Total prevention costs	$ 13,300	0.95%	$ 49,700	3.11%	$ 83,300	5.55%	$ 29,400	1.73%

(*continued*)

	Glenwood Division		Lakes Division		Springs Division		Gilman Division	
	Amount	% of Revenue	Amount	% of Revenue	Amount	% of Revenue	Amount	% of Revenue
Appraisal costs:								
End-of-process sampling and testing	$ 3,500		$ 19,500		$ 21,400		$ 6,900	
Quality audits of products	6,100		11,900		17,600		8,700	
Vendor audits	4,100		10,100		9,800		7,300	
Total appraisal costs	$ 13,700	0.98%	$ 41,500	2.59%	$ 48,800	3.25%	$ 22,900	1.35%
Total costs of conformance	$ 27,000	1.93%	$ 91,200	5.70%	$132,100	8.80%	$ 52,300	3.08%
Costs of Nonconformance								
Internal failure costs:								
Quality-related downtime	$ 26,800		$ 8,300		$ 6,500		$ 22,600	
Scrap and rework	17,500		9,100		7,800		16,200	
Scrap disposal losses	31,200		7,200		3,600		19,900	
Total internal failure costs	$ 75,500	5.39%	$ 24,600	1.54%	$ 17,900	1.19%	$ 58,700	3.45%
External failure costs:								
Warranty claims	$ 22,600		$ 4,400		$ 2,500		$ 17,100	
Customer complaint processing	31,600		8,100		6,400		22,300	
Returned goods	29,900		5,600		3,100		19,800	
Total external failure costs	$ 84,100	6.01%	$ 18,100	1.13%	$ 12,000	0.80%	$ 59,200	3.48%
Total costs of nonconformance	$159,600	11.40%	$ 42,700	2.67%	$ 29,900	1.99%	$117,900	6.93%
Total costs of quality	$186,600	13.33%	$133,900	8.37%	$162,000	10.79%	$170,200	10.01%

Ratios of Nonfinancial Measures:	Glenwood Division	Lakes Division	Springs Division	Gilman Division
Number of sales to number of warranty claims	168 to 1	372 to 1	996 to 1	225 to 1
Number of products produced to number of products reworked	1,420 to 1	3,257 to 1	6,430 to 1	2,140 to 1
Change in throughput time (positive amount means time reduction)	(−4.615%)	2.163%	5.600%	(−1.241%)
Total number of deliveries to number of late deliveries	86 to 1	168 to 1	290 to 1	128 to 1

Required

1. Rank the divisions in order of their apparent product quality.
2. What three measures were most important in your rankings in **1**? Why?
3. Which division is most successful in its bid to improve quality? What measures illustrate its high-quality rating?

Manager insight ▶ 4. Consider the two divisions producing the lowest-quality products. What actions would you recommend to the management of each division? Where should their quality dollars be spent?

Alternate Problems

LO2 Costs and Nonfinancial Measures of Quality

P 5. The Janelle Company operates as three autonomous divisions. Each division has a general manager in charge of product development, production, and distribution. Management recently adopted total quality management, and the divisions now track, record, and analyze their costs and nonfinancial measures of quality. All three divisions are operating in highly competitive marketplaces. Sales and quality-related data for April are summarized below.

	East Division	Central Division	West Division
Annual sales	$8,500,000	$9,500,000	$13,000,000
Costs of quality			
Field testing	$ 51,600	$ 112,800	$ 183,950
Quality audits	17,200	79,100	109,650
Failure analysis	103,100	14,700	92,700
Quality training of employees	60,200	188,000	167,700
Scrap and rework	151,000	18,800	154,800
Quality-certified suppliers	34,400	94,000	108,200
Preventive maintenance	65,800	148,000	141,900
Warranty claims	107,500	42,300	106,050
Customer complaint processing	151,500	108,100	154,800
Process engineering	94,600	235,000	232,200
End-of-process sampling and testing	24,700	178,600	141,900
Scrap disposal losses	77,400	23,500	64,500
Returned goods	152,500	16,200	45,150
Product recalls	64,500	32,900	64,500
Total costs of quality	$1,156,000	$1,292,000	$ 1,768,000
Nonfinancial measures of quality			
Defective parts per million	3,410	1,104	1,940
Returned orders	7.40%	1.10%	3.20%
Customer complaints	62	12	30
Number of warranty claims	74	16	52

Required

1. Prepare an analysis of the costs of quality for the three divisions. Categorize the costs as (a) costs of conformance, with subsets of prevention costs and appraisal costs, or (b) costs of nonconformance, with subsets of internal failure costs and external failure costs. Compute the total costs for each category for each division.

2. For each division, compute the percentage of sales represented by prevention costs, appraisal costs, total costs of conformance, internal failure costs, external failure costs, total costs of nonconformance, and total costs of quality.
3. Interpret the cost-of-quality data for each division. Is each division's product of high or low quality? Explain your answers. Are the divisions headed in the right direction to be competitive?

Manager insight ▶

4. Evaluate the nonfinancial measures of quality in terms of customer satisfaction. Are the results consistent with your analysis in requirement 3? Explain your answers.

LO2 LO3 **Analysis of Nonfinancial Data**

P 6. Park Electronics Company is known for its high-quality products and on-time deliveries. Six months ago, it installed a computer-integrated manufacturing system in its Sensitive Components Department. The new equipment produces the entire component, so the finished product is ready to be shipped when needed. During the past eight-week period, the controller's staff gathered the data that appear below.

	Week							
	1	2	3	4	5	6	7	8
Average process time (hours)	10.90	11.10	10.60	10.80	11.20	11.80	12.20	13.60
Average setup time (hours)	2.50	2.60	2.60	2.80	2.70	2.40	2.20	2.20
Customer complaints	11	10	23	15	9	7	5	6
Delivery time (hours)	26.20	26.40	26.10	25.90	26.20	26.60	27.10	26.40
Equipment utilization rate (%)	96.20	96.10	96.30	97.20	97.40	96.20	96.40	95.30
Machine downtime (hours)	106.40	108.10	120.20	110.40	112.80	102.20	124.60	136.20
Machine maintenance time (hours)	64.80	66.70	72.60	74.20	76.80	66.60	80.40	88.20
On-time deliveries (%)	97.20	97.50	97.60	98.20	98.40	96.40	94.80	92.60
Production backlog (units)	10,246	10,288	10,450	10,680	10,880	11,280	11,350	12,100
Production cycle time (hours)	16.50	16.40	16.30	16.10	16.30	17.60	19.80	21.80
Purchase-order lead time (hours)	15.20	15.10	14.90	14.60	14.60	13.20	12.40	12.60
Warranty claims	4	8	2	1	6	4	2	3

Required

1. Analyze the performance of the Sensitive Components Department for the eight-week period. Focus on performance in the following areas: (a) production performance, (b) delivery cycle time (include computations of delivery cycle time and waste time), and (c) customer satisfaction. Carry your answers to two decimal places.
2. Summarize your findings in a report to the department's superintendent, André Park.

LO2 **Costs of Quality**

P 7. Creed Napier, the regional manager of E-Taxes, Inc., is evaluating the performance of four ecommerce tax preparation sites in her region. The following data for the past six months were presented to her by each site in accordance with the company's costs-of-quality standards of performance:

	Small Business Portal	Big Business Portal	Self-Employed Portal	Partnership Portal
Sales	$5,000,000	$10,000,000	$8,000,000	$6,000,000
Prevention costs	$ 62,000	$ 58,000	$ 16,000	$ 20,000
Appraisal costs	32,000	42,000	28,000	15,000
Internal failure costs	54,000	31,000	32,000	40,000
External failure costs	3,000	26,000	55,000	35,000
Total costs of quality	$ 171,000	$ 157,000	$ 131,000	$ 110,000

Required

1. For each site, compute the percentages of sales represented by prevention costs, appraisal costs, total costs of conformance, internal failure costs, external failure costs, total costs of nonconformance, and total costs of quality.
2. For each site, calculate the ratio of costs of conformance to costs of quality and the ratio of costs of nonconformance to costs of quality.

Manager insight ▶ 3. Interpret the cost-of-quality data for each site. Rank the sites in terms of quality.

LO2 LO3 Interpreting Measures of Quality

P 8. Travis Corporation has five divisions, each manufacturing a product line that competes in the global marketplace. The company is planning to compete for the Malcolm Baldrige Award, so management requires that each division record and report its efforts to achieve quality in its product line. The information below was submitted to the company's controller for the most recent six-month period.

	Division A	Division B	Division C	Division D	Division E
Total Revenue	$886,000	$1,040,000	$956,000	$1,225,000	$1,540,000
Costs of Quality					
Customer complaint processing	$ 10,400	$ 12,600	$ 12,300	$ 10,100	$ 15,600
Scrap and rework	26,800	13,500	38,700	11,900	34,800
Quality audits of products	13,600	28,400	6,300	25,600	11,700
Returned goods	18,700	11,400	38,400	11,300	36,000
Warranty claims	21,100	6,400	36,200	6,500	42,600
Quality training of employees	8,900	12,600	4,600	11,400	4,200
Preventive maintenance	11,300	18,700	8,300	13,600	6,300
Failure analysis	34,800	9,800	46,900	10,200	56,900
Inspection of materials	12,500	18,700	7,800	17,500	5,600
Nonfinancial Measures of Quality					
Number of warranty claims versus	22	12	46	12	62
number of sales	6,500	8,900	7,200	9,800	9,600
Number of products reworked versus	150	140	870	70	900
number of products manufactured	325,000	456,000	365,000	450,000	315,600
Throughput time in hours versus	6.20	8.50	6.80	9.20	11.60

Required

1. Prepare an analysis of the costs of quality for each division. Categorize the costs as costs of conformance or costs of nonconformance. Carry your answers to two decimal places.

2. For each division, compute the percentage of total revenue for each of the four cost-of-quality categories and the ratios for the nonfinancial data.
3. Rank the divisions in order of their apparent product quality.

Manager insight ▶ 4. What three measures were most important in your rankings in requirement **3**? Why?
5. Which division has been most successful in its bid to improve quality? What measures illustrate its high quality rating?
6. Consider the two divisions producing the lowest-quality products. What actions would you recommend to the management of each division? Where should their quality dollars be spent?

ENHANCING Your Knowledge, Skills, and Critical Thinking

LO1 **MIS and Ethics**

C 1. Three months ago, Maxwell Enterprises hired a consultant, Stacy Slone, to assist in the design and installation of a new management information system for the company. Mike Cams, one of Maxwell's systems design engineers, was assigned to work with Slone on the project. During the three-month period, Slone and Cams met six times and developed a tentative design and installation plan for the MIS. Before the plan was to be unveiled to top management, Cams asked his supervisor, Todd Bowman, to look it over and comment on the design.

Included in the plan was the consolidation of three engineering functions into one. Both of the supervisors of the other two functions had seniority over Bowman, so he believed that the design would lead to his losing his management position. He communicated this to Cams and ended his comments with the following statement: "If you don't redesign the system to accommodate all three of the existing engineering functions, I will give you an unsatisfactory performance evaluation for this year!"

How should Cams respond to Bowman's assertion? Should he handle the problem alone, keeping it inside the company, or communicate the comment to Slone? Outline Carns's options, and be prepared to discuss them in class.

LO2 LO3 **Evaluating Performance Measures**

C 2. Ahern Company and Siedle Company compete in the same industry. Each company is located in a large midwestern city, and each employs between 300 and 350 people. Both companies have adopted a total quality management approach, and both want to improve their ability to compete in the marketplace. They have installed common performance measures to help track their quest for quality and a competitive advantage.

During the most recent three-month period, Ahern Company and Siedle Company generated the data that follow.

Performance Measures	Ahern Company Financial	Ahern Company Nonfinancial	Siedle Company Financial	Siedle Company Nonfinancial
Production performance				
Equipment utilization rate		89.4%		92.1%
Machine downtime (in machine hours)		720		490
Delivery cycle time				
On-time deliveries		92.1%		96.5%
Purchase-order lead time (hours)		17		18
Production cycle time (hours)		14		16
Waste time (hours)		3		2
Customer satisfaction				
Customer complaints		28		24
Scrap and rework costs	$14,390		$13,680	
Field service costs	9,240		7,700	

1. For each measure, indicate which company has the better performance.
2. Which company is more successful in achieving a total quality environment and an improved competitive position? Explain your answer.

LO2 LO3 **Reports on Quality Data**

C 3. Jim Macklin is chief executive officer of Red Cliff Machinery, Inc. The company adopted a JIT operating environment five years ago. Since then, each segment of the company has been converted, and a complete computer-integrated manufacturing system operates in all parts of the company's five plants. Processing of Red Cliff Machinery's products now averages less than four days once the materials have been put into production.

Macklin is worried about customer satisfaction and has asked you, as the controller, for some advice and help. He has also asked the Marketing Department to perform a quick survey of customers to determine weak areas in customer relations. Here is a summary of four customers' replies:

Customer A: Customer for five years; waits an average of six weeks for delivery; located 1,200 miles from plant; returns an average of 3 percent of products; receives 90 percent on-time deliveries; never hears from sales person after placing order; likes quality or would go with competitor.

Customer B: Customer for seven years; waits an average of five weeks for delivery; orders usually sit in backlog for at least three weeks; located 50 miles from plant; returns about 5 percent of products; receives 95 percent on-time deliveries; has great rapport with sales person; sales person is why this customer is loyal.

Customer C: Customer for twelve years; waits an average of seven weeks for delivery; located 1,500 miles from plant; returns about 4 percent of products; receives 92 percent on-time deliveries; sales person is available but of little help in getting faster delivery; customer is thinking about dealing with another source for its product needs.

Customer D: Customer for fifteen years; very pleased with company's product; waits almost five weeks for delivery; located 120 miles from plant; returns only 2 percent of goods received; rapport with sales person is very good; follow-up service of sales person is excellent; would like delivery cycle time reduced to equal that of competitors; usually deals with three-week backlog.

1. Identify the areas of concern, and give at least three examples of reports that will help managers improve the company's response to customer needs.
2. Assume that you are asked to write a report that will provide information about customer satisfaction. In preparation for writing the report, answer the following questions:
   a. What kinds of information do you need to prepare this report?
   b. Why is this information relevant?
   c. Where would you find this information (i.e., what sources would you use)?
   d. When would you want to obtain this information?

LO4 Quality Measures and Techniques

C 4. **Motorola's** Total Customer Satisfaction (TCS) Teams are cross-functional teams that use customer-focused methods to solve quality and process problems. According to Motorola's website, one TCS Team success story involved an international supplier with quality and delivery problems. These problems required additional order expediting and rework and were causing customer dissatisfaction. The TCS Team's report to management disclosed the following:

- By evaluating and revising the product's design with input from the international supplier, the team created a more robust finished product.
- The team's adoption of process capability studies, together with continuous monitoring, resulted in improved quality for the international supplier.
- When sourcing was moved to a local supplier, the number of times the inventory turned over annually improved. It went from 26 to 52 times a year.
- Over the three-year life of the product, the team's changes resulted in $831,438 in cost savings.

1. From the TCS Team's report, identify the key issues involved in solving the international supplier's quality and process problems.
2. How could the team have applied the process-based techniques of benchmarking and process mapping to improve quality?

LO4 Cookie Company (Continuing Case)

C 5. In this chapter, in preparation for developing a website for your company, you will compare the quality of cookie manufacturers' websites. Visit three sites from the following list:

- www.CherylandCo.com
- www.DavidsCookies.com
- www.famous-amos.com
- www.Gojigourmet.com
- www.MrsFields.com

What features does each site offer its customers? Do the sites offer both pre- and post-sale assistance? In your opinion, how have these websites affected the way cookies are sold? What features will your company's website have?

CHAPTER

28

Financial Analysis of Performance

The Management Process

PLAN

▷ **Prepare forward-looking financial statements based on budgets and forecasts.**

PERFORM

▷ **Prepare financial statements.**

EVALUATE

▷ **Apply analysis tools and techniquesto the financial statements.**

▷ **Assess financial performance using various objectives and standards of comparison.**

REPORT

▷ **Publish financial statements and management analyses.**

Comparisons within and across financial statements help managers assess financial performance.

The purpose of financial reporting is to communicate to creditors, investors, and other interested parties the financial results of a business in a useful and understandable way. The fundamental responsibility for reporting those financial results rests with the business's management. When the financial statements are published in quarterly or annual reports, managers are required to analyze and discuss company performance results. External parties use these unaudited manager insights along with the audited financial statements to evaluate a company's financial performance and judge management effectiveness. Because financial measures play a key role in executive compensation, there is always the risk that they will be manipulated. External users of financial statements therefore need to be familiar with the analytical tools and techniques used in financial performance analysis and the assumptions that underlie them.

LEARNING OBJECTIVES

LO1 Describe the objectives, standards of comparison, sources of information, and compensation issues in measuring financial performance. (pp. 1272–1279)

LO2 Apply horizontal analysis, trend analysis, vertical analysis, and ratio analysis to financial statements. (pp. 1279–1286)

LO3 Apply ratio analysis to financial statements in a comprehensive evaluation of a company's financial performance. (pp. 1287–1294)

DECISION POINT ▸ A MANAGER'S FOCUS STARBUCKS CORPORATION

- ▸ What standards should be used to evaluate Starbucks' performance?
- ▸ What analytical tools are available to measure performance?
- ▸ How successful has the company's management been in creating value for shareholders?

Formed in 1985, **Starbucks** is today the world's leading roaster and retailer of specialty coffee. The company purchases and roasts whole coffee beans and sells them, along with a variety of freshly brewed coffees and other beverages, food items, and coffee-related merchandise, in its retail shops. It also produces and sells bottled coffee drinks, a line of premium ice creams, and, most recently, instant coffee products. Starbucks is one of the most recognized and respected brands in the world.

Like many other companies, Starbucks uses financial performance measures, primarily earnings per share, in determining compensation for top management. Earnings per share and some of the measures that drive earnings per share appear in the company's annual report and are shown in the Financial Highlights below.[1] By linking compensation to financial performance, Starbucks provides its executives with incentive to improve the company's performance. Compensation and financial performance are thus linked to increasing shareholders' value.

STARBUCKS' FINANCIAL HIGHLIGHTS
(In millions, except profit margin and earnings per share)

	2008	2007	2006	2005
Net revenues	$10,383.0	$9,411.5	$7,786.9	$6,369.3
Net earnings	$315.5	$672.6	$564.3	$494.4
Profit margin	3.0%	7.1%	7.2%	7.8%
Earnings per share—basic	$0.43	$0.90	$0.74	$0.63

Foundations of Financial Performance Measurement

LO1 Describe the objectives, standards of comparison, sources of information, and compensation issues in measuring financial performance.

Financial performance measurement, also called *financial statement analysis*, uses all the techniques available to show how important items in a company's financial statements relate to the company's financial objectives. Persons with a strong interest in measuring a company's financial performance fall into two groups:

1. A company's top managers, who set and strive to achieve financial performance objectives; middle-level managers of business processes; and lower-level employees who own stock in the company
2. Creditors and investors, as well as customers who have cooperative agreements with the company

Financial Performance Measurement: Management's Objectives

All the strategic and operating plans that management formulates to achieve a company's goals must eventually be stated in terms of financial objectives. A primary objective is to increase the wealth of the company's stockholders, but this objective must be divided into categories. A complete financial plan should have financial objectives and related performance objectives in all the following categories:

Financial Objective	*Performance Objective*
Liquidity	The company must be able to pay bills when due and meet unexpected needs for cash.
Profitability	It must earn a satisfactory net income.
Long-term solvency	It must be able to survive for many years.
Cash flow adequacy	It must generate sufficient cash through operating, investing, and financing activities.
Market strength	It must be able to increase stockholders' wealth.

One of management's primary responsibilities is to achieve the company's financial objectives. This requires:

- Monitoring key financial performance measures constantly for each objective listed above.
- Determining the cause of any deviations from the measures, and taking corrective action.
- Comparing actual performance with the key performance measures in monthly, quarterly, and annual reports.
- Providing information and data for long-term trend analyses.

Managers communicate financial plans, risks, and results on the company website, in published reports, and in press releases. Many of these reports are required by the Securities and Exchange Commission (SEC) for publicly traded companies. They are public documents and can be viewed by anyone.

Financial Performance Measurement: Creditors' and Investors' Objectives

Creditors and investors use financial performance evaluation to judge a company's past performance and present position. They also use it to assess a company's future potential and the risk connected with acting on that potential.

- An investor focuses on a company's potential earnings ability because that ability will affect the market price of the company's stock and the amount of dividends the company will pay.
- A creditor focuses on the company's potential debt-paying ability.

Past performance is often a good indicator of future performance. To evaluate a company's past performance, creditors and investors look at trends in past sales, expenses, net income, cash flow, and return on investment. To evaluate its current position, they look at its assets, liabilities, cash position, debt in relation to equity, and levels of inventories and receivables. Knowing a company's past performance and current position can be important in judging its future potential and the related risk. The risk involved in making an investment or loan depends on how easy it is to predict future profitability or liquidity.

- In return for taking a greater risk, investors often look for a higher expected return (an increase in market price plus dividends).
- Creditors who take a greater risk by advancing funds to a new company may demand a higher interest rate and more assurance of repayment (a secured loan, for instance). The higher interest rate reimburses them for assuming the higher risk.

Standards of Comparison

When analyzing financial statements, decision makers must judge whether the relationships they find in the statements are favorable or unfavorable. Three standards of comparison that they commonly use are rule-of-thumb measures, a company's past performance, and industry norms.

Rule-of-Thumb Measures Many managers, financial analysts, investors, and lenders apply general standards, or rule-of-thumb measures, to key financial ratios. For example, most analysts today agree that a current ratio (current assets divided by current liabilities) of 2:1 is acceptable.

In its *Industry Norms and Key Business Ratios*, the credit-rating firm of Dun & Bradstreet offers such rules of thumb as the following:

- ***Current debt to tangible net worth***: A business is usually in trouble when this relationship exceeds 80 percent.
- ***Inventory to net working capital***: Ordinarily, this relationship should not exceed 80 percent.

Although rule-of thumb measures may suggest areas that need further investigation, there is no proof that the levels they specify apply to all companies. A company with a current ratio higher than 2:1 may have a poor credit policy (causing accounts receivable to be too large), too much inventory, or poor cash management. Another company may have a ratio lower than 2:1 but still have excellent management in all three of those areas. Thus, rule-of-thumb measures must be used with caution.

> **Study Note**
> Rules of thumb evolve and change as the business environment changes. Not long ago, an acceptable current ratio was higher than today's 2:1.

Past Performance Comparing financial measures or ratios of the same company over time is an improvement over using rule-of-thumb measures. Such a comparison gives the analyst some basis for judging whether the measure or ratio is getting better or worse. Thus, it may be helpful in showing future trends. However, trends reverse at times, so such projections must be made with care.

Another problem with analyzing trends is that past performance may not be enough to meet a company's present needs. For example, even though a company improves its return on investment from 3 percent in one year to 4 percent the next year, the 4 percent return may not be adequate for the company's current needs. In addition, using a company's past performance as a standard of comparison is not helpful in judging its performance relative to that of other companies.

Industry Norms Using industry norms as a standard of comparison overcomes some of the limitations of comparing a company's measures or ratios over time. Industry norms show how a company compares with other companies in the same industry. For example, if companies in a particular industry have an average rate of return on investment of 8 percent, a 3 or 4 percent rate of return is probably not adequate. Industry norms can also be used to judge trends. Suppose that because of a downturn in the economy, a company's profit margin dropped from 12 percent to 10 percent, while the average drop in profit margin of other companies in the same industry was from 12 to 4 percent. By this standard, the company would have done relatively well. Sometimes, instead of industry averages, data for the industry leader or a specific competitor are used for analysis.

Using industry norms as a standard of comparison has three limitations:

1. Companies in the same industry may not be strictly comparable. For example, consider two companies in the oil industry. One purchases oil products and markets them through service stations. The other, an international company, discovers, produces, refines, and markets its own oil products. Because of the disparity in their operations, these two companies cannot be directly compared.
2. Many large companies have multiple segments and operate in more than one industry. Some of these **diversified companies**, or *conglomerates*, operate in many unrelated industries. The individual segments of a diversified company generally have different rates of profitability and different degrees of risk. In analyzing a diversified company's consolidated financial statements, it is often impossible to use industry norms as a standard because there simply are no comparable companies.

   ▶ The FASB provides a partial solution to this problem. It requires diversified companies to report profit or loss, certain revenue and expense items, and assets for each of their segments. Segment information may be

FOCUS ON BUSINESS PRACTICE

Look Carefully at the Numbers

In recent years, companies have increasingly used pro forma statements—statements as they would appear without certain items—as a way of presenting a better picture of their operations than would be the case in reports prepared under GAAP. In one quarter, **Amazon.com** reported a "pro forma net" loss of $76 million; under GAAP, its net loss was $234 million. Pro forma statements, which are unaudited, have come to mean whatever a company's management wants them to mean. As a result, the SEC has issued new rules that prohibit companies from giving more prominence to non-GAAP measures and from using terms that are similar to GAAP measures.[2] Nevertheless, companies still report pro forma results. A common practice of companies such as **Google**, **eBay**, and **Starbucks** is to provide in the notes to the financial statements income as it would be without the expense related to compensation for stock options.[3] Analysts should rely exclusively on financial statements that are prepared using GAAP and that are audited by an independent CPA.

reported for operations in different industries or different geographical areas, or for major customers.[4]

- Exhibit 28-1 shows how **Starbucks** reports data on sales, income, and assets for its United States, International, and Global Consumer Products Group (CPG) segments.
- These data allow the analyst to compute important profitability performance measures, such as profit margin, asset turnover, and return on assets, for each segment and to compare them with the appropriate industry norms.

3. Another limitation of industry norms is that even when companies in the same industry have similar operations, they may use different acceptable accounting procedures. For example, they may use different methods of valuing inventories and different methods of depreciating assets.

Study Note

Each segment of a diversified company represents an investment that the home office or parent company evaluates and reviews frequently.

Despite these limitations, if little information about a company's past performance is available, industry norms probably offer the best available standards for judging current performance—as long as they are used with care.

Sources of Information

The major sources of information about public corporations are reports published by the corporations themselves, reports filed with the SEC, business periodicals, and credit and investment advisory services.

Reports Published by the Corporation A public corporation's annual report is an important source of financial information. Management is responsible for publishing these reports. From a financial analyst's perspective, the main parts of an annual report are management's analysis of the past year's operations; the financial statements; the notes to the financial statements, which include a summary of significant accounting policies; the auditors' report; and financial highlights for a five- or ten-year period.

Most public corporations also publish **interim financial statements** each quarter and sometimes each month. These reports, which present limited information in the form of condensed financial statements, are not subject to a full audit by an independent auditor. The financial community watches interim statements closely for early signs of change in a company's earnings trend.

Reports Filed with the SEC Public corporations in the United States must file annual reports, quarterly reports, and current reports with the Securities and Exchange Commission (SEC). If they have more than $10 million in assets and more than 500 shareholders, they must file these reports electronically at *www.sec.gov/edgar.shtml*, where anyone can access them free of charge.

- Form 10-K: The SEC requires companies to file their annual reports on a standard form, called Form 10-K. Form 10-K contains more information than a company's annual report and is therefore a valuable source of information. Analysis and comments made by Starbuck's management in their Form 10-K are referenced throughout this chapter.
- Form 10-Q: Companies file their quarterly reports with the SEC on Form 10-Q. This report presents important facts about interim financial performance.
- Form 8-K: The current report, which is filed on Form 8-K, must be submitted to the SEC within a few days of the date of certain significant events, such as the sale or purchase of a division or a change in auditors. The current report is often the first indicator of significant changes that will affect a company's financial performance in the future.

EXHIBIT 28-1 Selected Segment Information for Starbucks Corporation

	United States	International	Global CPG	Unallocated Corporate	Total
(Dollar amounts in millions)					
Fiscal 2008:					
Net Revenues:					
Company-operated retail	$6,997.7	$1,774.2	$ —	$ —	$ 8,771.9
Specialty:					
Licensing	504.2	274.8	392.6	—	1,171.6
Foodservice and other	385.1	54.4	—	—	439.5
Total specialty	889.3	329.2	392.6	—	1,611.1
Total net revenues	7,887.0	2,103.4	392.6	—	10,383.0
Depreciation and amortization	401.7	108.8	—	38.8	549.3
Income (loss) from equity investees	(1.3)	54.2	60.7	—	113.6
Operating income/(loss)	528.1	110.0	205.3	(339.5)	503.9
Earnings/(loss) before income taxes	541.6	119.4	205.3	(406.8)	459.5
Equity method investments	(0.5)	223.6	44.8	—	267.9
Identifiable assets	2,362.9	1,272.7	116.0	1,921.0	5,672.6
Net impairment and disposition losses	275.1	19.0	—	30.9	325.0
Net capital expenditures	534.7	253.6	—	196.2	984.5
Fiscal 2007:					
Net Revenues:					
Company-operated retail	$6,560.9	$1,437.4	$ —	$ —	$ 7,998.3
Specialty:					
Licensing	439.1	220.9	366.3	—	1,026.3
Foodservice and other	349.0	37.9	—	—	386.9
Total specialty	788.1	258.8	366.3	—	1,413.2
Total net revenues	7,349.0	1,696.2	366.3	—	9,411.5
Depreciation and amortization	348.2	84.2	—	34.7	467.1
Income from equity investees	0.8	45.7	61.5	—	108.0
Operating income/(loss)	1,070.5	137.7	183.6	(337.9)	1,053.9
Earnings/(loss) before income taxes	1,079.7	147.2	183.6	(354.2)	1,056.3
Equity method investments	0.8	196.9	36.8	—	234.5
Identifiable assets	2,454.6	1,116.1	91.6	1,681.6	5,343.9
Net impairment and disposition losses	9.3	15.1	—	1.6	26.0
Net capital expenditures	779.2	189.8	—	111.3	1,080.3

Source: Data from Starbucks Corporation, Form 10-K, 2008.

Business Periodicals and Credit and Investment Advisory Services

Financial analysts must keep up with current events in the financial world.

- *Newspapers and magazines:* A leading source of financial news is the *Wall Street Journal.* It is the most complete financial newspaper in the United States and is published every business day. Online subscriptions are also available. Useful print periodicals that are published every week or every two weeks include *Forbes*, *Barron's*, *Fortune*, and the *Financial Times.*

- *Credit and investment advisory services*: The publications of Moody's Investors Service and Standard & Poor's provide details about a company's financial history. Data on industry norms, average ratios, and credit ratings are available from agencies like Dun & Bradstreet. Dun & Bradstreet's *Industry Norms and Key Business Ratios* offers an annual analysis of 14 ratios for each of 125 industry groups, classified as retailing, wholesaling, manufacturing, and construction. *Annual Statement Studies*, published by Risk Management Association (formerly Robert Morris Associates), presents many facts and ratios for 223 different industries. The publications of a number of other agencies are also available for a yearly fee.

An example of specialized financial reporting readily available to the public is *Mergent's Dividend Achievers*. It profiles companies that have increased their dividends consistently over the past ten years. A listing from that publication—for **PepsiCo Inc.**—is presented in Exhibit 28-2. As you can see, a wealth of information about the company, including the market action of its stock, its business operations, recent developments and prospects, and earnings and dividend data, is summarized on one page. We use the kind of data contained in Mergent's summaries in many of the analyses and ratios that we present later in this chapter.

Executive Compensation

As we noted earlier in the text, one purpose of the Sarbanes-Oxley Act of 2002 was to strengthen the corporate governance of public corporations. Under this act, a public corporation's board of directors must establish a **compensation committee** made up of independent directors to determine how the company's top executives will be compensated. The company must disclose the components of compensation and the criteria it uses to remunerate top executives in documents that it files with the SEC.

The components of **Starbucks**' compensation of executive officers are typical of those used by many companies:

- Annual base salary
- Incentive bonuses
- Stock option awards[5]

Incentive bonuses and stock option awards are based on financial performance measures that the compensation committee identifies as important to the company's long-term success. Many companies tie incentive bonuses to measures like growth in revenues and return on assets or return on equity. Starbucks bases 80 percent of its incentive bonus on an "earnings per share target approved by the compensation committee" and 20 percent on the executive's "specific individual performance." The Financial Highlights at the beginning of the chapter show that Starbucks' earnings per share increased from 2005 to 2007, but decreased in 2008.

From one vantage point, earnings per share is a "bottom-line" number that encompasses all the other performance measures. However, using a single performance measure as the basis for determining compensation has the potential of leading to practices that are not in the best interests of the company or its stockholders. For instance, management could boost earnings per share by reducing the number of shares outstanding (the denominator in the earnings per share equation) while not improving earnings. It could accomplish this by using cash to repurchase shares of the company's stock (treasury stock), rather than investing the cash in more profitable operations.

EXHIBIT 28-2 Listing from Mergent's Dividend Achievers

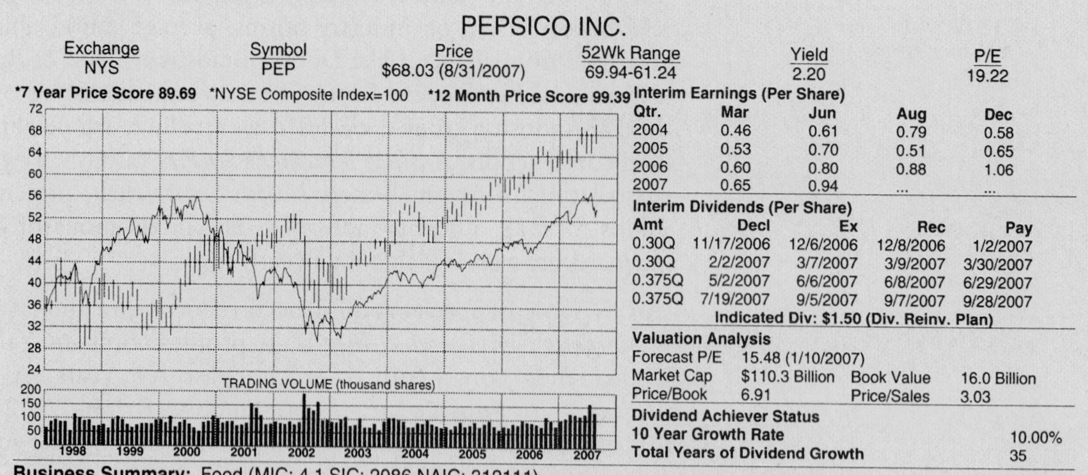

PEPSICO INC.

Exchange	Symbol	Price	52Wk Range	Yield	P/E
NYS	PEP	$68.03 (8/31/2007)	69.94-61.24	2.20	19.22

*7 Year Price Score 89.69 *NYSE Composite Index=100 *12 Month Price Score 99.39

Interim Earnings (Per Share)

Qtr.	Mar	Jun	Aug	Dec
2004	0.46	0.61	0.79	0.58
2005	0.53	0.70	0.51	0.65
2006	0.60	0.80	0.88	1.06
2007	0.65	0.94	...	...

Interim Dividends (Per Share)

Amt	Decl	Ex	Rec	Pay
0.30Q	11/17/2006	12/6/2006	12/8/2006	1/2/2007
0.30Q	2/2/2007	3/7/2007	3/9/2007	3/30/2007
0.375Q	5/2/2007	6/6/2007	6/8/2007	6/29/2007
0.375Q	7/19/2007	9/5/2007	9/7/2007	9/28/2007

Indicated Div: $1.50 (Div. Reinv. Plan)

Valuation Analysis

Forecast P/E	15.48 (1/10/2007)		
Market Cap	$110.3 Billion	Book Value	16.0 Billion
Price/Book	6.91	Price/Sales	3.03

Dividend Achiever Status

10 Year Growth Rate	10.00%
Total Years of Dividend Growth	35

Business Summary: Food (MIC: 4.1 SIC: 2086 NAIC: 312111)

PepsiCo is engaged in manufacturing, marketing and selling a range of salty, sweet and grain-based snacks, carbonated and non-carbonated beverages and foods. Co. is organized into four divisions: Frito-Lay North America (FLNA); PepsiCo Beverages North America (PBNA); PepsiCo International (PI); and Quaker Foods North America (QFNA). FLNA branded snacks include Lay's potato chips, Doritos tortilla chips and Rold Gold pretzels. PBNA's brands include Pepsi, Mountain Dew, Gatorade, Tropicana Pure Premium, and Lipton. PI's brands include Lay's, Walkers, Cheetos, Doritos, Ruffles, Gamesa and Sabritas. QFNA's brands include Quaker oatmeal, Rice-A-Roni and Near East side dishes.

Recent Developments: For the quarter ended June 16 2007, net income increased 13.2% to US$1.56 billion from US$1.38 billion in the year-earlier quarter. Revenues were US$9.61 billion, up 10.2% from US$8.71 billion the year before. Operating income was US$1.96 billion versus US$1.80 billion in the prior-year quarter, an increase of 8.8%. Direct operating expenses rose 12.4% to US$4.34 billion from US$3.86 billion in the comparable period the year before. Indirect operating expenses increased 8.3% to US$3.31 billion from US$3.05 billion in the equivalent prior-year period.

Prospects: Co. is seeing an increase in its net revenue, driven by robust snacks and beverage growth at its PepsiCo International division. Specifically, international snacks volume growth is being driven by double-digit growth in Russia and India, partially offset by low-single-digit declines at Sabritas in Mexico and Walkers in the U.K., while beverage volume growth is being fueled by double-digit growth in Pakistan, Russia, the Middle East and the U.K., partially offset by a mid-single-digit decline in Mexico and a double-digit decline in Thailand. Accordingly, Co. is raising its full year 2007 earnings guidance to at least $3.35 per share.

Financial Data

(US$ in Thousands)	6 Mos	3 Mos	12/30/2006	12/31/2005	12/25/2004	12/27/2003	12/28/2002	12/29/2001
Earnings Per Share	3.54	3.40	3.34	2.39	2.44	2.05	1.85	1.47
Cash Flow Per Share	3.86	3.95	3.70	3.45	2.99	2.53	2.65	2.39
Tang Book Value Per Share	5.71	5.51	5.50	5.20	4.84	3.82	4.93	2.17
Dividends Per Share	1.275	1.200	1.160	1.010	0.850	0.630	0.595	0.575
Dividend Payout %	36.02	35.32	34.73	42.26	34.84	30.73	32.16	39.12
Income Statement								
Total Revenue	16,957,000	7,350,000	35,137,000	32,562,000	29,261,000	26,971,000	25,112,000	26,935,000
EBITDA	4,233,000	1,769,000	8,399,000	7,732,000	6,848,000	6,269,000	6,077,000	5,189,000
Depn & Amortn	608,000	276,000	1,344,000	1,253,000	1,209,000	1,165,000	1,067,000	1,008,000
Income Before Taxes	3,590,000	1,473,000	6,989,000	6,382,000	5,546,000	4,992,000	4,868,000	4,029,000
Income Taxes	937,000	377,000	1,347,000	2,304,000	1,372,000	1,424,000	1,555,000	1,367,000
Net Income	2,653,000	1,096,000	5,642,000	4,078,000	4,212,000	3,568,000	3,313,000	2,662,000
Average Shares	1,665,000	1,673,000	1,687,000	1,706,000	1,729,000	1,739,000	1,789,000	1,807,000
Balance Sheet								
Total Assets	31,925,000	29,830,000	29,930,000	31,727,000	27,987,000	25,327,000	23,474,000	21,695,000
Current Liabilities	7,589,000	7,522,000	6,860,000	9,406,000	6,752,000	6,415,000	6,052,000	4,998,000
Long-Term Obligations	3,261,000	1,807,000	2,550,000	2,313,000	2,397,000	1,702,000	2,187,000	2,651,000
Total Liabilities	16,052,000	14,482,000	14,562,000	17,476,000	14,464,000	13,453,000	14,183,000	13,021,000
Stockholders' Equity	15,956,000	15,429,000	15,447,000	14,320,000	13,572,000	11,896,000	9,298,000	8,648,000
Shares Outstanding	1,621,000	1,631,000	1,638,000	1,656,000	1,679,000	1,705,000	1,722,000	1,756,000
Statistical Record								
Return on Assets %	18.73	18.84	18.35	13.44	15.84	14.66	14.71	13.34
Return on Equity %	37.96	37.90	38.01	28.77	33.17	33.76	37.02	33.58
EBITDA Margin %	24.96	24.07	23.90	23.75	23.40	23.24	24.20	19.26
Net Margin %	15.65	14.91	16.06	12.52	14.39	13.23	13.19	9.88
Asset Turnover	1.15	1.16	1.14	1.07	1.10	1.11	1.11	1.35
Current Ratio	1.29	1.16	1.33	1.11	1.28	1.08	1.06	1.17
Debt to Equity	0.20	0.12	0.17	0.16	0.18	0.14	0.24	0.31
Price Range	69.48-58.91	65.91-57.20	65.91-56.77	59.90-51.57	55.55-45.39	48.71-37.30	53.12-35.50	50.28-41.26
P/E Ratio	19.63-16.64	19.39-16.82	19.73-17.00	25.06-21.58	22.77-18.60	23.76-18.20	28.71-19.19	34.20-28.07
Average Yield %	1.99	1.93	1.90	1.82	1.66	1.43	1.29	1.25

Address: 700 Anderson Hill Road, Purchase, NY 10577-1444 **Telephone:** 914-253-2000 **Web Site:** www.pepsico.com	**Officers:** Steven S. Reinemund - Chmn., C.E.O. Indra K. Nooyi - Pres., C.F.O. **Transfer Agents:** The Bank of New York	**Investor Contact:** 914-253-3035 **No of Institutions:** 1292 **Shares:** 1,121,669,888 **% Held:** 68.49

Source: PepsiCo listing from *Mergent's Dividend Achievers Fall 2007: Featuring Second-Quarter Results for 2007.* Reprinted by permission of John Wiley & Sons Inc.

As you study the comprehensive financial analysis of Starbucks in the coming pages, consider that knowledge of performance measurement not only is important for evaluating a company but also leads to an understanding of the criteria by which a board of directors evaluates and compensates management.

STOP & APPLY >

Identify each of the following as (a) an objective of financial statement analysis, (b) a standard for financial statement analysis, (c) a source of information for financial statement analysis, or (d) an executive compensation issue:

1. A company's past performance
2. Investment advisory services
3. Assessment of a company's future potential
4. Incentive bonuses
5. Industry norms
6. Annual report
7. Creating shareholder value
8. Form 10-K

SOLUTION

1. b; 2. c; 3. a; 4. d; 5. b; 6. c; 7. d; 8. c

Tools and Techniques of Financial Analysis

LO2 Apply horizontal analysis, trend analysis, vertical analysis, and ratio analysis to financial statements.

To gain insight into a company's financial performance, one must look beyond the individual numbers to the relationship between the numbers and their change from one period to another. The tools of financial analysis—horizontal analysis, trend analysis, vertical analysis, and ratio analysis—are intended to show these relationships and changes. To illustrate how these tools are used, we devote the rest of this chapter to a comprehensive financial analysis of **Starbucks Corporation**.

Horizontal Analysis

Comparative financial statements provide financial information for the current year and the previous year. To gain insight into year-to-year changes, analysts use **horizontal analysis**, in which changes from the previous year to the current year are computed in both dollar amounts and percentages. The percentage change relates the size of the change to the size of the dollar amounts involved.

Study Note

It is important to ascertain the base amount used when a percentage describes an item. For example, inventory may be 50 percent of total current assets but only 10 percent of total assets.

Exhibits 28-3 and 28-4 present **Starbucks Corporation**'s comparative balance sheets and income statements and show both the dollar and percentage changes. The percentage change is computed as follows:

$$\text{Percentage Change} = 100 \times \left(\frac{\text{Amount of Change}}{\text{Base Year Amount}}\right)$$

The **base year** is always the first year to be considered in any set of data. For example, when comparing data for 2007 and 2008, 2007 is the base year. As the balance sheets in Exhibit 28-3 show, between 2007 and 2008, Starbucks' total current assets increased by $51.5 million, from $1,696.5 million to $1,748.0 million, or by 3.0 percent. This is computed as follows:

$$\text{Percentage Change} = 100 \times \frac{\$51.5 \text{ million}}{\$1{,}696.5 \text{ million}} = 3.0\%$$

EXHIBIT 28-3 Comparative Balance Sheets with Horizontal Analysis

Starbucks Corporation
Consolidated Balance Sheets
September 28, 2008, and September 30, 2007

(Dollar amounts in millions)	2008	2007	Increase (Decrease) Amount	Increase (Decrease) Percentage
		Assets		
Current assets:				
Cash and cash equivalents	$ 269.8	$ 281.3	$ (11.5)	(4.1)
Short-term investments	52.5	157.4	(104.9)	(66.6)
Accounts receivable, net	329.5	287.9	41.6	14.4
Inventories	692.8	691.7	1.1	0.2
Prepaid and other current assets	169.2	148.8	20.4	13.7
Deferred income taxes, net	234.2	129.4	104.8	81.0
Total current assets	$1,748.0	$1,696.5	$ 51.5	3.0
Long-term investments	374.0	279.9	94.1	33.6
Property, plant, and equipment, net	2,956.4	2,890.4	66.0	2.3
Other assets	261.1	219.4	41.7	19.0
Other intangible assets	66.6	42.1	24.5	58.2
Goodwill	266.5	215.6	50.9	23.6
Total assets	$5,672.6	$5,343.9	$328.7	6.2
		Liabilities and Shareholders' Equity		
Current liabilities:				
Commercial paper and short-term borrowings	$ 713.0	$ 710.3	$ 2.7	0.4
Accounts payable	324.9	390.8	(65.9)	(16.9)
Accrued compensation and related costs	253.6	292.4	(38.8)	(13.3)
Accrued occupancy costs	136.1	74.6	61.5	82.4
Accrued taxes	76.1	92.5	(16.4)	(17.7)
Insurance reserves	152.5	137.0	15.5	11.3
Other accrued expenses	164.4	160.3	4.1	2.6
Deferred revenue	368.4	296.9	71.5	24.1
Current portion of long-term debt	0.7	0.8	(0.1)	(12.5)
Total current liabilities	$2,189.7	$2,155.6	$ 34.1	1.6
Long-term debt and other liabilities	992.0	904.2	87.8	9.7
Shareholders' equity	2,490.9	2,284.1	206.8	9.1
Total liabilities and shareholders' equity	$5,672.6	$5,343.9	$328.7	6.2

Source: Data from Starbucks Corporation, Form 10-K, 2008.

When examining such changes, it is important to consider the dollar amount of the change as well as the percentage change in each component. For example, the difference between the percentage increase in goodwill, 23.6 percent, and total current assets, 3.0 percent, is about 20 percent. However, the dollar increase in goodwill is similar to the dollar increase in current assets ($50.9 million versus $51.5 million).

Starbucks' balance sheets for this period, illustrated in Exhibit 28-3, also show an increase in total assets of $328.7 million, or 6.2 percent. In addition,

EXHIBIT 28-4 Comparative Income Statements with Horizontal Analysis

Starbucks Corporation
Consolidated Income Statements
For the Years Ended September 28, 2008, and September 30, 2007

(Dollar amounts in millions except per share amounts)	2008	2007	Increase (Decrease) Amount	Increase (Decrease) Percentage
Net revenues	$10,383.0	$9,411.5	$ 971.5	10.3
Cost of sales, including occupancy costs	4,645.3	3,999.1	646.2	16.2
Gross margin	$ 5,737.7	$5,412.4	$ 325.3	6.0
Operating expenses				
Store operating expenses	$ 3,745.1	$3,215.9	$ 529.2	16.5
Other operating expenses	330.1	294.2	35.9	12.2
Depreciation and amortization expenses	549.3	467.2	82.1	17.6
General and administrative expenses	456.0	489.2	(33.2)	(6.8)
Restructuring charges	266.9	—	266.9	100.0
Total operating expenses	$ 5,347.4	$4,466.5	$ 880.9	19.7
Operating income	$ 390.3	$ 945.9	$(555.6)	(58.7)
Other income, net	122.6	148.4	(25.8)	(17.4)
Interest expense	(53.4)	(38.0)	(15.4)	40.5
Income before taxes	$ 459.5	$1,056.3	$(596.8)	(56.5)
Provision for income taxes	144.0	383.7	(239.7)	(62.5)
Income before cumulative change for FIN 47, net of taxes	$ 315.5	$ 672.6	$(357.1)	(53.1)
Cumulative effect of accounting change for FIN 47, net of taxes	—	—	—	0.0
Net income	$ 315.5	$ 672.6	$(357.1)	(53.1)
Per common share:				
Net income per common share before cumulative effect of change in accounting principle—basic	$ 0.43	$ 0.90	$ (0.47)	(52.2)
Cumulative effect of accounting change for FIN 47, net of taxes	—	—	—	0.0
Net income per common share—basic	$ 0.43	$ 0.90	$ (0.47)	(52.2)
Net income per common share before cumulative effect of change in accounting principle—diluted	$ 0.43	$ 0.87	$ (0.44)	(50.6)
Cumulative effect of accounting change for FIN 47, net of taxes	—	—	—	0.0
Net income per common share—diluted	$ 0.43	$ 0.87	$ (0.44)	(50.6)
Shares used in calculation of net income per common share—basic	731.5	749.8	(18.3)	(2.4)
Shares used in calculation of net income per common share—diluted	741.7	770.1	(28.4)	(3.7)

Source: Data from Starbucks Corporation, Form 10-K, 2008.

they show that shareholders' equity increased by $206.8 million, or 9.1 percent. All of this indicates that Starbucks is a growing company.

Starbucks' income statements in Exhibit 28-4 show that net revenues increased by $971.5 million, or 10.3 percent, while gross margin increased by $325.3 million, or 6.0 percent. This indicates that cost of sales grew faster than net revenues. Starbucks' total operating expenses increased by $880.9 million, or 19.7 percent, much faster than the 10.3 percent increase in net revenues. As a result, operating income declined by $555.6 million, or 58.7 percent, and net income decreased by $357.1 million, or 53.1 percent. In management's words,

> Approximately 260 basis points of the decrease in operating margin was a result of restructuring charges, primarily related to the significant U.S. store closures. Softness in U.S. revenues along with higher cost of sales including occupancy costs and store operating expenses were also significant drivers in the margin decline.[6]

Trend Analysis

Study Note

To reflect the general five-year economic cycle of the U.S. economy, trend analysis usually covers a five-year period. Starbucks analysis shows six years due to the economic downturn in 2008. Cycles of other lengths exist and are tracked by the National Bureau of Economic Research. Trend analysis needs to be of sufficient length to show a company's performance in both up and down markets.

Trend analysis is a variation of horizontal analysis. With this tool, the managers and analysts calculate percentage changes for several successive years instead of for just two years. Because of its long-term view, trend analysis can highlight basic changes in the nature of a business.

In addition to presenting comparative financial statements, many companies present a summary of key data for five or more years. Exhibit 28-5 shows a trend analysis of **Starbucks'** six-year summary of net revenues and operating income.

Trend analysis uses an **index number** to show changes in related items over time. For an index number, the base year is set at 100 percent. Other years are measured in relation to that amount. For example, the 2007 index for Starbucks' net revenues is figured as follows (dollar amounts are in millions):

$$\text{Index} = 100 \times \left(\frac{\text{Index Year Amount}}{\text{Base Year Amount}}\right)$$

$$= 100 \times \left(\frac{\$9{,}411.5}{\$4{,}075.5}\right) = 230.9\%$$

EXHIBIT 28-5
Trend Analysis

Starbucks Corporation
Net Revenues and Operating Income
Trend Analysis

	2008	2007	2006	2005	2004	2003
Dollar values (In millions)						
Net revenues	$10,383.0	$9,411.5	$7,786.9	$6,369.3	$5,294.2	$4,075.5
Operating income	390.3	945.9	800.0	703.9	549.5	386.3
Trend analysis (In percentages)						
Net revenues	254.8	230.9	191.1	156.3	129.9	100.0
Operating income	101.0	244.9	207.1	182.2	142.2	100.0

Source: Data from Starbucks Corporation, Form 10-K, 2008 and Form 10-K, 2007.

The trend analysis in Exhibit 28-5 shows that Starbucks' net revenues increased over the six-year period. Operating income grew faster than net revenues in every year except 2008 when it fell to 2003 levels.

In the words of Starbucks' management,

> We have just completed a very difficult fiscal 2008, and after 16 years of continuous growth as a public company, we were for the first time talking about slowing growth, store closures and cost reductions.[7]

Vertical Analysis

Vertical analysis shows how the different components of a financial statement relate to a total figure in the statement. The manager or analyst sets the total figure at 100 percent and computes each component's percentage of that total. The resulting financial statement, which is expressed entirely in percentages, is called a **common-size statement**. Vertical analysis and common-size statements are useful in comparing the importance of specific components in the operation of a business and in identifying important changes in the components from one year to the next.

Common-size balance sheets and common-size income statements for **Starbucks Corporation** are shown in financial statement form in Exhibits 28-6 and 28-7. (On the balance sheet, the total figure is total assets or total liabilities and stockholders' equity, and on the income statement, it is net revenues.) The main conclusions to be drawn from this analysis of Starbucks are that the company's assets consist largely of current assets and property, plant, and equipment and that the company finances assets primarily through current liabilities and a growing amount of long-term liabilities.

Looking at the common-size balance sheets in Exhibit 28-6, you can see that the composition of Starbucks' assets moved from current assets to long-term investments and goodwill. You can also see that the relationship of liabilities and

EXHIBIT 28-6
Common-Size Balance Sheets

Starbucks Corporation
Common-Size Balance Sheets
September 28, 2008, and September 30, 2007, and October 1, 2006

	2008	2007	2006
Assets			
Current assets	30.8%	31.7%	34.5%
Property, plant, and equipment, net	52.1	54.1	51.7
Long-term investments	6.6	5.2	5.1
Other assets	4.6	4.1	4.2
Goodwill	4.7	4.0	3.6
Other intangible assets	1.2	0.8	0.9
Total assets	100.0%	100.0%	100.0%
Liabilities and Shareholders' Equity			
Current liabilities	38.6	40.3%	43.7%
Long-term debt and other liabilities	17.5	16.9	6.0
Shareholders' equity	43.9	42.7	50.3
Total liabilities and shareholders' equity	100.0%	100.0%	100.0%

Note: Amounts do not precisely total 100 percent in all cases due to rounding.
Source: Data from Starbucks Corporation, Form 10-K, 2008 and Form 10-K, 2007.
Note: Not all items are presented.

EXHIBIT 28-7
Common-Size Income Statements

Starbucks Corporation
Common-Size Income Statements
For the Years Ended September 28, 2008 and September 30, 2007, and October 1, 2006

	2008	**2007**	**2006**
Net revenues	100.0%	100.0%	100.0%
Cost of sales, including occupancy costs	44.7	42.5	40.8
Gross margin	55.3%	57.5%	59.2%
Operating expenses:			
Store operating expenses	36.1%	34.2%	34.5%
Other operating expenses	3.2	3.1	3.3
Depreciation and amortization expenses	5.3	5.0	5.0
General and administrative expenses	4.4	5.2	6.2
Restructuring charges	2.5	—	—
Total operating expenses	51.5%	47.5%	48.9%
Operating income	3.8%	10.1%	10.3%
Other income, net	0.6	1.2	1.4
Income before taxes	4.4%	11.2%	11.6%
Provision for income taxes	1.4	4.1	4.2
Income before cumulative change for FIN 47, net of taxes	3.0%	7.1%	7.5%
Cumulative effect of accounting change for FIN 47, net of taxes	—	—	(0.2)
Net income	3.0%	7.1%	7.2%

Note: Amounts do not precisely total 100 percent in all cases due to rounding.
Source: Data from Starbucks Corporation, Form 10-K, 2008 and Form 10-K, 2007.

equity moved from stockholders' equity and current liabilities to long-term debt and other liabilities. The common-size income statements in Exhibit 28-7 show that Starbucks continues to reduce its general and administrative expenses from 2006 to 2008 while store operating expenses continue to increase. In management's words,

> Starbucks business is highly sensitive to increases and decreases in customer traffic. Increased customer visits create sales leverage, meaning that fixed expenses, such as occupancy costs, are spread across a greater revenue base, thereby improving operating margins. But the reverse is also true—sales deleveraging creates downward pressure on margins. The softness in U.S. revenues during fiscal 2008 impacted nearly all consolidated and U.S. segment operating expense line items when viewed as a percentage of sales.[8]

Common-size statements are often used to make comparisons between companies. They allow managers and analysts to compare the operating and financing characteristics of two companies of different size in the same industry. For example, a Starbuck's manager might want to compare Starbucks with other specialty coffee retailers like **Caribou Coffee** in terms of percentage of total assets financed by debt or in terms of operating expenses as a percentage of net revenues. Common-size statements would show those and other relationships. These statements can also be used to compare the characteristics of companies that report in different currencies.

Ratio Analysis

Ratio analysis identifies key relationships between the components of the financial statements. Ratios are useful tools for evaluating a company's financial position and operations and may reveal areas that need further investigation. To interpret ratios correctly, one must have a general understanding of the company and its environment, financial data for several years or for several companies, and an understanding of the data underlying the numerator and denominator.

Ratios can be expressed in several ways. For example, a ratio of net income of $100,000 to sales of $1,000,000 can be stated as follows:

1. Net income is 1/10, or 10 percent, of sales.
2. The ratio of sales to net income is 10 to 1 (10:1), or sales are 10 times net income.
3. For every dollar of sales, the company has an average net income of 10 cents.

STOP & APPLY >

Using 2007 as the base year, prepare a trend analysis of the following data for Sample Company, and tell whether the situation shown by the trends is favorable or unfavorable. (Round your answers to one decimal place.)

	2011	2010	2009	2008	2007
Net sales	$1,520	$980	$1,200	$880	$1,000
Cost of goods sold	620	600	540	700	600
General and administrative expenses	290	184	188	160	180
Operating income	610	196	472	20	220

Compute the amount and percentage changes for the following balance sheets for Sample Company, and comment on the changes from 2010 to 2011. (Round the percentage changes to one decimal place.)

Sample Company
Comparative Balance Sheets
December 31, 2011 and 2010

	2011	2010
Assets		
Current assets	$ 600	$ 800
Property, plant, and equipment (net)	10,500	7,200
Total assets	$11,100	$8,000
Liabilities and Stockholders' Equity		
Current liabilities	$ 1,200	$ 900
Long-term liabilities	5,000	3,000
Stockholders' equity	4,900	4,100
Total liabilities and stockholders' equity	$11,100	$8,000

(continued)

Express the partial comparative income statements for Sample Company that follow as common-size statements, and comment on the changes from 2010 to 2011. (Round computations to one decimal place.)

Sample Company
Partial Comparative Income Statements
For the Years Ended December 31, 2011 and 2010

	2011	2010
Net sales	$12,000	$10,000
Cost of goods sold	7,200	6,000
Gross margin	$ 4,800	$ 4,000
Selling and general expenses	4,000	3,800
Operating income	$ 800	$ 200

SOLUTION

Trend Analysis Solution

	2011	2010	2009	2008	2007
Net sales	152.0%	98.0%	120.0%	88.0%	100.0%
Cost of goods sold	103.3	100.0	90.0	116.7	100.0
General and administrative expenses	161.1	102.2	104.4	88.9	100.0
Operating income	277.3	89.1	214.5	9.1	100.0

Comment: No clear trends are apparent, as sales, expenses, and operating income fluctuated year to year.

Horizontal Analysis Solution

Sample Company
Comparative Balance Sheets
December 31, 2011 and 2010

	2011	2010	Increase (Decrease) Amount	Increase (Decrease) Percentage
Assets				
Current assets	$ 600	$ 800	$(200)	25.0%
Property, plant, and equipment (net)	10,500	7,200	3,300	45.8
Total assets	$11,100	$8,000	$3,100	38.8%
Liabilities and Stockholders' Equity				
Current liabilities	$ 1,200	$ 900	$ 300	33.3%
Long-term liabilities	5,000	3,000	2,000	66.7
Stockholders' equity	4,900	4,100	800	19.5
Total liabilities and stockholders' equity	$11,100	$8,000	$3,100	38.8%

Comment: All categories increased except for current assets. The largest increase was in long-term liabilities.

Vertical Analysis Solution

Sample Company
Partial Comparative Income Statements
For the Years Ended December 31, 2011 and 2010

	2011	2010
Net sales	100.0%	100.0%
Cost of goods sold	60.0	60.0
Gross margin	40.0%	40.0%
Selling and general expenses	33.3	38.0
Operating income	6.7%	2.0%

Comment: Operating income increased because expenses decreased as a percentage of sales.

Comprehensive Illustration of Ratio Analysis

LO3 Apply ratio analysis to financial statements in a comprehensive evaluation of a company's financial performance.

In this section, to illustrate how managers and analysts use ratio analysis in evaluating a company's financial performance, we perform a comprehensive ratio analysis of **Starbucks**' performance in 2006, 2007, and 2008. Compare the following excerpt from the discussion and analysis section of Starbucks' 2007 annual report with what you have already learned from manager analyses of the 2008 performance. These manager insights provide the context for our evaluation of the company's liquidity, profitability, long-term solvency, cash flow adequacy, and market strength:

> Starbucks achieved solid performance in fiscal 2007—meeting its targets for store openings, revenue growth, comparable store sales growth, and earnings per share—despite a challenging economic and operating environment, and significant cost increases from dairy. The Company completed the fiscal year with encouraging trends and momentum in its International business but faced increasing challenges in its U.S. business. While U.S. comparable store sales were within the Company's stated target range, it was accomplished through two price increases which offset flat-to-negative transaction count trends in the U.S. business. The pressure on traffic is consistent with similar trends reported across both the retail and restaurant industry. Management believes that the combination of the economic slowdown and the price increases implemented in fiscal 2007 to help mitigate significant cost pressures have impacted the frequency of customer visits to Starbucks stores.

Evaluating Liquidity

> **Study Note**
>
> When examining ratios in published sources, be aware that publishers often redefine the content of the ratios provided by the companies. While the general content is similar, variations occur. Be sure to ascertain and evaluate the information that a published source uses to calculate ratios.

As you know, liquidity is a company's ability to pay bills when they are due and to meet unexpected needs for cash. Because debts are paid out of working capital, all liquidity ratios involve working capital or some part of it. (Cash flow ratios are also closely related to liquidity.)

Exhibit 28-8 presents **Starbucks**' liquidity ratios in 2006, 2007, and 2008. The **current ratio** and the **quick ratio** are measures of short-term debt-paying ability. The principal difference between the two ratios is that the numerator of the current ratio includes inventories and prepaid expenses. Inventories take longer to convert to cash than the quick assets included in the numerator of the quick ratio. Starbucks' current ratio remained stable at 0.8 during 2006–2008. Its quick ratio was 0.4 in 2006 and remained stable at 0.3 during 2007 and 2008. These ratios indicate consistent cash management policies by Starbucks.

The **receivable turnover** measures the relative size of accounts receivable and the effectiveness of credit policies. The related ratio of **days' sales uncollected** expresses the average number of days between sales on account and the account payment. Starbucks' receivables appear to be slowing. The receivable turnover continues its trend downward from 37.5 times in 2006 to 36.7 times in 2007 to 33.6 times in 2008. Or, as expressed in days' sales uncollected, it is taking a day longer to collect from customers since 2006. The number of days is quite low because the majority of Starbucks' revenues are from cash sales.

The **inventory turnover** measures the relative size of inventories and generally how many times per year the inventory is restocked. The related ratio of **days' inventory on hand** expresses in general terms how long inventory generally stays on the shelf before it is sold. Starbuck's inventory turnover increased from 5.4 times in 2006 to 6.0 times in 2007 to 6.7 times in 2008. This resulted in a favorable decrease in days' inventory on hand, from 67.6 days in 2006 to 60.8 days in 2007 to 54.5 days in 2008.

The **operating cycle** is the time it takes to acquire and sell products and then to collect for them. It is computed by adding the days' sales uncollected to the

EXHIBIT 28-8 Liquidity Ratios of Starbucks Corporation (Dollar amounts in millions)

	2008	2007	2006
Current ratio: Measure of short-term debt-paying ability			
$\frac{\text{Current Assets}}{\text{Current Liabilities}}$	$\frac{\$1,748.0}{\$2,189.7} = 0.8$ times	$\frac{\$1,696.5}{\$2,155.6} = 0.8$ times	$\frac{\$1,529.8}{\$1,935.6} = 0.8$ times
Quick ratio: Measure of short-term debt-paying ability			
$\frac{\text{Cash + Marketable Securities + Receivables}}{\text{Current Liabilities}}$	$\frac{\$269.8 + \$52.5 + \$329.5}{\$2,189.7}$	$\frac{\$281.3 + \$157.4 + \$287.9}{\$2,155.6}$	$\frac{\$312.6 + \$141.0 + \$224.3}{\$1,935.6}$
	$\frac{\$651.8}{\$2,189.7} = 0.3$ times	$\frac{\$726.6}{\$2,155.6} = 0.3$ times	$\frac{\$677.9}{\$1,935.6} = 0.4$ times
Receivable turnover: Measure of relative size of accounts receivable and effectiveness of credit policies			
$\frac{\text{Net Sales}}{\text{Average Accounts Receivable}}$	$\frac{\$10,383.0}{(\$329.5 + \$287.9) \div 2}$	$\frac{\$9,411.5}{(\$287.9 + \$224.3) \div 2}$	$\frac{\$7,786.9}{(\$224.3 + \$190.8^{*})} \div 2$
	$\frac{\$10,383.0}{\$308.7} = 33.6$ times	$\frac{\$9,411.5}{\$256.1} = 36.7$ times	$\frac{\$7,786.9}{\$207.5} = 37.5$ times
Days' sales uncollected: Measure of average days taken to collect receivables			
$\frac{\text{Days in Year}}{\text{Receivable Turnover}}$	$\frac{365 \text{ days}}{33.6 \text{ times}} = 10.9$ days	$\frac{365 \text{ days}}{36.7 \text{ times}} = 9.9$ days	$\frac{365 \text{ days}}{37.5 \text{ times}} = 9.7$ days
Inventory turnover: Measure of relative size of inventory			
$\frac{\text{Costs of Goods Sold}}{\text{Average Inventory}}$	$\frac{\$4,645.3}{(\$692.8 + \$691.7) \div 2}$	$\frac{\$3,999.1}{(\$691.7 + \$636.2) \div 2}$	$\frac{\$3,178.8}{(\$636.2 + \$546.3^{*}) \div 2}$
	$\frac{\$4,645.3}{\$692.3} = 6.7$ times	$\frac{\$3,999.1}{\$663.9} = 6.0$ times	$\frac{\$3,178.8}{\$591.3} = 5.4$ times
Days' inventory on hand: Measure of average days taken to sell inventory			
$\frac{\text{Days in Year}}{\text{Inventory Turnover}}$	$\frac{365 \text{ days}}{6.7 \text{ times}} = 54.5$ days	$\frac{365 \text{ days}}{6.0 \text{ times}} = 60.8$ days	$\frac{365 \text{ days}}{5.4 \text{ times}} = 67.6$ days
Payables turnover: Measure of relative size of accounts payable			
$\frac{\text{Costs of Goods Sold +/− Change in Inventory}}{\text{Average Accounts Payable}}$	$\frac{\$4,645.3 + \$1.1}{(\$324.9 + \$390.8) \div 2}$	$\frac{\$3,999.1 + \$55.4}{(\$390.8 + \$340.9) \div 2}$	$\frac{\$3,178.8 + \$89.9^{*}}{(\$340.9 + \$221.0) \div 2}$
	= 13.0 times	= 11.1 times	= 11.6 times
Days' payable: Measure of average days taken to pay accounts payable			
$\frac{\text{Days in Year}}{\text{Payables Turnover}}$	$\frac{365 \text{ days}}{13.0 \text{ times}} = 28.1$ days	$\frac{365 \text{ days}}{11.1 \text{ times}} = 32.9$ days	$\frac{365 \text{ days}}{11.6 \text{ times}} = 31.5$ days

*Figures for 2005 are from the balance sheet in Starbucks' Form 10-K, 2006.

Source: Data from Starbucks Corporation, Form 10-K, 2008, Form 10-K, 2007, and Form 10-K, 2006.

days' inventory on hand. Starbucks' operating cycle continues its positive trend primarily because of improving inventory management. It has decreased from 77.3 days in 2006 (9.7 days + 67.6 days) to 70.7 days in 2007 (9.9 days + 60.8 days) to 65.3 days (10.9 days + 54.5 days) in 2008.

Related to the operating cycle is the **payables turnover**, which is the number of days a company takes to pay its accounts payable. The related ratio of **days' payable** expresses the average number of days it takes a company to pay its bills. Starbucks' payables turnover varied from 11.6 times in 2006 to 11.1 times in 2007 to 13.0 times, or, stated in terms of days' payable, it took about 31.5 days in 2006, 32.9 days in 2007, and 28.1 days in 2008 for Starbucks to pay its accounts payables.

If the days' payable is subtracted from the operating cycle, you can determine a company's financing period—the number of days that financing is required. Starbucks' financing period continues to shrink from 45.8 days in 2006 (77.3 days − 31.5 days) to 37.8 days in 2007 (70.7 days − 32.9 days) to 37.2 days (65.3 days − 28.1 days) in 2008. Overall, the company's liquidity improved.

Evaluating Profitability

Study Note

In accounting literature, profit is expressed in different ways—for example, as income before income taxes, income after income taxes, or operating income. To draw appropriate conclusions from profitability ratios, you must be aware of the content of net income data.

Managers, investors, and creditors are interested in evaluating not only a company's liquidity but also its profitability—that is, its ability to earn a satisfactory income. Profitability is closely linked to liquidity because earnings ultimately produce the cash flow needed for liquidity. Exhibit 28-9 shows **Starbucks'** profitability ratios in 2006, 2007, and 2008.

Profit margin focuses on income statement results and measures how well a company manages its costs per dollar of sales. **Asset turnover** focuses on how efficiently balance sheet assets are used to produce sales. **Return on assets** combines these two ratios to measure the earning power of a business. Starbucks' profit margin decreased from 7.2 to 7.1 to 3.0 percent between 2006 and 2008. Its asset turnover remained relatively stable at 2.0 times in 2006 and 1.9 times

EXHIBIT 28-9 Profitability Ratios of Starbucks Corporation (Dollar amounts in millions)

	2008	2007	2006
Profit margin: Measure of net income produced by each dollar of sales			
$\frac{\text{Net Income}}{\text{Net Sales}}$	$\frac{\$315.5}{\$10{,}383.0} = 3.0\%$	$\frac{\$672.6}{\$9{,}411.5} = 7.1\%$	$\frac{\$564.3}{\$7{,}786.9} = 7.2\%$
Asset turnover: Measure of how efficiently assets are used to produce sales			
	$\frac{\$10{,}383.0}{(\$5{,}672.6 + \$5{,}343.9) \div 2}$	$\frac{\$9{,}411.5}{(\$5{,}343.9 + \$4{,}428.9) \div 2}$	$\frac{\$7{,}786.9}{(\$4{,}428.9 + \$3{,}513.7^*) \div 2}$
$\frac{\text{Net Sales}}{\text{Average Total Assets}}$	$\frac{\$10{,}383.0}{\$5{,}508.3} = 1.9 \text{ times}$	$\frac{\$9{,}411.5}{\$4{,}886.4} = 1.9 \text{ times}$	$\frac{\$7{,}786.9}{\$3{,}971.3} = 2.0 \text{ times}$
Return on assets: Measure of overall earning power or profitability			
$\frac{\text{Net Income}}{\text{Average Total Assets}}$	$\frac{\$315.5}{\$5{,}508.3} = 5.7\%$	$\frac{\$672.6}{\$4{,}886.4} = 13.8\%$	$\frac{\$564.3}{\$3{,}971.3} = 14.2\%$
Return on equity: Measure of the profitability of stockholders' investments			
$\frac{\text{Net Income}}{\text{Average Stockholders' Equity}}$	$\frac{\$315.5}{(\$2{,}490.9 + \$2{,}284.1) \div 2}$	$\frac{\$672.6}{(\$2{,}284.1 + \$2{,}228.5) \div 2}$	$\frac{\$564.3}{(\$2{,}228.5 + \$2{,}090.3) \div 2}$
	$\frac{\$315.5}{\$2{,}387.5} = 13.2\%$	$\frac{\$672.6}{\$2{,}256.3} = 29.8\%$	$\frac{\$564.3}{\$2{,}159.4} = 26.1\%$

*Figures for 2005 are from the five-year selected financial data in Starbucks' Form 10-K, 2006.

Source: Data from Starbucks Corporation, Form 10-K, 2008, Form 10-K, 2007, and Form 10-K, 2006.

in 2007 and 2008. The result is a decrease in the company's earning power, or return on assets, from 14.2 percent in 2006 to 13.8 percent in 2007 to 5.7 percent in 2008. The computations that follow show the relationship among these three profitability ratios.

Profit Margin			*Asset Turnover*		*Return on Assets**
$\frac{\text{Net Income}}{\text{Net Sales}}$		×	$\frac{\text{Net Sales}}{\text{Average Total Assets}}$	=	$\frac{\text{Net Income}}{\text{Average Total Assets}}$
2006	7.2%	×	2.0 times	=	14.4%
2007	7.1	×	1.9	=	13.5
2008	3.0	×	1.9	=	5.7

Study Note

The analysis of both asset turnover and return on assets is improved if only productive assets are used in the calculations. For example, when investments in unfinished new plant construction or in plants that are now obsolete or nonoperating are removed from the asset base, the result is a better picture of the productivity of assets.

Return on equity measures the earning power of a company's stockholders investment. Starbucks' return on equity had mixed results for its shareholders of 26.1 percent in 2006 to 29.8 percent in 2007 to 13.2 percent in 2008.

A word of caution: Although we have used net income in computing profitability ratios for Starbucks, net income is not always a good indicator of a company's sustainable earnings. For instance, if a company has discontinued operations, income from continuing operations may be a better measure of sustainable earnings. For a company that has one-time items on its income statement—such as restructurings, gains, or losses—income from operations before these items may be a better measure. Some managers and analysts like to use earnings before interest and taxes, or EBIT, for the earnings measure because it excludes the effects of the company's borrowings and the tax rates from the analysis. Whatever figure one uses for earnings, it is important to try to determine the effects of various components on future operations.

Evaluating Long-Term Solvency

Long-term solvency has to do with a company's ability to survive for many years. The aim of evaluating long-term solvency is to detect early signs that a company is headed for financial difficulty. Increasing amounts of debt in a company's capital structure mean that the company is becoming more heavily leveraged. This condition may have a negative effect on long-term solvency because it represents increasing legal obligations to pay interest periodically and the principal at maturity. Failure to make those payments can result in bankruptcy. Alternatively, if interest rates are low, many companies will elect to borrow to finance operations to grow business and earn a healthy return, but only if they can earn a return on assets greater than the cost of interest.

Study Note

Liquidity is a firm's ability to meet its current obligations; solvency is its ability to meet maturing obligations as they come due without losing the ability to continue operations.

Declining profitability and liquidity ratios are key indicators of possible failure. Two other ratios that analysts consider when assessing long-term solvency are debt to equity and interest coverage, which are shown in Exhibit 28-10. The **debt to equity ratio** measures capital structure and leverage by showing the amount of a company's assets provided by creditors in relation to the amount provided by stockholders. **Starbucks**' debt to equity ratio increased from .99 times in 2006 to 1.3 times in 2007 and 2008, representing an increased reliance on debt financing. Recall from Exhibit 28-6 that Starbucks' long-term debt and other liabilities more than doubled. However, the company has little short-term debt and a strong current ratio. Starbucks' long-term solvency is not in danger.

If debt is risky, why have any? The answer is that the level of debt is a matter of balance. Despite its riskiness, debt is a flexible means of financing certain

*The small difference in the computations of return on assets in Exhibit 28-9 and the computations below results from the rounding of the ratios.

FOCUS ON BUSINESS PRACTICE

What's the Best Way to Measure Performance for Management Compensation?

Efforts to link management compensation to performance measures and the creation of shareholder wealth are increasing. **Starbucks** uses earning per share (EPS) for this purpose. Some other companies, including **Walgreens**, use a better approach. Walgreens' use of return on invested capital, which is closely related to return on assets, shows whether or not management is employing the assets profitably. Better still would be to compare the company's return on assets to its cost of debt and equity capital, as does **Target**.[9] Many analysts believe that this measure, which is called economic value added (EVA), is superior to EPS. If the return on assets exceeds the cost of financing the assets with debt and equity, then management is indeed creating value for the shareholders.

business operations. The interest paid on debt is tax-deductible, whereas dividends on stock are not. Because debt usually carries a fixed interest charge, the cost of financing can be limited, and leverage can be used to advantage. If a company can earn a return on assets greater than the cost of interest, it makes an overall profit. In addition, being a debtor in periods of inflation has advantages because the debt, which is a fixed dollar amount, can be repaid with cheaper dollars. However, the company runs the risk of not earning a return on assets equal to the cost of financing the assets, thereby incurring a loss.

The **interest coverage ratio** measures the degree of protection creditors have from default on interest payments. As shown in Exhibit 28-10, Starbucks' interest coverage declined from 108.9 times in 2006 to 28.8 in 2007 to 9.6 in 2008 due to large increases in interest. Interest coverage is still at a safe level but deteriorating rapidly.

Study Note

Because of innovative financing plans and other means of acquiring assets, lease payments and similar types of fixed obligations should be considered when evaluating long-term solvency.

Evaluating the Adequacy of Cash Flows

Because cash flows are needed to pay debts when they are due, cash flow measures are closely related to liquidity and long-term solvency. Exhibit 28-11 presents **Starbucks**' cash flow adequacy ratios in 2006, 2007, and 2008. **Cash flow yield** shows the cash-generating ability of a company's operations; it is measured by dividing cash flows from operating activities by net income. Starbucks' net cash flows from operating activities went from $1,1316.6 million in 2006 to $1,331.2 million in 2007 to $1,258.7 million in 2008. Its cash flow yield was stable at 2.0 times in 2006 and 2007 but rose to 4.0 times in 2008.

EXHIBIT 28-10 Long-term Solvency Ratios of Starbucks Corporation (Dollar amounts in millions)

	2008	2007	2006
Debt to equity ratio: Measure of capital structure and leverage			
Total Liabilities / Stockholders' Equity	$3,181.7 / $2,490.9 = 1.3 times	$3,059.8 / $2,284.1 = 1.3 times	$2,200.4 / $2,228.5 = .99 times
Interest coverage ratio: Measure of creditors' protection from default on interest payments			
(Income Before Income Taxes + Interest Expense) / Interest Expense	($459.5 + $53.4) / $53.5 = 9.6 times	($1,056.3 + $38.0) / $38.0 = 28.8 times	($906.3 + $8.4) / $8.4 = 108.9 times

Source: Starbucks Corporation, Form 10-K, 2008 and Form 10-K, 2007.

EXHIBIT 28-11 Cash Flow Adequacy Ratios of Starbucks Corporation (Dollar amounts in millions)

	2008	2007	2006
Cash flow yield: Measure of the ability to generate operating cash flows in relation to net income			
$\frac{\text{Net Cash Flows from Operating Activities}}{\text{Net Income}}$	$\frac{\$1,258.7}{\$315.5} = 4.0$ times	$\frac{\$1,331.2}{\$672.6} = 2.0$ times	$\frac{\$1,131.6}{\$564.3} = 2.0$ times
Cash flows to sales: Measure of the ability of sales to generate operating cash flows			
$\frac{\text{Net Cash Flows from Operating Activities}}{\text{Net Sales}}$	$\frac{\$1,258.7}{\$10,383.0} = 12.1\%$	$\frac{\$1,331.2}{\$9,411.5} = 14.1\%$	$\frac{\$1,131.6}{\$7,786.9} = 14.5\%$
Cash flows to assets: Measure of the ability of assets to generate operating cash flows			
$\frac{\text{Net Cash Flows from Operating Activities}}{\text{Average Total Assets}}$	$\frac{\$1,258.7}{(\$5,672,6 + \$5,343.9) \div 2}$	$\frac{\$1,331.2}{(\$5,343.9 + \$4,428.9) \div 2}$	$\frac{\$1,131.6}{(\$4,428.9 + \$3,513.7^{*}) \div 2}$
	$\frac{\$1,258.7}{\$5,508.3} = 22.9\%$	$\frac{\$1,331.2}{\$4,886.4} = 27.2\%$	$\frac{\$1,131.6}{\$3,971.3} = 28.5\%$
Free cash flow: Measure of cash remaining after providing for commitments			
Net Cash Flows from Operating Activities − Dividends − Net Capital Expenditures**	$1,258.7 − $0 − $984.5	$1,331.2 − $0 − $1,080.3 = $274.2	$1,131.6* − $0 − $771.2 = $250.9 = $360.4

*The 2005 figure is from the five-year selected financial data in Starbucks' Form 10-K, 2006.

**Net capital expenditures are called "net additions to property, plant and equipment" on Starbucks' statements of cash flows.

Source: Data from Starbucks Corporation, Form 10-K, 2008, Form 10-K, 2007, and Form 10-K, 2006.

The largest contributor to net cash flow from operating activities is depreciation expense. In 2008, $604.5 million in depreciation was added back. This is almost half of Starbucks' 2008 net cash flows from operating activities.

Cash flows to sales and **cash flows to assets** measure the ability of sales or assets to generate operating cash flow. Cash flows to sales continue to trend downward from 14.5 to 14.1 to 12.1 percent from 2006 to 2008. Cash flows to assets also continue to decrease from 28.5 to 27.2 to 22.9 percent over the three-year period. This means the company's net sales and average total assets increased faster than the cash flows provided by its operations.

Free cash flow is the cash remaining after providing for commitments such as dividends and net capital expenditures. As shown in Exhibit 28-11, free cash flow for Starbucks appears to be on the rebound to $274.2 million in 2008 after declining from $360.4 million in 2006 to $250.9 million in 2007. One factor is reduced spending on net capital expenditures (the difference between purchases and sales of plant assets).

Another factor in Starbucks' free cash flows is that the company pays no dividends. In top management's words regarding future liquidity and cash flows: "We generate strong cash flows and have solid liquidity, and we are executing rigorous cost-containment initiatives to improve our bottom line.[10]

Study Note

When the computation for free cash flow uses "net capital expenditures" in place of "purchases of plant assets minus sales of plant assets," it means that the company's sales of plant assets were too small or immaterial to be broken out.

EXHIBIT 28-12 Market Strength Ratios of Starbucks Corporation

	2008	2007	2006
Price/earnings (P/E) ratio: Measure of investors' confidence in a company			
$\frac{\text{Market Price per Share}}{\text{Earnings per Share}}$	$\frac{\$15.25^*}{\$0.43} = 35.5$ times	$\frac{\$27.08^*}{\$0.90} = 30.1$ times	$\frac{\$33.78^*}{\$0.74} = 45.6$ times
Dividends yield: Measure of a stock's current return to an investor			
$\frac{\text{Dividents per Share}}{\text{Market Price per Share}}$	Starbucks does not pay a dividend.		

*Market price is the average for the fourth quarter reported in Starbucks' annual report.

Source: Data from Starbucks Corporation, Form 10-K, 2008, and Form 10-K 2007.

Evaluating Market Strength

Market price is the price at which a company's stock is bought and sold. It indicates how investors view the potential return and risk connected with owning the stock. Market price by itself is not very informative, however, because companies have different numbers of shares outstanding, different earnings, and different dividend policies. Thus, market price must be related to earnings by considering the price/earnings (P/E) ratio and the dividends yield. Those ratios for **Starbucks** appear in Exhibit 28-12. We computed them by using the average market prices of Starbucks' stock during the fourth quarter of 2006, 2007, and 2008.

The **price/earnings (P/E) ratio**, which measures investors' confidence in a company, is the ratio of the market price per share to earnings per share. The P/E ratio is useful in comparing the earnings of different companies and the value of a company's shares in relation to values in the overall market. With a higher P/E ratio, the investor obtains less underlying earnings per dollar invested. Starbucks' P/E ratio fluctuated from 45.6 times in 2006 to 30.1 times in 2007 to 35.5 times in 2008, reflecting investor uneasiness in the stock market and the economy. Starbuck's stock price continued to slide from about $34 in 2006 to about $15 in 2008. Starbucks earnings per share had mixed results of $0.74 in 2006, $0.90 in 2007, and $0.43 in 2008. In the 2008 Form 10-K management discussion and analysis of results, management stated, "Restructuring charges and costs associated with the execution of the transformation agenda impacted EPS by approximately $0.28 per share in fiscal 2008."

The **dividends yield** measures a stock's current return to an investor in the form of dividends. Because Starbucks pays no dividends, we can conclude that those who invest in the company expect their return to come from increases in the stock's market value.

STOP & APPLY >

The Corner Cup, a local coffee bistro, engaged in the transactions listed in the first column of the following table. Opposite each transaction is a ratio and space to mark the effect of each transaction on the ratio. Place an X in the appropriate column to show whether the transaction increased, decreased, or had no effect on the ratio.

(continued)

Transaction	Ratio	Effect: Increase	Effect: Decrease	Effect: None
a. Accrued salaries.	Current ratio			
b. Purchased inventory.	Quick ratio			
c. Increased allowance for uncollectible accounts.	Receivable turnover			
d. Purchased inventory on credit.	Payables turnover			
e. Sold treasury stock.	Profit margin			
f. Borrowed cash by issuing bond payable.	Asset turnover			
g. Paid wages expense.	Return on assets			
h. Repaid bond payable.	Debt to equity			
i. Accrued interest expense.	Interest coverage			
k. Sold merchandise on account.	Return on equity			
l. Recorded depreciation expense.	Cash flow yield			
m. Sold equipment.	Free cash flow			

SOLUTION

Transaction	Ratio	Effect: Increase	Effect: Decrease	Effect: None
a. Accrued salaries.	Current ratio		X	
b. Purchased inventory.	Quick ratio		X	
c. Increased allowance for uncollectible accounts.	Receivable turnover	X		
d. Purchased inventory on credit.	Payables turnover		X	
e. Sold treasury stock.	Profit margin			X
f. Borrowed cash by issuing bond payable.	Asset turnover		X	
g. Paid wages expense.	Return on assets		X	
h. Repaid bond payable.	Debt to equity	X		
i. Accrued interest expense.	Interest coverage		X	
k. Sold merchandise on account.	Return on equity	X		
l. Recorded depreciation expense.	Cash flow yield	X		
m. Sold equipment.	Free cash flow	X		

A LOOK BACK AT ▶ STARBUCKS CORPORATION

To assess a company's financial performance, managers, stockholders, creditors, and other interested parties use measures that are linked to creating shareholder value. The Financial Highlights at the beginning of the chapter show that **Starbucks'** revenues, earnings, profit margin, and earnings per share appear highly sensitive to customer volume and economic ups and downs. However, but for a comprehensive view of the company's performance, users of Starbucks' financial statements must consider the following questions:

- What standards should be used to evaluate Starbucks' performance?
- What analytical tools are available to measure performance?
- How successful has the company's management been in creating value for shareholders?

Starbucks' performance should be compared with the performance of other companies in the same industry—the food and beverage specialty retail business. In addition,

Starbucks' performance in the current year should be compared with its performance in past years. To make this comparison, analysts employ horizontal or trend analysis, vertical analysis, and ratio analysis.

This chapter's comprehensive ratio analysis of Starbucks clearly shows the company's financial condition as stable for liquidity measures, with signs of weakness in 2008 in its profitability, long-term solvency, and cash flow adequacy ratios. This performance resulted in a decrease in earnings per share to $0.43 in 2008 after an increase in earnings per share from 2006 to 2007 of $0.74 to $0.90. Shareholder value appears in decline as evidenced by the 2006–2008 downward trend in share price from $34 to $27 to $15.

At Starbucks' 2008 annual meeting, CEO Howard Schultz summed up his management's analysis this way:

> Despite the challenging economic environment, Starbucks is profitable, has a strong balance sheet and generates solid cash from operations. Our customers' connection with, and trust in the Starbucks brand remains at a high level. We are laser-focused on delivering the finest quality coffee and getting the customer experience right every time.[11]

As for the future, Starbucks has two objectives: to increase profits in existing stores and to make strategic investments in key initiatives—for example, entering the instant coffee market. "We've been putting our feet into the shoes of our customers and responding directly to their needs," said Schultz. "Our customers are telling us they want value and quality and we will deliver that in a way that is both meaningful to them and authentic to Starbucks.[12]

Review Problem

Comparative Analysis of Two Companies

LO3

Suppose a company like **Starbucks** decided to analyze the coffee vending machine business as a new way to deliver value and convenience to customers. To learn more about selling hot beverages from machines in office buildings and schools, management decides to perform a comprehensive financial analysis of two successful cold beverage vending machine companies: Quik Cup and Big Taste. The balance sheets and income statements of Quik Cup and Big Taste are presented on the following pages.

The following information pertaining to 2010 is also available:

1. Quik Cup's statement of cash flows shows that it had net cash flows from operations of $2,200,000. Big Taste's statement of cash flows shows that its net cash flows from operations were $3,000,000.
2. Net capital expenditures were $2,100,000 for Quik Cup and $1,800,000 for Big Taste.
3. Quik Cup paid dividends of $500,000, and Big Taste paid dividends of $600,000.
4. The market prices of the stocks of Quik Cup and Big Taste were $30 and $20, respectively.

Financial information pertaining to prior years is not readily available.

Required

Perform a comprehensive ratio analysis of both Quik Cup and Big Taste following the steps outlined here. Assume that all notes payable of these two companies are current liabilities and that all their bonds payable are long-term liabilities. Show dollar amounts in thousands, use end-of-year balances for averages, assume no change in inventory, and round all ratios and percentages to one decimal place.

1. Prepare an analysis of liquidity.
2. Prepare an analysis of profitability.
3. Prepare an analysis of long-term solvency.
4. Prepare an analysis of cash flow adequacy.

5. Prepare an analysis of market strength.
6. In each analysis, indicate the company that apparently had the more favorable ratio. (Consider differences of .1 or less to be neutral.)
7. In what ways would having access to prior years' information aid this analysis?

A primary objective in management's use of financial performance measurement is to increase the wealth of the company's stockholders. Creditors and investors use financial performance measurement to judge a company's past performance and current position, as well as its future potential and the risk associated with it. Creditors use the information gained from their analyses to make reliable loans that will be repaid with interest. Investors use the information to make investments that will provide a return that is worth the risk.

	A	B	C
1	**Balance Sheets**		
2	**December 31, 2010**		
3	(In thousands)		
4		**Quik Cup**	**Big Taste**
5	**Assets**		
6	Cash	$ 2,000	$ 4,500
7	Accounts receivable (net)	2,000	6,500
8	Inventory	2,000	5,000
9	Property, plant, and equipment (net)	20,000	35,000
10	Other assets	4,000	5,000
11	Total assets	$30,000	$56,000
12			
13	**Liabilities and Stockholders' Equity**		
14	Accounts payable	$ 2,500	$ 3,000
15	Notes payable	1,500	4,000
16	Bonds payable	10,000	30,000
17	Common stock, $1 par value	1,000	3,000
18	Additional paid-in capital	9,000	9,000
19	Retained earnings	6,000	7,000
20	Total liabilities and stockholders' equity	$30,000	$56,000
21			

	A	B	C
1	**Income Statements**		
2	**For the Year Ended December 31, 2010**		
3	(In thousands, except per share amounts)		
4		**Quik Cup**	**Big Taste**
5	Net sales	$53,000	$86,000
6	Costs and expenses		
7	Cost of goods sold	$37,000	$61,000
8	Selling expenses	7,000	10,000
9	Administrative expenses	4,000	5,000
10	Total costs and expenses	$48,000	$76,000
11	Income from operations	$ 5,000	$10,000
12	Interest expense	1,400	3,200
13	Income before income taxes	$ 3,600	$ 6,800
14	Income taxes	1,800	3,400
15	Net income	$ 1,800	$ 3,400
16	Earnings per share	$ 1.80	$ 1.13
17			

Answers to Review Problem

	A	B	C	D
1	**Ratio Name**	**Quik Cup**	**Big Taste**	**6. Company with More Favorable Ratio**
2	**1. Liquidity analysis**			
3	a. Current ratio	$\frac{\$2,000 + \$2,000 + \$2,000}{\$2,500 + \$1,500}$	$\frac{\$4,500 + \$6,500 + \$5,000}{\$3,000 + \$4,000}$	Big Taste
4		$= \frac{\$6,000}{\$4,000} = 1.5$ times	$= \frac{\$16,000}{\$7,000} = 2.3$ times	
5	b. Quick ratio	$\frac{\$2,000 + \$2,000}{\$2,500 + \$1,500}$	$= \frac{\$11,000}{\$7,000} = 1.6$ times	Big Taste
6	c. Receivable turnover	$\frac{\$53,000}{\$2,000} = 26.5$ times	$\frac{\$86,00}{\$6,500} = 13.2$ times	Quik Cup
7	d. Days' sales uncollected	$\frac{365 \text{ days}}{26.5 \text{ times}} = 13.8$ days	$\frac{365 \text{ days}}{13.2 \text{ times}} = 27.6$ days	Quik Cup
8	e. Inventory turnover	$\frac{\$37,000}{\$2,000} = 18.5$ times	$\frac{\$61,000}{\$5,000} = 12.2$ times	Quik Cup
9	f. Days' inventory on hand	$\frac{365 \text{ days}}{18.5 \text{ times}} = 19.7$ days	$\frac{365 \text{ days}}{12.2 \text{ times}} = 29.9$ days	Quik Cup
10	g. Payables turnover	$\frac{\$37,000}{\$2,500} = 14.8$ times	$\frac{\$61,000}{\$3,000} = 20.3$ times	Big Taste
11	h. Days' payable	$\frac{365 \text{ days}}{20.3 \text{ times}} = 18.30$ days	$\frac{365 \text{ days}}{20.3 \text{ times}} = 18.0$ days	Big Taste
12	*Note:* This analysis indicates the company with the apparently more favorable ratio.			
13	Class discussion may focus on conditions under which different conclusions may be drawn.			

	A	B	C	D
1	**Ratio Name**	**Quik Cup**	**Big Taste**	**6. Company with More Favorable Ratio**
2	**2. Profitability analysis**			
3	a. Profit margin	$\frac{\$1,800}{\$53,000} = 3.4\%$	$\frac{\$3,400}{\$86,000} = 4.0\%$	Big Taste
4	b. Asset turnover	$\frac{\$53,000}{\$30,000} = 1.8$ times	$\frac{\$86,000}{\$56,000} = 1.5$ times	Quik Cup
5	c. Return on assets	$\frac{\$1,800}{\$30,000} = 6.0\%$	$\frac{\$1,800}{\$30,000} = 6.0\%$	Neutral
6	d. Return on equity	$\frac{\$1,800}{\$1,000 + \$9,000 + \$6,000}$ $= \frac{\$1,800}{\$16,000} = 11.3\%$	$\frac{\$3,400}{\$3,000 + \$9,000 + \$7,000}$ $= \frac{\$3,400}{\$19,000} = 17.9\%$	Big Taste

	A	B	C	D
1	**Ratio Name**	**Quik Cup**	**Big Taste**	**6. Company with More Favorable Ratio**
2	**3. Long-term solvency analysis**			
3	a. Debt to equity ratio	$\frac{\$2,500 + \$1,500 + \$10,000}{\$1,000 + \$9,000 + \$6,000}$	$\frac{\$3,000 + \$4,000 + \$30,000}{\$3,000 + \$9,000 + \$7,000}$	Quik Cup
4		$= \frac{\$14,000}{\$16,000} = 0.9$ time	$= \frac{\$37,000}{\$19,000} = 1.9$ times	
5	b. Interest coverage ratio	$\frac{\$3,600 + \$1,400}{\$1,400}$	$\frac{6,800 + \$3,200}{\$3,200}$	Quik Cup
6		$= \frac{\$5,000}{\$1,400} = 3.6$ times	$= \frac{\$10,000}{\$3,200} = 3.1$ times	

	A	B	C	D
1	**Ratio Name**	**Quik Cup**	**Big Taste**	**6. Company with More Favorable Ratio**
2	**4. Cash flow adequacy analysis**			
3	a. Cash flow yield	$\frac{\$2,200}{\$1,800} = 1.2$ times	$\frac{\$2,200}{\$1,800} = 1.2$ times	Quik Cup
4	b. Cash flows to sales	$\frac{\$2,200}{\$53,000} = 4.2\%$	$\frac{\$3,000}{\$86,000} = 3.5\%$	Quik Cup
5	c. Cash flows to assets	$\frac{\$2,200}{\$30,000} = 7.3\%$	$\frac{3,000}{\$56,000} = 5.4\%$	Quik Cup
6	d. Free cash flow	$2,200 − $500 − $2,100	$3,000 − $600 − $1,800	Big Taste
7		= **($400)**	= **$600**	

	A	B	C	D
1	**Ratio Name**	**Quik Cup**	**Big Taste**	**6. Company with More Favorable Ratio**
2	**5. Market strength analysis**			
3	a. Price/earnings ratio	$\frac{\$30}{\$1.80} = 16.7$ times	$\frac{\$20}{\$1.13} = 17.7$ times	Big Taste
4	b. Dividends yield	$\frac{\$500,000 \div 1,000,000}{\$30}$	$\frac{\$600,000 \div 3,000,000}{\$20}$	
5		$= \frac{\$0.50}{\$30} = 1.7\%$	$= \frac{\$0.20}{\$20} = 1/0\%$	Quik
6	7. Prior years' information would be helpful in two ways. First, turnover, return, and cash flows to assets ratios could be based on average amounts. Second, a trend analysis could be performed for each company.			

LO1 Describe the objectives, standards of comparison, sources of information, and compensation issues in measuring financial performance.

A primary objective in management's use of financial performance measurement is to increase the wealth of the company's stockholders. Creditors and investors use financial performance measurement to judge a company's past performance and current position, as well as its future potential and the risk associated with it. Creditors use the information gained from their analyses to make reliable loans that will be repaid with interest. Investors use the information to make investments that will provide a return that is worth the risk.

Three standards of comparison commonly used in evaluating financial performance are rule-of-thumb measures, a company's past performance, and industry norms. Rule-of-thumb measures are weak because of a lack of evidence that they can be widely applied. A company's past performance can offer a guideline for measuring improvement, but it is not helpful in judging performance relative to the performance of other companies. Although the use of industry norms overcomes this last problem, its disadvantage is that firms are not always comparable, even in the same industry.

The main sources of information about public corporations are reports that the corporations publish themselves, such as annual reports and interim financial statements; reports filed with the SEC; business periodicals; and credit and investment advisory services.

In public corporations, a committee made up of independent directors appointed by the board of directors determines the compensation of top executives. Although earnings per share can be regarded as a "bottom-line" number that encompasses all the other performance measures, using it as the sole basis for determining executive compensation may lead to management practices that are not in the best interests of the company or its stockholders.

LO2 Apply horizontal analysis, trend analysis, vertical analysis, and ratio analysis to financial statements.

Horizontal analysis involves the computation of changes in both dollar amounts and percentages from year to year.

Trend analysis is an extension of horizontal analysis in that it calculates percentage changes for several years. The analyst computes the changes by setting a base year equal to 100 and calculating the results for subsequent years as percentages of the base year.

Vertical analysis uses percentages to show the relationship of the component parts of a financial statement to a total figure in the statement. The resulting financial statements, which are expressed entirely in percentages, are called common-size statements.

Ratio analysis is a technique of financial performance evaluation that identifies key relationships between the components of the financial statements. To interpret ratios correctly, the analyst must have a general understanding of the company and its environment, financial data for several years or for several companies, and an understanding of the data underlying the numerators and denominators.

LO3 Apply ratio analysis to financial statements in a comprehensive evaluation of a company's financial performance.

A comprehensive ratio analysis includes the evaluation of a company's liquidity, as well as its profitability, long-term solvency, cash flow adequacy, and market strength. The ratios for measuring these characteristics are illustrated in Exhibits 28-8 through 28-12.

REVIEW of Concepts and Terminology

The following concepts and terms were introduced in this chapter:

Base year 1279 (LO2)

Common-size statement 1283 (LO2)

Compensation committee 1277 (LO1)

Diversified companies 1274 (LO1)

Financial performance measurement 1272 (LO1)

Free cash flow 1292 (LO3)

Horizontal analysis 1279 (LO2)

Index number 1282 (LO2)

Interim financial statements 1275 (LO1)

Operating cycle 1287 (LO3)

Ratio analysis 1285 (LO2)

Trend analysis 1282 (LO2)

Vertical analysis 1283 (LO2)

Key Ratios

Asset turnover 1289 (LO3)

Cash flows to assets 1292 (LO3)

Cash flows to sales 1292 (LO3)

Cash flow yield 1291 (LO3)

Current ratio 1287 (LO3)

Days' inventory on hand 1287 (LO3)

Days' payable 1289 (LO3)

Days' sales uncollected 1287 (LO3)

Debt to equity ratio 1290 (LO3)

Dividends yield 1293 (LO3)

Interest coverage ratio 1291 (LO3)

Inventory turnover 1287 (LO3)

Payables turnover 1289 (LO3)

Price/earnings (P/E) ratio 1293 (LO3)

Profit margin 1289 (LO3)

Quick ratio 1287 (LO3)

Receivable turnover 1287 (LO3)

Return on assets 1289 (LO3)

Return on equity 1290 (LO3)

CHAPTER ASSIGNMENTS

BUILDING Your Basic Knowledge and Skills

Short Exercises

LO1 **Objectives and Standards of Financial Performance Evaluation**

SE 1. Indicate whether each of the following items is (a) an objective or (b) a standard of comparison of financial statement analysis:

1. Industry norms
2. Assessment of a company's past performance
3. The company's past performance
4. Assessment of future potential and related risk
5. Rule-of-thumb measures

LO1 **Sources of Information**

SE 2. For each piece of information in the list that follows, indicate whether the best source would be (a) reports published by the company, (b) SEC reports, (c) business periodicals, or (d) credit and investment advisory services.

1. Current market value of a company's stock
2. Management's analysis of the past year's operations
3. Objective assessment of a company's financial performance
4. Most complete body of financial disclosures
5. Current events affecting the company

LO2 **Trend Analysis**

SE 3. Using 2009 as the base year, prepare a trend analysis for the following data, and tell whether the results suggest a favorable or unfavorable trend. (Round your answers to one decimal place.)

	2011	2010	2009
Net sales	$158,000	$136,000	$112,000
Accounts receivable (net)	43,000	32,000	21,000

LO2 **Horizontal Analysis**

SE 4. The comparative income statements and balance sheets of Sarot, Inc., appear on the opposite page. Compute the amount and percentage changes for the income statements, and comment on the changes from 2009 to 2010. (Round the percentage changes to one decimal place.)

LO2 **Vertical Analysis**

SE 5. Express the comparative balance sheets of Sarot, Inc. (shown on the opposite page) as common-size statements, and comment on the changes from 2009 to 2010. (Round computations to one decimal place.)

LO3 **Liquidity Analysis**

SE 6. Using the information for Sarot, Inc., in **SE 4** and **SE 5**, compute the current ratio, quick ratio, receivable turnover, days' sales uncollected, inventory turnover, days' inventory on hand, payables turnover, and days' payable for 2009 and 2010. Inventories were $16,000 in 2008, $20,000 in 2009, and $28,000 in 2010. Accounts receivable were $24,000 in 2008, $32,000 in 2009, and $40,000 in 2010. Accounts payable were $36,000 in 2008, $40,000 in 2009, and $48,000

Sarot, Inc.
Comparative Income Statements
For the Years Ended December 31, 2010 and 2009

	2010	2009
Net sales	$720,000	$580,000
Cost of goods sold	448,000	352,000
Gross margin	$272,000	$228,000
Operating expenses	160,000	120,000
Operating income	$112,000	$108,000
Interest expense	28,000	20,000
Income before income taxes	$ 84,000	$ 88,000
Income taxes expense	28,000	32,000
Net income	$ 56,000	$ 56,000
Earnings per share	$ 2.80	$ 2.80

Sarot, Inc.
Comparative Balance Sheets
December 31, 2010 and 2009

	2010	2009
Assets		
Current assets	$ 96,000	$ 80,000
Property, plant, and equipment (net)	520,000	400,000
Total assets	$616,000	$480,000
Liabilities and Stockholders' Equity		
Current liabilities	$ 72,000	$ 88,000
Long-term liabilities	360,000	240,000
Stockholders' equity	184,000	152,000
Total liabilities and stockholders' equity	$616,000	$480,000

in 2010. The company had no marketable securities or prepaid assets. Comment on the results. (Round computations to one decimal place.)

LO3 Profitability Analysis

SE 7. Using the information for Sarot, Inc., in **SE 4** and **SE 5**, compute the profit margin, asset turnover, return on assets, and return on equity for 2009 and 2010. In 2008, total assets were $400,000 and total stockholders' equity was $120,000. Comment on the results. (Round computations to one decimal place.)

LO3 Long-term Solvency Analysis

SE 8. Using the information for Sarot, Inc., in **SE 4** and **SE 5**, compute the debt to equity ratio and the interest coverage ratio for 2009 and 2010. Comment on the results. (Round computations to one decimal place.)

LO3 Cash Flow Adequacy Analysis

SE 9. Using the information for Sarot, Inc., in **SE 4**, **SE 5**, and **SE 7**, compute the cash flow yield, cash flows to sales, cash flows to assets, and free cash flow for 2009 and 2010. Net cash flows from operating activities were $84,000 in 2009 and $64,000 in 2010. Net capital expenditures were $120,000 in 2009 and

$160,000 in 2010. Cash dividends were $24,000 in both years. Comment on the results. (Round computations to one decimal place.)

LO3 **Market Strength Analysis**

SE 10. Using the information for Sarot, Inc., in **SE 4**, **SE 5**, and **SE 9**, compute the price/earnings (P/E) ratio and dividends yield for 2009 and 2010. The company had 20,000 shares of common stock outstanding in both years. The price of Sarot's common stock was $60 in 2009 and $40 in 2010. Comment on the results. (Round computations to one decimal place.)

Exercises

LO1 LO2 **Discussion Questions**

E 1. Develop brief answers to each of the following questions:

1. Why is it essential that management compensation, including bonuses, be linked to financial goals and strategies that achieve shareholder value?
2. How are past performance and industry norms useful in evaluating a company's performance? What are their limitations?
3. In a five-year trend analysis, why do the dollar values remain the same for their respective years while the percentages usually change when a new five-year period is chosen?

LO3 **Discussion Questions**

E 2. Develop brief answers to each of the following questions:

1. Why does a decrease in receivable turnover create the need for cash from operating activities?
2. Why would ratios that include one balance sheet account and one income statement account, such as receivable turnover or return on assets, be questionable if they came from quarterly or other interim financial reports?
3. What is a limitation of free cash flow in comparing one company to another?

LO1 **Issues in Financial Performance Evaluation: Objectives, Standards, Sources of Information, and Executive Compensation**

E 3. Identify each of the following as (a) an objective of financial statement analysis, (b) a standard for financial statement analysis, (c) a source of information for financial statement analysis, or (d) an executive compensation issue:

1. Average ratios of other companies in the same industry
2. Assessment of the future potential of an investment
3. Interim financial statements
4. Past ratios of the company
5. SEC Form 10-K
6. Assessment of risk
7. A company's annual report
8. Linking performance to shareholder value

LO1 **Standards for Financial Performance Evaluation**

E 4. **Standard & Poor's** Ratings Group, the large financial company that evaluates the riskiness of companies' debt, downgraded its rating of **General Motors** and **Ford Motor Co.** debt to "junk" bond status because of concerns about the companies' profitability and cash flows. Despite aggressive cost cutting, both companies still face substantial future liabilities for health care and pension obligations. They are losing money or barely breaking even on auto operations that concentrate on slow-selling SUVs. High gas prices and competition force them to sell the cars at a discount.[13]

What standards do you think Standard & Poor's would use to evaluate Ford's progress? What performance measures would Standard & Poor's most likely use in making its evaluation?

LO1 Using Segment Information

E 5. Refer to Exhibit 28-1, which shows the segment information of **Starbucks Corporation**. In what business segments does Starbucks operate? What is the relative size of its business segments in terms of sales and income in the most recent year shown? Which segment is most profitable in terms of return on assets?

LO1 Using Investors' Services

E 6. Refer to Exhibit 28-2, which contains the **PepsiCo Inc.** listing from Mergent's *Handbook of Dividend Achievers.* Assume that an investor has asked you to assess PepsiCo's recent history and prospects. Write a memorandum to the investor that addresses the following points:

1. PepsiCo's earnings history. What has been the general relationship between PepsiCo's return on assets and its return on equity over the last seven years? What does this tell you about the way the company is financed? What figures back up your conclusion?
2. The trend of PepsiCo's stock price and price/earnings (P/E) ratio for the seven years shown.
3. PepsiCo's prospects, including developments likely to affect the company's future.

LO2 Trend Analysis

E 7. Using 2006 as the base year, prepare a trend analysis of the following data, and tell whether the situation shown by the trends is favorable or unfavorable. (Round your answers to one decimal place.)

	2010	2009	2008	2007	2006
Net sales	$25,520	$23,980	$24,200	$22,880	$22,000
Cost of goods sold	17,220	15,400	15,540	14,700	14,000
General and administrative expenses	5,280	5,184	5,088	4,896	4,800
Operating income	3,020	3,396	3,572	3,284	3,200

LO2 Horizontal Analysis

E 8. Compute the amount and percentage changes for the following balance sheets for Davis Company, and comment on the changes from 2009 to 2010. (Round the percentage changes to one decimal place.)

Davis Company
Comparative Balance Sheets
December 31, 2010 and 2009

	2010	2009
Assets		
Current assets	$ 18,600	$ 12,800
Property, plant, and equipment (net)	109,464	97,200
Total assets	$128,064	$110,000
Liabilities and Stockholders' Equity		
Current liabilities	$ 11,200	$ 3,200
Long-term liabilities	35,000	40,000
Stockholders' equity	81,864	66,800
Total liabilities and stockholders' equity	$128,064	$110,000

LO2 **Vertical Analysis**

E 9. Express the partial comparative income statements for Davis Company that follow as common-size statements, and comment on the changes from 2009 to 2010. (Round computations to one decimal place.)

Davis Company
Partial Comparative Income Statements
For the Years Ended December 31, 2010 and 2009

	2010	2009
Net sales	$212,000	$184,000
Cost of goods sold	127,200	119,600
Gross margin	$ 84,800	$ 64,400
Selling expenses	$ 53,000	$ 36,800
General expenses	25,440	18,400
Total operating expenses	$ 78,440	$ 55,200
Operating income	$ 6,360	$ 9,200

LO3 **Liquidity Analysis**

E 10. Partial comparative balance sheet and income statement information for Smith Company is as follows:

	2011	2010
Cash	$ 27,200	$ 20,800
Marketable securities	14,400	34,400
Accounts receivable (net)	89,600	71,200
Inventory	108,800	99,200
Total current assets	$240,000	$225,600
Accounts payable	$ 80,000	$ 56,400
Net sales	$645,120	$441,440
Cost of goods sold	435,200	406,720
Gross margin	$209,920	$ 34,720

In 2009, the year-end balances for Accounts Receivable and Inventory were $64,800 and $102,400, respectively. Accounts Payable was $61,200 in 2009 and is the only current liability. Compute the current ratio, quick ratio, receivable turnover, days' sales uncollected, inventory turnover, days' inventory on hand, payables turnover, and days' payable for each year. (Round computations to one decimal place.) Comment on the change in the company's liquidity position.

LO3 **Operating Cycle**

E 11. Using the information for Smith Company in **E 10**, compute the operating cycle and finance period for both years. Comment on the change in the company's operating cycle and required days of financing from 2010 to 2011.

LO3 **Turnover Analysis**

E 12. Modern Suits Rental has been in business for four years. Because the company has recently had a cash flow problem, management wonders whether there is a problem with receivables or inventories. Selected figures from the company's financial statements (in thousands) follow.

	2011	2010	2009	2008
Net sales	$288.0	$224.0	$192.0	$160.0
Cost of goods sold	180.0	144.0	120.0	96.0
Accounts receivable (net)	48.0	40.0	32.0	24.0
Merchandise inventory	56.0	44.0	32.0	20.0
Accounts payable	26.0	20.0	16.0	10.0

Compute the receivable turnover, inventory turnover, and payables turnover for each of the four years, and comment on the results relative to the cash flow problem that the firm has been experiencing. Merchandise inventory was $22,000, accounts receivable were $22,000, and accounts payable were $8,000 in 2007. (Round computations to one decimal place.)

LO3 **Profitability Analysis**

E 13. Barr Company had total assets of $320,000 in 2008, $340,000 in 2009, and $380,000 in 2010. The company's debt to equity ratio was .67 times in all three years. In 2009, Barr had net income of $38,556 on revenues of $612,000. In 2010, it had net income of $49,476 on revenues of $798,000. Compute the profit margin, asset turnover, return on assets, and return on equity for 2009 and 2010. Comment on the apparent cause of the increase or decrease in profitability. (Round the percentages and other ratios to one decimal place.)

LO3 **Long-term Solvency and Market Strength Ratios**

E 14. An investor is trying to decide whether to invest in the long-term bonds and common stock of Companies P and R. Both companies operate in the same industry. Both also pay a dividend per share of $4 and have a yield of 5 percent on their long-term bonds. Other data for the two companies are as follows:

	Company P	Company R
Total assets	$2,400,000	$1,080,000
Total liabilities	1,080,000	594,000
Income before income taxes	288,000	129,600
Interest expense	97,200	53,460
Earnings per share	3.20	5.00
Market price of common stock	40.00	47.50

Compute the debt to equity, interest coverage, and price/earnings (P/E) ratios, as well as the dividends yield, and comment on the results. (Round computations to one decimal place.)

LO3 **Cash Flow Adequacy Analysis**

E 15. Using the following data from the financial statements of Bali, Inc., compute the company's cash flow yield, cash flows to sales, cash flows to assets, and free cash flow. (Round computations to one decimal place.)

Net sales	$1,600,000
Net income	176,000
Net cash flows from operating activities	228,000
Total assets, beginning of year	1,445,000
Total assets, end of year	1,560,000
Cash dividends	60,000
Net capital expenditures	149,000

Problems

LO2 Horizontal and Vertical Analysis

P 1. Robert Corporation's condensed comparative balance sheets and condensed comparative income statements for 2011 and 2010 follow.

Robert Corporation
Comparative Balance Sheets
December 31, 2011 and 2010

	2011	2010
Assets		
Cash	$ 40,600	$ 20,400
Accounts receivable (net)	117,800	114,600
Inventory	287,400	297,400
Property, plant, and equipment (net)	375,000	360,000
Total assets	$820,800	$792,400
Liabilities and Stockholders' Equity		
Accounts payable	$133,800	$238,600
Notes payable (short-term)	100,000	200,000
Bonds payable	200,000	—
Common stock, $10 par value	200,000	200,000
Retained earnings	187,000	153,800
Total liabilities and stockholders' equity	$820,800	$792,400

Robert Corporation
Comparative Income Statements
For the Years Ended December 31, 2011 and 2010

	2011	2010
Net sales	$1,638,400	$1,573,200
Cost of goods sold	1,044,400	1,004,200
Gross margin	$ 594,000	$ 569,000
Operating expenses		
Selling expenses	$ 238,400	$ 259,000
Administrative expenses	223,600	211,600
Total operating expenses	$ 462,000	$ 470,600
Income from operations	$ 132,000	$ 98,400
Interest expense	32,800	19,600
Income before income taxes	$ 99,200	$ 78,800
Income taxes expense	31,200	28,400
Net income	$ 68,000	$ 50,400
Earnings per share	$ 3.40	$ 2.52

Required

1. Prepare schedules showing the amount and percentage changes from 2010 to 2011 for the comparative income statements and the balance sheets.
2. Prepare common-size income statements and balance sheets for 2010 and 2011.

Manager insight ▶

3. Comment on the results in requirements **1** and **2** by identifying favorable and unfavorable changes in the components and composition of the statements.

LO3 Comprehensive Ratio Analysis

P 2. Data for Robert Corporation in 2011and 2010 follow. These data should be used in conjunction with the data in **P 1**.

	2011	2010
Net cash flows from operating activities	($98,000)	$72,000
Net capital expenditures	$20,000	$32,500
Dividends paid	$22,000	$17,200
Number of common shares	20,000	20,000
Market price per share	$18	$30

Selected balances at the end of 2009 were accounts receivable (net), $103,400; inventory, $273,600; total assets, $732,800; accounts payable, $193,300; and stockholders' equity, $320,600. All Robert's notes payable were current liabilities; all its bonds payable were long-term liabilities.

Required

Perform a comprehensive ratio analysis. Round all answers to one decimal place.

1. Prepare a liquidity analysis by calculating for each year the (a) current ratio, (b) quick ratio, (c) receivable turnover, (d) days' sales uncollected, (e) inventory turnover, (f) days' inventory on hand, (g) payables turnover, and (h) days' payable.
2. Prepare a profitability analysis by calculating for each year the (a) profit margin, (b) asset turnover, (c) return on assets, and (d) return on equity.
3. Prepare a long-term solvency analysis by calculating for each year the (a) debt to equity ratio and (b) interest coverage ratio.
4. Prepare a cash flow adequacy analysis by calculating for each year the (a) cash flow yield, (b) cash flows to sales, (c) cash flows to assets, and (d) free cash flow.
5. Prepare a market strength analysis by calculating for each year the (a) price/earnings (P/E) ratio and (b) dividends yield.

User insight ▶

6. After making the calculations, indicate whether each ratio improved or deteriorated from 2010 to 2011 (use *F* for favorable and *U* for unfavorable and consider changes of 0.1 or less to be neutral).

LO3 Effects of Transactions on Ratios

P 3. Sung Corporation, a clothing retailer, engaged in the transactions listed in the first column of the table that follows. Opposite each transaction is a ratio and space to mark the effect of each transaction on the ratio.

Transaction	Ratio	Effect: Increase	Effect: Decrease	Effect: None
a. Issued common stock for cash.	Asset turnover			
b. Declared cash dividend.	Current ratio			
c. Sold treasury stock.	Return on equity			
d. Borrowed cash by issuing note payable.	Debt to equity ratio			
e. Paid salaries expense.	Inventory turnover			
f. Purchased merchandise for cash.	Current ratio			
g. Sold equipment for cash.	Receivable turnover			
h. Sold merchandise on account.	Quick ratio			
i. Paid current portion of long-term debt.	Return on assets			
j. Gave sales discount.	Profit margin			
k. Purchased marketable securities for cash.	Quick ratio			
l. Declared 5% stock dividend.	Current ratio			
m. Purchased a building.	Free cash flow			

Required

User insight ▶ Place an X in the appropriate column to show whether the transaction increased, decreased, or had no effect on the indicated ratio.

LO3 Comprehensive Ratio Analysis

P 4. The condensed comparative income statements of Tola Corporation follow. The corporation's condensed comparative balance sheets are presented on the next page. All figures are given in thousands of dollars, except earnings per share and market price per share. Additional data for Tola Corporation in 2011 and 2010 are as follows:

	2011	2010
Net cash flows from operating activities	$32,000	$49,500
Net capital expenditures	$59,500	$19,000
Dividends paid	$15,700	$17,500
Number of common shares	15,000	15,000
Market price per share	$40	$60

Tola Corporation
Comparative Income Statements
For the Years Ended December 31, 2011 and 2010

	2011	2010
Net sales	$400,200	$371,300
Cost of goods sold	227,050	198,100
Gross margin	$173,150	$173,200
Operating expenses		
Selling expenses	$ 65,050	$ 52,300
Administrative expenses	70,150	57,750
Total operating expenses	$135,200	$110,050
Income from operations	$ 37,950	$ 63,150
Interest expense	12,500	10,000
Income before income taxes	$ 25,450	$ 53,150
Income taxes expense	7,000	17,500
Net income	$ 18,450	$ 35,650
Earnings per share	$ 1.23	$ 2.38

Tola Corporation
Comparative Balance Sheets
December 31, 2011 and 2010

	2011	2010
Assets		
Cash	$ 15,550	$ 13,600
Accounts receivable (net)	36,250	21,350
Inventory	61,300	53,900
Property, plant, and equipment (net)	288,850	253,750
Total assets	$401,950	$342,600
Liabilities and Stockholders' Equity		
Accounts payable	$ 52,350	$ 36,150
Notes payable	25,000	25,000
Bonds payable	100,000	55,000
Common stock, $10 par value	150,000	150,000
Retained earnings	74,600	76,450
Total liabilities and stockholders' equity	$401,950	$342,600

Balances of selected accounts at the end of 2009 were accounts receivable (net), $26,350; inventory, $49,700; accounts payable, $32,400; total assets, $323,900; and stockholders' equity, $188,300. All of the bonds payable were long-term liabilities.

Required

Perform a comprehensive analyses. Round percentages and ratios to one decimal place.

1. Prepare a liquidity analysis by calculating for each year the (a) current ratio, (b) quick ratio, (c) receivable turnover, (d) days' sales uncollected, (e) inventory turnover, (f) days' inventory on hand, (g) payables turnover, and (h) days' payable.
2. Prepare a profitability analysis by calculating for each year the (a) profit margin, (b) asset turnover, (c) return on assets, and (d) return on equity.
3. Prepare a long-term solvency analysis by calculating for each year the (a) debt to equity ratio and (b) interest coverage ratio.
4. Prepare a cash flow adequacy analysis by calculating for each year the (a) cash flow yield, (b) cash flows to sales, (c) cash flows to assets, and (d) free cash flow.
5. Prepare an analysis of market strength by calculating for each year the (a) price/earnings (P/E) ratio and (b) dividends yield.
6. User insight ▶ After making the calculations, indicate whether each ratio improved or deteriorated from 2010 to 2011 (use *F* for favorable and *U* for unfavorable and consider changes of 0.1 or less to be neutral).

LO3 Comprehensive Ratio Analysis of Two Companies

P 5. Agnes Ball is considering an investment in the common stock of a chain of retail department stores. She has narrowed her choice to two retail companies, Fast Corporation and Style Corporation, whose income statements and balance sheets are presented below.

During the year, Fast Corporation paid a total of $50,000 in dividends. The market price per share of its stock is currently $60. In comparison, Style Corporation paid a total of $114,000 in dividends, and the current market price of its stock is $76 per share. Fast Corporation had net cash flows from operations of $271,500 and net capital expenditures of $625,000. Style Corporation had net cash flows from operations of $492,500 and net capital expenditures of $1,050,000. Information for prior years is not readily available. Assume that all notes payable are current liabilities and all bonds payable are long-term liabilities and that there is no change in inventory.

Income Statements

	Fast	Style
Net sales	$12,560,000	$25,210,000
Costs and expenses		
Cost of goods sold	$ 6,142,000	$14,834,000
Selling expenses	4,822,600	7,108,200
Administrative expenses	986,000	2,434,000
Total costs and expenses	$11,950,600	$24,376,200
Income from operations	$ 609,400	$ 833,800
Interest expense	194,000	228,000
Income before income taxes	$ 415,400	$ 605,800
Income taxes expense	200,000	300,000
Net income	$ 215,400	$ 305,800
Earnings per share	$ 4.31	$ 10.19

Balance Sheets

	Fast	Style
Assets		
Cash	$ 80,000	$ 192,400
Marketable securities (at cost)	203,400	84,600
Accounts receivable (net)	552,800	985,400
Inventory	629,800	1,253,400
Prepaid expenses	54,400	114,000
Property, plant, and equipment (net)	2,913,600	6,552,000
Intangibles and other assets	553,200	144,800
Total assets	$4,987,200	$9,326,600
Liabilities and Stockholders' Equity		
Accounts payable	$ 344,000	$ 572,600
Notes payable	150,000	400,000
Income taxes payable	50,200	73,400
Bonds payable	2,000,000	2,000,000
Common stock, $20 par value	1,000,000	600,000
Additional paid-in capital	609,800	3,568,600
Retained earnings	833,200	2,112,000
Total liabilities and stockholders' equity	$4,987,200	$9,326,600

Required

Conduct a comprehensive ratio analysis for each company. Compare the results. Round percentages and ratios to one decimal place, and consider changes of .1 or less to be indeterminate.

1. Prepare a liquidity analysis by calculating for each company the (a) current ratio, (b) quick ratio, (c) receivable turnover, (d) days' sales uncollected, (e) inventory turnover, (f) days' inventory on hand, (g) payables turnover, and (h) days' payable.
2. Prepare a profitability analysis by calculating for each company the (a) profit margin, (b) asset turnover, (c) return on assets, and (d) return on equity.
3. Prepare a long-term solvency analysis by calculating for each company the (a) debt to equity ratio and (b) interest coverage ratio.
4. Prepare a cash flow adequacy analysis by calculating for each company the (a) cash flow yield, (b) cash flows to sales, (c) cash flows to assets, and (d) free cash flow.
5. Prepare an analysis of market strength by calculating for each company the (a) price/earnings (P/E) ratio and (b) dividends yield.
6. User insight ▶ Compare the two companies by inserting the ratio calculations from **1** through **5** in a table with the following column headings: Ratio, Name, Fast, Style, and Company with More Favorable Ratio. Indicate in the last column which company had the more favorable ratio in each case.
7. User insight ▶ How could the analysis be improved if information about these companies' prior years were available?

Alternate Problems

LO2 Horizontal and Vertical Analysis

P 6. Spain Corporation's condensed comparative balance sheets and condensed comparative income statements for 2011 and 2010 follow.

Spain Corporation
Comparative Balance Sheets
December 31, 2011 and 2010

	2011	2010
Assets		
Cash	$ 50,000	$ 60,000
Accounts receivable (net)	120,000	100,000
Inventory	400,000	300,000
Property, plant, and equipment (net)	330,000	40,000
Total assets	$900,000	$800,000
Liabilities and Stockholders' Equity		
Accounts payable	$200,000	$200,000
Notes payable (short-term)	100,000	200,000
Bonds payable	100,000	—
Common stock, $20 par value	200,000	200,000
Retained earnings	300,000	200,000
Total liabilities and stockholders' equity	$900,000	$800,000

Spain Corporation
Comparative Income Statements
For the Years Ended December 31, 2011 and 2010

	2011	2010
Net sales	$1,300,000	$1,200,000
Cost of goods sold	630,000	600,000
Gross margin	$ 670,000	$ 600,000
Operating expenses		
Selling expenses	$ 100,000	$ 100,000
Administrative expenses	400,000	300,000
Total operating expenses	$ 500,000	$ 400,000
Income from operations	$ 170,000	$ 200,000
Interest expense	30,000	20,000
Income before income taxes	$ 140,000	$ 180,000
Income taxes expense	40,000	50,000
Net income	$ 100,000	$ 130,000
Earnings per share	$ 10.00	$ 13.00

Required

1. Prepare schedules showing the amount and percentage changes from 2010 to 2011 for the comparative income statements and the balance sheets.
2. Prepare common-size income statements and balance sheets for 2010 and 2011.

User insight ▶ 3. Comment on the results in requirements **1** and **2** by identifying favorable and unfavorable changes in the components and composition of the statements.

LO3 Comprehensive Ratio Analysis

P 7. Data for Spain Corporation in 2011and 2010 follow. These data should be used in conjunction with the data in **P 6**.

	2011	2010
Net cash flows from operating activities	($50,000)	$26,000
Net capital expenditures	$10,000	$20,000
Dividends paid	$10,000	$12,000
Number of common shares	10,000	10,000
Market price per share	$20	$25

Selected balances at the end of 2009 were accounts receivable (net), $90,000; inventory, $270,000; total assets, $750,000; accounts payable, $150,000; and stockholders' equity, $350,000. All Spain's notes payable were current liabilities; all its bonds payable were long-term liabilities.

Required

Perform a comprehensive ratio analysis. Round all answers to one decimal place.

1. Prepare a liquidity analysis by calculating for each year the (a) current ratio, (b) quick ratio, (c) receivable turnover, (d) days' sales uncollected, (e) inventory turnover, (f) days' inventory on hand, (g) payables turnover, and (h) days' payable.
2. Prepare a profitability analysis by calculating for each year the (a) profit margin, (b) asset turnover, (c) return on assets, and (d) return on equity.
3. Prepare a long-term solvency analysis by calculating for each year the (a) debt to equity ratio and (b) interest coverage ratio.

4. Prepare a cash flow adequacy analysis by calculating for each year the (a) cash flow yield, (b) cash flows to sales, (c) cash flows to assets, and (d) free cash flow.
5. Prepare a market strength analysis by calculating for each year the (a) price/earnings (P/E) ratio and (b) dividends yield.

User insight ▶

6. After making the calculations, indicate whether each ratio improved or deteriorated from 2010 to 2011 (use *F* for favorable and *U* for unfavorable and consider changes of 0.1 or less to be neutral).

LO3 **Effects of Transactions on Ratios**

P 8. Alp Corporation engaged in the transactions listed in the first column of the following table. Opposite each transaction is a ratio and space to indicate the effect of each transaction on the ratio.

Transaction	Ratio	Effect		
		Increase	Decrease	None
a. Issued common stock for cash.	Asset turnover			
b. Borrowed cash by issuing a note payable.	Debt to equity ratio			
c. Purchase merchandise for cash.	Current ratio			
d. Pay salary expense.	Inventory turnover			
e. Sold equipment for cash.	Receivable turnover			
f. Sold merchandise on account.	Quick ratio			
g. Paid current portion of long-term debt.	Return on assets			
h. Issued stock dividend.	Current ratio			
i. Issued bonds payable.	Asset turnover			
j. Accrued salaries.	Current ratio			
k. Declared cash dividend.	Current ratio			
l. Sold treasury stock.	Profit margin			
m. Recorded depreciation for the year.	Cash flow yield			

Required

User insight ▶ Place an X in the appropriate column to show whether the transaction increased, decreased, or had no effect on the indicated ratio.

LO3 **Comprehensive Ratio Analysis**

P 9. The condensed comparative income statements and balance sheets of UK Corporation are presented on the next page. All figures are given in thousands of dollars, except earnings per share and market price per share. Additional data for UK Corporation in 2011 and 2010 are as follows:

	2011	2010
Net cash flows from operating activities	\$100,000	\$80,000
Net capital expenditures	\$80,000	\$50,000
Dividends paid	\$30,000	\$25,000
Number of common shares	20,000	20,000
Market price per share	\$70	\$50

Balances of selected accounts at the end of 2009 were accounts receivable (net), \$15,000; inventory, \$50,000; accounts payable, \$24,000; total assets, \$250,000; and stockholders' equity, \$200,000. All of the bonds payable were long-term liabilities.

UK Corporation
Comparative Income Statements
For the Years Ended December 31, 2011 and 2010

	2011	2010
Net sales	$400,000	$360,000
Cost of goods sold	200,000	200,000
Gross margin	$200,000	$160,000
Operating expenses		
Selling expenses	$ 50,000	$ 40,000
Administrative expenses	60,000	70,000
Total operating expenses	$110,000	$110,000
Income from operations	$ 90,000	$ 50,000
Interest expense	15,000	10,000
Income before income taxes	$ 75,000	$ 40,000
Income taxes expense	10,000	6,000
Net income	$ 65,000	$ 34,000
Earnings per share	$ 3.25	$ 1.70

UK Corporation
Comparative Balance Sheets
December 31, 2011 and 2010

	2011	2010
Assets		
Cash	$ 25,000	$ 20,000
Accounts receivable (net)	21,000	18,000
Inventory	49,000	52,000
Property, plant, and equipment (net)	205,000	200,000
Total assets	$300,000	$290,000
Liabilities and Stockholders' Equity		
Accounts payable	$ 50,000	$ 30,000
Notes payable	10,000	—
Bonds payable	10,000	40,000
Common stock, $10 par value	200,000	200,000
Retained earnings	30,000	20,000
Total liabilities and stockholders' equity	$300,000	$290,000

Required

Perform a comprehensive ratio analysis. Round percentages and ratios to one decimal place.

1. Prepare a liquidity analysis by calculating for each year the (a) current ratio, (b) quick ratio, (c) receivable turnover, (d) days' sales uncollected, (e) inventory turnover, (f) days' inventory on hand, (g) payables turnover, and (h) days' payable.
2. Prepare a profitability analysis by calculating for each year the (a) profit margin, (b) asset turnover, (c) return on assets, and (d) return on equity.
3. Prepare a long-term solvency analysis by calculating for each year the (a) debt to equity ratio and (b) interest coverage ratio.
4. Prepare a cash flow adequacy analysis by calculating for each year the (a) cash flow yield, (b) cash flows to sales, (c) cash flows to assets, and (d) free cash flow.

5. Prepare an analysis of market strength by calculating for each year the (a) price/earnings (P/E) ratio and (b) dividends yield.

User insight ▶ 6. After making the calculations, indicate whether each ratio improved or deteriorated from 2010 to 2011 (use *F* for favorable and *U* for unfavorable and consider changes of 0.1 or less to be neutral).

LO3 **Comprehensive Ratio Analysis of Two Companies**

P 10. Caitlin Cleary is considering an investment in the common stock of a chain of souvenir stores. She has narrowed her choice to two companies, Dover Corporation and Calais Corporation, whose income statements and balance sheets are presented here.

During the year, Dover Corporation paid a total of $50,000 in dividends. The market price per share of its stock is currently $60. In comparison, Calais Corporation paid a total of $114,000 in dividends, and the current market price of its stock is $76 per share. Dover Corporation had net cash flows from operations of $271,500 and net capital expenditures of $625,000. Calais Corporation had net cash flows from operations of $492,500 and net capital expenditures of $1,050,000. Information for prior years is not readily available. Assume that all notes payable are current liabilities and all bonds payable are long-term liabilities and that there is no change in inventory.

Income Statements

	Dover	Calais
Net sales	$13,000,000	$25,000,000
Costs and expenses		
Cost of goods sold	$ 6,000,000	$14,000,000
Selling expenses	4,000,000	7,000,000
Administrative expenses	1,000,000	3,000,000
Total costs and expenses	$11,000,000	$24,000,000
Income from operations	$ 2,000,000	$ 1,000,000
Interest expense	200,000	150,000
Income before income taxes	$ 1,800,000	$ 850,000
Income taxes expense	800,000	150,000
Net income	$ 1,000,000	$ 600,000
Earnings per share	$ 10.00	$ 10.00

Balance Sheets

	Dover	Calais
Assets		
Cash	$ 80,000	$ 180,000
Marketable securities (at cost)	200,000	20,000
Accounts receivable (net)	600,000	900,000
Inventory	700,000	1,300,000
Prepaid expenses	20,000	120,000
Property, plant, and equipment (net)	2,000,000	6,000,000
Intangibles and other assets	400,000	480,000
Total assets	$4,000,000	$9,000,000

(Continued)

	Dover	Calais
Liabilities and Stockholders' Equity		
Accounts payable	$ 200,000	$ 600,000
Notes payable	700,000	400,000
Income taxes payable	80,000	70,000
Bonds payable	1,000,000	2,000,000
Common stock, $10 par value	1,000,000	600,000
Additional paid-in capital	120,000	2,330,000
Retained earnings	900,000	3,000,000
Total liabilities and stockholders' equity	$4,000,000	$9,000,000

Required

Conduct a comprehensive ratio analysis for each company. Compare the results. Round percentages and ratios to one decimal place, and consider changes of 0.1 or less to be indeterminate.

1. Prepare a liquidity analysis by calculating for each company the (a) current ratio, (b) quick ratio, (c) receivable turnover, (d) days' sales uncollected, (e) inventory turnover, (f) days' inventory on hand, (g) payables turnover, and (h) days' payable.
2. Prepare a profitability analysis by calculating for each company the (a) profit margin, (b) asset turnover, (c) return on assets, and (d) return on equity.
3. Prepare a long-term solvency analysis by calculating for each company the (a) debt to equity ratio and (b) interest coverage ratio.
4. Prepare a cash flow adequacy analysis by calculating for each company the (a) cash flow yield, (b) cash flows to sales, (c) cash flows to assets, and (d) free cash flow.
5. Prepare an analysis of market strength by calculating for each company the (a) price/earnings (P/E) ratio and (b) dividends yield.

User insight ▶

6. Compare the two companies by inserting the ratio calculations from **1** through **5** in a table with the following column headings: Ratio, Name, Dover, Calais, and Company with More Favorable Ratio. Indicate in the last column which company had the more favorable ratio in each case.

User insight ▶

7. How could the analysis be improved if information about these companies' prior years were available?

ENHANCING Your Knowledge, Skills, and Critical Thinking

LO1 Executive Compensation

C1. Executive compensation is often based on meeting certain targets for revenue growth, earnings, earnings per share, return on assets, or other performance measures. But what if performance is not living up to expectations? Some companies are simply changing the targets. For instance, **Sun Microsystems**' proxy as quoted in the *Wall Street Journal* states that "due to economic challenges experienced during the last fiscal year, our earnings per share and revenues are significantly below plan. As such, the Bonus Plan was amended to reduce the target bonus to 50% of the original plan and base the target bonus solely on the third and fourth quarters."[14] Sun Microsystems was not alone. Other companies, such as **AT&T Wireless**, **Estee Lauder**, and **UST**, also lowered targets for executive bonuses.

Do you think it is acceptable to change the bonus targets for executives during the year if the year turns out to be not as successful as planned? What if an unexpected, world-shaking event occurs and has a negative effect on business, such as 9/11 had on the airline industry? What are three standards of comparison? Which of these might justify changing the bonus targets during the year?

LO1 Using Investors' Services

C 2. Go to the website for **Moody's Investors Service**. Click on "ratings," which will show revisions of debt ratings issued by Moody's in the past few days. Choose a rating that has been upgraded or downgraded and read the short press announcement related to it. What reasons does Moody's give for the change in rating? What is Moody's assessment of the future of the company or institution? What financial performance measures are mentioned in the article? Summarize your findings and be prepared to share them in class.

LO3 Analyzing the Airline Industry

C 3. Divide into groups. Assume your group is analyzing the fate of the larger airlines, such as **United** and **American**. You have the following information:

a. Between 1999 and now, the long-term debt, including lease obligations, of the largest airlines more than doubled.
b. The price of fuel has increased by one-third.
c. Passenger loads are only now getting back to pre-9/11 levels.
d. Severe price competition from discount airlines exists.

Identify the ratios that you consider most important to consider in assessing the future of the large airlines and discuss the effect of each of the above factors on the ratios. Be prepared to present all or part of your findings in class.

LO3 Comparison of International Companies' Operating Cycles

C 4. Ratio analysis enables one to compare the performance of companies whose financial statements are presented in different currencies. Selected data from 2006 for two large pharmaceutical companies—one American, **Pfizer, Inc.**, and one Swiss, **Roche**—are presented next (in millions).[15]

	Pfizer, Inc. (U.S.)	Roche (Swiss)
Net sales	$48,371	SF42,041
Cost of goods sold	7,640	10,616
Accounts receivable	9,392	8,960
Inventories	6,111	5,592
Accounts payable	2,019	2,213

For each company, calculate the receivable turnover, days' sales uncollected, inventory turnover, days' inventory on hand, payables turnover, and days' payable. Then determine the operating cycle and days of financing required for each company. (Accounts receivable in 2005 were $9,103 for Pfizer and SF7,698 for Roche. Inventories in 2005 were $5,478 for Pfizer and SF5,041 for Roche. Accounts payable in 2005 were $2,073 for Pfizer and SF2,373 for Roche.) Prepare a memo containing your analysis of the operating cycles of these companies.

LO2 LO3 Effect of a One-Time Item on a Loan Decision

C 5. Apple a Day, Inc., and Unforgettable Edibles, Inc. are food catering businesses that operate in the same metropolitan area. Their customers include *Fortune* 500 companies, regional firms, and individuals. The two firms reported similar profit margins for the current year, and both base bonuses for managers on the achievement of a target profit margin and return on equity. Each firm has submitted a loan request to you, a loan officer for City National Bank. They have provided you with the following information:

	Apple a Day	Unforgettable Edibles
Net sales	$625,348	$717,900
Cost of goods sold	25,125	287,080
Gross margin	$400,223	$430,820
Operating expenses	281,300	371,565
Operating income	$118,923	$ 59,255
Gain on sale of real estate	—	81,923
Interest expense	(9,333)	(15,338)
Income before income taxes	$109,590	$125,840
Income taxes expense	25,990	29,525
Net income	$ 83,600	$ 96,315
Average stockholders' equity	$312,700	$390,560

1. Perform a vertical analysis and prepare a common-size income statement for each firm. Compute profit margin and return on equity.
2. Discuss these results, the bonus plan for management, and loan considerations. Identify the company that is the better loan risk.

LO2 Cookie Company (Continuing Case)

C 6. In this segment of our continuing case, you will use the following data to analyze trends in your company's financial performance over the past five years.

Cookie Company
Five-Year Summary of Operations and Other Related Data

	2011	2010	2009	2008	2007
Summary of operations					
Sales	$9,000	$8,000	$ 7,000	$6,500	$5,000
Cost of products sold	6,700	5,500	5,000	4,700	3,000
Interest expense	300	120	50	70	50
Provision for income taxes	400	380	350	230	150
Net income (before special items)	1,600	2,000	1,600	1,500	1,800
Other related data					
Dividends paid: common	46	40	35	30	20
Total assets	5,000	4,000	3,000	2,500	2,000
Total debt	2,000	1,000	500	750	500
Shareholders' equity	3,000	3,000	2,500	1,750	1,500

Prepare a trend analysis for your company using 2007 as the base year, and discuss the results. Identify important trends, state whether the trends are favorable or unfavorable, and discuss significant relationships among the trends.

APPENDIX

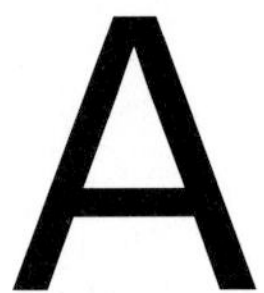

Accounting for Investments

Many companies invest in the stock or debt securities of other firms. They may do so for several reasons. A company may temporarily have excess funds on which it can earn a return, or investments may be an integral part of its business, as in the case of a bank. A company may also invest in other firms for the purpose of partnering with or controlling them.

Management Issues Related to Investments

The issues of recognition, valuation, classification, and disclosure apply to accounting for investments.

Recognition Recognition of investments as assets follows the general rule for recording transactions that we described earlier in the text. Purchases of investments are recorded on the date on which they are made, and sales of investments are reported on the date of sale. At the time of the transaction, there is either a transfer of funds or a definite obligation to pay. Income from investments is reported as other income on the income statement. Any gains or losses on investments are also reported on the income statement. Gains and losses appear as adjustments in the operating activities section of the statement of cash flows. The cash amounts of purchases and sales of investments appear in the investing activities section of the statement of cash flows.

Valuation Like other purchase transactions, investments are valued according to the *cost principle*—that is, they are valued in terms of their cost at the time they are purchased. The cost, or purchase price, includes any commissions or fees. However, after the purchase, the value of investments on the balance sheet is adjusted to reflect subsequent conditions. These conditions may reflect changes in the market value or fair value of the investments, changes caused by the passage of time (as in amortization), or changes in the operations of the investee companies. Long-term investments must be evaluated annually for any impairment or decline in value that is more than temporary. If such an impairment exists, a loss on the investment must be recorded.

IFRS

Under a new accounting standard, the goal of which is to bring U.S. standards more in line with international financial reporting standards, companies may elect to measure investments at fair value. Recall that *fair value* is defined as the *exchange price* associated with an actual or potential business transaction between market participants. This option applies to all types of investments except in the case of a subsidiary that is consolidated into the statements of the parent company. Generally, companies can elect the investment to which to apply fair value, but having done so, they cannot change the use of fair value in the future. Fair value can be determined when there is a ready market for the security, but determination is more problematic when a ready market does not exist. In the latter case, the fair value must be estimated through a method such as net present value.[1]

Classification Investments in debt and equity securities are classified as either short-term or long-term. *Short-term investments*, also called *marketable securities*, have a maturity of more than 90 days but are intended to be held only until cash is needed for current operations. (As we pointed out in an earlier chapter, investments with a maturity of *less* than 90 days are classified as cash equivalents.) Long-term investments are intended to be held for more than one year. *Long-term investments* are reported in the investments section of the balance sheet, not in the current assets section. Although long-term investments may be just as marketable as short-term assets, management intends to hold them for an indefinite time.

Short-term and long-term investments must be further classified as trading securities, available-for-sale securities, or held-to-maturity securities.[2]

- *Trading securities* are debt or equity securities bought and held principally for the purpose of being sold in the near term.
- *Available-for-sale securities* are debt or equity securities that do not meet the criteria for either trading or held-to-maturity securities. They may be short-term or long-term depending on what management intends to do with them.
- *Held-to-maturity securities* are debt securities that management intends to hold until their maturity date.

Figure 1 illustrates the classification of short-term and long-term investments. Table 1 shows the relationship between the percentage of ownership in a company's stock and the investing company's level of control, as well as the classifications and accounting treatments of these stock investments. These classifications are important because each one requires a different accounting treatment.

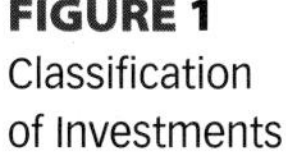
FIGURE 1
Classification of Investments

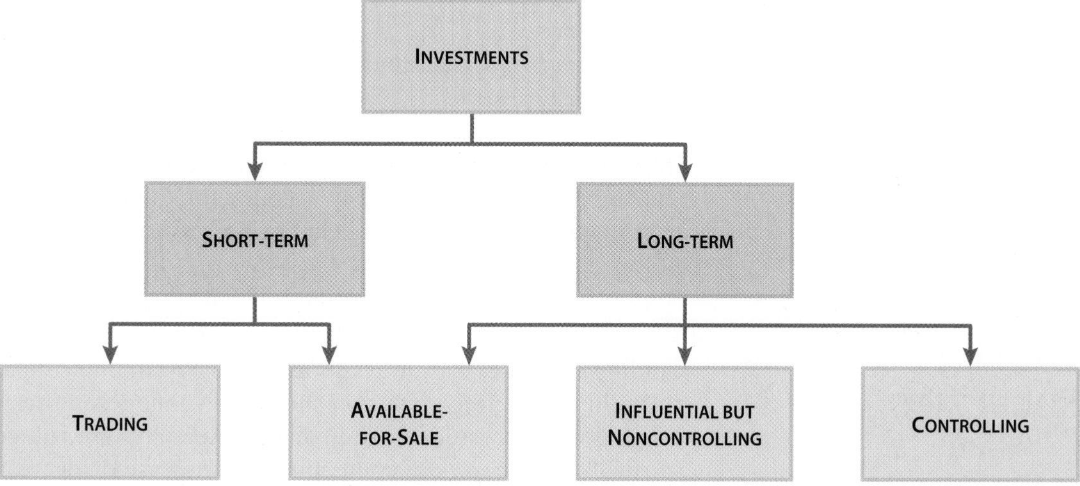

TABLE 1
Accounting for Equity Investments

Level of Control	Percentage of Ownership	Classification	Accounting Treatment
Noninfluential and noncontrolling	Less than 20%	Short-term investments—trading securities	Recorded at cost initially; cost adjusted after purchase for changes in market value; unrealized gains and losses reported on income statement
		Short-term or long-term investments—available-for-sale securities	Recorded at cost initially; cost adjusted for changes in market value with unrealized gains and losses to stockholders' equity
Influential but noncontrolling	Between 20% and 50%	Long-term investments	Equity method: recorded at cost initially; cost subsequently adjusted for investor's share of net income or loss and for dividends received
Controlling	More than 50%	Long-term investments	Financial statements consolidated

In general, the percentage of ownership in another company's stock has the following effects:

- ***Noninfluential and noncontrolling investment:*** A firm that owns less than 20 percent of the stock of another company has no influence on the other company's operations.
- ***Influential but noncontrolling investment:*** A firm that owns between 20 to 50 percent of another company's stock can exercise *significant influence* over that company's operating and financial policies, even though it holds 50 percent or less of the voting stock. Indications of significant influence include representation on the board of directors, participation in policymaking, exchange of managerial personnel, and technological dependency between the two companies.
- ***Controlling investment:*** A firm that owns more than 50 percent of another company's stock.

Disclosure Companies provide detailed information about their investments and the manner in which they account for them in the notes to their financial statements. Such disclosures help users assess the impact of the investments.

Trading Securities

Trading securities are always short-term investments and are frequently bought and sold to generate profits on short-term changes in their prices. They are classified as current assets on the balance sheet and are valued at fair value, which is usually the same as market value. An increase or decrease in the fair value of a company's total trading portfolio (the group of securities it holds for trading purposes) is included in net income in the accounting period in which the increase or decrease occurs.

For example, suppose Jackson Company buys 10,000 shares of **IBM** for $900,000 ($90 per share) and 10,000 shares of **Microsoft** for $300,000 ($30 per share) on October 25, 2010. The purchase is made for trading purposes—that is, Jackson's management intends to realize a gain by holding the shares for only a short period. The entry in journal form to record the investment at cost is as follows:

Purchase

A	= L	+ OE
+1,200,000		
−1,200,000		

2010			
Oct. 25	Short-Term Investments	1,200,000	
	Cash		1,200,000
	Investment in stocks for trading ($900,000 + $300,000 = $1,200,000)		

Assume that at year end, IBM's stock price has decreased to $80 per share and Microsoft's has risen to $32 per share. The trading portfolio is now valued at $1,120,000:

Security	*Market Value*	*Cost*	*Gain (Loss)*
IBM (10,000 shares)	$ 800,000	$ 900,000	
Microsoft (10,000 shares)	320,000	300,000	
Totals	$1,120,000	$1,200,000	($80,000)

Because the current fair value of the portfolio is $80,000 less than the original cost of $1,200,000, the following adjusting entry is needed:

Year-End Adjustment

A	= L	+ OE
−80,000		−80,000

2010			
Dec. 31	Unrealized Loss on Investments	80,000	
	Allowance to Adjust Short-Term Investments to Market		80,000
	Recognition of unrealized loss on trading portfolio		

Study Note

The Allowance to Adjust Short-Term Investments to Market account is never changed when securities are sold. It changes only when an adjusting entry is made at year end.

The unrealized loss will appear on the income statement as a reduction in income. The loss is unrealized because the securities have not been sold; if unrealized gains occur, they are treated the same way. The Allowance to Adjust Short-Term Investments to Market account appears on the balance sheet as a contra-asset, as follows:

Short-term investments (at cost)	$1,200,000
Less allowance to adjust short-term investments to market	80,000
Short-term investments (at market)	$1,120,000

or, more simply,

Short-term investments (at market value, cost is $1,200,000)	$1,120,000

If Jackson sells its 10,000 shares of Microsoft for $35 per share on March 2, 2011, a realized gain on trading securities is recorded as follows:

Sale

A	=	L	+	OE
+350,000				+50,000
−300,000				

2011			
Mar. 2	Cash	350,000	
	Short-Term Investments		300,000
	Realized Gain on Sale of Investments		50,000
	Sale of 10,000 shares of Microsoft for $35 per share; cost was $30 per share		

The realized gain will appear on the income statement. Note that the realized gain is unaffected by the adjustment for the unrealized loss at the end of 2010. The two transactions are treated independently. If the stock had been sold for less than cost, a realized loss on investments would have been recorded. Realized losses also appear on the income statement.

Now let's assume that during 2011, Jackson buys 4,000 shares of **Apple Computer** at $32 per share and has no transactions involving its shares of IBM. Also assume that by December 31, 2011, the price of IBM's stock has risen to $95 per share, or $5 per share more than the original cost, and that Apple's stock price has fallen to $29, or $3 less than the original cost. We can now analyze Jackson's trading portfolio as follows:

Security	*Market Value*	*Cost*	*Gain (Loss)*
IBM (10,000 shares)	$ 950,000	$ 900,000	
Apple (4,000 shares)	116,000	128,000	
Totals	$1,066,000	$1,028,000	$38,000

The market value of Jackson's trading portfolio now exceeds the cost by $38,000 ($1,066,000 − $1,028,000). This amount represents the targeted ending balance for the Allowance to Adjust Short-Term Investments to Market account. Recall that at the end of 2010, that account had a credit balance of $80,000, meaning that the market value of the trading portfolio was less than the cost. Because no entries are made to the account during 2011, it retains its balance until adjusting entries are made at the end of the year. The adjustment for 2011 must be $118,000—enough to result in a debit balance of $38,000 in the allowance account:

Year-End Adjustment

A	=	L	+	OE
+118,000				+118,000

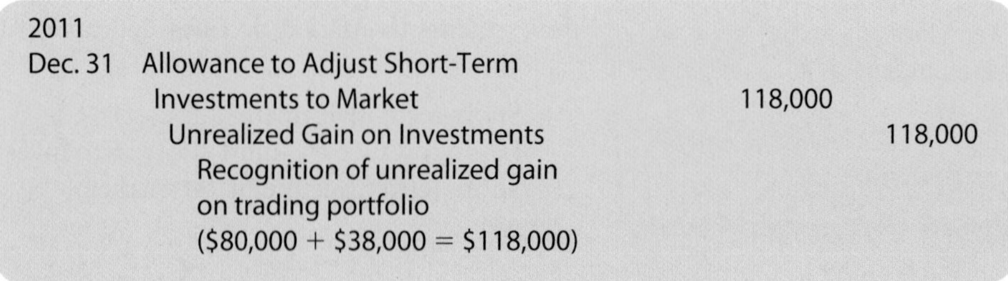

2011			
Dec. 31	Allowance to Adjust Short-Term Investments to Market	118,000	
	Unrealized Gain on Investments		118,000
	Recognition of unrealized gain on trading portfolio ($80,000 + $38,000 = $118,000)		

The 2011 ending balance of Jackson's allowance account can be determined as follows:

ALLOWANCE TO ADJUST SHORT-TERM INVESTMENTS TO MARKET

Dec. 31, 2011 Adj.	118,000	Dec. 31, 2010 Bal.	80,000
Dec. 31, 2011 Bal.	38,000		

The balance sheet presentation of short-term investments is as follows:

Short-term investments (at cost)	$1,028,000
Plus allowance to adjust short-term investments to market	38,000
Short-term investments (at market)	$1,066,000

or, more simply,

Short-term investments (at market value, cost is $1,028,000)	$1,066,000

If the company also has held-to-maturity securities that will mature within one year, they are included in short-term investments at cost adjusted for the effects of interest.

Available-for-Sale Securities

Short-term available-for-sale securities are accounted for in the same way as trading securities with two exceptions: (1) An unrealized gain or loss is reported as a special item in the stockholders' equity section of the balance sheet, not as a gain or loss on the income statement; (2) if a decline in the value of a security is considered permanent, it is charged as a loss on the income statement.

Long-Term Investments in Equity Securities

As indicated in Table 1, the accounting treatment of long-term investments in equity securities, such as common stock, depends on the extent to which the investing company can exercise control over the other company.

Noninfluential and Noncontrolling Investment As noted earlier, available-for-sale securities are debt or equity securities that cannot be classified as trading or held-to-maturity securities. When long-term equity securities are involved, a further criterion for classifying them as available for sale is that they be noninfluential and noncontrolling investments of less than 20 percent of the voting stock. Accounting for long-term available-for-sale securities requires using the *cost-adjusted-to-market method*. With this method, the securities are initially recorded at cost and are thereafter adjusted periodically for changes in market value by using an allowance account.[3]

Available-for-sale securities are classified as long-term if management intends to hold them for more than one year. When accounting for long-term available-for-sale securities, the unrealized gain or loss resulting from the adjustment is not reported on the income statement. Instead, the gain or loss is reported as a special item in the stockholders' equity section of the balance sheet and in the disclosure of comprehensive income.

At the end of each accounting period, the total cost and the total market value of these long-term stock investments must be determined. If the total market value is less than the total cost, the difference must be credited to a contra-asset account called Allowance to Adjust Long-Term Investments to Market. Because of the long-term nature of the investment, the debit part of the entry, which represents a decrease in value below cost, is treated as a temporary decrease and does not appear as a loss on the income statement. It is shown in a contra-stockholders' equity account called Unrealized Loss on Long-Term Investments.* Thus, both of these accounts are balance sheet accounts. If the market value exceeds the cost, the allowance account is added to Long-Term Investments, and the unrealized gain appears as an addition to stockholders' equity.

*If the decrease in market value of a long-term investment is deemed permanent or if the investment is deemed impaired, the decline or impairment is recorded by debiting a loss account on the income statement instead of the Unrealized Loss account.

When a company sells its long-term investments in stock, the difference between the sale price and the cost of the stock is recorded and reported as a realized gain or loss on the income statement. Dividend income from such investments is recorded by a debit to Cash and a credit to Dividend Income. For example, assume the following facts about the long-term stock investments of Nardini Corporation:

June 1, 2010	Paid cash for the following long-term investments: 10,000 shares of Herald Corporation common stock (representing 2 percent of outstanding stock) at $25 per share; 5,000 shares of Taza Corporation common stock (representing 3 percent of outstanding stock) at $15 per share.
Dec. 31, 2010	Quoted market prices at year end: Herald common stock, $21; Taza common stock, $17
Apr. 1, 2011	Change in policy required the sale of 2,000 shares of Herald common stock at $23.
July 1, 2011	Received cash dividend from Taza equal to $0.20 per share.
Dec. 31, 2011	Quoted market prices at year end: Herald common stock, $24; Taza common stock, $13.

Study Note

Nardini's sale of stock on April 1, 2011, was the result of a *change in policy*. This illustrates that intent is often the only difference between long-term investments and short-term investments.

Entries to record these transactions are as follows:

Investment

A	= L +	OE
+325,000		
−325,000		

2010			
June 1	Long-Term Investments	325,000	
	Cash		325,000
	Investments in Herald common stock (10,000 shares × $25 = $250,000) and Taza common stock (5,000 shares × $15 = $75,000)		

Year-End Adjustment

A	= L +	OE
−30,000		−30,000

2010			
Dec. 31	Unrealized Loss on Long-Term Investments	30,000	
	Allowance to Adjust Long-Term Investments to Market		30,000
	To record reduction of long-term investment to market		

This adjustment involves the following computations:

Company	*Shares*	*Market Price*	*Total Market*	*Total Cost*
Herald	10,000	$21	$210,000	$250,000
Taza	5,000	17	85,000	75,000
			$295,000	$325,000

Total Cost − Total Market Value = $325,000 − $295,000 = $30,000

Other entries are as follows:

Sale

A	= L +	OE
+46,000		−4,000
−50,000		

2011			
Apr. 1	Cash	46,000	
	Realized Loss on Sale of Investments	4,000	
	Long-Term Investments		50,000
	Sale of 2,000 shares of Herald common stock 2,000 × $23 = $46,000 2,000 × $25 = 50,000 Loss $ 4,000		

Dividend Received

A	= L +	OE
+1,000		+1,000

2011			
July 1	Cash	1,000	
	Dividend Income		1,000
	Receipt of cash dividend from Taza stock 5,000 × $0.20 = $1,000		

Year-End Adjustment

A	= L +	OE
+12,000		+12,000

2011			
Dec. 31	Allowance to Adjust Long-Term Investment to Market	12,000	
	Unrealized Loss on Long-Term Investments		12,000
	To record the adjustment in long-term investment so it is reported at market		

The adjustment equals the previous balance ($30,000 from the December 31, 2010, entry) minus the new balance ($18,000), or $12,000. The new balance of $18,000 is the difference at the present time between the total market value and the total cost of all investments. It is figured as follows:

Company	*Shares*	*Market Price*	*Total Market*	*Total Cost*
Herald	8,000	$24	$192,000	$200,000
Taza	5,000	13	65,000	75,000
			$257,000	$275,000

Total Cost − Total Market Value = $275,000 − $257,000 = $18,000

The Allowance to Adjust Long-Term Investments to Market and the Unrealized Loss on Long-Term Investments are reciprocal contra accounts, each with the same dollar balance, as shown by the effects of these transactions on the T accounts:

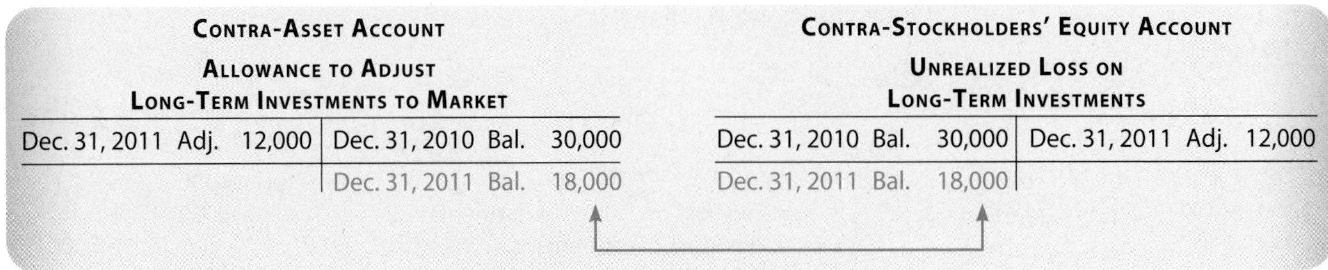

CONTRA-ASSET ACCOUNT ALLOWANCE TO ADJUST LONG-TERM INVESTMENTS TO MARKET	
Dec. 31, 2011 Adj. 12,000	Dec. 31, 2010 Bal. 30,000
	Dec. 31, 2011 Bal. 18,000

CONTRA-STOCKHOLDERS' EQUITY ACCOUNT UNREALIZED LOSS ON LONG-TERM INVESTMENTS	
Dec. 31, 2010 Bal. 30,000	Dec. 31, 2011 Adj. 12,000
Dec. 31, 2011 Bal. 18,000	

The Allowance account reduces long-term investments by the amount by which the cost of the investments exceeds market; the Unrealized Loss account reduces stockholders' equity by a similar amount. The opposite effects will exist if market value exceeds cost, resulting in an unrealized gain.

Influential but Noncontrolling Investment As we have noted, ownership of 20 percent or more of a company's voting stock is considered sufficient to influence the company's operations. When that is the case, the *equity method* should be used to account for the stock investment. The equity method presumes that an investment of 20 percent or more is not a passive investment and that the investor should therefore share proportionately in the success or failure of the company. The three main features of this method are as follows:

1. The investor records the original purchase of the stock at cost.
2. The investor records its share of the company's periodic net income as an increase in the Investment account, with a corresponding credit to an income account. Similarly, it records its share of a periodic loss as a decrease in the Investment account, with a corresponding debit to a loss account.
3. When the investor receives a cash dividend, the asset account Cash is increased, and the Investment account is decreased.

To illustrate the equity method, suppose that on January 1 of the current year, ITO Corporation acquired 40 percent of Quay Corporation's voting common stock for $180,000. With this share of ownership, ITO can exert significant influence over Quay's operations. During the year, Quay reported net income of $80,000 and paid cash dividends of $20,000. ITO recorded these transactions as follows:

Investment

A	=	L	+	OE
+180,000				
−180,000				

Investment in Quay Corporation	180,000	
Cash		180,000
Investments in Quay Corporation common stock		

Recognition of Income

A	=	L	+	OE
+32,000				+32,000

Investment in Quay Corporation	32,000	
Income, Quay Corporation Investment		32,000
Recognition of 40% of income reported by Quay Corporation 40% × $80,000 = $32,000		

Receipt of Cash Dividend

A	= L + OE
+8,000	
−8,000	

	Dr.	Cr.
Cash	8,000	
Investment in Quay Corporation		8,000
Cash dividend from Quay Corporation 40% × \$20,000 = \$8,000		

The balance of the Investment in Quay Corporation account after these transactions is \$204,000, as shown here:

Investment in Quay Corporation			
Investment	180,000	Dividend Received	8,000
Share of Income	32,000		
Bal.	204,000		

The share of income is reported as a separate line item on the income statement as a part of income from operations. The dividends received affect cash flows from operating activities on the statement of cash flows. The reported income (\$32,000) exceeds the cash received by \$24,000.

Controlling Investment When a controlling interest exists—usually when one company owns more than 50 percent of the voting stock of another company—consolidated financial statements are required. The investing company is the *parent company*; the other company is a *subsidiary*. Because a parent company and its subsidiaries are separate legal entities, each prepares separate financial statements. However, because of their special relationship, they are viewed for external financial reporting purposes as a single economic entity. For this reason, the FASB requires that they combine their financial statements into a single set of statements called *consolidated financial statements*. The concepts and procedures related to the preparation of consolidated financial statements are the subject of more advanced courses.

Investments in Debt Securities

As noted in previous chapters, debt securities are considered financial instruments because they are claims that will be paid in cash. When a company purchases debt securities, it records them at cost plus any commissions and fees. Like investments in equity securities, short-term investments in debt securities are valued at fair value at the end of the accounting period and are accounted for as trading securities or available-for-sale securities. However, the accounting treatment is different if they qualify as held-to-maturity securities.

Held-to-Maturity Securities As we noted earlier, held-to-maturity securities are debt securities that management intends to hold to their maturity date. Such securities are recorded at cost and are valued on the balance sheet at cost adjusted for the effects of interest. For example, suppose that on December 1, 2010, Webber Company pays \$97,000 for U.S. Treasury bills, which are short-term debt of the federal government. The bills will mature in 120 days at \$100,000. Webber would make the following entry:

A	= L + OE
+97,000	
−97,000	

2010		Dr.	Cr.
Dec. 1	Short-Term Investments	97,000	
	Cash		97,000
	Purchase of U.S. Treasury bills that mature in 120 days		

At Webber's year end on December 31, the entry to accrue the interest income earned to date would be as follows:

2010			
Dec. 31	Short-Term Investments	750	
	Interest Income		750
	Accrual of interest on U.S. Treasury bills $3,000 × 30/120 = $750		

On December 31, the U.S. Treasury bills would be shown on the balance sheet as a short-term investment at their amortized cost of $97,750 ($97,000 + $750). When Webber receives the maturity value on March 31, 2011, the entry is as follows:

A = L + OE
+100,000 +2,250
−97,750

2011			
Mar. 31	Cash	100,000	
	Short-Term Investments		97,750
	Interest Income		2,250
	Receipt of cash at maturity of U.S. Treasury bills and recognition of related income		

Long-Term Investments in Bonds

Like all investments, investments in bonds are recorded at cost, which, in this case, is the price of the bonds plus the broker's commission. When bonds are purchased between interest payment dates, the purchaser must also pay an amount equal to the interest that has accrued on the bonds since the last interest payment date. Then, on the next interest payment date, the purchaser receives an interest payment for the whole period. The payment for accrued interest should be recorded as a debit to Interest Income, which will be offset by a credit to Interest Income when the semiannual interest is received.

Subsequent accounting for a corporation's long-term bond investments depends on the classification of the bonds. If the company plans to hold the bonds until they are paid off on their maturity date, they are considered held-to-maturity securities. Except in industries like insurance and banking, it is unusual for companies to buy the bonds of other companies with the express purpose of holding them until they mature, which can be in 10 to 30 years. Thus, most long-term bond investments are classified as available-for-sale securities, meaning that the company plans to sell them at some point before their maturity date. Such bonds are accounted for at fair value, much as equity or stock investments are; fair value is usually the market value. When bonds are intended to be held to maturity, they are accounted for not at fair value but at cost, adjusted for the amortization of their discount or premium. The procedure is similar to accounting for long-term bond liabilities, except that separate accounts for discounts and premiums are not used.

& REVIEW >

- What is the role of fair value in accounting for investments?
- What is the difference between trading securities, available-for-sale securities, and held-to-maturity securities?
- Why are the level and percentage of ownership important in accounting for equity investments?
- How are trading securities valued at the balance sheet date?
- What are unrealized gains and losses on trading securities? On what statement are they reported?
- How does accounting for available-for-sale securities differ from accounting for trading securities?
- At what value are held-to-maturity securities shown on the balance sheet?

Problems

Trading Securities

P 1. Omar Corporation, which has begun investing in trading securities, engaged in the following transactions:

Jan. 6 Purchased 7,000 shares of Quaker Oats stock, $30 per share.
Feb. 15 Purchased 9,000 shares of EG&G, $22 per share.

At year end on June 30, Quaker Oats was trading at $40 per share, and EG&G was trading at $18 per share.

Record the entries in journal form for the purchases. Then record the necessary year-end adjusting entry. (Include a schedule of the trading portfolio cost and market in the explanation.) Also record the entry for the sale of all the EG&G shares on August 20 for $16 per share. Is the last entry affected by the June 30 adjustment?

Methods of Accounting for Long-Term Investments

P 2. Teague Corporation has the following long-term investments:

1. 60 percent of the common stock of Ariel Corporation
2. 13 percent of the common stock of Copper, Inc.
3. 50 percent of the nonvoting preferred stock of Staffordshire Corporation
4. 100 percent of the common stock of its financing subsidiary, EQ, Inc.
5. 35 percent of the common stock of the French company Rue de le Brasseur
6. 70 percent of the common stock of the Canadian company Nova Scotia Cannery

For each of these investments, tell which of the following methods should be used for external financial reporting, and why:

a. Cost-adjusted-to-market method
b. Equity method
c. Consolidation of parent and subsidiary financial statements

Long-Term Investments

P 3. Fulco Corporation has the following portfolio of long-term available-for-sale securities at year end, December 31, 2011:

Company	Percentage of Voting Stock Held	Cost	Year-End Market Value
A Corporation	4	$ 80,000	$ 95,000
B Corporation	12	375,000	275,000
C Corporation	5	30,000	55,000
Total		$485,000	$425,000

Both the Unrealized Loss on Long-Term Investments account and the Allowance to Adjust Long-Term Investments to Market account currently have a balance of $40,000 from the last accounting period. Prepare T accounts with a beginning balance for each of these accounts. Record the effects of the above information on the accounts, and determine the ending balances.

Long-Term Investments: Cost-Adjusted-to-Market and Equity Methods

P 4. On January 1, Rourke Corporation purchased, as long-term investments, 8 percent of the voting stock of Taglia Corporation for $250,000 and 45 percent of the voting stock of Curry Corporation for $2 million. During the year, Taglia Corporation had earnings of $100,000 and paid dividends of $40,000. Curry Corporation had earnings of $300,000 and paid dividends of $200,000. The market value did not change for either investment during the year. Which of these investments should be accounted for using the cost-adjusted-to-market method? Which should be accounted for using the equity method? At what amount should each investment be carried on the balance sheet at year end? Give a reason for each choice.

Held-to-Maturity Securities

P 5. Dale Company experiences heavy sales in the summer and early fall, after which time it has excess cash to invest until the next spring. On November 1, 2011, the company invested $194,000 in U.S. Treasury bills. The bills mature in 180 days at $200,000. Prepare entries in journal form to record the purchase on November 1; the adjustment to accrue interest on December 31, which is the end of the fiscal year; and the receipt of cash at the maturity date of April 30.

Comprehensive Accounting for Investments

P 6. Gulf Coast Corporation is a successful oil and gas exploration business in the southwestern United States. At the beginning of 2011, the company made investments in three companies that perform services in the oil and gas industry. The details of each of these investments follow.

Gulf Coast purchased 100,000 shares of Marsh Service Corporation at a cost of $16 per share. Marsh has 1.5 million shares outstanding and during 2011 paid dividends of $0.80 per share on earnings of $1.60 per share. At the end of the year, Marsh's shares were selling for $24 per share.

Gulf Coast also purchased 2 million shares of Crescent Drilling Company at $8 per share. Crescent has 10 million shares outstanding. In 2011, Crescent paid a dividend of $0.40 per share on earnings of $0.80 per share. During the year, the president of Gulf Coast was appointed to Crescent's board of directors. At the end of the year, Crescent's stock was selling for $12 per share.

In another action, Gulf Coast purchased 1 million shares of Logan Oil Field Supplies Company's 5 million outstanding shares at $12 per share. The president of Gulf Coast sought membership on Logan's board of directors but was rebuffed when a majority of shareholders stated they did not want to be associated with Gulf Coast. Logan paid a dividend of $0.80 per share and reported a net income of only \$0.40 per share for the year. By the end of the year, its stock price had dropped to \$4 per share.

Required

1. For each investment, make entries in journal form for (a) initial investment, (b) receipt of cash dividend, and (c) recognition of income (if appropriate).
2. What adjusting entry (if any) is required at the end of the year?
3. Assuming that Gulf Coast sells its investment in Logan after the first of the year for \$6 per share, what entry would be made?
4. Assuming no other transactions occur and that the market value of Gulf Coast's investment in Marsh exceeds cost by \$2,400,000 at the end of the second year, what adjusting entry (if any) would be required?

User insight ▶
5. What principal factors were considered in determining how to account for Gulf Coast's investments? Should they be shown on the balance sheet as short-term or long-term investments? What factors affect this decision?

Long-Term Investments: Equity Method

P 7. Rylander Corporation owns 35 percent of the voting stock of Waters Corporation. The Investment account on Rylander's books as of January 1, 2011, was \$720,000. During 2011, Waters reported the following quarterly earnings and dividends:

Quarter	Earnings	Dividends Paid
1	\$160,000	\$100,000
2	240,000	100,000
3	120,000	100,000
4	(80,000)	100,000
	\$440,000	\$400,000

Because of the percentage of voting shares Rylander owns, it can exercise significant influence over the operations of Waters Corporation. Therefore, Rylander Corporation must account for the investment using the equity method.

Required

1. Prepare a T account for Rylander Corporation's investment in Waters, and enter the beginning balance, the relevant entries for the year in total, and the ending balance.

User insight ▶
2. What is the effect and placement of the entries in requirement **1** on Rylander Corporation's earnings as reported on the income statement?

User insight ▶
3. What is the effect and placement of the entries in requirement **1** on the statement of cash flows?

User insight ▶
4. How would the effects on the statements differ if Rylander's ownership represented only a 15 percent share of Waters?

APPENDIX

B Present Value Tables

TABLE 1 Present Value of $1 to Be Received at the End of a Given Number of Time Periods

Periods	1%	2%	3%	4%	5%	6%	7%	8%	9%	10%	12%
1	0.990	0.980	0.971	0.962	0.952	0.943	0.935	0.926	0.917	0.909	0.893
2	0.980	0.961	0.943	0.925	0.907	0.890	0.873	0.857	0.842	0.826	0.797
3	0.971	0.942	0.915	0.889	0.864	0.840	0.816	0.794	0.772	0.751	0.712
4	0.961	0.924	0.888	0.855	0.823	0.792	0.763	0.735	0.708	0.683	0.636
5	0.951	0.906	0.883	0.822	0.784	0.747	0.713	0.681	0.650	0.621	0.567
6	0.942	0.888	0.837	0.790	0.746	0.705	0.666	0.630	0.596	0.564	0.507
7	0.933	0.871	0.813	0.760	0.711	0.665	0.623	0.583	0.547	0.513	0.452
8	0.923	0.853	0.789	0.731	0.677	0.627	0.582	0.540	0.502	0.467	0.404
9	0.914	0.837	0.766	0.703	0.645	0.592	0.544	0.500	0.460	0.424	0.361
10	0.905	0.820	0.744	0.676	0.614	0.558	0.508	0.463	0.422	0.386	0.322
11	0.896	0.804	0.722	0.650	0.585	0.527	0.475	0.429	0.388	0.350	0.287
12	0.887	0.788	0.701	0.625	0.557	0.497	0.444	0.397	0.356	0.319	0.257
13	0.879	0.773	0.681	0.601	0.530	0.469	0.415	0.368	0.326	0.290	0.229
14	0.870	0.758	0.661	0.577	0.505	0.442	0.388	0.340	0.299	0.263	0.205
15	0.861	0.743	0.642	0.555	0.481	0.417	0.362	0.315	0.275	0.239	0.183
16	0.853	0.728	0.623	0.534	0.458	0.394	0.339	0.292	0.252	0.218	0.163
17	0.844	0.714	0.605	0.513	0.436	0.371	0.317	0.270	0.231	0.198	0.146
18	0.836	0.700	0.587	0.494	0.416	0.350	0.296	0.250	0.212	0.180	0.130
19	0.828	0.686	0.570	0.475	0.396	0.331	0.277	0.232	0.194	0.164	0.116
20	0.820	0.673	0.554	0.456	0.377	0.312	0.258	0.215	0.178	0.149	0.104
21	0.811	0.660	0.538	0.439	0.359	0.294	0.242	0.199	0.164	0.135	0.093
22	0.803	0.647	0.522	0.422	0.342	0.278	0.226	0.184	0.150	0.123	0.083
23	0.795	0.634	0.507	0.406	0.326	0.262	0.211	0.170	0.138	0.112	0.074
24	0.788	0.622	0.492	0.390	0.310	0.247	0.197	0.158	0.126	0.102	0.066
25	0.780	0.610	0.478	0.375	0.295	0.233	0.184	0.146	0.116	0.092	0.059
26	0.772	0.598	0.464	0.361	0.281	0.220	0.172	0.135	0.106	0.084	0.053
27	0.764	0.586	0.450	0.347	0.268	0.207	0.161	0.125	0.098	0.076	0.047
28	0.757	0.574	0.437	0.333	0.255	0.196	0.150	0.116	0.090	0.069	0.042
29	0.749	0.563	0.424	0.321	0.243	0.185	0.141	0.107	0.082	0.063	0.037
30	0.742	0.552	0.412	0.308	0.231	0.174	0.131	0.099	0.075	0.057	0.033
40	0.672	0.453	0.307	0.208	0.142	0.097	0.067	0.046	0.032	0.022	0.011
50	0.608	0.372	0.228	0.141	0.087	0.054	0.034	0.021	0.013	0.009	0.003

Table 1 is used to compute the value today of a single amount of cash to be received sometime in the future. To use Table 1, you must first know (1) the time period in years until funds will be received, (2) the stated annual rate of interest, and (3) the dollar amount to be received at the end of the time period.

Example—Table 1. What is the present value of \$30,000 to be received 25 years from now, assuming a 14 percent interest rate? From Table 1, the required multiplier is 0.038, and the answer is:

$$\$30{,}000 \times 0.038 = \$1{,}140$$

The factor values for Table 1 are:

$$\text{PV Factor} = (1 + r)^{-n}$$

14%	15%	16%	18%	20%	25%	30%	35%	40%	45%	50%	Periods
0.877	0.870	0.862	0.847	0.833	0.800	0.769	0.741	0.714	0.690	0.667	1
0.769	0.756	0.743	0.718	0.694	0.640	0.592	0.549	0.510	0.476	0.444	2
0.675	0.658	0.641	0.609	0.579	0.512	0.455	0.406	0.364	0.328	0.296	3
0.592	0.572	0.552	0.516	0.482	0.410	0.350	0.301	0.260	0.226	0.198	4
0.519	0.497	0.476	0.437	0.402	0.328	0.269	0.223	0.186	0.156	0.132	5
0.456	0.432	0.410	0.370	0.335	0.262	0.207	0.165	0.133	0.108	0.088	6
0.400	0.376	0.354	0.314	0.279	0.210	0.159	0.122	0.095	0.074	0.059	7
0.351	0.327	0.305	0.266	0.233	0.168	0.123	0.091	0.068	0.051	0.039	8
0.308	0.284	0.263	0.225	0.194	0.134	0.094	0.067	0.048	0.035	0.026	9
0.270	0.247	0.227	0.191	0.162	0.107	0.073	0.050	0.035	0.024	0.017	10
0.237	0.215	0.195	0.162	0.135	0.086	0.056	0.037	0.025	0.017	0.012	11
0.208	0.187	0.168	0.137	0.112	0.069	0.043	0.027	0.018	0.012	0.008	12
0.182	0.163	0.145	0.116	0.093	0.055	0.033	0.020	0.013	0.008	0.005	13
0.160	0.141	0.125	0.099	0.078	0.044	0.025	0.015	0.009	0.006	0.003	14
0.140	0.123	0.108	0.084	0.065	0.035	0.020	0.011	0.006	0.004	0.002	15
0.123	0.107	0.093	0.071	0.054	0.028	0.015	0.008	0.005	0.003	0.002	16
0.108	0.093	0.080	0.060	0.045	0.023	0.012	0.006	0.003	0.002	0.001	17
0.095	0.081	0.069	0.051	0.038	0.018	0.009	0.005	0.002	0.001	0.001	18
0.083	0.070	0.060	0.043	0.031	0.014	0.007	0.003	0.002	0.001		19
0.073	0.061	0.051	0.037	0.026	0.012	0.005	0.002	0.001	0.001		20
0.064	0.053	0.044	0.031	0.022	0.009	0.004	0.002	0.001			21
0.056	0.046	0.038	0.026	0.018	0.007	0.003	0.001	0.001			22
0.049	0.040	0.033	0.022	0.015	0.006	0.002	0.001				23
0.043	0.035	0.028	0.019	0.013	0.005	0.002	0.001				24
0.038	0.030	0.024	0.016	0.010	0.004	0.001	0.001				25
0.033	0.026	0.021	0.014	0.009	0.003	0.001					26
0.029	0.023	0.018	0.011	0.007	0.002	0.001					27
0.026	0.020	0.016	0.010	0.006	0.002	0.001					28
0.022	0.017	0.014	0.008	0.005	0.002						29
0.020	0.015	0.012	0.007	0.004	0.001						30
0.005	0.004	0.003	0.001	0.001							40
0.001	0.001	0.001									50

TABLE 2 Present Value of $1 Received Each Period for a Given Number of Time Periods

Periods	1%	2%	3%	4%	5%	6%	7%	8%	9%	10%	12%
1	0.990	0.980	0.971	0.962	0.952	0.943	0.935	0.926	0.917	0.909	0.893
2	1.970	1.942	1.913	1.886	1.859	1.833	1.808	1.783	1.759	1.736	1.690
3	2.941	2.884	2.829	2.775	2.723	2.673	2.624	2.577	2.531	2.487	2.402
4	3.902	3.808	3.717	3.630	3.546	3.465	3.387	3.312	3.240	3.170	3.037
5	4.853	4.713	4.580	4.452	4.329	4.212	4.100	3.993	3.890	3.791	3.605
6	5.795	5.601	5.417	5.242	5.076	4.917	4.767	4.623	4.486	4.355	4.111
7	6.728	6.472	6.230	6.002	5.786	5.582	5.389	5.206	5.033	4.868	4.564
8	7.652	7.325	7.020	6.733	6.463	6.210	5.971	5.747	5.535	5.335	4.968
9	8.566	8.162	7.786	7.435	7.108	6.802	6.515	6.247	5.995	5.759	5.328
10	9.471	8.983	8.530	8.111	7.722	7.360	7.024	6.710	6.418	6.145	5.650
11	10.368	9.787	9.253	8.760	8.306	7.887	7.499	7.139	6.805	6.495	5.938
12	11.255	10.575	9.954	9.385	8.863	8.384	7.943	7.536	7.161	6.814	6.194
13	12.134	11.348	10.635	9.986	9.394	8.853	8.358	7.904	7.487	7.103	6.424
14	13.004	12.106	11.296	10.563	9.899	9.295	8.745	8.244	7.786	7.367	6.628
15	13.865	12.849	11.938	11.118	10.380	9.712	9.108	8.559	8.061	7.606	6.811
16	14.718	13.578	12.561	11.652	10.838	10.106	9.447	8.851	8.313	7.824	6.974
17	15.562	14.292	13.166	12.166	11.274	10.477	9.763	9.122	8.544	8.022	7.120
18	16.398	14.992	13.754	12.659	11.690	10.828	10.059	9.372	8.756	8.201	7.250
19	17.226	15.678	14.324	13.134	12.085	11.158	10.336	9.604	8.950	8.365	7.366
20	18.046	16.351	14.878	13.590	12.462	11.470	10.594	9.818	9.129	8.514	7.469
21	18.857	17.011	15.415	14.029	12.821	11.764	10.836	10.017	9.292	8.649	7.562
22	19.660	17.658	15.937	14.451	13.163	12.042	11.061	10.201	9.442	8.772	7.645
23	20.456	18.292	16.444	14.857	13.489	12.303	11.272	10.371	9.580	8.883	7.718
24	21.243	18.914	16.936	15.247	13.799	12.550	11.469	10.529	9.707	8.985	7.784
25	22.023	19.523	17.413	15.622	14.094	12.783	11.654	10.675	9.823	9.077	7.843
26	22.795	20.121	17.877	15.983	14.375	13.003	11.826	10.810	9.929	9.161	7.896
27	23.560	20.707	18.327	16.330	14.643	13.211	11.987	10.935	10.027	9.237	7.943
28	24.316	21.281	18.764	16.663	14.898	13.406	12.137	11.051	10.116	9.307	7.984
29	25.066	21.844	19.189	16.984	15.141	13.591	12.278	11.158	10.198	9.370	8.022
30	25.808	22.396	19.600	17.292	15.373	13.765	12.409	11.258	10.274	9.427	8.055
40	32.835	27.355	23.115	19.793	17.159	15.046	13.332	11.925	10.757	9.779	8.244
50	39.196	31.424	25.730	21.482	18.256	15.762	13.801	12.234	10.962	9.915	8.305

Table 2 is used to compute the present value of a *series* of *equal* annual cash flows.

Example—Table 2. Arthur Howard won a contest on January 1, 2010, in which the prize was $30,000, payable in 15 annual installments of $2,000 each December 31, beginning in 2010. Assuming a 9 percent interest rate, what is the present value of Howard's prize on January 1, 2010? From Table 2, the required multiplier is 8.061, and the answer is:

$$\$2,000 \times 8.061 = \$16,122$$

The factor values for Table 2 are:

$$\text{PVa Factor} = \frac{1 - (1 + r)^{-n}}{r}$$

14%	15%	16%	18%	20%	25%	30%	35%	40%	45%	50%	Periods
0.877	0.870	0.862	0.847	0.833	0.800	0.769	0.741	0.714	0.690	0.667	1
1.647	1.626	1.605	1.566	1.528	1.440	1.361	1.289	1.224	1.165	1.111	2
2.322	2.283	2.246	2.174	2.106	1.952	1.816	1.696	1.589	1.493	1.407	3
2.914	2.855	2.798	2.690	2.589	2.362	2.166	1.997	1.849	1.720	1.605	4
3.433	3.352	3.274	3.127	2.991	2.689	2.436	2.220	2.035	1.876	1.737	5
3.889	3.784	3.685	3.498	3.326	2.951	2.643	2.385	2.168	1.983	1.824	6
4.288	4.160	4.039	3.812	3.605	3.161	2.802	2.508	2.263	2.057	1.883	7
4.639	4.487	4.344	4.078	3.837	3.329	2.925	2.598	2.331	2.109	1.922	8
4.946	4.772	4.607	4.303	4.031	3.463	3.019	2.665	2.379	2.144	1.948	9
5.216	5.019	4.833	4.494	4.192	3.571	3.092	2.715	2.414	2.168	1.965	10
5.453	5.234	5.029	4.656	4.327	3.656	3.147	2.752	2.438	2.185	1.977	11
5.660	5.421	5.197	4.793	4.439	3.725	3.190	2.779	2.456	2.197	1.985	12
5.842	5.583	5.342	4.910	4.533	3.780	3.223	2.799	2.469	2.204	1.990	13
6.002	5.724	5.468	5.008	4.611	3.824	3.249	2.814	2.478	2.210	1.993	14
6.142	5.847	5.575	5.092	4.675	3.859	3.268	2.825	2.484	2.214	1.995	15
6.265	5.954	5.669	5.162	4.730	3.887	3.283	2.834	2.489	2.216	1.997	16
6.373	6.047	5.749	5.222	4.775	3.910	3.295	2.840	2.492	2.218	1.998	17
6.467	6.128	5.818	5.273	4.812	3.928	3.304	2.844	2.494	2.219	1.999	18
6.550	6.198	5.877	5.316	4.844	3.942	3.311	2.848	2.496	2.220	1.999	19
6.623	6.259	5.929	5.353	4.870	3.954	3.316	2.850	2.497	2.221	1.999	20
6.687	6.312	5.973	5.384	4.891	3.963	3.320	2.852	2.498	2.221	2.000	21
6.743	6.359	6.011	5.410	4.909	3.970	3.323	2.853	2.498	2.222	2.000	22
6.792	6.399	6.044	5.432	4.925	3.976	3.325	2.854	2.499	2.222	2.000	23
6.835	6.434	6.073	5.451	4.973	3.981	3.327	2.855	2.499	2.222	2.000	24
6.873	6.464	6.097	5.467	4.948	3.985	3.329	2.856	2.499	2.222	2.000	25
6.906	6.491	6.118	5.480	4.956	3.988	3.330	2.856	2.500	2.222	2.000	26
6.935	6.514	6.136	5.492	4.964	3.990	3.331	2.856	2.500	2.222	2.000	27
6.961	6.534	6.152	5.502	4.970	3.992	3.331	2.857	2.500	2.222	2.000	28
6.983	6.551	6.166	5.510	4.975	3.994	3.332	2.857	2.500	2.222	2.000	29
7.003	6.566	6.177	5.517	4.979	3.995	3.332	2.857	2.500	2.222	2.000	30
7.105	6.642	6.234	5.548	4.997	3.999	3.333	2.857	2.500	2.222	2.000	40
7.133	6.661	6.246	5.554	4.999	4.000	3.333	2.857	2.500	2.222	2.000	50

Table 2 is the columnar sum of Table 1. Table 2 applies to *ordinary annuities,* in which the first cash flow occurs one time period beyond the date for which the present value is computed.

An *annuity due* is a series of equal cash flows for N time periods, but the first payment occurs immediately. The present value of the first payment equals the face value of the cash flow; Table 2 then is used to measure the present value of $N - 1$ remaining cash flows.

Example—Table 2. Determine the present value on January 1, 2010, of 20 lease payments; each payment of $10,000 is due on January 1, beginning in 2010. Assume an interest rate of 8 percent.

Present Value = Immediate Payment + Present Value of 19 Subsequent Payments at 8%
= $10,000 + ($10,000 × 9.604) = $106,040

ENDNOTES

Chapter 1

1. *Statement of Financial Accounting Concepts No. 1*, "Objectives of Financial Reporting by Business Enterprises" (Norwalk, Conn.: Financial Accounting Standards Board, 1978), par. 9.
2. Ibid.
3. CVS Caremark Corporation, *Annual Report*, 2007.
4. John D. Stoll, "GM Sees a Cash Burn in 2007," *The Wall Street Journal*, January 12–14, 2007.
5. Madhav Rajan, "The Choice of Performance Measures in Annual Bonus Contracts," *The Accounting Review*, April 1997.
6. National Commission on Fraudulent Financial Reporting, *Report of the National Commission on Fraudulent Financial Reporting* (Washington, D.C.: 1987), p. 2.
7. Target Corporation, *Annual Report*, 2007.
8. "Gallup: Accounting Reputation in Recovery," telberg .com, August 22, 2005.
9. Robert Johnson, "The New CFO," *Crain's Chicago Business*, July 19, 2004.
10. Curtis C. Venschoor, "Corporate Performance Is Closely Tied to a Strong Ethical Commitment," *Journal of Business and Society*, Winter 1990; Verschoor, "Does Superior Governance Still Lead to Better Financial Performance?" *Strategic Finance*, October 2004.
11. *Accounting Principles Board Statement No. 4*, "Basic Concepts and Accounting Principles Underlying Financial Statements of Business Enterprises" (New York: AICPA, 1970), par. 138.
12. John D. McKinnon, "US-EU Deal Paves Way for Accounting-Rule Shift," *The Wall Street Journal*, May 1, 2007.
13. *Statement Number 1C*, "Standards of Ethical Conduct for Management Accountants" (Montvale, N.J.: Institute of Management Accountants, 1983; revised 1997).
14. CVS Caremark Corporation, *Annual Report*, 2007.
15. Costco Wholesale Corporation, *Annual Report*, 2006.
16. Southwest Airlines Co., *Annual Report*, 1996.
17. Queen Sook Kim, "Lechters Inc. Files for Chapter 11, Arranges Financing," *The Wall Street Journal*, May 22, 2001.
18. RIM Limited, *Annual Report*, 2007.
19. John D. Stoll, "GM Sees a Cash Burn in 2007," *The Wall Street Journal*, January 12–14, par. 9.

Chapter 2

1. Jeremy Herron, "Boeing Stock Soars on China Order," *The Seattle Times*, April 12, 2006.
2. The Boeing Company, *Annual Report*, 2006.
3. *Statement of Financial Accounting Standards No. 157*, "Fair Value Measurements" (Norwalk, Conn.: Financial Accounting Standards Board, 2007).
4. Intel Corporation, *Annual Report*, 2006.
5. The Boeing Company, *Annual Report*, 2006.
6. Gary McWilliams, "EDS Accounting Change Cuts Past Earnings by $2.24 Billion," *The Wall Street Journal*, October 28, 2003.
7. The Boeing Company, *Annual Report*, 2006.
8. Ibid.
9. Mellon Bank, *Annual Report*, 2006.
10. Nike, Inc., *Annual Report*, 2006.

Chapter 3

1. Netflix, Inc., *Annual Report*, 2007.
2. Ibid.
3. "Microsoft Settles with SEC," *CBSNews.com*, June 5, 2002.
4. Christopher Lawton and Don Clark, "Dell to Restate 4 Years of Results," *The Wall Street Journal*, August 17, 2007.
5. Securities and Exchange Commission, *Staff Accounting Bulletin No. 10*, 1999.
6. Ken Brown, "Wall Street Plays Numbers Games with Savings, Despite Reforms," *The Wall Street Journal*, July 22, 2003.
7. Netflix, Inc., *Annual Report*, 2007.
8. Ibid.
9. Lyric Opera of Chicago, *Annual Report*, 2007.
10. The Walt Disney Company, *Annual Report*, 2006.

Chapter 4

1. Dell Computer Corporation, Presentation, February 28, 2008.
2. *Financial Accounting Series No. 1570-100*, "Conceptual Framework for Financial Reporting: The Objective of Financial Reporting and Qualitative Characteristics and Constraints of Decision-Useful Financial Reporting Information" (Norwalk, Conn.: Financial Accounting Standards Board, May 29, 2008), p. 1.
3. *Statement of Financial Accounting Concepts No. 2*, "Qualitative Characteristics of Accounting Information" (Norwalk, Conn.: Financial Accounting Standards Board, 1980), par. 20.
4. *Financial Accounting Series No. 1570-100*, "Conceptual Framework for Financial Reporting: The Objective of Financial Reporting and Qualitative Characteristics and Constraints of Decision-Useful Financial Reporting Information" (Norwalk, Conn.: Financial Accounting Standards Board, May 29, 2008), chapters 1 and 2.
5. Dell Computer Corporation, *Form 10-K*, 2008.
6. "Ex-Chief of WorldCom Is Found Guilty in $11 Billion Fraud," *The New York Times*, March 16, 2005.
7. *Accounting Principles Board Opinion No. 20*, "Accounting Changes" (New York: AICPA, 1971), par. 17.
8. www.fasb.org, July 12, 2008.
9. Securities and Exchange Commission, *Staff Accounting Bulletin No. 99*, 1999.
10. Ray J. Groves, "Here's the Annual Report. Got a Few Hours?" *The Wall Street Journal Europe*, August 26–27, 1994.
11. Roger Lowenstein, "Investors Will Fish for Footnotes in 'Abbreviated' Annual Reports," *The Wall Street Journal*, September 14, 1995.

12. Securities and Exchange Commission, "Rules and Regulations." *Federal Register*, vol. 73, no. 3, January 4, 2008.
13. Belverd E. Needles, Jr., Mark Frigo, and Marian Powers, "Performance Measures and Executive Compensation: Practices of High-Performance Companies," *Studies in Financial and Managerial Accounting* (London: JAI Elsevier Science Ltd.), vol. 18, 2008.
14. Albertson's Inc., *Annual Report*, 2004; Great Atlantic & Pacific Tea Company, *Annual Report*, 2004.

Chapter 5

1. Costco Wholesale Corporation, *Annual Report*, 2007.
2. Helen Shaw, "Former NBC Treasurer Arrested," *CFO .com*, January 25, 2007.
3. Costco Wholesale Corporation, *Annual Report*, 2007.
4. Joel Millman, "Here's What Happens to Many Lovely Gifts After Santa Rides Off," *The Wall Street Journal*, December 26, 2001.
5. Matthew Rose, "Magazine Revenue at Newsstands Falls in Worst Year Ever," *The Wall Street Journal*, May 15, 2001.
6. American Institute of Certified Public Accountants, *Professional Standards*, vol. 1 (New York: AICPA June 1, 1999), Sec. AU 322.07.
7. KPMG Peat Marwick, "1998 Fraud Survey," 1998.
8. Elizabeth Woyke, "Attention Shoplifters," *BusinessWeek*, September 11, 2006.
9. Costco Wholesale Corporation, *Annual Report*, 2007.
10. Ibid.
11. Amy Merrick, "Starbucks Accuses Employee, Husband of Embezzling $3.7 Million from Firm," *The Wall Street Journal*, November 20, 2000.
12. Sid R. Ewer, "A Roundtrip Ticket to Trouble," *Strategic Finance*, April 2004.

Chapter 6

1. Toyota Motor Corporation, *Annual Report*, 2007.
2. Ibid.
3. Gary McWilliams, "Whirlwind on the Web," *BusinessWeek*, April 7, 1997.
4. Karen Lundebaard, "Bumpy Ride," *The Wall Street Journal*, May 21, 2001.
5. American Institute of Certified Public Accountants, *Accounting Trends & Techniques* (New York: AICPA, 2007).
6. Toyota Motor Corporation, *Annual Report*, 2007.
7. "Cisco's Numbers Confound Some," *International Herald Tribune*, April 19, 2001.
8. "Kmart Posts $67 Million Loss Due to Markdowns," *The Wall Street Journal*, November 10, 2000.
9. Ernst & Young, *U.S. GAAP vs. IFRS: The Basics*, 2007.
10. American Institute of Certified Public Accountants, *Accounting Trends & Techniques* (New York: AICPA, 2007).
11. "SEC Case Judge Rules Crazy Eddie Principals Must Pay $72.7 Million," *The Wall Street Journal*, May 11, 2000.
12. American Institute of Certified Public Accountants, *Accounting Trends & Techniques* (New York: AICPA, 2007).
13. ExxonMobil Corporation, *Annual Report*, 2006.
14. Ibid.
15. Yamaha Motor Company, Ltd., *Annual Report*, 2007; Pioneer Corporation, *Annual Report*, 2007.

Chapter 7

1. Nike, Inc., *Annual Report*, 2007.
2. Peter Coy and Michael Arndt, "Up a Creek with Lots of Cash," *BusinessWeek*, November 12, 2001.
3. "So Much for Detroit's Cash Cushion," *BusinessWeek*, November 5, 2001.
4. Jesse Drucker, "Sprint Expects Loss of Subscribers," *The Wall Street Journal*, September 24, 2002.
5. Deborah Solomon and Damian Paletta, "U.S. Drafts Sweeping Plans to Fight Crisis as Turmoil Worsens in Credit Markets," *The Wall Street Journal*, September 19, 2008.
6. Circuit City Stores, Inc., *Annual Report*, 2004.
7. Heather Timmons, "Do Household's Numbers Add Up?" *BusinessWeek*, December 10, 2001.
8. Steve Daniels, "Bank One Reserves Feed Earnings," *Crain's Chicago Business*, December 15, 2003.
9. Jonathon Weil, "Accounting Scheme Was Straightforward but Hard to Detect," *The Wall Street Journal*, March 20, 2003.
10. Nike, Inc., *Annual Report*, 2007.
11. Ibid.
12. American Institute of Certified Public Accountants, *Accounting Trends & Techniques* (New York: AICPA, 2007).
13. Tom Lauricella, Shefali Anand, and Valerie Bauerlein, "A $34 Billion Cash Fund to Close Up," *The Wall Street Journal*, December 11, 2007.
14. Jathon Sapsford, "As Cash Fades, America Becomes a Plastic Nation," *The Wall Street Journal*, July 23, 2004.
15. American Institute of Certified Public Accountants, *Accounting Trends & Techniques* (New York: AICPA, 2007).
16. "Bad Loans Rattle Telecom Vendors," *BusinessWeek*, February 19, 2001.
17. Scott Thurm, "Better Debt Bolsters Bottom Lines," *The Wall Street Journal*, August 18, 2003.
18. Information based on promotional brochures of Mitsubishi Corp.
19. Elizabeth McDonald, "Unhatched Chickens," *Forbes*, February 19, 2001.
20. Fosters Group Limited, *Annual Report*, 2007; Heineken N.V., *Annual Report*, 2007.
21. Rhonda L. Rundle and Paul Davies, "Hospitals Administer Antidote for Bad Debt," *The Wall Street Journal*, May 4, 2004.

Chapter 8

1. Microsoft, *Annual Report*, 2007.
2. Pamela L. Moore, "How Zerox Ran Short of Black Ink," *BusinessWeek*, October 30, 2000.
3. Mark Heinzel, Deborah Solomon, and Joanne S. Lublin, "Nortel Board Fires CEO and Others," *The Wall Street Journal*, April 29, 2004.
4. Hershey Foods Corporation, *Annual Report*, 2008.
5. Goodyear Tire & Rubber Company, *Annual Report*, 2006.
6. 2008 NSBA Small & Medium-Sized Business Survey, p. 13.
7. www.nytimes.com, February 19, 2007.

8. "Press Room," *www.webfyer.com*, January 4, 2010.
9. Hershey Foods Corporation, *Annual Report*, 2007.
10. *Statement of Financial Accounting Standards No. 5*, "Accounting for Contingencies" (Norwalk, Conn.: Financial Accounting Standards Board, 1975).
11. American Institute of Certified Public Accountants, *Accounting Trends & Techniques* (New York: AICPA, 2007).
12. Microsoft, *Annual Report*, 2007.
13. American Institute of Certified Public Accountants, *Accounting Trends & Techniques* (New York: AICPA, 2007).
14. *Statement of Financial Accounting Standards No. 157*, "Fair Value Measures" (Norwalk, Conn.: Financial Accounting Standards Board, 1975).
15. "Clarifications on Fair Value Accounting," U.S. Security and Exchange Commission, *Release 2008-234*, October 1, 2008.
16. WorldCom (MCI), *Annual Report*, 2004.
17. Advertisement, *Chicago Tribune*, December 2007.
18. Sun Microsystems Inc., *Annual Report*, 2007; Cisco Systems, Inc., *Annual Report*, 2007.
19. General Motors Corporation, *Annual Report*, 2006.
20. Advertisement, *Chicago Tribune*, 2000.

Chapter 9

1. Apple Computer, Inc., *Annual Report*, 2007.
2. *Statement of Financial Accounting Standards No. 144*, "Accounting for the Impairment or Disposal of Long-Lived Assets" (Norwalk, Conn.: Financial Accounting Standards Board, 2001).
3. Sharon Young, "Large Telecom Firms, After WorldCom Moves, Consider Writedowns," *The Wall Street Journal*, March 18, 2003.
4. Edward J. Riedl, "An Examination of Long-Lived Asset Impairments," *The Accounting Review*, vol. 79, No. 3, pp. 823–852.
5. *Statement of Financial Accounting Standards No. 34*, "Capitalization of Interest Cost" (Norwalk, Conn.: Financial Accounting Standards Board, 1979).
6. American Institute of Certified Public Accountants, *Accounting Trends & Techniques* (New York: AICPA, 2007).
7. Ibid.
8. Jonathan Weil, "Oil Reserves Can Sure Be Slick," *The Wall Street Journal*, March 11, 2004.
9. *Statement of Financial Accounting Standards No. 25*, "Suspension of Certain Accounting Requirements for Oil and Gas Producing Companies" (Norwalk, Conn.: Financial Accounting Standards Board, 1979).
10. *Statement of Financial Accounting Standards No. 142*, "Goodwill and Other Intangible Assets" (Norwalk, Conn.: Financial Accounting Standards Board, 2001), par. 11–17.
11. "The Top 100 Brands," *BusinessWeek Online*, 2008.
12. The New York Times Company, *Annual Report*, 2006.
13. General Motors Corporation, *Annual Report*, 2006.
14. Abbott Laboratories, *Annual Report*, 2006.
15. *Statement of Financial Accounting Standards No. 2*, "Accounting for Research and Development Costs" (Norwalk, Conn.: Financial Accounting Standards Board, 1974), par. 12.
16. *Statement of Financial Accounting Standards No. 86*, "Accounting for the Costs of Computer Software to Be Sold, Leased, or Otherwise Marketed" (Norwalk, Conn.: Financial Accounting Standards Board, 1985).
17. General Mills, Inc., *Annual Report*, 2007; H. J. Heinz Company, *Annual Report*, 2007; Cisco Systems, *Annual Report*, 2007.
18. *Statement of Financial Accounting Standards No. 142*, "Goodwill and Other Intangible Assets" (Norwalk, Conn.: Financial Accounting Standards Board, 2001), par. 11–17.
19. Southwest Airlines Co., *Annual Report*, 2002.
20. Costco Wholesale Corporation, *Annual Report*, 2007.
21. IBM Corporation, *Annual Report*, 2007.
22. Hilton Hotels Corporation, *Annual Report*, 2006; Marriott International, Inc., *Annual Report*, 2006.
23. "Stock Gives Case the Funds He Needs to Buy New Technology," *BusinessWeek*, April 15, 1996.

Chapter 10

1. McDonald's Corporation, *Annual Report*, 2007.
2. Ibid.
3. Lee Hawkins, Jr., "S&P Cuts Rating on GM and Ford to Junk Status," *The Wall Street Journal*, May 6, 2005.
4. David Reilly and Silvia Ascarelli, "History Is Made (Again) in Convertibles Boom," *The Wall Street Journal*, July 9, 2003.
5. *Statement of Financial Accounting Standards No. 13*, "Accounting for Leases" (Norwalk, Conn.: Financial Accounting Standards Board, 1976), par. 10.
6. *Statement of Financial Accounting Standards No. 158*, "Employers' Accounting for Defined Benefit Pension and Other Postretirement Plans" (Norwalk, Conn.: Financial Accounting Standards Board, 2007).
7. General Motors Corporation, *Form 10-K*, 2007.
8. Deborah Soloman, "After Pension Fund Debacle, San Diego Is Mired in Probes," *The Wall Street Journal*, October 10, 2005.
9. Mary Williams Walsh, "$58 Billion Shortfall for New Jersey Retiree Care," *The New York Times*, July 25, 2007.
10. *Statement of Financial Accounting Standards No. 106*, "Employers' Accounting for Postretirement Benefits Other Than Pensions" (Norwalk, Conn.: Financial Accounting Standards Board, 1990).
11. General Motors Corporation, *Annual Report*, 2007.
12. Adapted from quotations in *The Wall Street Journal Online*, December 18, 2007.
13. Bill Barnhart, "Bond Bellwether," *Chicago Tribune*, December 4, 1996.
14. *Accounting Principles Board, Opinion No. 21*, "Interest on Receivables and Payables" (New York: AICPA, 1971).
15. Continental Airlines, *Annual Report*, 2007.
16. Tom Sullivan and Sonia Ryst, "Kodak $1 Billion Issue Draws Crowds," *The Wall Street Journal*, October 8, 2003.
17. *The Wall Street Journal Online*, December 19, 2007.
18. "How Borrowing Yields Dividends at Many Firms," *The Wall Street Journal*, March 27, 2007.
19. Amazon.com, *Annual Report*, 2007.

Chapter 11

1. Google, Inc., *Form S-1* (Registration Statement), 2004; *Annual Report*, 2007.
2. Microsoft Corporation, *Annual Report*, 2007.

3. Deborah Solomon, "AT&T Slashes Dividends 83%, Cuts Forecasts," *The Wall Street Journal*, December 21, 2002.
4. Abbott Laboratories, *Annual Report*, 2004.
5. Google, Inc., *Form S-1* (Registration Statement), 2004.
6. Microsoft Corporation, *Annual Report*, 2007.
7. American Institute of Certified Public Accountants, *Accounting Trends & Techniques* (New York: AICPA, 2006).
8. *Statement of Accounting Standards No. 123*, "Stock-Based Payments" (Norwalk, Conn.: Financial Accounting Standards Board, 1995; amended 2004).
9. Google, Inc., *Form S-1* (Registration Statement), 2004, p. 136.
10. David Henry, "How the Options Mess Got So Ugly and Expensive," *BusinessWeek*, September 11, 2006.
11. Joseph Weber, "One Share, Many Votes," *BusinessWeek*, March 29, 2004; "A Class (B) Act," *BusinessWeek*, May 28, 2007.
12. Michael Rapoport and Jonathan Weil, "More Truth-in-Labeling for Accounting Carries Liabilities," *The Wall Street Journal*, August 23, 2003.
13. "The FASB's Basic Ownership Approach and a Reclassification of Preferred Stock as a Liability," *www.CFO.com*, July 18, 2008.
14. American Institute of Certified Public Accountants, *Accounting Trends & Techniques* (New York: AICPA, 2006).
15. David Henry, "The Dirty Little Secret About Buybacks," *BusinessWeek*, January 23, 2006; Peter A. McKay and Justin Lahart, "Boom in Buybacks Helps Lift Stocks to Record Heights," *The Wall Street Journal*, July 18, 2007.
16. Marissa Marr, "DreamWorks Shares Rise 38% on First Day," *The Wall Street Journal*, October 10, 2004; *Yahoo Finance*, December 26, 2007.
17. Tom Herman, "Preferreds' Rich Yields Blind Some Investors to Risks," *The Wall Street Journal*, March 24, 1992.
18. IBM Corporation, *Annual Report*, 2006.
19. Stanley Ziemba, "USAir Defers Dividends on Preferred Stock," *Chicago Tribune*, September 30, 1994.
20. Susan Carey, "US Airways to Redeem Preferred Owned by Berkshire Hathaway," *The Wall Street Journal*, February 4, 1998.

Chapter 12

1. eBay, Inc., *Annual Report*, 2007.
2. *Statement of Financial Accounting Standards No. 157*, "Fair Value Measurements" (Norwalk, Conn.: Financial Accounting Standards Board, 2007); *Statement of Financial Accounting Standards No. 159*, "The Fair Value Option for Financial Assets and Financial Liabilities" (Norwalk, Conn.: Financial Accounting Standards Board, 2007).
3. *Statement of Financial Accounting Standards No. 115*, "Accounting for Certain Investments in Debt and Equity Securities" (Norwalk, Conn.: Financial Accounting Standards Board, 1993).
4. Holman W. Jenkins, Jr., "Mark to Meltdown," *The Wall Street Journal*, March 3, 2008.
5. eBay, Inc., *Annual Report*, 2007.
6. Jalal Soroosh and Jack T. Ciesielski, "Accounting for Special Purpose Entities Revised," FASB Interpretation (46R), *The CPA Journal*, July 2004.
7. Greg Steinmetz and Cacilie Rohwedder, "SAP Insider Probe Points to Reforms Needed in Germany," *The Wall Street Journal*, May 8, 1997.
8. Kathryn Kranhold and Deborah Solomon, "GE Restates Several Years of Earnings," *The Wall Street Journal*, May 9, 2005.
9. eBay, Inc., *Annual Report*, 2007.
10. *Statement of Financial Accounting Standards No. 115*, "Accounting for Certain Investments in Debt and Equity Securities" (Norwalk, Conn.: Financial Accounting Standards Board, 1993).
11. eBay, Inc., *Annual Report*, 2007.
12. *Statement of Financial Accounting Standards No. 94*, "Consolidation of All Majority-Owned Subsidiaries" (Norwalk, Conn.: Financial Accounting Standards Board, 1987).
13. eBay, Inc., *Annual Report*, 2007.
14. *Statement of Financial Accounting Standards No. 160*, "Noncontrolling Interest in Consolidated Financial Statements" (Norwalk, Conn.: Financial Accounting Standards Board, 2007).
15. *Accounting Principles Board, Opinion No. 16*, "Business Combinations" (New York: AICPA, 1970).
16. eBay, Inc., *Annual Report*, 2007.
17. Ibid.
18. Dell Computer Corporation, *Annual Report*, 2007.
19. DreamWorks Animation, *SEC Form 10-Q*, 2006.
20. Microsoft Corporation, *Annual Report*, 2007.

Chapter 13

1. Motorola, Inc., *Annual Report*, 2007.
2. Cited in *The Week in Review* (Deloitte Haskins & Sells), February 28, 1985.
3. "After Charge for Licensing, McDonald's Posts a Record Loss," *The New York Times*, July 25, 2007; Christina Cheddar Berk, "Campbell's Profit Jumps 31 Percent," *The Wall Street Journal*, November 22, 2005.
4. "Up to the Minute, Down to the Wire," *Twentieth Century Mutual Funds Newsletter*, 1996.
5. American Institute of Certified Public Accountants, *Accounting Trends & Techniques* (New York: AICPA, 2007).
6. Elizabeth MacDonald, "Pro Forma Puff Jobs," *Forbes*, December 9, 2002.
7. Gary M. Entwistle, Glenn D. Felham, and Chima Mbagwu, "Financial Reporting Regulation and the Reporting of Pro Forma Earnings," *Accounting Horizons*, March 2006.
8. *Statement of Financial Accounting Standards No. 145*, "Recission and Amendments of Various Statements" (Norwalk, Conn.: Financial Accounting Standards Board, 2002).
9. Jesse Drucker, "Motorola's Profit: Special Again?" *The Wall Street Journal*, October 15, 2002.
10. *Statement of Accounting Standards No. 109*, "Accounting for Income Taxes" (Norwalk, Conn.: Financial Accounting Standards Board, 1992).
11. American Institute of Certified Public Accountants, *Accounting Trends & Techniques* (New York: AICPA, 2007).
12. *Accounting Principles Board, Opinion No. 15*, "Earnings per Share" (New York: AICPA, 1969), par. 12.
13. *Statement of Financial Accounting Standards No. 128*, "Earnings per Share and the Disclosure of Information About Capital Structure" (Norwalk, Conn.: Financial Accounting Standards Board, 1997).

14. *Statement of Financial Accounting Standards No. 130*, "Reporting Comprehensive Income" (Norwalk, Conn.: Financial Accounting Standards Board, 1997).
15. American Institute of Certified Public Accountants, *Accounting Trends & Techniques* (New York: AICPA, 2007).
16. American Institute of Certified Public Accountants, *Accounting Research Bulletin No. 43* (New York: AICPA, 1953), chapter 7, sec. B, par. 10.
17. Ibid., par. 13.
18. Nike, *Annual Report*, 2007.
19. Robert O'Brien, "Tech's Chill Fails to Stem Stock Splits," *The Wall Street Journal*, June 8, 2000.
20. *YahooFinance.com*, 2007.
21. "Technology Firms Post Strong Earnings but Stock Prices Decline Sharply," *The Wall Street Journal*, January 21, 1988; Donald R. Seace, "Industrials Plunge 57.2 Points—Technology Stocks' Woes Cited," *The Wall Street Journal*, January 21, 1988.

Chapter 14

1. Amazon.com, *Form 10-K*, 2007.
2. Ian McDonald, "Cash Dilemma: How to Spend It," *The Wall Street Journal*, May 24, 2006; Ian McDonald, "Companies Are Rolling in Cash. Too Bad," *The Wall Street Journal*, August 20, 2006.
3. "Deadweight on the Markets," *BusinessWeek*, February 19, 2001.
4. "Free Cash Flow Standouts," *Upside Newsletter*, October 3, 2005.
5. Gary Slutsker, "Look at the Birdie and Say: 'Cash Flow,'" *Forbes*, October 25, 1993.
6. Jonathan Clements, "Yacktman Fund Is Bloodied but Unbowed," *The Wall Street Journal*, November 8, 1993.
7. Amazon.com, *Form 10-K*, 2007.
8. Jeffery Laderman, "Earnings, Schmearnings—Look at the Cash," *BusinessWeek*, July 24, 1989.
9. Amazon.com, Inc., *Form 10-K*, 2007.
10. American Institute of Certified Public Accountants, *Accounting Trends & Techniques* (New York: AICPA, 2006).
11. Martin Peers and Robin Sidel, "WorldCom Causes Analysts to Evaluate EBITDA's Role," *The Wall Street Journal*, July 15, 2002.
12. Richard Passov, "How Much Cash Does Your Company Need?" *Harvard Business Review*, November 2003.
13. "Cash Flow Shortfall in Quarter May Lead to Default on Loan," *The Wall Street Journal*, September 4, 2001.
14. Enron Corporation, *Press Release*, October 16, 2001.
15. Sony Corporation, *Annual Report*, 2007; Panasonic, *Annual Report*, 2007.
16. Dean Foust, "So Much Cash, So Few Dividends," *BusinessWeek*, January 20, 2003.

Chapter 15

1. "Wal-Mart CEO Pleased with Sales," *Fort Meyers News-Press*, January 5, 2006.
2. http://imanet.org/about_ethics_statement.asp.
3. http://walmartstores.com/FactsNews/FactSheets/click on link to "The Company of the Future: Fact Sheet."
4. Andrew Ross Sorkin, "Albertsons Nears Deal, Yet Again, to Sell Itself," *The New York Times*, January 23, 2006.
5. Securities and Exchange Commission, "Final Rule: Certification of Disclosure in Companies' Quarterly and Annual Reports," August 28, 2002, http://www.sec.gov/rules/final/33-8124.htm.
6. Andra Gumbus and Susan D. Johnson, "The Balanced Scorecard at Futura Industries," *Strategic Finance*, July 2003.
7. http://walmartstores.com/FactsNews/FactSheets/click on link to "The Company of the Future: Fact Sheet."
8. Securities and Exchange Commission, "Final Rule: Certification of Disclosure in Companies' Quarterly and Annual Reports," August 28, 2002, http://www.sec.gov/rules/final/33-8124.htm.
9. Curtis C. Verschoor, "Economic Crime Results from Unethical Culture," *Strategic Finance*, March 2009.

Chapter 19

1. Lance Thompson, "Examining Methods of VBM," *Strategic Finance*, December 2002.
2. "Just in Time, Toyota Production System & Lean Manufacturing," http://www.strategosinc.com/just_in_time.htm.
3. Dan Morse, "Tennessee Producer Tries New Tactic in Sofas: Speed," *The Wall Street Journal*, November 19, 2002.

Chapter 20

1. http://investor.google.com/conduct.html.

Chapter 21

1. Omar Aguilar, "How Strategic Performance Management Is Helping Companies Create Business Value," *Strategic Finance*, January 2003.
2. Jeremy Hope and Robin Frase, "Who Needs Budgets?" *Harvard Business Review*, February 2003.

Chapter 22

1. PEAKS Resorts, www.peakscard.com.
2. Marc J. Epstein and Jean-François Manzoni, "The Balanced Scorecard and Tableau de Bord: Translating Strategy into Action," *Management Accounting*, August 1997.
3. Kerry A. McDonald, "Meyners Does a Reality Check," *Journal of Accountancy*, February 2006.
4. V. G. Narayanan and Ananth Raman, "Aligning Incentives in Supply Chains," *Harvard Business Review*, November 2004.

Chapter 23

1. David E. Keys and Anton Van Der Merwe, "Gaining Effective Organizational Control with RCA," *Strategic Finance*, May 2002.
2. IRobot Corporation website: http://www.irobot.com.

Chapter 24

1. Stephanie Miles, "What's a Check?" *The Wall Street Journal*, October 21, 2002, p. R5.
2. Alan Fuhrman, "Your e-Banking Future," *Strategic Finance*, April 2002.
3. Motorola Internet and Networking Group, "Why Motorola?" www.motorola.com/MIMS/ISG/ING/quality.

Chapter 25

1. Paulette Thomas, "Case Study: Electronics Firm Ends Practice Just in Time," *The Wall Street Journal*, October 29, 2002.
2. From a speech by Jim Croft, vice president of finance and administration of the Field Museum, Chicago, November 14, 2000.

Chapter 26

1. Christopher Lawton, Anheuser-Busch Rolls Out the Price Jump," *The Wall Street Journal*, October 23, 2002.

Chapter 28

1. Starbucks Corporation, *Annual Report*, 2008.
2. David Henry, "The Numbers Game," *BusinessWeek*, May 14, 2001.
3. Jonathan Weil, "'Pro forma' in Earnings Reports? . . . As If," *The Wall Street Journal,* April 24, 2003.
4. *Statement of Financial Accounting Standards No.131,* "Segment Disclosures" (Norwalk, Conn.: Financial Accounting Standards Board, 1997).
5. Starbucks Corporation, *Annual Report*, 2008.
6. Starbucks Corporation, *Form 10-K*, 2008.
7. Ibid.
8. Starbucks Corporation, *Form 10-K*, 2008, shareholders' letter.
9. Target Corporation, *Proxy Statement*, May 18, 2005.
10. Starbucks Corporation, *Form 10-K*, 2008, shareholders' letter.
11. Starbucks Financial Release, "Starbucks Details Strategy for Profitable Growth," March 18, 2009.
12. Ibid.
13. Lee Hawkins Jr., "S&P Cuts Rating on GM and Ford to Junk Status," *The Wall Street Journal*, May 6, 2005.
14. Jesse Drucker, "Performance Bonus Out of Reach? Move the Target," *The Wall Street Journal*, April 29, 2003.
15. Pfizer, Inc., *Annual Report*, 2005; Roche Group, *Annual Report*, 2005.

COMPANY INDEX

SUBJECT INDEX